America Reads

ROBERT C. POOLEY, General Editor

Projection in Literature
Counterpoint in Literature
Outlooks Through Literature
Exploring Life Through Literature
The United States in Literature
England in Literature

ROBERT C. POOLEY *Professor of English, University of Wisconsin. Director, Wisconsin English-Language-Arts Curriculum Project. First Chairman of the Board of Trustees of the Research Foundation of the National Council of Teachers of English. First recipient of the W. Wilbur Hatfield Award for extraordinary contributions to the teaching of English.*

JESSE HILTON STUART *Formerly one-room rural teacher, high school English teacher, Kentucky and Ohio Public Schools; city and county high school principal, city and county superintendent, Kentucky Public Schools. Author of over thirty volumes: novels, biography, autobiography, poetry, and short story collections. Lecturer to high school, university, and teacher groups in America. Lecture Specialist for the U.S. State Department to secondary, university, and teacher groups throughout the world.*

LILLIAN ZELLHOEFER WHITE *Formerly Head of the Department of English, Mark Keppel High School, Alhambra, California; formerly instructor in English, State University College, Cortland, New York. Author of* In This Our Life, *a book of poetry.*

JAY CLINE *Chairman of the English Department, Modesto High School, Modesto, California.*

Reading Advisor, **OLIVE S. NILES,** *Director of Reading, Public Schools of Springfield, Massachusetts.*

Composition Guide by **DON OTTO,** *Saint Cloud State College, Saint Cloud, Minnesota.*

Consultant for this revision, **STEPHEN DUNNING,** *University of Michigan.*

ROBERT C. POOLEY

JESSE STUART

LILLIAN WHITE

JAY CLINE

OLIVE S. NILES

Outlooks *through* Literature

SCOTT, FORESMAN AND COMPANY

This book designed by

DONALD MARVINE

with major illustrations by

Peter Amft
Robert Christiansen
Ben Denison
Howard Mueller
Tak Murakami
Susan Perl
Phil Renaud
George Roth
Ronald Searle
George Suyeoka

design illustrations by

Al Camasto

cover photo by Robert Amft

PRINTED IN THE UNITED STATES OF AMERICA. REGIONAL OFFICES OF SCOTT, FORESMAN AND COMPANY ARE LOCATED IN ATLANTA, DALLAS, GLENVIEW, PALO ALTO, AND OAKLAND, N.J.

Contents

Unit 1

The Short Story

Biography and Autobiography

Unit 2

Unit 3

A Book of Poetry

Romeo and Juliet

William Shakespeare

Unit 4

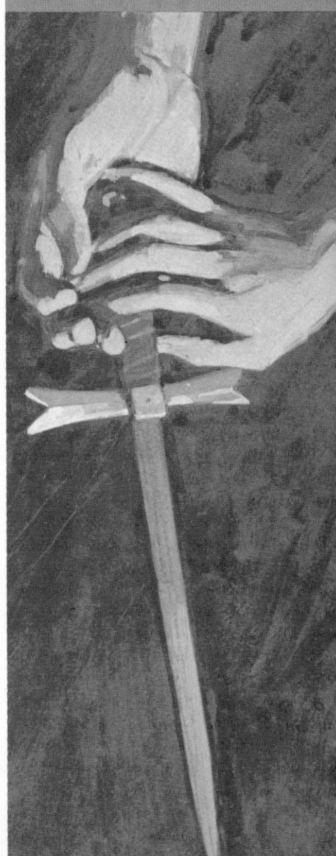

Classical Heritage

Unit 5

A Tale of Two Cities

Charles Dickens

Unit 7

At Random

COMPOSITION GUIDE

AUTHOR'S CRAFTS

POETRY CRAFTS

SUPPLEMENTARY ARTICLES

Almost every short story is centered around some kind of conflict: a conflict between characters, a conflict within a character, or a conflict between the main character and some abstract force such as nature. In addition to conflict, every short story in this unit has, to some degree, the following basic elements:

(1) PLOT: *what happens; the sequence of events around which a story is woven.*

(2) SETTING: *the time, place, and general background of the story.*

(3) CHARACTERS: *the individuals who appear in the story.*

(4) THEME: *the basic idea of the story; the center of interest; what the story is about.*

The major emphasis in this unit centers on the interrelationship of conflict, plot, setting, characters, and theme and their contributions to the short story as a type of literature.

J. W. ENGER PHOTO

Unit 1

The Short Story

"It is fear, Mr. Holmes. It is terror." These words were enough to challenge the Master Detective, Sherlock Holmes, to an immediate investigation, some rapid deductions, and a brilliant solution.

The Adventure of the Speckled Band

SIR ARTHUR CONAN DOYLE

On glancing over my notes of the seventy-odd cases in which I have during the last eight years studied the methods of my friend Sherlock Holmes, I find none which presented more singular features than that which was associated with the well-known family of the Roylotts of Stoke Moran.[1] The events in question occurred in the early days of my association with Holmes, when we were sharing rooms as bachelors in Baker Street.[2]

It was early in April in the year '83 that I woke one morning to find Sherlock Holmes standing, fully dressed, by the side of my bed. He was a late riser as a rule, and as the clock showed me that it was only a quarter past seven, I blinked up at him in some surprise, and perhaps just a little resentment, for I was myself regular in my habits.

"Very sorry to rouse you up, Watson," said he.

"What is it, then—a fire?" I asked.

"No; a client. It seems that a young lady has arrived in a considerable state of excitement, who insists upon seeing me. She is waiting now in the sitting room. Now, when young ladies wander about the metropolis at this hour of the morning, I presume that it is something very pressing which they have to communicate. Should it prove to be an interesting case, you would, I am sure, wish to follow it from the outset. I thought, at any rate, that I should give you the chance."

"My dear fellow, I would not miss it for anything."

I had no keener pleasure than in following Holmes in his professional investigations, and in admiring the rapid deductions, as swift as intuitions,[3] and yet always founded on a logical basis, with which he unraveled the problems which were submitted to him. I rapidly threw on my clothes, and accompanied my friend down to the sitting room. A lady dressed in black and heavily veiled, who had been sitting in the window, rose as we entered.

---

1. *Stoke Moran,* the name of the Roylott estate. **2. *Baker Street.*** Holmes' number on this actual London Street was 221B. **3. *Admiring the rapid deductions, as swift as intuitions.*** Dr. Watson admires Holmes' ability to think through a problem quickly and draw a correct conclusion; Holmes could do this as speedily as those who get quick flashes of truth without stopping to reason at all.

"Good morning, madam," said Holmes, cheerily. "My name is Sherlock Holmes. This is my intimate friend and associate, Dr. Watson, before whom you can speak as freely as before myself. Ha! I am glad to see that my housekeeper, Mrs. Hudson, has had the good sense to light the fire. Pray draw up to it, and I shall order you a cup of hot coffee, for I observe that you are shivering."

"It is not cold which makes me shiver," said the woman, in a low voice, changing her seat as requested.

"What, then?"

"It is fear, Mr. Holmes. It is terror." She had raised her veil; and we could see that she was indeed in a pitiable state of agitation, her face all drawn and gray, with restless, frightened eyes, like those of some hunted animal. Her features and her figure were those of a woman of thirty, but her hair was shot with premature gray, and her expression was weary and haggard. Sherlock Holmes ran her over with one of his quick, all-comprehensive glances.

"You must not fear," said he, soothingly. "We shall set matters right, I have no doubt. You have come in by train this morning, I see."

"You know me, then?"

"No, but I observe the second half of a return ticket in the palm of your left glove. You must have started early, and yet you had a good drive in a dogcart,[4] along heavy roads, before you reached the station."

The lady gave a violent start, and stared in bewilderment at my companion.

"There is no mystery, my dear madam," said he, smiling. "The left arm of your jacket is spattered with mud in no less than seven places. The marks are perfectly fresh. There is no vehicle save a dogcart which throws up mud in that way, and then only when you sit on the left-hand side of the driver."[5]

"Whatever your reasons may be, you are perfectly correct," said she. "I started from home before six, reached the railway station of Leatherhead at twenty past, and came in by the first train to Waterloo.[6] Sir, I can stand this strain no longer; I shall go mad if it continues. I have no one to turn to—none, save only one, who cares for me, and he, poor fellow, can be of little aid. I have heard of you, Mr. Holmes, from Mrs. Farintosh, whom you helped in the hour of her sore need. It was from her that I had your address. Oh, sir, do you not think that you could help me, too, and at least throw a little light through the dense darkness which surrounds me? At present it is out of my power to reward you for your services, but in a month or six weeks I shall be married, with the control of my own income, and then at least you shall not find me ungrateful."

Holmes turned to his desk and drew out a small case-book, which he consulted.

"I can only say, madam, that I shall be happy to devote the same care to your case as I did to that of your friend. As to reward, my profession is its own reward; but you are at liberty to defray whatever expenses I may be put to, at the time which suits you best. And now I beg you will lay before us everything that may help us in forming an opinion upon the matter."

"My name is Helen Stoner," replied our visitor, "and I am living with my stepfather, who is the last survivor of one of the oldest Saxon families[7] in England, the Roylotts of Stoke Moran, in Surrey."

Holmes nodded his head. "The name is familiar to me," said he.

"The family was at one time among the richest in England, and the estates extended many miles. In the last century, however, four successive heirs were of a dissolute and wasteful disposition, and the family ruin was eventually completed by a gambler in the days of the Regency.[8] Nothing was left

4. ***dogcart,*** a small open carriage. 5. ***the left-hand side of the driver.*** In England the driver sits at the right and drives on the left side of the road. 6. ***Waterloo,*** a famous railway station in London. 7. ***Saxon families.*** The Saxons were among the earliest inhabitants of England. 8. ***the Regency,*** the period from 1811 to 1820 in English history.

save a few acres of ground, and the two-hundred-year-old house, which is itself crushed under a heavy mortgage. The last squire dragged out his existence there, living the horrible life of an aristocratic pauper; but his only son, my stepfather, seeing that he must adapt himself to the new conditions, obtained an advance from a relative, which enabled him to take a medical degree, and went out to Calcutta, where, by his professional skill and his force of character, he established a large practice. In a fit of anger, however, caused by some robberies which had been perpetrated in the house, he beat his native butler to death, and narrowly escaped a capital sentence.[9] As it was, he suffered a long term of imprisonment, and afterward returned to England a morose and disappointed man.

"When Dr. Roylott was in India, he married my mother, Mrs. Stoner, the young widow of Major General Stoner, of the Bengal Artillery.[10] My sister Julia and I were twins, and we were only two years old at the time of my mother's remarriage. She had a considerable sum of money—not less than £1000 a year[11]—and this she bequeathed to Dr. Roylott entirely while we resided with him, with a provision that a certain annual sum should be allowed to each of us in the event of our marriage. Shortly after our return to England my mother died—she was killed eight years ago in a railway accident. Dr. Roylott then abandoned his attempts to establish himself in practice in London, and took us to live with him in the old ancestral house at Stoke Moran. The money which my mother had left was enough for all our wants, and there seemed to be no obstacle to our happiness.

"But a terrible change came over our stepfather about this time. Instead of making friends and exchanging visits with our neighbors, who had at first been overjoyed to see a Roylott of Stoke Moran back in the old family seat, he shut himself up in his house, and seldom came out save to indulge in ferocious quarrels with whoever might cross his path. Violence of temper approaching to mania has been hereditary in the men of the family, and in my stepfather's case it had, I believe, been intensified by his long residence in the tropics. A series of disgraceful brawls took place, two of which ended in the police court, until at last he became the terror of the village, and the folks would fly at his approach, for he is a man of immense strength and is absolutely uncontrollable in his anger.

"Last week he hurled the local blacksmith over a parapet into a stream, and it was only by paying over all the money which I could gather together that I was able to avert another public exposure. He had no friends at all save the wandering gypsies, and he would give these vagabonds leave to encamp upon the few acres of bramble-covered land which represent the family estate, and would accept in return the hospitality of their tents, wandering away with them sometimes for weeks on end. He has a passion also for Indian animals, which are sent over to him by a correspondent, and he has at this moment a cheetah and a baboon, which wander freely over his grounds, and are feared by the villagers almost as much as their master.

"You can imagine from what I say that my poor sister Julia and I had no great pleasure in our lives. No servant would stay with us, and for a long time we did all the work of the house. Julia was but thirty at the time of her death, and yet her hair had already begun to whiten, even as mine has."

"Your sister is dead, then?"

"She died just two years ago, and it is of her death that I wish to speak to you. You can understand that, living the life which I have described, we were little likely to see anyone of our own age and position. We

9. a capital sentence, a sentence of death. ***10. Bengal*** (beng gôl′) ***Artillery,*** famous British Army unit stationed in eastern India. ***11. £1000 a year,*** an income of one thousand pounds, or about $5000 a year at the time of the story, a pound being worth about five dollars at that time.

had, however, an aunt, my mother's maiden sister, Miss Honoria Westphail, who lives near Harrow, and we were occasionally allowed to pay short visits at this lady's house. Julia went there at Christmas two years ago, and met there a major of marines, to whom she became engaged. My stepfather learned of the engagement when my sister returned, and offered no objection to the marriage; but within a fortnight of the day which had been fixed for the wedding, the terrible event occurred which has deprived me of my only companion."

Sherlock Holmes had been leaning back in his chair with his eyes closed and his head sunk in a cushion, but he half opened his lids now and glanced across at his visitor.

"Pray be precise as to details," said he.

"It is easy for me to be so, for every event of that dreadful time is seared into my memory. The manor house is, as I have already said, very old; and only one wing is now inhabited. The bedrooms in this wing are on the ground floor, the sitting rooms being in the central block of the buildings. Of these bedrooms the first is Dr. Roylott's, the second my sister's, and the third my own. There is no communication between them, but they all open out into the same corridor. Do I make myself plain?"

"Perfectly so."

"The windows of the three rooms are full length and open out upon the lawn. That fatal night Dr. Roylott had gone to his room early, though we knew that he had not retired to rest, for my sister was troubled by the smell of the strong Indian cigars which it was his custom to smoke. She left her room, therefore, and came into mine, where she sat for some time, chatting about her approaching wedding. At eleven o'clock she rose to leave me, but she paused at the door and looked back.

" 'Tell me, Helen,' said she, 'have you ever heard anyone whistle in the dead of the night?'

" 'Never,' said I.

" 'I suppose that you could not possibly whistle, yourself, in your sleep?'

" 'Certainly not. But why?'

" 'Because during the last few nights I have always, about three in the morning, heard a low, clear whistle. I am a light sleeper, and it has awakened me. I cannot tell where it came from—perhaps from the next room, perhaps from the lawn. I thought that I would just ask you whether you had heard it.'

" 'No, I have not. It must be those wretched gypsies in the plantation.'

" 'Very likely. And yet if it were on the lawn, I wonder that you did not hear it also.'

" 'Ah, but I sleep more heavily than you.'

" 'Well, it is of no great consequence, at any rate.' She smiled back at me and closed my door, and a few moments later I heard her key turn in the lock of her own door."

"Indeed," said Holmes. "Was it your custom always to lock yourselves in at night?"

"Always."

"And why?"

"I think that I mentioned to you that the doctor kept a cheetah and a baboon. We had no feeling of security unless our doors were locked."

"Quite so. Pray proceed with your statement."

"I could not sleep that night. A vague feeling of impending misfortune impressed me. My sister and I, you will recollect, were twins, and you know how subtle are the links which bind two souls which are so closely allied. It was a wild night. The wind was howling outside, and the rain was beating and splashing against the windows. Suddenly, amid all the hubbub of the gale, there burst forth the wild scream of a terrified woman. I knew that it was my sister's voice. I sprang from my bed, wrapped a shawl around me, and rushed into the corridor. As I opened my door, I seemed to hear a low whistle, such as my sister described, and a few moments later a clanging sound, as if a mass of metal had fallen.

"As I ran down the passage, my sister's door was unlocked, and revolved slowly upon its hinges. I stared at it horror-stricken, not knowing what was about to issue from it. By the light of the corridor lamp I saw my sister appear at the opening, her face blanched with terror, her hands groping for help, her whole figure swaying to and fro like that of a drunkard. I ran to her and threw my arms round her, but at that moment her knees seemed to give way and she fell to the ground. She writhed as one who is in terrible pain, and her limbs were dreadfully convulsed. At first I thought that she had not recognized me, but as I bent over her she suddenly shrieked out, in a voice which I shall never forget: 'Oh, my God! Helen! It was the band! The speckled band!' There was something else which she would fain have said, and she stabbed with her finger into the air in the direction of the doctor's room, but a fresh convulsion seized her and choked her words. I rushed out, calling loudly for my stepfather, and I met him hastening from his room in his dressing gown. When he reached my sister's side, she was unconscious, and though he poured brandy down her throat and sent for medical aid from the village, all efforts were in vain, for she slowly sank and died without having recovered her consciousness. Such was the dreadful end of my beloved sister."

"One moment," said Holmes; "are you sure about this whistle and metallic sound? Could you swear to it?"

"That was what the county coroner asked me at the inquiry. It is my strong impression that I heard it, and yet, among the crash of the gale and the creaking of an old house, I may possibly have been deceived."

"Was your sister dressed?"

"No, she was in her nightdress. In her right hand was found the charred stump of a match, and in her left a matchbox."

"Showing that she had struck a light and looked about her when the alarm took place. That is important. And what conclusions did the coroner come to?"

"He investigated the case with great care, for Dr. Roylott's conduct had long been notorious in the county, but he was unable to find any satisfactory cause of death. My evidence showed that the door had been fastened upon the inner side, and the windows were blocked by old-fashioned shutters with broad iron bars, which were secured every night. The walls were carefully sounded, and were shown to be quite solid all round, and the flooring was also thoroughly examined, with the same result. The chimney is wide, but is barred up by four large staples. It is certain, therefore, that my sister was quite alone when she met her end. Besides, there were no marks of any violence upon her."

"How about poison?"

"The doctors examined her for it, but without success."

"What do you think that this unfortunate lady died of, then?"

"It is my belief that she died of pure fear and nervous shock, though what it was that frightened her I cannot imagine."

"Were gypsies in the plantation at the time?"

"Yes, there are nearly always some of them there."

"Ah, and what did you gather from this allusion to a band—a speckled band?"

"Sometimes I have thought that it was merely the wild talk of delirium, sometimes that it may have referred to some band of people, perhaps to these very gypsies in the plantation. I do not know whether the spotted handkerchiefs which so many of them wear over their heads might have suggested the strange adjective she used."

Holmes shook his head like a man who is far from being satisfied.

"These are very deep waters," said he; "pray go on with your narrative."

"Two years have passed since then, and my life has been until lately lonelier than ever. A month ago, however, a dear friend, whom I have known for many years, has done me the honor to ask my hand in marriage. His name is Armitage—Percy Armitage—the second son of Mr. Armitage, of Crane Water, near Reading. My stepfather has offered no opposition to the match, and we are to be married in the course of the spring. Two days ago some repairs were started in the west wing of the building, and my bedroom wall has been pierced, so that I have had to move into the chamber in which my twin sister died, and to sleep in the very bed in which she slept.

"Imagine my thrill of terror when last night, as I lay awake, thinking over her terrible fate, I suddenly heard in the silence of the night the low whistle which had been the herald of her own death. I sprang up and lit the lamp, but nothing was to be seen in the room. I was too shaken to go to bed again, however; so I dressed, and as soon as it was daylight I slipped down, got a dogcart at the Crown Inn, which is opposite, and drove to Leatherhead, from whence I have come on this morning with the one object of seeing you and asking your advice."

"You have done wisely," said my friend. "But have you told me all?"

"Yes, all."

"Miss Stoner, you have not. You are screening your stepfather."

"Why, what do you mean?"

For an answer Holmes pushed back the frill of black lace which fringed the hand that lay upon our visitor's knee. Five little livid spots, the marks of four fingers and a thumb, were printed upon the white wrist.

"You have been cruelly used," said Holmes.

The lady colored deeply and covered over her injured wrist. "He is a hard man," she said, "and perhaps he hardly knows his own strength."

There was a long silence, during which Holmes leaned his chin upon his hands and stared into the crackling fire.

"This is a very deep business," he said, at last.

"There are a thousand details which I should desire to know before I decide upon our course of action. Yet we have not a moment to lose. If we were to come to Stoke Moran today, would it be possible for us to see over these rooms without the knowledge of your stepfather?"

"As it happens, he spoke of coming into town today upon some most important business. It is probable that he will be away all day, and that there would be nothing to disturb you. We have a housekeeper now, but she is old and foolish, and I could easily get her out of the way."

"Excellent. You are not averse to this trip, Watson?"

"By no means."

"Then we shall both come. What are you going to do yourself?"

"I have one or two things which I would wish to do now that I am in town. But I shall return by the twelve o'clock train, so as to be there in time for your coming."

"And you may expect us early in the afternoon. I have some small business matters to attend to. Will you not wait and breakfast?"

"No, I must go. My heart is lightened already since I have confided my trouble to you. I shall look forward to seeing you again this afternoon." She dropped her thick black veil over her face and glided from the room.

"And what do you think of it all, Watson?" asked Holmes, after seeing her out.

"It seems to me to be a most dark and sinister business."

"Dark enough and sinister enough."

"Yet if the lady is correct in saying that the flooring and walls are sound, and that the door, window, and chimney are impassable, then her sister must have been undoubtedly alone when she met her mysterious end."

"What becomes, then, of these nocturnal whistles, and what of the very peculiar words of the dying woman?"

"I cannot think."

"When you combine the ideas of whistles

at night, the presence of a band of gypsies who are on intimate terms with this old doctor, the fact that we have every reason to believe that the doctor has an interest in preventing his stepdaughter's marriage, the dying allusion to a band, and, finally, the fact that Miss Helen Stoner heard a metallic clang, which might have been caused by one of those metal bars which secured the shutters falling back into its place, I think that there is good ground to think that the mystery may be cleared along those lines."

"But what, then, did the gypsies do?"

"I cannot imagine."

"I see many objections to any such theory."

"And so do I. It is precisely for that reason that we are going to Stoke Moran this day. I want to see whether the objections are fatal, or if they may be explained away. But what in the name of the devil!"

The ejaculation had been drawn from my companion by the fact that our door had been suddenly dashed open, and that a huge man had framed himself in the aperture. His costume was a peculiar mixture of the professional and of the agricultural,[12] having a black top hat, a long frock coat, and a pair of high gaiters, with a hunting crop swinging in his hand. So tall was he that his hat actually brushed the crossbar of the doorway, and his breadth seemed to span it across from side to side. A large face, seared with a thousand wrinkles, burned yellow with the sun, and marked with every evil passion, was turned from one to the other of us, while his deep-set eyes, and his high, thin, fleshless nose, gave him somewhat the resemblance to a fierce old bird of prey.

"Which of you is Holmes?" asked this apparition.

"My name, sir; but you have advantage of me," said my companion quietly.

"I am Dr. Grimesby Roylott, of Stoke Moran."

"Indeed, Doctor," said Holmes blandly. "Pray take a seat."

"I will do nothing of the kind. My stepdaughter has been here. I have traced her. What has she been saying to you?"

"It is a little cold for the time of the year," said Holmes.

"What has she been saying to you?" screamed the old man, furiously.

"But I have heard that the crocuses promise well," continued my companion, imperturbably.

"Ha! You put me off, do you?" said our new visitor, taking a step forward and shaking his hunting crop. "I know you, you scoundrel! I have heard of you before. You are Holmes, the meddler."

My friend smiled.

"Holmes, the busybody!"

His smile broadened.

"Holmes, the Scotland Yard Jack-in-office!"[13]

Holmes chuckled heartily. "Your conversation is most entertaining," said he. "When you go out, close the door, for there is a decided draft."

"I will go when I have said my say. Don't you dare to meddle with my affairs. I know that Miss Stoner has been here. I traced her! I am a dangerous man to fall foul of! See here." He stepped forward, seized the poker, and bent it into a curve with his huge brown hands.

"See that you keep yourself out of my grip," he snarled; and hurling the twisted poker into the fireplace, he strode out of the room.

"He seems a very amiable person," said Holmes, laughing. "I am not quite so bulky, but if he had remained I might have shown him that my grip was not much more feeble than his own." As he spoke he picked up the steel poker, and with a sudden effort straightened it out again.

"Fancy his having the insolence to con-

---

12. ***of the professional and of the agricultural,*** of the kinds of clothes worn by businessmen and by farmers.
13. ***the Scotland Yard Jack-in-office,*** an insolent person in authority at Scotland Yard. Scotland Yard is the famous headquarters of the London police. As a matter of fact, Holmes was not directly connected with Scotland Yard and avoided its officials as much as possible.

found me with the official detective force! This incident gives zest to our investigation, however, and I only trust that our little friend will not suffer from her imprudence in allowing this brute to trace her. And now, Watson, we shall order breakfast, and afterward I shall walk down to Doctors' Commons,[14] where I hope to get some data which may help us in this matter."

It was nearly one o'clock when Sherlock Holmes returned from his excursion. He held in his hand a sheet of blue paper, scrawled over with notes and figures.

"I have seen the will of the deceased wife," said he. "To determine its exact meaning, I have been obliged to work out the present prices of the investments with which it is concerned. The total income, which at the time of the wife's death was little short of £1100, is now, through the fall in agricultural prices, not more than £750. Each daughter can claim an income of £250, in case of marriage. It is evident, therefore, that if both girls had married, this beauty would have had a mere pittance, while even one of them would cripple him to a very serious extent. My morning's work has not been wasted, since it has proved that he has the very strongest motives for standing in the way of anything of the sort. And now, Watson, this is too serious for dawdling, especially as the old man is aware that we are interesting ourselves in his affairs; so if you are ready, we shall call a cab and drive to Waterloo. I should be very much obliged if you would slip your revolver into your pocket. An Eley's No. 2 is an excellent argument with gentlemen who can twist steel pokers into knots. That and a toothbrush are, I think, all that we need."

At Waterloo we were fortunate in catching a train for Leatherhead, where we hired a trap at the station inn, and drove for four or five miles through the lovely Surrey lanes. My companion sat in front of the trap, his arms folded, his hat pulled down over his eyes, and his chin sunk upon his breast, buried in the deepest thought. Suddenly, however, he started, tapped me on the shoulder, and pointed over the meadows.

"Look there!" said he.

A heavily timbered park stretched up in a gentle slope, thickening into a grove at the highest point. From amid the branches there jutted out the gray gables and high rooftree of a very old mansion.

"Stoke Moran?" said he.

"Yes, sir, that be the house of Dr. Grimesby Roylott," remarked the driver.

"There is some building going on there," said Holmes; "that is where we are going."

"There's the village," said the driver, pointing to a cluster of roofs some distance to the left; "but if you want to get to the house, you'll find it shorter to get over this stile, and so by the footpath over the fields. There it is where the lady is walking."

"And the lady, I fancy, is Miss Stoner," observed Holmes, shading his eyes. "Yes, I think we had better do as you suggest."

We got off, paid our fare, and the trap rattled back on its way to Leatherhead.

"I thought it as well," said Holmes, as we climbed the stile, "that this fellow should think we had come here as architects or on some definite business. It may stop his gossip. Good afternoon, Miss Stoner. You see that we have been as good as our word."

Our client of the morning had hurried forward to meet us with a face which spoke her joy. "I have been waiting so eagerly for you!" she cried, shaking hands with us warmly. "All has turned out splendidly. Dr. Roylott has gone to town, and it is unlikely that he will be back before evening."

"We have had the pleasure of making the doctor's acquaintance," said Holmes, and in a few words he sketched out what had occurred. Miss Stoner turned white to the lips as she listened.

14. Doctors' Commons, a group of buildings in London where various legal documents were filed. Actually, these buildings no longer stood at the time of this story.

"Good heavens!" she cried. "He has followed me, then."

"So it appears."

"He is so cunning that I never know when I am safe from him. What will he say when he returns?"

"He must guard himself, for he may find that there is someone more cunning than himself upon his track. You must lock yourself up from him tonight. If he is violent, we shall take you away to your aunt's at Harrow. Now, we must make the best use of our time, so kindly take us at once to the rooms which we are to examine."

The building was of gray, lichen-blotched stone,[15] with a high central portion, and two curving wings, like the claws of a crab, thrown out on each side. In one of these wings the windows were broken, and blocked with wooden boards, while the roof was partly caved in, a picture of ruin. The central portion was in little better repair, but the right-hand block was comparatively modern, and the blinds in the windows, with the blue smoke curling up from the chimneys, showed that this was where the family resided. Some scaffolding had been erected against the end wall, and the stonework had been broken into, but there were no signs of any workmen at the moment of our visit. Holmes walked slowly up and down the ill-trimmed lawn, and examined with deep attention the outsides of the windows.

"This, I take it, belongs to the room in which you used to sleep, the center one to your sister's, and the one next to the main building to Dr. Roylott's chamber?"

"Exactly so. But I am now sleeping in the middle one."

"Pending the alterations, as I understand. By the way, there does not seem to be any very pressing need for repairs at that end wall."

"There were none. I believe that it was an excuse to move me from my room."

"Ah! that is suggestive. Now, on the other side of this narrow wing runs the corridor from which these three rooms open. There are windows in it, of course?"

"Yes, but very small ones. Too narrow for anyone to pass through."

"As you both locked your doors at night, your rooms were unapproachable from that side. Now, would you have the kindness to go into your room and bar your shutters."

Miss Stoner did so, and Holmes, after a careful examination through the open window, endeavored in every way to force the shutter open, but without success. There was no slit through which a knife could be passed to raise the bar. Then with his lens he tested the hinges, but they were of solid iron, built firmly into the massive masonry. "Hum!" said he, scratching his chin in some perplexity. "My theory certainly presents some difficulties. No one could pass these shutters if they were bolted. Well, we shall see if the inside throws any light upon the matter."

A small side door led into the whitewashed corridor from which the three bedrooms opened. Holmes refused to examine the third chamber; so we passed at once to the second, that in which Miss Stoner was now sleeping, and in which her sister had met with her fate. It was a homely little room with a low ceiling and a gaping fireplace, after the fashion of old country houses. A brown chest of drawers stood in one corner, a narrow white-counterpaned bed in another, and a dressing table on the left-hand side of the window. These articles, with two small wickerwork chairs, made up all the furniture in the room, save for a square of Wilton carpet in the center. The baseboards and the paneling of the walls were of brown, worm-eaten oak, so old and discolored that it may have dated from the original building of the house. Holmes drew one of the chairs into a corner and sat silent, while his eyes traveled round and round and up and down, taking in every detail of the apartment.

---

15. lichen-blotched **(lī′ken blocht)** ***stone,*** stone stained by the growth of mosslike plants.

"Where does that bell communicate with?" he asked, at last, pointing to a thick bell rope which hung down beside the bed, the tassel actually lying upon the pillow.

"It goes to the housekeeper's room."

"It looks newer than the other things."

"Yes, it was only put there a couple of years ago."

"Your sister asked for it, I suppose?"

"No, I never heard of her using it. We used always to get what we wanted for ourselves."

"Indeed, it seemed unnecessary to put so nice a bell-pull there. You will excuse me for a few minutes while I satisfy myself as to this floor." He threw himself down upon his face with his lens in his hand, and crawled swiftly backward and forward, examining minutely the cracks between the boards. Then he did the same with the woodwork with which the chamber was paneled. At last he walked over to the bed, and spent some time in staring at it, and in running his eye up and down the wall. At last he took the bell rope in his hand and gave it a brisk tug.

"Why, it's a dummy," said he.

"Won't it ring?"

"No; it is not even attached to a wire. This is very interesting. You can see now that it is fastened to a hook just above where the little opening for the ventilator is."

"How very absurd! I never noticed that before."

"Very strange!" muttered Holmes, pulling at the rope. "There are one or two very singular points about this room. For example, what a fool a builder must be to open a ventilator into another room, when, with the same trouble, he might have communicated with the outside air!"

"That is also quite modern," said the lady.

"Done about the same time as the bell rope?" remarked Holmes.

"Yes, there were several little changes carried out about that time."

"They seem to have been of a most interesting character–dummy bell ropes, and ventilators which do not ventilate. With your permission, Miss Stoner, we shall now carry our researches into the inner apartment."

Dr. Grimesby Roylott's chamber was larger than that of his stepdaughter, but was as plainly furnished. A camp bed, a small wooden shelf full of books, mostly of a technical character, an armchair beside the bed, a plain wooden chair against the wall, a round table, and a large iron safe were the principal things which met the eye. Holmes walked slowly round and examined each and all of them with the keenest interest.

"What's in here?" he asked, tapping the safe.

"My stepfather's business papers, I think."

"Oh! you have seen inside, then?"

"Only once, some years ago. I remember that it was full of papers."

"There isn't a cat in it, for example?"

"What a strange idea!"

"Well, look at this!" He took up a small saucer of milk which stood on the top of the safe.

"No; we don't keep a cat. But there is a cheetah and a baboon."

"Ah, yes, of course! Well, a cheetah is just a big cat, and yet a saucer of milk does not go very far in satisfying its wants, I dare say. There is one point which I should wish to determine." He squatted down in front of the wooden chair, and examined the seat of it with the greatest attention.

"Thank you. That is quite settled," said he, rising and putting his lens in his pocket.

"Hello! Here is something interesting!"

The object which had caught his eye was a small dog lash which lay on a corner of the bed. The lash, however, was curled upon itself, and tied so as to make a loop of whipcord.

"What do you make of that, Watson?"

"It's a common enough lash. But I don't know why it should be tied."

"That is not quite so common, is it? Ah, me! it's a wicked world, and when a clever man turns his brain to crime, it is the worst of all. I think that I have seen enough now, Miss Stoner, and with your permission we shall walk out upon the lawn."

I had never seen my friend's face so grim or his brow so dark as it was when we turned from the scene of this investigation. We had walked several times up and down the lawn, neither Miss Stoner nor myself liking to break in upon his thoughts before he roused himself from his reverie.

"It is very essential, Miss Stoner," said he, "that you should absolutely follow my advice in every respect."

"I shall most certainly do so."

"The matter is too serious for any hesitation. Your life may depend upon your compliance. Now, in the first place, both my friend and I must spend the night in your room."

Both Miss Stoner and I gazed at him in astonishment.

"Yes, it must be so. Let me explain. I believe that that is the village inn over there?"

"Yes, that is the Crown."

"Very good. Your windows would be visible from there?"

"Certainly."

"You must confine yourself to your room, on pretense of a headache, when your stepfather comes back. Then when you hear him retire for the night, you must open the shutters of your window, undo the hasp, put your lamp there as a signal to us, and then withdraw quietly with everything which you are likely to want into the room which you used to occupy. I have no doubt that, in spite of the repairs, you could manage there for one night."

"Oh, yes, easily."

"The rest you will leave in our hands."

"But what will you do?"

"We shall spend the night in your room, and we shall investigate the cause of this noise which has disturbed you."

"I believe, Mr. Holmes, that you have already made up your mind," said Miss Stoner.

"Perhaps I have."

"Then, for pity's sake, tell me what was the cause of my sister's death."

"I should prefer to have clearer proofs before I speak."

"You can at least tell me whether my own thought is correct, and if she died from some sudden fright."

"No, I do not think so. I think that there was probably some more tangible cause. And now, Miss Stoner, we must leave you, for if Dr. Roylott returned and saw us, our journey would be in vain. Good-by, and be brave, for if you will do what I have told you, you may rest assured that we shall soon drive away the dangers that threaten you."

Sherlock Holmes and I had no difficulty in engaging a bedroom and sitting room at the Crown Inn. They were on the upper floor, and from our window we could command a view of the avenue gate and of the inhabited wing of Stoke Moran. At dusk we saw Dr. Grimesby Roylott drive past, and a few minutes later we saw a sudden light spring up at the manor house as the lamp was lit in one of the sitting rooms.

"Do you know, Watson," said Holmes, as we sat together in the gathering darkness, "I have really some scruples as to taking you tonight. There is a distinct element of danger."

"Can I be of assistance?"

"Your presence might be invaluable."

"Then I shall certainly come."

"It is very kind of you."

"You speak of danger. You have evidently seen more in these rooms than was visible to me."

"No, but I fancy that I may have deduced a little more. I imagine that you saw all that I did."

"I saw nothing remarkable save the bell rope, and what purpose that could answer I confess is more than I can imagine."

"You saw the ventilator, too?"

"Yes, but I do not think that it is such a very unusual thing to have a small opening

between two rooms. It was so small that a rat could hardly pass through."

"I knew that we should find a ventilator before ever we came to Stoke Moran."

"My dear Holmes!"

"Oh yes, I did. You remember in her statement she said that her sister could smell Dr. Roylott's cigar. Now, of course that suggested at once that there must be a communication between the two rooms. It could only be a small one, or it would have been remarked upon at the coroner's inquiry. I deduced a ventilator."

"But what harm can there be in that?"

"Well, there is at least a curious coincidence of dates. A ventilator is made, a cord is hung, and a lady who sleeps in the bed dies. Does not that strike you?"

"I cannot as yet see any connection."

"Did you observe anything very peculiar about that bed?"

"No."

"It was clamped to the floor. Did you ever see a bed fastened like that before?"

"I cannot say that I have."

"The lady could not move her bed. It must always be in the same relative position to the ventilator and to the rope—for so we may call it, since it was clearly never meant for a bell-pull."

"Holmes," I cried, "I seem to see dimly what you are hinting at! We are only just in time to prevent some subtle and horrible crime."

"Subtle enough and horrible enough. When a doctor does go wrong, he is the first of criminals. He has nerve and he has knowledge. This man strikes deep; but I think, Watson, that we shall be able to strike deeper still. But we shall have horrors enough before the night is over; for goodness' sake let us have a quiet pipe, and turn our minds for a few hours to something more cheerful."

About nine o'clock the lights at Stoke Moran were extinguished, and all was dark at the manor house. Two hours passed slowly away, and then, suddenly, just at the

stroke of eleven, a single bright light shone out in front of us.

"That is our signal," said Holmes, springing to his feet; "it comes from the middle window."

As we passed out, he exchanged a few words with the landlord, explaining that we were going on a late visit to an acquaintance, and that it was possible that we might spend the night there. A moment later we were out on the dark road, a chill wind blowing in our faces, and one yellow light twinkling in front of us through the gloom to guide us on our somber errand.

There was little difficulty in entering the grounds, for unrepaired breaches gaped in the old park wall. Making our way among the trees, we reached the lawn, crossed it, and were about to enter through the window, when out from a clump of laurel bushes there darted what seemed to be a hideous and distorted child, who threw itself upon the grass with writhing limbs and then ran swiftly across the lawn into the darkness.

"My God!" I whispered. "Did you see it?"

Holmes was for the moment as startled as I. His hand closed like a vise upon my wrist in his agitation. Then he broke into a low laugh, and put his lips to my ear.

"It is a nice household," he murmured. "That is the baboon."

I had forgotten the doctor's strange pets. There was a cheetah, too; perhaps we might find it upon our shoulders at any moment. I confess that I felt easier in my mind when, after following Holmes' example and slipping off my shoes, I found myself inside the bedroom. My companion noiselessly closed the shutters, moved the lamp onto the table, and cast his eyes round the room. All was as we had seen it in the daytime. Then creeping up to me and making a trumpet of his hand, he whispered into my ear again so gently that it was all that I could do to distinguish the words:

"The least sound would be fatal to our plans."

I nodded to show that I had heard.

"We must sit without a light. He would see it through the ventilator."

I nodded again.

"Do not go asleep! Your very life may depend upon it. Have your pistol ready in case we should need it. I will sit on the side of the bed, and you in that chair."

I took out my revolver and laid it on the corner of the table.

Holmes had brought up a long, thin cane and this he placed upon the bed beside him. By it he laid the box of matches and the stump of a candle. Then he turned down the lamp, and we were left in darkness.

How shall I ever forget that dreadful vigil? I could not hear a sound, not even the drawing of a breath, and yet I knew that my companion sat open-eyed, within a few feet of me, in the same state of nervous tension in which I was myself. The shutters cut off the least ray of light, and we waited in absolute darkness. From outside came the occasional cry of a night bird, and once at our very window a long-drawn, catlike whine, which told us that the cheetah was indeed at liberty. Far away we could hear the deep tones of the parish clock, which boomed out every quarter of an hour. How long they seemed, those quarters! Twelve struck, and one and two and three, and still we sat, waiting for whatever might befall.

Suddenly there was the momentary gleam of a light up in the direction of the ventilator, which vanished immediately, but was succeeded by a strong smell of burning oil and heated metal. Someone in the next room had lit a dark lantern.[16] I heard a sound of movement, and then all was silent, though the smell grew stronger. For half an hour I sat with straining ears. Then suddenly another sound became audible—a very gentle, soothing sound, like that of a small jet of steam escaping continually from a kettle. The instant that we heard it, Holmes sprang from the bed, struck a match, and lashed furiously with his cane at the bell-pull.

"You see it, Watson?" he yelled.

But I saw nothing. At the moment when Holmes struck the light I heard a low, clear whistle, but the sudden glare flashing into my weary eyes made it impossible for me to tell what it was at which my friend lashed so savagely. I could, however, see that his face was deadly pale, and filled with horror and loathing.

He had ceased to strike, and was gazing up at the ventilator, when suddenly there broke from the silence of the night the most horrible cry to which I have ever listened. It swelled up louder and louder, a hoarse yell of pain and fear and anger all mingled in the one dreadful shriek. They say that away down in the village, and even in the distant parsonage, that cry raised the sleepers from their beds. It struck cold to our hearts.

"What can it mean?" I gasped.

"It means that it is all over," Holmes answered. "And perhaps, after all, it is for the best. Take your pistol, and we will enter Dr. Roylott's room."

With a grave face he lit the lamp and led the way down the corridor. Twice he struck at the chamber door without any reply from within. Then he turned the handle and entered, I at his heels, with the cocked pistol in my hand.

It was a singular sight which met our eyes. On the table stood a dark lantern with the shutter half open, throwing a brilliant beam of light upon the iron safe, the door of which was ajar. Beside this table, on the wooden chair, sat Dr. Grimesby Roylott, clad in a long gray dressing gown, his bare ankles protruding beneath, and his feet thrust into red heelless Turkish slippers. Across his lap lay the short stock with the long lash which we had noticed during the day. His chin was cocked upward and his eyes were fixed in a dreadful, rigid stare at

16. ***dark lantern,*** lantern whose light can be hidden by a cover of dark glass.

the corner of the ceiling. Round his brow he had a peculiar yellow band, with brownish speckles, which seemed to be bound tightly round his head. As we entered, he made neither sound nor motion.

"The band! the speckled band!" whispered Holmes.

I took a step forward. In an instant his strange headgear began to move, and there reared itself from among his hair the squat diamond-shaped head and puffed neck of a loathsome serpent.

"It is a swamp adder!" cried Holmes; "the deadliest snake in India. He has died within ten seconds of being bitten. In truth, the schemer falls into the pit which he digs for another. Let us thrust this creature back into its den, and we can then remove Miss Stoner to some place of shelter, and let the county police know what has happened."

As he spoke, he drew the dog whip swiftly from the dead man's lap, and throwing the noose round the reptile's neck, he drew it from its horrid perch and threw it into the iron safe, which he closed upon it.

Such are the true facts of the death of Dr. Grimesby Roylott, of Stoke Moran. It is not necessary that I should prolong a narrative which has already run to too great a length, by telling how we broke the sad news to the terrified girl, how we conveyed her by the morning train to the care of her good aunt at Harrow, of how the slow process of official inquiry came to the conclusion that the doctor met his fate while indiscreetly playing with a dangerous pet. The little which I had yet to learn of the case was told me by Sherlock Holmes as we traveled back next day.

"I had," said he, "come to an entirely erroneous conclusion, which shows, my dear Watson, how dangerous it always is to reason from insufficient data. The presence of the gypsies, and the use of the word *band,* which was used by the poor girl, no doubt to explain the appearance which she had caught a hurried glimpse of by the light of her match, were sufficient to put me upon an entirely wrong scent. I can only claim the merit that I instantly reconsidered my position when, however, it became clear to me that whatever danger threatened an occupant of the room could not come either from the window or the door.

"My attention was speedily drawn, as I have already remarked, to this ventilator, and to the bell rope which hung down to the bed. The discovery that this was a dummy, and that the bed was clamped to the floor, instantly gave rise to the suspicion that the rope was there as a bridge for something passing through the hole and coming to the bed. The idea of a snake instantly occurred to me, and when I coupled it with my knowledge that the doctor was furnished with a supply of creatures from India, I felt that I was probably on the right track. The idea of using a form of poison which could not possibly be discovered by any chemical test was just such a one as would occur to a clever and ruthless man who had had an Eastern training. The rapidity with which such a poison would take effect would also, from his point of view, be an advantage. It would be a sharp-eyed coroner, indeed, who could distinguish the two little dark punctures which would show where the poison fangs had done their work. Then I thought of the whistle. Of course he must recall the snake before the morning light revealed it to the victim. He had trained it, probably by the use of the milk which we saw, to return to him when summoned. He would put it through this ventilator at the hour that he thought best, with the certainty that it would crawl down the rope and land on the bed. It might or might not bite the occupant; perhaps she might escape every night for a week, but sooner or later she must fall a victim.

"I had come to these conclusions before ever I had entered his room. An inspection of his chair showed me that he had been in the habit of standing on it, which of course would be necessary in order that he should reach the ventilator. The sight of the safe, the saucer of milk, and the loop of whipcord was enough to finally dispel any doubts which may have remained. The metallic clang heard by Miss Stoner was obviously caused by her stepfather hastily closing the door of his safe upon its terrible occupant. Having once made up my mind, you know the steps which I took in order to put the matter to the proof. I heard the creature hiss, and I instantly lit the light and attacked it."

"With the result of driving it through the ventilator."

"And also with the result of causing it to turn upon its master at the other side. Some of the blows of my cane came home, and roused its snakish temper, so that it flew upon the first person it saw. In this way I am no doubt indirectly responsible for Dr. Grimesby Roylott's death, and I cannot say that it is likely to weigh very heavily upon my conscience."

COULD THIS REALLY HAVE HAPPENED?

Many men have devoted the better part of their lives to careful research covering the life and cases of the most famous of all fictional detectives—Sherlock Holmes. For example, Dr. W. T. Williams, a British naturalist, made a detailed study of the animals which Holmes encountered in his various cases, and his findings concerning the snake in "The Adventure of the Speckled Band" are among the most interesting.

Holmes describes this snake as " . . . a swamp adder, the deadliest snake in India." Naturalists today know nothing about such a species, so they have tried to classify the reptile by Holmes' descriptions of its behavior, including its response to Dr. Roylott's low whistle, fondness for milk, and nocturnal jaunts up and down the bellrope. From the scientific point of view these actions seem quite impossible. In the first place, snakes are deaf, and in the second, they are not fond of milk; therefore, responses to these two stimuli are improbable. Even more unbelievable is the bellrope incident. Even if a snake were forced to climb down such a rope, there are few who could be expected to climb up again, even with the greatest amount of training.

After extensive research, Dr. Williams and other naturalists tentatively decided that this snake was an ordinary Indian cobra. The Indian cobra is active, one of the more intelligent species, and could *possibly* climb up a bellrope. The cobra also possesses a deadly venom and, in accordance with Watson's statement "there reared itself . . . the squat diamond-shaped head of a loathsome serpent," the Indian cobra rears up almost vertically when aroused.

The information which these researchers have gathered does not satisfactorily answer all of the scientific questions or rule out the possibility that this rope-climbing snake could have been one of several other species. The mystery of the speckled band still exists!

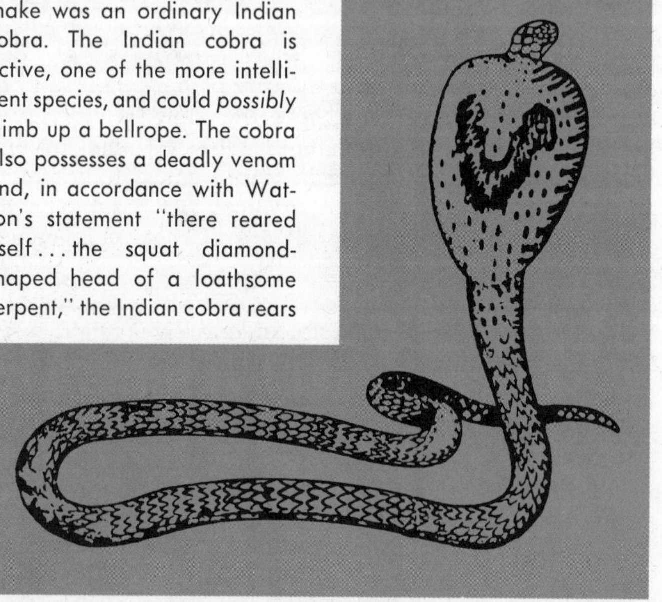

WHAT DO YOU SAY?

1. What were the first examples of Holmes' sharp powers of observation?

2. (a) What specific recent incident in Helen Stoner's life caused her to seek help from the detective? *(b)* What connection did this recent incident have with her sister's death two years previously?

3. (a) How did Holmes go about reassuring himself that his deduction as to Dr. Roylott's motive for the crime was correct? *(b)* What particular clue, furnished by Miss Stoner, misled Holmes at first?

4. (a) Why was it important that Holmes know the exact setting for the crime? *(b)* Is the setting usually important in solving a crime? Why?

5. (a) One test of a good detective story is the willingness of the author to play fair with the reader by giving him all the evidence needed to solve the crime—the same evidence that is available to the detective. Is all of the necessary evidence presented to the reader in this story? *(b)* Were you able to solve the crime? If so, at what stage?

AUTHOR'S CRAFT

Plot

One author writing about short stories has said, "When a story involves a conflict between two opposing forces, it is said to have a ***plot.***" Almost every short story has some kind of conflict. So you might conclude, and correctly, that most short stories have plots. However, not all short stories have plots developed to the same degree. One short story may have so little plot that you may wonder if it is really a story. Many modern short stories are of this type. A second story may have a very definite plot, that is, an easily recognizable series of events leading to a high point, or ***climax,*** after which the major problem is resolved. Which of these two kinds of stories is "The Adventure of the Speckled Band"?

Every good mystery or detective story, including "The Adventure of the Speckled Band," has a well-defined plot with considerable suspense, which is the chief source of interest and pleasure in this type of story. Can you outline the plot, that is, write down in simple statements all the major actions or events in A. Conan Doyle's story?

In addition to creating an excellent plot, Doyle has increased interest and believability in his stories by having them told, not by the detective himself, but by a narrator. Why do you think the author chose to have his stories told in this way? What are the advantages in using a narrator? What are the qualities of the narrator who tells the Sherlock Holmes stories?

KNOW YOUR WORDS

Prefixes

The prefixes "in-," "un-," "dis-," and "non-" often carry the meaning of ***not*** or ***the opposite of.*** For example: ***inaction*** is the opposite of ***action; undressed*** is the opposite of ***dressed;*** etc. Add one of these four negative prefixes to one word in each sentence below so that the sentence will have the opposite of its present meaning.

1. He was contented in his new job.
2. His voice was audible above the drone of the motors.
3. The new drug he bought was toxic.
4. I am grateful for all you have done.

SIR ARTHUR CONAN DOYLE

Arthur Conan Doyle, author of some sixty books, hoped to be remembered for his novels, but he is best known as the creator of one of the most popular fictional characters in literature. Sherlock Holmes was first presented to the public in 1887 in a novel, ***A Study in Scarlet.*** However, the detective did not become famous until the publication in 1891 of ***The Adventures of Sherlock Holmes,*** which ran serially in a British magazine, a complete story appearing in each issue. Recognizing the success of these stories, Arthur Conan Doyle gave up the medical career for which he had been educated and devoted his entire time to writing. His written defense of England's position in the Boer War in South Africa was rewarded by knighthood, and in 1902 Arthur Conan Doyle became Sir Arthur Conan Doyle. Although he eventually stopped writing detective stories because he found them "tiresome and of little value," his millions of readers continue to find them exciting and satisfying.

The Cask of Amontillado

Edgar Allan Poe, the creator of the short story in America, believed that there should not be one word in a short story that does not contribute to the one final effect of the story on the reader. Poe's own skill in creating a "single effect" is clearly shown in this story.

The thousand injuries of Fortunato I had borne as I best could; but when he ventured upon insult, I vowed revenge. You, who so well know the nature of my soul, will not suppose, however, that I gave utterance to a threat. *At length* I would be avenged; this was a point definitively settled—but the very definitiveness with which it was resolved precluded the idea of risk. I must not only punish, but punish with impunity. A wrong is unredressed when retribution overtakes its redresser. It is equally unredressed when the avenger fails to make himself felt as such to him who has done the wrong.

It must be understood that neither by word nor deed had I given Fortunato cause to doubt my good-will. I continued, as was my wont, to smile in his face, and he did not perceive that my smile *now* was at the thought of his immolation.

He had a weak point—this Fortunato—although in other regards he was a man to be respected and even feared. He prided himself on his connoisseur-ship in wine. Few Italians have the true virtuoso spirit.[1] For the most part their enthusiasm is adopted to suit the time and opportunity—to practice imposture upon the British and Austrian millionaires. In painting and gemmary[2] Fortunato, like his countrymen, was a quack—but in the matter of old wines he was sincere. In this respect I did not differ from him materially; I was skillful in the Italian vintages myself, and bought largely whenever I could.

It was about dusk, one evening during the supreme madness of the carnival season, that I encountered my friend. He accosted me with excessive warmth, for he had been drinking much. The man wore motley. He had on a tight-fitting parti-striped dress, and his head was surmounted by the conical cap and bells. I was so pleased to see him that I thought I should never have done wringing his hand.

I said to him, "My dear Fortunato, you are luckily met. How remarkably well you are looking today! But I have received a pipe[3] of what passes for Amontillado, and I have my doubts."

"How?" said he. "Amontillado? A pipe? Impossible! And in the middle of the carnival!"

"I have my doubts," I replied; "and I was silly enough to pay the full Amontillado price without consulting you in the matter. You were not to be found, and I was fearful of losing a bargain."

"Amontillado!"

"I have my doubts."

"Amontillado!"

"And I must satisfy them."

"Amontillado!"

---

1. ***virtuoso spirit,*** ability to judge works of art skillfully.
2. ***gemmary,*** the art of cutting fine gems or setting them in jewelry.
3. ***pipe,*** a large cask.

"As you are engaged, I am on my way to Luchesi. If anyone has a critical turn, it is he. He will tell me—"

"Luchesi cannot tell Amontillado from Sherry."

"And yet some fools will have it that his taste is a match for your own."

"Come, let us go."

"Whither?"

"To your vaults."

"My friend, no; I will not impose upon your good nature. I perceive you have an engagement. Luchesi—"

"I have no engagement—come."

"My friend, no. It is not the engagement, but the severe cold with which I perceive you are afflicted. The vaults are insufferably damp. They are incrusted with niter."

"Let us go, nevertheless. The cold is merely nothing. Amontillado! You have been imposed upon. And as for Luchesi, he cannot distinguish Sherry from Amontillado."

Thus speaking, Fortunato possessed himself of my arm. Putting on a mask of black silk, and drawing a roquelaire[4] closely about my person, I suffered him to hurry me to my palazzo.[5]

There were no attendants at home; they had absconded to make merry in honor of the time. I had told them that I should not return until the morning, and had given them explicit orders not to stir from the house. These orders were sufficient, I well knew, to insure their immediate disappearance, one and all, as soon as my back was turned.

I took from their sconces two flambeaus, and giving one to Fortunato, bowed him through several suites of rooms to the archway that led into the vaults. I passed down a long and winding staircase, requesting him to be cautious as he followed. We came at length to the foot of the descent, and stood together on the damp ground of the catacombs of the Montresors.

The gait of my friend was unsteady, and the bells upon his cap jingled as he strode.

"The pipe," said he.

"It is farther on," said I; "but observe the white web-work which gleams from these cavern walls."

He turned toward me, and looked into my eyes with two filmy orbs that distilled the rheum of intoxication.

"Niter?" he asked at length.

"Niter," I replied. "How long have you had that cough?"

"Ugh! ugh! ugh!—ugh! ugh! ugh!—ugh! ugh! ugh!—ugh! ugh! ugh!—ugh! ugh! ugh!"

My poor friend found it impossible to reply for many minutes.

"It is nothing," he said, at last.

"Come," I said, with decision, "we will go back; your health is precious. You are rich, respected, admired, beloved; you are happy, as once I was. You are a man to be missed. For me it is no matter. We will go back; you will be ill, and I cannot be responsible. Besides, there is Luchesi—"

"Enough," he said; "the cough is a mere nothing; it will not kill me. I shall not die of a cough."

"True—true," I replied; "and, indeed, I had no intention of alarming you unnecessarily—but you should use all proper caution. A draft of this Medoc will defend us from the damps."

Here I knocked off the neck of a bottle which I drew from a long row of its fellows that lay upon the mold.

"Drink," I said, presenting him the wine.

He raised it to his lips with a leer. He paused and nodded to me familiarly, while his bells jingled.

"I drink," he said "to the buried that repose around us."

"And I to your long life."

He again took my arm, and we proceeded. "These vaults," he said, "are extensive."

"The Montresors," I replied, "were a great and numerous family."

"I forget your arms."

---

4. roquelaire, short cloak. *5. palazzo,* home of a wealthy person.

"A huge human foot d'or, in a field azure[6]; the foot crushes a serpent rampant whose fangs are embedded in the heel."

"And the motto?"

"*Nemo me impune lacessit.*"[7]

"Good!" he said.

The wine sparkled in his eyes and the bells jingled. My own fancy grew warm with the Medoc. We had passed through walls of piled bones, with casks and puncheons intermingling, into the inmost recesses of the catacombs. I paused again, and this time I made bold to seize Fortunato by an arm above the elbow.

"The niter!" I said; "see, it increases. It hangs like moss upon the vaults. We are below the river's bed. The drops of moisture trickle among the bones. Come, we will go back ere it is too late. Your cough—"

"It is nothing," he said; "let us go on. But first, another draft of the Medoc."

I broke and reached him a flagon of De Grave. He emptied it at a breath. His eyes flashed with a fierce light. He laughed and threw the bottle upwards with a gesticulation I did not understand.

I looked at him in surprise. He repeated the movement—a grotesque one.

"You do not comprehend?" he said.

"Not I," I replied.

"Then you are not of the brotherhood."

"How?"

"You are not of the masons."

"Yes, yes," I said, "yes, yes."

"You? Impossible! A mason?"

"A mason," I replied.

"A sign," he said.

"It is this," I answered, producing a trowel from beneath the folds of my roquelaire.

"You jest," he exclaimed, recoiling a few paces. "But let us proceed to the Amontillado."

"Be it so," I said, replacing the tool beneath the cloak, and again offering him my arm. He leaned upon it heavily. We continued our route in search of the Amontillado. We passed through a range of low arches, descended, passed on, and, descending again, arrived at a deep crypt, in which the foulness of the air caused our flambeaus rather to glow than flame.

At the most remote end of the crypt there appeared another less spacious. Its walls had been lined with human remains, piled to the vault overhead, in the fashion of the great catacombs of Paris. Three sides of this interior crypt were still ornamented in this manner. From the fourth the bones had been thrown down, and lay promiscuously upon the earth, forming at one point a mound of some size. Within the wall thus exposed by the displacing of the bones, we perceived a still interior recess, in depth about four feet, in width three, in height six or seven. It seemed to have been constructed for no especial use within itself, but formed merely the interval between two of the colossal supports of the roof of the catacombs, and was backed by one of their circumscribing walls of solid granite.

It was in vain that Fortunato, uplifting his dull torch, endeavored to pry into the depth of the recess. Its termination the feeble light did not enable us to see.

"Proceed," I said; "herein is the Amontillado. As for Luchesi—"

"He is an ignoramus," interrupted my friend, as he stepped unsteadily forward, while I followed immediately at his heels. In an instant he had reached the extremity of the niche, and finding his progress arrested by the rock, stood stupidly bewildered. A moment more and I had fettered him to the granite. In its surface were two iron staples, distant from each other about two feet, horizontally. From one of these depended a short chain, from the other a padlock. Throwing the links about his waist, it was but the work of a few seconds to secure it. He was too much astounded to resist. Withdrawing the key, I stepped back from the recess.

---

6. *foot d'or...azure,* golden foot against a blue background. 7. ***Nemo me impune lacessit*** (nē′mō mē im pū′nē la kes′sit). No one safely challenges me. [*Latin*]

"Pass your hand," I said, "over the wall; you cannot help feeling the niter. Indeed it is *very* damp. Once more let me *implore* you to return. No? Then I must positively leave you. But I must first render you all the little attentions in my power."

"The Amontillado!" ejaculated my friend, not yet recovered from his astonishment.

"True," I replied; "the Amontillado."

As I said these words, I busied myself among the pile of bones of which I have before spoken. Throwing them aside, I soon uncovered a quantity of building stone and mortar. With these materials and with the aid of my trowel, I began vigorously to wall up the entrance of the niche.

I had scarcely laid the first tier of the masonry when I discovered that the intoxication of Fortunato had in a great measure worn off. The earliest indication I had of this was a low moaning cry from the depth of the recess. It was *not* the cry of a drunken man. There was then a long and obstinate silence. I laid the second tier, and the third, and the fourth; and then I heard the furious vibrations of the chain. The noise lasted for several minutes, during which, that I might hearken to it with the more satisfaction, I ceased my labors and sat down upon the bones. When at last the clanking subsided, I resumed the trowel, and finished without interruption the fifth, the sixth, and the seventh tier. The wall was now nearly upon a level with my breast. I again paused, and holding the flambeaus over the mason work, threw a few feeble rays upon the figure within.

A succession of loud and shrill screams, bursting suddenly from the throat of the chained form, seemed to thrust me violently back. For a brief moment I hesitated —I trembled. Unsheathing my rapier, I began to grope with it about the recess; but the thought of an instant reassured me. I placed my hand upon the solid fabric of the catacombs, and felt satisfied. I reapproached the wall. I replied to the yells of him who clamored. I re-echoed—I aided—I surpassed them in volume and in strength. I did this, and the clamorer grew still.

It was now midnight, and my task was drawing to a close. I had completed the eighth, the ninth, and the tenth tier. I had finished a portion of the last and the eleventh; there remained but a single stone to be fitted and plastered in. I struggled with its weight; I placed it partially in its destined position. But now there came from out the niche a low laugh that erected the hairs upon my head. It was succeeded by a sad voice, which I had difficulty in recognizing as that of the noble Fortunato. The voice said—

"Ha! ha! ha!—he! he! he!—a very good joke indeed—an excellent jest. We will have many a rich laugh about it at the palazzo—he! he! he!—over our wine—he! he! he!"

"The Amontillado!" I said.

"He! he! he!—he! he! he!—yes, the Amontillado. But is it not getting late? Will not they be awaiting us at the palazzo—the Lady Fortunato and the rest? Let us be gone."

"Yes," I said "let us be gone."

"For the love of God, Montresor."

"Yes," I said "for the love of God."

But to these words I hearkened in vain for a reply. I grew impatient. I called aloud—

"Fortunato!"

No answer. I called again—

"Fortunato!"

No answer still. I thrust a torch through the remaining aperture and let it fall within. There came forth in return only a jingling of the bells. My heart grew sick—on account of the dampness of the catacombs. I hastened to make an end of my labor. I forced the last stone into its position; I plastered it up. Against the new masonry I reerected the old rampart of bones. For the half of a century no mortal has disturbed them. *In pace requiescat.*[8]

8. ***In pace requiescat*** (in pa′ke re′kwi es′kat). May he rest in peace. [*Latin*]

"EDGARS"

Each spring throngs of moviegoers and television stay-at-homes become interested in which motion pictures and actors will receive "Oscars," or which television shows and stars will be awarded "Emmies." The climactic point arrives when the awards in each category are distributed, and the happy winners clutch their coveted prizes.

Meanwhile, in New York City, a distinguished group of the leading mystery writers in America meet for the same purpose—to bestow their annual awards, "Edgars," upon writers in various mystery categories for their outstanding accomplishments. These writers are members of the Mystery Writers of America, a nonprofit organization founded in 1945 to promote and improve the status of mystery writers and make available to them any helpful or rewarding information. Their appropriate slogan is—"Crime does not pay—enough!" The master of the mystery story, Edgar Allan Poe, has been adopted by this organization as their "patron saint," and the annual awards dinner is held in the spring, on, or near, the approximate anniversary of his pioneer mystery thriller "The Murders in the Rue Morgue." The "Edgars," ten-inch ceramic busts of Poe, are awarded in the writing categories, and the "Ravens," ceramic replicas of Poe's famous poetic creation, are awarded in related categories of the mystery field, such as publishing and illustrating.

PHOTOS MYSTERY WRITERS OF AMERICA

Nominations are made by ballots from mystery writers across the country, critics, other authorities, and, finally, by the Mystery Writers of America Awards Committee. The names of the winners are kept in deepest secrecy until the dinner. The various categories in which "Edgars" are presented include: Best Novel, Best First Novel, Best Short Story, Best Motion Picture, Best Hour and Half-Hour Television Shows, and Best Juvenile Mystery.

The publicity and prestige of the "Edgars" are equal to those of the motion picture "Oscars," and the distinguished audiences of both look forward to future award presentations.

WHAT DO YOU SAY?

1. What two conditions does Montresor say must be fulfilled for a satisfactory revenge? Does he succeed in fulfilling these conditions?

2. Point out the contrast between Montresor's revenge and "the supreme madness of the carnival season."

3. *(a)* Are the evils which we are told were committed by Fortunato ever explained? *(b)* Do you feel that Fortunato is a wicked man? *(c)* For which character do you have more sympathy? Why?

4. What is particularly appropriate about the coat of arms of the Montresor family?

5. (a) At what point does Montresor indicate a brief feeling of remorse for his actions? *(b)* How does he explain this feeling?

6. (a) What is the "single effect" that Poe wished to produce in this story? *(b)* How does telling the story in the first person add to this effect?

AUTHOR'S CRAFT

Setting

Whether or not you have ever taken part in a play, you know that a play always has a ***setting.*** Probably you have thought of the setting as the background against which the play takes place —***where*** and ***when*** the action occurs. Just as in a play, a short story has a background, a ***where*** and a ***when.*** But often the setting of a short story as well as of a play is much more important than just a place and time for the plot to unfold. For example, the setting of a story may be used to help create a particular emotion or response in the reader. This technique was used frequently and successfully by Edgar Allan Poe. Poe stated that his aim in many of his stories was "to achieve in the reader a powerful emotional effect." To do this, Poe used every possible detail of setting to create an atmosphere which would arouse a particular emotion in the reader. What atmosphere has Poe created in "The Cask of Amontillado"? What emotion is aroused? List some of the details of setting he has used to create the atmosphere.

What does the setting of "The Adventure of the Speckled Band" contribute to that story? How important is it to the plot development? Is the setting used to create an atmosphere or does it help shape events in the plot?

Irony

Also to create his single impression, Poe has used with great effectiveness a device called ***irony.*** The kind of irony you probably are most familiar with is ***verbal irony.*** Verbal irony means saying the opposite of what you really mean or think. The morning you overslept, slipped on the rug at the top of the stairs, and then said to your family, "I can tell this is going to be a wonderful day," you were using verbal irony or being ***ironical.*** In "The Cask of Amontillado" when Montresor implores Fortunato to turn back because of his health, Montresor is being ironical. Explain this example of irony. What other ironical remarks can you find in Poe's story?

A second kind of irony is the irony of ***situation*** or ***fate.*** When an event contrary to what would naturally be expected happens, the event or situation is ironical. If, for example, you were to go on an expedition to photograph a rare mountain goat, spend many days looking for one, finally use up your last roll of film on other subjects, and on your way back come face to face with three mountain goats, you would be experiencing the irony of fate or situation. In "The Cask of Amontillado" is the fact that Montresor succeeds in walling up Fortunato ironical? Why or why not? If a part of the vault had caved in and buried Montresor, would this have been ironical? Explain. In "The Adventure of the Speckled Band" what was ironical about the fate of Dr. Roylott?

EDGAR ALLAN POE

Shortly before his tragic death in 1849, at the age of forty, Edgar Allan Poe wrote, "I do believe God gave me a spark of genius, but he quenched it in misery." Both the genius and the misery are reflected in Poe's stories and poems.

Born of actor parents who died before he was three years old, Edgar was taken in by the wealthy Allan family of Virginia. His moodiness as a boy and the early indulgence of his foster parents may have been responsible for his later misbehavior which caused him to be withdrawn or expelled from both the University of Virginia and West Point. After his dismissal from West Point for gross neglect of duty, Poe, also rejected by the Allans, turned to journalism. Besides publishing independently when he could afford it, Poe was employed at various times on the staff of several literary magazines. Although his work was successful, there was little money, and he could not continue to hold a job because of his excessive drinking and general poor health. When Poe was twenty-six, he married his young cousin Virginia, who inspired some of his most beautiful poetry. He continued to write, free-lancing, editing, and acting as literary critic, a new rôle in American literary circles, but he could not make enough money to meet the heavy expenses of his own illness and his wife's. Virginia died in poverty after a long illness, and two years later Poe himself died.

Poe was one of the first American writers to be received with enthusiasm in Europe, and he had much influence on both American and European authors. Among his most familiar short stories are "The Telltale Heart," "The Pit and the Pendulum," "A Descent into the Maelstrom," "The Gold Bug," and "The Purloined Letter."

Bargain

A. B. GUTHRIE, Jr.

ORNING IN A MINING CAMP" BY OSCAR E. BERNINGHAUS. COURTESY C. R. SMITH

Often the outcome of a conflict depends on the use of brain rather than brawn. You saw this theory in operation in the story by Edgar Allan Poe. You will recognize it again in this story. As Mr. Baumer, the central character in "Bargain," says, "Is good to know to read."

Mr. Baumer and I had closed the Moon Dance Mercantile Company and were walking to the post office, and he had a bunch of bills in his hand ready to mail. There wasn't anyone or anything much on the street because it was suppertime. A buckboard and a saddle horse were tied at Hirschs' rack, and a rancher in a wagon rattled for home ahead of us, the sound of his going fading out as he prodded his team. Freighter Slade stood alone in front of the Moon Dance Saloon, maybe wondering whether to have one more before going to supper. People said he could hold a lot without showing it except in being ornerier even than usual.

Mr. Baumer didn't see him until he was almost on him, and then he stopped and fingered through the bills until he found the right one. He stepped up to Slade and held it out.

Slade said, "What's this, Dutchie?"

Mr. Baumer had to tilt his head up to talk to him. "You know vat it is."

Slade just said, "Yeah?" You never could tell from his face what went on inside his skull. He had dark skin and shallow cheeks and a thick-growing mustache that fell over the corners of his mouth.

"It is a bill," Mr. Baumer said. "I tell you before it is a bill. For twenty-vun dollars and fifty cents."

"You know what I do with bills, don't you, Dutchie?" Slade asked.

Mr. Baumer didn't answer the question. He said, "For merchandise."

Slade took the envelope from Mr. Baumer's hand and squeezed it up in his fist and let it drop on the plank sidewalk. Not saying anything, he reached down and took Mr. Baumer's nose between the knuckles of his fingers and twisted it up into his eyes. That was all. That was all at the time. Slade half turned and slouched to the door of the bar and let himself in. Some men were laughing in there.

Mr. Baumer stooped and picked up the bill and put it on top of the rest and smoothed it out for mailing. When he straightened up I could see tears in his eyes from having his nose screwed around.

He didn't say anything to me, and I didn't say anything to him, being so much younger and feeling embarrassed for him. He went into the post office and slipped the bills in the slot, and we walked on home together. At the last, at the crossing where I had to leave him, he remembered to say, "Better study, Al. Is good to know to read and write and figure." I guess he felt he had to push me a little, my father being dead.

I said, "Sure. See you after school tomorrow"—which he knew I would anyway. I had been working in the store for him during the summer and after classes ever since pneumonia took my dad off.

Three of us worked there regularly, Mr. Baumer, of course, and me and Colly Coleman, who knew enough to drive the delivery wagon but wasn't much help around the store except for carrying orders out to the rigs[1] at the hitchpost and handling heavy things like the whisky barrel at the back of the store which Mr. Baumer sold quarts and gallons out of.

The store carried quite a bit of stuff—sugar and flour and dried fruits and canned goods and such on one side and yard goods

1. ***rigs,*** carriages with their horses.

and coats and caps and aprons and the like of that on the other, besides kerosene and bran and buckets and linoleum and pitchforks in the storehouse at the rear—but it wasn't a big store like Hirsch Brothers up the street. Never would be, people guessed, going on to say, with a sort of slow respect, that it would have gone under long ago if Mr. Baumer hadn't been half mule and half beaver. He had started the store just two years before and, the way things were, worked himself close to death.

He was at the high desk at the end of the grocery counter when I came in the next afternoon. He had an eyeshade on and black sateen protectors on his forearms, and his pencil was in his hand instead of behind his ear and his glasses were roosted on the nose that Slade had twisted. He didn't hear me open and close the door or hear my feet as I walked back to him, and I saw he wasn't doing anything with the pencil but holding it over paper. I stood and studied him for a minute, seeing a small, stooped man with a little paunch bulging through his unbuttoned vest. He was a man you wouldn't remember from meeting once. There was nothing in his looks to set itself in your mind unless maybe it was his chin, which was a small, pink hill in the gentle plain of his face.

While I watched him, he lifted his hand and felt carefully of his nose. Then he saw me. His eyes had that kind of mistiness that seems to go with age or illness, though he wasn't really old or sick, either. He brought his hand down quickly and picked up the pencil, but he saw I still was looking at the nose, and finally he sighed and said, "That Slade."

Just the sound of the name brought Slade to my eye. I saw him slouched in front of the bar, and I saw him and his string coming down the grade from the buttes, the wheel horses held snug and the rest lined out pretty, and then the string[2] leveling off and Slade's whip lifting hair from a horse that wasn't up in the collar. I had heard it said that Slade could make a horse scream with that whip. Slade's name wasn't Freighter, of course. Our town had nicknamed him that because that was what he was.

"I don't think it's any good to send him a bill, Mr. Baumer," I said. "He can't even read."

"He could pay yet."

"He don't pay anybody," I said.

"I think he hate me," Mr. Baumer went on. "That is the thing. He hate me for coming not from this country. I come here, sixteen years old, and learn to read and write, and I make a business, and so I think he hate me."

"He hates everybody."

Mr. Baumer shook his head. "But not to pinch the nose. Not to call Dutchie."

The side door squeaked open, but it was only Colly Coleman coming in from a trip so I said, "Excuse me, Mr. Baumer, but you shouldn't have trusted him in the first place."

"I know," he answered, looking at me with his misty eyes. "A man make mistakes. I think some do not trust him, so he will pay me because I do. And I do not know him well then. He only came back to town three-four months ago, from being away since before I go into business."

"People who knew him before could have told you," I said.

"A man make mistakes," he explained again.

"It's not my business, Mr. Baumer, but I would forget the bill."

His eyes rested on my face for a long minute, as if they didn't see me but the problem itself. He said, "It is not twenty-vun dollars and fifty cents now, Al. It is not that any more."

"What is it?"

He took a little time to answer. Then he brought his two hands up as if to help him shape the words. "It is the thing. You see, it is the thing."

---

2. *string,* a group of horses driven in single or double file.

I wasn't quite sure what he meant.

He took his pencil from behind the ear where he had put it and studied the point of it. "That Slade. He steal whisky and call it evaporation. He sneak things from his load. A thief, he is. And too big for me."

I said, "I got no time for him, Mr. Baumer, but I guess there never was a freighter didn't steal whisky. That's what I hear."

It was true, too. From the railroad to Moon Dance was fifty miles and a little better—a two-day haul in good weather, heck knew how long in bad. Any freight string bound home with a load had to lie out at least one night. When a freighter had his stock tended to and maybe a little fire going against the dark, he'd tackle a barrel of whisky or of grain alcohol[3] if he had one aboard, consigned to Hirsch Brothers or Mr. Baumer's or the Moon Dance Saloon or the Gold Leaf Bar. He'd drive a hoop out of place, bore a little hole with a nail or bit and draw off what he wanted. Then he'd plug the hole with a whittled peg and pound the hoop back. That was evaporation. Nobody complained much. With freighters you generally took what they gave you, within reason.

"Moore steals it, too," I told Mr. Baumer. Moore was Mr. Baumer's freighter.

"Yah," he said, and that was all, but I stood there for a minute, thinking there might be something more. I could see thought swimming in his eyes, above that little hill of chin. Then a customer came in, and I had to go wait on him.

Nothing happened for a month, nothing between Mr. Baumer and Slade, that is, but fall drew on toward winter and the first flight of ducks headed south and Mr. Baumer hired Miss Lizzie Webb to help with the just-beginning Christmas trade, and here it was, the first week in October, and he and I walked up the street again with the monthly bills. He always sent them out. I guess he had to. A bigger store, like Hirschs', would wait on the ranchers until their beef or wool went to market.

Up to a point things looked and happened almost the same as they had before, so much the same that I had the crazy feeling I was going through that time again. There was a wagon and a rig tied up at Hirschs' rack and a saddle horse standing hipshot[4] in front of the harness shop. A few more people were on the street now, not many, and lamps had been lit against the shortened day.

It was dark enough that I didn't make out Slade right away. He was just a figure that came out of the yellow wash of light from the Moon Dance Saloon and stood on the board walk and with his head made the little motion of spitting. Then I recognized the lean, raw shape of him and the muscles flowing down into the sloped shoulders, and in the settling darkness I filled the picture in—the dark skin and the flat cheeks and the peevish eyes and the mustache growing rank.

There was Slade and here was Mr. Baumer with his bills and here I was, just as before, just like in the second go-round of a bad dream. I felt like turning back, being embarrassed and half scared by trouble even when it wasn't mine. Please, I said to myself, don't stop, Mr. Baumer! Don't bite off anything! Please, shortsighted the way you are, don't catch sight of him at all! I held up and stepped around behind Mr. Baumer and came up on the outside so as to be between him and Slade where maybe I'd cut off his view.

But it wasn't any use. All along I think I knew it was no use, not the praying or the walking between or anything. The act had to play itself out.

Mr. Baumer looked across the front of me and saw Slade and hesitated in his step and came to a stop. Then in his slow, business way, his chin held firm against his mouth, he began fingering through the bills, squinting to make out the names. Slade had

---

3. grain alcohol, a liquid made from grain and used in intoxicating beverages, medicine, etc. *4. hipshot,* with one hip lower than the other.

turned and was watching him, munching on a cud of tobacco like a bull waiting.

"You look, Al," Mr. Baumer said without lifting his face from the bills. "I cannot see so good."

So I looked, and while I was looking Slade must have moved. The next I knew Mr. Baumer was staggering ahead, the envelopes spilling out of his hands. There had been a thump, the clap of a heavy hand swung hard on his back.

Slade said, "Haryu, Dutchie?"

Mr. Baumer caught his balance and turned around, the bills he had trampled shining white between them and, at Slade's feet, the hat that Mr. Baumer had stumbled out from under.

Slade picked up the hat and scuffed through the bills and held it out. "Cold to be goin' without a sky-piece," he said.

Mr. Baumer hadn't spoken a word. The lampshine from inside the bar caught his eyes, and in them it seemed to me a light came and went as anger and the uselessness of it took turns in his head.

Two men had come up on us and stood watching. One of them was Angus McDonald, who owned the Ranchers' Bank, and the other was Dr. King. He had his bag in his hand.

Two others were drifting up, but I didn't have time to tell who. The light came in Mr. Baumer's eyes, and he took a step ahead and swung. I could have hit harder myself. The first landed on Slade's cheek without hardly so much as jogging his head, but it let hell loose in the man. I didn't know he could move so fast. He slid in like a practiced fighter and let Mr. Baumer have it full in the face.

Mr. Baumer slammed over on his back, but he wasn't out. He started lifting himself. Slade leaped ahead and brought a boot heel down on the hand he was lifting himself by. I heard meat and bone under that heel and saw Mr. Baumer fall back and try to roll away.

Things had happened so fast that not until then did anyone have a chance to get between them. Now Mr. McDonald pushed at Slade's chest, saying, "That's enough, Freighter. That's enough now," and Dr. King lined up, too, and another man I didn't know, and I took a place, and we formed a kind of screen between them. Dr. King turned and bent to look at Mr. Baumer.

"Damn fool hit me first," Slade said.

"That's enough," Mr. McDonald told him again while Slade looked at all of us as if he'd spit on us for a nickel. Mr. McDonald went on, using a half-friendly tone, and I knew it was because he didn't want to take Slade on any more than the rest of us did. "You go on home and sleep it off, Freighter. That's the ticket."

Slade just snorted.

From behind us Dr. King said, "I think you've broken this man's hand."

"Lucky for him I didn't kill him," Slade answered. "Damn Dutch penny-pincher!" He fingered the chew out of his mouth. "Maybe he'll know enough to leave me alone now."

Dr. King had Mr. Baumer on his feet. "I'll take him to the office," he said.

Blood was draining from Mr. Baumer's nose and rounding the curve of his lip and dripping from the sides of his chin. He held his hurt right hand in the other. But a thing was that he didn't look beaten even then, not the way a man who has given up looks beaten. Maybe that was why Slade said, with a show of that fierce anger, "You stay away from me! Hear? Stay clear away, or you'll get more of the same!"

Dr. King led Mr. Baumer away, Slade went back into the bar, and the other men walked off, talking about the fight. I got down and picked up the bills, because I knew Mr. Baumer would want me to, and mailed them at the post office dirty as they were. It made me sorer, someway, that Slade's bill was one of the few that wasn't marked up. The cleanness of it seemed to say that there was no getting the best of him.

Mr. Baumer had his hand in a sling the next day and wasn't much good at waiting on the trade. I had to hustle all afternoon and so didn't have a chance to talk to him even if he had wanted to talk. Mostly he stood at his desk, and once, passing it, I saw he was practicing writing with his left hand. His nose and the edges of the cheeks around it were swollen some.

At closing time I said, "Look, Mr. Baumer, I can lay out of school a few days until you kind of get straightened out here."

"No," he answered as if to wave the subject away. "I get somebody else. You go to school. Is good to learn."

I had a half notion to say that learning hadn't helped him with Slade. Instead, I blurted out that I would have the law on Slade.

"The law?" he asked.

"The sheriff or somebody."

"No, Al," he said. "You would not."

I asked why.

"The law, it is not for plain fights," he said. "Shooting? Robbing? Yes, the law come quick. The plain fights, they are too many. They not count enough."

He was right. I said, "Well, I'd do something anyhow."

"Yes," he answered with a slow nod of his head. "Something you vould do, Al." He didn't tell me what.

Within a couple of days he got another man to clerk for him—it was Ed Hempel, who was always finding and losing jobs—and we made out. Mr. Baumer took his hand from the sling in a couple or three weeks, but with the tape on it it still wasn't any use to him. From what you could see of the fingers below the tape it looked as if it never would be.

He spent most of his time at the high desk, sending me or Ed out on the errands he used to run, like posting and getting the mail. Sometimes I wondered if that was because he was afraid of meeting Slade. He could just as well have gone himself. He wasted a lot of hours just looking at nothing, though I will have to say he worked hard at learning to write left-handed.

Then, a month and a half before Christmas, he hired Slade to haul his freight for him.

Ed Hempel told me about the deal when I showed up for work. "Yessir," he said, resting his foot on a crate in the storeroom where we were supposed to be working. "I tell you he's throwed in with Slade. Told me this morning to go out and locate him if I could and bring him in. Slade was at the saloon, o' course, and says to hell with Dutchie, but I told him this was honest-to-God business, like Baumer had told me to, and there was a quart of whisky right there in the store for him if he'd come and get it. He was out of money, I reckon, because the quart fetched him."

"What'd they say?" I asked him.

"Search me. There was two or three people in the store and Baumer told me to wait on 'em, and he and Slade palavered back by the desk."

"How do you know they made a deal?"

Ed spread his hands out. "'Bout noon, Moore came in with his string, and I heard Baumer say he was makin' a change. Moore didn't like it too good, either."

It was a hard thing to believe, but there one day was Slade with a pile of stuff for the Moon Dance Mercantile Company, and that was proof enough with something left for boot.

Mr. Baumer never opened the subject up with me, though I gave him plenty of chances. And I didn't feel like asking. He didn't talk much these days but went around absent-minded, feeling now and then of the fingers that curled yellow and stiff out of the bandage like the toes on the leg of a dead chicken. Even on our walks home he kept his thoughts to himself.

I felt different about him now, and was sore inside. Not that I blamed him exactly. A hundred and thirty-five pounds wasn't much to throw against two hundred. And who could tell what Slade would do on a bellyful of whisky? He had promised Mr. Baumer more of the same, hadn't he? But I didn't feel good. I couldn't look up to Mr. Baumer like I used to and still wanted to. I didn't have the beginning of an answer when men cracked jokes or shook their heads in sympathy with Mr. Baumer, saying Slade had made him come to time.

Slade hauled in a load for the store, and another, and Christmas time was drawing on and trade heavy, and the winter that had started early and then pulled back came on again. There was a blizzard and then a still cold and another blizzard and afterwards a sunshine that was ice-shine on the drifted snow. I was glad to be busy, selling overshoes and sheep-lined coats and mitts and socks as thick as saddle blankets and Christmas candy out of buckets and hickory nuts and the fresh oranges that the people in our town never saw except when Santa Claus was coming.

One afternoon when I lit out from class the thermometer on the school porch read 42° below. But you didn't have to look at it to know how cold the weather was. Your nose and fingers and toes and ears and the bones inside you told you. The snow cried when you stepped on it.

I got to the store and took my things off and scuffed my hands at the stove for a minute so's to get life enough in them to tie a parcel. Mr. Baumer—he was always polite to me—said, "Hello, Al. Not so much to do today. Too cold for customers." He shuddered a little, as if he hadn't got the chill off even yet, and rubbed his broken hand with the good one. "Ve need Christmas goods," he said, looking out the window to the furrows that wheels had made in the snow-banked street, and I knew he was thinking of Slade's string, inbound from the railroad, and the time it might take even Slade to travel those hard miles.

Slade never made it at all.

Less than an hour later our old freighter, Moore, came in, his beard white and stiff with frost. He didn't speak at first but

PHOTO COURTESY HISTORICAL SOCIETY OF MONTANA, HELENA

looked around and clumped to the stove and took off his heavy mitts, holding his news inside him.

Then he said, not pleasantly, "Your new man's dead, Baumer."

"My new man?" Mr. Baumer said.

"Who the hell do you think? Slade. He's dead."

All Mr. Baumer could say was, "Dead!"

"Froze to death, I figger," Moore told him while Colly Coleman and Ed Hempel and Miss Lizzie and I and a couple of customers stepped closer.

"Not Slade," Mr. Baumer said. "He know too much to freeze."

"Maybe so, but he sure's God's froze now. I got him in the wagon."

We stood looking at one another and at Moore. Moore was enjoying his news, enjoying feeding it out bit by bit so's to hold the stage. "Heart might've given out for all I know."

The side door swung open, letting in a cloud of cold and three men who stood, like us, waiting on Moore. I moved a little and looked through the window and saw Slade's freight outfit tied outside with more men around it. Two of them were on a wheel of one of the wagons, looking inside.

"Had a extra man, so I brought your stuff in," Moore went on. "Figgered you'd be glad to pay for it."

"Not Slade," Mr. Baumer said again.

"You can take a look at him."

Mr. Baumer answered no.

"Someone's takin' word to Connor to bring his hearse. Anyhow I told 'em to. I carted old Slade this far. Connor can have him now."

Moore pulled on his mitts. "Found him there by the Deep Creek crossin', doubled up in the snow an' his fire out." He moved toward the door. "I'll see to the horses, but your stuff'll have to set there. I got more'n enough work to do at Hirschs'."

Mr. Baumer just nodded.

I put on my coat and went out and waited my turn and climbed on a wagon wheel and looked inside, and there was Slade piled on some bags of bran. Maybe because of being frozen, his face was whiter than I ever saw it, whiter and deader, too, though it never had been lively. Only the mustache seemed still alive, sprouting thick like greasewood from alkali. Slade was doubled up all right, as if he had died and stiffened leaning forward in a chair.

I got down from the wheel, and Colly and then Ed climbed up. Moore was unhitching, tossing off his pieces of information while he did so. Pretty soon Mr. Connor came up with his old hearse, and he and Moore tumbled Slade into it, and the team that was as old as the hearse made off, the tires squeaking in the snow. The people trailed on away with it, their breaths leaving little ribbons of mist in the air. It was beginning to get dark.

Mr. Baumer came out of the side door of the store, bundled up, and called to Colly and Ed and me. "We unload," he said. "Already is late. Al, better you get a couple lanterns now."

We did a fast job, setting the stuff out of the wagons on to the platform and then carrying it or rolling it on the one truck that the store owned and stowing it inside according to where Mr. Baumer's good hand pointed.

A barrel was one of the last things to go in. I edged it up and Colly nosed the truck under it, and then I let it fall back. "Mr. Baumer," I said, "we'll never sell all this, will we?"

"Yah," he answered. "Sure we sell it. I get it cheap. A bargain, Al, so I buy it."

I looked at the barrel head again. There in big letters I saw "Wood Alcohol[5]—Deadly Poison."

"Hurry now," Mr. Baumer said. "Is late." For a flash and no longer I saw through the mist in his eyes, saw, you might say, that hilly chin repeated there. "Then ve go home, Al. Is good to know to read."

5. *Wood Alcohol,* like grain alcohol in many ways but made from wood, used often as fuel, and poisonous to drink.

WHAT DO YOU SAY?

1. In the very first paragraph of this story, the author gives us important information about the setting and characters. Turn back to this paragraph and find answers to the following questions: *(a)* In what occupation are Mr. Baumer and the narrator apparently engaged? *(b)* What time of day is it? *(c)* What section of the country is suggested in the description? *(d)* What period of time is suggested? *(e)* What two significant facts do you learn about Freighter Slade?

2. *(a)* If you were asked to outline the plot of this story, what would you list as the first step? *(b)* Where is the first instance of conflict?

3. *(a)* At what point do you begin sympathizing with Mr. Baumer? *(b)* Disliking Slade?

4. On page 29, column 1, paragraph 2, the narrator tells us that Mr. Baumer "lifted his hand and felt carefully of his nose." Later on, the narrator pictures Mr. Baumer touching his injured fingers. What purpose do you think the author has in introducing these two details?

5. When do you think Mr. Baumer gets his idea for revenge—when the narrator first mentions the fact that Slade can't read, or later? Cite evidence for your answer.

6. *(a)* In what ways does the narrator try to justify Slade's actions? *(b)* What do you think is the narrator's purpose in doing this? *(c)* The author's purpose? *(d)* Why does this attempted justification have no effect on Baumer?

7. What is the major significance of Mr. Baumer's learning to write with his left hand?

8. *(a)* How does Mr. Baumer interest Slade in working for him? *(b)* What does this tell you about Mr. Baumer's knowledge of human nature?

9. *(a)* What is the significance of the title of this story? *(b)* What is ironical about the ending of the story?

AUTHOR'S CRAFT

Characterization

If you have discussed the preceding questions, you already know many things about the element of *characterization* in a short story. Characterization is the technique used by an author to make his characters come alive for the reader. You have learned something about the importance of plot and setting to a short story. You have learned that some short stories have very little plot; sometimes the setting for a story is very significant and sometimes it is simply a background for plot and characters.

There are some short stories in which characters or just one character may be the most important element in the story. "Bargain" does not completely fit this category, since this story has not only a very definite plot but also a setting which is used both to help create an atmosphere and to help shape the plot. However, in "Bargain" the author has made his characters, especially Mr. Baumer, come very much alive for the reader.

An author may reveal a character in several ways: (1) he may directly describe the character's appearance and personality; (2) he may describe the character's actions; (3) he may tell us what the character says; (4) he may combine all of these ways. In "Bargain" what ways has the author used to reveal the character of Mr. Baumer? Of Freighter Slade? Of the narrator? In which of the three stories you have read so far in this unit are the characters least developed as individuals?

A. B. GUTHRIE, JR.

The fact that Mr. Guthrie's own experiences in the West have provided the ideas for many of his stories is revealed by the author himself. "In my introduction to ***The Big It,*** which includes the story 'Bargain,'" says Mr. Guthrie, "I said that every story in the collection had some basis in fact. 'Bargain' was no exception. An illiterate freighter did die years ago some forty miles from my hometown because he could not read. He tapped a barrel plainly marked Wood Alcohol. The problem, once I heard of the incident, was to put the incident into the frame of fiction."

Mr. Guthrie, born in Indiana, was reared in Montana, where he developed his love for the West. After graduating from the University of Montana in 1923, he became a "cub" reporter for a newspaper in Lexington, Kentucky, and later rose to the position of editor. Encouraged by the reception given his novel ***The Big Sky*** in 1947, Mr. Guthrie left the newspaper and concentrated on his writing, and in 1950 he received the Pulitzer Prize for his novel ***The Way West.***

The Most Dangerous Game

RICHARD CONNELL

"Off there to the right—somewhere—is a large island," said Whitney. "It's rather a mystery—"

"What island is it?" Rainsford asked.

"The old charts call it 'Ship-Trap Island,'" Whitney replied. "A suggestive name, isn't it? Sailors have a curious dread of the place. I don't know why. Some superstition—"

"Can't see it," remarked Rainsford, trying to peer through the dank tropical night that was palpable as it pressed its thick, warm blackness in upon the yacht.

"You have good eyes," said Whitney, with a laugh, "and I've seen you pick off a moose moving in the brown fall bush at four hundred yards; but even you can't see four miles or so through a moonless Caribbean night."

"Nor four yards," admitted Rainsford. "Ugh! It's like moist black velvet."

"It will be light enough in Rio," promised Whitney. "We should make it in a few days. I hope the jaguar guns have come. We'll have some good hunting up the Amazon. Great sport, hunting."

"The best sport in the world," agreed Rainsford.

"For the hunter," amended Whitney. "Not for the jaguar."

"Don't talk rot, Whitney," said Rainsford. "You're a big-game hunter, not a philosopher. Who cares how a jaguar feels?"

"Perhaps the jaguar does," observed Whitney.

"Bah! They've no understanding."

"Even so, I rather think they understand one thing—fear. The fear of pain and the fear of death."

"Nonsense," laughed Rainsford. "This hot weather is making you soft, Whitney. Be a realist. The world is made up of two classes—the hunters and the hunted. Luckily, you and I are hunters. Do you think we've passed that island yet?"

"I can't tell in the dark. I hope so."

"Why?" asked Rainsford.

"The place has a reputation—a bad one. It's gotten into sailor lore, somehow. Didn't you notice that the crew's nerves seemed a bit jumpy today?"

"They were a bit strange, now you mention it. Even Captain Nielsen—"

"Yes, even that tough-minded old Swede, who'd go up to the devil himself and ask him for a light. All I could get out of him

"Tonight," said the General, "we will hunt—you and I."

was: 'This place has an evil name among seafaring men, sir.' Then he said to me, very gravely: 'Don't you feel anything?'—as if the air about us was actually poisonous. Now, you mustn't laugh when I tell you this—I did feel something like a sudden chill.

"There was no breeze. The sea was as flat as a plate-glass window. We were drawing near the island then. What I felt was a —a mental chill; a sort of sudden dread."

"Pure imagination," said Rainsford. "One superstitious sailor can taint the whole ship's company with his fear."

"Maybe. But sometimes I think sailors have an extra sense that tells them when they are in danger. Sometimes I think evil is a tangible thing—with wave lengths, just as sound and light have. An evil place can, so to speak, broadcast vibrations of evil. Anyhow, I'm glad we're getting out of this zone. Well, I think I'll turn in now, Rainsford."

"I'm not sleepy," said Rainsford. "I'm going to smoke another pipe up on the afterdeck."

"Good night, then, Rainsford. See you at breakfast."

"Right. Good night, Whitney."

Rainsford, reclining in a steamer chair, indolently puffed on his favorite brier. The sensuous drowsiness of the night was on him. "It's so dark," he thought, "that I could sleep without closing my eyes; the night would be my eyelids—"

An abrupt sound startled him. Off to the right he had heard it, and his ears, expert in such matters, could not be mistaken. Again he heard the sound, and again. Somewhere, off in the blackness, someone had fired a gun three times.

Rainsford sprang up and moved quickly to the rail, mystified. He strained his eyes in the direction from which the reports had come, but it was like trying to see through a blanket. He leaped upon the rail and balanced himself there, to get greater elevation; his pipe, striking a rope, was knocked from his mouth. He lunged for it; a short, hoarse cry came from his lips as he realized he had reached too far and had lost his balance. The cry was pinched off short as the blood-warm waters of the Caribbean Sea closed over his head.

He struggled up to the surface and tried to cry out, but the wash from the speeding yacht made him gag and strangle. Desperately he struck out with strong strokes after the receding lights of the yacht, but he stopped before he had swum fifty feet. A certain cool-headedness had come to him; it was not the first time he had been in a tight place. There was a chance that his cries could be heard by someone aboard the yacht, but that chance was slender, and grew more slender as the yacht raced on. He wrestled himself out of some of his clothes, and shouted with all his power. The lights of the yacht became faint and ever-vanishing fireflies; then they were blotted out entirely by the night.

Rainsford remembered that the shots had come from the right; and doggedly he swam in that direction, swimming with slow, deliberate strokes, conserving his strength. For a seemingly endless time he fought the sea. He began to count his strokes; he could do possibly a hundred more and then—

Rainsford heard a sound. It came out of the darkness, a high, screaming sound, the sound of an animal in an extremity of anguish and terror.

He did not recognize the animal that made the sound; he did not try to; with fresh vitality he swam toward the sound. He heard it again; then it was cut short by another noise, crisp, staccato.

"Pistol shot," muttered Rainsford, swimming on.

Ten minutes of determined effort brought another sound to his ears—the most welcome he had ever heard—the muttering and growling of the sea breaking on a rocky shore. He was almost on the rocks before he saw them. With his remaining strength he dragged himself from the swirling waters. Jagged crags appeared to jut up into the opaqueness; he forced himself upward, hand over hand. Gasping, his hands raw, he reached a flat place at the top. Dense jungle came down to the very edge of the cliffs. What perils that tangle of trees and underbrush might hold for him did not concern Rainsford just then. All he knew was that he was safe from the sea, and that utter weariness was on him. He flung himself down and tumbled headlong into the deepest sleep of his life.

When he opened his eyes, he knew from the position of the sun that it was late in the afternoon. Sleep had given him new vigor; a sharp hunger was picking at him. He looked about him, almost cheerfully.

"Where there are pistol shots, there are men. Where there are men, there is food," he thought. But what kind of men, he wondered, in so forbidding a place? An unbroken front of snarled and ragged jungle fringed the shore. He saw no sign of a trail through the closely knit web of weeds and trees; it was easier to go along the shore, and he floundered along by the water. Not far from where he had landed, he stopped.

Some wounded thing, by the evidence a large animal, had thrashed about in the underbrush; the jungle weeds were crushed down and the moss was lacerated; one patch of weeds was stained crimson. A small, glittering object not far away caught Rainsford's eye and he picked it up. It was an empty cartridge.

"A twenty-two," he remarked. "That's odd. It must have been a fairly large animal, too. The hunter had his nerve with him to tackle it with a light gun. It's clear that the brute put up a fight. I suppose the first three shots I heard was when the hunter flushed his quarry[1] and wounded it. The last shot was when he trailed it here and finished it."

He examined the ground closely and found what he had hoped to find—the print of hunting boots. They pointed along the cliff in the direction he had been going. Eagerly he hurried along, now slipping on a rotten log or a loose stone, but making headway; night was beginning to settle down.

Bleak darkness was blacking out the sea and jungle when Rainsford sighted the lights. He came upon them as he turned a

1. *flushed his quarry,* drove the pursued animal out of its hiding place.

crook in the coast line, and his first thought was that he had come upon a village, for there were many lights. But as he forged along he saw to his great astonishment that all the lights were in one enormous building—a lofty structure with pointed towers plunging upward into the gloom. His eyes made out the shadowy outlines of a palatial château; it was set on a high bluff, and on three sides of it cliffs dived down to where the sea licked greedy lips in the shadows.

"Mirage," thought Rainsford. But it was no mirage, he found, when he opened the tall spiked iron gate. The stone steps were real enough; the massive door with a leering gargoyle for a knocker was real enough; yet about it all hung an air of unreality.

He lifted the knocker; and it creaked up stiffly, as if it had never before been used. He let it fall, and it startled him with its booming loudness. He thought he heard steps within; the door remained closed. Again Rainsford lifted the heavy knocker, and let it fall. The door opened suddenly, and Rainsford stood blinking in the river of glaring gold light that poured out. The first thing his eyes discerned was the largest man he had ever seen—a gigantic creature, solidly made and black-bearded almost to the waist. In his hand the man held a long-barreled revolver, and he was pointing it straight at Rainsford's heart. Out of the snarl of beard two small eyes regarded Rainsford.

"Don't be alarmed," said Rainsford with a smile which he hoped was disarming. "I'm no robber. I fell off a yacht. My name is Sanger Rainsford of New York City."

The menacing look in the eyes did not change. The revolver pointed as rigidly as if the giant were a statue. He gave no sign that he understood Rainsford's words, or that he had even heard them. He was dressed in uniform, a black uniform trimmed with gray astrakhan.

"I'm Sanger Rainsford of New York," Rainsford began again. "I fell off a yacht. I am hungry."

The man's only answer was to raise with his thumb the hammer of his revolver. Then Rainsford saw the man's free hand go to his forehead in a military salute, and he saw him click his heels together and stand at attention. Another man was coming down the broad marble steps, an erect, slender man in evening clothes. He advanced to Rainsford and held out his hand.

In a cultivated voice marked by a slight accent that gave it added precision and deliberateness, he said: "It is a very great pleasure and honor to welcome Mr. Sanger Rainsford, the celebrated hunter, to my home."

Automatically Rainsford shook the man's hand.

"I've read your book about hunting snow leopards in Tibet, you see," explained the man. "I am General Zaroff."

Rainsford's first impression was that the man was singularly handsome; his second was that there was an original, almost bizarre quality about the general's face. He was a tall man past middle age, for his hair was a vivid white; but his thick eyebrows and pointed military mustache were as black as the night from which Rainsford had come. His eyes, too, were black and very bright. He had high cheekbones, a sharp-cut nose, a spare, dark face, the face of a man used to giving orders, the face of an aristocrat. Turning to the giant in uniform, the general made a sign. The giant put away his pistol, saluted, withdrew.

"Ivan is an incredibly strong fellow," remarked the general, "but he has the misfortune to be deaf and dumb. A simple fellow, but, I'm afraid, like all his race, a bit of a savage."

"Is he Russian?"

"He is a Cossack,"[2] said the general, and his smile showed red lips and pointed teeth. "So am I."

"Come," he said, "we shouldn't be chatting here. We can talk later. Now you want

2. ***He is a Cossack*** (kos'ak). The Cossacks, who lived in southern Russia, were noted for their love of fighting and their excellent horsemanship.

clothes, food, rest. You shall have them. This is a most restful spot."

Ivan had reappeared, and the general spoke to him with lips that moved but gave forth no sound.

"Follow Ivan, if you please, Mr. Rainsford," said the general. "I was about to have my dinner. I'll wait for you. You'll find that my clothes will fit you, I think."

It was to a huge, beam-ceilinged bedroom with a canopied bed big enough for six men that Rainsford followed the silent giant. Ivan laid out an evening suit, and Rainsford, as he put it on, noticed that it came from a London tailor who ordinarily cut and sewed for none below the rank of duke.

The dining room to which Ivan conducted him was in many ways remarkable. There was a medieval magnificence about it; it suggested a baronial hall of feudal times with its oaken panels, its high ceiling, its vast refectory table where twoscore men could sit down to eat. About the hall were mounted heads of many animals—lions, tigers, elephants, moose, bears; larger or more perfect specimens Rainsford had never seen. At the great table the general was sitting alone.

"You'll have a cocktail, Mr. Rainsford," he suggested. The cocktail was surpassingly good; and, Rainsford noted, the table appointments were of the finest—the linen, the crystal, the silver, the china.

They were eating *borsch*.[3] Half apologetically General Zaroff said: "We do our best to preserve the amenities of civilization here. Please forgive any lapses. We are well off the beaten track, you know."

Rainsford was finding the general a most thoughtful and affable host, a true cosmopolite. But there was one small trait of the general's that made Rainsford uncomfortable. Whenever he looked up from his plate he found the general studying him, appraising him narrowly.

"Perhaps," said General Zaroff, "you were surprised that I recognized your name. You see, I read all books on hunting published in English, French, and Russian. I have but one passion in my life, Mr. Rainsford, and that is the hunt."

"You have some wonderful heads here," said Rainsford as he ate a particularly well-cooked filet mignon.[4] "That Cape buffalo is the largest I ever saw."

"Oh, that fellow. Yes, he was a monster."

"Did he charge you?"

"Hurled me against a tree," said the general. "Fractured my skull. But I got the brute."

"I've always thought," said Rainsford, "that the Cape buffalo is the most dangerous of all big game."

For a moment the general did not reply; he was smiling his curious red-lipped smile. Then he said slowly: "No. You are wrong, sir. The Cape buffalo is not the most dangerous big game." He sipped his wine. "Here in my preserve on this island," he said in the same slow tone, "I hunt more dangerous game."

Rainsford expressed his surprise. "Is there big game on this island?"

The general nodded. "The biggest."

"Really?"

"Oh, it isn't here naturally, of course. I have to stock the island."

"What have you imported, general?" Rainsford asked. "Tigers?"

The general smiled. "No," he said. "Hunting tigers ceased to interest me some years ago. I exhausted their possibilities, you see. No thrill left in tigers, no real danger. I live for danger, Mr. Rainsford."

The general took from his pocket a gold cigarette case and offered his guest a long black cigarette with a silver tip; it was perfumed and gave off a smell like incense.

"We will have some capital hunting, you and I," said the general. "I shall be most glad to have your society."

"But what game—" began Rainsford.

---

3. *borsch* (bôrsh), a rich red soup, colored with beet juice and served with sour cream. **4. *filet mignon*** (fi lā′ min′yon), broiled steak of the finest cut.

"I'll tell you," said the general. "You will be amused, I know. I think I may say, in all modesty, that I have done a rare thing. I have invented a new sensation. May I pour you another glass of port, Mr. Rainsford?"

"Thank you, general."

The general filled both glasses, and said: "God makes some men poets. Some He makes kings, some beggars. Me He made a hunter. My hand was made for the trigger, my father said. He was a very rich man with a quarter of a million acres in the Crimea,[5] and he was an ardent sportsman. When I was only five years old, he gave me a little gun to shoot sparrows with. When I shot some of his prize turkeys with it, he did not punish me; he complimented me on my marksmanship. I killed my first bear when I was ten. My whole life has been one prolonged hunt. I went into the army—it was expected of noblemen's sons—and for a time commanded a division of Cossack cavalry, but my real interest was always the hunt. I have hunted every kind of game in every land. It would be impossible for me to tell you how many animals I have killed."

The general puffed at his cigarette.

"After the debacle in Russia[6] I left the country, for it was imprudent for an officer of the Czar to stay there. Many noble Russians lost everything. I, luckily, had invested heavily in American securities. Naturally, I continued to hunt—grizzlies in your Rockies, crocodiles in the Ganges,[7] rhinoceroses in East Africa. It was in Africa that the Cape buffalo hit me and laid me up for six months. As soon as I recovered I started for the Amazon to hunt jaguars, for I had heard they were unusually cunning. They weren't." The Cossack sighed. "I was bitterly disappointed. I was lying in my tent with a splitting headache one night when a terrible thought pushed its way into my mind. Hunting was beginning to bore me! And hunting, remember, had been my life. I have heard that in America businessmen often go to pieces when they give up the business that has been their life."

"Yes, that's so," said Rainsford.

The general smiled. "I had no wish to go to pieces," he said. "I must do something. Now, mine is an analytical mind, Mr. Rainsford. Doubtless that is why I enjoy the problems of the chase."

"No doubt, General Zaroff."

"So," continued the general, "I asked myself why the hunt no longer fascinated me. You are much younger than I am, Mr. Rainsford, and have not hunted as much; but you perhaps can guess the answer."

"What was it?"

"Simply this: hunting had ceased to be what you call 'a sporting proposition.' It had become too easy. I always got my quarry. Always. There is no greater bore than perfection."

The general lit a fresh cigarette.

"No animal had a chance with me any more. That is no boast; it is a mathematical certainty. The animal had nothing but his legs and his instinct. Instinct is no match for reason. When I thought of this it was a tragic moment for me, I can tell you."

Rainsford leaned across the table, absorbed in what his host was saying.

"It came to me as an inspiration what I must do," the general went on.

"And that was?"

The general smiled the quiet smile of one who has faced an obstacle and surmounted it with success. "I had to invent a new animal to hunt," he said.

"A new animal? You're joking."

"Not at all," said the general. "I never joke about hunting. I needed a new animal. I found one. So I bought this island, built this house, and here I do my hunting. The island is perfect for my purposes—there are jungles with a maze of trails in them, hills, swamps—"

---

5. the Crimea (krī mē′ə or kri mē′ə), a peninsula in southwestern Russia, jutting down into the Black Sea. ***6. the debacle*** (dā bä′kəl or di bak′əl) ***in Russia.*** In the Russian Revolution of 1917 the government of the Czar was overthrown, the property of the nobles confiscated, and most of the nobility driven into exile. ***7. Ganges*** (gan′jēz), a river in India regarded by the Hindus as being sacred.

"But the animal, General Zaroff?"

"Oh," said the general, "it supplies me with the most exciting hunting in the world. No other hunting compares with it for an instant. Every day I hunt, and I never grow bored now, for I have a quarry with which I can match my wits."

Rainsford's bewilderment showed in his face.

"I wanted the ideal animal to hunt," explained the general. "So I said: 'What are the attributes of an ideal quarry?' And the answer was, of course: 'It must have courage, cunning, and, above all, it must be able to reason.' "

"But no animal can reason," objected Rainsford.

"My dear fellow," said the general, "there is one that can."

"But you can't mean—" gasped Rainsford.

"And why not?"

"I can't believe you are serious, General Zaroff. This is a grisly joke."

"Why should I not be serious? I am speaking of hunting."

"Hunting? Good God, General Zaroff, what you speak of is murder."

The general laughed with entire good nature. He regarded Rainsford quizzically. "I refuse to believe that so modern and civilized a young man as you seem to be harbors romantic ideas about the value of human life. Surely your experiences in the recent war—"[8]

"Did not make me condone cold-blooded murder," finished Rainsford stiffly.

Laughter shook the general. "How extraordinarily droll you are!" he said. "One does not expect nowadays to find a young man of the educated class, even in America, with such a naïve, and, if I may say so, mid-Victorian[9] point of view. Ah, well, I'll wager you'll forget your notions when you go hunting with me. You've a genuine new thrill in store for you, Mr. Rainsford."

"Thank you, I'm a hunter, not a murderer."

"Dear me," said the general, quite unruffled, "again that unpleasant word. But I think I can show you that your scruples are quite ill-founded."

"Yes?"

"Life is for the strong, to be lived by the strong, and, if needs be, taken by the strong. The weak of the world were put here to give the strong pleasure. I am strong. Why should I not use my gift? If I wish to hunt, why should I not? I hunt the scum of the earth—sailors from tramp ships—lascars,[10] blacks, Chinese, whites, mongrels—a thoroughbred horse or hound is worth more than a score of them."

"But they are men," said Rainsford hotly.

"Precisely," said the general. "That is why I use them. It gives me pleasure. They can reason, after a fashion. So they are dangerous."

"But where do you get them?"

The general's left eyelid fluttered down in a wink. "This island is called Ship-Trap," he answered. "Sometimes an angry god of the high seas sends them to me. Sometimes, when Providence is not so kind, I help Providence a bit. Come to the window with me."

Rainsford went to the window and looked out toward the sea.

"Watch! Out there!" exclaimed the general, pointing into the night. Rainsford's eyes saw only blackness, and then, as the general pressed a button, far out to sea Rainsford saw the flash of lights.

The general chuckled. "They indicate a channel," he said, "where there's none: giant rocks with razor edges crouch like a sea monster with wide-open jaws. They can crush a ship as easily as I crush this nut." He dropped a walnut on the hardwood floor and brought his heel grinding down on it. "Oh, yes," he said, casually, as if in answer to a question, "I have electricity. We try to be civilized here."

"Civilized? And you shoot down men?"

---

8. ***the recent war,*** World War I. 9. ***mid-Victorian,*** old-fashioned; dating from the days of Queen Victoria, whose reign (1837-1901) was characterized by strictness in behavior. 10. ***lascars*** (las'kərz), native Malayan or East Indian sailors employed on European vessels.

A trace of anger was in the general's black eyes, but it was there for only a second; then he said, in his most pleasant manner: "Dear me, what a righteous young man you are! I assure you I do not do the thing you suggest. That would be barbarous. I treat these visitors with every consideration. They get plenty of good food and exercise. They get into splendid physical condition. You shall see for yourself tomorrow."

"What do you mean?"

"We shall visit my training school," smiled the general. "It's in the cellar. I have about a dozen pupils down there now. They're from the Spanish bark *San Lucar* that had the bad luck to go on the rocks out there. A very inferior lot, I regret to say. Poor specimens and more accustomed to the deck than to the jungle."

He raised his hand, and Ivan brought thick Turkish coffee. Rainsford, with an effort, held his tongue in check.

"It's a game, you see," pursued the general blandly. "I suggest to one of them that we go hunting. I give him a supply of food and an excellent hunting knife. I give him three hours' start. I am to follow, armed only with a pistol of the smallest caliber and range. If my quarry eludes me for three whole days, he wins the game. If I find him"—the general smiled—"he loses."

"Suppose he refuses to be hunted?"

"Oh," said the general, "I give him his option, of course. He need not play that game if he doesn't wish to. If he does not wish to hunt, I turn him over to Ivan. Ivan once had the honor of serving as official knouter to the Great White Czar,[11] and he has his own ideas of sport. Invariably, Mr. Rainsford, invariably they choose the hunt."

"And if they win?"

The smile on the general's face widened. "To date I have not lost," he said.

Then he added, hastily: "I don't wish you to think me a braggart, Mr. Rainsford. Many of them afford only the most elementary sort of problem. Occasionally I strike a tartar.[12] One almost did win. I eventually had to use the dogs."

"The dogs?"

"This way, please. I'll show you."

The general steered Rainsford to a window. The lights from the windows sent a flickering illumination that made grotesque patterns on the courtyard below, and Rainsford could see moving about there a dozen or so huge black shapes; as they turned toward him, their eyes glittered greenly.

"A rather good lot, I think," observed the general. "They are let out at seven every night. If anyone should try to get into my house—or out of it—something extremely regrettable would occur to him." He hummed a snatch of a gay French song.

"And now," said the general, "I want to show you my new collection of heads. Will you come with me to the library?"

"I hope," said Rainsford, "that you will excuse me tonight, General Zaroff. I'm really not feeling at all well."

"Ah, indeed?" the general inquired solicitously. "Well, I suppose that's only natural after your long swim. You need a good, restful night's sleep. Tomorrow you'll feel like a new man, I'll wager. Then we'll hunt, eh? I've one rather promising prospect—"

Rainsford was hurrying from the room.

"Sorry you can't go with me tonight," called the general. "I expect rather fair sport—a big, strong black. He looks resourceful— Well, good night, Mr. Rainsford; I hope you have a good night's rest."

The bed was good, and the pajamas of the softest silk, and he was tired in every fiber of his being; nevertheless Rainsford could not quiet his brain with the opiate of sleep. He lay, eyes wide open. Once he thought he heard stealthy steps in the corridor outside his room. He sought to throw open the door; it would not open. He went

---

11. Ivan ... knouter (nout′ər) *to the Great White Czar* (zär). During the reign of Alexander III (1881-1894), Ivan was the official flogger of those doomed to be lashed with a knout, a terrible whip made of plaited leather thongs and wire.

12. strike a tartar. The General means that sometimes he encounters a man who isn't easily manageable.

to the window and looked out. His room was high up in one of the towers. The lights of the château were out now, and it was dark and silent, but there was a fragment of sallow moon, and by its wan light he could see, dimly, the courtyard; there, weaving in and out in the pattern of shadow, were black, noiseless forms; the hounds heard him at the window and looked up, expectantly, with their green eyes. Rainsford went back to the bed and lay down. By many methods he tried to put himself to sleep. He had achieved a doze when, just as morning began to come, he heard, far off in the jungle, the faint report of a pistol.

General Zaroff did not appear until luncheon. He was dressed faultlessly in the tweeds of a country squire. He was solicitous about the state of Rainsford's health.

"As for me," sighed the general, "I do not feel so well. I am worried, Mr. Rainsford. Last night I detected traces of my old complaint."

To Rainsford's questioning glance the general said: "Ennui. Boredom."

Then, taking a second helping of crêpes suzette,[13] the general explained: "The hunting was not good last night. The fellow lost his head. He made a straight trail that offered no problems at all. That's the trouble with these sailors; they have dull brains to begin with, and they do not know how to get about in the woods. They do excessively stupid and obvious things. It's most annoying. Will you have another glass of wine, Mr. Rainsford?"

"General," said Rainsford firmly, "I wish to leave this island at once."

The general raised his eyebrows; he seemed hurt. "But, my dear fellow," he protested, "you've only just come. You've had no hunting—"

"I wish to go today," said Rainsford. He saw the dead black eyes of the general on him, studying him. General Zaroff's face suddenly brightened.

He filled Rainsford's glass from a dusty bottle.

"Tonight," said the general, "we will hunt —you and I."

Rainsford shook his head. "No, general," he said. "I will not hunt."

The general shrugged his shoulders and delicately ate a hothouse grape. "As you wish, my friend," he said. "The choice rests entirely with you. But may I not venture to suggest that you will find my idea of sport more diverting than Ivan's?"

He nodded toward the corner to where the giant stood, scowling, his thick arms crossed on his hogshead of a chest.

"You don't mean—" cried Rainsford.

"My dear fellow," said the general, "have I not told you I always mean what I say about hunting? This is really an inspiration. I drink to a foeman worthy of my steel—at last."

The general raised his glass, but Rainsford sat staring at him.

"You'll find this game worth playing," the general said enthusiastically. "Your brain against mine. Your woodcraft against mine. Your strength and stamina against mine. Outdoor chess! And the stake is not without value, eh?"

"And if I win—" began Rainsford huskily.

"I'll cheerfully acknowledge myself defeated if I do not find you by midnight of the third day," said General Zaroff. "My sloop will place you on the mainland near a town."

The general read what Rainsford was thinking.

"Oh, you can trust me," said the Cossack. "I will give you my word as a gentleman and a sportsman. Of course, you in turn must agree to say nothing of your visit here."

"I'll agree to nothing of the kind," said Rainsford.

"Oh," said the general, "in that case— But why discuss that now? Three days hence we can discuss it over a bottle of wine, unless—"

13. *crêpes suzette* (krāp′ sü zet′), a thin, sweet pancake, rolled with various hot sauces.

The general sipped his port.

Then a businesslike air animated him. "Ivan," he said to Rainsford, "will supply you with hunting clothes, food, a knife. I suggest you wear moccasins; they leave a poorer trail. I suggest, too, that you avoid the big swamp in the southeast corner of the island. We call it Death Swamp. There's quicksand there. One foolish fellow tried it. The deplorable part of it was that Lazarus followed him. You can imagine my feelings, Mr. Rainsford. I loved Lazarus; he was the finest hound in my pack. Well, I must beg you to excuse me now. I always take a siesta after lunch. You'll hardly have time for a nap, I fear. You'll want to start, no doubt. I shall not follow till dusk. Hunting at night is so much more exciting, don't you think? *Au revoir,*[14] Mr. Rainsford, *au revoir.*"

General Zaroff, with a deep, courtly bow, strolled from the room. From another door came Ivan. Under one arm he carried khaki hunting clothes, a haversack of food, a leather sheath containing a long-bladed hunting knife; his right hand rested on a cocked revolver thrust in the crimson sash about his waist. . . .

Rainsford had fought his way through the bush for two hours. "I must keep my nerve. I must keep my nerve," he said through tight teeth.

He had not been entirely clear-headed when the château gates snapped shut behind him. His whole idea at first was to put distance between himself and General Zaroff; and, to this end, he had plunged along, spurred on by something very much like panic. Now he had got a grip on himself, had stopped, and was taking stock of himself and the situation.

He saw that straight flight was futile; inevitably it would bring him face to face with the sea. He was in a picture with a frame of water, and his operations, clearly, must take place within that frame.

"I'll give him a trail to follow," muttered Rainsford, and he struck off from the rude path he had been following into the trackless wilderness. He executed a series of intricate loops; he doubled on his trail again and again, recalling all the lore of the fox hunt, and all the dodges of the fox. Night found him leg-weary, with hands and face lashed by the branches, on a thickly wooded ridge. He knew it would be insane to blunder on through the dark, even if he had the strength. His need for rest was imperative and he thought: "I have played the fox, now I must play the cat of the fable."[15] A big tree with a thick trunk and outspread branches was nearby, and, taking care to leave not the slightest mark, he climbed up, and stretching out on one of the broad limbs, after a fashion, rested. Rest brought him new confidence and almost a feeling of security. Even so zealous a hunter as General Zaroff could not trace him there, he told himself; only the devil himself could follow that complicated trail through the jungle after dark. But, perhaps, the general was a devil—

An apprehensive night crawled slowly by like a wounded snake, and sleep did not visit Rainsford, although the silence of a dead world was on the jungle. Toward morning when a dingy gray was varnishing the sky, the cry of some startled bird focused Rainsford's attention in that direction. Something was coming through the bush, coming slowly, carefully, coming by the same winding way Rainsford had come. He flattened himself down on the limb, and through a screen of leaves almost as thick as tapestry, he watched. The thing that was approaching was a man.

It was General Zaroff. He made his way along with his eyes fixed in utmost concentration on the ground before him. He paused, almost beneath the tree, dropped to his knees and studied the ground.

---

14. ***Au revoir*** (ō rə vwär′), good-by; till I see you again. [French] 15. ***I have played the fox . . . cat of the fable.*** Rainsford means that he has used craft; now he must, like a cat at a mousehole, employ watchful waiting.

Rainsford's impulse was to hurl himself down like a panther, but he saw that the general's right hand held something metallic—a small automatic pistol.

The hunter shook his head several times, as if he were puzzled. Then he straightened up and took from his case one of his black cigarettes; its incense-like smoke floated up to Rainsford's nostrils.

Rainsford held his breath. The general's eyes had left the ground and were traveling inch by inch up the tree. Rainsford froze there, every muscle tensed for a spring.

But the sharp eyes of the hunter stopped before they reached the limb where Rainsford lay; a smile spread over his brown face. Very deliberately he blew a smoke ring into the air; then he turned his back on the tree and walked carelessly away, back along the trail he had come. The swish of the underbrush against his hunting

boots grew fainter and fainter.

The pent-up air burst hotly from Rainsford's lungs. His first thought made him feel sick and numb. The general could follow a trail through the woods at night; he could follow an extremely difficult trail; he must have uncanny powers; only by the merest chance had the Cossack failed to see his quarry.

Rainsford's second thought was even more terrible. It sent a shudder of cold horror through his whole being. Why had the general smiled? Why had he turned back?

Rainsford did not want to believe what his reason told him was true, but the truth was as evident as the sun that by now had pushed through the morning mists. The general was playing with him! The general was saving him for another day's sport! The Cossack was the cat; *he* was the mouse. Then it was that Rainsford knew the full meaning of terror.

"I will not lose my nerve. I will not."

He slid down from the tree, and struck off again into the woods. His face was set and he forced the machinery of his mind to function. Three hundred yards from his hiding place he stopped where a huge dead tree leaned precariously on a smaller, living one. Throwing off his sack of food, Rainsford took his knife from its sheath and began to work with all his energy.

The job was finished at last, and he threw himself down behind a fallen log a hundred feet away. He did not have to wait long. The cat was coming again to play with the mouse.

Following the trail with the sureness of a bloodhound, came General Zaroff. Nothing escaped those searching black eyes, no crushed blade of grass, no bent twig, no mark, no matter how faint, in the moss. So intent was the Cossack on his stalking that he was upon the thing Rainsford had made before he saw it. His foot touched the protruding bough that was the trigger. Even as he touched it, the general sensed his danger and leaped back with the agility of an ape. But he was not quite quick enough; the dead tree, delicately adjusted to rest on the cut living one, crashed down and struck the general a glancing blow on the shoulder as it fell; but for his alertness, he must have been smashed beneath it. He staggered, but he did not fall; nor did he drop his revolver. He stood there, rubbing his injured shoulder; and Rainsford, with fear again gripping his heart, heard the general's mocking laugh ring through the jungle.

"Rainsford," called the general, "if you are within sound of my voice, as I suppose you are, let me congratulate you. Not many men know how to make a Malay mancatcher. Luckily, for me, I too, have hunted in Malacca.[16] You are proving interesting, Mr. Rainsford. I am going now to have my wound dressed; it's only a slight one. But I shall be back. I shall be back."

When the general had gone, Rainsford took up his flight again. It was flight now, a desperate, hopeless flight that carried him on for some hours. Dusk came, then darkness, and still he pressed on. The ground grew softer under his moccasins;

16. *Malacca* (mə lak′ə), an area in the southwestern part of the Malay Peninsula.

the vegetation grew ranker, denser; insects bit him savagely. Then, as he stepped forward, his foot sank into the ooze. He tried to wrench it back, but the muck sucked viciously at his foot as if it were a giant leech. With a violent effort, he tore his foot loose. He knew where he was now. Death Swamp and its quicksand.

His hands were tight closed as if his nerve were something tangible that someone in the darkness was trying to tear from his grip. The softness of the earth had given him an idea. He stepped back from the quicksand a dozen feet or so and, like some huge prehistoric beaver, he began to dig.

Rainsford had dug himself in in France when a second's delay meant death. That had been a pleasant pastime compared to his digging now. The pit grew deeper; when it was above his shoulders, he climbed out and from some hard saplings cut stakes and sharpened them to a fine point. These stakes he planted in the bottom of the pit with the points sticking up. With flying fingers he wove a rough carpet of weeds and branches, and with it he covered the mouth of the pit. Then, wet with sweat and aching with tiredness, he crouched behind the stump of a lightning-charred tree.

He knew his pursuer was coming; he heard the padding sound of feet on the soft earth, and the night breeze brought him the perfume of the general's cigarette. It seemed to Rainsford that the general was coming with unusual swiftness; he was not feeling his way along, foot by foot. Rainsford, crouching there, could not see the general, nor could he see the pit. He lived a year in a minute. Then he felt an impulse to cry aloud with joy, for he heard the sharp crackle of the breaking branches as the cover of the pit gave way; he heard the sharp scream of pain as the pointed stakes found their mark. He leaped up from his place of concealment. Then he cowered back. Three feet from the pit a man was standing, with an electric torch in his hand.

"You've done well, Rainsford," the voice of the general called. "Your Burmese tiger pit[17] has claimed one of my best dogs. Again you score. I think, Mr. Rainsford, I'll see what you can do against my whole pack. I'm going home for a rest now. Thank you for a most amusing evening."

At daybreak Rainsford, lying near the swamp, was awakened by a sound that made him know that he had new things to learn about fear. It was a distant sound, faint and wavering; but he knew it. It was the baying of a pack of hounds.

Rainsford knew he could do one of two things. He could stay where he was and wait. That was suicide. He could flee. That was postponing the inevitable. For a moment he stood there, thinking. An idea that held a wild chance came to him, and, tightening his belt, he headed away from the swamp. The baying of the hounds drew nearer, then still nearer, nearer, ever nearer. On a ridge Rainsford climbed a tree. Down a watercourse, not a quarter of a mile away, he could see the bush moving. Straining his eyes, he saw the lean figure of General Zaroff; just ahead of him Rainsford made out another figure whose wide shoulders surged through the tall jungle weeds; it was the giant Ivan, and he seemed pulled forward by some unseen force; Rainsford knew that Ivan must be holding the pack in leash.

They would be on him any minute now. His mind worked frantically. He thought of a native trick he had learned in Uganda.[18] He slid down the tree. He caught hold of a springy young sapling and to it he fastened his hunting knife, with the blade pointing down the trail; with a bit of wild grapevine he tied back the sapling. Then he ran for his life. The hounds raised their voices as they hit the fresh scent. Rainsford knew now how an animal at bay feels.

He had to stop to get his breath. The baying of the hounds stopped abruptly;

---

17. ***Burmese*** (bėr′mēz) ***tiger pit,*** a deep pit covered by brush for trapping tigers in Burma. 18. ***Uganda*** (ū gan′də or ü gän′dä), a British territory in eastern Africa.

and Rainsford's heart stopped, too. They must have reached the knife.

He shinned excitedly up a tree and looked back. His pursuers had stopped. But the hope that was in Rainsford's brain when he had climbed died, for he saw in the shallow valley that General Zaroff was still on his feet. But Ivan was not. The knife, driven by the recoil of the springing tree, had not wholly failed.

Rainsford had hardly tumbled to the ground when the pack took up the cry again.

"Nerve, nerve, nerve!" he panted, as he dashed along. A blue gap showed between the trees dead ahead. Ever nearer drew the hounds. Rainsford forced himself on toward that gap. He reached for it. It was the shore of the sea. Across a cove he could see the gloomy gray stone of the chateau. Twenty feet below him the sea rumbled and hissed. Rainsford hesitated. He heard the hounds. Then he leaped far out into the sea.

When the general and his pack reached the place by the sea, the Cossack stopped. For some minutes he stood regarding the blue-green expanse of water. He shrugged his shoulders. Then he sat down, took a drink of brandy from a silver flask, lit a perfumed cigarette, and hummed a bit from *Madame Butterfly*.[19]

General Zaroff had an exceedingly good dinner in his great paneled dining hall that evening. With it he had a bottle of his rarest wine. Two slight annoyances kept him from perfect enjoyment. One was the thought that it would be difficult to replace Ivan; the other was that his quarry had escaped him; of course the American hadn't played the game—so thought the general as he tasted his after-dinner liqueur. In his library he read, to soothe himself, from the works of Marcus Aurelius.[20] At ten he went up to his bedroom. He was deliciously tired, he said to himself, as he locked himself in. There was a little moonlight; so, before turning on his light, he went to the window and looked down at the courtyard. He could see the great hounds, and he called: "Better luck another time," to them. Then he switched on the light.

A man, who had been hiding in the curtains of the bed, was standing there.

"Rainsford!" screamed the general. "How did you get here?"

"Swam," said Rainsford. "I found it quicker than walking through the jungle."

The general sucked in his breath and smiled. "I congratulate you," he said. "You have won the game."

Rainsford did not smile. "I am still a beast at bay," he said, in a low, hoarse voice. "Get ready, General Zaroff."

The general made one of his deepest bows. "I see," he said. "Splendid! One of us is to furnish a repast for the hounds. The other will sleep in this very excellent bed. On guard, Rainsford."

He had never slept in a better bed, Rainsford decided.

---

19. Madame Butterfly, a tragic opera by Puccini (pü chē′ni). *20. Marcus Aurelius* (mär′kəs ô rē′li əs), a Roman emperor (161-180 A.D.) and famous philosopher.

WHAT DO YOU SAY?

1. What do you think is the main purpose of the shipboard conversation between Rainsford and Whitney?

2. How does "taking sides" with one of the two opposing forces in this conflict increase the suspense?

3. (a) In the dinner conversation between Rainsford and General Zaroff, the latter comments, "We do our best to preserve the amenities of civilization here." Why is this ironical? *(b)* What is the irony of Rainsford's situation?

4. To enjoy fully a story of suspense, we must feel that the actions and characters are possible. *(a)* Do you think that the general is a "possible" character? *(b)* Could anyone actually have his philosophy of hunting? Defend your answer.

5. (a) Do you think Rainsford's point of view at the beginning of the story changes because of his experience? *(b)* What do you think his future ideas on hunting will be?

AUTHOR'S CRAFT

Short-story elements

A short story, being short, does not have room to develop completely many conflicts, and many characters or characters in detail, and a distinct setting or atmosphere. Instead, as you have already learned, the author of a short story usually chooses to emphasize one of the elements and to develop the remaining ones to a lesser degree. What element do you think has been emphasized in each of the first three stories in this unit? In "The Most Dangerous Game" which element do you think has been given the most emphasis? It would be safe to guess that your chief interest was in the very exciting plot. If, however, you are much interested in people, you may have found General Zaroff almost as fascinating as the plot. What ways has the author used to characterize him?

How important is the setting to the story? Does it play a major or minor role in the total effect? Does it contribute more to the atmosphere or to the unfolding of the plot?

In reviewing the relative importance of the elements of plot, setting, and characters in "The Most Dangerous Game," you are likely to conclude that the author has given a great deal of attention to all three elements, integrating them into an unforgettable story.

KNOW YOUR WORDS

Using the right words

When you read this story, were you aware of how the author chose combinations of words which would help the reader feel the suspense and terror of the situation? One of the two sentences in each group below contains especially effective words or phrases taken from the story. Number your paper from one to ten and next to each number write the letter of that sentence and also the effective words or phrases. Be prepared to explain why you chose as you did.

1. *(a)* The night was like moist black velvet.
   (b) It was a dark night.
2. *(a)* Sailors have a curious dread of the place.
   (b) Sailors are extremely frightened of the place.
3. *(a)* The cry stopped short as the lukewarm waters closed over his head.
   (b) The cry was pinched off as the blood-warm waters closed over his head.
4. *(a)* Dense jungle came down to the very edge of the cliffs.
   (b) Many plants and bushes grew on the edge of the cliffs.
5. *(a)* Bleak darkness was blacking out the sea and jungle when Rainsford sighted the lights.
   (b) It was almost dark when Rainsford saw the lights.
6. *(a)* The menacing look in the eyes did not change.
   (b) The odd expression in the eyes did not change.
7. *(a)* A long night crawled by like an ancient turtle.
   (b) An apprehensive night crawled by like a wounded snake.
8. *(a)* Giant rocks with razor edges crouch like a sea monster with wide-open jaws.
   (b) Giant rocks with sharp edges lie like an animal with wide-open jaws.
9. *(a)* There was a fragment of sallow moon.
   (b) There was a fragment of new moon.
10. *(a)* The muck held tightly to his foot as if it were a giant leech.
    (b) The muck sucked viciously at his foot as if it were a giant leech.

RICHARD CONNELL

Richard Connell was born in Dutchess County, New York, in 1893, and at the age of ten had already started his writing career—as a baseball reporter for his father's newspaper. He attended Georgetown College for one year, left to be secretary to his father, a congressman, and, in 1915, finished his education at Harvard, where he was editor of the college newspaper and yearbook.

Before Connell decided to become a free-lance writer, he worked on a newspaper and as an ad writer in New York. He also served in France during World War I. In 1919 he began his career as a free-lance writer and produced short stories, novels, and many motion-picture scripts. Mr. Connell lived in California from 1925 until his death in Beverly Hills in 1949.

EDMUND WARE

An Underground Episode

Have you ever felt you had to volunteer to do something you were very much afraid to do?

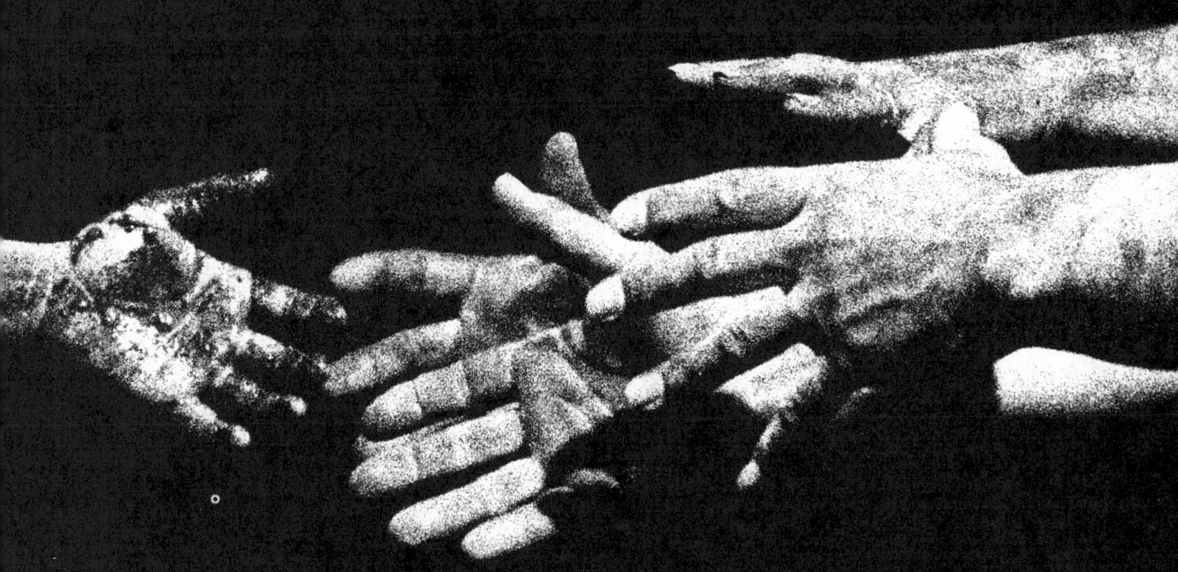

Three figures leaned against the slanting rain—Alamo Laska, Nick Christopher, and the boy who had run away from home. They rested on their long-handled shovels and, as they gazed into the crater which by their brawn they had hollowed in the earth, the blue clay oozed back again, slowly devouring the fruits of their toil.

Laska, the nomad, thought of the wild geese winging southward to warm bayous. Nick's heart, under the bone and muscle of his great chest, swelled with sweet thoughts of his wife and child who lived in a foreign city across an ocean. The boy felt the sting of rain against his cheeks and dreamed of his mother who seemed lovely and far away.

It was Sunday. The regular deep-trench gang lounged in their warm boarding house, while out on the job the three men toiled alone. They breathed heavily, and the gray steam crawled upon their backs, for it was cold.

"Look at 'er filling in," growled Laska, "faster than a man could dig."

"Mud's get inna pipe," said Nick. "The Inspector make us tear him out if she fill any more."

Backed close to the edge of the crater stood a giant trench-digging machine. In the dusk it appeared as a crouched and shadowy animal—silent, gloomy, capable. But a broken piston had crippled its engines and they were swathed in tarpaulin.

A long gray mound stretched away from the crater opposite the machine. Buried thirty feet below the mound was the new-laid sewer pipe. From the bottom of the pit at the machine, the pipe ran a hundred yards horizontally under the surface, opening in a manhole. This hundred yards of new-laid pipe was the reason for the three men digging in the rain. They had dug eleven hours trying to uncover the open end of the pipe in order to seal it against the mud. But rain and ooze and storm had bested them. The bank had caved, and the mud had crawled into the mouth of the pipe, obstructing it.

"It's getting dark fast," said Laska, "an' we're licked."

"We can't do nothing more," said the boy.

Nick Christopher scraped the mud from his shovel. He looked up into the whirlpools of the sky. "In a year I go old country. I see my wife. I see my kid."

"Nick," said Laska, "go over to the shanty and get a couple of lanterns and telephone Stender. Tell him if he don't want the Inspector on our neck to get out here quick with a gang."

Nick stuck his shovel in the mud and moved away across the plain toward the shanty.

The cold had crept into the boy. It frightened him, and in the darkness his eyes sought Laska's face. "How could we clean out the pipe, even when the gang got down to it?"

"Maybe we could flush her out with a fire hose," said Laska.

"There's no water plug within a mile."

Laska said nothing. The boy waited for him to reply, but he didn't. Picking up his damp shirt, the boy pulled it on over his head. He did not tuck in the tails, and they flapped in the wind, slapping against him. He looked like a gaunt, serious bird, striving to leave the ground. He was bareheaded, and his yellow hair was matted and stringy with dampness. His face was thin, a little sunken, and fine drops of moisture clung to the fuzz on his cheeks. His lips were blue with cold. He was seventeen.

Laska stared into the pit. It was too dark to see bottom, but something in the black hole fascinated him. "If we could get a rope

---

through the pipe we could drag sandbags through into the manhole. That would clean her out in good shape."

"How could we get a rope through?"

"I dunno. Stender'll know." Laska walked over to the digging machine and leaned against its towering side. The rain had turned to sleet. "It's cold," he said.

The boy followed Laska, and went close to him for warmth and friendship. "How *could* we get a rope through?"

Laska's shoulders lifted slowly. "You'll see. You'll see. You'll see when Stender gets here. Say, it's freezing."

After a long time of waiting, a yellow light flamed into being in the shanty, and they heard the muffled scraping of boots on the board floor. The shanty door opened. A rectangle of light stood out sharply.

Swart figures crossed and re-crossed the lighted area, pouring out into the storm.

"Ho!" called Laska.

"Ho!" came the answer, galloping to them in the wind.

They heard the rasping of caked mud on dungarees, the clank of shovels, the voice of Stender, the foreman. Lanterns swung like yellow pendulums. Long-legged shadows reached and receded.

The diggers gathered about the rim of the pit, staring. Stender's face showed in the lantern light. His lips were wrinkled, as if constantly prepared for blasphemy. He was a tall, cursing conqueror. Orders shot from his throat, and noisily the men descended into the pit and began to dig. They drew huge, gasping breaths like mired beasts fighting for life.

The boy watched, his eyes bulging in the dark. Hitherto he had thought very briefly of sewers, regarding them as unlovely things. But Laska and Nick and Stender gave them splendor and importance. The deep-trench men were admirable monsters. They knew the clay, the feel and pattern of it, for it had long been heavy in their minds and muscles. They were big in three dimensions and their eyes were black and barbarous. When they ate it was with rough and tumble relish, and as their bellies fattened, they spoke tolerantly of enemies. They played lustily with a view to satiation. They worked stupendously. They were diggers in clay, transformed by lantern light into a race of giants.

Through the rain came Stender, his black slicker crackling. "They're down," he said. "Angelo just struck the pipe."

Laska grunted.

Stender blew his nose with his fingers, walked away and climbed down into the hole. They lost sight of him as he dropped over the rim. The sound of digging had ceased and two or three men on the surface rested on their shovels, the light from below gleaming in their flat faces. Laska and the boy knew that Stender was examining the pipe. They heard him swearing at what he had found.

After a moment he clambered up over the rim and held up a lantern. His cuddy, gripped firmly between his teeth, was upside down to keep out the wet.

"Someone's got to go through the pipe," he said, raising his voice. "There's fifty bucks for the man that'll go through the pipe into the manhole with a line tied to his foot. Fifty bucks!"

There was a moment of quiet. The men thought of the fifty dollars, and furtively measured themselves against the deed at hand. It seemed to the boy that he was the only one who feared the task. He did not think of the fifty dollars, but thought only of the fear.

Three hundred feet through a rathole, eighteen inches in diameter. Three hundred feet of muck, of wet black dark, and no turning back. But, if he did not volunteer, they would know that he was afraid. The boy stepped from behind Laska and said uncertainly: "I'll go, Stender," and he wished he might snatch back the words; for, looking about him, he saw that not a man among those present could have wedged his shoulders into the mouth of an eighteen-inch pipe. He was the only volunteer. They had known he would be the only one.

Stender came striding over holding the lantern above his head. He peered into the boy's face. "Take off your clothes," he said.

"Take off my clothes?"

"That's what I said."

"You might get a buckle caught in a joint," said Laska. "See?"

The boy saw only that he had been trapped very cunningly. At home he could have been openly fearful, for at home everything about him was known. There, quite simply, he could have said: "I won't do it. I'm frightened. I'll be killed." But here the diggers in clay were lancing him with looks. And Laska was bringing a ball of line, one end of which would be fastened to his ankle.

"Just go in a sweater," said Laska. "A sweater an' boots over your woolens. We'll be waiting for you at the manhole."

He wanted so desperately to dive off into the night that he felt his legs bracing for a spring, and a tight feeling in his throat. Then, mechanically, he began to take off his clothes. Nick had gone clumping off to the shanty and shortly he returned with a pair of hip boots. "Here, kid. I get 'em warm for you inna shanty."

He thrust his feet into the boots, and Laska knelt and tied the heavy line to his ankle. "Too tight?"

"No. It's all right, I guess."

"Well—come on."

They walked past Stender who was pacing up and down among the men. They slid down into the crater, deepened now by the diggers. They stood by the partly covered mouth of the pipe. They were thirty feet below the surface of the ground.

Laska reached down and tugged at the knot he had tied in the line, then he peered into the mouth of the tube. He peered cautiously, as if he thought it might be inhabited. The boy's glance wandered up the wet sides of the pit. Over the rim a circle of bland yellow faces peered at him. Sleet tinkled against lanterns, spattered down and stung his flesh.

"Go ahead in," said Laska.

The boy blanched.

"Just keep thinking of the manhole, where you'll come out," said Laska.

The boy's throat constricted. He seemed to be bursting with a pressure from inside. He got down on his belly in the slush-ice and mud. It penetrated slowly to his skin, and spread over him. He put his head inside the mouth of the pipe, drew back in horror. Some gibbering words flew from his lips. His voice sounded preposterously loud. Laska's voice was already shopworn with distance. "You can make it! Go ahead."

He lay on his left side, and, reaching out with his left arm, caught a joint and drew himself in. The mud oozed up around him, finding its way upon him, welling up against the left side of his face. He pressed his right cheek against the ceiling of the pipe to keep the muck from covering his mouth and nose. Laska's voice was far and muffled. Laska was in another world—a sane world of night, of storm, and the mellow glow of lanterns.

"Are you makin' it all right, kid?"

The boy cried out, his ears ringing with his cry. It reëchoed from the sides of the pipe. The sides hemmed him, pinned him, closed him in on every side with their paralyzing circumference.

There is no darkness like the darkness underground that miners know. It borrows something from night, from tombs, from places used by bats. Such fluid black can terrify a flame, and suffocate, and drench a mind with madness. There is a fierce desire to struggle, to beat one's hands against the prison. The boy longed to lift his pitiful human strength against the walls. He longed to claw at his eyes in the mad certainty that more than darkness curtained them.

He had moved but a few feet on his journey when panic swept him. Ahead of him the mud had built into a solid wave. Putting forth his left hand, he felt a scant two inches between the wave's crest and the ceiling of the pipe. There was nothing to do but go back. If he moved ahead, it meant death by suffocation. He tried to back away, but caught his toe in a joint of the pipe. He was entombed! In an hour he would be a body. The cold and dampness would kill him before they could dig down to him. Nick and Laska would pull him from the muck, and Laska would say: "Huh, his clock's stopped."

He thrashed with delirious strength against his prison. He felt the skin tearing from the backs of his hands as he flailed the rough walls. And some gods must have snickered, for above the walls of the pipe were thirty feet of unyielding clay, eight thousand miles of earth below. A strength, a weight, a night, each a thousand times his most revolting dream, leaned upon the boy, depressing, crushing, stamping him out. The ground gave no cry of battle. It did no bleeding, suffered no pain, uttered no groans. It flattened him silently. It swallowed him in its foul despotism. It dropped its merciless weight upon his mind. It was so inhuman, so horribly incognizant of the God men swore had made it.

In the midst of his frenzy, when he had beaten his face against the walls until it bled, he heard a ringing voice he knew was real, springing from human sympathy. It was Laska, calling: "Are you all right, kid?"

In that instant the boy loved Laska as he loved his life. Laska's voice sheered the weight from him, scattered the darkness, brought him new balance and a hope to live.

"Fine!" he answered in a cracking yell. He yelled again, loving the sound of his voice, and thinking how foolish yelling was in such a place.

With his left hand he groped ahead and found that the wave of mud had settled, leveled off by its own weight. He drew his body together, pressing it against the pipe. He straightened, moved ahead six inches. His fingers found a loop of oakum dangling from a joint, and he pulled himself on, his left arm forward, his right arm behind over his hip, like a swimmer's.

He had vanquished panic, and he looked ahead to victory. Each joint brought him twenty inches nearer his goal. Each twenty inches was a plateau which enabled him to vision a new plateau—the next joint. The joints were like small deceitful rests upon a march.

He had been more than an hour on the way. He did not know how far he had gone, a third, perhaps even a half of the distance. He forgot the present, forgot fear, wet, cold, blackness; he lost himself in dreaming of the world of men outside the prison.

He did not know how long he had been counting the joints, but he found himself whispering good numbers: "Fifty-one, fifty-two, fifty-three. . . ." Each joint, when he thought of it, appeared to take up a vast time of squirming in the muck, and the line dragged heavily behind his foot.

Suddenly, staring into the darkness so that it seemed to bring a pain to his eyes, he saw a pallid ray. He closed his eyes, opened them, and looked again. The ray was real, and he uttered a whimper of relief. He knew that the ray must come from Stender's lantern. He pictured Stender and a group of the diggers huddled in the manhole, waiting for him. The men and the manhole grew magnificent in his mind, and he thought of them worshipfully.

"Seventy-six, seventy-seven, seventy-eight. . . ."

The ray grew slowly, like a worth-while thing. It took an oval shape, and the oval grew fat, like an egg, then round. It was a straight line to the manhole and the mud had thinned.

Through the pipe, into the boy's ears, a voice rumbled like a half-hearted thunder. It was Stender's voice: "How you makin' it?"

"Oh, just fine!" His cry came pricking back into his ears like a shower of needles.

There followed a long span of numbness. The cold and wet had dulled his senses, so that whenever the rough ceiling of the pipe ripped his face, he did not feel it; so that struggling in the muck became an almost pleasant and normal thing, since all elements of fear and pain and imagination had been removed. Warmth and dryness became alien to him. He was a creature native to darkness, foreign to light.

The round yellow disk before him gave him his only sense of living. It was a sunlit landfall, luring him on. He would close his eyes and count five joints, then open them quickly, cheering himself at the perceptible stages of progress.

Then, abruptly, it seemed, he was close to the manhole. He could hear men moving. He could see the outline of Stender's head as Stender peered into the mouth of the pipe. Men kneeled, pushing each other's heads to one side, in order to watch him squirm toward them. They began to talk excitedly. He could hear them breathing, see details—and Stender and Laska reached in. They got their hands upon him. They hauled him to them, as if he were something they wanted to inspect scientifically. He felt as if they thought he was a rarity, a thing of great oddness. The light dazzled him. It began to move around and around, and to dissolve into many lights, some of which danced locally on a bottle. He heard Stender's voice:

"Well, he made it all right. What do you know?"

"Here, kid," said Laska, holding the bottle to his mouth. "Drink all of this that you can hold."

He could not stand up. He believed calmly that his flesh and bones were constructed of putty. He could hear no vestige of the song of victory he had dreamed of hearing. He looked stupidly at his hands, which bled painlessly. He could not feel his arms and legs at all. He was a vast sensation of lantern light and the steam of human beings breathing in a damp place.

Faces peered at him. The faces were curious, and surprised. He felt a clouded, uncomprehending resentment against them. Stender held him up on one side, Laska on the other. They looked at each other across him. Suddenly Laska stooped and gathered him effortlessly into his arms.

"You'll get covered with mud," mumbled the boy.

"If he didn't make it all right," said Stender. "Save us tearing out the pipe."

"Forget the pipe," said Laska.

The boy's wet head fell against Laska's chest. He felt the rise and fall of Laska's muscles, and knew that Laska was climbing with him up the iron steps inside the manhole. Night wind smote him. He buried his head deeper against Laska. Laska's body became a mountain of warmth. He felt a heavy sighing peace, like a soldier who has been comfortably wounded and knows that war for him is over.

WHAT DO YOU SAY?

1. (a) What do we learn about the boy as the story opens? *(b)* What details provide the setting in which we find him?

2. (a) What circumstances lead to the boy's volunteering to go through the pipe? *(b)* Explain why he is led to volunteer: by forces within him; by forces around him.

3. (a) What one incident after the boy had started through the pipe brought him the greatest comfort? *(b)* What is the relation of that incident to the final paragraph of the story?

4. (a) You have learned that one of the skills of a storyteller is the ability to create a powerful emotional reaction in the reader. How well does Mr. Ware accomplish this goal? *(b)* What were your principal emotions as you read the story? *(c)* What particular details caused these emotions?

5. (a) Explain what Stender implies by the words, "If he didn't make it all right." *(b)* Why does Laska respond, "Forget the pipe"?

KNOW YOUR WORDS

Synonyms

From the synonyms (words having the same meaning) listed below, choose the one that might be used to replace the italicized word in each sentence. You may use the Glossary or a dictionary for help.

senselessly	uncivilized	unaware
wrapped	withdrew	indignation
tributary	desolate	
trace	oppression	

1. Laska, the nomad, thought of the wild geese winging southward to warm ***bayous.***
2. They were big in three dimensions and their eyes were black and ***barbarous.***
3. He felt a clouded, uncomprehending ***resentment*** against them.
4. A broken piston had crippled its engines, and they were ***swathed*** in tarpaulin.
5. He looked like a ***gaunt,*** serious bird, striving to leave the ground.
6. Long-legged shadows reached and ***receded.***
7. His voice sounded ***preposterously*** loud.
8. It swallowed him in its foul ***despotism.***
9. It was so inhuman, so horribly ***incognizant*** of the God men swore had made it.
10. He could hear no ***vestige*** of the song of victory he had dreamed of hearing.

EDMUND WARE (SMITH)

"When I was sixteen, I ran away from home and went west to become a cowboy and ride horses, sitting 'tall in the saddle,' " says Edmund Ware. "But what I actually did was dig postholes across a large portion of Montana.

" 'An Underground Episode is a true story of my experience during the construction of a tunnel sewer in Ecorse, Michigan. It emerges from fact into fiction with but a few distortions and/or exaggerations. I wrote the story nearly fifteen years after it happened to me—but the episode was so deeply engraved in my memory that the actual writing took only a couple of hours. I feel that the story exemplifies the power of appeal to all the senses, so that the reader hears, sees, smells, feels, and tastes just as I did while undergoing the ordeal of crawling through the pipe."

This author, whose full name is Edmund Ware Smith, actually has a New England background that he claims "over qualifies me as a Yankee." He was born in Connecticut, brought up in Massachusetts, lived in Vermont and New Hampshire, and now lives in Maine. He attended several schools and colleges but received no degrees. Of this experience he says, "If I had a diploma, it would be a mounted trout."

Mr. Smith, who spends six months of each year in a cabin in the Maine woods, is still writing stories, essays, and books that appeal to the senses—especially to the senses of nature lovers. Such books of Mr. Smith's as ***Further Adventures of the One-Eyed Poacher, Treasury of the Maine Woods,*** and ***For Maine Only*** not only appeal to the senses but add meaning to his "mounted trout diploma."

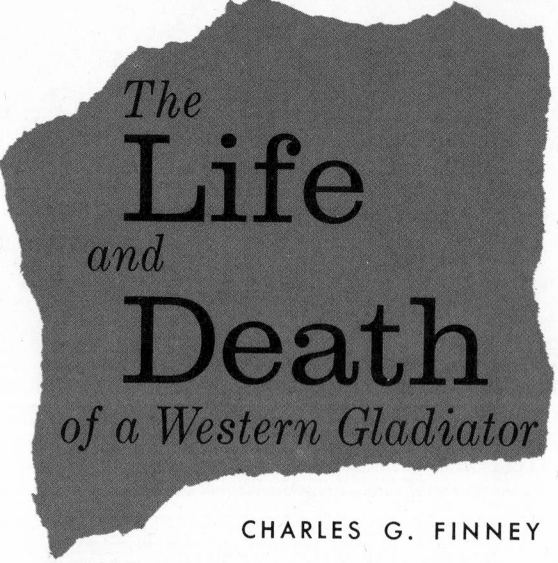

The Life and Death of a Western Gladiator

CHARLES G. FINNEY

We are constantly aware of the chances in life which bring luck to some and misfortune to others. But what are the odds in life for an animal?

He was born on a summer morning in the shady mouth of a cave. Three others were born with him, another male and two females. Each was about five inches long and slimmer than a lead pencil.

Their mother left them a few hours after they were born. A day after that his brother and sisters left him also. He was all alone. Nobody cared whether he lived or died. His tiny brain was very dull. He had no arms or legs. His skin was delicate. Nearly everything that walked on the ground or burrowed in it, that flew in the air or swam in the water or climbed trees was his enemy. But he didn't know that. He knew nothing at all. He was aware of his own existence, and that was the sum of his knowledge.

The direct rays of the sun could, in a short time, kill him. If the temperature dropped too low he would freeze. Without food he would starve. Without moisture he would die of dehydration. If a man or a horse stepped on him he would be crushed. If anything chased him he could run neither very far nor very fast.

Thus it was at the hour of his birth. Thus it would be, with modifications, all his life.

But against these drawbacks he had certain qualifications that fitted him to be a competitive creature of this world and equipped him for its warfare. He could exist a long time without food or water. His very smallness at birth protected him when

he most needed protection. Instinct provided him with what he lacked in experience. In order to eat he first had to kill; and he was eminently adapted for killing. In sacs in his jaws he secreted a virulent poison. To inject that poison he had two fangs, hollow and pointed. Without that poison and those fangs he would have been among the most helpless creatures on earth. With them he was among the deadliest.

He was, of course, a baby rattlesnake, a desert diamondback, named Crotalus atrox by the herpetologists Baird and Girard and so listed in the *Catalogue of North American Reptiles* in its issue of 1853. He was grayish brown in color with a series of large dark diamond-shaped blotches on his back. His tail was white with five black cross-bands. It had a button on the end of it.

Little Crotalus lay in the dust in the mouth of his cave. Some of his kinfolk lay there too. It was their home. That particular tribe of rattlers had lived there for scores of years.

The cave had never been seen by a white man.

Sometimes as many as two hundred rattlers occupied the den. Sometimes the numbers shrunk to as few as forty or fifty.

The tribe members did nothing at all for each other except breed. They hunted singly; they never shared their food. They derived some automatic degree of safety from their numbers, but their actions were never concerted toward using their numbers to any end. If an enemy attacked one of them, the others did nothing about it.

Young Crotalus' brother was the first of the litter to go out into the world and the first to die. He achieved a distance of fifty feet from the den when a Sonoran racer,[1] four feet long and hungry, came upon him. The little rattler, despite his poison fangs, was a tidbit. The racer, long skilled in such arts, snatched him up by the head and swallowed him down. Powerful digestive juices in the racer's stomach did the rest. Then the racer, appetite whetted, prowled around until it found one of Crotalus' little sisters. She went the way of the brother.

Nemesis of the second sister was a chaparral cock. This cuckoo, or road runner as it is called, found the baby, amid some rocks, uttered a cry of delight, scissored it by the neck, shook it until it was almost lifeless, banged and pounded it upon a rock until life had indeed left it, and then gulped it down.

---

1. *Sonoran racer,* one of a group of large, slender snakes, with smooth scales and very agile movements.

Crotalus, somnolent in a cranny of the cave's mouth, neither knew nor cared. Even if he had, there was nothing he could have done about it.

On the fourth day of his life he decided to go out into the world himself. He rippled forth uncertainly, the transverse plates on his belly serving him as legs.

He could see things well enough within his limited range, but a five-inch-long snake can command no great field of vision. He had an excellent sense of smell. But, having no ears, he was stone deaf. On the other hand, he had a pit, a deep pock mark between eye and nostril. Unique, this organ was sensitive to animal heat. In pitch blackness, Crotalus, by means of the heat messages recorded in his pit, could tell whether another animal was near and could also judge its size. That was better than an ear.

The single button on his tail could not, of course, yet rattle. Crotalus wouldn't be able to rattle until that button had grown into three segments. Then he would be able to buzz.

He had a wonderful tongue. It looked like an exposed nerve and was probably exactly that. It was forked, and Crotalus thrust it in and out as he traveled. It told him things that neither his eyes nor his nose nor his pit told him.

Snake fashion, Crotalus went forth, not knowing where he was going, for he had never been anywhere before. Hunger was probably his prime mover. In order to satisfy that hunger he had to find something smaller than himself and kill it.

He came upon a baby lizard sitting in the sand. Eyes, nose, pit, and tongue told Crotalus it was there. Instinct told him what it was and what to do. Crotalus gave a tiny one-inch strike and bit the lizard. His poison killed it. He took it by the head and swallowed it. Thus was his first meal.

During his first two years Crotalus grew rapidly. He attained a length of two feet; his tail had five rattles on it and its button. He rarely bothered with lizards any more, preferring baby rabbits, chipmunks, and round-tailed ground squirrels. Because of his slow locomotion he could not run down these agile little things. He had to contrive instead to be where they were when they would pass. Then he struck swiftly, injected his poison, and ate them after they died.

At two he was formidable. He had grown past the stage where a racer or a road runner could safely tackle him. He had grown to the size where other desert dwellers—coyotes, foxes, coatis, wildcats—knew it was better to leave him alone.

And, at two, Crotalus became a father, his life being regulated by cycles. His cycles were plant-like. The peach tree does not "know" when it is time to flower, but flower it does because its cycle orders it to do so.

In the same way, Crotalus did not "know" when it was time for young desert diamondback rattlers to pair off and breed. But his cycle knew. He found "her" on a rainy morning.

Of that physical union six new rattlesnakes were born. Thus Crotalus, at two, had carried out his major primary function: he had reproduced his kind. In two years he had experienced everything that was reasonably possible for desert diamondback rattlesnakes to experience except death.

He had not experienced death for the simple reason that there had never been an opportunity for anything bigger and stronger than himself to kill him. Now, at two, because he was so formidable, that opportunity became more and more unlikely.

He grew more slowly in the years following his initial spurt. At the age of twelve he was five feet long. Few of the other rattlers in his den were older or larger than he.

He had a castanet of fourteen segments. It had been broken off occasionally in the past, but with each new molting a new segment appeared.

His first skin-shedding back in his babyhood had been a bewildering experience. He did not know what was happening. His eyes clouded over until he could not see. His skin thickened and dried until it cracked in places. His pit and his nostrils ceased to function. There was only one thing to do and that was to get out of that skin.

Crotalus managed it by nosing against the bark of a shrub until he forced the old skin down over his head, bunching it like the rolled top of a stocking around his neck. Then he pushed around among rocks and sticks and branches, literally crawling out of his skin by slow degrees. Wriggling free at last, he looked like a brand new snake. His skin was bright and satiny, his eyes and nostrils were clear, his pit sang with sensation.

For the rest of his life he was to molt three or four times a year. Each time he did it he felt as if he had been born again.

At twelve he was a magnificent reptile. Not a single scar defaced his rippling symmetry. He was diabolically beautiful and deadly poison.

His venom was his only weapon, for he had no power of constriction. Yellowish in color, his poison was odorless and tasteless. It was a highly complex mixture of proteids, each in itself direly toxic. His venom worked on the blood. The more poison he injected with a bite, the more dangerous the wound. The pain rendered by his bite was instantaneous, and the shock accompanying it was profound. Swelling began immediately, to be followed by a ghastly oozing. Injected directly into a large vein, his poison brought death quickly, for the victim died when it reached his heart.

At the age of twenty Crotalus was the oldest and largest rattler in his den. He was six feet long and weighed thirteen pounds. His whole world was only about a mile in radius. He had fixed places where he avoided the sun when it was hot and he was away from his cave. He knew his hunting grounds thoroughly, every game trail, every animal burrow.

He was a fine old machine, perfectly adapted to his surroundings, accustomed to a life of leisure and comfort. He dominated his little world.

The mighty seasonal rhythms of the desert were as vast pulsations, and the lives of the rattlesnakes were attuned to them. Spring sun beat down, spring rains fell, and, as the plants of the desert ended their winter hibernations, so did the vipers in their lair. The plants opened forth and budded; the den "opened" too, and the snakes crawled forth. The plants fertilized each other, and new plants were born. The snakes bred, and new snakes were produced. The desert was repopulated.

In the autumn the plants began to close; in the same fashion the snake den began to close, the reptiles returned to it, lay like lingering blossoms about its entrance for a while, then disappeared within it when winter came. There they slept until summoned forth by a new spring.

Crotalus was twenty years old. He was in the golden age of his viperhood.

But men were approaching. Spilling out of their cities, men were settling in that part of the desert where Crotalus lived. They built roads and houses, set up fences, dug for water, planted crops.

They homesteaded the land. They brought new animals with them—cows, horses, dogs, cats, barnyard fowl.

The roads they built were death traps for the desert dwellers. Every morning new dead bodies lay on the roads, the bodies of the things the men had run over and crushed in their vehicles.

That summer Crotalus met his first dog. It was a German shepherd which had been reared on a farm in the Midwest and there had gained the reputation of being a snake-killer. Black snakes, garter snakes, pilots,[2] water snakes; it delighted in killing them all. It would seize them by the middle, heedless of their tiny teeth, and shake them violently until they died.

---

2. *pilots,* a name used to refer to black, pine, or copperhead snakes.

This dog met Crotalus face to face in the desert at dusk. Crotalus had seen coyotes aplenty and feared them not. Neither did the dog fear Crotalus, although Crotalus then was six feet long, as thick in the middle as a motorcycle tire, and had a head the size of a man's clenched fist. Also this snake buzzed and buzzed and buzzed.

The dog was brave, and a snake was a snake. The German shepherd snarled and attacked. Crotalus struck him in the underjaw; his fangs sank in almost half an inch and squirted big blobs of hematoxic poison into the tissues of the dog's flesh.

The shepherd bellowed with pain, backed off, groveled with his jaws in the desert sand, and attacked again. He seized Crotalus somewhere by the middle of his body and tried to flip him in the air and shake him as, in the past, he had shaken slender black snakes to their death. In return, he received another poison-blurting stab in his flank and a third in the belly and a fourth in the eye as the terrible, writhing snake bit wherever it could sink its fangs.

The German shepherd had enough. He dropped the big snake and in sick, agonizing bewilderment crawled somehow back to his master's homestead and died.

The homesteader looked at his dead dog and became alarmed. If there was a snake around big enough to kill a dog that size, it could also kill a child and probably a man. It was something that had to be eliminated.

The homesteader told his fellow farmers, and they agreed to initiate a war of extermination against the snakes.

The campaign during the summer was sporadic. The snakes were scattered over the desert, and it was only by chance that the men came upon them. Even so, at summer's end, twenty-six of the vipers had been killed.

When autumn came the men decided to look for the rattlers' den and execute mass slaughter. The homesteaders had become desert-wise and knew what to look for.

They found Crotalus' lair without too much trouble—a rock outcropping on a slope that faced the south. Cast-off skins were in evidence in the bushes. Bees flew idly in and out of the den's mouth. Convenient benches and shelves of rock were at hand where the snakes might lie for a final sunning in the autumn air.

They killed the three rattlers they found at the den when they first discovered it. They made plans to return in a few more days when more of the snakes had congregated. They decided to bring along dynamite with them and blow up the mouth of the den so that the snakes within would be sealed there forever and the snakes without would have no place to find refuge.

On the day the men chose to return nearly fifty desert diamondbacks were gathered at the portals of the cave. The men shot them, clubbed them, smashed them with rocks. Some of the rattlers escaped the attack and crawled into the den.

Crotalus had not yet arrived for the autumn rendezvous. He came that night. The den's mouth was a shattered mass of rock, for the men had done their dynamiting well. Dead members of his tribe lay everywhere. Crotalus nosed among them, tongue flicking as he slid slowly along.

There was no access to the cave any more. He spent the night outside among the dead. The morning sun warmed him and awakened him. He lay there at full length. He had no place to go.

The sun grew hotter upon him and instinctively he began to slide toward some dark shade. Then his senses warned him of some animal presence near by; he stopped, half coiled, raised his head and began to rattle. He saw two upright figures. He did not know what they were because he had never seen men before.

"That's the granddaddy of them all," said one of the homesteaders. "It's a good thing we came back." He raised his shotgun.

WHAT DO YOU SAY?

1. Although this story is fiction, it is based upon fact. What details particularly impressed you as revealing the author's knowledge of his subject?

2. (a) What is a gladiator? (Consult your dictionary if you are not familiar with the word.) *(b)* Why is the author's use of this word in his title appropriate?

3. (a) Why does Crotalus live for so many years? *(b)* Why are his brothers and sisters not living? *(c)* Explain the part that chance plays in these facts.

4. (a) Relate the circumstances which lead to the death of Crotalus. *(b)* What has happened to the environment in which he has lived? *(c)* Who or what is to blame for his death?

5. (a) At the end of the story are you glad or sad at the death of Crotalus? *(b)* Find lines in which the author's choice of words creates sympathy for the snake.

6. (a) You have learned that not all short stories have plots developed to the same degree. Would you say that this story has a highly developed plot? Why or why not? *(b)* The title of this story states its main idea, or theme, and the entire story consists of one major conflict. What is this conflict?

KNOW YOUR WORDS

Understanding definitions

From the list of meanings, pick the correct one for each of the italicized words in the sentences. Number your paper from one through ten and write the correct definition opposite the number of the sentence.

manage	slow in understanding
stimulated	removal of water
partial alterations	nimble
finely sensitive	devilishly

zoologists who deal with reptiles
one who punishes another for evil deeds

1. His tiny brain was very ***dull.***
2. His skin was ***delicate.***
3. Without moisture he would die of ***dehydration.***
4. Thus it would be, with ***modifications,*** all his life.
5. He was named Crotalus atrox by the ***herpetologists.***
6. Then the racer, appetite ***whetted,*** prowled around until it found one of Crotalus' little sisters.
7. ***Nemesis*** of the second sister was a chaparral cock.
8. Because of his slow locomotion he could not run down these ***agile*** little things.
9. He had to ***contrive,*** instead, to be where they were when they would pass.
10. He was ***diabolically*** beautiful and deadly poisonous.

CHARLES G. FINNEY

Mr. Finney has written numerous short stories for leading magazines, as well as several novels. He established himself as an author in 1934 when his novel ***The Circus of Dr. Lao*** was awarded the American Booksellers Association prize for the most original novel of the year. Finney has lived in Tucson, Arizona, for the past thirty years and is employed by the Arizona Daily Star as a proofreader, night telegraph editor, and copy reader.

When asked what in particular had prompted him to write "Life and Death of a Western Gladiator," Mr. Finney replied: "Since a toddler, I have always been accused (probably justly so) of writing about nothing but snakes and soldiers. Anyhow, in 1958 I began to wonder how such a bizarrely beautiful thing as a rattlesnake could survive in the first place; it has no feet, no fins, no feathers, no fur, no hands, no wings—only a mouth full of poison; and the result of such ponderings led me to write 'The Life and Death of a Western Gladiator.' "

After you, my dear Alphonse

SHIRLEY JACKSON

Mrs. Wilson was just taking the gingerbread out of the oven when she heard Johnny outside talking to someone.

"Johnny," she called, "you're late. Come in and get your lunch."

"Just a minute, Mother," Johnny said. "After you, my dear Alphonse."

"After *you*, my dear Alphonse," another voice said.

"No, after *you*, my dear Alphonse," Johnny said.

Mrs. Wilson opened the door. "Johnny," she said, "you come in this minute and get your lunch. You can play after you've eaten."

Johnny came in after her, slowly. "Mother," he said, "I brought Boyd home for lunch with me."

"Boyd?" Mrs. Wilson thought for a moment. "I don't believe I've met Boyd. Bring him in, dear, since you've invited him. Lunch is ready."

"Boyd!" Johnny yelled. "Hey, Boyd, come on in!"

"I'm coming. Just got to unload this stuff."

"Well, hurry, or my mother'll be sore."

"Johnny, that's not very polite to either your friend or your mother," Mrs. Wilson said. "Come sit down, Boyd."

As she turned to show Boyd where to sit, she saw he was a Negro boy, smaller than Johnny but about the same age. His arms were loaded with split kindling wood. "Where'll I put this stuff, Johnny?" he asked.

Mrs. Wilson turned to Johnny. "Johnny," she said, "what did you make Boyd do? What is that wood?"

"Dead Japanese," Johnny said mildly. "We stand them in the ground and run over them with tanks."

"How do you do, Mrs. Wilson?" Boyd said.

"How do you do, Boyd? You shouldn't let Johnny make you carry all that wood. Sit down now and eat lunch, both of you."

"Why shouldn't he carry the wood, Mother? It's his wood. We got it at his place."

"Johnny," Mrs. Wilson said, "go on and eat your lunch."

"Sure," Johnny said. He held out the dish of scrambled eggs to Boyd. "After you, my dear Alphonse."

"After *you*, my dear Alphonse," Boyd said.

"After *you*, my dear Alphonse," Johnny said. They began to giggle.

"Are you hungry, Boyd?" Mrs. Wilson asked.

"Yes, Mrs. Wilson."

"Well, don't you let Johnny stop you. He always fusses about eating, so you just see that you get a good lunch. There's plenty of food here for you to have all you want."

"Thank you, Mrs. Wilson."

"Come on, Alphonse," Johnny said. He pushed half the scrambled eggs on to Boyd's plate. Boyd watched while Mrs. Wilson put a dish of stewed tomatoes beside his plate.

"Boyd don't eat tomatoes, do you Boyd?" Johnny said.

"*Doesn't* eat tomatoes, Johnny. And just because you don't like them, don't say that about Boyd. Boyd will eat *anything*."

"Bet he won't," Johnny said, attacking his scrambled eggs.

"Boyd wants to grow up and be a big strong man so he can work hard," Mrs. Wilson said. "I'll bet Boyd's father eats stewed tomatoes."

"My father eats anything he wants to," Boyd said.

"So does mine," Johnny said. "Sometimes he doesn't eat hardly anything. He's a little guy, though. Wouldn't hurt a flea."

"Mine's a little guy too," Boyd said.

"I'll bet he's strong, though," Mrs. Wilson said. She hesitated. "Does he . . . work?"

"Sure," Johnny said. "Boyd's father works in a factory."

"There, you see?" Mrs. Wilson said. "And he certainly has to be strong to do that—all that lifting and carrying at a factory."

"Boyd's father doesn't have to," Johnny said. "He's a foreman."

Mrs. Wilson felt defeated. "What does your mother do, Boyd?"

"My mother?" Boyd was surprised. "She takes care of us kids."

"Oh. She doesn't work, then?"

"Why should she?" Johnny said through a mouthful of eggs. "You don't work."

"You really don't want any stewed tomatoes, Boyd?"

"No, thank you, Mrs. Wilson," Boyd said.

"No, thank you, Mrs. Wilson, no, thank you, Mrs. Wilson, no, thank you, Mrs. Wilson," Johnny said. "Boyd's sister's going to work, though. She's going to be a teacher."

"That's a fine attitude for her to have, Boyd." Mrs. Wilson restrained an impulse to pat Boyd on the head. "I imagine you're all very proud of her?"

"I guess so," Boyd said.

"What about all your other brothers and sisters? I guess all of you want to make just as much of yourselves as you can."

"There's only me and Jean," Boyd said. "I don't know yet what I want to be when I grow up."

"We're going to be tank drivers, Boyd and me," Johnny said.

"Zoom." Mrs. Wilson caught Boyd's glass of milk as Johnny's napkin ring, suddenly transformed into a tank, plowed heavily across the table.

"Look, Johnny," Boyd said. "Here's a foxhole. I'm shooting at you."

Mrs. Wilson, with the speed born of long experience, took the gingerbread off the shelf and placed it carefully between the tank and the foxhole.

"Now eat as much as you want to, Boyd," she said. "I want to see you get filled up."

"Boyd eats a lot, but not as much as I do," Johnny said. "I'm bigger than he is."

"You're not much bigger," Boyd said. "I can beat you running."

Mrs. Wilson took a deep breath. "Boyd," she said. Both boys turned to her. "Boyd, Johnny has some suits that are a little too small for him, and a winter coat. It's not new, of course, but there's lots of wear in it still. And I have a few dresses that your mother or sister could probably use. Your mother can make them over into lots of things for all of you, and I'd be very happy to give them to you. Suppose before you leave I make up a big bundle and then you and Johnny can take it over to your mother right away . . ." Her voice trailed off as she saw Boyd's puzzled expression.

"But I have plenty of clothes, thank you," he said. "And I don't think my mother knows how to sew very well, and anyway I guess we buy about everything we need. Thank you very much, though."

"We don't have time to carry that old stuff around, Mother," Johnny said. "We got to play tanks with the kids today."

Mrs. Wilson lifted the plate of gingerbread off the table as Boyd was about to take another piece. "There are many little boys like you, Boyd, who would be very grateful for the clothes someone was kind enough to give them."

"Boyd will take them if you want him to, Mother," Johnny said.

"I didn't mean to make you mad, Mrs. Wilson," Boyd said.

"Don't think I'm angry, Boyd. I'm just disappointed in you, that's all. Now let's not say anything more about it."

She began clearing the plates off the table, and Johnny took Boyd's hand and pulled him to the door. "'Bye, Mother," Johnny said. Boyd stood for a minute, staring at Mrs. Wilson's back.

"After you, my dear Alphonse," Johnny said, holding the door open.

"Is your mother still mad?" Mrs. Wilson heard Boyd ask in a low voice.

"I don't know," Johnny said. "She's screwy sometimes."

"So's mine," Boyd said. He hesitated. "After *you*, my dear Alphonse."

WHAT DO YOU SAY?

1. To understand this story fully, you must be aware of the assumptions Mrs. Wilson makes. Early in the story, for example, Mrs. Wilson wrongly assumes that Johnny "made" Boyd carry the kindling wood into the house. *(a)* What assumption is behind Mrs. Wilson's insistence that Boyd "get a good lunch" (page 65, column 1, paragraph 8)? *(b)* Why does she hesitate before asking Boyd if his father works (page 65, column 1, paragraph 18? *(c)* What other assumptions do Mrs. Wilson's statements and questions reveal?

2. In what ways does Boyd's family differ from Mrs. Wilson's stereotyped notions of what Negroes are like?

3. Do you think Mrs. Wilson learns any kind of lesson from her meeting with Boyd? Defend your answer with logical arguments based on what you know about her character.

4. When this story was first published, in 1943, most readers remembered a comic strip called ***Alphonse and Gaston.*** The most conspicuous point of humor in the strip was the absurd and exaggerated politeness with which Alphonse and Gaston treated each other. "After you, my dear Alphonse" became a popular expression that was used humorously to insist another person take precedence over the speaker in some way. What might Miss Jackson have been trying to suggest about the relationship between Mrs. Wilson and Boyd by entitling the story "After You, My Dear Alphonse"?

SHIRLEY JACKSON

In her writing, Shirley Jackson (1919-1965) explored the dark regions of human action and personality. Much of her work deals with seemingly good, ordinary people who suddenly reveal unexpected and ugly traits. Beneath their often grotesque surfaces these stories conceal some very accurate comments on mankind. But away from her typewriter, Shirley Jackson was a Vermont housewife and mother of four who enjoyed suburban living and domestic duties. Life in her fourteen-room house was hectic and humorous; it furnished her with material for two partly-fictional memoirs which chronicle the antics of her completely engaging family.

A single incident can completely alter the lives of human beings. In the following story, a famous French writer tells of the effect of one such incident on the lives of a young French woman and her husband.

The Necklace

Guy de Maupassant

She was one of those pretty and charming girls who, as if by a mistake of destiny, are born in a family of clerks.[1] She had no dowry, no expectations, no means of becoming known, understood, loved, wedded by any rich and distinguished man; and so she let herself be married to a petty clerk in the Bureau of Public Instruction.

She was simple in her dress because she could not be elaborate, but she was as unhappy as if she had fallen from a higher rank, for with women there is no distinction of higher and lower: their beauty, their grace, and their natural charm fill the place of birth and family. Natural delicacy, instinctive elegance, a lively wit, are the ruling forces in the social realm, and make daughters of the common people the equals of the finest ladies.

She suffered ceaselessly, feeling herself born for all the refinements and luxuries of life. She suffered from the poverty of her home as she looked at the dirty walls, the worn-out chairs, the ugly curtains. All those things of which another woman of her station would have been quite unconscious tortured her and made her indignant. The sight of the country girl who was maid-of-all-works in her humble household filled her almost with desperation.

1. *clerks,* office workers.

She dreamed of echoing halls hung with Oriental draperies and lighted by tall bronze candelabra, while two tall footmen in knee-breeches drowsed in great armchairs by reason of the heating stove's oppressive warmth. She dreamed of splendid parlors furnished in rare old silks, of carved cabinets loaded with priceless curiosities, and of entrancing little boudoirs just right for afternoon chats with bosom friends—men famous and sought after, the envy and the desire of all the other women.

When she sat down to dinner at a little table covered with a cloth three days old, and looked across at her husband as he uncovered the soup and exclaimed with an air of rapture, "Oh, the delicious stew! I know nothing better than that," she dreamed of dainty dinners, of shining silverware, of tapestries which peopled the walls with antique figures and strange birds in fairy forests; she dreamed of delicious viands served in wonderful dishes, of whispered gallantries heard with a sphinxlike smile as you eat the pink flesh of a trout or the wing of a bird.

She had no dresses, no jewels, nothing; and she loved only that, she felt made for that. She was filled with a desire to please, to be envied, to be bewitching and sought after. She had a rich friend, a former schoolmate at the convent, whom she no longer wished to visit because she suffered so much when she came home. For whole days at a time she wept without ceasing in bitterness and hopeless misery.

Now, one evening her husband came home with a triumphant air, holding in his hand a large envelope.

"There," said he, "there is something for you."

She quickly tore open the paper and drew out a printed card, bearing these words:

"The Minister of Public Instruction and Mme.[2] Georges Rampouneau request the honor of M.[3] and Mme. Loisel's company at the palace of the Ministry, Monday evening, January 18th."

Instead of being overcome with delight, as her husband expected, she threw the invitation on the table with disdain, murmuring:

"What do you wish me to do with that?"

"Why, my dear, I thought you would be pleased. You never go out, and it is such a fine opportunity, this! I had awful trouble getting it. Everyone wants to go; it is very select, and they are not giving many invitations to clerks. You will see the whole official world."

She looked at him with irritation, and said, impatiently:

"What do you wish me to put on my back if I go?"

He had not thought of that. He stammered:

"Why, the dress you go to the theatre in. It seems all right to me."

He stopped, stupefied, distracted, on seeing that his wife was crying. Two great tears descended slowly from the corners of her eyes toward the corners of her mouth. He stuttered:

"What's the matter? What's the matter?"

By a violent effort she subdued her feelings and replied in a calm voice, as she wiped her wet cheeks:

"Nothing. Only I have no dress and consequently I cannot go to this ball. Give your invitation to some friend whose wife is better equipped than I."

He was in despair. He replied:

"Let us see, Mathilde. How much would it cost, a suitable dress, which you could wear again on future occasions, something very simple?"

She reflected for some seconds, computing the cost, and also wondering what sum she could ask without bringing down upon herself an immediate refusal and an astonished exclamation from the economical clerk.

---

2. Mme., Madame. **3. M.,** Monsieur (mə syoeʹ), Mr. or Sir. [French]

At last she answered hesitatingly:

"I don't know exactly, but it seems to me that with four hundred francs[4] I could manage."

He turned a trifle pale, for he had been saving just that sum to buy a gun and treat himself to a little hunting the following summer, in the country near Nanterre,[5] with a few friends who went there to shoot larks of a Sunday.

However, he said:

"Well, I think I can give you four hundred francs. But see that you have a pretty dress."

The day of the ball drew near, and Madame Loisel seemed sad, unhappy, anxious. Her dress was ready, however. Her husband said to her one evening:

"What is the matter? Come, you've been looking queer these last three days."

And she replied:

"It worries me that I have no jewels, not a single stone, nothing to put on. I shall look wretched enough. I would almost rather not go to the party."

He answered:

"You might wear natural flowers. They are very fashionable this season. For ten francs you can get two or three magnificent roses."

She was not convinced.

"No; there is nothing more humiliating than to look poor among women who are rich."

But her husband cried:

"How stupid of you! Go and find your friend Madame Forestier and ask her to lend you some jewels. You are intimate enough with her for that."

She uttered a cry of joy.

"Of course. I had not thought of that."

The next day she went to her friend's house and told her distress. Madame Forestier went to her handsome wardrobe, took out a large casket, brought it back, opened it, and said to Madame Loisel:

"Choose, my dear."

She saw first of all some bracelets, then a pearl necklace, then a Venetian cross, gold and precious stones of wonderful workmanship. She tried on the ornaments before the glass, hesitated, could not make up her mind to part with them, to give them back. She kept asking:

"Have you nothing else?"

"Why, yes. See, I do not know what will please you."

All at once she discovered, in a black satin box, a splendid diamond necklace, and her heart began to beat with immoderate desire. Her hands trembled as she took it. She fastened it around her throat, over her high-necked dress, and stood lost in ecstasy as she looked at herself.

"Would you lend me that,—only that?"

"Why, yes, certainly."

She sprang upon the neck of her friend, embraced her rapturously, then fled with her treasure.

The day of the ball arrived. Madame Loisel was a success. She was prettier than all the others, elegant, gracious, smiling, and crazy with joy. All the men stared at her, asked her name, tried to be introduced. All the cabinet officers wished to waltz with her. The minister noticed her.

She danced with intoxication, with passion, made drunk with pleasure, forgetting all in the triumph of her beauty, in the glory of her success, in a sort of mist of happiness, the result of all this homage, all this admiration, all these awakened desires, this victory so complete and so sweet to the heart of woman.

She left about four o'clock in the morning. Her husband had been sleeping since midnight in a little deserted anteroom with three other gentlemen, whose wives were having a good time.

He threw about her shoulders the wraps which he had brought for her to go out in,

---

4. four hundred francs, about eighty dollars. *5. Nanterre* (nän tãr′).

the modest wraps of common life, whose poverty contrasted sharply with the elegance of the ballroom toilet. She felt this and wished to escape, that she might not be noticed by the other women who were enveloping themselves in costly furs.

Loisel held her back.

"Wait here, you will catch cold outside. I will go and find a cab."

But she would not listen to him, and rapidly descended the stairs. When they were at last in the street, they could find no carriage, and began to look for one, crying after the cabmen they saw passing at a distance.

They walked down toward the Seine[6] in despair, shivering with cold. At last they found on the quay one of those ancient nocturnal coupés that one sees in Paris only after dark, as if they were ashamed to display their wretchedness during the day.

They were put down at their door in the Rue des Martyrs, and sadly mounted the steps to their apartments. It was all over, for her. And as for him, he reflected that he must be at his office at ten o'clock.

She took off the wraps which enveloped her shoulders before the glass, to take a final look at herself in all her glory. But suddenly she uttered a cry. She no longer had the necklace about her neck!

Her husband, already half undressed, inquired:

"What is the matter?"

She turned madly toward him.

"I have—I have—I no longer have Madame Forestier's necklace."

He stood up distracted.

"What!—how!—it is impossible!"

They looked in the folds of her dress, in the folds of her cloak, in the pockets, everywhere. They could not find a trace of it.

He asked:

"You are sure you still had it when you left the ball?"

"Yes. I felt it in the vestibule at the palace."

"But if you had lost it in the street we should have heard it fall. It must be in the cab."

"Yes. That's probably it. Did you take the number?"

"No. And you, you did not notice it?"

"No."

They looked at each other thunderstruck. At last Loisel put on his clothes again.

"I am going back," said he, "over every foot of the way we came, to see if I shall not find it."

So he started. She remained in her ball dress without strength to go to bed, sitting on a chair, with no fire, her mind a blank.

Her husband returned about seven o'clock. He had found nothing.

He went to police headquarters, to the newspapers to offer a reward, to the cab companies, everywhere, in short, where a suspicion of hope led him.

She watched all day, in the same state of blank despair before this frightful disaster.

Loisel returned in the evening with cheeks hollow and pale; he had found nothing.

"You must write to your friend," said he, "that you have broken the clasp of her necklace and that you are having it repaired. It will give us time to turn around."

She wrote at his dictation.

At the end of a week they had lost all hope.

And Loisel, looking five years older, declared:

"We must consider how to replace this ornament."

The next day they took the box which had contained it, and went to the place of the jeweller whose name they found inside. He consulted his books.

"It was not I, madame, who sold the necklace; I must simply have furnished the casket."

Then they went from jeweller to jeweller, looking for an ornament like the other, con-

---

6. ***Seine*** (sān), a river which runs through Paris.

sulting their memories, both sick with chagrin and anguish.

They found, in a shop at the Palais-Royal,[7] a string of diamonds which seemed to them exactly what they were looking for. It was worth forty thousand francs. They could have it for thirty-six thousand.

So they begged the jeweller not to sell it for three days. And they made an arrangement that he should take it back for thirty-four thousand francs if the other were found before the end of February.

Loisel had eighteen thousand francs which his father had left him. He would borrow the rest.

He did borrow, asking a thousand francs of one, five hundred of another, five louis[8] here, three louis there. He gave notes, made ruinous engagements, dealt with usurers, with all the tribe of money-lenders. He compromised the rest of his life, risked his signature without knowing if he might not be involving his honor, and, terrified by the anguish yet to come, by the black misery about to fall upon him, by the prospect of physical privation and every mental torture, he went to get the new necklace, and laid down on the dealer's counter thirty-six thousand francs.

When Madame Loisel took the ornament back to Madame Forestier, the latter said coldly:

"You should have returned it sooner, for I might have needed it."

She did not open the case, to the relief of her friend. If she had detected the substitution, what would she have thought? What would she have said? Would she have taken her friend for a thief?

Madame Loisel now knew the horrible life of the needy; moreover, all at once she took her part heroically. They must pay this frightful debt. She would pay it. They dismissed their maid, they gave up their apartment, they rented another under the roof.

She came to know the drudgery of housework, the odious cares of the kitchen. She washed the dishes, using her rosy nails on the greasy pots and the bottoms of the saucepans. She washed the dirty linen, the shirts and the dishcloths, which she hung to dry on a line; she carried the garbage down to the street every morning, and carried up the water, stopping at each landing to rest. And, dressed like a woman of the people, she went to the fruiterer's, the grocer's, the butcher's, her basket on her arm, bargaining, abusing, defending sou[9] by sou her miserable money.

Each month they had to pay some notes, renew others, obtain more time.

The husband worked evenings neatly footing up the account books of some tradesman, and often far into the night he sat copying manuscript at five sous a page.

And this life lasted ten years.

At the end of ten years they had paid everything,—everything, with the exactions of usury and the accumulations of compound interest.

Madame Loisel seemed old now. She had become the woman of impoverished households—strong and hard and rough. With hair half combed, with skirts awry, and reddened hands, she talked loud as she washed the floor with great swishes of water. But sometimes, when her husband was at the office, she sat down near the window and thought of that evening at the ball so long ago, when she had been so beautiful and so fêted.

What would have happened if she had not lost that necklace? Who knows, who knows? How strange life is, how changeful! How little a thing is needed for us to be lost or to be saved!

But one Sunday, as she was going for a walk in the Champs Élysées[10] to refresh

---

7. ***Palais-Royal*** (pä lā′ rwä al′), a shopping district in Paris. 8. ***five louis*** (lü wē′), gold coins worth about twenty francs (four dollars) each. 9. ***sou*** (sü), one twentieth of a franc; about one cent. 10. ***Champs Élysées*** (shäN zā lē zā′), a fashionable avenue in Paris.

herself after the labors of the week, all at once she saw a woman walking with a child. It was Madame Forestier, still young, still beautiful, still charming.

Madame Loisel was agitated. Should she speak to her? Why, of course. And now that she had paid she would tell her all. Why not?

She went up.

"Bonjour,[11] Jeanne."

The other, astonished to be addressed so familiarly by this woman of the people, did not recognize her. She stammered:

"But–madame–I do not know you. You must have made a mistake."

"No, I am Mathilde Loisel."

Her friend uttered a cry.

"Oh! my poor Mathilde, how changed you are!"

"Yes, I have had days hard enough since I saw you, days wretched enough–and all because of you!"

"Me? How so?"

"You remember that necklace of diamonds that you lent me to wear to the ministerial ball?"

"Yes. Well?"

"Well, I lost it."

"How? But you returned it to me."

"I returned to you another exactly like it. These ten years we've been paying for it. You know it was not easy for us, who had nothing. At last it is over, and I am very glad."

Madame Forestier stood staring at her.

"You say that you bought a necklace of diamonds to replace mine?"

"Yes; you did not notice it, then? They were very like."

And she smiled with a proud and naïve pleasure.

Madame Forestier, deeply moved, took both her hands.

"Oh, my poor Mathilde! Why, my necklace was paste. It was worth five hundred francs at most."

---

*11. **Bonjour*** (bᴏɴ zhür′), good morning; good day. [French]

WHAT DO YOU SAY?

1. *(a)* What are Madame Loisel's outstanding traits? *(b)* At the beginning of the story what is her attitude toward her situation in life? *(c)* What is it that she desires? *(d)* After the necklace is lost, how does her personality change? *(e)* Do your feelings about her also change? Explain.

2. *(a)* What sort of person is M. Loisel? *(b)* How does he feel about his wife? Cite passages which show his feelings.

3. What does the necklace represent to Madame Loisel?

4. What connection is there between the paste necklace and the society to which Madame Loisel wishes to belong?

5. *(a)* Explain the role that irony of situation plays in this story. *(b)* What comment about life is the author making?

6. *(a)* Does this story seem true to life? Explain. *(b)* Would this story have been better if the author had contrived a happy ending? Why or why not?

GUY DE MAUPASSANT

Henri René Albert Guy de Maupassant was born in France in 1850. As a youth Maupassant became acquainted with the French novelist Gustave Flaubert, though at the time he himself seems to have had little interest in pursuing a literary career. Maupassant served in the French Army during the Franco-Prussian War, and afterward entered the French civil service. Encouraged by Flaubert, Maupassant began to write, and in 1881 published his first volume of short stories. Before his death in 1893, he had published more than thirty volumes of short stories, novels, plays, and travel essays.

Maupassant's fiction frequently deals with the subjects he knew best: the Norman peasantry, the Franco-Prussian War, and lower civil service officials. His concern for clarity and precise, accurate detail is apparent in his writings, as is his desire to present his subjects with as much objectivity and frankness as possible.

Facing the rattlesnakes was difficult enough. Helping at the odd burial was almost too much. The age-old conflict between city and country living is renewed.

INDIAN Burial

DEAN DONER

During the summer of 1932, I spent two months with my mother's sister, Edith Johnson, and her family on their farm in Ridley Bottom, a valley on the Missouri River in central South Dakota. At Ridley Bottom the bluffs withdraw from the north side of the river in a sweeping arc, creating a valley seven miles long and two miles across at the widest. The bluffs are gumbo hills,[1] covered with sagebrush, buffalo grass, and rocks, but the valley itself has a rich overlay of flood silt. In 1932, there were four farms in the valley, as well as an old, deserted mission, with a small cemetery beside it, established for a Sioux tribe that had lived in the valley before it was moved to a reservation. The only passage between the Bottom and the prairie beyond the bluffs was a dirt road that plunged precipitously down a bare bluff at the east end of the valley. When it rained, this road was impassable.

The Johnsons had a new five-room yellow stucco house, set into the cliff beside the valley road just where it reached the Bottom. Previously, they had lived in a crumbling log cabin, and the increased space probably accounted for my invitation to visit them. I was an only child and, at least in terms of South Dakota, a city child, since I lived in the town of Brookings,[2] and I'm sure that Aunt Edith and Uncle Edwin, as well as my parents, believed that a summer on the farm would be good for me.

---

1. gumbo hills, hills that have soil which contains much silt and becomes sticky when wet. ***2. Brookings,*** a town in eastern South Dakota.

I did not want to go; I had seen Ridley Bottom several times when my parents and I stopped there briefly on trips across the state, and neither the farm nor the Johnsons themselves offered sufficient attraction to make me want to give up the summer plans I had made with my friends at home. However, I don't remember that I was consulted at all. It was apparently assumed that I would welcome this opportunity, just as it seems to have been assumed that my cousin Ansel and I—probably because we were both eleven—were bound to find pleasure in each other's company.

The family ate in the kitchen—a large room with a long, narrow, oil-cloth-covered table in the center. Uncle Edwin sat at the end of the table nearest the living-room door. He never talked during a meal. He simply ate, his hands and his jaws moving constantly. When he was through eating, he got up immediately and left the kitchen. I remember watching his hands as they reached out for what he wanted. They were always scrubbed and shining, but there was dirt deeply ingrained in a network of cuts and wrinkles, and his fingernails were usually black. The white skin of his head contrasted sharply with his bronzed face and with the triangle of sunburn on his neck where his shirt lay open. He was bald, and always wore a hat outdoors.

Aunt Edith sat at the opposite end of the table, next to the cookstove, her face a steamy red, her hair straggling down her neck, her eyes bright and observant. She was an uncorseted and unpowdered image of my mother, and her appearance gave me at least a bit of comfort by thus being a tie to my own home. Her cooking, though, was very different from my mother's. I could eat Aunt Edith's chicken and her fresh bread, but the rest of her food I found nearly inedible. Everything tasted the same—a combination of greasiness and strong seasoning.

My four cousins and I sat along the sides of the table. Edward and Robert, eighteen and seventeen, had already moved into the adult world of farmwork. Judith, nine, was a pigtailed tomboy who wore glasses, and who—alone of all the Johnsons—chattered endlessly. Ansel, of course, was the cousin I was expected to play with, but, though it seemed that no adult recognized the fact, we were almost opposite types. I was large, slow, and unimaginative, having been carefully reared toward small-town respectability. I was certainly as willing as any boy to rise to the challenge of an adventure, but, at least in comparison with my cousin, I lacked some essential sixth sense—an ability to recognize or invent adventures, and to shape and drive them to a point of ultimate daring. Ansel was small, bright, and intense, with an almost military stance, and he seemed overwhelmingly sure of himself. He had, furthermore, a kind of magic touch that invested his days with greatness, and he seemed to have amassed a wealth of experience that he owned like a man. After a day spent hunting rattlesnakes, for example, Ansel would sit across from me at the supper table with such an air of accomplishment and self-satisfaction that I would look at him with wonder. I don't remember ever thinking that I liked or disliked him. He was too far beyond my experience of eleven-year-old boys for that, and he seemed to me strange, and rather hopelessly adult.

In the evening, a kerosene lamp would be placed on the round table in the living room, and Ansel and Judith and I would play rummy or some other card game. Uncle Edwin would open the Pierre[3] newspaper, which had come in the day's mail, and promptly fall asleep on the leather sofa. His head would roll back, his mouth would open, and he would snore. Slowly a large collection of insects would appear around the lamp, and each of them, it seemed, paused in its frenzied circlings to crawl on me. I was used to a house that in summer was always cool, dark, and closed against the hot wind of Dakota. My mother's life

3. ***Pierre,*** the capital of South Dakota.

was an unremitting battle against forces outside her house that tried to get in—dust and insects and heat. If a miller or a fly was seen in our house, my mother did not rest until it was dead.

The Johnsons, however, not only had made their peace with the forces of nature but felt a kind of impatient contempt for anyone who had not. They ignored insects, and I alone battled the ones that nightly circled the lamp. But the family did notice my squirming and slapping. Could I not sit still, someone would ask.

"Well, the bugs . . ." I would begin, and then Aunt Edith would say, "Why don't you move over away from the light?"

"Then we can't play cards any more," Ansel would say, slapping his hand down and gathering up the deck. Judith would groan and sigh elaborately.

Often, in the afternoons, Ansel, Judith, and I would go swimming in the Missouri, a treacherous and muddy river, with a swift current in the center where the water was deep. The Johnsons had all learned to swim in the river, but I was used to a Y.M.C.A. pool, and I was afraid of the river's dark speed. Nonetheless, I ventured two or three times beyond the sandy shallows into the main stream, or at least to the edge of it. The first time I felt the current suddenly grab me like a strong hand, it seemed that my breath had been pulled out of my lungs, and I frantically flailed my arms, making my way back to calm side water. Shaking and dripping, I came out onto the bank, and Ansel walked over to me. His dark-brown eyes glared with a cold, adult look. "Are you trying to kill yourself?" he asked.

I was astounded at the severity of his tone. "I just went to the edge of the current," I said.

"It's stupid to swim out there when you don't know how. If you get in trouble, don't expect *me* to rescue you."

He walked to the edge of the river, plunged in, and swam to a sandbar about twenty feet into the current. There he lay down and closed his eyes, while I had to stay in the shallows with Judith. It was humiliating.

In nothing else was I as anxious to impress Ansel as in our rattlesnake-hunting expeditions, probably because I was more afraid of the snakes than I was of any other thing in Ridley Bottom. The Missouri River bluffs are inhabited by thousands of rattlesnakes. Not even the Johnsons had made their peace with the snakes, though they claimed that one rarely saw a rattler in the valley itself; six or seven times a year, perhaps, a snake would be found somewhere on the farm and killed. The boys all had impressive collections of rattles, trophies gathered not only from the snakes they had killed on the farm but also from the ones they had bagged during their shooting expeditions on the bluffs. Robert and Edward, in their day, had been content simply to shoot at snakes sunning themselves on a ledge, but Ansel characteristically thought of a way to improve on this game.

"We'll find whole dens of them under the big rocks," he said to me one day when we were out along the bluffs, his eyes shining at the inspiration of his scheme. Holding the gun he was carrying in one hand, he began scrambling among some boulders, tugging at each one and kicking loose those he could move. I followed cautiously. I didn't want to hunt rattlesnakes at all, of course, but when Ansel came to a large boulder he couldn't move by himself, he beckoned me forward. "Turn that rock over," he commanded, and he stationed himself to one side, ready to shoot. I hadn't really imagined what it would be like to uncover a nest of snakes. When I finally managed to tug the stone out of place and saw below me a mass of hissing rattlers, I screamed, let the rock go bounding down the hill, and went racing after it, rolling and crawling and running. I knew I was screaming, but the wind seemed to snatch my cries away. Behind me, though, I could hear Ansel whooping with laughter, and then his gun went off several times. Suddenly, I felt a sharp sting on my leg, and, having reached the road in the valley, I ran toward the farmhouse, yelling that I had been bitten. It turned out that I had been grazed by one of Ansel's bullets, which must have ricocheted off a rock.

This incident produced a family council that evening, at which Aunt Edith laid down the law. The others were not to frighten me, she said, and I was not to be forced to do anything I didn't want to do. Furthermore, she added, the boys must remember that I was from the city and hadn't yet learned some things they had known all their lives. As she spoke, I was utterly miserable. I wanted to explain that no one had forced me to do anything, but I could not speak. While I sat silent at the long table and watched the Johnsons look at me, and look away, and look at me again, I felt the shock of my own identity. Never before had I thought of myself as someone whom other people had to worry about just because I was—or because they thought I was—a certain kind of human being. I realized that I was someone who raised all sorts of problems—at least for the Johnsons. And I also realized that because I hadn't been born a Johnson in the first place, I was doomed to a shameful inadequacy. Many important things seemed to be missing from my character. It wasn't only that I lacked knowledge and courage; I was wanting in some indefinable quality that made life in Ridley Bottom easy and natural—a quality that the Johnsons all automatically possessed and that, for some mysterious reason, I could never, never possess, no matter what I did. My faults lay not in my actions but in me.

After the talk that evening, I slipped out of the house and went across the farmyard and sat on the edge of the horse trough. The night was filled with restless noises from the barns and from the woods down by the river. I remember that there was only a fingernail of a moon, and I remember also that, feeling desperate in that dark and hated place, I hoped a rattlesnake would come along and bite me. I would let it, I thought. It would make no difference at all. I would let it bite me and not tell anyone. Actually, I don't suppose I stayed out there very long. The mosquitoes were thick around the watering trough, and I finally went back in the house and crawled into bed. I did lie awake a long time, though, thinking about my own room at home and listening to the snores of the Johnson family.

Only once after that did Ansel force me to do anything I didn't want to do. The incident involved Little Bear, an ancient and recalcitrant Sioux who lived in an old log cabin up in one of the draws set into the bluffs. Even Aunt Edith would have known that no family rules held for Ansel if they conflicted with his devotion to this old man. More than anything else, it was Ansel's knowledge about and love for the Indians that made him seem strangely adult to me. I knew nothing as thoroughly as he knew the Sioux's customs and history, and I did not care for anything—certainly not for anything abstract—as passionately as he cared that honor be paid to the Sioux. He had been taught that their way of life had been noble and far better suited to the conditions of the plains than the civilization of the white men who had usurped them. The intensity with which Ansel embraced these ideas must have startled even his father, who had taught them to him.

All of Ansel's heightened love for things Indian had been concentrated in his devotion to Little Bear. The old Indian was past taking care of himself, yet he refused to go to a reservation, and Ansel acted as if he were the old man's sole provider and protector. I knew that Uncle Edwin and the other farmers in the valley kept Little Bear supplied with discarded clothing and that they stopped in to see him two or three times a month, but Ansel pretended to believe that his own three trips a week, carrying food his mother had packed, were the only succor the old man had. Generally I went with Ansel on these expeditions, and as we walked up the draw, he would lecture to me about the greatness of Little Bear and the glory of the Sioux nation.

I knew nothing about the Sioux nation, but it was impossible for me to see Little Bear as anything but an ugly old man, not much more than tanned-leather skin and bones, who lived in the most overpoweringly foul-smelling shack I had ever been in. The first few times I went with Ansel to see him, early in the summer, Little Bear was able to hobble outdoors, and we would sit on a bench on the north side of the cabin. He ignored me, for the most part, which was all right with me, since I had nothing to say to him. Ansel didn't talk much, either. Little Bear didn't want conversation; he wanted an audience, and we were perfectly suited to that role. He was a profane old man, but I doubt whether his language hurt us. Half the time, we couldn't understand his mumbled words, and when we could, the tales he told were so disconnected that they made little sense. I know now that he wasn't telling us true stories of his youth; his mind had slipped back to tales he had heard of the days before the white man came.

"I counted coup on[4] three Crows in one day," he said once, chortling to himself. "The Crows made the mistake of stealing horses." He bent over, coughing and cackling, and slapped his knee. "I was just a boy, but—heh, heh!—I ran in and struck 'em, and they never touched me." The rest of the story was lost in Little Bear's appreciation of whatever memories he had evoked. Ansel was unbelievably polite to him. He seemed content to sit for hours and listen to gibberish. I was not only bored but hot, and usually thirsty, and the flies and the stench of the cabin and of the old man himself made me miserable.

Later in the summer, Little Bear became too weak to leave his pallet, and then Ansel would squat on the floor next to the Indian's head. I refused to stay in the cabin, and would either wait for Ansel outside or walk back to the farm.

Two weeks before I was to go home, we visited Little Bear on an afternoon when the temperature must have reached a hundred and ten, as it can in Dakota, and the usual strong, dry wind was not blowing. The sun burned down on the valley, and the dust from our heels hung in the air behind us. By the time we had trudged along the road and then climbed into the draw where the cabin was, I was panting for air. Ansel, though he carried his gun and a paper sack of canned food, was his usual stiff little militaristic self, and this afternoon he came smartly to attention in the doorway before going in. The sun had made me slightly sick, and my eyes seemed hot and dry and gritty. I decided that I had to have a drink of water, and I started toward the spring at the head of the draw. There was also a bit of shade there, for a few stunted and scraggly trees grew near the spring.

I was walking slowly, searching the dry, dusty grass for snakes, when I heard a sudden crackle of twigs behind me. I jumped and turned around. It was Ansel. He was marching toward me, a look of stern importance on his face. He stood a moment in silence, stiff-shouldered and scowling.

"He's dead," he said.

"Little Bear?" I asked.

He ignored me. I stood a moment in silence also. It seemed appropriate, and I didn't know what else to do. Ansel was squinting at the area round the spring.

"We'd better get Uncle Edwin," I said, and started down the path toward the valley road.

Ansel caught my arm. "No," he said. "We don't want anybody. We can do this alone."

"Do what? We ought to get Uncle Edwin."

"We're going to give him an Indian burial. He was a great Indian chief, and he should have an Indian burial."

---

4. counted coup on, took the scalps of.

"He wasn't a chief at all," I said.

Ansel tightened his fingers on my elbow. "He was a great Indian, true to the last, and he *wants* an Indian burial."

I jerked my arm loose. Ansel had the gleam in his eyes that he got when he was thinking fast, inspired.

"We can't bury that old Indian," I said. "We don't have any shovels. Besides, I'm not going to bury anyone. You have to report deaths. Anybody knows that. It's the law. You have to report deaths to the sheriff or somebody."

"White man's laws," Ansel said. He turned again and squinted at the spring, hands on his hips, moving in the stiff, jerking fashion he adopted whenever he took command. "You'll have to help," he said. "I can't do it alone." Then he turned and scowled at me. "But I wish it was somebody else," he added. "Little Bear didn't like you."

"Well, I didn't like Little Bear, either," I said.

"It doesn't make any difference who you like or don't like," Ansel said. "You're going to have to help me."

"We don't have any shovels," I repeated. "We can't bury him."

"That's all you know about it," Ansel said. "You don't know anything. You don't even know how Indians buried their dead. They put them in trees. Indians who didn't die in battle were wrapped in their blankets with their belongings and put in trees. You didn't even know that." He gave me a shove. "We're going to put Little Bear in that broken cottonwood over by the spring. Come on." He shoved me again toward the cabin.

Not until we got to the door did I find the courage to protest. "I'm not going to touch that old dead Indian. I'm not going to put him in any tree."

Before I knew what had happened, Ansel had twisted my right arm behind my back and pushed me against the side of the house. "Look you!" he said. "You're going to help me give Little Bear a proper burial, and you're going to be a man about it, you big sissy. I'll make you be a man once while you're here, or I'll kill you. If you act like a baby, I'll kill you. If you start down that path, I'll shoot you in the back."

He was half a head shorter than I, and at least twenty pounds lighter. I knew that he was harder and stronger, but my first thought was to push him away and walk back to the farmhouse. I was sure he wouldn't hurt me, much less shoot me. That exaggeration was simply a part of Ansel's usual heightened sense of the dramatic. But when I looked at his face, about five inches from my own, I became terrified. No one, it seemed to me, could possibly make his eyes flash with so much hate and power just to exaggerate and dramatize an adventure. I suddenly realized that Ansel couldn't be trusted to know the limits of his own imaginings. In my terror, I yelled, "All right, I'll help you bury your old Indian!"

Little Bear was lying on his pallet, his head to one side, a toothless grin stiff on his face and his eyes open. Ansel immediately began scurrying about. He arranged Little Bear on a blanket and began gathering up the Indian's junk. It made a poor showing; there was a rusty gun, a few strings of beads, and some old clothes, all of which Ansel threw onto the blanket beside the body. Then he hesitated a moment, but finally he quickly reached out and tried to close Little Bear's eyes. The lids wouldn't shut, and he hurriedly folded the blanket over the body, bringing the ends up so that we could carry it in a sort of hammock.

I suppose that from the moment I walked inside the cabin, I didn't really think about what I was doing. I merely followed Ansel's directions. I didn't touch the body but only grasped the two corners of the blanket above Little Bear's feet. When we lifted him, I had a moment of panic, for the body was heavier than I had expected. Actually, Little Bear must have weighed no more than ninety pounds by the time he died, and we were able to carry him without too much trouble, but I had never experienced before the peculiarly inert weight dead things have, and I almost lost my hold on the blanket.

We got him out of the cabin, all right, and started up the slope toward the head of the draw. Halfway there, my mind began working again. Perhaps it was the effect of the sunshine and fresh air. In any case, I started to shake, and soon I stumbled and dropped my end of the blanket. Ansel lowered his end gently to the ground. I didn't dare say anything. I just stood there, shaking and looking at Ansel. I suppose my silence must have made him realize that I was desperate.

"We'll rest a minute," he said. He glanced down at the valley road, probably to make sure that no one was in sight, then sat down at my feet, pulled out a stalk of dried grass, and began chewing it.

"See that tree over there?" he asked. "We'll put him in the crotch of that tree."

"I don't believe the Indians ever buried their dead in trees," I said.

"Yes, they did," he said. "Some Indians built scaffolds for their dead, but the Hunkpapa Sioux didn't have enough wood for that. They put them in trees, if there were any trees around."

"Well, I think Uncle Edwin should help."

"No."

"If you don't want him to, then you know you're doing wrong," I said.

"Of course he wouldn't do it, stupid! He'd take Little Bear in to town, and they'd bury him in a pauper's grave, or they'd take him to the reservation and bury him. Little Bear hated the reservation. They don't know that. I'm the only one who knows what he liked. He was my brother, and I'm going to bury him."

I was silent. I looked down at the top of Ansel's head, then along the draw to where the valley road crossed the brown expanse of burned grass, and beyond to the green line of trees marking the river. The air was absolutely still, and heavy with heat. I could feel fear collecting inside me like a heavy ball in the pit of my stomach. I was afraid of Ansel, of his wild imagination and exaggerations, but it seemed a point of honor that I protest at least once more. "You weren't his brother," I said.

He jumped up and grabbed my shirt. "I was, too! I was, too, his brother!" he said fiercely. "Little Bear adopted me into the tribe. He initiated me. One whole day I laid naked in the sun. I couldn't move—not for ants or flies or snakes or anything. One whole day I laid out in the sun, and I didn't even move a finger. You couldn't do that if you tried for a million years. So shut up. Little Bear initiated me, and adopted me as his brother. And now I'm going to bury him the right way, because there isn't anybody left in his family but me." He let go of my shirt and stood panting in front of me. "I shouldn't have told you that," he said. "I wasn't supposed to tell anybody." He stood a moment in silence, then marched over and picked up the blanket under Little Bear's head. "You keep it to yourself," he said. "Come on. Let's go."

When I picked up the other end of the blanket, I got a good hold on only one corner. The gun and beads fell out, and the body started to slip sidewise.

"Grab him. Let those things go," Ansel ordered. "We'll get them later."

We carried the body up the draw and laid it beside the cottonwood. Ansel walked around the tree, deciding which way to get the body wedged into the crotch. "Be careful," he said. "This is a big rattlesnake den." I examined the ground all around me. "We'll come in from this direction. I'll put his head up in the crotch, and then I'll get up there and pull while you push."

The tree looked as though it had been hit by lightning. About a foot above my head, the trunk was split, and a branch had been partly torn off. We lifted the body as high as our arms would reach, and Ansel got the shoulders started into the crotch. Then he climbed up above the crotch, and, with him tugging and me shoving, we were able to work the body up and in until it was firmly wedged. The blanket, of course, had been stripped off. Ansel picked it up and began trying to throw it over Little Bear. He sent me back to collect the gun and the beads. I was happy to get away even for a moment. As I was picking up the beads, Ansel yelled for me to go back to the cabin and see if I could find anything else to put with the body.

"What kind of things?" I asked.

"Anything," he answered.

I left the gun and the beads on the ground and went down to the cabin. Never had it smelled so foul. I stood in the doorway, trying to spot some object within easy reach that I could take—something that would satisfy Ansel. To my right was an orange crate, full of cans of food, and three brown paper sacks, which I knew contained salt, sugar, and flour. Hanging on the wall over it was a blackened frying pan. I reached for the pan and found a rosary underneath it, hung on the same nail. I didn't know what it was, but when I saw the cross hanging from it, I knew that I had found something that would be appropriate. I suppose that sometime during his stay in the valley Little Bear must have been converted.[5] I was glad to have found something so easily. Over behind the pallet I saw another orange crate filled with junk, and I started toward it.

The instant I stepped on the bed, I heard a warning rattle. I jumped away. A snake was curled on the pile of dirty blankets at the foot of the pallet. It flashed through my mind that the snake had killed Little Bear and that it might have been hidden in the blankets when I had gone to pick up the Indian's feet. And if there is one snake, I thought, there must be others, either in the orange crate or under the pillow at my feet or behind me along the wall. I flung the frying pan and the rosary at the snake, leaped for the door, and raced down the hill toward the road. Behind me I heard Ansel yelling, and just as I tripped on a stone, I heard what sounded like a shot.

I rolled over and looked back at Ansel. He didn't have his gun at all—it was propped against a wall of the cabin—but was standing under the tree holding a broken-off branch, which, I then realized, he must have struck against the trunk, to frighten me. He was standing just below the crotch where the Indian's body lay, and he had never looked so stern, so completely and coldly contemptuous.

Slowly I got up and walked on down the slope toward the valley road. Gradually, tears began to roll down my hot cheeks, until, by the time I could see the Johnsons' farm, I was sobbing in great, heaving cries. I didn't want to go back to the farm crying, and since I couldn't get to the river except through the farmyard, I found myself with no place to go, no place to hide, in all that sun-baked, treeless valley. There was nothing I could do but lie down in the dirt road and sob.

I have no idea how long I cried. At length I became aware again of the sun, and of the flies, and of the dirt in my mouth and the mud streaked on my face by the tears. I sat up, beat the flies away, and tried to wipe my face with my handkerchief. It occurred to me, now I was away from Ansel and Little Bear, that I had done something no adult would have done. There was no courage or honor involved in carrying that dead Indian up into a rattlesnake den and shoving him into a tree. That was not brave. It was ridiculous. If I had not been so alone, so separated from the Johnsons' life and so afraid of their scorn, Ansel would never have been able to make me weak and frightened enough to do what he had forced me to. Because I hated and feared Ridley Bottom, I had done things I would never have ordinarily done. I didn't understand how the two ideas fitted together, but I knew that it was so.

While I was sitting there, I heard Ansel coming down the road. To my relief, he walked right past me without a word, and I didn't look up until he was fifteen or twenty feet beyond me. He carried his gun in one hand and some rattles in the other.

I continued to sit in the road until I was sure that the Johnsons had started eating supper. Then I walked on to the farm and went to the horse trough, under the windmill, to wash my face and hands. The water was cold, and I scooped up handfuls of it and splashed it on my face. Suddenly I stopped and looked at my hands. They had carried a dead Indian, I thought in wonder. I dipped them into the water and looked at them again.

A breeze was just starting up, and overhead the windmill creaked around once or twice, stopped, and then slowly started to turn again. I could hear the horses down in the barn knocking against their stalls, and

5. ***must . . . converted,*** changed from unbelief to Christianity or from one religion to another.

the pigs grunting and rooting in the pigpens. There seemed to be an immense stillness over the place, even though the windmill was creaking, and I could hear the animal noises and the birds in the cottonwoods by the river calling and talking as they settled in the branches for the night.

Through the kitchen window I could see the kerosene lamp on the table and the shadows of the people around it. Between them and me, between the house and the horse trough, the distance of a city block, there wasn't a blade of grass. Around the house itself there wasn't even a tree.

I looked at my hands again. They seemed somehow different to me; they had changed during the summer without my noticing it. They were broadened and rough, and, like Uncle Edwin's, they had grime in the cracks; they scarcely seemed to be mine any more. And when I looked again at that house, I had a strange rush of feeling for the Johnsons, something I had never felt before for anyone or anything—a feeling that I hadn't willed into existence but that seemed to rise out of some part of me I didn't know existed. I saw the Johnsons as people separate from me, people who went on living in that barren place when I was not there, during blizzards in the winter and floods in the spring. And, oddly, the fact that they were wholly separate from me made them seem suddenly much more important and kinder and less strange than I had believed them to be. I had never thought about Ridley Bottom as being Ansel's whole life, or as being, really, his home. I suddenly realized, too, that I didn't care what Ansel had told or not told the family about our afternoon or why I was late for supper.

I wiped my hands on my shirttail and started toward the house. Then I stopped, picked up a stone, looked around, and threw it at the windmill. It hit the scaffold, and it made, I thought, a magnificent metallic ring. Confidently, I turned and ran toward the house.

WHAT DO YOU SAY?

1. How did the Johnson family differ from the narrator's family in their way of living?

2. (a) Compare the character and habits of Ansel with those of the narrator. *(b)* How does the rattlesnake incident emphasize the contrast between the two boys?

3. Why does Aunt Edith's lecture make the storyteller miserable?

4. State the importance of this sentence to the story as a whole: "The Johnsons, however, not only had made their peace with the forces of nature but felt a kind of impatient contempt for anyone who had not."

5. (a) In the Indian burial incident, for what attitudes and actions would you blame Ansel? *(b)* For what attitudes and actions would you blame the narrator? *(c)* With which boy do you chiefly sympathize? Why?

6. What is the key word in the last paragraph that indicates the narrator has solved his problem?

AUTHOR'S CRAFT

Fact and fiction

When you read a first-person story, that is, one told by an "I," do you tend to believe the story is ***true,*** or at least more true than a story told in the third person? Several authors you have met so far in this unit have told us their stories were based on personal experience. Yet not all these stories were told by an "I." So you cannot judge by "who" tells the story whether it is all—or even partly—true. Dean Doner in commenting on the "truth" of his story "Indian Burial" explains: "The story told in 'Indian Burial' did not really happen. I never helped put a dead Indian up into a tree, and, so far as I know, no boy ever did. But there are true elements in the story.

"In the first place, the setting is more or less real. It is the Oahe valley on the Missouri River just north of Pierre, South Dakota. I never saw the valley while I was a child, but it is where my wife lived as a girl, and she and I went to see it once just after the Oahe dam was begun, for we wanted to see it before it was flooded. From this visit—and from my wife's stories—I re-created the scene. I did not know my wife when we were children, but she has told me about the life she and her brothers and sisters lived in the valley. They all learned to swim in the Missouri River, which is a treacherous place to swim. They also learned to climb among the rocks on the gumbo bluffs, turn the rocks over and shoot the rattlesnakes they found beneath. My wife also told me about how she, her brothers, and her sisters used to think that the 'town kids' who came out to play were 'sissies.' Now, when I was a child there was a sharp distinction between 'town kids' and 'country kids.' I was a 'town kid.' I had never visited in Oahe Valley, but I had visited some cousins who lived on a farm in another section of South Dakota. And my experience was the same: my cousins would try to scare me with snakes and wild tales, and they thought, I am sure, that I was a 'town sissy.'

"Then from my wife's grandmother and her father I had heard stories of the early customs of the Indians, including the practice of building platforms on which to 'bury' the dead. Sometimes Indians used trees instead of platforms. Using that custom as something which might truly frighten a 'town sissy,' I made up the rest of the story—the part about Ansel's taking care of the old Indian. I took an experience which was 'real' and which was 'universal' and put my wife's stories and my own memories together to produce a setting and a situation. In a way, you see, the story never happened at all. But in a way, it does try to say something which is true about different kinds of people and about what their actions mean.

"All stories are 'autobiographical' in that they convey the writer's understanding of reality, but the first-person story is no more literally true than the third-person story.

"Incidents themselves are meaningless, whether they are incidents in fiction or in life. The meaning of a story is only what it means ***to some observer.*** This is true also for events that happen in life. Something that happens in a school corridor means different things to different people. So when a writer tells a story, he tries to show the reader what something means to him. To do this, he creates a situation which seems to him 'real.' It is important for the student to realize that when he reads a story he is not doing something unconnected with his 'real' life. When he reads a story, a person is doing exactly what he does in every moment of his life: he is observing an incident and trying to understand it.

"There is, however, a little difference between a story and real life. In real life incidents happen to us without a plan. When we turn the corner of a corridor, we have no control over what is going to happen to us next. We may meet Roger or we may meet Mary or the corridor may just be empty. In fiction, the writer controls what is happening. A story which tried to be absolutely faithful to life would be too long, too disorganized, and probably too boring. That is, there would be too many empty corridors. So the writer takes situations and arranges them in a pattern of developing action. Someone once called fiction 'a lie which is true.' We know what he meant. Things can't really happen in life as neatly as they do in a story. But in choosing incidents and arranging them in a story, the writer tries to re-create a 'true' experience."

Select a true incident in your life on which you might base a story. What additional situations might you "make up" in attempting to "re-create a 'true' experience"?

DEAN DONER

"I was born in Brookings, South Dakota, in 1923. I attended the Brookings public schools. For a good many years I thought I would be a pianist. But I was also always interested in writing, and I worked on the student newspaper in high school. I started college at South Dakota State College, but in my sophomore year I entered the Army Air Force during the Second World War. After the war I graduated from South Dakota State and entered the University of Iowa, for I wanted to study at Iowa's famous Writers' Workshop. I took a Master of Fine Arts and a Ph.D. at Iowa. Then I taught for three years at the University of Idaho. Since 1953 I have been teaching English at Purdue University. I teach courses in creative writing and modern fiction."

JAMES HURST

The Scarlet Ibis

"... pride is a wonderful, terrible thing, a seed that bears two vines, life and death."

It was in the clove of seasons,[1] summer was dead but autumn had not yet been born, that the ibis lit in the bleeding tree. The flower garden was stained with rotting brown magnolia petals and ironweeds grew rank amid the purple phlox. The five o'clocks by the chimney still marked time, but the oriole nest in the elm was untenanted and rocked back and forth like an empty cradle. The last graveyard flowers were blooming, and their smell drifted across the cotton field and through every room of our house, speaking softly the names of our dead.

It's strange that all this is still so clear to me, now that that summer has long since fled and time has had its way. A grindstone stands where the bleeding tree stood, just outside the kitchen door, and now if an oriole sings in the elm, its song seems to die up in the leaves, a silvery dust. The flower garden is prim, the house a gleaming white, and the pale fence across the yard stands straight and spruce. But sometimes (like right now), as I sit in the cool, green-draped parlor, the grindstone begins to turn, and time with all its changes is ground away—and I remember Doodle.

Doodle was just about the craziest brother a boy ever had. Of course, he wasn't a crazy crazy like old Miss Leedie, who was in love with President Wilson and wrote him a letter every day, but was a nice crazy, like someone you meet in your dreams. He was born when I was six and was, from the outset, a disappointment. He seemed all head, with a tiny body which was red and shriveled like an old man's. Everybody thought he was going to die—everybody except Aunt Nicey, who had delivered him. She said he would live because he was born in a caul and cauls were made from Jesus' nightgown. Daddy had Mr. Heath, the carpenter, build a little mahogany coffin for him. But he didn't die, and when he was three months old Mama and Daddy decided they might as well name him. They named him William Armstrong, which was like tying a big tail on a small kite. Such a name sounds good only on a tombstone.

I thought myself pretty smart at many things, like holding my breath, running, jumping, or climbing the vines in Old Woman Swamp, and I wanted more than anything else someone to race to Horsehead Landing, someone to box with, and someone to perch with in the top fork of the great pine behind the barn, where across the fields and swamps you could see the sea. I wanted a brother. But Mama, crying, told me that even if William Armstrong lived, he would never do these things with me. He might not, she sobbed, even be "all there." He might, as long as he lived, lie on the rubber sheet in the center of the bed in the front bedroom where the white marquisette curtains billowed out in the afternoon sea breeze, rustling like palmetto fronds.

It was bad enough having an invalid

---

1. ***clove of seasons,*** the interval between two seasons.

brother, but having one who possibly was not all there was unbearable, so I began to make plans to kill him by smothering him with a pillow. However, one afternoon as I watched him, my head poked between the iron posts of the foot of the bed, he looked straight at me and grinned. I skipped through the rooms, down the echoing halls, shouting, "Mama, he smiled. He's all there! He's all there!" and he was.

When he was two, if you laid him on his stomach, he began to try to move himself, straining terribly. The doctor said that with his weak heart this strain would probably kill him, but it didn't. Trembling, he'd push himself up, turning first red, then a soft purple, and finally collapse back onto the bed like an old worn-out doll. I can still see Mama watching him, her hand pressed tight across her mouth, her eyes wide and unblinking. But he learned to crawl (it was his third winter), and we brought him out of the front bedroom, putting him on the rug before the fireplace. For the first time he became one of us.

As long as he lay all the time in bed, we called him William Armstrong, even though it was formal and sounded as if we were referring to one of our ancestors, but with his creeping around on the deerskin rug and beginning to talk, something had to be done about his name. It was I who renamed him. When he crawled, he crawled backwards, as if he were in reverse and couldn't change gears. If you called him, he'd turn around as if he were going in the other direction, then he'd back right up to you to be picked up. Crawling backward made him look like a doodlebug,[2] so I began to call him Doodle, and in time even Mama and Daddy thought it was a better name than William Armstrong. Only Aunt Nicey disagreed. She said caul babies should be treated with special respect since they might turn out to be saints. Renaming my brother was perhaps the kindest thing I ever did for him, because nobody expects much from someone called Doodle.

Although Doodle learned to crawl, he showed no signs of walking, but he wasn't idle. He talked so much that we all quit listening to what he said. It was about this time that Daddy built him a go-cart and I had to pull him around. At first I just paraded him up and down the piazza, but then he started crying to be taken out into the yard and it ended up by my having to lug him wherever I went. If I so much as picked up my cap, he'd start crying to go with me and Mama would call from wherever she was, "Take Doodle with you."

He was a burden in many ways. The doctor had said that he mustn't get too excited, too hot, too cold, or too tired and that he must always be treated gently. A long list of don'ts went with him, all of which I ignored once we got out of the house. To discourage his coming with me, I'd run with him across the ends of the cotton rows and careen him around corners on two wheels. Sometimes I accidentally turned him over, but he never told Mama. His skin was very sensitive, and he had to wear a big straw hat whenever he went out. When the going got rough and he had to cling to the sides of the go-cart, the hat slipped all the way down over his ears. He was a sight. Finally, I could see I was licked. Doodle was my brother and he was going to cling to me forever, no matter what I did, so I dragged him across the burning cotton field to share with him the only beauty I knew, Old Woman Swamp. I pulled the go-cart through the saw-tooth fern, down into the green dimness where the palmetto fronds whispered by the stream. I lifted him out and set him down in the soft rubber grass beside a tall pine. His eyes were round with wonder as he gazed about him, and his little hands began to stroke the rubber grass. Then he began to cry.

"For heaven's sake, what's the matter?" I asked, annoyed.

2. *doodlebug,* an insect characterized by its backward crawling motion.

"It's so pretty," he said. "So pretty, pretty, pretty."

After that day Doodle and I often went down into Old Woman Swamp. I would gather wildflowers, wild violets, honeysuckle, yellow jasmine, snakeflowers, and water lilies, and with wire grass we'd weave them into necklaces and crowns. We'd bedeck ourselves with our handiwork and loll about thus beautified, beyond the touch of the everyday world. Then when the slanted rays of the sun burned orange in the tops of the pines, we'd drop our jewels into the stream and watch them float away toward the sea.

There is within me (and with sadness I have watched it in others) a knot of cruelty borne by the stream of love, much as our blood sometimes bears the seed of our destruction, and at times I was mean to Doodle. One day I took him up to the barn loft and showed him his casket, telling him how we all had believed he would die. It was covered with a film of Paris green[3] sprinkled to kill the rats, and screech owls had built a nest inside it.

Doodle studied the mahogany box for a long time, then said, "It's not mine."

"It is," I said. "And before I'll help you down from the loft, you're going to have to touch it."

"I won't touch it," he said sullenly.

"Then I'll leave you here by yourself," I threatened, and made as if I were going down.

Doodle was frightened of being left. "Don't go leave me, Brother," he cried, and he leaned toward the coffin. His hand, trembling, reached out, and when he touched the casket he screamed. A screech owl flapped out of the box into our faces, scaring us and covering us with Paris green. Doodle was paralyzed, so I put him on my shoulder and carried him down the ladder, and even when we were outside in the bright sunshine, he clung to me, crying, "Don't leave me. Don't leave me."

When Doodle was five years old, I was embarrassed at having a brother of that age who couldn't walk, so I set out to teach him. We were down in Old Woman Swamp and it was spring and the sick-sweet smell of bay flowers hung everywhere like a mournful song. "I'm going to teach you to walk, Doodle," I said.

He was sitting comfortably on the soft grass, leaning back against the pine. "Why?" he asked.

I hadn't expected such an answer. "So I won't have to haul you around all the time."

"I can't walk, Brother," he said.

"Who says so?" I demanded.

"Mama, the doctor—everybody."

"Oh, you can walk," I said, and I took him by the arms and stood him up. He collapsed onto the grass like a half-empty flour sack. It was as if he had no bones in his little legs.

"Don't hurt me, Brother," he warned.

"Shut up. I'm not going to hurt you. I'm going to teach you to walk." I heaved him up again, and again he collapsed.

This time he did not lift his face up out of the rubber grass. "I just can't do it. Let's make honeysuckle wreaths."

"Oh yes you can, Doodle," I said. "All you got to do is try. Now come on," and I hauled him up once more.

It seemed so hopeless from the beginning that it's a miracle I didn't give up. But all of us must have something or someone to be proud of, and Doodle had become mine. I did not know then that pride is a wonderful, terrible thing, a seed that bears two vines, life and death. Every day that summer we went to the pine beside the stream of Old Woman Swamp, and I put him on his feet at least a hundred times each afternoon. Occasionally I too became discouraged because it didn't seem as if he was trying, and I would say, "Doodle, don't you *want* to learn to walk?"

He'd nod his head, and I'd say, "Well, if you don't keep trying, you'll never learn."

3. *Paris green,* a poisonous emerald-green powder used to kill insects.

Then I'd paint for him a picture of us as old men, white-haired, him with a long white beard and me still pulling him around in the go-cart. This never failed to make him try again.

Finally one day, after many weeks of practicing, he stood alone for a few seconds. When he fell, I grabbed him in my arms and hugged him, our laughter pealing through the swamp like a ringing bell. Now we knew it could be done. Hope no longer hid in the dark palmetto thicket but perched like a cardinal in the lacy toothbrush tree, brilliantly visible. "Yes, yes," I cried, and he cried it too, and the grass beneath us was soft and the smell of the swamp was sweet.

With success so imminent, we decided not to tell anyone until he could actually walk. Each day, barring rain, we sneaked into Old Woman Swamp, and by cotton-picking time Doodle was ready to show what he could do. He still wasn't able to walk far, but we could wait no longer. Keeping a nice secret is very hard to do, like holding your breath. We chose to reveal all on October eighth, Doodle's sixth birthday, and for weeks ahead we mooned around the house, promising everybody a most spectacular surprise. Aunt Nicey said that, after so much talk, if we produced anything less tremendous than the Resurrection, she was going to be disappointed.

At breakfast on our chosen day, when Mama, Daddy, and Aunt Nicey were in the dining room, I brought Doodle to the door in the go-cart just as usual and had them turn their backs, making them cross their hearts and hope to die if they peeked. I helped Doodle up, and when he was standing alone I let them look. There wasn't a sound as Doodle walked slowly across the room and sat down at his place at the table. Then Mama began to cry and ran over to him, hugging him and kissing him. Daddy hugged him too, so I went to Aunt Nicey, who was thanks praying in the doorway, and began to waltz her around. We danced together quite well until she came down on my big toe with her brogans, hurting me so badly I thought I was crippled for life.

Doodle told them it was I who had taught him to walk, so everyone wanted to hug me, and I began to cry.

"What are you crying for?" asked Daddy, but I couldn't answer. They did not know that I did it for myself; that pride, whose slave I was, spoke to me louder than all their voices, and that Doodle walked only because I was ashamed of having a crippled brother.

Within a few months Doodle had learned to walk well and his go-cart was put up in the barn loft (it's still there) beside his little mahogany coffin. Now, when we roamed off together, resting often, we never turned back until our destination had been reached, and to help pass the time, we took up lying. From the beginning Doodle was a terrible liar and he got me in the habit. Had anyone stopped to listen to us, we would have been sent off to Dix Hill.

My lies were scary, involved, and usually pointless, but Doodle's were twice as crazy. People in his stories all had wings and flew wherever they wanted to go. His favorite lie was about a boy named Peter who had a pet peacock with a ten-foot tail. Peter wore a golden robe that glittered so brightly that when he walked through the sunflowers they turned away from the sun to face him. When Peter was ready to go to sleep, the peacock spread his magnificent tail, enfolding the boy gently like a closing go-to-sleep flower, burying him in the gloriously iridescent, rustling vortex. Yes, I must admit it. Doodle could beat me lying.

Doodle and I spent lots of time thinking about our future. We decided that when we were grown we'd live in Old Woman Swamp and pick dog-tongue for a living. Beside the stream, he planned, we'd build us a house of whispering leaves and the swamp birds would be our chickens. All day long (when we weren't gathering dog-tongue) we'd swing through the cypresses on the rope vines, and if it rained we'd huddle beneath an umbrella tree and play stickfrog. Mama and Daddy could come and live with us if they wanted to. He even came up with the idea that he could marry Mama and I could marry Daddy. Of course, I was old enough to know this wouldn't work out, but the picture he painted was so beautiful and serene that all I could do was whisper Yes, yes.

Once I had succeeded in teaching Doodle to walk, I began to believe in my own infallibility and I prepared a terrific development program for him, unknown to Mama and Daddy, of course. I would teach him to run, to swim, to climb trees, and to fight. He, too, now believed in my infallibility, so we set the deadline for these accomplishments less than a year away, when, it had been decided, Doodle could start to school.

That winter we didn't make much progress, for I was in school and Doodle suffered from one bad cold after another. But when spring came, rich and warm, we raised our sights again. Success lay at the end of summer like a pot of gold, and our campaign got off to a good start. On hot days, Doodle and I went down to Horsehead Landing and I gave him swimming lessons or showed him how to row a boat. Sometimes we descended into the cool greenness of Old Woman Swamp and climbed the rope vines or boxed scientifically beneath the pine where he had learned to walk. Promise hung about us like the leaves, and wherever we looked, ferns unfurled and birds broke into song.

That summer, the summer of 1918, was blighted. In May and June there was no rain and the crops withered, curled up, then died under the thirsty sun. One morning in July a hurricane came out of the east, tipping over the oaks in the yard and splitting the limbs of the elm trees. That afternoon it roared back out of the west, blew the fallen oaks around, snapping their roots and tearing them out of the earth like a hawk at the entrails of a chicken. Cotton bolls were wrenched from the stalks and lay like green walnuts in the valleys between the rows, while the cornfield leaned over uniformly so that the tassels touched the ground. Doodle and I followed Daddy out into the cotton field, where he stood, shoulders sagging, surveying the ruin. When his chin sank down onto his chest, we were frightened, and Doodle slipped his hand into mine. Suddenly Daddy straightened his shoulders, raised a giant knuckly fist, and with a voice that seemed to rumble out of the earth itself began cursing heaven, hell, the weather, and the Republican Party. Doodle and I, prodding each other and giggling, went back to the house, knowing that everything would be all right.

And during that summer, strange names were heard through the house: Château-Thierry, Amiens, Soissons, and in her blessing at the supper table, Mama once said, "And bless the Pearsons, whose boy Joe was lost at Belleau Wood."[4]

So we came to that clove of seasons. School was only a few weeks away, and Doodle was far behind schedule. He could barely clear the ground when climbing up the rope vines and his swimming was certainly not passable. We decided to double our efforts, to make that last drive and reach our pot of gold. I made him swim until he turned blue and row until he couldn't lift an oar. Wherever we went, I purposely walked fast, and although he kept up, his face turned red and his eyes became glazed. Once, he could go no further, so he collapsed on the ground and began to cry.

"Aw, come on, Doodle," I urged. "You can do it. Do you want to be different from everybody else when you start school?"

"Does it make any difference?"

"It certainly does," I said. "Now, come on," and I helped him up.

As we slipped through dog days, Doodle

---

4. ***Château-Thierry*** (sha tō′ tyār′i or shä tō′ tye rē′), ***Amiens*** (am′i ənz or ä myaɴ′), ***Soissons*** (swä sôn′), ***Belleau*** (bel′ō) ***Wood,*** French locations in or near which World War I battles were fought.

began to look feverish, and Mama felt his forehead, asking him if he felt ill. At night he didn't sleep well, and sometimes he had nightmares, crying out until I touched him and said, "Wake up, Doodle. Wake up."

It was Saturday noon, just a few days before school was to start. I should have already admitted defeat, but my pride wouldn't let me. The excitement of our program had now been gone for weeks, but still we kept on with a tired doggedness. It was too late to turn back, for we had both wandered too far into a net of expectations and had left no crumbs behind.

Daddy, Mama, Doodle, and I were seated at the dining-room table having lunch. It was a hot day, with all the windows and doors open in case a breeze should come. In the kitchen Aunt Nicey was humming softly. After a long silence, Daddy spoke. "It's so calm, I wouldn't be surprised if we had a storm this afternoon."

"I haven't heard a rain frog," said Mama, who believed in signs, as she served the bread around the table.

"I did," declared Doodle. "Down in the swamp."

"He didn't," I said contrarily.

"You did, eh?" said Daddy, ignoring my denial.

"I certainly did," Doodle reiterated, scowling at me over the top of his iced-tea glass, and we were quiet again.

Suddenly, from out in the yard, came a strange croaking noise. Doodle stopped eating, with a piece of bread poised ready for his mouth, his eyes popped round like two blue buttons. "What's that?" he whispered.

I jumped up, knocking over my chair, and had reached the door when Mama called, "Pick up the chair, sit down again, and say excuse me."

By the time I had done this, Doodle had excused himself and had slipped out into the yard. He was looking up into the bleeding tree. "It's a great big red bird!" he called.

The bird croaked loudly again, and Mama and Daddy came out into the yard. We shaded our eyes with our hands against the hazy glare of the sun and peered up through the still leaves. On the topmost branch a bird the size of a chicken, with scarlet feathers and long legs, was perched precariously. Its wings hung down loosely, and as we watched, a feather dropped away and floated slowly down through the green leaves.

"It's not even frightened of us," Mama said.

"It looks tired," Daddy added. "Or maybe sick."

Doodle's hands were clasped at his throat, and I had never seen him stand still so long. "What is it?" he asked.

Daddy shook his head. "I don't know, maybe it's—"

At that moment the bird began to flutter, but the wings were uncoördinated, and amid much flapping and a spray of flying feathers, it tumbled down, bumping through the limbs of the bleeding tree and landing at our feet with a thud. Its long, graceful neck jerked twice into an S, then straightened out, and the bird was still. A white veil came over the eyes and the long white beak unhinged. Its legs were crossed and its clawlike feet were delicately curved at rest. Even death did not mar its grace, for it lay on the earth like a broken vase of red flowers, and we stood around it, awed by its exotic beauty.

"It's dead," Mama said.

"What is it?" Doodle repeated.

"Go bring me the bird book," said Daddy.

I ran into the house and brought back the bird book. As we watched, Daddy thumbed through its pages. "It's a scarlet ibis," he said, pointing to a picture. "It lives in the tropics—South America to Florida. A storm must have brought it here."

Sadly, we all looked back at the bird. A scarlet ibis! How many miles it had traveled to die like this, in *our* yard, beneath the bleeding tree.

"Let's finish lunch," Mama said, nudging us back toward the dining room.

"I'm not hungry," said Doodle, and he knelt down beside the ibis.

"We've got peach cobbler for dessert," Mama tempted from the doorway.

Doodle remained kneeling. "I'm going to bury him."

"Don't you dare touch him," Mama warned. "There's no telling what disease he might have had."

"All right," said Doodle. "I won't."

Daddy, Mama, and I went back to the dining-room table, but we watched Doodle through the open door. He took out a piece of string from his pocket and, without touching the ibis, looped one end around its neck. Slowly, while singing softly *Shall We Gather at the River,*[5] he carried the bird around to the front yard and dug a hole in the flower garden, next to the petunia bed. Now we were watching him through the front window, but he didn't know it. His awkwardness at digging the hole with a shovel whose handle was twice as long as he was made us laugh, and we covered our mouths with our hands so he wouldn't hear.

When Doodle came into the dining room, he found us seriously eating our cobbler. He was pale and lingered just inside the screen door. "Did you get the scarlet ibis buried?" asked Daddy.

Doodle didn't speak but nodded his head.

"Go wash your hands, and then you can have some peach cobbler," said Mama.

"I'm not hungry," he said.

"Dead birds is bad luck," said Aunt Nicey poking her head from the kitchen door. "Specially *red* dead birds!"

As soon as I had finished eating, Doodle

5. ***Shall We Gather at the River,*** a popular hymn sung in many churches a generation or so ago.

and I hurried off to Horsehead Landing. Time was short, and Doodle still had a long way to go if he was going to keep up with the other boys when he started school. The sun, gilded with the yellow cast of autumn, still burned fiercely, but the dark green woods through which we passed were shady and cool. When we reached the landing, Doodle said he was too tired to swim, so we got into a skiff and floated down the creek with the tide. Far off in the marsh a rail was scolding, and over on the beach locusts were singing in the myrtle trees. Doodle did not speak and kept his head turned away, letting one hand trail limply in the water.

After we had drifted a long way, I put the oars in place and made Doodle row back against the tide. Black clouds began to gather in the southwest, and he kept watching them, trying to pull the oars a little faster. When we reached Horsehead Landing, lightning was playing across half the sky and thunder roared out, hiding even the sound of the sea. The sun disappeared and darkness descended, almost like night. Flocks of marsh crows flew by, heading inland to their roosting trees, and two egrets, squawking, arose from the oyster-rock shallows and careened away.

Doodle was both tired and frightened, and when he stepped from the skiff he collapsed onto the mud, sending an armada of fiddler crabs rustling off into the marsh grass. I helped him up, and as he wiped the mud off his trousers, he smiled at me ashamedly. He had failed and we both knew it, so we started back home, racing the storm. We never spoke (What are the words that can solder cracked pride?), but I knew he was watching me, watching for a sign of mercy. The lightning was near now, and from fear he walked so close behind me he kept stepping on my heels. The faster I walked, the faster he walked, so I began to run. The rain was coming, roaring through the pines, and then like a bursting Roman candle, a gum tree ahead of us was shattered by a bolt of lightning. When the deafening peal of thunder had died, and in the moment before the rain arrived, I heard Doodle, who had fallen behind, cry out, "Brother, Brother, don't leave me! Don't leave me!"

The knowledge that Doodle's and my plans had come to naught was bitter, and that streak of cruelty within me awakened. I ran as fast as I could, leaving him far behind with a wall of rain dividing us. The drops stung my face like nettles, and the wind flared the wet glistening leaves of the bordering trees. Soon I could hear his voice no more.

I hadn't run too far before I became tired, and the flood of childish spite evanesced as well. I stopped and waited for Doodle. The sound of rain was everywhere, but the wind had died and it fell straight down in parallel paths like ropes hanging from the sky. As I waited, I peered through the downpour, but no one came. Finally I went back and found him huddled beneath a red nightshade bush beside the road. He was sitting on the ground, his face buried in his arms, which were resting on his drawn-up knees. "Let's go, Doodle," I said.

He didn't answer, so I placed my hand on his forehead and lifted his head. Limply, he fell backwards onto the earth. He had been bleeding from the mouth, and his neck and the front of his shirt were stained a brilliant red.

"Doodle! Doodle!" I cried, shaking him, but there was no answer but the ropy rain. He lay very awkwardly, with his head thrown far back, making his vermilion neck appear unusually long and slim. His little legs, bent sharply at the knees, had never before seemed so fragile, so thin.

I began to weep, and the tear-blurred vision in red before me looked very familiar. "Doodle!" I screamed above the pounding storm and threw my body to the earth above his. For a long long time, it seemed forever, I lay there crying, sheltering my fallen scarlet ibis from the heresy of rain.

WHAT DO YOU SAY?

1. Explain why Doodle is different from other boys' brothers.

2. How do you feel about the narrator's attitude toward Doodle?

3. *(a)* Describe the progress that the narrator makes with Doodle. Is this really progress? Explain your answer. *(b)* Find the place in the story where the narrator explains, "Doodle walked only because I was ashamed of having a crippled brother." What motive made him keep after Doodle? What word best describes the motive?

4. *(a)* Outline the circumstances leading to the death of Doodle. *(b)* How much is the narrator to blame? Do you blame him or do you pity him? Explain your reactions.

AUTHOR'S CRAFT

Symbolism

In everyday life we are so accustomed to some symbols that we forget that they are symbols. We see a striped pole and know at once that it stands before a barber shop; a large clock or watch suspended over the sidewalk symbolizes a jeweler's shop; a cross on a spire symbolizes a Christian church; the Star of David is an honored symbol of the Jews. From these familiar examples we can conclude that a symbol is something that stands for or represents something else.

Writers frequently use symbols for the effective presentation of ideas. The color red, for example, is often associated with courage. Do you think red was used to symbolize courage in this story? Or was it an accident that the ibis was a *scarlet* ibis? Was the kind of bird, or the color of the bird, or the fact that the bird was a "stranger" to the area most important? Why do you think the author chose this particular bird to help him tell his story?

Mr. Hurst has given us his own answers:

"I wanted a bird," he said, "to represent Doodle—not Doodle's physical self, but his spirit. Certainly, Doodle inside had much more to admire than his outside. It was Doodle inside which was so rare, so courageous, so beautiful." (Explain in your own words how Doodle was beautiful inside. Look back through the story to find lines that indicate his spirit.)

"This bird must be destined to die," continues the author, "as Doodle was to die. A local bird, in order to die, would have to be sick. Was the ibis sick? Was Doodle inside sick? If the ibis had been back in a mangrove swamp, would it have died? Could not perhaps Doodle in another society have survived?" (What commentary do you think the author is making on our society? In what kind of a society do you think Doodle might have survived?)

"The ancient Egyptians worshiped the ibis because, they said, it destroyed the crocodiles. In their liturgy, it took second place only to the phoenix. So I chose as my symbol a scarlet ibis, the most beautiful and rare member of the ibis family, exotic to the point of bizarrerie.

"To further my symbolism, Doodle unconsciously identifies himself with the scarlet ibis and at the very end his outside comes to resemble the bird when he dies in the same position the bird died, with the front of his shirt stained with blood."

Did you attach any significance to the year in which the story is set? Hurst had a very definite purpose in choosing this particular setting: "The story was set in 1918 so that World War I would loom in the background, amid the other misfortunes, i.e., the drouth and the storm. A major cause of wars is the desire to transform others into one's own image, and Doodle's and his brother's struggle resembles on a minute, personal scale, the great war." (Were you aware of the importance of this setting to the meaning of the story?)

Finally, what do you think *is* the meaning of the story? The author tells us that there are three sentences very important to the meaning:

—There is within me (and with sadness I have watched it in others) a knot of cruelty borne by the stream of love, much as our blood sometimes bears the seed of our destruction.

—Pride is a wonderful, terrible thing, a seed that bears two vines, life and death.

—Brother, Brother, don't leave me. Don't leave me.

"This last sentence," the author continues, "could almost be called Doodle's theme and I hear it as the classic cry of all mankind wishing to belong and never to be lonely."

A Reading Problem

JEAN STAFFORD

One of the great hardships of my childhood—and there were many, as many, I suppose, as have ever plagued a living creature—was that I could never find a decent place to read. If I tried to read at home in the living room, I was constantly pestered by someone saying, "For goodness' sake, Emily, move where it's light. You're going to ruin your eyes and no two ways about it," or "You ought to be outdoors with the other youngsters getting some roses in your cheeks." Of course, I knew how to reply to these kill-joy injunctions; to the first I said, "They're *my* eyes," and to the second, "Getting some brains in my head is more important than getting any so-called roses in my cheeks." But even when I had settled the hash of that Paul Pry[1]—mother, usually, but sometimes a visiting aunt, or even a bossy neighbor—I was cross and could no longer concentrate. The bedroom I shared with my sister Stella was even worse, because Stella was always in it, making an inventory of her free samples out loud, singing Camp Fire Girl songs, practicing ballet steps and giggling whenever she made a mistake; she was one of the most vacant people I have ever known.

At one certain time of year, I could read up in the mountains, in any number of clearings and dingles and amphitheatres, and that was in the fall. But in the winter it was too cold, and in the spring there were wood ticks, and in the summer there were snakes. I had tried a pinewoods I was very fond of for several weeks one summer, but it was no good, because at the end of every paragraph I had to get up and stamp my feet and shout and describe an agitated circle on the ground with a stick to warn the rattlers to stay away from me.

The public library was better, but not much. The librarian, Mrs. Looby, a fussbudgety old thing in a yellow wig and a hat planted with nasturiums, was so strict about the silent rule that she evicted children who popped their gum or cracked

1. *Paul Pry,* an overly-inquisitive individual, originally a character in a comedy by John Poole.

their knuckles, and I was a child who did both as a matter of course and constantly. Besides, she was forever coming into the children's section like a principal making rounds, and leaning over you to see what you were reading; half the time she disapproved and recommended something else, something either so dry you'd go to sleep reading it or so mushy you'd throw up. Moreover, our dog, Reddie, loved to follow me to the library, and quite often instead of waiting outside under the lilac bush, as he was supposed to do, he would manage to get in when someone opened the door. He didn't come to see me; he came to tease Mrs. Looby, who abominated anything that walked on four legs. He would sit on his haunches in front of her desk, wagging his tail and laughing, with his long pink tongue hanging out. "Shoo!" Mrs. Looby would scream, waving her hands at him. "Emily Vanderpool, you get this pesky dog of yours out of here this minute! The very idea! Quick, Emily, or I'll call the dogcatcher! I'll call the dogcatcher! I will positively call the dogcatcher if a dog ever comes into my library again." I had to give up the library altogether after one unlucky occasion when Reddie stood on his hind legs and put his paws on top of her high desk. She had had her back to him, and, thinking she heard a customer, she turned, saying in her library whisper, "Good afternoon, and what may I do for you this afternoon?," and faced the grinning countenance of my dog. That time, in her wrath and dismay, she clutched her head in her hands and dislodged her hat and then her wig, so that a wide expanse of baldness showed, and everyone in the children's section dived into the stacks and went all to pieces.

For a while after that, I tried the lobby of the downtown hotel, the Goldmoor, where the permanent residents, who were all old men, sat in long-waisted rocking chairs, rocking and spitting tobacco juice into embossed cuspidors and talking in high, offended, lonesome voices about their stomach aches and their insomnia and how the times had changed. All in the world the old duffers had left was time, which, hour after hour, they had to kill. People like that, who are bored almost to extinction, think that everyone else is, too, and if they see someone reading a book, they say to themselves, "I declare, here's somebody worse off than I am. The poor soul's really hard up to have to depend on a book, and its my bounden Christian duty to help him pass the time," and they start talking to you. If you want company on the streetcar or the bus or the interurban, open a book and you're all set. At first, the old men didn't spot me, because I always sat in one of the two bow windows in a chair that was half hidden by a potted sweet-potato plant, which, according to local legend, dated from the nineteenth century—and well it might have, since it was the size of a small-size tree. My chair was crowded in between this and a table on which was a clutter of seedy Western souvenirs—a rusted, beat-up placer pan with samples of ore in it, some fossils and some arrowheads, a tomahawk, a powder horn, and the shellacked tail of a beaver that was supposed to have been trapped by a desperado named Mountain Jim Nugent, who had lived in Estes Park[2] in the seventies. It was this tabletop historical museum that made me have to give up the hotel, for one day, when I was spang in the middle of *Hans Brinker,* two of the old men came over to it to have a whining, cantankerous argument about one of the rocks in the placer pan, which one maintained was pyrites and the other maintained was not. (That was about as interesting as their conversations ever got.) They were so angry that if they hadn't been so feeble, I think they would have

2. *Estes Park,* a small town in northern Colorado, the state in which this story is set. Other Colorado communities Miss Stafford mentions are Watkins, Adams, Mangol, and Niwot.

thrown the rocks at each other. And then one of them caught sight of me and commenced to cackle. "Lookit what we got here," he said. "A little old kid in a middy reading windies[3] all by her lonesome." I had been taught to be courteous to my elders, so I looked up and gave the speaker a sickly smile and returned to my book, which now, of course, I could not follow. His disputant became his ally, and they carried on, laughing and teasing me as if I were a monkey that had suddenly entered their precincts for the sole purpose of amusing them. They asked me why I wasn't at the movies with my sweetheart, they asked me how I'd like to be paddled with the stiff old beaver tail of Mountain Jim's, and they asked me to sing them a song. All the other old men, delighted at this small interruption in their routine of spitting and complaining, started rubbernecking in my direction, grinning and chuckling, and a couple of them came shuffling over to watch the fun. I felt as if I had a fever of a hundred and five, because of the blush that spread over my entire person, including my insides. I was not only embarrassed, I was as mad as anything to be hemmed in by this phalanx of giggling old geezers who looked like a flock of turkey gobblers. "Maybe she ran away from home," said one of them. "Hasn't been any transients in this hotel since that last Watkins fella. Fella by the name of Fletcher. Is your name Fletcher, Missy?" Another said, "I think it's mighty nice of her to come and pay us a call instead of going to the show with her best beau," and when a third said, "I bet I know where there's a Hershey bar not a thousand miles from here," I got up and, in a panic, ducked through the lines and fled; taking candy from a strange old man was the quickest way to die like a dog from poison.

So the hotel after that was out. Then I tried the depot, but it was too dirty and noisy; a couple of times I went and sat in the back of the Catholic church, but it was dark there, and besides I didn't feel right about it, because I was a United Presbyterian in good standing. Once, I went into the women's smoking room in the library at the college, but it was full of worried-looking old-maid summer-school students who came back year after year to work on their Master's degrees in Education, and they asked me a lot of solemn questions, raising their voices as if I were deaf. Besides, it was embarrassing to watch them smoke; they were furtive and affected, and they coughed a good deal. I could smoke better than that and I was only ten; I mean the one time I had smoked I did it better—a friend and I each smoked a cubeb she had pinched from her tubercular father.

But at last I found a peachy place—the visitors' waiting room outside the jail in the basement of the courthouse. There were seldom any visitors, because there were seldom any prisoners, and when, on rare occasions, there were, the visitors were too edgy or too morose to pay any heed to me. The big, cool room had nothing in it but two long benches and a wicker table, on which was spread out free Christian Science literature. The sheriff, Mr. Starbird, was very sympathetic with me, for he liked to read himself and that's what he did most of the time (his job was a snap; Adams was, on the whole, a law-abiding town) in his office that adjoined the waiting room; he read and read, not lifting his eyes from Sax Rohmer[4] even when he was rolling a cigarette. Once, he said he wished his own daughters, Laverne, thirteen, and Ida, sixteen, would follow my example, instead of, as he put it, "rimfirin' around the county with paint on their faces and spikes on their heels and not caring two hoots for anything on God's green earth except

3. ***windies,*** a chiefly Western slang term meaning "tall tales." 4. ***Sax Rohmer,*** pseudonym of Englishman Arthur Wade, creator of Dr. Fu Manchu, a diabolically ingenious Oriental villain, who was unsuccessfully pursued through dozens of books and several films by English hero Nayland Smith. The sheriff is an avid Fu Manchu fan.

what's got on pants." Mr. Starbird and I became good friends, although we did not talk much, since we were busy reading. One time, when we were both feeling restless, he locked me up in a cell so I could see how it felt; I kind of liked it. And another time he put handcuffs on me, but they were too big.

At the time I discovered the jail, in the first hot days in June, I was trying to memorize the books of the Bible. If I got them by heart and could name them off in proper order and without hesitating or mispronouncing, I would be eligible to receive an award of a New Testament at Sunday school, and if there was one thing I liked, it was prizes. So every day for several weeks I spent the whole afternoon more or less in jail, reading whatever fun thing I had brought along *(Rebecca of Sunnybrook Farm, Misunderstood Betsy, Trudy Goes to Boarding School)* and then working away at I Samuel, II Samuel, I Kings, II Kings, whispering so as not to disturb Mr. Starbird. Sometimes, on a really hot day, he would send out for two bottles of Dr. Pepper.[5]

One blistering Saturday, when I was as limp as a rag after walking through the sun down the hill and into the hot valley where the courthouse was, I got to the stairs leading to the waiting room and was met by the most deafening din of men yelling and bars rattling and Mr. Starbird hollering "Quiet there!" at the top of his voice. I was shocked and scared but very curious, and I went on down the steps, hearing the vilest imaginable language spewing out from the direction of the cells. I had just sat down on the edge of one of the benches and was opening *Tom Sawyer Abroad* when Mr. Starbird, bright red in the face, came in, brushing his hands. Two sweating deputies followed him. "Not today, Emily," said Mr. Starbird when he saw me. "We got some tough customers today, worse luck. And me with a new Fu."

The prisoners were moonshiners, he told me as he led me by the arm to the stairs, whose still up in the mountains had been discovered, because they had drunk too much of their own rotgut and had got loose-tongued and had gone around bragging at the amusement park up at the head of the canyon. There were five of them, and they had had to be disarmed of sawed-off shot guns, although, as Mr. Starbird modestly pointed out, this wasn't much of a job, since they had been three sheets in the wind. "Whew!" said the sheriff. "They got a breath on em like the whole shootin' match of St. Louis before the Volstead Act."[6] I told him I didn't mind (it would give me considerable prestige with my brother and my friends to be on hand if one of them should try to make a break, and I would undoubtedly get my name in the paper ("Emily Vanderpool, daughter of Mr. and Mrs. Peter Vanderpool, witnessed the attempted escape of the desperate criminals. Emily is to receive an award at the United Presbyterian Church on July 29th"), but Mr. Starbird told me, a little sharply, to go on now, and I had no choice but to go.

Go where? I had exhausted every possibility in town. I thought of going to the Safeway,[7] where my father was the manager, and asking him if I could read in his office, but I knew how that would go over on a busy Saturday when the farmers and the mountain people were in town buying potatoes and side meat; my father didn't have Mr. Starbird's temperament. Then, vaguely, I considered the front porch of a haunted house at the top of Carlyle Hill but rejected it when I remembered a recent rumor that there was a nest of bats under the eaves; I didn't want them in my hair, using my pigtails to swing on. I wasn't too

---

5. Dr. Pepper, a soft drink. *6. Volstead Act,* a federal law passed in 1919 which defined intoxicating liquors as beverages containing "one-half of one per centum or more of alcohol by volume." The act, which took its name from U.S. Congressman Andrew J. Volstead, was the first step in the struggle to enforce the eighteenth amendment to the Constitution regarding prohibition of intoxicating beverages. *7. Safeway,* name of a Western supermarket chain.

sure I could read anyhow, because I was so excited over the prisoners, but it was far too hot to roller-skate, too hot to explore the dump—too hot, indeed, for anything but sitting quietly beside the lockup.

I started in the direction of home in a desultory way, stopping at every drinking fountain, window-shopping, going methodically through the ten-cent stores, looking for money in the gutters. I walked down the length of the main street, going toward the mountains, over whose summits hung a pale heat haze; the pavement was soft, and when it and the shimmering sidewalk ended, I had to walk in the red dirt road, which was so dusty that after a few steps my legs, above the tops of my socks, looked burned—not sunburned, *burned*.

At the outskirts of town, beside the creek, there was a tourist camp where funny-looking people pitched tents and filled up the wire trash baskets with tin cans; sometimes, on a still night, you could hear them singing state songs, and now and again there was the sound of an accordion or a harmonica playing a jig. Today there was only one tent up in the grounds, a sagging, ragged white one, and it looked forlorn, like something left behind. Nearby was parked a Model T, dark red with rust where its sky-blue paint had worn through, and to it was attached a trailer; I knew how hot the leather seat of that car would be and I could all but hear the sun beating on the top of it like hail-stones. There wasn't a soul in sight, and there wasn't a sound nearby except for a couple of magpies ranting at each other in the trees and the occasional digestive croak of a bullfrog. Along the creek, there was a line of shady cottonwoods, and I decided to rest there for a while and cool off my feet in the water.

After I had washed as well as I could, I leaned back against the tree trunk, my feet still in the water, and opened the Bible to the table of contents, and then I closed my eyes so that I wouldn't cheat; I started reciting, softly and clearly and proud of myself. I had just got to Ezra,[8] having gone so far very fast and without a hitch, when a noise caused me to fling back my eyelids and to discover that a man's big foot in a high buttoned shoe had materialized on the ground beside me. Startled, I looked up into the bearded face of a tall man in black clothes (black suit, black string tie, black-rimmed eyeglasses, black hat—the hat was dented in such a way that it looked like a gravy boat) and into the small brown eyes of a girl about Stella's age, who wore a tennis visor and a long, dirty white thing that looked like her nightgown.

"Greetings, Christian soldier," said the man, in a deep, rich Southern accent, and he offered me a large, warty hand, "Evangelist Gerlash is the name, and this is my girl, Opal."

Opal put her hand on my head and said, "Peace."

"Same to you," I said awkwardly, and took my feet out of the water. "You can have this tree if you want. I was just leaving."

I started to get up, but Evangelist Gerlash motioned me to stay where I was, and he said, "It uplifts my heavy heart and it uplifts Opal's to find a believer in our wanderings through this godless world. All too seldom do we find a person applying themself to the Book. Oh, sister, keep to this path your youthful feet have started on and shun the Sodoms *and* the Gomorrahs *and* the Babylons!"[9]

My youthful feet were so wet I was having a struggle to put on my socks, and I thought, Peace! That's all he knows about it. There's not an inch of peace or privacy in this whole town.

"Seek truth and *not* the fleshpots!" said the man. "Know light, *not* license! 'A little

---

8. ***Ezra,*** the fifteenth Book in the Authorized Version of the Old Testament. 9. ***Sodoms and Gomorrahs and the Babylons.*** As recorded in the Book of Genesis, the Lord rained fire and brimstone upon the cities of Sodom and Gomorrah to punish them for their sinfulness. Babylon, a city noted for its wickedness, is mentioned many times in the Bible.

child shall lead them,' says the Book you hold in your small hands, as yet unused to woman's work. Perhaps *you* are that very child."

"Amen," said Opal, and with this they both sat down, tailor-fashion,[10] on the bank of the stream. For some time, nothing more was said. The Gerlashes complacently scrutinized me, as if I were the very thing they had been looking for, and then they looked at each other in a congratulatory way, while I, breaking out in an itching rash of embarrassment, tried to think of an urgent bit of business that would excuse me from their company without being impolite. I could think only of the dentist or of a dancing class, but I was dressed for neither; some weeks before, my Uncle Will M'Kerrow, who lived in Ridley, Missouri, had gone to a sale at the Army and Navy store in St. Joe and had bought presents for me and my brother and my two sisters, and today I was wearing mine—khaki knickers and a khaki shirt and a cavalry hat. I had perked up the hat by twining a multi-colored shoe lace around the band; the other shoelace I had cut in two to tie the ends of my pigtails; over my heart was sewn a red "C," a school letter that I had got in the spring for collateral reading. The dentist, Dr. Skeen, a humorist, would have died laughing if he had seen me in these A.E.F. regimentals,[11] and Miss Jorene Roy, the dancing teacher, would have had kittens. Although the Gerlashes had no way of knowing the personality of either of them, I was so unskillful at useful lies, and believed so firmly that my mind could be read, that I did not dare pretend I was going to have a cavity filled or to assume the five ballet positions. I said nothing and waited for an inspiration to set me free. People who talked Bible talk like this made me ashamed for them.

Evangelist Gerlash was immensely tall, and his bones had only the barest wrapper of flesh; he made me think of a tree with the leaves off, he was so angular and gnarled, and even his skin was something like bark, rough and pitted and scarred. His wild beard was the color of a sorrel horse, but his long hair was black, and so were the whiskers on the backs of his hands that imperfectly concealed, on the right one, a tattoo of a peacock. His intense and watchful brown eyes were flecked with green, and so were Opal's. Opal's hair was the color of her father's beard and it fell ropily to her shoulders; it needed a good brushing, and probably a fine comb wouldn't have done it any harm.

Presently, the evangelist took his beard between his hands and squeezed as if he were strangling it, and he said, "We have had a weary journey, sister."

"You said a mouthful," said Opal, and hugely yawned.

"We come all the way from Arkansas this trip," said her father. "We been comin' since May."

"I liked it better last summer," said Opal, "up in Missouri and Iowa. I don't like this dry. Mountains give me the fantods."[12] She looked over her shoulder up at the heat-ridden range and shuddered violently.

"We been roving like gypsies of the Lord, warning the wicked and helping the sick," her father went on. "We are pleased to meet up with a person who goes to the source of goodness and spiritual health. In other words, we are glad to make the acquaintance of a *friend*." And, still wringing his beard, he gave me an alarming smile that showed a set of sharp, efficient teeth. "Yes, sir, it gladdens me right down to the marrowbone to see a little girl on a summer day reading the word of God instead of messing with the vanities of this world *or* robbing the honest farmer of his watermelon *or* sassing her Christian mother."

"We stopped in nineteen towns and preached up a storm," said Opal. "You got any gum on you?"

---

10. tailor-fashion, with the ankles crossed and the knees apart. *11. A.E.F. regimentals,* American Expeditionary Force clothing, or, clothing worn by soldiers in World War I. *12. give me the fantods,* make me restless, uneasy.

Fascinated by the Gerlashes, although the piety the evangelist assigned to me discomfited me, since I was no more reading the Bible than your cat, I took a package of Beech-Nut out of the pocket of my knickers, and along with it came my hand-me-down Ingersoll that hadn't run for two years. Opal took a stick of gum, and her father, with his eye on my watch, said, "Don't mind if I do," and also took a stick. "That's a dandy timepiece you got there. Remember that nice old gold turnip I used to have, Opie?"

"Yeah," said Opal scornfully. "I remember you hocked that nice old gold turnip."

"Possessions are a woe and a heavy load of sin," said her father, and reached out for my watch. But after he had held it to his ear and fiddled with the stem for a while, he gave it back, saying "*Was* a dandy timepiece. Ain't nothing now but a piece of tin and isinglass." Then he returned to his thesis. "I reckon this is the one and only time I or Opal has come across a person, let alone a child, drinking at the wellspring of enlightenment." And he gave me his hand to shake again.

"Amen," said Opal.

There followed a drawling antiphonal recitative[13] that related the Gerlash situation. In the winter, they lived in a town called Hoxie, Arkansas, where Evangelist Gerlash clerked in the Buttorf drugstore and preached and baptized on the side. ("Hoxie may be only a wide space in the road," said Opal, "but she don't have any homely mountains.") Mrs. Gerlash, whom Abraham had untimely gathered to his bosom the winter before, had been a hymn singer and an organ player and had done a little preaching herself. Opal, here, had got the word the day she was born, and by the time she was five and a half years old she could preach to a fare-thee-well against the Catholics and the Wets.[14] She was also an A-1 douser and was renowned throughout the Wonder State.[15] In the summer, they took to the road as soon as Opal was out of school, and went camping and preaching and praying (and dousing if there was a call for it) and spreading the truth all over the country. Last year, they had gone through the Middle West up as far as Chicago (here Opal, somewhat to her father's impatience, digressed to tell me the story of Mrs. O'Leary's cow[16]), and the year before they had gone through New England; on earlier trips they had covered Florida and Georgia. One of these days, they were going to set up shop in New York City, though they understood the tourist-camp situation there was poor. Sometimes they found hospitality and sometimes they didn't, depending on the heathens per capita. Sometimes, the Christian citizens lent them a hall, and they put up a sign on the front door saying, "The Bible Tabernacle"; often, in such a receptive community, they were invited to supper and given groceries by the believers. But sometimes they had to do their saving of souls in a public park or in a tourist camp. ("Not much business in this one," said Opal, gazing ruefully at their solitary tent.) Mr. Buttorf, the druggist in Hoxie, always said he wasn't going to keep Gerlash one more day if he didn't quit this traipsing around three months of the year, but the Lord saw to it that right after Labor Day Buttorf came to his senses and hired him again. They had arrived in Adams this morning, and if they found fertile ground, they meant to stay a week, sowing the seeds of righteousness. Evangelist Gerlash would be much obliged to learn from me what sort of town this was; he said he guessed nobody could give him the lay of the land—spiritually speaking—any better than a Bible-reading girl like me.

"But first," he said, "tell Opal and I a

---

13. ***antiphonal recitative.*** Gerlash and Opal alternated speaking in a sort of chant. 14. ***Wets,*** persons in favor of allowing the sale of alcoholic beverages. 15. ***Wonder State,*** since 1923, the official nickname of Arkansas. 16. ***Mrs. O'Leary's cow.*** According to legend, the Chicago fire of 1871 began when a cow belonging to one Mrs. O'Leary kicked over a lantern setting the barn on fire.

little something about yourself, sister." He took a black notebook out of the pocket of his black coat and took a stubby pencil out of his hatband, licked it, and began to ask me questions. All the time he was taking down my dossier, Opal rocked gently back and forth, hugging herself and humming "Holy, Holy, Holy." I was much impressed by her, because her jaws, as she diligently chewed her gum, were moving in the opposite direction to her trunk; I was sure she would be able to pat her head and rub her stomach at the same time.

It never occurred to me that I didn't have to answer questions put to me by adults (except for the old men in the Goldmoor, who were not serious)—even strange ones who had dropped out of nowhere. Besides, I was always as coöperative as possible with clergymen, not knowing when my number might come up. The evangelist's questions were harmless enough, but some of them were exceedingly strange. In between asking my name and my age and my father's occupation, he would say, "Which do you think is the Bible Sabbath—Saturday or Sunday?" and "Do you know if the Devil is a bachelor or is he a married man?" When to these hard, interesting questions I replied that I did not know, Opal left off her humming and said, "Amen."

When he had got from me all the data he wanted, he said "I bet you this here town is a candidate for brimstone. I bet you it's every bit as bad as that one out on the plains we were at for two weeks in a hall. Heathens they were, but *scared,* so they give us a hall. That Mangol."

"Mudhole is what I call it," said Opal.

Her father chuckled. "Opal makes jokes," he explained. Then he said, "That was the worst town we come across in all our travels, sister, and somewheres on me I've got a clipping from the Mangol daily showing what I told the folks down there. I wouldn't be surprised if the same situation was here in Adams, being in the same state with Mangol and not too far away from Mangol and having that college that is bound to sow free-thinking. Forewarned is forearmed is what I always say. I may have a good deal of hard work to do here." He began to fish things out of his pockets, and you never saw such a mess—a knife, a plug of chewing tobacco, a thin bar of soap, envelopes with arithmetic on them, a handkerchief I am not going to describe, any number of small pamphlets and folded-up handbills. Finally, he handed me a clipping. It said,

ANOTHER SOUR, GASSY STOMACH
VICTIM SAYS GASTRO-PEP
GAVE RELIEF

There was a picture of an indignant-looking man with a pointed head and beetling brows and a clenched jaw, who testified:

"For 3 years I had been a Great Victim of stomach gas and indigestion," said Mr. Homer Wagman, prominent Oklahoma citizen of 238 Taos Street, Muskogee. "My liver was sluggish, I would get bloated up and painful and had that tired dragged out feeling all the time. Recently a friend told me about Gastro-Pep so I decided to give it a trial. After taking 3 bottles of this medicine my WHOLE SYSTEM has gone through such a change that I can hardly believe it! Now my gas and stomach discomfort are relieved and I can eat my meals without suffering. I sleep like a schoolboy." Advt.

I did not know what I was reading, but I didn't like it anyway, since it had so nasty a sound; I didn't mind hearing about broken legs or diphtheria, but I hated any mention of anyone's insides. I started to read it for the second time, trying to think of something intelligent or complimentary to say to Evangelist Gerlash, and I must have made a face, because he leaned over me, adjusting his glasses, and said, "Oops! Hold on! Wrong write-up," and snatched the clipping out of my hand. I'm not absolutely sure, but I think Opal winked at me. Her father shuffled through his trash again and finally handed me another clipping, which, this time, was not an advertisement. The headline was:

GERLASH LOCATES HELL IN HEART OF CITY OF MANGOL

and the story beneath it ran:

"Hell is located right in the heart of the city of Mangol but will not be in operation until God sets up His Kingdom here in the earth," declared Evangelist Gerlash last night to another capacity crowd in the Bible Tabernacle.

"There are some very bad trouble spots in the city of Mangol that no doubt would be subjects of Hell right now," continued the evangelist and said, "but there are so many good people and places in this city that overshadow the bad that God has decided to postpone Hell in Mangol until the time of the harvest and the harvest, God says, 'is the end of the world' (Matthew 13:39).

"Hell, when started by God with eternal fire that comes from God out of Heaven and ignites the entire world, including this city will be an interesting place. It will be a real play of fireworks, so hot that all the elements of earth will melt; too hot all over to find a place for any human creature to live. God is not arranging this fireworks for any human creature and therefore, if you or I ever land in this place, it is because we choose to go there."

Evangelist Gerlash and his daughter, Opal Gerlash, 12, of Hoxie, Arkansas, have been preaching on alternate nights for the last week at the Bible Tabernacle, formerly the Alverez Feed and Grain Store at 1919 Prospect Street. Tonight Opal Gerlash will lecture on the subject, "Are You Born Again by Jumping, Rolling, Shouting, or Dancing?"

I read this with a good deal more interest than I had read of Mr. Wagman's renascence, although as Evangelist Gerlash's qualifications multiplied, my emotion waned. I had assumed from the headline, which made the back of my neck prickle, that he had some hot tips on the iniquities of that flat, dull little prairie town of Mangol that now and again we drove through when we were taking a trip to the southwest; the only thing I had ever noticed about it was that I had to hold my nose as we went through it, because the smell of sugar beets was so powerfully putrid. The city of Mangol had a population of about six hundred.

Nevertheless, though the evangelist did not scare or awe me, I had to be polite, and so, handing back the clipping, I said, "When do you think the end of the world is apt to be?" Opal had stopped her humming and swaying, and both she and her father were staring at me with those fierce brown eyes.

"In the autumn of the world," said Evangelist Gerlash sepulchrally, and Opal said, as she could be counted on to do, "Amen."

"Yeah, I know," I said. "But what autumn? What year?" He and Opal simultaneously bowed their heads in silent prayer. Both of them thoughtfully chewed gum.

Then Opal made a speech. "The answer to this and many other questions will be found in Evangelist Gerlash's inspirational hundred-and-twelve-page book entitled *Gerlash on the Bible*. Each and every one of you will want to read about the seven great plagues to smite the people of the world just before the end. Upon who will they fall? Have they begun? What will it mean to the world? In this book, on sale for the nominal sum of fifty cents or a half dollar, Evangelist Gerlash lets the people in on the ground floor regarding the law of God." From one of the deep sleeves of her kimono—for that was what that grimy garment was—Opal withdrew a paper-bound book with a picture of her father on the front of it, pointing his finger at me.

"Fifty cents, a half dollar," said the author, "Which is to say virtually free, gratis, and for nothing."

Up the creek a way, a bullfrog made a noise that sounded distinctly like "Gerlash."

"What makes Mangol so much worse than anyplace else?" I asked, growing more and more suspicious now that the conversation had taken so mercantile a turn.

But the Gerlashes were not giving out information free. "You will find the answer to this and many other questions in the book," said Opal. "Such as 'Can Wall Street Run God's Business?' "

"Why does the Devil go on a sitdown strike for a thousand years?" said her father.

"*What?*" said I.

"Who will receive the mark of the beast?" said Opal.

"Repent!" commanded Evangelist Gerlash. "Watch! Hearken!"

"Ger-lash," went the bullfrog.

"Will Hell burn forever?" cried Opal. "Be saved from the boiling pits! Take out insurance against spending eternity on a griddle!"

"Thy days are numbered," declared her father.

Opal said, "Major Hagedorn, editor of the Markston *Standard,* in his editorial said, 'This man Gerlash is as smart as chain lightning and seems to know his Bible forwards and backwards.'" All this time, she was holding up the book, and her father, on the cover of it, was threatening to impale me on his accusing finger.

"Perhaps our sister doesn't have the wherewithal to purchase this valuable book, or in other words the means to her salvation," he said, at last, and gave me a look of profound sadness, as if he had never been so sorry for anyone in his life. I said it was true I didn't have fifty cents (who ever heard of anyone ten years old going around with that kind of money?), and I offered to trade my Bible for *Gerlash on the Bible,* since I was interested in finding out whether the Devil was a bachelor or had a wife. But he shook his head. He began to throttle his beard again, and he said, "Does a dove need a kite? Does a giraffe need a neck? Does an Eskimo need a fur coat? Does Gerlash need a Bible?"

"Gerlash is a regular walking encyclopedia on the Bible," said Opal.

"One of the biggest trouble spots in the world is Mangol, Colorado," said Evangelist Gerlash. "No reason to think for a minute the contamination won't spread up here like a plague of locusts. Don't you think you had ought to be armed, Christian soldier?"

"Yes, I do," I said, for I had grown more and more curious. "But I don't have fifty cents."

"Considering that you are a Christian girl and a Bible reader," said the man, "I think we could make a special price for you. I reckon we could let you have it for twenty-five cents. O.K., Opal?"

Opal said rapidly, "Gastro-Pep contains over thirty ingredients. So it is like taking several medicines at once. And due to the immense volume in which it sells, the price of Gastro-Pep is reasonable, so get it now. Tonight!"

Evangelist Gerlash gave his daughter a sharp look. And, flustered, she stammered, "I mean, owing to the outstanding nature of Gerlash's information, the price of this *in*valuable book is a mere nothing. The truth in this book will stick and mark you forever."

"You want this book bad, don't you, sister Emily Vanderpool?" asked her father. "You are a good girl, and good girls are entitled to have this book, which is jampacked with answers to the questions that have troubled you for years. You can't tell me your mammy and pappy are so mean that they wouldn't give their little girl a quarter for *Gerlash on the Bible.* Why don't you skedaddle over to home and get the small sum of twenty-five cents off your Christian ma?" He opened his notebook and checked my address. "Over to 125 Belleview Avenue."

"I'm hungry," said Opal. "I could eat me a horse."

"Never mind you being hungry," said her father, with a note of asperity in his mushy voice. "Don't you doubt me, sister Vanderpool," he went on, "when I tell you your innocent life is in danger. Looky here, when I got a call to go and enlighten the children of darkness in Mangol, just down the line from here, I got that call like a clap of thunder and I knew I couldn't waste no time. I went and I studied every den of vice in the city limits and some outside the city limits. It's bad, sister. For twenty-five cents, you and your folks can be prepared for when the Mangolites come a-swarming into this town." He glanced again at his notebook. "While you're getting the purchase price of my book, please ask your pure-hearted mother if I might have the loan of her garage to preach the word of God in. Are you folks centrally located?"

"My brother's got his skunk skins drying in it," I said. "You couldn't stand the smell."

"Rats!" said Evangelist Gerlash crossly, and then sternly he said, "You better shake a leg, sister. This book is offered for a limited time only."

"I can't get a quarter," I said. "I already owe her twenty cents."

"What're you going to have for supper?" asked Opal avidly. "I could eat a bushel of roasting ears.[17] We ain't had a meal in a dog's age—not since that old handout in Niwot."

"Alas, too true," said her father. "Do you hear that, my sister Emily? You look upon a hungry holy man of God and his girl who give to the poor and save no crust for himself. Fainting for the want of but a crumb from the rich man's groaning board, we drive ourself onwards, bringing light to where there is darkness and comfort to where there is woe. Perhaps your good Christian mother and father would give us an invite to their supper tonight, in exchange for which they and theirs would gladly be given this priceless book, free of charge, signed by hand."

"Well, gosh," I said, working my tennis shoes on over my wet socks, "I mean . . . Well, I mean I don't know."

"Don't know what?" said that great big man, glowering at me over the tops of his severe spectacles. "Don't you go and tell me that a good Bible-reading girl like you has got kin which are evolutionists and agnostics and infidels who would turn two needy ministers of God away from their door. To those who are nourished by the Law of the Lord, a crust now and then is sufficient to keep body and soul together. I don't suppose Opal and I have had hot victuals for a good ten days, two weeks." A piteous note crept into his versatile voice, and his brown eyes and his daughter's begot a film of tears. They did look awfully hungry, and I felt guilty the way I did when I was eating a sandwich and Reddie was looking up at me like a martyr of old.

"Didn't she say her daddy ran a grocery store?" asked Opal, and her father, consulting my vital statistics, smiled broadly.

"There's nothing the matter with *your* ears, Opie," he said. And then, to me, "How's about it, sister? How's about you going down to this Safeway store and getting Opal and I some bread and some pork chops and like that?"

"Roasting ears," said Opal. "And a mushmelon."

It had suddenly occurred to me that if I could just get up and run away, the incident would be finished, but Evangelist Gerlash was clairvoyant, and, putting two firmly restraining hands on my shoulders and glaring at me straight in the eye, he said, "We don't have a thing in the world tonight to do but show up at 125 Belleview Avenue round about suppertime."

"I'd rather cook out," said Opal. "I'd rather she brought the groceries."

Her father bent his head into his hands, and there was a great sob in his voice when he said, "I have suffered many a bitter disappointment in this vale of tears, but I suppose the bitterest is right now here in Adams, Colorado, where, thinking I had found a child of light, she turned out to be a mocker, grinding under her heel shod in gold the poor and the halt.[18] Oh, sister, may you be forgiven on the Day of Judgment!"

---

17. ***roasting ears,*** sweet corn suitable for roasting. 18. ***halt,*** crippled, lame.

"Whyn't you go get us some eats?" said Opal, cajoling. "If you get us some eats, we won't come calling. If we come calling, like as not we'll spend the night."

"Haven't slept in a bed since May," said her father, snuffling.

"We don't shake easy," said Opal, with an absolutely shameless grin.

My mother had a heart made of butter, and our spare room was forever occupied by strays, causing my father to scold her to pieces after they'd gone, and I knew that if the Gerlashes showed up at our house (and plainly they would) with their hard-luck story and their hard-luck looks, and all their devices for saving souls, she would give them houseroom and urge them to stay as long as they liked, and my father would not simmer down for a month of Sundays.

So I got up and I said, "All right, I'll go get you a sack of groceries." I had a nebulous idea that my father might let me buy them on time or might give me a job as a delivery boy until I had paid for them.

To my distress, the Gerlashes got up, too, and the evangelist said, "We'll drive you down to Main Street, sister, and sit outside, so there won't be no slip-up."

"It's Saturday!" I cried. "You can't find a place to park."

"Then we'll just circle round and round the block."

"But I can't get into a car with strangers," I protested.

"Strangers!" exclaimed Evangelist Gerlash. "Why, sister, we're friends now. Don't you know all about Opal and I? Didn't we lay every last one of our cards on the table right off the bat?" He took my arm in his big, bony hand and started to propel me in the direction of the Ford, and just then, like the Mounties to the rescue, up came Mr. Starbird's official car, tearing into the camp-grounds and stopping, with a scream from the brakes, right in front of me and the Gerlashes. A man in a deputy's uniform was in the front seat beside him.

"Why, Emily," said Mr. Starbird as he got out of the car and pushed his hat back from his forehead. "I thought you went on home after that ruckus we had. You'll be glad to hear those scalawags are going off to the pen tomorrow, so you can come back to jail any time after 10 A.M."

Opal giggled, but her father shivered and looked as if a rabbit had just run over his grave. "We're getting outa here," he said to her under his breath, and started at a lope toward his car.

"That's them all right," said the man in the deputy's uniform. "They set up shop in the feed store, and when they wasn't passing out mumbo-jumbo about the world going up in firecrackers, they was selling that medicine. Medicine! Ninety per cent wood alcohol and ninety per cent fusel oil. Three cases of jake-leg[19] and God knows how many workers passed out in the fields."

Mr. Starbird and the deputy had closed in on the Gerlashes. Mr. Starbird said, "I don't want any trouble with you, Mister. I just want you to get out of Adams before I run you out on a rail. We got plenty of our own preachers and plenty of our own bootleggers, and we don't need any extra of either one. Just kindly allow me to impound this so-called medicine and then you shove. What kind of a bill of goods were they trying to sell you, Emily, kid?"

The deputy said, "That's another of their lines. We checked on them after they left Mangol, checked all the way back to Arkansas. They get some sucker like a kid or an idiot and give them this spiel and promise they'll go to Heaven if they'll just get them some grub or some money or my Aunt Geraldine's diamond engagement ring or whatever."

I said nothing. I was thrilled, and at the same time I was mortally embarrassed for the Gerlashes. I was sorry for them, too, because, in spite of their predicament, they looked more hungry than anything else.

---

19. jake-leg, liquor that is sold illegally.

Opal said, "If we went to jail, we could eat," but her father gave her a whack on the seat and told her "Hush up, you," and the procession, including myself, clutching my Bible and *Tom Sawyer Abroad*, moved toward the tent and the Model T. The sheriff took two cases of medicine out of the tent and put them in his car, and then we stood there watching the Gerlashes strike camp and put all their bivouac gear into the trailer. They worked swiftly and competently, as if they were accustomed to sudden removals. When they were finished, Opal got into the front seat and started to cry. "Whyn't we ever have something to eat?" said the child preacher.

Mr. Starbird, abashed by the dirty girl's tears, took out his wallet and gave her a dollar. "Don't you spend a red cent of it in Adams," he said. "You go on and get out of town and then get some food."

Evangelist Gerlash, having cranked the car, making a noise like a collision, climbed into the driver's seat, and grinned at the sight of the dollar. "I have cast my bread upon the waters and I am repaid one hundredfold," he said. "And you, in casting your bread upon the waters, you, too, will be repaid one hundredfold."

"Amen," said Opal, herself again, no longer crying.

"Now beat it," said Mr. Starbird.

"And give Mangol a wide berth," said the deputy.

The car shook as if it were shaking itself to death, and it coughed convulsively, and then it started up with a series of jerks and detonations, and disappeared in a screen of dust and black smoke.

Mr. Starbird offered to give me a lift home, and I got into the front seat beside him while the deputy from Mangol got in back. On the way up the hill, Mr. Starbird kept glancing at me and then smiling.

"I've never known a girl quite like you, Emily," he said. "Memorizing the books of the Bible in the hoosegow, wearing a buck-private hat."

I blushed darkly and felt like crying, but I was pleased when Mr. Starbird went on to say, "Yes, sir, Emily, you're going to go places. What was the book you were reading down at my place when you were wearing your father's Masonic fez?"[20] I grew prouder and prouder. "It isn't every girl of ten years of age who brushes up against some moonshiners with a record as long as your arm in the very same day that a couple of hillbilly fakers try to take her for a ride. Why, Emily, do you realize that if it hadn't of been for you, we might not have got rid of those birds till they'd set up shop and done a whole lot of mischief?"

"Really?" I said, not quite sure whether he was teasing me, and grinned, but did so looking out the window, so Mr. Starbird wouldn't see me.

Was I lucky that day! On the way home, I saw about ten people I knew, and waved and yelled at them, and when I was getting out in front of my house, Virgil Meade, with whom I had had an on-again off-again romance for some time and to whom I was not currently speaking, was passing by and he heard the sheriff say, "Come on down to jail tomorrow and we'll get some Dr. Pepper."

The sheriff's valedictory gave me a great prestige in the neighborhood, but it also put an end to my use of the jail as a library, because copycats began swarming to the courthouse and making so much racket in the waiting room that Mr. Starbird couldn't hear himself think, let alone follow Fu Manchu. And after a few weeks he had to post a notice forbidding anyone in the room except on business. Privately, he told me that he would just as lief let me read in one of the cells, but he was afraid word would leak out and it might be bad for my reputation. He was as sorry, he said, as he could be.

He wasn't half as sorry as I was. The snake season was still on in the mountains;

20. ***Masonic fez,*** a red felt hat worn by members of the Freemasonry, an international secret society.

Mrs. Looby hated me; Aunt Joey was visiting, and she and Mother were using the living room to cut out Butterick[21] patterns in; Stella had just got on to pig Latin and never shut her mouth for a minute. All the same, I memorized the books of the Bible, and I won the New Testament, and I'll tell you where I did my work—in the cemetery, under a shady tree, sitting beside the grave of an infant kinswoman of the sheriff, a late-nineteenth-century baby called Primrose Starbird.

---

21. ***Butterick,*** brand name of a dress pattern.

WHAT DO YOU SAY?

1. *(a)* What problems does Emily have to confront and what people must she battle whenever she tries to read? *(b)* Who is the one person who sympathizes with her? *(c)* Why does he do so and how does he show his sympathy?

2. Relate the events leading up to Emily's desperate retreat into the woods.

3. *(a)* What picture of himself does Gerlash want to give? *(b)* How does he try to do this? *(c)* Show how his attempts are foiled, however inadvertently, by his daughter. *(d)* What does the contrast between Opal and Gerlash add to the humor of the story?

4. *(a)* In your opinion, what is funniest about "A Reading Problem"? *(b)* Does the humor in the story arise from an observation of life or from a distortion of it? Explain.

5. *(a)* Is this a purely humorous story, or are there undertones of sadness in it? *(b)* If the latter, from what does the sadness arise?

6. In this story—often in a single sentence—the narrator mixes a very dignified vocabulary with a good many slang terms. For instance, in describing the librarian's reactions to finding a grinning Reddie at her desk, she says: ". . . in her wrath and dismay, she clutched her head in her hands and dislodged her hat and then her wig, so that a wide expanse of baldness showed, and everyone in the children's section dived into the stacks and went all to pieces." *(a)* Find other examples of such intermingling of formal and informal language. *(b)* Is the manner in which the narrator uses language appropriate to the nature of the story? Why or why not?

7. When the events described in "A Reading Problem" took place, Emily was ten years old. How old does she seem to be when she is telling the story? In answering this question, consider the language she uses and the attitudes she displays toward Opal, Gerlash, and her younger self.

8. *(a)* What contribution to the story is made by the setting? *(b)* Is the setting essential, or could the story have happened elsewhere, and at another time?

JEAN STAFFORD

Jean Stafford first won the critics' acclaim for her novel ***Boston Adventure*** and furthered their respect with two more full-length books: ***The Mountain Lion*** and ***The Catherine Wheel.*** Her short stories regularly appear in ***The New Yorker*** magazine and she has seldom missed making the list of prize-winners in the annual ***O. Henry*** and ***Best American Short Stories*** collections. She seems to take her success rather calmly: "It's gratifying, but in a way it isn't important. I just want to write as well as I can, as honestly and truthfully."

Miss Stafford was born in California in 1915 and spent most of her childhood there. The family later moved to Colorado, and she was educated at the University of Colorado. Before beginning ***Boston Adventure,*** she completed several other novels; but, because these works did not come up to her self-imposed standards, she subsequently abandoned them. During this period of apprenticeship she taught at Stephens College, then worked for the ***Southern Review.*** All of her works are characterized by careful craftsmanship, an eloquent style, and an understanding of the people she writes about.

The Third Ingredient

O. HENRY

The (so-called) Vallambrosa Apartment House[1] is not an apartment house. It is composed of two old-fashioned, brownstone-front residences welded into one. The parlor floor of one side is gay with the wraps and headgear of a modiste; the other is lugubrious with the sophistical promises and grisly display of a painless dentist. You may have a room there for two dollars a week or you may have one for twenty dollars. Among the Vallambrosa's roomers are stenographers, musicians, brokers, shopgirls, space-rate writers, art students, wire tappers, and other people who lean far over the banister rail when the doorbell rings.

This treatise shall have to do with but two of the Vallambrosians—though meaning no disrespect to the others.

At six o'clock one afternoon Hetty Pepper came back to her third-floor rear $3.50 room in the Vallambrosa with her nose and chin more sharply pointed than usual. To be discharged from the department store where you have been working four years, and with only fifteen cents in your purse, does have a tendency to make your features appear more finely chiseled.

And now for Hetty's thumbnail biography, while she climbs the two flights of stairs.

She walked into the Biggest Store one morning four years before with seventy-five other girls, applying for a job behind the waist department counter. The phalanx of wage earners formed a bewildering scene of beauty, carrying a total mass of blond hair sufficient to have justified the horseback gallops of a hundred Lady Godivas.

The capable, cool-eyed, impersonal, young, bald-headed man whose task it was to engage six of the contestants, was

---

1. ***Vallambrosa Apartment House.*** Vallombrosa (väl′lōm-brō′sä) or "shady valley" is a resort near Florence, Italy, noted for its beauty. O. Henry apparently misspells the name to emphasize its inappropriate use.

aware of a feeling of suffocation as if he were drowning in a sea of frangipani,[2] while white clouds, hand-embroidered, floated about him. And then a sail hove in sight. Hetty Pepper, homely of countenance, with small, contemptuous, green eyes and chocolate-colored hair, dressed in a suit of plain burlap and a common-sense hat, stood before him with every one of her twenty-nine years of life unmistakably in sight.

"You're on!" shouted the bald-headed young man, and was saved. And that is how Hetty came to be employed in the Biggest Store. The story of her rise to an eight-dollar-a-week salary is the combined stories of Hercules, Joan of Arc, Una,[3] Job, and Little Red Ridinghood. You shall not learn from me the salary that was paid her as a beginner. There is a sentiment growing about such things, and I want no millionaire store-proprietors climbing the fire escape of my tenement house to throw dynamite bombs into my skylight boudoir.

The story of Hetty's discharge from the Biggest Store is so nearly a repetition of her engagement as to be monotonous.

In each department of the store there is an omniscient, omnipresent, and omnivorous person carrying always a mileage book and a red necktie, and referred to as a "buyer." The destinies of the girls in his department who live on (see Bureau of Victual Statistics)—so much per week are in his hands.

This particular buyer was a capable, cool-eyed, impersonal, young, bald-headed man. As he walked along the aisles of his department, he seemed to be sailing on a sea of frangipani, while white clouds, machine-embroidered floated around him. Too many sweets bring surfeit. He looked upon Hetty Pepper's homely countenance, emerald eyes, and chocolate-colored hair as a welcome oasis of green in a desert of cloying beauty. In a quiet angle of a counter he pinched her arm kindly, three inches above the elbow. She slapped him three feet away with one good blow of her muscular and not especially lily-white right. So, now you know why Hetty Pepper came to leave the Biggest Store at thirty minutes' notice, with one dime and a nickel in her purse.

This morning's quotations list the price of rib beef at six cents per (butcher's) pound. But on the day that Hetty was "released" by the B. S. the price was seven and one half cents. That fact is what makes this story possible. Otherwise, the extra four cents would have——

But the plot of nearly all the good stories in the world is concerned with shorts who were unable to cover, so you can find no fault with this one.

Hetty mounted with her rib beef to her $3.50 third-floor back. One hot, savory beef stew for supper, a night's good sleep, and she would be fit in the morning to apply again for the tasks of Hercules, Joan of Arc, Una, Job, and Little Red Ridinghood.

In her room she got the graniteware stewpan out of the 2 × 4-foot china—er—I mean earthenware closet, and began to dig down in a rats' nest of paper bags for the potatoes and onions. She came out with her nose and chin just a little sharper pointed.

There was neither a potato nor an onion. Now, what kind of a beef stew can you make out of simply beef? You can make oyster soup without oysters, turtle soup without turtles, coffeecake without coffee, but you can't make a beef stew without potatoes and onions.

But rib beef alone, in an emergency, can make an ordinary pine door look like a wrought-iron gambling-house portal to the wolf. With salt and pepper and a tablespoonful of flour (first well stirred in a little cold water) 'twill serve—'tis not so deep as a lobster à la Newburg nor so wide

2. ***frangipani*** (fran′ji pan′i), a perfume with a jasmine fragrance. 3. ***Una*** (ü′nə), a lovely lady who personified Truth. She is the central figure in Book I of *The Faerie Queen*, an epic poem written by the Englishman Edmund Spenser (1552?-1599).

as a church festival doughnut; but 'twill serve.

Hetty took her stewpan to the rear of the third-floor hall. According to the advertisements of the Vallambrosa there was running water to be found there. Between you and me and the water meter, it only ambled or walked through the faucets; but technicalities have no place here. There was also a sink where house-keeping roomers often met to dump their coffee grounds and glare at one another's kimonos.

At this sink Hetty found a girl with heavy, gold-brown, artistic hair and plaintive eyes, washing two large Irish potatoes. Hetty knew the Vallambrosa as well as anyone not owning "double hextra-magnifying eyes" could compass its mysteries. The kimonos were her encyclopedia, her *Who's What?*, her clearing house of news, of goers and comers. From a rose-pink kimono edged with Nile green she had learned that the girl with the potatoes was a miniature painter living in a kind of attic —or "studio," as they prefer to call it—on the top floor. Hetty was not certain in her mind what a miniature was; but it certainly wasn't a house; because house painters, although they wear splashy overalls and poke ladders in your face on the street, are known to indulge in a riotous profusion of food at home.

The potato girl was quite slim and small, and handled her potatoes as an old bachelor uncle handles a baby who is cutting teeth. She had a dull, shoemaker's knife in her right hand, and she had begun to peel one of the potatoes with it.

Hetty addressed her in the punctiliously formal tone of one who intends to be cheerfully familiar with you in the second round.

"Beg pardon," she said, "for butting into what's not my business, but if you peel them potatoes, you lose out. They're new Bermudas. You want to scrape 'em. Lemme show you."

She took a potato and the knife, and began to demonstrate.

"Oh, thank you," breathed the artist. "I didn't know. And I *did* hate to see the thick peeling go; it seemed such a waste. But I thought they always had to be peeled. When you've got only potatoes to eat, the peelings count, you know."

"Say, kid," said Hetty, staying her knife, "you ain't up against it, too, are you?"

The miniature artist smiled starvedly.

"I suppose I am. Art—or, at least, the way I interpret it—doesn't seem to be much in demand. I have only these potatoes for my dinner. But they aren't so bad boiled and hot, with a little butter and salt."

"Child," said Hetty, letting a brief smile soften her rigid features. "Fate has sent me and you together. I've had it handed to me in the neck, too; but I've got a chunk of meat in my room as big as a lap dog. And I've done everything to get potatoes except pray for 'em. Let's me and you bunch our commissary departments and make a stew of 'em. We'll cook it in my room. If we only had an onion to go in it! Say, kid, you haven't got a couple of pennies that've slipped down into the lining of your last winter's sealskin, have you? I could step down to the corner and get one at old Giuseppe's stand. A stew without an onion is worse'n a matinée without candy."

"You may call me Cecilia," said the artist. "No, I spent my last penny three days ago."

"Then we'll have to cut the onion out instead of slicing it in," said Hetty. "I'd ask the janitress for one, but I don't want 'em hep just yet to the fact that I'm pounding the asphalt for another job. But I wish we did have an onion."

In the shopgirl's room the two began to prepare their supper. Cecilia's part was to sit on the couch helplessly and beg to be allowed to do something, in the voice of a cooing ringdove. Hetty prepared the rib beef, putting it in cold salted water in the stew pan and setting it on the one-burner gas stove.

"I wish we had an onion," said Hetty, as she scraped the two potatoes.

On the wall opposite the couch was pinned a flaming, gorgeous advertising picture of one of the new ferryboats of the P. U. F. F. Railroad that had been built to cut down the time between Los Angeles and New York City one eighth of a minute.

Hetty, turning her head during her continuous monologue, saw tears running from her guest's eyes as she gazed on the idealized presentment of the speeding, foam-girdled transport.

"Why, say, Cecilia, kid," said Hetty, poising her knife, "is it as bad art as that? I ain't a critic; but I thought it kind of brightened up the room. Of course, a manicure painter could tell it was a bum picture in a minute. I'll take it down if you say so, I wish to the holy Saint Potluck we had an onion."

But the miniature miniature painter had tumbled down, sobbing, with her nose indenting the hard-woven drapery of the couch. Something was here deeper than the artistic temperament offended at crude lithography.

Hetty knew. She had accepted her role long ago. How scant the words with which we try to describe a single quality of a human being! When we reach the abstract, we are lost. The nearer to Nature that the babbling of our lips comes, the better do we understand. Figuratively (let us say), some people are Bosoms, some are Hands, some are Heads, some are Muscles, some are Feet, some are Backs for burdens.

Hetty was a Shoulder. Hers was a sharp sinewy shoulder; but all her life people had laid their heads upon it, metaphorically or actually, and had left there all or half their troubles. Looking at Life anatomically, which is as good a way as any, she was preordained to be a Shoulder. There were few truer collarbones anywhere than hers.

Hetty was only thirty-three, and she had not yet outlived the little pang that visited her whenever the head of youth and beauty leaned upon her for consolation. But one glance in her mirror always served as an instantaneous painkiller. So she gave one pale look into the crinkly old looking glass on the wall above the gas stove, turned down the flame a little lower from the bubbling beef and potatoes, went over to the couch, and lifted Cecilia's head to its confessional.

"Go on and tell me, honey," she said. "I know now that it ain't art that's worrying you. You met him on a ferryboat, didn't you? Go on, Cecilia, kid, and tell your—your Aunt Hetty about it."

But youth and melancholy must first spend the surplus of sighs and tears that waft and float the bark of romance to its harbor in the delectable isles. Presently, through the stringy tendons that formed the bars of the confessional, the penitent—or was it the glorified communicant of the sacred flame—told her story without art or illumination.

"It was only three days ago. I was coming back on the ferry from Jersey City. Old Mr. Schrum, an art dealer, told me of a rich man in Newark who wanted a miniature of his daughter painted. I went to see him and showed him some of my work. When I told him the price would be fifty dollars, he laughed at me like a hyena. He said an enlarged crayon twenty times the size would cost him only eight dollars.

"I had just enough money to buy my ferry ticket back to New York. I felt as if I didn't want to live another day. I must have looked as I felt, for I saw *him* on the row of seats opposite me looking at me as if he understood. He was nice-looking, but oh, above everything else, he looked kind. When one is tired or unhappy or hopeless, kindness counts more than anything else.

"When I got so miserable that I couldn't fight against it any longer, I got up and walked slowly out the rear door of the ferryboat cabin. No one was there, and I slipped quickly over the rail and dropped into the water. Oh, friend Hetty, it was cold, cold!

"For just one moment I wished I was

back in the old Vallambrosa, starving and hoping. And then I got numb, and didn't care. And then, I felt that somebody else was in the water close by me, holding me up. *He* had followed me, and jumped in to save me.

"Somebody threw a thing like a big, white doughnut at us, and he made me put my arms through the hole. Then the ferryboat backed, and they pulled us on board. Oh, Hetty, I was so ashamed of my wickedness in trying to drown myself; and besides, my hair had all tumbled down and was sopping wet, and I was such a sight.

"And then some men in blue clothes came around; and *he* gave them his card, and I heard him tell them he had seen me drop my purse on the edge of the boat outside the rail, and in leaning over to get it I had fallen overboard. And then I remembered having read in the papers that people who try to kill themselves are locked up in cells with people who try to kill other people, and I was afraid.

"But some ladies on the boat took me downstairs to the furnace-room and got me nearly dry and did up my hair. When the boat landed, *he* came and put me in a cab. He was all dripping himself, but laughed as if he thought it was all a joke. He begged me, but I wouldn't tell him my name nor where I lived, I was so ashamed."

"You were a fool, child," said Hetty kindly. "Wait till I turn the light up a bit. I wish to Heaven we had an onion."

"Then he raised his hat," went on Cecilia, "and said, 'Very well. But I'll find you anyhow. I'm going to claim my rights of salvage.' Then he gave money to the cab driver and told him to take me where I wanted to go, and walked away. What is 'salvage,' Hetty?"

"The edge of a piece of goods that ain't hemmed," said the shopgirl. "You must have looked pretty well frazzled out to the little hero boy."

"It's been three days," moaned the miniature painter, "and he hasn't found me yet."

"Extend the time," said Hetty. "This is a big town. Think of how many girls he might have to see soaked in water with their hair down before he would recognize you. The stew's getting on fine—but oh, for an onion! I'd even use a piece of garlic if I had it."

The beef and potatoes bubbled merrily, exhaling a mouth-watering savor that yet lacked something, leaving a hunger on the palate, a haunting, wistful desire for some lost and needful ingredient.

"I came near drowning in that awful river," said Cecilia, shuddering.

"It ought to have more water in it," said Hetty; "the stew, I mean. I'll go get some at the sink."

"It smells good," said the artist.

"That nasty old North River?" objected Hetty. "It smells to me like soap factories and wet setterdogs—oh, you mean the stew. Well, I wish we had an onion for it. Did he look like he had money?"

"First, he looked kind," said Cecilia. "I'm sure he was rich; but that matters so little. When he drew out his billfold to pay the cabman, you couldn't help seeing hundreds and thousands of dollars in it. And I looked over the cab doors and saw him leave the ferry station in a motorcar; and the chauffeur gave him his bearskin to put on, for he was sopping wet. And it was only three days ago."

"What a fool!" said Hetty, shortly.

"Oh, the chauffeur wasn't wet," breathed Cecilia. "And he drove the car away very nicely."

"I mean *you*," said Hetty. "For not giving him your address."

"I never give my address to chauffeurs," said Cecilia, haughtily.

"I wish we had one," said Hetty, disconsolately.

"What for?"

"For the stew, of course—oh, I mean an onion."

Hetty took a pitcher and started to the sink at the end of the hall.

A young man came down the stairs from above just as she was opposite the lower step. He was decently dressed, but pale and haggard. His eyes were dull with the stress of some burden of physical or mental woe. In his hand he bore an onion—a pink, smooth, solid, shining onion as large around as a ninety-eight-cent alarm clock.

Hetty stopped. So did the young man. There was something Joan of Arcish, Herculean, and Unaish in the look and pose of the shoplady—She had cast off the roles of Job and Little Red Ridinghood. The young man stopped at the foot of the stairs and coughed distractedly. He felt marooned, held up, attacked, assailed, levied upon, sacked, assessed, panhandled, browbeaten, though he knew not why. It was the look in Hetty's eyes that did it. In them he saw the Jolly Roger fly to the masthead and an able seaman with a dirk between his teeth scurry up the ratlines and nail it there. But as yet he did not know that the cargo he carried was the thing that had caused him to be so nearly blown out of the water without even a parley.

"*Beg* your pardon," said Hetty, as sweetly as her dilute, acetic acid tones permitted, "but did you find that onion on the stairs? There was a hole in the paper bag; and I've just come out to look for it."

The young man coughed for half a minute. The interval may have given him the courage to defend his own property. Also, he clutched his pungent prize greedily, and, with a show of spirit, faced his grim waylayer.

"No," he said huskily, "I didn't find it on the stairs. It was given to me by Jack Bevens, on the top floor. If you don't believe it, ask him. I'll wait until you do."

"I know about Bevens," said Hetty sourly. "He writes books and things up there for the paper-and-rags man. We can hear the postman guy him all over the house when he brings them thick envelopes back. Say—do you live in the Vallambrosa?"

"I do not," said the young man. "I come to see Bevens sometimes. He's my friend. I live two blocks west."

"What are you going to do with the onion?—begging your pardon," said Hetty.

"I'm going to eat it."

"Raw?"

"Yes; as soon as I get home."

"Haven't you got anything else to eat with it?"

The young man considered briefly.

"No," he confessed; "there's not another scrap of anything in my diggings to eat. I think old Jack is pretty hard up for grub in his shack, too. He hated to give up the onion, but I worried him into parting with it."

"Man," said Hetty, fixing him with her world-sapient eyes, and laying a bony but impressive finger on his sleeve, "you've known trouble, too, haven't you?"

"Lots," said the onion owner, promptly. "But this onion is my own property, honestly come by. If you will excuse me, I must be going."

"Listen," said Hetty, paling a little with anxiety. "Raw onion is a mighty poor diet. And so is a beef stew without one. Now, if you're Jack Bevens' friend, I guess you're nearly right. There's a little lady—a friend of mine—in my room there at the end of the hall. Both of us are out of luck; and we had just potatoes and meat between us. They're stewing now. But it ain't got any soul. There's something lacking to it. There's certain things in life that are naturally intended to fit and belong together. One is pink cheesecloth and green roses, and one is ham and eggs, and one is Irish and trouble. And the other one is beef and potatoes *with* onions. And still another one is people who are up against it and other people in the same fix."

The young man went into a protracted paroxysm of coughing. With one hand he hugged his onion to his bosom.

"No doubt; no doubt," said he, at length. "But, as I said, I must be going because——"

Hetty clutched his sleeve firmly.

"Don't eat raw onions, Little Brother. Chip it in toward the dinner and line yourself inside with the best stew you ever licked a spoon over. Must two ladies knock a young gentleman down and drag him inside for the honor of dining with 'em? No harm shall befall you, Little Brother. Loosen up and fall into line."

The young man's pale face relaxed into a grin.

"Believe I'll go you," he said, brightening. "If my onion is good as a credential, I'll accept the invitation gladly."

"It's good as that, but better as seasoning," said Hetty. "You come and stand outside the door till I ask my friend if she has any objections. And don't run away with that letter of recommendation before I come out."

Hetty went into her room and closed the door. The young man waited outside.

"Cecilia, kid," said the shopgirl, oiling the sharp saw of her voice as well as she could, "there's an onion outside. With a young man attached. I've asked him in to dinner. You ain't going to kick, are you?"

"Oh, dear!" said Cecilia, sitting up and patting her artistic hair. She cast a mournful glance at the ferryboat poster on the wall.

"Nit," said Hetty. "It ain't him. You're up against real life now. I believe you said your hero friend had money and automobiles. This is a poor skeezicks that's got nothing to eat but an onion. But he's easy-spoken and not a freshy. I imagine he's been a gentleman, he's so low down now. And we need the onion. Shall I bring him in? I'll guarantee his behavior."

"Hetty, dear," sighed Cecilia, "I'm so hungry. What difference does it make whether he's a prince or a burglar? I don't care. Bring him in if he's got anything to eat with him."

Hetty went back into the hall. The onion man was gone. Her heart missed a beat, and a gray look settled over her face except on her nose and cheekbones. And the tides of life flowed in again, for she saw him leaning out of the front window at the other end of the hall. She hurried there. He was shouting to someone below. The noise of the street overpowered the sound of her footsteps. She looked down over his shoulder, saw whom he was speaking to and heard his words. He pulled himself in from the window sill and saw her standing over him. Hetty's eyes bored into him like two steel gimlets.

"Don't lie to me," she said, calmly. "What were you going to do with that onion?"

The young man suppressed a cough and faced her resolutely. His manner was that of one who had been bearded sufficiently.

"I was going to eat it," said he with emphatic slowness; "just as I told you before."

"And you have nothing else to eat at home?"

"Not a thing."

"What kind of work do you do?"

"I am not working at anything just now."

"Then why," said Hetty, with her voice set on its sharpest edge, "do you lean out of windows and give orders to chauffeurs in green automobiles in the street below?"

The young man flushed, and his dull eyes began to sparkle.

"Because, madam," said he, in accelerando tones, "I pay the chauffeur's wages and I own the automobile—and also this onion—this onion, madam." He flourished the onion within an inch of Hetty's nose. The shoplady did not retreat a hair's-breadth.

"Then why do you eat onions," she said, with biting contempt, "and nothing else?"

"I never said I did," retorted the young man, heatedly. "I said I had nothing else to eat where I live. I am not a delicatessen storekeeper."

"Then why," pursued Hetty, inflexibly, "were you going to eat a raw onion?"

"My mother," said the young man, "always made me eat one for a cold. Pardon my referring to a physical infirmity; but you may have noticed that I have a very, very severe cold. I was going to eat the onion and go to bed. I wonder why I am standing here and apologizing to you for it."

"How did you catch this cold?" went on Hetty, suspiciously.

The young man seemed to have arrived at some extreme height of feeling. There were two modes of descent open to him—a burst of rage or a surrender to the ridiculous. He chose wisely; and the empty hall echoed his hoarse laughter.

"You're a dandy," said he. "And I don't blame you for being careful. I don't mind telling you. I got wet. I was on a North River ferry a few days ago when a girl jumped overboard. Of course, I—"

Hetty extended her hand, interrupting his story.

"Give me the onion," she said.

The young man set his jaw a trifle harder.

"Give me the onion," she repeated.

He grinned, and laid it in her hand.

Then Hetty's infrequent, grim, melancholy smile showed itself. She took the young man's arm and pointed with her other hand to the door of her room.

"Little Brother," she said, "go in there. The little fool you fished out of the river is there waiting for you. Go on in. I'll give you three minutes before I come. Potatoes is in there waiting. Go on in, Onions."

After he had tapped at the door and entered, Hetty began to peel and wash the onion at the sink. She gave a gray look at the gray roofs outside, and the smile on her face vanished by little jerks and twitches. "But it's us," she said, grimly, to herself, "it's *us* that furnishes the beef."

WHAT DO YOU SAY?

1. (a) At what point in "The Third Ingredient" did you begin to anticipate the ending? *(b)* What clues point toward the outcome?

2. Coincidence plays a large part in "The Third Ingredient." The picture of the P. U. F. F. ferryboat on Hetty's wall, for example, provokes Cecilia's tearful story. *(a)* Mention other events that seem pure coincidence. *(b)* Would you classify the event that creates the ending as something that might happen naturally or as a coincidence? Explain.

3. O. Henry uses both irony of situation and verbal irony in this story. *(a)* What is ironic in Hetty's securing a job at the Biggest Store? *(b)* Point out other humorous examples of irony of situation. *(c)* Why is the fact that Hetty's apartment house is named the "Vallambrosa" an example of verbal irony? *(d)* Locate other examples of verbal irony.

4. O. Henry often uses language to create a humorous effect; for example, he states that the onion carried by the young man was "as large around as a ninety-eight-cent alarm clock." Point out other examples of amusing language.

5. (a) Do Hetty, Cecilia, and the young man emerge as real individuals or as character types? *(b)* What effect does O. Henry's reliance upon coincidence have on his character development?

6. (a) Cite details which show that this story is located in New York City. *(b)* Is the setting important to the action, or could the story have taken place anywhere?

O. HENRY

William Sydney Porter, who wrote under the pen name O. Henry, is the author of over 250 short stories and one of America's most widely read writers. O. Henry was born in North Carolina in 1862 and attended school there. He worked for a Houston, Texas, newspaper, and, later, for a bank in Austin, Texas. While working in this bank, O. Henry was accused of embezzlement, and he further incriminated himself by fleeing to Honduras. When news of his wife's illness reached him, he returned to the United States, and was tried and convicted of the crime. In prison, he began writing under the name O. Henry and, upon his release, settled in New York and continued to write. He died in 1910.

By The Waters of Babylon

STEPHEN VINCENT BENÉT

The title of this story probably comes from a poem by Algernon Charles Swinburne beginning,

"By the waters of Babylon we sat down
and wept,
Remembering thee,"

but the source of the reference lies in the Old Testament story of the captivity in Babylon of the Children of Israel about 600 B.C. When you have finished reading this imaginative story you will have discovered the meaning of the title and the significance of the words, "we sat down and wept, Remembering thee."

The north and the west and the south are good hunting ground, but it is forbidden to go east. It is forbidden to go to any of the Dead Places except to search for metal and then he who touches the metal must be a priest or the son of a priest. Afterwards, both the man and the metal must be purified. These are the rules and the laws; they are well made. It is forbidden to cross the great river and look upon the place that was the Place of the Gods—this is most strictly forbidden. We do not even say its

---

TO OF BRONZE STATUE HUGO HERDEG

name though we know its name. It is there that spirits live, and demons—it is there that there are the ashes of the Great Burning. These things are forbidden—they have been forbidden since the beginning of time.

My father is a priest; I am the son of a priest. I have been in the Dead Places near us, with my father—at first, I was afraid. When my father went into the house to search for the metal, I stood by the door and my heart felt small and weak. It was a dead man's house, a spirit house. It did not have the smell of man, though there were old bones in a corner. But it is not fitting that a priest's son should show fear. I looked at the bones in the shadow and kept my voice still.

Then my father came out with the metal —a good, strong piece. He looked at me with both eyes but I had not run away. He gave me the metal to hold—I took it and did not die. So he knew that I was truly his son and would be a priest in my time. That was when I was very young—nevertheless, my brothers would not have done it, though they are good hunters. After that, they gave me the good piece of meat and the warm corner by the fire. My father watched over me—he was glad that I should be a priest. But when I boasted or wept without a reason, he punished me more strictly than my brothers. That was right.

After a time, I myself was allowed to go into the dead houses and search for metal. So I learned the ways of those houses—and if I saw bones, I was no longer afraid. The bones are light and old—sometimes they will fall into dust if you touch them. But that is a great sin.

I was taught the chants and the spells—I was taught how to stop the running of blood from a wound and many secrets. A priest must know many secrets—that was what my father said. If the hunters think we do all things by chants and spells, they may believe so—it does not hurt them. I was taught how to read in the old books and how to make the old writings—that was hard and took a long time. My knowledge made me happy—it was like a fire in my heart. Most of all, I liked to hear of the Old Days and the stories of the gods. I asked myself many questions that I could not answer, but it was good to ask them. At night, I would lie awake and listen to the wind—it seemed to me that it was the voice of the gods as they flew through the air.

We are not ignorant like the Forest People—our women spin wool on the wheel, our priests wear a white robe. We do not eat grubs from the tree, we have not forgotten the old writings, although they are hard to understand. Nevertheless, my knowledge and my lack of knowledge burned in me—I wished to know more. When I was a man at last, I came to my father and said, "It is time for me to go on my journey. Give me your leave."

He looked at me for a long time, stroking his beard, then he said at last, "Yes. It is time." That night, in the house of the priesthood, I asked for and received purification. My body hurt but my spirit was a cool stone. It was my father himself who questioned me about my dreams.

He bade me look into the smoke of the fire and see—I saw and told what I saw. It was what I have always seen—a river, and, beyond it, a great Dead Place and in it the gods walking. I have always thought about that. His eyes were stern when I told him—he was no longer my father but a priest. He said, "This is a strong dream."

"It is mine," I said, while the smoke waved and my head felt light. They were singing the Star song in the outer chamber and it was like the buzzing of bees in my head.

He asked me how the gods were dressed and I told him how they were dressed. We know how they were dressed from the book, but I saw them as if they were before me. When I had finished, he threw the sticks three times and studied them as they fell.

"This is a very strong dream," he said. "It may eat you up."

"I am not afraid," I said and looked at him with both eyes. My voice sounded thin in my ears but that was because of the smoke.

He touched me on the breast and the forehead. He gave me the bow and the three arrows.

"Take them," he said. "It is forbidden to travel east. It is forbidden to cross the river. It is forbidden to go to the Place of the Gods. All these things are forbidden."

"All these things are forbidden," I said, but it was my voice that spoke and not my spirit. He looked at me again.

"My son," he said. "Once I had young dreams. If your dreams do not eat you up, you may be a great priest. If they eat you, you are still my son. Now go on your journey."

I went fasting, as is the law. My body hurt but not my heart. When the dawn came, I was out of sight of the village. I prayed and purified myself, waiting for a sign. The sign was an eagle. It flew east.

Sometimes signs are sent by bad spirits. I waited again on the flat rock, fasting, taking no food. I was very still—I could feel the sky above me and the earth beneath. I waited till the sun was beginning to sink. The three deer passed in the valley, going east—they did not mind me or see me. There was a white fawn with them—a very great sign.

I followed them, at a distance, waiting for what would happen. My heart was troubled about going east, yet I knew that I must go. My head hummed with my fasting—I did not even see the panther spring upon the white fawn. But, before I knew it, the bow was in my hand. I shouted and the panther lifted his head from the fawn. It is not easy to kill a panther with one arrow but the arrow went through his eye and into his brain. He died as he tried to spring—he rolled over, tearing at the ground. Then I knew I was meant to go east—I knew that was my journey. When the night came, I made my fire and roasted meat.

It is eight suns' journey to the east and a man passes by many Dead Places. The Forest People are afraid of them but I am not. Once I made my fire on the edge of a Dead Place at night and, next morning, in the dead house, I found a good knife, little rusted. That was small to what came afterward but it made my heart feel big. Always when I looked for game, it was in front of my arrow, and twice I passed hunting parties of the Forest People without their knowing. So I knew my magic was strong and my journey clean, in spite of the law.

Toward the setting of the eighth sun, I came to the banks of the great river. It was half-a-day's journey after I had left the god-road—we do not use the god-roads now for they are falling apart into great blocks of stone, and the forest is safer going. A long way off, I had seen the water through trees but the trees were thick. At last, I came out upon an open place at the top of a cliff. There was the great river below, like a giant in the sun. It is very long, very wide. It could eat all the streams we know and still be thirsty. Its name is Ou-dis-sun, the Sacred, the Long. No man of my tribe had seen it, not even my father, the priest. It was magic and I prayed.

Then I raised my eyes and looked south. It was there, the Place of the Gods.

How can I tell what it was like—you do not know. It was there, in the red light, and they were too big to be houses. It was there with the red light upon it, mighty and ruined. I knew that in another moment the gods would see me. I covered my eyes with my hands and crept back into the forest.

Surely, that was enough to do, and live. Surely it was enough to spend the night upon the cliff. The Forest People themselves do not come near. Yet, all through the night, I knew that I should have to cross the river and walk in the places of the gods, although the gods ate me up. My magic did not help me at all and yet there was a fire in my bowels, a fire in my mind. When the sun rose, I thought, "My journey has been clean. Now I will go home from my journey." But, even as I thought so, I knew I could not. If I went to the Place of the Gods, I would surely die, but, if I did not go, I could never be at peace with my spirit again. It is better to lose one's life than one's spirit, if one is a priest and the son of a priest.

Nevertheless, as I made the raft, the tears ran out of my eyes. The Forest People could have killed me without fight, if they had come upon me then, but they did not come. When the raft was made, I said the sayings for the dead and painted myself for death. My heart was cold as a frog and my knees like water, but the burning in my mind would not let me have peace. As I pushed the raft from the shore, I began my death song—I had the right. It was a fine song.

"I am John, son of John," I sang "My
people are the Hill People. They
are the men.
I go into the Dead Places but I am not
slain.
I take the metal from the Dead Place but
I am not blasted.
I travel upon the god-roads and am not
afraid. E-yah! I have killed the
panther, I have killed the fawn!
E-yah! I have come to the great river.
No man has come there before.
It is forbidden to go east, but I have gone,
forbidden to go on the great river,
but I am there.
Open your hearts, you spirits and hear
my song. Now I go to the Place of
the Gods, I shall not return.
My body is painted for death and my
limbs weak, but my heart is big as
I go to the Place of the Gods!"

All the same, when I came to the Place of the Gods, I was afraid, afraid. The current of the great river is very strong—it gripped my raft with its hands. That was magic, for the river itself is wide and calm. I could feel evil spirits about me, in the bright morning; I could feel their breath on my neck as I was swept down the stream. Never have I been so much alone—I tried to think of my knowledge, but it was a squirrel's heap of winter nuts. There was no strength in my knowledge any more and I felt small and naked as a new-hatched bird—alone upon the great river, the servant of the gods.

Yet, after a while, my eyes were opened and I saw. I saw both banks of the river—I saw that once there had been god-roads across it, though now they were broken and fallen like broken vines. Very great they were, and wonderful and broken—broken in the time of the Great Burning when the fire fell out of the sky. And always the current took me nearer to the Place of the Gods, and the huge ruins rose before my eyes.

I do not know the customs of rivers—we are the People of the Hills. I tried to guide my raft with the pole but it spun around. I thought the river meant to take me past the Place of the Gods and out into the Bitter Water of the legends. I grew angry then—my heart felt strong. I said aloud, "I am a priest and the son of a priest!" The gods heard me—they showed me how to paddle with the pole on one side of the raft. The current changed itself—I drew near to the Place of the Gods.

When I was very near, my raft struck and turned over. I can swim in our lakes—I swam to the shore. There was a great spike of rusted metal sticking out into the river—I hauled myself up upon it and sat there, panting. I had saved my bow and two arrows and the knife I found in the Dead Place but that was all. My raft went whirling downstream toward the Bitter Water. I looked after it, and thought if it had trod me under, at least I would be safely dead. Nevertheless, when I had dried my bowstring and restrung it, I walked forward to the Place of the Gods.

It felt like ground underfoot; it did not burn me. It is not true what some of the tales say, that the ground there burns forever, for I have been there. Here and there were the marks and stains of the Great Burning, on the ruins, that is true. But they were old marks and old stains. It is not true either, what some of our priests say, that it is an island covered with fogs and enchantments. It is not. It is a great Dead Place—greater than any Dead Place we know. Everywhere in it there are god-roads, though most are cracked and broken. Everywhere there are the ruins of the high towers of the gods.

How shall I tell what I saw? I went carefully, my strung bow in my hand, my skin ready for danger. There should have been the wailings of spirits and the shrieks of demons, but there were not. It was very silent and sunny where I had landed—the wind and the rain and the birds that drop seeds had done their work—the grass grew in the cracks of the broken stone. It is a fair island—no wonder the gods built there. If I had come there, a god, I also would have built.

How shall I tell what I saw? The towers are not all broken—here and there one still stands, like a great tree in a forest, and the birds nest high. But the towers themselves look blind, for the gods are gone. I saw a fish-hawk, catching fish in the river. I saw a little dance of white butterflies over a great heap of broken stones and columns. I went there and looked about me—there was a carved stone with cut-letters, broken in half. I can read letters but I could not understand these. They said UBTREAS. There was also the shattered image of a man or a god. It had been made of white stone and he wore his hair tied back like a woman's. His name was ASHING, as I read on the cracked half of a stone. I thought it wise to pray to ASHING, though I do not know that god.

How shall I tell what I saw? There was no smell of man left, on stone or metal. Nor were there many trees in that wilderness of stone. There are many pigeons, nesting and dropping in the towers—the gods must have loved them, or, perhaps, they used them for sacrifices. There are wild cats that roam the god-roads, green-eyed, unafraid of man. At night they wail like demons but they are not demons. The wild dogs are more dangerous, for they hunt in a pack, but them I did not meet till later. Everywhere there are the carved stones, carved with magical numbers or words.

I went North—I did not try to hide myself. When a god or a demon saw me, then I would die, but meanwhile I was no longer afraid. My hunger for knowledge burned in me—there was so much that I could not understand. After awhile, I knew that my belly was hungry. I could have hunted for my meat, but I did not hunt. It is known that the gods did not hunt as we do—they got their food from enchanted boxes and jars. Sometimes these are still found in the Dead Places—once, when I was a child and foolish, I opened such a jar and tasted it and found the food sweet. But my father found out and punished me for it strictly, for, often, that food is death. Now, though, I had long gone past what was forbidden, and I entered the likeliest towers, looking for the food of the gods.

I found it at last in the ruins of a great temple in the mid-city. A mighty temple it must have been, for the roof was painted like the sky at night with its stars—that much I could see, though the colors were faint and dim. It went down into great caves and tunnels—perhaps they kept their slaves there. But when I started to climb down, I heard the squeaking of rats, so I did not go—rats are unclean, and there must have been many tribes of them, from the squeaking. But near there, I found food, in the heart of a ruin, behind a door that still opened. I ate only the fruits from the jars—they had a very sweet taste. There was drink, too, in bottles of glass—the drink of the gods was strong and made my head swim. After I had eaten and drunk, I slept on the top of a stone, my bow at my side.

When I woke, the sun was low. Looking

down from where I lay, I saw a dog sitting on his haunches. His tongue was hanging out of his mouth; he looked as if he were laughing. He was a big dog, with a gray-brown coat, as big as a wolf. I sprang up and shouted at him but he did not move—he just sat there as if he were laughing. I did not like that. When I reached for a stone to throw, he moved swiftly out of the way of the stone. He was not afraid of me; he looked at me as if I were meat. No doubt I could have killed him with an arrow, but I did not know if there were others. Moreover, night was falling.

I looked about me—not far away there was a great, broken god-road, leading North. The towers were high enough, but not so high, and while many of the dead-houses were wrecked, there were some that stood. I went toward this god-road, keeping to the heights of the ruins, while the dog followed. When I had reached the god-road, I saw that there were others behind him. If I had slept later, they would have come upon me asleep and torn out my throat. As it was, they were sure enough of me; they did not hurry. When I went into the dead-house, they kept watch at the entrance—doubtless they thought they would have a fine hunt. But a dog cannot open a door and I knew, from the books, that the gods did not like to live on the ground but on high.

I had just found a door I could open when the dogs decided to rush. Ha! They were surprised when I shut the door in their faces—it was a good door, of strong metal. I could hear their foolish baying beyond it but I did not stop to answer them. I was in darkness—I found stairs and climbed. There were many stairs, turning around till my head was dizzy. At the top was another chamber—on one side of it was a bronze door that could not be opened, for it had no handle. Perhaps there was a magic word to open it but I did not have the word. I turned to the door in the opposite side of the wall. The lock of it was broken and I opened it and went in.

Within, there was a place of great riches. The god who lived there must have been a powerful god. The first room was a small ante-room—I waited there for some time, telling the spirits of the place that I came in peace and not as a robber. When it seemed to me that they had had time to hear me, I went on. Ah, what riches! Few, even, of the windows had been broken—it was all as it had been. The great windows that looked over the city had not been broken at all though they were dusty and streaked with many years. There were coverings on the floors, the colors not greatly faded, and the chairs were soft and deep. There were pictures upon the walls, very strange, very wonderful—I remember one of a bunch of flowers in a jar—if you came close to it, you could see nothing but bits of color, but if you stood away from it, the flowers might have been picked yesterday. It made my heart feel strange to look at this picture—and to look at the figure of a bird, in some hard clay, on a table and see it so like our birds. Everywhere there were books and writings, many in tongues that I could not read. The god who lived there must have been a wise god and full of knowledge. I felt I had right there, as I sought knowledge also.

Nevertheless, it was strange. There was a washing-place but no water—perhaps the gods washed in air. There was a cooking-place but no wood, and though there was a machine to cook food, there was no place to put fire in it. Nor were there candles or lamps—there were things that looked like lamps but they had neither oil nor wick. All these things were magic, but I touched them and lived—the magic had gone out of them. Let me tell one thing to show. In the washing-place, a thing said "Hot" but it was not hot to the touch—another thing said "Cold" but it was not cold. This must have been a strong magic but the magic was gone. I do not understand—they had ways—I wish that I knew.

It was close and dry and dusty in their

house of the gods. I have said the magic was gone but that is not true—it had gone from the magic things but it had not gone from the place. I felt the spirits about me, weighing upon me. Nor had I ever slept in a Dead Place before—and yet, tonight, I must sleep there. When I thought of it, my tongue felt dry in my throat, in spite of my wish for knowledge. Almost I would have gone down again and faced the dogs, but I did not.

I had not gone through all the rooms when the darkness fell. When it fell, I went back to the big room looking over the city and made fire. There was a place to make fire and a box with wood in it, though I do not think they cooked there. I wrapped myself in a floor-covering and slept in front of the fire—I was very tired.

Now I tell what is very strong magic. I woke in the midst of the night. When I woke, the fire had gone out and I was cold. It seemed to me that all around me there were whisperings and voices. I closed my eyes to shut them out. Some will say that I slept again, but I do not think that I slept. I could feel the spirits drawing my spirit out of my body as a fish is drawn on a line.

Why should I lie about it? I am a priest and the son of a priest. If there are spirits, as they say, in the small Dead Places near us, what spirits must there not be in that great Place of the Gods? And would not they wish to speak? After such long years? I know that I felt myself drawn as a fish is drawn on a line. I had stepped out of my body—I could see my body asleep in front of the cold fire, but it was not I. I was drawn to look out upon the city of the gods.

It should have been dark, for it was night, but it was not dark. Everywhere there were lights—lines of light—circles and blurs of light—ten thousand torches would not have been the same. The sky itself was alight—you could barely see the stars for the glow in the sky. I thought to myself "This is strong magic" and trembled. There was a roaring in my ears like the rushing of rivers. Then my eyes grew used to the light and my ears to the sound. I knew that I was seeing the city as it had been when the gods were alive.

That was a sight indeed—yes, that was a sight: I could not have seen it in the body—my body would have died. Everywhere went the gods, on foot and in chariots—there were gods beyond number and counting and their chariots blocked the streets. They had turned night to day for their pleasure—they did not sleep with the sun. The noise of their coming and going was the noise of many waters. It was magic what they could do—it was magic what they did.

I looked out of another window—the great vines of their bridges were mended and the god-roads went East and West. Restless, restless, were the gods and always in motion! They burrowed tunnels under rivers—they flew in the air. With unbelievable tools they did giant works—no part of the earth was safe from them, for, if they wished a thing, they summoned it from the other side of the world. And always, as they labored and rested, as they feasted and made love, there was a drum in their ears—the pulse of the giant city, beating and beating like a man's heart.

Were they happy? What is happiness to the gods? They were great, they were mighty, they were wonderful and terrible. As I looked upon them and their magic, I felt like a child—but a little more, it seemed to me, and they would pull down the moon from the sky. I saw them with wisdom beyond wisdom and knowledge beyond knowledge. And yet not all they did was well done—even I could see that—and yet their wisdom could not but grow until all was peace.

Then I saw their fate come upon them and that was terrible past speech. It came upon them as they walked the streets of their city. I have been in the fights with the Forest People—I have seen men die. But this was not like that. When gods war with gods, they use weapons we do not know. It was fire falling out of the sky and a mist that poisoned. It was the time of the Great Burning and the Destruction. They ran about like ants in the streets of their city—poor gods, poor gods! Then the towers began to fall. A few escaped—yes, a few. The legends tell it. But, even after the city had become a Dead Place, for many years the poison was still in the ground. I saw it happen, I saw the last of them die. It was darkness over the broken city and I wept.

All this, I saw. I saw it as I have told it, though not in the body. When I woke in the morning, I was hungry, but I did not think first of my hunger for my heart was perplexed and confused. I knew the reason for the Dead Places but I did not see why it had happened. It seemed to me it should not have happened, with all the magic they had. I went through the house looking for an answer. There was so much in the house I could not understand—and yet I am a priest and the son of a priest. It was like being on one side of the great river, at night, with no light to show the way.

Then I saw the dead god. He was sitting in his chair, by the window, in a room I had not entered before and, for the first moment, I thought that he was alive. Then I saw the skin on the back of his hand—it was like dry leather. The room was shut, hot and dry—no doubt that had kept him as he was. At first I was afraid to approach him—then the fear left me. He was sitting looking out over the city—he was dressed in the clothes of the gods. His age was neither young nor old—I could not tell his age. But there was wisdom in his face and great sadness. You could see that he would have not run away. He had sat at his window, watching his city die—then he himself had died. But it is better to lose one's life than one's spirit—and you could see from the face that his spirit had not been lost. I knew, that, if I touched him, he would fall into dust—and yet, there was something unconquered in the face.

That is all of my story, for then I knew he was a man—I knew then that they had been men, neither gods nor demons. It is a great knowledge, hard to tell and believe. They were men—they went a dark road, but they were men. I had no fear after that—I had no fear going home, though twice I fought off the dogs and once I was hunted for two days by the Forest People. When I saw my father again, I prayed and was purified. He touched my lips and my breast, he said, "You went away a boy. You come back a man and a priest." I said, "Father, they were men! I have been in the Place of the Gods and seen it! Now slay me, if it is the law—but still I know they were men."

He looked at me out of both eyes. He said, "The law is not always the same shape—you have done what you have done. I could not have done it my time, but you came after me. Tell!"

I told and he listened. After that, I wished to tell all the people but he showed me otherwise. He said, "Truth is a hard deer to hunt. If you eat too much truth at once, you may die of the truth. It was not idly that our fathers forbade the Dead Places." He was right—it is better that the truth should come little by little. I have learned that, being a priest. Perhaps, in the old days, they ate knowledge too fast.

Nevertheless, we make a beginning. It is not for the metal alone we go to the Dead Places now—there are the books and the writings. They are hard to learn. And the magic tools are broken—but we can look at them and wonder. At least, we make a beginning. And, when I am chief priest we shall go beyond the great river. We shall go to the Place of the Gods—the place newyork—not one man but a company. We shall look for the images of the gods and find the god ASHING and the others—the gods Licoln and Biltmore and Moses. But they were men who built the city, not gods or demons. They were men. I remember the dead man's face. They were men who were here before us. We must build again.

WHAT DO YOU SAY?

1. *(a)* As this story opens you realize that the time is not the present. When did you get the first hint that the time is in the future? *(b)* By what facts and incidents is the time made clear?

2. *(a)* To what city of the past does the young priest go? *(b)* How do you know what it is and where it is? *(c)* To what actual river does **Ou-dis-sun** refer? What clues help you identify it? *(d)* Who or what are ASHING and UBTREAS? *(e)* To what building do you think the "mighty temple" with "great caves and tunnels" refers?

3. *(a)* Why do you suppose it is forbidden to go East? *(b)* What is meant by the Dead Places?

4. *(a)* Tell what the young priest finds in the Place of the Gods. *(b)* What conclusions does he draw? *(c)* What does he tell his father?

5. The last words of the story are, "We must build again." What symbolic value attaches to these words?

6. *(a)* Could you call this story a modern parable (story used to teach a moral lesson)? If so, what is its lesson? *(b)* How does the title help you to interpret the story?

STEPHEN VINCENT BENÉT

The younger son in a family of writers, Stephen Vincent Benét was born July 22, 1898, in Bethlehem, Pennsylvania. He began to show literary interests before he had learned to read, and at the age of thirteen he won his first literary recognition, a three-dollar prize in a poetry contest. Benét was educated in California and Georgia, and attended Yale, where he received his B.A. and M.A. degrees. His first volume of verse was published when he was seventeen, and in 1929 ***John Brown's Body,*** a long narrative poem on the Civil War, won a Pulitzer Prize for poetry. "*The Devil and Daniel Webster,*" a short prose piece which has become a minor American classic, was his next great success.

Stephen Vincent Benét died on March 13, 1943, but his name lives on through his short stories and poems. Many of his works are characterized by an intense feeling of patriotism, and they vary in form from the ballad to a series of science fantasy poems. The best examples of the greatest of his literary powers are his short American folk tales.

The Fifty-first Dragon

HEYWOOD BROUN

When romantic fantasy and commonplace fact are brought together deliberately, a good setting for humor is created. Note in this story how the most extraordinary unreality is made to seem perfectly matter-of-fact.

Of all the pupils at the knight school Gawaine le Coeur-Hardy was among the least promising. He was tall and sturdy, but his instructors soon discovered that he lacked spirit. He would hide in the woods when the jousting[1] class was called, although his companions and members of the faculty sought to appeal to his better nature by shouting to him to come out and break his neck like a man. Even when they told him that the lances were padded, the horses no more than ponies and the field unusually soft for late autumn, Gawaine refused to grow enthusiastic. The Headmaster and the Assistant Professor of Pleasaunce were discussing the case one spring afternoon and the Assistant Professor could see no remedy but expulsion.

"No," said the Headmaster, as he looked out at the purple hills which ringed the school, "I think I'll train him to slay dragons."

"He might be killed," objected the Assistant Professor.

"So he might," replied the Headmaster brightly, but he added, more soberly, "we must consider the greater good. We are responsible for the formation of this lad's character."

"Are the dragons particularly bad this year?" interrupted the Assistant Professor. This was characteristic. He always seemed restive when the head of the school began to talk ethics and the ideals of the institution.

"I've never known them worse," replied the Headmaster. "Up in the hills to the south last week they killed a number of peasants, two cows and a prize pig. And if this dry spell holds there's no telling when they may start a forest fire simply by breathing around indiscriminately."

"Would any refund on the tuition fee be necessary in case of an accident to young Coeur-Hardy?"

"No," the principal answered, judicially, "that's all covered in the contract. But as a matter of fact he won't be killed. Before I send him up in the hills I'm going to give him a magic word."

"That's a good idea," said the Professor. "Sometimes they work wonders."

From that day on Gawaine specialized in dragons. His course included both theory and practice. In the morning there were long lectures on the history, anatomy, manners and customs of dragons. Gawaine did not distinguish himself in these studies. He had a marvelously versatile gift for forgetting things. In the afternoon he showed to better advantage, for then he would go down to the South Meadow and practice with a battle-ax. In this exercise he was truly impressive, for he had enormous strength as well as speed and grace. He even developed a deceptive display of ferocity. Old alumni say that it was a thrilling sight to see Gawaine charging across the field toward the dummy paper dragon which had been set up for his practice. As he ran he would brandish his ax and shout, "A murrain on thee!"[2] or some other vivid

---

1. ***jousting,*** fighting with lances on horseback. 2. ***A murrain*** (mėr′ən) ***on thee!*** A plague on you! An archaic expression.

bit of campus slang. It never took him more than one stroke to behead the dummy dragon.

Gradually his task was made more difficult. Paper gave way to papier-mâché[3] and finally to wood, but even the toughest of these dummy dragons had no terrors for Gawaine. One sweep of the ax always did the business. There were those who said that when the practice was protracted until dusk and the dragons threw long, fantastic shadows across the meadow, Gawaine did not charge so impetuously nor shout so loudly. It is possible there was malice in this charge. At any rate, the Headmaster decided by the end of June that it was time for the test. Only the night before a dragon had come close to the school grounds and had eaten some of the lettuce from the garden. The faculty decided that Gawaine was ready. They gave him a diploma and a new battle-ax and the Headmaster summoned him to a private conference.

"Sit down," said the Headmaster. "Have a cigarette."

Gawaine hesitated.

"Oh, I know it's against the rules," said the Headmaster. "But after all, you have received your preliminary degree. You are no longer a boy. You are a man. Tomorrow you will go out into the world, the great world of achievement."

Gawaine took a cigarette. The Headmaster offered him a match, but he produced one of his own and began to puff away with a dexterity which quite amazed the principal.

"Here you have learned the theories of life," continued the Headmaster, resuming the thread of his discourse, "but after all, life is not a matter of theories. Life is a matter of facts. It calls on the young and the old alike to face these facts, even though they are hard and sometimes unpleasant. Your problem, for example, is to slay dragons."

"They say that those dragons down in the south wood are five hundred feet long," ventured Gawaine, timorously.

"Stuff and nonsense!" said the Headmaster. "The curate saw one last week from the top of Arthur's Hill. The dragon was sunning himself down in the valley. The curate didn't have an opportunity to look at him very long because he felt it was his duty to hurry back to make a report to me. He said the monster—or shall I say, the big lizard?—wasn't an inch over two hundred feet. But the size has nothing at all to do with it. You'll find the big ones even easier than the little ones. They're far slower on their feet and less aggressive, I'm told. Besides, before you go I'm going to equip you in such fashion that you need have no fear of all the dragons in the world."

"I'd like an enchanted cap," said Gawaine.

"What's that?" asked the Headmaster, testily.

"A cap to make me disappear," explained Gawaine.

The Headmaster laughed indulgently. "You mustn't believe all those old wives' stories," he said. "There isn't any such thing. A cap to make you disappear, indeed! What would you do with it? You haven't even appeared yet. Why, my boy, you could walk from here to London, and nobody would so much as look at you. You're nobody. You couldn't be more invisible than that."

Gawaine seemed dangerously close to a relapse into his old habit of whimpering. The Headmaster reassured him: "Don't worry; I'll give you something much better than an enchanted cap. I'm going to give you a magic word. All you have to do is to repeat this magic charm once and no dragon can possibly harm a hair of your head. You can cut off his head at your leisure."

He took a heavy book from the shelf behind his desk and began to run through it. "Sometimes," he said, "the charm is a whole phrase or even a sentence. I might, for instance, give you 'To make the'—no, that

---

3. ***papier-mâché*** (pā'pər-mə shā'), a mixture of paper pulp and a stiffener. It can be molded when wet and becomes hard when dry.

might not do. I think a single word would be best for dragons."

"A short word," suggested Gawaine.

"It can't be too short or it wouldn't be potent. There isn't so much hurry as all that. Here's a splendid magic word: 'Rumplesnitz.' Do you think you can learn that?"

Gawaine tried and in an hour or so he seemed to have the word well in hand. Again and again he interrupted the lesson to inquire, "And if I say 'Rumplesnitz' the dragon can't possibly hurt me?" And always the Headmaster replied, "If you only say 'Rumplesnitz,' you are perfectly safe."

Toward morning Gawaine seemed resigned to his career. At daybreak the Headmaster saw him to the edge of the forest and pointed him to the direction in which he should proceed. About a mile away to the southwest a cloud of steam hovered over an open meadow in the woods and the Headmaster assured Gawaine that under the steam he would find a dragon. Gawaine went forward slowly. He wondered whether it would be best to approach the dragon on the run as he did in his practice in the South Meadow or to walk slowly toward him, shouting "Rumplesnitz" all the way.

The problem was decided for him. No sooner had he come to the fringe of the meadow than the dragon spied him and began to charge. It was a large dragon and yet it seemed decidedly aggressive in spite of the Headmaster's statement to the contrary. As the dragon charged it released huge clouds of hissing steam through its nostrils. It was almost as if a gigantic teapot had gone mad. The dragon came forward so fast and Gawaine was so frightened that he had time to say "Rumplesnitz" only once. As he said it, he swung his battle-ax and off popped the head of the dragon. Gawaine had to admit that it was even easier to kill a real dragon than a wooden one if only you said "Rumplesnitz."

Gawaine brought the ears home and a small section of the tail. His school mates and the faculty made much of him, but the Headmaster wisely kept him from being spoiled by insisting that he go on with his work. Every clear day Gawaine rose at dawn and went out to kill dragons. The Headmaster kept him at home when it rained, because he said the woods were damp and unhealthy at such times and that he didn't want the boy to run needless risks. Few good days passed in which Gawaine failed to get a dragon. On one particularly fortunate day he killed three, a husband and wife and a visiting relative. Gradually he developed a technique. Pupils who sometimes watched him from the hill-tops a long way off said that he often allowed the dragon to come within a few feet before he said "Rumplesnitz." He came to say it with a mocking sneer. Occasionally he did stunts. Once when an excursion party from London was watching him he went into action with his right hand tied behind his back. The dragon's head came off just as easily.

As Gawaine's record of killings mounted higher the Headmaster found it impossible to keep him completely in hand. He fell into the habit of stealing out at night and engaging in long drinking bouts at the village tavern. It was after such a debauch that he rose a little before dawn one fine August morning and started out after his fiftieth dragon. His head was heavy and his mind sluggish. He was heavy in other respects as well, for he had adopted the somewhat vulgar practice of wearing his medals, ribbons and all, when he went out dragon hunting. The decorations began on his chest and ran all the way down to his abdomen. They must have weighed at least eight pounds.

Gawaine found a dragon in the same meadow where he had killed the first one. It was a fair-sized dragon, but evidently an old one. Its face was wrinkled and Gawaine thought he had never seen so hideous a countenance. Much to the lad's disgust, the monster refused to charge and Gawaine was obliged to walk toward him. He whistled as he went. The dragon regarded him hopelessly, but craftily. Of course it had heard of Gawaine. Even when the lad raised his battle-ax the dragon made no move. It knew that there was no salvation in the quickest thrust of the head, for it had been informed that this hunter was protected by an enchantment. It merely waited, hoping something would turn up.

Gawaine raised the battle-ax and suddenly lowered it again. He had grown very pale and he trembled violently.

The dragon suspected a trick. "What's the matter?" it asked with false solicitude.

"I've forgotten the magic word," stammered Gawaine.

"What a pity," said the dragon. "So that was the secret. It doesn't seem quite sporting to me, all this magic stuff, you know. Not cricket, as we used to say when I was a little dragon; but after all, that's a matter of opinion."

Gawaine was so helpless with terror that the dragon's confidence rose immeasurably and it could not resist the temptation to show off a bit.

"Could I possibly be of any assistance?" it asked. "What's the first letter of the magic word?"

"It begins with an 'r,'" said Gawaine weakly.

"Let's see," mused the dragon, "that doesn't tell us much, does it? What sort of a word is this? Is it an epithet, do you think?"

Gawaine could do no more than nod.

"Why, of course," exclaimed the dragon, "reactionary Republican."

Gawaine shook his head.

"Well, then," said the dragon, "we'd better get down to business. Will you surrender?"

With the suggestion of a compromise Gawaine mustered up enough courage to speak.

"What will you do if I surrender?" he asked.

"Why, I'll eat you," said the dragon.

"And if I don't surrender?"

"I'll eat you just the same."

"Then it doesn't mean any difference, does it?" moaned Gawaine.

"It does to me," said the dragon with a smile. "I'd rather you didn't surrender. You'd taste much better if you didn't."

The dragon waited for a long time for Gawaine to ask "Why?" but the boy was too frightened to speak. At last the dragon had to give the explanation without his cue line. "You see," he said, "if you don't surrender you'll taste better because you'll die game."

This was an old and ancient trick of the dragon's. By means of some such quip he was accustomed to paralyze his victims with laughter and then to destroy them. Gawaine was sufficiently paralyzed as it was, but laughter had no part in his helplessness. With the last word of the joke the dragon drew back his head and struck. In that second there flashed into the mind of Gawaine the magic word "Rumplesnitz," but there was no time to say it. There was time only to strike and, without a word, Gawaine met the onrush of the dragon with a full swing. He put all his back and shoulders into it. The impact was terrific and the head of the dragon flew almost a hundred yards and landed in a thicket.

Gawaine did not remain frightened very long after the death of the dragon. His mood was one of wonder. He was enormously puzzled. He cut off the ears of the monster almost in a trance. Again and again he thought to himself, "I didn't say 'Rumplesnitz'!" He was sure of that and yet there was no question that he had killed the dragon. In fact, he had never killed one so utterly. Never before had he driven a head for anything like the same distance. Twenty-five yards was perhaps his best previous record. All the way back to the knight school he kept rumbling about in his mind seeking an explanation for what had occurred. He went to the Headmaster immediately and after closing the door told him what had happened. "I didn't say 'Rumplesnitz,'" he explained with great earnestness.

The Headmaster laughed. "I'm glad you've found out," he said. "It makes you ever so much more of a hero. Don't you see that? Now you know that it was you who killed all these dragons and not that foolish word 'Rumplesnitz.'"

Gawaine frowned. "Then it wasn't a magic word after all?" he asked.

"Of course not," said the Headmaster, "you ought to be too old for such foolishness. There isn't any such thing as a magic word."

"But you told me it was magic," protested Gawaine. "You said it was magic and now you say it isn't."

"It wasn't magic in a literal sense," answered the Headmaster, "but it was much more wonderful than that. The word gave you confidence. It took away your fears. If I hadn't told you that, you might have been killed the very first time. It was your battle-ax did the trick."

Gawaine surprised the Headmaster by his attitude. He was obviously distressed by the explanation. He interrupted a long philosophic and ethical discourse by the Headmaster with "If I hadn't of hit 'em all mighty hard and fast any one of 'em might have crushed me like a, like a—" He fumbled for a word.

"Egg shell," suggested the Headmaster.

"Like a egg shell," assented Gawaine, and he said it many times. All through the evening meal people who sat near him heard him muttering, "Like a egg shell, like a egg shell."

The next day was clear, but Gawaine did not get up at dawn. Indeed, it was almost noon when the Headmaster found him cowering in bed, with the clothes pulled over

THE FACTS ABOUT A FANTASY

Most of the associations we make with the word "dragon" come from this short passage in the *Bible:*

> . . . he [an angel] laid hold on the dragon, that old serpent, which is the devil, and Satan, and bound him a thousand years.

To Christians of the Middle Ages the dragon was the symbol of sin, paganism, and Satan. The legendary dragon of Christianity was a physical combination of other creatures associated with evil—the lion's claws, eagle's wings, and serpent's tail. On early maps the unexplored areas were represented as being the homes of these mythical creatures.

In "The Fifty-first Dragon" the author whimsically modifies the Christian association of the dragon with evil. However, the legendary characteristics of the dragon, such as its tremendous size, its ability to breathe fire and spout steam, and to swallow people and animals alive, are still present.

his head. The principal called the Assistant Professor of Pleasaunce, and together they dragged the boy toward the forest.

"He'll be all right as soon as he gets a couple more dragons under his belt," explained the Headmaster.

The Assistant Professor of Pleasaunce agreed. "It would be a shame to stop such a fine run," he said. "Why, counting that one yesterday, he's killed fifty dragons."

They pushed the boy into a thicket above which hung a meager cloud of steam. It was obviously quite a small dragon. But Gawaine did not come back that night or the next. In fact, he never came back. Some weeks afterward brave spirits from the school explored the thicket, but they could find nothing to remind them of Gawaine except the metal parts of his medals. Even the ribbons had been devoured.

The Headmaster and the Assistant Professor of Pleasaunce agreed that it would be just as well not to tell the school how Gawaine had achieved his record and still less how he came to die. They held that it might have a bad effect on school spirit. Accordingly, Gawaine has lived in the memory of the school as its greatest hero. No visitor succeeds in leaving the building today without seeing a great shield which hangs on the wall of the dining hall. Fifty pairs of dragons' ears are mounted upon the shield and underneath in gilt letters is "Gawaine le Coeur-Hardy," followed by the simple inscription, "He killed fifty dragons." The record has never been equaled.

WHAT DO YOU SAY?

1. (a) What details in the story read like the ordinary events in a boys' school? *(b)* In what other way does the author make the background of the story seem real and factual?

2. (a) What details seem to you to belong to what is called "romance"? *(b)* Does the author treat these details seriously or does he make them appear ridiculous? Give some examples.

3. (a) What is the significance of the magic word given to Gawaine? *(b)* How does it affect Gawaine's success? *(c)* What happens when he learns that the word is not magic? *(d)* When the Headmaster explains the magic word and its purpose, what suggestion does this make to you about the effect of believing something? *(e)* How does Gawaine react to the knowledge?

4. (a) This story is an ***allegory,*** a story told to explain or teach something. What do you think the author is trying to teach? *(b)* How can this story be applied to every individual?

KNOW YOUR WORDS

Synonyms and antonyms

From the word lists below choose a synonym and an antonym (word meaning the opposite) for each of these words: ***enthusiastic, restive, deceptive, ferocity, impetuously, dexterity.*** You may use a dictionary if necessary.

zealous	lively	authentic
gentleness	facility	clumsiness
slowly	inactive	eagerly
indifferent	brutality	fallacious

HEYWOOD BROUN

Heywood Broun, American journalist, essayist, and novelist, was born in Brooklyn, New York, on December 7, 1888. He gained his first writing experience at the Horace Mann School in New York City, a boys' preparatory school. After attending Harvard for four years, Broun withdrew to work in the sports department of a New York newspaper, where he became well known for his baseball stories. In 1912 he transferred to another New York paper and began his famous column "It Seems to Me," which appeared in a number of papers during the following years.

During World War I, Broun served as a war correspondent, and, in 1931 he wrote a musical comedy entitled ***Shoot the Works.*** Among his other accomplishments are the founding of the American Newspaper Guild and a series of excellent lectures on drama. In his last years, Broun published and edited a weekly newspaper, ***Broun's Nutmeg,*** in Stamford, Connecticut. He died on December 18, 1939. The depth, power, warmth, and imagination of this man are clearly visible in his writing.

JESSE STUART

The Slip-over Sweater

Can a young man respect, admire, and completely trust one girl and at the same time be infatuated with another? If so, to which girl does he owe his first loyalty?

"Now, if you don't get the sweater," Grace said as she followed me up the narrow mountain path, "you mustn't feel too bad. Everybody in Gadsen High School knows that you've made your letters. Just because you don't wear them like the other boys—"

Grace stopped talking before she finished the last sentence. And I knew why. But I didn't say anything—not right then. I stopped a minute to look down over the cliffs into the gorge where the mountain water swirled over the rocks, singing a melancholy song without words. Grace walked over and stood beside me. And I knew the sound of the roaring water did the same thing to her that it did to me. We stood there watching this clear blue mountain water hit and swirl over the giant water-beaten rocks, splashing into spray as it had done for hundreds of years before we were born.

The large yellow-gold leaves sifted slowly down from the tall poplars. And the leaves fell like big soft red raindrops from low bushy-topped sourwoods to ferny ground. Dark frostbitten oak leaves slithered down among the lacework of tree branches to the leaf-carpeted ground. Two of these oak leaves dropped onto Grace's ripe-wheat-colored hair. And a big yellow-gold poplar leaf fell and stuck to my shirt. They were a little damp, for they fell from a canopy of leaves where there was no sun.

Gold poplar leaves would look good in Jo-Anne Burton's chestnut-colored hair, I thought. And how pretty the dark oak leaves would look on her blouse. I was sorry she wasn't with me instead of Grace. I could just see Jo-Anne standing there with the red and yellow leaves falling on her.

I would say, "Gee, you look wonderful with those golden leaves in your dark hair."

"Do you think so?" she would answer. And I could imagine her smile and her even, white teeth. She was always gay and laughing.

I didn't say anything to Grace, but Grace knew how I felt about Jo-Anne. Grace and I had gone to Plum Grove grade school together for eight years. I had carried her books from the time I could remember. And then we started walking five miles across the mountains to Gadsen High School together. When we started to Gadsen, I was still carrying her books. I'd carried them down and up this mountain for three years. But I was not carrying her books this year and I wouldn't be again, for Gadsen was a bigger school than Plum Grove and there were many more girls. But there was only one for me, and Grace knew who she was. She was the prettiest and the most popular girl in Gadsen High School. When she was a sophomore, she was elected May Queen.

Grace knew why I wanted the slip-over sweater. It wasn't just to show the letters and the three stripes on the sleeve I'd won playing football three years for the Gadsen Tigers. Grace knew that Roy Tomlinson had a slip-over sweater and that he was trying to beat my time with Jo-Anne Burton. Grace had heard about Jo-Anne asking me one day why I didn't get a sweater.

"You've got a small waist and broad shoulders," Jo-Anne had said, "and you'd look wonderful in a slip-over sweater!"

I hadn't cared about having a sweater until Jo-Anne had said this to me. Now I wanted it more than anything on earth. I wanted a good one, of the style, color, and brand the other boys had bought. Then I could have my G and the three stripes sewed on, as my teammates had done. They let their favorite girls wear their sweaters. Jo-Anne was wearing Roy Tomlinson's, and that hurt me.

Grace probably knew I was thinking of Jo-Anne now. And as she stood beside me, with the leaves falling onto her dress, I couldn't keep from thinking how they would look on Jo-Anne.

Why we had stopped at this high place every morning and evening for three years, I didn't know. But it was from here on the

---

"The Slip-over Sweater" by Jesse Stuart. Reprinted from *The Woman's Home Companion*, January 1949, by permission of the author.

coldest days in winter, when the gorge below was a mass of ice, that we listened to the water singing its lonesome song beneath the ice. And here in early April we watched spring come back to the mountains.

We knew which trees leafed first. And even before the leaves came back we found trailing arbutus that had sprung up beside the cliffs and bloomed. Then came the percoon that sprang from the loamy coves where old logs had lain and rotted. It was the prettiest of all wildwood flowers and its season was short. Grace and I had taken bouquets of this to our high-school teachers before a sprig of green had come to the town below.

Grace shook the multicolored leaves from her hair and dress when we silently turned to move away. And I brushed the leaves from my shirt sleeves and trousers. We started up the mountain as we had done for the past three years—only I used to take Grace's arm. Now I walked in front and led the way. If there was a snake across the path, I took care of him. I just protected Grace as any boy would protect a girl he had once loved but had ceased to love since he had found another girl who meant more to him than anyone else in the world.

"If I had the money," Grace said after our long silence, "I'd let you have it, Shan, to buy your sweater."

"I'll get the money some way," I said.

Not another word was spoken while we climbed toward the ridge. But I did a lot of thinking. I was trying to figure out how I could buy that sweater. I was not going to hunt and trap wild animals any more and sell their skins just to get clothing for my own skin. Books had changed me since I'd gone to high school. I'd never have the teacher send me home because I had polecat scent on me. I'd always bought my schoolbooks and my clothes by hunting and trapping. But I'd not done it this year and I'd not do it again. I was determined about that. Books had made me want to do something in life—for my girl. And I knew now that I wanted to be a schoolteacher and teach math in Gadsen High School. And that's what I'd do.

When Grace started from the path across to her home, a big log house on Seaton Ridge, she said good-by. And I said good-by to her. These were the only words spoken. We used to linger a long time at this spot by a big oak tree. I looked over at the heart cut in the bark of the oak. Her initials and mine were cut side by side inside the heart. Now, if I'd had my knife, I would have gone over and shaved those initials and the heart from the oak bark. Now I hoped that she would find some boy she could love as much as I loved Jo-Anne.

When I first realized I had to get that sweater for Jo-Anne, I had thought about asking Pa for ten dollars. But I knew he wouldn't have it, for he raised light Burley tobacco,[1] like Grace's father, and it hadn't been a good season. Pa had not made enough to buy winter clothes for my four brothers and six sisters. And another thing, I'd never in my life asked him for money. I'd made my own way. I'd told my father I'd do this if he'd only let me go to high school. He wasn't much on education. But he agreed to this, and I'd stick to my end of the bargain.

That night I thought about the people I knew. I wondered if I could borrow from one of them. I didn't like to borrow but I'd do anything to get Jo-Anne to take off Roy Tomlinson's sweater and put mine on in place of it. Most of the people I knew did not have the money, though.

At noon the next day the idea came to me: what are banks for? Their job is to lend money to needy people—and that's why I walked straight to the Citizens' State Bank at lunch time. I was a citizen, a student at Gadsen High School; and I needed money. I'd just tell him I wanted very much to buy myself a sweater so I could put my school

1. ***light Burley*** (bėr′li) ***tobacco***, a thin tobacco, light-colored when cured. It is used as a base for nearly all American tobacco mixtures.

letter on it and my three stripes—and be like the other high-school boys. I wouldn't mention Jo-Anne.

I stood nervously at the window. Mr. Cole was a big heavy man with blue eyes and a pleasant smile. "Something I can do for you?" he asked politely.

"Yes, sir," I stammered. "I'd like to have ten dollars."

"You want to borrow it?" he asked.

"Yes, sir." Now the worst was over.

"You go to high school, don't you?"

"Yes, sir."

"Thought I'd seen you around here," he said. "You're the star player on the Gadsen Tigers—you're Mick Stringer's boy."

"Yes, sir," I said.

"What's your first name?" He started making out a note for me.

"Shan," I said, "Shan Stringer."

He shoved the note forward for me to sign. And he didn't ask for anyone to go my security.[2] If he had, I don't know who I could have got to sign. I wasn't old enough to borrow money at the bank. But it just seemed to me as if Mr. Cole read my mind. He knew I wanted the money badly. So he gave me nine dollars and seventy-five cents and took a quarter for interest.

"This note will be due in three months," he said. "This is October twenty-eighth. Come back January twenty-eighth. And if you can't pay it then, I'll let you renew for another three months. Then we'll expect all or partial payment."

"Thank you, Mr. Cole."

I hurried to Womack Brothers' store and bought the sweater. It had a red body with white sleeves—the Gadsen High colors. I would have Mom sew the white G on the front and the red stripes on the sleeves as soon as I got home. I was the happiest boy in the world. Gadsen High School had always been a fine place, but now it was wonderful. I loved everybody, but I worshiped Jo-Anne Burton.

That afternoon when Grace and I walked through the town and came to the mountain path, we talked more than we had in a long time. But I didn't mention what was in the package I was carrying. We stopped at our place on the cliffs and looked down at the swirling waters in the gorge. The dashing water did not sound melancholy to me. It was swift dance music like a reel from old Scotland. Even the trees above us with their arms interlaced were in love. All the world was in love because I had got what I wanted and I was in love.

The next morning Grace was waiting for me beside the old oak where we had cut our initials. Grace was all right, I thought. She was almost sure to be valedictorian of our class; and she was good-looking, too. But she didn't have the kind of beauty Jo-Anne had. Jo-Anne was not only beautiful—she was always happy, laughing and showing her pretty teeth. She wasn't one of the best students in the class—her grades were not high at all. But she was friendly with everybody and as free as the wind. Her clothes were always pretty, and they fitted her much better than Grace's did. I loved the way she wore her clothes. I loved everything about Jo-Anne. She held my love as firmly as the mountain loam held the roots of the wild flowers and the big trees.

"Why are you taking that bundle back to school?" Grace asked.

"Oh, just to be carrying something," I said.

Grace laughed as though she thought I was very funny.

We got to school early. When I had a chance to speak to Jo-Anne alone, I told her what I had.

"Oh, Shan!" she exclaimed. "Oh, you're a darling!"

"Brand new," I said. "You'll like it, Jo-Anne."

"Oh, I know I'll love it," she said. "I'll put it right on!"

I handed her the package, and she hurried off. I was never happier in my life.

2. *to go my security,* to sign the note also, indicating that he would pay the money if Shan were unable to do so.

When she came back she was smiling at me, her eyes dancing. She walked over to Roy Tomlinson and handed a package to him. Everybody standing around was looking at Jo-Anne in the new sweater with the three stripes on the sleeve—the only sweater in the school with three stripes. Was Jo-Anne proud! And was I proud!

"Do you like it on me?" she asked as she walked up to me.

"Do I like it?" I said. "I love it."

She smiled happily, and I was glad that Roy could see now that I was the one Jo-Anne loved. And everybody knew now that I was in love with her. Roy would probably wonder, I was thinking, how I was able to buy that sweater. He had probably thought that he would be able to keep Jo-Anne with his sweater and his two stripes because I'd never be able to buy one for her. But Roy would never know how I got it—that would be a secret between Mr. Cole, the banker, and me.

While the girls were admiring the sweater and many of my teammates were looking on, I glanced over at Roy. He stood by, not saying a word, just looking at the sweater that had replaced his. I hadn't expected him to react that way, and it bothered me. That noon Grace came up to where we had gathered in front of the auditorium, and she was wearing Roy Tomlinson's sweater.

"Boy!" Jim Darby exclaimed. "Look at Grace! Doesn't that sweater look swell on her!"

"She isn't the same girl!" Ed Patton said.

I stared at Grace. I didn't realize a sweater could make such a difference. Her clothes had never become her. But this sweater did! There were many whispers and a lot of excitement as we flocked into the auditorium. I was watching Grace move through the crowd in her new sweater when Jo-Anne edged over close to me.

"You do like this sweater on me, don't you, Shan?" she asked.

"Sure do, Jo-Anne," I said. And I walked proudly beside her into the auditorium.

That afternoon, after I had said good-by to Jo-Anne, I looked around for Grace. She was just saying her good-by to Roy. When she turned toward me, I could see that she was as proud of that sweater as she could be. And Roy stood there looking after us as we started toward the mountain together.

We stopped at the gorge, but we didn't stay very long. Grace did most of the talking and I did the listening, but I didn't hear quite everything she said. I was wild with joy, for I was thinking about Jo-Anne wearing my new red sweater.

At every football game Jo-Anne sat on the front bleacher and yelled for me. And Grace yelled for Roy Tomlinson. Once when I made an eighty-five-yard run for a touchdown, Jo-Anne came up to me after the game and kissed me. I could outkick, outpass, and outrun Roy Tomlinson. And I didn't brag when I said it. He earned another stripe that season, and so did I. Grace sewed Roy's third stripe on his sweater with pride. She kept the sweater clean as a pin. I'll have to admit she kept it cleaner than Jo-Anne kept mine.

When Grace was almost sure to be valedictorian, Roy Tomlinson could hardly stand the idea of our walking over the mountain together. He walked with us to the edge of Gadsen. But he never climbed the mountain and looked down at the gorge. He could just as well have come along. His going with her didn't bother me, not exactly. She did of course seem close to me—like a sister. As we walked along together, I saw the trees along the ridge where we had had our playhouses and grapevine swings. I saw the coves where we had gathered bouquets of trailing arbutus and percoon. And those initials on the oak reminded me of the days when we were little.

It was in the basketball season, just before the regional tournament, when I received a notice from the bank that my note was due. With the other little expenses I had at school, even twenty-five cents wasn't easy to get.

If the interest is hard to get, I thought, what will I do about the principal? What if I have to take the sweater from Jo-Anne and sell it to make a payment on the principal?

But when my mother let me have fifty cents and I paid the interest, I felt much better and didn't think about it again during the basketball season. Jo-Anne came to every game and was always urging everybody else to come. She was as proud of me and the way I played as I was proud of her and the way she looked in my sweater.

Grace was never so talkative and gay and popular as Jo-Anne, and I was always glad to hear anyone pay Grace compliments. One day I heard Harley Potters say, "You know, Grace Hinton is a beautiful girl. Think, she comes five miles to school and five miles home and makes the highest grades in her class. There's something to a girl that would go through all kinds of weather and do that."

I thought so, too. All through the winters when snow was on the ground and the winds blew harshly on the mountain, she and I had walked back and forth to school. I had walked in front and had broken the path through new-fallen snow. I had done that even when we went to Plum Grove. We had walked through the rain and sleet together, and I couldn't remember a day that she had not been good-natured. And I knew she had the durability and the toughness of a storm-battered mountain oak. I didn't believe there was another girl in Gadsen High School who could have done what Grace had done. And now to the Gadsen boys and girls she was as pretty as a cove sapling. Yet I was sure I would never go back to Grace. I'd always love Jo-Anne.

I only hoped that Roy Tomlinson appreciated Grace. I got a little tired of looking at his sweater so often. Sometimes I wondered if I were jealous of him for making his third stripe. But I couldn't have been, because I had four—and I had the most popular and beautiful girl in the world. I decided I was tired of looking at it just because Grace never wore anything else. I could hardly remember what Grace's clothes had looked like before.

When the bitter cold of January and February passed away, the melted snow ran down the gorge in deep foaming waters, and I grew as melancholy as the song of the swollen little winter river. Jo-Anne didn't know what was worrying me. Sometimes I wished she would ask, but she never did. And that hurt me, too. If I didn't always smile at something she said, she acted impatient with me. I'm sure I could not have told her about the note due in April, if she had asked. But I looked for some kind of sympathy, because I thought I needed it and that she loved me so much she would want to cheer me up. Instead, she kept asking me if I didn't love her and if I did, why didn't I show it the way all the other boys did?

So I tried my best to cheer up. I didn't want to lose her, but I did have to figure out some way to make money. I couldn't hunt now even if I did change my mind about killing animals. Spring was on the way, and animal pelts weren't good now.

One day Grace said to me, "What is the matter with you, Shan?" That was in late March as we were watching the blue melted snow waters roll down the gorge where the white dogwood sprays bent down to touch them. "I know something is bothering you."

"No, it isn't," I said. "I'm all right."

"If I can ever help you, I'll be glad to," she said. "Just let me know."

Her words made me feel better. I didn't want to tell her that I'd never been in debt before and that a debt worried me to death. So I didn't say anything.

After the snow had melted from the mountain, I grew more despondent. Neither the sight of Jo-Anne nor of Grace could cheer me. My grades went down, and some of the teachers asked me what had happened to me. Everyone around me seemed happy, for April had come again, and Jo-

Anne seemed gayer than ever. Several of my teammates had their eyes on her constantly; that only made me more despondent.

Grace coaxed me again one day to tell her what was wrong. "You always used to like spring on the mountain," she said.

Then I decided I had to tell somebody my trouble, and she was the one to tell. "Grace," I confessed, "I need money—ten dollars!"

"I don't have it," Grace said quietly. "If I did, you could have it. But that doesn't help. Maybe I'll think of a way—"

I didn't think she would; but it made me feel better—just to have someone to share my worry.

On April eighteenth something happened to me that the whole school witnessed. We were gathering at the auditorium for assembly period when Jo-Anne handed my sweater back to me!

"I'm tired of it," she said, without the pretty smile on her lips. "And I'm tired of your ways. You go around with your lower lip drooping as if the world had turned upside down and smashed you. You never have anything to say. You've just become a bore, and everybody knows it." She left me standing there with my sweater in my hand.

I was stunned. I couldn't speak. My face grew hot, and I felt everybody looking at me. When I looked up, I saw Grace and Roy standing at the other side of the auditorium. They were looking in my direction, and Grace suddenly started to talk to Roy, neither looking my way again. I don't know how I got through the rest of that day at school.

After school I didn't wait for Grace. I hurried out and away from them all. But just as I started up the mountain, Grace overtook me.

"I've thought of something, Shan. I know a way to get ten dollars."

I looked at her without speaking. I was still stunned.

"You know there's a big price at Dave Darby's store for roots and hides and poultry," she said, speaking quickly. "I noticed that sign yesterday. And you know the coves above the gorges are filled with ginseng, yellowroot, and May-apple root."

She waited for me to speak. I walked in silence for a while, thinking it was all too late now—thinking I'd sell my sweater for whatever I could get for it.

"When is the note due?" she asked.

"Ten more days," I said. "April twenty-eighth."

"We'll have it by then," she said.

We, I thought. I looked at her and thought of Jo-Anne. Jo-Anne was pretty and gay and popular, but her face had changed in my mind. I began to wonder if all that gaiety was real—and what she had meant by "love." I was too puzzled to think anything out clearly.

Grace and I walked along silently. We didn't stop at the gorge because Grace had suggested that we go into the cove. I just followed along and started to hunt ginseng after Grace had started.

I never saw anyone before who could find three-prong and four-prong ginseng like Grace. We found patches of yellowroot and May apple. We filled our lunch pails with these precious roots; and I took them home, strung them the way Mom used to string apples and shuckbeans to dry, and hung them on nails driven on the wall above our stove.

We stopped every evening that week and gathered wild roots, and I brought them home to dry. On April twenty-seventh, one day before my note was due—and I had already received the notice—I took a small paper sack of dried May-apple roots, a small sack of yellowroot, and more than a pound of the precious ginseng roots to Dave Darby. When he was through weighing the roots, he did some figuring. Then he said, "It all comes to sixteen dollars if you trade it out in the store."

"How much if I take cash?"

"Fifteen dollars," he said.

"Let me have the cash."

I went straight to the Citizens' State Bank and paid off my note. And I had five dollars for Grace. I never felt better, not even when I was so much in love with Jo-Anne.

As I walked home with Grace, I told her how much the roots had brought. "This is not your half," I said as I gave her the five dollars; "but we'll dig more until we get your share. I paid my note."

"Wonderful," she said, smiling at me.

I looked at Grace. Whatever had been wrong with me, I wondered. Why hadn't I seen before that she had beauty such as Jo-Anne could never have? Grace was as beautiful as our mountain was in April, prettier than a blossom of wild phlox or a mountain daisy. She was as solid as the jutting cliffs, I thought, and as durable as the mountain oaks.

"Now ask me if there is anything more I want from you," I said as I took her arm to help her up the mountain toward the gorge and the wild-root coves.

"What is it?" she asked quickly.

"Take off Roy Tomlinson's sweater," I said. "I'm awfully tired of looking at it."

"But what will I do without it?" she said. "It keeps me warm."

I didn't answer. I started to pull off mine. Then I felt her hand on my arm. "No, Shan," she said. "Keep it a while. I couldn't wear it yet."

We stood silently on the mountain path and looked at each other. "I couldn't wear it yet," she had said. And that was all the promise I needed. I knew how fine she was; and I was proud that she would not discard Roy Tomlinson's sweater as Jo-Anne had done, without a word to him first.

I didn't know what she was thinking as we started down the path, and she didn't know what I was thinking. I didn't ask her; she didn't ask me. But I was thinking that our high-school days would soon be over and I could build a house, if she'd want it there, right on Seaton Ridge on the path that leads from her family's house to mine.

WHAT DO YOU SAY?

1. *(a)* What do you learn about Shan and Grace at the very opening of the story? *(b)* What opinion do you form of Grace's character?

2. *(a)* Explain the part that Jo-Anne plays in Shan's wanting a slip-over sweater. *(b)* How does Shan manage to buy a sweater?

3. *(a)* Why does Jo-Anne want to wear Shan's sweater? *(b)* Explain why Grace suddenly appears in Roy Tomlinson's sweater. *(c)* What do you learn about the two girls from these facts?

4. *(a)* How does Shan manage to pay off his note at the bank? *(b)* What part does Grace play in this? *(c)* List the events that lead Shan to appreciate the real quality of Grace.

5. *(a)* If this story seems real to you, how does the author create such a feeling? *(b)* Select from the story incidents, descriptions, and conversations that seem to you to reflect actual experiences. *(c)* What have you learned about the motives of people from this story? *(d)* Did the ending of the story please you? Why or why not?

KNOW YOUR WORDS

Using specific words

An author can make his story more interesting to the reader by choosing exact, specific words instead of general words. One of the two words following each number below is a specific word, the other is a general word. Number your paper to fifteen and after each number write the general word first and the specific word after it.

1. poplar, forest
2. Grace, girl
3. sports, football
4. clothing, sweater
5. Gadsen, town
6. dollar, money
7. distance, mile
8. animal, polecat
9. emotion, sympathy
10. arbutus, plant
11. percoon, flower
12. music, reel
13. winter, season
14. root, ginseng
15. April, spring

PHOTO BY EARL PALMER

MY EXCITING ADVENTURES IN WRITING

By

JESSE STUART

I have been writing as long as I can remember. When I entered the one-room Plum Grove Rural School, where one teacher taught all the classes in eight grades in a six-hour day, I learned to write. Hand writing was magic. I began to put little stories, rhymes, and items on paper. And I remember students in my class laughed when I read my themes. They thought they were funny. And when they laughed, this pleased me. Writing was an exciting thing for me when I was a small boy.

In high school I wrote themes which later became short stories and I wrote poems which my classmates liked. In college I wrote articles, stories, and poems. Many of my stories written then were later published in magazines and are included in my published collections. Many of my poems were published in the college paper and in small magazines. And, while an undergraduate, I won first place in our college poetry and short story contests. I got a bigger thrill out of this than if I had taken a first place in the two miles in a track meet. I never got a first on the two miles. I got seconds and thirds.

On planes, trains, and buses I have written poems. In my hotel rooms I have written stories. I have written them out in the fields on the farm. I have written them at home. I didn't know any editor would take them. And, now, a bibliographer has compiled a book on the stories, poems, essays, articles, and books I have had accepted. In May 1960 the count was 2200 acceptances. And each one of these acceptances gave me a thrill. I believe when I am no longer happy over an acceptance, I will be through as a writer.

When my collection of poems, ***Man with a Bull-Tongue Plow,*** was published in 1934, I walked on the wind. I couldn't believe a book of sonnets, many of which I had written on leaves from trees with little sticks for pencils when I didn't have paper, had been accepted. I wrote these for recreation and enjoyment in eleven months. This acceptance was the greatest thrill of my life up to then. I let whatever was past be past and sought the new always. I was more interested in writing new books than I was in the books I had written and published. I have never been able to read one of my books after it has been published. I am through with it. The joy of its creation and the excitement of its birth are over for me.

After many excitements of having poems, stories, articles, and books published, I wrote a book about how important teachers and schools are. I titled it ***The Thread That Runs So True.*** This book wasn't given much of a chance when first published, but when the National Education Association selected it as the "best book of 1949," I walked on the wind again. Being a teacher, I was really overjoyed that the people of my profession thought this well of *The Thread.*

Then another surprise came which wasn't enjoyable but one I had to accept. I had a heart attack. But I found a bright side to this. I had lived fully and enjoyed life. I had lived longer than Keats, Shelley, Byron, Burns, Poe, and other favorite authors. I had received honors, degrees, and awards, all of which had been great to me! Other writers had received greater ones. I had read about these. I had wondered if they had been as excited over their writing acceptances and honors as I had been. I wondered if they had found writing as exciting an adventure as I had found it. I wondered if they had found life as exciting as I had found it.

I had been given one chance in a thousand to live. I spent days, weeks, months in bed. I had to learn to walk again. I wondered if I would ever be able to use my hands again. They had been good, strong, fast hands. Now they were so stiff I could hardly use them. Instead of using a rubber ball to squeeze in my hands to give them exercise, my doctors gave me permission to try to hold a pencil and write. At first, I was permitted to write only a page per day. As my hands grew better my journal increased.

I lay in bed most of the time. Later I was permitted to take little walks. My world was my home, yard, and farm. At the end of the year my journal was very large. When my editor visited me I showed him my journal. He was impressed. He said, "Here is a fine book!" Talk about excitement again! I wasn't through as a writer and a teacher. Out of this struggle to live again had come *The Year of My Rebirth.* A short time ago, I had lain in bed and wondered if death, which came to all, would be as exciting an adventure as life had been.

With a new lease on life, everything meant much more to me now than it had before. I became principal of McKell High School for a year, but it was a load that taxed my strength. Then I taught for a summer at the University of Nevada.

When we returned from Nevada, I answered a long distance call. It was a very long distance call. I was offered a teaching position at American University at Cairo, and I accepted. After arriving there, I asked who had recommended me. I was told that my book *The Thread That Runs So True* had recommended me! This was a new experience, a new enjoyment which was one of the extras that had come directly from writing.

I went to teach, relax, and enjoy myself in this quiet land of antiquity. We lived in the center of the capital of Egypt and the United Arab Republic. Life was so exciting here I forgot I had ever had any kind of illness. I never dreamed anything could happen in my homeland that could be as exciting as the life my wife, daughter, and I were living here.

But a message came by cable in March 1961. And this was the biggest of all surprises. I had a time believing this message which said I had won the Academy of the American Poets Award, for "distinguished service to poetry." I had had three books and over 1600 poems published, but my honors for poetry had been meager. After receiving this distinguished award, I didn't feel like walking on the wind. I was stunned. And after I read the names of the well-known American poets, novelists, and scholars who thought enough of my poems to give me this, I felt humble and I wept.

Now, if any writer in America or any country in the world, past or present or in the future, has ever had, has now, or ever will have a more exciting life and time than I have had as a writer and teacher, I would like to shake his hand. I have never expected anything. I won't let myself. I cannot dream of myself as being one to be honored. I think of the one-room shack where I was born, my mother, with a second-grade education, and my coal-mining father, who couldn't read and write. And I think of the opportunities I have been given in America. The adventures in my life have been one exciting event following another from the time I entered the one-room school at Plum Grove.

UNIT 1 REVIEW

1. In this unit, you have studied three major elements of a short story: *plot, setting,* and *characterization.* You learned that authors frequently emphasize one of these elements. Name two stories in which you think plot is the dominant element; two that emphasize setting, and two that stress characterization. In "The Most Dangerous Game" setting, plot, and characterization are combined to achieve an over-all effect. Select another story from this unit in which you feel the three elements are of relatively equal importance and explain your choice.

2. Much of the effectiveness of Poe's story, "The Cask of Amontillado" depends upon the element *irony.* Find examples of irony in "The Most Dangerous Game" and "The Adventure of the Speckled Band." Do any other stories in the unit contain an element of irony?

3. The story "The Scarlet Ibis" demonstrates the use of *symbolism.* Which of the other stories in this unit contain symbolism? You may wish to refer to the "Author's Craft" article on page 95.

4. Some of the methods used by writers to create humor are: *incongruity,* two ideas or qualities which do not logically belong together ("She wore riding boots with her prom dress"); *exaggeration* or *overstatement* ("I've told you a million times"); and *understatement* ("He was somewhat hungry after five days with no food"). Find examples of incongruity, exaggeration and understatement in "A Reading Problem" and "The Fifty-first Dragon."

5. The author of "Indian Burial" has combined fact and fiction through the use of a true setting and an imaginary plot. Select other stories in this unit which you feel might be combinations of fact and fiction and explain your choice. Choose at least three stories which are probably pure fiction and explain why they appear to be so.

SUGGESTED READING

ARNOLD, ELLIOTT, *Blood Brother.* (Duell) Against the background of the old West, Cochise, an Apache chief, and Tom Jeffords, an Indian agent, became friends and attempt to establish peace between the Indians and the White men.

ASHMUN, MARGARET, *Modern Short Stories.* (Macmillan) A collection of twenty-one short stories.

BALMER, EDWIN and PHILIP WYLIE, *When Worlds Collide.* (Lippincott) Faced with the destruction of the earth by a collision with another heavenly body approaching through space, the inhabitants design and build a spaceship in which a few of them can escape the disaster.

CRONIN, ARCHIBALD JOSEPH, *The Green Years.* (Little) A small Scottish town provides the setting for the story of Robert Shannon, an Irish orphan, and his attempts to adjust to life in a new country.

DOYLE, SIR ARTHUR CONAN, *The Adventures of Sherlock Holmes.* (Harper •Collier, Dolphin) Readers who enjoyed "The Adventure of the Speckled Band" will want to read this collection of tales about London's most famous sleuth.

FERRIS, HELEN, *The Brave and the Fair.* (Winston) Girls particularly will enjoy this collection of stories about courageous young women during America's pioneer days.

GUTHRIE, ALFRED BERTRAM, *The Big Sky; an Edition for Younger Readers.* (Houghton) Young Boone Caudill runs away from his vicious father and begins a new life on the western frontier.

HARTE, BRET, *The Luck of Roaring Camp and Other Tales.* (Dodd •Dolphin) A collection of tales, both humorous and sad, about life in the Old West.

HAYCRAFT, HOWARD and JOHN BEECROFT, *Ten Great Mysteries.* (Doubleday) This collection includes two full length novels as well as short stories by Erle Stanley Gardner, Agatha Christie, and Ellery Queen.

HENRY, O., *The Best Short Stories of O. Henry.* (Modern Library) A collection of thirty-eight stories by the master of the "surprise ending." *Pocket Book of O. Henry Stories* (•Washington Square).

LANE, ROSE WILDER, *Let the Hurricane Roar.* (Longmans) In this story of pioneer life, Charles and Caroline meet the rigorous challenge of the Dakota country with its crop failures, fierce storms, and loneliness.

MAUPASSANT, GUY DE, *The Odd Number; Thirteen Tales.* (Harper) A collection of stories by a French writer, an acknowledged master of the short story form. *Portable Maupassant* (•Viking).

POE, EDGAR ALLAN, *The Complete Tales and Poems.* (Modern Library) Sixty-nine tales of mystery and terror are included in this volume. *Tales and Poems of Edgar Allan Poe* (•Washington Square).

SAROYAN, WILLIAM, *My Name is Aram.* (Harcourt) A collection of stories about an American-born Armenian boy and his family.

SCOGGIN, MARGARET C., *Chucklebait; Funny Stories for Everyone* (Knopf).

SPEARE, ELIZABETH G., *The Witch of Blackbird Pond.* (Houghton) In this historical narrative, young Kit Tyler finds prejudice and suspicion in a colonial Connecticut town and becomes the object of a witch-hunt.

STREET, JAMES, *Goodbye, My Lady.* (Lippincott) Young Skeeter's life in the Mississippi swamp is primitive and lonely until he finds Lady, a very unusual dog.

STUART, JESSE, *Hie to the Hunters.* (McGraw) Fourteen-year-old Did runs away from his city home to live with his friend, Sparkle, in a mountain cabin and gains insight into a completely different way of life.

ULLMAN, JAMES RAMSEY, *Banner in the Sky.* (Lippincott) The story of a young man's attempt to climb the Citadel, the highest mountain in Switzerland.

•paperback

A *biography* is the life history of one person, written by another, while an *autobiography* is a person's own life history, written by himself. These two classes of non-fiction, along with histories, sermons, essays, and some poetry, made up practically all of America's early literature. Biography and autobiography still form a large part of the literature published each year, and many are as widely read and enjoyed as the most popular works of current fiction.

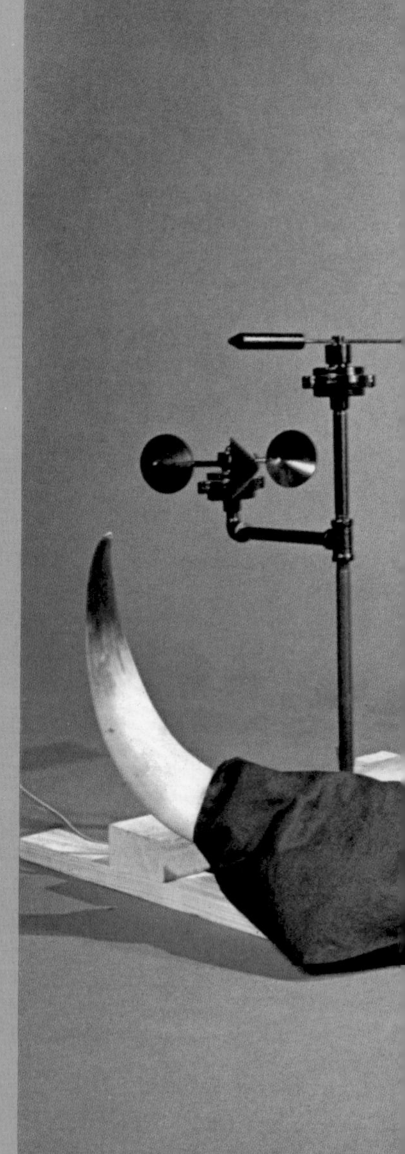

PHOTO BY JAMES BALLARD

Unit 2

Biography and Autobiography

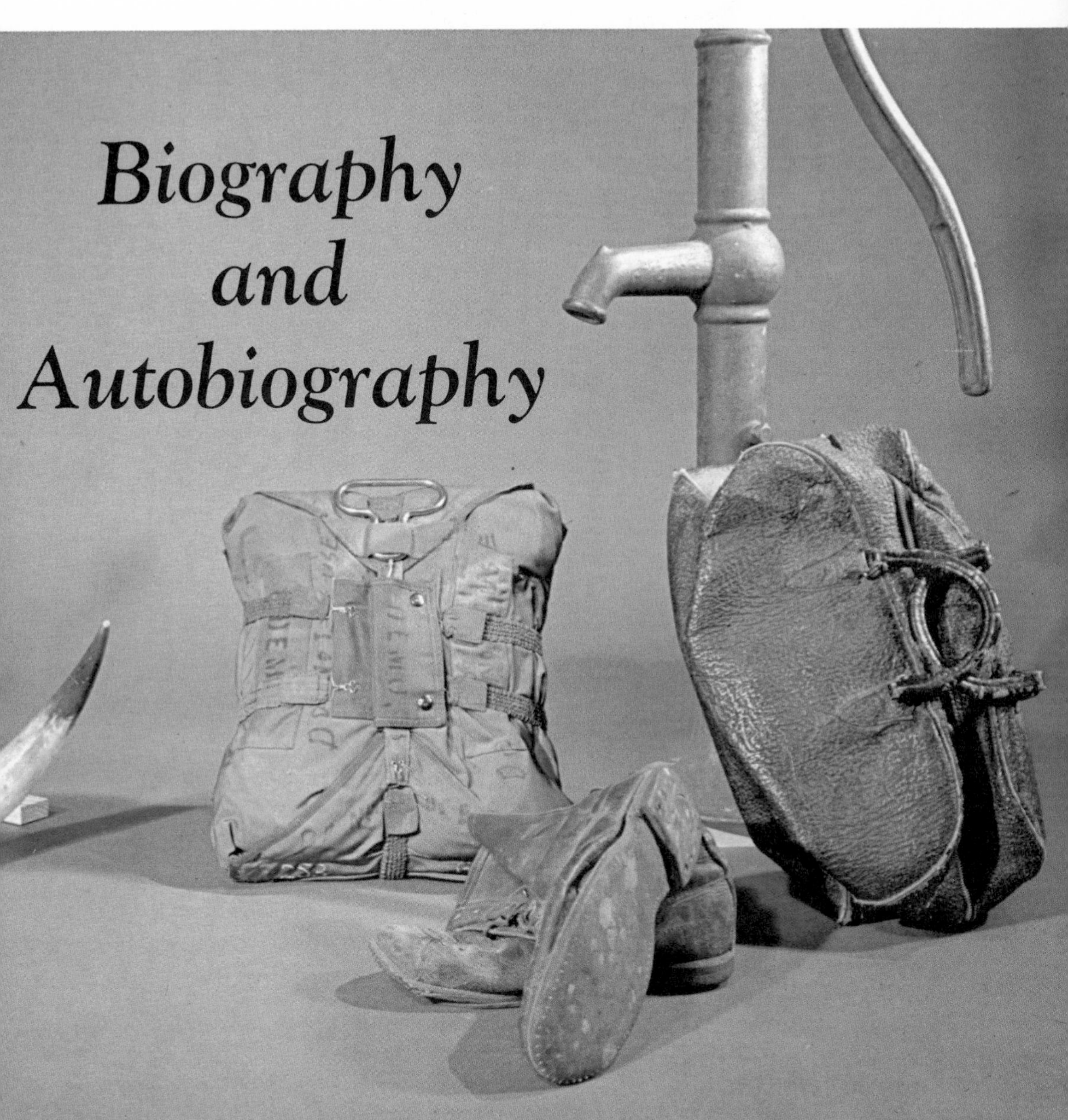

Walter Havighurst

From: GEORGE ROGERS CLARK, Soldier in the West

Surveyor, explorer, and brilliant military commander against the Indians and British during the Revolutionary War, George Rogers Clark is credited with the winning of the Old West—that vast region of America between the Allegheny Mountains and the Mississippi River.

Clark was born in Virginia on November 19, 1752, and at the age of nineteen left his home in Albemarle County to become a surveyor along the Ohio River frontier. By 1778, however, he had become a military leader and was enlisted by the Council of Virginia to conduct an ambitious campaign to capture the British strongholds of Vincennes, Cahokia, and Kaskaskia in the Indiana territory.

Colonel Clark and his men were successful in carrying out their mission and had settled in for the winter at Kaskaskia, when they received word that the British, under the leadership of Lt. Governor Henry Hamilton, had managed to recapture Vincennes. In this selection, which is taken from a biography of Clark, you will meet him at Kaskaskia and accompany him on his nearly impossible march to recover the lost fort during the bitter winter of 1779.

CHAPTER 11: *Flames on a Winter Night*

In the desolate Illinois winter Kaskaskia huddled on its gray riverbank under a cold gray sky. Behind the little farmhouses cornstalks rattled in the wind; the pastures were gray, the orchards bare and rocking. As Clark stared from the blockhouse, a thin curtain of snow blurred the eastern plain. Weeks had passed, with no word from the spies he had sent across the prairie. He paced the puncheon floor and stood again at the porthole, as though his narrowed eyes could see across 200 bleak and frozen miles to the banks of the Wabash. But he could not see. He could only wait and wonder—about the fate of Captain Helm[1] and his small garrison, about the loyalty of the French citizens of Vincennes, about the strength of the British in the fort and the Indians camped on the commons. In those gray days Kaskaskia was besieged by winter and by worry. Was Hamilton even now marching across the desolate land?

A commander cannot wait for a blow to fall; he must make ready to parry or absorb it. So Clark set out over the iron roads to Cahokia: he could not protect that defenseless town, but he could instruct the French habitants about their conduct under siege or capture. His party moved briskly, mounted on shaggy ponies and bouncing in two-wheeled carts. But they never reached Cahokia.

Twelve miles the hoofbeats drummed on the Old Fort Chartres Road,[2] between tattered cornfields and wheat stubble powdered with snow, and in the chilling dusk they reached the village of Prairie du Rocher.[3] In that quiet place, in the empty

---

1. ***Captain Helm,*** Leonard Helm, who had been put in command of Vincennes with only twenty men to hold the fort.
2. ***Fort Chartres*** (chä'trə) ***Road,*** the road to Cahokia.
3. ***Prairie du Rocher*** (prā'rē dü rō shā').

winter season, the arrival of visitors was an event. After a smoking supper Clark's party was entertained at a ball. The fiddler twanged his strings and feet tapped briskly on the timbered floor. A cold wind moaned outside the windows, but firelight leapt in the chimney and a bowl of spiced cider steamed on the hearth. Clark danced a quadrille and talked with the French farmers around the smoking punch bowl. For a little while even a commander could forget the siege of winter and the weight of war.

At midnight the fiddle strings were lilting and French voices raised the refrain of a *voyageurs'* song, rhythmic as the dip of canoe paddles in swift water:

Lon, lon, laridon daine!
Lon, lon, laridon dai!

Now there was hot buttered rum and crisp-crusted French bread with mellow cheese. Suddenly the door burst open. A bitter wind swept the room and a mist of snow, fine and sharp like sand, stung the faces of the dancers.

Into the hall came a man gray with cold and grim with his message. He went straight to Clark in the ruddy light of the hearth fire. At that moment the fiddler's strings went silent and all the voices were still. Then came the stunning message—Governor Hamilton, the "Hair-buyer General,"[4] was within three miles of Kaskaskia, leading 800 troops and Indians against the fort. Kaskaskia must even now be in his possession.

The hall filled with murmur, with confusion, with alarm, and then, suddenly, it was strained with silence. Every eye was on the commander, where the firelight washed his rugged features and gleamed like copper in his hair. In that stillness the wind moaned overhead and the windows rattled.

Clark turned to his officers. "Saddle the horses. We must gain the fort before they gather their attack."

The voices murmured again, anxious now, begging the commander not to ride into the arms of the enemy. Already the town must be in British hands. They urged him to fly to the Mississippi, to cross the river to safety on the Spanish side,[5] to take refuge in the friendly town of St. Louis. Clark shook his head. In war a commander sought not to save his life but to risk it when that was necessary. He must not turn his back on the enemy but go to meet them. Now he called to the fiddler, "Strike up the music!" and to the company he said, "On with the dance. The horses are not yet ready."

At that display of spirit the young Frenchmen were fired with boldness. They ran out to get their own ponies, to ride with the Americans in the face of an overwhelming enemy. While the fiddler played, Clark wrote a hurried message to Major Bowman[6] at Cahokia. Soon an officer reported the horses ready. With a last word to the villagers Clark led his men outside.

In the cold wind under a starless sky, that file of horsemen pounded over the frozen road toward Kaskaskia. Each man had a blanket rolled behind his saddle. Clark had instructed them in a border stratagem: if they found the fort under attack, they would wrap themselves in blankets and mingle with the enemy. At the gate of the fort they would give the recognition signal and immediately join in its defense.

For two hours they raced through darkness with a thin snow blowing, and as he neared Kaskaskia, Clark listened for the din of battle. There was only the uneasy wind and the creak of saddle leather—no crash and bang of gunfire, no piercing war whoops, no flickering torches or fiery arrows in the sky. They reined their horses and jogged into the quiet street, with the houses sleeping and the fort hunched darkly on the hill. With a creak of timber the gate swung open; all was in order there. From the blockhouse Clark peered over the vague

---

4. ***Governor Hamilton, the "Hair-Buyer General."*** This British commander was said to have offered Indians a cash bounty for American scalps. 5. ***the Spanish side,*** the west bank of the Mississippi River, where many Spanish people lived. 6. ***Major Bowman,*** in command of the American troops at Cahokia.

dark prairie. Perhaps the attack was delayed in this bad weather; perhaps the British general was waiting for daylight. Perhaps he was giving the Americans time to withdraw, so that he could march unresisted into an empty fort. In that case Clark would disappoint him.

Before daybreak he sent men with smoking torches to burn the houses nearest to the fort; he would leave no cover for the enemy's attack. Soon a fierce light washed the faces of the defenders, standing at their cannon, crouching at loopholes with rifles ready. Outside the stockade frantic citizens milled in the snowy street. When Clark threatened to burn all houses containing stores of food that the enemy might seize, French householders streamed into the fort with boxes, baskets, barrels. Quickly the fort was provisioned, and with their stores inside, the citizens grew anxious to defend it. From the portholes they watched gray day break on the snowy prairie.

With full daylight the thin snow stopped, the wind died down. It was good weather for an attacking army, but no army came. Instead, from the other direction, over the Old Fort Chartres Road from Cahokia, galloped a file of men under Major Bowman. They brought cheering news. The approaching British force had not been Hamilton's great army; it was but a scouting force of forty men, sent out to raid Kaskaskia and to capture Colonel Clark. That band had lost the way and given up the mission. At this moment they were hurrying back toward Vincennes.

After that fearful and defiant night Kaskaskia waited tensely for a new attack. Clark's scouts rode off toward Vincennes, but they did not return. Apparently they were captured, and Clark was left to worry and wonder about the enemy's movements. At last, on a cold day in late January, 1779, a single horesman rode in from the frozen prairie. So came to Kaskaskia a Spanish merchant, Colonel Francis Vigo,[7] who traded in all the Illinois towns and across the river at St. Louis. He rode straight to the fort, and a sentry led him into the commander's office.

A slight, shrewd, swarthy man with black eyes in a deeply wrinkled face, he stood before the young red-haired commander. Francis Vigo was a native of Sardinia in the blue Mediterranean; he had come to New Orleans as a young soldier in the Spanish army. Later he had located in St. Louis as a fur trader, traveling to and from the prairie posts. He was liked by the Indians and respected by the French; he made a fortune. A shrewd and knowing trader, he was also a man of wholehearted warmth and generosity.

Now he gave Clark fresh news from Vincennes: General Hamilton was there, making himself comfortable during the harsh season, with a large quantity of arms and ammunition, a warehouse full of supplies, and a force of British regulars, French volunteers, and tribal warriors. Some of the Indians he had sent to raid Kentucky, some of the regulars he had ordered back to Detroit. But his entire army of 700 men would reassemble in the spring to march against the Americans. Meanwhile his men were repairing the fort, patrolling the town, scouting the approaches—though they had no fear of attack from Clark's outnumbered men.

At this report Clark paced the room with long, devouring strides. When he turned to the wrinkled Spaniard, his blue eyes were smoldering. Did Vigo judge that an attack would take Hamilton by surprise?

Attack? Did Colonel Clark mean an American attack? In this season? The prairies were desolate, the bottom lands were flooded. Vincennes was a stronghold surrounded with a moat of ice and water. How would Clark get his army there?

The commander had his answer ready. They would march, wade, swim.

---

7. *Vigo* (vē′gō).

The merchant's face grew more wrinkled than ever. An American attack. The weak surprising the strong.... Then his shrewd black eyes began to burn. He understood the strategy of trade—catch the other off his guard, take him by surprise. In the fateful contest of war the same strategy might win.

Now the little merchant, still huddled in his great coat, was nodding his head. If the Americans could get there undiscovered, at a time when the British would least expect attack, they might capture Vincennes and make prisoners of their enemies. Yes—if they could attack without warning, if they could take them by surprise....

Alone again, Clark peered out at the winter prairie. He stood quiet at the porthole, but his thoughts were seething. This was the kind of situation that fired his mind and roused his will. A weak force and a strong enemy. An unlikely time, a bold attack, a strategy of secrecy and daring. But his own troops were depleted by illness and desertion; he had hardly one full company. He turned to a big map on the wall and studied the Wabash Valley with Fort Vincennes marked out in bold black ink. His big fists clenched. At this moment he would have bound himself to seven years' imprisonment or slavery to have 500 troops for a fortnight's service. But he had barely 150 men. He might go to Kentucky to raise more volunteers; there was no time for that. He might send to Fort Pitt[8]; that would take longer still. There was just one course—to attack the enemy without hesitation or delay, to do by daring what he could not do by reason. He would be defeated if he waited in Kaskaskia for Hamilton's campaign. He could be no more than defeated at Vincennes. And if he won.... If he won. ... If he won....

As he considered it, the very audacity of his purpose gave him confidence. He thought now, step by step: *The season being so formidable*—slush ice drifting in the rivers, the prairie sodden with melting snow, the swamps swollen to miles of sullen water, the bottoms drowned in a numbing waist-deep flood. It was a favorable season for a forced march into enemy country; the very madness of it made it favorable. *No enemy would suppose*—it was out of all order and logic, it was beyond all reason that a weak force would cross a flooded country in a bleak season to attack a stronghold. *An enemy off their guard*—in this desolation they would not even send out spies, and their scouting parties would huddle over the fire in some half-faced camp, not thinking it worth while to watch for an invasion. *A desperate situation needs a desperate resolution*—there was no alternative. The more he thought of it the more inevitable his plan became.

That night he called his captains and told them. They were silent, doubtful, fearful. He talked a little more, acknowledging the hardships and dangers of the march. But the season being so hostile, no enemy would suppose that an attack could come over an impassable country. An enemy off guard is an enemy half beaten; surprise is stronger than an arsenal. Slowly the doubting captains began to speak. "Yes, the time is favorable."..."Yes, we can capture the 'Hair-buyer'!"

Boldness is a strong contagion. Now all Kaskaskia came to life with courage and resolve. French volunteers offered to join the desperate march. Citizens brought provisions, blankets, boots, caps, mufflers, mittens. Clark would need stores of ammunition for his attack and a cannon to breach the heavy walls of the fort. With funds borrowed from Merchant Vigo, he bought a Mississippi flatboat, mounted six small cannon on the deck, and loaded the cabin with supplies. This was the *Willing*, the first gunboat on the western rivers. Aboard it marched Captain John Rogers, Clark's cousin, and forty men, mostly from Cahokia. On the gray fourth day of February,

---

8. *Fort Pitt,* the site of the present city of Pittsburgh.

shortly after noon, they pushed into the current of the swollen Kaskaskia River. They would go down the Mississippi, up the Ohio, up the Wabash. Below Vincennes they would hide in the river thickets, waiting the arrival of Clark's regiment across the prairies.

While the *Willing* disappeared around a bend of the river, Clark sat in his office writing a message to Governor Patrick Henry[9]. "*...I know the case is desperate; but Sir, we must either quit the country or attack.... Great things have been effected by a few men well conducted. Perhaps we may be fortunate.*"

It was a hazardous, perilous plan, against enormous odds. That night George Rogers Clark sat late beside the fire. *Perhaps we may be fortunate....*

COURTESY OF THE CLARK MEMORIAL, VINCENNES, INDIANA PHOTO BY JAMES BALLARD

CHAPTER 12: *The Gaunt Regiment*

On the fifth day of February, 1779, while drums rolled in the fort yard, the citizens of Kaskaskia lined the street below. In the stockade Father Gibault[10] raised his hand; the drums ceased and the priest said a simple, heartfelt blessing. As the drums rolled again, Clark's regiment filed out the fort gate in a thin cold rain. It was mid-afternoon; all morning the captains had been busy, inspecting the men's clothing, ammunition, and provisions, tallying the pack ponies and their loads of tents, baggage, and supplies. Now in mingled French and English the townsfolk cried out their last farewells.

The men marched steadily, followed by the plodding pack train. Soon they were on the empty prairie. Behind them, in the cold seep of the rain, lay the huddled houses of Kaskaskia; behind was Merchant Vigo who had counted out money for the campaign, the old men who had given rifle balls and powder, the women who had stitched twenty flags for their soldiers to raise from the roofs and bastions of Vincennes. Be-

9. ***message to Governor Patrick Henry.*** Clark is writing to urge the famous Patrick Henry, now governor of Virginia, to send a large force of men to help him overcome the British. 10. ***Father Gibault,*** Father Pierre Gibault (pēär zhi bō′), a missionary priest who aided Clark by winning the French citizens' support of the Americans.

hind was the warmth of familiar hearth fires; ahead lay 200 miles of soaking prairie and drowned bottom land, and at the end a superior enemy waited in a massive fort. Hour after hour they tramped on. Some remembered what was behind them, some thought of what was ahead. Some, perhaps, just marched. Long-striding Virginians and Kentuckians in deerskin jackets, dark-eyed French-Americans in matchcoats and mackinaws, they marched together in the rain. In all they were 130 men.

Six miles out on the prairie the winter dusk came down. They made their camp on desolate ground; they ate a cold supper washed down with smoking tea. They huddled over reluctant fires, trying to dry their boots and mackinaws. They rolled in their blankets and slept on sodden earth; before daylight they were on their way again. Hour after hour they slogged through mud and mire under a sky the color of wet ashes. A file of stubborn, plodding men, they made twenty-seven miles before they pitched their square camp in the winter dusk, baggage in the middle, sentries posted all around. The third day brought great flat plains of standing water, and the rain kept falling. With a kind of incredulity the men remembered when sunlight washed a green and fragrant prairie; now they gave up thought of warmth and dryness. They splashed on toward a watery horizon.

But the commander kept their spirits burning. Each day he sent out mounted hunters at the sign of game. They came back with quarters of venison and buffalo, and at the end of the day's march one of the four companies gave a feast. They ate like a war party on a triumphant raid. Tearing juicy flesh from bones, grinning with greasy bearded faces, gulping down their burning whisky ration, they feasted together. Clark passed from one supper fire to another, a hulking, mud-smeared man with a gruff humor, sampling the joints of smoking meat and nodding approval of the cooking. He was a commander with a kind of triumph in him, not seeming to think of the hardships, the hazards, the desperate test ahead. So, feasting and laughing, singing rowdy songs and whooping like savages, the men forgot the misery of the march. The hot food roused their blood, and the whooping raised their courage. They were young men, in a wild new country, on a mission of daring.

During the day's march Clark often gave his horse to the hunters and fell in with the men. Sometimes he swung along in silence, his big feet sloshing up and down. But he was mysteriously aware of the army's spirit. He knew when the men were grim with weariness and when their thoughts went ahead with uncertainty and fear. At those times his ragged voice lifted a song or raised a war whoop, and gradually the other voices took it up until the whole wretched regiment sang and shouted under the desolate sky. At weary stretches of mud he set out on a lumbering run, challenging them all to a footrace. At the edge of swollen creeks he held his rifle high and lunged into the water with a savage war cry. So he kept them going; they took fire, like wet faggots, from his own nerve and will. They finished the day's march and devoured their food like a gaunt wolf pack in the firelight. They held numb and swollen hands to the blaze; the leather steamed and stiffened on their feet. They slept in sodden blankets and they did not complain.

On February 13, a week away from Kaskaskia, they reached the Little Wabash. That small river was now a vast flood, five miles across, with the drowned bottoms of the Embarrass River and the swollen Wabash beyond. They were sixty-three forbidding miles from Vincennes. From that camp Clark stared at the gray water, knee-deep, waist-deep, sometimes shoulder-deep. Now a third of his men were shaking with chills and fever. It was five miles to the hills on the opposite shore, and over all that plain of water the cold rain kept falling. Clark ordered his strongest men to take axes, to fell poplar logs, to hollow out canoes. In the first crude craft he sent a party ahead to build a landing platform on the distant shore. Into other canoes they loaded their sick and their baggage. Then they were ready to march.

Clark took the lead, plunging into waist-deep water, lifting his long rifle overhead. The men splashed after him. In that numbing water he kept their courage alive. Time after time he promised land ahead; when the water rose about his waist, he broke into the strains of "A Soldier's Life" or "Billy of the Wild Woods" or "A Man Who Wouldn't Hoe Corn." At last they reached the wooded shore. They landed their baggage and helped their sick ashore. Provisions were short, but Clark was more concerned with secrecy than hunger. He ordered short rations and no firing of guns.

They made a cheerful camp, laughing over their nightmare march, repeating a dozen times how in deep water the drummer boy had crawled onto his drum and floated on it like a raft. Strengthened by hardship, made bold by difficulty, they thought nothing could stop them. Now they spoke of the formidable Wabash as a creek; they would find a way to cross it. And when they reached Vincennes—. Before the fires died down, there was talk of marching on Detroit.

That night, lying sleepless in a wet blanket, Clark had his own grim realization. They were now in the enemy's country, a flooded valley behind them, their horses abandoned, with no possibility of retreat. He wondered about the Wabash: could the *Willing* ascend a flooded river in time to keep their rendezvous below Vincennes?

Next day they marched through endless swamps and creek bottoms. Hour after hour they stumbled through freezing mud and splashed through ice-skimmed water. It was long after dark before they stumbled on dry ground and made their desolate camp. The day that followed, and the day that followed that, were the same. At night they gnawed a handful of parched corn and slept with exhaustion.

On the evening of February 17 they reached the Embarrass River at a point nine miles from Vincennes. Those nine miles were a vast drowned bottom, broken by islanded hills and ridges. Gaunt with fatigue and hunger they marched along the Embarrass to its juncture with the Wabash. They marched grimly. Clark and his captains shouted, but the men slogged on in silence. Mud, mud, mud, mud . . . water, water, water, water . . . cold, cold, cold, cold . . . war, war, war, war. . . . In a weary, aching trance they kept moving, one foot lifting, then another, one stride more.

So they reached the Wabash. Now Vincennes was upstream, still nine miles away, across the swollen channel and the drowned bottom lands. They had no rations left—not even a rind of bacon or a handful of corn. Here they were to meet the *Willing;* but the flooded Wabash lay empty between the wooded hills.

"Camp Hunger" the men called it. Clark promptly had a pair of axmen hollowing out a log, and in that canoe he sent a party downstream to find the *Willing.* The rest waited, remembering the bushels of corn and the stacks of dried buffalo meat they had loaded on the gunboat. They watched in silence while the canoe came back, and the gaunt faces of the paddlers told the news before they voiced it. The *Willing* had not arrived. (The gunboat had been delayed by floodwater and was now at the mouth of the Wabash, 100 miles away.)

It was a hungry night. In the cold gray daybreak they heard a boom of cannon—the morning gun from the frowning fort at Vincennes. At that moment General Hamilton was sitting down to a hot and hearty breakfast, but Clark gave his men no time to think of food. He kept them chopping trees and lacing logs together with fox vines from the branches; on those makeshift rafts he sent men toward Vincennes to steal boats. They poled the rafts away, and too soon they returned. A mile away they had found a camp of Indians around four large campfires; they dared not go farther for fear of being discovered. Again Clark sent men down river, to look for the *Willing*. He paced the muddy shore while his gaunt troops chewed the bark of slippery elm to quiet their stomach pains. They had not tasted food for two days.

Weak as they were, Clark kept his axmen hollowing canoes. All morning their blades hacked and thudded on wet poplar logs. At noon the river sentries brought in a captured boat, and five astonished Frenchmen were led to the commander. They answered Clark's questions readily, declaring that no one in Vincennes suspected the presence of American troops in the Wabash country. That evening a hunter came in with fresh-killed venison. One deer for 130 men—it made their hunger violent.

Next morning in the leaden dawn they ferried the Wabash, and still they were cut off from the town by miles of flooded lowland. With a muttered "March!" Clark plunged into knee-deep water. The men waded after him. All day the gray rain fell, all day they floundered on, pushing their canoes through drowned timber and across desolate bays of flood. The five Frenchmen from Vincennes were amazed at this march; they had told Clark it was impossible to reach Vincennes without a fleet of boats. When Clark asked the location of the nearest dry land, they described a sugar camp, a grove of maple trees on a rounded hill. A canoe went ahead through submerged thickets, but it could not find a passage. Then Clark went forward, wading into the deepening stream. It was cold as ice.

Waist-deep in sullen water, he turned to his men. They watched him in silence, eyes fearful and beaten, faces gaunt and hollow. Some were shaking with chills, some were dazed with fever; in all of them hunger was gnawing like an animal. Suddenly Clark raised his powder horn. He poured a pinch of precious gunpowder into his wet hand and smeared the black mixture on his face. His voice went up in a frenzied, yowling war whoop; in it sounded hunger, grimness, desperation, but it ended in a fierce defiance. He turned then and lunged into the stream. For a moment the men stared blankly, eyes dead as cinders in their famished faces. Then one man blacked his own cheeks and plunged in. Another followed, and another; the gaunt regiment was moving. Ahead of them Clark lifted his rifle. His ragged voice began a song, and behind him, in a thin and growing chorus, the men joined in. They were a wretched, starving, and exhausted army—singing.

At last they felt firm ground beneath their feet. They followed it through a chaos of brush and bending willow branches. It led to a half acre of mounded land, covered with bare maple trees. They made their camp in the sugar grove. It was a cold night but they slept like dead.

In the morning the Frenchmen from Vincennes pointed to the broad Horseshoe Plain—not a plain now but a gray sea covering a great sickle bend of the Wabash. The sky had cleared in the night and a yellow sun rose over the floodlands. Clark stood among his silent men. This was the final march, he told them. In two hours they would see the roofs of Vincennes. There could be no weakness now.

He stationed Major Bowman in the rear with orders to shoot any man who faltered or turned back. Then he led the way. Out in the desolate Horseshoe Plain there were no half-drowned bushes to grasp at, no trees to cling to. Clark ordered canoes to carry the weakest men, to land them on the far shore, and to return for others. The rest struggled on, arms around each other's shoulders, floundering toward the land. There was no singing now. Even the commander kept silent, but he kept advancing. When at last they reached a brushy ridge, they would have sunk down, numb and exhausted, but Clark kept them on their feet.

They chopped branches and started fires. The strong men dragged the weak around and around the burning embers until their clothing had dried and the blood was brisk in their veins.

When a sentry reported a craft on the water, Clark sent a party after it. They captured a large canoe paddled by Indian women; in it were buffalo meat, corn, tallow, and a nest of blackened kettles. Hungry eyes glittered while the kettles warmed on the fire. Broth was fed to the weak and fevered men; all of them had a ration of corn. It was not a feast, but it was a taste of food; it quickened sluggish blood and put strength into exhausted muscles. With new spirit they pushed on.

In canoes and afoot they crossed another mile of floodland and came to the brushy knob of Warrior's Island, with sunlight slanting through its winter trees. From there Clark gazed across two miles of flat and open country to Post Vincennes—the houses scattered along the river, the timbered church and the long stockade of the fort with its five frowning blockhouses catching the rays of the sinking sun. Around him stood his men, staring at the goal of their impossible march.

"THE FALL OF FORT SACKVILLE" BY FREDERICK C. YOHN, INDIANA HISTORICAL BUREAU. PHOTO BY JAMES BALLARD

WHAT DO YOU SAY?

1. *(a)* What is the mood in the first paragraph of this selection? *(b)* What particular words and phrases establish this mood? *(c)* How does the mood change between paragraphs one and three? *(d)* Where else in the selection are there vivid changes in mood?

2. *(a)* What did Clark feel to be the best strategy in waging war? *(b)* How did he put that strategy into practice?

3. *(a)* What are some examples of ways in which Clark inspired his men to follow him? *(b)* How would you describe Clark as a commander?

4. *(a)* Although this selection from Clark's biography does not include the outcome of his goal to take Vincennes, what was your impression of the results of this struggle? *(b)* Where is the outcome implied?

AUTHOR'S CRAFT

Biographical presentation

If you had read this selection without knowing that it was from a biography of a real person, you might easily have mistaken it for a fictional adventure story. This would have been understandable, because the author of this biography has used a style of presentation that is commonly found in novels and short stories. Instead of presenting the facts of Clark's life in history-book fashion, Mr. Havighurst has skillfully woven them into a framework of vivid narrative description and dialogue that makes a reader see, hear, and feel what is taking place.

When you met Colonel Clark in the first paragraph, for example, you saw him pace the floor, narrow his eyes, and peer out the porthole of the blockhouse. You were aware of the atmosphere of uneasiness and suspense as Clark wondered about the spies he had sent across the prairie, the loyalty of the French citizens, and the British troops that might march on the fort at any time. Similarly, the author made you see the setting in which the action was to begin—the desolate Illinois winter, Kaskaskia huddled on the gray riverbank, the bare frozen cornfields, pastures, and orchards behind the tiny farmhouses, and the thin curtain of snow.

The development of ***setting, atmosphere,*** and ***suspense*** contributes much to a biography, because these elements form the background against which the subject of the biography is seen. However, a biographer must take great care to insure the accuracy of his description. For example, he must not invent a river in his setting if there was none, any more than a historian would invent a fake battle scene. A biographer must provide the ***real*** background of which his subject was once a part.

Similarly, a biographer must develop an honest and complete portrait of his subject, as Mr. Havighurst has done. Colonel Clark was more than just a strong and courageous commander, and the author has shown Clark dancing the quadrille and talking with the French farmers around the punch bowl. Other aspects of his character and personality are also revealed in the story. Skim through the selection to find specific examples of the following character traits: sense of humor, kindness, strength, courage, understanding, determination, unselfishness. How well does this author achieve his aim—an accurate portrait of a ***real person,*** who lived in a ***real place*** and took part in ***real events?***

KNOW YOUR WORDS

Image-making words

Effective writing greatly depends upon the selection of "image" words—words that help a reader see, smell, hear, taste, and feel. In each of the following sentences select the italicized word that produces the more appropriate image and explain why it is more appropriate.

1. Clark peered out the ***(window, porthole)*** of the blockhouse.
2. The winter was a ***(harsh, difficult)*** season.
3. He paced the floor, taking giant ***(steps, strides).***
4. The ***(musician, fiddler)*** struck up a tune.
5. Clark's ***(ragged, tired)*** voice was heard throughout the column.
6. They stopped to look at the man with the ***(serious, grim)*** expression on his face.
7. The winter night was ***(frigid, cold).***
8. The troops ***(rode, jogged)*** into town.
9. It was only the ***(moan, sound)*** of the wind.
10. A single ***(sentry, soldier)*** stood watch.

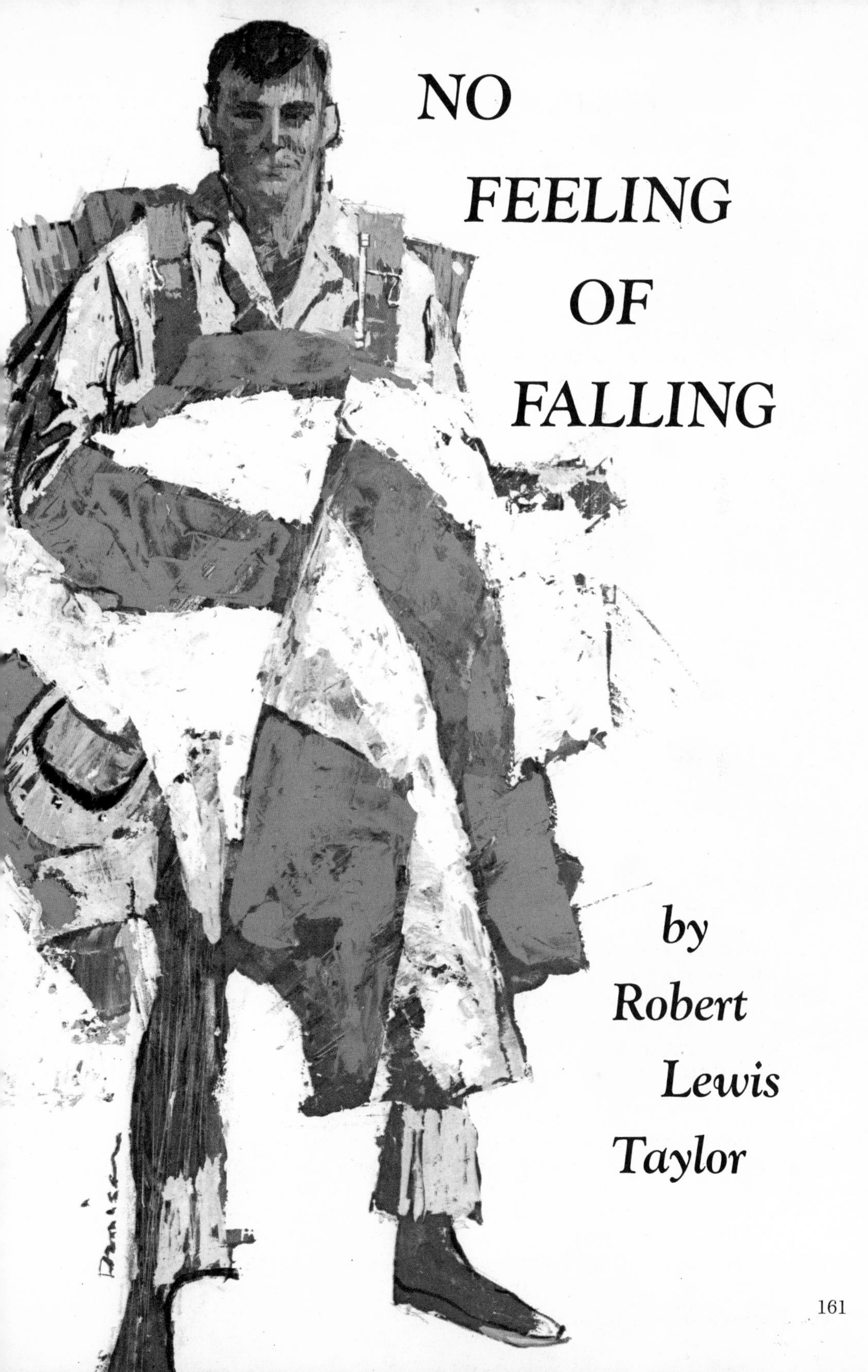

NO FEELING OF FALLING

by Robert Lewis Taylor

Until a few years ago, parachuting in the United States was something engaged in only by members of the military and, perhaps, a few people noted for their daring. But this was before a young French-American named Jacques André Istel began his campaign to bring sport parachuting to the attention of the American public.

Jacques André Istel, a twenty-nine-year-old French-American with a Princeton education and a distinguished family background of banking and international finance, is the nation's leading parachutist. It is scarcely too much to say that Istel *is* the parachute movement in the United States. He has been the United States team captain, trainer, and organizer at the international meets we have lately been entering (with growing success), and, together with his sidekick, Lewis B. Sanborn, a former carpenter who looks as though he might have stepped out of Harvard Yard, he has led in our scoring. Istel is a naturalized citizen with a perpetually gnawing sense of obligation to his adopted land, and he wishes to pay off his debt by seeing all adults under eighty parachute from airplanes, many of them several times daily. Toward this alarming goal he is progressing, or jumping, with astonishing celerity. A number of years ago, he took over a dozing organization called the National Parachute Jumpers-Riggers, a kind of amateur sports group with minus thirty members (that is, thirty members who had long since let their dues lapse), and converted it into the Parachute Club of America, a non-profit organization that now has a paid-up and fervent membership of eight hundred and fifty-nine. In addition, he has urged into being, by the naked force of his bristling personality, forty sports parachute clubs, at such centers as Ivy League colleges and West Point, and has made certain nervous inroads on the thinking of the military—no small feat, as the late General Billy Mitchell and the present Admiral Hyman Rickover and Lieutenant General James M. Gavin[1] would probably be happy to affirm. It is a melancholy thought to Istel that his most clamorous followers, the inmates of penitentiaries, must go unattended. He has received any number of requests to form clubs among prisoners in some of the leading penal institutions, but thus far he has had little or no encouragement from the wardens.

Istel is the proprietor of an outfit called Parachutes, Inc., which is in the business of designing innovations and refining safety features for the (until now) slightly disreputable old crutch of flying. More specifically, Istel and Sanborn design and sell the kind of chutes they think people should use, and delegate the manufacturing to the Pioneer Parachute Company, of Manchester, Connecticut, which, under the direction of a former parachutist named Lyman Ford, has been making chutes since 1938. Today, Istel is an earnest, careful, and conservative businessman, but this was not always so. His business is conducted in a venerable and properly sedate stone mansion at Bedford Village, New York, in a setting far above the highroad, surrounded by evergreens, and lulled by the chirp and squeak of woods creatures. The long, crazily winding private drive leading to the house, however, is strewn with the bones of expensive cars—testimony to Istel's impetuous past—including an eight-thousand-dollar Mercedes 300 SL that he smashed while trying to see if he could gain the heights under conditions of ice. The Mercedes (insured) had been bought by Istel for a Parisian friend; the mansion was bought by

---

1. ***Billy Mitchell,*** an American airforce officer whose charges of poor management against the Navy and War departments led to a court-martial resulting in his five year suspension from the service. ***Admiral Hyman Rickover,*** the naval officer in charge of the nuclear propulsion division in the development of atomic submarines who was several times denied promotion, finally achieving the rank of Admiral in 1953. ***Lieutenant General James M. Gavin,*** an officer who resigned from the army in 1958 to protest against what he considered to be a decline in army strength and prestige.

Istel's father in 1954 in a gesture of despairing resignation. It would be difficult to overstate the chilly hostility with which the elder Istel viewed his son's aversion to Wall Street and romance with parachutes after his graduation from Princeton, in 1949. For a brief period, memorable chiefly for its vivid episodes of protest, the boy toiled in the New York and Paris money markets. His choler was not unlike that of a dinosaur writhing and bawling in the ensnaring gumbo of primordia. Then he burst loose, and his father, putting his faith in the braking power of austere country living, provided the Bedford house. In 1952, Istel married a beautiful girl named Claudia Beardslee, the daughter of a Pennsylvania professor and minister, and when, after a spell of peripatetic housekeeping, she finally settled down with Istel in a house of her own, it was in a twenty-seven-room mansion with, literally, no more furniture than a double bed. A stove and a refrigerator came with the place, and that was all. To her occasional queries along the line of "Jacques, why don't we get a few things, maybe even a chair?" her husband always replied, "You can't make any money with furniture." He at length consented to borrow a dining set from a friend who was leaving for Spain, and he reclaimed his Princeton-room desk to form the nucleus of his company's personal effects. This kind of Spartanism has paid off. Having long struggled against a hurtful lack of capital and the ill will of multitudes who thought they knew more about Istel's specialty than Istel did, Parachutes, Inc., is beginning to take on a rosier fiscal hue, and the prospect is that the sky's the limit, so to speak. A straw in the upper-level wind is the fact that he and Sanborn (his treasurer and spiritual partner) have landed a fat contract to supply parachutes to the Marine Corps.

Istel is, of course, a fanatic, but, like many fanatics, he is about as right as it's possible to get without being offensive. He is bitterly chagrined that the United States stood by while a feverish parachute movement gathered steam (and military approval) in the Iron Curtain countries. He is convinced that we have a great deal of catching up to do, and he means to see that we do it, at whatever cost to his person, his purse, and his pride. For the accomplishment of these and kindred aims, the head of Parachutes, Inc., is magnificently equipped. He has the unabashed drive of a young adult gorilla in especially fine condition. The fact is that Istel is not unsimian in appearance—in an agreeable and even a hypnotic way—largely because of his posture, which at nearly all times is the crouching stance of a man about to do a swan dive out of an airplane. The illusion is heightened by his facial expression, an arrangement described by his school yearbook as "fiendish" (but actually the intense look of a young man in a hurry), and by his powerful, sloping shoulders, his deep chest, and his rolling, Dutch-sailor's gait. Istel has jet-black hair trimmed in a crew cut that droops slightly forward, and he wears the standard Eastern-college uniform of oxford-gray or khaki trousers with tweed jacket. Altogether, at twenty-nine he still manages to look like an undergraduate, if one of unique character and purpose. Quite possibly it is supererogatory to record that a career parachutist is in good, hard shape, but in Istel's case a special point might be made of it. Early each morning, he bounds out of bed and does fifty push-ups and a long series of spine-crunching bends from a sitting position on the floor. Then he drives to a nearby airport and gets in several parachute jumps before breakfast. The regimen might well kill the average professional pug in a matter of weeks. At the outbreak of war in Korea, Istel enlisted as a private in the Marine Corps, considering this to be another means of earning his citizenship, and rapidly advanced to the rank of second lieutenant, in charge of a weapons company at Camp Pendleton, California. It was a group in which there had previously been

a notable tendency to sag. Istel ended all that. He pepped the fellows up by having them do long hikes while carrying forty-pound mortar tubes in addition to their regular packs, to iron out the kinks, and made them sing French marching songs, to offset the pull. No comparable mixture has been seen in any modern force except the French Foreign Legion, in which Istel has never served. Anyhow, the combination worked. Istel went to Korea with a very springy and melodious (and bilingual) company, and it was, besides, a happy company. Of this period he recently said, with undue modesty, "I believe I was a pretty good Marine officer." Certainly the old company members, some of them perhaps a trifle bow-legged and apt to burst into hysterical snatches of French song in moments of crisis, continue to write to him, and not a few belong to one or another of his sports parachute clubs.

Istel's conditioning has helped bring about what is thus far unquestionably his greatest parachuting gift to America—sky diving. The general sport, or (in the military) the tactical exercise, of parachuting has always been divided into two types—the free fall and the static-line jump. In the former, one merely hurls oneself out of a plane and pulls the ripcord at one's leisure, preferably with an eye on the altitude. The static-line jump, used mainly for a group of men parachuting in sequence, automatically takes care of the pull by means of a long cord, to which each man's chute is attached before he leaves the aircraft. Istel has revolutionized the whole concept of free-fall parachuting in America. In 1955, having made a number of wildly informal jumps over a period of several years, he went to Vienna as the official United States delegate (appointed by the National Aeronautic Association) to a parachuting conference sponsored by a society called the Fédération Aéronautique Internationale.[2]

2. ***Fédération Aéronautique Internationale*** (fā dā räs'yoN ā rô nô tēk' äN ter nä'sēyô näl), the international agency which governs world parachute jumping and is responsible for making the arrangements for international jumping contests.

The object of the Vienna huddle was to plan a world meet, to be held the next year in Moscow, and when Istel was asked what part the United States might play, he unshyly declared that we would, of course, be represented "with a full team." This came as a pleasurable shock to everybody, and particularly to Istel himself, an hour or so later, back in his hotel. The United States *had* no team, he reflected with mild consternation, or any part of a team, and, what's more, Istel was unable to think of a sole American, aside from himself, who might be warmed up and run out onto the field. Parachuting in this country was in low repute—on a level with cockfighting and riding over Niagara Falls in a barrel. Nevertheless, he charged forward to find out what the European nations were doing in the sport, and was electrified to learn that they were doing a great deal—so much, in fact, that he decided he needed some expert instruction. Accordingly, on his way home from Vienna he stopped off in Paris, where he was able to talk the parachuting champion of France, Sam Chasak, into giving him lessons. Chasak was patiently helpful; with his assistant, Gerard Van de Meersch, a Belgian nobleman who had thrown up a hereditary business to become a parachute instructor, he put the eager Istel through a number of thrillingly novel paces. Istel came home and announced to aviation people everywhere that it was possible for a person to dive out of an airplane and soar like a bird—fully under control, changing his course and his body positions, making a planned flight—for as long as two hundred seconds, or more than three minutes, before pulling the ripcord. This, in essence, is sky diving, the pivot of the sports parachute movement. Beyond doubt, it provides one of the oddest physical sensations available to the human being, its oddness resting chiefly on the fact that there is scarcely any sensation at all. One has no feeling of falling. The air rushes by, the earth tilts below, like movies shot from

a rocket, and the jumper attains his maximum velocity—over a hundred miles an hour—in a very few seconds. After that, it is simply a matter of floating unencumbered, released for once from any awareness of man's lifelong thralldom to gravity. "You feel free, somewhat the way you do in skiing," Istel says. "Space loses its meaning. Your important dimension is time." The truth is that a jumper, unless he is careful, can forget that he is aloft, and vulnerable, and headed in a hurry toward the implacable reckoning of earth.

Istel, now one of the world's leading practitioners of the art of sky diving, felt that his epochal declaration to America, as important in its way as Revere's gallop or Sam Morse's announcement of telegraphy, did not elicit a suitable response. The prevailing sentiment was "The boy's obviously an ass." Istel has never been daunted, and the enveloping apathy only encouraged him to bull ahead and assemble his United States parachute team, in accordance with his promise in Vienna. At the Tushino Airport, in Moscow, in August of 1956, he was on hand with a six-man team (including one alternate), which had been gathered and trained amidst adversities that might have exhausted the fortitude of Lincoln. In a parachute meet, the object is to land directly on a target, with points awarded for form and style in the air, much as in a high-diving competition. Istel's team finished sixth in a field of ten competing nations. Czechoslovakia was first and Russia second, followed by Bulgaria, France, and Yugoslavia; the American team beat Poland, Rumania, Hungary, and Israel. At the Coupe du Monde,[3] an international meet in Paris involving ten predominantly non-Iron Curtain nations, Istel's team finished second, defeated only by France, and at the next World Championship, held a few weeks afterward, in Czechoslovakia, the United States wound up, as at Moscow, in sixth place, but on this occasion fourteen countries were represented and, what is more significant, we beat France, which for years has gone in for parachuting with about the same zeal that Norway shows for skiing. Istel regards these achievements as among the hollower of his triumphs. In his main theatre of combat—specifically, the United States military vs. Istel, on the subject of parachuting—he has recently won some decisive skirmishes. After being ordered to Fort Bragg a while back to demonstrate his theories, he was asked to help write a code of regulations for the Army governing free-fall parachuting, and the Air Force officially petitioned him to send it all his literature. The Special Services branch of the Army is now buying his parachutes, and the Army and the Air Force, jointly, invited him to make use of Fort Bragg as a training ground for the United States team entered in the Czechoslovakian meet. Istel is only temporarily impressed by such events. When he first checked in at Fort Bragg and, as a preliminary gesture, addressed a large roomful of ripely skeptical brass, he thanked everybody politely for the invitation and went on to say, in his pleasantly accented Princetonian English, "Gentlemen, I wish you to know that up to this time the United States parachute team has received better treatment in Moscow than it has in certain important quarters in the U.S. It is a great pleasure to finally be taken in at home."

Istel richly qualifies as a candidate for Emerson's description of Henry David Thoreau—"a protestant *à outrance*."[4] From all reports, including those of his dearest kin, Istel has been a handful almost from his birth, which took place in Paris on January 28, 1929. His father, André Istel, was at the time a partner in the private banking house of Schlumberger, Istel,

3. Coupe du Monde (küp dü mōNd). ***4. "a protestant à outrance"*** (ä ô träNs), one who is excessively dedicated to making protests and to criticism. Emerson, a nineteenth century American writer, used the expression to describe Thoreau, one of his contemporaries, noted for his non-conformity and devotion to causes.

Noyer & Cie.,[5] and he has since acquired further financial interests, both in this country and abroad. He is at present chairman of the board of four investment companies. Two of them, the Istel Fund and the Pallas Corporation, are in the United States; one, Dominion Equity Investments, Ltd., is in Canada; and the fourth is in France. Jacques is quick to agree that his father has led an energetic and useful life, too, even though it has touched very slightly—or as slightly as M. Istel could manage—on parachuting. The elder Istel holds a degree in electrical engineering, but he never got around to plying that trade and is uncertain now whether he could successfully splice a frayed extension cord. He was sidetracked first of all by the French diplomatic service, which persuaded him to become a consular agent in Vancouver. Then, in 1914, when the war began, he enlisted as a private soldier and was soon proposed for the Croix de Guerre[6] for leaping out of a forward shell hole during a gas attack, tearing off his gas mask, and crying the alarm back to his comrades. A slight cough caused by that episode plagues him to this day. André Istel's extraordinary mental gifts were soon recognized as being wasted in shell holes, and he finished up the war as secretary of the Inter-Allied Aviation Committee. Jacques Istel's ancestry on both sides is marked by exceptional spirit and capability and distinction. His mother, the former Yvonne Crémieux[7] was so beloved in her Parisian neighborhood that in the Second World War, when she and her family retired south under German pressure, her neighbors removed the furniture from her house and hid it. All of it—and even her laundry, beautifully done and neatly wrapped—was returned to her in 1944. One of her brothers, Raymond Crémieux, was a hero of the 1914-18 war and among the few French aviators who were shot down

5. ***Schlumberger, . . . and Cie.,*** Schlumberger, . . . and Company. 6. ***Croix de Guerre*** (krwä də gār′), a French military decoration. 7. ***Yvonne Crémieux*** (ē von′ krā mū′).

three times. His aerial maneuvers over the German lines were conducted so nonchalantly near the earth that there was some question whether one of his involuntary descents had not been accomplished by a hurled rock.

The advent of Jacques in the Istel household introduced a disturbing note that has steadily endured. He himself recalls the period of his early childhood as one of crushing boredom. The major part of his first schooling was managed by tutors, none of whom had the durability to stay with the job very long. In the end, a private school was induced to accommodate him for one day a week, and his mother handled the rest. For recreation, he was led, or dragged, by a governess to a nearby park, where he spent a couple of hours each day under hot pursuit by nannies brandishing sticks and rolled-up periodicals. Finally, his mother, a woman of perception, saw that the boy did not have enough to occupy what was clearly an uncommonly active mind, and when he was nine she sent him off to visit an uncle who lived on a country estate. On the first day (which proved to be the last) of his stay, the child invented an ingenious game called *"bombardier"* and knocked out a hundred and seventy-five panes of a hothouse, or all the panes the hothouse contained. His mother wearily suspended his allowance for two years and used it to replace the glass, completing the task a week before the Germans marched across the border. As the Germans pressed on toward Paris, Mme. Istel, together with Jacques, his younger brother, Yves André, and his sister Geneviève, fled, dodging and hiding, into Spain and then Portugal, where they eventually found passage to the United States. Her husband, who happened to be in this country when France fell, was appointed an adviser to General de Gaulle, and, with the first passport issued by the Free French government, began commuting between Washington and London, to buy aircraft. An older brother of Jacques, Jean Francois,[8] fought with the French Army, fell captive to the Germans, made a brilliant and daring escape to Canada, enlisted in the R.C.A.F., and died of an illness before getting into aerial combat. A friend of the Istel and Crémieux families has remarked, "For people who—all except Jacques of course—speak and behave with such mildness by nature, they turn into the most improbable tigers in times of military need."

When America's future parachuting champion arrived in New York, aged eleven, his parents resolved to lodge him in a good strong school; that is, one with a reasonable chance of holding him. They at length selected Stony Brook, a boys' school of excellent reputation on Long Island. The establishment was, and is, no more zealously devoted to discipline than the average boarding school, but most of its masters were young and muscular, and fully able to cope with newcomers of any dynamic impetus. As things turned out, the fuss was largely unnecessary. Istel settled into Stony Brook life with joy and coöperation, comparatively speaking, and began to be unbored for the first time he could remember. When he took his seat in the first form, he was unable to speak a word of English, but this by no means excluded him from conversation. He spoke right up in French, whether anybody could understand him or not. By good fortune, he picked up English in a hurry.

Istel, who stayed at Stony Brook until he was sixteen and ready for college, became one of the most popular boys in the history of the school. Though he meshed tractably with the school machinery, he remained supercharged with energy, and he spent many of his spare hours doing odd jobs on the campus—raking leaves, mowing lawns—to raise money. Jacques' father, a wise and observant parent, foresaw that overloading a boy of his son's calibre with cash would be like pouring gasoline on a

8. ***Jean François*** (zhon frän′swä).

hotly burning fire. Young Istel's allowance at school began with the tidy sum of ten cents a week and rose, over the years, to a dollar. Speaking of his limited budget, Istel recently said, "It may well have prevented me from being hanged." Early in his Stony Brook years, he was understood to be the champion talker of his class, and probably in the annals of the school, and he was called upon to deliver the salutatorian's address at his graduation. His yearbook, class of '45, presents him as the student most likely to succeed, and is sprinkled with those scribbled lyric partings of friends. Prophetically, from Ed: "To a Frenchman that always takes a double dare, lots of everything." And from Bill: "Good luck to a fellow 'long-distance hitchhiker,' Sincerely, your pal." This reference to travel alludes to an extracurricular sport that Istel developed during his Stony Brook phase. In the summers, he struck out, usually alone, to see the country. This was accomplished without much in the line of a parental blessing. In those years, his father was occupied in advising General de Gaulle financially and, as a French delegate to the Bretton Woods conference,[9] was engaged in helping to set up the World Bank. Usually, Jacques hitchhiked, picking up jobs here and there along the route, but he once took a thousand-mile bicycle trip through New England, sleeping in barns. On this tour, he gained lucrative employment as a concrete mixer in Vermont. One day, he and a colleague were called in on an emergency job at an expensive hotel; a chimney had tumbled down. By a regrettable coincidence, Istel stalked through the dining room, in costume and carrying a hod, at the very time when his parents (off on a vacation, unknown to him) were having lunch. He was tickled to death to see them. "Hello, Mama and Papa!" he cried in a voice that rang through the room. "*Comment ca va?*"[10] The 1945 Stony Brook yearbook sped Istel on his way to Princeton with the following astute description: "Mix: One able body, three parts genius, one part recklessness, and a few quarts of hot French blood, and you have Jack Istel. . . . He is a fellow who will try anything once . . . and his fun-loving exterior hides a serious personality."

Istel, having achieved a certain unconventionality through his impecunious meanderings over the nation, arrived at Princeton wearing blue jeans and a leather jacket. College seemed little more than a stumbling block on the road to progress; he felt ready for the world. The truth is that Princeton was not at its best for a sixteen-year-old freshman in 1945. A good many of those on the campus were returned veterans, who looked upon newly enrolled children with, at best, an avuncular interest—impersonal, aloof, and tinged with a superiority obtained from four years of travel, fighting, and a close acquaintance with gore. During his first two years at Princeton, Istel was miserable, wallowing through a course of economics decreed by his father as the prelude to a career in banking, missing the intimacy of Stony Brook, and wishing, usually, that he was off hitchhiking or pouring concrete in Vermont. His old boredom settled on him again. In his junior year, he became a member of the Terrace Club and played on its chess team, but otherwise he made little effort to participate in campus activities. Today, Istel has no regrets about his lackadaisical stint in college. He considers that his younger brother, Yves André, who was valedictorian at Lawrenceville and went on to have a distinguished Princeton career, upheld the family tradition well enough to serve for two.

At the moment of Jacques Istel's Princeton commencement, he was sleeping in a haystack in England. Deciding not to wait around for the ceremony, he had embarked

---

9. ***Bretton Woods Conference,*** a forty-four nation conference held in July, 1944 for the purpose of outlining plans for post-war reconstruction and future development. 10. ***Comment ca va?*** (kô mäɴ′ sä vä′), How is everything going?

on a hitchhiking trip of importance. He went steerage to England, covered the British Isles, removed to Scandinavia, which he viewed with thoroughness, and then casually thumbed on down into North Africa. When he returned to New York, his father, irate at last, collared him and dragged him, almost by the use of leg irons, into Wall Street. Now began young Istel's travail in the wilderness; it was easily the low point of his life. For a brief spell, he was sent to Paris as a combination student and employee at his father's banking house, but Paris offered really stupendous ways of avoiding bank work, and the partners, including André Istel, soon agreed that as a Paris banker the boy would be far more effective in New York. He returned to Wall Street. To offset his anguish, he began surreptitiously taking flying lessons at Armonk. He soloed after seven hours, and qualified for a private license. At this time, his parents noticed that he seemed, somehow, much happier. They were delighted. Partly as a reward, his father dispatched him on a business mission to Vancouver, for the purpose of selling a large tract of timberland—a transaction running into hundreds of thousands of dollars. To the amazement of everybody concerned except Jacques, he brought off the deal smoothly. André Istel was now in a quandary: obviously Jacques should be recompensed, but was it safe to hand him a large sum of money? Finally, as a compromise, he wired his son eight hundred dollars. From the parents' standpoint, the move was uniquely ill-advised. Jacques promptly bought a second-hand airplane and embarked on what ranks as probably the most ramshackle transcontinental flight on record. The chief trouble was that he knew very little about the plane. To start with, bad weather en route to Seattle forced him to land, against a red signal and roars of protest, at an intermediate Air Force base. He took off again for Portland, and was soon reported missing. Eventually, he showed up in Sacramento, from where, uneasily, he telephoned home to explain. His father's conversation consisted, in its entirety, of "If there are high mountains between here and there, sell the plane. That's an order." "They are very low mountains, Papa," the boy said, and hung up. He proceeded to Winslow, Arizona, where his father, who had been pursuing him by person-to-person long-distance calls, caught up with him and threatened to disinherit him. "I didn't mind about the money," Istel says, "but it did worry me to upset Papa." However, it was not for nothing that Istel had been salutatorian at Stony Brook. When he got in his licks during the phone conversation, he talked both himself and his plane free. Then he headed east. At dusk, he thought it might be fun to try some night flying, since he had received no instruction in it, and he followed a lighted highway for some distance. Then, unhappily, he became entangled in a flight of B-25's and suffered a very brisk cursing. Out of gas, he came down in a potato field near Effingham, Illinois, nosed over, and broke his propeller. The farmers of the area proving tolerantly helpful, he was off again, the prop repaired, in a day and a half. With his radio out of whack, he landed at La Guardia Airport sandwiched between two squawking Constellations.

To Istel, the Korean War came not only as a patriotic opportunity but as a welcome respite. When he attempted to enlist in the Marine Corps, immediately on the announcement of hostilities, he ran into citizenship troubles. He had put in for naturalization, but approximately three months more had to elapse before his papers could come through. In the interim, he made his first parachute jump—one of the genuinely significant actions of his life. The thought of parachutes had occurred to Istel when, without any such aid, he got entangled with the B-25's. Since then, he had read up on the exercise, and he was now determined to give it a try. From his studies, he had learned that there existed an amateur sports group, the National Parachute Jumpers-Riggers, and that its head, and sole guiding genius, was a man named Joe Crane, who lived in Mineola, Long Island. Crane, then as now the greatly revered patriarch of United States parachutists, was running a parachute-maintenance company (by law, emergency parachutes must be repacked every sixty days), and had been making jumps since the old barnstorming days of aviation. Istel called on him with a request to rent a chute. Crane vehemently denounced the offhand project as premature. On leaving, with the rented chute, Istel repaired to an airport at Deer Park, Long Island, hired a pilot, soared into the blue, and leaped out. The jump turned out to be ragged and inaccurate but uncomplicated by fractures, and Istel was ready for more. His next jump was also uneventful, but his third landed him in Westchester County Court. In this episode, Istel came down in a tree on the Saxon Woods golf course; that is, he was left dangling in it, an object of attention. The trees overhung the Hutchinson River Parkway, upon which traffic was securely tied up for about two hours. As luck would have it, Westchester carried on its books an ordinance that specifically prohibited anybody from descending by parachute onto the Saxon Woods golf course. Istel was fined twenty-five dollars and was made the subject of a scalding editorial in a New Rochelle paper. Undismayed by this setback, he began planning more jumps, but at that point his citizenship came through and he hurried into the Marines.

Not very surprisingly for a man of action, Istel found his military service the most soothing and enjoyable experience of his life to date. He liked in particular the grinding physical regimen, which seemed mild by contrast to much of his hitchhiking, and, besides, it was in this period that he married. During one of his Princeton vacation rambles, which took him to Mexico, he had mixed concrete with a young divinity student, Alvord Beardslee, who impressed him so favorably that Istel finally said, "See here, if you have a sister like you, I want to marry her." Beardslee acknowledged that he did have a sister, named Claudia, and Istel later visted the family at their home, in Bethlehem, Pennsylvania, where the father, Claude Beardslee, was the chaplain of Lehigh University. In the course of his Marine Corps training, at the Great Lakes Naval Training Station, Istel telephoned Miss Beardslee and asked if she would care to come out and get married; he had just bought a "home," he said. The wedding of Istel and his fiancée took place in the base chapel, with no members of their families present, and afterward he escorted her to his newly purchased residence, which turned out to be a trailer. They were very happy in it until he went to Korea, as a second lieutenant, in 1953. Though Istel put in many requests for front-line action, he never saw combat, for medical reasons, and also because the war ended shortly after he arrived. It was discovered that he had a sizable bone tumor in his pelvis, and he shipped back to Oakland, California, where his wife joined him and rented an apartment. Technically, he was lodged in a naval hospital, but he became such a pesky nuisance, hobbling all over the place, asking questions, attempting to read his own X-rays, and pinching medical books, that he was permitted to come and go as he pleased. The apartment his wife had rented plagued Istel as being painfully civilized, so he bought a pup tent and moved them to a mountaintop near town. There they lived for three weeks, or until Istel could abstract his X-rays and mail them to a noted surgeon friend in New York for scrutiny. The surgeon's message, contained in a telegram, was "Have the tumor removed." Istel was sent to the naval hospital at St. Albans, Long Island, and there the operation was performed. A four-inch piece of bone was grafted in, but it was eventually resorbed; Istel now has no bone in part of his pelvis. This hiatus would appear to be a serious handicap for the average parachutist, but Istel sees it only as a mildly interesting challenge.

When Istel's incision had healed and his discharge from the service had come through, he and his wife took a Mexican vacation. On their return to New York, he was spiritually bruised to learn that he was expected to reënter Wall Street. This time, however, his sentence proved to be short-lived. Oddly, it was not airplanes but automobiles that removed Istel from the investment world. A friend in Paris wanted a Mercedes 300 SL, a sports racer that could then be bought only with dollars. Istel got him one, and lost little time wrecking it on the icy upsloping drive of his Bedford Village home. With the insurance money (and with the friend's permission), he bought another Mercedes, a model identical to the one that had won a recent Pan-American road race, in Mexico. When the second racer arrived, Istel eyed it with interest, plus a familiar, yeasty feeling of exploration. Finally, at around 2 A.M., he knuckled under, climbed in the car, and headed for the New Jersey Turnpike. It turned out to be an eventful night. On the turnpike approach, Istel was warned for driving at sixty miles an hour. Meekly, he promised to reform, and entered the turnpike gates. Then he gave the racer the works. Frequently, along the road, police cars took up the chase, but Istel, in his souped-up Mercedes, was doing a hundred and twenty-five miles an hour by the radar check, and they understandably headed for the pit to regroup. A credo of the New Jersey State Police is that there are several ways of skinning a cat. The runaway was finally stopped with a full-scale roadblock, somewhere near Camden. Hauled into a hastily convened court, Istel was contrite. He told the authorities the truth: he hadn't wanted to inconvenience anybody; his motive had been simple and scientific—he had wished to see how fast the car would go. His candor may have reduced his punishment, which amounted to a two hundred-dollar fine and a suspension of his driver's privileges in New Jersey for two years. The story had priceless ingredients for the newspapers: rich banker's son, Princeton, late hours, exotic car, the "international set," unheard-of speed on a public thoroughfare, and a juicy pronouncement by the court. Istel has checked carefully, and he believes that he made the front page of nearly every large journal in America. When his father called him in to the New York company office, the parental message was more thoughtful than angry. "You're a good boy, Jacques," said André Istel. "Certainly you're an interesting boy. But I must tell you that I can at last see clearly that your heart is not in the investment-banking business. Whatever your future business ventures may be, I wish you the best of luck in them. *Au revoir*.[11]"

Not long after this rupture, which Istel sees as being similar in tone to Edmond Dantès' escape from the Château d'If,[12] he began his real career, with parachutes. All along, something had been lacking, some foreordained channel into which he could pour his overflowing vitality. For a while, he worked for a New Jersey company called Air Associates, which dealt in aircraft supplies and electronic equipment, but his heart and his mind were aloft. It was probably the Vienna parachuting conference, to which Istel, at Joe Crane's suggestion, went as the United States delegate, that urged him down the correct path. When he came back, he was fired with zeal not only to raise a team for the impending championships in Moscow but to improve American parachuting in general, including that of the military, to the level of parachuting in Europe.

---

11. ***Au revoir*** (ō rə vwär'), Good-bye. 12. ***Edmond Dantès'*** (dɑN tes') ***escape from the Château d'If*** (dēf), the hero of Alexandre Dumas' novel ***The Count of Monte Cristo.*** Unjustly imprisoned as a young man, Dantès escapes and carries on an elaborate plan of revenge.

Istel considers, rightly, that few people understand how difficult a task he faced. In the minds of most Americans, the sport was tainted with the sleazy carnival air of the old barn-storming days, when migrant daredevils made jumps, for a fee, at county fairs. Besides, as Istel points out, people associated parachuting with crisis and disaster; it was a step to be taken at great risk—the last resort, when all else had failed. He wishes now that he had been paid a dollar, or even a franc, each time somebody said, "You seem like a bright young man. You could earn a fine living. Why do you go around making parachute jumps?" Despite this black wall of prejudice, a few Americans, over the years since the Wright brothers, had sporadically continued to jump, largely in a scientific or sporting way. At the world contest held in France in 1954, the United States was represented by one man, Fred Mason, an Army sergeant who jumped from an English plane using a French parachute. Operating entirely on his own hook, against full teams from other nations, he finished in twenty-first place, a few notches from the bottom. None of the American military or diplomatic people in attendance bothered to shake his hand; he was, though, cordially treated by his competitors. Mason died in a glider crash in 1955; his widow sent Istel thirty dollars to help raise funds for the Czechoslovakian meet.

Istel's first move toward forming a United States team was to obtain, from the highly coöperative Joe Crane, lists of those who might be in any sense qualified, and interested in competing. From these were winnowed twelve men—nearly all of them busy making a living—to whom Istel wrote an exceedingly attractive invitation, as follows: "Please inform the undersigned if you would care to try out, at your own expense, for a United States parachute team to go to the Moscow world championship, also at your own expense." By this time, Istel had risen to the eminence of vice-president of

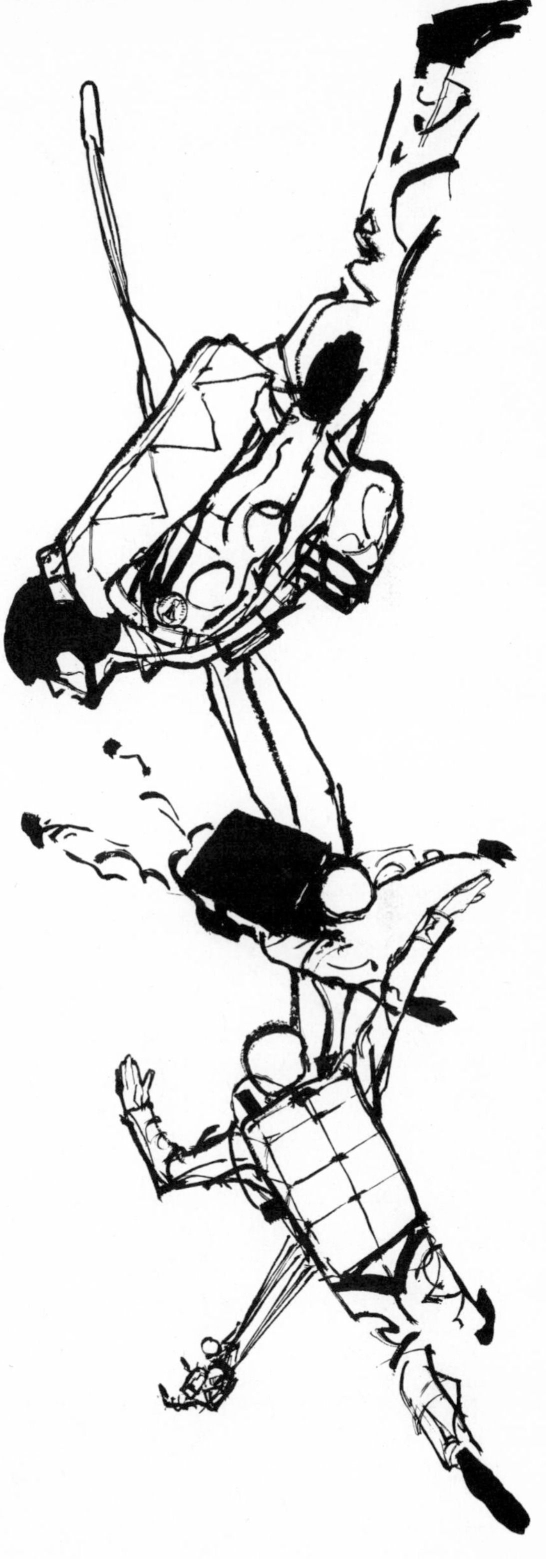

the National Parachute Jumpers-Riggers, and his voice carried authority. The response was stunning. Out of the twelve, seven knocked off their jobs and showed up in New York; several had borrowed money for the trip. Sky diving, upon which the whole burden of European performance rested, was unknown to any American except Istel. He showed his candidates some French parachuting films he had imported; then, with their help, he began making talks here and there, coaxing, wheedling, explaining, and pushing his project forward. He told how, at the European meets, a person left a plane, assumed a stable position, roughly in the form of a swan dive, and underwent intricate gyrations. In sum, Istel, again calling on his salutatorian skill, spread the word on parachuting. He explained that a falling body attains its top speed—about a hundred and twenty miles an hour—in twelve seconds; that fourteen thousand five hundred feet is perhaps the maximum altitude at which one may jump safely without oxygen; that to extend a free fall past sixty seconds one should start at an altitude of twelve thousand five hundred feet; and that twenty-two hundred feet is considered by experts a good safe minimum for pulling the cord. He explained (somewhat reluctantly) that in a free fall a soaring parachutist, like an airplane, runs a chance of going into a spin that is apt to reach a rate of a hundred and eighty revolutions per minute, but added that this can be stopped by certain movements of the arms and legs.

By March, 1956—five months before the Moscow meet—Istel had obtained, free, parachutes from the Pioneer Parachute Company; an airplane lent by Cessna[13]; stopwatches from Bulova; some funds from Air Associates, the business he worked for; and a few private donations. He then talked the McGuire Air Force Base, in New Jersey, into letting his group live at the field while in training. As the weeks of practice went on, the costs proved so high that the team was finally subsisting on a small hamburger daily per man. At one point, a team member, to help out, went to Freehold, New Jersey, and won thirty dollars driving a car in a road race.

The Moscow meet, and the sixth place that his team won, was a point of departure for Istel. Afterward, besides setting to work organizing jumping contests in this country and training men for future events in Europe, he hatched his scheme for designing the world's best chute, based on a modification of the "sleeve"—a pillowcase affair that at the outset controls the opening of a chute, so the parachutist will not get tangled in the lines, and, in addition, reduces the opening shock. The idea of a parachute sleeve had been dreamed up by the Germans, refined by the English, redesigned by the French, and taken up by the Russians, who soon felt that they had invented it, along with airplanes, and birds. Istel's head buzzed with innovations; he was on fire to get a business started. He broached the matter of financing to his father, and, getting virtually nowhere, began looking around for outside help, even if it should prove to be only moral. Today, Istel agrees that his father's stand was typically farsighted. In substance, it was "If a parachute company can be made profitable, it should be proved so without a subsidy." In any event, André Istel put in a little money, and then, giving his son a hearty pat, sat back to watch developments. At this time, the elder Istels, despite all the parachuting, were jubilant at a species of metamorphosis that had overtaken Jacques. Almost overnight, he had become a serious, unreckless, businesslike citizen, dedicated to an ideal and clearly finished with such trivia as driving racing cars a hundred and twenty-five miles an hour on the New Jersey Turnpike. At one of the domestic meets, Jacques met Lewis B. Sanborn, a young Ohio carpenter whose thoughts, like Istel's, were centered on para-

13. **Cessna,** the Cessna Aircraft Company.

chutes. In 1956, they borrowed some money and formed a company, Parachutes, Inc., with headquarters in the Bedford Village house. Then they devised what may well be the best chute extant. Lyman Ford's Pioneer Parachute Company agreed to manufacture the equipment for them. To Istel, the military was, of course, his best potential market; he took to haunting the labyrinthine corridors of the Pentagon, but his arguments fell flat. This was an authentic pity, for Parachutes, Inc., had something valuable to sell, as has been amply demonstrated since those days. Among other things, Istel rejected the age-old notion that the cloth used in all chutes must be porous, to cut down the opening shock. His modification of the European sleeve all but removed the jerky shock of opening. His subsequent employment of nonporous cloth softened the landing to the equivalent of jumping from a five-foot-high bookcase. With Istel's chutes, jumpers often make landings standing up. Istel and Sanborn also altered the Russian version of the "blank-gore" chute (a chute lacking one panel of cloth) to increase the lateral speed of the parachute; made a multitude of minor changes; and incorporated a shoulder snap that instantly freed half the parachute's lines from a landed jumper. A part of the argument Istel advanced to the armed services was that sky diving—the controlled, hawk-like flight of free fall—could be wonderfully useful in planting men for espionage, or other purposes, in terrain that required accuracy of descent. All these pleas were, at the start of Parachutes, Inc., unavailing, despite the fact that Istel and Sanborn continued to win acclaim all over the world. They had become moderately famous, but their message was locally viewed as ignorant.

To whoop up his sport, Istel launched a campaign to make parachuting popular in colleges. His first real opportunity came on the train he was taking to Fort Bragg to demonstrate sky diving. Istel on a train (and elsewhere) is a sociable fellow inclined to wander and chat, and at one point he sat down beside a well-dressed stranger and said. "How are you? My name is Jacques Istel. Would you care to hear a few things about parachutes?" The man responded, weakly, that he didn't mind, he supposed, and Istel moved into high vocal gear. The stranger turned out to be Whitney Griswold, the president of Yale, and before the train hit the next station, Istel had persuaded him that Yale was not likely to endure without a sports parachute club. To Griswold's astonishment, Istel arrived in New Haven very shortly thereafter, in accordance with a declaration he had made on the train; delivered a stirring, if unsettling, address; and organized the club. It flourishes today, with a steadily growing membership. Similar clubs thrive at Princeton, Harvard, West Point, and other colleges across the land, and, now, at many military bases. Early in 1957, in order to standardize all this, Istel transformed the old National Parachute Jumpers-Riggers into a dynamic society called the Parachute Club of America, of which Joe Crane is the head. Istel changed the rules, worked out safety regulations, established a membership, laid down strict qualifications for joining, and collected dues. Crane is immensely entertained by Istel, and considers him a heaven-sent boon to a sport that was all but moribund here. Istel, for his part, while happily serving under Crane in an official way, blandly transacts a great deal of the organization business on his own hook. For this purpose, he periodically has Crane sign a thick sheaf of stationery, upon which Istel composes club letters. Istel in print is clear, trenchant, and emphatic, but is also inclined to wax a trifle feverish. Crane is often surprised at the sprightly answers he gets to letters of which he had no knowledge whatever.

These are great days for Istel; things are moving forward apace. At long last, he and the military are singing a sweet duet, with the Army and the Marines buying his parachutes, the Air Force soliciting his views on sky diving, and sports clubs springing up like mushrooms at service posts. Occasional little rifts, differing viewpoints, still appear. Not long ago, a large aviation company told Istel that no man could sky-dive from a plane while wearing a fifteen-pound camera strapped to his helmet; his neck, they said, would instantly snap. Istel, with camera attached, was in the air inside of a week, and took some startling pictures, in midflight, of a sky diver who had preceded him a moment before. One of the most fervent and sincere young men alive, Istel believes passionately that parachuting can play a great part in keeping American youth in the paths of righteousness. He hopes soon to establish parachuting centers here on the order of ski centers, where people can go for tutelage and recreation, as they can now do in France. Moreover, he feels that he is exploring a vast and silent new medium, the deep blue well of the sky, and who knows what may come of it? He realizes that he still has a long way to go; until lately, for example, the Civil Aeronautics Administration declined to consider the issuance of parachuting regulations for independent jumpers, or, indeed, to have anything to do with parachuting at all—a state of affairs that Istel bitterly deplored, since about eight people a year were being killed in ill-advised and untrained jumps, usually from a failure to pull the ripcord in time, if at all. In the spring of 1957, the Parachute Club of America issued safety regulations to every jumper on its lists, but it was not until December of 1958 that the C.A.A. finally came around to recognizing the existence of parachuting; it will soon issue the Parachute Club regulations, as the authoritative word on the subject, to all its offices. Ever since the club drew up its code, not one jumper governed by its rules has hit the ground too hard. Istel has often received help from high places. Tom Lanphier, assistant to the president of Convair[14] and the man who, during the war, shot down Admiral Yamamoto,[15] gives him frequent counsel and assistance. So do Jacqueline Cochran, the noted aviatrix; her husband, Floyd Odlum, the financier; and, now, many excellent Army, Air Force, and Marine officers of high rank. Istel's parents look upon this phase of their son's success with quiet pride; André Istel, to his amazement, has even conceived the notion that Jacques may be as commercially astute as the next man.

The social life of a parachutist is inclined to be narrowly channelled, as Istel's wife ruefully attests. They still live in the Bedford Village house—with, by now, an infant daughter, Claudia—and their guests, in the main, are members of the sports clubs, whom he invites, often in large numbers, to come in with sleeping bags and bunk on the floor of his house after meets. Mrs. Istel has a recurring dream in which the sky—her sky—is clogged with swaying bodies and striped nylon. They pour down like snowflakes, growing thicker in proportion to her increasing speed as she tries to elude them—a dilemma like that of the sorcerer's apprentice.[16]

Istel is at his best at the World Championships—gala affairs, hugely attended in Europe, with the flags of all competing nations flying in symmetrical rows on the field, and an air of both fiesta and solemnity, like that at the Olympic Games. When he lines up for official congratulations, with Sanborn and their team, in the smart white jumper's costume with the United States emblem—the Stars and Stripes—sewn on the breast, his face wears an expression of pride. Unknown to Istel, it is also the look of an exemplary young American who has indeed earned his citizenship.

---

14. Convair. Derived from Consolidated Vultee Aircraft, a company which manufactures planes, the term *Convair* is also used to designate types of aircraft as in *Convair B-36.* ***15. Admiral Yamamoto*** (yä mä mō′tō), the Japanese officer who led the attack on Pearl Harbor. ***16. sorcerer's apprentice,*** a magician's helper in a musical composition by Paul Dukas. The apprentice creates a magic spell but is unable to control or stop it.

WHAT DO YOU SAY?

1. What aspects of Istel's character and personality are revealed in this sketch of his life?

2. *(a)* Evaluate Istel as a Marine officer. *(b)* Was he similar to or different from George Rogers Clark as a commander? Explain your answer. *(c)* If the situations of the two men had been reversed, Istel leading the march on Vincennes and Clark parachuting, how do you think each would have handled the situation?

3. What event actually pulled Istel—and the United States—into international competition in parachuting?

4. Istel has combined his sporting interests and business career. *(a)* Which seems to take precedence? *(b)* What changes in attitude has Istel undergone since he first started parachuting?

5. How does this selection differ from the previous one in its mood and in the attitude of its author?

AUTHOR'S CRAFT

Character sketch

You probably finished "No Feeling of Falling" with the impression that it was very different from the Clark biography. The fact is, the piece you have just read cannot properly be classified as a biography at all. It is actually a close relative of biography which is sometimes referred to as a ***character sketch.***

One difference between a character sketch and a book-length biography is in their development. A complete biography usually begins with the subject's birth and continues with his life, year by year—although several years may be condensed into a fairly short space, while others may be covered in more detail.

The author of a character sketch, however, is not confined to a consecutive development of his subject's life history. He may begin where he chooses and may cover any segments of his subject's life he chooses, because his aim is not to develop a complete life history, but to develop one or more phases of the person's character or personality. In "No Feeling of Falling," for example, Mr. Taylor has chosen to develop the character of Jacques André Istel in relationship to his activities as a parachutist.

A good character sketch, however, does share one very important feature with a well-developed biography. Each event, action, or scene described contributes something to the development of the character of the person about whom the author is writing.

For example, the description of the auto-strewn driveway leading up to Istel's mansion tells the reader something about his character, as does the description of his early morning push-ups, spine-crunching bends, and several parachute jumps before breakfast. But the author does not include a great many routine details that would add nothing to the development of Istel's character. Such details would do no more than clutter the picture and increase the length of the manuscript; so a good author avoids meaningless description through careful ***selection*** and ***condensation*** of his material. Find at least three details other than those mentioned above that reveal something about Istel's character.

KNOW YOUR WORDS

Discriminating between words similar in sound

Mr. Taylor's writing is an excellent example of how less common words can be used to help create a distinctive style of writing that is vivid and entertaining. A beginning writer, however, may encounter many pitfalls in trying to use more difficult words without carefully determining their meanings. One common error is to confuse words that sound somewhat alike but are quite different in meaning.

The following sentences include pairs of words that might sometimes be confused because of their similar sound. Choose the correct word for each sentence. Then write a sentence using the other word correctly.

1. Mr. Istel was ***(delegated, relegated)*** to represent France at the conference.
2. Many of Istel's actions left him ***(venerable, vulnerable)*** to criticism.
3. Istel managed to ***(elude, delude)*** his pursuers.
4. Istel has revolutionized the ***(percept, precept)*** of free-fall parachuting.
5. Istel's ***(regimen, regiment)*** is extremely rigorous.
6. In its beginning stages, Istel's program met with ***(hostility, hospitality)*** in the United States.

THE GREAT DAY

Helen Keller

UNITED PRESS INTERNATIONAL PHOTO

Helen Keller was less than two years old when she was stricken with a disease that left her deaf and blind, and for the next five years she remained in this dark, lonely world without even the ability to speak. Then came the great day when Anne Sullivan arrived from the Perkins Institute for the Blind.

The most important day I remember in all my life is the one on which my teacher, Anne Mansfield Sullivan, came to me. I am filled with wonder when I consider the immeasurable contrast between the two lives which it connects. It was the third of March, 1887, three months before I was seven years old.

On the afternoon of that eventful day, I stood on the porch, dumb, expectant. I guessed vaguely from my mother's signs and from the hurrying to and fro in the house that something unusual was about to happen; so I went to the door and waited on the steps. The afternoon sun penetrated the mass of honeysuckle that covered the porch, and fell on my upturned face. My fingers lingered almost unconsciously on the familiar leaves and blossoms which had just come forth to greet the sweet Southern spring. I did not know what the future held of marvel or surprise for me. Anger and bitterness had preyed upon me continually for weeks, and a deep languor had succeeded this passionate struggle.

Have you ever been at sea in a dense fog, when it seemed as if a tangible white darkness shut you in, and the great ship, tense and anxious, groped her way toward the shore with plummet and sounding line,[1] and you waited with beating heart for something to happen? I was like that ship before my education began, only I was without compass or sounding line, and had no way of knowing how near the harbor was. "Light! Give me light!" was the wordless cry of my soul, and the light of love shone on me in that very hour.

1. *plummet and sounding line,* a weight and a line used to find the depth of water.

I felt approaching footsteps.[2] I stretched out my hand as I supposed to my mother. Someone took it, and I was caught up and held close in the arms of her who had come to reveal all things to me, and, more than all things else, to love me.

The morning after my teacher came she led me into her room and gave me a doll. The little blind children at the Perkins Institution had sent it, and Laura Bridgman[3] had dressed it; but I did not know this until afterward. When I had played with it a little while, Miss Sullivan slowly spelled into my hand[4] the word "d-o-l-l." I was at once interested in this finger play and tried to imitate it. When I finally succeeded in making the letters correctly, I was flushed with childish pleasure and pride. Running downstairs to my mother, I held up my hand and made the letters for *doll*. I did not know that I was spelling a word or even that words existed; I was simply making my fingers go in monkeylike imitation. In the days that followed I learned to spell in this uncomprehending way a great many words, among them *pin, hat, cup* and a few verbs like *sit, stand,* and *walk*. But my teacher had been with me several weeks before I understood that everything has a name.

One day, while I was playing with my new doll, Miss Sullivan put my big rag doll into my lap also, spelled "d-o-l-l" and tried to make me understand that "d-o-l-l" applied to both. Earlier in the day we had had a tussle over the words "m-u-g" and "w-a-t-e-r." Miss Sullivan had tried to impress it upon me that "m-u-g" is *mug* and that "w-a-t-e-r" is *water,* but I persisted in confounding the two. In despair she had dropped the subject for the time, only to renew it at the first opportunity. I became impatient at her repeated attempts and, seizing the new doll, I dashed it upon the floor. I was keenly delighted when I felt the fragments of the broken doll at my feet. Neither sorrow nor regret followed my passionate outburst. I had not loved the doll. In the still, dark world in which I lived there was no strong sentiment or tenderness. I felt my teacher sweep the fragments to one side of the hearth, and I had a sense of satisfaction that the cause of my discomfort was removed. She brought me my hat, and I knew I was going out into the warm sunshine. This thought, if a wordless sensation may be called a thought, made me hop and skip with pleasure.

We walked down the path to the well-house, attracted by the fragrance of the honeysuckle with which it was covered. Someone was drawing water, and my teacher placed my hand under the spout. As the cool stream gushed over one hand, she spelled into the other the word *water,* first slowly, then rapidly. I stood still, my whole attention fixed upon the motions of her fingers. Suddenly I felt a misty consciousness as of something forgotten—a thrill of returning thought; and somehow the mystery of language was revealed to me. I knew then that "w-a-t-e-r" meant the wonderful cool something that was flowing over my hand. That living word awakened my soul, gave it light, hope, joy, set it free! There were barriers still, it is true, but barriers that could in time be swept away.

I left the well-house eager to learn. Everything had a name, and each name gave birth to a new thought. As we returned to the house, every object which I touched seemed to quiver with life. That was because I saw everything with the strange, new sight that had come to me. On entering the door, I remembered the doll I had broken. I felt my way to the hearth and picked up the pieces. I tried vainly to put them together. Then my eyes filled with tears; for I realized what I had done, and for the first time I felt repentance and sorrow.

---

2. ***felt approaching footsteps,*** felt the vibrations caused by Miss Sullivan's footsteps as she approached. 3. ***Laura Bridgman,*** a blind deaf-mute who attended the Perkins Institute for the Blind and who later became an influential teacher at the school. 4. ***spelled into my hand.*** Miss Sullivan used the manual alphabet, forming the letters with her fingers on Helen's palm.

I learned a great many new words that day. I do not remember what they all were; but I do know that *mother, father, sister, teacher* were among them—words that were to make the world blossom for me, "like Aaron's rod, with flowers."[5] It would have been difficult to find a happier child than I was as I lay in my crib at the close of that eventful day and lived over the joys it had brought me, and for the first time longed for a new day to come.

---

5. ***like Aaron's rod, with flowers.*** When the Israelites in the wilderness rebelled against Aaron's leadership, Moses placed in the tabernacle the rods belonging to the twelve tribal princes. The next morning Aaron's rod was discovered to have put forth almond buds and blossoms. This miracle was interpreted to signify that Aaron should continue as leader.

WHAT DO YOU SAY?

1. Although Helen was deaf and blind, her other senses were more acute than usual. Give illustrations of this from the story.

2. *(a)* What was the first word that came to have real meaning to Helen? *(b)* How did Anne Sullivan teach her this word and its meaning?

3. Describe the change in Helen's attitude and behavior after the above incident had taken place.

4. Do you feel that Miss Keller presents a true, complete picture of herself? Be prepared to give reasons for your answers.

AUTHOR'S CRAFT

Autobiography

Biographies and autobiographies are very similar to one another in their general method of development, but there are some differences, which you may have noticed for yourself as you read "The Great Day." For one thing, you were probably aware of the more intimate style and presentation in this autobiography of Helen Keller. Since she herself was the author, her thoughts, feelings, and actions could be described by the "I" of the story rather than a third person observer. And because of this, a reader often feels closer to the subject of the story than is possible in a biography.

The sources of autobiography also differ from those of biography. While a biographer must gather his material from such sources as letters, journals, manuscripts, conversations, and other biographies, an autobiographer relies upon his own recollections and perhaps personal records such as diaries.

However, an autobiographer is faced with special problems that are not always so difficult for a biographer. For example, a person writing his own life history may find it extremely difficult to be ***objective*** about himself. A person may tend to forget his mistakes, minimize his shortcomings, and exaggerate his strong points, or he may do the opposite. A good autobiographer must at all times be aware of this tendency and attempt to develop an honest picture of himself.

Helen Keller has avoided a one-sided picture of herself in a number of ways. She has stated the facts of her great achievement simply and without appearing to congratulate herself for what she accomplished; and she has not given the impression that she learned to talk all by herself, but has shown gratitude for the understanding and help given her by Anne Sullivan, her teacher. Similarly, Miss Keller has not implied that she was always a good, well-mannered child, but has told the reader about her temper tantrums and her periods of sulkiness. Together, these facets of Helen Keller's personality have contributed to the reader's image of a great and compassionate lady.

As you read the next three selections, keep in mind the qualities of a good autobiography in an attempt to decide how well the authors achieve their purpose.

KNOW YOUR WORDS

The appeal to the senses

Helen Keller describes her excitement when the mystery of language was at last revealed to her. She learned that everything had a name. However, some "names" or words would have little or no meaning for a blind and deaf person. Which of the following words would have no significance for Helen Keller? Explain why not.

1. smoke
2. lilacs
3. carmine
4. noisy
5. fog
6. stream
7. tears
8. stars
9. shriek
10. distance
11. picture
12. breeze

Booker T. Washington was never quite sure exactly when he was born, although he thought it might have been 1858 or 1859. Careful records of the birth dates of slaves were not kept on the Virginia plantation where Washington began his life. But from the time he was a few years old, he did know one thing. Above all, he desired an education.

MY STRUGGLE FOR AN EDUCATION

Booker T. Washington

One day, while at work in the coal mine, I happened to overhear two miners talking about a great school for colored people somewhere in Virginia. This was the first time that I had ever heard anything about any kind of school or college that was more pretentious than the little colored school in our town.

In the darkness of the mine I noiselessly crept as close as I could to the two men who were talking. I heard one tell the other that not only was the school established for the members of my race, but that opportunities were provided by which poor but worthy students could work out all or a part of the cost of board, and at the same time be taught some trade or industry.

As they went on describing the school, it seemed to me that it must be the greatest place on earth, and not even Heaven presented more attractions for me at that time than did the Hampton Normal and Agricultural Institute in Virginia, about which these men were talking. I resolved at once to go to that school, although I had no idea where it was, or how many miles away, or how I was going to reach it; I remembered only that I was on fire constantly with one ambition, and that was to go to Hampton. This thought was with me day and night. . . .

In the fall of 1872, I determined to make an effort to get there; although, as I have stated, I had no definite idea of the direction in which Hampton was, or of what it would cost to go there. I do not think that anyone thoroughly sympathized with me in my ambition to go to Hampton unless it was my mother, and she was troubled with a grave fear that I was starting out on a "wild-goose chase." At any rate, I got only a half-hearted consent from her that I might start. The small amount of money that I had earned had been consumed by my stepfather and the remainder of the family, with the exception of a very few dollars, and so I had very little with which to buy clothes and pay my traveling expenses. My brother John helped me all that he could; but, of course, that was not a great deal, for his work was in the coal mine, where he did not earn much, and most of what he did earn went in the direction of paying the household expenses. . . .

Finally the great day came, and I started for Hampton. I had only a small cheap satchel that contained what few articles of clothing I could get. My mother at the time was rather weak and broken in health. I hardly expected to see her again, and thus our parting was all the more sad. She, however, was very brave through it all. . . .

EBONY MAGAZINE

The distance from Malden to Hampton is about five hundred miles. I had not been away from home many hours before it began to grow painfully evident that I did not have enough money to pay my fare to Hampton. . . . By walking, begging rides both in wagons and in the cars,[1] in some way, after a number of days, I reached the city of Richmond, Virginia, about eighty-two miles from Hampton. When I reached there, tired, hungry, and dirty, it was late in the night.

I had never been in a large city, and this rather added to my misery. When I reached Richmond, I was completely out of money. I had not a single acquaintance in the place; and, being unused to city ways, I did not know where to go. I applied at several places for lodging, but they all wanted money, and that was what I did not have. Knowing nothing better to do, I walked the streets. In doing this I passed by many food stands where fried chicken and half-moon apple pies were piled high and made to present a most tempting appearance. At that time it seemed to me that I would have promised all that I expected to possess in the future to have gotten hold of one of those chicken legs or one of those pies. But I could not get either of these, nor anything else to eat.

I must have walked the streets till after midnight. At last I became so exhausted that I could walk no longer. I was tired, I was hungry, I was everything but discouraged. Just about the time when I reached extreme physical exhaustion, I came upon a portion of a street where the board sidewalk was considerably elevated. I waited for a few minutes till I was sure that no passers-by could see me, and then crept under the sidewalk and lay for the night upon the ground, with my satchel of clothing for a pillow. Nearly all night I could hear the tramp of feet over my head.

The next morning I found myself somewhat refreshed, but I was extremely hungry, because it had been a long time since I had had sufficient food. As soon as it became light enough for me to see my surroundings, I noticed that I was near a large ship, and that this ship seemed to be unloading a cargo of pig iron. I went at once to the vessel and asked the captain to permit me to help unload the vessel in order to get money for food. The captain, a white man, who seemed to be kind-hearted, consented. I worked long enough to earn money for my breakfast, and it seems to me, as I remember it now, to have been about the best breakfast I have ever eaten.

My work pleased the captain so well that he told me if I desired I could continue working for a small amount per day. This I was very glad to do. I continued working on this vessel for a number of days. After

1. *the cars.* Dr. Washington is speaking here of railroad cars, not automobiles.

buying food with the small wages I had received, there was not much left to add to the amount I must get to pay my way to Hampton. In order to economize in every way possible so as to be sure to reach Hampton in a reasonable time, I continued to sleep under the same sidewalk that gave me shelter the first night I was in Richmond. . . .

When I had saved what I considered enough money with which to reach Hampton, I thanked the captain of the vessel for his kindness, and started again. Without any unusual occurrence I reached Hampton, with a surplus of exactly fifty cents with which to begin my education. To me it had been a long, eventful journey; but the first sight of the large, three-story, brick school building seemed to have rewarded me for all that I had undergone in order to reach the place. . . . It seemed to me to be the largest and most beautiful building I had ever seen. The sight of it seemed to give me new life. I felt that a new kind of existence had now begun—that life would now have a new meaning. I felt that I had reached the promised land, and I resolved to let no obstacle prevent me from putting forth the highest effort to fit myself to accomplish the most good in the world.

As soon as possible after reaching the grounds of the Hampton Institute, I presented myself before the head teacher for assignment to a class. Having been so long without proper food, a bath, and change of clothing, I did not, of course, make a very favorable impression upon her, and I could see at once that there were doubts in her mind about the wisdom of admitting me as a student. I felt that I could hardly blame her if she got the idea that I was a worthless loafer or tramp. For some time she did not refuse to admit me, neither did she decide in my favor, and I continued to linger about her, and to impress her in all the ways I could with my worthiness. In the meantime I saw her admitting other students, and that added greatly to my discomfort, for I felt, deep down in my heart, that I could do as well as they, if I could only get a chance to show what was in me.

After some hours had passed, the head teacher said to me, "The adjoining recitation room needs sweeping. Take the broom and sweep it."

It occurred to me at once that here was my chance. Never did I receive an order with more delight. . . .

I swept the recitation room three times. Then I got a dusting cloth, and I dusted it four times. All the woodwork around the walls, every bench, table, and desk, I went over four times with my dusting cloth. Besides, every piece of furniture had been moved and every closet and corner in the room had been thoroughly cleaned. I had the feeling that in large measure my future depended upon the impression I made upon the teacher in the cleaning of that room. When I was through, I reported to the head teacher. She was a "Yankee" woman who knew just where to look for dirt. She went into the room and inspected the floor and closets; then she took her handkerchief and rubbed it on the woodwork about the walls, and over the table and benches. When she was unable to find one bit of dirt on the floor, or a particle of dust on any of the furniture, she quietly remarked, "I guess you will do to enter this institution."

I was one of the happiest souls on earth. The sweeping of that room was my college examination, and never did any youth pass an examination for entrance into Harvard or Yale that gave him more genuine satisfaction. I have passed several examinations since then, but I have always felt that this was the best one I ever passed. . . .

The sweeping of the recitation room in the manner that I did it seems to have paved the way for me to get through Hampton. Miss Mary F. Mackie, the head teacher, offered me a postion as janitor. This, of course, I gladly accepted, because it was a place where I could work out nearly all the cost of my board. The work was hard and taxing, but I stuck to it. I had a large number of rooms to care for, and had to work late into the night, while at the same time I had to rise by four o'clock in the morning, in order to build the fires and have a little time in which to prepare my lessons. . . .

I have spoken of the impression that was made upon me by the buildings and general appearance of the Hampton Institute, but I have not spoken of that which made the greatest and most lasting impression upon me, and that was a great man—the noblest, rarest human being that it has ever been my privilege to meet. I refer to the late General Samuel C. Armstrong. . . . One might have removed from Hampton all the buildings, classrooms, teachers, and industries, and given the men and women there the opportunity of coming into daily contact with General Armstrong, and that alone would have been a liberal education. The older I grow, the more I am convinced that there is no education which one can get from books and costly apparatus that is equal to that which can be gotten from contact with great men and women. Instead of studying books so constantly, how I wish that our schools and colleges might learn to study men and things! . . .

While I was a student at Hampton, the dormitories became so crowded that it was impossible to find room for all who wanted to be admitted. In order to help remedy the difficulty, the General conceived the plan of putting up tents to be used as rooms. As soon as it became known that General Armstrong would be pleased if some of the older students would live in the tents during the winter, nearly every student in school volunteered to go.

I was one of the volunteers. The winter that we spent in those tents was an intensely cold one, and we suffered severely—how much I am sure General Armstrong never knew, because we made no complaints. . . .

The charge for my board at Hampton was ten dollars per month. I was expected to pay a part of this in cash and to work out the remainder. To meet this cash payment, as I have stated, I had just fifty cents when I reached the institution. Aside from a very few dollars that my brother John was able to send me once in a while, I had no money with which to pay my board. I was determined from the first to make my work as janitor so valuable that my services would be indispensable. This I succeeded in doing to such an extent that I was soon informed that I would be allowed the full cost of my board in return for my work. The cost of tuition was seventy dollars a year. This, of course, was wholly beyond my ability to provide. If I had been compelled to pay the seventy dollars for tuition, in addition to providing for my board, I would have been compelled to leave the Hampton School. General Armstrong, however, very kindly got Mr. S. Griffitts Morgan, of New Bedford, Massachusetts, to defray the cost of my tuition during the whole time that I was at Hampton. . . .

After having been for a while at Hampton, I found myself in difficulty because I did not have books and clothing. Usually, however, I got around the trouble about books by borrowing from those who were more fortunate than myself. As to clothes, when I reached Hampton I had practically nothing. Everything that I possessed was in a small hand satchel. My anxiety about clothing was increased because of the fact that General Armstrong made a personal inspection of the young men in ranks, to see that their clothes were clean. Shoes had to be polished, there must be no buttons off the clothing, and no grease spots. To wear one suit of clothes continually, while at work and in the schoolroom, and at the same time keep it clean, was rather a hard problem for me to solve. In some way I managed to get on till the teachers learned that I was in earnest and meant to succeed, and then some of them were kind enough to see that I was partly supplied with second-hand clothing that had been sent in barrels from the North. . . .

I was among the youngest of the students who were in Hampton at that time. Most of the students were men and women—some as old as forty years of age. As I now recall the scene of my first year, I do not believe that one often has the opportunity of coming into contact with three or four hundred men and women who were so tremendously in earnest as these men and women were. Every hour was occupied in study or work. Nearly all had had enough actual contact with the world to teach them the need of education. Many of the older ones were, of course, too old to master the textbooks very thoroughly, and it was often sad to watch their struggles; but they made up in earnestness much of what they lacked in books. Many of them were as poor as I was, and, besides having to wrestle with their books, they had to struggle with a poverty which prevented their having the necessities of life. Many of them had aged parents who were dependent upon them, and some of them were men who had wives whose support in some way they had to provide for.

The great and prevailing idea that seemed to take possession of everyone was to prepare himself to lift up the people at his home. No one seemed to think of himself.

WHAT DO YOU SAY?

1. *(a)* What was young Washington's "entrance examination" for entering Hampton Institute? *(b)* How did his performance reflect his character?

2. Which of the two autobiographies you have read seemed to portray the author's personality more vividly? Explain your answer by specific illustrations.

3. *(a)* Apart from his actual studies, what lessons did Washington learn at Hampton? *(b)* How might these lessons have benefited him in later years?

4. One purpose of a biography or autobiography is simply to record the life history of a person, but both may have secondary purposes. *(a)* What secondary purpose do you think this selection might have? *(b)* How would you compare this secondary purpose with the secondary purpose of the Keller autobiography? *(c)* With the Clark biography? *(d)* With the Istel character sketch?

KNOW YOUR WORDS

Formal and informal words

Words and expressions can often be classified as ***formal*** or ***informal*** in tone. For example, consider the following sentence: "Jerry and I were up and down several times since neither of us had skated before, but we still had a convivial experience." The formal-sounding ***convivial experience*** seems out of place here because of the general, informal tone of the rest of the sentence, and a ***good time*** would be a much better expression to use.

In the following sentences, the words in italics seem somewhat formal and not in keeping with the rest of the words and with the subject matter. Replace each of these words with one of the more informal words or phrases from the list given below.

spent	***own***	***enough***	***let***	***wanted***
save money	***vowed***	***told***	***forced***	***common***

1. His family had ***consumed*** most of the money he had made.
2. He didn't ***possess*** a second suit of clothes.
3. On the way to Hampton, Washington did not even have ***sufficient*** food.
4. He asked the captain to ***permit*** him [to] work.
5. Washington, above all, ***desired*** to learn.
6. He had to ***economize*** in even the simplest ways.
7. Still, Washington ***resolved*** that he would get an education.
8. He was ***informed*** that he could be janitor for the school.
9. Even with the help given him, he was ***compelled*** to live simply.
10. The ***prevailing*** desire of all the students was to lift up the people at home.

One of the most vivid eras of American history is that of the Great Westward Movement, during which thousands of people banded together to form wagon trains headed for California. In April, 1846, one such wagon train left from Springfield, Illinois, but of its eighty-odd members, only forty-five survived to reach their destination. Others perished during the bitter winter months when they were stranded at Donner Lake (named after the leader of the party) because of heavy snowfall that prevented them from passing through the Sierra Nevada Mountains. The following narrative by one of the survivors, Virginia Reed Murphy, is based on an earlier letter she had written to a cousin in Springfield.

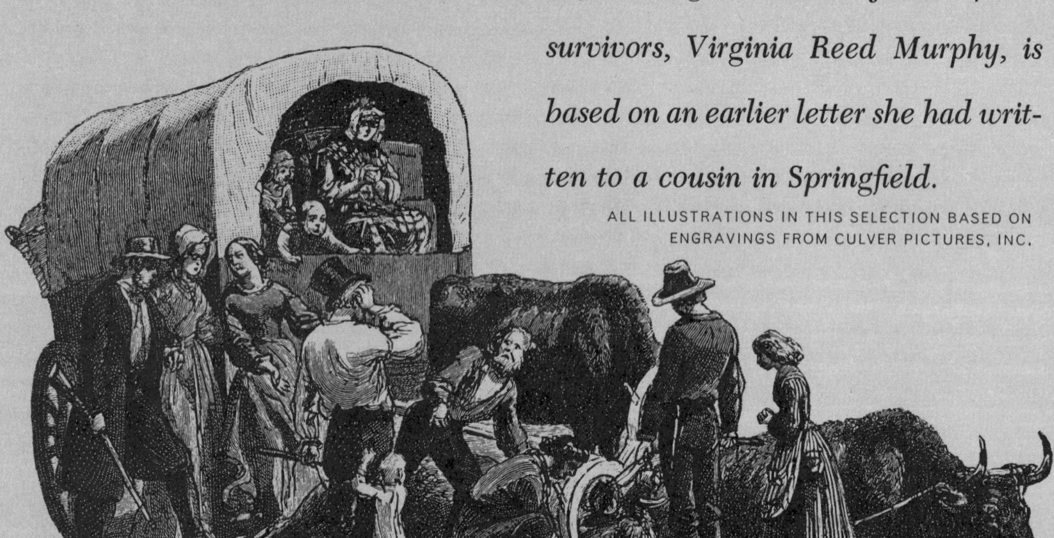

DEATH AT DONNER LAKE

Virginia Reed Murphy

Snow was already falling, although it was only the last week in October. Winter had set in a month earlier than usual. All trails and roads were covered, and our only guide was the summit which it seemed we would never reach. Despair drove many nearly frantic. Each family tried to cross the mountains but found it impossible to do so. When it was seen that the wagons could not be dragged through the snow, their goods and provisions were packed on oxen and another start was made, men and women walking in snow up to their waists, carrying their children in their arms, and trying to drive their cattle. The Indians said they could find no road; so a halt was called, and Stanton[1] went ahead with the guides and came back and reported that we could get across if we kept right on, but that it would be impossible if snow fell. He was in favor of a forced march until the other side of the summit should be reached, but some of our party were so tired and exhausted with the day's labor that they declared they could not take another step; so the few who knew the danger that the night might bring yielded to the many, and we camped within three miles of the summit.

That night came the dreaded snow. Around the campfires under the trees great feathery flakes came whirling down. The air was so full of them that one could see objects only a few feet away. The Indians knew we were doomed, and one of them wrapped his blanket about him and stood all night under a tree. We children slept soundly on our cold bed of snow with a soft white mantle falling over us so thickly that every few moments my mother would have to shake the shawl—our only covering —to keep us from being buried alive. In the morning the snow lay deep on mountain and valley. With heavy hearts we turned back to a cabin that had been built by the Murphy-Schallenberger party[2] two years before. We built more cabins and prepared as best we could for the winter. That camp, which proved the camp of death to many in our company, was made on the shore of a lake, since known as Donner Lake. The Donners were camped in Alder Creek Valley below the lake, and were, if possible, in a worse condition than ourselves. The

1. ***Stanton,*** a bachelor from Chicago, who assumed part of the leadership after Reed was forced to leave the party due to a quarrel in which a man was killed. 2. ***Murphy-Schallenberger Party,*** a group of pioneers who crossed the Sierra Nevada Mountains in 1844 without losing a single person.

snow came on so suddenly that they had no time to build cabins, but hastily put up brush sheds, covering them with pine boughs.

Three double cabins were built at Donner Lake, which were known as the Breen Cabin, the Murphy Cabin, and the Reed-Graves Cabin. The cattle were all killed, and the meat was placed in snow for preservation. My mother had no cattle to kill, but she made arrangements for some, promising to give two for one in California. Stanton and the Indians made their home in my mother's cabin.

Many attempts were made to cross the mountains, but all who tried were driven back by the pitiless storms. Finally a party was organized, since known as the Forlorn Hope. They made snowshoes, and fifteen started—ten men and five women—but only seven lived to reach California; eight men perished. They were over a month on the way, and the horrors endured by that Forlorn Hope no pen can describe nor imagination conceive. The noble Stanton was one of the party, and perished the sixth day out, thus sacrificing his life for strangers. I can find no words in which to express a fitting tribute to the memory of Stanton.

The misery endured during those four months at Donner Lake in our little dark cabins under the snow would fill pages and make the coldest heart ache. Christmas was near, but to the starving its memory gave no comfort. It came and passed without observance, but my mother had determined weeks before that her children should have a treat on this one day. She had laid away a few dried apples, some beans, a bit of tripe, and a small piece of bacon. When this hoarded store was brought out, the delight of the little ones knew no bounds. The cooking was watched carefully, and when we sat down to our Christmas dinner, Mother said, "Children, eat slowly, for this one day you can have all you wish." So bitter was the misery relieved by that one bright day that I have never since sat down to a Christmas dinner without my thoughts going back to Donner Lake.

The storms would often last ten days at a time, and we would have to cut chips from the logs inside which formed our cabins in order to start a fire. We could scarcely walk, and the men had hardly strength to procure wood. We would drag ourselves through the snow from one cabin to another, and some mornings snow would have to be shoveled out of the fireplace before a fire could be made. Poor little children were crying with hunger, and mothers were crying because they had so little to give their children. We seldom thought of bread, we had been without it so long. Four months of such suffering would fill the bravest hearts with despair. . . .

Time dragged slowly along till we were no longer on short allowance but were simply starving. Mother determined to make an effort to cross the mountains. She could not see her children die without trying to get them food. It was hard to leave them, but she felt that it must be done. She told them she would bring them bread, so they were willing to stay, and with no guide but a compass we started—my mother, Eliza,[3] Milt Elliott,[4] and myself. Milt wore snowshoes, and we followed in his tracks. We were five days in the mountains; Eliza

3. *Eliza,* a young girl who was employed by the Reeds to cook and care for the children. 4. *Milt Elliott,* one of Reed's wagon-drivers.

gave out the first day and had to return, but we kept on and climbed one high mountain after another only to see others higher still ahead. Often I would have to crawl up the mountains, being too tired to walk. The nights were made hideous by the screams of wild beasts heard in the distance. Again, we would be lulled to sleep by the moan of the pine trees, which seemed to sympathize with our loneliness. One morning we awoke to find ourselves in a well of snow. During the night, while in the deep sleep of exhaustion, the heat of the fire had melted the snow and our little camp had gradually sunk many feet below the surface until we were literally buried in a well of snow. The danger was that any attempt to get out might bring an avalanche upon us, but finally steps were carefully made and we reached the surface. My foot was badly frozen, so we were compelled to return, and just in time, for that night a storm came on, the most fearful of the winter, and we should have perished had we not been in the cabins.

We now had nothing to eat but raw hides and they were on the roof of the cabin to keep out the snow; when prepared for cooking and boiled they were simply a pot of glue. When the hides were taken off our cabin and we were left without shelter, Mr. Breen gave us a home with his family, and Mrs. Breen prolonged my life by slipping me little bits of meat now and then when she discovered that I could not eat the hide. Death had already claimed many in our party, and it seemed as though relief never would reach us. Baylis Williams,[5] who had been in delicate health before we left Springfield, was the first to die; he passed away before starvation had really set in. . . .

On his arrival at Sutter's Fort[6] my father made known the situation of the emigrants, and Captain Sutter offered at once to do everything possible for their relief. He furnished horses and provisions, and my father

5. ***Baylis Williams,*** employee of the Reeds and brother of Eliza. 6. ***Sutter's Fort,*** the site of Sacramento, California.

with Mr. McClutchen[7] started for the mountains, coming as far as possible with horses and then with packs on their backs proceeding on foot; but they were finally compelled to return. Captain Sutter was not surprised at their defeat. He stated that there were no able-bodied men in that vicinity, all having gone down the country with Frémont[8] to fight the Mexicans. He advised my father to go to Yerba Buena,[9] now San Francisco, and make his case known to the naval officer in command. My father was in fact conducting parties there —when the seven members of the Forlorn Hope arrived from across the mountains. Their famished faces told the story. Cattle were killed and men were up all night, drying beef and making flour by hand mills, nearly two hundred pounds being made in one night, and a party of seven, commanded by Captain Reasen P. Tucker, were sent to our relief by Captain Sutter and the alcalde,[10] Mr. Sinclair. On the evening of February 19, 1847, they reached our cabins, where all were starving. They shouted to attract attention. Mr. Breen clambered up the icy steps from our cabin, and soon we heard the blessed words, "Relief, thank God, relief!" There was joy at Donner Lake that night, for we did not know the fate of the Forlorn Hope; and we were told that relief parties would come and go until all were across the mountains. But with the joy sorrow was strangely blended. There were tears in other eyes than those of children; strong men sat down and wept. For the dead were lying about on the snow, some even unburied, since the living had not had strength to bury their dead. When Milt Elliott died—our faithful friend who seemed so like a brother—my mother and I dragged him up out of the cabin and covered him with snow. Commencing at his feet, I patted the pure white snow down softly until I reached his face. Poor Milt! It was hard to cover that face from sight forever, for with his death our best friend was gone.

On the twenty-second of February the first relief started with a party of twenty-three—men, women and children. My mother and her family were among the number. It was a bright, sunny morning, and we felt happy; but we had not gone far when Patty and Tommy gave out. They were not able to stand the fatigue, and it was not thought safe to allow them to proceed; so Mr. Glover[11] informed Mama that they would have to be sent back to the cabins to await the next expedition. What language can express our feelings? My mother said that she would go back with her children—that we would all go back together. This the relief party would not permit, and Mr. Glover promised Mama that as soon as they reached Bear Valley he himself would return for her children. . . . Mr. Glover returned with the children and, providing them with food, left them in the care of Mr. Breen.

With sorrowful hearts we traveled on, walking through the snow in single file. The men wearing snowshoes broke the way, and we followed in their tracks. At night we lay down on the snow to sleep, to awake to find our clothing all frozen, even to our shoestrings. At break of day we were again on the road, owing to the fact that we could make better time over the frozen snow. The sunshine, which it would seem would have been welcome, only added to our misery. The dazzling reflection of the snow was very trying to the eyes, while its heat melted our frozen clothing, making [it] cling to our bodies. My brother was too small to step in the tracks made by the men, and in order to travel he had to place his knee on the little hill of snow after each step and climb over. Mother coaxed him

7. ***Mr. McClutchen.*** McClutchen had gone with Reed when Reed had been sent away from the party. 8. ***Frémont,*** the leader of two pioneer parties to California, and the first man to make a complete circuit of the West. He fought against the Mexicans in California in an attempt to annex this territory to the United States. 9. ***Yerba Buena*** (yer′bə or yėr′bə bwā′nə). 10. ***alcalde*** (al kal′di), in regions of former Spanish influence, a mayor, judge, or justice-of-the-peace. 11. ***Mr. Glover,*** one of the first volunteers for the first relief party.

along, telling him that every step he took he was getting nearer Papa and nearer something to eat. He was the youngest child that walked over the Sierra Nevada. On our second day's journey John Denton[12] gave out and declared it would be impossible for him to travel, but he begged his companions to continue their journey. A fire was built and he was left lying on a bed of freshly-cut pine boughs, peacefully smoking. He looked so comfortable that my little brother wanted to stay with him, but when the second relief party reached him, poor Denton was past waking. His last thoughts seemed to have gone back to his childhood's home, as a little poem was found by his side, the pencil apparently just dropped from his hand.

Captain Tucker's party on their way to the cabins had lightened their packs of a sufficient quantity of provisions to supply the sufferers on their way out. But when we reached the place where the cache had been made by hanging the food on a tree, we were horrified to find that wild animals had destroyed it; and again starvation stared us in the face. But my father was hurrying over the mountains and met us in our hour of need with his hands full of bread. He had expected to meet us on this day and had stayed up all night, baking bread to give us. He brought with him fourteen men. Some of his party were ahead, and when they saw us coming they called out: "Is Mrs. Reed with you? If she is, tell her Mr. Reed is here." We heard the call; Mother knelt on the snow, while I tried to run to meet Papa.

When my father learned that two of his children were still at the cabins, he hurried on, so fearful was he that they might perish before he reached them. He seemed to fly over the snow, and made in two days the distance we had been five in traveling, and was overjoyed to find Patty and Tommy alive. He reached Donner Lake on the first of March and what a sight met his gaze! The famished little children and the deathlike look of all made his heart ache. He filled Patty's apron with biscuits which she carried around, giving one to each person. He had soup made for the infirm and rendered every assistance possible to the sufferers. Leaving them with about seven days' provisions, he started out with a party of seventeen, all that were able to travel. Three of his men were left at the cabins to procure wood and assist the helpless. My father's party (the second relief) had not traveled many miles when a storm broke upon them. With the snow came a perfect hurricane. The crying of half-frozen children, the lamenting of the mothers, and the suffering of the whole party was heartrending; and above all could be heard the shrieking of the storm king. One who has never witnessed a blizzard in the Sierra can form no idea of the situation. All night my father and his men worked unceasingly through the raging storm, trying to erect shelter for the dying women and children. At times the hurricane would burst forth with such violence that he felt alarmed on account of the tall timber surrounding the camp. The party were destitute for food, all supplies that could be spared having been left

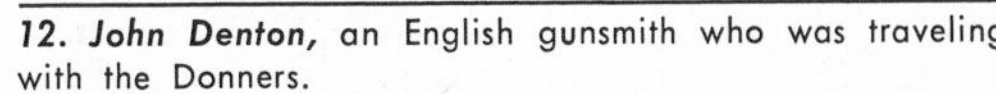

12. ***John Denton,*** an English gunsmith who was traveling with the Donners.

with those at the cabins. The relief party had cached provisions on their way over to the cabins, and my father had sent three of the men forward for food before the storm set in, but they could not return. Thus, again, death stared all in the face. At one time the fire was nearly gone; had it been lost, all would have perished. Three days and nights they were exposed to the fury of the elements. Finally my father became snow-blind and could do no more, and he would have died but for the exertions of William McClutchen and Hiram Miller,[13] who worked over him all night. From this time forward the toil and responsibility rested upon McClutchen and Miller.

The storm at last ceased, and these two determined to set out over the snow and send back relief to those not able to travel. Hiram Miller picked up Tommy and started. Patty thought she could walk, but gradually everything faded from her sight, and she too seemed to be dying. All other sufferings were now forgotten, and everything was done to revive the child. My father found some crumbs in the thumb of his woolen mitten; warming and moistening them between his own lips, he gave them to her and thus saved her life, and afterward she was carried along by different ones in the company. Patty was not alone in her travels. Hidden away in her bosom was a tiny doll which she had carried day and night through all of our trials. Sitting before a nice, bright fire at Woodworth's Camp, she took dolly out to have a talk, and told her of all her new happiness.

---

13. ***Hiram Miller,*** one of George Donner's wagon-drivers who had gone to Oregon with the Bryant-Boggs party and then south to California.

WHAT DO YOU SAY?

1. *(a)* What was the Forlorn Hope? *(b)* What were its results?

2. *(a)* Which decision of the party brought on the tragic consequences that took place at Donner Lake? *(b)* Why was this decision made?

3. *(a)* Why did the Reeds leave their cabin and move in with the Breens? *(b)* What did the author show of the character of the Breens?

4. *(a)* Has the development of Virginia Reed's character and personality been achieved in "Death at Donner Lake"? *(b)* Can this selection properly be classified as an autobiography? Explain your answer.

5. *(a)* Did you find references in this selection that were confusing to you? *(b)* If you were rewriting this story in the role of a biographer, what changes or additions would you make?

KNOW YOUR WORDS

Shades of meaning

Although ***synonyms*** are words with similar meaning, they cannot always be interchanged with one another, because they may have different ***shades of meaning.*** For example, ***stride, strut,*** and ***stroll*** are synonyms for ***walk,*** but they do not describe the same kind of walk. Each has a shade of meaning that produces a special visual picture.

Complete the following exercise by selecting the synonyms that are closer in meaning to the italicized words. Consult a dictionary to help you understand the shades of meaning.

1. The Indians said they could ***find*** no road.
   (a) perceive *(b)* discover
2. Some of our party were ***exhausted.***
   (a) weary *(b)* spent
3. The few who knew the danger of the night ***yielded*** to the many.
   (a) submitted *(b)* conceded
4. The cattle were ***killed*** for food.
   (a) slain *(b)* slaughtered
5. The little children were ***famished.***
   (a) hungry *(b)* starved
6. We had nothing to eat but raw hides, and they were on the roof of the ***cabin.***
   (a) house *(b)* hut
7. Even strong men ***wept.***
   (a) cried *(b)* wailed
8. The sunshine only added to our ***misery.***
   (a) wretchedness *(b)* unhappiness
9. Three men were left to ***procure*** wood.
   (a) gain *(b)* obtain
10. She took dolly out and told her of her new ***happiness.***
    (a) gaiety *(b)* joy

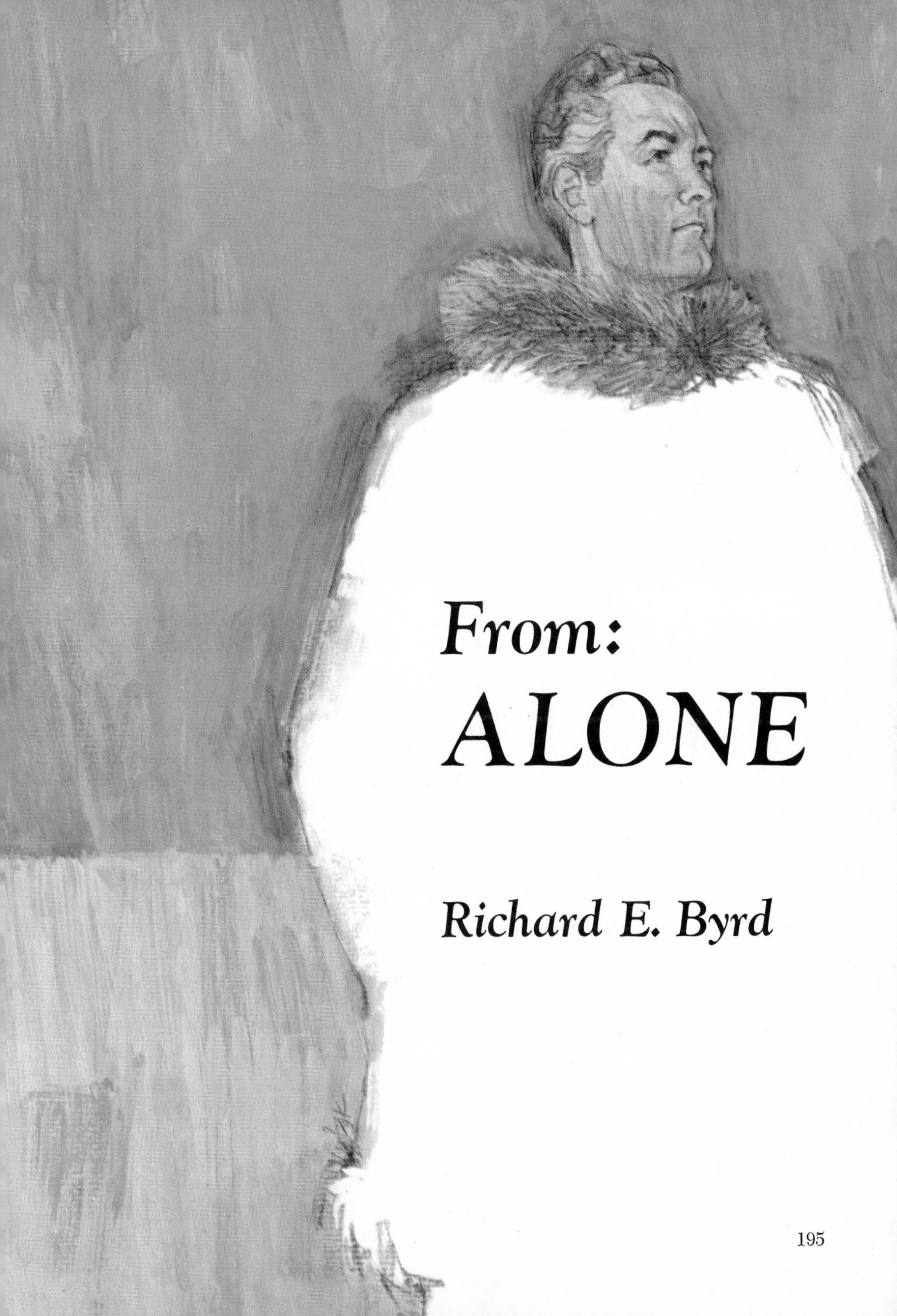

From: ALONE

Richard E. Byrd

In 1928, Admiral Richard E. Byrd, already a veteran of Arctic exploration, helped establish on the Ross Sea, Little America, the first Antarctic outpost. Five years later he returned to Antarctica to establish, for the purpose of making weather observations, another base, even more remote from civilization. This base, Bolling Advance Weather Base, was located on the Ross Ice Barrier, 123 miles south of the main base at Little America. It consisted of one small half-buried hut, numerous weather instruments, and enough bare necessities of life to sustain one man through the polar winter. The following selection is taken from the autobiographical journal that Admiral Byrd kept during his isolated four and a half months' stay at Advance Base.

During the four and a half months I occupied Advance Base alone, I kept a fairly complete diary. Nearly every night, before turning in, I sat down and wrote a thoroughgoing account of the day's doings. Yet, I have been surprised and puzzled, on reading the entries four years later to find that not more of the emotions and circumstances which I have always associated with the first few days alone were actually committed to paper. For afterwards, it seemed that I was never busier. Although I was up mornings before 8 o'clock and rarely went to bed before midnight, the days weren't half long enough for me to accomplish the things I set out to do. A fagged mind in the midst of a task has little patience with autobiographical trifles. As witness:

MARCH 29

. . . Last night, when I finished writing, I noticed a dark patch spreading over the floor from under the stove. A bad leak had opened up the fuel line. Worried about the fire risk, I shut off the stove and searched all through my gear for a spare line. I couldn't find one, which annoyed me; but I finally succeeded in stopping the leak with adhesive tape borrowed from the medical chest. Result: I was up until 4 o'clock this morning, most of the time damned cold, what with the fire out and the temperature at 58° below zero. The cold metal stripped the flesh from three fingers of one hand.

(Later) This being the twenty-second anniversary of the death of Captain Robert Falcon Scott,[1] I have been reading again his immortal diary. He died on this same Barrier, at approximately the same latitude as that of Advance Base. I admire him as I admire few other men; better than most, perhaps, I can appreciate what he went through. . . .

---

1. ***Captain Robert Falcon Scott,*** an Antarctic explorer who led an expedition in 1912. The entire party perished on the return trek.

MARCH 30

There will be no peace until I know that the tractor party has reached Little America. I blame myself for having kept them so long. Well, the radio schedule two days hence will tell the story. I've been occupied with putting the tunnels to rights, and not succeeding very well on account of my shoulder.[2] A fearful amount of lifting remains to be done. So far, I've managed with one hand by using my hip as a fulcrum. . . .

MARCH 31

. . . It's been a deuce of a job to wake up without an alarm clock. And this is puzzling, because I've always been able to fix my mind on the time at which I should awaken, and wake up at that time, almost to the minute. I was born with that gift, and it has stood me in good stead when I dash around the country on lecture tours, leaping from hotels to trains on split-second schedules. But now the gift has simply vanished, perhaps because I am putting too much pressure on it. At night, in the sleeping bag, I whisper to myself: Seven-thirty. Seven-thirty. That's the time you must get up. Seven-thirty. But I've been missing it cleanly—yesterday by nearly an hour, and this morning by half an hour. . . .

April came in on Easter Sunday. It came in blowing and snowing, bringing a southeaster which laced the air with drift but shot the temperature up from —48° to —25° before the day was done. Not a pleasant day, but decidedly on the warmish side, after March's cold. In the morning at 10 o'clock, I attempted the first radio contact with Little America. Considering my inexperience, the fact that it was successful—at least in that I managed to make myself understood—set me up enormously. For, if any contingency truly disturbed me, it was the chance of my losing radio contact with Little America. Not on my account, but on the expedition's account generally. In spite of the orders I had given and the promises made to respect them,[3] I knew in my own heart that both might be ignored if Little America was out of touch with me for long. And, if Little America chose to act, an appalling tragedy might easily result. Realizing how much depended upon my ability to hold communication, I was oppressed by the thought I might fail through sheer ignorance. Dyer had shown me how to make repairs, and Waite had coached me in operating the set; but, whenever I looked at the complications of tubes, switches, and coils, my heart misgave me. I scarcely knew the Morse code. Fortunately Little America could talk to me by radio telephone. So I wasn't obliged to decipher hot outpourings of dots and dashes from skillful operators. But reply I must in dots and dashes, and that I doubted I could do.

Two hours before the schedule I made ready. The gasoline-driven generator which powered the transmitter stood in an alcove, about halfway down the food tunnel, from which a six-inch ventilator pipe went through to the surface. Of course, it couldn't be run in the shack on account of the fumes. To drive the chill out of the metal I brought the engine indoors and put it on the chair, close to the stove. There the engine stood for an hour and a half, dripping with moisture. Then I filled the tank with a mixture of gasoline and lubricating oil, hurried the engine back to the alcove and tried to start it before the metal chilled. I cranked it after the fashion of an outboard motor, using a cord with a wooden handle

2. ***not succeeding . . . shoulder.*** While helping the men from Little America stow the sledges, Byrd had fallen and wrenched his shoulder. 3. ***In spite of the orders . . . to respect them.*** Realizing that darkness and blizzards made traveling unusually dangerous, Byrd had ordered the men at Little America not to come for him until a month after the sun returned even if they lost radio contact with him.

at one end and a knot at the other. The knot slipped into a notch in the small fly-wheel; and, after taking a couple of turns around the wheel, I'd pull hard, spinning the engine. That morning it started off on the first spin. By then it was nearly 10 o'clock, and I had to leg it back into the hut to meet the schedule on time.

The receiver was tuned for 100 meters. The tubes glowed when I threw the switch, and the dial readings showed that everything was as it should be. I waited five minutes or so for the tubes to warm up. Precisely at 10 o'clock, as I clamped on the headphones, I heard Dyer's clear, modulated voice saying: "KFZ calling KFY. This is KFZ calling KFY. Will you please come in?" Excited, as nervous as a student pilot on his first solo hop, I cut in the transmitter and keyed: "OK, KFZ. All well. How are trail parties?" Or at least that was what I tried to spell out. The dot-dash equivalents were as confusing and unfamiliar as Arabic, and in the middle of a sentence I forgot completely what I was supposed to be sending.

Nevertheless, Charlie Murphy came on a moment later with the news that both the Advance Base crew and Innes-Taylor's[4] party were safely at Little America. "All hands are well," he continued. After a few more remarks I heard him say, "Is everything all right with you?"

I was encouraged to make a more elaborate answer. "Great, working hard. Wind here thirty miles. Snowing. Think blow coming."

Murphy chuckled, "I think John got most of that. No snow here as yet, but an easterly is making with lots of drift."

The contact lasted only twenty minutes. The schedule days were confirmed: Sundays, Tuesdays, and Thursdays, at 10 o'clock, with daily emergency schedules to take effect at the same hour whenever my regular schedule was missed. Just before we signed off, Charlie said, "Dyer rates you D minus on your debut, but I think you deserve better than that."

To this I retorted, "Yes, world's finest radio operator south of Lat. 80°."

That night I wrote in my diary: ". . .The fact that the tractor party and Innes-Taylor's party are safely at Little America has raised my spirits to a new high. This is wonderful news. For the first time, after the months of struggle and anxiety, Little America is at last buttoned up for the winter, and so am I. If we both obey our common sense, nothing untoward need happen. I am free to take stock of my own situation and to make the most of the experience that is to be mine. I realize at this moment more than ever before how much I have been wanting something like this. I must confess feeling a tremendous exhilaration."

APRIL 6

I am sleeping fairly well, which is a blessing. But I still can't seem to wake up when I want to—missed by three quarters of an hour this morning—which is a nuisance. I don't know why I've lost the faculty; I'll have to regain it somehow. When the long night comes, I shall have no light to awaken me.

I'm keeping the skylights cleared of snow to enjoy what little daylight remains. But all three are frosted over most of the time. When the temperature at the ceiling passes freezing, the frost melts; and the drip-drip-drip makes little ice stalagmites on the floor, which is always cold. I've proved, with a thermometer, that when I'm sitting down the temperature at the level of my feet is anywhere from 10° to 30° colder than at my head . . . .

4. *Innes-Taylor,* a captain in Byrd's company who had led a base-laying trek for the future spring operations. His party then helped the Advance Base crew to set up the equipment needed by Admiral Byrd for his stay at Advance Base, after which both parties returned to Little America.

APRIL 7

The six months' day is slowly dying, and the darkness is descending very gently. Even at midday the sun is only several times its diameter above the horizon. It is cold and dull. At its brightest it scarcely gives light enough to throw a shadow. A funeral gloom hangs in the twilight sky. This is the way the world will look to the last man when it dies.

APRIL 8

Were it not for my lame shoulder and the difficulties caused by the weather instruments (which were designed for a warmer place), I should be making much better progress in preparing myself for the oncoming darkness. Unpredictable things, small but often annoying, make continuous demands upon my time. For example, I find that even when there is no drift, the three-and-one-half inch outlet ventilator fills every three or four days with ice (or rather with what looks like névé, which is between snow and ice). It's due, I think, to condensation. Anyhow, I've got to watch that. Good ventilation I must have at any cost. The pipe being held in place by friction, I just pull it out of the hole, carry it below, and lay it on the stove to thaw. The icy stuff won't pound out. It has to be melted.

Just to complicate matters, the same trouble is developing in the topside end of the stovepipe. Around dinner time (or whenever the stove is running hot) the ice melts, and the water runs through a hole in the elbow. Luckily, the register, which stands directly underneath, has a glass top; otherwise it would have been out of commission long ago. I have tied a can under the elbow to catch the water. Nevertheless, I'm rather worried about the blockage in the pipe; unless the fumes from the stove escape to the surface, I shall have trouble. . . .

* * *

Thus the first part of April hurried like a man on an errand. I was occupied with all kinds of small projects. Aside from the Escape Tunnel,[5] the hardest task was putting the food and fuel tunnels to rights. These two parallel corridors, it will be remembered, ran out from the veranda and were separated by a three-foot wall of snow. Both were dark as dungeons; whenever I worked in them it was by the light of a storm lantern or flashlight. In the artificial light, though, they acquired a breathless radiance. The ice crystals, which were thickening on the canvas roofing, glistened like candelabra; and the walls glowed with a sharp, blue nakedness.

In the fuel tunnel were four fifty-gallon kerosene drums, weighing about five hundred pounds each, which we set in individual recesses. Besides this, I had 360 gallons of Stoddard solvent for the stove, which came in handy twelve-gallon drums weighing about ninety pounds each. In addition I had about ninety gallons of gasoline for the radio generator, in two large drums at the far end of the tunnel. Except for the fact that the drums all stood upright so as to prevent leakage from the bungs, the place used to remind me sometimes of a French wine cellar, especially the shadows cast by my figure as I moved about in front of the lantern.

The food tunnel, which opened directly in front of the door, was a different sort of place. There the walls were formed by the boxes of foodstuffs themselves. Wanting something, I simply had to pry open the sides with a chisel and take out whatever I needed, leaving the empty box as a permanent wall. What disturbed me was the haphazard manner in which the boxes had

---

5. ***Escape Tunnel.*** To avoid being trapped in the shack in case the trapdoor became stuck, Byrd hollowed an escape tunnel leading from the food tunnel to the outside.

been stowed. Here and there the walls were bulging out; the beans were hopelessly mixed with the canned meats, tomato juice, and boxes of odds and ends; and the roof was caving in. All this offended my growing sense of neatness. During my spare time I set about rearranging the whole setup.

I didn't try to rush the job. If the polar regions have taught me anything, it is patience. I rarely spent more than an hour on any one job, preferring to shift to something else. In that way I was able to show a little progress each day on all the important jobs, and at the same time keep from becoming bored with any one. This was a way of bringing variety into an existence which would be basically monotonous.

* * *

Not that the materials for variety were ever lacking to a mind capable of forgetting what civilization was like. The sheer rigorousness of the Barrier took care of that. At times I felt as if I were the last survivor of an Ice Age, striving to hold on with the flimsy tools bequeathed by an easy-going, temperate world. Cold does queer things. At 50° below zero a flashlight dies out in your hand. At —55° kerosene will freeze, and the flame will dry up on the wick. At —60° rubber turns brittle. One day, I remember, the antenna wire snapped in my hands when I tried to bend it to make a new connection. Below —60° cold will find the last microscopic touch of oil in an instrument and stop it dead. If there is the slightest breeze, you can hear your breath freeze as it floats away, making a sound like that of Chinese firecrackers. As does the morning dew, rime coats every exposed object. And if you work too hard and breathe too deeply, your lungs will sometimes feel as if they were on fire.

Cold—even April's relatively moderate cold—gave me plenty to think about. The novocaine in my medical kit froze and shattered the glass tubes. So did the chemicals in the fire bombs. Two cases of tomato juice shattered their bottles. Whenever I brought canned food inside the shack I had to let it stand all day near the stove to thaw. On very cold days the kerosene and Stoddard solvent flowed like cylinder oil; I dug a deep hole in the tunnel floor for my can to lengthen the drop in the rubber hose which I used as a syphon. Frost was forever collecting on the electrical contact points of the wind vane and wind cups. Some days I climbed the twelve-foot anemometer pole two and three times to clean them. It was a bitter job, especially on blustery nights. With my legs twined around the slender pole, my arms flung over the cleats, and my free hands trying to scrape the contact point clean with a knife and at the same time hold a flashlight to see, I qualified for the world's coldest flagpole sitter. I seldom came down from that pole without a frozen finger, toe, nose, or cheek.

The shack was always freezingly cold in the morning. I slept with the door open. When I arose the inside temperature (depending upon the surface weather) might be anywhere from 10° to 40° below zero. Frost coated the sleeping bag where my breath had condensed during the night; my socks and boots, when I picked them up, were so stiff with frozen sweat that I first had to work them between my hands. A pair of silk gloves hung from a nail over the bunk, where I could grab them the first thing. Yet, even with their protection, my fingers would sting and burn from the touch of the lamp and stove as I lighted them. The old flesh had sloughed off the tips, and the new flesh for a while was insufferably tender. So I had my troubles. Some came from my own inadequacies. At first I had a devil of a time with the weather instruments. The traces became horribly blotched, the pens stuck, and the instruments themselves stopped without rhyme or reason. But, one way or another, I usually managed to contrive a cure. I learned how to thin the ink with glycerine to keep it from freezing, and how to cut the oil in the instruments with gasoline and rub the delicate parts with graphite which wasn't affected so much by the cold.

Yet, in playing Admirable Crichton[6] to myself, I was far from distinguished. Many of my Advance Base concoctions wouldn't have passed Captain's Inspection. In the Navy phrase, they were generally no better than "lash-up." As to that, I plead *nolo contendere*[7] and throw myself on the court's mercy. An officer, I was learning to do things again with my hands. My standards were humble. If anything, I was again a worshiping disciple of the God of 2.5 of Naval Academy days, the god of the hairs-breadth passing grade, as personified by Tecumseh,[8] at whose bust we midshipmen used to chip penny offerings as we marched to examinations. By Academy standards, I should have "bilged out" of Advance Base on cooking alone.

Breakfast didn't count. I rarely took more than tea and a whole-wheat biscuit. Lunch was habitually an out-of-the-can affair, consisting usually of tomato juice, Eskimo biscuits, and frequently a cold meat or fish—either corned beef, tongue, or sardines. These I prepared in masterly fashion. But supper, by rights the high spot in an explorer's day, the hot meal toward which a cold and hungry man looks with mounting anticipation—this meal for a while was a daily fiasco.

I have only to close my eyes to witness again the succession of culinary disasters. Consider what my diary designated as The Corn Meal Incident. Into a boiler I dumped what seemed a moderate quantity of meal, added a little water, and stood it on the stove to boil. That simple formula gave birth to a Hydra-headed monster. The stuff began to swell and dry up, swell and dry up, with fearful blowing and sucking noises. All innocently I added water, more water, and still more water. Whereupon the boiler erupted like Vesuvius. All the pots and pans within reach couldn't begin to contain the corn meal that overflowed. It oozed over the stove. It spattered the ceiling. It covered me from head to foot. If I hadn't acted resolutely, I might have been drowned in corn meal. Seizing the container in my mittened hands, I rushed it to the door and hurled it far into the food tunnel. There it continued to give off deadly golden lava until the cold finally stilled the crater.

There were other disasters of the same order. There was the Dried Lima Beans Incident of April 10th. ("It's amazing," the diary reports soberly, "how much water lima beans can absorb, and how long it takes them to cook. At supper time I had enough half-cooked lima beans to feed a ship's company.") My first jelly dessert bounced like a rubber ball under my knife; the flapjacks had to be scraped from the pan with a chisel. ("And you, the man who sat at a thousand banquets," goes the accusing entry of April 12th.) I dreaded banquets before I went to Advance Base; and I have come to dread them since. But in April's dark hours I ransacked my memory, trying to remember what they were like. All that I could recall was filet mignon spiced and darkened to the color of an old cavalry boot; or lobster thermidor; or squabs perched on triangles of toast; or chicken salad heaped on billowing lettuce. All these were far beyond the simple foods in my larder. When I did experiment, the results filled the shack with pungent burning smells and coated the skillets with awful gummy residues. But, in spite of the missing cook book, the record was not one of unmitigated failure. Resolved to make a last stand, I took the surviving chicken, hung it for two days from a nail over the stove to

---

6. ***Admirable Crichton*** (krī'tən), title-character of Sir James Barrie's play about an English butler whose qualities of leadership and resourcefulness emerge when he is cast away on a desert island with the aristocratic family for which he works. 7. ***nolo contendere*** (nō'lō kən ten'də rē), a Latin term used in criminal cases which is equivalent to the plea of guilty but without the defendant's admission of guilt. 8. ***If anything, I was . . . Tecumseh,*** a reference to the passing grade point (2.5) at the United States Naval Academy. The statue outside the Naval Academy is not of Tecumseh, a Shawnee Indian chief, but of a Delaware chief, Tamenend.

thaw, boiled it all one day, seasoned it with salt and pepper, and served. The soup, which was an unexpected by-product, was delicious; that night I broached a bottle of cider and drank a toast to Escoffier.[9]

* * *

Thus April moved along. Each night, as the last formal act of the day, I crossed off another date on the big calendar on the wall, and each morning consulted the calendar the first thing, to make sure that I hadn't forgotten. Above me the day was dying; the night was rising in its place. Ever since late in February, when the sun had rolled down from its lofty twenty-four-hour circuit around the sky, it had been setting a little earlier at night, rising a little later in the morning. Now, with less than a fortnight of daylight left in this latitude, it was just a monstrous ball which could barely hoist itself free from the horizon. It would wheel along for a few hours, obscured by mist, then sink out of sight in the north not long after noon. I found myself watching it as one might watch a departing lover.

APRIL 21

The morning is the hardest time. It is hard enough anywhere for a man to begin the day's work in darkness; where I am it is doubly difficult. One may be a long time realizing it, but cold and darkness deplete the body gradually; the mind turns sluggish; and the nervous system slows up in its responses. This morning I had to admit to myself that I was lonely. Try as I may, I find I can't take my loneliness casually; it is too big. But I must not dwell on it. Otherwise I am undone.

At home I usually awaken instantly, in full possession of my faculties. But that's not the case here. It takes me some minutes to collect my wits; I seem to be groping in cold reaches of interstellar space, lost and bewildered. The room is a non-dimensional darkness, without shadow or substance; even after all these days I sometimes ask myself: Where am I? What am I doing here? I discover myself straining, as if trying to hear something in a place where no sound could possibly exist. Ah, yes. Tick-tick, tick-tick-tick, tick. The busy, friendly voices of the register and thermograph on the shelves, each distinct and dramatic—sounds I can understand and follow, even as a mariner emerging from the darkness of the boundless ocean can recognize and follow a coast by the bell buoys offshore.

As I dread getting up, I just lie and listen to these sharp, clean beats, letting them form little conversations, little rhythms, even short stories in my mind. They have a pleasant, narcotizing effect. The slightest move, disturbing the nice temperature balance in the sleeping bag, sends a blast of frosty air down my back or stomach. My skin crawls at the thought of touching foot to the deck. But up I must for the 8 A.M. observation; and so I lie there, mustering resolve for a wrenching heave into the dark. Clear of the bag, I feel around on the shelf at the head of the bunk until I locate the silk gloves which I wear to protect my fingers while handling cold metal. After putting these on, I light the lantern, which hangs from a nail over the bunk. The wick, hard with frost, seldom takes fire easily. The flame catches and goes out, catches and goes out. Then, as it steadies on the wick, the light gradually pushes a liquid arc into the room, bringing my possessions one by one into its wavering yellow orbit. I suppose it is really a gloomy light. Things on the opposite wall are scarcely touched by it. But to me that feeble burning is a daily miracle. With light the day begins, the mind escapes from darkness, and numbness leaves the body. I sleep in my underclothes, with my pants and shirt and socks

9. *Escoffier* (es kô fyā'), a famous French chef and a noted writer on cookery (1847-1935).

heaped upon the table. Needless to say, I dress faster than a fireman. . . .

Thus the Advance Base day began. The next day, exactly a month after I flew from Little America, I sat down and wrote—at odd moments during the day—exactly what I did from waking to sleeping. The whole entry ran close to 3,500 words. The day happened to be a Sunday, but the flow of the hours at Advance Base was no different from that of any other day. Since the entry describes a typical day, at least for this period, I have decided to include it, except for slight editing against repetition:

APRIL 22

. . . After dressing, the first thing I do, of course, and that right lively, is to start the stove. The fuel is usually somewhat congealed, and it takes ten minutes or so for enough to run from the tank to fill the burner. I crave hot tea in the morning; for, rather than wait for the stove to warm up, I heat a quart of water (ice, of course) with meta tablets, which are inch-long wafers of solidified alcohol. I dump half a dozen of these in a can, and set the pan of ice in a metal rack over the hot blue flame.

The silence during these first minutes of the day is always depressing. It seems real, as if a gloomy critic were brooding in the shadows, on the verge of saying something unpleasant. Sharing his mood, I merely grunt a good morning. My exercises help to snap me out of this. Stretched out flat on the bunk, I go through fifteen minutes of various kinds of muscle stretchings. By the time I've finished, the water is hot. I brew about a pint of tea in a big porcelain cup, and dump in lots of sugar and powdered milk. After a sip or two, I put the cup over the flame, and hold it there until it gets piping hot; so hot, in fact, that it burns the mouth and throat. Thus fortified, I am ready for the observation.

A few minutes before 8 o'clock, I noted the barometric pressure (28.79 inches). A quick glance at the inside thermograph, just before I buttoned on my canvas windbreaker, showed a topside temperature in the minus forties. I heated the flashlight a minute or two over the stove; that would keep the batteries from freezing. Without bothering to turn the switch, I went into the pitch-black veranda, and up the ladder. That little route I knew by heart: a step past the door, two to the left, six rungs up.

The trapdoor stuck a little. The violence of my second heave sent a shower of crystals down my neck, making me shiver. It was still very dark, but an impalpable fog lay close to the surface, giving the day a gray look; and a relentless flutter of snow was in my face. I still use the words "day" and "night" having no equivalents for the divisions whose differences are only in time; "day" seems a meaningless description of the soggy pall which this morning lay over the Barrier. As I looked about, I was conscious only of solitude and my own forlornness.

The thermograph in the shelter showed a minimum temperature of 48.5° below zero and a maximum of 46° since the last observation. I reset the pin in the minimum thermometer and brushed out the rime and snow with a whisk broom which I carried in my pocket. Altogether I was not on the surface more than five minutes, counting the time spent taking notes on cloudiness, mist, drift, precipitation, and the rest of it; but it was long enough for me to decide that a blow was in the making.

Although the fire had not yet driven the cold out of the room, the place seemed snug and pleasant when I returned. The first thing I did was to light a candle, which I put on the table to brighten the middle of the room. While still standing up with my coat on, I jotted down on a piece of scratch paper the data I had gathered topside—I felt too cold to sit down. Meanwhile I polished off another pint of tea. Except for a biscuit, which was hard as rock, this was my breakfast.

8:30 o'clock. Some of the ice in the water bucket had melted; before I fetched in another snow block from the veranda, I poured enough water into a basin to wash my hands. Now was the time to decide what to have for supper and to begin thawing it. My choice was pea soup, seal meat, and stewed corn. From the meat box I took a five-inch slab of seal, black and unappetizing, which I hung from a nail over the stove to thaw. The can of corn I lifted from the cold deck to the shelf close behind the stove. The four-gallon gravity tank on the stove needs filling every three days; today is a filling day. I shut off the flame, unshipped the tank, and carried it into the fuel tunnel, a matter of thirty-five feet or so to the farthest drum. A stick driven into the wall served as a peg for the lantern. By its dim light I found the rubber siphon coiled over one of the drums. I had to suck on this for dear life to start the flow; and, while waiting for the tank to fill, I examined the roof to make sure that it wasn't caving again. Everything was holding nicely.

Just about 9 o'clock, I commenced the usual rigmarole of preparations for the radio schedule. I finished barely in time to pop topside for the 10 A.M. auroral "ob."[10] Nothing doing—heavy clouds still. As I tuned in the receiver, Dyer was calling KFY. Today's was an interesting conversation. The general objectives of the big exploration campaign in the spring had been set up before I left Little America, but certain revisions in the plan seemed desirable after closer scrutiny; and these Charlie Murphy took up, after discussions with Poulter, June, Innes-Taylor, Rawson, Siple, and the scientific staff. With the suggested revisions I was in accord.

Just before we shut down, Dyer gave me a time tick, which he had picked up from either the U.S. Naval Observatory or Greenwich, I've forgotten which. "When I say 'now,'" Dyer warned, "it will be 10:53 o'clock. You have thirty-five seconds to go ...Twenty seconds...Ten seconds...Now." One chronometer, I found, was running 2 minutes, 10 seconds fast, the other 31 seconds fast, the third was 1 minute, 20 seconds slow. I noted the facts in my records. I must know the exact time in order to synchronize my observations with those at Little America. After that I carefully wound all three chronometers.

After the schedule I had an hour to devote to the Escape Tunnel. It's just about a third done—thirteen feet, to be exact. I'm far behind my schedule of a foot a day, but my lame shoulder has been something of a handicap. This morning I finished cutting shelves in the sides for superfluous books. Later on I expect to build alcoves in the tunnel for other gear. There isn't an inch of blank space anywhere in the shack. That's because I've been bringing in so much stuff from the boxes in the tunnel. Looking around, I was almost horrified at the amount of clothing, food, tools, gear, and other things it takes to support even one man and a scientific station here. Much of the stuff could just as well remain outside; but I suppose I'd get bored trotting in and out every time I want something....

* * *

The hour between 12 and 1 o'clock was, as always, the busiest. Exactly at noon I inked the register pens, changed the sheet, and wound the clock (the tracing had turned irregular, which meant that the contact points were foul).

So, topside, armed with a flashlight looped around my neck, a whisk broom, and an open knife in the chest pocket of my parka. Reaching the top of the pole, I whipped off the reindeer-skin mittens, which were also on a cord around my neck, and fell to work on the wind vane. I lifted it off its seat, brushed the snow out of the

10. "ob," an abbreviated term for observing or gathering of data.

cups, and scraped the contact points clean, all the while cursing the cold torturing my fingers and face.

My wrist watch showed 1 o'clock. No necessity for an auroral observation—still overcast. But time to wind the inside thermograph and change the recording sheet. After that, lunch. I am half through Somerset Maugham's *Of Human Bondage*, and I read a chapter as I ate. A meal eaten alone and in silence is no pleasure. So I fell into the habit of reading while I ate. In that way I can lose myself completely for a time. The days I don't read I feel like a barbarian brooding over a chunk of meat.

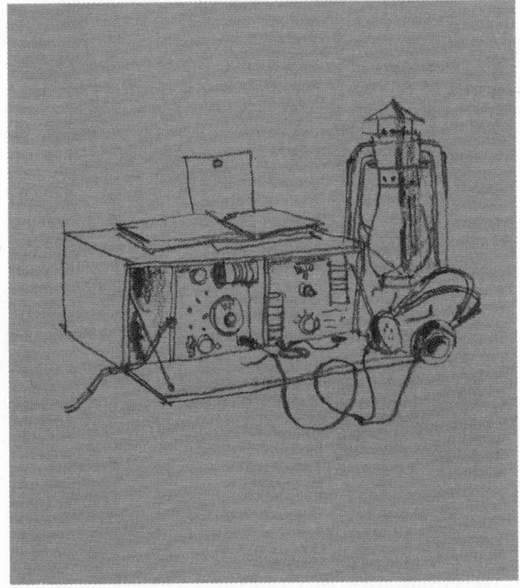

A moment ago there came a tremendous boom, as if tons of dynamite had exploded in the Barrier. [From seismic soundings taken the following summer we learned that Advance Base was underlaid by a stratum of ice and snow about seven hundred feet thick. The presence of this perpetual carapace of ice throughout most of Antarctica is one of the principal features which differentiate it from the Arctic, where, with few exceptions, the ground is uncovered during the summer.] The sound was muffled by distance; yet, it was inherently ominous breaking through the silence. But I confess that any sound which interrupts the evenness of this place is welcome. I had the feeling that the Barrier was moving slightly. The handle of the lantern rattled against the tin base. The flashlight, hanging from a nail on a shelf in front of me, seemed to sway a little. This is what is known as a Barrier quake—a subsidence of great areas of snow contracting from cold.

Half an hour of shoveling drift was on the afternoon program. Before I went topside, I picked up the slop pail, already half frozen from standing on the floor. I was careful to dump it to leeward so that a mound wouldn't be formed to catch drift. Put in my half hour leveling off the snow around the shack. Not so difficult today. The snow lies a couple feet deep on the roof, but for the time being does not seem to be deepening. After finishing that I pulled the ventilator up through the roof, and carried it below to thaw on the stove. For once it was fairly free of ice. After a few minutes on the stove, the ice loosened; and I was able to jar it out with a hammer. The chunk of seal over the stove was steadily dripping drops of blood and water.

Then I had an hour to myself. I spent part of it entering my rough meteorological notes on U.S. Weather Bureau form Number 1083. Then I tinkered with the handle of the victrola, which had come unscrewed the night before. Just before 4 o'clock I put on my windproofs and went topside for the auroral "ob." The overcast had thinned a little, and the snow had stopped; but, beyond a pale, trembling glow in the dark edging of cloud, there was no sign of the aurora. A quiet day for the auroral department, I said to myself, and went walking.

Because of the fog and the threat of blizzard in the air, I decided not to go very far. It is my practice to walk between an hour and two hours a day—when I have time. The walk gives me change and it also provides another means of exercise. Starting out, I usually stop every few steps and do a knee bend or stoop or any one of a

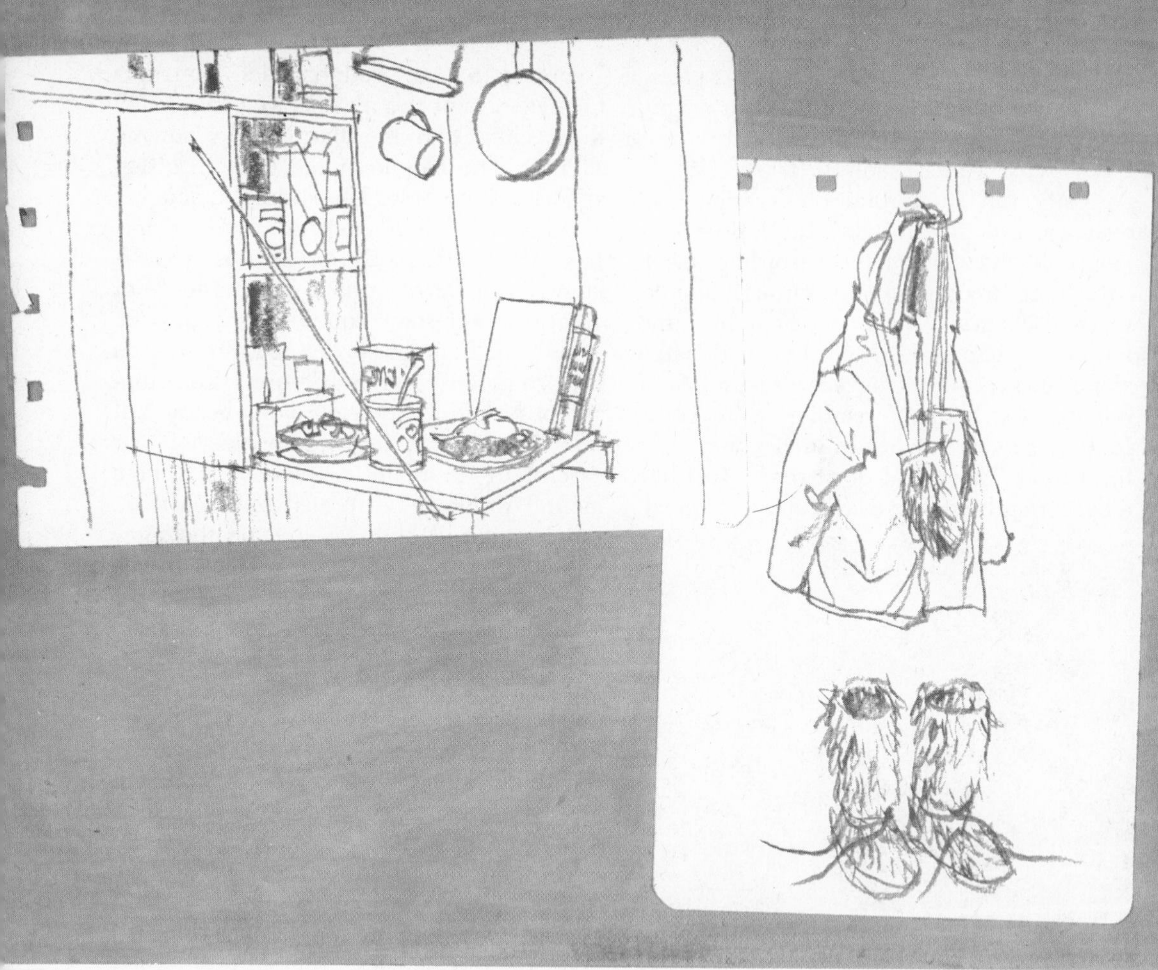

dozen exercises I enjoy. Today, however, I favored myself. My lungs hurt a little when I breathe, and I may have frosted them[11] on the 18th a little more than I realized.

The last half of the walk is the best part of the day, the time when I am most nearly at peace with myself and circumstances. Thoughts of life and the nature of things flow smoothly and so naturally as to create an illusion that one is swimming harmoniously in the broad current of the cosmos. During this hour I undergo a sort of intellectual levitation, although my thinking is usually on earthy, practical matters. Last night, before turning in, I read, in Santayana's *Soliloquies in England,* an essay on friendship. I thought of that and the structure of social relationships and the mechanics of friendship as they have operated in my life. The negative aspects—the betrayals, the disappointments, and the bitternesses—I shut out entirely. Only by ruthlessly exorcising the disillusioning and unpleasant thoughts can I maintain any feeling of real detachment, any sense of being wholly apart from selfish concerns.

I made many turns back and forth before I decided to go below. It was very dark then, too dark to see the upperworks of the

11. ***I may have frosted them . . .*** This event occurred while Byrd was in the process of hollowing out his escape tunnel.

hut or even the anemometer pole until I was hard by; so I finished the walk by flashlight. On the way down the ladder, I noticed that one of the rungs had sprung, and made a mental note to fix that tomorrow. After getting rid of my heavy clothes, I set about the afternoon ritual of lighting the gasoline pressure lamp. Anyhow, I have made it a ritual. Its light is twice as strong as that of the storm lantern; it reaches every corner of the room. But I have forced myself to use it sparingly because it consumes a lot of gasoline, and, also, because it gives off certain disagreeable fumes. But I find that I crave light as a thirsting man craves water; and just the fact of having this lantern alive in the night hours makes an immense difference.

The water in the bucket was hot when I dipped my finger—just right for the soup. Making a great clatter of pans and whistling out of tune anything that came to my lips, I got the supper ready: hot pea soup (made from a stick of dried peas, called erbswurst); fried young seal, which was very tender; plus corn, tea, powdered milk, and canned peaches for dessert. Excellent, all of it. Just before dessert I went topside for the 7 P.M. auroral "ob." Sky had cleared quite a bit. A vague, luminous belt lay sprawled through the northeast and southwest quarters of the sky, but it had little color or life. The data were dutifully entered in the records; structure H.A. (made up of homogeneous quiet arcs); intensity 2; altitude, about 35° above the horizon. Slight glow about 10° to the right, in the direction of Little America.

When I had finished the peaches, I pushed my book and the dishes to one side, got out the deck of cards, and played two or three hands of Canfield. No luck. At a dollar a point, I lost $15 to my imaginary banker. And then my only real luxury—music. I wound up the battered green victrola, slipped on a Strauss waltz, "Wine, Women and Song," released the brake, and jumped simultaneously for the dishes. The idea is to finish the dishes before the phonograph runs down. The machine has a double-length spring, and I've rigged a rude sort of repeater which plays a small record four or five times on one winding. Tonight, though, no sound came out. Cause: frozen oil in the works. I stood the machine on a corner of the stove. In a little while the record began to turn, very slowly at first, making lugubrious notes, then faster and faster. I transferred it to the table and fell to on the dishes, going like mad. Tonight they outlasted the record by fifteen seconds: a very poor showing indeed, although I credit the defeat to the head start the phonograph got while it was warming up on the stove.

While adding to this diary, I suddenly realized that I had almost forgotten the 8 P.M. "ob." Hurriedly threw on a coat, cap, and mittens, and scrambled topside. Still cloudy; the pin in the minimum thermometer stood at 50° below zero; the wind was still in the northwest and very light. But I could still smell a blizzard. I was glad to return to the snugness of the shack.

Except for the 10 P.M. auroral "ob," my day's work was finished. I spent the few remaining hours playing the phonograph and completing this entry.... The day is about to end. I have just finished my nightly bath, or, rather, third of a bath; for each night I wash a different third of my body. I don't know how I came to decide upon that arbitrary division, unless it was that I discovered my conscience could be placated by performing the ritual in installments. Anyhow, I started bathing this way during my first stay at Little America, and have found it satisfactory. I really don't get dirty. The Barrier is as clean as the top of Mount Everest, but habits must be satisfied, and the truth is that I find the bath a diversion. And my body always feels refreshed afterwards.

It is now close to midnight. In a moment I shall go to bed. I know exactly what I shall do. With a pencil stroke, I shall cross this day off the calendar; then fetch snow and alcohol tablets for the morning tea, and, finally, make sure that the instruments are functioning properly. This inspection over, I shall take a quick glance from the hatch to see whether anything unusual is happening in the auroral department. After battening down the trapdoor, I shall undress, turn down the pressure lantern, put out the fire, open the door, and jump for the sleeping bag, leaving the storm lantern burning over my head. That part of the routine is automatic. As long as heat remains in the shack, I shall read; tonight it will be the second volume of the *Life of Alexander*, which I've nearly finished. That part is by choice. When my hands turn numb, I'll reach up and blow out the lantern, but not until I have first made sure that the flashlight is somewhere in the sleeping bag, where my body will keep the battery warm.

I don't try to force myself to sleep, as I sometimes do at home. My whole life here in a sense is an experiment in harmony, and I let the bodily processes achieve a natural equilibrium. As a rule, it doesn't take me long to go to sleep. But a man can live a lifetime in a few half-dreaming moments of introspection between going to bed and falling asleep: a lifetime reordered and edited to satisfy the ever-changing demands of the mind.

OPERATION DEEP FREEZE

When Admiral Richard E. Byrd manned the Advance Base weather station back in 1934, the vast area of ice and snow of Antarctica was still unexplored. Since the time of the Advance Base expedition, scientific interest in Antarctica has rapidly increased. Exploration of the continent and scientific analysis of data obtained there were the project of the 1957-1958 International Geophysical Year and the United States Navy's supporting mission "Operation Deep Freeze." Many permanent stations have been set up, resulting in improvements in communication methods and equipment which have greatly aided scientists, both in obtaining data and in sharing their "finds" with the rest of the world.

What do the activities in Antarctica mean? What is the importance of this rugged mass of land and ice which, until recently, was inhabited only by penguins, seals, and other wild creatures? First, there has been a continuation of the work begun by Byrd, obtaining information on weather and atmospheric conditions. Scientists also have learned a great deal about Antarctica itself, its geological features and its history as written in the rocks and the many fossils which have been uncovered. With the discovery of coal in Antarctica, the continent is now being looked upon as a possible source for raw materials and minerals.

In spite of the advances, it is really too early to evaluate fully the importance of Antarctica; the answer to this question lies in the future. Before leading his fifth and final mission to Antarctica in 1955, Admiral Byrd stated, ". . . I believe, as the scientists do, that the things we can learn there will have a profound effect upon the lives of us all."

WHAT DO YOU SAY?

1. (a) What similarity in theme does this autobiography have with the three preceding autobiographies? *(b)* Has the author succeeded in presenting an objective view of himself and his experiences? Quote lines to support your answer.

2. (a) How does Byrd constantly remind you that the purpose of his stay at Advance Base was scientific? *(b)* How does he prevent technical details from becoming monotonous? *(c)* What seemed to be the most difficult part of his experience?

3. Choose several details of Byrd's experiences and explain what these details reveal about his personality and character.

4. In recording his stay at Advance Base, Byrd reveals besides scientific data his philosophy, a sense of humor, and an ability to use colorful comparisons and picturesque language. Find examples of each of these elements.

AUTHOR'S CRAFT

Selection and condensation

For the autobiographer as well as for the biographer, ***selection*** and ***condensation*** of material are important problems. But it is an even more difficult problem for the autobiographer than for the biographer. Just as a person may have difficulty in presenting an objective view of himself, he may also have difficulty in estimating the importance of events in his life. What might seem vivid and important to him might seem trivial and uninteresting to a reader.

Admiral Byrd faced this problem in writing ***Alone,*** the autobiographical record of his stay at the Bolling Advance Weather Base in Antarctica. The journal that he kept during that time provided the basis for this fragmentary autobiography. But Byrd was a scientist on a mission, and the journal was lengthy and contained many personal references and technical details that would have held little meaning for most people. So, he found himself in the position of most other autobiographers. He had to select and condense the material that would be of interest and meaning to the public for which he was writing. The result, of course, was a vivid and exciting account of his lonely existence on a new American frontier. What sort of details not included in his autobiography do you think Byrd may have had in his original journal?

UNIT 2 REVIEW

1. In this unit you learned that an important element of both biography and autobiography is the careful selection of details which reveal the subject's character. From each of the autobiographies of Helen Keller, Booker T. Washington, and Admiral Byrd, select at least three details which help to reveal aspects of the subjects' personalities. Refer if necessary to the "Author's Craft" articles on pages 160 and 177.

2. (a) What prose elements are common to both biographies and short stories? (b) What are the differences? (c) Explain how a short story could be partly biographical or autobiographical.

3. In the biography of George Rogers Clark, the author carefully and accurately develops the background and setting against which Clark's character is revealed. In the autobiographies of Admiral Byrd, Booker T. Washington, Helen Keller, and Virginia Reed, how important is the setting in helping to reveal their characters?

4. (a) In what ways does a character sketch differ from a biography or autobiography? (b) From the selections in this unit, find an example of a character sketch. Explain why your example fits into this category.

5. (a) The six people in this unit differ from each other in their personalities and in their experiences. Explain why each of them provides a good subject for a biography. (b) Could a biography be written about anyone? Why or why not?

SUGGESTED READING

ANDERSON, MARIAN, *My Lord, What A Morning.* (Viking) The author describes her childhood in Philadelphia and her long struggle to become a concert singer.

BRICKHILL, PAUL, *Reach for the Sky.* (Norton) Having lost both legs in an air crash, British aviator Douglas Bader succeeds in overcoming his handicap to become a hero of World War II.

BUCK, PEARL S., *My Several Worlds.* (Day) Excitement is the keynote of this autobiography in which Pearl Buck describes her childhood in China and her efforts to promote international understanding between the Chinese and other peoples.

COUSINS, NORMAN, *Dr. Schweitzer of Lambaréné.* The ideals of Dr. Albert Schweitzer and his love for humanity are vividly portrayed in this intimate picture of his work in Africa.

DAUGHERTY, JAMES, *Daniel Boone.* (Viking) The frontier provides the background for the biography of the famous pioneer whose courage and fortitude helped to build America.

DOOLEY, THOMAS A., *Dr. Tom Dooley's Three Great Books.* (Farrar, Strauss • Signet Books) In *Deliver Us From Evil, The Edge of Tomorrow,* and *The Night They Burned the Mountain,* Dr. Dooley describes his experiences as a medical missionary in Laos.

EWEN, DAVID, *The Story of Irving Berlin.* (Holt) The biography of one of America's most famous song writers.

FORBES, ESTHER, *Paul Revere and the World He Lived In.* (Houghton) Against the background of the American Revolution, Paul Revere is brought to life in a setting that accurately pictures the people, places, and events of his time.

FRANK, ANNE, *The Diary of A Young Girl.* (Doubleday • Pocket Books, Inc.) A young Jewish girl describes her life in Holland during the Nazi regime.

GILBRETH, FRANK BUNKER AND ERNESTINE GILBRETH CAREY, *Cheaper by the Dozen.* (Crowell • Bantam Books) The antics of the twelve Gilbreth children and their efficiency-loving father are humorously portrayed by two of the "dozen."

GRAHAM, SHIRLEY AND GEORGE D. LIPSCOMB, *Dr. George Washington Carver: Scientist.* (Messner) The authors present a human portrait of the life and achievements of Dr. Carver, who was born the son of a slave and who rose above nearly overwhelming odds to become a scientist.

GUNTHER, JOHN, *Death Be Not Proud.* (Harper • Pyramid Books) In this memoir to his seventeen-year-old son, the author reveals a boy's courage and quiet heroism in the face of great pain.

KUGELMASS, J. ALVIN, *Roald Amundsen.* (Messner) In this biography of the first man to explore the polar regions, the author describes Amundsen's early training and his adventures as an explorer.

MARSHALL, CATHARINE, *A Man Called Peter.* (McGraw) Written by his wife, this story presents a personal portrait of Peter Marshall, minister and chaplain of the United States Senate.

STUART, JESSE, *The Thread That Runs So True* (Scribner • Scribner Library) The author describes his career as a teacher, from his first class in a one-room school in Kentucky through increasingly responsible positions.

TWAIN, MARK, *The Autobiography of Mark Twain.* (Harper) Compiled from his own writings, this autobiography provides insights into nineteenth-century American life as well as into the life and personality of a great American humorist.

WAITE, HELEN ELMIRE, *How Do I Love Thee?* (Macrae Smith) The story of the English poet, Elizabeth Barrett, and of her marriage to Robert Browning.

• paperback

In defining poetry, Emily Dickinson, two of whose poems you will read in this unit, said:

"If I read a book and it makes my whole body so cold no fire can ever warm me, I know that is poetry. If I feel physically as if the top of my head were taken off, I know that is poetry. These are the only ways I know it. Is there any other way?"

There are other ways to know poetry. There are, perhaps, as many ways as there are readers. And there are many elements that contribute to poetry as a type of literature. A poem may tell a story, a poem may sing. It may have action, mood, tone, rhyme. One poem may have all these elements. You may or may not learn to recognize all of the elements that contribute to a poem, but if any one of the poems in this unit makes you feel happy, or sad, or thoughtful, or just pleased, you will have experienced poetry.

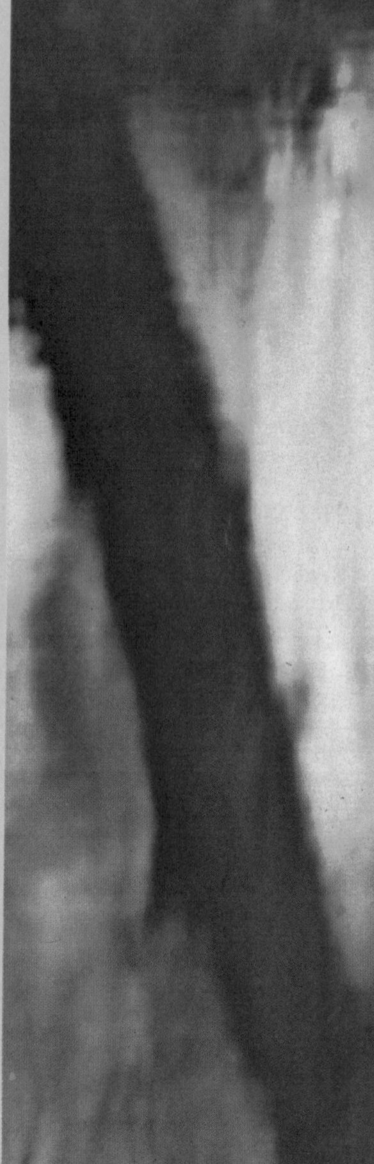

Unit 3

A BOOK OF POETRY

DANIEL FARBER FROM RAPHO-GUILLUMETTE

GUNGA DIN

Rudyard Kipling

You may talk o' gin and beer
When you're quartered safe out 'ere,[1]
An' you're sent to penny-fights an' Aldershot it,[2]
But when it comes to slaughter
You will do your work on water,
An' you'll lick the bloomin' boots of 'im that's got it.
Now in Injia's sunny clime,
Where I used to spend my time
A-servin' of 'Er Majesty the Queen,
Of all them blackfaced crew
The finest man I knew
Was our regimental *bhisti,*[3] Gunga Din.
It was "Din! Din! Din!
You limpin' lump o' brick dust, Gunga Din!
Hi! *Slippy hitherao!*[4]
Water, get it! *Panee lao*[5]
You squidgy-nosed old idol, Gunga Din."

The uniform 'e wore
Was nothin' much before,
An' rather less than 'arf o' that be'ind,

1. out 'ere, here in England. ***2. Aldershot it,*** live as one does in Aldershot, a large military camp in Hampshire, England. ***3. bhisti*** (bēs'ti), water carrier. ***4. Slippy hitherao*** (hiTH'ər-ä'ō), mock dialect for "slip here." ***5. Panee lao*** (pô'ni-lä'ō), bring water quickly.

For a piece o' twisty rag
An' a goatskin water bag
Was all the field equipment 'e could find.
When the sweatin' troop train lay
In a sidin' through the day,
Where the 'eat would make your bloomin' eyebrows crawl,
We shouted "*Harry By!*"[6]
Till our throats were bricky-dry,
Then we wopped 'im 'cause 'e couldn't serve us all.
It was "Din! Din! Din!
You 'eathen, where the mischief 'ave you been?
You put some *juldee*[7] in it
Or I'll marrow[8] you this minute
If you don't fill up my helmet, Gunga Din!"

6. ***Harry By,*** O Brother. 7. ***juldee*** (jul′dē), speed. 8. ***marrow,*** beat.

'E would dot an' carry one
Till the longest day was done;
An' 'e didn't seem to know the use o' fear.
If we charged or broke or cut,
You could bet your bloomin' nut,
'E'd be waitin' fifty paces right flank rear.
With 'is *mussick*[9] on 'is back,
'E would skip with our attack,
An' watch us till the bugles made "Retire,"
An' for all 'is dirty 'ide
'E was white, clear white, inside
When 'e went to tend the wounded under fire!
It was "Din! Din! Din!"
With the bullets kickin' dust spots on the green;
When the cartridges ran out,
You could hear the front ranks shout,
"Hi! ammunition mules an' Gunga Din!"

I sha'nt forgit the night
When I dropped be'ind the fight
With a bullet where my belt plate should 'a' been.
I was chokin' mad with thirst,
An' the man that spied me first
Was our good old grinnin', gruntin' Gunga Din.
'E lifted up my 'ead,
An' 'e plugged me where I bled,
An' 'e guv me 'arf a pint o' water green.
It was crawlin' and it stunk,
But of all the drinks I've drunk,
I'm gratefullest to one from Gunga Din.
It was "Din! Din! Din!
'Ere's a beggar with a bullet through 'is spleen;
'E's chawin' up the ground,
An' 'e's kickin' all around;
For Gawd's sake, git the water, Gunga Din!"

RUDYARD KIPLING

The first few years of Kipling's life were spent in India where his father was head of the Bombay school of art. Though he was sent to England for his education, the boy returned to India at the age of seventeen and went to work as a reporter. In 1889 Kipling returned to England and continued his journalistic career. Three years later he published ***Barrack-Room Ballads,*** one of his best-known volumes of poetry. In 1907 he was awarded the Nobel prize for literature.

In his novels, poems, travel sketches, and short stories, Kipling is particularly noted for his portrayals of the people of India and of the British soldiers stationed there.

9. ***mussick*** (mus'ək), leather water bag.

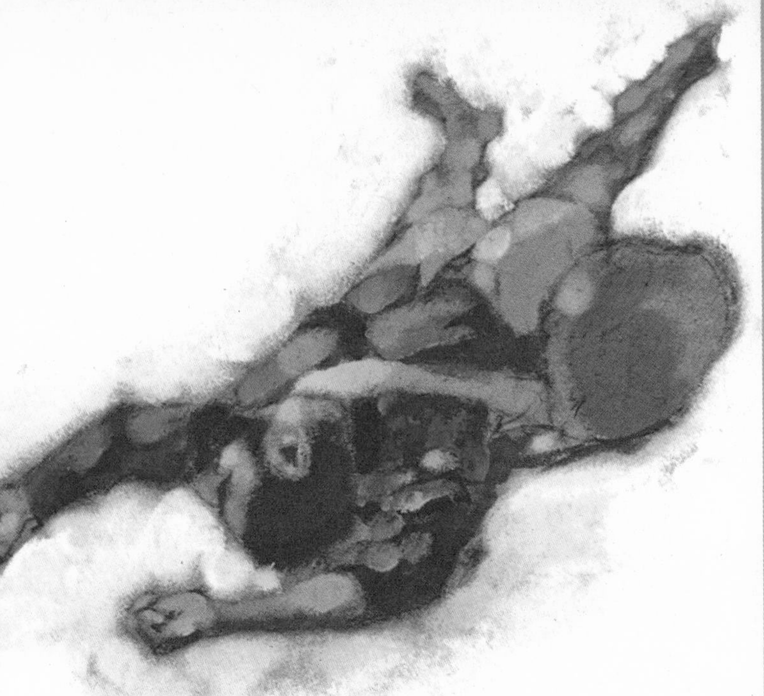

'E carried me away
To where a *dooli*[10] lay,
An' a bullet come an' drilled the beggar clean.
'E put me safe inside,
An' just before 'e died,
"I 'ope you liked your drink," sez Gunga Din.
So I'll meet 'im later on
In the place where 'e is gone—
Where it's always double drill and no canteen.[11]
'E'll be squattin' on the coals
Givin' drink to poor damned souls,
An' I'll get a swig in hell from Gunga Din!
Yes, Din! Din! Din!
You Lazarushian-leather[12] Gunga Din!
Though I've belted you and flayed you,
By the livin' Gawd that made you,
You're a better man than I am, Gunga Din!

WHAT DO YOU SAY?

1. What is the narrator's attitude toward Gunga Din? Quote at least 3 lines to support your answer.

2. ***(a)*** What are the appearance and character of Gunga Din? ***(b)*** In your estimation was he a hero? Why or why not?

3. ***(a)*** What elements of a short story does this poem have? ***(b)*** Which line actually begins the unfolding of the story? ***(c)*** What purpose do the lines preceding this serve?

4. In line 10 who are the "blackfaced crew"?

5. ***(a)*** What impression do you get of the narrator? ***(b)*** Quote several lines that contribute to this impression.

6. What, do you think, is the theme of the poem?

10. dooli (dü'li), a stretcher, usually covered. ***11. no canteen,*** no place or time for refreshments. ***12. Lazarushian-leather,*** old British army slang for "tough and dark-skinned."

ALLEN-A-DALE

Sir Walter Scott

Allen-a-Dale has no fagot for burning,
Allen-a-Dale has no furrow for turning,
Allen-a-Dale has no fleece for the spinning,
Yet Allen-a-Dale has red gold for the winning.
Come, read me my riddle! come, hearken my tale!
And tell me the craft of bold Allen-a-Dale.

The Baron of Ravensworth prances in pride,
And he views his domains upon Arkindale side;
The mere for his net, and the land for his game,
The chase for the wild, and the park for the tame;
Yet the fish of the lake, and the deer of the vale,
Are less free to Lord Dacre than Allen-a-Dale!

Allen-a-Dale was ne'er belted a knight,[1]
Though his spur be as sharp, and his blade be as bright;
Allen-a-Dale is no baron or lord,
Yet twenty tall yeomen will draw at his word;
And the best of our nobles his bonnet will vail,[2]
Who at Rere-cross on Stanmore meets Allen-a-Dale.

Allen-a-Dale to his wooing is come;
The mother, she ask'd of his household and home:
"Though the castle of Richmond stand fair on the hill,
My hall," quoth bold Allen, "shows gallanter still;
'Tis the blue vault of heaven, with its crescent so pale,
And with all its bright spangles," said Allen-a-Dale.

The father was steel, and the mother was stone;
They lifted the latch, and they bade him be gone;
But loud, on the morrow, their wail and their cry:
He had laugh'd on the lass with his bonny black eye,
And she fled to the forest to hear a love-tale,
And the youth it was told by was Allen-a-Dale!

*1. **belted a knight,*** made a knight. *2. **his bonnet will vail,*** will take off his hat.

SIR WALTER SCOTT

As a child, Scott was stricken with infantile paralysis and was sent to live with his grandfather in the Border Country of Scotland. Here he became acquainted with Scottish folk ballads and legends which were to provide a source of inspiration for his poetry and novels.

After a year's study at the University of Edinburgh, from which he withdrew because of illness, Scott studied law in his father's office and was admitted to the bar in 1792. In 1802, Scott published ***Minstrelsy of the Scottish Border***, a collection of ballads. This was followed by such popular verse tales as ***Lady of the Lake***, the novel ***Ivanhoe***, and many shorter poems, all of which show Scott's love for his native land as well as his skill as a storyteller.

WHAT DO YOU SAY?

1. Both "Gunga Din" and "Allen-a-Dale" focus on one main character. What other similarities are there in the two poems?

2. ***(a)*** What is the "red gold" in line 4? ***(b)*** Can you answer the riddle in the first stanza of the poem?

3. Of what other fictional character does Allen-a-Dale remind you?

4. Using clues found in the poem, describe where and how Allen-a-Dale lived.

5. To whom does the "his" in line 17 refer?

6. What is the attitude of the noblemen toward Allen-a-Dale?

7. The last two stanzas of the poem tell the story of Allen-a-Dale's romance. ***(a)*** How do the girl's mother and father react to his wooing? ***(b)*** Was Allen-a-Dale's suit successful?

NARRATIVE POETRY

In your discussion of "Gunga Din" you learned that this poem has all the elements of a short story. It has a setting, plot, characters, theme. It also has conflict and suspense. "Gunga Din" is really a short story in compact form. It is a story-poem or ***narrative.*** Narrative poems have always been popular because they tell an exciting story with a minimum of words, because they move quickly and are often dramatic, and because of the appeal of rhythm and rhyme. Reread a stanza of "Gunga Din" and listen to its fast-moving rhythm and sound appeal.

The earliest form of narrative poem, still popular today, is the ***folk ballad.*** The word ***ballad*** means "a simple song" or "a story in verse." No one knows where or when folk ballads originated, but they have been sung for many hundreds of years. The authors of the old folk ballads are unknown, for ballads were sung long before printing was known. They were passed along from person to person and generation to generation and country to country. But regardless of its origin, the most important features of the ballad are its dramatic and musical qualities. The ballad has a quickly unfolding plot and a lively, lilting rhythm with a definite pattern. The old folk ballad usually treated a simple theme dealing with love, hate, and death.

So popular have been the old ballads with both readers and poets that many recognized authors have written their own ballads styling them after the old folk ballad. A ballad by a known author is called a ***literary ballad.*** "Allen-a-Dale" is a literary ballad. Which of the characteristics of the folk ballad does "Allen-a-Dale" have? Both "Gunga Din" and "Allen-a-Dale" are narrative poems. You have already discussed in what ways they are alike. In what ways do they differ?

THE FLUTE

by

Wilfrid

Gibson

"Good-night!" he sang out cheerily:
"Good-night!" and yet again: "Good-night!"

And I was gay that night to be
Once more in my clean countryside,
Among the windy hills and wide.
Six days of city slush and mud,
Of hooting horn, and spattering wheel,
Made me rejoice again to feel
The tingling frost that fires the blood,
And sets life burning keen and bright;
And down the ringing road to stride
The eager swinging stride that braces
The straining thews from hip to heel:
To breathe again the wind that sweeps
Across the grassy, Northern steeps,
From crystal deeps and starry spaces.

And I was glad again to hear
The old man's greeting of good cheer:
For every night for many a year
At that same corner we had met,
Summer and Winter, dry and wet:
And though I never once had heard
The old man speak another word,
His cheery greeting at the bend
Seemed like the welcome of a friend.
But, as we neared to-night, somehow,
I felt that he would stop and speak—
Though he went by: and when I turned,
I saw him standing in the road,
And looking back, with hand to brow,
As if to shade old eyes, grown weak
Awaiting the long sleep they'd earned:
Though, as again towards him I strode,
A friendly light within them burned.
And then, as I drew nigh, he spoke
With shaking head, and voice that broke:
"I've missed you these last nights," he said:
"And I have not so many now
That I can miss friends easily . . .
Ay: friends grow scarce, as you grow old:
And roads are rough: and winds are cold:
And when you feel you're losing hold,
Life does not go too merrily."

And then he stood with nodding head,
And spoke no more. And so I told
How I had been, six days and nights,
Exiled from pleasant sounds and sights.
And now, as though my voice had stirred
His heart to speech, he told right out,
With quickening eye and quavering word,
The things I care to hear about,
The little things that make up life:
How he'd been lonesome, since his wife
Had died, some thirty year ago:
And how he trudged three mile or so
To reach the farmstead where he worked,
And three mile back to his own door . . .
For he dwelt outby on the moor:
And every day the distance irked
More sorely still his poor, old bones;
And all the road seemed strewn with stones
To trip you up, when you were old—
When you were old, and friends were few:
How, since the farmstead had been sold,
The master and the men were new,
All save himself; and they were young;
And Mistress had a raspy tongue:
So, often, he would hardly speak
A friendly word from week to week
With any soul. Old friends had died,
Or else had quit the countryside:
And since his wife was taken, he
Had lived alone, these thirty year:
And there were few who cared to hear
An old man's jabber . . . and too long
He'd kept me, standing in the cold,
With his long tongue, and such a song
About himself! And I would be . . .

I put my arm through his; and turned
To go upon his way with him:
And once again that warm light burned
In those old eyes, so weak and dim:
While, with thin, piping voice, he told
How much it meant to him each night
To change a kindly word with me:
To think that he'd at least one friend
Who'd maybe miss him, in the end.

Then, as we walked, he said no more:
And, silent, in the starry light,
Across the wide, sweet-smelling bent,
Between the grass and stars we went
In quiet, friendly company:
And, all the way, we only heard
A chirrup where some partridge stirred,
And ran before us through the grass,
To hide his head till we should pass.

At length we reached the cottage-door:
But when I stopped, and turned to go,
His words came falteringly and slow:
If I would step inside, and rest,
I'd be right welcome: not a guest
Had crossed his threshold, thirty year . . .
He'd naught but bread and cheese and beer
To offer me . . . but, I'd know best . . .
He spoke with hand upon the latch;
And when I answered, opened wide
The cottage-door, and stepped inside;
And, as I followed, struck a match,
And lit a tallow-dip: and stirred
The banked-up peats into a glow:
And then with shuffling step and slow
He moved about: and soon had set
Two mugs of beer, and bread and cheese:
And while we made a meal off these,
The old man never spoke a word;
But, brooding in the ingle-seat,
With eyes upon the kindling peat,
He seemed a while to quite forget
He was not sitting by himself
To-night, like any other night;

When, as in the dim candle-light
I glanced around me, with surprise
I saw upon the rafter-shelf
A flute, nigh hidden in the shade.

And when I asked him if he played,
The light came back into his eyes:
Ay, ay, he sometimes piped a bit,
But not so often since she died.
And then, as though old memories lit
His poor, old heart, and made it glad,
He told how he, when quite a lad,
Had taught himself: and they would play
On penny whistles all the day—
He and the miller's son, beside
The millpool, chirping all they knew,
Till they could whistle clean and true:
And how, when old enough to earn,
They both saved up to buy a flute:
And they had played it, turn for turn:
But Jake was dead, this long while back . . .
Ah! if I'd only heard him toot,
I'd know what music meant. Ay, ay . . .
He'd play me something, bye-and-bye;
Though he was nought to Jake . . . and now
His breath was scant, and fingering slack . . .
He used to play to her at night
The melodies that she liked best,
While she worked on: she'd never rest
By daylight, or by candle-light . . .
And then, with hand upon his brow,
He brooded, quiet in his chair,
With eyes upon the red peat-glare;
Until, at length, he roused himself,
And reached the flute down from the shelf;
And, carrying it outside the door,
I saw him take a can, and pour
Fresh water through the instrument,
To make it sweet of tone, he said.
Then in his seat, so old and bent,
With kindling eyes and swaying head,
He played the airs he used to play
To please his wife, before she died.

And as I watched his body sway
In time and tune, from side to side—
So happy, just to play and please
With old familiar melodies—
His eyes grew brighter and more bright,
As though they saw some well-loved sight:
And, following his happy gaze,
I turned, and saw, without amaze,
A woman standing, young and fair,
With hazel eyes, and thick, brown hair
Brushed smoothly backward from the brow,
Beside the table that but now,
Save for the empty mugs, was bare.
Upon it she had spread a sheet,
And stood there, ironing a shirt,
Her husband's, as he played to her
Her favorite tunes, so old and sweet.
I watched her move with soundless stir;
Then stand with listening eyes, and hold
The iron near her glowing cheek,
Lest it, too hot, should do some hurt,
And she, so careful not to burn
The well-darned shirt, so worn and old.

Then, something seemed to make me turn
To look at the old man again:
And, as I looked, the playing stopped;
And now I saw that he had dropped
Into his brooding mood once more,
With eyes again grown dull and weak.
He seemed the oldest of old men
Who grope through life with sight worn dim:
And, even as I looked at him,
Too full of tender awe to speak,
I knew once more the board was bare,
With no young woman standing there
With hazel eyes and thick, brown hair.

And so, at last, I rose, and took
His hand: and as he clasped mine tight,
I saw again that friendly look
Fill his old weary eyes with light,
And wish me, without words, good-night.
And in my heart, that look glowed bright
Till I reached home across the moor.

And, at the corner of the lane,
Next night, I heard the old voice cry
In greeting, as I struggled by,
Head-down against the wind and rain.
And so each night, until one day,
His master chanced across my way:
But, when I spoke of him, he said:
Did I not know the man was dead,
And had been dead a week or so?
One morn he'd not turned up to work,
And never having known him shirk,
And hearing that he lived alone,
He thought it best himself to go
And see what ailed: and coming there,
He found the old man in his chair,
Stone-dead beside the cold hearthstone.
It must be full a week, or more . . .
Ay, just two weeks, come Saturday,
He'd found him; but he must have died
O'ernight—(the night I heard him play!)
And they had found, dropt by his side,
A broken flute upon the floor.

Yet, every night, his greeting still
At that same corner of the hill,
Summer and Winter, wet or dry,
'Neath cloud, or moon, or cold starlight,
Is waiting to welcome me:
And ever as I hurry by,
The old voice sings out cheerily:
"Good-night!" and yet again, "Good-night!"

WILFRID GIBSON

Wilfrid Wilson Gibson was born in Northern England in 1878. As a young boy he began writing poetry and, with the exception of his military service during World War I, poetry has been his profession since. His first volume of verse, ***Urlyn the Harper***, was published in 1902, but he did not achieve prominence as a poet until his war poems appeared. Since that time he has written many books of poems as well as plays and dialogues. His poems are mainly concerned with the portrayal of common people and the problems of industrialization.

WHAT DO YOU SAY?

1. (a) Identify the narrative elements in this poem. ***(b)*** State the clues that identify the country the poem describes.
2. How do lines 17-18 explain the first two lines of the poem?
3. What effect does the old man's playing of the flute have on the narrator?
4. Why, though the old man is dead, can the narrator still "hear" the greeting at the corner of the lane?
5. Skim back over the poem and notice how the poet uses ***and*** as he narrates one detail after another. Does this device tend to make the poem formal or informal in feeling?

THE COURAGE THAT MY MOTHER HAD

Edna St. Vincent Millay

The courage that my mother had
Went with her, and is with her still:
Rock from New England quarried;
Now granite in a granite hill.

The golden brooch my mother wore
She left behind for me to wear;
I have no thing I treasure more:
Yet, it is something I could spare.

Oh, if instead she'd left to me
The thing she took into the grave!—
That courage like a rock, which she
Has no more need of, and I have.

PHOTO BY LOUIS MARIANO

THE POET AT SEVEN

by Donald Justice

And on the porch, across the upturned chair,
The boy would spread a dingy counterpane
Against the length and majesty of the rain,
And on all fours crawl under it like a bear
To lick his wounds in secret in his lair;
And afterwards, in the windy yard again,
One hand cocked back, release his paper plane
Frail as a May fly to the faithless air.
And summer evenings he would whirl around
Faster and faster till the drunken ground
Rose up to meet him; or sometimes would squat
Among the foul weeds of the vacant lot,
Waiting for dusk and someone dear to come
And whip him down the street, but gently, home.

EDNA ST. VINCENT MILLAY

Edna St. Vincent Millay once said, "I see things with my own eyes just as if they were the first eyes that ever saw, and then I set about to tell, as best I can, just what I see." What she saw was a paradoxical world of happiness and heartbreak, and in her poetry she reveals her reactions to this world.

She was born in 1892 in Rockland, Maine. Her first major poem, "Renascence," was published in 1912 when the author was only nineteen. From the 1920's until her death in 1950 she wrote many volumes of poetry and several verse plays. Her collection of poems, ***The Harp-Weaver***, won the 1923 Pulitzer Prize.

DONALD JUSTICE

Donald Justice, born in Florida in 1925, is among the younger poets of this generation. His poems are perceptive, and his work is quickly gaining recognition in poetry circles. Donald Justice's first complete collection of poetry, ***The Summer Anniversaries***, was published in 1959. Other of his poems have appeared in ***Poetry Magazine*** and in the ***New Yorker***. Mr. Justice currently teaches creative writing in the Poetry Workshop of Iowa State University.

WHAT DO YOU SAY?

"The Courage. . . ."

1. (a) What two of her mother's possessions does the poet mention? ***(b)*** What value does she place on each? ***2. (a)*** To what does the poet compare her mother's courage? ***(b)*** Why is this comparison especially suitable? ***(c)*** This comparison is stated in both the first and third stanzas. What lines make the comparison?

"The Poet at Seven"

1. (a) What does the boy spread across the chair? ***(b)*** How does he feel about the rain?
2. (a) In what way is the boy compared to a bear? ***(b)*** What "wounds" do you think the boy might be licking? ***(c)*** Does the poet state what these are?
3. In line 10, is the ground really "drunken"? Explain.
4. What lines suggest that the boy is happy and secure?
5. What does the title mean to you?

MELORA VILAS

Stephen Vincent Benét

Melora Vilas, rising by candlelight,
Looked at herself in the bottom of the tin basin
And wished that she had a mirror.
                                        Now Spring was here,
She could kneel above the well of a forest pool
And see the shadow hidden under the water,
The intent brown eyes, the small face cut like a heart.
She looked at the eyes and the eyes looked back at her,
But just when it seemed they could start to talk to each other—
"What are you like? Who are you?"—
                                        a ripple flawed
The deep glass and the shadow trembled away.

If she only had a mirror, maybe she'd know
Something, she didn't know what, but something important,
Something like knowing your skin and you were alive
On a good day, something as drenched as sleep,
As wise as sleep, as piercing as the bee's dagger.
But she'd never know it unless she could get a mirror
And they'd never get a mirror while they were hiders.
They were bound to be hiders as long as the war kept on.
Pop was that way. She remembered roads and places.
She was seventeen. She had seen a lot of places,
A lot of roads. Pop was always moving along.
Everybody she'd ever known was moving along.
—Dusty wagons full of chickens and children,
Full of tools and quilts, Rising Sun and Roses of Sharon,
Mahogany dressers out of Grandmother's house,
Tin plates, cracked china, a couple of silver spoons,
Moving from State to State behind tired, scuffed horses
Because the land was always better elsewhere.

Next time they'd quit. Next stop they'd settle right down.
Next year they'd have time to rub up the mahogany dresser.
Next place, Mom could raise the flowers she wanted to raise.
But it never began. They were always moving along.

She liked Kansas best. She wished they'd go back to Kansas.
She liked the smell of the wind there.
But Pop hadn't wanted to join with the Free-Soilers
And then the slavery men had shot up the town
And killed the best horse they had. That had settled Pop.
He said something about a plague on both of your houses
And moved along. So now they were hiders here
And whenever you wanted to ask Pop about the war
All he said was that same old thing about the plague.
She mustn't call him Pop—that was movers'-talk.
She must call him Father, the way Mom, Mother wanted.
But it was hard to remember. Mom talked a lot
About old times back in the East and Grandmother's house.
She couldn't remember an East. The East wasn't real.
There was only the dusty road and moving along.
Although she knew that Mom had worn a silk dress
And gone to a ball, once. There was a picture of Pop
And Mom, looking Eastern, in queer old Eastern clothes.
They weren't white trash. She knew how to read and figure.
She'd read *Macbeth* and *Beulah* and *Oliver Twist*.[1]
She liked *Beulah* best but *Macbeth* would have suited Pop.
Sometimes she wondered what had happened to them,
When Mother used to live in Grandmother's house
And wear silk dresses, and Father used to read Latin—
When had they started to go just moving along,
And how would it feel to live in Grandmother's house?

But it was so long ago, so hard to work out
And she liked it this way—she even liked being hiders.
It was exciting, especially when the guns
Coughed in the sky as they had all yesterday,
When Bent hid out in the woods to keep from recruiters,
And you knew there were armies stumbling all around you,
Big, blundering cows of armies, snuffling and tramping
The whole scuffed world with their muddy, lumbering hoofs,
Except the little lost brushpile where you were safe.
There were guns in the sky again today. Big armies.
An army must be fine to look at.
But Pop
Would never let her do it or understand.
An army or a mirror. She didn't know
Which she'd rather find, but whenever she thought of it
The mirror generally won. You could keep a mirror yourself.

WHAT DO YOU SAY?

1. What two things does Melora Vilas use for a mirror?
2. What is the color of her eyes? The shape of her face? Her age?
3. ***(a)*** Why did Melora Vilas want a mirror so very much? ***(b)*** What kept her from getting a mirror?
4. What do you learn in lines 17-32 about her family and their present situation?
5. You know from the poem that a war is going on. What clues can you find as to which war it is?
6. Line 38 contains a famous quotation from Shakespeare. To whom do you think Pop is referring in the words "both your houses"?
7. What do you learn in lines 44-58 about the background of the Vilas family?
8. ***(a)*** In line 63, who do you suppose "Bent" is? ***(b)*** Where is Melora's hiding place?
9. Melora Vilas found an army and a mirror almost equally exciting. Why did she usually choose the mirror?
10. This selection is from a long narrative poem in which many people and their lives are revealed. What is your impression of the particular person described here?

1. ***Macbeth,*** a play by William Shakespeare; ***Beulah,*** a novel by Augusta Jane Wilson (1835-1909); ***Oliver Twist,*** a novel by Charles Dickens.

THE BALLAD OF WILLIAM SYCAMORE

Stephen Vincent Benét

My father, he was a mountaineer,
His fist was a knotty hammer;
He was quick on his feet as a running deer,
And he spoke with a Yankee stammer.

My mother, she was merry and brave,
And so she came to her labor,
With a tall green fir for her doctor grave
And a stream for her comforting neighbor.

And some are wrapped in the linen fine,
And some like a godling's scion[1];
But I was cradled on twigs of pine
In the skin of a mountain lion.

And some remember a white, starched lap
And a ewer with silver handles;
But I remember a coonskin cap
And the smell of bayberry candles.

The cabin logs, with the bark still rough,
And my mother who laughed at trifles,
And the tall, lank visitors, brown as snuff,
With their long, straight squirrel-rifles.

I can hear them dance, like a foggy song,
Through the deepest one of my slumbers,
The fiddle squeaking the boots along
And my father calling the numbers.[2]

BRONZE BY FREDERIC REMINGTON COURTESY ART INSTITUTE OF CHICAGO PHOTOS BY JAMES BALLARD

1. like a godling's scion (sī′ən), like the descendant of a god. ***2. calling the numbers,*** calling out the steps for the square dancers to follow.

The quick feet shaking the puncheon-floor,
And the fiddle squealing and squealing,
Till the dried herbs rattled above the door
And the dust went up to the ceiling.

There are children lucky from dawn till dusk,
But never a child so lucky!
For I cut my teeth on "Money Musk"[3]
In the Bloody Ground of Kentucky![4]

When I grew tall as the Indian corn,
My father had little to lend me,
But he gave me his great, old powder-horn
And his woodsman's skill to befriend me.

3. ***"Money Musk,"*** a tune often played for square dances.
4. ***Bloody Ground of Kentucky.*** Kentucky is often referred to as "the dark and bloody ground" because of the struggles of various Indian tribes to possess this rich land.

With a leather shirt to cover my back,
And a redskin nose to unravel
Each forest sign,[5] I carried my pack
As far as a scout could travel.

Till I lost my boyhood and found my wife,
A girl like a Salem clipper![6]
A woman straight as a hunting-knife
With eyes as bright as the Dipper!

We cleared our camp where the buffalo feed,
Unheard-of streams were our flagons;
And I sowed my sons like the apple-seed
On the trail of the Western wagons.

They were right, tight boys, never sulky or slow,
A fruitful, a goodly muster.
The eldest died at the Alamo.[7]
The youngest fell with Custer.[8]

5. ***a redskin nose . . . forest sign,*** an Indian's knowledge of woodcraft. 6. ***like a Salem clipper,*** as trim and graceful as one of the fast sailing ships (clippers) that were the pride of such Eastern seaports as Salem, Massachusetts. 7. ***Alamo*** (al'ə mō *or* ä'lə mō), a famous mission at San Antonio, Texas. On March 6, 1836, the small garrison of Americans holding it was completely destroyed by an overwhelming force of Mexicans. 8. ***Custer*** (kus'tər), an American army officer and Indian fighter. In June 1876, he made his famous "last stand" against the Sioux Indians at the Little Big Horn River in what is now Montana. He and 264 of his men were killed.

The letter that told it burned my hand.
Yet we smiled and said, "So be it!"
But I could not live when they fenced the land,
For it broke my heart to see it.

I saddled a red, unbroken colt
And rode him into the day there;
And he threw me down like a thunderbolt
And rolled on me as I lay there.

The hunter's whistle hummed in my ear
As the city-men tried to move me,
And I died in my boots like a pioneer
With the whole wide sky above me.

Now I lie in the heart of the fat, black soil,
Like the seed of a prairie-thistle;
It has washed my bones with honey and oil
And picked them clean as a whistle.

And my youth returns, like the rains of Spring,
And my sons, like the wild-geese flying;
And I lie and hear the meadow-lark sing
And have much content in my dying.

Go play with the towns you have built of blocks,
The towns where you would have bound me!
I sleep in my earth like a tired fox,
And my buffalo have found me.

WHAT DO YOU SAY?

1. ***(a)*** What kind of boyhood did William Sycamore have? ***(b)*** Did he consider himself fortunate or unfortunate? Explain.

2. What gifts did his father give him?

3. ***(a)*** What was the one experience in William Sycamore's life he could not endure? ***(b)*** What reasons does he give for being content in his dying?

4. How is this poem like "Melora Vilas"?

5. ***(a)*** How many of the ballad characteristics (page 219) does this poem have? ***(b)*** Why is this a literary ballad?

THE WHIPPING
Robert Hayden

The old woman across the way
        is whipping the boy again
and shouting to the neighborhood
        her goodness and his wrongs.

Wildly he crashes through elephant ears,
        pleads in dusty zinnias,
while she in spite of crippling fat,
        pursues and corners him.

She strikes and strikes the shrilly circling
        boy till the stick breaks
in her hand. His tears are rainy weather
        to woundlike memories:

My head gripped in bony vise
        of knees, the writhing struggle
to wrench free, the blows, the fear
        worse than blows that hateful

Words could bring, the face that I
        no longer knew or loved . . .
Well, it is over now, it is over,
        and the boy sobs in his room,

And the woman leans muttering against
        a tree, exhausted, purged—
avenged in part for lifelong suffering
        she has had to bear.

WHAT DO YOU SAY?

1. In this poem, someone observes a scene which stirs up personal memories. ***(a)*** Describe the scene the speaker sees. ***(b)*** What recollections does the scene bring to his mind?
2. The speaker gives no indication as to what the boy has done wrong. Does he seem to feel the boy is deserving of so harsh a punishment? Find evidence in the poem to support your answer.
3. ***(a)*** What is the "lifelong suffering" (line 23) the woman has borne? ***(b)*** Why, according to the speaker, does she beat the boy? ***(c)*** Does the speaker seem to feel any sympathy for the woman? Explain.
4. Can we accept, without question, the speaker's description of the scene and his explanation of it, or should we consider his personal feelings before doing so? Why?

ROBERT HAYDEN

Robert Hayden, who was born and educated in Michigan, currently teaches creative writing and English at Fisk University. In his poetry, Hayden emphasizes the language of common speech, the exact word, the precise image. Frequently, he deals with characters in dramatic action, but, as in "The Whipping," he suggests rather than states their predicaments by using images to reflect the emotions of a character. The subject matter of his work reveals his love for people and his concern for their problems.

FIGURATIVE LANGUAGE

All literature, if it is effective, induces images in the minds of its readers. Since most poems are briefer than most short stories and other types of literature, the poet must present a picture clearly and quickly with a minimum of words. To do this he makes extensive use of devices used by all authors, ***figures of speech.***

There are many kinds of figures of speech, or ***figurative language,*** but the three kinds most often found in poetry are: ***simile, metaphor,*** and ***personification.***

In "The Ballad of William Sycamore" the poet states that his father was "quick on his feet as a running deer." What the poet means, of course, is that his father was swift in his movements, but by comparing him to a deer, the poet intensifies the reader's impression of the father. This figure of speech in which two ***unlike*** objects are compared by the use of the words ***like*** or ***as*** is called a ***simile.*** What unlike things are being compared in the following two similes?

When I grew tall as the Indian corn,

a girl like a Salem clipper.

A ***metaphor*** is very much like a simile in that it also compares two things of unlike nature, as: "His fist was a knotty hammer." The poet is comparing his father's fist to a hammer. However, he makes the comparison ***without*** using the words ***like*** or ***as.*** So, a ***metaphor*** is an ***implied***, or suggested, comparison. What are the implied comparisons in the following line?

The father was steel, and the mother was stone;

Change these metaphors into similes.

A third common figure of speech also involves the idea of comparison. An object is given one or more characteristics of a human being. The name of this figure of speech is a clue to its meaning. ***Personification*** means the giving to inanimate objects, animals, or ideas the qualities or characteristics of a person—the ability to speak, act, or feel. These characteristics may be either stated outright or suggested. In the following lines, there is an example of personification:

It was exciting, especially when the guns
Coughed in the sky.

What objects are given what characteristics of a person?

What is personified in this line from "The Poet at Seven"?

till the drunken ground rose up to meet him.

Find examples of ***simile, metaphor,*** and ***personification*** in the following lines:

Now I lie in the heart of the fat, black soil,
Like the seed of a prairie thistle;
It has washed my bones with honey and oil
And picked them clean as a whistle.

KNOW YOUR WORDS
Context clues

When you are able to determine the meaning of a new word from the way it is used in a sentence, you are using ***context clues.*** Frequently we make use of this method of word detecting without realizing we are doing it. It is not always necessary to turn to the dictionary to find the meaning of a new word. We can often determine the author's meaning by examining the information surrounding the new word.

For example, one line from "Gunga Din" reads, "Though I've belted you and flayed you." You undoubtedly know the meaning of "belted"; that is, "to hit." Since the next word is "and," it is natural to expect that the word "flayed" also means some kind of abuse, although you may not know exactly what kind. However, you can continue reading the poem without stopping to look up the word because you have a general understanding of its meaning from context clues.

The following lines from "The Flute" contain context clues to the meaning of "tallow-dip." What are the clues?

And, as I followed, he struck a match,
And lit a tallow-dip.

Later on in this poem, you are told that the light in the room is "candlelight." At this point the meaning of "tallow-dip" becomes quite clear from the context.

What can you figure out about the meaning of "counterpane" from the following lines?

And on the porch, across the upturned chair,
The boy would spread a dingy counterpane
Against the length and majesty of the rain,
And on all fours crawl under it. . . .

Look up the word "counterpane" in the glossary. What additional information does it give?

SECTION 2
NATURE

GOD'S WORLD

by

Edna St. Vincent Millay

O World, I cannot hold thee close enough!
  Thy winds, thy wide grey skies!
  Thy mists, that roll and rise!
Thy woods, this autumn day, that ache and sag
And all but cry with color! That gaunt crag
To crush! To lift the lean of that black bluff!
World, World, I cannot get thee close enough!

Long have I known a glory in it all,
  But never knew I this;
  Here such a passion is
As stretcheth me apart,—Lord, I do fear
Thou'st made the world too beautiful this year;
My soul is all but out of me,—let fall
No burning leaf; prithee, let no bird call.

WHAT DO YOU SAY?

1. This poem is obviously a very emotional reaction on the part of the poet to the beauty of nature. What words in particular give the emotional tone to the poem?
2. In the last two lines the poet fears that a leaf may fall or a bird may call. Why does she not want this to happen?
3. The first stanza of this poem is called an ***apostrophe.*** An apostrophe is a figure of speech in which an inanimate object, an abstract quality, or an absent person is addressed as though it were alive and present. Explain the use of ***apostrophe*** in this poem.

A WANDERER'S SONG

by John Masefield

A wind's in the heart of me, a fire's in my heels,
I am tired of brick and stone and rumbling wagon-wheels;
I hunger for the sea's edge, the limits of the land,
Where the wild old Atlantic is shouting on the sand.

Oh I'll be going, leaving the noises of the street,
To where a lifting foresail-foot is yanking at the sheet[1];
To a windy, tossing anchorage where yawls and ketches ride,
Oh I'll be going, going, until I meet the tide.

And first I'll hear the sea-wind, the mewing of the gulls,
The clucking, sucking of the sea about the rusty hulls,
The songs at the capstan in the hooker warping out,[2]
And then the heart of me'll know I'm there or there-about.

Oh I am tired of brick and stone, the heart of me is sick,
For windy green, unquiet sea, the realm of Moby Dick[3];
And I'll be going, going, from the roaring of the wheels,
For a wind's in the heart of me, a fire's in my heels.

PHOTO BY GUNNAR BERNEHOLM

1. foresail foot . . . sheet, the bottom of the lowest sail is tugging at the rope which controls the angle at which the sail is set. *2. hooker warping out,* movement of the ship (hooker) by ropes fastened to something fixed. *3. Moby Dick,* the great white whale in Herman Melville's novel of the same name.

JOHN MASEFIELD

At the age of thirteen, John Masefield began training to become a seaman, and two years later he became an apprentice on board a sailing ship which rounded Cape Horn. After a serious illness, Masefield abandoned the life of a sailor and went to New York where he worked, at various times, in a bakery, a livery stable, and a saloon.

During his stay in New York, Masefield became interested in literature, and, in addition to reading avidly, he began to write poems and stories based on his sea experiences. His first book of poetry, ***Salt-Water Poems and Ballads***, was published in 1902.

In 1930, Masefield became Poet Laureate of England, a position which he held until his death in 1967.

WHAT DO YOU SAY?

1. The author points up his longing for the sea by making the qualities of the sea contrast with "brick" and "stone." What qualities does the sea have that brick and stone do not?

2. Note the words ***mewing, clucking, sucking.*** These words themselves actually sound like the sounds they express, just as "hiss" sounds like a hiss. This device is called ***onomatopoeia*** (on′ə mat′ə pē′ə). What other example of onomatopoeia can you find in the last stanza?

SARA TEASDALE

The poem "Barter" might well represent Sara Teasdale's approach to life. It expresses a theme common to many of her lyrics. Although Miss Teasdale sought "loveliness" in her life, in reality she found life very difficult to adjust to.

Born in 1884 in St. Louis, Missouri, of a wealthy family, sheltered and unable to accept responsibilty, Miss Teasdale spent much of her life traveling in search of security. Her most published volume of poetry, ***Love Song,*** demonstrates her lyric ability.

ROBERT FROST

America's "New England poet," Robert Frost, was born in San Francisco in 1874. His father died when the boy was ten, and his mother moved her family to Massachusetts. After high school, Frost entered Dartmouth College but left after only three months. He tried teaching, newspaper work, and farming. After attending Harvard for two years, Frost turned once more to farming. When this venture failed, Frost and his family sailed for England. His first two volumes of poetry, ***A Boy's Will*** and ***North of Boston,*** were published in England, and on his return to the United States in 1915, he found his reputation had preceded him.

As a four-time Pulitzer Prize winner, Frost was greatly in demand as a lecturer and teacher and gained the title of America's "teacher-at-large." Until his death in 1963, he traveled throughout the country, teaching, lecturing, and reading his poetry, devoting what leisure time he could find to his Vermont farm.

Frost's subjects include almost every phase of human life. Perhaps the man and his work are best summarized in a statement by President John F. Kennedy.

"There are many kinds of courage—bravery under fire, the courage to risk reputation and friendship and career for convictions which are deeply held. But perhaps the rarest courage of all . . . is the courage to wage a silent battle to illuminate the nature of man and the world in which he lives.

"This is Robert Frost's courage. . . ."

LYRIC POETRY

You have learned that a narrative poem like "Gunga Din" tells a story. It has all the elements of a short story. You know without analyzing the reasons that the poem "God's World" is very different from "Gunga Din" and from "The Ballad of William Sycamore."

"God's World" does not have a plot or characters and it tells no story. It describes the poet's feelings at a particular moment. It is an example of a ***lyric*** poem. A lyric is the expression of personal feelings on a subject or about an experience. The poet tries to express himself in such a way that the reader shares his emotion.

The poet's emotion may be one of longing, happiness, quietness, frustration, exuberance, or melancholy, but the emotion is always intense or deeply felt. The kind of emotion and the poet's feeling about it contribute to the overall ***tone,*** or spirit, of the poem.

"The Courage That My Mother Had" and "God's World" are both lyrics by the same author. They both express deep personal emotions, but they are quite different in ***tone.*** What is the tone of each?

Why is "A Wanderer's Song" classified as a lyric? In what way is it similar to the two poems by Edna St. Vincent Millay? How does it differ in tone?

BARTER
by Sara Teasdale

Life has loveliness to sell,
All beautiful and splendid things,
Blue waves whitened on a cliff,
Soaring fire that sways and sings,
And children's faces looking up
Holding wonder like a cup.

Life has loveliness to sell,
Music like a curve of gold,
Scent of pine trees in the rain,
Eyes that love you, arms that hold,
And for your spirit's still delight,
Holy thoughts that star the night.

Spend all you have for loveliness,
Buy it and never count the cost;
For one white singing hour of peace
Count many a year of strife well lost,
And for a breath of ecstasy
Give all you have been, or could be.

A YOUNG BIRCH
by Robert Frost

The birch begins to crack its outer sheath
Of baby green and show the white beneath,
As whosoever likes the young and slight
May well have noticed. Soon entirely white
To double day and cut in half the dark
It will stand forth, entirely white in bark,
And nothing but the top a leafy green—
The only native tree that dares to lean,
Relying on its beauty, to the air.
(Less brave perhaps than trusting are the fair.)
And someone reminiscent will recall
How once in cutting brush along the wall
He spared it from the number of the slain,
At first to be no bigger than a cane,
And then no bigger than a fishing pole,
But now at last so obvious a bole
The most efficient help you ever hired
Would know that it was there to be admired,
And zeal would not be thanked that cut it down
When you were sick in bed or out of town.
It was a thing of beauty and was sent
To live its life out as an ornament.

WHAT DO YOU SAY?

"Barter"

1. The word "barter" suggests a trade between two people—a seller and a buyer. In this poem, who is the "seller" and who is the "buyer"?
2. What things does the author find particularly lovely?
3. According to the author, what should one "barter" for loveliness?
4. Point out several effective figures of speech in the poem.

"A Young Birch"

1. ***(a)*** What does the poet do in the first seven lines of this poem? ***(b)*** What makes the day seem twice as bright and the night seem only half as dark?
2. ***(a)*** What do lines 8-10 suggest about the appearance of the birch tree? ***(b)*** How is the tree personified in these lines?
3. Who is the "someone reminiscent" in line 11?
4. Why would "the most efficient help" not dare to cut down the tree?
5. "Barter" and "A Young Birch" are both lyrics. How do they differ?

THE DAFFODILS
by William Wordsworth

I wandered lonely as a cloud
That floats on high o'er vales and hills,
When all at once I saw a crowd,
A host, of golden daffodils;
Beside the lake, beneath the trees,
Fluttering and dancing in the breeze.

Continuous as the stars that shine
And twinkle on the milky way,
They stretched in never-ending line
Along the margin of a bay:
Ten thousand saw I at a glance,
Tossing their heads in sprightly dance.

The waves beside them danced; but they
Out-did the sparkling waves in glee:
A poet could not but be gay,
In such a jocund company:
I gazed—and gazed—but little thought
What wealth the show to me had brought:

For oft, when on my couch I lie
In vacant or in pensive mood,
They flash upon that inward eye
Which is the bliss of solitude;
And then my heart with pleasure fills,
And dances with the daffodils.

WILLIAM WORDSWORTH

William Wordsworth reveals in his poetry the romance of the commonplace and the beauty of nature. He was born in 1770 in the Lake District of England. During his school days, Wordsworth remained aloof from other students, preferring solitary walks to companionship. His guardians had wanted him to enter the ministry, but Wordsworth had other ideas.

He became a great sympathizer with the French in their revolution and lived in France for a period of time. When Wordsworth, upon becoming disillusioned with the "Reign of Terror," returned to England, his constant companions were his sister and Samuel Taylor Coleridge, with whom Wordsworth wrote ***Lyrical Ballads.*** Although the book and its authors were at first criticized, in the later years of his life, Wordsworth was recognized as one of the outstanding poets of England. He died in 1850.

WHAT DO YOU SAY?

1. ***(a)*** What words does the poet use to personify the daffodils? ***(b)*** Try to summarize in your own words the appearance of the daffodils.

2. Wordsworth once wrote that poetry "takes its origin from emotion recollected in tranquillity." How is this idea expressed in the last stanza of "The Daffodils"?

STARS

by

Sara Teasdale

Alone in the night
On a dark hill
With pines around me
Spicy and still;

And a heaven full of stars
Over my head,
White and topaz
And misty-red;

Myriads with beating
Hearts of fire
That aeons
Cannot vex or tire;

Up the dome of heaven
Like a great hill,
I watch them marching
Stately and still,

And I know that I
Am honored to be
Witness
Of so much majesty.

WHAT DO YOU SAY?

1. How does this poem compare with "The Daffodils" in tone?

2. What is the similarity in theme between this poem and "Barter"?

SENSORY IMAGERY

When a writer uses words that have a special appeal to one or more of the senses, he is using ***sensory imagery.*** He appeals to the reader's sight, hearing, smell, touch, taste, and feeling in order to communicate his own feelings more vividly.

Appeal to sight, or ***visual imagery,*** is the most frequently used sensory image. For example, "a heaven full of stars . . . White and topaz And misty-red" is an obvious appeal to the sense of sight. "With pines around me Spicy and still" has an appeal to sight and to what other sense?

"My heart with pleasure fills, And dances with the daffodils" is an appeal to the sense of feeling. "I wandered lonely as a cloud" appeals to what sense?

In creating sound, or ***auditory imagery,*** the poet uses several special devices. You have already learned about one of them, ***onomatopoeia,*** in which words actually sound like what they mean. Another device is found in the following line:

Soaring fire that sways and sings

Notice that three of the words begin with ***s.*** When two or more words close together begin with the same consonant sound, the resulting sound effect is called ***alliteration.*** How has the poet made use of alliteration in the first two lines of "God's World" (p. 234)?

A third device used to create sound imagery is called ***assonance.*** Read the following line aloud:

A host of golden daffodils

What particular sound is outstanding? It is the ***o*** in *host* and *golden.* When the same vowel sound is accented and repeated in a line, the resulting sound imagery is called ***assonance.*** The following line from "A Wanderer's Song" demonstrates all three poetic devices used to create sound or auditory imagery. Point them out.

The clucking, sucking of the sea about the rusty hulls.

PHOTO BY AL CAMASTO

CENTRAL PARK TOURNEY

by Mildred Weston

Cars
In the Park
With long spear lights
Ride at each other
Like armored knights;
Rush,
Miss the mark,
Pierce the dark,
Dash by!
Another two
Try.

Staged
In the Park
From dusk
To dawn,
The tourney goes on:
Rush,
Miss the mark,
Pierce the dark,
Dash by!
Another two
Try.

WHAT DO YOU SAY?

1. Which kind of sensory imagery makes the greatest appeal in this poem? Quote lines or phrases to support your answer.

2. What is the connection between lines 5 and 6 and the title?

3. Read the poem aloud. Explain in your own words why the particular accent in the lines, or the rhythm, of this poem is appropriate to the meaning.

FOG

by

Carl

Sandburg

The fog comes
on little cat feet.

It sits looking
over harbor and city
on silent haunches
and then moves on.

ASSOCIATED PRESS WIRE PHOTO

CARL SANDBURG

Carl Sandburg, American poet and biographer, was born in Galesburg, Illinois, in 1878. The family was very poor, and Carl left school at thirteen to work at unskilled laboring jobs. He enlisted in the Spanish-American War, and, upon his return, attended Lombard College in Galesburg but did not receive his degree. He was later given honorary degrees from three institutions. Sandburg began his journalistic career after college and worked on both magazines and newspapers, and toured the country on lectures as well.

Sandburg wrote not only poetry, but children's books and biography. His biography of Abraham Lincoln, a six-volume work, is one of the great biographies of modern times, and Sandburg spent fifteen years making this dream into a reality. To earn his living while writing this masterpiece, he toured the country with his banjo or guitar, sang folksongs, and read his poetry. His honors and awards were many, including two Pulitzer Prizes. Through his poetry Sandburg earned the right to be called the authentic voice of the Middle West.

WHAT DO YOU SAY?

1. Point out words or phrases that indicate three distinct steps in the movement of the fog.
2. This poem is called an ***extended metaphor.*** You remember that a metaphor is an implied comparison. What is the meaning of ***extended metaphor?***
3. Why is the comparison of fog and a cat a particularly good one?
4. How many kinds of sensory imagery can you find in these six lines?

WIND SONG by Carl Sandburg

"Wind Song" from ***Smoke and Steel*** by Carl Sandburg. Copyright 1920 by Harcourt, Brace and World, Inc., New York, renewed 1948 by Carl Sandburg. By permission of the publishers.

Long ago I learned how to sleep,
In an old apple orchard where the wind swept by
counting its money and throwing it away,
In a wind-gaunt orchard where the limbs forked out
and listened or never listened at all,
In a passel of trees where the branches trapped the
wind into whistling, "Who, who are you?"
I slept with my head in an elbow on a summer after-
noon and there I took a sleep lesson.
There I went away saying: I know why they sleep,
I know how they trap the tricky winds.
Long ago I learned how to listen to the singing wind
and how to forget and how to hear the deep whine,
Slapping and lapsing under the day blue and the night
stars:
Who, who are you?

Who can ever forget
listening to the wind go by
counting its money
and throwing it away?

THE SKATERS by John Gould Fletcher

"The Skaters" from ***Preludes and Symphonies*** by John Gould Fletcher. Reprinted by permission of Mrs. John Gould Fletcher.

Black swallows swooping or gliding
In a flurry of entangled loops and curves;
The skaters skim over the frozen river.
And the grinding click of their skates as they impinge upon the
surface,
Is like the brushing together of thin wing-tips of silver.

A WINTER LYRIC by Louis Untermeyer

"A Winter Lyric" from ***These Times*** by Louis Untermeyer. Copyright 1917 by Harcourt, Brace and World, Inc., New York; renewed 1945 by Louis Untermeyer. Reprinted by permission of the publishers.

The winter winds were swift and stinging,
The day was growing old and dark;
And yet within the icy park
Birds in the leafless trees were singing.

Somehow the cold was not so clinging,
And homing people stopped to stare
At all the brave hearts clustered there—
Birds in the leafless trees! And singing!

Yes, Spring is sweet with new songs ringing,
And Summer's pageant moves all men;
But my heart leaps to Winter when
Birds in the leafless trees are singing.

JOHN GOULD FLETCHER

John Gould Fletcher was born in 1886 in Little Rock, Arkansas. He once stated that by the age of ten he had "already shown a marked fondness for reading poetry." At the age of seventeen he entered Harvard where he devoted much of his time to reading and writing poetry. During his last year in college, Fletcher decided to become a writer. A year later he went to Europe where he could devote his full efforts to writing. He settled in London in 1909 and between that time and his return to the United States in 1914, he had published five volumes of poetry.

His later works include an autobiography, ***Life is My Song***, and ***Selected Poems*** which received the Pulitzer Prize in 1939.

LOUIS UNTERMEYER

Poet, critic, and editor, Louis Untermeyer was born in 1885 in New York City where, he says, he "was raised and miseducated." After leaving high school he entered his father's jewelry manufacturing business but left it in 1923 and went to Europe for two years. Upon his return to the United States, he purchased a large farm in the New York Adirondacks and divided his time between writing, lecturing, and farming.

In addition to writing poetry, Untermeyer has written several biographies and edited numerous poetry anthologies. In 1956 he received a gold medal from the Poetry Society of America and in 1961 was appointed Consultant in Poetry for the Library of Congress.

WHAT DO YOU SAY?

1. Each of the three lyrics on the previous page has a very dominant appeal to a different sense. What is the dominant sensory appeal in each?

2. ***(a)*** In "Wind Song" the author reveals an emotional experience he has enjoyed. What did he learn from listening to the wind? ***(b)*** What does he mean by "counting its money and throwing it away" (line 2)?

3. In line 6 of "Wind Song" what does "they" refer to?

4. ***(a)*** In "The Skaters," to whom does "black swallows" refer? ***(b)*** What is this figure of speech called?

5. Point out examples of alliteration and assonance in the first line of "A Winter Lyric." Find other examples throughout the poem.

6. ***(a)*** In "A Winter Lyric" what season does the poet prefer? ***(b)*** Why does he prefer it?

READING POETRY ALOUD

The same skills you use in understanding prose apply to understanding poetry. One difference between the two forms, however, is that most poetry is intended for the ear as well as for the eye. Not until you enjoy reading poetry aloud or enjoy hearing it read aloud can you really appreciate all that poetry has to offer.

Such characteristics of poetry as figures of speech, sensory imagery, rhythm, and rhyme become completely exciting only when they are heard. This is ***why*** poetry should be read aloud. But ***how*** should it be read?

Poetry should be read aloud so as to bring out the meaning and feeling intended by the poet. Look at the three poems on the facing page. They are very different in appearance. The length of their lines varies; they have different themes; they have different rhythms—so, of course, they would not be read aloud in the same way. Before you can correctly read any one of these poems aloud, you must know what mood the poet intended, what the lines mean, what, in other words, the poet is saying. Your voice must then reflect what is appropriate to the meaning of the words. If the meaning of one line is not completed until the next line you would not pause at the end of the first line any more than you would say: "I am going (pause) downtown." In reading "Wind Song" you would not read in line 4, ". . . the branches trapped the (pause) wind into whistling," simply because "the" is at the end of a line.

In "The Skaters" the poet's intention is to re-create the sight and feeling of skaters. Thus in reading these lines aloud, you would want to imitate the swooping and gliding of the skaters with a smooth continuous reading. Turn back to page 240. Why would this poem be read aloud very differently from "The Skaters"? In what ways would it be read differently?

"A Winter Lyric" is a good poem to practice reading aloud. The ideas are easy to follow; the emphasis falls naturally on the important words. Practice reading aloud all three of these poems until you can communicate the mood and meaning of the poet.

SECTION 3
PRINCIPLES

DUST OF SNOW

by Robert Frost

The way a crow
Shook down on me
The dust of snow
From a hemlock tree

Has given my heart
A change of mood
And saved some part
Of a day I had rued.

WHAT DO YOU SAY?

1. What does the poet say in the first six lines?
2. ***(a)*** Why is it important that you understand the meaning of the word "rued" in the last line? ***(b)*** What context clue gives you some idea of its meaning?
3. In what way was the poet's mood changed?

WE NEVER KNOW HOW HIGH WE ARE

by Emily Dickinson

We never know how high we are
  Till we are called to rise;
And then, if we are true to plan,
  Our statures touch the skies.

The heroism we recite
  Would be a daily thing,
Did not ourselves the cubits warp
  For fear to be a king.

CHARTLESS

by Emily Dickinson

I never saw a moor,
I never saw the sea;
Yet know I how the heather looks,
And what a wave must be.

I never talked with God,
Nor visited in heaven;
Yet certain am I of the spot
As if the chart were given.

EMILY DICKINSON

Emily Dickinson was born in 1830 in Amherst, Massachusetts. Though her father, a prominent lawyer, was sternly and almost Puritanically religious, as a child Emily was happy and fun-loving, with a sense of humor and an enthusiastic interest in people. After attending Mt. Holyoke College for a year she returned to the family home in Amherst and, for some unknown reason, withdrew from almost all social contacts.

Having had four poems rejected by the ***Atlantic Monthly,*** she refused to publish any of her verses. During her lifetime, only seven of her more than eighteen hundred poems were published. These were submitted secretly and anonymously by her friends. After her death in 1886, her poems were collected and edited by her sister and a friend of the family, her first published volume appearing in 1890.

Louis Untermeyer refers to her poetry with its startling and unusual imagery as a "blend of whimsicality and wisdom."

WHAT DO YOU SAY?

1. In your own words, what is the poet saying in each of these two poems?
2. (a) What does the poet mean by "plan" in line 3 of the first poem? ***(b)*** Line 7 could mean: (1) Our measurements warp us, or (2) We, ourselves, warp our own measurements. Which meaning fits the general sense of the poem?
3. What one word expresses what Miss Dickinson says in "Chartless"?

ALFRED NOYES

Alfred Noyes was one of the rare poets who enjoyed not only critical acclaim, but almost instant popularity with the general public. Born in 1880 in Staffordshire, England, the major part of his boyhood was spent near the sea. During his college days at Oxford, he was noted for his athletic ability rather than for his literary skill. His first book, ***The Loom of Years,*** was published when Noyes was twenty-two. In 1913 he traveled to the United States where, for nine years, he was professor of English literature at Princeton. Except for frequent visits to the United States, the rest of his life was spent in England.

He is remembered primarily for his verse narratives and ballads. Among his most famous poems are "The Barrel-Organ" and "The Highwayman."

WHAT DO YOU SAY?

1. The effectiveness of this poem lies in the contrasts the poet has used. What are the contrasts?

2. (a) How many times in the poem is the theme stated? ***(b)*** It is possible to interpret blindness figuratively rather than literally in this poem. What is the meaning of the poem if "blindness" is interpreted figuratively?

JOURNEY BY NIGHT
A Blind Man's Prayer
by Alfred Noyes

Thou who never canst err, for Thyself art the Way;
Thou whose infinite kingdom is flooded with day;
Thou whose eyes behold all, for Thyself art the Light,
Look down on us gently who journey by night.

By the pity revealed in Thy loneliest hour,
Forsaken, self-bound and self-emptied of power;
Thou who, even in death, hadst all heaven in sight,
Look down on us gently who journey by night.

On the road to Emmaus,[1] they thought Thou wast dead,
Yet they saw Thee and knew in the breaking of bread,
Though the day was far spent, in Thy face there was light.
Look down on us gently who journey by night.

THE FOOL'S PRAYER
by Edward R. Sill

The royal feast was done; the king
   Sought some new sport to banish care,
And to his jester cried: "Sir Fool,
   Kneel now, and make for us a prayer!"

The jester doffed his cap and bells,
   And stood the mocking court before;
They could not see the bitter smile
   Behind the painted grin he wore.

1. Emmaus (em ā′əs). Following his resurrection, Jesus appeared to two men on the road to the Biblical city of Emmaus.

He bowed his head, and bent his knee
  Upon the monarch's silken stool;
His pleading voice arose: "O Lord,
  Be merciful to me, a fool!

"No pity, Lord, could change the heart
  From red with wrong to white as wool;
The rod must heal the sin: but, Lord,
  Be merciful to me, a fool!

" 'T is not by guilt the onward sweep
  Of truth and right, O Lord, we stay;
'T is by our follies that so long
  We hold the earth from heaven away.

"These clumsy feet, still in the mire,
  Go crushing blossoms without end;
These hard, well-meaning hands we thrust
  Among the heart-strings of a friend.

"The ill-timed truth we might have kept—
  Who knows how sharp it pierced and stung?
The word we had not sense to say—
  Who knows how grandly it had rung?

"Our faults no tenderness should ask,
  The chastening stripes must cleanse them all;
But for our blunders—oh, in shame
  Before the eyes of heaven we fall.

"Earth bears no balsam for mistakes;
  Men crown the knave, and scourge the tool
That did his will; but Thou, O Lord,
  Be merciful to me, a fool!"

The room was hushed; in silence rose
  The king, and sought his gardens cool,
And walked apart, and murmured low,
  "Be merciful to me, a fool!"

EDWARD ROWLAND SILL

Edward Rowland Sill was born in Connecticut in 1841. His parents died when he was young and he was raised by an uncle in Ohio. While at Yale, from which he was graduated in 1861, he served as editor of the college literary magazine. After his graduation he taught both in California and in the East.

He eventually returned to Ohio, where he died in 1887. Only one volume of his poems was printed during his lifetime and, discouraged by its poor reception, he printed two more only for private distribution among his friends. His two best known poems are "The Fool's Prayer" and "Opportunity."

WHAT DO YOU SAY?

1. The first stanza of this poem presents the setting; a royal court, a king, and a clown. At this point there is no indication of the tone or mood or theme. With what word of stanza 2 do we have the first indication of the tone of the poem?
2. As "the fool" recites his prayer, he excuses "us" for some things but feels there are other things we must take the blame for. For which things may we be excused and for which must we suffer most? Why?
3. Of the people present to whom does the fool's prayer particularly apply?

POLONIUS' ADVICE TO LAERTES

William Shakespeare

Those friends thou hast, and their adoption tried,
Grapple them to thy soul with hoops of steel;
But do not dull thy palm with entertainment
Of each new-hatched, unfledged comrade. Beware
Of entrance to a quarrel; but, being in,
Bear 't that the opposed may beware of thee.
Give every man thy ear, but few thy voice;
Take each man's censure, but reserve thy judgment.
Costly thy habit as thy purse can buy,
But not expressed in fancy; rich, not gaudy;
For the apparel oft proclaims the man . . .
Neither a borrower nor a lender be;
For loan oft loses both itself and friend,
And borrowing dulls the edge of husbandry.
This above all: to thine own self be true,
And it must follow, as the night the day,
Thou canst not then be false to any man.

WHAT DO YOU SAY?

1. The title of this selection gives you its theme but does not tell you that this is a father's advice to his son. There are seven different pieces of advice in the 17 lines. State all seven in your own words.
2. Which piece of advice is a climax to, or includes, all the others?

STEPHEN CRANE

Stephen Crane, born in 1871, the fourteenth child in his family, lived only twenty-nine years. But this brief span was enough for his dynamic imagination and spirit to explode into a half dozen novels, scores of short stories and poems, and one history. Indicative of his great energy is the fact that he wrote ***The Red Badge of Courage***, his famous Civil War novel, in ten days and nights. He absorbed life around him, projecting what he found into what he wrote. He died of tuberculosis while completing a newspaper assignment in Germany.

Stephen Crane

A MAN SAW A BALL OF GOLD IN THE SKY

A man saw a ball of gold in the sky;
He climbed for it,
And eventually he achieved it—
It was clay.

Now this is the strange part:
When the man went to the earth
And looked again,
Lo, there was the ball of gold.
Now this is the strange part:
It was a ball of gold.
Ay, by the heavens, it was a ball of gold.

WHAT DO YOU SAY?

1. State the theme of this poem in one sentence.
2. You have learned how authors use symbolism to express their ideas. ***(a)*** What does the "ball of gold" symbolize? ***(b)*** How is the symbolism continued in the next three lines?
3. What is the significance of the man's finding "the ball of gold" again?

GRASS
Carl Sandburg

Pile the bodies high at Austerlitz[1] and Waterloo.[2]
Shovel them under and let me work—
I am the grass; I cover all.

And pile them high at Gettysburg[3]
And pile them high at Ypres[4] and Verdun.[5]
Shovel them under and let me work.
Two years, ten years, and passengers ask the conductor:
What place is this?
Where are we now?

I am the grass.
Let me work.

1. ***Austerlitz*** (ôs′tər lits), town of Moravia, Czechoslovakia; scene of Napoleon's victory, December 2, 1805. 2. ***Waterloo,*** village of Brabant province, Belgium; scene of Napoleon's defeat, June 18, 1815. 3. ***Gettysburg,*** borough and county seat of Adams county, Pennsylvania; a bloody Civil War battle was fought here July 1-3, 1863. 4. ***Ypres*** (ē′pr), town in Belgium which was the scene of many World War I battles. 5. ***Verdun*** (vér dun′), town in France which was the site of many World War I battles.

THERE WILL COME SOFT RAINS (War Time)
Sara Teasdale

There will come soft rains and the smell of the ground,
And swallows circling with their shimmering sound;

And frogs in the pools singing at night,
And wild plum-trees in tremulous white.

Robins will wear their feathery fire
Whistling their whims on a low fence-wire;

And not one will know of the war, not one
Will care at last when it is done.

Not one would mind, neither bird nor tree,
If mankind perished utterly;

And Spring herself, when she woke at dawn,
Would scarcely know that we were gone.

WHAT DO YOU SAY?

1. ***(a)*** What is the tone of each of these poems? ***(b)*** State the theme common to both poems.
2. ***(a)*** What figure of speech is presented in the last two lines of "There Will Come Soft Rains"? ***(b)*** What kinds of sensory imagery do you find in both poems?

AT WOODWARD'S GARDENS

by Robert Frost

A boy, presuming on his intellect,
Once showed two little monkeys in a cage
A burning-glass they could not understand
And never could be made to understand.
Words are no good: to say it was a lens
For gathering solar rays would not have helped.
But let him show them how the weapon worked.
He made the sun a pin-point on the nose
Of first one, then the other till it brought
A look of puzzled dimness to their eyes
That blinking could not seem to blink away.
They stood arms laced together at the bars,
And exchanged troubled glances over life.
One put a thoughtful hand up to his nose
As if reminded—or as if perhaps
Within a million years of an idea.
He got his purple little knuckles stung.
The already known had once more been confirmed
By psychological experiment,
And that were all the finding to announce
Had the boy not presumed too close and long.
There was a sudden flash of arm, a snatch,
And the glass was the monkeys', not the boy's.
Precipitately they retired back cage
And instituted an investigation
On their part, though without the needed insight.
They bit the glass and listened for the flavor.
They broke the handle and the binding off it.
Then none the wiser, frankly gave it up,
And having hid it in their bedding straw
Against the day of prisoners' ennui,
Came dryly forward to the bars again
To answer for themselves: Who said it mattered
What monkeys did or didn't understand?
They might not understand a burning-glass.
They might not understand the sun itself.
It's knowing what to do with things that counts.

WIDE WORLD PHOTO

WHAT DO YOU SAY?

1. What was the boy's purpose in showing the burning-glass to the monkeys?
2. What caused the monkey to get his knuckles stung (line 17)?
3. What is the meaning of lines 18-19?
4. What image does line 27 create in your mind?
5. Why, according to the author, did the monkeys hide the glass?
6. What point is the author making in this poem?

WORD ORDER

Lines of poetry are often packed with meaning and expressed in a concise, almost abbreviated, manner. In order to determine exactly what the lines mean, the reader must rephrase, adding words as well as changing the order of words.

The seventh line of "At Woodward's Gardens" reads "But let him show them how the weapon worked." The poet is really saying "Perhaps the monkeys could understand the glass [note that he calls it a weapon] if he could show them how it works." Studying a poem often requires this kind of rephrasing. Rephrase line 21: "Had not the boy presumed too close and long"; and line 31 "Against the day of prisoners' ennui." You will probably need to reread the lines that immediately precede and follow these two lines and you may have to use the dictionary.

Now turn back to the selection, "Polonius' Advice to Laertes," on page 248. The first two lines read: "Those friends thou hast, and their adoption tried, Grapple them to thy soul with hoops of steel." If you were making a prose statement out of these lines you would probably say, "With hoops of steel, grapple the friends you know are friends." What is the difference in the order of words in these two sentences? "Neither a borrower nor a lender be" (line 12) in everyday conversation would probably be said, "Do not be either a borrower or a lender."

Most sentences begin with the subject, followed by the verb and object. Frequently, to achieve conciseness and to maintain patterns of rhyme and rhythm, poets change or ***invert*** the natural order of words. Thus, in order to understand the meaning, you must rephrase the sentence, putting the words in their natural order. What would be the natural order of the words in the following line: "to thine own self be true"? How would you rephrase this line from "God's World," "But never knew I this"? Because such rephrasing almost always destroys the poetic effect of the lines and is a device for getting ***meaning*** only, the study of such a poem must ***always*** be concluded with a rereading of the entire poem, exactly as the poet wrote it.

SECTION 4
VISIONS

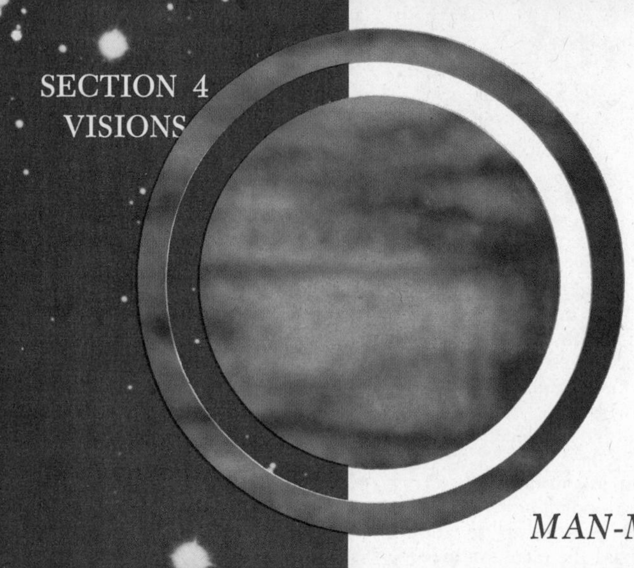

MAN-MADE SATELLITE

Louis Ginsberg

Closer to neighbor wheeling constellations,
At last the man-made satellite is hurled,
Adventuring amid uncharted spaces,
Yet tethered to the rolling of the world.

Now finite man with all his infinite dreaming
At last has launched undaunted symbol of
The grandeur of his visionary power
Toward archipelagoes of suns above.

This voyager in interstellar vastness,
What questions does this man-made moon now ferry?
What signals does it semaphore and beacon?
What riddle does this satellite now query?

And even as this little orb in splendor,
When will the glory of man's mind, elate,
Also launch up his heart above the murky,
The thick and earthly atmosphere of hate?

LOUIS GINSBERG

Louis Ginsberg was born in Newark, New Jersey, in 1896. After graduating from Rutgers College, he received his Master's Degree from Columbia University. Since that time he has taught high-school English in Paterson, New Jersey. His first volume of verses, ***The Attic of the Past and Other Poems,*** was published in 1921, followed by a second collection of poems, ***The Everlasting Minute.*** His poems have also appeared in various periodicals including ***The Atlantic Monthly*** and ***The Saturday Review.***

WHAT DO YOU SAY?

1. How is the satellite still tethered to the world?
2. In stanza 2 what is the symbol of the grandeur of man's power?
3. ***(a)*** How does the tone of this poem change in the fourth stanza? ***(b)*** What question does the author ask?

THE SECRET OF MARS

John Gould Fletcher

Some men assert that the planet Mars is
uninhabited, but this is not true, for I have
been there and seen it.
Many centuries ago, the Martians fought
their last great war; many centuries ago
they organized a life scientifically perfect.
But for all that, they were not content;
and their planet, like their hearts, began
growing colder every year.
Then one day they suddenly decided to build
a great tower to a forgotten God; and because
they were weary of their machines, they
decided that no stone of it should be cut by
anything else but hammer and chisel and
human hands.
Centuries they must have labored, for the
building as it stands is immense in desolation.
It is surrounded with a forest of columns
for many miles; at the intersection of
enormous aisles, poised above the glory of
huge leaping arches, stands the lantern
tower unfinished, ten thousand feet high.
Upon the pavement below it lies the body
of the last workman, his trowel uplifted, and
his hand ready to place a stone. His form
is still perfect, for it is frozen in death.
On the tower rests the treasure of the
perpetual snow; you would not say that Mars
is uninhabited, could you hear the groans
that the settling stone makes at sunrise or
when the evening drifts swiftly across the
barren planet.

WHAT DO YOU SAY?

1. (a) In what way was the Martian civilization perfect? ***(b)*** What was lacking?
2. (a) Why did they build the great tower by hand? ***(b)*** Describe the building.
3. What eventually happened to the race?
4. In what sense is the word "treasure" used in line 27?
5. What now inhabits Mars?
6. In what way is this poem similar to "Grass" by Carl Sandburg?

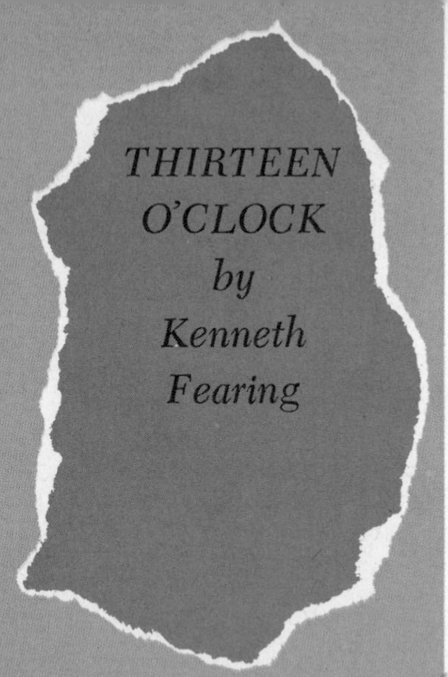

Why do they whistle so loud, when they walk past the graveyard late at night?
Why do they look behind them when they reach the gates?
Why do they have any gates? Why don't they go through the wall?
But why, O why do they make that horrible whistling sound?

GO AWAY, LIVE PEOPLE, STOP HAUNTING THE DEAD.

If they catch you, it is said, they make you rap, rap, rap on a table all night,
And blow through a trumpet and float around the room in long white veils,
While they ask you, and ask you: Can you hear us, Uncle Ted?
Are you happy, Uncle Ted? Should we buy or should we sell? Should we marry, Uncle Ted?
What became of Uncle Ned, Uncle Ted, and is he happy, and ask him if he knows what became of Uncle Fred?

KEEP AWAY, LIVE PEOPLE, KEEP FAR AWAY,
STAY IN THE WORLD'S OTHER WORLD WHERE YOU REALLY BELONG. YOU WILL PROBABLY BE MUCH HAPPIER THERE.

And who knows what they are hunting for, always looking, looking, looking with sharp bright eyes where they ought to have sockets?
Whoever saw them really grin with their teeth?
Who knows why they worry, or what they scheme, with a brain where there should be nothing but good, damp air?

STAY AWAY, LIVE PEOPLE, STAY AWAY, STAY AWAY,
YOU MEAN NO HARM, AND WE AREN'T AFRAID OF YOU, AND WE DON'T BELIEVE SUCH PEOPLE EXIST,
BUT WHAT ARE YOU LOOKING FOR? WHO DO YOU WANT?
WHO? WHO? WHO? O WHO?

KENNETH FEARING

Kenneth Fearing was born in Oak Park, Illinois, in 1902. After graduating from the University of Wisconsin, he worked at various occupations including that of salesman, newspaper reporter, and free-lance writer. His first volume of poetry, ***Angel Arms,*** was published in 1929, followed by several other volumes in the succeeding years. In addition to writing poetry, Fearing wrote several novels. He died in 1961.

Fearing once stated that his favorite authors were those "who can write exciting books." There is usually a high degree of suspense and tension in his own work, even in his descriptions of common-place people and events.

WHAT DO YOU SAY?

1. Where do you find the first clue as to who is speaking in this poem?
2. What things do "live" people do that annoy those in the other world?
3. Point out several particularly vivid images.
4. What is humorously ironic in the last stanza?
5. Why is the title especially appropriate to the theme?

THE WITCH
by
Sara Henderson Hay

It pleases me to give a man three wishes,
Then trick him into wasting every one;
To set the simpering goosegirl on the throne
While the true Princess weeps among the ashes.
I like to come unbidden to the christening,
Cackling a curse on the young princeling's head,
To slip a toad into the maiden's bed,
To conjure up the briers, the glass slope glistening.

And I am near, oh nearer than you've known.
You cannot shut me in a fairy book.
It was my step you heard, mine and my creatures',
Soft at your heel; and if you lean and look
Long in your mirror, you will see my features
Inextricably mingled with your own.

WHAT DO YOU SAY?

1. ***(a)*** To what is the speaker referring in the first eight lines? ***(b)*** What line in the poem makes this clear?
2. What lines tell you how and where to find the witch?

The Rime of the Ancient Mariner

THE RIME OF THE ANCIENT MARINER

Samuel Taylor Coleridge

ARGUMENT[1]

How a Ship, having passed the Line,[2] was driven by storms to the cold country toward the South Pole; and how from thence she made her course to the Tropical Latitude of the Great Pacific Ocean; and of the strange things that befell; and in what manner the ancient Mariner came back to his own country.

PART THE FIRST

An ancient Mariner meeteth three Gallants bidden to a wedding feast, and detaineth one.

It is an ancient Mariner,
And he stoppeth one of three.
"By thy long gray beard and glittering eye,
Now wherefore stopp'st thou me?

"The Bridegroom's doors are opened wide,
And I am next of kin;
The guests are met, the feast is set—
May'st hear the merry din."

He[3] holds him with his skinny hand,
"There was a ship," quoth he.
"Hold off! unhand me, graybeard loon!"
Eftsoons[4] his hand dropt he.

The wedding Guest is spellbound by the eye of the old seafaring man, and constrained to hear his tale.

He holds him with his glittering eye;
The Wedding Guest stood still,
And listens like a three years' child—
The Mariner hath his will.

The Wedding Guest sat on a stone—
He cannot choose but hear;
And thus spake on that ancient man,
The bright-eyed Mariner.

"The ship was cheered, the harbor cleared;
Merrily did we drop
Below the kirk, below the hill,
Below the lighthouse top.

The Mariner tells how the ship sailed southward with a good wind and fair weather till it reached the Line.

"The Sun came up upon the left;
Out of the sea came he!
And he shone bright, and on the right
Went down into the sea.

1. ***Argument,*** meaning here "a summary." In 1798, when "The Rime of the Ancient Mariner" was first published in ***Lyrical Ballads,*** by Samuel Taylor Coleridge and William Wordsworth, the reader was given no reading helps except the Argument. In later editions, Coleridge added the "Gloss," or prose summary, which is printed alongside the poem. 2. ***the Line,*** the Equator. 3. ***He,*** the Mariner. 4. ***Eftsoons*** (eft sünz′), immediately. (Archaic)

"Higher and higher every day,
Till over the mast at noon—"
The Wedding Guest here beat his breast;
For he heard the loud bassoon.

THE WEDDING GUEST HEARETH THE BRIDAL MUSIC; BUT THE MARINER CONTINUETH HIS TALE.

The Bride hath paced into the hall;
Red as a rose is she;
Nodding their heads before her goes
The merry minstrelsy.

The Wedding Guest he beat his breast,
Yet he cannot choose but hear;
And thus spake on that ancient man,
The bright-eyed Mariner.

THE SHIP DRAWN BY STORM TOWARD THE SOUTH POLE.

"And now the Storm Blast came, and he
Was tyrannous and strong;
He struck with his o'ertaking wings,
And chased us south along.

"With sloping masts and dipping prow,
As who pursued with yell and blow
Still treads the shadow of his foe,
And forward bends his head,[5]
The ship drove fast, loud roared the blast,
And southward aye we fled.

"And now there came both mist and snow,
And it grew wondrous cold;
And ice, mast-high, came floating by
As green as emerald.

THE LAND OF ICE, AND OF FEARFUL SOUNDS, WHERE NO LIVING THING WAS TO BE SEEN;

"And through the drifts the snowy clifts[6]
Did send a dismal sheen;
Nor shapes of men nor beasts we ken—
The ice was all between.

"The ice was here, the ice was there,
The ice was all around;
It cracked and growled, and roared and howled;
Like noises in a swound![7]

5. ***As who . . . head,*** as a person, who, pursued so closely that he is running in his enemy's shadow, bends forward in an effort to attain greater speed. 6. ***snowy clifts,*** towering icebergs. 7. ***Like noises in a swound,*** like the roaring that a fainting person hears in his ears.

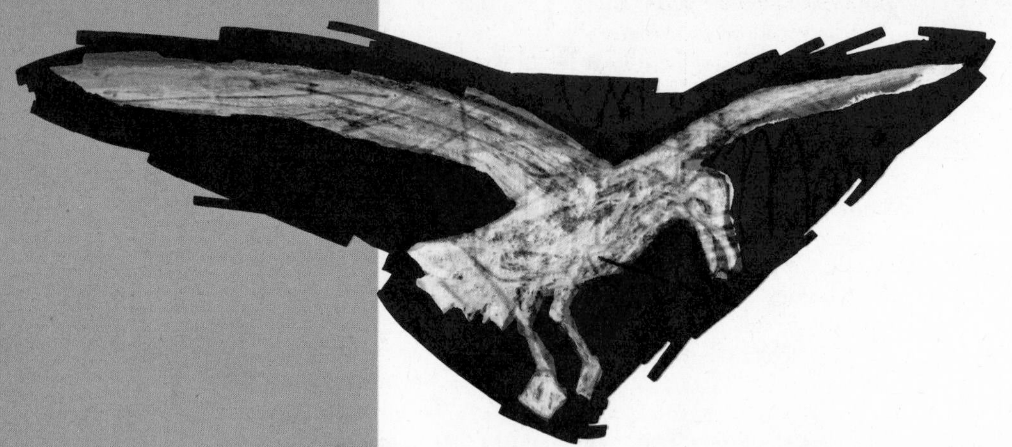

TILL A GREAT SEA BIRD CALLED THE ALBATROSS CAME THROUGH THE SNOW-FOG, AND WAS RECEIVED WITH GREAT JOY AND HOSPITALITY.

"At length did cross an Albatross;
  Thorough[8] the fog it came;
As if it had been a Christian soul,
  We hailed it in God's name.

"It ate the food it ne'er had eat,
  And round and round it flew.
The ice did split with a thunder-fit;
  The helmsman steered us through!

AND LO! THE ALBATROSS PROVETH A BIRD OF GOOD OMEN, AND FOLLOWETH THE SHIP AS IT RETURNED NORTHWARD, THROUGH FOG AND FLOATING ICE.

"And a good south wind sprung up behind;
  The Albatross did follow,
And every day, for food or play,
  Came to the mariners' hollo!

"In mist or cloud, on mast or shroud,
  It perched for vespers nine[9];
Whiles all the night, through fog-smoke white,
  Glimmered the white moonshine."

THE ANCIENT MARINER INHOSPITABLY KILLETH THE PIOUS BIRD OF GOOD OMEN.

"God save thee, ancient Mariner,
  From the fiends that plague thee thus!—
Why look'st thou so?"—"With my crossbow
  I shot the Albatross."

PART THE SECOND

"The Sun now rose upon the right;
  Out of the sea came he,
Still hid in mist, and on the left
  Went down into the sea.

"And the good south wind still blew behind,
  But no sweet bird did follow,
Nor any day, for food or play,
  Came to the mariners' hollo!

8. Thorough (thə′ rō), through. *9. for vespers nine,* for nine evenings.

His shipmates cry out against the ancient Mariner for killing the bird of good luck.

"And I had done a hellish thing,
And it would work 'em woe;
For all averred I had killed the bird
That made the breeze to blow.
'Ah, wretch!' said they, 'the bird to slay,
That made the breeze to blow!'

But when the fog clears off, they justify the same, and thus make themselves accomplices in the crime.

"Nor dim nor red, like God's own head,
The glorious Sun uprist[10];
Then all averred I had killed the bird
That brought the fog and mist.
' 'Twas right,' said they, 'such birds to slay,
That bring the fog and mist.'

The fair breeze continues; the ship enters the Pacific Ocean and sails northward, even till it reaches the Line.

"The fair breeze blew, the white foam flew,
The furrow followed free;
We were the first that ever burst
Into that silent sea.

The ship hath been suddenly becalmed.

"Down dropt the breeze, the sails dropt down;
'Twas sad as sad could be;
And we did speak only to break
The silence of the sea!

"All in a hot and copper sky,
The bloody Sun, at noon,
Right up above the mast did stand,
No bigger than the Moon.

"Day after day, day after day,
We stuck, nor breath nor motion;
As idle as a painted ship
Upon a painted ocean.

And the Albatross begins to be avenged.

"Water, water, everywhere,
And all the boards did shrink;
Water, water, everywhere,
Nor any drop to drink.

"The very deep did rot—O Christ!
That ever this should be!
Yea, slimy things did crawl with legs
Upon the slimy sea.

"About, about, in reel and rout
The death fires[11] danced at night;
The water, like a witch's oils,
Burnt green, and blue, and white.

A spirit had followed them; one of the invisible inhabitants of this planet,

"And some in dreams assurèd were
Of the spirit that plagued us so;

10. uprist, uprose. ***11. death fires,*** lights sometimes called St. Elmo's fire. Caused by a discharge of atmospheric electricity, they are often seen on masts of sailing ships. Sailors formerly feared them.

NEITHER DEPARTED SOULS NOR ANGELS; CONCERNING WHOM THE LEARNED JEW JOSEPHUS AND THE PLATONIC CONSTANTINOPOLITAN, MICHAEL PSELLUS,[12] MAY BE CONSULTED. THEY ARE VERY NUMEROUS, AND THERE IS NO CLIMATE OR ELEMENT WITHOUT ONE OR MORE.

Nine fathom deep he had followed us
From the land of mist and snow.

"And every tongue, through utter drought,
Was withered at the root;
We could not speak, no more than if
We had been choked with soot.

"Ah! well-a-day!—what evil looks
Had I from old and young!
Instead of the cross, the Albatross
About my neck was hung."

THE SHIPMATES IN THEIR SORE DISTRESS WOULD FAIN THROW THE WHOLE GUILT ON THE ANCIENT MARINER; IN SIGN WHEREOF THEY HANG THE DEAD SEA BIRD ROUND HIS NECK.

PART THE THIRD

"There passed a weary time. Each throat
Was parched, and glazed each eye.
A weary time! a weary time!
How glazed each weary eye!
When, looking westward, I beheld
A something in the sky.

THE ANCIENT MARINER BEHOLDETH A SIGN IN THE ELEMENT AFAR OFF.

"At first it seemed a little speck,
And then it seemed a mist;
It moved, and moved, and took at last
A certain shape, I wist.[13]

"A speck, a mist, a shape, I wist!
And still it neared and neared;
As if it dodged a water sprite,
It plunged and tacked and veered.

AT ITS NEARER APPROACH, IT SEEMETH HIM TO BE A SHIP; AND AT A DEAR RANSOM HE FREETH HIS SPEECH FROM THE BONDS OF THIRST.

"With throats unslaked, with black lips baked
We could nor laugh nor wail;
Through utter drought all dumb we stood!
I bit my arm, I sucked the blood,
And cried, 'A sail! a sail!'

A FLASH OF JOY;

"With throats unslaked, with black lips bake
Agape they heard me call;
Gramercy![14] they for joy did grin,
And all at once their breath drew in,
As they were drinking all.

AND HORROR FOLLOWS. FOR CAN IT BE A SHIP THAT COMES ONWARD WITHOUT WIND OR TIDE?

" 'See! see!' I cried, 'she tacks no more!
Hither to work us weal[15];
Without a breeze, without a tide,
She steadies with upright keel!'

"The western wave was all aflame,
The day was well-nigh done!

12. the learned Jew Josephus (jō sē′fəs) ... *Michael Psellus* (sel′əs). Josephus (37-95) was a historian. Psellus (1018-1079) was a theologian, born in Constantinople, who admired Plato, the famous ancient Greek philosopher. *13. wist,* knew or discovered. (Archaic) *14. Gramercy* (grə mėr′si), many thanks. (Archaic) *15. to work us weal* (wēl), to bring us good.

"Almost upon the western wave
Rested the broad bright Sun;
When that strange shape drove suddenly
Betwixt us and the Sun.

IT SEEMETH HIM BUT THE SKELETON OF A SHIP.

"And straight the Sun was flecked with bars
(Heaven's Mother send us grace!),
As if through a dungeon grate he peered,
With broad and burning face.

" 'Alas!' thought I, and my heart beat loud,
'How fast she nears and nears!
Are those *her* sails that glance in the Sun,
Like restless gossameres?

AND ITS RIBS ARE SEEN AS BARS ON THE FACE OF THE SETTING SUN. THE SPECTER WOMAN AND HER DEATH MATE, AND NO OTHER ON BOARD THE SKELETON SHIP.

" 'Are those *her* ribs through which the Sun
Did peer, as through a grate?
And is that Woman all her crew?
Is that a Death?[16] and are there two?
Is Death that Woman's mate?'

LIKE VESSEL, LIKE CREW!

"Her lips were red, her looks were free,[17]
Her locks were yellow as gold;
Her skin was as white as leprosy;
The Nightmare Life-in-Death was she,
Who thicks man's blood with cold.

DEATH AND LIFE-IN-DEATH HAVE DICED FOR THE SHIP'S CREW, AND SHE (THE LATTER) WINNETH THE ANCIENT MARINER.

"The naked hulk alongside came,
And the twain were casting dice;
'The game is done! I've won! I've won!'
Quoth she, and whistles thrice.

NO TWILIGHT WITHIN THE COURTS OF THE SUN.[18]

"The Sun's rim dips; the stars rush out;
At one stride comes the dark;
With far-heard whisper, o'er the sea,
Off shot the specter bark.

AT THE RISING OF THE MOON,

"We listened and looked sideways up!
Fear at my heart, as at a cup,
My lifeblood seemed to sip!

"The stars were dim, and thick the night;
The steersman's face by his lamp gleamed
white;
From the sails the dew did drip—
Till clomb above the eastern bar
The hornèd Moon,[19] with one bright star
Within the nether tip.

ONE AFTER ANOTHER

"One after one, by the star-dogged Moon,
Too quick for groan or sigh,

16. a Death, a skeleton. *17. her looks were free.* The Specter Woman's manner is bold and brazen. *18. the courts of the sun,* those far northern lands where the sun shines most of the day and night. *19. Till clomb . . . Moon,* until the crescent moon climbed (clomb) high above the eastern horizon (bar).

Each turned his face with a ghastly pang,
And cursed me with his eye.

His shipmates drop down dead,

"Four times fifty living men
(And I heard nor sigh nor groan),
With heavy thump, a lifeless lump,
They dropped down one by one.

But Life-in-Death begins her work on the ancient Mariner.

"The souls did from their bodies fly—
They fled to bliss or woe!
And every soul, it passed me by,
Like the whizz of my crossbow!"

PART THE FOURTH

The Wedding Guest feareth that a Spirit is talking to him;

"I fear thee, ancient Mariner!
I fear thy skinny hand!
And thou art long, and lank, and brown,
As is the ribbed sea sand.

But the ancient Mariner assureth him of his bodily life, and proceedeth to relate his horrible penance.

"I fear thee and thy glittering eye
And thy skinny hand, so brown."
"Fear not, fear not, thou Wedding Guest!
This body dropt not down.

"Alone, alone, all, all alone,
Alone on a wide, wide sea!
And never a saint took pity on
My soul in agony.

He despiseth the creatures of the calm,

"The many men, so beautiful!
And they all dead did lie;
And a thousand thousand slimy things
Lived on; and so did I.

And envieth that they should live, and so many lie dead,

"I looked upon the rotting sea,
And drew my eyes away;
I looked upon the rotting deck,
And there the dead men lay.

"I looked to Heaven, and tried to pray;
But or ever a prayer had gusht,
A wicked whisper came, and made
My heart as dry as dust.

"I closed my lids, and kept them close,
And the balls like pulses beat;
For the sky and the sea, and the sea and the sky
Lay like a load on my weary eye,
And the dead were at my feet.

But the curse liveth for him in the eye of the dead men.

"The cold sweat melted from their limbs;
Nor rot nor reek did they;
The look with which they looked on me
Had never passed away.

In his loneliness and fixedness he yearneth toward the journeying Moon, and the stars that still sojourn, yet still move onward; and everywhere the blue sky belongs to them, and is their appointed rest and their native country and their own natural homes, which they enter unannounced, as lords that are certainly expected and yet there is a silent joy at their arrival.

"An orphan's curse would drag to Hell
A spirit from on high;
But oh! more horrible than that
Is a curse in a dead man's eye!
Seven days, seven nights, I saw that curse,
And yet I could not die.

"The moving Moon went up the sky,
And nowhere did abide;
Softly she was going up,
And a star or two beside–

"Her beams bemocked the sultry main,[20]
Like April hoarfrost spread;
But where the ship's huge shadow lay,
The charmèd water burnt alway
A still and awful red.

By the light of the Moon he beholdeth God's creatures of the great calm,

"Beyond the shadow of the ship,
I watched the water snakes;
They moved in tracks of shining white,
And when they reared, the elfish light
Fell off in hoary flakes.

"Within the shadow of the ship
I watched their rich attire;
Blue, glossy green, and velvet black,
They coiled and swam; and every track
Was a flash of golden fire.

Their beauty and their happiness.

He blesseth them in his heart.

"O happy living things! no tongue
Their beauty might declare;
A spring of love gushed from my heart;
And I blessed them unaware!
Sure my kind saint took pity on me,
And I blessed them unaware.

The spell begins to break.

"The selfsame moment I could pray;
And from my neck so free
The Albatross fell off, and sank
Like lead into the sea."

PART THE FIFTH

"Oh, sleep! it is a gentle thing,
Beloved from pole to pole!

20. ***Her beams . . . main.*** The moonbeams looked cool in contrast to the fiery sea.

To Mary Queen the praise be given!
She sent the gentle sleep from Heaven,
That slid into my soul.

BY THE GRACE OF THE HOLY MOTHER, THE ANCIENT MARINER IS REFRESHED WITH RAIN.

"The silly[21] buckets on the deck,
That had so long remained,
I dreamt that they were filled with dew;
And when I awoke, it rained.

"My lips were wet, my throat was cold,
My garments all were dank,
Sure I had drunken in my dreams,
And still my body drank.

"I moved, and could not feel my limbs;
I was so light—almost
I thought that I had died in sleep,
And was a blessed ghost.

HE HEARETH SOUNDS AND SEETH STRANGE SIGHTS AND COMMOTIONS IN THE SKY AND THE ELEMENT.

"And soon I heard a roaring wind;
It did not come anear;
But with its sound it shook the sails
That were so thin and sere.

"The upper air burst into life!
And a hundred fire-flags sheen[22];
To and fro they were hurried about;
And to and fro, and in and out,
The wan stars danced between.

"And the coming wind did roar more loud,
And the sails did sigh like sedge;
And the rain poured down from one
black cloud;
The Moon was at its edge.

"The thick, black cloud was cleft, and still
The Moon was at its side;
Like waters shot from some high crag,
The lightning fell with never a jag,
A river steep and wide.

THE BODIES OF THE SHIP'S CREW ARE INSPIRED, AND THE SHIP MOVES ON;

"The loud wind never reached the ship,
Yet now the ship moved on!
Beneath the lightning and the Moon
The dead men gave a groan.

"They groaned, they stirred, they all uprose;
Nor spake, nor moved their eyes;
It had been strange, even in a dream,
To have seen those dead men rise.

21. silly, simple. ***22. fireflags sheen***, flashes of lightning shone bright.

"The helmsman steered, the ship moved on;
  Yet never a breeze up-blew.
The mariners all 'gan work the ropes,
  Where they were wont to do;
They raised their limbs like lifeless tools—
  We were a ghastly crew.

"The body of my brother's son
  Stood by me, knee to knee;
The body and I pulled at one rope,
  But he said naught to me."

BUT NOT BY THE SOULS OF THE MEN, NOR BY DEMONS OF EARTH OR MIDDLE AIR, BUT BY A BLESSED TROOP OF ANGELIC SPIRITS, SENT DOWN BY THE INVOCATION OF THE GUARDIAN SAINT.

"I fear thee, ancient Mariner!"
  "Be calm, thou Wedding Guest!
'Twas not those souls that fled in pain,
Which to their corses[23] came again,
  But a troop of spirits blest;

"For when it dawned—they dropped their
    arms
  And clustered round the mast;
Sweet sounds rose slowly through their mouths;
  And from their bodies passed.

"Around, around, flew each sweet sound,
  They darted to the Sun;
Slowly the sounds came back again,
  Now mixed, now one by one.

"Sometimes a-dropping from the sky
  I heard the skylark sing;
Sometimes all little birds that are,
How they seemed to fill the sea and air
  With their sweet jargoning!

23. corses, corpses.

"And now 'twas like all instruments,
  Now like a lonely flute;
And now it is an angel's song,
  That makes the heavens be mute.

"It ceased; yet still the sails made on
  A pleasant noise till noon,
A noise like of a hidden brook
  In the leafy month of June,
That to the sleeping woods all night
  Singeth a quiet tune.

"Till noon we quietly sailed on.
  Yet never a breeze did breathe;
Slowly and smoothly went the ship,
  Moved onward from beneath.

THE LONESOME SPIRIT FROM THE SOUTH POLE CARRIES ON THE SHIP AS FAR AS THE LINE, IN OBEDIENCE TO THE ANGELIC TROOP, BUT STILL REQUIRETH VENGEANCE.

"Under the keel nine fathom deep,
  From the land of mist and snow,
The spirit slid; and it was he
  That made the ship to go.
The sails at noon left off their tune,
  And the ship stood still also.

"The Sun, right up above the mast,
  Had fixed her to the ocean,
But in a minute she 'gan stir,
  With a short, uneasy motion—
Backwards and forwards half her length
  With a short, uneasy motion.

"Then like a pawing horse let go,
  She made a sudden bound;
It flung the blood into my head,
  And I fell down in a swound.

"How long in that same fit I lay,
  I have not to declare;
But ere my living life returned
I heard and in my soul discerned
  Two voices in the air.

THE POLAR SPIRIT'S FELLOW DEMONS, THE INVISIBLE INHABITANTS OF THE ELEMENT, TAKE PART IN HIS WRONG; AND TWO OF THEM RELATE, ONE TO THE OTHER, THAT PENANCE LONG AND HEAVY FOR THE ANCIENT MARINER HATH BEEN ACCORDED TO THE POLAR SPIRIT, WHO RETURNETH SOUTHWARD.

" 'Is it he?' quoth one, 'Is this the man?
  By Him who died on cross,
With his cruel bow he laid full low
  The harmless Albatross.

" 'The spirit who bideth by himself
  In the land of mist and snow,
He loved the bird that loved the man
  Who shot him with his bow.'

"The other was a softer voice,
  As soft as honeydew;
Quoth he, 'The man hath penance done
  And penance more will do.' "

PART THE SIXTH

First Voice
" 'But tell me, tell me! speak again,
  Thy soft response renewing—
What makes that ship drive on so fast?
  What is the Ocean doing?'

Second Voice
" 'Still as a slave before his lord,
  The Ocean hath no blast;
His great bright eye most silently
  Up to the Moon is cast—

" 'If he may know which way to go;
  For she guides him smooth or grim.
See, brother, see! how graciously
  She looketh down on him.'

THE MARINER HATH BEEN CAST INTO A TRANCE; FOR THE ANGELIC POWER CAUSETH THE VESSEL TO DRIVE NORTHWARD FASTER THAN HUMAN LIFE COULD ENDURE.

First Voice
" 'But why drives on that ship so fast,
  Without or[24] wave or wind?'

Second Voice
" 'The air is cut away before,
  And closes from behind.

" 'Fly, brother, fly! more high, more high,
  Or we shall be belated;
For slow and slow that ship will go,
  When the Mariner's trance is abated.'

THE SUPERNATURAL MOTION IS RETARDED; THE MARINER AWAKES, AND HIS PENANCE BEGINS ANEW.

"I woke, and we were sailing on
  As in a gentle weather.
'Twas night, calm night, the Moon was high;
  The dead men stood together.

"All stood together on the deck,
  For a charnel dungeon[25] fitter;
All fixed on me their stony eyes
  That in the Moon did glitter.

"The pang, the curse, with which they died,
  Had never passed away;
I could not draw my eyes from theirs,
  Nor turn them up to pray.

24. or, either. ***25. charnel*** (chär′nəl) ***dungeon,*** burial vault.

THE CURSE IS FINALLY EXPIATED.

"And now this spell was snapt; once more
I viewed the ocean green,
And looked far forth, yet little saw
Of what had else been seen—

"Like one that on a lonesome road
Doth walk in fear and dread,
And having once turned round, walks on,
And turns no more his head,
Because he knows a frightful fiend
Doth close behind him tread.

"But soon there breathed a wind on me,
Nor sound nor motion made;
Its path was not upon the sea,
In ripple or in shade.

"It raised my hair, it fanned my cheek
Like a meadow gale of spring—
It mingled strangely with my fears,
Yet it felt like a welcoming.

"Swiftly, swiftly flew the ship,
Yet she sailed softly, too;
Sweetly, sweetly blew the breeze—
On me alone it blew.

AND THE ANCIENT MARINER BEHOLDETH HIS NATIVE COUNTRY.

"Oh! dream of joy! is this indeed
The lighthouse top I see?
Is this the hill? Is this the kirk?
Is this mine own countree?

"We drifted o'er the harbor bar,
And I with sobs did pray—
'O let me be awake, my God!
Or let me sleep alway.'

"The harbor bay was clear as glass,
So smoothly it was strewn!
And on the bay the moonlight lay,
And the shadow of the Moon.

"The rock shone bright, the kirk no less,
That stands above the rock;
The moonlight steeped in silentness
The steady weathercock.

The angelic spirits leave the dead bodies,

"And the bay was white with silent light,
Till rising from the same,
Full many shapes, that shadows were,
In crimson colors came.

And appear in their own forms of light.

"A little distance from the prow
Those crimson shadows were;
I turned my eyes upon the deck—
Oh, Christ! what I saw there!

"Each corse lay flat, lifeless and flat,
And, by the holy rood![26]
A man all light, a seraph man,
On every corse there stood.

"This seraph band, each waved his hand—
It was a heavenly sight!
They stood as signals to the land,
Each one a lovely light;

"This seraph band, each waved his hand;
No voice did they impart—
No voice; but oh! the silence sank
Like music on my heart.

"But soon I heard the dash of oars,
I heard the Pilot's cheer;
My head was turned perforce away,
And I saw a boat appear.

"The Pilot, and the Pilot's boy,
I heard them coming fast;
Dear Lord in Heaven! it was a joy
The dead men could not blast.

"I saw a third—I heard his voice;
It is the Hermit good!
He singeth loud his godly hymns
That he makes in the wood.
He'll shrieve my soul,[27] he'll wash away
The Albatross's blood."

PART THE SEVENTH

The Hermit of the wood

"This hermit good lives in that wood
Which slopes down to the sea;

26. the holy rood (rüd), the cross of Christ. *27. He'll shrieve* (shrīv) *my soul.* The Hermit of the wood will hear the Ancient Mariner's confession and, after listening to the tale of his wrongdoings, will impose a penance upon him. When this penance is carried out, the Mariner will secure peace and forgiveness for his sins.

How loudly his sweet voice he rears!
He loves to talk with marineres
That come from a far countree.

"He kneels at morn, and noon, and eve—
He hath a cushion plump;
It is the moss that wholly hides
The rotted old oak stump.

"The skiff boat neared; I heard them talk:
'Why, this is strange, I trow![28]
Where are those lights so many and fair
That signal made but now?'

APPROACHETH THE SHIP WITH WONDER.

" 'Strange, by my faith!' the Hermit said—
'And they answered not our cheer!
The planks look warped! and see those sails
How thin they are and sere!
I never saw aught like to them,
Unless perchance it were

" 'Brown skeletons of leaves that lag
My forest brook along;
When the ivy tod[29] is heavy with snow;
And the owlet whoops to the wolf below
That eats the she-wolf's young.'

" 'Dear Lord! it hath a fiendish look'—
(The Pilot made reply)
'I am a-feared'—'Push on, push on!'
Said the Hermit cheerily.

"The boat came closer to the ship,
But I nor spake nor stirred;
The boat came close beneath the ship,
And straight a sound was heard.

THE SHIP SUDDENLY SINKETH.

"Under the water it rumbled on,
Still louder and more dread;
It reached the ship, it split the bay;
The ship went down like lead.

THE ANCIENT MARINER IS SAVED IN THE PILOT'S BOAT.

"Stunned by that loud and dreadful sound,
Which sky and ocean smote,
Like one that hath been seven days drowned
My body lay afloat;
But swift as dreams, myself I found
Within the Pilot's boat.

"Upon the whirl, where sank the ship,
The boat spun round and round;

28. I trow (trō *or* trou), I think. ***29. the ivy tod,*** a clump of ivy.

And all was still, save that the hill
  Was telling of the sound.

"I moved my lips—the Pilot shrieked
  And fell down in a fit;
The holy Hermit raised his eyes
  And prayed where he did sit.

"I took the oars; the Pilot's boy,
  Who now doth crazy go,
Laughed loud and long, and all the while
  His eyes went to and fro.
'Ha! ha!' quoth he, 'full plain I see,
  The Devil knows how to row.'

"And now, all in my own countree,
  I stood on the firm land!
The Hermit stepped forth from the boat,
  And scarcely he could stand.

THE ANCIENT MARINER EARNESTLY ENTREATETH THE HERMIT TO SHRIEVE HIM; AND THE PENANCE OF LIFE FALLS ON HIM,

" 'O shrieve me, shrieve me, holy man!'
  The Hermit crossed his brow.
'Say quick,' quoth he, 'I bid thee say—
  What manner of man art thou?'

"Forthwith this frame of mine was wrenched
  With a woeful agony,
Which forced me to begin my tale;
  And then it left me free.

AND EVER AND ANON THROUGHOUT HIS FUTURE LIFE AN AGONY CONSTRAINETH HIM TO TRAVEL FROM LAND TO LAND,

"Since then, at an uncertain hour,
  That agony returns;
And till my ghastly tale is told,
  This heart within me burns.

"I pass, like night, from land to land;
  I have strange power of speech;
That moment that his face I see,
I know the man that must hear me—
  To him my tale I teach.

"What loud uproar bursts from that door!
  The wedding guests are there;
But in the garden bower the bride
  And bridemaids singing are;
And hark the little vesper bell,
  Which biddeth me to prayer!

"O Wedding Guest! this soul hath been
  Alone on a wide, wide sea;
So lonely 'twas that God himself

Scarce seemèd there to be.

"O sweeter than the marriage feast,
'Tis sweeter far to me,
To walk together to the kirk
With a goodly company!—

AND TO TEACH, BY HIS OWN EXAMPLE, LOVE AND REVERENCE TO ALL THINGS THAT GOD MADE AND LOVETH.

"To walk together to the kirk,
And all together pray,
While each to his great Father bends,
Old men, and babes, and loving friends,
And youths, and maidens gay!

"Farewell, farewell! but this I tell
To thee, thou Wedding Guest!
He prayeth well who loveth well
Both man and bird and beast.

"He prayeth best who loveth best
All things both great and small;
For the dear God who loveth us,
He made and loveth all."

The Mariner, whose eye is bright,
Whose beard with age is hoar,
Is gone; and now the Wedding Guest
Turned from the Bridegroom's door.

He went like one that hath been stunned,
And is of sense forlorn;
A sadder and a wiser man,
He rose the morrow morn.

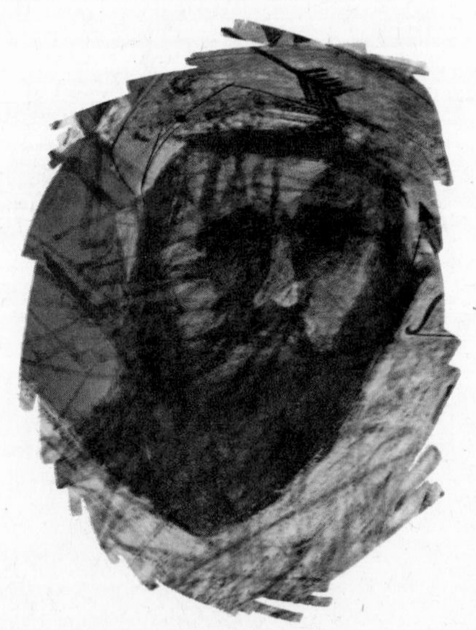

SAMUEL TAYLOR COLERIDGE

Born in 1772 at Ottery St. Mary, in Derbyshire, England, Coleridge very early showed signs of genius. He loved to read, and for hours at a time would lose himself in fantastic dreams in which he figured as a hero of long ago.

In 1791 Coleridge entered Cambridge University; but soon tiring of it, he ran away and joined the army, where he became popular through his ability to write charming love letters for the soldiers to copy and send their sweethearts. Although he later returned to the university, he never completed his course there.

In 1795 Coleridge met the poet William Wordsworth. The two men were soon absorbed in plans for writing a book of poems together. ***Lyrical Ballads***, which appeared in 1798, contained nineteen poems by Wordsworth and only four by Coleridge. But among the four was "The Rime of the Ancient Mariner," which has become one of the most greatly admired poems in the English language.

WHAT DO YOU SAY?

1. The first five stanzas of this poem give the setting. In your own words explain what has happened up to this point.

2. (a) What interrupts the Mariner's tale? ***(b)*** How do lines 31-38 affect the Mariner's tale?

3. (a) What is the dominant imagery in lines 51-62? ***(b)*** What technique is used to express the imagery?

4. What effect did the albatross have on the weather and general welfare of the ship (lines 63-78)?

5. Who is speaking in lines 79-80?

6. Does the Mariner explain why he shot the albatross?

7. (a) Why do the sailors at first chastise the Ancient Mariner and then approve his killing the bird? ***(b)*** Why do they then accuse him once more?

8. What poetic device is used in lines 232-235?

9. (a) Why does the Ancient Mariner bless the water snakes? ***(b)*** What happens as a result?

10. How does the ship eventually get under way again?

11. (a) In what way does the mood of the poem change in lines 350-376? ***(b)*** What does this change contribute to the poem as a whole?

12. How do the Pilot and the Pilot's boy react to the Ancient Mariner?

13. How does the Ancient Mariner select his listeners?

14. Why are lines 614-617 often quoted?

UNIT 3 REVIEW

1. Write a statement that expresses the content of the poem below.

2. Is the poem a lyric or a narrative?

3. What is the tone of the poem?

4. Find examples of auditory imagery, visual imagery, and imagery of touch or feeling.

5. In the poem what metaphor is used for *death*?

6. Point out examples of: (1) similes, (2) personification, (3) alliteration, (4) assonance, (5) onamatopoeia.

From MY SISTER'S SLEEP
by Dante Gabriel Rossetti

She fell asleep on Christmas Eve.
 At length the long-ungranted shade
 Of weary eyelids overweighed
The pain naught else might yet relieve.

Our mother, who had leaned all day
 Over the bed from chime to chime,
 Then raised herself for the first time,
And as she sat her down, did pray.

Her little worktable was spread
 With work to finish. For the glare
 Made by her candle, she had care
To work some distance from the bed.

Without, there was a cold moon up,
 Of winter radiance sheer and thin;
 The hollow halo it was in
Was like an icy crystal cup.

Through the small room, with subtle sound
 Of flame, by vents the fireshine drove
 And reddened. In its dim alcove
The mirror shed a clearness round.

I had been sitting up some nights,
 And my tired mind felt weak and blank;
 Like a sharp strengthening wine it drank
The stillness and the broken lights.

Twelve struck. That sound, by dwindling years
 Heard in each hour, crept off; and then
 The ruffled silence spread again,
Like water that a pebble stirs.

Our mother rose from where she sat;
Her needles, as she laid them down,
Met lightly, and her silken gown
Settled—no other noise than that.

Just then in the room over us
There was a pushing back of chairs,
As some who had sat unawares
So late, now heard the hour, and rose.

With anxious softly-stepping haste
Our mother went where Margaret lay,
Fearing the sounds o'erhead—should they
Have broken her long watched-for rest!

She stooped an instant, calm, and turned,
But suddenly turned back again;
And all her features seemed in pain
With woe, and her eyes gazed and yearned.

For my part, I but hid my face,
And held my breath, and spoke no word.
There was none spoken; but I heard
The silence for a little space.

Our mother bowed herself and wept;
And both my arms fell, and I said,
"God knows I knew that she was dead."
And there, all white, my sister slept.

SUGGESTED READING

ADSHEAD, GLADYS L. AND ANNIS DUFF, eds., *An Inheritance of Poetry.* (Houghton) A collection of sonnets, ballads, and lyrics from England and America.

BENET, STEPHEN VINCENT, *John Brown's Body.* (Rinehart) This famous narrative poem gives a vivid sketch of the Civil War and its effect upon people of the time.

FROST, ROBERT, *Complete Poems of Robert Frost, 1949.* (Holt) One of America's most famous poets presents this collection of poems which reveal his outstanding wit and wisdom. A good introduction to Frost's poetry is provided by *The Road Not Taken.* (Holt)

HAMPSON, ALFRED LEETE, ed., *Poems for Youth.* (Little) Hampson has selected a group of poems by Emily Dickinson which have a special appeal for young people.

KIPLING, RUDYARD, *Rudyard Kipling's Verse.* (Doubleday) A complete collection of Kipling's published poetry is found in this volume.

LEACH, MACEDWARD, *The Ballad Book.* (Harper) Two hundred and fifty favorite English, Scotch, and American ballads have been gathered together in this volume.

MASEFIELD, JOHN, *Salt-water Poems and Ballads.* (Macmillan) Songs of youth and of the sea.

MATTHIESSEN, F. O., ed., *The Oxford Book of American Verse.* (Oxford) A representative selection of poems by fifty-one American poets from colonial times to the present.

MILLAY, EDNA ST. VINCENT, *Edna St. Vincent Millay's Poems Selected for Young People.* (Harper) Containing poems from almost all of her works published prior to 1929, this is another book with a special appeal for young people.

NASH, OGDEN, *Selected Verse.* (Modern Library) One hundred and sixty-five poems by America's wizard of wit.

PLOTZ, HELEN, *Imagination's Other Place: Poems of Science and Mathematics.* (Crowell) A collection of poems about science and well-known scientists.

QUILLER-COUCH, SIR ARTHUR, ed., *The Oxford Book of English Verse.* (Oxford) A collection of poems by English writers from 1300 to the end of the nineteenth century.

SANDBURG, CARL, *Complete Poems.* (Harcourt) This collection includes six volumes of Sandburg's poetry.

TEASDALE, SARA, *The Collected Poems,* (Macmillan) Poems from eight of the author's books are represented in this volume.

UNTERMEYER, LOUIS, ed., *The Magic Circle.* (Harcourt) Over a hundred poems about people, bravery, and our American heritage.

UNTERMEYER, LOUIS, ed., *Modern American and Modern British Poetry.* (Harcourt) Almost eight hundred poems by well-known contemporary poets.

Because the dramatic instinct in people is universal, drama is one of the oldest and most popular types of literature. Yet, a play is simply a story written to be acted out upon a stage. As in a story, a problem is presented which must be solved. Thus there is a plot, there are characters, there is a setting and a theme. But unlike a story, a play has no descriptive passages to explain what the characters do or what they think. This understanding must come through the dialogue, that is, what the characters say, and the action, what the characters do. Thus, a play is a story brought to life by real people upon the stage.

Because you cannot actually see the stage in the play you are about to read, the illustrations will help you to visualize the characters, feel the conflict, and become aware of the effect of setting. To enjoy fully drama as a type of literature you must lose yourself in the spirit of the theater, becoming at once both audience and actor.

Unit 4

INTRODUCTION TO ROMEO AND JULIET

Only a few basic facts, derived from documents and records of the time, are known about William Shakespeare, the foremost dramatist of his own day and one of the greatest writers of all times. He was born in the town of Stratford, England, in April, 1564, the son of a glove-maker. It is probable that he attended the town's free grammar school where, as was the custom, he studied the Greek and Latin classics. The next definite information we have about him is that, at the age of eighteen, he married Anne Hathaway.

Several years after his marriage, Shakespeare left Stratford and went to London where he soon made a name for himself as an actor and where he began writing plays. In 1594, he was listed as a member of the Lord Chamberlain's Company (after 1603 called the King's Men). Among the members of this troupe were some of the greatest actors of the time, and it is very likely that Shakespeare, in developing the characters of his plays, took into consideration the talents of the actors who were to portray them on the stage. By this time Shakespeare was well established as a playwright as well as an actor, and his plays apparently enjoyed tremendous popularity with the theater-going public. In 1598 he is cited by a critic as the best author of both tragedy and comedy for the stage.

The Lord Chamberlain's Company continued to prosper. In 1599, the group erected the famous Globe Theater, the theater in which Shakespeare's greatest plays were probably first produced, and in 1608, the company acquired control of the Blackfriars, the only theater of the time built within the city limits. Shakespeare was a stockholder in both these ventures, suggesting that he had a head for business as well as for acting and writing.

About 1612, having written thirty-seven plays and having become a wealthy man, Shakespeare retired to Stratford where he died on April 23, 1616. The poetic powers of William Shakespeare and the plight of young romantic lovers lost in a world which doesn't understand them, have been combined to create a play which has endured over three centuries, has been performed by the greatest actors of each generation, and receives as much acclaim as when it was first performed.

The plot of *Romeo and Juliet,* as were many of Shakespeare's plots, was borrowed from other sources. The basic theme appears as early as the fourth century B.C. in a tale by a Greek writer. The idea of ill-fated lovers was also immensely popular among Italian writers of the 15th and 16th centuries. But the direct source of *Romeo and Juliet* was a long narrative poem written in 1562 by an English writer, Arthur Brooke. Shakespeare rewrote the story emphasizing certain events and eliminating others, and developing the characters in much greater detail. However, Brooke's original plot included lively action, social conflict, intense passion, and the clash between youth and age. All these, Shakespeare kept.

While it is important in reading *Romeo and Juliet* to appreciate the author's powers of poetic description and the intrigue of the plot, the most important idea to keep in mind is that *Romeo and Juliet* is neither a poem nor a story but a play. First and foremost Shakespeare was a dramatist. To enjoy the reading of *Romeo and Juliet* we must visualize it upon the stage with real actors interpreting real characters in real conflicts.

The Characters of the Play

ESCALUS (es'kə ləs), *Prince of Verona.*

MONTAGUE (mon'tə gū)
CAPULET (kap'ū let) } *heads of two feuding households.*

LADY MONTAGUE
LADY CAPULET } *their wives.*

ROMEO, *the son of the Montagues.*

JULIET, *daughter of the Capulets.*

MERCUTIO (mėr kū'shi ō), *kinsman of Prince Escalus and friend of Romeo.*

BENVOLIO (ben vōl'i ō), *nephew of Montague and friend of Romeo.*

TYBALT (tib'əlt), *nephew of Capulet's wife.*

PARIS, *kinsman of Prince Escalus and a suitor of Juliet.*

FRIAR LAURENCE, *counselor of Romeo.*

FRIAR JOHN, *a trusted messenger of Friar Laurence.*

NURSE, *servant and friend of Juliet.*

OLD MAN, *a member of the Capulet family.*

BALTHASAR (bal thə sär'), *servant of Romeo.*

SAMPSON
GREGORY } *servants of Capulet.*

ABRAHAM, *servant of Montague.*

PETER, *servant of Juliet's nurse.*

APOTHECARY

MASKERS, MUSICIANS, WATCHMEN, PAGES, OFFICERS, CITIZENS, and ATTENDANTS.

Prologue

CHORUS *(spoken by a single actor).* Two households,
both alike in dignity,
In fair Verona, where we lay our scene,
From ancient grudge break to new mutiny,[1]
Where civil blood makes civil hands unclean.[2]
From forth the fatal loins of these two foes
A pair of star-crossed[3] lovers take their life,
Whose misadventured piteous overthrows
Do with their death bury their parents' strife.
The fearful passage[4] of their death-marked love,
And the continuance of their parents' rage,
Which, but[5] their children's end, naught could remove,
Is now the two hours' traffic of our stage,
The which if you with patient ears attend,
What here shall miss, our toil shall strive to mend.
(Exit.)

1. ***mutiny,*** rioting.
2. ***Where civil blood . . . unclean,*** where citizens' hands are soiled with one another's blood.
3. ***star-crossed,*** ill-fated. In Shakespeare's day it was commonly believed that the stars controlled people's lives.
4. ***fearful passage,*** progress that is full of fear.
5. ***but,*** except for.

Act one

Scene 1: A public square in Verona.

Enter SAMPSON *and* GREGORY, *servants of the house of* CAPULET, *armed with swords and bucklers.*[1]

SAMPSON. Gregory, on my word, we'll not carry coals.[2] I mean an[3] we be in choler,[4] we'll draw.

GREGORY. Ay, while you live, draw your neck out o' the collar.[5]

SAMPSON *(with mock belligerence).* I strike quickly, being moved.

GREGORY. But thou art not quickly moved to strike.

SAMPSON. A dog of the house of Montague moves me.

GREGORY. To move is to stir; and to be valiant is to stand; therefore, if thou art moved, thou runn'st away.

SAMPSON. A dog of that house shall move me to stand; I will take the wall of[6] any man of Montague's.

GREGORY. The quarrel is between our masters and us their men.

SAMPSON. 'Tis all one. I will show myself a tyrant.

GREGORY *(warningly).* Draw thy sword! Here comes two of the house of the Montagues.

1. ***bucklers,*** small shields.
2. ***carry coals,*** endure insults.
3. ***an,*** if.
4. ***in choler,*** angry.
5. ***collar,*** a halter used by the hangman.
6. ***take the wall of,*** figurative for "get the better of."

ROTH

SAMPSON. My naked weapon is out; quarrel, I will back thee.

GREGORY. How! Turn thy back and run?

SAMPSON. Fear me not.[7]

GREGORY. No, marry[8]; I fear thee!

SAMPSON. Let us take the law of our sides; let *them* begin.

GREGORY. I will frown as I pass by, and let them take it as they list.[9]

SAMPSON. Nay, as they dare. I will bite my thumb[10] at them; which is a disgrace to them if they bear it.

Enter ABRAHAM *and* BALTHASAR, *servants of the* MONTAGUES.

ABRAHAM. Do you bite your thumb at us, sir?

SAMPSON. I do bite my thumb, sir.

ABRAHAM. Do you bite your thumb at *us*, sir?

SAMPSON *(aside to* GREGORY*)*. Is the law of our side if I say "Ay"?

GREGORY. No.

SAMPSON *(to* ABRAHAM*)*. No, sir, I do not bite my thumb at you, sir; but I bite my thumb, sir.

GREGORY *(to* ABRAHAM*)*. Do you quarrel, sir?

ABRAHAM. Quarrel, sir? No, sir.

SAMPSON. If you do, sir, I am for you. I serve as good a man as you.

ABRAHAM. No better.

SAMPSON. Well, sir.

Enter BENVOLIO, *a nephew of* MONTAGUE *and hence a first cousin of* ROMEO.

GREGORY *(aside to* SAMPSON*)*. Say "better"; here comes one of my master's kinsmen.

SAMPSON. Yes, better, sir.

ABRAHAM. You lie.

SAMPSON. Draw, if you be men. Gregory, remember thy swashing[11] blow. *(The four* SERVANTS *fight.)*

BENVOLIO. Part, fools! *(He beats down their swords.)*

Enter TYBALT, *a hot-headed youth, nephew of* LADY CAPULET *and first cousin of* JULIET.

TYBALT *(contemptuously)*. What, art thou drawn among these heartless hinds?[12]
Turn thee, Benvolio, look upon thy death.

BENVOLIO *(quietly)*. I do but keep the peace. Put up thy sword,
Or manage it to part these men with me.

TYBALT *(scornfully)*. What, drawn, and talk of peace? I hate the word

7. ***Fear me not.*** Don't mistrust me.

8. ***marry,*** by the Virgin Mary; a mild oath.

9. ***list,*** wish.

10. ***bite my thumb,*** an insulting gesture.

11. ***swashing,*** crushing.

12. ***heartless hinds,*** cowardly servants.

As I hate hell, all Montagues, and thee. *(They fight.)*
Have at thee,[13] coward!

Enter several of both houses, who join the fray; then enter CITIZENS *with clubs or other weapons.*

FIRST CITIZEN. Clubs, bills, and partisans![14] Strike! Beat them down!
Down with the Capulets! Down with the Montagues!

Enter CAPULET *in his gown*[15] *and* LADY CAPULET.

CAPULET *(who cannot resist joining in the quarrel).* What noise is this? Give me my long sword, ho!

LADY CAPULET *(scornfully).* A crutch,[16] a crutch! Why call you for a sword?

CAPULET. My sword, I say! Old Montague is come,
And flourishes his blade in spite[17] of me.

Enter MONTAGUE *and* LADY MONTAGUE.

MONTAGUE. Thou villain Capulet! Hold me not, let me go.

LADY MONTAGUE. Thou shalt not stir one foot to seek a foe.

Enter PRINCE ESCALUS, *head of Verona's government, with* ATTENDANTS.

ESCALUS *(sternly).* Rebellious subjects, enemies to peace,
Profaners of this neighbor-stainèd steel—
Will you not hear? What, ho! You men, you beasts,
That quench the fire of your pernicious rage
With purple fountains issuing from your veins,
On pain of torture, from those bloody hands
Throw your mistempered weapons to the ground,
And hear the sentence of your movèd prince.
Three civil brawls, bred of an airy word
By thee, old Capulet, and Montague,
Have thrice disturbed the quiet of our streets.
If ever you disturb our streets again,
Your lives shall pay the forfeit of the peace.[18]
For this time, all the rest depart away.
You, Capulet, shall go along with me;
And, Montague, come you this afternoon
To know our further pleasure in this case,
To old Freetown, our common judgment place.
Once more, on pain of death, all men depart.
(Exeunt[19] *all but* MONTAGUE, LADY MONTAGUE, *and* BENVOLIO.*)*

MONTAGUE. Who set this ancient quarrel new abroach?[20]
(To BENVOLIO.*)* Speak, nephew. Were you by when it began?

BENVOLIO. Here were the servants of your adversary,

13. ***Have at thee.*** I shall attack you; be on your guard.

14. ***bills . . . partisans,*** long-handled spears with sharp cutting blades.

15. ***gown,*** dressing gown.

16. ***crutch.*** Lady Capulet implies that a crutch is better suited to her aged husband than a sword.

17. ***spite,*** defiance.

18. ***forfeit of the peace,*** penalty for disturbing the peace.

19. ***Exeunt,*** the plural form of ***exit.***

20. ***set . . . new abroach,*** reopened or started again this old quarrel.

And yours, close fighting ere I did approach.
I drew to part them; in the instant came
The fiery Tybalt, with his sword prepared,
Which, as he breathed defiance to my ears,
He swung about his head and cut the winds,
Who, nothing hurt withal,[21] hissed him in scorn.
While we were interchanging thrusts and blows,
Came more and more and fought on part and part,
Till the prince came, who parted either part.

LADY MONTAGUE. O, where is Romeo? Saw you him today?
Right glad I am he was not at this fray.

BENVOLIO. Madam, an hour before the worshiped sun
Peered forth the golden window of the east,
A troubled mind drave me to walk abroad;
Where, underneath the grove of sycamore
That westward rooteth from the city's side,
So early walking did I see your son.
Towards him I made, but he was ware of me
And stole into the covert of the wood.
I, measuring his affections[22] by my own,
That most are busied when they're most alone,
Pursued my humor,[23] not pursuing his,
And gladly shunned who gladly fled from me.

MONTAGUE. Many a morning hath he there been seen,
With tears augmenting the fresh morning's dew,
Adding to clouds more clouds with his deep sighs.
But all so soon as the all-cheering sun
Should in the farthest east begin to draw
The shady curtains from Aurora's[24] bed,
Away from light steals home my heavy[25] son,
And private in his chamber pens himself,
Shuts up his windows, locks fair daylight out,
And makes himself an artificial night.
Black and portentous must this humor prove,
Unless good counsel may the cause remove.

BENVOLIO. My noble uncle, do you know the cause?

MONTAGUE. I neither know it nor can learn of him.

BENVOLIO. Have you importuned him by any means?

MONTAGUE. Both by myself and many other friends;
But he, his own affections' counselor,
Is to himself—I will not say how true—
But to himself so secret and so close,[26]
So far from sounding and discovery,[27]
As is the bud bit with an envious[28] worm,
Ere he can spread his sweet leaves[29] to the air,
Or dedicate his beauty to the sun.
Could we but learn from whence his sorrows grow,
We would as willingly give cure as know.

21. ***Who . . . withal,*** the winds, hurt not at all by Tybalt's swinging of his sword.

22. ***affections,*** wishes, feelings.

23. ***humor,*** mood, whim.

24. ***Aurora,*** goddess of the dawn.

25. ***heavy,*** sad.

26. ***close,*** not inclined to talk.

27. ***sounding and discovery,*** responding to efforts to understand his views.

28. ***envious,*** malicious.

29. ***Ere . . . leaves,*** before the bud can open its sweet leaves.

Enter ROMEO *absorbed in thought.*

BENVOLIO. See where he comes; so please you, step aside.
I'll know his grievance or be much denied.[30]
MONTAGUE. I would thou wert so happy by thy stay[31]
To hear true shrift.[32] Come, madam, let's away.
(Exeunt MONTAGUE *and* LADY MONTAGUE.*)*
BENVOLIO. Good morrow, cousin.[33]
ROMEO. Is the day so young?
BENVOLIO. But new struck nine.
ROMEO. Ay me! Sad hours seem long.
Was that my father that went hence so fast?
BENVOLIO. It was. What sadness lengthens Romeo's hours?
ROMEO. Not having that which, having, makes them short.
BENVOLIO. In love?
ROMEO. Out—
BENVOLIO. Of love?
ROMEO. Out of her favor where I am in love.
BENVOLIO. Alas, that Love, so gentle in his view,
Should be so tyrannous and rough in proof![34]
ROMEO. Alas, that Love, whose view is muffled still,[35]
Should, without eyes, see pathways to his will!
Where shall we dine? O me! What fray was here?
Yet tell me not, for I have heard it all.
Here's much to do with hate, but more with love.
Why, then, O brawling love! O loving hate!
O heavy lightness, serious vanity[36];
Misshapen chaos of well-seeming forms!
Feather of lead, bright smoke, cold fire, sick health!
Still-waking[37] sleep, that is not what it is!
This love feel I, that feel no love in this.[38]
Dost thou not laugh?
BENVOLIO. No, coz,[39] I rather weep.
ROMEO. Good heart, at what?
BENVOLIO. At thy good heart's oppression.
ROMEO. Why, such is love's transgression.
Griefs of mine own lie heavy in my breast,
Which thou wilt propagate, to have it pressed[40]
With more of thine; this love that thou hast shown
Doth add more grief to too much of mine own.
Farewell, my coz.
BENVOLIO. Soft! I will go along;
An if you leave me so, you do me wrong.
ROMEO. Tut, I have lost myself; I am not here.
This is not Romeo; he's some otherwhere.
BENVOLIO. Tell me in sadness,[41] who is that you love.
ROMEO. In sadness, cousin, I do love a woman.
BENVOLIO *(smiling).* I aimed so near when I supposed you loved.

30. ***be much denied.*** He will find it difficult to refuse me an answer.
31. ***happy by thy stay,*** fortunate in your waiting.
32. ***To hear true shrift,*** as to hear true confession.
33. ***Good morrow, cousin.*** Good morning, cousin (any relative).
34. ***in proof,*** on trial.
35. ***view . . . still,*** sight is blindfolded always.
36. ***vanity,*** frivolity.
37. ***Still-waking,*** always awake.
38. ***that feel . . . in this,*** that cannot take any pleasure in this love.
39. ***coz,*** a short form of *cousin.*
40. ***pressed,*** oppressed.
41. ***sadness,*** seriousness.

ROMEO. A right good mark-man! And she's fair I love.
BENVOLIO. A right fair mark, fair coz, is soonest hit.
ROMEO. Well, in that hit you miss. She'll not be hit
With Cupid's arrow. She hath Dian's wit[42];
From Love's weak childish bow she lives unharmed.
She will not stay the siege of loving terms,[43]
Nor bide the encounter of assailing eyes;
O, she is rich in beauty, only poor
That, when she dies, with beauty dies her store.[44]
BENVOLIO. Then she hath sworn that she will still live
chaste?
ROMEO. She hath, and in that sparing makes huge waste,
For beauty starved[45] with her severity
Cuts beauty off from all posterity.
She is too fair, too wise, wisely too fair,
To merit bliss by making me despair.
She hath forsworn to love, and in that vow
Do I live dead that live to tell it now.
BENVOLIO. Be ruled by me: forget to think of her.
ROMEO. O, teach me how I should forget to think!
BENVOLIO. By giving liberty unto thine eyes;
Examine other beauties.
ROMEO. 'Tis the way
To call hers exquisite, in question more.[46]
These happy masks that kiss fair ladies' brows,
Being black, put us in mind they hide the fair;
He that is strucken blind cannot forget
The precious treasure of his eyesight lost.
Farewell. Thou canst not teach me to forget.
BENVOLIO. I'll pay that doctrine,[47] or else die in debt.
(Exeunt.)

42. ***Dian's wit,*** the wisdom of the goddess Diana.

43. ***She will not . . . terms.*** She will not listen to avowals of love.

44. ***with beauty . . . store.*** She will die without children, and therefore her beauty will die with her.

45. ***starved,*** killed.

46. ***in question more,*** into greater consideration.

47. ***pay that doctrine,*** teach Romeo to forget.

CONSIDERING THE PROLOGUE AND SCENE 1

1. *(a)* Name the heads of the two households, or families, mentioned in the first line of the Prologue. *(b)* Identify the following characters who appear in Scene 1: Tybalt, Benvolio, Romeo, Escalus.

2. *(a)* What atmosphere does the Prologue suggest will be most strongly stressed in the play? *(b)* Choose words, phrases, or sentences from the Prologue that most clearly indicate this atmosphere.

3. What do you think was Shakespeare's purpose in beginning the action of the play with the quarrel between the servants rather than with the clash between Benvolio and Tybalt?

4. *(a)* What threat does Prince Escalus make against the "enemies of peace"? *(b)* Do you think this threat will or will not end the conflict between the feuding families? State your reasons.

5. *(a)* What is Romeo's mood in this first scene and what has caused it? *(b)* How, according to Benvolio, might Romeo alter that mood? *(c)* How does Romeo react to Benvolio's suggestion? Why?

ROTH.

Scene 2: A street in Verona.

Enter CAPULET, PARIS, *and* SERVANT.

CAPULET *(addressing* PARIS*)*. But Montague is bound[1] as well as I,
In penalty alike; and 'tis not hard, I think,
For men so old as we to keep the peace.

PARIS. Of honorable reckoning[2] are you both;
And pity 'tis you lived at odds so long.
But now, my lord, what say you to my suit?

CAPULET. But saying o'er what I have said before:
My child is yet a stranger in the world;
She hath not seen the change of fourteen years.
Let two more summers wither in their pride,
Ere we may think her ripe to be a bride.
The earth hath swallowed all my hopes but she;
She is the hopeful lady of my earth.[3]
But woo her, gentle Paris, get her heart;
My will to her consent is but a part.[4]
An she agree, within her scope of choice
Lies my consent and fair according voice.
This night I hold an old accustomed feast,
Whereto I have invited many a guest,
Such as I love, and you, among the store,
One more, most welcome, makes my number more.
At my poor house look to behold this night
Earth-treading stars that make dark heaven light:
Such comfort as do lusty young men feel
When well-appareled April on the heel
Of limping winter treads, even such delight
Among fresh female buds shall you this night
Inherit[5] at my house; hear all, all see,
And like her most whose merit most shall be.
Come, go with me. *(To* SERVANT, *giving him a paper.)* Go, sirrah,[6] trudge about
Through fair Verona; find those persons out
Whose names are written there, and to them say
My house and welcome on their pleasure stay.

(Exeunt CAPULET *and* PARIS.*)*

SERVANT *(peering at the paper)*. I am sent to find those persons whose names are here writ, and can never find what names the writing person hath here writ. I must to the learned!

Enter BENVOLIO *and* ROMEO.

BENVOLIO. Tut, man, one fire burns out another's burning,

1. ***bound,*** obliged to keep the peace.

2. ***reckoning,*** reputation.

3. ***hopeful lady of my earth,*** center of my existence.

4. ***My will . . . part.*** My wishes are of secondary importance to her consent.

5. ***Inherit,*** enjoy.

6. ***sirrah,*** customary form of address to servants.

One pain is lessened by another's anguish.
Take thou some new infection to thy eye,
And the rank poison of the old will die.

ROMEO. Your plantain leaf[7] is excellent for that.

BENVOLIO. For what, I pray thee?

ROMEO. For your broken shin.

BENVOLIO. Why, Romeo, art thou mad?

ROMEO. Not mad, but bound more than a madman is;
Shut up in prison, kept without my food,
Whipped and tormented and—God-den,[8] good fellow.

SERVANT. God gi' god-den. I pray, sir, can you read?

ROMEO. Ay, mine own fortune in my misery.

SERVANT. Perhaps you have learned it without book; but, I pray, can you read anything you see?

ROMEO. Ay, if I know the letters and the language.

SERVANT. Ye say honestly; rest you merry![9]

(He thinks ROMEO *is not taking him seriously, and starts to leave.)*

ROMEO. Stay, fellow; I can read. *(He reads the paper.)* "Signior Martino and his wife and daughters; County Anselme and his beauteous sisters; the lady widow of Vitruvio; Signior Placentio and his lovely nieces; Mercutio and his brother Valentine; mine uncle Capulet, his wife and daughters; my fair niece Rosaline; Livia; Signior Valentio and his cousin Tybalt; Lucio and the lively Helena."

(He returns the paper to the SERVANT.*)*

A fair assembly; whither should they come?

SERVANT. Up.

ROMEO. Wither?

SERVANT. To supper; to our house.

ROMEO. Whose house?

SERVANT. My master's.

ROMEO. Indeed, I should have asked you that before.

SERVANT. Now I'll tell you without asking. My master is the great rich Capulet; and if you be not of the house of Montagues, I pray come and crush a cup[10] of wine. Rest you merry!

(Exit.)

BENVOLIO. At this same ancient[11] feast of Capulet's
Sups the fair Rosaline whom thou so lovest,
With all the admirèd beauties of Verona.
Go thither, and, with unattainted[12] eye,
Compare her face with some that I shall show,
And I will make thee think thy swan a crow.

ROMEO. One fairer than my love! The all-seeing sun
Ne'er saw her match since first the world begun.

7. ***plantain leaf,*** used as a salve for bruises.

8. ***God-den,*** a greeting like "good evening;" literally, "God give you a good evening."

9. ***rest you merry!*** May you continue happy.

10. ***crush a cup,*** have a drink; a slang term like "crack a bottle" today.

11. ***ancient,*** customary.

12. ***unattainted,*** unprejudiced, impartial.

BENVOLIO. Tut, you saw her fair, none else being by,
But weigh your lady against some other maid
That I will show you shining at this feast,
And she shall scant show well that now shows best.
ROMEO. I'll go along, no such sight to be shown,
But to rejoice in splendor of mine own.[13]
(Exeunt.)

13. ***splendor of mine own,*** the beauty of the lady I love.

CONSIDERING ACT ONE, SCENE 2

1. *(a)* In his talk with Capulet, what proposal does Paris make? *(b)* What is Capulet's reaction to that proposal?

2. What do you think Shakespeare's purpose was in having the Capulets plan a party?

3. *(a)* Quote arguments used by Benvolio in attempting to persuade Romeo to attend the party. *(b)* What reason does Romeo give for deciding to go to the party after all?

Scene 3: A room in Capulet's house.

Enter LADY CAPULET *and* NURSE.

LADY CAPULET. Nurse, where's my daughter? Call her forth to me.
NURSE. I'll bid her come. What, lamb! What, ladybird!
God forbid! Where's this girl? What, Juliet!

Enter JULIET.

JULIET. How now! Who calls?
NURSE. Your mother.
JULIET. Madam, I am here. What is your will?
LADY CAPULET. This is the matter:—Nurse, give leave[1] awhile,
We must talk in secret.—Nurse, come back again;
I have remembered me, thou's[2] hear our counsel.
Thou know'st my daughter's of a pretty age.
NURSE. Faith, I can tell her age unto an hour.
LADY CAPULET. She's not fourteen.
NURSE. I'll lay fourteen of my teeth—
And yet, to my teen[3] be it spoken, I have but four—
She is not fourteen. How long is it now
To Lammastide?[4]
LADY CAPULET. A fortnight and odd days.
NURSE. Even or odd, of all days in the year,
Come Lammas Eve at night shall she be fourteen.

1. ***give leave,*** leave us alone.
2. ***thou's,*** thou shalt.
3. ***teen,*** sorrow, grief.
4. ***Lammastide,*** August 1.

Susan and she—God rest all Christian souls!—
Were of an age. Well, Susan is with God;
She was too good for me. But, as I said,
On Lammas Eve at night shall she be fourteen;
That shall she, marry; I remember it well.
'Tis since the earthquake[5] now eleven years;
And she was weaned—I never shall forget it—
Of all the days of the year, upon that day.
My lord and you were then at Mantua:—
Nay, I do bear a brain[6]; but, as I said,
Since that time it is eleven years;
For then she could stand alone. Nay, by the rood,[7]
She could have run and waddled all about,
For even the day before, she broke her brow.[8]
And then my husband—God be with his soul!
A'[9] was a merry man—took up the child.
"Yea," quoth he, "dost thou fall upon thy face?
Thou wilt fall backward when thou hast more wit,
Wilt thou not, Jule?" and, by my holidame,[10]
The pretty wretch left crying and said "Ay."
To see, now, how a jest shall come about!
I warrant, an I should live a thousand years,
I never should forget it: "Wilt thou not, Jule?" quoth he;
And, pretty fool, it stinted[11] and said "Ay."

LADY CAPULET. Enough of this; I pray thee, hold thy peace.

NURSE. Yes, madam; yet I cannot choose but laugh
To think it should leave crying and say "Ay."

JULIET. And stint thou, too, I pray thee, Nurse, say I.

NURSE. Peace, I have done. God mark thee to His grace!
Thou wast the prettiest babe that e'er I nursed;
An I might live to see thee married once,
I have my wish.

LADY CAPULET. Marry, that "marry" is the very theme
I came to talk of. Tell me, daughter Juliet,
How stands your disposition to be married?

JULIET. It is an honor that I dream not of.

LADY CAPULET. Well, think of marriage now; by my count,
I was your mother much upon these years[12]
That you are now a maid. Thus, then, in brief:
The valiant Paris seeks you for his love.

NURSE. A man, young lady! Lady, such a man
As all the world—why, he's a man of wax.[13]

LADY CAPULET. Verona's summer hath not such a flower.

NURSE. Nay, he's a flower; in faith, a very flower.

LADY CAPULET *(to* JULIET*)*. What say you? Can you love the gentleman?
This night you shall behold him at our feast.

5. ***earthquake,*** possibly a reference to a famous earthquake in 1580—eleven years earlier than it is thought Shakespeare may have been writing the play (1591).

6. ***bear a brain,*** have a good brain or memory.

7. ***rood,*** Holy Cross.

8. ***even . . . brow,*** just the day before she cut her forehead.

9. ***A',*** he.

10. ***by my holidame,*** a mild oath.

11. ***stinted,*** stopped crying.

12. ***much upon these years,*** almost at the same age.

13. ***a man of wax,*** as handsome as if modeled in wax.

Read o'er the volume of young Paris' face
And find delight writ there with beauty's pen;
Speak briefly; can you like of Paris' love?
JULIET. I'll look to like, if looking liking move.[14]

14. *I'll look . . . move.* I am ready to look on him favorably—if mere eyesight can inspire liking.

Enter a SERVANT.

SERVANT. Madam, the guests are come, supper served up, you called, my young lady asked for, the nurse cursed in the pantry, and everything in extremity. I must hence to wait; I beseech you, follow straight.[15]

15. *straight,* immediately.

LADY CAPULET. We follow thee. (*Exit* SERVANT.) Juliet,
the county stays.[16]
NURSE. Go girl, seek happy days. (*Exeunt.*)

16. *the county stays,* Count Paris awaits you.

CONSIDERING ACT ONE, SCENE 3

1. *(a)* What subject does Lady Capulet want to take up with Juliet? *(b)* How is their conversation postponed for a considerable time?

2. Which of these terms accurately describe the nurse: ***garrulous, refined, reserved, ready to give advice***? Point out supporting evidence for your choices.

3. What is Juliet's attitude toward marrying Paris?

Scene 4: A street in Verona that same evening.

Enter ROMEO, MERCUTIO, BENVOLIO, *with five or six* MASKERS, TORCHBEARERS, *and* OTHERS.

ROMEO. What, shall we on without apology?
BENVOLIO. We'll measure them a measure,[1] and be gone.
ROMEO. Give me a torch; I am not for this ambling[2];
Being but heavy, I will bear the light.
MERCUTIO. Nay, gentle Romeo, we must have you dance.
ROMEO. Not I, believe me. You have dancing shoes
With nimble soles; I have a soul of lead
So stakes me to the ground I cannot move.
MERCUTIO. You are a lover; borrow Cupid's wings,
And soar with them above a common bound.[3]
ROMEO. I am too sore enpierced with his shaft
To soar with his light feathers; and so bound,
I cannot bound a pitch[4] above dull woe.
Under love's heavy burden do I sink.

1. ***measure . . . measure,*** perform a dance.
2. ***ambling,*** dancing in an affected manner.
3. ***bound,*** leap.
4. ***pitch,*** any distance.

MERCUTIO. And, to sink in it, should you burden love—
Too great oppression for a tender thing.
ROMEO *(sighing)*. Is love a tender thing? It is too rough,
Too rude, too boisterous, and it pricks like thorn.
MERCUTIO. If love be rough with you, be rough with love.
Give me a case[5] to put my visage in:
A visor for a visor![6] *(Puts on a mask.)* What care I
What curious eye doth quote[7] deformities?
BENVOLIO. Come, knock and enter; and no sooner in
But every man betake him to his legs.
ROMEO. A torch for me. Let wantons light of heart
Tickle the senseless rushes[8] with their heels;
For I am proverbed with a grandsire phrase[9];
I'll be a candle-holder,[10] and look on.
MERCUTIO. Come, we burn daylight,[11] ho!
ROMEO. Nay, that's not so.
MERCUTIO. I mean, sir, in delay
We waste our lights in vain, like lamps by day.
ROMEO. We mean well in going to this mask, sir;
But 'tis no wit to go.
MERCUTIO. Why, may one ask?
ROMEO. I dreamed a dream tonight.[12]
MERCUTIO. And so did I.
ROMEO. Well, what was yours?
MERCUTIO. That dreamers often lie.
ROMEO. In bed asleep while they do dream things true.
MERCUTIO. O, then, I see Queen Mab[13] hath been with you.
She is the fairies' midwife, and she comes
In shape no bigger than an agate stone
On the forefinger of an alderman,
Drawn with a team of little atomies[14]
Athwart men's noses as they lie asleep;
Her wagon spokes made of long spinners'[15] legs,
The cover of the wings of grasshoppers,
The traces of the smallest spider's web,
The collars of the moonshine's watery beams,
Her whip of cricket's bone, the lash of film,[16]
Her wagoner[17] a small gray-coated gnat,
Not half so big as a round little worm
Pricked from the lazy finger of a maid.[18]
Her chariot is an empty hazel nut
Made by the joiner squirrel or old grub,
Time out o' mind the fairies' coachmakers.
And in this state[19] she gallops night by night
Through lovers' brains, and then they dream of love;
O'er lawyers' fingers, who straight dream on fees;
O'er ladies' lips who straight on kisses dream,
Which oft the angry Mab with blisters plagues,

5. ***case,*** mask.
6. ***A visor . . . visor,*** a mask for an ugly, masklike face.
7. ***quote,*** take notice of.
8. ***senseless rushes,*** unfeeling fibers used as floor coverings.
9. ***proverbed . . . phrase,*** taught by an old saying.
10. ***candle-holder,*** spectator.
11. ***burn daylight,*** to light a candle while the sun is shining; figuratively used of wasting time, as Mercutio explains.
12. ***tonight,*** last night.
13. **Queen Mab,** the fairy queen.
14. ***atomies,*** tiny creatures.
15. ***spinners',*** spiders'.
16. ***film,*** delicate, light thread.
17. ***wagoner,*** coachman.
18. ***worm . . . maid.*** It was popularly believed that worms breed in the fingers of the idle.
19. ***state,*** pomp, dignity.

Because their breaths with sweetmeats tainted are.
Sometime she gallops o'er a courtier's nose,
And then dreams he of smelling out a suit[20];
Sometime she driveth o'er a soldier's neck,
And then dreams he of cutting foreign throats,
Of breaches, ambuscadoes, Spanish blades,[21]
Of healths five-fathom deep; and then anon
Drums in his ear, at which he starts and wakes,
And being thus frighted swears a prayer or two
And sleeps again. This is that very Mab
That plaits the manes of horses in the night,
And bakes the elf locks in foul sluttish hairs,[22]
Which once untangled much misfortune bodes;
This is she—

ROMEO. Peace, peace, Mercutio, peace!
Thou talk'st of nothing.

MERCUTIO. True, I talk of dreams,
Which are the children of an idle brain,
Begot of nothing but vain fantasy,
Which is as thin of substance as the air
And more inconstant than the wind, who woos
Even now the frozen bosom of the north,
And, being angered, puffs away from thence,
Turning his face to the dew-dropping south.

BENVOLIO. This wind you talk of blows us from ourselves;
Supper is done, and we shall come too late.

ROMEO. I fear, too early; for my mind misgives
Some consequence yet hanging in the stars[23]
Shall bitterly begin his fearful date[24]
With this night's revels and expire[25] the term
Of a despisèd life closed in my breast
By some vile forfeit of untimely death.
But He that hath the steerage of my course,
Direct my sail! On, lusty gentlemen.

(Exeunt.)

20. ***smelling out a suit,*** seeing an opportunity to gain royal favor.

21. ***ambuscadoes, Spanish blades,*** surprise attacks with swords made of fine steel from Toledo, in Spain.

22. ***bakes . . . hairs,*** mats together and tangles the hair.

23. ***misgives . . . stars,*** forebodes some future misfortune not yet determined.

24. ***his fearful date,*** its dreaded time.

25. ***expire,*** bring to an end.

CONSIDERING ACT ONE, SCENE 4

1. Although Mercutio and Romeo are close friends, they differ strongly in their attitudes toward life. How are their contrasting moods brought out in this scene?

2. Does Mercutio's long Queen Mab speech make any contribution to *(a)* advancing the plot of the play, *(b)* understanding the characters? On what grounds, if any, might it be defended?

Scene 5: A spacious room in Capulet's house.

MUSICIANS *waiting. Enter* CAPULET, LADY CAPULET, *with* JULIET, *the* NURSE, TYBALT, *and others of the* CAPULET *clan, mingling with, and talking to, the* GUESTS *and the* MASKERS.

CAPULET. *(As he speaks, the conversation dies down.)* Welcome, gentlemen! Ladies that have their toes
Unplagued with corns will have a bout[1] with you.
Ah ha, my mistresses! Which of you all
Will now deny to dance? She that makes dainty,[2]
She, I'll swear, hath corns; am I come near ye now?[3]
Welcome, gentlemen! I have seen the day
That I have worn a visor and could tell
A whispering tale in a fair lady's ear,
Such as would please. 'Tis gone, 'tis gone, 'tis gone.
You are welcome, gentlemen! Come, musicians, play.
A hall, a hall![4] Give room, and foot it, girls.
(Music plays, and they dance.)
(To SERVANTS.*)* More light, you knaves, and turn the tables up,[5]
And quench the fire, the room is grown too hot.
(To an elderly kinsman.) Nay, sit, nay, sit, good cousin Capulet,
For you and I are past our dancing days.
How long is 't now since last yourself and I
Were in a mask?

SECOND CAPULET. By'r lady,[6] thirty years.

CAPULET. What, man! 'Tis not so much, 'tis not so much.
'Tis since the nuptial of Lucentio,
Come Pentecost as quickly as it will,
Some five and twenty years, and then we masked.

SECOND CAPULET. 'Tis more, 'tis more, his son is elder, sir;
His son is thirty.

CAPULET. Will you tell me that?
His son was but a ward two years ago.

*(*ROMEO, *who has been trying to locate* ROSALINE, *catches a fleeting glimpse of* JULIET, *whose beauty dazzles him. He halts a passing* SERVANT.*)*

ROMEO. What lady is that, which doth enrich the hand
Of yonder knight?

SERVANT. I know not, sir.[7]

ROMEO. O, she doth teach the torches to burn bright!
It seems she hangs upon the cheek of night
Like a rich jewel in an Ethiope's ear;
Beauty too rich for use, for earth too dear![8]

1. ***have a bout,*** dance a turn.

2. ***makes dainty,*** affectedly hesitates to dance.

3. ***am . . . now?*** Have I hit home to the truth?

4. ***A hall, a hall!*** Make room!

5. ***turn the tables up.*** The tables were flat leaves hinged together and placed on trestles. When they were folded, they took little space.

6. ***By'r lady,*** by the Virgin Mary; a mild oath.

7. ***I know not, sir.*** The servant has been hired for the party and does not know Juliet.

8. ***dear,*** precious.

ROTH

So shows a snowy dove trooping with crows,
As yonder lady o'er her fellows shows.
The measure done, I'll watch her place of stand,
And, touching hers, make blessèd my rude hand.
Did my heart love till now? Forswear it, sight!
For I ne'er saw true beauty till this night.

TYBALT *(who has been standing near* ROMEO*)*. This by his voice, should be a Montague.
Fetch me my rapier, boy. What, dares the slave
Come hither, covered with an antic face,
To fleer[9] and scorn at our solemnity?[10]
Now, by the stock and honor of my kin,
To strike him dead I hold it not a sin.

CAPULET *(overhearing* TYBALT*)*. Why, how now, kinsman! Wherefore storm you so?

TYBALT. Uncle, this is a Montague, our foe,
A villain that is hither come in spite,
To scorn at our solemnity this night.

CAPULET. Young Romeo, is it?

TYBALT. 'Tis he, that villain Romeo.

CAPULET. Content thee, gentle coz, let him alone;
He bears him like a portly[11] gentleman;
And, to say truth, Verona brags of him
To be a virtuous and well-governed youth.
I would not for the wealth of all the town
Here in my house do him disparagement;
Therefore be patient, take no note of him.
It is my will, the which if thou respect,
Show a fair presence and put off these frowns,
An ill-beseeming semblance for a feast.

TYBALT. It fits when such a villain is a guest;
I'll not endure him.

CAPULET *(sternly)*. He shall be endured.
What, goodman boy![12] I say, he shall. Go to[13];
Am I the master here, or you? Go to.
You'll not endure him! God shall mend my soul![14]
You'll make a mutiny among my guests!

TYBALT *(grumbling)*. Why, Uncle, 'tis a shame.

CAPULET. Go to, go to.
You are a saucy boy; is't so, indeed?
This trick may chance to scathe[15] you, I know what.
You must contrary me![16] Marry, 'tis time.
(To GUESTS.*)* Well said, my hearts![17] *(To* TYBALT.*)* You are a princox[18]; go.
Be quiet, or— *(To* SERVANTS.*)* More light, more light! *(To* TYBALT.*)* For shame!
I'll make you quiet. *(To* GUESTS.*)* What, cheerly, my hearts!

9. ***fleer,*** sneer.
10. ***solemnity,*** celebration.
11. ***portly,*** of good carriage.
12. ***goodman boy,*** a scornful term.
13. ***Go to,*** come now (a reproof).
14. ***God . . . soul!*** God save me!
15. ***scathe,*** injure.
16. ***You must contrary me!*** You insist on opposing my wishes!
17. ***Well said, my hearts!*** You have danced well, good fellows!
18. ***princox,*** a saucy youngster.

TYBALT. Patience perforce[19] with willful choler meeting
Makes my flesh tremble in their different greeting.[20]
I will withdraw; but this intrusion shall,
Now seeming sweet, convert to bitter gall.
(Exit.)

19. ***Patience perforce,*** imposed patience or restraint.
20. ***different greeting,*** opposition.

ROMEO *(to* JULIET.*)* If I profane with my unworthiest hand
This holy shrine, the gentle fine[21] is this:
My lips, two blushing pilgrims, ready stand
To smooth that rough touch with a tender kiss.

21. ***gentle fine,*** mild penance.

JULIET. Good pilgrim,[22] you do wrong your hand too much,
Which mannerly devotion shows in this;
For saints have hands that pilgrims' hands do touch,
And palm to palm is holy palmers' kiss.

22. ***pilgrim.*** Romeo was masquerading as a palmer—a pilgrim who had visited the Holy Land.

ROMEO. Have not saints lips, and holy palmers too?
JULIET. Ay, pilgrim, lips that they must use in prayer.
ROMEO. O, then, dear saint, let lips do what hands do;
They pray, grant thou, lest faith turn to despair.
JULIET. Saints do not move, though grant for prayers' sake.
ROMEO. Then move not, while my prayer's effect I take.
Thus from my lips, by yours, my sin is purged.
(His lips touch hers.)
JULIET. Then have my lips the sin that they have took.
ROMEO. Sin from my lips? O trespass sweetly urged!
Give me my sin again.
JULIET. You kiss by the book.[23]

23. ***by the book,*** according to rule.

NURSE *(who has made her way through the crowds to find* JULIET*).* Madam, your mother craves a word with you.
ROMEO *(aside to the* NURSE*).* What is her mother?
NURSE *(aside to* ROMEO*).* Marry, bachelor,
Her mother is the lady of the house,
And a good lady, and a wise and virtuous.
I nursed her daughter, that you talked withal[24];
I tell you, he that can lay hold of her
Shall have the chinks.[25]
ROMEO. Is she a Capulet?
O dear[26] account! My life is my foe's debt.[27]

24. ***withal,*** with.
25. ***chinks,*** money (inherited by Juliet from her father).
26. ***dear,*** costly.
27. ***my foe's debt,*** a debt due my foe, which he may or may not take, as he wishes.

BENVOLIO *(coming forward).* Away, be gone; the sport is at the best.
ROMEO. Ay, so I fear; the more is my unrest.
CAPULET *(addressing the guests who are about to take their leave).* Nay, gentlemen, prepare not to be gone;
We have a trifling foolish banquet towards.[28]
Is it e'en so? Why, then, I thank you all;
I thank you, honest gentlemen; good night.
(To a SERVANT.*)* More torches here! Come on, then, let's to bed.
Ah, sirrah, by my fay,[29] it waxes late;
I'll to my rest.

28. ***foolish banquet towards,*** a simple dessert about to be served.
29. ***fay,*** faith.

(BENVOLIO *and* ROMEO *join the departing guests;* NURSE *stands near* JULIET.)

JULIET. Come hither, Nurse. What is yond gentleman?
NURSE. The son and heir of old Tiberio.
JULIET. What's he that now is going out of door?
NURSE. Marry, that, I think, be young Petrucio.
JULIET. What's he that follows there, that would not dance?
NURSE. I know not. *(The* NURSE *does know, but tries to keep* JULIET *from learning that the man is* ROMEO*—and a* MONTAGUE.*)*
JULIET. Go, ask his name. If he is married,
My grave is like to be my wedding bed.
NURSE *(seeing that it is useless to hide* ROMEO*'s identity).*
His name is Romeo, and a Montague,
The only son of your great enemy.
JULIET. My only love sprung from my only hate!
Too early seen unknown, and known too late!
Prodigious[30] birth of love it is to me,
That I must love a loathèd enemy.
NURSE. What's this? What's this?
JULIET. A rhyme I learned even now
Of one I danced withal.

(A call off-stage: "Juliet.")

NURSE. Anon, anon!
Come, let's away; the strangers all are gone.

(Exeunt.)

30. ***Prodigious,*** suggesting bad luck.

CONSIDERING ACT ONE, SCENE 5

1. *(a)* What is the general atmosphere as the scene opens? *(b)* How is that atmosphere affected by Tybalt's attitude toward Romeo? *(c)* What is the atmosphere as the scene ends?

2. In line 35, page 302, Romeo asks, "Did my heart love till now?" How would you answer his question? Give reasons for your answer.

3. Having fallen deeply in love, Romeo and Juliet kiss and part. Then each makes a surprising discovery. *(a)* What is that discovery? *(b)* How does the discovery affect both Romeo and Juliet?

LOOKING BACK—AND AHEAD

1. Make a brief outline of the most important events that have taken place in Act One.

2. Before starting to read Act Two, list several things that you think may happen now.

Act two

Scene 1: A lane outside the wall of Capulet's orchard.

Enter ROMEO.

ROMEO. Can I go forward when my heart is here?
Turn back, dull earth,[1] and find thy center[2] out.
(He climbs the wall and leaps down within it.)

1. ***dull earth,*** Romeo himself.
2. ***thy center,*** Juliet.

Enter BENVOLIO *and* MERCUTIO.

BENVOLIO *(calling to the hidden* ROMEO*).* Romeo! My cousin Romeo!
MERCUTIO. He is wise,
And, on my life, hath stolen him home to bed.
BENVOLIO. He ran this way, and leaped this orchard wall.
Call, good Mercutio.
MERCUTIO *(jestingly).* Nay, I'll conjure too.
Romeo! Humors![3] Madman! Passion! Lover!
Appear thou in the likeness of a sigh;
Speak but one rhyme, and I am satisfied;
Cry but "Ay me"; pronounce but "love" and "dove."
(To BENVOLIO.*)* He heareth not, he stirreth not, he moveth not;
The ape[4] is dead, and I must conjure him.
(Calls jestingly to ROMEO.*)* I conjure thee by Rosaline's bright eyes,
By her high forehead and her scarlet lip,
That in thy likeness thou appear to us!
BENVOLIO. An if he hear thee, thou wilt anger him.
MERCUTIO. This cannot anger him; my invocation
Is fair and honest,[5] and in his mistress' name
I conjure only but to raise up him.
BENVOLIO. Come, he hath hid himself among these trees,
To be consorted with the humorous night[6];
Blind is his love and best befits the dark.
MERCUTIO. If love be blind, love cannot hit the mark.
Romeo, good night. I'll to my truckle bed[7];
This field bed[8] is too cold for me to sleep.
Come, shall we go?
BENVOLIO. Go, then; for 'tis in vain
To seek him here that means not to be found. *(Exeunt.)*

3. ***Humors!*** Whims.

4. ***ape.*** Used as a term of endearment.

5. ***honest,*** honorable.

6. ***consorted . . . night,*** associated with the moist night.

7. ***truckle bed,*** a small bed that can be run under a larger one.
8. ***field bed,*** the ground.

CONSIDERING ACT TWO, SCENE 1

1. Why does Romeo hide from Benvolio and Mercutio?
2. Do you think Benvolio and Mercutio realize that Romeo has found a new love? Quote lines to support your answer.

Scene 2: A beautiful orchard in the Capulets' grounds, with a balcony of the house prominently placed outside Juliet's bedroom.

Enter ROMEO.

ROMEO. He jests at scars that never felt a wound.[1]
(Catching sight of JULIET *at her dimly lighted window.)*
But soft, what light through yonder window breaks?
It is the east, and Juliet is the sun.
Arise, fair sun, and kill the envious moon,
Who is already sick and pale with grief,
That thou her maid art far more fair than she.
Be not her maid, since she is envious.

JULIET *steps out onto the balcony.*

It is my lady. O, it is my love!
O, that she knew she were!
She speaks, yet she says nothing. What of that?
Her eye discourses; I will answer it.
I am too bold, 'tis not to me she speaks;
Two of the fairest stars in all the heaven,
Having some business, do entreat her eyes
To twinkle in their spheres[2] till they return.
What if her eyes were there, they in her head?
The brightness of her cheek would shame those stars
As daylight doth a lamp; her eyes in heaven
Would through the airy region stream so bright
That birds would sing and think it were not night.
See how she leans her cheek upon her hand!
O, that I were a glove upon that hand,
That I might touch that cheek!

JULIET. Ay me!

ROMEO. She speaks.
O, speak again, bright angel, for thou art
As glorious to this night, being o'er my head,
As is a wingèd messenger of heaven
Unto the white-upturnèd wondering eyes
Of mortals that fall back to gaze on him
When he bestrides the lazy-pacing clouds
And sails upon the bosom of the air.

JULIET *(unaware that she is being overheard).* O Romeo,
Romeo, wherefore art thou Romeo?
Deny thy father and refuse thy name;
Or, if thou wilt not, be but sworn my love,
And I'll no longer be a Capulet.

ROMEO *(aside).* Shall I hear more, or shall I speak at this?

1. ***He jests . . . wound.*** Romeo has overheard the jests made by Mercutio, who, Romeo says, has never known the pangs of love.

2. ***spheres,*** the hollow, transparent globes in which, it was believed, the stars and other planets were set.

JULIET. 'Tis but thy name that is my enemy;
Thou art thyself, though not a Montague.[3]
What's Montague? It is nor hand nor foot,
Nor arm, nor face, nor any other part
Belonging to a man. O, be some other name!
What's in a name? That which we call a rose
By any other name would smell as sweet;
So Romeo would, were he not Romeo called,
Retain that dear perfection which he owes[4]
Without that title. Romeo, doff thy name,
And for that name, which is no part of thee,
Take all myself.

ROMEO *(speaking loudly enough to be heard by* JULIET*).*
I take thee at thy word.
Call me but love, and I'll be new baptized;
Henceforth I never will be Romeo.

JULIET. What man art thou that thus bescreened in night
So stumblest on my counsel?[5]

ROMEO. By a name
I know not how to tell thee who I am.
My name, dear saint, is hateful to myself,
Because it is an enemy to thee;
Had I it written, I would tear the word.

JULIET. My ears have not yet drunk a hundred words
Of thy tongue's utterance, yet I know the sound.
Art thou not Romeo and a Montague?

ROMEO. Neither, fair saint, if either thee dislike.

JULIET. How camest thou hither, tell me, and wherefore?
The orchard walls are high and hard to climb,
And the place death, considering who thou art,
If any of my kinsmen find thee here.

ROMEO. With love's light wings did I o'erperch[6] these walls;
For stony limits cannot hold love out,
And what love can do, that dares love attempt;
Therefore thy kinsmen are no let[7] to me.

JULIET. If they do see thee, they will murder thee.

ROMEO. Alack, there lies more peril in thine eye
Than twenty of their swords; look thou but sweet,
And I am proof[8] against their enmity.

JULIET. I would not for the world they saw thee here.

ROMEO. I have night's cloak to hide me from their sight;
And but thou love me,[9] let them find me here.
My life were better ended by their hate
Than death prorogued,[10] wanting of[11] thy love.

JULIET. By whose direction found'st thou out this place?

ROMEO. By love, who first did prompt me to inquire;
He lent me counsel and I lent him eyes.

3. ***though . . . Montague,*** even if you were not a Montague.

4. ***owes,*** owns.

5. ***counsel,*** secret thoughts.

6. ***o'erperch,*** fly over and perch beyond.

7. ***let,*** hindrance.

8. ***proof,*** safeguarded by armor.

9. ***but thou love me,*** unless you love me.

10. ***prorogued,*** postponed.

11. ***wanting of,*** lacking.

I am no pilot; yet, wert thou as far
As that vast shore washed with the farthest sea,
I would adventure for such merchandise.
JULIET. Thou know'st the mask of night is on my face,
Else would a maiden blush bepaint my cheek
For that which thou hast heard me speak tonight.
Fain[12] would I dwell on form,[13] fain, fain deny
What I have spoke; but farewell compliment![14]
Dost thou love me? I know thou will say "Ay,"
And I will take thy word. Yet, if thou swear'st,
Thou mayst prove false; at lovers' perjuries,
They say, Jove[15] laughs. O gentle Romeo,
If thou dost love, pronounce it faithfully;
Or if thou think'st I am too quickly won,
I'll frown and be perverse and say thee nay,
So thou wilt woo; but else, not for the world.
In truth, fair Montague, I am too fond,[16]
And therefore thou mayst think my 'havior light.
But trust me, gentleman, I'll prove more true
Than those that have more cunning to be strange.[17]
I should have been more strange, I must confess,
But that thou overheard'st, ere I was ware,
My true love's passion; therefore pardon me,
And not impute this yielding to light love,
Which the dark night hath so discovered.[18]
ROMEO. Lady, by yonder blessèd moon I swear
That tips with silver all these fruit tree tops—
JULIET. O, swear not by the moon, the inconstant moon,
That monthly changes in her circled orb,
Lest that thy love prove likewise variable.
ROMEO. What shall I swear by?
JULIET. Do not swear at all;
Or, if thou wilt, swear by thy gracious self,
Which is the god of my idolatry,
And I'll believe thee.
ROMEO. If my heart's dear love—
JULIET. Well, do not swear. Although I joy in thee,
I have no joy of this contract tonight;
It is too rash, too unadvised,[19] too sudden,
Too like the lightning, which doth cease to be
Ere one can say "It lightens." Sweet, good night!
This bud of love, by summer's ripening breath,
May prove a beauteous flower when next we meet.
Good night, good night! As sweet repose and rest
Come to thy heart as that within my breast.
ROMEO. O, wilt thou leave me so unsatisfied?
JULIET. What satisfaction canst thou have tonight?
ROMEO. The exchange of thy love's faithful vow for mine.

12. ***Fain,*** gladly.
13. ***dwell on form,*** stick to formalities.
14. ***compliment,*** ceremony, formal manners.
15. ***Jove,*** ruler of the gods and men.
16. ***fond,*** foolish.
17. ***strange,*** reserved, distant.
18. ***discovered,*** revealed.
19. ***unadvised,*** heedless.

JULIET. I gave thee mine before thou didst request it,
And yet I would it were to give again.
ROMEO. Wouldst thou withdraw it? For what purpose, love?
JULIET. But to be frank,[20] and give it thee again.
And yet I wish but for the thing I have.
My bounty is as boundless as the sea,
My love as deep; the more I give to thee,
The more I have, for both are infinite.
(NURSE calls "Juliet" from inside the bedroom.)
I hear some noise within; dear love, adieu!
Anon, good Nurse! Sweet Montague, be true.
Stay but a little, I will come again.
(JULIET goes into her bedroom.)

ROMEO. O blessèd, blessèd night! I am afeard,
Being in night, all this is but a dream,
Too flattering-sweet to be substantial.

(JULIET returns to the balcony.)
JULIET. Three words, dear Romeo, and good night indeed.
If that thy bent of love[21] be honorable,
Thy purpose marriage, send me word tomorrow,
By one that I'll procure to come to thee,
Where and what time thou wilt perform the rite;
And all my fortunes at thy foot I'll lay
And follow thee my lord throughout the world.
NURSE *(within the bedroom).* Madam!
JULIET. I come, anon.—But if thou meanest not well,
I do beseech thee—
NURSE *(within and more persistently).* Madam!
JULIET. By and by[22] I come—
To cease thy suit, and leave me to my grief.
Tomorrow will I send.
ROMEO. So thrive my soul—
JULIET. A thousand times good night!
(JULIET goes inside for a few moments.)
ROMEO. A thousand times the worse, to want thy light.
Love goes toward love as schoolboys from their books,
But love from love, toward school with heavy looks.

(JULIET reappears.)
JULIET. Hist! Romeo, hist! O, for a falconer's voice,
To lure this tassel-gentle[23] back again!
Bondage is hoarse, and may not speak aloud[24];
Else would I tear the cave where Echo[25] lies,
And make her airy tongue more hoarse than mine
With repetition of my Romeo's name.

20. ***frank,*** generous.

21. ***thy bent of love,*** the intentions of your love.

22. ***By and by,*** at once.

23. ***tassel-gentle,*** a male hawk.

24. ***Bondage . . . speak aloud,*** I am bound down by the necessity of not being overheard.

25. ***Echo,*** a nymph who pined away for a handsome youth until only her voice was left.

ROMEO. It is my soul that calls upon my name.
How silver-sweet sound lovers' tongues by night,
Like softest music to attending ears!
JULIET. Romeo!
ROMEO. My dear?
JULIET. At what o'clock tomorrow
Shall I send to thee?
ROMEO. At the hour of nine.
JULIET. I will not fail; 'tis twenty years till then.
I have forgot why I did call thee back.
ROMEO. Let me stand here till thou remember it.
JULIET. I shall forget, to have thee still stand there,
Remembering how I love thy company.
ROMEO. And I'll still stay, to have thee still forget,
Forgetting any other home but this.
JULIET. 'Tis almost morning; I would have thee gone,
And yet no further than a wanton's bird,
Who lets it hop a little from her hand,
Like a poor prisoner in his twisted gyves,
And with a silk thread plucks it back again,
So loving-jealous of his liberty.
ROMEO. I would I were thy bird.
JULIET. Sweet, so would I;
Yet I should kill thee with much cherishing.
Good night, good night! Parting is such sweet sorrow
That I shall say good night till it be morrow.
(She goes into her room.)
ROMEO. Sleep dwell upon thine eyes, peace in thy breast!
Would I were sleep and peace, so sweet to rest!
Hence will I to my ghostly[26] father's cell,
His help to crave, and my dear hap[27] to tell. *(Exit.)*

26. ***ghostly,*** spiritual.
27. ***dear hap,*** good fortune.

CONSIDERING ACT TWO, SCENE 2

1. How has Romeo's attitude toward life changed since he has met Juliet?

2. A collection of famous quotations includes lines from thirteen speeches in this scene alone. Choose several lines that you would include in your own collection of favorite quotations.

Scene 3: Friar Laurence's cell.

Enter FRIAR LAURENCE *with a basketful of herbs believed to be health-giving.*

FRIAR LAURENCE. The gray-eyed morn smiles on the frowning night,

Check'ring the eastern clouds with streaks of light,
And fleckèd darkness like a drunkard reels
From forth day's path and Titan's[1] fiery wheels.
Now, ere the sun advance his burning eye,
The day to cheer and night's dank dew to dry,
I must up-fill this osier cage[2] of ours
With baleful weeds and precious-juicèd flowers,
Many for many virtues excellent,
None but for some[3] and yet all different.
O, mickle[4] is the powerful grace[5] that lies
In herbs, plants, stones, and their true qualities;
For naught so vile that on the earth doth live
But to the earth some special good doth give,
Nor aught so good but strained from that fair use
Revolts from true birth,[6] stumbling on abuse.
Virtue itself turns vice, being misapplied,
And vice sometime's by action dignified.

1. *Titan's.* Titan, the sun god, was descended from a race of giants called Titans.

2. *osier cage,* willow basket.

3. *None but for some.* No plant entirely lacks value.
4. *mickle,* much.
5. *grace,* virtue, worth.

6. *Revolts . . . birth,* betrays its own special purpose.

ROMEO *enters and stands by the door unseen.*

Within the infant rind of this small flower
Poison hath residence and medicine power;
For this, being smelt, with that part cheers each part,[7]
Being tasted, slays all senses with the heart.[8]
Two such opposèd kings encamp them still
In man as well as herbs—grace and rude will[9];
And where the worser is predominant,
Full soon the canker[10] death eats up that plant.

7. *that part . . . part.* Its odor refreshes all parts of the body.
8. *with the heart,* by stopping the heart.
9. *rude will,* violent, lustful disposition.

10. *canker,* cankerworm, which destroys plants.

(ROMEO *advances and speaks.)*

ROMEO. Good morrow, Father.
FRIAR LAURENCE. Benedicite![11]
What early tongue so sweet saluteth me?
Young son, it argues a distempered head
So soon to bid good morrow[12] to thy bed.
Care keeps his watch in every old man's eye,
And where care lodges, sleep will never lie;
But where unbruisèd youth with unstuffed brain[13]
Doth couch his limbs, there golden sleep doth reign.
Therefore thy earliness doth me assure
Thou art up-roused by some distemperature;
Or if not so, then here I hit it right—
Our Romeo hath not been in bed tonight.
ROMEO. That last is true; the sweeter rest was mine.
FRIAR LAURENCE. God pardon sin! Wast thou with Rosaline?
ROMEO. With Rosaline, my ghostly father? No;
I have forgot that name, and that name's woe.
FRIAR LAURENCE. That's my good son; but where hast thou been then?

11. *Benedicite* (ben′ə dis′ə ti), God bless us.

12. *good morrow,* farewell.

13. *unstuffed brain,* mind unoccupied with busy thoughts and cares.

ROMEO. I'll tell thee, ere thou ask it me again.
I have been feasting with mine enemy,
Where on a sudden one hath wounded me,
That's by me wounded; both our remedies
Within thy help and holy physic[14] lies.
I bear no hatred, blessèd man, for, lo,
My intercession likewise steads[15] my foe.
FRIAR LAURENCE. Be plain, good son, and homely in thy drift[16];
Riddling[17] confession finds but riddling shrift.[18]
ROMEO. Then plainly know my heart's dear love is set
On the fair daughter of rich Capulet.
As mine on hers, so hers is set on mine,
And all combined,[19] save what thou must combine
By holy marriage. When and where and how
We met, we wooed, and made exchange of vow,
I'll tell thee as we pass; but this I pray,
That thou consent to marry us today.
FRIAR LAURENCE. Holy Saint Francis, what a change is here!
Is Rosaline, whom thou didst love so dear,
So soon forsaken? Young men's love then lies
Not truly in their hearts, but in their eyes.
Jesu Maria, what a deal of brine
Hath washed thy sallow cheeks for Rosaline!
How much salt water thrown away in waste,
To season love, that of it doth not taste!
The sun not yet thy sighs from heaven clears,
Thy old groans ring yet in my ancient ears;
Lo, here upon thy cheek the stain doth sit
Of an old tear that is not washed off yet:
If e'er thou wast thyself and these woes thine,
Thou and these woes were all for Rosaline.
And art thou changed? Pronounce this sentence then:
Women may fall when there's no strength in men.
ROMEO. Thou chid'st[20] me oft for loving Rosaline.
FRIAR LAURENCE. For doting, not for loving, pupil mine.
ROMEO. And bad'st me bury love.
FRIAR LAURENCE. Not in a grave,
To lay one in, another out to have.
ROMEO. I pray thee, chide me not; she whom I love now
Doth grace for grace and love for love allow;
The other did not so.
FRIAR LAURENCE. O, she knew well
Thy love did read by rote[21] and could not spell.
But come, young waverer, come, go with me,
In one respect I'll thy assistant be;
For this alliance may so happy prove
To turn your households' rancor to pure love.

14. *physic,* medicine.

15. *steads,* helps.

16. *homely . . . drift,* simple and direct in your speech.

17. *Riddling,* like a riddle.

18. *shrift,* absolution.

19. *all combined,* the arrangement is complete.

20. *chid'st,* scolded.

21. *did read by rote,* merely repeated conventional expressions of love.

ROMEO. O, let us hence; I stand on[22] sudden haste.
FRIAR LAURENCE. Wisely and slow; they stumble that run fast.

(ROMEO *and the* FRIAR *go out.*)

22. ***I stand on,*** I am in a position demanding.

CONSIDERING ACT TWO, SCENE 3

1. Think of several adjectives you might use in describing Friar Laurence. Justify each one.

2. *(a)* What proposal does Romeo make to the friar? *(b)* What doubts does the friar have about Romeo's proposal? *(c)* Why does Friar Laurence finally accept Romeo's proposal?

Scene 4: A street in Verona on the morning after the ball.

Enter MERCUTIO *and* BENVOLIO.

MERCUTIO. Where the devil should this Romeo be?
Came he not home tonight?[1]
BENVOLIO. Not to his father's; I spoke with his man.
MERCUTIO. Ah, that same pale hard-hearted wench, that Rosaline,
Torments him so that he will sure run mad.
BENVOLIO. Tybalt, the kinsman of old Capulet,
Hath sent a letter to his father's house.
MERCUTIO. A challenge, on my life.
BENVOLIO. Romeo will answer it.
MERCUTIO. Any man that can write may answer a letter.
BENVOLIO. Nay, he will answer the letter's master, how he dares, being dared.

MERCUTIO. Alas, poor Romeo! He is already dead, stabbed with a white wench's black eye, shot through the ear with a love song; the very pin[2] of his heart cleft with the blind bow-boy's butt-shaft[3]; and is he a man to encounter Tybalt?

BENVOLIO. Why, what is Tybalt?

MERCUTIO. More than Prince of Cats,[4] I can tell you. O, he is the courageous captain of compliments.[5] He fights as you sing, keeps time, distance, and proportion[6]; rests me his minim rest,[7] one, two, and the third in your bosom; the very butcher of a silk button,[8] a duelist, a duelist; a gentleman of the very first house,[9] of the first and second cause.[10] Ah, the immortal passado![11] the punto reverso![12] the hai![13]

1. ***tonight,*** last night.

2. ***pin,*** the center of a target.
3. ***butt-shaft,*** an unbarbed arrow. Mercutio suggests that Cupid needed only the least powerful weapon to overcome Romeo.
4. ***Prince of Cats,*** a play on Tybalt's name. In a collection of fables the name of the Prince of Cats was Tibert or Tibalt.
5. ***captain of compliments,*** master of rules of ceremony in dueling.
6. ***time, distance, and proportion,*** technical fencing terms.
7. ***minim rest,*** a half rest in music.
8. ***butcher . . . button,*** one who can select and cut off any button of his adversary.
9. ***of the very first house,*** of first rank as a duelist.
10. ***of the first . . . cause,*** ready to quarrel over anything—or nothing.
11. ***passado*** (pə sä′dō), a step forward or aside in thrusting.
12. ***punto reverso*** (pun′tō ri vėr′sō), a backhanded thrust from the left side of the body.
13. ***hai*** (hā), a home thrust.

Enter ROMEO, *who shows no sign of his former moodiness.*

BENVOLIO. Here comes Romeo, here comes Romeo!

MERCUTIO. Signior Romeo, bon jour![14] There's a French salutation to your French slop.[15] You gave us the counterfeit[16] fairly last night.

ROMEO. Good morrow to you both. What counterfeit did I give you?

MERCUTIO. The slip,[17] sir, the slip; can you not conceive?

ROMEO. Pardon, good Mercutio, my business was great; and in such a case as mine a man may strain courtesy.

(He laughs and claps MERCUTIO *on the shoulder.)*

MERCUTIO. Why, is not this better now than groaning for love? Now art thou sociable, now art thou Romeo.

Enter NURSE *and* PETER, *her servant. He is carrying a large fan.*

ROMEO. Here's goodly gear![18]

MERCUTIO. A sail, a sail!

BENVOLIO. Two, two; a shirt and a smock.[19]

NURSE. Peter!

PETER. Anon!

NURSE. My fan, Peter.

MERCUTIO. Good Peter, to hide her face, for her fan's the fairer face.

NURSE. God ye good morrow,[20] gentlemen.

MERCUTIO. God ye good den, fair gentlewoman.

NURSE. Gentlemen, can any of you tell me where I may find the young Romeo?

ROMEO. I can tell you; but young Romeo will be older when you have found him than he was when you sought him. I am the youngest of that name, for fault[21] of a worse.

NURSE. If you be he, sir, I desire come confidence[22] with you.

BENVOLIO. She will indite[23] him to some supper.

MERCUTIO. Romeo, will you come to your father's? We'll to dinner thither.

ROMEO. I will follow you.

MERCUTIO. Farewell, ancient lady; farewell. *(Singing.)* "Lady, lady, lady."

(Exeunt MERCUTIO *and* BENVOLIO.*)*

NURSE. Marry, farewell! I pray you, sir, what saucy merchant[24] was this, that was so full of his ropery?[25]

ROMEO. A gentleman, Nurse, that loves to hear himself talk, and will speak more in a minute than he will stand to[26] in a month.

14. ***Signior*** (se'nyor) . . . ***bon jour*** (bôN zhür'), Sir Romeo, good day.
15. ***slop,*** large breeches (a French style).
16. ***gave . . . counterfeit,*** played us a trick.
17. ***slip,*** a counterfeit coin.
18. ***gear,*** business.
19. ***shirt . . . smock,*** indicating a man and a woman.
20. ***God . . . morrow,*** God give you a good morning.
21. ***fault,*** lack.
22. ***confidence,*** the nurse's blunder for ***conference.***
23. ***indite.*** Imitating the nurse, Benvolio jokingly misuses ***indite*** for ***invite.***
24. ***merchant,*** fellow.
25. ***ropery,*** roguery.
26. ***stand to,*** maintain.

NURSE. An a' speak anything against me, I'll take him down, an a' were lustier than he is, and twenty such Jacks[27]; and if I cannot, I'll find those that shall. Scurvy knave! I am none of his flirt-gills.[28] *(To* PETER.*)* And thou must stand by, too, and suffer every knave to abuse me at his pleasure?

PETER. I saw no man abuse you at his pleasure. If I had, my weapon should quickly have been out, I warrant you. I dare draw as soon as another man if I see occasion in a good quarrel, and the law on my side.

NURSE. Now, afore God, I am so vexed that every part about me quivers. Scurvy knave! Pray you, sir, a word; and, as I told you, my young lady bade me inquire you out. What she bade me say, I will keep to myself; but first let me tell ye, if ye should lead her into a fool's paradise, as they say, it were a very gross kind of behavior, as they say. For the gentlewoman is young; and, therefore, if you should deal double with her, truly it were an ill thing to be offered to any gentlewoman, and very weak dealing.

ROMEO. Nurse, commend me to thy lady and mistress. I protest[29] unto thee—

NURSE. Good heart, and, i' faith, I will tell her as much. Lord, Lord, she will be a joyful woman.

ROMEO. What wilt thou tell her, Nurse? Thou dost not mark me.[30]

NURSE. I will tell her, sir, that you do protest; which, as I take it, is a gentlemanlike offer.

ROMEO. Bid her devise
Some means to come to shrift this afternoon;
And there she shall at Friar Laurence' cell
Be shrived and married. Here *(offers money)* is for thy pains.

NURSE. No, truly, sir, not a penny.

ROMEO. Go to[31]; I say you shall.

NURSE *(taking the money and pocketing it).* This afternoon, sir? Well, she shall be there.

ROMEO. And stay, good Nurse, behind the abbey wall.
Within this hour my man shall be with thee,
And bring thee cords made like a tackled stair[32];
Which to the high topgallant[33] of my joy
Must be my convoy[34] in the secret night.
Farewell; be trusty, and I'll quit[35] thy pains.
Farewell; commend me to thy mistress.

NURSE. Now God in heaven bless thee! Hark you, sir.

ROMEO. What say'st thou, my dear Nurse?

NURSE. Is your man secret?[36] Did you ne'er hear say,
Two may keep counsel, putting one away?

27. *Jacks,* rascals.

28. *flirt-gills,* flirtatious women.

29. *protest,* vow.

30. *mark me,* pay attention to what I say.

31. *Go to,* say nothing more.

32. *tackled stair,* rope ladder.

33. *topgallant,* summit, height.

34. *convoy,* means of conducting me.

35. *quit,* reward.

36. *secret,* trustworthy.

ROMEO. I warrant thee, my man's as true as steel.

NURSE. Well, sir, my mistress is the sweetest lady— Lord, Lord, when 'twas a little prating thing! O, there is a nobleman in town, one Paris, that would fain lay knife aboard[37]; but she, good soul, had as lief see a toad, a very toad, as see him. I anger her sometimes and tell her that Paris is the properer[38] man; but, I'll warrant you, when I say so, she looks as pale as any clout[39] in the versal[40] world. Doth not rosemary and Romeo begin both with a letter?[41]

ROMEO. Ay, Nurse; what of that? Both with an R.

NURSE. Ah, mocker! That's the dog's name[42]; R is for the — No; I know it begins with some other letter; and she hath the prettiest sententious[43] of it, of you and rosemary, that it would do you good to hear it.

ROMEO. Commend me to thy lady.

NURSE. Ay, a thousand times. *(Exit* ROMEO.*)* Peter!

PETER. Anon!

NURSE. Peter, take my fan, and go before, and apace.

(Exeunt.)

37. ***fain . . . aboard,*** gladly seize, in the manner of a pirate, what he desires.

38. ***properer,*** handsomer.

39. ***clout,*** rag.

40. ***versal,*** universal.

41. ***a letter,*** the same letter.

42. ***the dog's name.*** The sound of the letter ***R*** was thought to resemble a dog's snarl.

43. ***sententious,*** the nurse's error for ***sayings.***

CONSIDERING ACT TWO, SCENE 4

1. *(a)* What examples of humor can you point out in this scene? *(b)* Everything seems to be going well—except for a certain threat. What is that threat?

2. Outline the steps the nurse is to take in carrying out Romeo's instructions.

3. Identify Paris, to whom the nurse refers in line 117. What have we learned about him in earlier scenes?

Scene 5: Capulet's orchard.

Enter JULIET.

JULIET *(with ever rising anxiety).* The clock struck nine when I did send the nurse;
In half an hour she promised to return.
Perchance she cannot meet him—that's not so.
O, she is lame! Love's heralds should be thoughts,
Which ten times faster glide than the sun's beams,
Driving back shadows over louring hills.
Therefore do nimble-pinioned doves draw love,[1]
And therefore hath the wind-swift Cupid wings.
Now is the sun upon the highmost hill
Of this day's journey, and from nine till twelve

1. ***nimble-pinioned . . . love.*** Quick moving doves drew Venus, goddess of love.

Is three long hours, yet she is not come.
Had she affections and warm youthful blood,
She would be as swift in motion as a ball;
My words would bandy[2] her to my sweet love,
And his to me.
But old folks, many feign as they were dead–
Unwieldy, slow, heavy, and pale as lead.
O God, she comes!

Enter NURSE *and* PETER.

O honey Nurse, what news?
Hast thou met with him? Send thy man away.

NURSE. Peter, stay at the gate.

(Exit PETER.*)*

JULIET. Now, good, sweet Nurse,—O Lord, why look'st thou sad?
Though news be sad, yet tell them[3] merrily;
If good, thou shamest the music of sweet news
By playing it to me with so sour a face.

NURSE. I am aweary; give me leave awhile.
Fie, how my bones ache! What a jaunce[4] have I had!

JULIET. I would thou hadst my bones, and I thy news.
Nay, come, I pray thee, speak; good, good Nurse, speak.

NURSE. Jesu, what haste? Can you not stay awhile?
Do you not see that I am out of breath?

JULIET *(with exasperation)*. How art thou out of breath when thou hast breath
To say to me that thou art out of breath?
The excuse that thou dost make in this delay
Is longer than the tale thou dost excuse.[5]
Is thy news good, or bad? Answer to that;
Say either, and I'll stay the circumstance.[6]
Let me be satisfied: is 't good or bad?

NURSE. Well, you have made a simple choice; you know not how to choose a man. Romeo? No, not he; though his face be better than any man's, yet his leg excels all men's; and for a hand, and a foot, and a body, though they be not to be talked on, yet they are past compare. He is not the flower of courtesy, but, I'll warrant him, as gentle as a lamb. Go thy ways, wench; serve God. What, have you dined at home?

JULIET. No, no. But all this did I know before.
What says he of our marriage? What of that?

NURSE. Lord, how my head aches! What a head have I!
It beats as it would fall in twenty pieces.
My back—O my back, my back!
Beshrew[7] your heart for sending me about
To catch my death with jauncing up and down!

2. *bandy,* hurry.

3. *news . . . them. News* was often used in the plural.

4. *jaunce,* rough jaunt.

5. *excuse,* put off by making excuses.

6. *stay the circumstance,* await details.

7. *Beshrew,* ill luck to.

JULIET. I' faith, I am sorry that thou art not well.
(Beseechingly.) Sweet, sweet, sweet Nurse, tell me, what says my love?

NURSE. Your love says, like an honest gentleman, and a courteous, and a kind, and a handsome, and I warrant, a virtuous— Where is your mother?

JULIET. Where is my mother! Why, she is within;
Where should she be? How oddly thou repliest!—
"Your love says, like an honest gentleman,
Where is your mother?"

NURSE. O God's lady dear!
Are you so hot? Marry, come up, I trow[8];
Is this the poultice for my aching bones?
Henceforward do your messages yourself.

JULIET. Here's such a coil![9] Come, what says Romeo?

NURSE. Have you got leave to go to shrift today?

JULIET. I have.

NURSE. Then hie[10] you hence to Friar Laurence' cell;
There stays a husband to make you a wife.
Now comes the wanton blood up in your cheeks;
They'll be in scarlet straight at any news.
Hie you to church; I must another way
To fetch a ladder, by the which your love
Must climb a bird's nest soon when it is dark:
I am the drudge, and toil in your delight.
Go; I'll to dinner; hie you to the cell.

JULIET. Hie to high fortune! Honest Nurse, farewell.
(They go out in opposite directions.)

8. ***Marry . . . I trow.*** Come, now; you are too impatient, I declare.

9. ***coil,*** commotion, ado.

10. ***hie,*** hasten.

Scene 6: Friar Laurence's cell.

Enter FRIAR LAURENCE *and* ROMEO.

FRIAR LAURENCE. So smile the heavens upon this holy act
That after hours with sorrow chide us not!

ROMEO. Amen, amen! But come what sorrow can,
It cannot countervail[1] the exchange of joy
That one short minute gives me in her sight.
Do thou but close our hands with holy words,
Then love-devouring death do what he dare;
It is enough I may but call her mine.

FRIAR LAURENCE. These violent delights have violent ends
And in their triumph die, like fire and powder,
Which as they kiss consume.[2] The sweetest honey
Is loathsome in his own deliciousness
And in the taste confounds[3] the appetite.
Therefore love moderately; long love doth so;
Too swift arrives as tardy as too slow.

1. ***countervail,*** balance, equal.

2. ***These violent delights . . . consume.*** In lines 9-11 Friar Laurence expresses a premonition of evil.

3. ***confounds,*** destroys.

Enter JULIET.

Here comes the lady. O, so light a foot
Will ne'er wear out the everlasting flint.[4]
A lover may bestride the gossamer[5]
That idles in the wanton summer air,
And yet not fall; so light is vanity.[6]
JULIET. Good even[7] to my ghostly confessor.
FRIAR LAURENCE. Romeo shall thank thee, daughter, for us both.
JULIET. As much to him,[8] else is his thanks too much.
ROMEO. Ah, Juliet, if the measure of thy joy
Be heaped like mine, and that[9] thy skill be more
To blazon[10] it, then sweeten with thy breath
This neighbor air, and let rich music's tongue
Unfold the imagined happiness that both
Receive in either by this dear encounter.
JULIET. Conceit,[11] more rich in matter than in words,
Brags of his substance, not of ornament.
They are but beggars that can count their worth;
But my true love is grown to such excess
I cannot sum up sum of half my wealth.
FRIAR LAURENCE. Come, come with me, and we will make short work;
For, by your leaves, you shall not stay alone
Till holy church incorporate two in one.

(Exeunt.)

4. ***wear out . . . flint.*** The friar is suggesting the roughness of life's journey.
5. ***gossamer,*** cobweb.
6. ***so light is vanity,*** so unsubstantial are the illusions of love.
7. ***even,*** evening.
8. ***As much to him,*** the same greeting to him.
9. ***that,*** if.
10. ***blazon,*** proclaim.
11. ***Conceit,*** imagination, understanding.

CONSIDERING ACT TWO, SCENES 5 AND 6

1. Quote lines from Scene 5 that bring out especially well Juliet's desperate effort to wring the news from the nurse.

2. In what ways are the nurse's speeches in Scene 5 consistent (or inconsistent) with the impressions you have gained of her in earlier scenes?

3. What is the attitude of Friar Laurence toward the lovers' insistence that he marry them without delay?

LOOKING BACK—AND AHEAD

1. Write a brief outline of the events in Act Two.

2. All seems to be going smoothly with Romeo and Juliet. On the other hand, do you find suggestions in Scene 6 that indicate that their happiness may not continue? Cite specific lines to uphold your answer.

JULIET'S MAIL

Not long ago it was announced that Ettore Solimani, the custodian of "Juliet's tomb" in Verona, was to be retired at the age of sixty-seven. During the past two decades he had, by his own account, received—and answered—some 10,000 letters from people seeking advice on their love problems and addressed to "The Secretary of Juliet." Despite the announcement of his retirement, letters have continued to come in to him, and he has answered them as conscientiously as ever.

More than twenty years ago, when Solimani took over as watchman for the old church of a former Franciscan convent and an adjoining modern cloister, a travelers' guidebook carried this note: "The cloister contains a medieval trough baselessly called the ***Tomba di Giulietta,*** or the Tomb of Juliet. The whole scene is prosaic and unattractive." To relieve that atmosphere, Solimani planted a weeping willow in the courtyard and bred white doves to add a further romantic touch.

As to the tomb itself, about the size and shape of a bathtub, it may have been used for many years as a trough on a farm.

As the myth of Juliet's tomb spread, pilgrims began to flock to Verona to see the romantic relic. But a recent visitor, skeptical, demanded proof that there are as many lovesick people in the world as Solimani claimed. In answer, he showed the visitor a large trunk filled with letters seeking advice on the writers' love problems.

Solimani says the letter-writing to Juliet started casually. It seems to have begun when a young woman struck up a conversation years ago with the then new custodian and soon poured out her heart, complaining of an unresponsive lover. Other visitors, neglected, began to mutter and Solimani broke off the talk, suggesting: "Why don't you write Juliet?" The young woman did write, and thousands have followed her example. In the beginning, only a few letters came in, but, after a lull during World War II, correspondence swelled. Magazine and newspaper articles in Italy and abroad made "The Secretary of Juliet, Verona," known as an emergency address for people unhappy in love, and during the past few years the mailman has brought an average of five letters daily. Each has been answered promptly by Solimani, offering sympathetic advice in the name of Juliet.

Based on a story by Paul Hofmann from the *New York Times Magazine*, May 25, 1958.

Act three

Scene 1: A public place in Verona.

Enter MERCUTIO, BENVOLIO, PAGE, *and* SERVANTS.

BENVOLIO. I pray thee, good Mercutio, let's retire.
The day is hot, the Capulets abroad,
And, if we meet, we shall not 'scape a brawl;
For now, these hot days, is the mad blood stirring.

MERCUTIO. Thou art like one of those fellows that when he enters the confines of a tavern claps his sword upon the table and says "God send me no need of thee!" and by the operation of the second cup[1] draws it on the drawer,[2] when indeed there is no need.

BENVOLIO. Am I like such a fellow?

MERCUTIO. Come, come, thou art as hot a Jack[3] in thy mood[4] as any in Italy, and as soon moved to be moody, and as soon moody to be moved.

BENVOLIO. And what to?[5]

MERCUTIO. Nay, an there were two such, we should have none shortly, for one would kill the other. Thou! Why, thou wilt quarrel with a man that hath a hair more, or a hair less, in his beard than thou hast. Thou wilt quarrel with a man for cracking nuts, having no other reason but because thou hast hazel eyes. Thy head is as full of quarrels as an egg is full of meat. Thou hast quarreled with a man for coughing in the street, because he hath wakened thy dog that hath lain asleep in the sun. Didst thou not fall out with a tailor for wearing his new doublet before Easter? And yet thou wilt tutor me from quarreling!

BENVOLIO. An I were so apt to quarrel as thou art, any man should buy the fee-simple[6] of my life for an hour and a quarter.

MERCUTIO. The fee-simple! O simple!

BENVOLIO. By my head, here come the Capulets.

MERCUTIO. By my heel, I care not.

Enter TYBALT *and other* CAPULETS.

TYBALT. Follow me close, for I will speak to them.
Gentlemen, good den; a word with one of you.

MERCUTIO. And but one word with one of us? Couple it with something; make it a word and a blow.

1. ***by . . . the second cup,*** by the time the second cup of wine begins to affect him.
2. ***drawer,*** one who draws wine from its container.
3. ***Jack,*** fellow.
4. ***mood,*** ill humor.
5. ***what to,*** moved to what.
6. ***fee-simple,*** absolute ownership.

TYBALT. You shall find me apt enough to that, sir, an you will give me occasion.

MERCUTIO. Could you not take some occasion without giving?

TYBALT. Mercutio, thou consort'st with[7] Romeo—

MERCUTIO. Consort! 'Zounds,[8] consort!

BENVOLIO. We talk here in the public haunt of men.
Either withdraw unto some private place,
And reason coldly of your grievances,
Or else depart[9]; here all eyes gaze on us.

MERCUTIO. Men's eyes were made to look, and let them gaze;
I will not budge for no man's pleasure, I.

Enter ROMEO.

TYBALT *(to* BENVOLIO*)*. Well, peace be with you, sir. Here comes my man.[10]

MERCUTIO. But I'll be hanged, sir, if he wear your livery.[11]
Marry, go before to field, he'll be your follower[12];
Your worship in that sense may call him "man."

TYBALT. Romeo, the hate I bear thee can afford
No better term than this—thou art a villain.

ROMEO. Tybalt, the reason that I have to love thee
Doth much excuse the appertaining rage
To such a greeting[13]; villain am I none.
Therefore, farewell; I see thou know'st me not.

TYBALT *(contemptuously)*. Boy, this shall not excuse the injuries
That thou hast done me; therefore turn and draw.

ROMEO. I do protest, I never injured thee,
But love thee better than thou canst devise,
Till thou shalt know the reason of my love.
And so, good Capulet—which name I tender[14]
As dearly as my own—be satisfied.

MERCUTIO. O calm, dishonorable, vile submission!

(He draws his sword.)

Tybalt, you rat catcher,[15] will you walk?[16]

TYBALT. What wouldst thou have with me?

MERCUTIO. Good King of Cats, nothing but one of your nine lives; that I mean to make bold withal,[17] and, as you shall use me hereafter, dry-beat the rest of the eight.[18] Will you pluck your sword out of his pilcher[19] by the ears? Make haste, lest mine be about your ears ere it be out.

TYBALT *(drawing)*. I am for you.

ROMEO. Gentle Mercutio, put thy rapier up.

MERCUTIO. Come, sir, your passado.

*(*TYBALT *and* MERCUTIO *fight.)*

7. ***consort'st with,*** accompany or wait upon.
8. ***'Zounds,*** a form of the oath "by God's wounds."

9. ***depart,*** separate.

10. ***my man.*** Tybalt speaks insultingly of Romeo as though Romeo were his servant.
11. ***if . . . livery,*** if Romeo wears the uniform (livery) of Tybalt's servants.
12. ***go . . . follower.*** If you went to the field of encounter, Romeo would follow you quickly enough.

13. ***appertaining rage . . . greeting,*** rage suitable to such a greeting.

14. ***tender,*** cherish.

15. ***rat catcher,*** an allusion to Tybalt as Prince of Cats.
16. ***walk,*** step aside with me.

17. ***that . . . withal.*** That one life I intend to take at once.

18. ***dry-beat . . . eight,*** soundly beat your other eight lives.
19. ***his pilcher,*** its scabbard.

ROMEO. Draw, Benvolio; beat down their weapons.
Gentlemen, for shame, forbear this outrage!
Tybalt, Mercutio, the prince expressly hath
Forbidden bandying in Verona streets.
Hold, Tybalt! Good Mercutio!

(TYBALT, *reaching under* ROMEO*'s arm, stabs* MERCUTIO, *and flies with his followers.)*

MERCUTIO. I am hurt.
A plague o' both your houses! I am sped.[20]
BENVOLIO. What, art thou hurt?
MERCUTIO. Ay, ay, a scratch, a scratch; marry, 'tis enough.
Where is my page? Go, villain,[21] fetch a surgeon.

(Exit PAGE.*)*

ROMEO. Courage, man; the hurt cannot be much.

MERCUTIO. No, 'tis not so deep as a well, nor so wide as a church door; but 'tis enough, 'twill serve. Ask for me tomorrow, and you shall find me a grave man.[22] I am peppered,[23] I warrant, for this world. A plague o' both your houses! 'Zounds, a dog, a rat, a mouse, a cat, to scratch a man to death! A braggart, a rogue, a villain, that fights by the book of arithmetic![24] Why the devil came you between us? I was hurt under your arm.

ROMEO. I thought all for the best.
MERCUTIO. Help me into some house, Benvolio,
Or I shall faint. A plague o' both your houses!
They have made worms' meat of me; I have it,
And soundly too. Your houses!

*(*MERCUTIO *is helped off by* BENVOLIO *and some* SERVANTS.*)*

ROMEO. This gentleman, the prince's near ally,[25]
My very[26] friend, hath got his mortal hurt
In my behalf; my reputation stained
With Tybalt's slander—Tybalt, that an hour
Hath been my kinsman! O sweet Juliet,
Thy beauty hath made me effeminate
And in my temper softened valor's steel!

Reënter BENVOLIO.

BENVOLIO. O Romeo, Romeo, brave Mercutio's dead!
That gallant spirit hath aspired[27] the clouds,
Which too untimely here did scorn the earth.
ROMEO. This day's black fate on moe[28] days doth depend[29];
This but begins the woe others must end.

Reënter TYBALT.

BENVOLIO. Here comes the furious Tybalt back again.
ROMEO. Alive, in triumph—and Mercutio slain!
Away to heaven, respective lenity,[30]
And fire-eyed fury be my conduct[31] now!

20. ***sped,*** done for.

21. ***villain,*** a form of address to a servant.

22. ***a grave man.*** Thus Mercutio puns with his last breath.

23. ***peppered.*** Mercutio means that receiving the one wound is as serious as being peppered with many wounds.

24. ***book of arithmetic,*** a textbook on fencing.

25. ***ally,*** kinsman.

26. ***very,*** true.

27. ***aspired,*** soared to.

28. ***moe,*** more.

29. ***depend,*** hang over threateningly.

30. ***respective lenity,*** considerate mildness.

31. ***conduct,*** guide.

ROTH

Now, Tybalt, take the villain back again
That late thou gavest me; for Mercutio's soul
Is but a little way above our heads,
Staying for thine to keep him company:
Either thou, or I, or both, must go with him.

TYBALT. Thou wretched boy, that didst consort him here,
Shalt with him hence.

ROMEO. This shall determine that.

(They fight. TYBALT *falls dead.)*

BENVOLIO. Romeo, away, be gone!
The citizens are up, and Tybalt slain.
Stand not amazed[32]; the prince will doom thee death
If thou art taken; hence, be gone, away!

ROMEO. O, I am fortune's fool![33]

BENVOLIO. Why dost thou stay?

(Exit ROMEO.*)*

Enter several CITIZENS.

FIRST CITIZEN. Which way ran he that killed Mercutio?
Tybalt, that murderer, which way ran he?

BENVOLIO. There lies that Tybalt.

FIRST CITIZEN. Up, sir, go with me;
I charge thee in the prince's name, obey.

Enter PRINCE ESCALUS, *attended;* MONTAGUE, CAPULET, THEIR WIVES, *and* OTHERS.

PRINCE. Where are the vile beginners of this fray?

BENVOLIO. O noble Prince, I can discover[34] all
The unlucky manage[35] of this fatal brawl.
There lies the man, slain by young Romeo,
That slew thy kinsman, brave Mercutio.

LADY CAPULET. Tybalt, my cousin! O my brother's child!
O Prince! O cousin! Husband! O, the blood is spilt
Of my dear kinsman! Prince, as thou art true,
For blood of ours shed blood of Montague.
O cousin, cousin!

PRINCE. Benvolio, who began this bloody fray?

BENVOLIO. Tybalt, here slain, whom Romeo's hand did slay;
Romeo that spoke him fair, bade him bethink
How nice[36] the quarrel was, and urged withal
Your high displeasure. All this, uttered
With gentle breath, calm look, knees humbly bowed,
Could not take truce[37] with the unruly spleen[38]
Of Tybalt deaf to peace, but that he tilts[39]
With piercing steel at bold Mercutio's breast,
Who, all as hot, turns deadly point to point,
And, with a martial scorn, with one hand beats
Cold death aside, and with the other sends

32. ***amazed,*** stupefied.

33. ***fortune's fool,*** the plaything or pawn of fate.

34. ***discover,*** reveal.

35. ***manage,*** conduct.

36. ***nice,*** trivial.

37. ***take truce,*** make peace.

38. ***unruly spleen,*** ungovernable rage.

39. ***tilts,*** strikes.

It back to Tybalt, whose dexterity
Retorts[40] it. Romeo he cries aloud,
"Hold, friends; friends, part," and, swifter than his
tongue,
His agile arm beats down their fatal points,
And 'twixt them rushes; underneath whose arm
An envious thrust from Tybalt hit the life
Of stout[41] Mercutio, and then Tybalt fled;
But by and by comes back to Romeo,
Who had but newly entertained[42] revenge,
And to 't they go like lightning, for ere I
Could draw to part them, was stout Tybalt slain,
And, as he fell, did Romeo turn and fly.
This is the truth, or let Benvolio die.

LADY CAPULET. He is a kinsman to the Montague;
Affection makes him false; he speaks not true.
Some twenty of them fought in this black strife,
And all those twenty could but kill one life.
I beg for justice, which thou, Prince, must give.
Romeo slew Tybalt; Romeo must not live.

PRINCE. Romeo slew him, he slew Mercutio;
Who now the price of his dear blood doth owe?

MONTAGUE. Not Romeo, Prince; he was Mercutio's friend.
His fault concludes but what the law should end—
The life of Tybalt.

PRINCE. And for that offense
Immediately we do exile him hence.
I have an interest in your hate's proceeding,
My blood[43] for your rude brawls doth lie a-bleeding;
But I'll amerce[44] you with so strong a fine
That you shall all repent the loss of mine.[45]
I will be deaf to pleading and excuses;
Nor tears nor prayers shall purchase out abuses.[46]
Therefore use none. Let Romeo hence in haste,
Else, when he's found, that hour is his last.
Bear hence this body and attend our will.
Mercy but murders, pardoning those that kill. *(Exeunt.)*

40. ***Retorts,*** returns.

41. ***stout,*** brave.

42. ***entertained,*** harbored thoughts of.

43. ***My blood,*** the blood of my kin.

44. ***amerce,*** punish by fine.

45. ***mine,*** my blood.

46. ***purchase out abuses,*** exempt misdeeds from penalty.

CONSIDERING ACT THREE, SCENE 1

1. *(a)* Who renews the quarreling and feuding between the Montagues and the Capulets? *(b)* Which character attempts to serve as peacemaker? Why is he unsuccessful? *(c)* Why does Romeo refuse Tybalt's first challenge to fight?

2. Why does Romeo finally assume personal responsibility for avenging Mercutio's death? In your opinion, is Romeo's decision justified—or should he have left Tybalt's punishment to Prince Escalus? Give reasons for your answer.

Scene 2: Capulet's orchard.

Enter JULIET.

JULIET. Gallop apace, you fiery-footed steeds,
Toward Phoebus'[1] lodging; such a wagoner
As Phaëthon[2] would whip you to the west,
And bring in cloudy night immediately.
Come, night; come, Romeo; come, thou day in night,
For thou wilt lie upon the wings of night
Whiter than new snow on a raven's back.
Come, gentle night, come, loving, black-browed night,
Give me my Romeo, and, when he shall die,
Take him and cut him out in little stars,
And he will make the face of heaven so fine
That all the world will be in love with night
And pay no worship to the garish sun.
O, here comes my nurse,
And she brings news; and every tongue that speaks
But Romeo's name speaks heavenly eloquence.

Enter NURSE *with the rope-ladder that* ROMEO *had directed her to make ready.*

Now, Nurse, what news? What, hast thou there the cords
That Romeo bid thee fetch?

NURSE. Ay, ay, the cords.
(She throws down the ladder.)

JULIET. Ay me! What news? Why dost thou wring thy hands?

NURSE. Ah, well-a-day![3] He's dead, he's dead, he's dead!
We are undone, lady, we are undone!
Alack the day! He's gone, he's killed, he's dead!

JULIET. Can heaven be so envious?

NURSE. Romeo can,
Though heaven cannot. O Romeo, Romeo!
Who ever would have thought it? Romeo!

JULIET. What devil art thou, that dost torment me thus?
This torture should be roared in dismal hell.
Hath Romeo slain himself? Say thou but "Ay"
And that bare vowel "I" shall poison more
Than the death-darting eye of cockatrice.[4]
I am not I, if there be such an I,
Or those eyes shut that make thee answer "Ay."
If he be slain, say "Ay"; or, if not, "No."
Brief sounds determine of my weal or woe.[5]

NURSE. I saw the wound, I saw it with mine eyes—
God save the mark![6]—here on his manly breast.

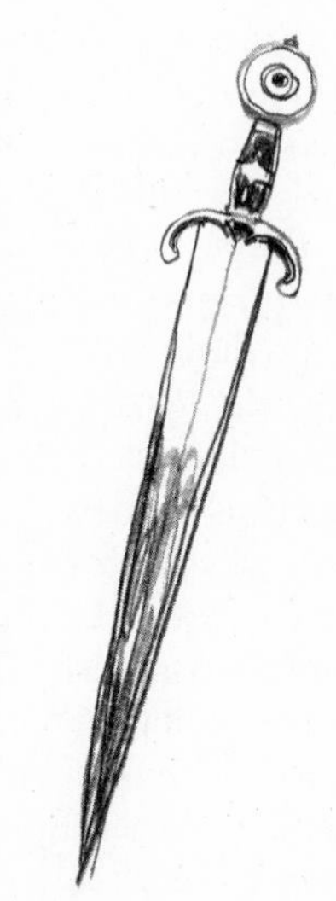

1. ***Phoebus*** (fē′bəs), the sun god.
2. ***Phaëthon*** (fā′ə thon). He was allowed to drive the chariot of the sun for a day. Too weak to control the horses, he nearly destroyed the universe.
3. ***well-a-day,*** alas.
4. ***cockatrice,*** a fabled serpent which could kill with its glance.
5. ***determine . . . woe,*** decide my well-being or my sorrow.
6. ***God . . . mark,*** God have mercy on us.

A piteous corse,[7] a bloody piteous corse;
Pale, pale as ashes, all bedaubed in blood,
All in gore-blood[8]; I swounded[9] at the sight.

JULIET. O, break, my heart! Poor bankrupt, break at once!
To prison, eyes; ne'er look on liberty!
Vile earth, to earth resign[10]; end motion[11] here;
And thou and Romeo press one heavy bier!

NURSE. O Tybalt, Tybalt, the best friend I had!
O courteous Tybalt; honest gentleman!
That ever I should live to see thee dead!

JULIET. What storm is this that blows so contrary?
Is Romeo slaughtered, and is Tybalt dead?
My dear-loved cousin, and my dearer lord?
Then, dreadful trumpet,[12] sound the general doom!
For who is living if those two are gone?

NURSE. Tybalt is gone, and Romeo banished;
Romeo that killed him, he is banished.

JULIET. O God! Did Romeo's hand shed Tybalt's blood?

NURSE. It did, it did; alas the day, it did!

JULIET. O serpent heart, hid with a flowering face!
Did ever dragon keep[13] so fair a cave?
O nature, what hadst thou to do in hell,
When thou didst bower[14] the spirit of a fiend
In mortal paradise of such sweet flesh?
Was ever book containing such vile matter
So fairly bound? O, that deceit should dwell
In such a gorgeous palace!

NURSE. There's no trust,
No faith, no honesty in men; all perjured,
All forsworn,[15] all naught, all dissemblers.
Ah, where's my man? Give me some aqua vitae[16];
These griefs, these woes, these sorrows make me old.
Shame come to Romeo!

JULIET. Blistered be thy tongue
For such a wish! He was not born to shame.
Upon his brow shame is ashamed to sit;
For 'tis a throne where honor may be crowned
Sole monarch of the universal earth.
O, what a beast was I to chide at him!

NURSE. Will you speak well of him that killed your cousin?

JULIET. Shall I speak ill of him that is my husband?
Ah, poor my lord, what tongue shall smooth thy name,
When I, thy three-hours' wife, have mangled it?
But, wherefore, villain, didst thou kill my cousin?
That villain cousin would have killed my husband.
Back, foolish tears, back to your native spring,
Your tributary drops belong to woe,
Which you, mistaking, offer up to joy.

7. ***corse,*** corpse.

8. ***gore-blood,*** clotted blood.

9. ***swounded,*** swooned.

10. ***Vile earth . . . resign.*** Miserable body, resign yourself to death.

11. ***motion,*** human activity.

12. ***dreadful trumpet,*** the trumpet proclaiming doomsday, or the end of the world.

13. ***keep,*** guard.

14. ***bower,*** give lodging to.

15. ***forsworn,*** untrue to one's sworn oath.

16. ***aqua vitae*** (ak′wə vī′tē), spirits to restore calmness.

My husband lives, that Tybalt would have slain;
And Tybalt's dead, that would have slain my husband.
All this is comfort; wherefore weep I then?
Some word there was, worser than Tybalt's death,
That murdered me. I would forget it fain[17];
But, O, it presses to my memory,
Liked damnèd guilty deeds to sinners' minds:
"Tybalt is dead, and Romeo—banishèd";
That "banishèd," that one word "banishèd,"
Hath slain ten thousand Tybalts. Tybalt's death
Was woe enough, if it had ended there.
Or, if sour woe delights in fellowship,
And needly[18] will be ranked with other griefs,
Why followed not, when she said "Tybalt's dead,"
Thy father or thy mother, nay, or both,
Which modern lamentation[19] might have moved?
But with a rearward[20] following Tybalt's death,
"Romeo is banishèd"—to speak that word
Is father, mother, Tybalt, Romeo, Juliet,
All slain, all dead. "Romeo is banishèd!"—
There is no end, no limit, measure, bound,
In that word's death; no words can that woe sound.
Where is my father, and my mother, Nurse?

NURSE. Weeping and wailing over Tybalt's corse.
Will you go to them? I will bring you thither.

JULIET. Wash they his wounds with tears? Mine shall be spent,
When theirs are dry, for Romeo's banishment.
Take up those cords. Poor ropes, you are beguiled,
Both you and I, for Romeo is exiled.

NURSE. Hie to your chamber. I'll find Romeo
To comfort you. I wot[21] well where he is.
Hark ye, your Romeo will be here at night;
I'll to him. He is hid at Laurence' cell.

JULIET. O, find him! Give this ring to my true knight,
And bid him come to take his last farewell. *(Exeunt.)*

17. *fain,* gladly.

18. *needly,* of necessity.

19. *modern lamentation,* ordinary grief.

20. *rearward,* a guard following at the rear of a group.

21. *wot,* know.

Scene 3: Friar Laurence's cell.

Enter FRIAR LAURENCE.

FRIAR LAURENCE. Romeo, come forth; come forth, thou fearful[1] man.
Affliction is enamored of thy parts[2]
And thou art wedded to calamity.

Enter ROMEO.

1. *fearful,* full of fear.

2. *Affliction . . . parts.* Misfortune thrives on the qualities (parts) you are showing—self-pity and despair.

ROMEO. Father, what news? What is the prince's doom?
What sorrow craves acquaintance at my hand,
That I yet know not?
FRIAR LAURENCE. Too familiar
Is my dear son with such sour company.
I bring thee tidings of the prince's doom.
ROMEO. What less than doomsday is the prince's doom?
FRIAR LAURENCE. A gentler judgment vanished[3] from his lips—
Not body's death, but body's banishment.
ROMEO. Ha, banishment! Be merciful, say "death";
For exile hath more terror in his look,
Much more than death. Do not say "banishment."
FRIAR LAURENCE. Hence from Verona art thou banishèd.
Be patient, for the world is broad and wide.
ROMEO. There is no world without Verona walls,
But purgatory, torture, hell itself.
Hence—banishèd is banished from the world,
And world's exile[4] is death. Then banishèd
Is death mistermed. Calling death "banishment,"
Thou cut'st my head off with a golden ax
And smilest upon the stroke that murders me.
FRIAR LAURENCE. O deadly sin! O rude unthankfulness!
Thy fault our law calls death, but the kind prince,
Taking thy part, hath rushed aside[5] the law,
And turned that black word death to banishment.
This is dear[6] mercy, and thou seest it not.
ROMEO. 'Tis torture, and not mercy. Heaven is here,
Where Juliet lives; and every cat and dog
And little mouse, every unworthy thing,
Live here in heaven and may look on her,
But Romeo may not; he is banishèd.
Hadst thou no poison mixed, no sharp-ground knife,
No sudden mean[7] of death, though ne'er so mean,[8]
But "banishèd" to kill me?—"Banishèd"?
O Friar, the damnèd use that word in hell;
Howlings attend it. How has thou the heart,
Being a divine, a ghostly confessor,
A sin-absolver, and my friend professed,
To mangle me with that word "banishèd"?
FRIAR LAURENCE. Thou fond[9] mad man, hear me but speak a word.
ROMEO. O, thou wilt speak again of banishment.
FRIAR LAURENCE. I'll give thee armor to keep off that word;
Adversity's sweet milk, philosophy,
To comfort thee, though thou art banishèd.
ROMEO. Yet "banishèd"? Hang up philosophy!
Unless philosophy can make a Juliet,

3. ***vanished,*** issued.

4. ***world's exile,*** exile from the world that is everything to me—the world where Juliet dwells.

5. ***rushed aside,*** thrust aside; dodged.

6. ***dear,*** rare, unusual.

7. ***mean,*** means.

8. ***mean,*** base, vile.

9. ***fond,*** foolish.

Displant a town, reverse a prince's doom,
It helps not, it prevails not. Talk no more.
FRIAR LAURENCE. O, then I see that madmen have no ears.
ROMEO. How should they, when that wise men have no eyes?
FRIAR LAURENCE. Let me dispute[10] with thee of thy estate.[11]
ROMEO. Thou canst not speak of that thou dost not feel.
Wert thou as young as I, Juliet thy love,
An hour but married, Tybalt murdered,
Doting like me and like me banishèd,
Then mightst thou speak, then mightst thou tear thy hair,
And *(flinging himself full length upon the floor and sobbing)* fall upon the ground, as I do now,
Taking the measure of an unmade grave.
(The NURSE *knocks on the door.)*
FRIAR LAURENCE. Arise; one knocks. Good Romeo, hide thyself.
ROMEO. Not I; unless the breath of heart-sick groans,
Mistlike, infold me from the search of eyes.
(The NURSE *knocks again.)*
FRIAR LAURENCE. Hark, how they knock! Who's there? Romeo, arise;
Thou wilt be taken.–Stay awhile! Stand up.
(Louder knocking.)
Run to my study.–By and by! God's will,
What simpleness is this!–I come, I come!
(Knocking continues.)
Who knocks so hard? Whence come you? What is your will?
NURSE *(speaking off-stage).* Let me come in, and you shall know my errand.
I come from Lady Juliet.
FRIAR LAURENCE. Welcome, then.

Enter NURSE.

NURSE. O holy Friar, O, tell me, holy Friar,
Where is my lady's lord, where's Romeo?
FRIAR LAURENCE. There on the ground, with his own tears made drunk.
NURSE. O, he is even in my mistress' case,[12]
Just in her case! O woeful sympathy![13]
Piteous predicament! Even so lies she,
Blubbering and weeping, weeping and blubbering.
Stand up, stand up; stand, an you be a man.
For Juliet's sake, for her sake, rise and stand.
(ROMEO *rises.)*
ROMEO. Nurse!

10. ***dispute,*** reason, discuss.
11. ***estate,*** situation, condition.

12. ***O, he is . . . case.*** Romeo is in the same state as Juliet.
13. ***woeful sympathy,*** sad agreement.

NURSE. Ah sir! ah sir! Well, death's the end of all.
ROMEO. Spakest thou of Juliet? How is it with her?
Doth she not think me an old[14] murderer,
Now I have stained the childhood of our joy
With blood removed but little from her own?
Where is she? And how doth she? And what says
My concealed lady[15] to our canceled love?
NURSE. O, she says nothing, sir, but weeps and weeps,
And now falls on her bed, and then starts up,
And Tybalt calls, and then on Romeo cries,
And then down falls again.
ROMEO. As if that name,
Shot from the deadly level[16] of a gun,
Did murder her; as that name's cursèd hand
Murdered her kinsman. O, tell me, Friar, tell me,
In what vile part of this anatomy
Doth my name lodge? Tell me that I may sack
The hateful mansion.

(ROMEO *draws his sword.)*

FRIAR LAURENCE. Hold thy desperate hand.
Art thou a man? Thy form cries out thou art;
Thy tears are womanish; thy wild acts denote
The unreasonable fury of a beast—
Unseemly woman in a seeming man,
Or ill-beseeming[17] beast in seeming both!
Thou hast amazed me. By my holy order,
I thought thy disposition better tempered.
Hast thou slain Tybalt? Wilt thou slay thyself?
And slay thy lady too that lives in thee,
By doing damnèd hate upon thyself?
Why rail'st thou on[18] thy birth, the heaven, and earth—
Since birth, and heaven, and earth, all three do meet
In thee at once, which thou at once wouldst lose?
What, rouse thee, man! Thy Juliet is alive,
For whose dear sake thou wast but lately dead;
There[19] art thou happy. Tybalt would kill thee,
But thou slew'st Tybalt; there art thou happy too.
The law that threatened death becomes thy friend
And turns it to exile; there art thou happy.
But, like a misbehaved and sullen wench,
Thou pouts upon thy fortune and thy love.
Take heed, take heed, for such die miserable.
Go, get thee to thy love, as was decreed,
Ascend her chamber, hence and comfort her.
But look thou stay not till the watch be set,[20]
For then thou canst not pass to Mantua,
Where thou shalt live till we can find a time
To blaze[21] your marriage, reconcile your friends,

14. ***an old,*** a real or actual.

15. ***concealed lady,*** secretly married wife.

16. ***level,*** line of fire.

17. ***ill-beseeming,*** unsuitable, inappropriate.

18. ***Why rail'st thou on,*** why do you complain about.

19. ***There,*** in this respect.

20. ***watch be set,*** watchmen have taken their stand at the gates of Verona.

21. ***blaze,*** announce.

Beg pardon of the prince, and call thee back
With twenty hundred thousand times more joy
Than thou went'st forth in lamentation.
Go before, Nurse. Commend me to thy lady,
And bid her hasten all the house to bed,
Which heavy sorrow makes them apt unto.[22]
Romeo is coming.

NURSE. O Lord, I could have stayed here all the night
To hear good counsel. O, what learning is!
My lord, I'll tell my lady you will come.

ROMEO. Do so, and bid my sweet prepare to chide.

NURSE. Here is a ring she bid me give you, sir.
Hie you, make haste, for it grows very late.

(Exit NURSE.*)*

ROMEO. How well my comfort is revived by this!

FRIAR LAURENCE. Go hence; good night; and here stands
all your state—[23]
Either be gone before the watch be set,
Or by the break of day disguised from hence.
Sojourn in Mantua; I'll find out your man,[24]
And he shall signify from time to time
Every good hap[25] to you that chances here.
Give me thy hand; 'tis late. Farewell; good night.

ROMEO. But that a joy past joy calls out on me,
It were a grief, so brief to part with thee.
Farewell. *(Exeunt.)*

22. ***apt unto,*** inclined to.

23. ***here stands . . . state,*** your fortune depends on acting exactly as follows.

24. ***your man,*** Romeo's servant, Balthasar.

25. ***hap,*** occurrence.

CONSIDERING ACT THREE, SCENES 2 AND 3

1. *(a)* What are Juliet's first reactions to the tragic news brought to her by the nurse? *(b)* How do we know that, despite everything, Juliet will remain true to Romeo?

2. Scene 2 has shown how Juliet reacts to misfortune; Scene 3 shows how Romeo reacts to misfortune. Which of them makes the more favorable impression on you? Why?

3. *(a)* What arguments does the friar use in attempting to convince Romeo that his despair is not justified? *(b)* According to the friar, what steps should now be taken to safeguard Romeo? What is Romeo's reaction to the friar's suggestions?

Scene 4: A room in Capulet's house.

Enter LORD *and* LADY CAPULET *and* PARIS.

CAPULET *(to* PARIS*)*. Things have fallen out, sir, so unluckily
That we have had no time to move our daughter.[1]
Look you, she loved her kinsman Tybalt dearly,

1. ***move our daughter,*** talk to Juliet about marrying you.

And so did I.—Well, we were born to die.
'Tis very late, she'll not come down tonight;
I promise you, but for your company,
I would have been abed an hour ago.

PARIS. These times of woe afford no time to woo.
Madam, good night; commend me to your daughter.

LADY CAPULET. I will, and know her mind early tomorrow;
Tonight she is mewed up to her heaviness.[2]

CAPULET. Sir Paris, I will make a desperate tender[3]
Of my child's love. I think she will be ruled
In all respects by me; nay, more, I doubt it not.
Wife, go you to her ere you go to bed;
Acquaint her here of my son[4] Paris' love,
And bid her, mark you me, on Wednesday next—
But soft! What day is this?

PARIS. Monday, my lord.

CAPULET. Monday? Ha, ha! Well, Wednesday is too soon.
O' Thursday let it be; o' Thursday, tell her,
She shall be married to this noble earl.
Will you be ready? Do you like this haste?
We'll keep no great ado—a friend or two;
For, hark you, Tybalt being slain so late,[5]
It may be thought we held him carelessly,[6]
Being our kinsman, if we revel much.
Therefore we'll have some half a dozen friends,
And there an end. But what say you to Thursday?

PARIS. My lord, I would that Thursday were tomorrow.

CAPULET. Well, get you gone; o' Thursday be it, then.
(To LADY CAPULET.*)* Go you to Juliet ere you go to bed,
Prepare her, wife, against[7] this wedding day.
Farewell, my lord. Light to my chamber, ho!
Afore me,[8] it is so very very late
That we may call it early by-and-by.
Good night. *(Exeunt.)*

2. ***mewed . . . heaviness,*** confined in her room with her grief.
3. ***desperate tender,*** rash offer.
4. ***son,*** prospective son-in-law.
5. ***late,*** recently.
6. ***held him carelessly,*** regarded him too lightly.
7. ***against,*** for.
8. ***Afore me,*** by my life!

Scene 5: Capulet's orchard.

Enter ROMEO *and* JULIET, *at the window of her bedroom.*

JULIET. Wilt thou be gone? It is not yet near day.
It was the nightingale, and not the lark,[1]
That pierced the fearful hollow of thine ear;
Nightly she sings on yond pomegranate tree.
Believe me, love, it was the nightingale.

ROMEO. It was the lark, the herald of the morn,
No nightingale. Look, love, what envious streaks

1. ***nightingale . . . lark.*** The nightingale's song is associated with the night, the lark's song with dawn.

Do lace[2] the severing[3] clouds in yonder east.
Night's candles are burnt out, and jocund day
Stands tiptoe on the misty mountain tops.
I must be gone and live, or stay and die.

JULIET. Yond light is not daylight, I know it, I;
It is some meteor that the sun exhales,
To be to thee this night a torchbearer
And light thee on thy way to Mantua.
Therefore stay yet; thou need'st not to be gone.

ROMEO. Let me be ta'en, let me be put to death;
I am content, so thou wilt have it so.
I have more care[4] to stay than will to go.
Come, death, and welcome! Juliet wills it so.
How is 't, my soul? Let's talk; it is not day.

JULIET. It is, it is; hie hence, be gone, away!
It is the lark that sings so out of tune,
Straining harsh discords and unpleasing sharps.[5]
O, now be gone; more light and light it grows.

ROMEO. More light and light; more dark and dark our woes!

Enter the NURSE, *to the bedchamber.*

NURSE *(urgently).* Madam!

JULIET. Nurse?

NURSE. Your lady mother is coming to your chamber.
The day is broke; be wary, look about. *(Exit.)*

JULIET. Then, window, let day in and let life out.

ROMEO. Farewell, farewell! One kiss, and I'll descend.
(He starts down the ladder.)

JULIET. Art thou gone so, love, lord, ay, husband, friend?[6]
I must hear from thee every day in the hour,
For in a minute there are many days.
O, by this count I shall be much in years
Ere I again behold my Romeo!

ROMEO. Farewell!
I will omit no opportunity
That may convey my greetings, love, to thee.

JULIET. O, think'st thou we shall ever meet again?

ROMEO. I doubt it not; and all these woes shall serve
For sweet discourses in our time to come.

JULIET. O God, I have an ill-divining[7] soul!
Methinks I see thee, now thou art below,
As one dead in the bottom of a tomb.
Either my eyesight fails, or thou look'st pale.

ROMEO. And trust me, love, in my eye so do you.
Dry sorrow drinks our blood.[8] Adieu, adieu! *(Exit.)*

JULIET. O fortune, fortune! All men call thee fickle;
If thou art fickle, what dost thou with him
That is renowned for faith? Be fickle, fortune,

2. ***lace,*** stripe, streak.
3. ***severing,*** scattering.
4. ***care,*** concern, desire.
5. ***sharps,*** high notes.
6. ***friend,*** lover.
7. ***ill-divining,*** anticipating evil.
8. ***Dry sorrow . . . blood.*** It was believed that sorrow dried up the blood.

For then I hope thou wilt not keep him long,
But send him back.

LADY CAPULET *(off-stage)*. Ho, daughter! Are you up?

JULIET. Who is 't that calls? Is it my lady mother?
Is she not down[9] so late, or up so early?
What unaccustomed cause procures her hither?[10]

9. *down,* in bed.

10. *procures her hither,* leads her to come this way.

Enter LADY CAPULET.

LADY CAPULET. Why, how now, Juliet!

JULIET. Madam, I am not well.

LADY CAPULET. Evermore weeping for your cousin's death?
What, wilt thou wash him from his grave with tears?
An if thou couldst, thou couldst not make him live;
Therefore, have done. Some grief shows much of love,
But much of grief shows still some want of wit.

JULIET. Yet let me weep for such a feeling[11] loss.

11. *feeling,* deeply felt.

LADY CAPULET. So shall you feel the loss, but not the friend
Which you weep for.

JULIET. Feeling so the loss,
I cannot choose but ever weep the friend.

LADY CAPULET. Well, girl, thou weep'st not so much for his death
As that the villain lives which slaughtered him.

JULIET. What villain, madam?

LADY CAPULET. That same villain Romeo.

JULIET *(aside)*. Villain and he be many miles asunder.—
(Aloud.) God pardon him! I do, with all my heart;
And yet no man like[12] he doth grieve my heart.

12. *like,* so much as.

LADY CAPULET. That is because the traitor murderer lives.

JULIET. Ay, madam, from the reach of these my hands.
Would none but I might venge[13] my cousin's death!

13. *venge,* avenge.

LADY CAPULET. We will have vengeance for it, fear thou not;
Then weep no more. I'll send to one in Mantua,
Where that same banished runagate doth live,
Shall give him such an unaccustomed dram
That he shall soon keep Tybalt company;
And then, I hope, thou wilt be satisfied.

JULIET. Indeed, I never shall be satisfied
With Romeo till I behold him—dead[14]—
Is my poor heart so for a kinsman vexed.
Madam, if you could find out but a man
To bear a poison, I would temper[15] it,
That Romeo should, upon receipt thereof,
Soon sleep in quiet. O, how my heart abhors
To hear him named, and cannot come to him,
To wreak the love I bore my cousin
Upon his body that hath slaughtered him!

14. *dead.* Juliet arranges her words in such a way that Lady Capulet will mistakenly think that Juliet wishes to see Romeo dead.

15. *temper,* mix. Juliet continues to speak in a way that misleads her mother.

LADY CAPULET. Find thou the means, and I'll find such a man.
But now I'll tell thee joyful tidings, girl.
JULIET. And joy comes well in such a needy time;
What are they,[16] I beseech your ladyship?
LADY CAPULET. Well, well, thou hast a careful[17] father, child,
One who, to put thee from thy heaviness,
Hath sorted out[18] a sudden day of joy,
That thou expect'st not nor I looked not for.
JULIET. Madam, in happy time, what day is that?
LADY CAPULET. Marry, my child, early next Thursday morn,
The gallant, young, and noble gentleman,
The County Paris, at Saint Peter's Church,
Shall happily make thee there a joyful bride.
JULIET *(with vigorous spirit).* Now, by Saint Peter's Church and Peter too,
He shall *not* make me there a joyful bride.
I wonder at this haste, that I must wed
Ere he that should be husband comes to woo.
I pray you, tell my lord and father, madam,
I will not marry yet, and when I do, I swear
It shall be Romeo, whom you know I hate,
Rather than Paris. These are news indeed!
LADY CAPULET *(angrily).* Here comes your father, tell him so yourself,
And see how he will take it at your hands.

Enter CAPULET *and the* NURSE.

CAPULET. How now! A conduit,[19] girl? What, still in tears?
Evermore showering? In one little body
Thou counterfeit'st a bark, a sea, a wind;
For still thy eyes, which I may call the sea,
Do ebb and flow with tears; the bark thy body is,
Sailing in this salt flood; the winds, thy sighs,
Who, raging with thy tears, and they with them,
Without a sudden calm, will overset
Thy tempest-tossèd body. How now, wife!
Have you delivered to her our decree?
LADY CAPULET. Ay, sir, but she will none,[20] she gives you thanks.
I would the fool were married to her grave!
CAPULET. Soft! Take me with you,[21] take me with you, wife.
How! Will she none? Doth she not give us thanks?
Is she not proud? Doth she not count her blest,
Unworthy as she is, that we have wrought
So worthy a gentleman to be her bridegroom?
JULIET. Not proud you have, but thankful that you have.

16. ***they,*** the "joyful tidings," in line 94.
17. ***careful,*** taking care to ensure your well-being.
18. ***sorted out,*** chosen.
19. ***conduit,*** fountain.
20. ***will none,*** refuses "our decree," in the preceding line.
21. ***Take me with you.*** Let me understand you.

ROTH

Proud can I never be of what I hate,
But thankful even for hate that is meant love.
CAPULET. How now, how now, choplogic![22] What is this?
"Proud," and "I thank you," and "I thank you not";
And yet "not proud." Mistress minion,[23] you,
Thank me no thankings, nor proud me no prouds,
But fettle[24] your fine joints 'gainst[25] Thursday next,
To go with Paris to Saint Peter's Church,
Or I will drag thee on a hurdle[26] thither.
Out, you green-sickness[27] carrion! Out, you baggage,[28]
You tallow-face!
LADY CAPULET *(to* CAPULET*)*. Fie, fie! What, art you mad?
JULIET *(kneeling)*. Good father, I beseech you on my knees,
Hear me with patience but to speak a word.
CAPULET. Hang thee, young baggage, disobedient wretch!
I tell thee what: get thee to church o' Thursday
Or never after look me in the face.
Speak not, reply not, do not answer me;
My fingers itch.[29] Wife, we scarce thought us blest
That God had lent us but this only child;
But now I see this one is one too much,
And that we have a curse in having her.
Out on her, hilding![30]
NURSE. God in heaven, bless her!
You are to blame, my lord, to rate[31] her so.
CAPULET. And why, my lady wisdom? Hold your tongue,
Good prudence[32]; smatter[33] with your gossips, go.
NURSE. I speak no treason.
CAPULET. O, God ye god-den.
NURSE. May not one speak?
CAPULET. Peace, you mumbling fool!
Utter your gravity[34] o'er a gossip's bowl,
For here we need it not.
LADY CAPULET. You are too hot.
CAPULET. God's bread![35] It makes me mad:
Day, night, hour, tide, time, work, play,
Alone, in company—still my care hath been
To have her matched; and having now provided
A gentleman of noble parentage,
Of fair demesnes, youthful, and nobly trained,
Stuffed, as they say, with honorable parts,[36]
Proportioned as one's thought would wish a man—
And then to have a wretched puling fool,
A whining mammet,[37] in her fortune's tender,[38]
To answer "I'll not wed; I cannot love,
I am too young; I pray you, pardon me."
But, an you will not wed, I'll pardon you;
Graze where you will, you shall not house with me.

22. ***choplogic,*** quibbler, one who argues unfairly.
23. ***minion,*** darling, favored person.
24. ***fettle,*** make ready.
25. ***'gainst,*** in preparation for.
26. ***hurdle,*** a conveyance for transporting criminals.
27. ***green-sickness,*** an anemic ailment of young women.
28. ***baggage,*** worthless woman.
29. ***My fingers itch,*** that is, to choke or strike you.
30. ***hilding,*** good-for-nothing.
31. ***rate,*** berate, scold.
32. ***Good prudence,*** my wise one! Capulet is speaking ironically.
33. ***smatter,*** chatter.
34. ***gravity,*** wisdom.
35. ***God's bread,*** by the sacrament; a mild oath.
36. ***parts,*** qualities, abilities.
37. ***mammet,*** doll.
38. ***in . . . tender,*** offer of good fortune.

Look to 't, think on 't; I do not use to jest.[39]
Thursday is near; lay hand on heart, advise.[40]
An you be mine, I'll give you to my friend;
An you be not, hang, beg, starve, die in the streets,
For, by my soul, I'll ne'er acknowledge thee,
Nor what is mine shall never do thee good.
Trust to 't, bethink you; I'll not be forsworn.
(Exit CAPULET.*)*

JULIET. Is there no pity sitting in the clouds,
That sees into the bottom of my grief?
O sweet my mother, cast me not away!
Delay this marriage for a month, a week;
Or, if you do not, make the bridal bed
In that dim monument where Tybalt lies.

LADY CAPULET. Talk not to me, for I'll not speak a word.
Do as thou wilt, for I have done with thee.
(Exit, leaving JULIET *and the* NURSE *alone.)*

JULIET. O God!—O Nurse, how shall this be prevented?
My husband is on earth, my faith in heaven[41];
How shall that faith return again to earth
Unless that husband send it me from heaven
By leaving earth? Comfort me, counsel me.
Alack, alack, that heaven should practice stratagems[42]
Upon so soft a subject as myself!
What say'st thou? Hast thou not a word of joy?
Some comfort, Nurse.

NURSE. Faith, here it is.
Romeo is banished; and all the world to nothing,[43]
That he dares ne'er come back to challenge[44] you;
Or, if he do, it needs must be by stealth.
Then, since the case so stands as now it doth,
I think it best you married with the County.
O, he's a lovely gentleman!
Romeo's a dishclout to him[45]; an eagle, madam,
Hath not so green,[46] so quick, so fair an eye
As Paris hath. Beshrew[47] my very heart,
I think you are happy in this second match,
For it excels your first; or, if it did not,
Your first is dead, or 'twere as good he were
As living here and you no use of him.

JULIET. Speakest thou from thy heart?

NURSE. And from my soul too;
Or else beshrew them both.

JULIET. Amen!

NURSE. What?

JULIET. Well, thou hast comforted me marvelous much.
Go in, and tell my lady I am gone,

39. ***I do not . . . jest.*** I am unaccustomed to jesting.
40. ***advise,*** consider carefully.
41. ***faith in heaven.*** Juliet refers to her marriage vows.
42. ***practice stratagems,*** contrive dreadful deeds.
43. ***all . . . nothing.*** The odds are all the world to nothing.
44. ***challenge,*** lay claim to.
45. ***to him,*** compared to him.
46. ***green.*** Green eyes were much admired in Shakespeare's day.
47. ***Beshrew,*** curse.

Having displeased my father, to Laurence' cell,
To make confession and to be absolved.
NURSE. Marry, I will; and this is wisely done. *(Exit.)*
JULIET. Ancient damnation![48] O most wicked fiend!
Is it more sin to wish me thus forsworn,
Or to dispraise my lord with that same tongue
Which she hath praised him with above compare
So many thousand times? Go, counselor;
Thou and my bosom[49] henceforth shall be twain.
I'll to the friar to know his remedy.
If all else fail, myself have power to die. *(Exit.)*

48. Ancient damnation, wicked old devil.

49. bosom, confidence.

CONSIDERING ACT THREE, SCENES 4 AND 5

1. *(a)* Point out evidence that Capulet has wrongly assumed that Juliet will be "ruled in all respects" by his wishes. *(b)* What is Capulet's reaction to Juliet's stand?

2. *(a)* What is the attitude of Lady Capulet toward Juliet's defiance? *(b)* What is the nurse's advice to Juliet, and what is Juliet's reaction to that advice?

3. What does Juliet plan to do now?

LOOKING BACK—AND AHEAD

1. Continue your outline of the play, listing the most important events that take place in Act Three.

2. Shakespeare not only tells us what his characters do, he also makes clear why (wisely or unwisely) they act as they do. Complete each of the following statements based on Act Three: *(a)* Because Tybalt slays Mercutio, Romeo __________. *(b)* Because Romeo avenges Mercutio's death, the prince sentences him to __________. (c) Because Juliet is eager to learn what plans Romeo has made for their marriage, she __________. *(d)* Because the nurse is a great talker, Juliet finds it almost impossible to __________. *(e)* Because Romeo cannot reconcile himself to being separated from Juliet, he threatens to __________.

3. On what note of foreboding does Act Three end?

Act four

Scene 1: Friar Laurence's cell.

Enter FRIAR LAURENCE *and* PARIS.

FRIAR LAURENCE. On Thursday, sir? The time is very short.
PARIS. My father[1] Capulet will have it so,
And I am nothing slow to slack his haste.[2]

1. My father, my prospective father-in-law.

2. nothing slow . . . haste, anxious to do nothing that might slow him down in his plans to hasten the marriage.

FRIAR LAURENCE. You say you do not know the lady's mind.
Uneven is the course; I like it not.

PARIS. Immoderately she weeps for Tybalt's death,
And therefore have I little talked of love;
For Venus smiles not in a house of tears.
Now, sir, her father counts it dangerous
That she doth give her sorrow so much sway,[3]
And in his wisdom hastes our marriage,
To stop the inundation of her tears;
Which, too much minded by herself alone,[4]
May be put from her by society.[5]
Now do you know the reason of this haste.

FRIAR LAURENCE *(speaking aside).* I would I knew not why
it should be slowed.
Look, sir, here comes the lady toward my cell.

3. ***doth give . . . sway,*** allows her sorrow (over Tybalt's death) to control her feelings.

4. ***minded . . . alone,*** dwelt on by her in privacy.

5. ***May be . . . society,*** may be remedied if she mingles with others.

Enter JULIET.

PARIS. Happily met, my lady and my wife!

JULIET. That may be, sir, when I may be a wife.

PARIS. That may be, must be, love, on Thursday next.

JULIET. What must be shall be.

FRIAR LAURENCE. That's a certain text.

PARIS. Come you to make confession to this father?

JULIET. To answer that, I should confess to you.

PARIS. Do not deny to him that you love me.

JULIET. I will confess to you that I love him.

PARIS. So will ye, I am sure, that you love me.

JULIET. If I do so, it will be of more price,
Being spoke behind your back, than to your face.

PARIS. Poor soul, thy face is much abused with tears.

JULIET. The tears have got small victory by that,
For it was bad enough before their spite.

PARIS. Thou wrong'st it, more than tears, with that report.

JULIET. That is no slander, sir, which is a truth;
And what I spake, I spake it to my face.

PARIS. Thy face is mine, and thou hast slandered it.

JULIET. It may be so, for it is not mine own.
Are you at leisure, holy father, now,
Or shall I come to you at evening mass?

FRIAR LAURENCE. My leisure serves me, pensive daughter,
now.
My lord, we must entreat the time alone.[6]

PARIS. God shield[7] I should disturb devotion!
Juliet, on Thursday early will I rouse ye.
Till then, adieu; and keep this holy kiss.

(Exit.)

JULIET. O, shut the door! And when thou hast done so,
Come weep with me—past hope, past cure, past help!

6. ***entreat . . . alone,*** request that you leave Juliet and me alone.

7. ***shield,*** forbid, prevent.

FRIAR LAURENCE. Ah, Juliet, I already know thy grief;
It strains me past the compass of my wits.[8]
I hear thou must, and nothing may prorogue it,
On Thursday next be married to this county.
JULIET. Tell me not, Friar, that thou hear'st of this,
Unless thou tell me how I may prevent it.
If, in thy wisdom, thou canst give no help,
Do thou but call my resolution wise,
And with this knife I'll help it presently.[9]
God joined my heart and Romeo's, thou our hands;
And ere this hand, by thee to Romeo sealed,
Shall be the label[10] to another deed,
Or my true heart with treacherous revolt
Turn to another, this shall slay them both.
Therefore, out of thy long-experienced time,
Give me some present counsel, or, behold,
'Twixt my extremes[11] and me this bloody knife
Shall play the umpire, arbitrating that
Which the commission[12] of thy years and art
Could to no issue of true honor bring.
Be not so long to speak; I long to die,
If what thou speak'st speak not of remedy.
FRIAR LAURENCE. Hold, daughter. I do spy a kind of hope,
Which craves as desperate an execution[13]
As that is desperate which we would prevent.
If, rather than to marry County Paris,
Thou hast the strength of will to slay thyself,
Then is it likely thou wilt undertake
A thing like death to chide away this shame,
That copest with[14] death himself to 'scape from it;
And, if thou darest, I'll give thee remedy.
JULIET. O, bid me leap, rather than marry Paris,
From off the battlements of yonder tower,
Or walk in thievish ways[15]; or bid me lurk
Where serpents are; chain me with roaring bears;
Or shut me nightly in a charnel house,[16]
O'ercovered quite with dead men's rattling bones,
With reeky[17] shanks and yellow chapless[18] skulls;
Or bid me go into a new-made grave
And hide me with a dead man in his shroud—
Things that, to hear them told, have made me tremble—
And I will do it without fear or doubt,
To live an unstained wife to my sweet love.
FRIAR LAURENCE. Hold, then; go home, be merry, give consent
To marry Paris. Wednesday is tomorrow;
Tomorrow night look that thou lie alone;
Let not thy nurse lie with thee in thy chamber.

8. *It strains . . . wits,* it exceeds the limits of my wisdom.

9. *presently,* at once.

10. *label,* the seal attached to a deed (a legal document) showing proof of ownership.

11. *extremes,* extreme difficulties.

12. *commission,* authority.

13. *execution,* carrying out.

14. *copest with,* bargains with.

15. *in thievish ways,* along highways where thieves hide out.

16. *charnel house,* a vault where the bodies of the dead were placed.

17. *reeky,* foul-smelling.

18. *chapless,* with the lower jaw missing.

Take thou this vial, being then in bed,
And this distillèd liquor drink thou off;
When presently through all thy veins shall run
A cold and drowsy humor,[19] for no pulse
Shall keep his native progress, but surcease[20];
No warmth, no breath, shall testify thou livest;
The roses in thy lips and cheeks shall fade
To paly ashes, thy eyes' windows fall
Like death when he shuts up the day of life.
Each part, deprived of supple government,[21]
Shall, stiff and stark and cold, appear like death,
And in this borrowed likeness of shrunk death
Thou shalt continue two and forty hours,
And then awake as from a pleasant sleep.
Now, when the bridegroom in the morning comes
To rouse thee from thy bed, there art thou dead;
Then, as a manner of our country is,
In thy best robes uncovered[22] on the bier
Thou shalt be borne to that same ancient vault
Where all the kindred of the Capulets lie.
In the meantime, against thou shalt awake,[23]
Shall Romeo by my letters know our drift,[24]
And hither shall he come, and he and I
Will watch thy waking, and that very night
Shall Romeo bear thee hence to Mantua.
And this shall free thee from this present shame,
If no inconstant toy,[25] nor womanish fear,
Abate thy valor in the acting it.

JULIET. Give me, give me! O, tell not me of fear!

FRIAR LAURENCE. Hold! Get you gone. Be strong and prosperous
In this resolve. I'll send a friar with speed
To Mantua, with my letters to thy lord.

JULIET. Love give me strength, and strength shall help afford.
Farewell, dear father! *(Exeunt.)*

19. ***humor,*** liquid.

20. ***surcease,*** cease.

21. ***supple government,*** control over the flexibility of the body.

22. ***uncovered,*** with your face uncovered.

23. ***against . . . awake,*** in preparation for your awakening.

24. ***drift,*** intentions.

25. ***inconstant toy,*** fickle, trifling fancy.

CONSIDERING ACT FOUR, SCENE 1

1. *(a)* Why does Paris call on Friar Laurence? *(b)* What is Juliet's reason for visiting the friar?

2. *(a)* How does Juliet's brief conversation with Paris reveal her attitude toward him? *(b)* Point out some double, or hidden, meanings in Juliet's remarks to Paris.

3. *(a)* Quote lines that reveal Juliet's desperate hope that the friar can devise a plan that will prevent her marriage to Paris. *(b)* Outline, step by step, the friar's plan. What is Juliet's reaction to that plan?

Scene 2: A hall in Capulet's house.

Enter CAPULET, LADY CAPULET, *the* NURSE, *and* SERVINGMEN.

CAPULET. So many guests invite as here are writ.
(Exit FIRST SERVANT.*)*
Sirrah, go hire me twenty cunning cooks.

SECOND SERVANT. You shall have none ill, sir; for I'll try if they can lick their fingers.

CAPULET. How canst thou try them so?

SECOND SERVANT. Marry, sir, 'tis an ill cook that cannot lick his own fingers; therefore he that cannot lick his fingers goes not with me.

CAPULET. Go, be gone. *(Exit* SECOND SERVANT.*)*
What, is my daughter gone to Friar Laurence?

NURSE. Ay, forsooth.

CAPULET. Well, he may chance to do some good on her.

NURSE. See where she comes from shrift with merry look.

Enter JULIET. *She is apparently in good spirits.*

CAPULET. How now, my headstrong! Where have you been gadding?

JULIET. Where I have learned me to repent the sin
Of disobedient opposition
To you and your behests, and am enjoined
By holy Laurence to fall prostrate here
And beg your pardon. *(She kneels.)* Pardon, I beseech you!
Henceforward I am ever ruled by you.

CAPULET. Send for the county; go tell him of this.
I'll have this knot knit up tomorrow morning.

JULIET. I met the youthful lord at Laurence' cell,
And gave him what becomèd[1] love I might,
Not stepping o'er the bounds of modesty.

CAPULET. Why, I am glad on 't; this is well. Stand up.
This is as 't should be. Let me see the county;
Ay, marry, go, I say, and fetch him hither.
Now, afore God, this reverend holy friar,
All our whole city is much bound[2] to him.

JULIET. Nurse, will you go with me into my closet,[3]
To help me sort such needful ornaments
As you think fit to furnish me[4] tomorrow?

LADY CAPULET. No, not till Thursday; there is time enough.

CAPULET. Go, Nurse, go with her. We'll to church tomorrow. *(Exeunt* JULIET *and* NURSE.*)*

LADY CAPULET. We shall be short in our provision;
'Tis now near night.

1. ***becomèd,*** suitable.

2. ***bound,*** indebted.

3. ***closet,*** private room.

4. ***furnish me,*** fit me out.

CAPULET. Tush, I will stir about,
And all things shall be well, I warrant thee, wife.
Go thou to Juliet, help to deck her up;
I'll not to bed tonight; let me alone;
I'll play the housewife for this once. What, ho!
They are all forth. Well, I will walk myself
To County Paris to prepare him up
Against tomorrow. My heart is wondrous light,
Since this same wayward girl is so reclaimed.
(Exeunt.)

Scene 3: Juliet's bedchamber.

Enter JULIET *and the* NURSE.

JULIET. Ay, those attires are best; but, gentle Nurse,
I pray thee, leave me to myself tonight,
For I have need of many orisons
To move the heavens to smile upon my state,
Which, well thou know'st, is cross[1] and full of sin.

Enter LADY CAPULET.

LADY CAPULET. What, are you busy, ho? Need you my help?
JULIET. No, madam; we have culled such necessaries
As are behoveful[2] for our state tomorrow.
So please you, let me now be left alone,
And let the nurse this night sit up with you,
For I am sure you have your hands full all
In this so sudden business.
LADY CAPULET. Good night;
Get thee to bed, and rest, for thou hast need.
(Exeunt LADY CAPULET *and the* NURSE.*)*
JULIET. Farewell! God knows when we shall meet again.
I have a faint cold fear thrills through my veins,[3]
That almost freezes up the heat of life;
I'll call them back again to comfort me.
Nurse!—What should she do here?
My dismal scene I needs must act alone.
Come, vial.
What if this mixture do not work at all?
Shall I be married then tomorrow morning?
No, no; this shall forbid it. Lie thou there.
(She lays down her dagger.)
What if it be a poison which the friar
Subtly hath ministered[4] to have me dead,
Lest in this marriage he should be dishonored
Because he married me before to Romeo?

1. ***cross,*** contrary.

2. ***behoveful,*** needed.

3. ***faint . . . veins,*** a feeling of coldness and faintness that courses through my veins.

4. ***ministered,*** applied or administered (something).

I fear it is, and yet methinks it should not,
For he hath still been tried[5] a holy man.
How if, when I am laid into the tomb,
I wake before the time that Romeo
Come to redeem me?—There's a fearful point!
Shall I not then be stifled in the vault,
To whose foul mouth no healthsome air breathes in,
And there die strangled ere my Romeo comes?
Or, if I live, is it not very like[6]
The horrible conceit[7] of death and night,
Together with the terror of the place—
As[8] in a vault, an ancient receptacle
Where, for these many hundred years, the bones
Of all my buried ancestors are packed;
Where bloody Tybalt, yet but green in earth,[9]
Lies festering in his shroud; where, as they say,
At some hours in the night spirits resort;—
Alack, alack, is it not like that I,
So early waking, what with loathsome smells,
And shrieks like mandrakes'[10] torn out of the earth,
That living mortals, hearing them, run mad:—
O, if I wake, shall I not be distraught,
Environed with all these hideous fears,[11]
And madly play with my forefathers' joints,
And pluck the mangled Tybalt from his shroud,
And, in this rage,[12] with some great kinsman's bone,
As with a club, dash out my desperate brains?
O, look! Methinks I see my cousin's ghost
Seeking out Romeo, that did spit his body
Upon a rapier's point.—Stay, Tybalt, stay!
Romeo, I come! This do I drink to thee.
(She drinks and falls upon her curtained bed.)

5. ***still been tried,*** always been proved to be.

6. ***like,*** likely.

7. ***conceit,*** idea.

8. ***As,*** namely.

9. ***green in earth,*** newly buried.

10. ***mandrakes,*** plants that resemble the human form. The mandrake was fabled to shrink and to cause madness when torn from the ground.

11. ***fears,*** objects of fear.

12. ***rage,*** madness.

CONSIDERING ACT FOUR, SCENES 2 AND 3

1. In carrying out the friar's instructions, how does Juliet resort to deceit? Do you think her deceit was justified? Why or why not?

2. ***(a)*** What questions and doubts come to Juliet's mind during the famous "potion" scene? ***(b)*** What are your feelings toward Juliet in this scene? Read lines that were especially effective in arousing those feelings.

Scene 4: A hall in Capulet's house.

Enter LADY CAPULET *and the* NURSE.

LADY CAPULET. Hold, take these keys, and fetch more spices, Nurse.

NURSE. They call for dates and quinces in the pastry.[1]

Enter CAPULET.

CAPULET. Come, stir, stir, stir! The second cock hath crowed,
The curfew bell hath rung, 'tis three o'clock.
Look to the bakèd meats,[2] good Angelica;
Spare not for cost.
NURSE. Get you to bed; faith, you'll be sick tomorrow
For this night's watching.[3]
CAPULET. No, not a whit. What! I have watched ere now
All night for lesser cause, and ne'er been sick.
LADY CAPULET. Ay; but I'll watch you from such watching now. *(Exeunt* LADY CAPULET *and* NURSE.*)*

Enter SERVANTS *carrying baskets of food.*

CAPULET. Now, fellow! What's there?
FIRST SERVANT. Things for the cook, sir, but I know not what.
CAPULET. Make haste, make haste. *(Exit* FIRST SERVANT.*)*
(To SECOND SERVANT.*)* Sirrah, fetch drier logs;
Call Peter, he will show thee where they are.
SECOND SERVANT. I have a head, sir, that will find out logs,
And never trouble Peter for the matter. *(Exit.)*
CAPULET. Mass,[4] and well said! A merry fellow, ha!
Thou shalt be loggerhead.[5] Good faith, 'tis day.
The county will be here with music straight,
For so he said he would. I hear him near.
(Music sounds off-stage.)
Nurse! Wife! What, ho! What, Nurse, I say!

Enter NURSE.

Go waken Juliet; go and trim her up.
I'll go and chat with Paris. Hie, make haste,
Make haste; the bridegroom he is come already;
Make haste, I say. *(Exeunt.)*

1. ***pastry,*** room in which pastry was made.
2. ***bakèd meats,*** pies, pastries.
3. ***For . . . watching,*** because of lying awake tonight.
4. ***Mass,*** by the Mass.
5. ***loggerhead,*** blockhead.

Scene 5: Juliet's bedchamber. The curtains are drawn around Juliet's bed.

Enter the NURSE.

NURSE *(urgently).* Mistress! What, mistress! Juliet! Fast,[1] I warrant her.
Why, lamb; why, lady! Fie, you slugabed!
Why, love, I say! *(She undraws the curtains around the bed.)* Madam! Sweetheart! Why, bride!
What, not a word? How sound is she asleep!

1. ***Fast,*** fast asleep.

I must needs wake her. Madam, madam, madam!
What, dressed, and in your clothes, and down again!
I must needs wake you. Lady! lady! lady!
Alas, alas! Help, help! My lady's dead!
O well-a-day, that ever I was born!
Some aqua vitae, ho! My lord! My lady!

Enter LADY CAPULET.

LADY CAPULET. What noise is here?
NURSE. O lamentable day!
LADY CAPULET. What is the matter?
NURSE. Look, look! O heavy day!
LADY CAPULET. O me, O me! My child, my only life,
Revive, look up, or I will die with thee!
Help, help! Call help!

Enter CAPULET.

CAPULET. For shame, bring Juliet forth; her lord is come.
NURSE. She's dead, deceased, she's dead; alack the day!
LADY CAPULET. Alack the day, she's dead, she's dead, she's dead!
CAPULET. Ha! Let me see her. Out, alas![2] She's cold;
Her blood is settled,[3] and her joints are stiff.
Life and these lips have long been separated.
Death lies on her like an untimely frost
Upon the sweetest flower of all the field.

2. *Out, alas,* an exclamation of grief.

3. *settled,* thickened.

Enter FRIAR LAURENCE *and* PARIS.

FRIAR LAURENCE. Come, is the bride ready to go to church?
CAPULET. Ready to go, but never to return.
Death is my son-in-law, Death is my heir;
My daughter he hath wedded. I will die
And leave him all. Life, living, all is Death's.
PARIS. Have I thought long to see this morning's face,[4]
And doth it give me such a sight as this?
LADY CAPULET. Accursed, unhappy, wretched, hateful day!
Most miserable hour that e'er time saw.
But one thing to rejoice and solace in,
And cruel Death hath catched it from my sight!
NURSE. O woe! O woeful, woeful, woeful day!
Most lamentable day, most woeful day,
That ever, ever, I did yet behold!
PARIS. Beguiled, divorced, wronged, spited, slain!
Most detestable Death, by thee beguiled,
By cruel cruel thee quite overthrown!
O love! O life; not life, but love in death!
CAPULET. O child! O child! My soul, and not my child!
Dead art thou, dead! Alack, my child is dead,
And with my child my joys are buried.

4. *thought long . . . face,* long looked forward to the dawn of this, my wedding day.

FRIAR LAURENCE. Peace, ho, for shame! Confusion's[5] cure
lives not
In these confusions. Heaven and yourself
Had part in this fair maid; now heaven hath all,
And all the better is it for the maid.
Your part in her you could not keep from death,
But heaven keeps his part in eternal life.
The most you sought was her promotion;
For 'twas your heaven she should be advanced[6];
And weep ye now, seeing she is advanced
Above the clouds, as high as heaven itself?
Dry up your tears, and stick your rosemary[7]
On this fair corse; and, as the custom is,
In all her best array bear her to church.

CAPULET. All things that we ordained festival,[8]
Turn from their office to black funeral—
Our instruments to melancholy bells,
Our wedding cheer to a sad burial feast,
Our solemn hymns to sullen[9] dirges change;
Our bridal flowers serve for a buried corse,
And all things change them to the contrary.

FRIAR LAURENCE. Sir, go you in; and, madam, go with him;
And go, Sir Paris; everyone prepare
To follow this fair corse unto her grave.
The heavens do lour upon you for some ill[10];
Move them no more by crossing their high will.
(Exeunt CAPULET, LADY CAPULET, PARIS, *and* FRIAR.*)*

5. ***Confusion's,*** destruction's.

6. ***advanced,*** lifted up, promoted.

7. ***rosemary,*** symbol of immortality and enduring love; therefore, used at both funerals and weddings.

8. ***ordained festival,*** intended to be gay and festive.

9. ***sullen,*** mournful.

10. ***ill,*** sin committed by you.

CONSIDERING ACT FOUR, SCENES 4 AND 5

1. Why may the hustle and bustle of preparation for the wedding feast be described as ***ironical?***

2. How does Scene 5 indicate that an important step in the friar's plan has worked out just as he had hoped it would?

3. *(a)* What are your feelings toward Lord and Lady Capulet as they lament the "death" of their daughter? Explain why you feel as you do. *(b)* Why had Juliet not taken the nurse into her confidence concerning the friar's plan?

LOOKING BACK—AND AHEAD

1. Add your outline of the important events in Act Four to your previous outlines.

2. Point out ways in which Juliet has shown strength and courage in Act Four.

3. Do you think that Friar Laurence's plan will continue to work out well? Why or why not?

Act five

Scene 1: A street in Mantua, where Romeo is living.

ROMEO *enters.*

ROMEO. If I may trust the flattering truth of sleep,[1]
My dreams presage some joyful news at hand.
My bosom's lord[2] sits lightly in his throne,
And all this day an unaccustomed spirit
Lifts me above the ground with cheerful thoughts.
I dreamt my lady came and found me dead—
Strange dream that gives a dead man leave[3] to think!—
And breathed such life with kisses in my lips
That I revived and was an emperor.
Ah me, how sweet is love itself possessed,
When but love's shadows[4] are so rich in joy!

Enter BALTHASAR.

News from Verona!—How now, Balthasar!
Dost thou not bring me letters from the friar?
How doth my lady? Is my father well?
How fares my Juliet? That I ask again,
For nothing can be ill if she be well.

BALTHASAR. Then she is well, and nothing can be ill.
Her body sleeps in Capel's monument,
And her immortal part with angels lives.
I saw her laid low in her kindred's vault,
And presently took post[5] to tell it you.
O, pardon me for bringing these ill news,
Since you did leave it for my office,[6] sir.

ROMEO. Is it even so? Then I defy you, stars![7]
Thou know'st my lodging; get me ink and paper,
And hire post horses; I will hence tonight.

BALTHASAR. I do beseech you, sir, have patience;
Your looks are pale and wild, and do import
Some misadventure.

ROMEO. Tush, thou art deceived.
Leave me, and do the thing I bid thee do.
Hast thou no letters to me from the friar?

BALTHASAR. No, my good lord.

ROMEO. No matter. Get thee gone,
And hire those horses; I'll be with thee straight.

(Exit BALTHASAR.*)*

Well, Juliet, I will be with thee tonight.
Let's see for means. O mischief, thou art swift
To enter in the thoughts of desperate men!
I do remember an apothecary—

1. ***flattering . . . sleep,*** pleasant dreams that seem true.

2. ***bosom's lord,*** heart.

3. ***gives . . . leave,*** allows a dead man.

4. ***shadows,*** unreal images of the imagination.

5. ***presently took post,*** soon set out with post horses.

6. ***office,*** duty.

7. ***Then . . . stars.*** Romeo defies the destiny that has fated him to live without Juliet.

And hereabouts he dwells—which late I noted
In tattered weeds,[8] with overwhelming[9] brows,
Culling of simples.[10] Meager were his looks,
Sharp misery had worn him to the bones;
And in his needy shop a tortoise hung,
An alligator stuffed, and other skins
Of ill-shaped fishes; and about his shelves
A beggarly account[11] of empty boxes,
Green earthen pots, bladders, and musty seeds,
Remnants of packthread[12] and old cakes of roses,[13]
Were thinly scattered to make up a show.
Noting this penury, to myself I said,
"An if a man did need a poison now
Whose sale is present[14] death in Mantua,
Here lives a caitiff[15] wretch would sell it him."
O, this same thought did but forerun my need,
And this same needy man must sell it me.
As I remember, this should be the house.
Being holiday, the beggar's shop is shut.
What, ho, apothecary!

Enter APOTHECARY.

APOTHECARY. Who calls so loud?
ROMEO. Come hither, man. I see that thou art poor.
Hold, there is forty ducats; let me have
A dram of poison, such soon-speeding gear[16]
As will disperse itself through all the veins
That the life-weary taker may fall dead
And that the trunk[17] may be discharged of breath
As violently as hasty powder fired
Doth hurry from the fatal cannon's maw.
APOTHECARY. Such mortal drugs I have; but Mantua's law
Is death to any he that utters them.[18]
ROMEO. Art thou so bare and full of wretchedness,
And fear'st to die? Famine is in thy cheeks,
Need and oppression starveth[19] in thine eyes,
Contempt and beggary hangs upon thy back;
The world is not thy friend, nor the world's law;
The world affords no law to make thee rich;
Then be not poor, but break it, and take this.
APOTHECARY. My poverty, but not my will, consents.
ROMEO. I pay thy poverty, and not thy will.
APOTHECARY. Put this in any liquid thing you will
And drink it off; and, if you had the strength
Of twenty men, it would dispatch you straight.
ROMEO. There is thy gold, worse poison to men's souls.
Farewell. Buy food, and get thyself in flesh.
Come, cordial[20] and not poison, go with me
To Juliet's grave, for there must I use thee. *(Exeunt.)*

8. ***weeds,*** clothes.
9. ***overwhelming,*** overhanging.
10. ***Culling of simples,*** selecting medicinal herbs.
11. ***beggarly account,*** poor array.
12. ***packthread,*** twine.
13. ***cakes of roses,*** rose petals caked together for use as a perfume.
14. ***present,*** immediate.
15. ***caitiff,*** poor.
16. ***soon-speeding gear,*** stuff that will begin to act quickly.
17. ***trunk,*** body.
18. ***any . . . utters them,*** anyone who distributes them.
19. ***starveth,*** show hunger.
20. ***cordial,*** a heart stimulant.

Scene 2: Friar Laurence's cell.

Enter FRIAR JOHN.

FRIAR JOHN. Holy Franciscan friar! Brother, ho!

Enter FRIAR LAURENCE.

FRIAR LAURENCE. This same should be the voice of Friar
John.
Welcome from Mantua. What says Romeo?
Or, if his mind be writ,[1] give me his letter.

FRIAR JOHN. Going to find a barefoot brother out,
One of our order, to associate[2] me,
Here in this city visiting the sick,
And finding him, the searchers[3] of the town,
Suspecting that we both were in a house
Where the infectious pestilence did reign,
Sealed up the doors, and would not let us forth,
So that my speed to Mantua there was stayed.

FRIAR LAURENCE. Who bare my letter, then, to Romeo?

FRIAR JOHN. I could not send it—here it is again—
Nor get a messenger to bring it thee,
So fearful were they of infection.

FRIAR LAURENCE. Unhappy fortune! By my brotherhood,
The letter was not nice[4] but full of charge
Of dear import,[5] and the neglecting it
May do much danger. Friar John, go hence;
Get me an iron crow,[6] and bring it straight
Unto my cell.

FRIAR JOHN. Brother, I'll go and bring it thee. *(Exit.)*

FRIAR LAURENCE. Now must I to the monument alone.
Within this three hours will fair Juliet wake.
She will beshrew me much that Romeo
Hath had no notice of these accidents[7];
But I will write again to Mantua,
And keep her at my cell till Romeo come;
Poor living corse, closed in a dead man's tomb! *(Exit.)*

1. ***if . . . writ,*** if he has sent a written message.

2. ***associate,*** accompany.

3. ***searchers,*** officials who sought out those suspected of having a highly contagious disease (the "infectious pestilence," in line 10).

4. ***nice,*** trivial.

5. ***Of dear import,*** having dreadful significance.

6. ***iron crow,*** crowbar.

7. ***accidents,*** happenings.

CONSIDERING ACT FIVE, SCENES 1 AND 2

1. *(a)* What is Romeo's mood at the beginning of Scene 1? *(b)* What causes Romeo's mood to change quickly?

2. What arguments does Romeo use in persuading the apothecary to sell him a dram of poison? Explain why you do or do not agree with these arguments.

3. *(a)* Why has Friar John been unable to deliver Friar Laurence's letter to Romeo? *(b)* Explain the irony of Romeo's indifferent comment, "No matter," when Balthasar tells him he has brought no letters from Friar Laurence.

Scene 3: The churchyard in Verona where the Capulets' tomb is located. It is nighttime.

Enter PARIS *and his* PAGE *bearing flowers and a torch.*

PARIS. Give me thy torch, boy; hence, and stand aloof.
Yet put it out, for I would not be seen.
(The PAGE *extinguishes the torch.)*
Under yond yew trees lay thee all along,[1]
Holding thine ear close to the hollow ground;
So shall no foot upon the churchyard tread—
Being loose, infirm, with digging up of graves—
But thou shalt hear it; whistle then to me,
As signal that thou hear'st something approach.
Give me those flowers. Do as I bid thee, go.

PAGE *(speaking aside).* I am almost afraid to stand alone
Here in the churchyard; yet I will adventure. *(He retires.)*

PARIS. Sweet flower, with flowers thy bridal bed I strew.
O woe! Thy canopy is dust and stones,
Which[2] with sweet[3] water nightly I will dew,
Or, wanting[4] that, with tears distilled by moans.
The obsequies that I for thee will keep
Nightly shall be to strew thy grave and weep.
(The PAGE *whistles off-stage.)*
The boy gives warning something doth approach.
What cursèd foot wanders this way tonight
To cross[5] my obsequies and true love's rite?
What, with a torch! Muffle[6] me, night, awhile. *(He retires.)*

Enter ROMEO *and* BALTHASAR *carrying tools to open the tomb. They cannot see* PARIS.

ROMEO. Give me that mattock[7] and the wrenching iron.
Hold, take this letter; early in the morning
See thou deliver it to my lord and father.
Give me the light. Upon thy life, I charge thee,
Whate'er thou hear'st or seest, stand all aloof,
And do not interrupt me in my course.
Why I descend into this bed of death
Is partly to behold my lady's face,
But chiefly to take thence from her dead finger
A precious ring—a ring that I must use
In dear employment. Therefore hence, be gone.
But if thou, jealous,[8] dost return to pry
In what I further shall intend to do,
By heaven I will tear thee joint by joint
And strew this hungry churchyard with thy limbs.
The time and my intents are savage, wild,
More fierce and more inexorable far
Than empty tigers or the roaring sea.

1. ***all along,*** at full length.
2. ***Which.*** The antecedent is "flowers," line 12.
3. ***sweet,*** perfumed.
4. ***wanting,*** lacking.
5. ***cross,*** interfere with.
6. ***Muffle,*** hide.
7. ***mattock,*** pickax.
8. ***jealous,*** suspicious.

BALTHASAR. I will be gone, sir, and not trouble you.
ROMEO. So shalt thou show me friendship. *(Offering money.)*
Take thou that.
Live and be prosperous, and farewell, good fellow.
BALTHASAR *(speaking aside).* For all this same, I'll hide me hereabout.
His looks I fear, and his intents I doubt.[9] *(He retires.)*
ROMEO. Thou detestable maw, thou womb of death,
Gorged with the dearest morsel of the earth,
Thus I enforce thy rotten jaws to open,
And, in despite,[10] I'll cram thee with more food!
(He succeeds in opening the tomb.)
PARIS. This is that banished haughty Montague
That murdered my love's cousin, with which grief,
It is supposed, the fair creature died,
And here is come to do some villainous shame
To the dead bodies. I will apprehend him.
(He comes forward.)
Stop thy unhallowed toil, vile Montague!
Can vengeance be pursued further than death?
Condemnèd villain, I do apprehend thee;
Obey and go with me, for thou must die.
ROMEO. I must indeed; and therefore came I hither.
Good gentle youth, tempt not a desperate man;
Fly hence, and leave me. Think upon these gone;
Let them affright thee. I beseech thee, youth,
Put not another sin upon my head,
By urging me to fury. O, be gone!
By heaven, I love thee better than myself;
For I come hither armed against myself.
Stay not, be gone; live, and hereafter say
A madman's mercy bade thee run away.
PARIS. I do defy thy conjurations,[11]
And apprehend thee for a felon here.
ROMEO. Wilt thou provoke me? Then have at thee, boy!
PAGE. O Lord, they fight! I will go call the watch. *(Exit.)*
PARIS. O, I am slain! *(He falls.)* If thou be merciful,
Open the tomb, lay me with Juliet. *(He dies.)*
ROMEO. In faith, I will. Let me peruse this face.
Mercutio's kinsman, noble County Paris!
What said my man when my betossèd soul
Did not attend[12] him as we rode? I think
He told me Paris should have married[13] Juliet.
Said he not so? Or did I dream it so?
Or am I mad, hearing him talk of Juliet,
To think it was so? O, give me thy hand,
One writ with me in sour misfortune's book!
I'll bury thee in a triumphant[14] grave;

9. ***doubt,*** suspect.

10. ***in despite,*** in defiance.

11. ***conjurations,*** solemn appeals.

12. ***attend,*** pay attention to.

13. ***should have married,*** was intended to marry.

14. ***triumphant,*** glorious, honorable.

A grave? O, no; a lantern,[15] slaughtered youth,
For here lies Juliet, and her beauty makes
This vault a feasting presence[16] full of light.
Death,[17] lie thou there, by a dead man interred.
(He lays PARIS *in the tomb, not far from* JULIET.*)*
How oft when men are at the point of death
Have they been merry, which their keepers call
A lightning[18] before death. O, how may I
Call this a lightning? O my love! my wife!
Death, that hath sucked the honey of thy breath,
Hath had no power yet upon thy beauty:
Thou art not conquered; beauty's ensign yet
Is crimson in thy lips and in thy cheeks,
And death's pale flag is not advancèd there.
Tybalt, liest thou there in thy bloody sheet?
O, what more favor can I do to thee
Than with that hand that cut thy youth in twain
To sunder his that was thine enemy?
Forgive me, cousin! Ah, dear Juliet,
Why art thou yet so fair? Shall I believe
That unsubstantial death is amorous,
And that the lean abhorrèd monster keeps
Thee here in the dark to be his paramour?
For fear of that, I still will stay with thee
And never from this palace of dim night
Depart again. Here, here will I remain
With worms that are thy chambermaids. O, here
Will I set up my everlasting rest,
And shake the yoke of inauspicious stars
From this world-wearied flesh. Eyes, look your last!
Arms, take your last embrace! And, lips, O you
The doors of breath, seal with a righteous kiss
A dateless[19] bargain to engrossing[20] death!
Come, bitter conduct, come, unsavory guide!
Thou desperate pilot, now at once run on
The dashing rocks thy seasick weary bark!
Here's to my love! *(He drinks the poison.)* O true
apothecary!
Thy drugs are quick. Thus with a kiss I die. *(Falls.)*

Enter, at the other end of the churchyard,
FRIAR LAURENCE, *with a lantern,*
crowbar, mattock, and spade.

FRIAR LAURENCE. Saint Francis be my speed![21] How oft
tonight
Have my old feet stumbled at graves![22] Who's there?

BALTHASAR. Here's one, a friend, and one that knows you
well.

15. ***lantern,*** a tower filled with many windows.
16. ***feasting presence,*** a splendid reception room in a regal mansion.
17. ***Death,*** the corpse of Paris.
18. ***lightning,*** a revival of spirit.
19. ***dateless,*** everlasting.
20. ***engrossing,*** all-demanding.
21. ***speed,*** protector.
22. ***stumbled at graves.*** This was an unlucky omen.

FRIAR LAURENCE. Bliss be upon you! Tell me, good my friend,
What torch is yond that vainly lends his light
To grubs and eyeless skulls? As I discern,
It burneth in the Capels' monument.
BALTHASAR. It doth so, holy sir; and there's my master,
One that you love.
FRIAR LAURENCE. Who is it?
BALTHASAR. Romeo.
FRIAR LAURENCE. How long hath he been there?
BALTHASAR. Full half an hour.
FRIAR LAURENCE. Go with me to the vault.
BALTHASAR. I dare not, sir.
My master knows not but I am gone hence,
And fearfully did menace me with death
If I did stay to look on his intents.
FRIAR LAURENCE. Stay, then; I'll go alone. Fear comes upon me;
O, much I fear some ill unlucky thing.
BALTHASAR. As I did sleep under this yew tree here,
I dreamt my master and another fought,
And that my master slew him.
FRIAR LAURENCE. Romeo! *(He goes forward.)*
Alack, alack, what blood is this which stains
The stony entrance of this sepulcher?
What mean these masterless and gory swords
To lie discolored by this place of peace?
(He enters the tomb.)
Romeo! O, pale! Who else? What, Paris too?
And steeped in blood? Ah, what an unkind hour
Is guilty of this lamentable chance!
The lady stirs. *(Slowly* JULIET *comes out of her trance.)*
JULIET. O comfortable[23] friar! Where is my lord?
I do remember well where I should be,
And there I am. Where is my Romeo?
(Off-stage noise of the WATCH *approaching.)*
FRIAR LAURENCE. I hear some noise. Lady, come from that nest.
Of death, contagion, and unnatural sleep.
A greater power than we can contradict
Hath thwarted our intents. Come, come away.
Thy husband in thy bosom there lies dead;
And Paris too. Come, I'll dispose of thee
Among a sisterhood of holy nuns.
Stay not to question, for the watch is coming;
Come, go, good Juliet. I dare no longer stay.
(He leaves JULIET *alone with her dead husband.)*
JULIET. Go, get thee hence, for I will not away.

23. *comfortable,* comforting.

(Exit FRIAR LAURENCE.*)*
What's here? A cup closed in my true love's hand?
Poison, I see, hath been his timeless[24] end.
O churl![25] Drunk all, and left no friendly drop
To help me after? I will kiss thy lips;
Haply[26] some poison yet doth hang on them,
To make me die with a restorative.[27] *(Kisses him.)*
Thy lips are warm.

FIRST WATCHMAN *(off-stage).* Lead, boy. Which way?

JULIET. Yea, noise? Then I'll be brief. O happy[28] dagger
(snatching ROMEO's *dagger.)*
This is thy sheath *(stabs herself);* there rust, and let me die.

(She falls on ROMEO's *body and dies.)*

Enter WATCH, *with the* PAGE *of* PARIS.

PAGE. This is the place; there, where the torch doth burn.

FIRST WATCHMAN. The ground is bloody; search about the churchyard.
Go, some of you; whoe'er you find, attach.[29]
Pitiful sight! Here lies the county slain,
And Juliet bleeding, warm, and newly dead,
Who here hath lain these two days buried.
Go, tell the prince; run to the Capulets;
Raise up the Montagues; some others search.
We see the ground whereon these woes[30] do lie,
But the true ground[31] of all these piteous woes
We cannot without circumstance descry.[32]

Enter some members of the WATCH, *with* BALTHASAR.

SECOND WATCHMAN. Here's Romeo's man; we found him in the churchyard.

FIRST WATCHMAN. Hold him in safety till the prince come hither.

Reënter FRIAR LAURENCE *and a third* WATCHMAN.

THIRD WATCHMAN. Here is a friar that trembles, sighs, and weeps.
We took this mattock and this spade from him
As he was coming from this churchyard side.

FIRST WATCHMAN. A great suspicion[33]; stay the friar too.

Enter PRINCE ESCALUS *and* ATTENDANTS.

PRINCE. What misadventure is so early up,
That calls our person from our morning's rest?

Enter LORD *and* LADY CAPULET.

CAPULET. What should it be that is so shrieked abroad?

LADY CAPULET. The people in the street cry "Romeo,"

24. ***timeless,*** untimely.
25. ***churl,*** miser.
26. ***Haply,*** perhaps.
27. ***To make . . . restorative.*** The very thing (a kiss) that had been a means of renewing good cheer when Romeo was alive, may now bring about Juliet's death.
28. ***happy,*** timely.
29. ***whoe'er . . . attach,*** arrest anyone you find.
30. ***woes,*** the bodies of Romeo and Juliet.
31. ***ground,*** cause.
32. ***circumstance descry,*** note the details.
33. ***A great suspicion,*** a most suspicious thing.

Some "Juliet," and some "Paris"; and all run
With open outcry toward our monument.

PRINCE. What fear is this which startles in our ears?

FIRST WATCHMAN. Sovereign, here lies the County Paris slain,
And Romeo dead, and Juliet, dead before,
Warm and new killed.

PRINCE. Search, seek, and know how this foul murder comes.

FIRST WATCHMAN. Here is a friar, and slaughtered Romeo's man,
With instruments upon them fit to open
These dead men's tombs.

CAPULET. O heavens! O wife, look how our daughter bleeds!
This dagger hath mista'en[34]—for, lo, his house[35]
Is empty on the back of Montague—
And it missheathed in my daughter's bosom!

LADY CAPULET. O me! This sight of death is as a bell
That warns[36] my old age to a sepulcher.

Enter MONTAGUE *and* OTHERS.

PRINCE. Come, Montague; for thou art early up
To see thy son and heir more early down.

MONTAGUE. Alas, my liege, my wife is dead tonight;
Grief of my son's exile hath stopped her breath.
What further woe conspires against mine age?

PRINCE. Look, and thou shalt see.

MONTAGUE. O thou untaught! What manners is in this,
To press before thy father to a grave?

PRINCE. Seal up the mouth of outrage[37] for a while,
Till we can clear these ambiguities
And know their spring,[38] their head, their true descent;
And then will I be general of your woes,
And lead you even to death. Meantime, forbear
And let mischance be slave to patience.[39]
Bring forth the parties of suspicion.

FRIAR LAURENCE. I am the greatest, able to do least,
Yet most suspected, as the time and place
Doth make against me, of this direful murder;
And here I stand, both to impeach and purge[40]
Myself condemned and myself excused.

PRINCE. Then say at once what thou dost know in this.

FRIAR LAURENCE. I will be brief, for my short date of breath
Is not so long as is a tedious tale.
Romeo, there dead, was husband to that Juliet,
And she, there dead, that Romeo's faithful wife.
I married them, and their stol'n marriage day

34. ***mista'en,*** mistaken its right target.
35. ***his house,*** its scabbard.
36. ***warns,*** orders.
37. ***mouth of outrage,*** outcry.
38. ***spring,*** source.
39. ***let mischance . . . patience.*** Let patience control your hasty reaction to these mishaps.
40. ***impeach and purge,*** accuse and free from blame.

ROTH

Was Tybalt's doomsday, whose untimely death
Banished the new-made bridegroom from this city,
For whom, and not for Tybalt, Juliet pined.
You, to remove that siege of grief from her,
Betrothed and would have married her perforce
To County Paris. Then comes she to me
And with wild looks bid me devise some mean
To rid her from this second marriage,
Or in my cell there would she kill herself.
Then gave I her, so tutored by my art,
A sleeping potion; which so took effect
As I intended, for it wrought on her
The form of death. Meantime I writ to Romeo
That he should hither come as this[41] dire night,
To help to take her from her borrowed[42] grave,
Being the time the potion's force should cease.
But he which bore my letter, Friar John,
Was stayed by accident, and yesternight
Returned my letter back. Then all alone
At the prefixèd hour of her waking,
Came I to take her from her kindred's vault,
Meaning to keep her closely[43] at my cell
Till I conveniently could send to Romeo.
But when I came, some minute ere the time
Of her awaking, here untimely lay
The noble Paris and true Romeo dead.
She wakes, and I entreated her come forth
And bear this work of heaven with patience.
But then a noise did scare me from the tomb,
And she, too desperate, would not go with me,
But, as it seems, did violence on herself.
All this I know; and to the marriage
Her nurse is privy[44]; and, if aught in this
Miscarried by my fault, let my old life
Be sacrificed, some hour before his time,
Unto the rigor of severest law.

PRINCE. We still have known thee for a holy man.
Where's Romeo's man? What can he say in this?

BALTHASAR. I brought my master news of Juliet's death;
And then in post[45] he came from Mantua
To this same place, to this same monument.
This letter he early bid me give his father,
And threatened me with death, going in the vault,
If I departed not and left him there.

PRINCE. Give me the letter; I will look on it.
Where is the county's page that raised the watch?
Sirrah, what made[46] your master in this place?

PAGE. He came with flowers to strew his lady's grave,

41. ***as this,*** this very.

42. ***borrowed,*** used temporarily.

43. ***closely,*** secretly.

44. ***privy,*** sharing secret knowledge of something.

45. ***in post,*** with the greatest possible speed.

46. ***made,*** did.

And bid me stand aloof, and so I did.
Anon comes one with light to ope the tomb,
And by and by my master drew on[47] him;
And then I ran away to call the watch.

PRINCE. This letter doth make good the friar's words,
Their course of love, the tidings of her death;
And here he writes that he did buy a poison
Of a poor 'pothecary, and therewithal
Came to this vault to die and lie with Juliet.
Where be these enemies? Capulet! Montague!
See, what a scourge is laid upon your hate,
That heaven finds means to kill your joys[48] with love!
And I, for winking at your discords, too,
Have lost a brace of kinsmen.[49] All are punished.

CAPULET. O brother Montague, give me thy hand.
This is my daughter's jointure,[50] for no more
Can I demand.

MONTAGUE. But I can give thee more;
For I will raise her statue in pure gold,
That while Verona by that name is known,
There shall no figure at such rate be set[51]
As that of true and faithful Juliet.

CAPULET. As rich shall Romeo's by his lady's lie,
Poor sacrifices of our enmity.

PRINCE. A glooming peace this morning with it brings;
The sun, for sorrow, will not show his head.
Go hence, to have more talk of these sad things;
Some shall be pardoned, and some punished,
For never was a story of more woe
Than this of Juliet and her Romeo. *(Exeunt.)*

47. ***drew on,*** approached.

48. ***your joys,*** your children.

49. ***brace of kinsmen,*** Mercutio and Paris.

50. ***jointure,*** dowry.

51. ***at such . . . set,*** be valued so greatly.

CONSIDERING ACT FIVE, SCENE 3

1. *(a)* Why has Paris come to the Capulets' tomb? *(b)* Why has Romeo also come there? *(c)* What mistaken idea do both Paris and Romeo have about Juliet? How has each of them gained that idea?

2. *(a)* Why does Paris feel justified in his determination to slay Romeo? *(b)* How does Romeo try to persuade Paris to leave? *(c)* What happens when Paris refuses to heed Romeo's plea?

3. *(a)* What two tragic discoveries does Friar Laurence make when he enters the tomb? *(b)* What does he urge Juliet to do when she awakens? *(c)* Why does he leave the tomb? Explain why you think he should or should not be blamed for leaving.

4. *(a)* How does Juliet first attempt to end her life and join her husband in death? *(b)* How does she eventually achieve her aim?

5. How, at long last, do old Montague and Capulet show that they have learned the price of enmity between their families?

6. Complete your outline of the important events in the play.

VARIATIONS ON A THEME

Shakespeare's ***Romeo and Juliet*** illustrates one of the most popular themes in literature—a tragic theme of young lovers who cannot marry because of bitterness and prejudice on the part of people around them. As you learned in the introduction, this play itself is a variation on a theme, for Shakespeare derived the idea from a poem by Arthur Brooke. In fact, the poem came from a short story by the Italian author, Matteo Bandello.

Similarly, Shakespeare's treatment of the tragic story has inspired others to use the theme, not only in writing, but in music and ballet as well. Among well-known works based on the play are an opera by Gounod, symphonic pieces by Berlioz and Tschaikovsky, and a ballet by Prokofieff.

However, the most recent Romeo and Juliet variation is probably the Broadway musical that opened in New York in September, 1957. Its title is ***West Side Story,*** a colorful, tension-filled production that has become one of the most popular hits in recent years. The musical was also made into a movie, which won the 1961 academy awards for best film of the year, best supporting actor, and best supporting actress.

As the curtain goes up, it is evident, however, that ***West Side Story*** is not a mere replica of ***Romeo and Juliet*** set to music. Indeed, it is difficult at first even to recognize Shakespeare's influence. His romantic settings of gardens and palaces have become dreary streets, alleys, and tenements in New York's westside Manhattan. Romeo has become "Tony," who works in "Doc's drugstore." And Juliet has become "Maria," who has recently arrived from her native Puerto Rico.

Most of the other principal characters are members of rival street gangs, the Jets, who were once led by Tony, and the Sharks, who are led by Maria's brother, Bernardo. The Jets have determined to drive the "foreign" gang from the streets, and from the first scene, the tension begins to mount, as the rivals taunt one another in a street skirmish.

When Maria and Tony meet and fall in love, Bernardo's hatred for Tony and the Jets increases, and he forbids his sister to see Tony again. However, the two lovers meet secretly and plan to be married. The story then moves toward a climax as the Jets and Sharks make plans for an all-out rumble, or street fight. Maria appeals to Tony to stop the fighting. But when he tries to reason with Bernardo, the scene bursts into violence and ends as Bernardo is stabbed by Tony.

Maria understands that the death of her brother was inadvertent, and she and Tony reaffirm their love and plan to start a new life. But tragically, Tony is led to believe that Maria herself has been killed in revenge. He runs into the street, shouting for his own death, and then sees Maria alive—but too late, for he is killed by a bullet from the shadows.

With Tony's death, another variation on the Romeo and

Juliet theme is completed. But the author and director of the show have reinforced the original theme with elements that make the production meaningful in terms of today's problems. The conflict is no longer between two families, but between people of different nationalities and races—a bitter conflict that is a major problem in practically all large cities and in many smaller ones.

In spite of its tragic overtones, ***West Side Story*** does not dwell wholly on themes of misery. There are tender love scenes such as the one pictured on the right. It was here on a tenement fire escape that Tony and Maria pledged their love. From this scene came the two popular love songs, "Maria" and "Tonight." Similarly, there are flashes of wit and humor. And even in the end, with Tony lying dead, the author adds a ray of hope to the story, for, in the face of tragedy, the Jets and Sharks forget their bitterness and together carry Tony's body to the waiting ambulance.

PHOTO BY HANK WALKER COURTESY ***LIFE***

UNIT 4 REVIEW

1. Some critics have maintained that a tragedy should never cover a period longer than a single day. Such a brief time limit was generally ignored by Shakespeare, who sometimes stretched a play (*Julius Caesar*, for example) over several years. He did, however, limit *Romeo and Juliet* to a period of only a few days. Trace the time-scheme of the play. On what day of the week does the action begin? You can find a clue by re-reading Act Three, Scene 4, in which Capulet asks, "What day is this?" and Paris replies, "Monday, my lord." How much time has elapsed between the opening of the play and this conversation between Capulet and Paris? What days are taken up by the events that occur during the remainder of the play?

2. Any first-rate dramatist is aware of the fact that an occasional change in the mood of a play—a dash of humor, say, in a tragedy, or a temporary threat of disaster in a comedy—tends to sharpen the spectators' enjoyment of the play. Shakespeare was unusually successful in providing such a change of pace in his plays. Point out some notable examples of Shakespeare's use of humorous characters and situations in *Romeo and Juliet* to relieve the atmosphere of tragedy that pervades the play as a whole.

3. Chance plays an important part in *Romeo and Juliet*. For example, when Capulet's servant happens to ask Romeo to read the list of guests to be invited to the party, Romeo learns that Rosaline's name is included. At once he decides to attend the party himself. How does his decision affect the development of the story? Cite other examples of the importance of chance in *Romeo and Juliet*. In each instance explain (1) what the chance is; (2) what effect the chance has upon the action in the play.

SUGGESTED READING

BARRIE, J. M., *The Plays of J. M. Barrie.* (Scribner) This collection contains twenty of Barrie's plays, including such favorites as *Peter Pan* and *What Every Woman Knows.*

CHASE, MARY, *Mrs. McThing.* (Oxford) Mrs. Larue and her son, Howay, find themselves in trouble when Mrs. McThing, a witch, attempts to obtain revenge for Mrs. Larue's ill-treatment of her daughter.

CHUTE, MARCHETTE, *An Introduction to Shakespeare.* (Dutton) The author presents an account of the theater of Shakespeare's day as well as studies of his plays as to sources, plot development, and theme. *Shakespeare of London.* (Dutton) In this book the author presents a biographical portrait of the man and a description of the society in which he lived.

CONNELLY, MARCUS, *The Green Pastures.* (Rinehart) This classic of the American stage portrays God's dealings with man from the Creation of the world through the Resurrection as seen from a Southern Negro's point of view.

GASSNER, JOHN, *Best American Plays, 1918-1958.* (Crown) Young readers will particularly enjoy such plays as *Harvey* and *Green Grow the Lilacs.*

HACKETT, WALTER, ed., *Radio Plays for Young People.* (Plays, Inc.) This collection of fifteen plays includes dramatized versions of stories and novels by well-known authors.

HAMMERSTEIN, OSCAR, *Six Plays by Rodgers and Hammerstein.* (Modern Library) *Oklahoma, South Pacific,* and *Carousel* are among the plays included in this volume.

HART, MOSS AND GEORGE S. KAUFMAN, *Six Plays by Kaufman and Hart.* (Random House) *You Can't Take It With You* and *The Man Who Came to Dinner* are two of the entertaining comedies presented in this book.

HODGES, C. WALTER, *Shakespeare and the Players.* (Coward-McCann) The growth and development of the theater is portrayed beginning with the days when traveling companies of players put on shows.

LINDSAY, HOWARD AND RUSSELL CROUSE, *Clarence Day's Life with Father and Life with Mother.* (Knopf) Clarence Day's humorous accounts of his family and their problems are presented in dramatized form.

SCHARY, DORE, *Sunrise at Campobello.* (Random House • Signet Books) The courage of Franklin Delano Roosevelt during his bout with polio is shown in this fine play.

SHAKESPEARE, WILLIAM. *As You Like It* and *A Midsummer Night's Dream.* These two comedies reveal an entirely different aspect of Shakespeare's many-sided view of life.

SHERWOOD, ROBERT EMMET, *Abe Lincoln in Illinois.* (Scribner) This Pulitzer Prize-winning play portrays the life of Abraham Lincoln from his first meeting with Ann Rutledge until his departure for Washington to assume his responsibilities as President of the United States.

VAN DRUTEN, JOHN, *I Remember Mama.* (Harcourt) This dramatized version of Kathryn Forbes' novel, *Mama's Bank Account,* presents the story of a Norwegian family living in San Francisco in the early 1900's.

WILDER, THORNTON, *Three Plays.* (Harper • Bantam Books) Contained in this volume are Wilder's best known plays, *The Skin of Our Teeth, The Matchmaker,* and *Our Town.*

•paperback

Since the beginnings of history, each century has had its craftsmen who have preserved in literature the problems, beliefs, and ideals of their times and cultures. A great part of ancient literature has been lost over the ages. Still more of it has faded from public attention and is of little interest except, perhaps, to scholars. But some of it has been destined to live on through the centuries. This literature has lived because it is of the highest acknowledged quality or excellence; that is, it is classical. Such are the writings of ancient Greece and Rome which you will read in this unit. You will read stories of gods and goddesses, tales of the Trojan War, essays from ancient times, and finally, a Greek play, which is still performed on the modern stage.

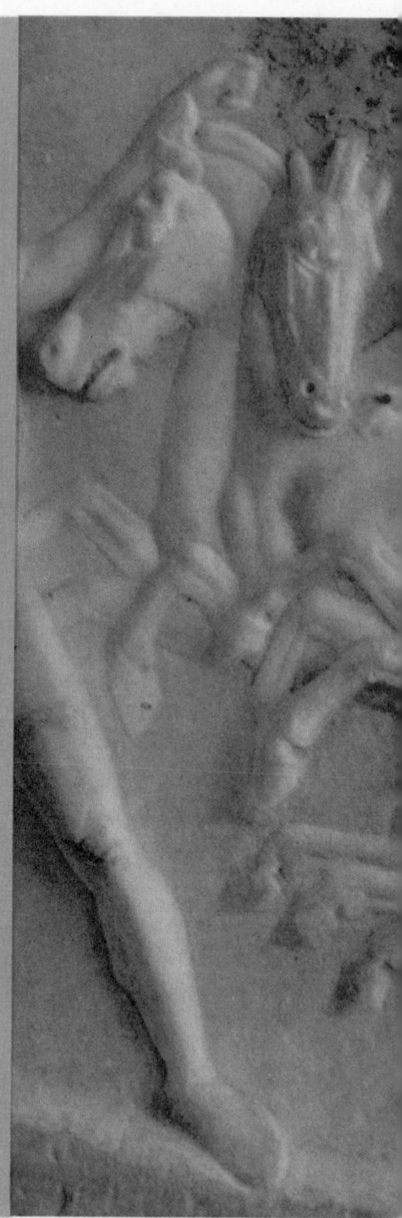

Unit 5

ARBLE FRIEZE, "BASILE CARRIED OFF BY ECHELOS" NATIONAL MUSEUM, ATHENS. COURTESY PARIS BOOK CENTER, INC., NEW YORK

LITERATURE OF GODS AND GODDESSES

As in the modern world, the ancient Greeks and Romans could not accept a hazy view of life and the natural universe, and like people today, they tried to explain the things they saw happening around them. But their explanations might seem strange to the modern mind, for the people of Greece and Rome in the centuries B.C. believed that their destinies were governed by the plottings of numerous gods and goddesses—deities who were charged with directing all human affairs, as well as the affairs of the universe.

For example, people fell in and out of love according to the whims of Venus, the goddess of love and beauty. Wars were started and directed by Mars. The sea was ruled by Neptune, who caused great storms when his wrath was aroused. The movements of the sun were governed by Apollo, and those of the moon by the goddess Diana. Not even by death did people escape the authority of the gods, for departed spirits were governed by Pluto, the god of the underworld. And ruling over all was the supreme deity, Jupiter. He was ruler of earth and sky and king of gods and men.

The deities themselves were not without problems, however. Each was charged with the proper governing of his particular segment of life or the universe. Thus, it was often necessary for a god or goddess to take on human form and descend from Mount Olympus to help straighten out the tangled affairs of humans. In fact, the gods and goddesses themselves were often found entangled in jealousies, conflicts, and injured feelings, because the Greeks and Romans credited their deities with certain human emotions and failings, as well as a divine nature.

The citizens of ancient Greece and Rome, then, were faced with the challenge of living their lives without offending one or another of their deities—quite a difficult task, considering the large number of gods, goddesses, and lesser deities who continually needed to be flattered and pacified. It is no wonder that a great amount of thought and attention was paid to religion in the ancient world. Neither is it any wonder that *myths* became a basic part of Greek and Roman literature, for it is these stories that tell of the deities, their adventures, their problems, and their effects on human life and the natural universe.

Many myths, like those that follow, were of Greek origin and were later adopted by the Romans, who believed in the Greek gods but gave them different names. Here, the myths are retold by an American scholar, Thomas Bulfinch. These same myths have found their way into the literature of many different countries and have also served as the basis for poems, stories, and dramas written by modern authors from many different parts of the world.

GLOSSARY

DEITIES

APOLLO, *God of the sun, poetry, and music, and father of* ORPHEUS.

CALLIOPE (kə lī′ə pi *or* kal′i ōp), *one of nine sister goddesses who were* MUSES, *or patrons, of poetry and song; also the mother of* ORPHEUS.

EURYDICE (ū rid′ə sē), *a nymph, or lesser goddess, wed to* ORPHEUS.

HYMEN, *God of marriage.*

JOVE, *also known as* JUPITER *or* ZEUS, *the chief among gods. Father of* PERSEUS.

MERCURY, *also known as* HERMES (hėr′mēz), *messenger of the gods.*

MINERVA, *also known as* ATHENE (ə thē′nə), *Goddess of wisdom.*

PLUTO, *God of the underworld and ruler of departed spirits.*

PROSERPINE (prō sėr′pə nē *or* pros′ər pīn), *Goddess of spring, who lived in the underworld as the wife of* PLUTO *during fall and winter, but who returned to the upper world during the spring and summer.*

SEA NYMPHS, *lesser deities who aided the gods in ruling the universe.*

MORTALS

ACRISIUS (ə kris′i əs), *grandfather of* PERSEUS.

CEPHEUS (sē′fūs *or* sē′fi əs), *king of the* AETHIOPIANS (ē thi ō′pi ənz), *husband of* CASSIOPEIA (kas′i ə pē′ə), *and father of* ANDROMEDA (an drom′ə də).

DANAE (dan′ā ē), *daughter of* ACRISIUS *and mother of* PERSEUS.

GORGONS (gôr′gənz), *three sisters with snakes for hair. This terrible aspect turned beholders to stone.* MEDUSA (mə dü′sa) *was a gorgon.*

THRACIAN (thrā′shən) MAIDENS, *musical maidens who were jealous of* ORPHEUS.

SPIRITS

DAUGHTERS OF DANAÜS (dan′ā əs), *sisters who had murdered their husbands and were forever sentenced to draw water through a sieve.*

FURIES, *avenging spirits who came to be known as snake-haired women.*

SISYPHUS (sis′ə fəs), *the once greedy king of Corinth who was condemned to roll to the top of a hill a heavy stone, which forever rolled back again.*

TANTALUS (tan′tə ləs), *a king who, for attempting to serve his son to the gods for dinner, was doomed to stand in water beneath a fruit-laden tree; but when he tried to drink or eat, the water and fruit always evaded his grasp.*

PLACES

ELYSIAN (i lizh′ən) FIELDS, *the paradise of the underworld.*

EREBUS (er′ə bəs), *the gloomy outer regions of the underworld.*

STYGIAN (stij′i ən) REALM, *the land of* HADES, *home of the dead, which lay past the river* STYX, *one of three rivers that separated the land of the dead from the land of the living.*

TARTARUS (tär′tə rəs), *another name for* HADES *and a place of punishment for unusually wicked souls.*

Orpheus and Eurydice

Retold by
Thomas Bulfinch

Orpheus was the son of Apollo and the Muse Calliope. He was presented by his father with a Lyre and taught to play upon it, which he did to such perfection that nothing could withstand the charm of his music. Not only his fellow-mortals but wild beasts were softened by his strains, and gathering round him laid by their fierceness, and stood entranced with his lay. Nay, the very trees and rocks were sensible to the charm. The former crowded round him and the latter relaxed somewhat of their hardness, softened by his notes.

"Orpheus and Eurydice" from ***Mythology*** by Thomas Bulfinch. Published by Thomas Y. Crowell Company, New York.

Hymen had been called to bless with his presence the nuptials of Orpheus with Eurydice; but though he attended, he brought no happy omens with him. His very torch smoked and brought tears into their eyes. In coincidence with such prognostics, Eurydice, shortly after her marriage, while wandering with the nymphs, her companions, was seen by the shepherd Aristæus, who was struck with her beauty and made advances to her. She fled, and in flying trod upon a snake in the grass, was bitten in the foot, and died.

Orpheus sang his grief to all who breathed the upper air, both gods and men, and, finding it all unavailing, resolved to seek his wife in the regions of the dead. He descended by a cave situated on the side of the promontory of Tænarus and arrived at the Stygian realm. He passed through crowds of ghosts and presented himself before the throne of Pluto and Proserpine. Accompanying the words with the lyre, he sung, "O deities of the underworld, to whom all we who live must come, hear my words, for they are true. I come not to spy out the secrets of Tartarus, nor to try my strength against the three-headed dog with snaky hair who guards the entrance. I come to seek my wife, whose opening years the poisonous viper's fang has brought to an untimely end. Love has led me here, Love, a god all powerful with us who dwell on the earth, and, if old traditions say true, not less so here. I implore you by these abodes full of terror, these realms of silence and uncreated things, unite again the thread of Eurydice's life. We all are destined to you, and sooner or later must pass to your domain. She too, when she shall have filled her term of life, will rightly be yours. But till then grant her to me, I beseech you. If you deny me I cannot return alone; you shall triumph in the death of us both."

As he sang these tender strains, the very ghosts shed tears. Tantalus, in spite of his thirst, stopped for a moment his efforts for water, the daughters of Danaüs rested from their task of drawing water in a sieve, and Sisyphus sat on his rock to listen. Then for the first time, it is said, the cheeks of the Furies were wet with tears. Proserpine could not resist, and Pluto himself gave way. Eurydice was called. She came from among the new-arrived ghosts, limping with her wounded foot. Orpheus was permitted to take her away with him on one condition, that he should not turn around to look at her till they should have reached the upper air. Under this condition they proceeded on their way, he leading, she following, through passages dark and steep, in total silence, till they had nearly reached the outlet into the cheerful upper world, when Orpheus, in a moment of forgetfulness, to assure himself that she was still following, cast a glance behind him, when instantly she was borne away. Stretching out their arms to embrace each other, they grasped only the air! Dying now a second time, she yet cannot reproach her husband, for how can she blame his impatience to behold her? "Farewell," she said, "a last farewell,"—and was hurried away, so fast that the sound hardly reached his ears.

Orpheus endeavored to follow her, and besought permission to return and try once more for her release; but the stern ferryman repulsed him and refused passage. Seven days he lingered about the brink, without food or sleep; then bitterly accusing of cruelty the powers of Erebus, he sang his complaints to the rocks and mountains, melting the hearts of tigers and moving the oaks from their stations. He held himself aloof from womankind, dwelling constantly on the recollection of his sad mischance. The Thracian maidens tried their best to captivate him, but he repulsed their advances. They bore with him as long as they could; but finding him insensible one day, one of them exclaimed, "See yonder our despiser!" and threw at him her javelin.

The weapon, as soon as it came within the sound of his lyre, fell harmless at his feet. So did also the stones that they threw at him. But the women raised a scream and drowned the voice of the music, and then the missiles reached him and soon were stained with his blood. The maniacs tore him limb from limb, and threw his head and his lyre into the river Hebrus, down which they floated, murmuring sad music, to which the shores responded a plaintive symphony. The Muses gathered up the fragments of his body and buried them at Libethra, where the nightingale is said to sing over his grave more sweetly than in any other part of Greece. His lyre was placed by Jupiter among the stars. His shade passed a second time to Tartarus, where he sought out his Eurydice and embraced her with eager arms. They roam the happy fields together now, sometimes he leading, sometimes she; and Orpheus gazes as much as he will upon her, no longer incurring a penalty for a thoughtless glance.

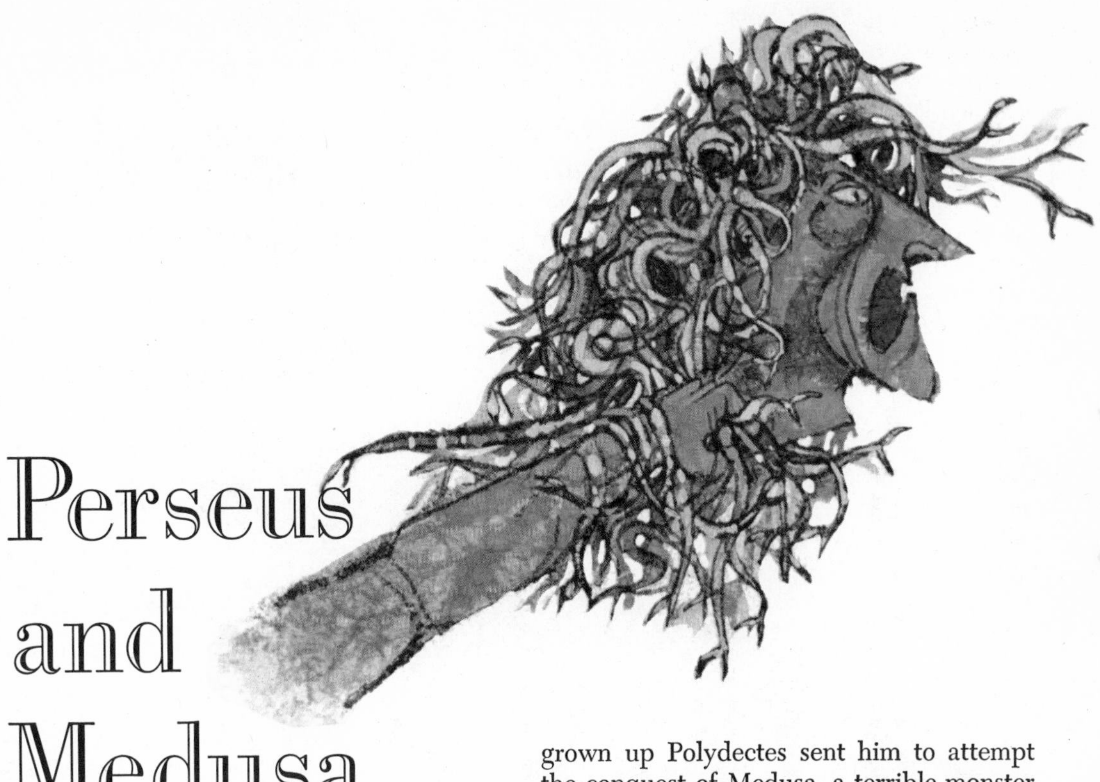

Perseus and Medusa

Retold by Thomas Bulfinch

Perseus was the son of Jupiter and Danaë. His grandfather Acrisius, alarmed by an oracle which had told him that his daughter's child would be the instrument of his death, caused the mother and child to be shut up in a chest and set adrift on the sea. The chest floated toward Seriphus, where it was found by a fisherman who conveyed the mother and infant to Polydectes, the king of the country, by whom they were treated with kindness. When Perseus was grown up Polydectes sent him to attempt the conquest of Medusa, a terrible monster who had laid waste the country. She was once a beautiful maiden whose hair was her chief glory, but as she dared to vie in beauty with Minerva, the goddess deprived her of her charms and changed her beautiful ringlets into hissing serpents. She became a cruel monster of so frightful an aspect that no living thing could behold her without being turned into stone. All around the cavern where she dwelt might be seen the stony figures of men and animals which had chanced to catch a glimpse of her and had been petrified with the sight. Perseus, favored by Minerva and Mercury, the former of whom lent him her shield and the latter his winged shoes, approached Medusa while she slept, and taking care not to look directly at her, but guided by her image reflected in the bright shield which he bore, he cut off her head and gave it to Minerva.

"Perseus and Medusa" from *Mythology* by Thomas Bulfinch. Published by Thomas Y. Crowell Company, New York.

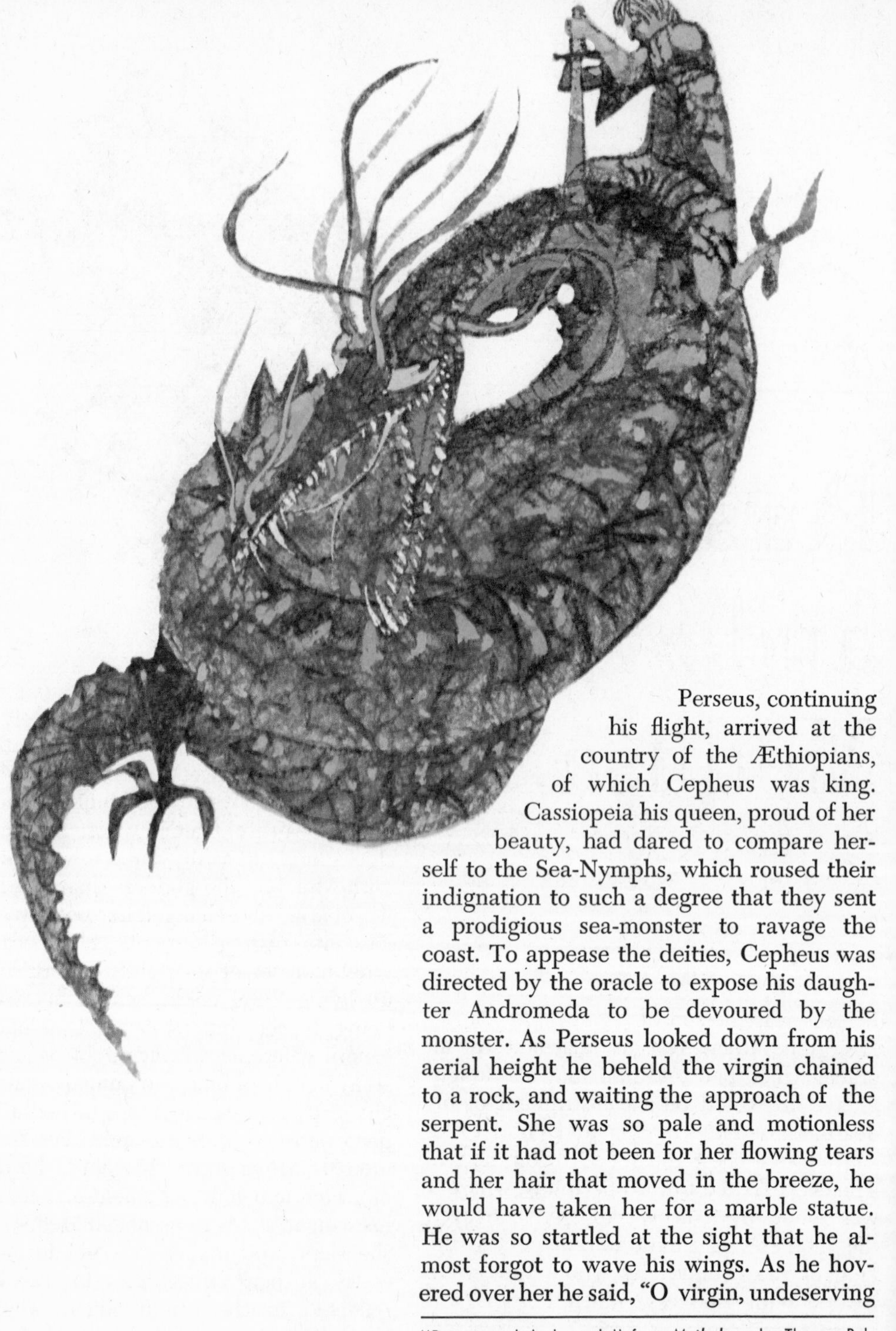

Perseus, continuing his flight, arrived at the country of the Æthiopians, of which Cepheus was king. Cassiopeia his queen, proud of her beauty, had dared to compare herself to the Sea-Nymphs, which roused their indignation to such a degree that they sent a prodigious sea-monster to ravage the coast. To appease the deities, Cepheus was directed by the oracle to expose his daughter Andromeda to be devoured by the monster. As Perseus looked down from his aerial height he beheld the virgin chained to a rock, and waiting the approach of the serpent. She was so pale and motionless that if it had not been for her flowing tears and her hair that moved in the breeze, he would have taken her for a marble statue. He was so startled at the sight that he almost forgot to wave his wings. As he hovered over her he said, "O virgin, undeserving

"Perseus and Andromeda" from *Mythology* by Thomas Bulfinch. Published by Thomas Y. Crowell Company, New York.

Perseus and Andromeda

Retold by Thomas Bulfinch

of those chains, but rather of such as bind fond lovers together, tell me, I beseech you, your name, and the name of your country, and why you are thus bound." At first she was silent from modesty, and, if she could, would have hid her face with her hands; but when he repeated his questions, for fear she might be thought guilty of some fault which she dared not tell, she disclosed her name and that of her country, and her mother's pride of beauty. Before she had done speaking, a sound was heard off upon the water, and the sea-monster appeared, with his head raised above the surface, cleaving the waves with his broad breast. The virgin shrieked, the father and mother who had now arrived at the scene, wretched both, but the mother more justly so, stood by, not able to afford protection, but only to pour forth lamentations and to embrace the victim. Then spoke Perseus: "There will be time enough for tears; this hour is all we have for rescue. My rank as the son of Jove and my renown as the slayer of the Gorgon might make me acceptable as a suitor; but I will try to win her by services rendered, if the gods will only be propitious. If she be rescued by my valor, I demand that she be my reward." The parents consent (how could they hesitate?) and promise a royal dowry with her.

And now the monster was within the range of a stone thrown by a skilful slinger, when with a sudden bound the youth soared into the air. As an eagle, when from his lofty flight he sees a serpent basking in the sun, pounces upon him and seizes him by the neck to prevent him from turning his head round and using his fangs, so the youth darted down upon the back of the monster and plunged his sword into its shoulder. Irritated by the wound, the monster raised himself in the air, then plunged into the depth; then, like a wild boar surrounded by a pack of barking dogs, turned swiftly from side to side, while the youth eluded its attacks by means of his wings. Wherever he can find a passage for his sword between the scales he makes a wound, piercing now the side, now the flank, as it slopes towards the tail. The brute spouts from his nostrils water mixed with blood. The wings of the hero are wet with it, and he dares no longer trust to them. Alighting on a rock which rose above the waves, and holding on by a projecting fragment, as the monster floated near he gave him a death stroke. The people who had gathered on the shore shouted so that the hills reëchoed the sound. The parents, transported with joy, embraced their future son-in-law, calling him their deliverer and the savior of their house, and the virgin, both cause and reward of the contest, descended from the rock.

WHAT DO YOU SAY?

1. (a) Upon what condition was Eurydice permitted to return to the upper world? *(b)* Who allowed this? *(c)* How did Orpheus break the terms of the agreement? *(d)* Did his action reveal stupidity or great carelessness, or did it reveal a natural characteristic of human behavior? Explain.

2. *(a)* Was the underworld merely a place for the departed spirits of evil people who were to be punished? *(b)* Did all of the spirits there receive the same treatment? Explain your answer by citing specific examples.

3. The suffering souls that Orpheus first met in the underworld were undergoing rather unique forms of punishment that shared one general characteristic. What was the characteristic that these forms of torture had in common?

4. (a) Who was more courageous, Orpheus or Perseus? *(b)* Which of them was portrayed as a more convincing, or real, personality? *(c)* In what ways was he more real?

5. (a) In what way was Eurydice's death foreshadowed? *(b)* How did the element of prophecy enter into the Perseus and Medusa myth?

6. (a) What flaw in character did Medusa and Cassiopeia have in common? *(b)* What were the different consequences of the actions of Medusa and Cassiopeia toward the deities?

7. (a) What human characteristics were shown by Minerva? *(b)* By Pluto? *(c)* What characteristics marked them as gods?

8. (a) The three myths you have just read reveal ancient Greek ideas about the power of magic and the power of natural talent. In what ways were these ideas illustrated in the stories? *(b)* Which led to greater victory, the use of talent or the use of magic? Explain your answer.

AUTHOR'S CRAFT

Literary allusions

Not only are the myths of ancient Greece and Rome delightful reading in themselves, they are also important in understanding the ***literary allusions*** that often appear in stories, plays, and poetry. Literary allusions are brief, passing references to pieces of literature or the people, places, and events that appear in them. For example, what do you think is meant by the following sentence?

"She did so well in her examinations that you might have thought she was wearing Minerva's shield."

This sentence, of course, would make little sense if you knew nothing about Minerva. But it becomes more meaningful when you recall that this mythical figure was the goddess of wisdom and that her magic shield brought protection and success to its wearer.

Especially in poetry, allusions to classical mythology are used abundantly in describing commonplace events. For example, a poet might see lightning as ***Jove's mighty spear flashing through the sky,*** or a storm at sea as ***Neptune's heaving wrath.*** Similarly, springtime might be described as ***Proserpine's lilting song,*** and a peaceful countryside might be referred to as ***Elysian fields.*** A piece of literature becomes more meaningful and satisfying to a reader when the reader is familiar with the allusions that the author uses.

KNOW YOUR WORDS

Derivations

Many of our English words are derived from the names of the Greek and Roman gods. For example, the word ***cereal*** comes from **Ceres,** the Roman goddess of agriculture. Listed below are several mythological characters. Using a dictionary, locate an English word which has been derived from each of these names. Use each word in a sentence.

1. Tantalus
2. Mars
3. Hygeia, goddess of health
4. Juventus, god of youth
5. Luna, goddess of the moon (Diana)
6. Hypnos, god of sleep
7. Titans, a family of giants
8. Hercules, a Greek hero of tremendous physical strength
9. Mercury, messenger of the gods (Roman)
10. Hermes, messenger of the gods (Greek)
11. Plutus, god of riches
12. Cupid, god of love

LITERATURE OF LEGENDS AND HEROES

Another great portion of Greek and Roman literature is based on the popular histories of ancient heroes and their adventures. While these tales, like the myths, often involve gods and goddesses, divine interference, and magic, they are usually found to have at least some basis in actual history. For this reason such tales are classified as *legends* rather than as pure myth.

Into this category of the heroic legend falls one of the most popular themes of all times—that of the Trojan War and its heroes, who often take on godlike proportions. Although this story has many qualities of a myth, the city of Troy actually existed, and it fell to the Greeks about 1184 B.C., following a nine-year siege of war.

But it is the legendary account of the Trojan War that has held the fascination of readers through these many centuries. The great conflict is said to have started over a woman, the beautiful Helen, who was the wife of the Greek king, Menelaus. Through the action of the goddess Athena, Helen was persuaded to elope with the handsome young prince, Paris, the son of King Priam of Troy. The Greek chieftains set out to recapture Helen from the Trojans and to return her to her native shores. The three selections that follow recount the Battle of Troy and its aftermath.

The Surprise

by John Masefield

Although the tale of Troy was probably passed in story and song for several generations, the first written account of the war is found in the Iliad, *a long epic poem written by the Greek poet Homer, who is thought to have lived during the ninth century* B.C. *His poetic masterpiece has served as a basis for the work of many other writers, including the British poet John Masefield, who retells the last episode of the Trojan War.*

For nine years the Greeks laid siege to Troy but the city held fast. In the tenth year, force having failed, the Grecian leaders decided to try craft. Led by Ithaca's king, Odysseus (ō dis′i əs), *the Greeks secretly constructed a huge wooden horse which was hollow inside and was furnished with a trap door. Through this door climbed a band of Grecian soldiers. The remaining Greeks then boarded their ships as though they intended to sail home. Actually they sailed to a nearby island.*

The Trojans believed that the Greeks had at last given up. Joyfully, they flung open the city gates and swarmed out over the surrounding plain. There they spied the wooden horse and, proclaiming it a trophy of war, they dragged it into the city.

Meanwhile, the Greek ships had returned, and the Greek soldiers landed to play their part in the ruse that had been planned to surprise the Trojans.

You have heard the story of the Horse of Troy.
We left him on the sea-beach when we sailed.
We sailed all day, but when the darkness fell
The captains ordered all the fleet ashore.
We beached the black ships out of sight of Troy.

Then quietly the captains of the hundreds[1]
Were told that a surprise would be attempted.
Orders were given: then most stringent watch
Was made, lest any traitor should give warning.

We supped and slept, till somewhere after midnight,
Then roused, and tied bleached linen on our arms,[2]
And took short spears and swords: no other weapons:
And forth we went by fifties toward Troy.
Absolute silence upon pain of death
The order was: we crept along like ghosts.
Soon we were in the Plain among the graves
Of men half-buried, whom we used to know,
And how they died, a dozen known to me.
And Trojan bodies, too; familiar landmarks.
It was all cold and windy, with bright stars,
No moon, dry summer going, and the wind
Beating the withered grass and shriveled leaves.
Then we were at the ford and passing through.
I remember water gurgling at a flag-root.

Beyond the ford we were in Trojan land.
There was the black mass of the walls of Troy
With towers (and a light in one of them).
No other sign of life, except a glow,

1. ***captains of the hundreds.*** The Greek army was organized in hundreds. 2. ***tied . . . our arms,*** for purposes of identification.

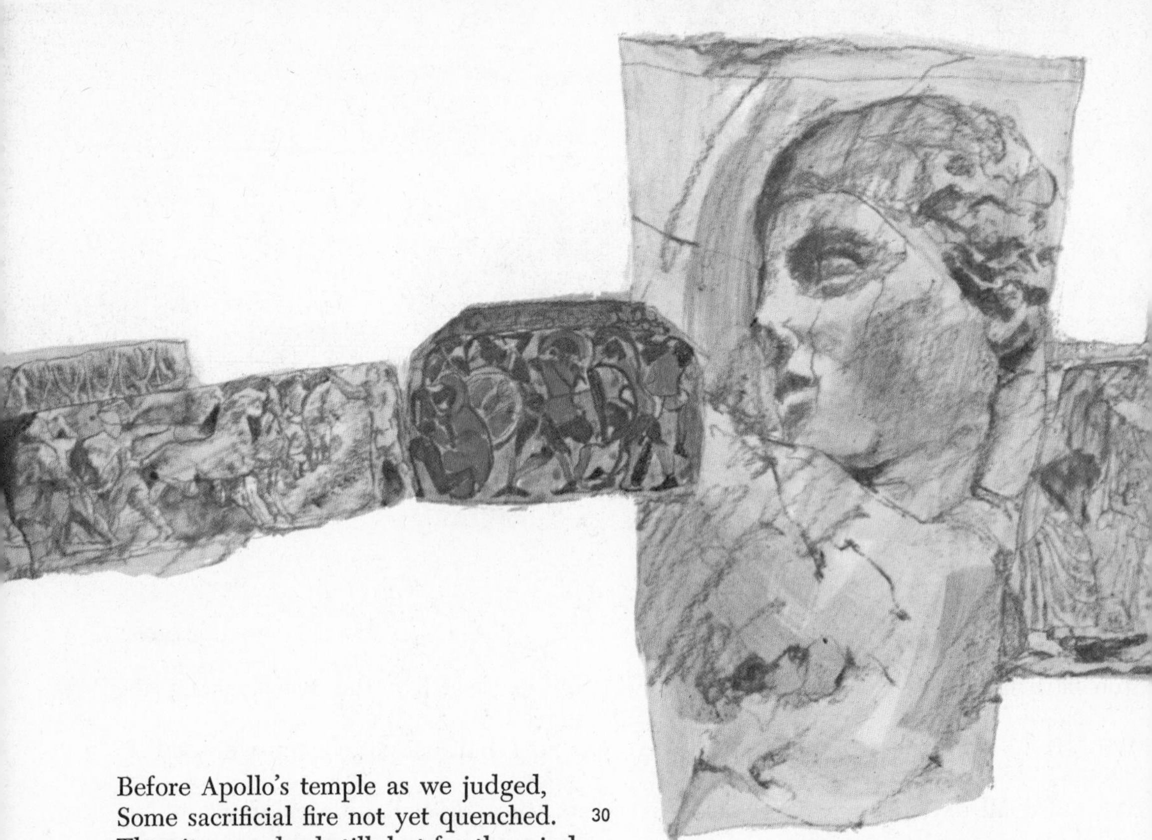

Before Apollo's temple as we judged,
Some sacrificial fire not yet quenched.
The city was dead still, but for the wind.

They halted us below the wagon track
Between the Spartans and the Ithacans.[3]
And there we huddled in the bitter cold,
Wondering what had happened in the city
And why the city should be still as death:
Whether the Horse were burning in the fire
With all our men inside it sacrifice:
Whether the trap door in the Horse had jammed
So that they could not leave it: or perhaps
(We thought) the Horse is guarded in the temple,
Surrounded by men praying all night long.
Or had they ventured out, and all been killed?
And if the men were killed, the stratagem
Was surely known, and we half-armed and freezing,
Would be attacked at dawn and ridden down.
A temple bell jangled within the city,
A lesser bell tinkled; then all was silent.

And all this time the little owls from Ida[4]
Came hooting over us: and presently
A mighty, savage owl perched upon Troy[5]
And snapped his iron lips, and flapped, and screamed,
Almost one saw the yellow of his eyes.
Then he launched forth, stealing into the air.
It seemed like many ages in the cold

3. ***They halted us . . . Ithacans.*** The soldiers were halted near a road, on either side of which were encamped Greek soldiers, the Spartans and the Ithacans. 4. ***Ida,*** a mountain overlooking the city of Troy. 5. ***a mighty savage owl . . . Troy.*** The owl was the symbol of Athene who favored the Greeks. Thus, its presence on the gates of Troy symbolized woe to its defenders.

Before the whisper reached the Ithacans
To creep a little nearer to the wall.
When they had passed, unchallenged, others went.
Word passed that there were sentries on the wall.
And though the orders were against all speech,
Yet whispers let us know that Diomed[6]
Was at the South Gate underneath the tower,[7]
With the picked fighters.
Hours seemed to pass
While we froze slowly in our companies.
My eyes were so accustomed to the dark
That I could see the great wall with its ramparts,
A tower, and a gate, close-fastened, brazen,
With men of ours heaped near it like to stones.

Then there was whispering in the ranks behind me:
A captain whispered, "Who knows Diomed?
Do you?" I whispered, "Yes."
"Why, then," he whispered,
"Creep forward there, and find him by the gate
Under the tower with the forward party.
Tell him *King Agamemnon*[8] *is convinced*
That this has failed, and that we must withdraw.
Be ready to fall back as we retire."

I crept the seventy yards up to the front.
One whispered, "Diomed is on the right,
Nearest the wall." I found him lying there
And whispered him the message of the King.

---

6. ***Diomed*** (dī′ə med), leader of an advance party of Grecian warriors. 7. ***South Gate . . . tower.*** The city was surrounded by a high wall surmounted by a rampart. Beside each gate in the wall were square towers for defense. 8. ***King Agamemnon*** (ag′ə mem′non), older brother of Menelaus and commander-in-chief of the Greeks.

"What?" he said, "What? Withdraw from where we are?
Who says so? What authority have you?"
I told him, "Verbal orders from a captain."
"Lie still," he said, "and not another word.
I'll learn of your authority when day dawns."

Then suddenly there came a little noise.
Someone within the gate was lifting down
The heavy bars that barred it, one by one.
Each of us nudged his fellow and drew breath.
Diomed stood: we others raised ourselves.
One half the narrow brazen door moved back,
Showing a dark gash that grew wider and lighter;
A lamp wavered and flickered in a lane,
The damp glistened on wallwork; a man peered
Round the half-opened door; and "Sst, Sst, Sst,"
He hissed. It was Odysseus, from the Horse.

Diomed signaled to us: he himself
Was first within the gate: I helped him there
To lay the gate wide open to our men.
Then we pressed in, up the steep narrow lane
Past the still flickering lamp, over a Trojan
Sentry or watchman, newly murdered there,
Killed by Odysseus: no one challenged us.
We were in Troy: the city was surprised.

The dogs had all been killed some weeks before,
There were no watchdogs. When we reached the Ways,[9]
The Wide Ways running round within the walls,
Some horses, tethered there, whinnied and stamped,
And drowsy horse-boys mumbled in their sleep,
But no one challenged; Troy was in a drowse
In the deep morning sleep before the dawn
Now faint upon the distant tops of Ida.

And we were seen by watchmen on the tower
On that side Troy, but none of them suspected
That we were Greeks: they thought that we were Lycians,
Old allies of the Trojans, mustering
Up to the temples for a sacrifice
Before we marched from Troia[10] to our homes.

We were within the second ring of road,[11]
Outside King Priam's palace[12] and the temples,
Before a sentry challenged us, and then
It was too late for the alarm to help.
The man paused at the turning of his beat,
Looked round and saw us, gave a cry, then challenged,
Then died, stabbed through the throat by Diomed.

My party rushed into Apollo's temple
And burst into the palace to the guards
Sleeping in quarters, some of them half drunk,
All without arms: we herded them like sheep.

And by the time the guards were bound, the city
Was lit with blazing thatches, and awake,

---

9. ***the Ways.*** The walled city was circular. Just within the wall ran a wide avenue (Ways) that encircled the city. 10. ***Lycians*** (lish′i ənz) . . . ***Troia*** (trō′yə). The Lycians, who lived south of the Trojans, had been their allies in the war. When the watchmen heard the noises of men moving, they thought that it was the Lycians marching in a body to the temples to offer sacrifices before leaving Troia (Troy). 11. ***second ring of road.*** A second avenue encircled the principal buildings, temples, and the king's palace. 12. ***King Priam's*** (prī′əmz) ***palace.*** King Priam was the king of Troy and the father of Paris.

Dawn coming, fire burning, women screaming,
And war-cries, and loud trumpets and clashed armor.
There was hard fighting in a dozen spots.

We came out of the guard-room by a gate
Into a blaze all red with fire flying:
A palace court it was, the inner court,
Where Menelaus and his Spartan spearmen
Were killing Priam's sons.
Just as we reached the court a dozen spearmen
Were all attacking young Deiphobus.[13]

I knew the lad by sight, for he had come
On embassy to Agamemnon once,
And Menelaus meant to have him killed
And flung to the camp-dogs, because of Helen.

There he was, fighting for his life with twelve.

A fine young man, like Hektor[14] in the face,
A bright, clean-cut face, tanned with sun and wind,
Smiling and cool and swift with parry on parry.
He had been surprised: he had no body-armor,
Nothing but spear and shield, and there he stood,
Checking each thrust, swift, marvelously.
One minute
He stood, matchless in skill in the red glare,
Then someone crept above and stabbed him down.

The city was all ours in the hour.
Many were killed in fighting; many more
Escaped, during the burning and confusion,
Out, to the mountains, by the Eastern gate.
The rest we took: some of the prisoners,
The little children and old men and women,
We drove out of the gates into the wild.
The rest we kept: young women skilled in crafts
And men who might make slaves.
We made
them quench
The fires that were burning here and there
And then we sacked the city utterly.

When we had sacked her utterly, we forced
Our Trojan slaves to lever down the ramparts
Over the walls,[15] until the city seemed
A mound of fallen stones and roofless houses.
We lit the wreck.

Then as we sailed for home with slaves and plunder,
We saw the ruins burning, and the smoke
Streaming across the sunburnt Trojan plain.
With all that world of murder on our backs
We bore our load of misery from Asia.

---

13. ***Deiphobus*** (di if′ō bəs), son of King Priam. 14. ***Hektor,*** the oldest son of Priam and the greatest of the Trojan warriors. He had been killed earlier in the war by the Greek warrior, Achilles (ə kil′ēz). 15. ***to lever down . . . walls,*** to knock down and level off the fortifications.

WHAT DO YOU SAY?

1. *(a)* Is "The Surprise" told from the Greek or the Trojan point of view? *(b)* Who seems to be the narrator of the poem?

2. *(a)* What was the Trojan horse? *(b)* How was it used in capturing the city of Troy? *(c)* Who prevented the Greek troops from withdrawing before the trick had worked?

3. Does the author draw from the reader any sympathy for the Trojans? If so, in what way is this accomplished?

4. Point out particular passages in which the poet builds suspense. Explain why these passages seem particularly effective.

5. *(a)* Who were the chief Greek heroes in this story? *(b)* In what way did each of them contribute to the success of the battle?

6. In what way does the dialogue add to the effect of the poem?

Several centuries after the Iliad *had been written, a Latin poet named Virgil took up the Trojan theme in his epic poem,* The Aeneid. *While Homer wrote from the Greek point of view, Virgil approached the story from the viewpoint of Aeneas, who was one of the famous Trojan heroes.*

The Flight of Aeneas

By VIRGIL *translated by C. Day Lewis*

Then first the full horror of it all was borne in upon me. I stood
In a daze: the picture of my dear father came to mind,
As I watched King Priam, a man of the same age, cruelly wounded,
Gasping his life away; I pictured my Creusa[1]
Deserted, my home pillaged, and the fate of my little Ascanius.[2]
I glanced round, wishing to see what force of men was left me.
All were gone: utter exhaustion and sickness of heart
Had made them drop from the roof to the ground or into the flames.
Yes, I was now the one man left of my party. But just then,
Hugging close to the threshold of Vesta,[3] speechlessly hiding there,
I noticed the daughter of Tyndareus,[4] Helen. The blaze lit up
The whole scene as I wandered, peering this way and that.
Helen, the scourge of Troy and her own land alike,
In dread anticipation of Trojan wrath at Troy's
Downfall, of Greek revenge, of her cuckolded husband's anger,—
Helen, that hateful creature, was crouched by the altar, in hiding.
A fire broke out in my heart, a passion of rage to avenge
My country's fall and punish her crime by a crime upon her.
Was she going to get away with it? see Sparta again and her homeland?
Return as a queen, in triumph? be once more reunited
With husband, home, parents and children? use our Trojan
Ladies for her attendants and Trojan men for slaves?—
All this, with Priam put to the sword, and Troy in ashes,
And Troy's shore time and again bathed in a sweat of blood?
Not so, I said. For although to kill a woman earns one
No fame, and victory over a female wins no decorations,
I shall be praised for stamping out an iniquity, punishing
One who so richly deserves it; and I shall enjoy fulfilling
My soul with a flame of vengeance, appeasing my people's ashes.
Such were my thoughts, the insensate fury that drove me onward,
When to my view—and never before had I seen her so clear—

---

1. Creusa (krē ü'sə). ***2. Ascanius*** (as kān'i əs). ***3. Vesta*** (ves'tə), goddess of the hearth. ***4. Tyndareus*** (tin dār'i əs).

My gentle mother[5] appeared: all glowing with light she came
Through the gloom, a goddess manifest, oh, high and handsome as
The heaven-dwellers know her. She laid a hand on mine,
Restraining me, then shaped these words with her rosy lips:—
My son, what anguish spurs you to this ungoverned rage?
What madness has driven all thought for love out of your heart?
Will you not first find out if your aged father, Anchises,[6]
Is where you left him, and whether your wife, Creusa, be still
Alive, and little Ascanius? A whole Greek army is surging
Round them on every side, and but for my guardian care
The flames would have got them by now, the fell sword drained their blood.
It is not the beauty of hated Helen, it is not Paris,
Though you hold him to blame—the gods, the gods, I tell you, are hostile,
It's they who have undermined Troy's power and sent it tumbling.
Jove supplies fresh courage and a victorious strength
To the Greeks, inciting the gods against the Trojan cause.
Escape then, while you may, my son, and end this ordeal.
I shall be with you, seeing you safe to your father's house.
She had spoken; and now she was vanished into the night's thick darkness.
Terrible shapes loom up, set against Troy, the shapes of
Heaven's transcendent will.
Then indeed I saw that all Ilium[7] was subsiding
Into the flames, and Neptune's Troy[8] quite overthrown.
Well, I went down from the roof, and divinely guided pressed on
Through flame and foe: the weapons gave way, the flames drew back for me.
But when I reached the door of my father's house, the ancestral
Home, my father Anchises, whom first I looked for, wishing
To get him away first to the safety of the hills—Anchises
Flatly refused to prolong his life, now Troy was finished,
Or to endure exile. He said:—
O you, whose blood

5. ***gentle mother,*** Venus, the goddess of love. 6. ***Anchises*** (an kī′sēz). 7. ***Ilium*** (il′i əm), Troy. 8. ***Neptune's Troy.*** Neptune, the god of the sea and brother of Zeus, as punishment for an attempted revolt against Zeus, was forced to help build the walls of Troy.

Is in the prime, who are strong enough to stand on your own feet,
Do you try for escape!
But as for me, if the gods had meant me to go on living,
They'd have preserved this place. Enough, more than enough
To have seen Troy ruined once and once have survived her capture.
Bid me farewell and leave, O leave this body of mine
Where it is! I shall find death in action. The foe will slay me
For pity, or spoils. And to bury me—that will not cost them much.
For years now I have been lingering, obnoxious to heaven and useless
To mankind, ever since the ruler of gods and men
Blasted me with the searing breath of his levin-flash.[9]
  So he went on saying. We could not shift him, although
We implored him with floods of tears—I, and my wife Creusa,
Ascanius and the whole household—not to ruin everything,
Not to add his weight to the doom which was heavy upon us.
He refused: obstinately he clung to his house and his purpose.
Once again I am moved to fight, yearning for death in my misery,
Since neither luck nor forethought offered a way out now.
"Father," I said, "did you really think I could run away
And leave you? Did so shameful a notion escape your lips?
If it's the will of heaven that nothing be left of our city,
And if your mind's made up that you and your family
Shall perish, as well as Troy, a door to that death is wide open:
Pyrrhus[10] is coming, all bathed in Priam's blood; he loves
Butchering sons in front of their fathers, fathers at the altar.
Was it for this, dear mother, you fetched me through fire and steel,—
That I should witness the enemy right in our house, witness
Ascanius and my father and my Creusa beside them
Lying slaughtered here in one another's blood?
To arms, my men! To arms! Their last hour calls the conquered.
Send me back to the Greeks! Let me go back and renew

---

9. levin-flash, lightning-flash. *10. Pyrrhus* (pir′əs), son of Achilles.

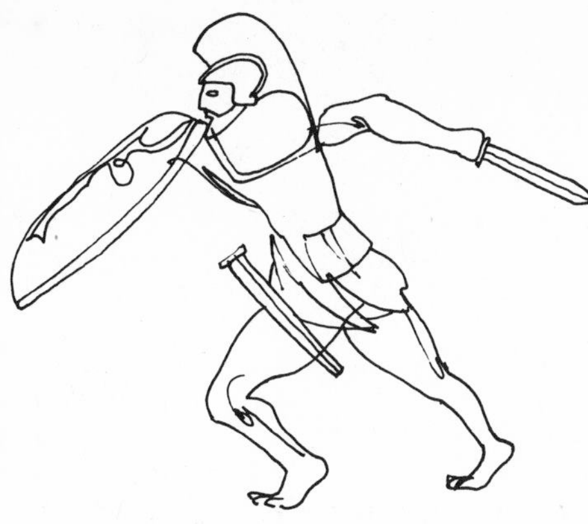

The fight! It must never be said we died unavenged this day!"
  My sword was at my side again; I was fitting my left arm
Through the strap of my shield, and on my way out of the house,
When Creusa clung to me at the door, gripping my ankles,
Holding little Ascanius up to his father, and crying:—
  If it's deathwards you go, take us with you! O take us, and come what may!
But if your experience tells you that something is to be gained by
Fighting, protect this house first! Think what you're leaving us to—
Ascanius, your father, and me who loved to be called your wife once!
  Loudly she cried these words, and filled the house with her crying.
Just then a miracle happened, a wonderful miracle.
Imagine it!—our hands and our sad eyes were upon
Ascanius, when we beheld a feathery tongue of flame
Luminously alight on his head, licking the soft curls
With fire that harmed them not, and playing about his temples.
Anxious, in great alarm, his mother and I hurried to
Beat out, put out with water, that holy blaze on his hair.
But father Anchises, greatly heartened, lifted his eyes up,
Stretched up his hands to heaven, with words of prayer, saying:—
  O god omnipotent, if any prayers can sway you,
Give ear to mine. One thing I ask: if by our goodness
We have deserved it, grant your aid, confirm this omen!
  The old man had hardly spoken when from our left hand came
A sudden crash of thunder, and a shooting star slid down
The sky's dark face, drawing a trail of light behind it.
We watched that star as it glided high over the palace roof,
And blazing a path, buried its brightness deep in the woods of
Ida; when it was gone, it left in its wake a long furrow
Of light, and a sulphurous smoke spread widely over the terrain.
That did convince my father. He drew himself upright,
Addressed the gods above, and worshipped the heaven-sent star:—

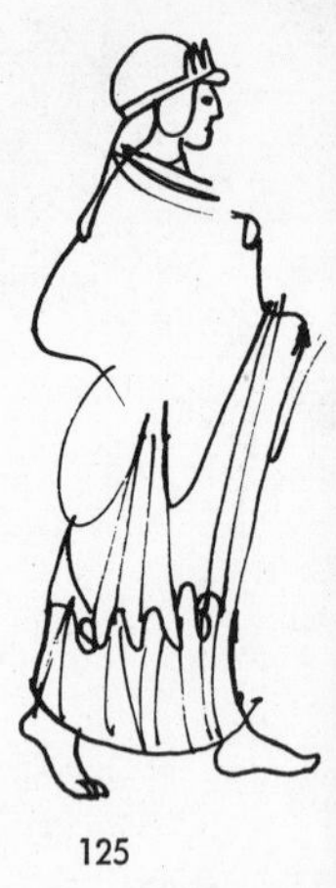

No more, no more lingering! I follow, I'm there, where you guide me!
Gods of our fathers, guard this family, guard my grandson!
This sign is yours, and Troy is still in your heavenly keeping.
Yea, I consent. I refuse no longer, my son, to go with you.

He had spoken; and now more clearly over the town the fire's roar
Was heard, and nearer rolled the tide of its conflagration.
"Quick, then, dear father," I said, "climb onto my back, and I will
Carry you on my shoulders—that's a burden will not be burdensome.
However things turn out, at least we shall share one danger,
One way of safety, both of us. Let little Ascanius walk
Beside me, and Creusa follow my steps at a distance.
And you, servants, pay careful attention to what I shall tell you.
As you go out of the city, you come to a mound with an ancient
Temple of Ceres upon it, secluded; nearby, an old cypress
Stands, which for many years our fathers preserved in reverence.
Let this be our rendezvous: we'll get there by different routes.
Do you, my father, carry the sacred relics and home-gods:[11]
Sinful for me to touch them, when I have just withdrawn
From battle, with blood on my hands, until in running water
I am purified."

With these words, I laid the pelt of a tawny lion
For covering over my broad shoulders and bowed neck;
Then stooped to lift my burden: Ascanius twined his fingers
In mine, hurrying to keep up with his father's longer stride.
My wife came on behind. We fared on, hugging the shadows.
I, who just now had faced the enemy volleys, the Greeks'
Concentrated attack, without turning a hair—I was scared by
Every breeze, alarmed by every sound, so strung up
Was I with anxiety for my burden and my companion.

And now I was nearing the gates and thinking that we had made it,
When on a sudden there came to my ears the sound of many

---

*11. **home-gods,*** images of the household gods, supposed to embody the spirits of ancestors.

Footsteps—or so it seemed. Then, peering into the gloom,
My father exclaimed:—
—Run! They're upon us! Run, Aeneas!
I can see the shine of their shields and the bronze accoutrements winking.
Well, I panicked. My wits were fuddled, were snatched away
By some malignant prompting. For even as I darted off
Into byways, off my course among streets I knew not—O god,
The anguish of it!—my wife Creusa, fate took her—did she
Stop there? or lose her way? Did she sink down in exhaustion?
We never knew. We never set eyes on her again.
I did not look back for the lost one, I did not give her a thought
Until we had reached the mound, the ancient, hallowed place
Of Ceres. Here at last, when all were assembled, one was
Missing, one had denied husband and son her company.
I was out of my mind. What mortal, what god did I not curse?
In all the city's ruin what bitterer thing did I see?
Commending Ascanius, Anchises and the Teucrian[12] home-gods
To my friends' care, and hiding them deep in the hollow vale,
I put on my shining armour, I made for the city once more.
To reconstruct those events, to retrace our path through Troy
And expose my life to its perils again—that was my purpose.
For a start, I returned to the shadowed gate in the city wall
By which I had sallied forth, noting my tracks and following them
Back through the night, straining my eyes to scan them. Everywhere
Dread and the sheer silence reduced my courage to nothing.
Next, I went home, in case—just on the chance that she might have
Gone there. The Greeks had broken in, the whole house was occupied.
That instant, gluttonous fire was fanned by the draught right up to
The roof top; flames burst out there, the blast of the heat roared skywards.
I went on, to revisit Priam's house and the citadel.
Here, in the empty colonnades of Juno's sanctuary,

12. ***Teucrian*** (tü'kri ən), Trojan: after Teucer the first king of Troy.

Phoenix and fell Ulysses were engaged on the duty allotted them,
Guarding the loot. To this point from all over Troy had plunder,
Salvaged from burning shrines, been brought: tables of gods,
Solid gold bowls and looted vestments were being piled up here
In heaps. Children and frightened mothers were standing about
In a long queue.
I dared (you will hardly believe it) to call out loud through the gloom
And fill the streets with shouting: sadly I cried "Creusa!"—
Called to her over and over again, but it was no good.
As I roamed on that endless, frenzied search through the city buildings,
There appeared before my eyes a piteous phantom, yes,
The very ghost of Creusa—a figure larger than life.
I was appalled: my hair stood on end, and my voice stuck
In my throat. It was she who spoke then, and thus relieved my pain:—
  Darling husband, it's madness of you to indulge your grief
Like this. These happenings are part of the divine
Purpose. It was not written that you should bring Creusa
Away with you; the great ruler of heaven does not allow it.
For you, long exile is destined, broad tracts of sea to be furrowed;
Then you will reach Hesperia,[13] where Lydian Tiber[14] flows
Gently through a land in good heart, and good men live.
There, your affairs will prosper; a kingdom, a royal bride
Await you. No more tears now for your heart's love, Creusa:
I shall not see the proud halls of the Myrmidons or Dolopes,[15]
Nor work as a slave for Greek women—I, who am Dardan[16]
And daughter-in-law to the goddess Venus.
No, the great Mother of the gods is going to keep me here.
Goodbye, Aeneas. Cherish our love in the son it gave us.
  With these words, though I wept and had so much to say
To her, she left me, fading out into thin air.
Three times I tried to put my arms round her neck, and three times

---

13. Hesperia (hes pãr′i a), Western Land, Italy. ***14. Tiber*** (tī′bər), a river in central Italy. ***15. Myrmidons or Dolopes,*** Greek peoples. The Myrmidons were followers of Achilles. ***16. Dardan,*** Trojan.

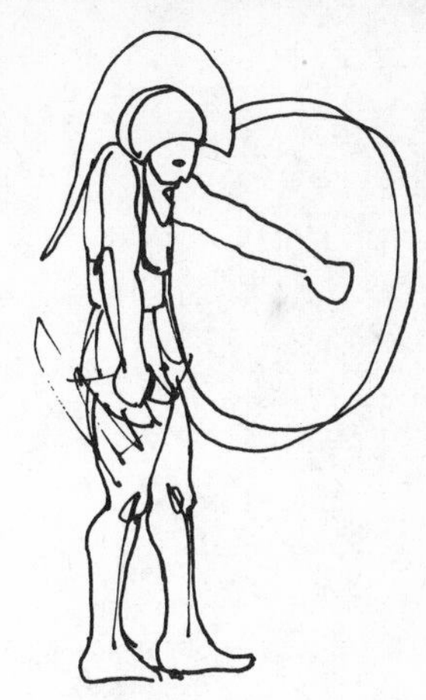

The phantom slipped my hands, my vain embrace: it was like
Grasping a wisp of wind or the wings of a fleeting dream.
So in the end I went back to my friends, the night being over.
I was astonished to find, when I got there, a great number
Of new arrivals come in, both women and men, a sorry
Concourse of refugees assembled for exile. From all sides
They'd rendezvous'd, their minds made up, their belongings ready
For me to lead them wherever I wished across the sea.
And now was the dawn star rising over the ridges of Ida,
Bringing another day. The Greeks were holding the gates of
The city in force. Troy was beyond all hope of aid.
I accepted defeat, picked up my father and made for the mountains.

WHAT DO YOU SAY?

1. *(a)* In what way does the point of view in this poem differ from that of the last? *(b)* Who is the narrator in this one? *(c)* What did he have to do with the war? *(d)* Did he seem to be more actively involved than the narrator in the previous poem? Explain.

2. *(a)* Who was responsible for and what means of persuasion was used in restraining Aeneas from killing Helen? *(b)* What did the goddess promise Aeneas if he would do what she asked?

3. *(a)* What unusual occurrence convinced Aeneas' father to flee with him? *(b)* What happened to Creusa during the family's flight from the city? *(c)* What did Creusa predict for Aeneas' future?

4. *(a)* Were the tragedies that befell Aeneas during the Trojan War caused only by the results of the war, or did the gods have a hand in them? *(b)* How did Aeneas finally accept his misfortune?

5. *(a)* In what way is the tone of this poem different from that of "The Surprise"? *(b)* In which one is there more physical action? *(c)* How do the two poems differ in rhythm?

6. *(a)* Did you feel the greater sympathy for Aeneas or for the narrator in "The Surprise"? Why? *(b)* In what sense were both men victims of the war?

In The House of Circe

By HOMER

translated by George Herbert Palmer

The story of the Trojan War would be incomplete without following up the Greek heroes who won the war. This is done in another of Homer's poems, the Odyssey, *which tells of the adventures of the Greek hero Odysseus on his homeward voyage. Although the distance was not long, the Greeks had now incurred the wrath of the gods, and their journey home took ten tragic years. In the next selection, the survivors have reached a small island where they encounter the goddess and sorceress Circe.*

Thence we sailed on with aching hearts, glad to be clear of death. And now we reached the island of Aeaea,[1] where fair-haired Circe[2] dwelt, a mighty goddess, human of speech. She was own sister of the sorcerer Aeetes.[3] Here we bore landward with our ship and ran in silence into a sheltering harbor, some god our guide.

Landing, we lay two days and nights, gnawing our hearts because of toil and trouble. But when the fair-haired dawn brought the third day, I took my spear and my sharp sword, and from the ship walked briskly up to a place of distant view, hoping to see some work of man or catch some voice. So climbing up, I took my stand on a rugged point of outlook. Smoke appeared rising from open ground at Circe's dwelling, through some oak thicket and a wood. Then for a time I doubted in my mind and heart whether to go and search the matter while I saw the flaring smoke. Reflecting thus, it seemed the better way first to return to the ship and to the shore, there give my men their dinner and send them forth to search.

But on my way, as I drew near to the curved ship, some god took pity on me all forlorn and sent a high-horned deer into my very path. From feeding in the wood he came to the stream to drink. As he stepped out I struck him in the spine midway along the back. The bronze spear pierced him through; down in the dust he fell with a moan, and his life flew away. Setting my foot upon him, I drew from the wound the brazen spear and laid it on the ground. Then I plucked twigs and osiers, and wove a rope a fathom long, twisted from end to end, with which I bound together the monstrous creature's legs. So with him upon my back I walked to the black ship and threw him down before it. Then with cheering words I aroused my men:

"We shall not, friends, however sad, go to the halls of Hades until our destined day. But while there still is food and drink in the swift ship, let us attend to eating."

So I spoke, and my words they quickly heeded. Thus all throughout the day till setting sun we sat and feasted on abundant meat and pleasant wine. And when the sun went down and darkness came, we laid us down to sleep upon the beach. Then as the early rosy-fingered dawn appeared, holding a counsel, I said to all my men:

"Suffering comrades, hearken to my words. Since we do not know the place of dusk or dawn,[4] let us at once consider if a wise course is left. I do not think there is; for I saw, on climbing to a rugged outlook, an island which the boundless deep encircles like a crown. Low in the sea the island lies. Midway across it I saw a smoke through some oak thickets and a wood."

As I thus spoke, their very souls were crushed, remembering the cruelty of the daring Cyclops,[5] the devourer of men. They cried aloud and let the big tears fall; but no good came to them for their lamenting.

Now the whole body of my mailed com-

"In the House of Circe" from Homer's *Odyssey,* translated by George Herbert Palmer. Reprinted by permission of the publisher, Houghton Mifflin Company.

1. *Aeaea* (ē ē'ə), an island in the Mediterranean Sea. **2. *Circe*** (sėr'si). **3. *Aeetes*** (ē ē'tēz). **4. *we do not know . . . dusk or dawn.*** We do not know west from east. Odysseus and his men had been sailing in unknown waters. **5. *Cyclops*** (sī'klops), one of a one-eyed race of giants.

panions I told off in two bands. One band I led, godlike Eurylochus[6] the other. Straightway we shook the lots in a bronze helmet, and the lot of bold Eurylochus leapt out the first. So he departed, two and twenty comrades following.

Within the glades they found the house of Circe, built of smooth stone upon commanding ground. All round about were mountain wolves and lions, which Circe had charmed by giving them evil drugs. These creatures did not spring upon my men, but stood erect, wagging their long tails, fawning. Still the men trembled at the sight of the strange beasts. They stood before the door of the fair-haired goddess, and in the house heard Circe singing with sweet voice while tending her great imperishable loom and weaving webs, fine, beautiful, and lustrous as are the works of gods.

Polites[7] was the first to speak, the nearest and the dearest of my companions:

"Ah, friends, somebody in the house is tending a great loom and singing sweetly. It is a goddess or some woman. Then let us quickly call to her."

He spoke. The others lifted up their voices and called. Suddenly coming forth, Circe opened the shining doors and bade them in. The rest all followed, heedless; only Eurylochus remained behind, suspicious of a snare. She led them in and seated them on couches and on chairs, and made a potion for them—cheese, barley, and yellow honey—but mingled with the food pernicious drugs, to make them quite forget their native land. Now after she had given the cup and they had drunk it off, straight with a wand she smote them and penned them up in sties. And they took on the heads, the voice, the bristles, and even the shape of swine. Yet was their reason as sound as heretofore. Thus, weeping, they were penned; and Circe flung them acorns, chestnuts, and cornel fruit,[8] such things as swine that wallow in the mire are wont to eat.

Eurylochus, at length, came back to the swift black ship to bring me tidings of his men and tell their bitter fate. Strive as he might, he could not speak a word, so stricken was he to the soul with great distress. His eyes were filled with tears; his heart felt anguish. But when we all in great amazement questioned him, then he described the loss of all his men:

"We went, as you commanded, noble Odysseus, through the thicket. We found within the glades a beautiful home, built of smooth stone upon commanding ground. There somebody was tending a great loom and singing loud. The others lifted up their voice and called; and suddenly coming forth, Circe opened the shining doors and bade them in. The rest all followed; but I remained behind, suspicious of a snare. They vanished, one and all. Not one appeared, though long I sat and watched."

So he spoke. I slung my silver-studded sword about my shoulders—large it was and made of bronze—and my bow with it, and bade him lead me back the selfsame way. But he, clasping my knees, entreated me:

"O heaven-descended man,[9] bring me not there against my will, but leave me here. For well I know you will never return, nor will you bring another of your comrades. Rather, with these now here, let us speed on, for we might yet escape the evil day."

So he spoke, and answering him said I:

"Eurylochus, remain then here yourself, eating and drinking by the black hollow ship. But I will go, for strong necessity is laid on me."

Saying this, I passed up from the ship and from the sea. But when, in walking up the solemn glades, I was about to reach the great house of the sorceress Circe, there I was met by Hermes of the golden wand,[10] in likeness of a youth—a time of life most winning. He thus addressed me:

---

*6. **Eurylochus*** (ū ril′ō kəs). *7. **Polites*** (pō·lī′tēz). *8. **cornel fruit,*** the fruit of a certain type of wild cherry. *9. **heaven-descended man.*** According to Greek mythology, Odysseus was a great-grandson of Hermes. *10. **Hermes of the golden wand.*** Hermes was usually pictured with a magic rod entwined with two serpents. This wand, called a caduceus (kə dü′si əs), is often used today as an emblem of the medical profession.

"Where are you going hapless man, along the hills alone, ignorant of the land? Your comrades yonder, at the house of Circe, are penned like swine and kept in fast-closed sties. You come to free them? Nay, I am sure you will, without my aid, return no more, but there, like all the rest, you too will stay. But come, I can keep you clear of harm and give you safety. Here, take this potent herb and go to Circe's house. This shall protect your life against the evil day. And I will tell you all the magic arts of Circe. She will prepare for you a potion and cast drugs into your food. But even so, she cannot harm you, because the potent herb which I shall give will not permit it. And let me tell you more. When Circe turns against you her long wand, then draw the sharp sword from your thigh and spring upon Circe as if you meant to slay her. She then will cower and bid you to lie down and rest. And do not you refuse the goddess' request, so that she may release your men and care for you. But bid her swear the blessed ones' great oath[11] that she is not meaning now to plot you a new woe."

As he thus spoke, he gave the herb, drawing it from the ground, and pointed out its nature. Black at the root it is, like milk its blossom, and the gods call it *moly*.

Hermes departed now to high Olympus along the woody island. I made my way to Circe's house, and as I went my heart grew very dark. But I stood at the gate of the fair-haired goddess, stood there and called, and the goddess heard my voice. Suddenly coming forth, she opened the shining doors and bade me in. I followed her with aching heart.

She led me in and placed me on a silver-studded chair, beautiful, richly wrought. Then she prepared a potion in a golden cup for me to drink, but put therein a drug, with a wicked purpose in her heart. Now after I had drunk it off, and yet it had not charmed me, smiting me with her wand, she spoke: "Off to the sty, and lie there with your fellows!"

She spoke. I drew my sharp blade and sprang upon her as if I meant to slay her. With a loud cry she cowered and clasped my knees, and sorrowfully said:

"Who are you? Of what people? Where is your town, your kindred? I marvel much that, drinking of these drugs, you were not charmed. None, no man else, ever withstood these drugs who tasted them. Surely you are adventurous Odysseus, who the god of the golden wand always declared would come upon his way from Troy. Nay, then, put up your sword and let us learn to trust each other."

So she spoke, and answering her I said: "Circe, why ask me to trust you when you have turned my comrades into swine within your halls and here detain me with treacherous purpose? I will never willingly unguard myself till you consent, goddess, to swear a solemn oath that you are not meaning now to plot me a new woe."

So I spoke, and straightway she took the oath that I required. Now she bade me retire to a bedchamber and there find refreshment in easeful sleep.

Renewed by sleep, I returned once more to Circe in the hall. Here four maids, Circe's attendants, plied their work. (They are the children of the springs and of the sacred streams that run into the sea.[12]) One threw upon the chairs beautiful cloths; purple she spread above, linen below. The next placed silver tables by the chairs and set forth golden baskets. A third stirred in a bowl the cheering wine—sweet wine in silver—and filled the golden cups. A fourth brought me water in a basin for my washing, and spread a polished table by my side. Then the grave housekeeper brought bread and placed it before me, setting out also food of many a kind, and bade me eat. But that pleased not my heart. I sat with other thoughts; my heart foreboded evil.

---

11. ***the blessed ones' great oath,*** a solemn oath made by gods and goddesses. 12. ***They are the children . . . into the sea.*** In Greek mythology, every body of water was inhabited by its own goddess or nymph.

When Circe marked me sitting thus, approaching me she said: "Why do you sit, Odysseus, thus, like one struck dumb, gnawing your heart and touch no food nor drink? Do you suspect some further guile? You have no cause for fear, for I have sworn to you a solemn oath."

So she spoke, and answering her I said: "Ah, Circe, what upright man could bring himself to taste of food or drink before he had released his friends and seen them with his eyes? But if you in sincerity will bid me drink and eat, then set them free."

So I spoke, and from the hall went Circe, wand in hand. She opened the sty doors, and forth she drove what seemed like swine. Passing along the line, Circe anointed each one with a counter charm. So from them fell the hair that Circe's accursed drug had made to grow. And once more they were men, men younger than before, much fairer, too, and taller to behold. They knew me, and each grasped my hand. From them all passionate sobs of joy burst forth.

Standing by my side the goddess said: "High-born son of Laertes,[13] ready Odysseus, go now to your swift ship and to the shore. First of all draw up your ship upon the land and store within the caves your goods and all your gear, and then come back yourself and bring your trusty comrades."

She spoke, and my high heart assented. I went to the swift ship and to the shore, and found by the swift ship my band of trusty comrades in bitter lamentation. And as when calves sport about the droves of cows returning from the pasture to the farmyard, all together they, with constant lowing, run about their mothers, so my men, when they caught sight of me, all bounded forth and pressed round, weeping. Through their sobs they said:

"Now you have come, O heaven-descended man, we are as glad as if we were approaching Ithaca, our native land. But tell about the loss of all our other comrades."

So they spoke. I in soft words made answer: "Let me now first of all draw up our ship upon the land and store within the caves our goods and all our gear. Then hasten all of you to follow me to the house of Circe."

So I spoke, and my words they quickly heeded. At the palace of Circe we found my other comrades merrily feasting. When the men saw and recognized each other, they wept aloud and the house rang around. And standing by my side the goddess said:

"High-born son of Laertes, ready Odysseus, let not this swelling grief rise further now. I myself know what hardships you have borne upon the swarming sea and how fierce men harassed you on the land. Come, then, eat food, drink wine, until you find once more that spirit in the breast which once was yours when you first left your native land of rugged Ithaca. Now, worn and spiritless, your thoughts still dwell upon your weary wandering. This many a day your heart has not been glad, for sorely have you suffered."

So she spoke, and our high hearts assented. Here, then, day after day, we sat in Circe's palace and feasted on abundant meat and pleasant wine. But when the full circle of a year had passed, I roused my men with smooth words: "Sleep now no more, but let us go our way."

So spoke I, and their lordly souls consented.

When we had gone down to the bright sea, we placed the mast and the sails in the black ship and climbed on board. And in the wake of our dark-prowed ship Circe sent a favoring breeze that filled the sails, a goodly escort.

---

13. ***Laertes*** (lā ėr′tēz), former king of Ithaca and father of Odysseus.

WHAT DO YOU SAY?

1. Were there greater evidences of myth in this selection than in the previous two? Give examples to support your answer.

2. (a) Who is the narrator in this story? *(b)* Does he take an active part in the plot?

(c) Is he more like the narrator in "The Surprise" or the narrator in "The Flight of Aeneas"?

3. (a) In what way did Circe lead the adventurers into a trap? *(b)* What happened to them? *(c)* How did Eurylochus escape the same fate?

4. Was Odysseus wholly heroic? Explain your answer.

5. (a) What instructions were given to Odysseus by Hermes? *(b)* What was Circe's reaction to Odysseus' actions toward her? *(c)* How might the outcome have been different if Odysseus had failed to carry out the instructions of the god? *(d)* What does this part of the story illustrate about the relations between the gods and mortals? *(e)* What does it illustrate about the relations between different deities themselves?

AUTHOR'S CRAFT

From old language into new

An obvious hurdle in studying classical literature is that of language. Although classical scholars may study these works in their original tongue, most people must depend upon others to put the compositions into a familiar language. This, of course, is the work of the translator.

The problems of translation become extremely great in rendering poetry from one language into another, for the translator then must contend not only with the translation of words and thoughts, but also with the translation of poetic elements such as rhythm, rhyme, alliteration, and meter. In fact, this rarely can be done with complete success, and a translator often must use a prose form in translating poetry into a different language. In spite of this, a skilled craftsman can preserve a part of the original poetic sound and effect. Compare the following translations of the same passage from "In the House of Circe."

> "Thence we sailed on with aching hearts,
> glad to be clear of death.
> And now we reached the island of Aeaea,
> where fair-haired Circe dwelt,
> A mighty goddess, human of speech. She was
> own sister of the sorceror Aeetes."

"Thence we sailed sadly on, glad to have escaped death, though we had lost our comrades, and came to the Aeaean island, where Circe lives, a great and cunning goddess, who is own sister to the Magician Aeetes—for they are both children of the sun by Perse, who is daughter to Oceanus."

In the second passage, the translator, Samuel Butler, has not attempted to reproduce a poetic effect, but has been more concerned with reproducing the exact text of the original poem. So, translations may vary, according to the purposes of the translator. Other translators may depart almost entirely from the language of the original composition and take on the rôle of storyteller, as in the following passage:

"With grief for their slain companions mixed with joy at their own escape, they pursued their way till they arrived at the Aeaean isle, where Circe dwelt, the daughter of the sun."

This is not truly a translation but a retelling of the story in the words of Thomas Bulfinch, the American scholar whose work you met in the myths in the first part of this unit.

The storyteller, then, is free to use his own choice of language, style, arrangement, and other matters of composition. But he still must follow the original text faithfully, without violating essential features that would change the basic meaning or effect of an original composition. Which of the three preceding selections resembles more closely the work of a storyteller than that of a translator? Which seems most successful as a translation of both the story and the poetic elements of an original composition?

KNOW YOUR WORDS

Figurative expressions

Many figurative expressions in use today had their origin in Greek myths and legends. For example, a beautiful girl might be described as being a "Helen of Troy." This expression would be meaningless to anyone who did not know the story of Helen and the Trojan War.

Each of the following sentences contains an allusion to Greek mythology. Explain the meaning of each sentence, relating it to the specific Greek legend.

1. The military leaders feared that the captured plans might turn out to be a ***Trojan horse.***
2. The child darted across the road in ***mercurial*** fashion.
3. His singing was worthy of ***Orpheus.***
4. The estate looked like the ***Elysian fields.***
5. The men were extremely tired after their ***odyssey.***

OF MEN AND IDEAS

It might seem thus far that the whole of ancient Greek and Roman literature centered about a fairy-tale world created by storytellers and poets. Nothing could be further from the truth, and for a different view of Greek classical literature, we now turn to the writings of the philosophers—thinkers and teachers to whom we owe a great many of our modern ideas about morals, ethics, education, and other human affairs.

One of the classical philosophers was an Athenian named Socrates, who lived from 469-399 B.C. He wrote no books and kept no schools. He called himself the Gadfly and simply wandered about the town, mingling with the crowds in the public squares, talking with people and asking questions. Through this continuous questioning he tried to arrive at underlying principles of truth.

However, Socrates introduced ideas and methods that clashed with established beliefs and at the age of seventy he was put to death. He was convicted of impiety and of corrupting the youth of Athens—charges that grew out of his refusal to worship the gods publicly and his encouragement of the young people to question existing ideas.

Since Socrates wrote nothing, it is from others that we must learn of him. Chief among those who tell of this philosopher is his friend and student, Plato, who is another familiar name in Greek literature. In the following two selections, Plato first gives his version of what Socrates said to the courtroom audience after he had received his sentence. Plato then gives his account of Socrates' final hours in prison.

Plato's "The Prophecy of Socrates" translated by Benjamin Jowett, reprinted by permission of Clarendon Press, Oxford. Fourth edition (1953).

The Prophecy of Socrates

By PLATO

translated by Benjamin Jowett

Not much time will be gained, O Athenians, in return for the evil name which you will get from the detractors of the city, who will say that you killed Socrates, a wise man; for they will call me wise, even although I am not wise, when they want to reproach you. If you had waited a little while, your desire would have been fulfilled in the course of nature. For I am far advanced in years, as you may perceive, and not far from death. I am speaking now not to all of you, but only to those who have condemned me to death. And I have another thing to say to them: You think that I was convicted because I had no words of the sort which would have procured my acquittal—I mean, if I had thought fit to leave nothing undone or unsaid. Not so; the deficiency which led to my conviction was not of words—certainly not. But I had not the boldness or impudence or inclination to address you as you would have liked me to do, weeping and wailing and lamenting, and saying and doing many things which you have been accustomed to hear from others, and which, as I maintain, are unworthy of me. I thought at the time that I ought not to do anything common or mean when in danger: nor do I now repent of the style of my defence; I would rather die having spoken after my manner, than speak in your manner and live. For neither in war nor yet at law ought I or any man to use every way of escaping death. Often in battle there can be no doubt that if a man will throw away his arms, and fall on his knees before his pursuers, he may escape death; and in other dangers there are other ways of escaping death, if a man is willing to say and do anything. The difficulty, my friends, is not to avoid death, but to avoid unrighteousness; for that runs faster than death. I am old and move slowly, and the slower runner has overtaken me, and my accusers are keen and quick, and the faster runner, who is unrighteousness, has overtaken them. And now I depart hence condemned by you to suffer the penalty of death,—they too go their ways condemned by the truth to suffer the penalty of villainy and wrong; and I must abide by my award—let them abide by theirs. I suppose that these things may be regarded as fated,—and I think that they are well.

And now, O men who have condemned me, I would fain prophesy to you; for I am about to die, and in the hour of death men are gifted with prophetic power. And I prophesy to you who are my murderers, that immediately after my departure punishment far heavier than you have inflicted on me will surely await you. Me you have killed because you wanted to escape the accuser, and not to give an account of your lives. But that will not be as you suppose: far otherwise. For I say that there will be more accusers of you than there are now; accusers whom hitherto I have restrained: and as they are younger they will be more inconsiderate with you, and you will be more offended at them. If you think that by killing men you can prevent someone from censuring your evil lives, you are mistaken; that is not a way of escape which is either possible or honourable; the easiest and noblest way is not to be disabling others, but to be improving yourselves. This is the prophecy which I utter before my departure to the judges who have condemned me.

Friends, who have acquitted me, I would like also to talk with you about the thing which has come to pass, while the magistrates are busy, and before I go to the place at which I must die. Stay then a little, for we may as well talk with one another while there is time. You are my friends, and I should like to show you the meaning of this event which has happened to me. O my judges—for you I may truly call judges—I should like to tell you of a wonderful circumstance. Hitherto the divine faculty of which the internal oracle is the source has constantly been in the habit of opposing me even about trifles, if I was going to make a slip or error in any matter; and now as you see there has come upon me that which may be thought, and is generally believed to be, the last and worst evil. But the oracle made no sign of opposition, either when I was leaving my house in the morning, or when I was on my way to the court, or while I was speaking, at anything which I was going to say; and yet I have often been stopped in the middle of a speech, but now in nothing I either said or did touching the matter in hand has the oracle opposed me. What do I take to be the explanation of this silence? I will tell you. It is an intimation that what has happened to me is a good, and that those of us who think that death is an evil are in error. For the customary sign would surely have opposed me had I been going to evil and not to good.

Let us reflect in another way, and we shall see that there is great reason to hope that death is a good; for one of two things —either death is a state of nothingness and utter unconsciousness, or, as men say, there is a change and migration of the soul from this world to another. Now, if you suppose that there is no consciousness, but a sleep like the sleep of him who is undisturbed even by dreams, death will be an unspeakable gain. For if a person were to select the night in which his sleep was undisturbed even by dreams, and were to compare with this the other days and nights of his life, and then were to tell us how many days and nights he had passed in the course of his life better and more pleasantly than this one, I think that any man, I will not say a private man, but even the great king will not find many such days or nights, when compared with the others. Now, if death be of such a nature, I say that to die is gain; for eternity is then only a single night. But if death is the journey to another place, and there, as men say, all the dead abide, what good, O my friends and judges, can be greater than this? If, indeed, when the pilgrim arrives in the world below, he is delivered from the professors of justice in this world, and finds the true judges who are said to give judgment there, Minos and Rhadamanthus and Aeacus and Triptolemus, and other sons of God who were righteous in their own life, that pilgrimage will be worth making. Above all, I shall then be able to continue my search into true and false knowledge; as in this world, so also in the next; and I shall find out who is wise, and who pretends to be wise, and is not. What would not a man give, O judges, to be able to examine the leader of the great Trojan expedition; or Odysseus or Sisyphus, or numberless others, men and women too! What infinite delight would there be in conversing with them and asking them questions! In another world they do not put a man to death for asking questions: assuredly not. For besides being happier than we are, they will be immortal, if what is said is true.

Wherefore, O judges, be of good cheer about death, and know of a certainty, that no evil can happen to a good man, either in life or after death. He and his are not neglected by the gods; nor has my own approaching end happened by mere chance. But I see clearly that the time had arrived when it was better for me to die and be released from trouble: wherefore the oracle gave no sign. For which reason, also, I am not angry with my condemners, or with my accusers; they have done me no harm, although they did not mean to do me any good; and for this I may gently blame them.

The hour of departure has arrived, and we go our ways—I to die, and you to live. Which is better God only knows.

The Death of Socrates

By PLATO

It seemed to us as if we were going to lose a father, and to be orphans for the rest of our life.

When Socrates had bathed, and his children had been brought to him—he had two sons quite little, and one grown up—and the women of his family were come, he spoke with them in Crito's[1] presence, and gave them his last commands. Then he sent the women and children away, and returned to us.

Presently the servant of the governing council which had condemned him to death came and stood before him and said, "I know that I shall not find you unreasonable like other men, Socrates. They are angry with me and curse me when I bid them drink the poison because the authorities make me do it. But I have found you all along the noblest and gentlest and best man that has ever come here; and now I am sure that you will not be angry with me, but with those who you know are to blame. And so farewell, and try to bear what must be as lightly as you can; you know why I have come." With that he turned away weeping, and went out.

Socrates looked up at him, and replied, "Farewell—I will do as you say." Then he turned to us and said, "How courteous the man is. And the whole time that I have been here, he has constantly come in to see me, and sometimes he has talked to me, and has been the best of men; and now, how generously he weeps for me. Come, Crito, let us obey him—let the poison be brought if it is ready; and if it is not ready, let it be prepared."

Crito replied: "Nay, Socrates, I think that the sun is still upon the hills—it has not set. Besides, I know that other men take the poison quite late, and eat and drink heartily, and even enjoy the company of their chosen friends, after the announcement has been made. So do not hurry, there is still time."

Socrates replied: "And those whom you speak of, Crito, naturally do so; for they think that they will be gainers by so doing. And I naturally shall not do so for I think that I should gain nothing by drinking the poison a little later, by my own contempt for so greedily saving up a life which is already spent. So do not refuse to do as I say."

Then Crito made a sign to his slave who was standing by, and the slave went out, and after some delay returned with the man who was to give the poison, carrying it prepared in a cup. When Socrates saw him, he asked, "You understand these things, my good sir, what have I to do?"

"You have only to drink this," he replied, "and to walk about until your legs feel heavy, and then lie down, and it will act of itself."

With that he handed the cup to Socrates,

1. **Crito,** follower of Socrates.

who took it quite cheerfully, without trembling, and without any change of colour or of feature, and looked up at the man with that fixed glance of his, and asked, "What say you to pouring out a libation to the gods from this draught? May I, or not?"

"We only prepare so much as we think sufficient, Socrates," he answered.

"I understand," said Socrates, "But I suppose that I may, and must, pray to the gods that my journey hence may be prosperous. That is my prayer—be it so."

With these words he put the cup to his lips and drank the poison quite calmly and cheerfully. Till then most of us had been able to control our grief fairly well. But when we saw him drinking, and then the poison finished, we could do so no longer. My tears came fast in spite of myself, and I covered my face and wept for myself—it was not for him, but at my own misfortune in losing such a friend. Even before that Crito had been unable to restrain his tears, and had gone away. And Apollodorus, who had never once ceased weeping the whole time, burst into a loud cry, and made us one and all break down by his sobbing and grief, except only Socrates himself.

"What are you doing, my friends?" he exclaimed. "I sent away the women chiefly in order that they might not offend in this way for I have heard that a man should die in silence. So calm yourselves and bear up."

When we heard that we were ashamed, and we ceased from weeping. But he walked about, until he said that his legs were getting heavy, and then he lay down on his back, as he was told. And the man who gave the poison began to examine his feet and legs from time to time. Then he pressed his foot hard, and asked if there was any feeling in it, and Socrates said, No. And then his legs, and so higher and higher, and showed us that he was cold and stiff.

And Socrates felt himself, and said that when it came to his heart, he should be gone. He was already growing cold about the groin, when he uncovered his face, which had been covered, and spoke for the last time.

"Crito," he said, "I owe a cock to Asclepius; do not forget to pay it."

"It shall be done," replied Crito. "Is there anything else that you wish?"

He made no answer to this question, but after a short interval there was a movement, and the man uncovered him, and his eyes were fixed. Then Crito closed his mouth, and his eyes.

Such was the end of our friend, a man, I think, who was the wisest and justest, and the best man I have ever known.

The Educated Man

By ISOCRATES (436-338 B.C.)

In contrast to Socrates, Isocrates considered writing to be an important process in education, and he wrote many speeches, essays, and letters. The following selection is typical of the theme and style of Isocrates.

Whom, then, do I call educated, since I exclude the arts and sciences and specialties? First, those who manage well the circumstances which they encounter day by day, and who possess a judgment which is

"The Educated Man" from ***Isocrates, Volume II, Oration V, "Panathenaicus,"*** translated by George Norlin (Loeb Classical Library). Reprinted by permission of the Harvard University Press.

accurate in meeting occasions as they arise and rarely misses the expedient course of action; next, those who are decent and honourable in their intercourse with all with whom they associate, tolerating easily and good-naturedly what is unpleasant or offensive in others and being themselves as agreeable and reasonable to their associates as it is possible to be; furthermore, those who hold their pleasures always under control and are not duly overcome by their misfortunes, bearing up under them bravely and in a manner worthy of our common nature; finally, and most important of all, those who are not spoiled by successes and do not desert their true selves and become arrogant, but hold their ground steadfastly as intelligent men, not rejoicing in the good things which have come to them through chance rather than in those which through their own nature and intelligence are theirs from their birth. Those who have a character which is in accord, not with one of these things, but with all of them—these, I contend, are wise and complete men, possessed of all the virtues.

WHAT DO YOU SAY?

The Prophecy of Socrates

1. *(a)* What prophecy did Socrates make? *(b)* To whom did he make this prophecy? *(c)* Was his prophecy fulfilled in his own age or in some later period of history?

2. *(a)* What did Socrates mean by his metaphors, the ***slower runner*** and the ***faster runner***? *(b)* Which runner overtook him? *(c)* Which overtook his judges? *(d)* Which did Socrates say was more to be feared? Why?

3. *(a)* What were the two concepts of death presented by Socrates? *(b)* Which of these ideas of death did he seem to prefer? *(c)* Why?

4. *(a)* If Socrates had chosen to avoid his penalty, what defense did he say he could have used? *(b)* In what way would this have differed from the defense he did use? *(c)* Why did he choose not to save himself?

5. *(a)* What interpretation did Socrates give to the silence of the 'oracle'? *(b)* What did he mean when he said that "no evil can happen to a good man, either in life or after death"? *(c)* In what ways was death a gain, according to his two concepts of death?

6. *(a)* In what ways did Socrates show that he was opposed to existing beliefs? *(b)* In what ways did he show that he supported existing beliefs? *(c)* Was there evidence that Socrates actually considered himself a wiser man than most others? Explain.

The Death of Socrates

1. Which lines in the selection show particularly well the calmness and strength with which Socrates approached death?

2. *(a)* In what way are Socrates' ideals reinforced by his refusal to await the setting of the sun before taking the poison? *(b)* In what spirit does Socrates drink the poison? *(c)* What is the attitude of his followers toward his death? *(d)* Do they share Socrates' own attitude and strength of character? Explain.

3. *(a)* What reference to ***gainers*** does Socrates make in this selection? *(b)* In what way does this reference reinforce ideas that were set forth in his speech after his trial?

4. *(a)* Which of Socrates' words in this selection seem to indicate that he was not guilty of the charges of impiety that were leveled against him? *(b)* What further light did these words shed upon Socrates' view of death?

5. In what ways was Socrates shown to be a man of practical, earthly character, as well as one of strength and lofty ideals?

The Educated Man

1. Did Isocrates agree with the modern concept that a well-educated person must be instructed in the fundamentals of the various arts and sciences? Explain.

2. *(a)* Are any of Isocrates' ideas still held in modern education? If so, in what ways? *(b)* Would Isocrates have favored the "self-educated" person who learns through practical experience? Support your answer with lines from the text.

3. Which of Isocrates' ideas seem especially close to those of Socrates?

4. Contrast the ideas of Isocrates and Socrates as presented in the three selections.

Every civilization has found a way to dramatize human beliefs, emotions, and desires. In earliest times, this action took the form of dances and lyrics. Following this, the ancient Greeks developed ritualistic ceremonies into the form of literature known as *drama.*

GREEK TRAGEDIES

Although comedies were performed in ancient Greece, few survive today, and it is the *tragedies* that are of special importance. These plays were first performed in connection with the worship of Dionysus, god of wine. At a great festival held each year in honor of this god, competing playwrights presented their plays and the winner was awarded a goat. Perhaps it was this prize itself that gave tragedy its name, for the word literally means *goat-song.*

To many people a tragedy is merely an unhappy sort of play in which one or more characters have a run of bad luck, eventually meeting a sad end. The ancient Greeks had no such simple idea, however, and to understand what tragedy was to the Greeks, it is necessary to review some basic concepts about which ancient Greek culture centered.

FATE AND PERSONAL FLAW

First of all, the Greeks believed that every person's life was ruled by a predetermined *fate*—a natural force set in motion by the gods and one that could not be altered under any circumstances. This concept was illustrated in the myths at the beginning of this unit.

Furthermore, it was believed that every person's fate held in store a personal allotment of unavoidable misery that would come about naturally. Misery in itself was not tragic but was something that every person expected.

The Greeks also believed, however, that Man possessed a certain freedom of will and action—a concept that was often touched upon by Socrates in his teachings. Through proper exercise of this personal freedom, a person could live out his fate with dignity, bringing upon himself no more than his allotted share of grief. On the other hand, a person always stood in danger of misusing this freedom. Through some tragic flaw in his own character, he might tempt fate in such a way that he would come to lose all personal dignity and bring upon himself more pain and suffering than his fate had originally held in store for him.

A Greek tragedy, then, is the story of the downfall of a basically good and noble individual who tempts fate because of some personal flaw in character, bringing upon himself extraordinary amounts of sorrow and suffering. Such a play is *Antigone*.

A CYCLE OF TRAGEDY

Although *Antigone* is a complete play in itself, it is closely associated with two other of Sophocles' plays, *Oedipus the King* and *Oedipus at Colonus*. These two plays deal with King Oedipus, who as a child had been separated from his parents. In later life, however, he fulfilled the dreadful prophecy that had been cast at his birth; unknowingly, he met and killed his father and later married his mother.

When he discovered the truth, Oedipus put out his own eyes and banished himself from his kingdom of Thebes. He wandered about many years, blinded and tormented, until he finally died in Colonus, as the oracle had prophesied.

Antigone begins after the death of Oedipus, but in a sense this story completes the cycle of tragedy that began with this great king of Thebes. The fate of Oedipus continues to be played out by his daughter, Antigone. She pursues her fate with dignity. Creon, the brother-in-law of Oedipus and the new king of Thebes, however, falls victim to personal pride, bringing upon himself untold amounts of misery. In terms of the Greek concept of tragedy, it is Creon who emerges as the tragic figure in this drama.

THE CHORUS

The chorus is an important feature of Greek drama. Often this chorus takes on the rôle of an actor and assumes an active part in the action of the play. The chorus was also used to interpret and retell past events, to comment on present actions, and to foretell the future. At other times, the chorus acts simply as spectators. In this rôle, they sometimes disapprove of the actions of the main character, but more often they support the chief character and are easily fooled into thinking that his beliefs and actions are always right. The chorus in *Antigone* is composed of the elders, or senior members, of the Theban community. Because of their age and experience, they are more likely to see events from the viewpoint of Creon, than from that of Antigone.

Antigone

BY SOPHOCLES

translated by

ELIZABETH WYCKOFF

ROTH

Characters

ANTIGONE (an tig′ə nē)
ISMENE (is mē′nē)
CHORUS of THEBAN ELDERS
CREON (krē′on)
A GUARD
HAEMON (hē′mən)
TEIRESIAS (tī rē′si əs)
A MESSENGER
EURYDICE (ū rid′ə sē)

SCENE: *Thebes, before the royal palace.* ANTIGONE *and* ISMENE *emerge from its great central door.*

ANTIGONE. My sister, my Ismene, do you know
of any suffering from our father sprung
that Zeus does not achieve for us survivors?
There's nothing grievous, nothing free from doom,
not shameful, not dishonored, I've not seen.
Your sufferings and mine.
And now, what of this edict which they say
the commander[1] has proclaimed to the whole people?
Have you heard anything? Or don't you know
that the foes' trouble comes upon our friends?

ISMENE. I've heard no word, Antigone, of our friends.
Not sweet nor bitter, since that single moment
when we two lost two brothers
who died on one day by a double blow.
And since the Argive army[2] went away
this very night, I have no further news
of fortune or disaster for myself.

ANTIGONE. I knew it well, and brought you from the house
for just this reason, that you alone may hear.

ISMENE. What is it? Clearly some news has clouded you.

ANTIGONE. It has indeed. Creon will give the one
of our two brothers honor in the tomb;
the other none.[3]
Eteocles,[4] with just entreatment treated,
as law provides he has hidden under earth
to have full honor with the dead below.
But Polyneices'[5] corpse who died in pain,
they say he[6] has proclaimed to the whole town
that none may bury him and none bewail,
but leave him unwept, untombed, a rich sweet sight
for the hungry birds' beholding.
Such orders they say the worthy Creon gives

1. ***the commander,*** Creon.

2. ***Argive army,*** the army which attacked Thebes; from Argos (är′gos), a city in southern Greece.

3. ***honor . . . the other none.*** In Greek mythology, the souls of unburied human beings could not cross the River Styx to the realm of the dead but were compelled to wander forever with no permanent resting place. Consequently, burial of the dead was an important sacred duty of surviving friends and relatives.

4. ***Eteocles*** (ē tē′ō klēz).

5. ***Polyneices*** (pol i nī′sēz).

6. ***he,*** Creon.

to you and me—yes, yes, I say to *me*—
and that he's coming to proclaim it clear
to those who know it not.
Further: he has the matter so at heart
that anyone who dares attempt the act
will die by public stoning in the town.
So there you have it and you soon will show
if you are noble, or fallen from your descent.
ISMENE. If things have reached this stage, what can I do,
poor sister, that will help to make or mend?
ANTIGONE. Think will you share my labor and my act.
ISMENE. What will you risk? And where is your intent?
ANTIGONE. Will you take up that corpse along with me?
ISMENE. To bury him you mean, when it's forbidden?
ANTIGONE. My brother, and yours, though you may wish
he were not.
I never shall be found to be his traitor.
ISMENE. O hard of mind! When Creon spoke against it!
ANTIGONE. It's not for him to keep me from my own.
ISMENE. Alas. Remember, sister, how our father
perished abhorred, ill-famed.
Himself with his own hand, through his own curse
destroyed both eyes.
Remember next his mother and his wife
finishing life in the shame of the twisted strings.[7]
And third two brothers on a single day,
poor creatures, murdering, a common doom
each with his arm accomplished on the other.
And now look at the two of us alone.
We'll perish terribly if we force law
and try to cross the royal vote and power.
We must remember that we two are women
so not to fight with men.
And that since we are subject to strong power
we must hear these orders, or any that may be worse.
So I shall ask of them beneath the earth
forgiveness, for in these things I am forced,
and shall obey the men in power. I know
that wild and futile action makes no sense.
ANTIGONE. I wouldn't urge it. And if now you wished
to act, you wouldn't please me as a partner.
Be what you want to; but that man shall I
bury. For me, the doer, death is best.
Friend shall I lie with him, yes friend with friend,
when I have dared the crime of piety.
Longer the time in which to please the dead
than that for those up here.
There shall I lie forever. You may see fit

7. ***his mother . . . twisted strings.*** Jocasta, realizing that she was both wife and mother to Oedipus, hanged herself.

to keep from honor what the gods have honored.
ISMENE. I shall do no dishonor. But to act
against the citizens. I cannot.
ANTIGONE. That's your protection. Now I go, to pile
the burial-mound for him, my dearest brother.
ISMENE. Oh my poor sister. How I fear for you!
ANTIGONE. For me, don't borrow trouble. Clear your fate.
ISMENE. At least give no one warning of this act;
you keep it hidden, and I'll do the same.
ANTIGONE. Dear God! Denounce me. I shall hate you more
if silent, not proclaiming this to all.
ISMENE. You have a hot mind over chilly things.
ANTIGONE. I know I please those whom I most should please.
ISMENE. If but you can. You crave what can't be done.
ANTIGONE. And so, when strength runs out, I shall give over.
ISMENE. Wrong from the start, to chase what cannot be.
ANTIGONE. If that's your saying, I shall hate you first,
and next the dead will hate you in all justice.
But let me and my own ill-counselling
suffer this terror. I shall suffer nothing
as great as dying with a lack of grace.
ISMENE. Go, since you want to. But know this: you go
senseless indeed, but loved by those who love you.
(ISMENE *returns to the palace;* ANTIGONE *leaves by one of the side entrances.*)

The CHORUS *now enters from the other side.*

CHORUS. Sun's own radiance, fairest light ever shone on the gates of Thebes,
then did you shine, O golden day's
eye, coming over Dirce's stream,[8]
on the Man who had come from Argos[9] with all his armor
running now in headlong fear as you shook his bridle free.
He was stirred by the dubious quarrel of Polyneices.[10]
So, screaming shrill,
like an eagle over the land he[11] flew,
covered with white-snow wing,
with many weapons,
with horse-hair crested helms.
He who had stood above our halls, gaping about our seven gates,
with that circle of thirsting spears.

8. ***Dirce's stream.*** Dirce (dėr′sē), the wife of a previous ruler of Thebes, was brutally murdered and her corpse thrown into a stream thereafter called by her name.
9. ***Man who had come from Argos,*** personification of the Argive army.
10. ***He was stirred . . . quarrel of Polyneices.*** The Argive army was aroused to battle by its leader, Polyneices.
11. ***he,*** Argive army.

ROTH

Gone, without our blood in his jaws,
before the torch took hold on our tower-crown.
Rattle of war at his back; hard the fight for the
dragon's foe.[12]
The boasts of a proud tongue are for Zeus to hate.
So seeing them streaming on
in insolent clangor of gold,
he struck with hurling fire him who rushed
for the high wall's top,[13]
to cry conquest abroad.
Swinging, striking the earth he fell
fire in hand, who in mad attack,
had raged against us with blasts of hate.
He failed. He failed of his aim.[14]
For the rest great Ares[15] dealt his blows about,
first in the war-team.
The captains stationed at seven gates
fought with seven[16] and left behind
their brazen arms as an offering
to Zeus who is turner of battle.
All but those wretches, sons of one man,
one mother's sons, who sent their spears
each against each and found the share
of a common death together.[17]
Great-named Victory[18] comes to us
answering Thebe's warrior-joy.
Let us forget the wars just done
and visit the shrines of the gods.
All, with night-long dance which Bacchus[19] will lead,
who shakes Thebe's acres.

CREON *enters from the palace.*

Now here he comes, the king of the land,
Creon, Menoeceus'[20] son,
newly named by the gods' new fate.
What plan that beats about his mind
has made him call this council-session,
sending his summons to all?

CREON. My friends, the very gods who shook the state
with mighty surge have set it straight again.
So now I sent for you, chosen from all,
first that I knew you constant in respect
to Laius'[21] royal power; and again
when Oedipus had set the state to rights,
and when he perished, you were faithful still
in mind to the descendants of the dead.
When they two perished by a double fate,
on one day struck and striking and defiled

12. ***Gone without our blood . . . dragon's foe.*** The Argive army has left without conquering us, without burning our city, in retreat ***(war at their backs);*** the fight was hard for the dragon's foe (the Argive army, Thebes being referred to as a dragon).

13. ***He struck . . . him who rushed for the high wall's top.*** An Argive chieftain was struck down by one of Zeus' thunderbolts when he tried to mount the wall of Thebes.

14. ***Swinging, striking . . . failed of his aim.*** The army led by Polyneices was unable to capture the city.

15. ***Ares*** (ãr′ēz), Mars, the god of war.

16. ***The captains stationed . . . fought with seven.*** Polyneices and the six Argive chiefs each attacked one of Thebes' seven gates which were successfully defended by seven Theban heroes.

17. ***those wretches . . . common death together.*** The war was finally ended by a combat between the two brothers, Polyneices and Eteocles, who killed each other.

18. ***Great-named Victory.*** After the death of Polyneices, the Argive army fled.

19. ***Bacchus*** (bak′əs), Dionysus (dī ə-nī′səs), the Greek god of wine. Thebes was under his special protection.

20. ***Menoeceus*** (men ā′si əs).

21. ***Laius*** (lā′əs), a former king of Thebes and father of Oedipus.

each by his own hand, now it comes that I
hold all the power and the royal throne
through close connection with the perished men.
You cannot learn of any man the soul,
the mind, and the intent until he shows
his practise of the government and law.
For I believe that who controls the state
and does not hold to the best plans of all,
but locks his tongue up through some kind of fear,
that he is worst of all who are or were.
And he who counts another greater friend
than his own fatherland, I put him nowhere.
So I—may Zeus all-seeing always know it—
could not keep silent as disaster crept
upon the town, destroying hope of safety.
Nor could I count the enemy of the land
friend to myself, not I who know so well
that she[22] it is who saves us, sailing straight,
and only so can we have friends at all.
With such good rules shall I enlarge our state.
And now I have proclaimed their brother-edict.
In the matter of the sons of Oedipus,
citizens, know: Eteocles who died,
defending this our town with champion spear,
is to be covered in the grave and granted
all holy rites we give the noble dead.
But his brother Polyneices whom I name
the exile who came back and sought to burn
his fatherland, the gods who were his kin,
who tried to gorge on blood he shared, and lead
the rest of us as slaves—
it is announced that no one in this town
may give him burial or mourn for him.
Leave him unburied, leave his corpse disgraced,
a dinner for the birds and for the dogs.
Such is my mind. Never shall I, myself,
honor the wicked and reject the just.
The man who is well-minded to the state
from me in death and life shall have his honor.

CHORUS. This resolution, Creon, is your own,
in the matter of the traitor and the true.
For you can make such rulings as you will
about the living and about the dead.

CREON. Now you be sentinels of the decree.

CHORUS. Order some younger man to take this on.

CREON. Already there are watchers of the corpse.

CHORUS. What other order would you give us, then?

CREON. Not to take sides with any who disobey.

22. *she,* Thebes or the Theban people.

CHORUS. No fool is fool as far as loving death.
CREON. Death is the price. But often we have known
men to be ruined by the hope of profit.

Enter, from the side, a GUARD.

GUARD. Lord, I can't claim that I am out of breath
from rushing here with light and hasty step,
for I had many haltings in my thought
making me double back upon my road.
My mind kept saying many things to me:
"Why go where you will surely pay the price?"
"Fool, are you halting? And if Creon learns
from someone else, how shall you not be hurt?"
Turning this over, on I dilly-dallied.
And so a short trip turns itself to long.
Finally, though, my coming here won out.
If what I say is nothing, still I'll say it.
For I come clutching to one single hope
that I can't suffer what is not my fate.
CREON. What is it that brings on this gloom of yours?
GUARD. I want to tell you first about myself.
I didn't do it, didn't see who did it.
It isn't right for me to get in trouble.
CREON. Your aim is good. You fence the fact around.
It's clear you have some shocking news to tell.
GUARD. Terrible tidings make for long delays.
CREON. Speak out the story, and then get away.
GUARD. I'll tell you. Someone left the corpse just now,
burial all accomplished, thirsty dust
strewn on the flesh, the ritual complete.
CREON. What are you saying? What man has dared
to do it?
GUARD. I wouldn't know. There were no marks of picks,
no grubbed-out earth. The ground was dry and hard,
no trace of wheels. The doer left no sign.
When the first fellow on the day-shift showed us,
we all were sick with wonder.
For he was hidden, not inside a tomb,
light dust upon him, enough to turn the curse,
no wild beast's track, nor track of any hound
having been near, nor was the body torn.
We roared bad words about, guard against guard,
and came to blows. No one was there to stop us.
Each man had done it, nobody had done it
so as to prove it on him—we couldn't tell.
We were prepared to hold to red-hot iron,
to walk through fire, to swear before the gods
we hadn't done it, hadn't shared the plan,

when it was plotted or when it was done.
And last, when all our sleuthing came out nowhere,
one fellow spoke, who made our heads to droop
low toward the ground. We couldn't disagree.
We couldn't see a chance of getting off.
He said we had to tell you all about it.
We couldn't hide the fact.
So he won out. The lot chose poor old me
to win the prize. So here I am unwilling,
quite sure you people hardly want to see me.
Nobody likes the bringer of bad news.

CHORUS. Lord, while he spoke, my mind kept on debating.
Isn't this action possibly a god's?

CREON. Stop now, before you fill me up with rage,
or you'll prove yourself insane as well as old.
Unbearable, your saying that the gods
take any kindly forethought for this corpse.
Would it be they had hidden him away,
honoring his good service, his who came
to burn their pillared temples and their wealth,
even their land, and break apart their laws?
Or have you seen them honor wicked men?
It isn't so.
No, from the first there were some men in town
who took the edict hard, and growled against me,
who hid the fact that they were rearing back,
not rightly in the yoke, no way my friends.
These are the people—oh it's clear to me—
who have bribed these men and brought about the deed.
No current custom among men as bad
as silver currency. This destroys the state;
this drives men from their homes; this wicked teacher
drives solid citizens to acts of shame.
It shows men how to practise infamy
and know the deeds of all unholiness.
Every least hireling who helped in this
brought about then the sentence he shall have.
But further, as I still revere great Zeus,
understand this, I tell you under oath,
if you don't find the very man whose hands
buried the corpse, bring him for me to see,
not death alone shall be enough for you
till living, hanging, you make clear the crime.
For any future grabbings you'll have learned
where to get pay, and that it doesn't pay
to squeeze a profit out of every source.

For you'll have felt that more men come to doom
through dirty profits than are kept by them.
GUARD. May I say something? Or just turn and go?
CREON. Aren't you aware your speech is most unwelcome?
GUARD. Does it annoy your hearing or your mind?
CREON. Why are you out to allocate my pain?
GUARD. The doer hurts your mind. I hurt your ears.
CREON. You are a quibbling rascal through and through.
GUARD. But anyhow I never did the deed.
CREON. And you the man who sold your mind for money!
GUARD. Oh! How terrible to guess, and guess at lies!
CREON. Go pretty up your guesswork. If you don't
show me the doers you will have to say
that wicked payments work their own revenge.
GUARD. Indeed, I pray he's found, but yes or no,
taken or not as luck may settle it,
you won't see me returning to this place.
Saved when I neither hoped nor thought to be,
I owe the gods a mighty debt of thanks.
(CREON *enters the palace. The* GUARD *leaves by the way he came.*)

CHORUS. Many the wonders but nothing walks stranger than man.
This thing crosses the sea in the winter's storm,
making his path through the roaring waves.
And she, the greatest of gods, the earth—
ageless she is, and unwearied—he wears her away
as the ploughs go up and down from year to year
and his mules turn up the soil.

Gay nations of birds he snares and leads,
wild beast tribes and the salty brood of the sea,
with the twisted mesh of his nets, this clever man.
He controls with craft the beasts of the open air,
walkers on hills. The horse with his shaggy mane
he holds and harnesses, yoked about the neck,
and the strong bull of the mountain.

Language, and thought like the wind
and the feelings that make the town,
he has taught himself, and shelter against the cold,
refuge from rain. He can always help himself.
He faces no future helpless. There's only death
that he cannot find an escape from. He has contrived
refuge from illnesses once beyond all cure.

Clever beyond all dreams
the inventive craft that he has

which may drive him one time or another to well or ill.
When he honors the laws of the land and the gods'
sworn right
high indeed is his city; but stateless the man
who dares to dwell with dishonor.[23] Not by my fire,
never to share my thoughts, who does these things.[24]

The GUARD *enters with* ANTIGONE.

My mind is split at this awful sight.
I know her. I cannot deny
Antigone is here.
Alas, the unhappy girl,
her unhappy father's child.
Oh what is the meaning of this?
It cannot be you that they bring
for breaking the royal law,
caught in open shame.

GUARD. This is the woman who has done the deed.
We caught her at the burying. Where's the king?

CREON *enters.*

CHORUS. Back from the house again just when
he's needed.

CREON. What must I measure up to? What has happened?

GUARD. Lord, one should never swear off anything.
Afterthought makes the first resolve a liar.
I could have vowed I wouldn't come back here
after your threats, after the storm I faced.
But joy that comes beyond the wildest hope
is bigger than all other pleasure known.
I'm here, though I swore not to be, and bring
this girl. We caught her burying the dead.
This time we didn't need to shake the lots;
mine was the luck, all mine.
So now, lord, take her, you, and question her
and prove her as you will. But I am free.
And I deserve full clearance on this charge.

CREON. Explain the circumstance of the arrest.

GUARD. She was burying the man. You have it all.

CREON. Is this the truth? And do you grasp its meaning?

GUARD. I saw her burying the very corpse
you had forbidden. Is this adequate?

CREON. How was she caught and taken in the act?

GUARD. It was like this: when we got back again
struck with those dreadful threatenings of yours,
we swept away the dust that hid the corpse.
We stripped it back to slimy nakedness.
And then we sat to windward on the hill

23. ***When he honors . . . dwell with dishonor.*** When he honors the gods they will reward him, but when he disregards their laws, he will be punished.

24. ***Not by my fire . . . who does these things.*** A man who does not honor the gods will never be welcome in my home.

so as to dodge the smell.
We poked each other up with growling threats
if anyone was careless of his work.
For some time this went on, till it was noon.
The sun was high and hot. Then from the earth
up rose a dusty whirlwind to the sky,
filling the plain, smearing the forest-leaves,
clogging the upper air. We shut our eyes,
sat and endured the plague the gods had sent.
So the storm left us after a long time.
We saw the girl. She cried the sharp and shrill
cry of a bitter bird which sees the nest
bare where the young birds lay.
So this same girl, seeing the body stripped,
cried with great groanings, cried a dreadful curse
upon the people who had done the deed.
Soon in her hands she brought the thirsty dust,
and holding high a pitcher of wrought bronze
she poured the three libations[25] for the dead.
We saw this and surged down. We trapped her fast;
and she was calm. We taxed her with the deeds
both past and present. Nothing was denied.
And I was glad, and yet I took it hard.
One's own escape from trouble makes one glad;
but bringing friends to trouble is hard grief.
Still, I care less for all these second thoughts
than for the fact that I myself am safe.

CREON. You there, whose head is drooping to the ground,
do you admit this, or deny you did it?

ANTIGONE. I say I did it and I don't deny it.

CREON (*to the* GUARD). Take yourself off wherever you
wish to go
free of a heavy charge.

CREON (*to* ANTIGONE). You—tell me not at length but
in a word.
You knew the order not to do this thing?

ANTIGONE. I knew, of course I knew. The word was plain.

CREON. And still you dared to overstep these laws?

ANTIGONE. For me it was not Zeus who made that order.
Nor did that Justice who lives with the gods below
mark out such laws to hold among mankind.
Nor did I think your orders were so strong
that you, a mortal man, could over-run
the gods' unwritten and unfailing laws.
Not now, nor yesterday's, they always live,
and no one knows their origin in time.
So not through fear of any man's proud spirit
would I be likely to neglect these laws,

25. ***three libations,*** pouring of wi
or water; an offering to the go
usually on behalf of the dead.

draw on myself the gods' sure punishment.
I knew that I must die; how could I not?
even without your warning. If I die
before my time, I say it is a gain.
Who lives in sorrows many as are mine
how shall he not be glad to gain his death?
And so, for me to meet this fate, no grief.
But if I left that corpse, my mother's son,
dead and unburied I'd have cause to grieve
as now I grieve not.
And if you think my acts are foolishness
the foolishness may be in a fool's eye.
CHORUS. The girl is bitter. She's her father's child.
She cannot yield to trouble; nor could he.
CREON. These rigid spirits are the first to fall.
The strongest iron, hardened in the fire,
most often ends in scraps and shatterings.
Small curbs bring raging horses back to terms.
Slave to his neighbor, who can think of pride?
This girl was expert in her insolence
when she broke bounds beyond established law.
Once she had done it, insolence the second,
to boast her doing, and to laugh in it.
I am no man and she the man instead
if she can have this conquest without pain.
She is my sister's child, but were she child
of closer kin than any at my hearth,
she and her sister should not so escape
their death and doom. I charge Ismene too.
She shared the planning of this burial.
Call her outside. I saw her in the house,
maddened, no longer mistress of herself.
The sly intent betrays itself sometimes
before the secret plotters work their wrong.
I hate it too when someone caught in crime
then wants to make it seem a lovely thing.
ANTIGONE. Do you want more than my arrest and death?
CREON. No more than that. For that is all I need.
ANTIGONE. Why are you waiting? Nothing that you say
fits with my thought. I pray it never will.
Nor will you ever like to hear my words.
And yet what greater glory could I find
than giving my own brother funeral?
All these would say that they approved my act
did fear not mute them.
(A king is fortunate in many ways,
and most, that he can act and speak at will.)
CREON. None of these others see the case this way.

ANTIGONE. They see, and do not say. You have them cowed.
CREON. And you are not ashamed to think alone?
ANTIGONE. No, I am not ashamed. When was it shame
to serve the children of my mother's womb?
CREON. It was not your brother who died against him, then?
ANTIGONE. Full brother, on both sides, my parents' child.
CREON. Your act of grace, in his regard, is crime.
ANTIGONE. The corpse below would never say it was.
CREON. When you honor him and the criminal just alike?
ANTIGONE. It was a brother, not a slave, who died.
CREON. Died to destroy this land the other guarded.
ANTIGONE. Death yearns for equal law for all the dead.
CREON. Not that the good and bad draw equal shares.
ANTIGONE. Who knows that this is holiness below?
CREON. Never the enemy, even in death, a friend.
ANTIGONE. I cannot share in hatred, but in love.
CREON. Then go down there, if you must love, and love
the dead. No woman rules me while I live.

(ISMENE *is brought from the palace under guard.*)

CHORUS. Look there! Ismene is coming out.
She loves her sister and mourns,
with clouded brow and bloodied cheeks,
tears on her lovely face.
CREON. You, lurking like a viper in the house,
who sucked me dry. I looked the other way
while twin destruction planned against the throne.
Now tell me, do you say you shared this deed?
Or will you swear you didn't even know?
ISMENE. I did the deed, if she agrees I did.
I am accessory and share the blame.
ANTIGONE. Justice will not allow this. You did not
wish for a part, nor did I give you one.
ISMENE. You are in trouble, and I'm not ashamed
to sail beside you into suffering.
ANTIGONE. Death and the dead, they know whose act it was.
I cannot love a friend whose love is words.
ISMENE. Sister, I pray, don't fence me out from honor,
from death with you, and honor done the dead.
ANTIGONE. Don't die along with me, nor make your own
that which you did not do. My death's enough.
ISMENE. When you are gone what life can be my friend?
ANTIGONE. Love Creon. He's your kinsman and your care.
ISMENE. Why hurt me, when it does yourself no good?
ANTIGONE. I also suffer, when I laugh at you.

ISMENE. What further service can I do you now?
ANTIGONE. To save yourself. I shall not envy you.
ISMENE. Alas for me. Am I outside your fate?
ANTIGONE. Yes. For you chose to live when I chose death.
ISMENE. At least I was not silent. You were warned.
ANTIGONE. Some will have thought you wiser. Some
will not.
ISMENE. And yet the blame is equal for us both.
ANTIGONE. Take heart. You live. My life died long ago.
And that has made me fit to help the dead.
CREON. One of these girls has shown her lack of sense
just now. The other had it from her birth.
ISMENE. Yes, lord. When people fall in deep distress
their native sense departs, and will not stay.
CREON. You chose your mind's distraction when you chose
to work out wickedness with this wicked girl.
ISMENE. What life is there for me to live without her?
CREON. Don't speak of her. For she is here no more.
ISMENE. But will you kill your own son's promised bride?
CREON. Oh, there are other furrows for his plough.
ISMENE. But where the closeness that has bound
these two?
CREON. Not for my sons will I choose wicked wives.
ISMENE. Dear Haemon, your father robs you of your
rights.
CREON. You and your marriage trouble me too much.
ISMENE. You will take away his bride from your own son?
CREON. Yes. Death will help me break this marriage off.
CHORUS. It seems determined that the girl must die.
CREON. You helped determine it. Now, no delay!
Slaves, take them in. They must be women now.[26]
No more free running.
Even the bold will fly when they see Death
drawing in close enough to end their life.
(ANTIGONE *and* ISMENE *are taken inside.*)
CHORUS. Fortunate they whose lives have no taste of pain.
For those whose house is shaken by the gods
escape no kind of doom. It extends to all the kin
like the wave that comes when the winds of Thrace[27]
run over the dark of the sea.
The black sand of the bottom is brought from the
depth;
the beaten capes sound back with a hollow cry.

Ancient the sorrow of Labdacus' house,[28] I know.
Dead men's grief comes back, and falls on grief.
No generation can free the next.
One of the gods will strike. There is no escape.

26. ***They must be women now.*** They are now prisoners and lose their aristocratic rank.

27. ***Thrace*** (thrās), a country to the northeast of Greece; today the northern part of Turkey.

28. ***Labdacus'*** (lab'də kəs) ***house,*** the ruling family of Thebes. Labdacus was the grandfather of Oedipus.

So now the light goes out
for the house of Oedipus, while the bloody knife
cuts the remaining root. Folly and Fury have done this.
What madness of man, O Zeus, can bind your power?
Not sleep can destroy it who ages all,
nor the weariless months the gods have set. Unaged
in time
monarch you rule of Olympus' gleaming light.
Near time, far future, and the past,
one law controls them all:
any greatness in human life brings doom.

Wandering hope brings help to many men.
But others she tricks from their giddy loves,
and her quarry knows nothing until he has walked
into flame.
Word of wisdom it was when someone said,
"The bad becomes the good
to him a god would doom."
Only briefly is that one from under doom.[29]

29. The bad . . . from under doom. When any man convinces himself that the evil he is doing is good, he will be doomed even more quickly. The Chorus makes this statement about Creon.

HAEMON *enters from the side.*

Here is your one surviving son.
Does he come in grief at the fate of his bride,
in pain that he's tricked of his wedding?

CREON. Soon we shall know more than a seer could
tell us.
Son, have you heard the vote condemned your bride?
And are you here, maddened against your father,
or are we friends, whatever I may do?

HAEMON. My father, I am yours. You keep me straight
with your good judgment, which I shall ever follow.
Nor shall a marriage count for more with me
than your kind leading.

CREON. There's my good boy. So should you hold at heart
and stand behind your father all the way.
It is for this men pray they may beget
households of dutiful obedient sons,
who share alike in punishing enemies,
and give due honor to their father's friends.
Whoever breeds a child that will not help
what has he sown but trouble for himself,
and for his enemies laughter full and free?
Son, do not let your lust mislead your mind,
all for a woman's sake, for well you know
how cold the thing he takes into his arms
who has a wicked woman for his wife.
What deeper wounding than a friend no friend?

Oh spit her forth forever, as your foe.
Let the girl marry somebody in Hades.
Since I have caught her in the open act,
the only one in town who disobeyed,
I shall not now proclaim myself a liar,
but kill her. Let her sing her song of Zeus
who guards the kindred.
If I allow disorder in my house
I'd surely have to licence it abroad.
A man who deals in fairness with his own,
he can make manifest justice in the state.
But he who crosses law, or forces it,
or hopes to bring the rulers under him,
shall never have a word of praise from me.
The man the state has put in place must have
obedient hearing to his least command
when it is right, and even when it's not.
He who accepts this teaching I can trust,
ruler, or ruled, to function in his place,
to stand his ground even in the storm of spears,
a mate to trust in battle at one's side.
There is no greater wrong than disobedience.
This ruins cities, this tears down our homes,
this breaks the battle-front in panic-rout.
If men live decently it is because
discipline saves their very lives for them.
So I must guard the men who yield to order,
not let myself be beaten by a woman.
Better, if it must happen, that a man
should overset me.
I won't be called weaker than womankind.

CHORUS. We think—unless our age is cheating us—
that what you say is sensible and right.

HAEMON. Father, the gods have given men good sense,
the only sure possession that we have.
I couldn't find the words in which to claim
that there was error in your late remarks.
Yet someone else might bring some further light.
Because I am your son I must keep watch
on all men's doing where it touches you,
their speech, and most of all, their discontents.
Your presence frightens any common man
from saying things you would not care to hear.
But in dark corners I have heard them say
how the whole town is grieving for this girl,
unjustly doomed, if ever woman was,
to die in shame for glorious action done.
She would not leave her fallen, slaughtered brother

there, as he lay, unburied, for the birds
and hungry dogs to make an end of him.
Isn't her real desert a golden prize?[30]
This is the undercover speech in town.
Father, your welfare is my greatest good.
What loveliness in life for any child
outweighs a father's fortune and good fame?
And so a father feels his children's faring.
Then, do not have one mind, and one alone
that only your opinion can be right.
Whoever thinks that he alone is wise,
his eloquence, his mind, above the rest,
come the unfolding, shows his emptiness.
A man, though wise, should never be ashamed
of learning more, and must unbend his mind.
Have you not seen the trees beside the torrent,
the ones that bend them saving every leaf,
while the resistant perish root and branch?
And so the ship that will not slacken sail,
the sheet drawn tight, unyielding, overturns.
She ends the voyage with her keel on top.
No, yield your wrath, allow a change of stand.
Young as I am, if I may give advice,
I'd say it would be best if men were born
perfect in wisdom, but that failing this
(which often fails) it can be no dishonor
to learn from others when they speak good sense.

30. ***Isn't her real desert a golde[n] prize?*** Doesn't she really deserve [a] golden prize rather than punishment[?]

CHORUS. Lord, if your son has spoken to the point
you should take his lesson. He should do the same.
Both sides have spoken well.
CREON. At my age I'm to school my mind by his?
This boy instructor is my master, then?
HAEMON. I urge no wrong. I'm young, but you should watch
my actions, not my years, to judge of me.
CREON. A loyal action, to respect disorder?
HAEMON. I wouldn't urge respect for wickedness.
CREON. You don't think she is sick with that disease?
HAEMON. Your fellow-citizens maintain she's not.
CREON. Is the town to tell me how I ought to rule?
HAEMON. Now there you speak just like a boy yourself.
CREON. Am I to rule by other mind than mine?
HAEMON. No city is property of a single man.
CREON. But custom gives possession to the ruler.
HAEMON. You'd rule a desert beautifully alone.
CREON. (*to the* CHORUS). It seems he's firmly on the woman's side.
HAEMON. If you're a woman. It is you I care for.

CREON. Wicked, to try conclusions with your father.
HAEMON. When you conclude unjustly, so I must.
CREON. Am I unjust, when I respect my office?
HAEMON. You tread down the gods' due. Respect is gone.
CREON. Your mind is poisoned. Weaker than a woman!
HAEMON. At least you'll never see me yield to shame.
CREON. Your whole long argument is but for her.
HAEMON. And you, and me, and for the gods below.
CREON. You shall not marry her while she's alive.
HAEMON. Then she shall die. Her death will bring another.
CREON. Your boldness has made progress. Threats, indeed!
HAEMON. No threat, to speak against your empty plan.
CREON. Past due, sharp lessons for your empty brain.
HAEMON. If you weren't father, I should call you mad.
CREON. Don't flatter me with "father," you woman's slave.
HAEMON. You wish to speak but never wish to hear.
CREON. You think so? By Olympus, you shall not
revile me with these tauntings and go free.
Bring out the hateful creature; she shall die
full in his sight, close at her bridegroom's side.
HAEMON. Not at my side her death, and you will not
ever lay eyes upon my face again.
Find other friends to rave with after this.

(HAEMON *leaves, by one of the side entrances.*)

CHORUS. Lord, he has gone with all the speed of rage.
When such a man is grieved his mind is hard.
CREON. Oh, let him go, plan superhuman action.
In any case the girls shall not escape.
CHORUS. You plan for both the punishment of death?
CREON. Not her who did not do it. You are right.
CHORUS. And what death have you chosen for the other?
CREON. To take her where the foot of man comes not.
There shall I hide her in a hollowed cave
living, and leave her just so much to eat
as clears the city from the guilt of death.[31]
There, if she prays to Death, the only god
of her respect, she may manage not to die.
Or she may learn at last and even then
how much too much her labor for the dead.

(CREON *returns to the palace.*)

CHORUS. Love unconquered in fight, love who falls on our havings.[32]
You rest in the bloom of a girl's unwithered face.
You cross the sea, you are known in the wildest lairs.
Not the immortal gods can fly,
nor men of a day. Who has you within him is mad.

31. leave her . . . the guilt of death. Creon means that, since Antigone will die by suffocation, the gods will not hold him and his people responsible for her death.

32. Love unconquered . . . on our havings. In this speech of the Chorus, they state that love is all powerful, conquers rich and poor, just and unjust.

You twist the minds of the just. Wrong they pursue
and are ruined.
You made this quarrel of kindred before us now.
Desire looks clear from the eyes of a lovely bride:
power as strong as the founded world.
For there is the goddess at play with whom no man
can fight.

(ANTIGONE *is brought from the palace under guard.)*

Now I am carried beyond all bounds.
My tears will not be checked.
I see Antigone depart
to the chamber where all men sleep.

ANTIGONE. Men of my fathers' land, you see me go
my last journey. My last sight of the sun,
then never again. Death who brings all to sleep
takes me alive to the shore
of the river underground.[33]
Not for me was the marriage-hymn, nor will anyone
start the song
at a wedding of mine. Acheron[34] is my mate.

33. ***river underground,*** the River Styx.

34. ***Acheron*** (ak'ər on), a river in the underworld; the River of Woe.

CHORUS. With praise as your portion you go
in fame to the vault of the dead.
Untouched by wasting disease,
not paying the price of the sword,
of your own motion you go.
Alone among mortals will you descend
in life to the house of Death.

ANTIGONE. Pitiful was the death that stranger died,
our queen once, Tantalus' daughter.[35] The rock
it covered her over, like stubborn ivy it grew.
Still, as she wastes, the rain
and snow companion her.
Pouring down from her mourning eyes comes the
water that soaks the stone.
My own putting to sleep a god has planned like hers.

35. ***Tantalus' daughter,*** Niobe (nī'ō-bē), whose children were slain by the gods to punish her for her excessive pride. Overcome with grief, she turned into a stone from which tears continued to flow.

CHORUS. God's child and god she was.
We are born to death.
Yet even in death you will have your fame,
to have gone like a god to your fate,
in living and dying alike.

ANTIGONE. Laughter against me now.[36] In the name of our
fathers' gods,
could you not wait till I went? Must affront be thrown
in my face?
O city of wealthy men.
I call upon Dirce's spring,
I call upon Thebe's grove in the armored plain,
to be my witnesses, how with no friend's mourning,

36. ***Laughter against me now.*** Antigone mistakenly thinks that the Chorus, in comparing her to the gods, is making fun of her.

by what decree I go to the fresh-made prison-tomb.
Alive to the place of corpses, an alien still,
never at home with the living nor with the dead.

CHORUS. You went to the furthest verge
of daring, but there you found
the high foundation of justice, and fell.
Perhaps you are paying your father's pain.

ANTIGONE. You speak of my darkest thought, my pitiful father's fame,
spread through all the world, and the doom that haunts our house,
the royal house of Thebes.
My mother's marriage-bed.
Destruction where she lay with her husband-son,
my father. These are my parents and I their child.
I go to stay with them. My curse is to die unwed.
My brother, you found your fate when you found your bride,
found it for me as well. Dead, you destroy my life.

CHORUS. You showed respect for the dead.
So we for you: but power
is not to be thwarted so.
Your self-sufficiency has brought you down.

ANTIGONE. Unwept, no wedding-song, unfriended, now I go
the road laid down for me.
No longer shall I see this holy light of the sun.
No friend to bewail my fate.

CREON *enters from the palace.*

CREON. When people sing the dirge for their own deaths
ahead of time, nothing will break them off
if they can hope that this will buy delay.
Take her away at once, and open up
the tomb I spoke of. Leave her there alone.
There let her choose: death, or a buried life.
No stain of guilt upon us in this case,
but she is exiled from our life on earth.

ANTIGONE. O tomb, O marriage-chamber, hollowed out
house that will watch forever, where I go.
To my own people, who are mostly there;
Persephone has taken them to her.
Last of them all, ill-fated past the rest,
shall I descend, before my course is run.
Still when I get there I may hope to find
I come as a dear friend to my dear father,
to you, my mother, and my brother too.

ROTH

All three of you have known my hand in death.
I washed your bodies, dressed them for the grave,
poured out the last libation at the tomb.
Last, Polyneices knows the price I pay
for doing final service to his corpse.
And yet the wise will know my choice was right.
Had I had children or their father dead,
I'd let them moulder. I should not have chosen
in such a case to cross the state's decree.
What is the law that lies behind these words?
One husband gone, I might have found another,
or a child from a new man in first child's place,
but with my parents hid away in death,
no brother, ever, could spring up for me.
Such was the law by which I honored you.
But Creon thought the doing was a crime,
a dreadful daring, brother of my heart.
So now he takes and leads me out by force.
No marriage-bed, no marriage-song for me,
and since no wedding, so no child to rear.
I go, without a friend, struck down by fate,
live to the hollow chambers of the dead.
What divine justice have I disobeyed?
Why, in my misery, look to the gods for help?
Can I call any of them my ally?
I stand convicted of impiety,
the evidence my pious duty done.
Should the gods think that this is righteousness,
in suffering I'll see my error clear.
But if it is the others who are wrong
I wish them no greater punishment than mine.

CHORUS. The same tempest of mind
as ever, controls the girl.

CREON. Therefore her guards shall regret
the slowness with which they move.

ANTIGONE. That word comes close to death.

CREON. You are perfectly right in that.

ANTIGONE. O town of my fathers in Thebe's land,
O gods of our house.
I am led away at last.
Look, leaders of Thebes,
I am last of your royal line.
Look what I suffer, at whose command,
because I respected the right.

(ANTIGONE *is led away. The slow procession should begin during the preceding passage.*)

CHORUS. Danaë[37] suffered too.
She went from the light to the brass-built room,

37. Danaë, the mother of Perseus, who was shut up in a bronze chamber by her father when he learned from Apollo's priestess that her son would someday kill him.

chamber and tomb together. Like you, poor child,
she was of great descent, and more, she held and kept
the seed of the golden rain which was Zeus.[38]
Fate has terrible power.
You cannot escape it by wealth or war.
No fort will keep it out, no ships outrun it.

38. seed . . . was Zeus. Zeus came to her as a golden rain. From their union, Perseus was born.

Remember the angry king,
son of Dryas,[39] who raged at the god and paid,
pent in a rock-walled prison. His bursting wrath
slowly went down. As the terror of madness went,
he learned of his frenzied attack on the god.
Fool, he had tried to stop
the dancing women possessed of god,
the fire of Dionysus, the songs and flutes.

39. son of Dryas (drī'əs), Lycurgus (lī kėr'gəs), a Greek king who had opposed the worship of Dionysus and who was driven insane by the god to punish him for his sacrilege.

Where the dark rocks divide
sea from sea in Thrace
is Salmydessus whose savage god[40]
beheld the terrible blinding wounds
dealt to Phineus' sons by their father's wife.[41]
Dark the eyes that looked to avenge their mother.
Sharp with her shuttle she struck, and blooded her
hands.

40. savage god, Mars, whose birthplace was said to have been in Thrace.

41. terrible blinding wounds . . . their father's wife. Idaea, the second wife of King Phineus of Salmydessus (a Thracian city on the Black Sea), was jealous of the two sons of his former wife and blinded them with her weaving needle.

Wasting they wept their fate,
settled when they were born
to Cleopatra,[42] unhappy queen.
She was a princess too, of an ancient house,
reared in the cave of the wild north wind, her father.
Half a goddess but, child, she suffered like you.

42. Cleopatra, the daughter of Boreas, the north wind, and the first wife of Phineus.

Enter, from the side TEIRESIAS, *the blind prophet, led by a* BOY ATTENDANT.

TEIRESIAS. Elders of Thebes, we two have come one road,
two of us looking through one pair of eyes.
This is the way of walking for the blind.
CREON. Teiresias, what news has brought you here?
TEIRESIAS. I'll tell you. You in turn must trust the
prophet.
CREON. I've always been attentive to your counsel.
TEIRESIAS. And therefore you have steered this city
straight.
CREON. So I can say how helpful you have been.
TEIRESIAS. But now you are balanced on a razor's edge.
CREON. What is it? How I shudder at your words!
TEIRESIAS. You'll know, when you hear the signs that
I have marked.

I sat where every bird of heaven comes
in my old place of augury, and heard
bird-cries I'd never known.[43] They screeched about
goaded by madness, inarticulate.
I marked that they were tearing one another
with claws of murder. I could hear the wing-beats.
I was afraid, so straight away I tried
burnt sacrifice upon the flaming altar.
No fire caught my offerings. Slimy ooze
dripped on the ashes, smoked and sputtered there.
Gall burst its bladder, vanished into vapor;
the fat dripped from the bones and would not burn.
These are the omens of the rites that failed,
as my boy here has told me. He's my guide
as I am guide to others.
Why has this sickness struck against the state?
Through your decision.
All of the altars of the town are choked
with leavings of the dogs and birds; their feast
was on that fated, fallen Polyneices.
So the gods will have no offering from us,
not prayer, nor flame of sacrifice. The birds
will not cry out a sound I can distinguish,
gorged with the greasy blood of that dead man.
Think of these things, my son. All men may err
but error once committed, he's no fool
nor yet unfortunate, who gives up his stiffness
and cures the trouble he has fallen in.
Stubbornness and stupidity are twins.
Yield to the dead. Why goad him where he lies?
What use to kill the dead a second time?
I speak for your own good. And I am right.
Learning from a wise counsellor is not pain
if what he speaks are profitable words.

CREON. Old man, you all, like bowmen at a mark,
have bent your bows at me. I've had my share
of seers. I've been an item in your accounts.
Make profit, trade in Lydian silver-gold,
pure gold of India; that's your chief desire.
But you will never cover up that corpse.[44]
Not if the very eagles tear their food
from him, and leave it at the throne of Zeus.
I wouldn't give him up for burial
in fear of that pollution. For I know
no mortal being can pollute the gods.
O old Teiresias, human beings fall;
the clever ones the furthest, when they plead
a shameful case so well in hope of profit.

43. heard bird-cries I'd never known. The prophet Teiresias was able to interpret the calls of birds and received his prophecies from them.

44. Make profit . . . cover up that corpse. All of the gold of India is not enough to pay for Polyneices' burial.

TEIRESIAS. Alas!
What man can tell me, has he thought at all . . .
CREON. What hackneyed saw is coming from your lips?
TEIRESIAS. How better than all wealth is sound good counsel.
CREON. And so is folly worse than anything.
TEIRESIAS. And you're infected with that same disease.
CREON. I'm reluctant to be uncivil to a seer . . .
TEIRESIAS. You're that already. You have said I lie.
CREON. Well, the whole crew of seers are money-mad.
TEIRESIAS. And the whole tribe of tyrants grab at gain.
CREON. Do you realize you are talking to a king?
TEIRESIAS. I know. Who helped you save this town you hold?
CREON. You're a wise seer, but you love wickedness.
TEIRESIAS. You'll bring me to speak the unspeakable, very soon.
CREON. Well, speak it out. But do not speak for profit.
TEIRESIAS. No, there's no profit in my words for you.
CREON. You'd better realise that you can't deliver
my mind, if you should sell it, to the buyer.
TEIRESIAS. Know well, the sun will not have rolled its course
many more days, before you come to give
corpse for these corpses, child of your own loins.
For you've confused the upper and lower worlds.
You sent a life to settle in a tomb;
you keep up here that which belongs below
the corpse unburied, robbed of its release.
Not you, nor any god that rules on high
can claim him now.
You rob the nether gods of what is theirs.
So the pursuing horrors lie in wait
to track you down. The Furies sent by Hades
and by all gods will even you with your victims.
Now say that I am bribed! At no far time
shall men and women wail within your house.
And all the cities that you fought in war
whose sons had burial from wild beasts, or dogs,
or birds that brought the stench of your great wrong
back to each hearth, they move against you now.[45]
A bowman, as you said, I send my shafts,
now you have moved me, straight. You'll feel the wound.
Boy, take me home now. Let him spend his rage
on younger men, and learn to calm his tongue,
and keep a better mind than now he does.

(Exit.)

45. all the cities . . . move against you now. This prophecy of Teiresias later came true when the families of the slain Argive chiefs enlisted the aid of the Athenian king, Theseus, to obtain burial rites for their dead. The Athenian army marched against Thebes and conquered it.

CHORUS. Lord, he has gone. Terrible prophecies!
And since the time when I first grew grey hair
his sayings to the city have been true.
CREON. I also know this. And my mind is torn.
To yield is dreadful. But to stand against him.
Dreadful to strike my spirit to destruction.
CHORUS. Now you must come to counsel, and take advice.
CREON. What must I do? Speak, and I shall obey.
CHORUS. Go free the maiden from that rocky house.
Bury the dead who lies in readiness.
CREON. This is your counsel? You would have me yield?
CHORUS. Quick as you can. The gods move very fast
when they bring ruin on misguided men.
CREON. How hard, abandonment of my desire.
But I can fight necessity no more.
CHORUS. Do it yourself. Leave it to no one else.
CREON. I'll go at once. Come, followers, to your work.
You that are here round up the other fellows.
Take axes with you, hurry to that place
that overlooks us.
Now my decision has been overturned
shall I, who bound her, set her free myself.
I've come to fear it's best to hold the laws
of old tradition to the end of life.

(Exit.)

CHORUS. God of the many names,[46] Semele's golden child,
child of Olympian thunder, Italy's lord.
Lord of Eleusis, where all men come
to mother Demeter's plain.
Bacchus, who dwells in Thebes,
by Ismenus' running water,
where wild Bacchic women are at home,
on the soil of the dragon seed.[47]

Seen in the glaring flame, high on the double mount,
with the nymphs of Parnassus[48] at play on the hill,
seen by Kastalia's flowing stream.[49]
You come from the ivied heights,
from green Euboea's shore.[50]
In immortal words we cry
your name, lord, who watch the ways,
the many ways of Thebes.

This is your city, honored beyond the rest,
the town of your mother's miracle-death.[51]
Now, as we wrestle our grim disease,
come with healing step from Parnassus' slope
or over the moaning sea.

46. God of the many names. This and the following descriptions refer to Dionysus. The expression "Lord of Eleusis" refers to the mysterious religious rites which were held at the temple of Eleusis (ē lü'səs) to honor Dionysus and Ceres (Demeter).

47. on the soil of the dragon seed. Cadmus, the founder of Thebes, sowed dragon's teeth in the soil from which sprang men who helped him build the city.

48. Parnassus (pär nas'əs), one of the three mountains frequented by the Muses.

49. Kastalia's flowing stream. Kastalia (Castalia) was a spring near Thebes sacred to Ares.

50. Euboea's (ū bē'ə) ***shore,*** an island in the Aegean Sea just off the Greek mainland.

51. your mother's miracle-death. Zeus had promised Semele (sem'ə lē), Dionysus' mother, that he would grant her one wish. When she requested to see him in all his glory as the King of gods and men, Zeus reluctantly carried out his oath, knowing that the sight would cause her death.

Leader in dance of the fire-pulsing stars,
overseer of the voices of night,
child of Zeus, be manifest,
with due companionship of Maenad maids[52]
whose cry is but your name.

Enter one of those who left with CREON, *as* MESSENGER.

MESSENGER. Neighbors of Cadmus, and Amphion's[53]
house,
there is no kind of state in human life
which I now dare to envy or to blame.
Luck sets it straight, and luck she overturns
the happy or unhappy day by day.
No prophecy can deal with men's affairs.
Creon was envied once, as I believe,
for having saved this city from its foes
and having got full power in this land.
He steered it well. And he had noble sons.
Now everything is gone.
Yes, when a man has lost all happiness,
he's not alive. Call him a breathing corpse.
Be very rich at home. Live as a king.
But once your joy has gone, though these are left
they are smoke's shadow to lost happiness.

CHORUS. What is the grief of princes that you bring?
MESSENGER. They're dead. The living are responsible.
CHORUS. Who died? Who did the murder? Tell us now.
MESSENGER. Haemon is gone. One of his kin drew blood.
CHORUS. But whose arm struck? His father's or his own?
MESSENGER. He killed himself. His blood is on his father.
CHORUS. Seer, all too true the prophecy you told!
MESSENGER. This is the state of things. Now make
your plans.

Enter, from the palace, EURYDICE.

CHORUS. Eurydice is with us now, I see.
Creon's poor wife. She may have come by chance.
She may have heard something about her son.

EURYDICE. I heard your talk as I was coming out
to greet the goddess Pallas[54] with my prayer.
And as I moved the bolts that held the door
I heard of my own sorrow.
I fell back fainting in my women's arms.
But say again just what the news you bring.
I, whom you speak to, have known grief before.[55]

MESSENGER. Dear lady, I was there, and I shall tell,
leaving out nothing of the true account.
Why should I make it soft for you with tales

52. ***Maenad maids,*** women made mad with wine or the power of Dionysus.

53. ***Amphion,*** husband of Niobe.

54. ***Pallas*** (pal′əs), Athene.

55. ***I . . . have known grief before.*** The older son of Creon and Eurydice had been killed at the beginning of the war.

to prove myself a liar? Truth is right.
I followed your husband to the plain's far edge,
where Polyneices' corpse was lying still
unpitied. The dogs had torn him all apart.
We prayed the goddess of all journeyings,[56]
and Pluto, that they turn their wrath to kindness,
we gave the final purifying bath,
then burned the poor remains on new-cut boughs,
and heaped a high mound of his native earth.
Then turned we to the maiden's rocky bed,
death's hollow marriage-chamber.
But, still far off, one of us heard a voice
in keen lament by that unblest abode.
He ran and told the master. As Creon came
he heard confusion crying. He groaned and spoke:
"Am I a prophet now, and do I tread
the saddest of all roads I ever trod?
My son's voice crying! Servants, run up close,
stand by the tomb and look, push through the crevice
where we built the pile of rock, right to the entry.
Find out if that is Haemon's voice I hear
or if the gods are tricking me indeed."
We obeyed the order of our mournful master.
In the far corner of the tomb we saw
her, hanging by the neck, caught in a noose
of her own linen veiling.
Haemon embraced her as she hung, and mourned
his bride's destruction, dead and gone below,
his father's actions, the unfated marriage.
When Creon saw him, he groaned terribly,
and went toward him, and called him with lament:
"What have you done, what plan have you caught up,
what sort of suffering is killing you?
Come out, my child, I do beseech you, come!"
The boy looked at him with his angry eyes,
spat in his face and spoke no further word.
He drew his sword, but as his father ran,
he missed his aim. Then the unhappy boy,
in anger at himself, leant on the blade.
It entered, half its length, into his side.
While he was conscious he embraced the maiden,
holding her gently. Last, he gasped out blood,
red blood on her white cheek.
Corpse on a corpse he lies. He found his marriage.
Its celebration in the halls of Hades.
So he has made it very clear to men
that to reject good counsel is a crime.

(EURYDICE *returns to the house.*)

56. goddess of all journeyings, Hecate (hek'ə ti), goddess of the crossways. Artemis or Diana is frequently associated with her.

CHORUS. What do you make of this? The queen has gone
in silence. We know nothing of her mind.
MESSENGER. I wonder at her, too. But we can hope
that she has gone to mourn her son within
with her own women, not before the town.
She knows discretion. She will do no wrong.
CHORUS. I am not sure. This muteness may portend
as great disaster as a loud lament.
MESSENGER. I will go in and see if some deep plan
hides in her heart's wild pain. You may be right.
There can be heavy danger in mute grief.
(The MESSENGER *goes into the house.)*

CREON *enters with his followers. They*
are carrying HAEMON'S *body on a bier.*

CHORUS. But look, the king draws near.
His own hand brings
the witness of his crime,
the doom he brought on himself.
CREON. O crimes of my wicked heart,
harshness bringing death.
You see the killer, you see the kin he killed.
My planning was all unblest.
Son, you have died too soon.
Oh, you have gone away
through my fault, not your own.
CHORUS. You have learned justice, though it comes
too late.
CREON. Yes, I have learned in sorrow. It was a god who
struck,
who has weighted my head with disaster; he drove me
to wild strange ways,
his heavy heel on my joy.
Oh sorrows, sorrows of men.

(Re-enter the MESSENGER, *from*
a side door of the palace.)

MESSENGER. Master, you hold one sorrow in your hands
but you have more, stored up inside the house.
CREON. What further suffering can come on me?
MESSENGER. Your wife has died. The dead man's mother
in deed,
poor soul, her wounds are fresh.
CREON. Hades, harbor of all,
you have destroyed me now.
Terrible news to hear, horror the tale you tell.
I was dead, and you kill me again.
Boy, did I hear you right?

ROTH

Did you say the queen was dead,
slaughter on slaughter heaped?

(The central doors of the palace begin to open.)

CHORUS. Now you can see. Concealment is all over.

(The doors are open, and the corpse of EURYDICE *is revealed.)*

CREON. My second sorrow is here. Surely no fate remains
which can strike me again. Just now, I held my son
in my arms.
And now I see her dead.
Woe for the mother and son.

MESSENGER. There, by the altar, dying on the sword,
her eyes fell shut. She wept her older son
who died before, and this one. Last of all
she cursed you as the killer of her children.

CREON. I am mad with fear. Will no one strike
and kill me with cutting sword?
Sorrowful, soaked in sorrow to the bone!

MESSENGER. Yes, for she held you guilty in the death
of him before you, and the elder dead.

CREON. How did she die?

MESSENGER. Struck home at her own heart
when she had heard of Haemon's suffering.

CREON. This is my guilt, all mine. I killed you, I say it
clear.
Servants, take me away, out of the sight of men.
I who am nothing more than nothing now.

CHORUS. Your plan is good—if any good is left.
Best to cut short our sorrow.

CREON. Let me go, let me go. May death come quick,
bringing my final day.
O let me never see tomorrow's dawn.

CHORUS. That is the future's. We must look to now.
What will be is in other hands than ours.

CREON. All my desire was in that prayer of mine.

CHORUS. Pray not again. No mortal can escape
the doom prepared for him.

CREON. Take me away at once, the frantic man who killed
my son, against my meaning. I cannot rest.
My life is warped past cure. My fate has struck me
down.

*(*CREON *and his* ATTENDANTS *enter the house.)*

CHORUS. Our happiness depends
on wisdom all the way.
The gods must have their due.
Great words by men of pride
bring greater blows upon them.
So wisdom comes to the old.

WHAT DO YOU SAY?

1. (a) What was the conflict between Eteocles and Polyneices? *(b)* Who revealed it during the course of the play? *(c)* Which characters in the play does this conflict affect directly and which characters does it affect indirectly?

2. On one level, this play is a personal contest between Creon and Antigone, but their opposition also represents a basic conflict between the law of the state and the law of individual conscience. Which actions of Creon and Antigone illustrate this conflict?

3. (a) What was the attitude of Ismene toward Antigone? *(b)* Was the rôle of Ismene vital to the plot? *(c)* In what way does the characterization of Ismene contribute to the dramatic picture of Antigone?

4. (a) Who was Teiresias? *(b)* What was his function in the play?

5. What vital part does the Messenger have in this tragedy?

6. (a) How long is the time span of this play? *(b)* Is the action continuous, or is it interrupted by lapses of time? *(c)* Does the action take place in more than one setting? *(d)* How does the audience find out what happens "off stage," that is, in another location? What particular actions in *Antigone* are handled in this way?

7. Discuss the good and bad qualities of Creon as a father and Haemon as a son. Use specific references from the play.

8. (a) Was Creon basically an evil man? What was his tragic flaw? Explain. *(b)* Why must Creon be described as the tragic figure in this play rather than Antigone?

9. (a) At what point does the chorus sympathize with Creon? With Antigone? *(b)* What causes its change of attitude?

KNOW YOUR WORDS

Word origins

The words listed below have become a part of the English language, but each has its origin in the language of Greek drama and theater. List the *literal* meanings of these words in their original sense, and then use each one in its modern sense in the following sentences.

scene	*dithyramb*
proscenium	*Thespian*
tragedy	*theater*
comedy	*drama*
orchestra	

1. The most expensive seats are usually on the main floor in the ________.
2. The ________ framing the stage in the old theater was magnificently carved.
3. He had never tried acting, but his love of the theater made him a ________ at heart.
4. Although the play was funny in part, it could not truly be called a ________.
5. The orator's fiery speech was practically a ________.
6. Before the opening ________, an actor stepped on stage to deliver a prologue.
7. Strictly speaking, an auditorium is not exactly the same thing as a ________.
8. ________ is probably to be regarded as the highest form of dramatic composition.
9. Even though ________ is traditionally considered as a major division of literature, it might also be regarded as an art form in itself.

UNIT 5 REVIEW

1. In this unit you learned that certain works of classical literature may be classified as *myths*, while others may be classified as *legends*. (a) What is the major difference between the two? (b) Which selections in this unit are myths? (c) Which are regarded as legends? (d) Which are more realistic, or believable, from the modern viewpoint? Why?

2. (a) What are literary allusions? (b) In what way do they help a writer? (c) How does a wide knowledge of classical literature aid a reader?

3. (a) In what ways is a storyteller less restricted than a translator? (b) In what ways is a translator of prose less restricted than a translator of poetry?

4. Both Socrates and Isocrates were noted educators of their times. (a) Which man stressed the importance of good character and common sense? (b) Which stressed the importance of inquiry and self-examination? (c) In what other basic way did their methods of education differ? (d) Cite examples in modern education of the application of the ideas of Socrates and Isocrates.

5. The concept of *fate* was a central part of human life in ancient Greece. (a) What was the Greek concept of fate? (b) What might happen if a person tempted his fate? (c) In what way did Creon tempt his fate? What was the result?

6. (a) In what way are the elements of fate and personal flaw related to the Greek concept of tragedy? (b) Was extraordinary suffering, in itself, regarded as tragic, in the Greek sense? Explain. (c) Why would the Greeks not have accepted Antigone as a true tragic figure?

SUGGESTED READING

BAKER, GEORGE, *Paris of Troy.* (Ziff-Davis) The story of the Trojan War is retold from the point of view of a Trojan soldier, Achates.

COOLIDGE, OLIVIA E., *The Trojan War.* (Houghton) This account of the Trojan War, based upon the Iliad and the Odyssey, provides a good introduction to the Greek classics and to Greek mythology in general.

COSTAIN, THOMAS, *The Silver Chalice.* (Doubleday) In this historical narrative, a young artist, commissioned by the disciples of Jesus to create a container for the cup used at the Last Supper, attempts to carry out his assignment amidst Nero's persecution of the Christians.

DAVIS, WILLIAM STEARNS, *A Friend of Caesar's.* (Macmillan) The adventures of a young Roman nobleman during the declining years of the Roman Republic are recounted in this historical novel.

DOUGLAS, LLOYD C., *The Robe.* (Houghton • Bantam Books) This is the story of Marcellus, a young Roman soldier in charge of the Crucifixion, who wins Jesus' robe, and of the effect that his possession of the robe has upon him.

FITTS, DUDLEY, *Greek Plays in Modern Translation.* (Dial) Ten plays by the three major Greek dramatists are gathered together in this volume.

FOSTER, GENEVIEVE, *Augustus Caesar's World.* (Scribner) The people and events of the Roman empire between the years 44 B. C. and 14 A. D. are described.

HAMILTON, EDITH, *Mythology.* (Little • Mentor) The legends and myths of the Greek gods and heroes are retold in a manner both interesting and informative.

HOMER, *The Iliad,* tr. by Robert Graves. (Doubleday) *The Odyssey,* tr. by Robert Fitzgerald. (Doubleday) The story of the Trojan War and of Odysseus' return to his homeland provides interesting reading as well as insight into Greek beliefs and ideas.

MILLS, DOROTHY, *The Book of the Ancient Greeks.* (Putnam) The development of Greek civilization from the coming of the Greeks until the conquest of Greece by Rome is described in an interesting and factual manner. *The Book of the Ancient Romans.* (Putnam) The second book by Miss Mills gives an account of the Roman culture from its founding until its fall in 476 A. D.

SIENKIEWICZ, HENRYK, *Quo Vadis.* (Dodd • Bantam Books) The Roman Empire at the time of Nero provides the background for the story of Vinicius, a young Roman patrician, and Lygia, a beautiful foreign princess.

VIRGIL, *The Aeneid,* tr. by Michael Oakley. (Dutton) Following the fall of Troy, the Trojan hero, Aeneas, wanders throughout the Mediterranean world, finally arriving in Italy to become the founder of the Latin race.

WALLACE, LEW, *Ben Hur.* (Dodd • Dolphin) A young Jewish man, falsely accused of a crime by his former friend, is sentenced to life at the galleys. The account of his dramatic escape and his attempts to regain his property and locate his family is presented against the background of the Crucifixion.

• paperback

When you have learned what elements make up the short story, you also know what elements make up a novel, for the elements are the same: both are fiction; both are concerned with characters, plot, and setting; both involve theme and style. Then how does one distinguish between a short story and a novel? The novelist usually employs many more characters and describes many more places than does the writer of short fiction. He develops his characters in greater depth, showing more complex interrelationships of his characters as they move from scene to scene and from incident to incident. In other words, the short story writer writes of a battle, while the novelist portrays an entire revolution—as Charles Dickens has done in *A Tale of Two Cities*. In this novel you will meet many different types of characters, and in following them through many related incidents, you will be concerned with concepts with which great literature deals, concepts of love, death, freedom, oppression, justice, honor, and sacrifice.

Unit 6

A TALE OF TWO CITIES

Charles Dickens

INTRODUCTION TO A TALE OF TWO CITIES

The novel you are about to read is a classic written by a master storyteller. Classic literature has lasting qualities partly because it probes issues or suggests truths that are vitally important to many people over generations in time. Literary art, like any other kind, is an individual expression. Charles Dickens, author of *A Tale of Two Cities,* drew from history and from his own experience.

In his youth Dickens lived in slums and suffered poverty. When he was eleven his father was imprisoned for debt, and the boy had to go to work for a mere six shillings a week in a shoe-polish factory where long, hard hours of child labor were of no concern to the management or to the lawmakers. After his father's release from the humiliating imprisonment, Dickens received three years of schooling under a tyrannical schoolmaster. At sixteen he worked as an office boy in a law firm, where he had a chance to observe English courts. What he drew from such experiences and how he inevitably took the side of the underdog, you will observe in *A Tale of Two Cities.*

For source material to lay the setting and the action, Dickens studied Thomas Carlyle's history, *The French Revolution.* The French Revolution, which some people think was inspired by the success of the American Revolution, had ended—after a bloody decade—just sixty years before Dickens wrote this novel. Many old-timers remembered the way French masses exploded in rebellion against the aristocratic ruling class, who had pitilessly oppressed the common man.

Common people had been deprived of the basic rights that we today associate with democracy. They had no political liberty. They could not hold public meetings or speak freely. They could not worship as they pleased. Peasants bore an unfair and often crushing burden of taxation. They could turn to no one with their grievances. In fact, a nobleman with no more reason than a personal grudge could write a letter to the authorities and have a common man thrown into prison without benefit of trial.

At last, on July 14, 1789, the oppressed and hungry of Paris stormed the Bastille, where many prisoners were unjustly confined. Then other outbreaks swept France. With the battle cry "Liberty, Equality, Fraternity, or Death" the violent mob ruled with a lawless, vengeful, and fickle hand, the king and queen themselves finally being slain at the busy guillotine.

In *A Tale of Two Cities* Dickens' purpose was not to give the historian's balanced picture of the revolution, to show both sides; rather, his concern was to re-create the revolutionary atmosphere largely from the viewpoint of the revolutionists. Although Dickens despised social injustice, selfishness, privileged rank, sham, tyranny, and cruelty, he injected the novel with an ultimate note of optimism. While sympathizing with the downtrodden in their fears and hopes, he believed in man's ability to surmount periods of baseness, turmoil, and despair. He measured life in terms of human welfare, and he believed in orderly change through legal reforms. A dramatic writer, he created vivid characters, and he cast the characters in a historical setting with which he was in sympathy.

A main strength of the novel is its tightly knit plot. Dickens frequently introduces details that make the reader wonder. But the reader's curiosity, once aroused, will be satisfied—the puzzles will be solved one by one. All the details are important in the later unfolding of the plot. The tantalizing digressions, the later tying-together of details, the crises, the unexpected turns, all contribute to make *A Tale of Two Cities* a suspenseful and thrilling novel.

A TALE OF TWO CITIES

IN THREE BOOKS

BY

CHARLES DICKENS

BOOK THE FIRST: Recalled to Life

CHAPTER I
The Period

It was the best of times, it was the worst of times, it was the age of wisdom, it was the age of foolishness, it was the epoch of belief, it was the epoch of incredulity, it was the season of light, it was the season of darkness, it was the spring of hope, it was the winter of despair. We had everything before us, we had nothing before us, we were all going direct to heaven, we were all going direct the other way. In short, the period was so far like the present period that some of its noisiest authorities insisted on its being received, for good or for evil, in the superlative degree of comparison only.

There were a king with a large jaw and a queen with a plain face on the throne of England[1]; there were a king with a large jaw and a queen with a fair face on the throne of France.[2] In both countries it was clearer than crystal to the lords of the state preserves of loaves and fishes[3] that things in general were settled forever.

It was in the year of our Lord one thousand seven hundred and seventy-five.

France rolled with exceeding smoothness downhill, making paper money and spending it. There were trees, already marked by the Woodman, Fate, to be sawed into boards, to make a certain movable framework with a sack and a knife in it, terrible in history. In the rough outhouses of the lands adjacent to Paris, there were rude carts, which the Farmer, Death, had already set apart to be his tumbrils[4] of the Revolution. But that Woodman and that Farmer, though they work unceasingly, work silently, and no one heard them as they went about with muffled tread.

In England there was scarcely an amount of order and protection to justify much national boasting. Daring burglaries by armed

1. ***king with a large jaw . . . England,*** George III and Queen Charlotte Sophia. 2. ***king with a large jaw . . . France,*** Louis XVI and Marie Antoinette (an′twə net′). 3. ***lords of . . . fishes,*** the nobility. 4. ***tumbrils,*** farmers' carts used for carrying condemned persons to the guillotine.

men and highway robberies took place in the capital itself every night; families were publicly cautioned not to go out of town without removing their furniture to upholsterers' warehouses for security; the mail was waylaid by seven robbers, and the guard shot three dead, and then got shot dead himself by the other four, "in consequence of the failure of his ammunition"; after which the mail was robbed in peace. That magnificent potentate, the Lord Mayor of London, was made to stand and deliver on Turnham Green by one highwayman who despoiled the illustrious creature in sight of all his retinue; thieves snipped off diamond crosses from the necks of noble lords at Court drawing-rooms; musketeers went into St. Giles'[5] to search for contraband goods, and the mob fired on the musketeers, and the musketeers fired on the mob, and nobody thought any of these occurrences much out of the common way. In the midst of them, the hangman was in constant requisition; now stringing up long rows of miscellaneous criminals; now hanging a housebreaker on Saturday who had been taken on Tuesday; today taking the life of an atrocious murderer, and tomorrow of a wretched pilferer who had robbed a farmer's boy of sixpence.

All these things, and a thousand like them, came to pass in and close upon the dear old year one thousand seven hundred and seventy-five. Environed by them, while the Woodman and the Farmer worked unheeded, those two of the large jaws, and those other two of the plain and the fair faces, trod with stir enough and carried their divine rights[6] with a high hand. Thus did the year one thousand seven hundred and seventy-five conduct their Greatnesses and myriads of small creatures—the creatures of this chronicle among the rest—along the roads that lay before them.

---

5. *St. Giles'*, medieval church in the central part of London. **6. *divine rights*,** the prevailing eighteenth-century idea that a king received his royal authority from God and, therefore, was responsible only to God for his actions.

WHAT DO YOU SAY?

1. *(a)* What examples does Dickens give to show that in 1775 conditions were bad in France? In England? *(b)* How does he suggest that differences existed between upper and lower classes in both countries?

2. In what ways does this chapter serve as an introduction to the novel? (Note especially the last paragraph.)

3. What did you notice about the figurative language of the author in this opening chapter?

AUTHOR'S CRAFT

Style

After reading the fiction so far in this anthology, what would you say are the fundamental elements that writers put into their stories? If you were to make a list, it should include ***setting*** (where and when), ***plot*** (what), and ***characters*** (who). All these elements you studied in Unit 1. Your list might include also the ***theme,*** or main idea, of the story and the ***viewpoint*** of the writer. Certainly it should include ***style*** (how).

In an historical romance like ***A Tale of Two Cities,*** place, people, and plot are logically important, and in a novel they all can be developed. Dickens emphasizes all three, especially plot. Since he "slants" his story to conform with his sympathies for downtrodden people, he also stresses ***viewpoint.*** If you will read carefully, you will discern how Dickens reveals his own outlook, or viewpoint, through his distinctive use of language—in other words, through his ***style.***

The very first paragraph sets an atmosphere of contrasts that immediately interests the reader: it was the best and the worst, it was wise and it was foolish; we had everything and we had nothing. The second paragraph continues this contrast but also introduces a comparison between England and France. Notice the first sentence in this paragraph. How do the two parts of this sentence compare? The parallel construction of this sentence is a style technique used often by Dickens. The contrasts and comparisons continue through the descriptions of conditions in France and in England, and we begin to see the importance of the title expression "two cities."

One of the ways in which Dickens achieves a

richness of style within the comparisons and contrasts is by implying ideas through the use of the ***metaphor.*** Metaphorically he compares hope with spring, despair with winter. In what ways does he use ***personification?***

The last paragraph of this chapter not only summarizes the ideas in the preceding paragraphs but also strikes into the plot by suggesting that this novel will trace the lives of certain great and small people along the roads that lie ahead. In addition, this paragraph introduces another technique of Dickens' style, ***repetition.*** What particular point is repeated within the paragraph? What ideas introduced in earlier paragraphs are repeated here? What do you think is the value of repetition?

By contrasting the living conditions of two classes of people, by comparing the situations in two countries, by the use of figures of speech, parallelism, and repetition; through all these techniques of style, Dickens provides the reader with his viewpoint. Watch for these same techniques of style as you learn who the characters are and what happens to them.

CHAPTER II
The Mail

It was the Dover road[1] that lay, on a Friday night late in November, before the first of the persons with whom this history has business. The Dover road lay, as to him, beyond the Dover mail as it lumbered up Shooter's Hill. He walked uphill in the mire by the side of the mail as the rest of the passengers did; not because they had the least relish for walking exercise, under the circumstances, but because the hill and the harness and the mud and the mail were all so heavy that the horses had three times already come to a stop. Reins and whip and coachman and guard, however, in combination, had read that article of war which forbade a purpose otherwise strongly in favor of the argument that some brute animals are endued with Reason; and the team had capitulated and returned to their duty.

With drooping heads and tremulous tails they mashed their way through the thick mud, floundering and stumbling between whiles, as if they were falling to pieces at the larger joints. As often as the driver rested them and brought them to a stand with a wary "Wo-ho! so-ho then!" the near leader violently shook his head and everything upon it—like an unusually emphatic horse, denying that the coach could be got up the hill. Whenever the leader made this rattle the passenger started, as a nervous passenger might, and was disturbed in mind.

There was a steaming mist in all the hollows, and it had roamed in its forlornness up the hill, like an evil spirit, seeking rest and finding none. A clammy and intensely cold mist, it made its slow way through the air in ripples that visibly followed and overspread one another, as the waves of an unwholesome sea might do. It was dense enough to shut out everything from the light of the coach lamps but these its own workings and a few yards of road; and the reek of the laboring horses steamed into it, as if they had made it all.

Two other passengers besides the one were plodding up the hill by the side of the mail. All three were wrapped to the cheekbones and over the ears and wore jackboots.[2] Not one of the three could have said, from anything he saw, what either of the other two was like; and each was hidden under almost as many wrappers from the eyes of the mind, as from the eyes of the body, of his two companions. In those days travelers were very shy of being confidential on a short notice, for anybody on the road might be a robber or in league with robbers. As to the latter, when every posting house and alehouse could produce somebody in "the Captain's"[3] pay, ranging from the landlord to the lowest stable nondescript, it was the likeliest thing upon the cards. So the guard of the Dover mail

1. ***Dover Road,*** highway between London and the port city of Dover, a popular departure point for France even today. 2. **jackboots,** large strong boots reaching above the knees, formerly worn by cavalrymen. 3. ***"the Captain's,"*** the head robber's.

thought to himself, that Friday night in November one thousand seven hundred and seventy-five, lumbering up Shooter's Hill, as he stood on his own particular perch behind the mail, beating his feet, and keeping an eye and a hand on the arm-chest before him, where a loaded blunderbuss lay at the top of six or eight loaded horse pistols, deposited on a substratum of cutlass.

The Dover mail was in its usual genial position that the guard suspected the passengers, the passengers suspected one another and the guard, they all suspected everybody else, and the coachman was sure of nothing but the horses; as to which cattle he could with a clear conscience have taken his oath on the two Testaments that they were not fit for the journey.

The last burst carried the mail to the summit of the hill. The horses stopped to breathe again, and the guard got down to open the coach door to let the passengers in.

"Tst! Joe!" cried the coachman in a warning voice. "I say a horse at a canter coming up, Joe."

"*I* say a horse at a gallop, Tom," returned the guard, leaving his hold of the door, and mounting nimbly to his place.

"Gentlemen! In the King's name, all of you!"

With this hurried adjuration, Joe cocked his blunderbuss, and stood on the offensive.

The sound of a horse at a gallop came fast and furiously up the hill.

"So-ho!" the guard sang out, as loud as he could roar. "Yo there! Stand! I shall fire!"

The pace was suddenly checked, and, with much splashing and floundering, a man's voice called from the mist, "Is that the Dover mail?"

"Never you mind what it is!" the guard retorted. "What are you?"

"*Is* that the Dover mail?"

"Why do you want to know?"

"I want a passenger, if it is."

"What passenger?"

"Mr. Jarvis Lorry."

The passenger showed in a moment that it was his name. The guard, the coachman, and the two other passengers eyed him distrustfully.

"Keep where you are," the guard called to the voice in the mist, "because, if I should make a mistake, it could never be set right in your lifetime. Gentleman of the name of Lorry answer straight."

"What is the matter?" asked the passenger, then, with mildly quavering speech. "Who wants me? Is it Jerry?"

("I don't like Jerry's voice, if it is Jerry," growled the guard to himself. "He's hoarser than suits me, is Jerry.")

"Yes, Mr. Lorry."

"What is the matter?"

"A dispatch sent after you from over yonder. T. and Co."

The figures of a horse and rider came slowly through the eddying mist to the side of the mail, where the passenger stood. The rider stooped and handed the passenger a small, folded paper. The rider's horse was blown, and both horse and rider were covered with mud, from the hoofs of the horse to the hat of the man.

"Guard!" said the passenger, in a tone of quiet business confidence.

The watchful guard, with his right hand at the stock of his raised blunderbuss, his left at the barrel, and his eye on the horseman, answered curtly, "Sir."

"There is nothing to apprehend. I belong to Tellson's Bank. You must know Tellson's Bank in London. I am going to Paris on business. A crown to drink. I may read this?"

"If so be as you're quick, sir."

He opened it in the light of the coach lamp on that side, and read—first to himself and then aloud: " 'Wait at Dover for Mam'selle.' It's not long, you see, guard. Jerry, say that my answer was, RECALLED TO LIFE."

Jerry started in his saddle. "That's a blazing strange answer, too," said he, at his hoarsest.

"Take that message back, and they will know that I received this, as well as if I wrote. Make the best of your way. Good night."

With those words the passenger opened the coach door and got in; not at all assisted by his fellow passengers, who had expeditiously secreted their watches and purses in their boots, and were now making a general pretense of being asleep. The coach lumbered on again, with heavier wreaths of mist closing round it as it began the descent.

Jerry, left alone in the mist and darkness, dismounted meanwhile, not only to ease his spent horse, but to wipe the mud from his face, and shake the wet out of his hat brim, which might be capable of holding about half a gallon.

"After that there gallop, old lady, I won't trust your forelegs till I get you on the level," said this hoarse messenger, glancing at his mare. "'Recalled to life.' That's a blazing strange message. Much of that wouldn't do for you, Jerry! I say, Jerry! You'd be in a blazing bad way, if recalling to life was to come into fashion, Jerry!"

WHAT DO YOU SAY?

1. *(a)* What road is the setting here and what characters are introduced? *(b)* Why are the characters so suspicious of each other? *(c)* Can you relate this attitude to any of the ideas set forth in Chapter I?

2. What particular descriptions do you think make the scene most realistic?

3. *(a)* What do you think is the most important phrase in this chapter? *(b)* What makes you think it is important? *(c)* Do you have any idea at this point what it could possibly mean? *(d)* What is Jerry's reaction to the phrase?

CHAPTER III
The Night Shadows

A wonderful fact to reflect upon, that every human creature is constituted to be that profound secret and mystery to every other. A solemn consideration, when I enter a great city by night, that every one of those darkly clustered houses incloses its own secret; that every room in every one of them incloses its own secret; that every beating heart, in the hundreds of thousands of breasts there, is, in some of its imaginings, a secret to the heart nearest it! Something of the awfulness even of Death itself is referable to this. No more can I turn the leaves of this dear book that I loved, and vainly hope in time to read it all. No more can I look into the depths of this unfathomable water, wherein, as momentary lights glanced into it, I have had glimpses of buried treasure and other things submerged. It was appointed that the book should shut with a spring, forever and forever, when I had read but a page. It was appointed that the water should be locked in an eternal frost, when the light was playing on its surface, and I stood in ignorance on the shore. My friend is dead, my neighbor is dead, my love, the darling of my soul, is dead; it is the inexorable consolidation and perpetuation of the secret that was always in that individuality, and which I shall carry in mine to my life's end. In any of the burial places of this city through which I pass, is there a sleeper more inscrutable than its busy inhabitants are, in their innermost personality, to me, or than I am to them?

As to this, his natural and not to be alienated inheritance, the messenger on horseback had exactly the same possessions as the King, the first Minister of State, or the richest merchant in London. So with the three passengers shut up in the narrow compass of one lumbering old mail coach; they were mysteries to one another, as complete as if each had been in his own coach and six, or his own coach and sixty, with the breadth of a county between him and the next.

The messenger rode back at an easy trot, stopping pretty often at alehouses by the way to drink, but evincing a tendency to keep his own counsel and to keep his hat cocked over his eyes. He had eyes that assorted very well with that decoration, being of a surface black, with no depth in the color or form, and much too near together—as if they were afraid of being found out in something, singly, if they kept too far apart. They had a sinister expression, under an old cocked hat and over a great muffler for the chin and throat, which descended nearly to the wearer's knees. When he stopped for drink, he moved this muffler with his left hand, only while he poured his liquor in with his right; as soon as that was done, he muffled again.

"No, Jerry, no!" said the messenger, harping on one theme as he rode. "It wouldn't do for you, Jerry. Jerry, you honest tradesman, it wouldn't suit *your* line of business! Recalled—! Bust me if I don't think he'd been a-drinking!"

His message perplexed his mind to that degree that he was fain several times to take off his hat to scratch his head. Except on the crown, which was raggedly bald, he had stiff black hair, standing jaggedly all over it and growing downhill almost to his broad, blunt nose. It was so much more like the top of a strongly spiked wall than a head of hair, that the best of players at leapfrog might have declined him, as the most dangerous man in the world to go over.

While he trotted back with the message he was to deliver to the night watchman in his box at the door of Tellson's Bank by Temple Bar,[1] who was to deliver it to greater authorities within, the shadows of the night took such shapes to him as arose out of the message, and took such shapes to the mare as arose out of *her* private topics of uneasiness. They seemed to be numerous, for she shied at every shadow on the road.

What time, the mail coach lumbered, jolted, rattled, and bumped upon its tedious way, with its three fellow-inscrutables inside. To whom, likewise, the shadows of the night revealed themselves, in the forms their dozing eyes and wandering thoughts suggested.

Tellson's Bank had a run upon it in the mail. As the bank passenger nodded in his place with half-shut eyes, the little coach windows and the bulky bundle of opposite passenger, became the bank and did a great stroke of business. The rattle of the harness was the chink of money, and more drafts were honored in five minutes than even Tellson's, with all its foreign and home connection, ever paid in thrice the time. Then the strong rooms underground at Tellson's, with such of their valuable stores and secrets as were known to the passenger—and it was not a little that he knew about them—opened before him, and he went in among them with the great keys and the feebly burning candle, and found them safe and strong and sound and still, just as he had last seen them.

But, though the bank was almost always with him, and though the coach—in a confused way, like the presence of pain under an opiate—was always with him, there was another current of impression that never ceased to run, all through the night. He was on his way to dig someone out of a grave.

Now, which of the multitude of faces that showed themselves before him was the true face of the buried person, the shadows of the night did not indicate; but they were all the faces of a man of five and forty by years, and they differed principally in the passions they expressed, and in the ghastliness of their worn and wasted state. Pride, contempt, defiance, stubbornness, submission, lamentation, succeeded one another; so did varieties of sunken cheek, cadaverous color, emaciated hands, and figures. But the face was in the main one face, and every head was prematurely white. A hundred times the dozing passenger inquired of this specter:

"Buried how long?"

The answer was always the same: "Almost eighteen years."

---

1. ***Temple Bar,*** the gate built by Christopher Wren (c. 1672) on the site of one of the entrances to the city of London.

"You had abandoned all hope of being dug out?"

"Long ago."

"You know that you are recalled to life?"

"They tell me so."

"I hope you care to live?"

"I can't say."

"Shall I show her to you? Will you come and see her?"

The answers to this question were various and contradictory. Sometimes the broken reply was, "Wait! It would kill me if I saw her too soon." Sometimes it was given in a tender rain of tears, and then it was "Take me to her." Sometimes it was staring and bewildered, and then it was, "I don't know her. I don't understand."

After such imaginary discourse, the passenger in his fancy would dig and dig, dig—now with a spade, now with a great key, now with his hands—to dig this wretched creature out. Got out at last, with earth hanging about his face and hair, he would suddenly fall away to dust. The passenger would then start to himself, and lower the window, to get the reality of mist and rain on his cheek.

Yet even when his eyes were opened on the mist and rain, on the moving patch of light from the lamps, and the hedge at the roadside retreating by jerks, the night shadows outside the coach would fall into the train of the night shadows within. The real banking house by Temple Bar, the real business of the past day, the real strong rooms, the real express sent after him, and the real message returned, would all be there. Out of the midst of them the ghostly face would rise, and he would accost it again.

"Buried how long?"

"Almost eighteen years."

"I hope you care to live?"

"I can't say."

Dig—dig—dig—until an impatient movement from one of the two passengers would admonish him to pull up the window, draw his arm securely through the leather strap, and speculate upon the two slumbering forms, until his mind lost its hold of them, and they again slid away into the bank and the grave.

"Buried how long?"

"Almost eighteen years."

"You had abandoned all hope of being dug out?"

"Long ago."

The words were still in his hearing as just spoken—distinctly in his hearing as ever spoken words had been in his life—when the weary passenger started to the consciousness of daylight and found that the shadows of the night were gone.

He lowered the window and looked out at the rising sun. There was a ridge of plowed land, with a plow upon it where it had been left last night when the horses were unyoked; beyond, a quiet coppice wood, in which many leaves of burning red and golden yellow still remained upon the trees. Though the earth was cold and wet, the sky was clear, and the sun rose bright, placid, and beautiful.

"Eighteen years!" said the passenger, looking at the sun. "Gracious Creator of day! To be buried alive for eighteen years!"

WHAT DO YOU SAY?

1. (a) What is Dickens saying in paragraph one? *(b)* How does this general comment about life lead into the main action of the story? *(c)* What does this paragraph indicate about the author's view toward social class?

2. *(a)* Describe Jerry's appearance. *(b)* What is Jerry's mood? *(c)* How does his mood arouse your curiosity about him?

3. *(a)* From the details of Mr. Lorry's dream, what would you guess about his purpose in making his trip? *(b)* What phrases were repeated in his dream?

4. (a) What is the significance of the statement, "Tellson's Bank had a run upon it in the mail," and what is the significance of the entire paragraph? (Page 455, column 2, paragraph 1) *(b)* What lines in this and the following paragraphs tell you that Mr. Lorry is dreaming?

CHAPTER IV
The Preparation

When the mail got successfully to Dover, in the course of the forenoon, the head drawer[1] at the Royal George Hotel opened the coach door as his custom was. He did it with some flourish of ceremony, for a mail journey from London in winter was an achievement to congratulate an adventurous traveler upon.

By that time there was only one adventurous traveler left to be congratulated, for the two others had been set down at their respective roadside destinations. The mildewy inside of the coach was rather like a larger dog kennel. Mr. Lorry, the passenger, shaking himself out of it, a tangle of shaggy wrapper, flapping hat, and muddy legs, was rather like a larger sort of dog.

"There will be a packet to Calais,[2] tomorrow, drawer?"

"Yes, sir, if the weather holds and the wind sets tolerable fair. The tide will serve pretty nicely at about two in the afternoon, sir. Bed, sir?"

"I shall not go to bed till night; but I want a bedroom and a barber."

"And then breakfast, sir? Yes, sir."

The coffee room had no other occupant, that forenoon, than the gentleman in brown. His breakfast table was drawn before the fire, and as he sat, with its light shining on him waiting for the meal, he sat so still that he might have been sitting for his portrait.

Very orderly and methodical he looked, with a hand on each knee, and a loud watch ticking a sonorous sermon under his flapped waistcoat. He had a good leg, and was a little vain of it, for his brown stockings fitted sleek and close; his shoes and buckles, too, though plain, were trim. He wore an odd little sleek crisp flaxen wig, setting very close to his head; which wig, it is to be presumed, was made of hair, but which looked far more as though it was spun from filaments of silk or glass. His linen was as white as the tops of the waves that broke upon the neighboring beach or the specks of sail that glinted in the sunlight far at sea. A face habitually suppressed and quieted was still lighted up under the quaint wig by a pair of moist bright eyes that it must have cost their owner, in years gone by, some pains to drill to the composed and reserved expression of Tellson's Bank. He had a healthy color in his cheeks, and his face, though lined, bore few traces of anxiety. But perhaps the confidential bachelor clerks in Tellson's Bank were principally occupied with the cares of other people; and perhaps second-hand cares, like second-hand clothes, come easily off and on.

Completing his resemblance to a man who was sitting for his portrait, Mr. Lorry dropped off to sleep. The arrival of his breakfast roused him, and he said to the drawer, as he moved his chair to it:

"I wish accommodation prepared for a young lady who may come here at any time today. She may ask for Mr. Jarvis Lorry, or she may only ask for a gentleman from Tellson's Bank. Please to let me know."

"Yes, sir. Tellson's Bank in London, sir?"

"Yes."

"Yes, sir. We have oftentimes the honor to entertain your gentlemen in their traveling backwards and forwards betwixt London and Paris, sir. A vast deal of traveling, sir, in Tellson and Company's House."[3]

"Yes; we are quite a French House, as well as an English one."

"Yes, sir. Not much in the habit of such traveling yourself, I think, sir?"

"Not of late years. It is fifteen years since we—since I—came last from France."

"Indeed, sir? That was before my time here, sir. Before our people's time here, sir. The George was in other hands at that time, sir."

---

1. ***head drawer,*** chief doorman. 2. ***packet to Calais*** (ka lā'), a boat traveling regularly to Calais, a port city on the extreme northern coast of France. A packet carries passengers, mail, and goods. 3. ***Tellson and Company's House,*** bank or banking house with its headquarters in London but also operating a flourishing branch in Paris.

"I believe so."

"But I would hold a pretty wager, sir, that a House like Tellson and Company was flourishing, a matter of fifty, not to speak of fifteen, years ago?"

"You might treble that, and say a hundred and fifty, yet not be far from the truth."

"Indeed, sir!"

When Mr. Lorry had finished his breakfast, he went out for a stroll on the beach. The little narrow, crooked town of Dover hid itself away from the beach and ran its head into the chalk cliffs, like a marine ostrich. The beach was a desert of heaps of sea and stones tumbling wildly about, and the sea did what it liked, and what it liked was destruction. It thundered at the town, and thundered at the cliffs, and brought the coast down, madly.

As the day declined into the afternoon, and the air, which had been at intervals clear enough to allow the French coast to be seen, became again charged with mist and vapor, Mr. Lorry sat before the coffee-room fire, awaiting his dinner as he had awaited his breakfast. He had just poured out his last glassful of wine when a rattling of wheels came up the narrow street and rumbled into the inn yard.

He set down his glass untouched. "This is Mam'selle!" said he.

In a very few minutes the waiter came in to announce that Miss Manette had arrived from London, and would be happy to see the gentleman from Tellson's.

"So soon?"

Miss Manette had taken some refreshment on the road, and was extremely anxious to see the gentleman from Tellson's immediately, if it suited his convenience.

The gentleman from Tellson's had nothing left for it but to empty his glass with an air of stolid desperation, settle his odd little flaxen wig at the ears, and follow the waiter to Miss Manette's apartment. Mr. Lorry saw, standing to receive him by the table between them and the fire, a young lady of not more than seventeen, in a riding cloak, and still holding her straw traveling hat by its ribbon in her hand. As his eyes rested on a short, slight, pretty figure, a quantity of golden hair, a pair of blue eyes that met his own with an inquiring look, and a forehead with a singular capacity of lifting and knitting itself into an expression that was not quite one of perplexity, or wonder, or alarm, or merely of a bright, fixed attention, though it included all the four expressions—as his eyes rested on these things, a sudden vivid likeness passed before him, of a child whom he had held in his arms on the passage across that very Channel, one cold time, when the hail drifted heavily and the sea ran high. The likeness passed away, like a breath along the surface of the gaunt pier glass behind her, and he made his formal bow to Miss Manette. "Pray take a seat, sir." In a very clear and pleasant young voice; a little foreign in its accent, but a very little indeed.

"I kiss your hand, miss," said Mr. Lorry, with the manners of an earlier date, as he made his formal bow again, and took his seat.

"I received a letter from the Bank, sir, yesterday, informing me that some intelligence—or discovery—"

"The word is not material, miss; either word will do."

"—respecting the small property of my poor father, whom I never saw—so long dead—"

Mr. Lorry moved in his chair.

"—rendered it necessary that I should go to Paris, there to communicate with a gentleman of the Bank, so good as to be dispatched to Paris for the purpose."

"Myself."

"As I was prepared to hear, sir."

She curtsied to him. He made her another bow.

"I replied to the Bank, sir, that as it was considered necessary, by those who know, and who are so kind as to advise me, that I should go to France, and that as I am an orphan and have no friend who could go with me, I should esteem it highly if I might be permitted to place myself, during the journey, under that worthy gentleman's protection. The gentleman had left London, but I think a messenger was sent after him to beg the favor of his waiting for me here."

"I was happy," said Mr. Lorry, "to be entrusted with the charge. I shall be more happy to execute it."

"Sir, I thank you indeed. I thank you very gratefully. It was told me by the Bank that the gentleman would explain to me the details of the business, and that I must prepare myself to find them of a surprising nature. I have done my best to prepare myself, and I naturally have a strong and eager interest to know what they are."

"Naturally," said Mr. Lorry. "Yes—I—"

After a pause, he added, again settling the crisp flaxen wig at the ears:

"It is very difficult to begin."

He did not begin, but, in his indecision, met her glance. The young forehead lifted itself into that singular expression—but it was pretty and characteristic, besides being singular—and she raised her hand, as if with an involuntary action she caught at, or stayed, some passing shadow.

"Are you quite a stranger to me, sir?"

"Am I not?" Mr. Lorry opened his hands, and extended them outwards with an argumentative smile. He went on. "In your adopted country, I presume, I cannot do better than address you as a young English lady, Miss Manette?"

"If you please, sir."

"Miss Manette, I am a man of business. I have a business charge to acquit myself of. In your reception of it don't heed me any more than if I was a speaking machine—truly, I am not much else. I will, with your leave, relate to you the story of one of our customers."

"Story!"

He seemed willfully to mistake the word she had repeated when he added, in a hurry, "Yes, customers; in the banking business we usually call our connection our customers. He was a French gentleman; a scientific gentleman; a man of great acquirements—a Doctor."

"Not of Beauvais?"[4]

"Why, yes, of Beauvais. Like Monsieur Manette, your father, the gentleman was of Beauvais. Like Monsieur Manette, your father, the gentleman was of repute in Paris. I had the honor of knowing him there. Our relations were business relations, but confidential. I was at that time in our French House, and had been—oh! twenty years."

"At that time—I may ask, at what time, sir?"

"I speak, miss, of twenty years ago. He married—an English lady—and I was one of the trustees. His affairs, like the affairs of many other French gentlemen and French families, were entirely in Tellson's hands. In a similar way I am, or I have been, trustee of one kind or other for scores of our customers. These are mere business relations, miss; there is no friendship in them, no particular interest, nothing like sentiment. To go on—"

"But this is my father's story, sir; and I begin to think"—the curiously roughened forehead was very intent upon him—"that when I was left an orphan through my mother's surviving my father only two years, it was you who brought me to England. I am almost sure it was you."

Mr. Lorry took the hesitating little hand that confidingly advanced to take his, and he put it with some ceremony to his lips. He then conducted the young lady straightway to her chair again, and, holding the chair back with his left hand, and using his right by turns to rub his chin, pull his wig at the ears, or point what he said, stood looking down into her face while she sat looking up into his.

"Miss Manette, it *was* I. And you will see how truly I spoke of myself just now, in saying I had no feelings, and that all the

---

*4. **Beauvais*** (bō vā′), a city in northern France.

relations I hold with my fellow creatures are mere business relations, when you reflect that I have never seen you since. No; you have been the ward of Tellson's House since, and I have been busy with the other business of Tellson's House since.

"So far, miss—as you have remarked—this is the story of your regretted father. Now comes the difference. If your father had not died when he did—Don't be frightened! How you start!"

She did, indeed, start. And she caught his wrist with both her hands.

"Pray," said Mr. Lorry, in a soothing tone, bringing his left hand from the back of the chair to lay it on the supplicatory fingers that clasped him in so violent a tremble, "pray control your agitation—a matter of business. As I was saying—"

Her look so discomposed him that he stopped, wandered, and began anew.

"As I was saying: if Monsieur Manette had not died; if he had suddenly and silently disappeared; if he had been spirited away; if it had not been difficult to guess to what dreadful place, though no art could trace him; if he had an enemy in some compatriot who could exercise a privilege that I in my own time have known the boldest people afraid to speak of in a whisper, across the water there; for instance, the privilege of filling up blank forms for the consignment of anyone to the oblivion of a prison for any length of time; if his wife had implored the King, the Queen, the court, the clergy, for any tidings of him, and all quite in vain—then the history of your father would have been the history of this unfortunate gentleman, the Doctor of Beauvais."

"I entreat you to tell me more, sir."

"I will. I am going to. You can bear it?"

"I can bear anything but the uncertainty you leave me in at this moment."

"You speak collectedly, and you—*are* collected. That's good!" (Though his manner was less satisfied than his words.) "A matter of business. Regard it as a matter of business—business that must be done. Now if this doctor's wife, though a lady of great courage and spirit, had suffered so intensely from this cause before her little child was born—"

"The little child was a daughter, sir."

"A daughter. A—a—matter of business—don't be distressed. Miss, if the poor lady had suffered so intensely before her little child was born that she came to the determination of sparing the poor child the inheritance of any part of the agony she had known the pains of, by rearing her in the belief that her father was dead—No, don't kneel! In heaven's name, why should you kneel to me!"

"For the truth. O dear, good, compassionate sir, for the truth!"

"A—a matter of business. You confuse me, and how can I transact business if I am confused? Let us be clear-headed. If you could kindly mention now, for instance, what nine times ninepence are, or how many shillings in twenty guineas,[5] it would be so encouraging. I should be so much more at my ease about your state of mind."

Without directly answering to this appeal, she sat so still when he had very gently raised her, and the hands that had not ceased to clasp his wrists were so much more steady than they had been, that she communicated some reassurance to Mr. Jarvis Lorry.

"That's right, that's right. Courage! Business! You have business before you; useful business. Miss Manette, your mother took this course with you. And when she died—I believe broken-hearted—having never slackened her unavailing search for your father, she left you, at two years old, to grow to be blooming, beautiful, and happy, without the dark cloud upon you of living in uncertainty whether your father soon

---

5. ***nine times ninepence . . .guineas.*** Pence, shillings, and guineas—coins of bronze, silver, and gold, respectively—are units of English currency. Mr. Lorry makes this request of Miss Manette to reassure himself that he has not shocked her into a complete state of confusion.

wore his heart out in prison, or wasted there through many lingering years."

As he said the words he looked down, with an admiring pity, on the flowing, golden hair, as if he pictured to himself that it might have been already tinged with gray.

"You know that your parents had no great possession, and that what they had was secured to your mother and to you. There has been no new discovery of money or of any other property; but—"

He felt his wrist held closer, and he stopped. The expression in the forehead, which had so particularly attracted his notice, and which was now immovable, had deepened into one of pain and horror.

"But he has been—been found. He is alive. Greatly changed, it is too probable; almost a wreck, it is possible; though we will hope the best. Still, alive. Your father has been taken to the house of an old servant in Paris, and we are going there: I, to identify him if I can; you, to restore him to life, love, duty, rest, comfort."

A shiver ran through her frame, and from it through his.

She said, in a low, distinct, awe-stricken voice, as if she were saying it in a dream:

"I am going to see his ghost! It will be his ghost—not him!"

Mr. Lorry quietly chafed the hands that held his arm. "There, there, there! See now, see now! The best and the worst are known to you, now. You are well on your way to the poor wronged gentleman, and, with a fair sea voyage, and a fair land journey, you will be soon at his dear side."

She repeated in the same tone, sunk to a whisper, "I have been happy, yet his ghost has never haunted me!"

"Only one thing more," said Mr. Lorry, laying stress upon it as a wholesome means of enforcing her attention, "he has been found under another name; his own, long forgotten or long concealed. It would be worse than useless now to inquire which; worse than useless to seek to know whether he has been for years overlooked, or always designedly held prisoner. It would be worse than useless now to make any inquiries, because it would be dangerous. Better not to mention the subject, anywhere or in any way, and to remove him—for a while at all events—out of France. Even I, safe as an Englishman, and even Tellson's, important as they are to French credit, avoid all naming of the matter. I carry about me, not a scrap of writing openly referring to it. This is a secret service altogether. My credentials, entries, and memoranda are all comprehended in the one line, 'Recalled to Life,' which may mean anything. But what is the matter! She doesn't notice a word! Miss Manette!"

Perfectly still and silent, and not even fallen back in her chair, she sat utterly insensible. So close was her hold upon his arm that he feared to detach himself lest he hurt her; therefore he called loudly for assistance without moving.

A wild-looking woman, whom even in his agitation, Mr. Lorry observed to be all of red color, and to have red hair, and to be dressed in some extraordinary tight-fitting fashion, and to have on her head a most wonderful bonnet like a Stilton cheese,[6] came running into the room in advance of the inn servants, and settled the question of his detachment from the young lady, by laying a brawny hand upon his chest, and sending him flying back against the nearest wall.

("I really think this must be a man!" was Mr. Lorry's breathless reflection, simultaneously with his coming against the wall.)

"Why, look at you all!" bawled this figure, addressing the inn servants. "Why don't you go and fetch things? I'll let you know, if you don't bring smelling salts, cold water, and vinegar, quick, I will."

There was an immediate dispersal for these restoratives, and she softly laid the patient on a sofa, and tended her with great skill and gentleness, calling her "my bird!"

6. ***Stilton cheese,*** a round, rich, waxy white cheese veined with blue-green mold.

"And you in brown!" she said, indignantly turning to Mr. Lorry. "Couldn't you tell her what you had to tell her, without frightening her to death? Look at her, with her pretty pale face and her cold hands. Do you call *that* being a banker?"

Mr. Lorry was so exceedingly disconcerted by a question so hard to answer that he could only look on, at a distance.

"I hope she will do well now," said Mr. Lorry, "and that you accompany Miss Manette to France?"

"A likely thing, too!" replied the strong woman. "If it was ever intended that I should go across salt water, do you suppose Providence would have cast my lot in an island?"

This being another question hard to answer, Mr. Jarvis Lorry withdrew to consider it.

WHAT DO YOU SAY?

1. *(a)* How would you describe the appearance and manner of Mr. Jarvis Lorry? *(b)* Miss Manette?

2. *(a)* What story does Mr. Lorry tell Miss Manette? *(b)* By what method does he relate the story? *(c)* What does his method of telling the story reveal to you about Mr. Lorry?

3. What have you learned so far of the relationships of the three main characters in this chapter?

4. How does the author relieve the seriousness of this chapter?

CHAPTER V
The Wine Shop

A large cask of wine had been dropped and broken in the street. The accident had happened in getting it out of a cart. The cask had tumbled out with a run, the hoops had burst, and it lay on the stones just outside the door of the wine shop, shattered like a walnut shell.

All the people within reach had suspended their business, or their idleness, to run to the spot and drink the wine. Some men knelt down, made scoops of their two hands joined, and sipped, or tried to help women, who bent over their shoulders, to sip, before the wine had all run out between their fingers. Others, men and women, dipped in the puddles with little mugs of mutilated earthenware, or even with handkerchiefs from women's heads, which were squeezed dry into infants' mouths. Others devoted themselves to the sodden and lee-dyed pieces of the cask, licking and even champing the moister wine-rotted fragments with eager relish.

A shrill sound of laughter and of amused voices—voices of men, women, and children—resounded in the street while this wine game lasted. When the wine was gone, and the places where it had been most abundant were raked into a gridiron pattern by fingers, these demonstrations ceased, as suddenly as they had broken out.

The wine was red wine and had stained the ground of the narrow street in the suburb of Saint Antoine,[1] in Paris, where it was spilled. It had stained many hands, too, and many faces, and many naked feet, and many wooden shoes; and one tall joker, his head more out of a long squalid bag of a nightcap than in it, scrawled upon a wall with his finger dipped in muddy wine lees—BLOOD.

The time was to come when that wine, too, would be spilled on the street stones and when the stain of it would be red upon many there.

And now that the cloud settled on Saint Antoine, which a momentary gleam had driven from his sacred countenance, the darkness of it was heavy—cold, dirt, sickness, ignorance, and want were the lords in

1. *Saint Antoine* (an'twän), a poor suburb of Paris at the time of the story. Now within the city limits, the Rue St. Antoine still remains one of the principal streets in the poorest part of Paris.

VINS
Ronald Searle

waiting on the saintly presence—nobles of great power all of them; but, most especially the last. Samples of a people that had undergone a terrible grinding and regrinding in the mill, and certainly not in the fabulous mill which ground old people young, shivered at every corner, passed in and out at every doorway, looked from every window, fluttered in every vestige of a garment that the wind shook. The mill which had worked them down was the mill that grinds young people old; the children had ancient faces and grave voices; and upon them, and upon the grown faces, and plowed into every furrow of age and coming up afresh, was the sign Hunger. It was prevalent everywhere. Hunger was pushed out of the tall houses, in the wretched clothing that hung upon poles and lines; Hunger was patched into them with straw and rag and wood and paper; Hunger was repeated in every fragment of the small modicum of firewood that the man sawed off; Hunger stared down from the smokeless chimneys, and started up from the filthy street that had no offal, among its refuse, of anything to eat. Hunger was the inscription on the baker's shelves, written in every small loaf of his scanty stock of bad bread; at the sausage shop, in every dead-dog preparation that was offered for sale. Hunger rattled its dry bones among the roasting chestnuts in the turned cylinder; Hunger was shred into atomies in every farthing porringer of husky chips of potato, fried with some reluctant drops of oil.

Its abiding place was in all things fitted to it. A narrow, winding street, full of offense and stench, with other narrow, winding streets diverging, all peopled by rags and nightcaps, and all smelling of rags and nightcaps, and all visible things with a brooding look upon them that looked ill. In the hunted air of the people there was yet some wild beast thought of the possibility of turning at bay. Depressed and slinking though they were, eyes of fire were not wanting among them; nor compressed lips, white with what they suppressed; nor foreheads knitted into the likeness of the gallows rope they mused about enduring, or inflicting. The trade signs—and they were almost as many as the shops—were, all, grim illustrations of Want. The butcher and the porkman painted up only the leanest scrags of meat; the baker, the coarsest of meager loaves. The people rudely pictured as drinking in the wine shops croaked over their scanty measures of thin wine and beer, and were gloweringly confidential together. Nothing was represented in a flourishing condition save tools and weapons; but the cutler's knives and axes were sharp and bright, the smith's hammers were heavy, and the gunmaker's stock was murderous. The crippling stones of the pavement, with their many little reservoirs of mud and water, had no footways, but broke off abruptly at the doors. The kennel,[2] to make amends, ran down the middle of the street—when it ran at all; which was only after heavy rains, and then it ran, by many eccentric fits, into the houses. Across the streets, at wide intervals, one clumsy lamp was slung by a rope and pulley; at night, when the lamplighter had let these down, and lighted and hoisted them again, a feeble grove of dim wicks swung in a sickly manner overhead, as if they were at sea. Indeed they were at sea, and the ship and crew were in peril of tempest.

For the time was to come when the gaunt scarecrows of that region should have watched the lamplighter, in their idleness and hunger, so long as to conceive the idea of improving on his method, and hauling up men by those ropes and pulleys, to flare upon the darkness of their condition. But the time was not come yet; and every wind that blew over France shook the rags of the scarecrows in vain, for the birds, fine in song and feather, took no warning.[3]

---

2. ***kennel,*** a little channel; gutter. 3. ***the birds . . . warning.*** The French aristocracy, in high spirits and finely dressed, paid no attention to the suffering and rising discontent among the lower classes.

The wine shop was a corner shop, better than most others in its appearance and degree, and the master of the wine shop had stood outside it, in a yellow waistcoat and green breeches, looking on at the struggle for the lost wine. "It's not my affair," said he, with a final shrug of the shoulders. "The people from the market did it. Let them bring another."

This wine-shop keeper was a bull-necked, martial-looking man of thirty, and he should have been of a hot temperament, for, although it was a bitter day, he wore no coat. His shirt sleeves were rolled up, too, and his brown arms were bare to the elbows. Neither did he wear anything more on his head than his own crisply curling, short dark hair. He was a dark man altogether, with good eyes and a good bold breadth between them. Good-humored looking on the whole, but implacable looking, too; evidently a man of a strong resolution and a set purpose, a man not desirable to be met, rushing down a narrow pass with a gulf on either side, for nothing would turn the man.

Madame Defarge, his wife, sat in the shop behind the counter as he came in. Madame Defarge was a stout woman of his own age, with a watchful eye that seldom seemed to look at anything, a large hand heavily ringed, a steady face, strong features, and great composure of manner. There was a character about Madame Defarge, from which one might have predicted that she did not often make mistakes against herself in any of the reckonings over which she presided. Madame Defarge, being sensitive to cold, was wrapped in fur, and had a quantity of bright shawl twined about her head, though not to the concealment of her large earrings. Her knitting was before her, but she had laid it down to pick her teeth with a toothpick. She said nothing when her lord came in, but coughed just one grain of cough. This, in combination with the lifting of her darkly defined eyebrows over her toothpick by the breadth of a line, suggested to her husband he would do well to look round the shop, among the customers, for any new customer who had dropped in.

The wine-shop keeper accordingly rolled his eyes about until they rested upon an elderly gentleman and a young lady, who were seated in a corner. As he passed behind the counter, he took notice that the elderly gentleman said in a look to the young lady, "This is our man."

But he feigned not to notice the two strangers, and fell into discourse with the triumvirate of customers who were drinking at the counter.

"How goes it, Jacques?"[4] said one of these three to Monsieur Defarge. "Is all the spilt wine swallowed?"

"Every drop, Jacques," answered Monsieur Defarge.

When this interchange of Christian name was effected, Madame Defarge, picking her teeth with her toothpick, coughed another grain of cough, and raised her eyebrows by the breadth of another line.

"Gentlemen," said her husband, who had kept his bright eye observantly upon her, "good day. The chamber that you wished to see, and were inquiring for when I stepped out, is on the fifth floor. The doorway of the staircase gives on the little courtyard close to the left here. But, now that I remember, one of you has already been there and can show the way. Gentlemen, adieu!"

They paid for their wine and left the place. The eyes of Monsieur Defarge were studying his wife at her knitting, when the elderly gentleman advanced from his corner and begged the favor of a word.

"Willingly, sir," said Monsieur Defarge.

Their conference was very short, but very decided. Almost at the first word, Monsieur Defarge started and became deeply attentive. It had not lasted a minute, when he nodded and went out. The gentleman then

4. ***Jacques*** (zhäk), a French word for man or fellow; also a proper name (James in English). During the days preceding the revolution, this name was used as a password of the mysterious secret society, the ***Jacquerie,*** which some authorities believe to have planned and brought about the revolution.

beckoned to the young lady, and they, too, went out. Madame Defarge knitted with nimble fingers and saw nothing.

Mr. Jarvis Lorry and Miss Manette, emerging from the wine shop thus, joined Monsieur Defarge in the doorway to which he had directed his other company just before. It opened from a stinking little black courtyard and was the general public entrance to a great pile of houses, inhabited by a great number of people. In the gloomy entry to the gloomy, tile-paved staircase, Monsieur Defarge bent on one knee to the child of his old master, and put her hand to his lips. It was a gentle action, but not at all gently done; a remarkable transformation had come over him in a few seconds. He had no good humor in his face, nor any openness of aspect left, but had become a secret, angry, dangerous man.

"It is very high; it is a little difficult. Better to begin slowly." Thus, Monsieur Defarge, in a stern voice to Mr. Lorry as they began ascending the stairs.

"Is he alone?" the latter whispered.

"Alone! God help him, who should be with him!" said the other in the same low voice.

"Is he always alone, then?"

"Yes."

"Of his own desire?"

"Of his own necessity. As he was, when I first saw him after they found me and demanded to know if I would take him, and, at my peril be discreet—as he was then—so he is now."

"He is greatly changed?"

"Changed!"

The keeper of the wine shop stopped to strike the wall with his hand, and mutter a tremendous curse. No direct answer could have been half so forcible. Mr. Lorry's spirits grew heavier and heavier, as he and his two companions ascended higher and higher.

At last the top of the staircase was gained. There was yet an upper staircase, of a steeper inclination and of contracted dimensions, to be ascended before the garret story was reached. The keeper of the wine shop turned himself about here, and, carefully feeling in the pockets of the coat he carried over his shoulder, took out a key.

"The door is locked then, my friend?" said Mr. Lorry, surprised.

"Aye. Yes," was the grim reply of Monsieur Defarge.

"You think it necessary to keep the unfortunate gentleman so retired?"

"I think it necessary to turn the key." Monsieur Defarge whispered it closer in his ear and frowned heavily.

"Why?"

"Why! Because he has lived so long locked up that he would be frightened—rave—die—come to I know not what harm—if this door was left open."

"Is it possible!" exclaimed Mr. Lorry.

"Is it possible!" repeated Defarge, bitterly. "Yes. And a beautiful world we live in, when it *is* possible, and when many other such things are possible, and not only possible, but done—done, see you!—under that sky there, every day. Long live the Devil. Let us go on."

They went up slowly and softly. The staircase was short, and they were soon at the top. There, as it had an abrupt turn in it, they came all at once in sight of three men, bent down close together at the side of a door, intently looking into the room to which the door belonged, through some chinks or holes in the wall. On hearing footsteps close at hand, these three turned, rose, and showed themselves to be the three who had been drinking in the wine shop.

"I forgot them in the surprise of your visit," explained Monsieur Defarge. "Leave us, good boys."

The three glided by and went silently down.

There appearing to be no other door on that floor, and the keeper of the wine shop going straight to this one when they were left alone, Mr. Lorry asked in a whisper, with a little anger:

"Do you make a show of Monsieur Manette?"

"I show him to a chosen few."

"Is that well?"

"*I* think it is well."

"Who are the few? How do you choose them?"

"I choose men of my name—Jacques is my name—to whom the sight is likely to do good. Enough; you are English; that is another thing. Stay there, if you please."

With an admonitory gesture to keep them back, he struck twice or thrice upon the door—evidently with no other object than to make a noise there. With the same intention, he drew the key across it three or four times before he put it clumsily into the lock, and turned it as heavily as he could.

The door slowly opened inwardly under his hand, and he looked into the room and said something. A faint voice answered something.

He looked back over his shoulder and beckoned them to enter. Mr. Lorry got his arm securely around the daughter's waist and held her, for he felt that she was sinking. Rendered in a manner desperate, by her state and by the beckoning of their conductor, he lifted her a little, and hurried her into the room. He set her down just within the door, and held her, clinging to him.

Defarge drew out the key, closed the door, locked it on the inside, took out the key again, and held it in his hand. All this he did, methodically, and with as loud and harsh an accompaniment of noise as he could make. Finally, he walked across the room with a measured tread to where the window was. He stopped there and faced round.

The garret, built to be a depository for firewood and the like, was dim and dark; for the window, of dormer shape, was in truth a door in the roof, with a little crane over it for the hoisting up of stores from the street, and closing up the middle in two pieces, like any other door of French construction. To exclude the cold, one half of this door was fast closed, and the other was opened but a very little way. It was difficult, on first coming in, to see anything, and long habit alone could have slowly formed in anyone the ability to do any work requiring nicety in such obscurity. Yet work of that kind was being done in the garret; for, with his back toward the door and his face toward the window where the keeper of the wine shop stood looking at him, a white-haired man sat on a low bench, stooping forward and very busy, making shoes.

WHAT DO YOU SAY?

1. What evidence does the author present to show that people in Saint Antoine were living in "explosive" conditions?

2. *(a)* What do you infer about Madame Defarge from her actions? *(b)* In what physical occupation is she constantly engaged?

3. What had been Monsieur Defarge's relationship to Miss Manette's father in former years?

4. Point out several examples of ***personification*** in this chapter.

CHAPTER VI
The Shoemaker

"Good day!" said Monsieur Defarge, looking down at the white head that bent low over the shoemaking.

It was raised for a moment, and a very faint voice responded to the salutation, as if it were at a distance:

"Good day!"

"You are still hard at work, I see?"

After a long silence, the head was lifted for another moment, and the voice replied, "Yes—I am working." This time a pair of haggard eyes had looked at the questioner, before the face had dropped again.

"I want," said Defarge, who had not removed his gaze from the shoemaker, "to let in a little more light here. You can bear a little more?"

"I must bear it, if you let it in." (Laying the palest shadow of a stress upon the second word.)

The opened half-door was opened a little farther and secured at that angle for the time. A broad ray of light fell into the garret, and showed the workman with an unfinished shoe upon his lap, pausing in his labor. His few common tools and various scraps of leather were at his feet and on his bench. He had a white beard, raggedly cut but not very long, a hollow face, and exceedingly bright eyes. The hollowness and thinness of his face would have caused them to look large under his yet dark eyebrows and his confused white hair, though they had been really otherwise; but they were naturally large and looked unnaturally so. His yellow rags of shirt lay open at the throat and showed his body to be withered and worn.

He had put up a hand between his eyes and the light, and the very bones of it seemed transparent. So he sat, with a steadfastly vacant gaze, pausing in his work. He never looked at the figure before him, without first looking down on this side of himself, then on that, as if he had lost the habit of associating place with sound; he never spoke, without first wandering in this manner and forgetting to speak.

"Are you going to finish that pair of shoes today?" asked Defarge, motioning to Mr. Lorry to come forward.

"What did you say?"

"Do you mean to finish that pair of shoes today?"

"I can't say that I mean to. I suppose so. I don't know." Reminded of his work he bent over it again.

Mr. Lorry came silently forward, leaving the daughter by the door. When he had stood for a minute or two by the side of Defarge, the shoemaker looked up. He showed no surprise at seeing another figure, but the unsteady fingers of one of his hands strayed to his lips as he looked at it (his lips and his nails were of the same pale lead-color), and then the hand dropped to his work, and he once more bent over the shoe.

"You have a visitor, you see," said Monsieur Defarge.

"What did you say?"

"Here is a visitor."

The shoemaker looked up as before, but without removing a hand from his work.

"Come!" said Defarge. "Show monsieur that shoe you are working at."

Mr. Lorry took it in his hand.

"Tell monsieur what kind of shoe it is and the maker's name."

"It is a lady's shoe in the present mode. I never saw the mode. I have had a pattern in my hand." He glanced at the shoe with some little passing touch of pride.

"And the maker's name?" said Defarge.

"Did you ask me for my name?"

"Assuredly I did."

"One Hundred and Five, North Tower."

"Is that all?"

"One Hundred and Five, North Tower."

With a weary sound that was not a sigh nor a groan, he bent to work until the silence was again broken.

"You are not a shoemaker by trade?" said Mr. Lorry, looking steadfastly at him.

His haggard eyes turned to Defarge as if he would have transferred the question to him; but as no help came from that quarter, they turned back on the questioner when they had sought the ground.

"I am not a shoemaker by trade? No, I was not a shoemaker by trade. I—I learned it here. I taught myself. I asked leave to—"

He lapsed away for minutes. His eyes came slowly back at last to the face from which they had wandered; when they rested on it, he started and resumed, in the manner of a sleeper that moment awake.

"I asked leave to teach myself, and I got it with much difficulty after a long while, and I have made shoes ever since."

As he held out his hand for the shoe that

had been taken from him, Mr. Lorry said, still looking steadfastly in his face:

"Monsieur Manette, do you remember nothing of me?"

The shoe dropped to the ground, and he sat looking fixedly at the questioner.

"Monsieur Manette," Mr. Lorry laid his hand upon Defarge's arm, "do you remember nothing of this man? Look at him. Look at me. Is there no old banker, no old servant, no old time, rising in your mind?"

As the captive of many years sat looking fixedly, by turns, at Mr. Lorry and at Defarge, some long obliterated marks of an active intelligence in the middle of the forehead, gradually forced themselves through the black mist that had fallen on him. They were overclouded again, they were fainter, they were gone; but they had been there. And so exactly was the expression repeated on the fair young face of her who had crept to a point where she could see him, that it looked as though it had passed like a moving light from him to her.

Not a word was spoken, not a sound was made. She stood like a spirit beside him, and he bent over his work.

It happened, at length, that he had occasion to change the instrument in his hand for his shoemaker's knife. He had taken it up and was stooping to work again, when his eyes caught the skirt of her dress. He raised them and saw her face. The two spectators started forward, but she stayed them with a motion of her hand. She had no fear of his striking at her with the knife, though they had.

He stared at her with a fearful look, and in the pauses of his quick and labored breathing, he was heard to say:

"What is this?"

With the tears streaming down her face, she put her two hands to her lips and kissed them to him.

"You are not the gaoler's daughter?"

She sighed "No."

"Who are you?"

Not yet trusting of her voice, she sat down on the bench beside him; he laid the knife down softly, as he sat staring at her.

Her golden hair, which she wore in long curls, had been hurriedly pushed aside and fell down over her neck. Advancing his hand by little and little, he took it up and looked at it. In the midst of the action he went astray, and, with another deep sigh, fell to work at his shoemaking.

But not for long. She laid her hand upon his shoulder. After looking doubtfully at it, two or three times, as if to be sure that it was really there, he laid down his work, put his hand to his neck, and took off a blackened string with a scrap of folded rag attached to it. He opened this carefully on his knee, and it contained a very little quantity of hair: not more than one or two long golden hairs, which he had, in some old day, wound off upon his finger.

He took her hair into his hand again, and looked closely at it. "It is the same. How can it be!" He turned her full to the light and looked at her.

"She had laid her head upon my shoulder that night when I was summoned out—she had a fear of my going, though I had none—and when I was brought to the North Tower they found these upon my sleeve. 'You will leave me them? They can never help me to escape in the body, though they may in spirit.' Those were the words I said."

He formed this speech with his lips many times before he could utter it. But when he did find spoken words for it, they came to him coherently, though slowly.

"How was this?—*Was it you?*"

Once more the two spectators started, as he turned upon her with a frightful suddenness. But she sat perfectly still in his grasp and only said, in a low voice, "I entreat you, good gentlemen, do not come near us!"

"Hark!" he exclaimed. "Whose voice was that?"

His hands released her, as he uttered this cry, and went up to his white hair which they tore in a frenzy. It died out, as everything but his shoemaking did die out of him, and he refolded his little packet and tried to secure it in his breast; but he still looked at her and gloomily shook his head.

"No, no, no; you are too young, too blooming. It can't be. See what the prisoner is. No, no. She was—and he was—before the slow years of the North Tower—ages ago. What is your name, my gentle angel?"

"Oh, sir, at another time you shall know my name, and who my mother was, and who my father, and how I never knew their hard, hard history. But I cannot tell you at this time.

"If you hear in my voice any resemblance to a voice that once was sweet music in your ears, weep for it! If you touch, in touching my hair, anything that recalls a beloved head that lay on your breast when you were young and free, weep for it! If I bring back the remembrance of a home long desolate, while your poor heart pined away, weep for it, weep for it!"

He had sunk in her arms, and his face dropped on her breast, a sight so touching, yet so terrible in the tremendous wrong and suffering which had gone before it, that the two beholders covered their faces.

When the quiet of the garret had been long undisturbed, they came forward to raise the father and daughter from the ground. He had gradually dropped to the floor, and lay there in a lethargy, worn out. She had nestled down with him, that his head might lie upon her arm.

"If, without disturbing him," she said, raising her hand to Mr. Lorry as he stooped over them, after repeated blowings of his nose, "all could be arranged for our leaving Paris at once, so that, from the very door, he could be taken away—"

"But, consider. Is he fit for the journey?"

"More fit for that, I think, than to remain in this city, so dreadful to him."

"It is true," said Defarge, who was kneeling to hear. "More than that; Monsieur Manette is, for all reasons, best out of France. Say, shall I hire a carriage and post horses?"

"That's business," said Mr. Lorry, "and if business is to be done, I had better do it."

"Then be so kind," urged Miss Manette, "as to leave us here. You see how composed he has become, and you cannot be afraid to leave him with me now. If you will lock the door to secure us from interruption, I will take care of him until you return, and then we will remove him straight."

Both Mr. Lorry and Defarge were rather disinclined to this course, and in favor of one of them remaining. But, as there were not only carriage and horses to be seen to, but traveling papers, and as time pressed, for the day was drawing to an end, it came at last to their hastily dividing the business that was necessary to be done, and hurrying away to do it.

Then, the daughter laid her head down on the hard ground close to the father's side, and they both lay quiet, until a light gleamed through the chinks in the wall.

Mr. Lorry and Monsieur Defarge had made all ready for the journey and had brought with them, besides traveling cloaks and wrappers, bread and meat, wine, and hot coffee. Monsieur Defarge and Mr. Lorry roused the captive and assisted him to his feet.

In the submissive way of one long accustomed to obey under coercion, he ate and drank what they gave him to eat and drink, and put on the cloak and other wrappings that they gave him to wear. He readily responded to his daughter's drawing her arm through his, and took—and kept—her hand in both his own.

They began to descend; Monsieur Defarge going first with the lamp, Mr. Lorry closing the little procession. They had not traversed many steps of the long main staircase when the prisoner stopped, and stared at the roof and round at the walls.

That he had no recollection of his having been brought from his prison to that house was apparent. They heard him mutter, "One Hundred and Five, North Tower"; and when he looked about him, it evidently was

Ronald Searle

for the strong fortress walls which had long encompassed him.

No crowd was about the door; no people were at any of the windows; not even a chance passer-by was in the street. An unnatural silence and desertion reigned there. Only one soul was to be seen, Madame Defarge—who leaned against the doorpost, knitting, and saw nothing.

The prisoner had got into a coach, and his daughter had followed him, when Mr. Lorry's feet were arrested on the step by his asking, miserably, for his shoemaking tools and the unfinished shoes. Madame Defarge called to her husband that she would get them. She quickly brought them down and handed them in—and immediately afterwards leaned against the doorpost, knitting, and saw nothing.

Defarge got upon the box and gave the word "To the Barrier!"[1] The postilion cracked his whip, and they clattered away.

Under the overswinging lamps—swinging ever brighter in the better streets, and ever dimmer in the worse—and by lighted shops, gay crowds, illuminated coffee houses, and theater doors, to one of the city gates. Soldiers with lanterns, at the guardhouse there, "Your papers, travelers!" "See here then, Monsieur the Officer," said Defarge, getting down and taking him gravely apart, "these are the papers of monsieur inside, with the white head. They were consigned to me, with him, at the—." He dropped his voice, there was a flutter among the military lanterns, and one of them being handed into the coach by an arm in uniform, the eyes connected with the arm looked, not an everyday or an everynight look, at monsieur with the white head. "It is well. Forward!" from the uniform. "Adieu!" from Defarge. And so, under a short grove of feebler and feebler overswinging lamps, out under the great grove of stars.

Beneath that arch of unmoved and eternal lights the shadows of the night were broad and black. All through the cold and restless interval, until dawn, they whispered in the ears of Mr. Jarvis Lorry—sitting opposite the buried man who had been dug out, and wondering what subtle powers were forever lost to him, and what were capable of restoration—the old inquiry:

"I hope you care to be recalled to life?"

And the answer:

"I can't say."

---

1. ***the Barrier,*** the gate of Paris where travelers' identification was checked.

WHAT DO YOU SAY?

1. What is the meaning of Doctor Manette's removing a rag, attached to his neck, and taking from it two golden hairs?

2. What is the significance of "One Hundred and Five, North Tower"?

3. What is the connection between the incident of Miss Manette's attempt to make her father weep and the title of Book the First?

4. (a) How would you explain the fulfillment of Jarvis Lorry's message on the Dover mail? *(b)* What do the last three lines of the chapter make you wonder about?

TIMETABLE for Book the First

1757
Dr. Alexandre Manette is imprisoned in the Bastille.

1758
Lucie Manette is born.

1760
Lucie Manette's mother dies.

1775-1783
The American colonists fight for independence from England.

1775
The novel opens.

Lucie Manette and Jarvis Lorry take Dr. Manette from the Defarges, who have received him after his rescue from the Bastille.

BOOK THE SECOND: The Golden Thread

CHAPTER I
Five Years Later

Tellson's Bank by Temple Bar was an old-fashioned place, even in the year one thousand seven hundred and eighty. It was very small, very dark, very ugly, very incommodious. It was an old-fashioned place, moreover, in the moral attribute that the partners in the House were proud of its smallness, proud of its darkness, proud of its ugliness, proud of its incommodiousness. They were even boastful of its eminence in those particulars and were fired by an express conviction that, if it were less objectionable, it would be less respectable. This was no passive belief, but an active weapon which they flashed at more convenient places of business. Tellson's, they said, wanted no elbow room, Tellson's wanted no light, Tellson's wanted no embellishment. Noakes and Co.'s might, or Snooks Brothers' might, but Tellson's, thank heaven!—

Any one of these partners would have disinherited his son on the question of rebuilding Tellson's. In this respect the House was much on a par with the Country; which did very often disinherit its sons for suggesting improvements in laws and customs that had long been highly objectionable, but were only the more respectable.

Thus it had come to pass that Tellson's was the triumphant perfection of inconvenience. After bursting open a door of idiotic obstinacy with a weak rattle in its throat, you fell into Tellson's down two steps and came to your senses in a miserable little shop with two little counters, where the oldest of men made your check shake as if the wind rustled it, while they examined the signature by the dingiest of windows, which were always under a shower bath of mud from Fleet Street, and which were made the dingier by their own iron bars proper, and the heavy shadow of Temple Bar. If your business necessitated your seeing "the House," you were put into a species of Condemned Hold at the back, where you meditated on a misspent life, until the House came with its hands in its pockets, and you could hardly blink at it in the dismal twilight. Your money came out of, or went into, wormy old wooden drawers, particles of which flew up your nose and down your throat when they were opened and shut. Your bank notes had a musty odor, as if they were fast decomposing into rags again. Your plate was stowed away among the neighboring cesspools, and evil communications corrupted its good polish in a day or two. Your deeds got into extemporized strong rooms made of kitchens and sculleries. Your lighter boxes of family papers went upstairs into a Barmecide room,[1] that always had a great dining table in it and never had a dinner, and where, even in the year one thousand seven hundred and eighty, the first letters written to you by your old love, or by your little children, were but newly released from the horror of being ogled through the windows, by the heads exposed on Temple Bar.

But indeed, at that time, putting to death was a recipe much in vogue with all trades and professions, and not least of all with Tellson's. Death is Nature's remedy for all things, and why not Legislation's? Accordingly, the forger was put to Death; the utterer of a bad note was put to Death; the unlawful opener of a letter was put to Death; the holder of a horse at Tellson's door, who made off with it, was put to

1. ***Barmecide*** (bär′mə sīd) ***room,*** a room for pretended feasts with empty dishes. Barmecide was a wealthy man in the ***Arabian Nights*** who gave a beggar a pretended feast on empty dishes.

Death; the sounders of three-fourths of the notes in the whole gamut of Crime were put to Death. Not that it did the least good in the way of prevention—it might almost have been worth remarking that the fact was exactly the reverse—but, it cleared off—as to this world—the trouble of each particular case, and left nothing else connected with it to be looked after. Thus, Tellson's, in its day, like greater places of business, had taken so many lives that, if the heads laid low before it had been ranged on Temple Bar instead of being privately disposed of, they would probably have excluded what little light the ground floor had, in a rather significant manner.

Cramped in all kinds of dim cupboards and hutches at Tellson's, the oldest of men carried on the business gravely. When they took a young man into Tellson's London House, they hid him somewhere till he was old. They kept him in a dark place, like a cheese, until he had the full Tellson flavor and blue mold upon him. Then only was he permitted to be seen, spectacularly poring over large books.

Outside Tellson's—never by any means in it, unless called in—was an odd-job man, an occasional porter and messenger, who served as the live sign of the House. He was never absent during business hours, unless upon an errand, and then he was represented by his son, a grisly urchin of twelve, who was his express image. People understood that Tellson's, in a stately way, tolerated the odd-job man. The House had always tolerated some person in that capacity, and time and tide had drifted this person to the post. His surname was Cruncher and, on the youthful occasion of his renouncing by proxy the works of darkness, in the easterly parish church of Houndsditch, he had received the added appellation of Jerry.

The scene was Mr. Cruncher's private lodging in Hanging Sword Alley, Whitefriars;[2] the time, half-past seven of the clock on a windy March morning, Anno Domini seventeen hundred and eighty. (Mr. Cruncher himself always spoke of the year of our Lord as Anna Dominoes; apparently under the impression that the Christian era dated from the invention of a popular game, by a lady who had bestowed her name upon it.)

Mr. Cruncher's apartments were not in a savory neighborhood and were but two in number, even if a closet with a single pane of glass in it might be counted as one. But they were very decently kept. Early as it was, on the windy March morning, the room in which he lay abed was already scrubbed throughout; and between the cups and saucers arranged for breakfast, and the lumbering deal table, a very clean white cloth was spread.

Mr. Cruncher reposed under a patchwork counterpane. At first he slept heavily, but, by degrees, began to roll and surge in bed, until he rose above the surface, with his spiky hair looking as if it must tear the sheets to ribbons. At which juncture, he exclaimed, in a voice of dire exasperation:

"Bust me, if she ain't at it agin!"

A woman of orderly and industrious appearance rose from her knees in a corner, with sufficient haste and trepidation to show that she was the person referred to.

"What!" said Mr. Cruncher, looking out of bed for a boot. "You're at it agin, are you?"

After hailing the morn with this second salutation, he threw a boot at the woman as a third. It was a very muddy boot, and may introduce the odd circumstance connected with Mr. Cruncher's domestic economy, that whereas he often came home after banking hours with clean boots, he often got up next morning to find the same boots covered with clay.

"What," said Mr. Cruncher, varying his apostrophe after missing his mark—"what are you up to, Aggerawayter?"[3]

2. ***Hanging Sword Alley, Whitefriars,*** name of a street and district in London, frequented by criminals and evildoers. 3. ***Aggerawayter,*** Mr. Cruncher's garbled version of ***aggravator,*** his name for his wife when she displeased him with her too careful observance of religious duties.

"I was only saying my prayers."

"Saying your prayers! You're a nice woman! What do you mean by flopping yourself down and praying agin me?"

"I was not praying against you; I was praying for you."

"You weren't! And if you were, I won't be took the liberty with. Here! your mother's a nice woman, young Jerry, going a-praying agin your father's prosperity. You've got a dutiful mother, you have, my son. You've got a religious mother, you have, my boy; going and flopping herself down, and praying that the bread and butter may be snatched out of the mouth of her only child.

"I won't be prayed agin, I tell you. I can't afford it. I'm not a-going to be made unlucky by *your* sneaking. If you must go flopping yourself down, flop in favor of your husband and child, and not in opposition to 'em. B-u-u-ust me!" said Mr. Cruncher, who all this time had been putting on his clothes, "if I ain't, what with piety and one blowed thing and another, been choused this last week into as bad luck as ever a poor devil of a honest tradesman met with! Young Jerry, dress yourself, my boy, and while I clean my boots keep a eye upon your mother now and then, and if you see any signs of more flopping, give me a call. For, I tell you," here he addressed his wife once more, "I won't be gone agin, in this manner. I won't put up with it, Aggerawayter, and what do you say now!"

Growling, in addition, such phrases as, "Ah! yes! You're religious, too. You wouldn't put yourself in opposition to the interests of your husband and child, would you? Not you!" and throwing off other sarcastic sparks from the whirling grindstone of his indignation, Mr. Cruncher betook himself to his boot cleaning and his general preparation for business. In the meantime, his son, whose head was garnished with tenderer spikes, and whose young eyes stood close by one another, as his father's did, kept the required watch upon his mother. He greatly disturbed that poor woman at intervals, by darting out of his sleeping closet, where he made his toilet, with a suppressed cry of, "You are going to flop, mother—Halloa, father!" and, after raising this fictitious alarm, darting in again with an undutiful grin.

Mr. Cruncher's temper was not at all improved when he came to his breakfast. He resented Mrs. Cruncher's saying grace with particular animosity. "Now, Aggerawayter! What are you up to? At it agin?"

His wife explained that she had merely "asked a blessing."

"Don't do it!" said Mr. Cruncher, looking about, as if he rather expected to see the loaf disappear under the efficacy of his wife's petitions. "I ain't a-going to be blest out of house and home. I won't have my wittles blest off my table. Keep still!"

Exceedingly red-eyed and grim, as if he had been up all night at a party which had taken anything but a convivial turn, Jerry Cruncher worried his breakfast rather than ate it, growling over it like any four-footed inmate of a menagerie. Toward nine o'clock he smoothed his ruffled aspect, and, presenting as respectful and businesslike an exterior as he could overlay his natural self with, issued forth to the occupation of the day.

It could scarcely be called a trade, in spite of his favorite description of himself as "a honest tradesman." His stock consisted of a wooden stool, made out of a broken-backed chair cut down, which stool, young Jerry, walking at his father's side, carried every morning to beneath the banking-house window that was nearest Temple Bar; where, with the addition of the first handful of straw that could be gleaned from any passing vehicle to keep the cold and wet from the odd-job man's feet, it formed the encampment for the day. On this post of his, Mr. Cruncher was as well known to Fleet Street, and the Temple, as the Bar itself—and was almost as ill-looking.

Encamped at a quarter before nine, in

good time to touch his three-cornered hat to the oldest men as they passed in to Tellson's, Jerry took up his station on this windy March morning, with young Jerry standing by him, when not engaged in making forays through the Bar, to inflict bodily and mental injuries of an acute description on passing boys who were small enough for his amiable purpose. Father and son, extremely like each other, looking silently on at the morning traffic in Fleet Street, with their two heads as near to one another as the two eyes of each were, bore a considerable resemblance to a pair of monkeys. The resemblance was not lessened by the accidental circumstance, that the mature Jerry bit and spat out straw, while the twinkling eyes of the youthful Jerry were as restlessly watchful of him as of everything else in Fleet Street.

The head of one of the regular indoor messengers attached to Tellson's establishment was put through the door, and the word was given:

"Porter wanted!"

"Hooray, father! Here's an early job to begin with!"

Having thus given his parent God speed, young Jerry seated himself on the stool, entered on his reversionary interest in the straw his father had been chewing, and cogitated.

"Al-ways rusty! His fingers is al-ways rusty!" muttered young Jerry. "Where does my father get all that iron rust from? He don't get no iron rust here!"

WHAT DO YOU SAY?

1. *(a)* Describe Tellson's Bank in your own words. *(b)* Why did Tellson's choose to remain old-fashioned?

2. *(a)* Why do you think Jerry Cruncher is so set against his wife's praying? *(b)* Does the fact that she tells Jerry she is praying **for** him suggest anything to you? *(c)* What two other clues arouse your suspicions about Jerry Cruncher?

3. In what ways is young Jerry like his father?

CHAPTER II
A Sight

"You know the Old Bailey[1] well, no doubt?" said one of the oldest of clerks to Jerry Cruncher, the messenger.

"Ye-es, sir," returned Jerry, in something of a dogged manner. "I *do* know the Bailey."

"Just so. And you know Mr. Lorry."

"I know Mr. Lorry, sir, much better than I know the Bailey. Much better," said Jerry, not unlike a reluctant witness at the establishment in question, "than I, as a honest tradesman, wish to know the Bailey."

"Very well. Find the door where the witnesses go in, and show the doorkeeper this note for Mr. Lorry. He will then let you in."

"Into the court, sir?"

"Into the court."

"Am I to wait in the court, sir?"

"I am going to tell you. The doorkeeper will pass the note to Mr. Lorry, and you make any gesture that will attract Mr. Lorry's attention and show him where you stand. Then remain there until he wants you."

"Is that all, sir?"

"That's all. He wishes to have a messenger at hand. This is to tell him you are there."

As the ancient clerk deliberately folded and superscribed the note, Mr. Cruncher remarked:

"I suppose they'll be trying forgeries this morning?"

"Treason!"

"That's quartering," said Jerry. "Barbarous!"

"It is the law," remarked the ancient clerk, turning his surprised spectacles upon him. "It is the law."

"It's hard in the law to spile a man, I think. It's hard enough to kill him, but it's wery hard to spile him, sir."

"Not at all," returned the ancient clerk.

1. *Old Bailey,* the chief court in London for trying criminal cases.

"Speak well of the law. Take care of your chest and voice, my good friend, and leave the law to take care of itself."

"It's the damp, sir, what settles on my chest," said Jerry. "A damp way of earning a living mine is."

"Well," said the old clerk, "we all have our various ways of gaining a livelihood. Here is the letter. Go along." Jerry took the letter, and making his way through the crowd with the skill of a man accustomed to make his way quietly, found the door he sought and handed in his letter through a trap in it. After some delay and demur, the door grudgingly turned on its hinges a very little way and allowed Mr. Jerry Cruncher to squeeze himself into court.

"What's on?" he asked, in a whisper, of the man he found himself next to.

"The treason case."

"The quartering one, eh?"

"Ah!" returned the man, with a relish; "he'll be drawn on a hurdle to be half hanged, and then he'll be taken down and sliced before his own face, and then his inside will be taken out and burnt while he looks on, and then his head will be chopped off, and he'll be cut into quarters. That's the sentence."

"If he's found guilty, you mean to say?" Jerry added, by way of proviso.

"Oh! they'll find him guilty," said the other. "Don't you be afraid of that."

Mr. Cruncher's attention was here diverted to the doorkeeper, whom he saw making his way to Mr. Lorry, with the note in his hand. Mr. Lorry sat at a table, among the gentlemen in wigs; not far from a wigged gentleman, the prisoner's counsel, who had a great bundle of papers before him, and nearly opposite another wigged gentleman with his hands in his pockets, whose whole attention, when Mr. Cruncher looked at him then or afterwards, seemed to be concentrated on the ceiling of the court. After some gruff coughing and rubbing of his chin and signing with his hand, Jerry attracted the notice of Mr. Lorry, who had stood up to look for him, and who quietly nodded and sat down again.

The entrance of the Judge, and a consequent great stir and settling down in the court, stopped the dialogue. Presently the dock became the central point of interest. Two jailers, who had been standing there, went out, and the prisoner was brought in and put to the bar.

Everybody present, except the one wigged gentleman who looked at the ceiling, stared at him. Eager faces strained round pillars and corners to get a sight of him; spectators stood a-tiptoe, got upon ledges, stood upon next to nothing, to see every inch of him. Conspicuous among these latter, like an animated bit of the spiked wall of Newgate,[2] Jerry stood.

The object of all this staring was a young man of about five-and-twenty, well-grown and well-looking, with a sunburnt cheek and a dark eye. He was plainly dressed in black, or very dark gray, and his hair, which was long and dark, was gathered in a ribbon at the back of his neck; more to be out of his way than for ornament. He was quite self-possessed, bowed to the Judge, and stood quiet.

Silence in the court! Charles Darnay had yesterday pleaded not guilty to an indictment denouncing him—with infinite jingle and jangle—for that he was a false traitor to our serene, illustrious, excellent, and so forth, prince, our Lord the King, by reason of his having, on divers occasions, and by divers means and ways, assisted Lewis, the French King, in his wars against our said serene, illustrious, excellent, and so forth; that was to say, by coming and going, between the dominions of our said serene, illustrious, excellent, and so forth, and those of the said French Lewis, and wickedly, falsely, traitorously, and otherwise evil-adverbiously, revealing to the said French Lewis what forces our said serene, illustrious, excellent, and so forth, had in prepara-

2. ***Newgate,*** a famous London prison, near the Old Bailey.

tion to send to Canada and North America. Jerry made out that the jury were swearing in, and that Mr. Attorney General was making ready to speak.

The accused, who was—and who knew he was—being mentally hanged, beheaded, and quartered by everybody there, neither flinched from the situation nor assumed any theatrical air in it. He was quiet and attentive; watched the opening proceedings with a grave interest; and stood with his hands resting on the slab of wood before him, so composedly that they had not displaced a leaf of the herbs with which it was strewn as a precaution against jail air and jail fever.

Over the prisoner's head there was a mirror, to throw the light down upon him. He looked up and when he saw the glass, his face flushed and his hand pushed the herbs away.

About on a level with his eyes, there sat two persons upon whom his look immediately rested; so immediately, all the eyes that were turned upon him, turned to them.

The spectators saw in the two figures a young lady of little more than twenty and a gentleman who was evidently her father; a man of very remarkable appearance in respect of the absolute whiteness of his hair, and a certain indescribable intensity of face; a handsome man, not past the prime of life.

His daughter had one of her hands drawn through his arm, as she sat by him, and the other pressed upon it. She had drawn close to him, in her dread of the scene, and in her pity for the prisoner. This had been so very noticeable, so very powerfully and naturally shown, that starers who had had no pity for him were touched by her; and the whisper went about, "Who are they?"

"Witnesses."

"For which side?"

"Against."

"Against what side?"

"The prisoner's."

The Judge, whose eyes had gone in the general direction, recalled them, leaned back in his seat, and looked steadily at the man whose life was in his hand, as Mr. Attorney General rose to spin the rope, grind the ax, and hammer the nails into the scaffold.

WHAT DO YOU SAY?

1. Of what crime is Charles Darnay accused?

2. What is your impression of "the wigged gentleman who looked at the ceiling"?

3. (a) What is the atmosphere in the courtroom? Comment on the attitudes of the spectators, the judge, and Mr. Attorney General. *(b)* The chapter ends with this line: ". . . Mr. Attorney General rose to spin the rope, grind the ax, and hammer the nails into the scaffold." What, exactly, does Dickens mean by this line?

CHAPTER III
A *Disappointment*

Mr. Attorney General had to inform the jury that the prisoner before them, though young in years, was old in the treasonable practices which claimed the forfeit of his life. That this correspondence with the public enemy was not a correspondence of today, or of yesterday, or even of last year, or of the year before. That it was certain the prisoner had, for longer than that, been in the habit of passing and repassing between France and England, on secret business of which he could give no honest account. That, if it were in the nature of traitorous ways to thrive—which happily it never was—the real wickedness and guilt of his business might have remained undiscovered. That Providence, however, had put it into the heart of a person who was beyond fear and beyond reproach to ferret out the nature of the prisoner's schemes, and, struck with horror, to disclose them to his Majesty's Chief Secretary of State and most honorable Privy Council.[1] That this patriot would be produced before them. That his

1. Privy Council, a group of counselors selected by the King of England to advise him in matters of state.

position and attitude were, on the whole, sublime. That he had been the prisoner's friend, but, at once in an auspicious and an evil hour detecting his infamy, had resolved to immolate the traitor he could no longer cherish in his bosom, on the sacred altar of his country. That, if statues were decreed in Britain, as in ancient Greece and Rome, to public benefactors, this shining citizen would assuredly have had one. That, as they were not so decreed, he probably would not have one. That Virtue, as had been observed by the poets—in many passages which he well knew the jury would have at the tips of their tongues, whereat the jury's countenances displayed a guilty consciousness that they knew nothing about the passages—was in a manner contagious; more especially the bright virtue known as patriotism, or love of country. That the lofty example of this immaculate and unimpeachable witness for the Crown had communicated itself to the prisoner's servant, and engendered in him a holy determination to examine his master's table drawers and pockets, and secrete his papers. That he (Mr. Attorney General) was prepared to hear some disparagement attempted of this admirable servant; but that, in a general way, he preferred him to his (Mr. Attorney General's) brothers and sisters, and honored him more than his (Mr. Attorney General's) father and mother. That he called with confidence on the jury to come and do likewise. That the evidence of these two witnesses, coupled with the documents of their discovering that would be produced, would show the prisoner to have been furnished with lists of his Majesty's forces, and of their disposition and preparation, both by sea and land, and would leave no doubt that he had habitually conveyed such information to a hostile power. That these lists could not be proved to be in the prisoner's handwriting; but that it was all the same; that, indeed, it was rather the better for the prosecution, as showing the prisoner to be artful in his precautions. That the proof would go back five years, and would show the prisoner already engaged in these pernicious missions, within a few weeks before the date of the very first action fought between the British troops and the Americans. That, for these reasons, the jury, being a loyal jury (as he knew they were), and being a responsible jury (as *they* knew they were), must positively find the prisoner guilty, and make an end of him, whether they liked it or not. That they never could lay their heads upon their pillows; that they never could tolerate the idea of their wives laying their heads upon their pillows; that they never could endure the notion of their children laying their heads upon their pillows: in short, that there never more could be, for them or theirs, any laying of heads upon pillows at all, unless the prisoner's head was taken off. That head Mr. Attorney General concluded by demanding of them, in the name of everything he could think of with a round turn in it, and on the faith of his solemn asseveration that he already considered the prisoner as good as dead and gone.

When the Attorney General ceased, a buzz arose in the court as if a cloud of great blueflies were swarming about the prisoner, in anticipation of what he was soon to become. When toned down again, the unimpeachable patriot appeared in the witness box.

Mr. Solicitor General then, following his leader's lead, examined the patriot, John Barsad, gentleman. The story of his pure soul was exactly what Mr. Attorney General had described it to be—perhaps, if it had a fault, a little too exactly. Having released his noble bosom of its burden, he would have modestly withdrawn himself, but that the wigged gentleman with the papers before him, sitting not far from Mr. Lorry, begged to ask him a few questions. The wigged gentleman sitting opposite, still looking at the ceiling of the court.

Had he ever been a spy himself? No, he scorned the base insinuation. What did he live upon? His property. Where was his property? He didn't precisely remember where it was. What was it? No business of anybody's. Had he inherited it? Yes, he had. From whom? Distant relation. Very distant? Rather. Ever been in prison? Certainly not. Never in a debtors' prison? Didn't see what that had to do with it. Never in a debtors' prison?—Come, once again. Never? Yes. How many times? Two or three times. Not five or six? Perhaps. Of what profession? Gentleman. Ever been kicked? Might have been. Frequently? No. Ever kicked downstairs? Decidedly not; once received a kick on the top of a staircase, and fell downstairs. Kicked on that occasion for cheating at dice? Something to that effect was said by the intoxicated liar who committed the assault, but it was not true. Swear it was not true? Positively. Ever live by cheating at play? Never. Ever live by play? Not more than other gentlemen do. Ever borrow money of the prisoner? Yes. Ever pay him? No. Was not this intimacy with the prisoner, in reality a very slight one, forced upon the prisoner in coaches, inns, and packets? No. Sure he saw the prisoner with these lists? Certain. Knew no more about the lists? No. Had not procured them himself, for instance? No. Expect to get anything by this evidence? No. Not in regular government pay and employment, to lay traps? Oh, dear no. Or to do anything? Oh, dear no. Swear that? Over and over again. No motives but motives of sheer patriotism? None whatever.

The virtuous servant, Roger Cly, swore his way through the case at a great rate. He had taken service with the prisoner four years ago. He had asked the prisoner, aboard the Calais packet, if he wanted a handy fellow, and the prisoner had engaged him. He had not asked the prisoner to take the handy fellow as an act of charity—never thought of such a thing. He began to have suspicions of the prisoner soon afterwards. In arranging his clothes he had seen similar lists to these in the prisoner's pockets, over and over again. He had taken these lists from the drawer of the prisoner's desk. He had not put them there first. He had seen the prisoner show these identical lists to French gentlemen of Calais, and similar lists to French gentlemen, both at Calais and Boulogne.[2] He loved his country, couldn't bear it, and had given information. He had never been suspected of stealing a silver teapot; he had been maligned respecting a mustard-pot, but it turned out to be only a plated one. He had known the last witness seven or eight years; that was merely a coincidence. He didn't call it a particularly curious coincidence. Neither did he call it a curious coincidence that true patriotism was *his* only motive too. He was a true Briton, and hoped there were many like him.

The blueflies buzzed again, and Mr. Attorney General called Mr. Jarvis Lorry.

"Mr. Jarvis Lorry, are you a clerk in Tellson's Bank?"

"I am."

"On a certain Friday night in November one thousand seven hundred and seventy-five, did business occasion you to travel between London and Dover by the mail?"

"It did."

"Were there any other passengers in the mail?"

"Two."

"Mr. Lorry, look upon the prisoner. Was he one of those two passengers?"

"I cannot undertake to say that he was."

"Does he resemble either of these two passengers?"

"Both were so wrapped up, the night was so dark, and we were all so reserved that I cannot say even that."

"Mr. Lorry, look again upon the prisoner. Supposing him wrapped up as those two passengers were, is there anything to render it unlikely that he was one of them?"

"No."

"You will not swear, Mr. Lorry, that he was not one of them?"

2. **Boulogne** (bü lōn′), a seaport in northern France.

"No."

"So at least you say he may have been one of them?"

"Yes. Except that I remember them both to have been—like myself—timorous of highwaymen, and the prisoner has not a timorous air."

"Did you ever see a counterfeit of timidity, Mr. Lorry?"

"I certainly have seen that."

"Mr. Lorry, look once more upon the prisoner. Have you seen him, to your certain knowledge, before?"

"I have."

"When?"

"I was returning from France a few days afterwards, and, at Calais, the prisoner came on board the packet ship in which I returned, and made the voyage with me."

"At what hour did he come on board?"

"At a little after midnight."

"In the dead of the night. Was he the only passenger who came on board at that untimely hour?"

"He happened to be the only one."

"Never mind about 'happening,' Mr. Lorry. He was the only passenger who came on board in the dead of the night?"

"He was."

"Were you traveling with any companion?"

"With two companions. A gentleman and lady. They are here."

"Had you any conversation with the prisoner?"

"Hardly any. The weather was stormy, the passage rough, and I lay on a sofa, almost from shore to shore."

"Miss Manette!"

The young lady, to whom all eyes had turned before, and now turned again, stood up. Her father rose with her, and kept her hand drawn through his arm.

"Miss Manette, look upon the prisoner."

To be confronted with such pity, and such earnest youth and beauty, was far more trying to the accused than to be confronted with the crowd. His efforts to control and steady his breathing shook the lips from which the color rushed to his heart. The buzz of the great flies was loud again.

"Miss Manette, have you seen the prisoner before?"

"Yes, sir."

"Where?"

"On board of the packet ship just now referred to, sir, and on the same occasion."

"You are the young lady just now referred to?"

"Oh! most unhappily, I am!"

The plaintive tone of her compassion merged into the less musical voice of the Judge, as he said fiercely: "Answer the questions put to you, and make no remark upon them."

"Miss Manette, had you any conversation with the prisoner on that passage across the Channel?"

"Yes, sir."

"Recall it."

In the midst of a profound stillness, she faintly began:

"When the gentleman came on board—"

"Do you mean the prisoner?" inquired the Judge, knitting his brows.

"Yes, my Lord."

"Then say the prisoner."

"When the prisoner came on board, he noticed that my father," turning her eyes lovingly to him, "was in a very weak state of health. My father was so reduced that I was afraid to take him out of the air; I had made a bed for him on the deck near the cabin steps, and I sat at his side to take care of him. There were no other passengers that night but we four. The prisoner was so good as to advise me how I could shelter my father from the wind and weather, better than I had done. I had not known how to do it well, not understanding how the wind would set when we were out of the harbor. He did it for me. He expressed great gentleness and kindness for my father's state, and I am sure he felt it. That was the manner of our beginning to speak together."

"Let me interrupt you. Had he come on board alone?"

"No."

"How many were with him?"

"Two French gentlemen."

"Had they conferred together?"

"They had conferred together until it was necessary for the French gentlemen to be landed in their boat."

"Had any papers been handed about among them, similar to these lists?"

"Some papers had been handed about among them, but I don't know what papers."

"Like these in shape and size?"

"Possibly, but indeed I don't know, although they stood very near to me: they stood at the top of the cabin steps to have the light of the lamp that was hanging there; it was a dull lamp, they spoke very low, and I did not hear what they said, and saw only that they looked at papers."

"Now, to the prisoner's conversation, Miss Manette."

"The prisoner was as open in his confidence with me—which arose out of my helpless situation—as he was kind, and good, and useful to my father. I hope," bursting into tears, "I may not repay him by doing him harm today."

Buzzing from the blueflies.

"Miss Manette, if the prisoner does not perfectly understand that you give the evidence which you cannot escape giving with great unwillingness, he is the only person present in that condition. Please go on."

"He told me that he was traveling on business of a delicate and difficult nature, which might get people into trouble and that he was therefore traveling under an assumed name. He said that this business had taken him to France, and might take him backwards and forwards between France and England for a long time to come."

"Did he say anything about America, Miss Manette?"

"He tried to explain to me how that quarrel had arisen, and he said that, so far as he could judge, it was a wrong and foolish one on England's part. He added, in a jesting way, that perhaps George Washington might gain almost as great a name in history as George the Third. But there was no harm in his way of saying this; it was said laughingly and to beguile the time."

The Judge looked up from his notes to glare at the tremendous heresy about George Washington. Mr. Attorney General now signified to my Lord that he deemed it necessary to call the young lady's father, Doctor Manette; who was called accordingly.

"Doctor Manette, look upon the prisoner. Have you ever seen him before?"

"Once. When he called at my lodgings in London. Some three years ago."

"Can you identify him as your fellow passenger on board the packet, or speak to his conversation with your daughter?"

"Sir, I can do neither."

"Is there any particular and special reason for your being unable to do either?"

He answered, in a low voice, "There is."

"Has it been your misfortune to undergo a long imprisonment, without trial, or even accusation, in your native country, Doctor Manette?"

He answered in a tone that went to every heart, "A long imprisonment."

"Were you newly released on the occasion in question?"

"They tell me so."

"Have you no remembrance of the occasion?"

"None. My mind is a blank, from some time—I cannot even say what time—when I employed myself, in my captivity, in making shoes, to the time when I found myself living in London with my dear daughter here. She had become familiar to me, when a gracious God restored my faculties; but, I am quite unable even to say how she had become familiar. I have no remembrance of the process."

Mr. Attorney General sat down, and the father and daughter sat down together.

A singular circumstance then arose in the case. The object in hand being to show that the prisoner went down, with some fellow plotter untracked, in the Dover mail on that Friday night in November five years ago, and got out of the mail in the night, as a blind, at a place where he did not remain, but from which he traveled back some dozen miles or more, to a garrison and dockyard, and there collected information; a witness was called to identify him as having been at the precise time required, in the coffee room of an hotel in that garrison-and-dockyard town, waiting for another person. The prisoner's counsel was cross-examining this witness with no result, except that he had never seen the prisoner on any other occasion, when the wigged gentleman who had all this time been looking at the ceiling of the court, wrote a word or two on a little piece of paper, screwed it up, and tossed it to him. Opening this piece of paper in the next pause, the counsel looked with great attention and curiosity at the prisoner.

"You say again you are quite sure that it *was* the prisoner?"

The witness was quite sure.

"Did you ever see anybody very like the prisoner?"

Not so like, the witness said, as that he could be mistaken.

"Look well upon that gentleman, my learned friend there," pointing to him who had tossed the paper over, "and then look well upon the prisoner. How say you? Are they very like each other?"

Allowing for my learned friend's appearance being careless and slovenly if not debauched, they were sufficiently like each other to surprise, not only the witness, but everybody present, when they were thus brought into comparison. My Lord being prayed to bid my learned friend lay aside his wig, and giving no very gracious consent, the likeness became much more remarkable. My Lord inquired of Mr. Stryver, the prisoner's counsel, whether they were next to try Mr. Carton (name of my learned friend) for treason? But, Mr. Stryver replied to my Lord, no; but he would ask the witness to tell him whether what happened once might happen twice; whether he would have been so confident if he had seen this illustration of his rashness sooner, whether he would be so confident, having seen it. The upshot of which was to smash this witness like a crockery vessel, and shiver his part of the case to useless lumber.

Mr. Stryver now fitted the prisoner's case on the jury, like a compact suit of clothes, showing them how the patriot, Barsad, was a hired spy and traitor, one of the greatest scoundrels upon earth since accursed Judas. How the virtuous servant, Cly, was his friend and partner; how the watchful eyes of those forgers and false swearers had rested on the prisoner as a victim, because some family affairs in France, he being of French extraction, did require his making those passages across the Channel—though what those affairs were, a consideration for others who were near and dear to him forbade him, even for his life, to disclose. How the evidence that had been warped and wrested from the young lady, whose anguish in giving it they had witnessed, came to nothing, involving the mere little innocent gallantries and politenesses likely to pass between any young gentleman and young lady so thrown together—with the exception of that reference to George Washington, which was altogether too extravagant and impossible to be regarded in any other light than as a monstrous joke.

Mr. Stryver then called his few witnesses, and Mr. Cruncher had to attend while Mr. Attorney General turned the whole suit of clothes Mr. Stryver had fitted on the jury, inside out; showing how Barsad and Cly were even a hundred times better than he had thought them, and the prisoner a hundred times worse. Lastly, came my Lord himself, turning the suit of clothes, now inside out, now outside in, but on the whole decidedly trimming and shaping them into grave clothes for the prisoner.

And now, the jury turned to consider, and the great flies swarmed again.

Mr. Carton, who had so long sat looking at the ceiling of the court, changed neither his place nor his attitude, even in this excitement. While his learned friend, Mr. Stryver, whispered with those who sat near, and from time to time glanced anxiously at the jury; while all the spectators moved more or less, and grouped themselves anew; while even my Lord himself arose from his seat, and slowly paced up and down his platform; this one man sat leaning back, with his torn gown half off him, his untidy wig put on just as it had happened to light on his head after its removal, his hands in his pockets, and his eyes on the ceiling as they had been all day. Something especially reckless in his demeanor not only gave him a disreputable look, but so diminished the strong resemblance he undoubtedly bore to the prisoner that many of the lookers-on, taking note of him now, said to one another they would hardly have thought the two were so alike.

Yet this Mr. Carton took in more of the details of the scene than he appeared to take in; for now, when Miss Manette's head dropped upon her father's breast, he was the first to see it, and to say audibly: "Officer! look to that young lady. Help the gentleman to take her out. Don't you see she will fall!"

There was much commiseration for her as she was removed, and much sympathy with her father. It had evidently been a great distress to him to have the days of his imprisonment recalled. He had shown strong internal agitation when he was questioned, and that pondering or brooding look which made him old had been upon him, like a heavy cloud, ever since. As he passed out, the jury, who had turned back, spoke, through their foreman.

They were not agreed and wished to retire. My Lord—perhaps with George Washington on his mind—showed some surprise that they were not agreed, but signified his pleasure that they should retire under watch and ward, and retired himself. The trial had lasted all day, and the lamps in the court were now being lighted. It began to be rumored that the jury would be out a long while. The spectators dropped off to get refreshment, and the prisoner withdrew to the back of the dock and sat down.

Mr. Lorry, who had gone out when the young lady and her father went out, now reappeared, and beckoned to Jerry, who in the slackened interest, could easily get near him.

"Jerry, if you wish to take something to eat, you can. You will be sure to hear when the jury come in. Don't be a moment behind them, for I want you to take the verdict back to the bank. You are the quickest messenger I know, and will get to Temple Bar long before I can."

Jerry had just enough forehead to knuckle, in acknowledgment of this communication and a shilling.

An hour and a half limped heavily away in the thief-and-rascal crowded passages below, even though assisted off with mutton pies and ale. The hoarse messenger had dropped into a doze, when a loud murmur and a rapid tide of people setting up the stairs that led to the court, carried him along with them.

"Jerry! Jerry!" Mr. Lorry was already calling at the door when he got there.

"Here, sir! It's a fight to get back again. Here I am, sir!"

Mr. Lorry handed him a paper through the throng. "Quick! Have you got it?"

"Yes, sir."

Hastily written on the paper was the word "ACQUITTED."

"If you had sent the message, 'Recalled to Life,' again," muttered Jerry as he turned, "I should have known what you meant this time."

He had no opportunity of saying, or so much as thinking, anything else, until he was clear of the Old Bailey; for the crowd came pouring out with a vehemence that nearly took him off his legs, and a loud buzz swept into the street as if the baffled blue-flies were dispersing in search of other carrion.

WHAT DO YOU SAY?

1. *(a)* Who are the first two witnesses against Darnay? *(b)* How would you judge the prosecution's case, including the testimony supplied by these two witnesses? *(c)* How does the defense attorney manage to discredit the two witnesses?

2. Several times throughout the description of the trial the author refers to the "buzzing of blue flies." What idea does he convey with this figurative expression?

3. What fact saved the prisoner's life? Is there any direct clue at this point that this fact might be important in later events?

4. Although the prisoner, Charles Darnay, is acquitted by the jury, Dickens has titled this chapter "A Disappointment." Explain.

KNOW YOUR WORDS

Formal language

Dickens, in this chapter, helps to ridicule the English Court by the use of exaggerated, formal, and "flowery" words and phrases which he puts into the mouth of Mr. Attorney General. For example, the author has Mr. Attorney General, in introducing the witnesses John Barsad and Roger Cly, state:

"That he [John Barsad] had been the prisoner's friend, but, at once in an ***auspicious*** and an evil hour ***detecting*** his ***infamy,*** had resolved to ***immolate*** the traitor he could no longer ***cherish in his bosom,*** on the sacred altar of his country .... That the ***lofty*** example of this ***immaculate*** and ***unimpeachable*** witness for the Crown had communicated itself to the prisoner's servant [Roger Cly], and ***engendered*** in him a holy determination to examine his master's table drawers and pockets, and ***secrete*** his papers."

Rewrite the above two sentences, replacing the italicized words and phrases with simple synonyms. Use your glossary or a dictionary for any words you do not understand.

CHAPTER IV
Congratulatory

From the dimly lighted passages of the court the last sediment of the human stew that had been boiling there all day was straining off, when Doctor Manette, Lucie Manette, his daughter, Mr. Lorry, the solicitor for the defense, and its counsel, Mr. Stryver, stood gathered around Mr. Charles Darnay—just released—congratulating him on his escape from death.

It would have been difficult by a far brighter light, to recognize in Doctor Manette, intellectual of face and upright of bearing, the shoemaker of the garret in Paris. Yet no one could have looked at him twice, without looking again; even though the opportunity of observation had not extended to the mournful cadence of his low, grave voice, and to the abstraction that overclouded him fitfully, without any apparent reason. While one external cause, and that a reference to his long lingering agony, would always—as on the trial—evoke this condition from the depths of his soul, it was also in its nature to arise of itself, and to draw a gloom over him, as incomprehensible to those unacquainted with his story as if they had seen the shadow of the actual Bastille[1] thrown upon him by a summer sun, when the substance was three hundred miles away.

Only his daughter had the power of charming this black brooding from his mind. She was the golden thread that united him to a Past beyond his misery, and to a Present beyond his misery; and the sound of her voice, the light of her face, the touch of her hand, had a strong beneficial influence with him almost always. Not absolutely always, for she could recall some occasions on which her power had failed; but

1. ***Bastille*** (bas tēl′), an old fortress in Paris used as a prison especially for political offenders. Destroyed on July 14, 1789, the beginning of the French Revolution, the word ***bastille*** has come to mean any prison.

they were few and slight, and she believed them over.

Mr. Darnay had kissed her hand fervently and gratefully, and had turned to Mr. Stryver, whom he warmly thanked.

Mr. Stryver, a man of little more than thirty, but looking twenty years older than he was, stout, loud, red, bluff, and free from any drawback of delicacy, had a pushing way of shouldering himself, morally and physically, into companies and conversations, that argued well for his shouldering his way up in life.

He still had his wig and gown on, and he said, squaring himself at his late client to that degree that he squeezed the innocent Mr. Lorry clean out of the group: "I am glad to have brought you off with honor, Mr. Darnay. It was an infamous prosecution, grossly infamous; but not the less likely to succeed on that account."

"You have laid me under an obligation to you for life—in two senses," said his late client, taking his hand.

"I have done my best for you, Mr. Darnay; and my best is as good as another man's, I believe."

It clearly being incumbent on someone to say, "Much better," Mr. Lorry said it; perhaps not quite disinterestedly, but with the interested object of squeezing himself back again.

"You think so?" said Mr. Stryver. "Well! you have been present all day and you ought to know. You are a man of business, too."

"And as such," quoth Mr. Lorry, whom the counsel learned in the law had now shouldered back into the group, just as he had previously shouldered him out of it—"as such I will appeal to Doctor Manette, to break up this conference and order us all to our homes. Miss Lucie looks ill, Mr. Darnay has had a terrible day, we are worn out."

"Speak for yourself, Mr. Lorry," said Stryver; "I have a night's work to do yet. Speak for yourself."

"I speak for myself," answered Mr. Lorry, "and for Mr. Darnay, and for Miss Lucie, and—Miss Lucie, do you not think I may speak for us all?" He asked her the question pointedly, and with a glance at her father.

His face had become frozen, as it were, in a very curious look at Darnay; an intent look, deepening into a frown of dislike and distrust, not even unmixed with fear. With this strange expression on him his thoughts had wandered away.

"My father," said Lucie, softly laying her hand on his.

He slowly shook the shadow off, and turned to her.

"Shall we go home, my father?"

With a long breath, he answered, "Yes."

The friends of the acquitted prisoner had dispersed, under the impression—which he himself had originated—that he would not be released that night. The lights were nearly all extinguished in the passages, the iron gates were being closed with a jar and a rattle, and the dismal place was deserted until tomorrow morning's interest of gallows, pillory, whipping post, and branding iron, should repeople it. Walking between her father and Mr. Darnay, Lucie Manette passed into the open air. A hackney coach was called, and the father and daughter departed in it.

Mr. Stryver had left them in the passages, to shoulder his way back to the robing room. Another person, who had not joined the group, or interchanged a word with anyone of them, but who had been leaning against the wall where its shadow was darkest, had silently strolled out after the rest, and had looked on until the coach drove away. He now stepped up to where Mr. Lorry and Mr. Darnay stood upon the pavement.

"So, Mr. Lorry! Men of business may speak to Mr. Darnay now?"

Nobody had made any acknowledgment of Mr. Carton's part in the day's proceedings; nobody had known of it. He was unrobed, and was none the better for it in appearance.

"If you knew what a conflict goes on in the business mind when the business mind is divided between good-natured impulse and business appearances, you would be amused, Mr. Darnay."

Mr. Lorry reddened and said warmly, "You have mentioned that before, sir. We men of business who serve a House are not our own masters. We have to think of the House more than ourselves."

"*I* know, *I* know," rejoined Mr. Carton, carelessly. "Don't be nettled, Mr. Lorry. You are as good as another, I have no doubt; better, I dare say."

"And indeed, sir," pursued Mr. Lorry, not minding him, "I really don't know what you have to do with the matter. If you'll excuse me, as very much your elder, for saying so, I really don't know that it is your business."

"Business! Bless you, *I* have no business," said Mr. Carton.

"It is a pity you have not, sir."

"I think so, too."

"If you had," pursued Mr. Lorry, "perhaps you would attend to it."

"Lord love you, no!—I shouldn't," said Mr. Carton.

"Well, sir!" cried Mr. Lorry, thoroughly heated by his indifference, "business is a very good thing, and a very respectable thing. And, sir, if business imposes its restraints and its silences and impediments, Mr. Darnay as a young gentleman of generosity knows how to make allowance for that circumstance. Mr. Darnay, good night, God bless you, sir! I hope you have been this day preserved for a prosperous and happy life.—Chair there!"

Perhaps a little angry with himself, as well as with the barrister, Mr. Lorry bustled into the chair, and was carried off to Tellson's. Carton, who smelt of port wine, and did not appear to be quite sober, laughed then, and turned to Darnay:

"This is a strange chance that throws you and me together. This must be a strange night to you, standing alone here with your counterpart on these street stones?"

"I hardly seem yet," returned Charles Darnay, "to belong to this world again."

"I don't wonder at it; it's not so long since you were pretty far advanced on your way to another. You speak faintly."

"I begin to think I *am* faint."

"Then why the devil don't you dine? I dined, myself, while those numskulls were deliberating which world you should belong to—this, or some other. Let me show you the nearest tavern to dine well at."

Drawing his arm through his own, he took him down Ludgate Hill to Fleet Street, and so, up a covered way, into a tavern. Here they were shown into a little room, where Charles Darnay was soon recruiting his strength with a good plain dinner and good wine; while Carton sat opposite to him at the same table, with his separate bottle of port before him, and his fully half-insolent manner upon him.

"Do you feel yet that you belong to this terrestrial scheme again, Mr. Darnay?"

"I am frightfully confused regarding time and place; but I am so far mended as to feel that."

"It must be an immense satisfaction!"

He said it bitterly, and filled up his glass again, which was a large one.

"As to me, the greatest desire I have, is to forget that I belong to it. It has no good in it for me—except wine like this—nor I for it. So we are not much alike in that particular. Indeed, I begin to think we are not much alike in any particular, you and I."

Confused by the emotion of the day, and feeling his being there with this double of coarse deportment to be like a dream, Charles Darnay was at a loss how to answer; finally, answered not at all.

"Now your dinner is done," Carton presently said, "why don't you call a health, Mr. Darnay; why don't you give your toast?"

"What health? What toast?"

"Why, it's on the tip of your tongue. It ought to be, it must be, I'll swear it's there."

"Miss Manette, then!"

Looking his companion full in the face while he drank the toast, Carton flung his glass over his shoulder against the wall, where it shivered to pieces; then rang the bell, and ordered in another.

"That's a fair young lady to hand to a coach in the dark, Mr. Darnay!" he said, filling his new goblet.

A slight frown and a laconic "Yes," were the answer.

"That's a fair young lady to be pitied by and wept for by! How does it feel? Is it worth being tried for one's life, to be the object of such sympathy and compassion, Mr. Darnay?"

Again Darnay answered not a word.

"She was mightily pleased to have your message, when I gave it her. Not that she showed she was pleased, but I suppose she was."

The allusion served as a timely reminder to Darnay that this disagreeable companion, had, of his own free will, assisted him in the strait of the day. He turned the dialogue to that point, and thanked him for it.

"I neither want any thanks, nor merit any," was the careless rejoinder. "It was nothing to do, in the first place; and I don't know why I did it, in the second. Mr. Darnay, let me ask you a question."

"Willingly, and a small return for your good offices."

"Do you think I particularly like you?"

"Really, Mr. Carton," returned the other, oddly disconcerted, "I have not asked myself that question."

"But ask yourself the question now."

"You have acted as if you do; but I don't think you do."

"*I* don't think I do," said Carton. "I begin to have a very good opinion of your understanding."

"Nevertheless," pursued Darnay, rising to ring the bell, "there is nothing in that, I hope, to prevent my calling the reckoning, and our parting without ill-blood on either side."

Carton rejoining, "Nothing in life!" Darnay rang. "Do you call the whole reckoning?" said Carton. On his answering in the affirmative, "Then bring me another pint of wine, drawer, and wake me at ten."

The bill being paid, Charles Darnay rose and wished him good night. Without returning the wish, Carton rose too, with something of a threat of defiance in his manner, and said, "A last word, Mr. Darnay: you think I am drunk?"

"I think you have been drinking, Mr. Carton."

"Think? You know I have been drinking."

"Since I must say so, I know it."

"Then you shall likewise know why. I am a disappointed drudge, sir. I care for no man on earth, and no man on earth cares for me."

"Much to be regretted. You might have used your talents better."

"Maybe so, Mr. Darnay; maybe not. Don't let your sober face elate you, however; you don't know what it may come to. Good night!"

When he was left alone, this strange being took up a candle, went to a glass that hung against the wall, and surveyed himself minutely in it.

"Do you particularly like the man?" he muttered, at his own image; "why should you particularly like a man who resembles you? There is nothing in you to like; you know that. Ah, confound you! What a change you have made in yourself! A good reason for taking to a man, that he shows you what you have fallen away from, and what you might have been! Change places with him, and would you have been looked at by those blue eyes as he was, and commiserated by that agitated face as he was? Come on, and have it out in plain words! You hate the fellow."

He resorted to his pint of wine for consolation, drank it all in a few minutes, and fell asleep on his arms, with his hair straggling over the table, and a long winding sheet in the candle dripping down upon him.

WHAT DO YOU SAY?

1. Reread page 487, column 2, paragraph 2. Have you been given any reason so far for this reaction on the part of Dr. Manette? What, if anything, does it suggest to you?

2. What evidence can you find that Sydney Carton has become interested in Lucie Manette?

3. What is your reaction to Sydney Carton?

CHAPTER V
The Jackal

It had once been noted at the Bar that while Mr. Stryver was a glib man, and an unscrupulous, and a ready, and a bold, he had not that faculty of extracting the essence from a heap of statements, which is among the most striking and necessary of the advocate's accomplishments. But a remarkable improvement came upon him as to this. The more business he got, the greater his power seemed to grow of getting at its pith and marrow; and however late at night he sat carousing with Sydney Carton, he always had his points at his fingers' ends in the morning.

Sydney Carton, idlest and most unpromising of men, was Stryver's great ally. What the two drank together might have floated a king's ship. Stryver never had a case in hand anywhere but Carton was there, with his hands in his pockets, staring at the ceiling of the court; they went the same Circuit, and even there they prolonged their usual orgies late into the night, and Carton was rumored to be seen at broad day, going home stealthily and unsteadily to his lodgings, like a dissipated cat. At last it began to get about, among such as were interested in the matter, that although Sydney Carton would never be a lion, he was an amazing good jackal, and that he rendered suit and service to Stryver in that humble capacity.

"Ten o'clock, sir," said the man at the tavern, whom he had charged to wake him —"ten o'clock, sir."

"*What's* the matter?"

"Ten o'clock, sir."

"What do you mean? Ten o'clock at night?"

"Yes, sir. Your honor told me to call you."

"Oh! I remember. Very well, very well."

After a few dull efforts to get to sleep again, which the man dexterously combated by stirring the fire continuously for five minutes, he got up, tossed his hat on, and walked out. He turned into the Temple,[1] and having revived himself by twice pacing the pavements of King's Bench walk, turned into the Stryver chambers.

"You are a little late, Memory," said Stryver.

"About the usual time."

They went into a dingy room lined with books and littered with papers, where there was a blazing fire. A kettle steamed upon the hob, and in the midst of the wreck of papers a table shone, with plenty of wine upon it, and brandy, and rum, and sugar, and lemons.

"That was a rare point, Sydney, that you brought to bear upon the identification. How did you come by it? When did it strike you?"

"I thought he was rather handsome, and I should have been much the same sort of fellow, if I had had any luck."

Mr. Stryver laughed till he shook his precocious paunch.

"You and your luck, Sydney! Get to work, get to work."

Sullenly enough, the jackal loosened his dress, went into an adjoining room, and came back with a large jug of cold water, a basin, and a towel or two. Steeping the towels in the water, and partially wringing them out, he folded them on his head in a manner hideous to behold, sat down at the table, and said, "Now I am ready!"

"Not much boiling down to be done to-

1. ***Temple,*** the lodge of the Knights Templars in London of which only the Temple Church remains; at the time of the story and at present, the site is occupied by the inner Temple and Middle Temple, buildings belonging to English legal societies.

night, Memory," said Mr. Stryver, gaily, as he looked among his papers.

"How much?"

"Only two sets of them."

"Give me the worst first."

"There they are, Sydney. Fire away!"

The lion then composed himself on his back on a sofa on one side of the drinking table, while the jackal sat at his own paper-bestrewn table proper, on the other side of it, with the bottles and glasses ready to his hand. Two or three times the matter in hand became so knotty that the jackal found it imperative to get up, and steep his towels anew.

At length the jackal had got together a compact repast for the lion, and proceeded to offer it to him. The lion took it with care and caution, made his selections from it, and his remarks upon it, and the jackal assisted both. When the repast was fully discussed, the lion put his hands in his waistband and lay down to meditate. The jackal then applied himself to the collection of a second meal; this was administered to the lion in the same manner and not disposed of until three in the morning.

"And now we have done, Sydney, fill a bumper of punch," said Mr. Stryver.

The jackal removed the towels from his head, shook himself, yawned, shivered, and complied.

"You were very sound, Sydney, in the matter of those crown witnesses today. Every question told."

"I always am sound; am I not?"

"I don't gainsay it. What has roughened your temper? Put some punch to it and smooth it again."

With a deprecatory grunt, the jackal again complied.

"The old Sydney Carton of old Shrewsbury School," said Stryver, "the old seesaw Sydney."

"Ah!" returned the other, sighing; "yes! The same Sydney, with the same luck. Even then I did exercises for other boys, and seldom did my own."

"And why not?"

"God knows. It was my way, I suppose."

"Carton," said his friend, "your way is, and always was, a lame way. Look at me."

"Oh, botheration!" returned Sydney, with a lighter and more good-humored laugh, "don't *you* be moral!"

"How have I done what I have done?" said Stryver: "how do I do what I do?"

"Partly through paying me to help you, I suppose. You were always in the front rank, and I always behind."

"And whose fault was that?"

"Upon my soul, I am not sure that it was not yours. It's a gloomy thing, however, to talk about one's past, with day breaking. Turn me in some other direction."

"Well then! Pledge me to the pretty witness," said Stryver, holding up his glass.

"Pretty witness," he muttered, "who's your pretty witness?"

"The picturesque doctor's daughter, Miss Manette. Why, man, she was the admiration of the whole Court!"

"Rot the admiration of the whole Court! Who made the Old Bailey a judge of beauty? She was a golden-haired doll!"

"Do you know, Sydney," said Mr. Stryver, looking at him with sharp eyes, "I rather thought, at the time, that you sympathized with the golden-haired doll, and were quick to see what happened to the golden-haired doll?"

"Quick to see what happened! If a girl, doll or no doll, swoons within a yard or two of a man's nose, he can see it. I pledge you, but I deny the beauty. And now I'll have no more drink; I'll get to bed."

When his host followed him out on the staircase with a candle, to light him down the stairs, the day was coldly looking in through its grimy windows, the air was cold and sad, the dull sky overcast, the river dark and dim, the whole scene like a lifeless desert.

Waste forces within him and a desert all around, this man stood still on his way across a silent terrace, and saw for a moment, lying in the wilderness before him, a mirage of honorable ambition, self-denial, and perseverance. A moment, and it was gone. Climbing to a high chamber in a well of houses, he threw himself down in his clothes on a neglected bed, and its pillow was wet with wasted tears.

Sadly, sadly, the sun rose; it rose upon no sadder sight than the man of good abilities and good emotions, incapable of their directed exercise, incapable of his own help and his own happiness, sensible of the blight on him, and resigning himself to let it eat him away.

WHAT DO YOU SAY?

1. In what ways is Sydney Carton's relationship to Mr. Stryver like that of a jackal to a lion?

2. (a) What specific character traits of Sydney Carton does this chapter reveal? *(b)* How is he "his own worst enemy"?

3. For which of the two characters in this chapter does Dickens create sympathy? Quote lines to support your answer.

CHAPTER VI
Hundreds of People

The quiet lodgings of Doctor Manette were in a quiet street corner not far from Soho Square. On the afternoon of a certain fine Sunday, when the waves of four months had rolled over the trial for treason, Mr. Jarvis Lorry walked along the sunny streets from Clerkenwell where he lived, on his way to dine with the Doctor. After several relapses into business absorption, Mr. Lorry had become the Doctor's friend, and the quiet street corner was the sunny part of his life.

A quainter corner than the corner where the Doctor lived was not to be found in London. There was no way through it, and the front windows commanded a pleasant little vista of street that had a congenial air of retirement. It was a cool spot, a wonderful place for echoes, a very harbor from the raging streets.

Doctor Manette received such patients here as his old reputation, and its revival in the floating whispers of his story, brought him. His scientific knowledge and his skill in conducting ingenious experiments brought him otherwise into moderate request, and he earned as much as he wanted.

These things were within Mr. Jarvis Lorry's thoughts when he rang the doorbell on the fine Sunday afternoon.

"Doctor Manette at home?"

Expected home.

"Miss Lucie at home?"

Expected home.

"As I am at home myself, I'll go upstairs."

There were three rooms on a floor and, the doors by which they communicated being put open that the air might pass freely through them all, Mr. Lorry walked from one to another. The first was the best room and in it were Lucie's birds, flowers, books, desk, worktable, and box of water colors; the second the Doctor's consulting room, used also as the dining room; the third was the Doctor's bedroom, and there, in a corner, stood the disused shoemaker's bench and tray of tools, much as it had stood on the fifth floor of the house by the wine shop in Paris.

"I wonder," said Mr. Lorry, pausing in his looking about, "that he keeps that reminder of his sufferings about him!"

"And why wonder at that?" was the abrupt inquiry.

It proceeded from Miss Pross, the wild red woman, strong of hand, whose acquaintance he had first made at the Royal George Hotel at Dover, and had since improved.

"How do you do?" inquired that lady then.

"I am pretty well, I thank you," answered Mr. Lorry, with meekness; "how are you?"

"Nothing to boast of," said Miss Pross.

"Indeed?"

"Ah! indeed!" said Miss Pross. "I am very much put out about my Ladybird."

"May I ask the cause?"

"I don't want dozens of people who are not worthy of Ladybird to come looking after her," said Miss Pross.

"*Do* dozens come for that purpose?"

"Hundreds," said Miss Pross.

"Dear me!" said Mr. Lorry.

"I have lived with the darling—or the darling has lived with me, and paid me for it; which she certainly should never have done, you may take your affidavit, if I could have afforded to keep either myself or her for nothing—since she was ten years old. And it's really very hard," said Miss Pross.

Mr. Lorry knew Miss Pross to be very jealous, but he also knew her by this time to be, beneath the surface of her eccentricity, one of those unselfish creatures much nearer to the lower Angels than many ladies better got up by Nature and Art, who had balances at Tellson's.

"There never was nor will be but one man worthy of Ladybird," said Miss Pross; "and that was my brother Solomon, if he hadn't made a mistake in life."

Here again: Mr. Lorry's inquiries into Miss Pross' personal history had established the fact that her brother Solomon was a heartless scoundrel who had stripped her of everything she possessed, as a stake to speculate with, and had abandoned her in her poverty forevermore.

"As we happen to be alone for the moment, and are both people of business," he said, when they had got back to the drawing room and had sat down there in friendly relations, "let me ask you—does the Doctor, in talking with Lucie, never refer to the shoemaking time, yet?"

"Never."

"Do you suppose," Mr. Lorry went on, "that Doctor Manette has any theory of his own, preserved through all those years, relative to the cause of his being so oppressed; perhaps, even to the name of his oppressor?"

"I don't suppose anything but what Ladybird tells me."

"And that is—?"

"That she thinks he has."

"Now don't be angry at my asking all these questions, but is it not remarkable that Doctor Manette, unquestionably innocent of any crime as we are all well assured he is, should never touch upon that question?"

"Well! To the best of my understanding," said Miss Pross, softened by the tone of the apology, "he is afraid of the whole subject."

"Afraid?"

"It's plain enough, I should think, why he may be. It's a dreadful remembrance. Besides that, his loss of himself grew out of it. Not knowing how he lost himself, or how he recovered himself, he may never feel certain of not losing himself again."

It was a profounder remark than Mr. Lorry had looked for. "True," said he. "Yet a doubt lurks in my mind, Miss Pross, whether it is good for Doctor Manette to have that suppression always shut up within him. Indeed, it is this doubt that has led me to our present confidence."

"Can't be helped," said Miss Pross, shaking her head. "Touch that string, and he instantly changes for the worse. Better leave it alone. Sometimes he gets up in the dead of the night, and will be heard, by us overhead there, walking up and down, walking up and down, in his room. Ladybird has learned to know then that his mind is walking up and down in his old prison. She hurries to him, and they go on together, walking up and down, until he is composed. In silence they go walking up and down together, till her love and company have brought him to himself."

The corner has been mentioned as a wonderful corner for echoes; it had begun to echo so resoundingly to the tread of coming feet that it seemed that the very mention of that weary pacing to and fro had set it going.

"Here they are!" said Miss Pross, rising

to break up the conference, "and now we shall have hundreds of people pretty soon!"

On Sundays Miss Pross dined at the Doctor's table, but on other days persisted in taking her meals at unknown periods, either in the lower regions, or in her own room. On this occasion, Miss Pross, responding to Ladybird's pleasant face and efforts to please her, unbent exceedingly; so the dinner was very pleasant, too.

It was an oppressive day, and, after dinner, Lucie proposed that the wine should be carried out under the plane tree, and they should sit there in the air. As everything turned upon her, and revolved about her, they went out under the plane tree, and she carried the wine down for the special benefit of Mr. Lorry.

Still, the Hundreds of people did not present themselves. Mr. Darnay presented himself while they were sitting under the plane tree, but he was only One.

Doctor Manette received him kindly, and so did Lucie. But Miss Pross suddenly became afflicted with a twitching in the head and body, and retired into the house.

"Pray, Doctor Manette," said Mr. Darnay, as they sat under the plane tree—and he said it in pursuit of the topic in hand, which happened to be the old buildings of London —"have you seen much of the Tower?"[1]

"Lucie and I have been there; but only casually. We know that it teems with interest; little more."

"*I* have been there, as you remember," said Darnay, with a smile, though reddening a little angrily, "in another character, and not in a character that gives facilities for seeing much of it. They told me a curious thing when I was there."

"What was that?" Lucie asked.

"In making some alterations the workmen came upon an old dungeon, which had been for many years built up and forgotten. Upon a corner stone in an angle of the wall, one prisoner, who seemed to have gone to execution, had cut as his last work, three letters. At first they were read as D. I. C.; but, on being more carefully examined, the last letter was found to be G. There was no record or legend of any prisoner with those initials, and it was suggested that the letters were not initials, but the word, *Dig*. The floor was examined very carefully under the inscription, and, in the earth beneath a stone, were found the ashes of a paper, mingled with the ashes of a small leather bag. The unknown prisoner had written something, and hidden it away to keep it from the jailer."

"My father," exclaimed Lucie, "you are ill!"

He had suddenly started up, with his hand to his head. His manner and his look quite terrified them all.

"No, my dear, not ill. There are large drops of rain falling, and they made me start. We had better go in."

He recovered himself almost instantly. Rain was really falling in large drops, and he showed the back of his hand with raindrops on it. But he said not a single word in reference to the discovery that had been told of, and, as they went into the house, the business eye of Mr. Lorry either detected, or fancied it detected, on his face, as it turned toward Charles Darnay, the same singular look that had been upon it when it turned toward him in the passages of the court house. He recovered himself so quickly, however, that Mr. Lorry had doubts of his business eye.

Tea time, and Miss Pross making tea, with another fit of the jerks upon her, and yet no Hundreds of people. Mr. Carton had lounged in, but he made only Two. When the tea table was done with, they all moved to one of the windows, and looked out into the heavy twilight.

"The raindrops are still falling, large, heavy, and few," said Doctor Manette. "It comes slowly."

There was a great hurry in the streets, of people speeding away to get shelter be-

1. ***Tower,*** the Tower of London, ancient palace-fortress, used at various times as palace, prison, mint, and arsenal.

fore the storm broke; the wonderful corner for echoes resounded with the echoes of footsteps coming and going, yet not a footstep was there.

"A multitude of people, and yet a solitude!" said Darnay, when they had listened for a while.

"Is it not impressive, Mr. Darnay?" asked Lucie. "Sometimes I have sat here of an evening, until I have fancied—but even the shade of a foolish fancy makes me shudder tonight when all is so black and solemn—"

"Let us shudder, too. We may know what it is."

"It will seem nothing to you. I have sometimes sat here alone of an evening, listening, until I have made the echoes out to be the echoes of all the footsteps that are coming by-and-by into our lives."

"There is a great crowd coming one day into our lives, if that be so," Sydney Carton struck in, in his moody way. "And I hear them!" he added, after a peal of thunder. "Here they come, fast, fierce, and furious!"

It was the rush and roar of rain that stopped him, for no voice could be heard in it. A memorable storm of thunder and lightning broke with that sweep of water, and there was not a moment's interval in crash, and fire, and rain, until after the moon rose at midnight.

The great bell of Saint Paul's was striking one in the cleared air when Mr. Lorry, escorted by Jerry, high-booted and bearing a lantern, set forth on his return passage to Clerkenwell. There were solitary patches of road on the way between Soho and Clerkenwell, and Mr. Lorry, mindful of footpads, always retained Jerry for this service; though it was usually performed a good two hours earlier.

"What a night it has been! Almost a night, Jerry," said Mr. Lorry, "to bring the dead out of their graves."

"I never see the night myself, master—nor yet I don't expect to—what would do that," answered Jerry.

"Good night, Mr. Carton," said the man of business.

"Good night, Mr. Darnay. Shall we ever see such a night again, together!"

Perhaps. Perhaps, see the great crowd of people with its rush and roar, bearing down upon them, too.

WHAT DO YOU SAY?

1. How long after the trial does the action of this chapter take place?

2. *(a)* Establish the identity of each of the following characters (all of whom you have met earlier in the novel): Dr. Manette, Mr. Lorry, Miss Pross, Lucie Manette, Charles Darnay, Sydney Carton, Jerry Cruncher. *(b)* What new character, mentioned by Miss Pross, do you hear about for the first time in this chapter? *(c)* What reason do you suppose the author has for introducing his name into the story?

3. *(a)* How does Dr. Manette react to Charles' story about the prisoner in the tower of London? *(b)* How do you explain this reaction?

4. *(a)* What purpose do you think the footsteps, the echoes, the rainstorm, and the repeated reference to many people are meant to serve? *(b)* Upon what note does the chapter end?

CHAPTER VII
Monseigneur in Town

Monseigneur,[1] one of the great lords in power at the Court, held his fortnightly reception in his grand hotel in Paris. Monseigneur was in his inner room, his sanctuary of sanctuaries, the Holiest of Holiests to the crowd of worshipers in the suite of rooms without. Monseigneur was about to take his chocolate. Monseigneur could swallow a great many things with ease, and was by some few sullen minds supposed to be rapidly swallowing France; but his morn-

1. **Monseigneur** (môn se nyoer′), a French title of honor given to princes, bishops, and other persons of importance; here used to personify the French aristocracy. It later refers to a specific person bearing this title.

ing's chocolate could not so much as get into the throat of Monseigneur, without the aid of four strong men besides the Cook.

Yes. It took four men, all four ablaze with gorgeous decoration, and the Chief of them unable to exist with fewer than two gold watches in his pocket, emulative of the noble and chaste fashion set by Monseigneur, to conduct the happy chocolate to Monseigneur's lips. One lackey carried the chocolate pot into the sacred presence; a second milled and frothed the chocolate with the little instrument he bore for that function; a third presented the favored napkin; a fourth—he of the two gold watches—poured the chocolate out. It was impossible for Monseigneur to dispense with one of these attendants on the chocolate and hold his high place under the admiring heavens. Deep would have been the blot upon his escutcheon if his chocolate had been ignobly waited on by only three men; he must have died of two.

Monseigneur, having taken his chocolate, caused the doors of the Holiest of Holiests to be thrown open, and issued forth. Then, what submission, what cringing and fawning, what servility, what abject humiliation! As to bowing down in body and spirit, nothing in that way was left for heaven—which may have been one among other reasons why the worshipers of Monseigneur never troubled it.

Bestowing a word of promise here and a smile there, a whisper on one happy slave and a wave of the hand on another, Monseigneur affably passed through his rooms. Monseigneur turned, and came back again, and so in due course of time got himself shut up in his sanctuary by the chocolate sprites, and was seen no more.

The show being over, the flutter in the air became quite a little storm, and there was soon but one person left of all the crowd, and he, with his hat under his arm and his snuffbox in his hand, slowly passed among the mirrors on his way out.

"I devote you," said this person turning in the direction of the sanctuary, "to the Devil!"

With that he shook the snuff from his fingers as if he had shaken the dust from his feet, and quietly walked downstairs.

He was a man of about sixty, handsomely dressed, haughty in manner, and with a face like a fine mask. A face of a transparent paleness; every feature in it clearly defined; one set expression on it. The nose, beautifully formed otherwise, was very slightly pinched at the top of each nostril. In those two compressions, or dints, the only little change that the face ever showed, resided. They persisted in changing color sometimes, and they would be occasionally dilated and contracted by something like a faint pulsation; then they gave a look of treachery and cruelty to the whole countenance. Still, it was a handsome face, and a remarkable one.

Its owner went downstairs into the courtyard, got into his carriage, and drove away. Not many people had talked with him at the reception; he had stood in a little space apart, and Monseigneur might have been warmer in his manner. It appeared, under the circumstances, rather agreeable to him to see the common people dispersed before his horses, and often barely escaping from being run down. His man drove as if he were charging an enemy, and the furious recklessness of the man brought no check into the face, or to the lips, of the master.

With a wild rattle and clatter, the carriage dashed through streets and swept round corners, women screaming before it, and men clutching children out of its way. At last, swooping at a street corner by a fountain, one of its wheels came to a sickening little jolt, there was a loud cry from a number of voices, and the horses reared and plunged.

But for the latter inconvenience, the carriage probably would not have stopped; carriages were often known to drive on and leave their wounded behind, and why not? But the frightened valet had got down in a

hurry, and there were twenty hands at the horses' bridles.

"What has gone wrong?" said Monsieur, calmly looking out.

A tall man in a nightcap had caught up a bundle from among the feet of the horses, and had laid it on the basement of the fountain, and was down in the mud and wet, howling over it like a wild animal.

"Pardon, Monsieur the Marquis!" said a ragged and submissive man, "it is a child."

"Why does he make that abominable noise? Is it his child?"

"Excuse me, Monsieur the Marquis—it is a pity—yes."

The fountain was a little removed; for the street opened, where it was, into a space some ten or twelve yards square. As the tall man suddenly got up from the ground, and came running at the carriage, Monsieur the Marquis clapped his hand for an instant on his sword hilt.

"Killed!" shrieked the man, in wild desperation, extending both arms above his head, and staring at him. "Dead!"

The people closed round. Monsieur the Marquis ran his eyes over them as if they had been rats come out of their holes.

He took out his purse.

"It is extraordinary to me," said he, "that you people cannot take care of yourselves and your children. One or the other of you is forever in the way. How do I know what injury you have done my horses? See! Give him that."

He threw a gold coin for the valet to pick up, and all the heads craned forward that all the eyes might look down at it as it fell. The tall man called out again with a most unearthly cry, "Dead!"

He was arrested by the quick arrival of another man, for whom the rest made way. On seeing him the miserable creature fell upon his shoulder, sobbing and crying, and pointing to the fountain, where some women were stooping over the motionless bundle, and moving gently about it. They were as silent, however, as the men.

"I know all, I know all," said the last comer. "Be a brave man, my Gaspard! It is better for the poor little plaything to die so than to live. It has died in a moment without pain. Could it have lived an hour as happily?"

"You are a philosopher, you there," said the Marquis, smiling. "How do they call you?"

"They call me Defarge."

"Of what trade?"

"Monsieur the Marquis, vendor of wine."

"Pick up that, philosopher and vendor of wine," said the Marquis, throwing him another gold coin, "and spend it as you will. The horses there; are they right?"

Without deigning to look at the assemblage a second time, Monsieur the Marquis leaned back in his seat, and was just being driven away with the air of a gentleman who had accidentally broken some common thing, and had paid for it, and could afford to pay for it; when his ease was suddenly disturbed by a coin flying into his carriage, and ringing on its floor.

"Hold!" said Monsieur the Marquis. "Hold the horses! Who threw that?"

He looked to the spot where Defarge the vendor of wine had stood a moment before; but the wretched father was groveling on his face on the pavement in that spot, and the figure that stood beside him was the figure of a dark stout woman, knitting.

"You dogs!" said the Marquis, but smoothly, and with an unchanged front, except as to the spots on his nose: "I would ride over any of you very willingly, and exterminate you from the earth. If I knew which rascal threw at the carriage, and if that brigand were sufficiently near it, he should be crushed under the wheels."

So cowed was their condition and so long and hard their experience of what such a man could do to them, within the law and beyond it, that not a voice, or a hand, or even an eye was raised. Among the men, not one. But the woman who stood knitting looked up steadily, and looked the Marquis in the face. It was not for his dignity to notice it; his contemptuous eyes passed over her, and over all the other rats; and he leaned back in his seat again, and gave the word, "Go on!"

He was driven on, and other carriages came whirling by in quick succession; the Minister, the State-Projector, the Farmer General, the Doctor, the Lawyer, the Ecclesiastic, the Grand Opera, the Comedy, the whole Fancy Ball in a bright continuous flow, came whirling by. The rats had crept out of their holes to look on, and they remained looking on for hours; soldiers and police often passing between them and the spectacle, and making a barrier behind which they slunk, and through which they peeped. The father had long ago taken up his bundle and hidden himself away with it, when the women who had tended the bundle while it lay on the base of the fountain, sat there watching the running of the water and the rolling of the Fancy Ball—when the one woman who had stood conspicuous, knitting, still knitted on with the steadfastness of Fate. The water of the fountain ran, the swift river ran, the day ran into evening, so much life in the city ran into death according to rule, time and tide waited for no man, the rats were sleeping close together in their dark holes again, the Fancy Ball was lighted up at supper, all things ran their course.

WHAT DO YOU SAY?

1. *(a)* Why do you think the author describes in detail the episode of the hot chocolate? *(b)* How does this scene contrast with the scene at the fountain?

2. *(a)* Why is Monsieur the Marquis in a bad mood when he leaves the Grand Hotel? *(b)* Which man in the chapter has the most reason to seek revenge?

3. *(a)* Who is the woman who stood knitting? *(b)* In what situation did she appear earlier in the novel? *(c)* How would you judge she feels about the Marquis?

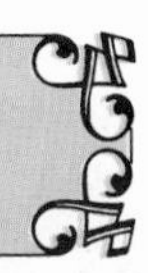

CHAPTER VIII
Monseigneur in the Country

A beautiful landscape with the corn bright in it, but not abundant. Patches of poor rye where corn should have been, patches of poor peas and beans, patches of most coarse vegetable substitutes for wheat. On inanimate nature, as on the men and women who cultivated it, a prevalent tendency toward an appearance of vegetating unwillingly—a dejected disposition to give up, and wither away.

Monsieur the Marquis in his traveling carriage (which might have been lighter), conducted by four post horses and two postilions, fagged up a steep hill. A blush on the countenance of Monsieur the Marquis was no impeachment of his high breeding; it was not from within; it was occasioned by an external circumstance beyond his control—the setting sun.

The sunset struck so brilliantly into the traveling carriage when it gained the hilltop that its occupant was steeped in crimson. "It will die out," said Monsieur the Marquis, glancing at his hands, "directly."

In effect, the sun was so low that it dipped at the moment. When the heavy drag had been adjusted to the wheel,[1] and the carriage slid down hill, with a cinderous smell, in a cloud of dust, the red glow departed quickly; the sun and the Marquis going down together; there was no glow left when the drag was taken off.

But there remained a broken country, bold and open, a little village at the bottom of the hill, a broad sweep and rise beyond it, a church tower, a windmill, a forest for the chase, and a crag with a fortress on it used as a prison. Round upon all these darkening objects as the night drew on, the Marquis looked, with the air of one who was coming near home.

---

1. ***When the heavy drag . . . the wheel,*** a weighted obstruction placed against the wheel of a carriage to prevent the carriage from going downhill too fast.

The village had its one poor street, with its poor brewery, poor tannery, poor tavern, poor stableyard for relay of post horses, poor fountain, all usual poor appointments. It had its poor people too. All its people were poor, and many of them were sitting at their doors, shredding spare onions and the like for supper, while many were at the fountain, washing leaves, and grasses, and any such small yieldings of the earth that could be eaten. Expressive signs of what made them poor were not wanting; the tax for the state, the tax for the church, the tax for the lord, tax local and tax general, were to be paid here and to be paid there, according to solemn inscription in the little village, until the wonder was that there was any village left unswallowed.

Few children were to be seen, and no dogs. As to the men and women, their choice on earth was stated in the prospect—Life on the lowest terms that could sustain it, down in the little village under the mill; or captivity and Death in the dominant prison on the crag.

Heralded by a courier in advance, and by the cracking of his postilions' whips, which twined snakelike about their heads, as if he came attended by the Furies,[2] Monsieur the Marquis drew up in his traveling carriage at the posting-house gate. It was hard by the fountain, and the peasants suspended their operations to look at him. Monsieur the Marquis cast his eyes over the submissive faces that drooped before him, when a grizzled mender of the roads joined the group.

"Bring me hither that fellow!" said the Marquis.

The fellow was brought, cap in hand, and the other fellows closed round to look and to listen, in the manner of the people at the Paris fountain.

"I passed you on the road?"

"Monseigneur, it is true. I had the honor of being passed on the road."

"Coming up the hill, and at the top of the hill, both?"

"Monseigneur, it is true."

"What did you look at, so fixedly?"

"Monseigneur, I looked at the man."

He stooped a little, and with his tattered blue cap pointed under the carriage.

"What man, pig? And why look there?"

"Pardon, Monseigneur; he swung by the chain of the shoe—the drag."

"Who?" demanded the traveler.

"Monseigneur, the man."

"May the Devil carry away these idiots! How do you call the man? You know all the men of this part of the country. Who was he?"

"Your clemency, Monseigneur! He was not of this part of the country. Of all the days of my life, I never saw him."

"Swinging by the chain? To be suffocated?"

"With your gracious permission, that was the wonder of it, Monseigneur. His head hanging over—like this!"

He turned himself sideways to the carriage, and leaned back, with his face thrown up to the sky, and his head hanging down; then recovered himself, fumbled with his cap, and made a bow.

"What was he like?"

"Monseigneur, he was whiter than the miller. All covered with dust, white as a specter, tall as a specter!"

The picture produced an immense sensation in the little crowd; but all eyes, without comparing notes with other eyes, looked at Monsieur the Marquis.

"Truly, you did well," said the Marquis, "to see a thief accompanying my carriages, and not open that great mouth of yours. Bah! Put him aside, Monsieur Gabelle!"

Monsieur Gabelle was the postmaster, and some other taxing functionary united; he had come out with great obsequiousness to assist at this examination, and had held the examined by his arm in an official manner.

"Bah! Go aside!" said Monsieur Gabelle.

2. *the Furies,* in Greek and Roman mythology, three female spirits who pursued and tormented evildoers.

"Lay hands on this stranger if he seeks your village tonight, and be sure his business is honest, Gabelle."

"Monseigneur, I devote myself to your orders."

"Did he run away, fellow?—where is that Accursed?"

The accursed was under the carriage with some half-dozen particular friends, pointing out the chain. Some half-dozen other particular friends hauled him out, and presented him breathless to Monsieur the Marquis.

"Did the man run away, Dolt, when we stopped for the drag?"

"Monseigneur, he precipitated himself over the hillside, head first, as a person plunges into the river."

"See to it, Gabelle. Go on!"

The half-dozen who were peering at the chain were still among the wheels; the wheels turned so suddenly they were lucky to save their skins and bones; they had very little else to save, or they might not have been so fortunate.

The burst with which the carriage started out of the village and up the rise beyond was soon checked by the steepness of the hill. Gradually it subsided to a footpace, swinging and lumbering upward among the many sweet scents of a summer night.

The scents rose all around him, and rose on the dusty, ragged, and toil-worn group at the fountain not far away; to whom the mender of roads still enlarged upon his man like a specter as long as they could bear it. By degrees, they dropped off one by one, and lights twinkled in little casements.

The shadow of a large high-roofed house, and of many overhanging trees, was upon Monsieur the Marquis by that time; and the shadow was exchanged for the light of a flambeau, as his carriage stopped, and the great door of his château was opened to him.

"Monsieur Charles, whom I expect, is he arrived from England?"

"Monseigneur, not yet."

WHAT DO YOU SAY?

1. Dickens frequently used direct means to prejudice the reader for or against a condition or a character. What are some outstanding examples in Chapters VII and VIII?

2. What is the most important plot fact in Chapter VIII?

3. Who is "Monsieur Charles" mentioned at the end of the chapter?

4. What do you think is Dickens' purpose in devoting two chapters to Monsieur the Marquis, a minor character?

CHAPTER IX
The Gorgon's Head

Monsieur the Marquis, his flambeau bearer going before, went up the staircase to a door in a corridor. This thrown open, admitted him to his private apartment of three rooms; his bed chamber and two others. High, vaulted rooms with cool uncarpeted floors, great dogs upon the hearths for the burning of wood, and all luxuries befitting the state of a marquis in a luxurious age and country. Monsieur the Marquis crossed a hall grim with old boar spears, swords, and knives of the chase; grimmer with heavy riding rods and riding whips, of which many a peasant, gone to his benefactor Death, had felt the weight when his lord was angry.

A supper table was laid for two, in the third of the rooms; a round room, in one of the château's four extinguisher-topped towers. A small lofty room, with its window wide open, and the wooden jalousie blinds closed, so that the dark night only showed in slight horizontal lines of black, alternating with their broad lines of stone color.

"My nephew," said the Marquis, glancing at the supper preparation; "they said he was not arrived."

Nor was he; but, he had been expected with Monseigneur.

"It is not probable he will arrive tonight. I shall be ready in a quarter of an hour."

In a quarter of an hour Monseigneur sat down alone to his sumptuous and choice supper. His chair was opposite to the window, and he was raising his glass of Bordeaux to his lips, when he put it down.

"What is that?" he calmly asked, looking with attention at the horizontal lines of black and stone color.

"Monseigneur? That?"

"Outside the blinds. Open the blinds." It was done.

"Well?"

"Monseigneur, it is nothing. The trees and the night are all that are here." The servant had thrown the blinds wide and stood, looking round for instruction.

"Good," said the imperturbable master. "Close them again."

That was done too, and the Marquis went on with his supper. He was halfway through it, when he again stopped with his glass in his hand, hearing the sound of wheels. It came on briskly, and came up to the front of the château.

"Ask who is arrived."

It was the nephew of Monseigneur.

He was to be told, said Monseigneur, that supper awaited him then and there, and that he was prayed to come to it. In a little while he came. He had been known in England as Charles Darnay.

Monseigneur received him in a courtly manner, but they did not shake hands.

"You left Paris yesterday, sir?" he said to Monseigneur, as he took his seat at table.

"Yesterday. And you?"

"I come direct."

"From London?"

"Yes."

"You have been a long time coming," said the Marquis, with a smile.

"On the contrary; I come direct."

"Pardon me! I mean not a long time on the journey; a long time intending the journey."

"I have been detained by"—the nephew stopped a moment in his answer—"various business."

"Without doubt," said the polished uncle.

So long as a servant was present no other words passed between them. When coffee had been served and they were alone together, the nephew opened a conversation.

"I have come back, sir, as you anticipate, pursuing the object that took me away. It carried me into great and unexpected peril; but it is a sacred object, and if it had carried me to death I hope it would have sustained me."

"Not to death," said the uncle.

"I doubt, sir," returned the nephew, "whether, if it had carried me to the utmost brink of death, you would have cared to stop me there."

The uncle made a graceful gesture of protest, so clearly a form of good breeding that it was not reassuring.

"Indeed, sir," pursued the nephew, "for anything I know, you may have expressly worked to give a more suspicious appearance to the circumstances that surrounded me."

"No, no, no," said the uncle, pleasantly.

"But, however that may be," resumed the nephew, glancing at him with deep distrust, "I know your diplomacy would stop me by any means and would know no scruple as to means."

"My friend, I told you so," said the uncle, with a fine pulsation in the two marks. "Do me the favor to recall that I told you so, long ago."

"I recall it."

"Thank you," said the Marquis—very sweetly indeed.

"In effect, sir," pursued the nephew, "I believe it to be at once your bad fortune, and my good fortune, that has kept me out of a prison in France here."

"I do not quite understand," returned the uncle, sipping his coffee. "Dare I ask you to explain?"

"I believe that if you were not in disgrace

with the Court, a letter *de cachet*[1] would have sent me to some fortress indefinitely."

"It is possible," said the uncle, with great calmness. "For the honor of the family, I could even resolve to incommode you to that extent. These little instruments of correction, these slight favors that might so incommode you, are sought by so many and granted to so few! It used not to be so, but France in all such things is changed for the worse."

"We have so asserted our station, both in the old time and in the modern time also," said the nephew, gloomily, "that I believe our name to be more detested than any name in France."

"Let us hope so," said the uncle. "Detestation of the high is the involuntary homage of the low. Meanwhile, I will preserve the honor of the family, if you will not. But you must be fatigued. Shall we terminate our conference for the night?"

"A moment more."

"An hour, if you please."

"Sir," said the nephew, "we have done wrong, and are reaping the fruits of wrong."

"*We* have done wrong?" repeated the Marquis.

"Our family, whose honor is of so much account to both of us, in such different ways. Even in my father's time, we did a world of wrong, injuring every human creature who came between us and our pleasure. Why need I speak of my father's time, when it is equally yours? Can I separate my father's twin brother from himself?"

"Death has done that!" said the Marquis.

"And has left me," answered the nephew, "bound to a system that is frightful to me, responsible for it, but powerless in it; seeking to execute the last request of my dear mother's lips, to have mercy and to redress; and tortured by seeking assistance and power in vain."

"Seeking them from me, my nephew," said the Marquis, "you will forever seek them in vain, be assured."

Every fine straight line in the clear whiteness of his face was cruelly, craftily, and closely compressed, while he stood looking quietly at his nephew, with his snuffbox in his hand. He touched him on the breast, as though his finger were the fine point of a small sword, with which, in delicate finesse, he ran him through the body, and said:

"My friend, I will die, perpetuating the system under which I have lived." He added then, after ringing a bell on the table, "But you are lost, Monsieur Charles, I see."

"This property and France are lost to me," said the nephew, sadly; "I renounce them."

"Are they yours to renounce? France may be, but the property? It is scarcely worth mentioning; but, is it yet?"

"I had no intention to claim it. If it passed to me from you, tomorrow, I would abandon it and live elsewhere. What is it but a wilderness of misery and ruin?"

"Hah!" said the Marquis, glancing round the luxurious room.

"If it ever becomes mine, it shall be put into hands qualified to free it—if such a thing is possible so that the miserable people who cannot leave it and who have been long wrung to the last point of endurance, may, in another generation, suffer less; but it is not for me. There is a curse on it, and on all this land."

"And you?" said the uncle.

"I must do, to live, what others of my countrymen, even with nobility at their backs, may have to do some day—work."

"In England, for example?"

"Yes. The family honor, sir, is safe from me in this country. The family name can suffer from me in no other, for I bear it in no other."

The ringing of the bell had caused the adjoining bedchamber to be lighted. It now shone brightly, through the door of com-

1. ***letter de cachet,*** usually ***lettre de cachet*** (let′ rə də kä shā′), a letter bearing the seal of the king of France, frequently an order for someone to be imprisoned or exiled. This royal order provided no opportunity for a hearing for its recipient, and often contained no mention of the crime of which he was accused or of a date for his release.

munication. The Marquis looked that way, and listened for the retreating step of his valet.

"England is very attractive to you, seeing how indifferently you have prospered there," he observed then, turning his calm face to his nephew with a smile.

"I have already said, for my prospering there, I may be indebted to you, sir. For the rest, it is my refuge."

"They say, those boastful English, that it is the refuge of many. You know a compatriot who has found a refuge there? A doctor?"

"Yes."

"With a daughter?"

"Yes."

"Yes," repeated the Marquis. "A doctor with a daughter. Yes. You are fatigued. I look to the pleasure of seeing you again in the morning. Good repose! Light Monsieur my nephew to his chamber there!—and burn Monsieur my nephew in his bed, if you will," he added to himself, before he summoned his valet to his own bedroom.

The valet come and gone, Monsieur the Marquis walked to and fro in his loose chamber robe, to prepare himself gently for sleep that hot, still night.

"I am cool now," said Monsieur the Marquis, "and may go to bed."

So, leaving only one light burning, he let his thin gauze curtains fall around him, and heard the night break its silence with a long sigh as he composed himself to sleep.

The fountain in the village flowed unseen and unheard, and the fountain at the château dropped unseen and unheard through three dark hours. Then the gray water of both began to be ghostly in the light, and the eyes of the stone faces of the château were opened.

Lighter and lighter, until at last the sun touched the tops of the still trees, and poured its radiance over the hill. In the glow the water of the château fountain seemed to turn to blood, and the stone faces crimsoned. The carol of the birds was loud and high, and, on the weather-beaten sill of the great window of the bedchamber of Monsieur the Marquis, one little bird sang its sweetest song with all its might. At this the nearest stone face seemed to stare amazed, and, with open mouth and dropped underjaw, looked awe-stricken.

Now the sun was full up, and movement began in the village. Casement windows opened, crazy doors were unbarred, and people came forth shivering—chilled, as yet, by the new sweet air. Then began the rarely lightened toil of the day among the village population. Some, to the fountain; some, to the fields; men and women here, to dig and delve; men and women there, to see to the poor livestock, and lead the bony cows out, to such pasture as could be found by the roadside. In the church and at the Cross, a kneeling figure or two; attendant on the latter prayers, the led cow, trying for a breakfast among the weeds at its foot.

The château awoke later, as became its quality, but awoke gradually and surely. First, the lonely boar spears and knives of the chase had been reddened as of old; then, had gleamed trenchant in the morning sunshine; now, doors and windows were thrown open, horses in their stables looked round over their shoulders at the light and freshness pouring in at doorways, leaves sparkled and rustled at iron-grated windows, dogs pulled hard at their chains, and reared impatient to be loosed.

All these trivial incidents belonged to the routine of life, and the return of morning. Surely, not so the ringing of the great bell of the château, nor the running up and down the stairs; nor the hurried figures on the terrace; nor the booting and tramping here and there and everywhere, nor the quick saddling of horses and riding away?

What winds conveyed this hurry to the grizzled mender of roads, already at work on the hilltop beyond the village, with his day's dinner—not much to carry—lying in a bundle that it was worth no crow's while to peck at, on a heap of stones? Had the birds, carrying some grains of it to a distance, dropped one over him as they sow chance seeds? Whether or no, the mender of roads ran, on the sultry morning, as if for his life, down the hill, knee-high in dust, and never stopped till he got to the fountain.

All the people of the village were at the fountain, standing about in their depressed manner, and whispering low, but showing no other emotions than grim curiosity and surprise. The led cows, hastily brought in and tethered to anything that would hold them, were looking stupidly on, or lying down chewing the cud of nothing particularly repaying their trouble, which they had picked up in their interrupted saunter. Some of the people of the château, and some of those of the posting house, and all the taxing authorities, were armed more or less and were crowded on the other side of the little street in a purposeless way, that was highly fraught with nothing.

Already the mender of roads had penetrated into the midst of a group of fifty particular friends, and was smiting himself in the breast with his blue cap. What did all this portend, and what portended the swift hoisting-up of Monsieur Gabelle behind a servant on horseback, and the conveying away of the said Gabelle—double-laden though the horse was—at a gallop.

It portended that there was one stone face too many up at the château.

The Gorgon had surveyed the building again in the night, and had added the one stone face wanting; the stone face for which it had waited through about two hundred years.

It lay back on the pillow of Monsieur the Marquis. It was like a fine mask, suddenly startled, made angry, and petrified. Driven home into the heart of the stone figure attached to it, was a knife. Round its hilt was a frill of paper, on which was scrawled:

"Drive him fast to his tomb. This, from JACQUES."

WHAT DO YOU SAY?

1. *(a)* In the conversation between Charles Darnay and his uncle, the Marquis, what was revealed about Charles Darnay's views? *(b)* How would you explain the contrast between Darnay and his uncle?

2. *(a)* Who do you think murdered the Marquis? *(b)* In Chapters VII and VIII you saw the conditions under which the peasants lived; how would you say the murder in Chapter IX is related to these conditions?

3. Upon the Marquis' death, to whom would his title now logically go?

4. In what way is Chapter IX a climax to Chapters VII and VIII?

AUTHOR'S CRAFT

Foreshadowing

One of the important techniques of storytelling is called **foreshadowing,** the "planting" of clues that relate to coming events. These clues, or half-hidden suggestions, whet the reader's interest by raising questions in his mind. He wants to race ahead to see what will happen. When he comes to the event and remembers the foreshadowing, he sees how the event has been made plausible and convincing, and is related to other events or actions.

Charles Dickens has given us in Chapter IX a good example of such foreshadowing. You will remember, in Chapter VII, the street scene, with the killing of the child and the crowd's reaction, and, in Chapter VIII, the suggestion that someone had clung to the under side of the Marquis' carriage as it left Paris. You do not know who this is or why he has done so. Now in Chapter IX the Marquis, comfortably beginning dinner in his chateau, thinks he hears a disturbance outside his window. The Marquis' servant opens the blinds, assures the Marquis no one is there, and closes the blinds. Again, you do not really know whether anyone was there or not. Later the reader understands the purpose of these actions: they foreshadow the murder of the Marquis.

Skim through Chapter VIII to see what you can find of possible foreshadowing related to events not yet seen in Chapter IX. Reread carefully the reactions of Doctor Manette, Darnay, Lucie, and Carton to the rainstorm. What is the mood in this brief scene? How does the scene open? Progress? Close? What great event would you guess it foreshadows? What words suggest that the lives of those present will be connected with the event? Note that foreshadowing always involves your curiosity. Only later, after the foreshadowed event has taken place, does the reader really *know* the technique has been used.

Earlier, in Chapter VI, Dickens makes a point of having Mr. Lorry reminded of the circumstances under which he had first met Miss Pross (note the appositive "the wild woman, strong of hand"). Lorry reacts to her "with meekness." Knowing Miss Pross' strength of hand and her loyalty to Lucie, you can assume that in some way these two characteristics will be important in a forthcoming event.

What facts so far have aroused your curiosity about Cruncher? What have you concluded about him? Cruncher's activities provide him with his one vital link to the plot. You will find out his avocation in Chapter XII; you will discover the plot link much later. And the most important foreshadowing in the whole novel will appear in Chapter XI.

CHAPTER X
Two Promises

More months, to the number of twelve, had come and gone, and Mr. Charles Darnay was established in England as a higher teacher of the French language who was conversant with French literature. In this age he would have been a professor; in that age he was a tutor. As a tutor, whose attainments made the student's way pleasant and profitable, and as an elegant translator who brought something to his work besides dictionary knowledge, young Mr. Darnay soon became known and encouraged. He was well acquainted, moreover, with the circumstances of his country, and those were of ever growing interest. So, with perseverance and untiring industry, he prospered. A certain portion of his time was passed at Cambridge, where he read with undergraduates. The rest of his time he passed in London.

He had loved Lucie Manette from the hour of his danger. He had never heard a sound so sweet and dear as the sound of her compassionate voice; he had never seen a face so tenderly beautiful as hers when it was confronted with his own on the edge of the grave that had been dug for him. But he had not yet spoken to her on the subject; the assassination at the deserted château far away had been done a year, and he had never yet, by so much as a single spoken word, disclosed to her the state of his heart.

It was again summer when, lately arrived in London from his college occupation, he turned into the quiet corner in Soho, bent on opening his mind to Doctor Manette. He knew Lucie to be out with Miss Pross.

He found the Doctor reading in his armchair. The energy which had at once supported him under his old sufferings had been gradually restored to him. He was now a very energetic man indeed, with great firmness of purpose, strength of resolution, and vigor of action. To him now entered Charles Darnay, at sight of whom he laid aside his book and held out his hand.

"Charles Darnay! I rejoice to see you. We have been counting on your return these three or four days past. Mr. Stryver and Sydney Carton were both here yesterday, and both made you out to be more than due."

"I am obliged to them for their interest in the matter," he answered. "Miss Manette—"

"Is well," said the Doctor, "and your return will delight us all. She has gone out but will soon be home."

"Doctor Manette, I knew she was from home. I took the opportunity of her being from home, to beg to speak to you."

There was a blank silence.

"Yes?" said the Doctor, with evident constraint. "Bring your chair here, and speak on."

He complied as to the chair, but appeared to find the speaking on less easy.

"I have had the happiness, Doctor Manette, of being so intimate here," he began, "for some year and a half, that I hope the topic on which I am about to touch may not—"

He was stayed by the Doctor's putting out his hand to stop him.

"Is Lucie the topic?"

"She is."

"It is hard for me to speak of her at any time. It is very hard for me to hear her spoken of in that tone of yours, Charles Darnay."

"It is a tone of fervent admiration, true homage, and deep love, Doctor Manette!" he said deferentially.

There was another blank silence before her father rejoined:

"Have you spoken to Lucie?"

"No."

"Nor written?"

"Never."

"It would be ungenerous to affect not to know that your self-denial is to be referred to your consideration for her father. Her father thanks you."

He offered his hand; but his eyes did not go with it.

"I know," said Darnay, respectfully, "how can I fail to know, Doctor Manette, I who have seen you together, that between you and Miss Manette there is an affection so unusual, so touching, that it can have few parallels, even in the tenderness between a father and child. I have known this, since I have known you."

Her father sat silent.

"Dear Doctor Manette, always knowing this, always seeing her and you with this hallowed light about you, I have forborne, and forborne, as long as it was in the nature of man to do it. I have felt, and do even now feel, that to bring my love between you, is to touch your history with something not quite so good as itself. But I love her. Heaven is my witness that I love her!"

"I believe it," answered her father, mournfully. "I have thought so before now. I believe it."

"But do not believe," said Darnay, upon whose ear the mournful voice struck with a reproachful sound, "that if my fortune were so cast as that, being one day so happy as to make her my wife, I must at any time put any separation between her and you, I could or would breathe a word of what I now say.

"No, dear Doctor Manette. Like you, a voluntary exile from France; like you, driven from it by its distractions, oppressions, and miseries; like you, striving to live away from it by my own exertions, and trusting in a happier future; I look only to sharing your fortunes, sharing your life and home, and being faithful to you to the death. Not to divide with Lucie her privilege as your child, companion, and friend; but to come in aid of it, and bind her closer to you if such a thing can be."

Her father rested his hands upon the arms of his chair, and looked up for the first time since the beginning of the conference. A struggle was evident in his face; a struggle with that occasional look which had a tendency in it to dark doubt and dread.

"You speak so feelingly and so manfully, Charles Darnay, that I thank you with all my heart, and will open all my heart—or nearly so. Have you any reason to believe that Lucie loves you?"

"None. As yet, none."

"Do you seek any promise from me?"

"I do seek that."

"What is it?"

"It is that if Miss Manette would bring to you at any time, on her part, such a confidence as I have ventured to lay before you, you will bear testimony to what I have said, and to your belief in it. I hope you may be able to think so well of me as to urge no influence against me. I say nothing more of my stake in this; this is what I ask. The condition on which I ask it, and which you have an undoubted right to require, I will observe immediately."

"I give the promise," said the Doctor, "without any condition. I believe your object to be, purely and truthfully, as you have stated it. I believe your intention is to perpetuate, and not to weaken, the ties between me and my other and far dearer self. If she should ever tell me that you are essential to her perfect happiness, I will give her to you. If there were—Charles Darnay, if there were—"

The young man had taken his hand gratefully; their hands were joined as the Doctor spoke:

"—any fancies, any reasons, any apprehensions, anything whatsoever, new or old, against the man she really loved—the direct responsibility thereof not lying on his head—they should all be obliterated for her sake. She is everything to me; more to me than suffering, more to me than wrong, more to me—Well! This is idle talk."

"Your confidence in me ought to be returned with full confidence on my part. My present name, though but slightly changed from my mother's, is not my own. I wish to tell you what that is, and why I am in England."

"Stop!" said the Doctor of Beauvais. "If your suit should prosper, if Lucie should love you, you shall tell me on your marriage morning. Do you promise?"

"Willingly."

"Give me your hand. She will be home directly. Go! God bless you!"

It was dark when Charles Darnay left him, and it was an hour later and darker when Lucie came home.

"My father!" she called to him. "Father dear!"

She heard a low hammering sound in his bedroom. She looked in at his door and came running back crying to herself, "What shall I do! What shall I do!"

Her uncertainty lasted but a moment; she hurried back, and tapped at his door, and softly called to him. The noise ceased at the sound of her voice, and he presently came out to her, and they walked up and down together for a long time.

She came down from her bed, to look at him in his sleep that night. He slept heavily, and his tray of shoemaking tools, and his old unfinished work, were all as usual.

WHAT DO YOU SAY?

1. *(a)* How long has it been since Darnay's return from France? *(b)* How has he been employed during this time?

2. *(a)* What are the "two promises" in this chapter? *(b)* Find the lines that reveal Dr. Manette's reaction to Darnay's wish to marry Lucie. Are you given any explanation for his reaction? Explain.

CHAPTER XI
The Fellow of No Delicacy

If Sydney Carton ever shone anywhere, he certainly never shone in the house of Doctor Manette. He had been there often during a whole year, and had always been the same moody and morose lounger there. When he cared to talk, he talked well; but the cloud of caring for nothing, which overshadowed him with such a fatal darkness, was very rarely pierced by the light within him.

And yet he did care something for the streets that environed that house, and for the stones that made their pavements. Many a night he vaguely and unhappily wandered there, when wine had brought no transitory gladness to him; many a dreary daybreak revealed his solitary figure lingering there.

On a day in August, Sydney's feet still trod those stones. From being irresolute and purposeless his feet became animated and took him to the Doctor's door.

He was shown upstairs, and found Lucie at her work, alone. She had never been quite at her ease with him, and received him with some little embarrassment. But, looking up at his face in the interchange of the first few commonplaces, she observed a change in it.

"I fear you are not well, Mr. Carton!"

"No. But the life I lead, Miss Manette, is not conducive to health. What is to be expected of, or by, such profligates?"

"Is it not—forgive me—a pity to live no better life?"

"God knows it is a shame!"

"Then why not change it?"

Looking gently at him again, she was surprised and saddened to see that there were tears in his eyes. There were tears in his voice too, as he answered:

"It is too late for that. I shall never be better than I am. I shall sink lower, and be worse. I am like one who died young. All my life might have been."

"No, Mr. Carton. I am sure that the best part of it might still be; I am sure that you might be much, much worthier of yourself."

"Say of you, Miss Manette, and although I know better—although in the mystery of my own wretched heart I know better—I shall never forget it!"

She was pale and trembling. He came to her relief with a fixed despair of himself which made the interview unlike any other that could have been holden.

"If it had been possible, Miss Manette, that you could have returned the love of the man you see before you—self-flung away, wasted, drunken, poor creature of misuse as you know him to be—he would have been conscious this day and hour, in spite of his happiness, that he would bring you to misery, bring you to sorrow and repentance, blight you, disgrace you, pull you down with him. I know very well that you can have no tenderness for me; I ask for none; I am even thankful that it cannot be."

"Without it, can I not save you, Mr. Carton? Can I not recall you—forgive me again!—to a better course? Can I in no way repay your confidence? I know this is a confidence," she modestly said, after a little hesitation, and in earnest tears, "I know you would say this to no one else. Can I turn it to no good account for yourself, Mr. Carton?"

He shook his head.

"The utmost good that I am capable of now, Miss Manette, I have come here to realize. Let me carry through the rest of my misdirected life the remembrance that I opened my heart to you, last of all the world; and that there was something left in me at this time which you could pity. I distress you; I draw fast to an end. Will you let me believe that the last confidence of my life was reposed in you and will be shared by no one?"

"If that will be a consolation to you, yes."

"Not even by the dearest one ever to be known to you?"

"Mr. Carton," she answered, after an agitated pause, "the secret is yours, not mine; and I promise to respect it."

"Thank you. And again, God bless you."

He put her hand to his lips, and moved toward the door.

He was so unlike what he had ever shown himself to be, and it was so sad to think how much he had thrown away, that Lucie Manette wept mournfully for him as he stood looking back at her.

"Be comforted!" he said, "I am not worth such feeling, Miss Manette. My last supplication of all, is this; it is useless to say it, I know, but it rises out of my soul. For you, and for any dear to you, I would do anything. I would embrace any sacrifice for you and for those dear to you. The time will come, the time will not be long in coming, when new ties will be formed about you—the dearest ties that will ever grace and gladden you. O Miss Manette, when the little picture of a happy father's face looks up in yours, when you see your own bright beauty springing up anew at your feet, think now and then that there is a man who would give his life, to keep a life you love beside you!"

He said, "Farewell!" said a last, "God bless you!" and left her.

WHAT DO YOU SAY?

1. *(a)* What new side of Sydney Carton's nature is revealed in this chapter? *(b)* How does his expression of devotion to Lucie compare with Darnay's in Chapter X?

2. What do you consider Carton's most significant remark to Lucie?

CHAPTER XII
The Honest Tradesman

To the eyes of Mr. Jeremiah Cruncher, sitting on his stool in Fleet Street with his son beside him, a vast number and variety of objects in movement were every day present. Time was, when a poet sat upon a stool in a public place, and mused in the sight of men. Mr. Cruncher, sitting on a stool in a public place, but not being a poet, mused as little as possible, and looked about him.

It fell out that he was thus engaged when an unusual concourse down Fleet Street westward attracted his attention. Looking that way, Mr. Cruncher made out that some kind of funeral was coming along, and that there was popular objection to this funeral, which engendered uproar.

The crowd approached; they were bawling and hissing round a dingy hearse and dingy mourning coach, in which there was only one mourner, with an increasing rabble surrounding the coach, deriding him, and incessantly calling out: "Yah! Spies! Tst! Spies!"

Funerals had at all times a remarkable attraction for Mr. Cruncher; he always pricked up his senses and became excited when a funeral passed Tellson's. Naturally, therefore, a funeral with this uncommon attendance excited him greatly, and he asked of the first man who ran against him:

"What is it, brother? What's it about?"

"*I* don't know," said the man. "Spies! Yaha! Tst! Spies!"

At length, a person better informed on the merits of the case tumbled against him, and from this person he learned that the funeral was the funeral of one Roger Cly.

"Was *he* a spy?" asked Mr. Cruncher.

"Old Bailey spy," returned his informant.

"Why, to be sure!" exclaimed Jerry, recalling the trial at which he had assisted. "I've seen him. Dead, is he?"

"Dead as mutton," returned the other, "and can't be too dead. Have 'em out, there! Spies! Pull 'em out! Spies!"

The idea was so acceptable, in the prevalent absence of any idea, that the crowd caught it up with eagerness, and loudly repeating the suggestion to have 'em out, and to pull 'em out, mobbed the two vehicles so closely that they came to a stop. On the crowd's opening the coach doors, the one mourner scuffled out of himself and was in their hands for a moment; but he was so alert and made such good use of his time that in another moment he was scouring away up a by-street, after shedding his cloak, hat, long hatband, white pocket handkerchief, and other symbolical tears.

These the people tore to pieces and scattered far and wide with great enjoyment, while the tradesmen hurriedly shut up their shops; for a crowd in those times stopped at nothing, and was a monster much dreaded. They had already got the length of opening the hearse to take the coffin out, when some brighter genius proposed, instead, its being escorted to its destination amidst general rejoicing. Practical suggestions being much needed, this suggestion, too, was received with acclamation, and the coach was immediately filled with eight inside and a dozen out, while as many people got on the roof of the hearse as could by any exercise of ingenuity stick upon it. Among the first of these volunteers was Jerry Cruncher himself, who modestly concealed his spiky head from the observation of Tellson's, in the further corner of the mourning coach.

The officiating undertakers made some protest against these changes in the cere-

Ronald Searle

monies; but, the river being alarmingly near, and several voices remarking on the efficacy of cold immersion in bringing refractory members of the profession to reason, the protest was faint and brief. The remodeled procession started, with a chimney sweep driving the hearse—advised by the regular driver, who was perched beside him under close inspection, for the purpose—and with a pieman, also attended by his cabinet minister, driving the mourning coach. A bear leader, a popular street character of the time, was impressed as an additional ornament, before the cavalcade had gone far down the Strand; and his bear, who was black and very mangy, gave quite an undertaking air to that part of the procession in which he walked.

Thus, with beer drinking, pipe smoking, song roaring, and infinite caricaturing of woe, the disorderly procession went its way, recruiting at every step, and all the shops shutting up about it. Its destination was the old church of Saint Pancras, far off in the fields. It got there in course of time; insisted on pouring into the burial ground; finally, accomplished the interment of the deceased Roger Cly in its own way, and highly to its own satisfaction.

The dead man disposed of, and the crowd being under the necessity of providing some other entertainment for itself, another brighter genius—or perhaps the same—conceived the humor of impeaching casual passers-by, as Old Bailey spies, and wreaking vengeance on them. Chase was given to some scores of inoffensive persons who had never been near the Old Bailey in their lives, in the realization of this fancy, and they were roughly hustled and maltreated. The transition to the sport of window breaking, and thence to the plundering of public houses, was easy and natural. At last, after several hours, when sundry summer houses had been pulled down, and some area railings had been torn up, to arm the more belligerent spirits, a rumor got about that the Guards were coming. Before this rumor, the crowd gradually melted away, and perhaps the Guards came, and perhaps they never came; and this was the usual progress of a mob.

Mr. Cruncher did not assist at the closing sports, but had remained behind in the churchyard, to confer and condole with the undertakers. The place had a soothing influence on him. He procured a pipe from a neighboring public house and smoked it, looking in at the railings and maturely considering the spot.

"Jerry," said Mr. Cruncher, apostrophizing himself in his usual way, "you see that there Cly that day, and you see with your own eyes that he was a young 'un and a straight made 'un."

Having smoked his pipe out and ruminated a little longer, he turned himself about, and made a short call upon his medical adviser—a distinguished surgeon.

Young Jerry relieved his father with dutiful interest, and reported no job in his absence. The bank closed, the ancient clerks came out, the usual watch was set, and Mr. Cruncher and his son went home to tea.

"Now, I tell you where it is!" said Mr. Cruncher to his wife, on entering. "If, as a honest tradesman, my wentures goes wrong tonight, I shall make sure that you've been praying agin me, and I shall work you for it just the same as if I seen you do it."

The dejected Mrs. Cruncher shook her head.

"Why, you're at it afore my face!" said Mr. Cruncher, with signs of angry apprehension.

"I am saying nothing."

"Well, then; don't meditate nothing. You might as well flop as meditate. You may as well go again' me one way as another. Drop it altogether."

"You were going out tonight?" asked his decent wife.

"Yes, I am."

"May I go with you, father?" asked his son, briskly.

"No, you mayn't. I'm a-going—as your

mother knows—a-fishing. That's where I'm going to. Going a-fishing."

"Your fishing rod gets rayther rusty don't it, father?"

"Never you mind."

"Shall you bring any fish home, father?"

"If I don't, you'll have short commons, tomorrow," returned that gentleman; "that's questions enough for you; I ain't a-going out till you've been long abed."

He devoted himself during the remainder of the evening to keeping a vigilant watch on Mrs. Cruncher, and sullenly holding her in conversation that she might be prevented from meditating any petitions to his disadvantage. The devoutest person could have rendered no greater homage to the efficacy of an honest prayer than he did in this distrust of his wife. It was as if a professed unbeliever in ghosts should be frightened by a ghost story.

Thus the evening wore away with the Cruncher family until Young Jerry was ordered to bed, and his mother, laid under similar injunctions, obeyed them. Mr. Cruncher did not start upon his excursion until nearly one o'clock. Toward that small and ghostly hour he rose up from his chair, took a key out of his pocket, opened a locked cupboard, and brought forth a sack, a crowbar of convenient size, a rope and chain, and other fishing tackle of that nature. Disposing these articles about him, he bestowed a parting defiance on Mrs. Cruncher, extinguished the light, and went out.

Young Jerry, who had only made a feint of undressing when he went to bed, was not long after his father. Under cover of the darkness he followed out of the room, followed down the stairs, followed down the court, followed out into the streets. He was in no uneasiness concerning his getting into the house again, for it was full of lodgers, and the door stood ajar all night.

Jerry had not gone far when he was joined by another disciple of Izaak Walton,[1] and the two trudged on together. Within half an hour another fisherman was picked up. They turned out of the road, and up a blind lane, of which a wall—some ten feet high—formed one side. Young Jerry saw his honored parent nimbly scaling an iron gate. He was soon over, and then the second fisherman got over, and then the third.

It was now Young Jerry's turn to approach the gate; which he did, holding his breath. Crouching down in a corner there, and looking in, he made out the three fishermen creeping through some rank grass, and all the gravestones in the churchyard—it was a large churchyard that they were in—looking on like ghosts in white. Then they began to fish.

They fished with a spade at first. Presently the honored parent appeared to be adjusting some instrument like a great corkscrew. Now they seemed to have got a bite. There was a screwing and complaining sound down below, and their bent figures were strained, as if by a weight. By degrees the weight came to the surface. Young Jerry knew what it would be; but when he saw it and saw his honored parent about to wrench it open, he was so frightened that he made off and never stopped until he had run a mile or more. He had a strong idea that the coffin he had seen was running after him; so that when the boy got to his own door he had reason for being half dead. And even then it would not leave him, but followed him upstairs with a bump on every stair, scrambled into bed with him, and bumped down on his breast when he fell asleep.

From his oppressed slumber, Young Jerry in his closet was awakened after daybreak and before sunrise by the presence of his father in the family room. Something had gone wrong with him; at least, Young Jerry inferred, from the circumstance of his holding Mrs. Cruncher by the ears, and knocking the back of her head against the headboard of the bed.

---

1. *Izaak Walton,* English writer [1593-1683] and author of *The Compleat Angler,* a book on fishing. His name has become synonymous with *fisherman.*

"I told you I would," said Mr. Cruncher, "and I did."

"Jerry, Jerry, Jerry!" his wife implored.

"You oppose yourself to the profit of the business," said Jerry, "and me and my partners suffer. You was to honor and obey; why the devil don't you?"

"I try to be a good wife, Jerry," the poor woman protested.

"Is it being a good wife to oppose your husband's business? Is it honoring your husband to dishonor his business? Is it obeying your husband to disobey him on the wital subject of his business?"

"You hadn't taken to the dreadful business then, Jerry."

"It's enough for you," retorted Mr. Cruncher, "to be the wife of a honest tradesman, and not to occupy your female mind with calculations when he took to his trade or when he didn't. A honoring and obeying wife would let his trade alone altogether. Call yourself a religious woman? If you're a religious woman, give me a irreligious one! You have no more nat'ral sense of duty than the bed of this here Thames River has of a pile, and similarly it must be knocked into you."

The altercation terminated in the honest tradesman's kicking off his clay-soiled boots, and lying down at his length on the floor. After taking a timid peep at him lying on his back, with his rusty hands under his head for a pillow, his son lay down too, and fell asleep again.

There was no fish for breakfast, and not much of anything else. Mr. Cruncher, out of spirits, and out of temper, kept an iron potlid by him as a projectile for the correction of Mrs. Cruncher, in case he should observe any symptoms of her saying Grace. He was brushed and washed at the usual hour and set off with his son to pursue his ostensible calling.

"Father," said Young Jerry, as they walked along, taking care to keep at arm's length and to have the stool well between them; "what's a resurrection-man?"

Mr. Cruncher came to a stop on the pavement before he answered, "How should I know?"

"I thought you knowed everything, father," said the artless boy.

"Hem! Well," returned Mr. Cruncher, going on again, and lifting off his hat to give his spikes free play, "he's a tradesman."

"What's his goods, father?" asked the brisk Young Jerry.

"His goods," said Mr. Cruncher, after turning it over in his mind, "is a branch of scientific goods."

"Persons' bodies, ain't it, father?" asked the lively boy.

"I believe it is something of that sort," said Mr. Cruncher.

"Oh, father, I should so like to be a resurrection-man when I'm quite growed up!"

Mr. Cruncher was soothed, but shook his head in a dubious and moral way. "It depends upon how you dewelop your talents. Be careful to dewelop your talents, and never to say no more than you can help to nobody, and there's no telling at the present time what you may not come to be fit for." As Young Jerry, thus encouraged, went on a few yards in advance, to plant the stool in the shadow of the Bar, Mr. Cruncher added to himself: "Jerry, you honest tradesman, there's hopes wot that boy will yet be a blessing to you, and a recompense to you for his mother!"

WHAT DO YOU SAY?

1. (a) Where have you met "the spy" Roger Cly before? *(b)* Who do you suppose is the "one mourner" at his funeral?

2. Is the description of the London mob realistic? Explain.

3. On Jerry Cruncher's return to the bank, he makes a call on his medical advisor. What is the significance of this action?

4. (a) At what point in the novel did you first surmise Jerry's "trade"? *(b)* What kind of luck did Jerry have on this particular "fishing" trip? How do you know?

CHAPTER XIII
Knitting

This had been the third morning in succession on which there had been early drinking at the wine shop of Monsieur Defarge. There had been more of early brooding than drinking; for many men had listened and whispered and slunk about there from the time of the opening of the door who could not have laid a piece of money on the counter to save their souls. These were to the full as interested in the place, however, as if they could have commanded whole barrels of wine; and they glided from seat to seat, and from corner to corner, swallowing talk in lieu of drink, with greedy looks.

Notwithstanding an unusual flow of company, the master of the wine shop was not visible. He was not missed; for, nobody who crossed the threshold looked for him, nobody asked for him, nobody wondered to see only Madame Defarge in her seat, presiding over the distribution of wine, with a bowl of battered small coins before her, as much defaced and beaten out of their original impress as the small coinage of humanity from whose ragged pockets they had come.

Thus, Saint Antoine, until high noontide, when two dusty men passed through his streets, of whom one was Monsieur Defarge, the other a mender of roads in a blue cap. All adust and athirst, the two entered the wine shop. Their arrival had lighted a kind of fire in the breast of Saint Antoine, fast spreading as they came along, which stirred and flickered in flames of faces at most doors and windows. Yet no one had followed them, and no man spoke when they entered the wine shop, though the eyes of every man there were turned upon them.

"Good-day, gentlemen!" said Monsieur Defarge.

It may have been a signal for loosening the general tongue. It elicited an answering chorus of "Good-day!"

"It is bad weather, gentlemen," said Defarge, shaking his head.

Upon which every man looked at his neighbor, and then all cast down their eyes and sat silent. Except one man, who got up and went out.

"My wife," said Defarge aloud, addressing Madame Defarge, "I have traveled certain leagues with this good mender of roads, called Jacques. I met him—by accident—a day and a half's journey out of Paris. He is a good child, this Jacques. Give him to drink, my wife!"

A second man got up and went out. Madame Defarge set wine before the mender of roads called Jacques, who doffed his blue cap to the company, and drank. In the breast of his blouse he carried some coarse dark bread; he ate of this between whiles, and sat munching and drinking near Madame Defarge's counter. A third man got up and went out.

Defarge refreshed himself with a draft of wine and stood waiting until the countryman had made his breakfast. He looked at no one present, and no one now looked at him; not even Madame Defarge, who had taken up her knitting, and was at work.

"Have you finished, friend?" he asked, in due season.

"Yes, thank you."

"Come, then! You shall see the apartment that I told you you could occupy. It will suit you to a marvel."

Out of the wine shop into the street, out of the street into a courtyard, out of the courtyard up a steep staircase, out of the staircase into a garret—formerly the garret where a white-haired man sat very busy, making shoes.

No white-haired man was there now; but the three men were there who had gone out of the wine shop singly, and had once looked in at him through the chinks in the wall.

Defarge closed the door and spoke in a subdued voice:

"Jacques One, Jacques Two, Jacques

Three! This is the witness encountered by appointment, by me, Jacques Four. He will tell you all. Speak, Jacques Five!"

The mender of roads, blue cap in hand, said, "Where shall I commence, monsieur?"

"Commence," was Monsieur Defarge's not unreasonable reply, "at the commencement."

"I saw him then, messieurs," began the mender of roads, "a year ago this running summer, underneath the carriage of the Marquis, hanging by the chain."

Jacques One struck in, and asked if he had ever seen the man before.

"Never," answered the mender of roads.

Jacques Three demanded how he afterwards recognized him then.

"By his tall figure," said the mender of roads. "When Monsieur the Marquis demands that evening, 'Say, what is he like?' I make response, 'Tall as a specter.'"

"You should have said, short as a dwarf," returned Jacques Two.

"But what did I know? The deed was not then accomplished. Observe! Under those circumstances even, I do not offer my testimony. Monsieur the Marquis indicates me with his finger, and says, 'To me! Bring that rascal!' My faith, messieurs, I offer nothing."

"He is right there, Jacques," murmured Defarge, to him who had interrupted. "Go on!"

"Good!" said the mender of roads, with an air of mystery.

"The tall man is lost, and he is sought—how many months? Nine, ten, eleven?"

"No matter, the number," said Defarge. "He is well hidden, but at last he is unluckily found. Go on!"

"I am again at work upon the hillside. I am collecting my tools to descend to my cottage in the village below, where it is already dark, when I raise my eyes, and see coming over the hill six soldiers. In the midst of them is a tall man with his arms bound—tied to his sides—like this!"

With the aid of his indispensable cap, he represented a man with his elbows bound fast at his hips, with cords that were knotted behind him.

"I stand aside, messieurs, to see the soldiers and their prisoner pass—for it is a solitary road, that, where any spectacle is well worth looking at—and at first, as they approach, I see no more than that they are six soldiers with a tall man bound, and that they are almost black to my sight. I see that they are covered with dust, and that the dust moves with them as they come, tramp, tramp! But when they advance quite near to me, I recognize the tall man, and he recognizes me. Ah, but he would be content to precipitate himself over the hillside once again, as on the evening he and I first encountered, close to the same spot!

"I do not show the soldiers that I recognize the tall man; he does not show the soldiers that he recognizes me; we do it, and we know it, with our eyes. 'Come on!' says the chief of that company, pointing to the village, 'bring him fast to his tomb!' and they bring him faster. I follow. His arms are swelled because of being bound so tight, his wooden shoes are large and clumsy, and he is lame. Because he is consequently slow, they drive him with their guns—like this!"

He imitated the action of a man's being impelled forward by the butt ends of muskets.

"As they descend the hill like madmen running a race, he falls. They laugh and pick him up again. His face is bleeding and covered with dust, but he cannot touch it; thereupon they laugh again. They bring him into the village; all the village runs to look; they take him past the mill, and up to the prison; all the village sees the prison gate open in the darkness of the night, and swallow him!

"All the village," pursued the mender of roads, "whispers by the fountain; in the morning, my tools upon my shoulder, I make a circuit by the prison on my way to my work. There I see him, high up, behind the bars of a lofty iron cage, bloody and dusty as last night, looking through. He has no hand free, to wave to me; I dare not call to him; he regards me like a dead man."

Defarge and the three glanced darkly at one another. The looks of all of them were dark, repressed, and revengeful, as they listened to the countryman's story; the manner of all of them, while it was secret, was authoritative too. They had the air of a rough tribunal; Jacques One and Two sitting on the old pallet bed, each with his chin resting on his hand, and his eyes intent on the road mender; Jacques Three equally intent, on one knee behind them, with his agitated hand always gliding over the network of fine nerves about his mouth and nose; Defarge standing between them and the narrator, whom he had stationed in the light of the window, by turns looking from him to them, and from them to him.

"Go on, Jacques," said Defarge.

"He remains up there in his iron cage some days. The village looks at him by stealth, for it is afraid. They whisper at the fountain that although condemned to death he will not be executed; they say that petitions have been presented in Paris, showing that he was enraged and made mad by the death of his child; they say that a petition has been presented to the King himself. What do I know? It is possible. Perhaps yes, perhaps no."

"Listen then, Jacques," Number One of that name sternly interposed. "Know that a petition was presented to the King and Queen. All here, yourself excepted, saw the King take it, in his carriage in the street, sitting beside the Queen. It is Defarge here, who, at the hazard of his life, darted out before the horses, with the petition in his hand."

"And once again listen, Jacques!" said the kneeling Number Three: his fingers ever wandering over and over those fine nerves, with a strikingly greedy air, as if he hungered for something—that was neither food nor drink; "the guard horse and foot, surrounded the petitioner, and struck him blows. You hear?"

"I hear, messieurs."

"Go on then," said Defarge.

"Again; on the other hand, they whisper at the fountain," resumed the countryman, "that he is brought down into our country to be executed on the spot, and that he will very certainly be executed. They even whisper that because he has slain Monseigneur, and because Monseigneur was the father of his tenants—serfs—what you will—he will be executed as a parricide.

"Well! Some whisper this, some whisper that; they speak of nothing else. At length, on Sunday night, when all the village is asleep, come soldiers, winding down from the prison. Workmen dig, workmen hammer, soldiers laugh and sing; in the morning by the fountain, there is raised a gallows forty feet high, poisoning the water."

The mender of roads pointed as if he saw the gallows somewhere in the sky.

"All work is stopped, all assemble there. At midday, the roll of drums. Soldiers have marched into the prison in the night, and he is in the midst of many soldiers. He is bound as before, and in his mouth there is a gag—tied so, with a tight string, making him look almost as if he laughed." He suggested it, by creasing his face with his two thumbs, from the corners of his mouth to his ears. "On the top of the gallows is fixed the knife, blade upwards, with its point in the air. He is hanged there forty feet high—and is left hanging, poisoning the water.

"It is frightful, messieurs. How can the women and the children draw water! Who can gossip of an evening, under that shadow!" He used his blue cap to wipe his face, on which the perspiration had started while he recalled the spectacle.

The hungry man gnawed one of his fingers as he looked at the other three, and his finger quivered with the craving that was on him.

"That's all, messieurs. I left at sunset—as

I had been warned to do—and I walked on, that night and half next day, until I met—as I was warned I should—this comrade. With him, I came on through the rest of yesterday and through last night. And here you see me!"

After a gloomy silence the first Jacques said, "Good! You have acted and recounted faithfully. Will you wait for us a little, outside the door?"

"Very willingly," said the mender of roads, whom Defarge escorted to the top of the stairs and, leaving seated there, returned.

"How say you, Jacques?" demanded Number One. "To be registered?"

"To be registered as doomed to destruction," returned Defarge.

"Magnificent!" croaked the man with the craving.

"The Château and all the race?" inquired the first.

"The Château and all the race," returned Defarge. "Extermination."

The hungry man repeated, in a rapturous croak, "Magnificent!" and began gnawing another finger.

"Are you sure," asked Jacques Two, of Defarge, "that no embarrassment can arise from our manner of keeping the register? Without doubt it is safe, for no one beyond ourselves can decipher it; but shall we always be able to decipher it—or, I ought to say, will she?"

"Jacques," returned Defarge, drawing himself up, "if madame my wife undertook to keep the register in her memory alone, she would not lose a word of it—not a syllable of it. Knitted, in her own stitches and her own symbols, it will always be as plain to her as the sun. It would be easier for the weakest poltroon that lives to erase himself from existence than to erase one letter of his name or crimes from the knitted register of Madame Defarge."

There was a murmur of confidence and approval, and then the man who hungered, asked: "Is this rustic to be sent back soon? I hope so. He is very simple; is he not a little dangerous?"

"He knows nothing," said Defarge; "I will take care of him, and set him on his road. He wishes to see the Court; let him see it on Sunday."

"What?" exclaimed the hungry man, staring. "Is it a good sign that he wishes to see royalty and nobility?"

"Jacques," said Defarge; "judiciously show a cat milk, if you wish her to thirst for it. Judiciously show a dog his natural prey, if you wish him to bring it down one day."

Nothing more was said, and the mender of roads, already dozing on the topmost stair, was advised to take some rest. He needed no persuasion, and was soon asleep.

Worse quarters than Defarge's wine shop could easily have been found in Paris for a provincial slave of that degree. Saving for a mysterious dread of madame by which he was constantly haunted, his life was very new and agreeable. But madame sat all day at her counter, so expressly unconscious of him, and so particularly determined not to perceive that his being there had any connection with anything below the surface, that he shook in his wooden shoes whenever his eye lighted on her. For he contended with himself that it was impossible to foresee what the lady might pretend next; and he felt assured that if she should take it into her brightly ornamented head to pretend that she had seen him do a murder and afterwards flay the victim, she would infallibly go through with it until the play was played out.

When Sunday came, the mender of roads was not enchanted to find that madame was to accompany monsieur and himself to Versailles.[1] It was additionally disconcerting to have madame still with her knitting in her

---

1. Versailles (vär sī'), a city twelve miles southwest of Paris and the seat of the principal royal dwelling, the Palace of Versailles, which is still associated with the glory that was France in the years from 1638 to 1793.

hands as the crowd waited to see the carriage of the King and Queen.

"What do you make, madame?" asked a man near her.

"Many things."

"For instance—"

"For instance," returned Madame Defarge, composedly, "shrouds."

The man moved a little farther away, as soon as he could, and the mender of roads fanned himself with his blue cap. Soon the large-faced King and the fair-faced Queen came in their golden coach, attended by a glittering multitude of laughing ladies and fine lords; the mender of roads cried, "Long live the King, Long live the Queen, Long live everybody!" until he absolutely wept with sentiment.

"Bravo!" said Defarge, clapping him on the back when it was over, like a patron; "you are a good boy!"

The mender of roads was now coming to himself, and was mistrustful of having made a mistake in his late demonstrations; but no.

"You are the fellow we want," said Defarge; "you make these fools believe it will last forever. Then they are the more insolent, and it is the nearer ended."

Madame Defarge nodded in confirmation.

"As to you," said she, "you would shout and shed tears for anything, if it made a show and a noise. Say! Would you not?"

"Truly, madame, I think so. For the moment."

"If you were shown a great heap of dolls, and were set upon them to pluck them to pieces and despoil them, for your own advantage, you would pick out the richest and gayest. Say. Would you not?"

"Truly yes, madame."

"Yes. And if you were shown a flock of birds, unable to fly, and were set upon them to strip them of their feathers, for your own advantage, you would set upon the birds of the finest feathers; would you not?"

"It is true, madame."

"You have seen both dolls and birds today," said Madame Defarge; "now go home!"

WHAT DO YOU SAY?

1. *(a)* Why did the five men meet in the garret above the wine shop? *(b)* What story did the road mender relate?

2. *(a)* What was Dickens' purpose in revealing in detail the execution of the Marquis' murderer? *(b)* For what does Jacques Three hunger? *(c)* What do his peculiar actions contribute to the emotional feeling of this chapter?

3. *(a)* After the road mender has given his testimony, what decision is reached? *(b)* What was the purpose of the secret register and how was it kept?

CHAPTER XIV
Still Knitting

Madame Defarge and monsieur her husband returned amicably to the bosom of Saint Antoine, while a speck in a blue cap toiled through the darkness, and through the dust, and down the weary miles, slowly tending toward where the château of Monsieur the Marquis, now in his grave, listened to the whispering trees.

The Defarges, husband and wife, came lumbering under the starlight, in their public vehicle, to that gate of Paris whereunto their journey tended. Monsieur Defarge alighted; knowing one or two of the soldiery there, and one of the police. The latter he was intimate with, and affectionately embraced. When Saint Antoine had again enfolded the Defarges in his dusky wings, Madame Defarge spoke to her husband:

"Say then; what did Jacques of the police tell thee?"

"Very little tonight, but all he knows. There is another spy commissioned for our quarter."

"Eh, well!" said Madame Defarge. "It is necessary to register him. How do they call that man?"

"He is English."

"So much the better. His name?"

"John Barsad," said Defarge.

"John Barsad," repeated madame, after murmuring it once to herself. "Good. His appearance; is it known?"

"Age, about forty years; height, about five feet nine; black hair; complexion dark; generally, rather handsome visage; eyes dark, face thin, long, and sallow; nose aquiline, but not straight, having a peculiar inclination toward the left cheek; expression, therefore, sinister."

"Eh, my faith. It is a portrait!" said madame, laughing. "He shall be registered tomorrow."

They turned into the wine shop, which was closed—for it was midnight—and where Madame Defarge immediately took her post at her desk, counted the small moneys, examined the stock, went through the entries in the book, made other entries of her own, checked the serving man in every possible way, and finally dismissed him to bed.

Next noontide saw the admirable woman in her usual place in the wine shop, knitting away assiduously. A rose lay beside her, and if she now and then glanced at the flower, it was with no infraction of her usual preoccupied air. There were a few customers, drinking or not drinking, standing or seated, sprinkled about.

A figure entering at the door threw a shadow on Madame Defarge which she felt to be a new one. She laid down her knitting, and began to pin her rose in her headdress, before she looked at the figure.

It was curious. The moment Madame Defarge took up the rose the customers ceased talking, and began gradually to drop out of the wine shop.

"Good day, madame," said the newcomer.

"Good day, monsieur."

She said it aloud, but added to herself, as she resumed her knitting: "Hah! Good day, age about forty, height about five feet nine, black hair, generally rather handsome visage, complexion dark, eyes dark, thin long and sallow face, aquiline nose but not straight, having a peculiar inclination toward the left cheek which imparts a sinister expression! Good day, one and all!"

"Have the goodness to give a little glass of old cognac."

"John," thought madame, checking off her work as her fingers knitted, and her eyes looked at the stranger. "Stay long enough, and I shall knit 'Barsad' before you go."

The spy, who was there to pick up any crumbs he could find, stood with an air of gossiping gallantry, leaning his elbow on Madame Defarge's little counter.

"A bad business this, madame, of Gaspard's execution. Ah! the poor Gaspard!" With a sigh of great compassion.

"My faith!" returned madame, coolly and lightly, "if people use knives for such purposes, they have to pay for it. He knew beforehand what the price of his luxury was; he has paid the price."

"I believe," said the spy, "there is much compassion and anger in this neighborhood, touching the poor fellow?"

"Is there?" asked madame, vacantly.

"Is there not?"

"—Here is my husband!" said Madame Defarge.

As the keeper of the wine shop entered, the spy saluted him by saying, with an engaging smile, "Good day, Jacques!" Defarge stopped short and stared at him.

"Good day, Jacques!" the spy repeated; with not quite so much confidence, or quite so easy a smile under the stare.

"You deceive yourself, monsieur," returned the keeper of the wine shop. "I am Ernest Defarge."

"It is all the same," said the spy, airily, but discomfited too; "good day!"

"Good day!" answered Defarge, drily.

"The pleasure of conversing with you, Monsieur Defarge, recalls to me," pursued the spy, "that I have the honor of cherishing some interesting associations with your name."

"Indeed!" said Defarge, with much indifference.

"Yes, indeed. When Doctor Manette was released, you, his old domestic, had the charge of him, I know. You see I am informed of the circumstances?"

"Such is the fact, certainly," said Defarge. He had it conveyed to him, in an accidental touch of his wife's elbow, as she knitted and warbled, that he would do best to answer, but with brevity.

"It was to you," said the spy, "that his daughter came; and it was from your care that his daughter took him, accompanied by Monsieur Lorry—of the bank of Tellson and Company—over to England."

"Such is the fact," repeated Defarge.

"Very interesting remembrances!" said the spy. "I have known Doctor Manette and his daughter, in England."

"Yes?" said Defarge.

"You don't hear much about them now?" said the spy. "She is going to be married."

"Going?" echoed madame. "She was pretty enough to have been married long ago. You English are cold, it seems to me."

"Oh! You know I am English?"

"I perceive your tongue is," returned madame, "and what the tongue is, I suppose the man is."

He did not take the identification as a compliment; but he made the best of it, and turned it off with a laugh. After sipping his cognac to the end, he added:

"Yes, Miss Manette is going to be married. But not to an Englishman; to one who, like herself, is French by birth. And speaking of Gaspard—ah, poor Gaspard!—she is going to marry the nephew of Monsieur the Marquis, for whom Gaspard was exalted to so many feet; in other words, the present Marquis. But he lives unknown in England, he is no Marquis there; he is Mr. Charles Darnay. D'Aulnais is the name of his mother's family."

Madame Defarge knitted steadily, but the intelligence had a palpable effect upon her husband. The spy would have been no spy if he had failed to see it. Having made, at least, this one hit, whatever it might prove to be worth, Mr. Barsad paid for what he had drunk, and left.

"Can it be true," said Defarge, in a low voice, "what he has said of Ma'amselle Manette?"

"As he has said it," retorted madame, lifting her eyebrows a little, "it is probably false. But it may be true."

"If it is, I hope, for her sake, Destiny will keep her husband out of France."

"Her husband's destiny," said Madame Defarge, with her usual composure, "will take him where he is to go, and will lead him to the end that is to end him. That is all I know."

"But it is very strange—now, at least, is it not very strange"—said Defarge, rather pleading with his wife to induce her to admit it, "that, after all our sympathy of Monsieur her father, and herself, her husband's name should be proscribed under your hand at this moment, by the side of that infernal dog's who has just left us?"

"Stranger things than that will happen when it does come," answered madame. "I have them both here, of a certainty; and they are both here for their merits; that is enough."

She rolled up her knitting when she had said those words and presently took the rose out of the handkerchief that was wound about her head.

In the evening, Madame Defarge with her work in her hand was accustomed to pass from place to place and from group to group; a Missionary—there were many like her—such as the world will do well never to breed again. And as Madame Defarge moved on from group to group, her husband smoked at his door, looking after her with admiration. "A great woman," said he, "a strong woman, a grand woman, a frightfully grand woman!"

WHAT DO YOU SAY?

1. *(a)* What was the subtle contest between Madame Defarge and John Barsad? *(b)* Which person ended by giving the other more information? *(c)* Where has Barsad appeared before in the novel?

2. Among the last six paragraphs, which sentences would you choose as likely foreshadowing of events to come?

CHAPTER XV
Nine Days

The marriage day was shining brightly, and they were ready outside the closed door of the Doctor's room, where he was speaking with Charles Darnay. They were ready to go to church; the beautiful bride, Mr. Lorry, and Miss Pross—to whom the event, through a gradual process of reconcilement to the inevitable would have been one of absolute bliss but for the yet lingering consideration that her brother Solomon should have been the bridegroom.

"And so," said Mr. Lorry, who could not sufficiently admire the bride, and who had been moving round her to take in every point of her quiet, pretty dress; "and so it was for this, my sweet Lucie, that I brought you across the Channel, such a baby! Lord bless me! How little I thought what I was doing! How lightly I valued the obligation I was conferring on my friend Mr. Charles!"

"You didn't mean it," remarked the matter-of-fact Miss Pross, "and therefore how could you know it? Nonsense!"

"Really? Well; but don't cry," said the gentle Mr. Lorry.

"I am not crying," said Miss Pross; "*you* are."

"I, my Pross?" (By this time, Mr. Lorry dared to be pleasant with her, on occasion.)

"You were, just now; I saw you do it, and I don't wonder at it. Such a present of plate as you made 'em is enough to bring tears into anybody's eyes. There's not a fork or a spoon in the collection that I didn't cry over, last night after the box came, till I couldn't see it."

"I am highly gratified," said Mr. Lorry. "Dear me! This is an occasion that makes a man speculate on all he has lost. Dear, dear, dear! To think that there might have been a Mrs. Lorry any time these fifty years almost!"

"Not at all!" From Miss Pross.

"You think there never might have been a Mrs. Lorry?" asked the gentleman of that name.

"Pooh!" rejoined Miss Pross; "you were a bachelor in your cradle."

"Well!" observed Mr. Lorry, beamingly adjusting his little wig, "that seems probable too."

"And you were cut out for a bachelor," pursued Miss Pross, "before you were put in your cradle."

"Then, I think," said Mr. Lorry, "that I was very unhandsomely dealt with, and that I ought to have had a voice in the selection of my pattern. Enough! Now, my dear Lucie," drawing his arm soothingly round her waist, "I hear them moving in the next room, and Miss Pross and I, as two formal folks of business, are anxious not to lose the final opportunity of saying something to you that you wish to hear. You leave your good father, my dear, in hands as earnest and as loving as your own; he shall be taken every conceivable care of; during the next fortnight, while you are in Warwickshire and thereabouts, even Tellson's shall go to the wall—comparatively speaking—before him. And when, at the fortnight's end, he comes to join you and your beloved husband, on your other fortnight's trip in Wales, you shall say that we have sent him to you in the best health and in the happiest frame. Now I hear Somebody's step coming to the door. Let me kiss my dear girl with an old-fashioned bachelor blessing before Somebody comes to claim his own."

The door of the Doctor's room opened,

and he came out with Charles Darnay. He was so deadly pale—which had not been the case when they went in together—that no vestige of color was in his face. But in the composure of his manner he was unaltered, except that to Mr. Lorry it disclosed some shadowy indication that the old air of avoidance and dread had lately passed over him, like a cold wind.

He gave his arm to his daughter, and took her downstairs to the chariot which Mr. Lorry had hired in honor of the day. The rest followed in another carriage, and soon, in a neighboring church, where no strange eyes looked on, Charles Darnay and Lucie Manette were happily married.

They returned home to breakfast, and all went well, and in due course the golden hair that had mingled with the poor shoemaker's white locks in the Paris garret, was mingled with them again in the morning sunlight, on the threshold of the door at parting.

It was a hard parting, though not for long. But her father said at last, gently disengaging himself from her enfolding arms, "Take her, Charles! She is yours!"

And her agitated hand waved to them from a chaise window, and she was gone.

The preparations having been very simple and few, the Doctor, Mr. Lorry, and Miss Pross, were left quite alone. It was when they returned into the welcome shade of the cool old hall that Mr. Lorry observed a great change to have come over the Doctor; as if the golden arm uplifted there had struck him a poisoned blow.

"I think," he whispered to Miss Pross, after anxious consideration, "we had best not speak to him just now, or at all disturb him. I must look in at Tellson's; so I will go there at once and come back presently. Then we will take him a ride into the country, and all will be well."

It was easier for Mr. Lorry to look in at Tellson's than to look out of Tellson's. He was detained two hours. When he came back to the Doctor's rooms, he was stopped by a low sound of knocking.

"Good God!" he said, with a start. "What's that?"

Miss Pross, with a terrified face, was at his ear. "O me! All is lost!" cried she, wringing her hands. "What is to be told to Ladybird? He is making shoes!"

Mr. Lorry said what he could to calm her, and went himself into the Doctor's room. The bench was turned toward the light, as it had been when he had seen the shoemaker at his work before, and he was very busy.

"Doctor Manette. My dear friend, Doctor Manette!"

The Doctor looked at him for a moment, half inquiringly, and bent over his work again.

He had laid aside his coat and waistcoat; his shirt was open at the throat, and even the old haggard, faded surface of face had come back to him. He worked hard—impatiently—as if in some sense of having been interrupted.

Mr. Lorry glanced at the work in his hand, and observed that it was a shoe of the old size and shape. He took up another that was lying by him, and asked what it was.

"A young lady's walking shoe," he muttered, without looking up. "It ought to have been finished long ago."

"But, Doctor Manette. Look at me."

He obeyed, in the old mechanically submissive manner.

"You know me, my dear friend? Think again. This is not your proper occupation. Think, dear friend!"

Nothing would induce him to speak more. He looked up, for an instant at a time, when he was requested to do so; but no persuasion would extract a word from him.

Two things at once impressed themselves on Mr. Lorry, as important above all others; the first, that this must be kept secret from Lucie; the second, that it must be kept secret from all who knew him. In conjunction with Miss Pross, he took immediate steps toward the latter precaution, by giving out that the Doctor was not well, and required a few days of complete rest.

In the hope of his recovery, Mr. Lorry resolved to watch him attentively, with as little appearance as possible of doing so. He therefore made arrangements to absent himself from Tellson's for the first time in his life, and took his post by the window in the same room.

He was not long in discovering that it was worse than useless to speak to him, since, on being pressed, he became worried. He abandoned that attempt on the first day, and resolved merely to keep himself always before him, as a silent protest against the delusion into which he had fallen, or was falling. He remained, therefore, in his seat near the window, reading and writing, and expressing in as many pleasant and natural ways as he could think of, that it was a free place.

Doctor Manette took what was given him to eat and drink, and worked on, that first day, until it was too dark to see. When he put his tools aside, Mr. Lorry rose and said:

"Will you go out?"

He looked down at the floor on either side of him in the old manner, looked up in the old manner, and repeated:

"Out?"

"Yes; for a walk with me. Why not?"

He made no effort to say why not, and said not a word more. But Mr. Lorry thought he saw that he was in some misty way asking himself, "Why not?" The sagacity of the man of business perceived an advantage here, and determined to hold it.

On the second day, Mr. Lorry saluted him cheerfully by his name, and spoke to him on topics that had been of late familiar to them. He returned no reply, but it was evident that he heard what was said, and that he thought about it, however confusedly. This encouraged Mr. Lorry to have Miss Pross in with her work, several times during the day; at those times, they quietly spoke of Lucie, and of her father then present, precisely in the usual manner, and as if there were nothing amiss. This was done without any demonstrative accompaniment, not long enough, or often enough to harass him; and it lightened Mr. Lorry's friendly heart to believe that he looked up oftener, and appeared to be stirred by some perception of inconsistencies surrounding him.

When it fell dark again, Mr. Lorry asked him as before.

"Dear Doctor, will you go out?"

As before, he repeated, "Out?"

"Yes; for a walk with me. Why not?"

This time Mr. Lorry feigned to go out when he could extract no answer from him, and, after remaining absent for an hour, returned. In the meanwhile, the Doctor had removed to the seat in the window, but, on Mr. Lorry's return, he slipped away to his bench.

The time went slowly on, and Mr. Lorry's hope darkened, and his heart grew heavier and heavier every day. The third day came and went, the fourth, the fifth. Five days, six days, seven days, eight days, nine days.

With a hope ever darkening, and with a heart always growing heavier and heavier, Mr. Lorry passed through this anxious time. The secret was well kept, and Lucie was unconscious and happy; but he could not fail to observe that the shoemaker, whose hand had been a little out at first, was growing dreadfully skillful, and that he had never been so intent on his work, and that his hands had never been so nimble and expert as in the dusk of the ninth evening.

WHAT DO YOU SAY?

1. *(a)* Where have you heard previously of Miss Pross' brother Solomon? *(b)* What purpose do you think the author has in introducing his name again?

2. *(a)* Regarding Dr. Manette's relapse, what connection do you find between this chapter and Chapter X? *(b)* What do you think really troubles the Doctor?

CHAPTER XVI
An Opinion

Worn out by anxious watching, Mr. Lorry fell asleep at his post. On the tenth morning of his suspense, he was startled by the shining of the sun into the room where a heavy slumber had overtaken him when it was dark night.

He rubbed his eyes and roused himself; but he doubted, when he had done so, whether he was not still asleep. For, going to the door of the Doctor's room and looking in, he perceived that the shoemaker's bench and tools were put aside again, and that the Doctor himself sat reading at the window. He was in his usual morning dress, and his face—which Mr. Lorry could distinctly see—though still very pale, was calmly studious and attentive.

Within a few minutes Miss Pross stood whispering at his side. If he had had any particle of doubt left, her talk would of necessity have resolved it; but he was by that time clear-headed, and had none. He advised that they should let the time go by until the regular breakfast hour, and should then meet the Doctor as if nothing unusual had occurred.

When the breakfast was done and cleared away, and he and the Doctor were left together, Mr. Lorry said, feelingly:

"My dear Manette, I am anxious to have your opinion, in confidence, on a very curious case in which I am deeply interested; that is to say, it is very curious to me; perhaps, to your better information it may be less so."

Glancing at his hands, which were discolored by his late work, the Doctor looked troubled, and listened attentively. He had already glanced at his hands more than once.

"Doctor Manette," said Mr. Lorry, touching him affectionately on the arm, "the case is the case of a particularly dear friend of mine. Pray advise me well for his sake—and above all, for his daughter's, my dear Manette."

"If I understand," said the Doctor, in a subdued tone, "some mental shock—?"

"Yes!"

"Be explicit," said the Doctor. "Spare no detail."

Mr. Lorry saw that they understood one another, and proceeded:

"My dear Manette, it is the case of an old and a prolonged shock. It is the case of a shock from which the sufferer recovered, by a process that he cannot trace himself—as I once heard him publicly relate in a striking manner. But, unfortunately, there has been"—he paused and took a deep breath—"a slight relapse."

The Doctor, in a low voice, asked, "Of how long duration?"

"Nine days and nights."

"How did it show itself? I infer," glancing at his hands again, "in the resumption of some old pursuit connected with the shock?"

"That is the fact."

"Now, did you ever see him," asked the Doctor, distinctly and collectedly, though in the same low voice, "engaged in that pursuit originally?"

"Once."

"And when the relapse fell on him, was he in most respects—or in all respects—as he was then?"

"I think in all respects."

"Does his daughter know of the relapse?"

"No. It has been kept from her. It is known only to myself, and to one other who may be trusted."

The Doctor grasped his hand, and murmured, "That was very kind." Neither of the two spoke for a little while.

"Now," said Mr. Lorry, gently, "to what would you refer this attack?"

"I believe," returned Doctor Manette, "that there had been a strong revival of the train of thought and remembrance that was the first cause of the malady. Some intense associations of a most distressing nature were vividly recalled, I think. It is probable that there had long been a dread lurking in his mind that those associations would be recalled—say, under certain circumstances—say, on a particular occasion. He tried to prepare himself in vain; perhaps the effort to prepare himself made him less able to bear it."

"Would he remember what took place in the relapse?" asked Mr. Lorry, with natural hesitation.

The Doctor looked desolately round the room, shook his head, and answered, in a low voice, "Not at all."

"Now, as to the future," hinted Mr. Lorry.

"As to the future," said the Doctor, recovering firmness, "I should have great hope. As it pleased heaven in its mercy to restore him so soon, I should have great hope. I should hope that the worst was over."

"That's good comfort. I am thankful!" said Mr. Lorry.

"I am thankful!" repeated the Doctor, bending his head with reverence.

"The occupation resumed under the influence of this passing affliction so happily recovered from," said Mr. Lorry, clearing his throat, "we will call—blacksmith's work. We will say, to put a case and for the sake of illustration, that he had been used, in his bad time, to work at a little forge. We will say that he was unexpectedly found at his forge again. Is it not a pity that he should keep it by him?"

The Doctor beat his foot nervously on the ground.

"He has always kept it by him," said Mr. Lorry, with an anxious look at his friend. "Now, would it not be better that he should let it go?"

"You see," said Doctor Manette, after an uneasy pause, "it is very hard to explain the workings of this poor man's mind. He once yearned so frightfully for that occupation, and it was so welcome when it came; no doubt it relieved his pain so much, by substituting the perplexity of the fingers for the perplexity of the brain, that he has never been able to bear the thought of putting it quite out of his reach. Even now, when he is more hopeful of himself than he has ever been, the idea that he might need that old employment, and not find it, gives him a sudden sense of terror, like that which strikes the heart of a lost child."

He looked like his illustration, as he raised his eyes to Mr. Lorry's face.

"I would not keep it," said Mr. Lorry, shaking his head; for he gained in firmness as he saw the Doctor disquieted. "I only want your authority. I am sure it does no good. Come! Give me your authority, like a dear good man. For his daughter's sake, my dear Manette!"

Very strange to see what a struggle there was within him!

"In her name, then, let it be done. But let it be removed when he is not there; let him miss his old companion after an absence."

Mr. Lorry readily engaged for that, and the conference was ended. They passed the day in the country, and the Doctor was quite restored. On the fourteenth day he went to join Lucie and her husband, and she had no suspicions.

On the night of the day on which he left the house, Mr. Lorry went into his room with a chopper, saw, chisel, and hammer, attended by Miss Pross carrying a light. There with closed doors, and in a mysterious and guilty manner, Mr. Lorry hacked the shoemaker's bench to pieces, while Miss Pross held the candle as if she were assisting at a murder—for which, indeed, in her grimness, she was no unsuitable figure. The burning of the body—previously reduced to pieces convenient for the purpose—was commenced without delay in the kitchen fire; and the tools, shoes, and leather were buried in the garden. So wicked do destruction and secrecy appear to honest minds that Mr. Lorry and Miss Pross, while engaged in the commission of their deed and in the removal of its traces, almost felt, and almost looked, like accomplices in a horrible crime.

WHAT DO YOU SAY?

1. *(a)* How does Mr. Lorry go about presenting his problem to Dr. Manette? *(b)* Why does he use this approach? *(c)* In the Doctor's diagnosis, what was the cause of his recent "attack"?

2. *(a)* What purpose did the making of shoes serve for Dr. Manette, both in prison and during his relapse? *(b)* How did Mr. Lorry finally persuade Dr. Manette to give up his shoemaker's bench and tools?

CHAPTER XVII
A Plea

When the newly married pair came home, the first person who appeared, to offer his congratulations, was Sydney Carton. They had not been at home many hours when he presented himself. He was not improved in habits, or in looks, or in manner; but there was a certain rugged air of fidelity about him, which was new to the observation of Charles Darnay.

He watched his opportunity of taking Darnay aside into a window, and of speaking to him when no one overheard.

"Mr. Darnay," said Carton, "I wish we might be friends."

"We are already friends, I hope."

"You are good enough to say so, as a fashion of speech; but, I don't mean any fashion of speech. Indeed, when I say I wish we might be friends, I scarcely mean quite that, either."

Charles Darnay—as was natural—asked him, in all good humor and good fellowship, what he did mean?

"Upon my life," said Carton, smiling, "I find that easier to comprehend in my own mind, than to convey to yours. However, let me try. You remember a certain famous occasion when I was more drunk than—than usual?"

"I remember a certain famous occasion when you forced me to confess that you had been drinking."

"I remember it too. The curse of those occasions is heavy upon me, for I always remember them. I hope it may be taken into account one day, when all days are at an end for me! Don't be alarmed; I am not going to preach."

"I am not at all alarmed. Earnestness in you is anything but alarming to me."

"Ah!" said Carton, with a careless wave of his hand, as if he waved that away. "On the drunken occasion in question—one of a large number, as you know—I was insufferable about liking you, and not liking you. I wish you would forget it."

"I forgot it long ago."

"Fashion of speech again! But, Mr. Darnay, oblivion is not so easy to me as you represent it to be to you. I have by no means forgotten it, and a light answer does not help me to forget it."

"If it was a light answer," returned Darnay, "I beg your forgiveness for it. I had no other object than to turn a slight thing, which to my surprise seems to trouble you too much, aside. I declare to you, on the faith of a gentleman, that I have long dismissed it from my mind. Good heaven, what was there to dismiss! Have I had nothing more important to remember, in the great service you rendered me that day?"

"As to the great service," said Carton, "I am bound to avow to you, when you speak of it in that way, that it was mere professional claptrap. I don't know that I cared what became of you, when I rendered it.—Mind! I say when I rendered it; I am speaking of the past."

"You make light of the obligation," returned Darnay, "but I will not quarrel with *your* light answer."

"Genuine truth, Mr. Darnay, trust me! I have gone aside from my purpose; I was speaking about our being friends. Now, you know me; you know I am incapable of all the higher and better flights of men. If you doubt it, ask Stryver, and he'll tell you so."

"I prefer to form my own opinion, without the aid of his."

"Well! At any rate you know me as a dissolute dog, who has never done any good, and never will."

"I don't know that you 'never will.'"

"But I do, and you must take my word for it. Well! If you could endure to have such a worthless fellow, and a fellow of such indifferent reputation, coming and going at odd times, I should ask that I might be permitted to come and go as a privileged person here; that I might be regarded as a useless—and I would add, if it were not for the resemblance I detected between you and me, an unornamental—piece of furniture, tolerated for its old service, and taken no notice of. I doubt if I should abuse the permission. It is a hundred to one if I should avail myself of it four times in a year. It would satisfy me, I dare say, to know that I had it."

"Will you try?"

"That is another way of saying that I am placed on the footing I have indicated. I thank you, Darnay. I may use that freedom with your name?"

"I think so, Carton, by this time."

They shook hands upon it, and Sydney turned away. Within a minute afterwards, he was, to all outward appearance, as unsubstantial as ever.

When he was gone, and in the course of an evening passed with Miss Pross, the Doctor, and Mr. Lorry, Charles Darnay made some mention of this conversation in general terms, and spoke of Sydney Carton as a problem of carelessness and recklessness. He spoke of him, in short, not bitterly or meaning to bear hard upon him, but as anybody might who saw him as he showed himself.

He had no idea that this could dwell in the thoughts of his fair young wife; but, when he afterwards joined her in their own rooms, he found her waiting for him with the old pretty lifting of the forehead strongly marked.

"We are thoughtful tonight!" said Darnay, drawing his arm about her.

"Yes, dearest Charles," with the inquiring and attentive expression fixed upon him; "we are rather thoughtful tonight, for we have something on our mind tonight."

"What is it, my Lucie?"

"Will you promise not to press one question on me, if I beg you not to ask it?"

"Will I promise? What will I not promise to my love?"

"I think, Charles, poor Mr. Carton deserves more consideration and respect than you expressed for him tonight."

"Indeed, my own? Why so?"

"That is what you are not to ask me. But I think—I know—he does."

"If you know it, it is enough. What would you have me do, my life?"

"I would ask you, dearest, to be very generous with him always, and very lenient on his faults when he is not by. I would ask you to believe that he has a heart he very, very seldom reveals, and that there are deep wounds in it. My dear, I have seen it bleeding."

"It is a painful reflection to me," said Charles Darnay, quite astounded, "that I should have done him any wrong. I never thought this of him."

"My husband, it is so. I fear he is not to be reclaimed; there is scarcely a hope that anything in his character or fortunes is reparable now. But I am sure that he is capable of good things, gentle things, even magnanimous things."

She looked so beautiful in the purity of her faith in this lost man that her husband could have looked at her as she was for hours.

"And, O my dearest love!" she urged, clinging nearer to him, "remember how strong we are in our happiness, and how weak he is in his misery!"

The supplication touched him home. "I will always remember it, dear heart! I will remember it as long as I live."

He bent over the golden head and put the rosy lips to his, and folded her in his arms.

WHAT DO YOU SAY?

1. (a) What was Sydney Carton's plea? *(b)* How do the Darnays react to it?

2. (a) What part of Sydney Carton's nature is revealed in this chapter? *(b)* Do you think Lucie's confidence in him is well placed? Explain.

CHAPTER XVIII
Echoing Footsteps

A wonderful corner for echoes, it has been remarked, that corner where the Doctor lived. Ever busily winding the golden thread which bound her husband, and her father, and herself, and her old directress and companion, in a life of quiet bliss, Lucie sat in the still house in the tranquilly resounding corner, listening to the echoing footsteps of years.

At first there were times, though she was a perfectly happy young wife, when her work would slowly fall from her hands, and her eyes would be dimmed. That time passed, and her little Lucie lay on her bosom. Then, among the advancing echoes, there was the tread of her tiny feet and the sound of her prattling words.

Ever winding the golden thread that bound them all together, Lucie heard in the echoes of years none but friendly and soothing sounds. Her husband's step was strong and prosperous among them; her father's firm and equal.

The echoes rarely answered to the actual tread of Sydney Carton. Some half-dozen times a year, at most, he claimed his privilege of coming in uninvited, and would sit among them through the evening, as he had once done often.

These were among the echoes to which Lucie, sometimes pensive, sometimes amused and laughing, listened in the echoing corner, until her little daughter was six years old.

But other echoes, from a distance, rumbled menacingly all through this space of time. And now, about little Lucie's sixth birthday, they began to have an awful sound, as of a great storm in France with a dreadful sea rising.

On a night in mid-July, one thousand seven hundred and eighty-nine, Mr. Lorry came in late, from Tellson's, and sat himself down by Lucie and her husband. It was a hot, wild night, and they were all reminded of the Sunday night when they had looked at the lightning from the same place.

"I began to think," said Mr. Lorry, pushing his brown wig back, "that I should have to pass the night at Tellson's. We have been so full of business all day, that we have not known which way to turn. There is such an uneasiness in Paris that we have actually a run of confidence upon us! Our customers over there seem not to be able to confide their property to us fast enough. There is positively a mania among some of them for sending it to England."

"That has a bad look," said Darnay.

"A bad look, you say, my dear Darnay? Yes, but we don't know what reason there is in it. Where is Manette?"

"Here he is," said the Doctor, entering.

"I am quite glad you are at home; for these hurries and forebodings by which I have been surrounded all day long have made me nervous. You are not going out?"

"No; I am going to play backgammon with you, if you like," said the Doctor.

"I don't think I do like. I am not fit to be pitted against you tonight. Is the tea board still there, Lucie?"

"Of course; it has been kept for you."

"Thank ye, my dear. The precious child is safe in bed?"

"And sleeping soundly."

"That's right; all safe and well! I don't know why anything should be otherwise than safe and well here, thank God; but I have been so put out all day, and I am not as young as I was! My tea, my dear! Thank ye. Now, let us sit quiet, and hear the echoes."

Headlong, mad, and dangerous footsteps to force their way into anybody's life, footsteps not easily made clean again if once stained red, the footsteps raging in Saint Antoine afar off, as the little circle sat in the dark London window.

A tremendous roar arose from the throat of Saint Antoine, and a forest of naked arms struggled in the air, all the fingers convulsively clutching at every weapon or semblance of a weapon no matter how far off.

Who gave them out, whence they last came, no eye in the throng could have told; but muskets were being distributed—so were cartridges, powder, ball, bars of iron and wood, knives, axes, pikes, every weapon ingenuity could devise. People who could lay hold of nothing else set themselves with bleeding hands to force stones and bricks out of their places in walls. Every pulse and heart in Saint Antoine was on high fever strain and at high fever heat. Every living creature there held life as of no account, and was demented with a passionate readiness to sacrifice it.

As a whirlpool of boiling waters has a center point, so all this raging circled round Defarge's wine shop, where Defarge himself, already begrimed with gunpowder and sweat, issued orders, issued arms, thrust this man back, dragged this man forward, disarmed one to arm another, labored and strove in the thickest of the uproar.

"Keep near me, Jacques Three," cried Defarge; "Jacques One and Two, separate and put yourselves at the head of as many patriots as you can. Where is my wife?"

"Here you see me!" said madame, composed as ever, but not knitting today. Madame's resolute right hand was occupied with an ax, and in her girdle were a pistol and a cruel knife.

"Where do you go, my wife?"

"I go," said madame, "with you at present. You shall see me at the head of women, by-and-by."

"Come, then!" cried Defarge, in a resounding voice. "Patriots and friends, we are ready! The Bastille!"

With a roar that sounded as if all the breath in France had been shaped into the detested word, the living sea rose, wave on wave, depth on depth, and overflowed the city to that point. Alarm bells ringing, drums beating, the sea raging and thundering on its new beach, the attack begun.

Deep ditches, double drawbridge, massive stone walls, eight great towers, cannon, muskets, fire, and smoke. Through the fire and through the smoke—in the fire and in the smoke, for the sea cast him up against a cannon, and on the instant he became a cannonier—Defarge of the wine shop worked like a manful soldier, two fierce hours.

Deep ditch, single drawbridge, massive stone walls, eight great towers, cannon, muskets, fire, and smoke. One drawbridge down! "Work, comrades all, work! Work, Jacques One, Jacques Two, Jacques One Thousand, Jacques Two Thousand, Jacques Five-and-Twenty Thousand; in the name of all the angels or the devils—which you prefer—work!" Thus Defarge of the wine shop, still at his gun, which had long grown hot.

"To me, women!" cried madame his wife. "What! We can kill as well as the men when the place is taken!" And to her, with a shrill, thirsty cry, trooping women variously armed, but all armed alike in hunger and revenge.

Cannon, muskets, fire and smoke; but, still the deep ditch, the single drawbridge, the massive stone walls, and the eight great towers. Slight displacements of the raging sea, made by the falling wounded. Flashing weapons, blazing torches, smoking wagonloads of wet straw, hard work at neighboring barricades in all directions, shrieks, volleys, execrations, bravery without stint, boom, smash, and rattle, and the furious sounding of the living sea; but, still the deep ditch, and the single drawbridge,

Ronald Searle

and the massive stone walls, and the eight great towers, and still Defarge of the wine shop at his gun, grown doubly hot by the service of four fierce hours.

A white flag from within the fortress, and a parley—suddenly the sea rose and swept Defarge of the wine shop over the lowered drawbridge, past the massive stone outer walls, in among the eight great towers surrendered!

So resistless was the force of the ocean bearing him on that even to draw his breath or turn his head was impracticable until he was landed in the outer courtyard of the Bastille. There, against a wall, he made a struggle to look about him. Jacques Three was nearly at his side; Madame Defarge, still heading some of her women, was visible in the inner distance, her knife in her hand. Everywhere was tumult, exultation, deafening and maniacal bewilderment, astounding noise, yet furious dumb show.

"The Prisoners!"

"The Records!"

"The secret cells!"

"The instruments of torture!"

"The Prisoners!"

Of all these cries, and ten thousand incoherencies, "The Prisoners!" was the cry most taken up by the sea that rushed in. When the foremost billows rolled past, bearing the prison officers with them, and threatening them all with instant death if any secret nook remained undisclosed, Defarge laid his hand on the breast of one of these men—a man who had a lighted torch in his hand—and got him between himself and the wall.

"Show me the North Tower!" said Defarge. "Quick!"

"I will faithfully," replied the man, "if you will come with me. But there is no one there."

"What is the meaning of One Hundred and Five, North Tower?" asked Defarge. "Quick!"

"The meaning, monsieur?"

"Does it mean a captive, or a place of captivity? Or do you mean that I shall strike you dead?"

"Kill him!" croaked Jacques Three, who had come close up.

"Monsieur, it is a cell."

"Show it me!"

"Pass this way, then."

The turnkey stopped at a low door, put a key in a clashing lock, swung the door slowly open, and said, as they all bent their heads and passed in:

"One Hundred and Five, North Tower!"

There was a small, heavily grated, unglazed window high in the wall, a stone screen before it, so that the sky could be only seen by stooping low and looking up. There was a small chimney, heavily barred across, a few feet within. There was a heap of old wood ashes on the hearth. There was a stool, and table, and a straw bed. There were the four blackened walls, a rusted iron ring in one of them.

"Pass that torch slowly along these walls, that I may see them," said Defarge to the turnkey.

The man obeyed, and Defarge followed the light closely with his eyes.

"Stop!—Look here, Jacques!"

"A. M.!" croaked Jacques Three, as he read greedily.

"Alexandre Manette," said Defarge in his ear, following the letters with his swart forefinger.

"What is that in your hand? A crowbar? Give it me!"

He had his gun in his own hand. He made a sudden exchange of the two instruments, and turning on the worm-eaten stool and table, beat them to pieces in a few blows.

"Hold the light higher!" he said, wrathfully, to the turnkey. "Look among those fragments with care, Jacques. And see! Here is my knife," throwing it to him; "rip open that bed, and search the straw. Hold the light higher, you!"

With a menacing look at the turnkey, he crawled upon the hearth, and, peering up the chimney, struck and prised at its sides with the crowbar. In a few minutes some mortar and dust came dropping down, which he averted his face to avoid; and in it, and in the old wood ashes, and in a crevice in the chimney into which his weapon had slipped or wrought itself, he groped with a cautious touch.

"Nothing in the wood, and nothing in the straw, Jacques?"

"Nothing."

"Let us collect them together, in the middle of the cell. So! Light them, you!"

The turnkey fired the little pile, which blazed high and hot. Stooping again to come out at the low-arched door, they left it burning, and retraced their way to the courtyard, until they were in the raging flood once more.

They found it surging and tossing, in quest of Defarge himself. Saint Antoine was clamorous to have its wine-shop keeper foremost in the guard upon the governor who had defended the Bastille and shot the people. Otherwise the governor would escape, and the people's blood—suddenly of some value, after many years of worthlessness—be unavenged.

In the howling universe of passion and contention that seemed to encompass this grim old officer conspicuous in his gray coat and red decoration, there was but one quite steady figure, and that was a woman's. "See, my husband!" she cried, pointing him out. "See Defarge!" She stood immovable close to the grim old officer, and remained immovable close to him; remained immovable close to him through the streets, as Defarge and the rest bore him along; remained immovable close to him when he was near his destination, and began to be struck at from behind; remained immovable close to him when the long gathering rain of stabs and blows fell heavy; was so close to him when he dropped dead, that, suddenly animated, she put her foot upon his neck, and with her cruel knife—long ready—hewed off his head.

Seven prisoners released, seven gory heads on pikes, the keys of the accursed fortress of the eight strong towers, some discovered letters and other memorials of prisoners of old time, long dead of broken hearts—such, and suchlike, the loudly echoing footsteps of Saint Antoine escort through the Paris streets in mid-July, one thousand seven hundred and eighty-nine. Now, heaven defeat the fancy of Lucie Darnay and keep these feet far out of her life! For they are headlong, mad, and dangerous; and in the years so long after the breaking of the cask at Defarge's wine-shop door, they are not easily purified when once stained red.

WHAT DO YOU SAY?

1. (a) In what ways is the passage of time indicated? *(b)* What two pictures in this chapter provide dramatic contrast? *(c)* How does Dickens weave them together?

2. *(a)* Does the author tell you for what Defarge searched in the prison cell? *(b)* Did he find it? Explain.

CHAPTER XIX
The Sea Still Rises

Haggard Saint Antoine had had only one exultant week in which to soften his modicum of hard and bitter bread to such extent as he could, with the relish of fraternal embraces and congratulations, when Madame Defarge sat at her counter, as usual, presiding over the customers. Madame Defarge wore no rose in her head, for the great brotherhood of Spies had become, even in one short week, extremely chary of trusting themselves to the saint's mercies. The lamps across his streets had a portentously elastic swing with them.

Madame Defarge, with her arms folded, sat in the morning light and heat, contemplating the wine shop and the street. In both, there were several knots of loungers, squalid and miserable, but now with a manifest sense of power enthroned on their distress. The raggedest nightcap, awry on the wretchedest head, had this crooked significance in it: "I know how hard it has grown for me, the wearer of this, to support life in myself; but do you know how easy it has grown for me, the wearer of this, to destroy life in you?" Every lean bare arm, that had been without work before, had this work always ready for it now, that it could strike. The fingers of the knitting women were vicious, with the experience that they could tear. There was a change in the appearance of Saint Antoine; the image had been hammering into this for hundreds of years, and the last finishing blows had told mightily on the expression.

Madame Defarge sat observing it, with such suppressed approval as was to be desired in the leader of the Saint Antoine women. One of her sisterhood knitted beside her. The short, rather plump wife of a starved grocer, and the mother of two children withal, this lieutenant had already earned the complimentary name of The Vengeance.

"Hark!" said The Vengeance. "Listen, then! Who comes?"

As if a train of powder laid from the outermost bound of the Saint Antoine Quarter to the wine shop door, had been suddenly fired, a fast spreading murmur came rushing along.

"It is Defarge," said madame. "Silence, patriots!"

Defarge came in breathless, pulled off a red cap he wore, and looked around him! "Listen, everywhere!" said madame again. "Listen to him!" Defarge stood, panting, against a background of eager eyes and open mouths, formed outside the door; all those within the wine shop had sprung to their feet.

"Say then, my husband. What is it?"

"News from the other world!"

"How, then?" cried madame, contemptuously. "The other world?"

"Does everybody here recall old Foulon, who told the famished people that they might eat grass, and who died, and went to hell?"

"Everybody!" from all throats.

"The news is of him. He is among us!"

"Among us!" from the universal throat again. "And dead?"

"Not dead! He feared us so much—and with reason—that he caused himself to be represented as dead, and had a grand mock funeral. But they have found him alive, hiding in the country, and have brought him in. I have seen him but now, on his way to the Hôtel de Ville, a prisoner. I have said that he had reason to fear us. Say all! *Had* he reason?"

Wretched old sinner of more than three score years and ten, if he had never known it yet, he would have known it in his heart of hearts if he could have heard the answering cry.

A moment of profound silence followed. Defarge and his wife looked steadfastly at one another. The Vengeance stooped, and the jar of a drum was heard as she moved it at her feet behind the counter.

"Patriots!" said Defarge, in a determined voice, "are we ready?"

Instantly Madame Defarge's knife was in her girdle; the drum was beating in the streets, as if it and a drummer had flown together by magic; and The Vengeance, uttering terrific shrieks, and flinging her arms about her head like all the forty Furies at once, was tearing from house to house, rousing the women.

The men were terrible, in the bloody minded anger with which they looked from windows, caught up what arms they had, and came pouring down into the streets; but the women were a sight to chill the boldest. From such household occupations as their bare poverty yielded, from their children, from their aged and their sick crouching on the bare ground famished and naked, they ran out with streaming hair, urging one another and themselves to madness with the wildest cries and actions. Villain Foulon taken, my sister! Old Foulon taken, my mother! Miscreant Foulon taken, my daughter! Then a score of others ran into the midst of these, beating their breasts, tearing their hair, and screaming, Foulon alive! Foulon who told the starving people they might eat grass! Foulon who told my old father he might eat grass, when I had no bread to give him! Foulon who told my baby it might suck grass, when these breasts were dry with want! O mother of God, this Foulon! O heaven, our suffering! Hear me, my dead baby and my withered father; I swear on my knees, on these stones, to avenge you on Foulon! Husbands and brothers, and young men, Give us the blood of Foulon, Give us the head of Foulon, Give us the heart of Foulon, Give us the body and soul of Foulon, Rend Foulon to pieces, and dig him into the ground, that grass may grow from him! With these cries, numbers of the women, lashed into blind frenzy, whirled about, striking and tearing at their own friends until they dropped into a passionate swoon, and were only saved by the men belonging to them from being trampled under foot.

Nevertheless, not a moment was lost; not a moment! This Foulon was at the Hôtel de Ville, and might be loosed. Never, if Saint Antoine knew his own sufferings, insults, and wrongs! Armed men and women flocked out of the Quarter so fast, and drew even these last dregs after them with such a force of suction that within a quarter of an hour there was not a human creature in Saint Antoine's bosom but a few old crones and the wailing children.

No. They were all by that time choking the Hall of Examination where this old man, ugly and wicked, was, and overflowing into the adjacent open space and streets. The Defarges, husband and wife, The Vengeance, and Jacques Three were in the first press, and at no great distance from him in the Hall.

"See!" cried madame, pointing with her knife. "See the old villain bound with ropes. That was well done to tie a bunch of grass upon his back. Ha, ha! That was well done. Let him eat it now!" Madame put her knife under her arm, and clapped her hands as at a play.

The people immediately behind Madame Defarge, explaining the cause of her satisfaction to those behind them, and those again explaining to others, and those to others, the neighboring streets resounded with the clapping of hands. Similarly, during two or three hours of drawl, and the winnowing of many bushels of words, Madame Defarge's frequent expressions of impatience were taken up, with marvelous quickness, at a distance; the more readily, because certain men who had by some wonderful exercise of agility climbed up the external architecture to look in from the windows knew Madame Defarge well and acted as a telegraph between her and the crowd outside the building.

At length the sun rose so high that it struck a kindly ray as of hope or protection, directly down upon the old prisoner's head. The favor was too much to bear; in an instant the barrier of dust and chaff that had stood surprisingly long went to the winds, and Saint Antoine had got him!

It was known directly, to the farthest confines of the crowd. Defarge had but sprung over a railing and a table and folded the miserable wretch in a deadly embrace —Madame Defarge had but followed and turned her hand in one of the ropes with which he was tied—The Vengeance and Jacques Three were not yet up with them, and the men at the windows had not yet swooped into the Hall, like birds of prey from their high perches—when the cry seemed to go up, all over the city, "Bring him out! Bring him to the lamp!"

Down, and up, and head foremost on the steps of the building; now, on his knees; now, on his feet; now, on his back; dragged, and struck at, and stifled by the bunches of grass and straw that were thrust into his face by hundreds of hands; torn, bruised, panting, bleeding, yet always entreating and beseeching for mercy; now full of vehement agony of action, with a small clear space about him as the people drew one another back that they might see; now a log of dead wood drawn through a forest of legs; he was hauled to the nearest street corner where one of the fatal lamps swung, and there Madame Defarge let him go—as a cat might have done to a mouse—and silently and composedly looked at him while they made ready, and while he besought her; the women passionately screeching at him all the time, and the men sternly calling out to have him killed with grass in his mouth. Once he went aloft, and the rope broke, and they caught him shrieking; twice he went aloft, and the rope broke, and they caught him shrieking; then the rope was merciful, and held him, and his head was soon upon a pike, with grass enough in the mouth for all Saint Antoine to dance at the sight of.

Nor was this the end of the day's bad work, for Saint Antoine so shouted and danced his angry blood up that it boiled again, on hearing when the day closed in that the son-in-law of the despatched, another of the people's enemies and insulters, was coming into Paris under a guard five hundred strong in cavalry alone. Saint Antoine wrote his crimes on flaring sheets of paper, seized him—would have torn him out of the breast of an army to bear Foulon company—set his head and heart on pikes, and carried the spoils of the day, in wolf procession, through the streets.

Not before dark night did the men and women come back to the children wailing and breadless. Then the miserable baker's shops were beset by long files of them, patiently waiting to buy bad bread; and while they waited with stomachs faint and empty, they beguiled the time by embracing one another on the triumphs of the day, and achieving them again in gossip. Gradually these strings of ragged people shortened and frayed away; and then poor lights began to shine in high windows, and slender fires were made in the streets, at which neighbors cooked in common, afterwards supping at their doors.

Scanty and insufficient suppers those, and innocent of meat, as of most other sauce to wretched bread. Yet human fellowship infused some nourishment into the flinty viands, and struck some sparks of cheerfulness out of them. Fathers and mothers who had had their full share in the worst of the day played gently with their meager children; and lovers, with such a world around them and before them, loved and hoped.

It was almost morning when Defarge's wine-shop parted with its last knot of customers, and Monsieur Defarge said to madame his wife while fastening the door:

"At last it is come, my dear!"

"Eh well!" returned madame. "Almost."

Saint Antoine slept, the Defarges slept; even The Vengeance slept with her starved grocer, and the drum was at rest. The drum's was the only voice in Saint Antoine that blood and hurry had not changed. The Vengeance, as custodian of the drum, could have wakened him up and had the same speech out of him as before the Bastille fell, or old Foulon was seized; not so with the hoarse tones of the men and women in Saint Antoine's bosom.

WHAT DO YOU SAY?

1. *(a)* In your opinion does Dickens justify the actions of the people of Saint Antoine? *(b)* Do you think he is sympathizing with them or criticizing them? Explain.

2. How do you feel about the actions of these people?

CHAPTER XX
Fire Rises

There was a change on the village where the fountain fell, and where the mender of roads went forth daily to hammer out of the stones on the highway such morsels of bread as might serve for patches to hold his poor ignorant soul and his poor reduced body together. The prison on the crag was not so dominant as of yore; there were soldiers to guard it, but not many; there were officers to guard the soldiers, but not one of them knew what his men would do—beyond this: that it would probably not be what he was ordered.

Far and wide lay a ruined country, yielding nothing but desolation. Every green leaf, every blade of grass and blade of grain, was as shriveled and poor as the miserable people. Everything was bowed down, dejected, oppressed, and broken. Habitations, fences, domesticated animals, men, women, children, and the soil that bore them—all worn out.

In these times, as the mender of roads worked, solitary, in the dust, not often troubling himself to reflect that dust he was and to dust he must return, being for the most part too much occupied in thinking how little he had for supper and how much more he would eat if he had it—in these times as he raised his eyes from his lonely labor, and viewed the prospect, he would see some rough figure approaching on foot, the like of which was once a rarity in those parts, but was now a frequent presence. As it advanced, the mender of roads would discern, without surprise, that it was a shaggy-haired man, of almost barbarian aspect, tall, in wooden shoes that were clumsy even to the eyes of a mender of roads, grim, rough, swart, steeped in the mud and dust of many highways, dank with the marshy moisture of many low grounds, sprinkled with the thorns and leaves and moss of many byways through woods.

Such a man came upon him, like a ghost, at noon in the July weather, as he sat on his heap of stones under a bank, taking such shelter as he could get from a shower of hail.

The man looked at him, looked at the village in the hollow, at the mill, and at the prison on the crag. When he had identified these objects in what benighted mind he had, he said, in a dialect that was just intelligible:

"How goes it, Jacques?"

"All well, Jacques."

"Touch then!" They joined hands, and the man sat down on the heap of stones.

"No dinner?"

"Nothing but supper now," said the mender of roads, with a hungry face.

"It is the fashion," growled the man. "I meet no dinner anywhere."

He took out a blackened pipe, filled it, lighted it with flint and steel, pulled at it until it was in a bright glow; then, suddenly held it from him and dropped something into it from between his finger and thumb, that blazed and went out in a puff of smoke.

"Touch then." It was the turn of the mender of roads to say it this time, after observing these operations. They again joined hands. "Tonight?" said the mender of roads.

"Tonight," said the man, putting the pipe in his mouth.

"Where?"

"Here."

He and the mender of roads sat on the heap of stones looking silently at one another, with the hail driving in between them like a pigmy charge of bayonets, until the sky began to clear over the village.

"Show me!" said the traveler then, moving to the brow of the hill.

"See!" returned the mender of roads, with extended finger. "You go down here, and straight through the street, and past the fountain—"

"To the devil with all that!" interrupted the other, rolling his eye over the landscape. "*I* go through no streets and past no fountains. Well?"

"Well! About two leagues beyond the summit of that hill above the village."

"Good. When do you cease to work?"

"At sunset."

"Will you wake me, before departing? I have walked two nights without resting. Let me finish my pipe, and I shall sleep like a child. Will you wake me?"

"Surely."

The wayfarer smoked his pipe out, put it in his breast, slipped off his great wooden shoes, and lay down on his back on the heap of stones. He was fast asleep directly, indifferent to showers of hail and intervals of brightness, to sunshine on his face and shadow, to the pattering lumps of dull ice on his body and the diamonds into which the sun changed them, until the sun was low in the west, and the sky was glowing. Then the mender of roads, having got his tools together and all things ready to go down into the village, roused him.

"Good!" said the sleeper, rising on his elbow. "Two leagues beyond the summit of the hill?"

"About."

"About. Good!"

The mender of roads went home, with the dust going on before him according to the set of the wind, and was soon at the fountain, squeezing himself in among the lean kine brought there to drink, and appearing even to whisper to them in his whispering to all the village. When the village had taken its poor supper, it did not creep to bed, as it usually did, but came out of doors again, and remained there. A curious contagion of whispering was upon it, and also, when it gathered together at the fountain in the dark, another curious contagion of looking expectantly at the sky in one direction only. Monsieur Gabelle, chief functionary of the place, became uneasy; went out on his housetop alone, and looked in that direction too; glanced down from behind his chimneys at the darkening faces by the fountain below, and sent word to the sacristan who kept the keys of the church, that there might be need to ring the tocsin by-and-by.

The night deepened. The trees environing the old château, keeping its solitary state apart, moved in a rising wind, as though they threatened the pile of building, massive and dark in the gloom. Up the two terrace flights of steps the rain ran wildly, and beat at the great door, like a swift messenger rousing those within; uneasy rushes of wind went through the hall, among the old spears and knives, and passed lamenting up the stairs, and shook the curtains of the bed where the last Marquis had slept. East, west, north, and south, through the woods, four heavy-treading, unkempt figures crushed the high grass and cracked the branches, striding on cautiously to come together in the courtyard. Four lights broke out there and moved away in different directions, and all was black again.

But not for long. Presently, the château began to make itself strangely visible by some light of its own, as though it were growing luminous. Then a flickering streak played behind the architecture of the front, picking out transparent places, and showing where balustrades, arches, and windows were. Then it soared higher, and grew broader and brighter. Soon, from a score of the great windows, flames burst forth, and the stone faces, awakened, stared out of fire.

A faint murmur arose about the house from the few people who were left there, and there was a saddling of a horse and riding away. There was spurring and splashing through the darkness, and bridle was drawn in the space by the village fountain, and the horse in a foam stood at Monsieur Gabelle's door. "Help, Gabelle! Help, everyone!" The tocsin rang impatiently, but other help—if that were any—there was none. The mender of roads and two hundred and fifty particular friends stood with folded arms at the fountain, looking at the pillar of fire in the sky. "It must be forty feet high," said they grimly; and never moved.

The rider from the château and the horse in a foam clattered away through the village and galloped up the stony steep to the prison on the crag. At the gate a group of officers were looking at the fire; removed from them, a group of soldiers. "Help, gentlemen—officers! The château is on fire; valuable objects may be saved from the flames by timely aid! Help, help!" The officers looked toward the soldiers who looked at the fire; gave no orders; and answered, with shrugs and biting of lips, "It must burn."

As the rider rattled down the hill again and through the street, the village was illuminating. The mender of roads and the two hundred and fifty particular friends, inspired as one man and woman by the idea of lighting up, had darted into their houses, and were putting candles in every dull little pane of glass. The general scarcity of everything occasioned candles to be borrowed in a rather peremptory manner of Monsieur Gabelle; and in a moment of reluctance and hesitation on that functionary's part, the mender of roads, once so submissive to authority, had remarked that carriages were good to make bonfires with, and that post horses would roast.

The château was left to itself to flame and burn. In the roaring and raging of the conflagration, a red-hot wind, driving straight from the infernal regions, seemed to be blowing the edifice away. With the rising and falling of the blaze, the stone faces showed as if they were in torment. When great masses of stone and timber fell, the face with the two dints in the nose became obscured; anon struggled out of the smoke again, as if it were the face of the cruel Marquis, burning at the stake and contending with the fire.

The château burned; the nearest trees, laid hold of by the fire, scorched and shriveled; trees at a distance, fired by the four fierce figures, begirt the blazing edifice with a new forest of smoke. Molten lead and iron boiled in the marble basin of the fountain; the water ran dry; the extinguished tops of the towers vanished like ice before the heat, and trickled down into four rugged wells of flame. Great rents and splits branched out in the solid walls, like crystallization; stupefied birds wheeled about and dropped into the furnace; four fierce figures trudged away, east, west, north, and south, along the night-enshrouded roads, guided by the beacon they had lighted, toward their next destination. The illuminated village had seized hold of the tocsin, and, abolishing the lawful ringer, rang for joy.

Not only that; but the village, light-headed with famine, fire, and bell-ringing, and bethinking itself that Monsieur Gabelle had to do with the collection of rent and taxes—though it was but a small installment of taxes, and no rent at all, that Gabelle had got in those latter days—became impatient for an interview with him, and, surrounding his house, summoned him to come forth for personal conference. Whereupon, Monsieur Gabelle did heavily bar his door, and retire to hold counsel with himself. The result of that conference was that Gabelle again withdrew himself to his housetop behind his stack of chimneys; this time resolved, if his door were broken in (he was a small Southern man of retaliative temperament), to pitch himself head foremost over the parapet, and crush a man or two below.

Probably, Monsieur Gabelle passed a long night up there, with the distant château for fire and candle, and the beating at his door, combined with the joy-ringing, for music; not to mention his having an ill-omened lamp slung across the road before his posting-house gate, which the village showed a lively inclination to displace in his favor. A trying suspense, to be passing a whole summer night on the brink of the black ocean, ready to take that plunge into it upon which Monsieur Gabelle had resolved! But, the friendly dawn appearing at last, and the rush candles of the village guttering out, the people happily dispersed, and Monsieur Gabelle came down bringing his life with him for that while.

Within a hundred miles, and in the light

of other fires, there were other functionaries less fortunate, that night and other nights, whom the rising sun found hanging across once peaceful streets, where they had been born and bred; also, there were other villagers and townspeople less fortunate than the mender of roads and his fellows, upon whom the functionaries and soldiery turned with success, and whom they strung up in their turn. But the fierce figures were steadily wending east, west, north, and south, be that as it would; and whosoever hung, fire burned. The altitude of the gallows that would turn to water and quench it, no functionary, by any stretch of mathematics, was able to calculate successfully.

WHAT DO YOU SAY?

1. Of what is the fire a symbol in this chapter?

2. (a) Judging by the plight of Monsieur Gabelle, how much authority would you say the government had at this point? *(b)* What was the situation in other parts of France?

CHAPTER XXI
Drawn to the Loadstone Rock

In such risings of fire and risings of sea—the firm earth shaken by the rushes of an angry ocean which had now no ebb, but was always on the flow, higher and higher, to the terror and wonder of the beholders on the shore—three years of tempest were consumed. Three more birthdays of little Lucie had been woven by the golden thread into the peaceful tissue of the life of her home.

Many a night and many a day had its inmates listened to the echoes in the corner, with hearts that failed them when they heard the thronging feet. For, the footsteps had become to their minds as the footsteps of a people, tumultuous under a red flag and with their country declared in danger, changed into wild beasts, by terrible enchantment long persisted in.

Monseigneur, as a class, had dissociated himself from the phenomenon of his not being appreciated: of his being so little wanted in France, as to incur considerable danger of receiving his dismissal from it and this life together. Like the fabled rustic who raised the devil with infinite pains, and was so terrified at the sight of him that he could ask the Enemy no question, but immediately fled; so, Monseigneur, after boldly reading the Lord's Prayer backwards for a great number of years, and performing many other potent spells for compelling the Evil One, no sooner beheld him in his terrors than he took to his noble heels.

The Court, from that exclusive inner circle to its outermost rotten ring of intrigue, corruption, and dissimulation, was all gone together. Royalty was gone; had been besieged in its Palace and "suspended" when the last tidings came over.

The August of the year one thousand seven hundred and ninety-two was come, and Monseigneur was by this time scattered far and wide.

As was natural, the headquarters and great gathering place of Monseigneur, in London, was Tellson's Bank. Spirits are supposed to haunt the places where their bodies most resorted, and Monseigneur without a guinea haunted the spot where his guineas used to be. Moreover, it was the spot to which such French intelligence as was most to be relied upon, came quickest. Again: Tellson's was a munificent house, and extended great liberality to old customers who had fallen from their high estate. Again: those nobles who had seen the coming storm in time, and anticipating plunder or confiscation, had made provident remittances to Tellson's, were always to be heard of there by their needy brethren. To which it must be added that every newcomer from France reported himself and his tidings at Tellson's, almost as a matter of course. For such variety of reasons, Tellson's was at that time, as to French intelligence, a kind of High Exchange; and this was so well known to the public, and the inquiries made there were in consequence so numerous, that Tellson's sometimes wrote the latest news out in a line or so and posted it in the Bank windows, for all who ran through Temple Bar to read.

On a steaming, misty afternoon, Mr. Lorry sat at his desk, and Charles Darnay stood leaning on it, talking with him in a low voice.

"But, although you are the youngest man that ever lived," said Charles Darnay, rather hesitating, "I must still suggest to you—"

"I understand. That I am too old?" said Mr. Lorry.

"Unsettled weather, a long journey, uncertain means of traveling, a disorganized country, a city that may not be even safe for you."

"My dear Charles," said Mr. Lorry, with cheerful confidence, "you touch some of the reasons for my going; not for my staying away. It is safe enough for me; nobody will care to interfere with an old fellow of hard upon fourscore. As to its being a disorganized city, if it were not, there would be no occasion to send somebody from our House here to our House there, who knows the city and the business, of old. As to uncertain traveling, the long journey, and winter weather, if I were not prepared to submit to a few inconveniences for the sake of Tellson's, after all these years, who ought to be?"

"I wish I were going myself," said Charles Darnay, somewhat restlessly, and like one thinking aloud.

"Indeed! You wish you were going yourself? And you a Frenchman born?"

"My dear Mr. Lorry, it is because I am a Frenchman born, that the thought has passed through my mind. One cannot help thinking one might be listened to, and might have the power to persuade to some restraint. Only last night, after you left us, when I was talking to Lucie—"

"When you were talking to Lucie," Mr. Lorry repeated. "I wonder you are not ashamed to mention Lucie! Wishing you were going to France at this time of day!"

"However, I am not going," said Charles Darnay, with a smile. "It is more to the purpose that you say you are."

"And I am, in plain reality. The truth is, my dear Charles, you can have no conception of the peril in which our books and papers over yonder are involved. The Lord above knows what the compromising consequences would be to numbers of people, if some of our documents were seized or destroyed; and they might be at any time, you know, for who can say that Paris is not set afire today, or sacked tomorrow! Now, a judicious selection from these and the burying of them, or otherwise getting of them out of harm's way, is within the power —without loss of precious time—of scarcely anyone but myself, if anyone. And shall I hang back, when Tellson's says this—Tellson's whose bread I have eaten these sixty years—because I am a little stiff about the joints? Why, I am a boy, sir, to half a dozen old codgers here!"

"How I admire the gallantry of your youthful spirit, Mr. Lorry."

"Tut! Nonsense, sir!—And, my dear Charles," said Mr. Lorry, "you are to remember that getting things out of Paris at this present time is next to an impossibility. Papers and precious matters were this very day brought to us here—I speak in strict confidence—by the strangest bearers you can imagine, every one of whom had his head hanging on by a single hair as he passed the Barriers. At another time our parcels would come and go, as easily as in businesslike Old England; but now, everything is stopped."

"And do you really go tonight?"

"I really go tonight, for the case has become too pressing to admit of delay."

"And do you take no one with you?"

"All sorts of people have been proposed to me, but I intend to take Jerry. Jerry has been my bodyguard on Sunday nights for a long time past, and I am used to him. Nobody will suspect Jerry of being anything but an English bulldog, or of having any design in his head but to fly at anybody who touches his master."

"I must say again that I heartily admire your gallantry and youthfulness."

"I must say again, nonsense! When I have executed this commission, I shall, perhaps, retire. Time enough to think about growing old."

The House approached Mr. Lorry, and laying a soiled and unopened letter before him, asked if he had yet discovered any traces of the person to whom it was addressed. The House laid the letter down so close to Darnay that he saw the direction—the more quickly because it was his own right name. The address, turned into English, ran:

"Very pressing. To Monsieur heretofore the Marquis St. Evrémonde, of France. Confided to the care of Messrs. Tellson and Co., Bankers, London, England."

On the marriage morning, Dr. Manette had made it his one urgent and express request to Charles Darnay that the secret of his name should be kept inviolate between them. Nobody else knew it to be his name; his own wife had no suspicion of the fact; Mr. Lorry could have none.

"No," said Mr. Lorry, in reply to the House; "I have referred it, I think, to everybody now here, and no one can tell me where this gentleman is to be found."

Darnay, unable to restrain himself any longer, said: "I know the fellow."

"Will you take charge of the letter?" said Mr. Lorry. "You know where to deliver it?"

"I do."

"Will you undertake to explain that we suppose it to have been addressed here, on the chance of our knowing where to forward it, and that it has been here some time?"

"I will do so. Do you start for Paris from here?"

"From here, at eight."

"I will come back, to see you off."

Darnay made the best of his way into the quiet of the Temple, opened the letter, and read it. These were its contents:

"Prison of the Abbaye, Paris
"June 21, 1792

MONSIEUR HERETOFORE
THE MARQUIS:

After having long been in danger of my life at the hands of the village, I have been seized, with great violence, and brought a long journey on foot to Paris. Nor is that all; my house has been destroyed—razed to the ground.

The crime for which I am imprisoned, Monsieur heretofore the Marquis, and for which I shall be summoned before the tribunal, and shall lose my life—without your so generous help—is, they tell me, treason against the majesty of the people, in that I have acted against them for an emigrant. It is in vain I represent that I have acted for them, and not against, according to your commands. It is in vain I represent that, before the sequestration of emigrant property,[1] I had remitted the imposts they had ceased to pay; that I had collected no rent. The only response is, that I have acted for an emigrant, and where is that emigrant?

Ah! most gracious Monsieur heretofore the Marquis, I send my desolate cry across the sea, hoping it may perhaps reach your ears through the great bank of Tilson.

For the love of heaven, of justice, of generosity, of the honor of your noble name, I supplicate you, Monsieur heretofore the Marquis, to succor and release me. My fault is that I have been true to you. Oh, Monsieur heretofore the Marquis, I pray you be you true to me!

From this prison of horror, whence I every hour tend nearer to destruction, I send you, Monsieur heretofore the Marquis, assurance of my dolorous and unhappy service.

"Your afflicted,
"GABELLE."

The latent uneasiness in Darnay's mind was aroused to vigorous life by this letter. The peril of an old servant and a good one, whose only crime was fidelity to himself and his family, stared him so reproachfully

---

1. ***the sequestration of emigrant property,*** the seizing and holding of property belonging to French aristocrats who left France at the beginning of the French Revolution and were, therefore, called emigrants.

in the face that, as he walked to and fro in the Temple considering what to do, he almost hid his face from the passers-by. He knew very well that in his love for Lucie, his renunciation of his social place had been incomplete.

But he had oppressed no man, imprisoned no man; he was so far from having exacted payment of his dues that he had relinquished them of his own will, thrown himself on a world with no favor in it, won his own private place there, and earned his own bread. Monsieur Gabelle had held the impoverished estate on written instructions to spare the people, to give them what little there was to give and no doubt he had put the fact in plea and proof, for his own safety, so that it could not but appear now.

This favored the desperate resolution Charles Darnay had begun to make, that he would go to Paris.

Yes. Like the mariner in the old story, the winds and streams had driven him within the influence of the Loadstone Rock,[2] and it was drawing him to itself, and he must go.

His resolution was made. He must go to Paris.

Yes. The Loadstone Rock was drawing him, and he must sail on, until he struck. He knew of no rock; he saw hardly any danger. The intention with which he had done what he had done presented it before him in an aspect that would be gratefully acknowledged in France on his presenting himself to assert it. Then that glorious vision of doing good, which is so often the sanguine mirage of so many good minds, arose before him, and he even saw himself with some influence to guide this raging Revolution that was running so fearfully wild.

As he walked to and fro with his resolution made, he considered that neither Lucie nor her father must know of it until he was gone. He walked to and fro, with thoughts very busy, until it was time to return to Tellson's and take leave of Mr. Lorry. As soon as he arrived in Paris he would present himself to this old friend, but he must say nothing of his intention now.

A carriage was ready at the Bank door, and Jerry was booted and equipped.

"I have delivered that letter," said Charles Darnay to Mr. Lorry. "I would not consent to your being charged with any written answer, but perhaps you will take a verbal one?"

"That I will, if it is not dangerous."

"Not at all. Though it is to a prisoner in the Abbaye."

"What is his name?" said Mr. Lorry.

"Gabelle."

"Gabelle. And what is the message?"

"Simply, that 'he has received the letter, and will come.' "

"Any time mentioned?"

"He will start tomorrow night."

"Any person mentioned?"

"No."

He helped Mr. Lorry to wrap himself in a number of coats and cloaks, and went out with him from the old Bank, into Fleet Street. "My love to Lucie, and to little Lucie," said Mr. Lorry at parting, "and take precious care of them till I come back."

That night—it was the fourteenth of August—he sat up late, and wrote two fervent letters; one was to Lucie, explaining the strong obligation he was under to go to Paris, and showing her the reasons that he had, for feeling confident that he could become involved in no personal danger there; the other was to the Doctor, confiding Lucie and their dear child to his care, and dwelling on the same topics with the strongest assurance. To both he wrote that he would dispatch letters immediately after his arrival.

The unseen force was drawing him fast. He left his two letters with a trusty porter, to be delivered half an hour before midnight, and no sooner; took horse for Dover; and began his journey. "For the love of heaven, of justice, of generosity, of the

2. *the Loadstone Rock,* a mythical rock which drew ships to their destruction by magnetic attraction of their iron parts.

honor of your noble name!" was the poor prisoner's cry with which he strengthened his sinking heart, as he left all that was dear on earth behind him, and floated away for the Loadstone Rock.

WHAT DO YOU SAY?

1. *(a)* What connection had Tellson's Bank with the French aristocratic class? ***(b)*** What drew Mr. Lorry to Paris? ***(c)*** What is the irony in Mr. Lorry's continued confidence in Jerry's innocent simplicity?

2. *(a)* What motive lay behind Darnay's decision to go to Paris? ***(b)*** How would you judge his reasoning?

3. Why is "Loadstone Rock" in the title of this chapter a metaphor?

AUTHOR'S CRAFT

Symbolism

Previously in **Outlooks** you have observed how writers sometimes suggest meaning to you through symbols: Hurst ("The Scarlet Ibis," page 87), Edna St. Vincent Millay ("The Courage That My Mother Had," page 224). Like the short story writer and the poet, the novelist, too, uses symbols. Here in ***A Tale of Two Cities*** you have an excellent opportunity to see symbolism at work.

Let us examine just a few of Dickens' word symbols. Dickens spent months trying to decide upon the best title for the novel. He made a trial list of possibilities, e.g., ***Two Generations, Memory Carton, Buried Alive, The Thread of Gold, The Doctor of Beauvais, Recalled to Life.*** Why do you think he finally arrived at ***A Tale of Two Cities?*** Reread the opening paragraphs of the book to determine what these two cities symbolize or "stand for."

The three Book titles within the novel are also symbolic. ***Recalled to Life,*** the first Book, concentrates upon getting Doctor Manette out of his eighteen years' imprisonment in the Bastille. This title suggests that the prison symbolizes death. Release from death is life. ***The Golden Thread,*** the second Book, relates to the influence of the blond Lucie upon the lives of certain other key characters. What is the symbolism of **Storm** in the title of Book the Third, ***The Track of a Storm?***

In Book the First, Chapter V, when the wine casks burst upon falling onto the street in the squalid Saint Antoine and one character writes BLOOD with a wine-drenched finger upon a wall, have you any doubt about this symbolic stroke? What symbolism did you find in these lines from Chapter VIII: "The sun struck so brilliantly into the traveling carriage when it reached the hilltop, that its occupant was steeped in crimson"?

So concerned with the power of symbols was Dickens that he even used the names of his characters to represent ideas. The very name Stryver, for instance, suggests someone who strives to forward his own interests, even if he has to depend, unscrupulously, upon other people's talents (such as Carton's). Dickens gave Gabelle the same name used for the hated tax on salt. The Vengeance symbolizes the capricious revolutionists' hungering for revenge as a sole, simple purpose in life, and she walks in the shadow of Madame Defarge, herself a powerful symbol, **de forge** meaning "the forge." How is Madame Defarge a forge for the revolution?

TIMETABLE for Book the Second

1780
Book the Second opens.

Charles Darnay goes on trial for treason in London. Later he visits his uncle, the Marquis, in France.

1781
Charles Darnay and Lucie Manette are married.

1789
The Bastille falls (July 14 becomes the French "Independence Day").

1790
French decree abolishes all titles of nobility.

1792
Duty draws both Jarvis Lorry and Charles Darnay to Paris on separate missions.

BOOK THE THIRD: The Track of a Storm

CHAPTER I
In Secret

The traveler fared slowly on his way, who fared toward Paris from England in the autumn of the year one thousand seven hundred and ninety-two.

A very few French leagues of his journey were accomplished when Charles Darnay began to perceive that for him along these country roads there was no hope of return until he should have been declared a good citizen at Paris. Whatever might befall now, he must on to his journey's end. Not a mean village closed upon him, not a common barrier dropped across the road behind him, but he knew it to be another iron door, in the series that was barred between him and England. He had been days upon his journey in France alone, when he went to bed tired out, in a little town on the high road, still a long way from Paris.

Nothing but the production of the afflicted Gabelle's letter from his prison of the Abbaye would have got him on so far. His difficulty at the guardhouse in this small place had been such that he felt his journey to have come to a crisis. And he was, therefore, as little surprised as a man could be, to find himself awakened at the small inn to which he had been remitted until morning, in the middle of the night. Awakened by a timid local functionary and three armed patriots in rough red caps and with pipes in their mouths.

"Emigrant," said the functionary, "I am going to send you on to Paris, under an escort."

"Citizen, I desire nothing more than to get to Paris, though I could dispense with the escort."

"Silence!" growled a red-cap, striking at the coverlet with the butt end of his musket.

"It is as the good patriot says," observed the functionary. "You must have an escort—and pay for it."

"I have no choice," said Charles Darnay.

"Choice! Listen to him!" cried the scowling red-cap. "As if it was not a favor to be protected!"

"It is always as the good patriot says," observed the functionary. "Rise and dress yourself, emigrant."

When they came to the town of Beauvais —which they did at eventide—Darnay could not conceal from himself that the aspect of affairs was alarming. An ominous crowd gathered to see him dismount at the posting yard, and many voices called loudly, "Down with the emigrant!"

"Emigrant, my friends! Do you not see me here, in France, of my own will?"

"You are a cursed emigrant," cried a farrier, making at him, hammer in hand; "and a cursed aristocrat!"

The postmaster interposed himself between this man and the rider's bridle and soothingly said, "Let him be; let him be! He will be judged at Paris."

"Judged!" repeated the farrier. "Aye! and condemned as a traitor." The crowd roared approval. Darnay said, as soon as he could make his voice heard:

"Friends, you are deceived. I am not a traitor."

"He lies!" cried the smith. "He is a traitor since the decree. His life is forfeit to the people."

At the instant when Darnay saw a rush in the eyes of the crowd, the postmaster shut and barred the gates. The crowd groaned; but no more was done.

"What is this decree that the smith spoke of?" Darnay asked the postmaster, when he had thanked him.

"Truly, a decree for selling the property of emigrants."

"When passed?"

"On the fourteenth."

"The day I left England!"

"Everyone says it is but one of several, and that there will be others—if there are not already—banishing all emigrants, and condemning all to death who return. That is what he meant when he said your life was not your own."

"But there are no such decrees yet?"

"What do I know!" said the postmaster, shrugging his shoulders; "there may be, or there will be."

Daylight at last found them before the wall of Paris. The Barrier was closed and strongly guarded when they rode up to it.

"Where are the papers of this prisoner?" demanded a resolute-looking man.

Naturally struck by the disagreeable word, Charles Darnay requested the speaker to take notice that he was a free traveler and French citizen, in charge of an escort which the disturbed state of the country had imposed upon him and which he had paid for.

"Where," repeated the same personage, "are the papers of this prisoner?"

The drunken patriot produced them. Casting his eyes over Gabelle's letter, the same personage showed surprise, and looked at Darnay with close attention.

He left escort and escorted without saying a word, and went into the guardroom.

When he had sat in his saddle some half-hour, Darnay found himself confronted by the same man in authority, who directed the guard to open the Barrier. Then he delivered to the escort a receipt for the escorted, and requested him to dismount. Darnay accompanied his conductor into a guardroom, where an officer of a coarse, dark aspect, presided.

"Citizen Defarge," said he to Darnay's conductor, "is this the emigrant Evrémonde?"

"This is the man."

"Your age, Evrémonde?"

"Thirty-seven."

"Married, Evrémonde?"

"Yes."

"Where is your wife, Evrémonde?"

"In England."

"Without doubt. You are consigned, Evrémonde, to the prison of La Force."

"Just heaven!" exclaimed Darnay. "Under what law and for what offense?"

The officer looked up from his slip of paper for a moment.

"We have new laws, Evrémonde, and new offenses, since you were here." He said it with a hard smile.

"I entreat you to observe that I have come here voluntarily, in response to that written appeal of a fellow countryman which lies before you. I demand no more than the opportunity to do so without delay. Is not that my right?"

"Emigrants have no rights, Evrémonde," was the stolid reply. The officer wrote until he had finished, read over to himself what he had written, sanded it, and handed it to Defarge, with the words, "In secret."

Defarge motioned to the prisoner that he must accompany him and a guard of two armed patriots.

"Is it you," said Defarge, in a low voice, as they went down the guardhouse steps, "who married the daughter of Doctor Manette, once a prisoner in the Bastille?"

"Yes," replied Darnay, looking at him with surprise.

"My name is Defarge, and I keep a wine shop in the Quarter Saint Antoine. Possibly you have heard of me."

"My wife came to your house to reclaim her father? Yes!"

The word "wife" seemed to serve as a gloomy reminder to Defarge to say with sudden impatience, "In the name of that sharp female La Guillotine, why did you come to France?"

"You heard me say why, a minute ago. Do you not believe it is the truth?"

"A bad truth for you," said Defarge.

Ronald Searle

"Indeed I am lost here. All is so changed. Will you render me a little help?"

"None." Defarge spoke, looking straight before him.

"Will you answer me a single question?"

"Perhaps. You can say what it is."

"In this prison that I am going to so unjustly, shall I have some free communication with the world outside?"

"You will see."

"I am not to be buried there, prejudged, and without any means of presenting my case?"

"You will see. But what then? Other people have been similarly buried in worse prisons, before now."

"But never by me, Citizen Defarge."

Defarge walked on in a steady and set silence. Darnay made haste to say:

"It is of the utmost importance to me—you know, Citizen, of how much importance—that I should be able to communicate to Mr. Lorry of Tellson's Bank, an English gentleman now in Paris, the fact that I have been thrown into the prison of La Force. Will you do that for me?"

"I will do," Defarge doggedly rejoined, "nothing for you. My duty is to my country and the People. I am the sworn servant of both. I will do nothing for you."

Charles Darnay felt it hopeless to entreat him further. That he had fallen among far greater dangers than those which had developed when he left England he knew now. Of unjust treatment in detention, and in cruel separation from his wife and child, he foreshadowed the likelihood; but, beyond this, he dreaded nothing distinctly. With this on his mind, he arrived at the prison of La Force.

"In secret," grumbled the jailer, looking at the written paper. "As if I was not already full to bursting! Come with me, emigrant."

The wicket opened on a staircase, leading upward. When they had ascended forty steps, the jailer opened a low door, and they passed into a solitary cell.

"Yours," said the jailer.

"Why am I confined alone?"

"How do I know!"

"I can buy pen, ink, and paper?"

"Such are not my orders. You will be visited, and can ask then. At present you may buy food, nothing more."

There were in the cell, a chair, a table, and a straw mattress. When the jailer was gone, Darnay thought, "Now am I left, as if I were dead." Stopping then, to look at the mattress, he thought, "And here in these crawling creatures is the first condition of the body after death."

WHAT DO YOU SAY?

1. In Chapter XXI of Book the Second, Darnay appears to be unaware of the dangers involved in his returning to Paris. Cite specific examples of the present change in his attitude.

2. (a) On what charge was Darnay arrested? *(b)* In Book the First, Doctor Manette had been unjustly arrested under the laws of the royal government. What does Darnay's arrest show about the "justice" of the new laws?

3. (a) What would you say are Defarge's real feelings toward Darnay? *(b)* Why does he not show his real feelings?

4. Compare Darnay's imprisonment in La Force with what you know of Doctor Manette's imprisonment in the Bastille. Are there similarities?

CHAPTER II
The Grindstone

Tellson's Bank, in the Saint Germain Quarter of Paris, was in a large house, approached by a courtyard and shut off from the street by a high wall and a strong gate.

What money would be drawn out of Tellson's henceforth, and what would lie there, forgotten; what plate and jewels would tarnish in Tellson's hiding places, while the depositors rusted in prisons, and when they should have violently perished; how many accounts with Tellson's, never to be balanced in this world, must be carried over into the next; no man could have said, that night, any more than Mr. Jarvis Lorry could, though he thought heavily of these questions.

"Thank God," said Mr. Lorry, clasping his hands, "that no one near and dear to me is in this dreadful town tonight. May He have mercy on all who are in danger!"

Soon afterwards, the bell at the great gate sounded, but he heard the gate clash again, and all was quiet. Then his door suddenly opened, and two figures rushed in, at sight of which he fell back in amazement.

Lucie and her father! Lucie with her arms stretched out to him, and with that old look of earnestness upon her face.

"What is this?" cried Mr. Lorry, breathless and confused. "What is the matter? Lucie! Manette! What has happened? What has brought you here? What is it?"

With the look fixed upon him, in her paleness and wildness, she panted imploringly, "O my dear friend! My husband!"

"Your husband, Lucie?"

"Here."

"Here, in Paris?"

"Has been here some days—three or four—I don't know how many. An errand of generosity brought him here unknown to us; he was stopped and sent to prison."

The old man uttered an irrepressible cry. Almost at the same moment the bell of the gate rang again, and a loud noise of feet and voices came pouring into the courtyard.

"What is that noise?" said the Doctor.

"Don't look!" cried Mr. Lorry. "Don't look out! Manette, for your life, don't touch the blind!"

The Doctor turned, with his hand upon the fastening of the window, and said, with a cool, bold smile:

"My dear friend, I have a charmed life in this city. I have been a Bastille prisoner. There is no patriot in Paris—in Paris? In France—who, knowing me to have been a prisoner in the Bastille, would touch me, except to overwhelm me with embraces. My old pain has given me a power that has brought us through the Barrier, gained us news of Charles there, and brought us here. I knew it would be so; I knew I could help Charles; I told Lucie so—What is that noise?" His hand was again upon the window.

"Don't look!" cried Mr. Lorry, absolutely desperate. "No, Lucie, my dear, nor you!" He got his arm around her, and held her. "Don't be so terrified, my love. I solemnly swear to you that I know of no harm having happened to Charles. What prison is he in?"

"La Force!"

"La Force! Lucie, my child, you will compose yourself now, to do exactly as I bid you; for more depends upon it than you can think, or I can say. There is no help for you in any action on your part tonight; you cannot possibly stir out. I say this, because what I must bid you to do for Charles' sake, is the hardest thing to do of all. You must instantly be obedient, still, and quiet. You must let me put you in a room at the back here. You must leave your father and me alone for two minutes, and you must not delay."

"I will be submissive to you. I see in your face that you know I can do nothing else. I know you are true."

The old man kissed her, hurried her into his room, and turned the key; then came hurrying back to the Doctor, partly opened the blind, put his hand upon the Doctor's arm, and looked out with him into the courtyard.

Looked out upon a throng of men and women; not enough in number to fill the courtyard; not more than forty or fifty in all. The people in possession of the house had let them in at the gate, and they had rushed in to work at the grindstone; it had evidently been set up there for their purpose, as in a convenient and retired spot.

But, such awful workers, and such awful work! The eye could not detect one creature in the group free from the smear of blood. Shouldering one another to get next at the

At the London trial in Book the Second, Chapter II, Jerry Cruncher spoke of "quartering" as "barbarous." Review in that chapter how an excited spectator described to Jerry his own version of the torture which would befall Charles Darnay if he were convicted of treason. If Darnay is convicted in Paris, the death penalty assigned to him will be carried out in a more humane way.

Dr. Joseph I. Guillotin, a surgeon and a member of the Revolutionary Assembly, proposed in 1789 that persons condemned to death be executed swiftly and mercifully by a beheading machine, which thereafter came to bear his name. Before the revolution only French nobles had the privilege of being decapitated for capital crimes; common people were hanged, broken on the wheel, burned at the stake, or tortured to death on the rack. Guillotin sought a quick, painless, uniform method of execution to be used democratically for all condemned persons, regardless of rank.

Decapitating machines of one design or another had been known in other countries: ancient Persia, Germany, and Italy during the Middle Ages, Scotland during the sixteenth and seventeenth centuries, and even France long before the revolution. The machine which was designed after Guillotin's suggestion had two tall posts separated by a crossbeam at the top. The inside edges of the posts were grooved to guide a heavy, slant-edged steel knife as it dropped from top to bottom. By means of a rope on a pulley, the knife was raised and then held suspended by a figure-eight claw fixed to the crossbeam. A pull on a cord released the blade.

The victim was strapped to a board and then laid horizontally on a table, which extended at right angles from the base of the upright posts. His neck was confined in a round opening between two planks, the upper one of which could be raised and then lowered. Since the falling blade would cover the round opening, the head would be severed from the body. In front of the opening was an oblong trough or basket to receive the head, and on the right of the table was a large wicker-work basket to receive the body.

During the revolution French people called the guillotine "the national razor." Victims "sneezed into the basket." Those who looked through the "little window" were cured of headaches forever. At one time it was fashionable for revolutionists to wear miniature guillotines suspended as charms from necklaces.

The guillotine was first used April 25, 1792, on a murderer named Nicholas Jacques Pelletier, and then between August 10 of that year and July 31, 1794, approximately 20,000 persons were executed. Though no longer used for political terrorism, the guillotine remains today the legal method of execution in France.

sharpening stone, were men stripped to the waist, the stain all over their bodies; men in rags, with the stain upon those rags; men set off with spoils of women's lace and silk and ribbon, the stain dyeing those trifles. Hatchets, knives, bayonets, swords, all brought to be sharpened, were red with it. And as the frantic wielders of these weapons snatched them from the stream of sparks and tore away into the streets, the same red hue was in their frenzied eyes —eyes which any unbrutalized beholder would have given twenty years of life to petrify with a well directed gun.

They drew back from the window, and the Doctor looked for explanation in his friend's ashy face.

"They are," Mr. Lorry whispered, glancing fearfully at the locked room, "murdering the prisoners. If you really have the power you think you have—as I believe you have—make yourself known to these devils, and get taken to La Force. It may be too late—I don't know!"

Doctor Manette pressed his hand, hastened bareheaded out of the room, and was in the courtyard when Mr. Lorry regained the blind.

His streaming white hair, his remarkable face, and the impetuous confidence of his manner, as he put the weapons aside like water, carried him in an instant to the heart of the concourse at the stone. For a few moments there was a pause, and a hurry, and a murmur, and the unintelligible sound of his voice; and then Mr. Lorry saw him, surrounded by all, and in the midst of a line of twenty men long, all linked shoulder to shoulder, and hand to shoulder, hurried out with cries of—"Live the Bastille prisoner! Help for the Bastille prisoner's kindred in La Force! Room for the Bastille prisoner in front there! Save the prisoner Evrémonde at La Force!" and a thousand answering shouts.

He closed the lattice again with a fluttering heart, closed the window and the curtain, hastened to Lucie, and told her that her father was assisted by the people, and gone in search of her husband. He found her child and Miss Pross with her; but, it never occurred to him to be surprised by their appearance until a long time afterwards, when he sat watching them in such quiet as the night knew.

Lucie had, by that time, fallen into a stupor on the floor at his feet, clinging to his hand. Miss Pross had laid the child down on his own bed, and her head had gradually fallen on the pillow beside her pretty charge. Oh, the long, long night, with the moans of the poor wife! And oh, the long, long night, with no return of her father and no tidings!

WHAT DO YOU SAY?

1. Why is Doctor Manette so confident of his power to help Charles Darnay?

2. What is the significance of the grindstone as Dickens describes it?

3. *(a)* What effect does the arrival of Lucie and Doctor Manette have on Mr. Lorry? *(b)* Is he glad to see them? Why or why not?

CHAPTER III
The Shadow

One of the first considerations which arose in the business mind of Mr. Lorry when business hours came round, was this—that he had no right to imperil Tellson's by sheltering the wife of an emigrant prisoner under the Bank roof. His own possessions, safety, life, he would have hazarded for Lucie and her child, without a moment's demur; but the great trust he held was not his own, and as to that business charge he was a strict man of business.

Noon coming, and the Doctor not returning, and every minute's delay tending to compromise Tellson's, Mr. Lorry advised with Lucie. She said that her father had spoken of hiring a lodging for a short term, in that Quarter, near the Banking house. As there was no business objection to this, and as he foresaw that even if it were all well with Charles, and he were to be released, he could not hope to leave the city, Mr. Lorry went out in quest of such a lodging and found a suitable one, high up in a removed by-street where the closed blinds in all the other windows of a high melancholy square of buildings marked deserted homes.

To this lodging he at once removed Lucie and her child, and Miss Pross; giving them what comfort he could, and much more than he had himself. He left Jerry with them, as a figure to fill a doorway that would bear considerable knocking on the head, and returned to his occupations. A disturbed and doleful mind he brought to bear upon them, and slowly and heavily the day lagged on with him.

It wore itself out, and wore him out with it, until the Bank closed. He was again alone in his room of the previous night, considering what to do next, when he heard a foot upon the stair. In a few moments a man stood in his presence, who addressed him by his name.

"Your servant," said Mr. Lorry. "Do you know me?"

He was a strongly made man with dark curling hair, from forty-five to fifty years of age. For answer he repeated, without any change of emphasis, the words:

"Do you know me?"

"I have seen you somewhere."

"Perhaps at my wine shop?"

"You come from Doctor Manette?"

"Yes. I come from Doctor Manette."

"And what says he? What does he send me?"

Defarge gave into his anxious hand an open scrap of paper. It bore the words in the Doctor's writing:

"Charles is safe, but I cannot safely leave this place yet. I have obtained the favor that the bearer has a short note from Charles to his wife. Let the bearer see his wife."

It was dated from La Force, within an hour.

"Will you accompany me," said Mr. Lorry, joyfully relieved, "to where his wife resides?"

"Yes," returned Defarge.

Scarcely noticing as yet in what a curiously reserved way Defarge spoke, Mr. Lorry went with him into the courtyard. There they found two women; one knitting.

"Madame Defarge!" said Mr. Lorry, who had left her in exactly the same attitude some seventeen years ago. "Does madame go with us?"

"Yes. That she may be able to recognize the faces and know the persons. It is for their safety."

Mr. Lorry led the way. Both the women followed; the second woman being The Vengeance.

They passed through the intervening streets as quickly as they might, ascended the staircase of the new domicile, were admitted by Jerry, and found Lucie weeping, alone. She was thrown into a transport by the tidings Mr. Lorry gave her of her husband, and clasped the hand that delivered his note—little thinking what it had been doing near him in the night, and might, but for a chance, have done to him.

"Dearest—Take courage. I am well, and your father has influence around me. You cannot answer this. Kiss our child for me."

That was all the writing. It was so much, however, to her who received it, that she turned from Defarge to his wife, and kissed one of the hands that knitted. It was a loving, thankful, womanly action, but the hand made no response—dropped cold and heavy, and took to its knitting again.

There was something in its touch that gave Lucie a check. She stopped in the act of putting the note in her bosom, and looked terrified at Madame Defarge. Madame Defarge met the lifted eyebrows and forehead with a cold, impassive stare.

"Is that his child?" said Madame Defarge, stopping in her work for the first time, and pointing her knitting needle at little Lucie as if it were the finger of Fate.

"Yes, madame," answered Mr. Lorry; "this is our poor prisoner's darling daughter, and only child."

The shadow attendant on Madame Defarge and her party seemed to fall so threatening and dark on the child that her mother instinctively kneeled on the ground beside her, and held her to her breast. The shadow attendant on Madame Defarge and her party seemed then to fall, threatening and dark, on both the mother and the child.

"What is it your husband says in that little letter?" asked Madame Defarge, with a lowering smile. "Influence; he says something touching influence?"

"That my father," said Lucie, hurriedly taking the paper from her breast, but with her alarmed eyes on her questioner and not on it, "has much influence around him."

"Surely it will release him!" said Madame Defarge. "Let it do so."

She resumed her knitting and went out. The Vengeance followed. Defarge went last and closed the door.

"Courage, my dear Lucie," said Mr. Lorry, as he raised her. "Courage, courage! So far all goes well with us—much, much better than it has of late gone with many poor souls. Cheer up, and have a thankful heart."

"I am not thankless, I hope, but that dreadful woman seems to throw a shadow on me and on all my hopes."

"Tut, tut!" said Mr. Lorry; "what is this despondency? A shadow indeed! No substance in it, Lucie."

But the shadow of the manner of these Defarges was dark, for all that, and in his secret mind it troubled him greatly.

WHAT DO YOU SAY?

1. *(a)* Why do the Defarges wish to visit Lucie? *(b)* What is the attitude of Madame Defarge toward Lucie during this visit?

2. The word "shadow" is used several times in relation to Madame Defarge. Do you think this word has a particular significance and, if so, what do you think it is?

KNOW YOUR WORDS

Understanding meanings

The italicized words in the sentences below illustrate the exactness of the Dickens vocabulary.

Number to 8, skipping three spaces between numbers. Provide for four column headings: ***Word, Part of Speech, Meaning, Use.*** Under ***Use*** compose a phrase or a sentence in which you use the word appropriately. Underline the word, changing the word form if you need to. Fill in all four columns. Use a dictionary.

1. Mr. Lorry "had no right to ***imperil*** Tellson's."
2. Mr. Lorry "would have ***hazarded***" his own possessions.
3. Mr. Lorry would have done so "without a moment's ***demur***."
4. Every minute's delay of the Doctor tended "to ***compromise*** Tellson's."
5. Mr. Lorry ***foresaw*** conditions which Charles might face.
6. Madame Defarge and The Vengeance ascended the staircase of the new ***domicile.***
7. Madame Defarge ***resumed*** her knitting.
8. "Tut, tut!" said Mr. Lorry. "What is this ***despondency?***"

CHAPTER IV
Calm in Storm

Doctor Manette did not return until the morning of the fourth day of his absence. Not until long afterwards, did Lucie know that eleven hundred defenseless prisoners had been killed by the populace. She only knew that there had been an attack upon the prisons, that all prisoners had been in danger, and that some had been dragged out by the crowd and murdered.

To Mr. Lorry, the Doctor communicated that the crowd had taken him through a scene of carnage to the prison of La Force. That, in the prison he had found a self-appointed Tribunal sitting, before which the prisoners were brought singly, and by which they were rapidly ordered to be put forth to be massacred, or to be released, or —in a few cases—to be sent back to their cells. That, presented by his conductors to this Tribunal, he had announced himself by name and profession as having been for eighteen years a secret and unaccused prisoner in the Bastille; that one of the body so sitting in judgment had risen and identified him, and that this man was Defarge.

That, hereupon, he had ascertained that his son-in-law was among the living prisoners, and had pleaded hard for his life and liberty. That, in the first frantic greetings lavished on himself as a notable sufferer under the overthrown system, it had been accorded to him to have Charles Darnay brought before the Court, and examined. That, he seemed on the point of being at once released, when the tide in his favor met with some unexplained check—not intelligible to the Doctor—which led to a few words of secret conference. That, the man sitting as President had then informed Doctor Manette that the prisoner must remain in custody, but should, for his sake, be held in safe custody. That, immediately, the prisoner was removed to the interior of the prison again; but that he, the Doctor, had then so strongly pleaded for permission to remain and assure himself that his son-in-law was, through no malice or mischance, delivered to the concourse whose murderous yells outside the gate had often drowned the proceedings, that he had obtained the permission and had remained until the danger was over.

Greater things than the Doctor had at that time to contend with would have yielded before his persevering purpose. While he kept himself in his place, as a physician, whose business was with all degrees of mankind, he used his influence so wisely that he was soon the inspecting physician of three prisons, and among them La Force. He could now assure Lucie that her husband was no longer confined alone; he saw her husband weekly, and brought sweet messages to her, straight from his lips; sometimes her husband himself sent a letter to her—though never by the Doctor's hand—but she was not permitted to write to him; for, among the many wild suspicions of plots in the prisons, the wildest of all pointed at emigrants who were known to have made friends abroad.

But though the Doctor never ceased trying to get Charles Darnay set at liberty, or at least to get him brought to trial, the public current of the time set too strong and fast for him. The new era began; the King was tried, doomed, and beheaded; the Republic of Liberty, Equality, Fraternity, or Death, declared for victory or death against the world in arms. Above all, one hideous figure grew familiar—the figure of the sharp female, La Guillotine.

It sheared off heads so many that it, and the ground it polluted, were a rotten red. It hushed the eloquent, struck down the powerful, abolished the beautiful and good. Twenty-two friends of high public mark it had lopped the heads off, in one morning, in as many minutes. The name of the strong man of Old Scripture[1] had descended to the functionary who worked it; but, so armed, he was stronger than his namesake, and blinder, and tore away the gates of God's own Temple every day.

Among these terrors, the Doctor walked with a steady head; confident in his power, cautiously persistent, never doubting that he would save Lucie's husband at last. Yet the current of the time swept by, so strong and deep, and carried the time away so fiercely, that Charles had lain in prison one year and three months.

Still the Doctor walked among the terrors with a steady head. No man better known than he, in Paris at that day; no man in a stranger situation. Silent, humane, indispensable in hospital and prison, using his art equally among assassins and victims, he was a man apart. In the exercise of his skill, the appearance and the story of the Bastille Captive removed him from all other men. He was not suspected or brought in

1. ***the strong man of Old Scripture.*** Samson, in the Old Testament, was famous for his tremendous physical strength.

question any more than if he had indeed been recalled to life some eighteen years before, or were a Spirit moving among mortals.

WHAT DO YOU SAY?

1. Cite an example of foreshadowing which suggests that things will not go well for Charles Darnay.

2. (a) In what ways has Doctor Manette managed to be useful? *(b)* What is the attitude of the people of Paris toward Doctor Manette?

CHAPTER V
The Wood Sawyer

One year and three months. During all that time Lucie was never sure, from hour to hour, but that the Guillotine would strike off her husband's head next day. Every day, through the stony streets, the tumbrils now jolted heavily, filled with Condemned. Lovely girls; bright women, brown-haired, black-haired, and gray; youths; stalwart men and old; gentle born and peasant born; all red wine for La Guillotine, all daily brought into light from the dark cellars of the loathsome prisons, and carried to her through the street to slake her devouring thirst. Liberty, Equality, Fraternity, or Death—the last, much the easiest to bestow, O Guillotine!

As soon as they were established in their new residence, she arranged the little household as exactly as if her husband had been there. Everything had its appointed place and its appointed time. Little Lucie she taught, regularly. The belief that they would soon be reunited—the little preparations for his speedy return, the setting aside of his chair and his book—these, and the solemn prayer at night for one dear prisoner especially, among the many unhappy souls in prison—were almost the only reliefs of her heavy mind.

Sometimes, at night on kissing her father, she would burst into the grief she had repressed all day, and say that her sole reliance, under heaven, was on him. He always resolutely answered: "Nothing can happen to him without my knowledge, and I know that I can save him, Lucie."

They had not made the round of their changed life many weeks, when her father said to her, one evening:

"My dear, there is an upper window in the prison, to which Charles can sometimes gain access at three in the afternoon. When he can get to it, he might see you in the street, he thinks, if you stood in a certain place that I can show you. But you will not be able to see him, my poor child, and even if you could, it would be unsafe for you to make a sign of recognition."

"O show me the place; I will go there every day."

From that time, in all weathers, she waited there two hours. As the clock struck two, she was there; at four she turned resignedly away. When it was not too inclement for her child to be with her, they went together; at other times she was alone; but she never missed a single day.

It was the dark and dirty corner of a small winding street. The hovel of a cutter of wood into lengths for burning was the only house at that end; all else was wall. On the third day of her being there, he noticed her.

"Good day, citizeness."

"Good day, citizen."

This mode of address was now prescribed by decree. It had been established voluntarily some time ago, among the more thorough patriots; but was now law for everybody.

"Walking here again, citizeness?"

"You see me, citizen!"

The wood sawyer, who was a little man with a redundancy of gesture—he had once been a mender of roads—cast a glance at the prison, pointed at the prison, and putting his ten fingers before his face to represent bars, peeped through them jocosely.

"But it's not my business," said he. And went on sawing his wood.

Next day he was looking out for her, and accosted her the moment she appeared.

"What? Walking here again, citizeness?"

"Yes, citizen."

"Ah! A child too! Your mother, is it not, my little citizeness?"

"Do I say yes, mamma?" whispered little Lucie, drawing close to her.

"Yes, dearest."

"Yes, citizen."

"Ah! But it's not my business. My work is my business. See my saw! I call it my Little Guillotine. La, la, la; La, la, la! And off his head comes!"

The billet fell as he spoke, and he threw it into a basket.

"I call myself the Samson of the firewood guillotine. See here again! Loo, loo, loo; Loo, loo, loo! And off her head comes. All the family!"

Lucie shuddered as he threw two more billets into his basket, but it was impossible to be there while the wood sawyer was at work, and not be in his sight. Thenceforth, to secure his good will, she always spoke to him first, and often gave him drink-money, which he readily received.

In all weathers, in the snow and frost of winter, in the bitter winds of spring, in the hot sunshine of summer, in the rains of autumn, and again in the snow and frost of winter, Lucie passed two hours of every day at this place. Her husband saw her—so she learned from her father—it might be once in five or six times; it might be twice or thrice running; it might be not for a week or a fortnight together. It was enough that he did see her when the chances served, and on that possibility she would have waited out the day, seven days a week.

These occupations brought her round to the December month, wherein her father walked among the terrors with a steady head. On a lightly snowing afternoon she arrived at the usual corner. It was a day of wild rejoicing, and festival. She had seen the houses, as she came along, decorated with little pikes, with little red caps stuck upon them; with tricolored ribbons; also, with the standard inscription Republic One and Indivisible. Liberty, Equality, Fraternity, or Death!

Presently she heard a troubled movement and a shouting coming along, which filled her with fear. A moment afterwards a throng of people came pouring around the corner by the prison wall. Some five hundred people were dancing like five thousand demons. There was no other music than their own singing. They danced to the popular Revolution song, keeping a ferocious time that was like a gnashing of teeth in unison. Men and women danced together, women danced together, men danced together.

They advanced, retreated, struck at one another's hands, clutched at one another's heads, spun round alone, caught one another and spun round in pairs, until many of them dropped. While those were down, the rest linked hand in hand, and all spun round together; then the ring broke, and in separate rings of two and four they turned and turned until they all stopped at once, began again, struck, clutched, and tore, and then reversed the spin, and all spun round another way. Suddenly they stopped again, paused, struck out the time afresh, formed into lines the width of the public way, and, with their heads low down and their hands high up, swooped screaming off. No fight could have been half so terrible as this dance. It was so emphatically a fallen sport —a healthy pastime changed into a means of angering the blood, bewildering the senses, and steeling the heart. Such grace as was in it made it the uglier, showing how warped and perverted all things good by nature were become.

This was the Carmagnole.[1] As it passed,

1. ***The Carmagnole,*** a bizarre dance and song popular among the French Revolutionists. The term was also used for the popular costume the Revolutionists wore—a jacket with a wide collar and metal buttons, a blue, white, and red waistcoat, and a red cap.

leaving Lucie frightened and bewildered in the doorway of the wood-sawyer's house, the feathery snow fell as quietly and lay as white and soft as if it had never been.

"O my father!" for he stood before her when she lifted up her eyes, "such a cruel, bad sight."

"I know, my dear, I know. I have seen it many times. Don't be frightened! Not one of them would harm you."

"I am not frightened for myself, my father. But when I think of my husband, and the mercies of these people—"

"We will set him above their mercies soon. I left him climbing to the window. There is no one here to see. You may kiss your hand toward that highest shelving roof."

"I do so, father, and I send him my soul with it!"

A footstep in the snow. Madame Defarge. "I salute you, citizeness," from the Doctor. "I salute you, citizen." Madame gone, like a shadow over the white road.

"Give me your arm, my love, with an air of cheerfulness for his sake. Charles is summoned for tomorrow."

"For tomorrow!"

"There is no time to lose. There are precautions to be taken, that could not be taken until he was actually summoned. You are not afraid?"

She could scarcely answer, "I trust in you."

"Do so. Your suspense is nearly ended, my darling; he shall be restored to you within a few hours; I have encompassed him with every protection. I must see Lorry.

"I must see Lorry," the Doctor repeated, turning her another way.

The stanch old gentleman was still in his trust; had never left it. He and his books were in frequent requisition as to property confiscated and made national. What he could save for the owners he saved. No better man living to hold fast by what Tellson's had in keeping, and to hold his peace.

WHAT DO YOU SAY?

1. What does the author mean by the sentence "Liberty, Equality, Fraternity, or Death—the last, much the easiest to bestow, O Guillotine"?

2. What major point does Dickens make through his description of the Carmagnole?

CHAPTER VI
Triumph

The dread Tribunal of five Judges, Public Prosecutor, and determined Jury, sat every day. Their lists went forth every evening, and were read out by jailers of various prisons to their prisoners. The standard jailer joke was, "Come and listen to the Evening Paper, you inside there!"

"Charles Evrémonde, called Darnay!"

So at last began the Evening Paper at La Force.

When a name was called, its owner stepped into a spot reserved for those announced as being thus fatally recorded. Charles Evrémonde, called Darnay, had reason to know the usage; he had seen hundreds pass away so.

The passage to the Conciergerie was short and dark; the night in its vermin-haunted cells was long and cold. Next day fifteen prisoners were put to the bar before Charles Darnay's name was called. All the fifteen were condemned, and the trials of the whole occupied an hour and a half.

"Charles Evrémonde, called Darnay," was at length arraigned.

His Judges sat upon the Bench in feathered hats; but the rough red cap and tricolored cockade was the headdress otherwise prevailing. Looking at the Jury and the turbulent audience, he might have thought that the usual order of things was reversed, and that the felons were trying the honest men. The lowest, cruelest, and worst populace of a city, directing spirits of the scene; noisily commenting, applauding, disapproving, anticipating, and precipitating the result, without a check.

Under the President sat Doctor Manette, in his usual quiet dress. As well as the prisoner could see, he and Mr. Lorry were the only men there, unconnected with the Tribunal, who wore their usual clothes, and had not assumed the coarse garb of the Carmagnole.

Charles Evrémonde, called Darnay, was accused by the public prosecutor as an emigrant, whose life was forfeit under the decree which banished all emigrants on pain of death. It was nothing that the decree bore date since his return to France. There he was, and there the decree; he had been taken in France, and his head was demanded.

"Take off his head!" cried the audience. "An enemy to the Republic!"

The President rang his bell to silence those cries and asked the prisoner whether it was not true that he had lived many years in England?

Undoubtedly it was.

Was he not an emigrant then? What did he call himself?

Not an emigrant, he hoped, within the spirit of the law.

Why not? the President desired to know.

Because he had voluntarily relinquished a title that was distasteful to him, and had left his country—before the word emigrant in the present acceptation by the Tribunal was in use—to live by his own industry in England, rather than on the industry of the overladen people of France.

What proof had he of this?

He handed in the names of two witnesses: Théophile Gabelle, and Alexandre Manette.

But he had married in England?

True, but not an English woman.

A citizeness of France?

Yes. By birth.

Her name and family?

"Lucie Manette, only daughter of Doctor Manette, the good physician who sits there."

This answer had a happy effect upon the audience. Cries in exaltation of the well-known good physician rent the hall. So capriciously were the people moved that tears immediately rolled down several ferocious countenances which had been glaring at the prisoner a moment before, as if with impatience to pluck him out into the streets and kill him.

On these few steps of his dangerous way, Charles Darnay had set his foot according to Doctor Manette's reiterated instructions. The same cautious counsel directed every step that lay before him, and had prepared every inch of his road.

The President asked why had he returned to France when he did, and not sooner?

He had not returned sooner because he had no means of living in France save those he had resigned; whereas, in England, he lived by giving instruction in the French language and literature. He had returned when he did, on the written entreaty of a French citizen, who represented that his life was endangered by his absence. He had come back to save a citizen's life and to bear his testimony, at whatever personal hazard. Was that criminal in the eyes of the Republic?

The populace cried enthusiastically, "No!" and the President rang his bell to quiet them. Which it did not, for they continued to cry "No!" until they left off, of their own will.

The President required the name of that citizen. The accused explained that the citizen was his first witness. He also referred with confidence to the citizen's letter, which he did not doubt would be found among the papers then before the President.

The Doctor had taken care that it should be there—had assured him that it would be there—and at this stage of the proceedings it was produced and read. Citizen Gabelle was called to confirm it, and did so. Citizen Gabelle hinted, with infinite delicacy, that in the pressure of business imposed on the Tribunal by the multitude of enemies of the Republic he had been slightly overlooked in his prison of the Abbaye until three days ago; when he had been summoned before it, and had been set at liberty on the Jury's declaring themselves satisfied that the accusation against him was answered, as to himself, by the surrender of the citizen Evrémonde, called Darnay.

Doctor Manette was next questioned. His high personal popularity, and the clearness of his answers, made a great impression; but as he proceeded, as he showed that the accused was his first friend on his release from his long imprisonment; that the accused had remained in England, always faithful and devoted to his daughter and himself in their exile; that, so far from being in favor with the Aristocrat government there, he had actually been tried for his life by it, as the foe of England and friend of the United States—as he brought these circumstances into view, with the greatest discretion and with the straightforward force of truth and earnestness, the Jury and the populace became one. At last, when he appealed by name to Monsieur Lorry, an English gentleman then and there present, who, like himself, had been a witness on that English trial and could corroborate his account of it, the Jury declared that they had heard enough, and that they were ready with their votes if the President were content to receive them.

At every vote—the Jurymen voted aloud and individually—the populace set up a shout of applause. All the voices were in the prisoner's favor, and the President declared him free. No sooner was the acquittal pronounced than tears were shed, and such fraternal embraces were bestowed upon the prisoner by as many of both sexes as could rush at him, that after his long and unwholesome confinement he was in danger of fainting from exhaustion.

His removal, to make way for other accused persons who were to be tried, rescued him from these caresses for the moment. Five were to be tried together, next, as enemies of the Republic. So quick was the Tribunal to compensate itself and the nation for a chance lost that these five came down to him before he left the place, condemned to die within twenty-four hours. The first of them told him so, with the customary prison sign of Death—a raised finger—and they all added in words, "Long live the Republic!"

The five had had, it is true, no audience to lengthen their proceedings, for when Darnay and Doctor Manette emerged from the gate, there was a great crowd about it. They put him into a great chair over which they had thrown a red flag, and to the back of it had bound a pike with a red cap on top. In this car of triumph, not even the Doctor's entreaties could prevent his being carried to his home on men's shoulders, with a confused sea of red caps heaving about him, and casting up to sight such wrecks of faces that he more than once misdoubted his mind being in confusion, and that he was in the tumbril on his way to the Guillotine.

In wild procession, they carried him thus into the courtyard of the building where he lived. Lucie's father had gone before to prepare her, and when her husband stood upon his feet, she dropped insensible in his arms.

As he held her to his heart, a few of the people fell to dancing. Instantly all the rest fell to dancing, and the courtyard overflowed with the Carmagnole. Then the Carmagnole absorbed them every one and whirled them away.

After grasping the Doctor's hand, as he stood victorious and proud before him; after grasping the hand of Mr. Lorry, who came panting in breathless from his struggle against the waterspout of the Carmagnole; after kissing little Lucie, who was lifted up to clasp her arms round his neck; and after embracing the ever zealous and faithful Pross; Charles took his wife in his arms, and carried her up to their rooms.

"Lucie! My own! I am safe."

"O dearest Charles, let me thank God for this on my knees as I have prayed to Him."

They all reverently bowed their heads and hearts. When she was again in his arms, he said to her:

"Now speak to your father, dearest. No other man in all France could have done what he has done for me."

She laid her head upon her father's breast, as she had laid his poor head on her breast, long, long ago. He was happy in the return he had made her, he was recompensed for his suffering, he was proud of his strength. "My darling," he remonstrated, "don't tremble so. I have saved him."

WHAT DO YOU SAY?

1. *(a)* How does the mob react to the evidence and testimony presented in the trial? *(b)* What seems to be the author's view regarding the fickleness of the mob?

2. *(a)* Whose testimony marks the turning point in the trial, bringing about Darnay's release? *(b)* How is the mob's reaction to this event related to their earlier reactions toward this man?

3. *(a)* How does this trial compare with Darnay's trial in Book the Second? *(b)* Which seems to be more just? Give reasons for your answer.

CHAPTER VII
A Knock at the Door

"I have saved him." It was not another of the dreams in which he had often come back; he was really here. And yet his wife trembled, and a vague fear was upon her.

Her father, cheering her, showed a compassionate superiority to this woman's weakness. No One Hundred and Five, North Tower, now! He had accomplished the task he had set himself, his promise was redeemed, he had saved Charles.

Their housekeeping was of a very frugal kind; not only because that was the safest way of life, but because they were not rich. Charles, throughout his imprisonment, had had to pay heavily for his bad food, and for his guard, and toward the living of the poorer prisoners. Partly on this account, and partly to avoid a domestic spy, they kept no servant; and Jerry—almost wholly transferred to them by Mr. Lorry—had become their daily retainer, and had his bed there every night.

For some months past, Miss Pross and Mr. Cruncher had discharged the office of purveyors; the former carrying the money; the latter, the basket. Every afternoon they fared forth, and made and brought home such purchases as were needful.

"There's all manner of things wanted," said Miss Pross, "and we shall have a time of it. We want wine, among the rest."

They went out, leaving Lucie, her husband, her father, and the child, by a bright fire. Mr. Lorry was expected back presently. Miss Pross had lighted the lamp, but had put it aside in a corner, that they might enjoy the firelight. All was quiet, and Lucie was more at ease than she had been.

"What is that?" she cried, all at once.

"My dear!" said her father, "command yourself. What a disordered state you are in! The least thing—nothing—startles you! *You*, your father's daughter!"

"I thought," said Lucie, with a pale face and in a faltering voice, "that I heard strange feet upon the stairs."

"My love, the staircase is as still as death."

As he said the word, a blow was struck upon the door.

"Oh father, father. What can this be! Hide Charles. Save him!"

"My child," said the Doctor, rising, and laying his hand upon her shoulder, "I *have* saved him. What weakness is this, my dear! Let me go to the door."

He took the lamp in his hand, crossed the two intervening outer rooms, and opened it. Four rough men in red caps, armed with sabers and pistols, entered the room.

Ronald Searle

"The Citizen Evrémonde, called Darnay," said the first.

"Who seeks him?" answered Darnay.

"I seek him. We seek him. I know you, Evrémonde. You are again the prisoner of the Republic."

He stood with his wife and child clinging to him.

"Tell me how and why am I again a prisoner?"

"It is enough that you return to the Conciergerie, and will know tomorrow. You are summoned for tomorrow."

Dr. Manette, who stood with the lamp in his hand, as if he were a statue made to hold it, put the lamp down, and, taking the speaker, not ungently, by the front of his red woolen shirt, said:

"You know him, you have said. Do you know me?"

"Yes, I know you, Citizen Doctor."

"We all know you, Citizen Doctor," said the other three.

He looked abstractedly from one to another, and said:

"Will you answer me then? How does this happen?"

"Citizen Doctor," said the first, reluctantly, "he has been denounced to the Section of Saint Antoine. This citizen," pointing out the second, "is from Saint Antoine."

The citizen here indicated nodded his head, and added:

"He is accused by Saint Antoine."

"Of what?" asked the Doctor.

"Citizen Doctor," said the first with his former reluctance, "ask no more. If the Republic demands sacrifices from you, without doubt you as a good patriot will be happy to make them. The Republic goes before all. The People is supreme. Evrémonde, we are pressed."

"One word," the Doctor entreated. "Will you tell me who denounced him?"

"It is against rule," answered the first; "but you can ask him of Saint Antoine here."

The Doctor turned his eyes upon that man, who moved uneasily on his feet, and at length said:

"Truly it is against rule. But he is denounced by the Citizen and Citizeness Defarge. And by one other."

"What other?"

"Do *you* ask, Citizen Doctor?"

"Yes."

"Then," said he of Saint Antoine, with a strange look, "you will be answered tomorrow. Now, I am dumb!"

WHAT DO YOU SAY?

1. *(a)* What unexpected new event occurs in this chapter? *(b)* Point out any previous warnings or clues that Darnay would be arrested again.
2. How do the men who have come to arrest Darnay feel about their job? How do you know?
3. Do you have any clues as to the identity of the third person to denounce Darnay?

CHAPTER VIII
A Hand at Cards

Happily unconscious of the new calamity at home, Miss Pross threaded her way along the narrow streets, and crossed the river by the bridge of the Pont-Neuf, reckoning in her mind the number of indispensable purchases she had to make. Mr. Cruncher, with the basket, walked at her side. They both looked to the right and to the left into most of the shops they passed, had a wary eye for all gregarious assemblages of people, and turned out of their road to avoid any very excited group of talkers. It was a raw evening, and the misty river, blurred to the eye with blazing lights and to the ear with harsh noises, showed where the barges were stationed in which the smiths worked, making guns for the Army of the Republic.

Having purchased a few small articles of grocery, and a measure of oil for the lamp, Miss Pross bethought herself of the wine they wanted. After peeping into several wine shops, she stopped at the sign of The Good Republican Brutus of Antiquity, where the aspect of things rather took her fancy.

As their wine was measuring out, a man parted from another man in a corner, and rose to depart. In going, he had to face Miss Pross. No sooner did he face her than Miss Pross uttered a scream and clapped her hands.

In a moment the whole company were on their feet. That somebody was assassinated by somebody vindicating a difference of opinion was the likeliest occurrence. Everybody looked to see somebody fall, but only saw a man and a woman standing staring at each other; the man with all the outward aspect of a Frenchman and a thorough Republican; the woman, evidently English.

"What is the matter?" said the man who had caused Miss Pross to scream; speaking in a vexed, abrupt voice—though in a low tone—and in English.

"Oh, Solomon, dear Solomon!" cried Miss Pross. "After not hearing of you for so long I find you here!"

"Don't call me Solomon. Do you want to be the death of me?" asked the man, in a furtive, frightened way.

Miss Pross burst into tears. "Have I ever been so hard with you that you ask me such a cruel question?"

"Then," said Solomon, "come out, if you want to speak to me. Pay for your wine, and come out. Who's this man?"

Miss Pross said through her tears, "Mr. Cruncher."

"Let him come out too," said Solomon. "Does he think me a ghost?"

Apparently, Mr. Cruncher did, to judge from his looks. He said not a word, however, and Miss Pross, exploring the depths of her reticule through her tears, paid for her wine. As she did so, Solomon turned to the followers of The Good Republican Brutus and offered a few words of explanation in French which caused them all to relapse into their former pursuits.

"Now," said Solomon, stopping at the dark street corner, "what do you want?"

"How dreadfully unkind in a brother nothing has ever turned my love away from!" cried Miss Pross, "to give me such a greeting, and show me no affection."

"There. Con-found it!" said Solomon, making a dab at Miss Pross' lips. "Now are you content?"

Miss Pross only shook her head and wept in silence.

"If you expect me to be surprised," said her brother Solomon, "I am not; I knew you were here; if you really don't want to endanger my existence—I half believe you do —go as soon as possible. I am busy. I am an official."

Mr. Cruncher, touching him on the shoulder, hoarsely and unexpectedly interposed with the following singular question:

"I say! Might I ask the favor? As to whether your name is John Solomon or Solomon John?"

The official turned toward him with sudden distrust.

"Come!" said Mr. Cruncher. "John Solomon or Solomon John? And regarding that name of Pross, likewise. That warn't your name over the water."

"What do you mean?"

"Well, I don't know all I mean, for I can't call to mind what your name was, over the water."

"No?"

"No. But I'll swear it was a name of two syllables."

"Barsad," said another voice, striking in.

"That's the name for a thousand pound!" cried Jerry.

The speaker who struck in was Sydney Carton. He had his hands behind him under the skirts of his riding coat, and he stood at Mr. Cruncher's elbow as negligently as he might have stood at the Old Bailey itself.

"Don't be alarmed, my dear Miss Pross. I arrived at Mr. Lorry's, to his surprise, yesterday evening. I present myself here, to beg a little talk with your brother. I wish for your sake Mr. Barsad was not a Sheep of the Prisons."

Sheep was a cant word of the time for a spy. The spy asked him how he dared—

"I'll tell you," said Sydney. "I lighted on you, Mr. Barsad, coming out of the Conciergerie an hour or more ago. You have a face to be remembered, and I remember faces well. Made curious by seeing you, and having a reason for associating you with the misfortunes of a friend, I walked into the wine shop here, close after you, and sat near you. I had no difficulty in deducing from your unreserved conversation, and the rumor openly going about, the nature of your calling. And gradually, what I had done seemed to shape into a purpose, Mr. Barsad."

"What purpose?" the spy asked.

"It might be dangerous to explain in the street. Could you favor me, in confidence, with some minutes of your company—at the office of Tellson's Bank?"

"Under a threat?"

"Oh! Did I say that?"

"Then why should I go there?"

"Really, Mr. Barsad, I can't say, if you can't."

Carton's negligent recklessness of manner came powerfully in aid of his quickness and skill, in such a business as he had in his secret mind, and with such a man as he had to do with. His practiced eye saw it, and made the most of it.

"I told you," said the spy, casting a reproachful look at his sister; "if trouble comes of this, it's your doing."

"Come, come, Mr. Barsad!" exclaimed Sydney. "Don't be ungrateful. But for my great respect for your sister, I might not have led up so pleasantly to a little proposal that I wish to make. Do you go with me to the Bank?"

"I'll hear what you have to say. Yes, I'll go."

"I propose that we first conduct your sister safely to the corner of her own street. Let me take your arm, Miss Pross. This is not a good city, at this time, for you to be out in, unprotected; and as your escort knows Mr. Barsad, I will invite him to Mr. Lorry's with us. Are we ready? Come then!"

Miss Pross to the end of her life remembered, that as she pressed her hands on Sydney's arm and looked up in his face, imploring him to do no hurt to Solomon, there was a braced purpose in the arm and a kind of inspiration in the eyes, which not only contradicted his light manner, but changed and raised the man. They left her at the corner of the street, and Carton led the way to Mr. Lorry's, which was within a few minutes' walk. John Barsad, or Solomon Pross, walked at his side.

Mr. Lorry had just finished his dinner, and showed the surprise with which he saw a stranger.

"Miss Pross' brother, sir," said Sydney, "Mr. Barsad."

"Barsad?" repeated the old gentleman, "Barsad? I have an association with the name—and with the face."

"I told you you had a remarkable face, Mr. Barsad," observed Carton, coolly. "Pray sit down."

As he took a chair himself, he supplied the link that Mr. Lorry wanted, by saying to him, "Witness at that trial." Mr. Lorry immediately remembered, and regarded his new visitor with an undisguised look of abhorrence.

"Mr. Barsad has been recognized by Miss Pross as the affectionate brother you have heard of," said Sydney. "I pass to worse news. Darnay has been arrested again."

Struck with consternation, the old gentleman exclaimed, "What do you tell me! I left him safe and free within these two hours, and am about to return to him!"

"Arrested for all that. When was it done, Mr. Barsad?"

"Just now, if at all."

"Mr. Barsad is the best authority possible, sir," said Sydney, "and I have it from Mr. Barsad's communication to a friend and brother Sheep over a bottle of wine that the arrest has taken place. There is no earthly doubt that he is retaken."

Mr. Lorry's business eye read in the speaker's face that it was loss of time to dwell upon the point. He commanded himself and was silently attentive.

"I trust," said Sydney, "the influence of Doctor Manette may stand him in as good stead tomorrow—you said he would be before the Tribunal tomorrow, Mr. Barsad?—"

"Yes; I believe so."

"—In as good stead tomorrow as today. But it may not be so. I own to you, I am shaken, Mr. Lorry, by Doctor Manette's not having had the power to prevent this arrest."

"He may not have known of it."

"But that very circumstance would be alarming, when we remember how identified he is with his son-in-law."

"That's true," Mr. Lorry acknowledged.

"In short," said Sydney, "this is a desperate time, when desperate games are played for desperate stakes. Let the Doctor play the winning game; I will play the losing one. Now, the stake I have resolved to play for, in case of the worst, is a friend in the Conciergerie. And the friend I purpose to myself to win is Mr. Barsad."

"You need have good cards, sir," said the spy.

"I'll run them over. I'll see what I hold —Mr. Lorry, I wish you'd give me a little brandy."

It was put before him, and he drank off a glassful. "Mr. Barsad," he went on, in the tone of one who really was looking over a hand at cards: "Sheep of the prisons, now turnkey, now prisoner, always spy and secret informer, represents himself to his employers under a false name. That's a very good card. Mr. Barsad, now in the employ of the republican French government, was formerly in the employ of the aristocratic English government, the enemy of France and freedom. That's an excellent card. Inference clear as day that Mr. Barsad, still in the pay of the English government, is the spy of Pitt, the treacherous foe of the Republic crouching in its bosom, the English traitor. That's a card not to be beaten. Have you followed my hand, Mr. Barsad?"

"Not to understand your play," returned the spy.

"I play my Ace, Denunciation of Mr. Barsad to the nearest Section Committee. Look over your hand, Mr. Barsad, and see what you have. Don't hurry."

It was a poorer hand than he suspected. Mr. Barsad saw losing cards in it that Sydney Carton knew nothing of. Thrown out of his honorable employment in England, he had crossed the Channel, and accepted service in France: first, as a tempter and an eavesdropper among his own countrymen there; gradually, as a tempter and an eavesdropper among the natives. He knew that under the overthrown government he had been a spy upon Saint Antoine and Defarge's wine shop; had received from the police such information concerning Doctor Manette's imprisonment, release, and history, as should serve him for an introduction to conversation with the Defarges; and tried them on Madame Defarge, and had broken down with them signally. He always remembered with fear and trembling that that terrible woman had knitted when he talked with her, and had looked ominously at him as her fingers moved. He had since seen her, in the Section of Saint Antoine, over and over again produce her knitted registers, and denounce people whose lives the guillotine then surely swallowed up. Once denounced, and on such grave grounds as had just now been suggested, he foresaw that the dreadful woman would produce against him that fatal register, and would quash his last chance of life. Besides that all secret men are men soon terrified, here were surely cards enough of one black suit, to justify the holder in growing livid as he turned them over.

"You scarcely seem to like your hand," said Sydney, with the greatest composure. "Do you play?"

"I think, sir," said the spy, as he turned to Mr. Lorry, "I may appeal to you to put it to this other gentleman, so much your junior, whether he can reconcile it to his station to play that Ace of which he has spoken."

"I play my Ace, Mr. Barsad," said Carton, "without any scruple, in a very few minutes."

"I should have hoped, gentlemen both," said the spy, "that your respect for my sister—"

"I could not better testify my respect for your sister than by finally relieving her of her brother," said Sydney Carton.

"You think not, sir?"

"I have thoroughly made up my mind about it."

The smooth manner of the spy received such a check from the inscrutability of Carton—who was a mystery to wiser and honester men than he—that it faltered here. While he was at a loss, Carton said, resuming his former air of contemplating cards:

"And indeed, now I think again, I have a strong impression that I have another good card here, not yet enumerated. That friend and fellow Sheep, who spoke of himself as pasturing in the country prisons; who was he?"

"French. You don't know him," said the spy, quickly.

"French, eh?" repeated Carton. "Well; he may be."

"Is," said the spy; "though it's not important."

"Though it's not important," repeated Carton, in the same mechanical way—"No. Yet I know the face."

"I think not. I am sure not. It can't be," said the spy.

"It—can't—be," muttered Sydney Carton, retrospectively. "Can't—be. Spoke good French. Yet like a foreigner?"

"Provincial," said the spy.

"No. Foreign!" cried Carton, striking his open hand on the table, as a light broke clearly on his mind. "Cly! Disguised, but the same man—at the Old Bailey."

"Now, you are hasty, sir," said Barsad, with a smile.

"Cly—who I will admit was a partner of mine—has been dead several years. He was buried in London, at the church of Saint Pancras-in-the-Fields. His unpopularity with the blackguard multitude prevented my following his remains, but I helped to lay him in his coffin."

Here Mr. Lorry became aware of a remarkable goblin shadow on the wall. He discovered it to be caused by a rising and stiffening of all the hair on Mr. Cruncher's head. Mr. Cruncher rose and stepped forward. Unseen by the spy, Mr. Cruncher stood at his side, and touched him on the shoulder like a ghostly bailiff.

"That there Roger Cly, master," said Mr. Cruncher, "so *you* put him in his coffin?"

"I did."

"Who took him out of it?"

Barsad leaned back and stammered, "What do you mean?"

"I mean," said Mr. Cruncher, "that he warn't never in it. I'll have my head took off, if he was ever in it."

The spy looked round at the two gentlemen; they both looked in unspeakable astonishment at Jerry.

"I tell you," said Jerry, "that you buried paving stones and earth in that there coffin. It was a take in. Me and two more knows it."

"How do you know it?"

"What's that to you?" growled Mr. Cruncher, "it's you I have got a old grudge again, is it, with your shameful impositions upon tradesmen! I'd catch hold of your throat and choke you for half a guinea."

Sydney Carton, who, with Mr. Lorry, had been lost in amazement at this turn of the business, here requested Mr. Cruncher to explain himself.

"At another time, sir," he returned, evasively, "the present time is ill-conwenient for explainin'. What I stand to is that he knows well wot that there Cly was never in that there coffin. Let him say he was and I'll catch hold of his throat and choke him for half a guinea or I'll out and announce him."

"I see one thing," said Carton. "I hold another card, Mr. Barsad. Impossible for you to outlive denunciation, when you are in communication with another aristocratic spy who has feigned death and come to life again! A plot of the foreigner against the Republic. A certain Guillotine card! Do you play?"

"No!" returned the spy. "I throw up. I confess that we were so unpopular with the mob that I got away from England at the risk of death, and that Cly never would have got away but for that sham. Though how this man knows it was a sham is a wonder of wonders to me."

"Never you trouble your head about this man," retorted the contentious Mr. Cruncher; "you'll have trouble enough with giving your attention to that gentleman."

The Sheep of the prisons turned from him to Sydney Carton, and said, with more decision, "You told me you had a proposal; what is it? Now, it is of no use asking too much of me. What do you want with me?"

"Not very much. You are a turnkey at the Conciergerie?"

"I tell you once for all, there is no such thing as an escape possible," said the spy, firmly.

"Why need you tell me what I have not asked? You are a turnkey at the Conciergerie?"

"I am sometimes."

"You can be when you choose."

"I can pass in and out when I choose."

Sydney Carton filled another glass with brandy, poured it slowly out upon the hearth, and watched it as it dropped. It being all spent, he said, rising:

"So far, we have spoken before these two, because it was as well that the merits of the cards should not rest solely between you and me. Let us have one final word alone."

WHAT DO YOU SAY?

1. How do past incidents play a part in the surprising turn of events in this chapter?

2. What kind of "hand" does Sydney Carton hold against Solomon Pross, alias John Barsad?

3. *(a)* What knowledge did Jerry Cruncher have (from Book the Second, Chapter XII) that made him important to the plot in this chapter? *(b)* How do Sydney Carton and John Barsad react to Jerry's information?

4. Cite specific statements in this chapter which show that Carton has a "plan."

CHAPTER IX
The Game Made

While Sydney Carton and the spy were in the adjoining dark room, Mr. Lorry looked at Jerry in considerable doubt and mistrust.

"Jerry," said Mr. Lorry. "Come here."

Mr. Cruncher came forward sideways, with one of his shoulders in advance of him.

"What have you been, besides a messenger?"

After some cogitation, accompanied with an intent look at his patron, Mr. Cruncher conceived the idea of replying, "Agricultooral character."

"My mind misgives me much," said Mr. Lorry, "that you have used the great house of Tellson's as a blind, and that you have had an unlawful occupation of an infamous description. If you have, don't expect me to keep your secret. Tellson's shall not be imposed upon."

"I hope, sir," pleaded the abashed Mr. Cruncher, "that a gentleman like yourself wot I've had the honor of odd jobbing till I'm gray at it, would think twice about harming of me, even if it wos so—I don't say it is, but even if it wos. And which it is to be took into account that if it wos, it wouldn't, even then, be all o' one side. There'd be two sides to it. There might be medical doctors at the present hour a-banking away like smoke at Tellson's, and a-cocking their medical eyes at that tradesman on the sly. Well, that 'ud be imposing, too, on Tellson's. For you cannot sarse the goose and not the gander. Then, wot with undertakers, and wot with parish clerks, and wot with sextons, and wot with private watchmen—all awaricious and all in it—a man wouldn't get much by it, even if it wos so. And wot little a man did get would never prosper with him, Mr. Lorry. He'd never have no good of it; he'd want all along to be out of the line, if he could see his way out, being once in—even if it wos so."

"Ugh!" cried Mr. Lorry, rather relenting, nevertheless. "I am shocked at the sight of you."

"Now, what I would humbly offer to you, sir," pursued Mr. Cruncher, "even if it wos so, which I don't say it is—"

"Don't prevaricate," said Mr. Lorry.

"No, I will *not*, sir," returned Mr. Cruncher, as if nothing were further from his thoughts or practice—"which I don't say it is—wot I would humbly offer to you, sir, would be this. A man don't see all this a-goin' on dreadful round him, without havin' his serious thoughts. And these here would be mine, if it wos so, entreatin' of you fur to bear in mind that wot I said just now, I up and said in the good cause when I might have kep' it back."

"That at least is true," said Mr. Lorry. "It may be that I shall yet stand your friend, if you deserve it, and repent in action—not in words. I want no more words."

Mr. Cruncher knuckled his forehead, as Sydney Carton and the spy returned. "Adieu, Mr. Barsad," said the former; "you have nothing to fear from me."

He sat down in a chair on the hearth. When they were alone, Mr. Lorry asked what he had done.

"Not much. If it should go ill with the prisoner, I have insured access to him, once."

Mr. Lorry's countenance fell.

"It is all I could do," said Carton. "To propose too much, would be to put this man's head under the ax, and, as he himself said, nothing worse could happen to him if he were denounced. It was the weakness of the position."

"But access to him," said Mr. Lorry, "if it should go ill before the Tribunal, will not save him."

"I never said it would."

Mr. Lorry's eyes sought the fire; he was an old man now, overborne with anxiety of late, and his tears fell.

"You are a good man and a true friend," said Carton, in an altered voice. "Forgive me if I notice that you are affected. I could not see my father weep, and sit by, careless. And I could not respect your sorrow more, if you were my father. You are free from that misfortune, however.

"To return to poor Darnay," said Carton. "Don't tell her of this interview, or this arrangement. It would not enable her to go to see him. She might think it was contrived, in case of the worst, to convey to him the means of anticipating the sentence."

Mr. Lorry had not thought of that, and he looked quickly at Carton to see if it were in his mind. It seemed to be; he returned the look, and evidently understood it.

"She might think a thousand things," Carton said, "and any of them would only add to her trouble. Don't speak of me to her. I had better not see her. I can do any little helpful work for her that my hand can find to do, without that. You are going to her, I hope? She must be very desolate tonight."

"I am going now, directly."

"I am glad of that. She has such a strong attachment to you and reliance on you. How does she look?"

"Anxious and unhappy, but very beautiful."

"Ah!"

It was a long, grieving sound, like a sigh —almost like a sob. It attracted Mr. Lorry's eyes to Carton's face, which was turned to the fire. A light, or a shade—the old gentleman could not have said which—passed from it as swiftly as a change will sweep over a hillside on a wild bright day, and he lifted his foot to put back one of the little flaming logs, which was tumbling forward. He wore the white riding coat and top boots, and the light of the fire touching their light surfaces made him look very pale, with his long brown hair, all untrimmed, hanging loose about him. His indifference to fire was sufficiently remarkable to elicit a word of remonstrance from Mr. Lorry; his boot was still upon the hot embers of the flaming log, when it had broken under the weight of his boot.

"I forgot it," he said.

Mr. Lorry's eyes were again attracted to his face. Taking note of the wasted air which clouded the naturally handsome features, and having the expression of prisoners' faces fresh in his mind, he was strongly reminded of that expression.

"And your duties here have drawn to an end, sir?" said Carton, turning to him.

"Yes. As I was telling you last night when Lucie came in so unexpectedly, I have at length done all that I can do here. I hoped to have left them in perfect safety, and then to have quitted Paris. I have my Leave to Pass. I was ready to go." They were both silent.

Carton terminated the conversation here, by rising to help him on with his outer coat. "I'll walk with you to her gate. You know my vagabond habits. If I should prowl about the streets a long time, don't be uneasy; I shall reappear in the morning. You go to the Court tomorrow?"

"Yes, unhappily."

"I shall be there, but only as one of the crowd. My spy will find a place for me. Take my arm, sir." Mr. Lorry did so, and they went out in the streets. A few minutes brought them to Mr. Lorry's destination. Carton left him there; but lingered at a little distance, turned back to the gate when it was shut, and touched it. He had heard of her going to the prison every day. "She came out here," he said, looking about him, "turned this way, must have trod on these stones often. Let me follow in her steps."

Sydney had not gone far when he stopped in the middle of the street under a glimmering lamp, and wrote with his pencil on a scrap of paper. Then, traversing with the decided step of one who remembered the way well, several dark and dirty streets, he stopped at a chemist's shop. A small, dim, crooked shop, kept in a tortuous, uphill thoroughfare, by a small, dim, crooked man.

Giving this citizen good night, as he confronted him at his counter, he laid the scrap of paper before him. "Whew!" the chemist whistled softly, as he read it.

Sydney Carton took no heed, and the chemist said:

"For you, citizen?"

"For me."

"You will be careful to keep them separate, citizen? You know the consequences of mixing them?"

"Perfectly."

Certain small packets were made and given to him. He put them, one by one, in the breast of his inner coat, counted out the money for them, and deliberately left the shop.

"There is nothing more to do," said he, glancing upward at the moon, "until tomorrow. I can't sleep."

It was not a reckless manner, the manner in which he said these words. It was the settled manner of a tired man, who had wandered and got lost, but at length struck his road and saw its end.

Long ago, when he had been famous as a youth of great promise, he had followed his father to the grave. His mother had died, years before. These solemn words, which had been read at his father's grave, arose in his mind as he went down the dark streets. "I am the resurrection and the life, saith the Lord; he that believeth in me, though he were dead, yet shall he live; and whosoever liveth and believeth in me, shall never die."

In a city dominated by the ax, alone at night, with natural sorrow rising in him for the sixty-three who had been that day put to death, and for tomorrow's victims then awaiting their doom in the prisons, and still of tomorrow's and tomorrow's, the chain of association that brought the words home might have been easily found. He did not seek it, but repeated them and went on.

Few coaches were abroad, for riders in coaches were liable to be suspected. But, the theaters were all well filled, and the people poured cheerfully out as he passed. At one of the theater doors, there was a little girl with a mother, looking for a way across the street through the mud. He carried the child over, and before the timid arm was loosed from his neck asked her for a kiss.

"I am the resurrection and the life, saith the Lord; he that believeth in me, though he were dead, yet shall he live; and whosoever liveth and believeth in me, shall never die."

Now that the night wore on, the words were in the echoes of his feet. Perfectly calm and steady, he sometimes repeated them to himself as he walked, but he heard them always.

The night wore out, and he stood upon the bridge listening to the water as it splashed the river walls of the Island of Paris. He walked by the stream and in the light and warmth of the sun fell asleep on the bank. When he awoke, he lingered yet a little longer, watching an eddy that turned and turned purposeless, until the stream absorbed it, and carried it on to the sea. —"Like me!"

A trading boat glided by him. As its silent track in the water disappeared, the prayer that had broken up out of his heart for a merciful consideration of all his poor blindnesses and errors, ended in the words, "I am the resurrection and the life."

Mr. Lorry was already out when he got back, and it was easy to surmise where the good old man was gone. Sydney Carton drank a little coffee, ate some bread, and, having washed and changed, went out to the place of trial.

The court was all astir and abuzz, when the black sheep—whom many fell away from in dread—pressed him into an obscure corner among the crowd. Mr. Lorry was there, and Doctor Manette. She was there, beside her father.

When her husband was brought in, she turned a look upon him, so sustaining, so encouraging, so full of admiring love and pitying tenderness, yet so courageous for his sake, that it called the healthy blood into his face, brightened his glance and animated his heart. If there had been any eyes to notice the influence of her look, on Sydney Carton, it would have been seen to be the same influence exactly.

Before that unjust Tribunal there was little or no order of procedure, insuring to any accused person any reasonable hearing. There could have been no such Revolution, if all laws, forms, and ceremonies had not first been so monstrously abused that the suicidal vengeance of the Revolution was to scatter them all to the winds.

Every eye was turned to the Jury. The same determined patriots and good republicans as yesterday and the day before, and tomorrow and the day after. A life-thirsting, cannibal-looking, bloody-minded Juryman, the Jacques Three of Saint Antoine. The whole Jury, as a jury of dogs empaneled to try the deer.

Every eye then turned to the five Judges and the Public Prosecutor. No favorable leaning in that quarter today. A fell, uncompromising, murderous business-meaning there.

Charles Evrémonde, called Darnay. Released yesterday. Reaccused and retaken yesterday. Indictment delivered to him last night. Suspected and denounced enemy of the Republic, aristocrat, one of a family of tyrants, one of a race proscribed, for that they had used their abolished privileges to

the infamous oppression of the people. Charles Evrémonde, called Darnay, in right of such proscription, absolutely dead in Law:

To this effect, the Public Prosecutor.

Was the accused openly denounced or secretly?

"Openly, President."

"By whom?"

"Three voices. Ernest Defarge, wine-vendor."

"Good."

"Thérèse Defarge, his wife."

"Good."

"Alexandre Manette, physician."

A great uproar took place in the court, and in the midst of it, Doctor Manette was seen, pale and trembling, standing where he had been seated.

"President, I indignantly protest that this is a forgery. You know the accused to be the husband of my daughter. My daughter, and those dear to her, are far dearer to me than my life. Who and where is the false conspirator who says I denounce the husband of my child?"

"Citizen Manette, be tranquil. To fail in submission to the authority of the Tribunal would be to put yourself out of Law. As to what is dearer to you than life, nothing can be so dear to a good citizen as the Republic."

Loud acclamations hailed this rebuke. The President rang his bell, and with warmth resumed:

"If the Republic should demand sacrifice of your child herself, you would have no duty but to sacrifice her. Listen to what is to follow. In the meanwhile, be silent!"

Frantic acclamations were again raised. Doctor Manette sat down, his lips trembling.

Defarge was produced, and rapidly expounded the story of the imprisonment, of his having been a mere boy in the Doctor's service, of the release, and of the state of the prisoner when released and delivered to him. This short examination followed, for the court was quick with its work.

"You did good service at the taking of the Bastille?"

"I believe so."

"Inform the Tribunal of what you did that day within the Bastille, citizen."

"I knew," said Defarge, looking down at his wife, "that this prisoner had been confined in cell One Hundred and Five, North Tower. As I serve my gun that day, I resolve to examine that cell. I mount to the cell, with a fellow citizen who is one of the Jury, directed by a jailer. I examine it very closely. In a hole in the chimney, where a stone has been worked out and replaced, I find this written paper. I confide this paper, in the writing of Doctor Manette, to the President."

"Let it be read."

In a dead silence and stillness—the prisoner under trial looking lovingly at his wife, his wife only looking from him to look with solicitude at her father, Doctor Manette keeping his eyes fixed on the reader, Madame Defarge never taking hers from the prisoner, Defarge never taking his from his wife, and all other eyes intent upon the Doctor, who saw none of them—the paper was read as follows.

WHAT DO YOU SAY?

1. What was the most important fact that Sydney Carton revealed to Mr. Lorry about his plans?

2. Why does Sydney Carton not want Lucie to know he has gained access to the prison?

3. Recount the conversation between Sydney Carton and the chemist.

4. (a) What Biblical quotation recurred in the chapter? *(b)* Is there a meaning in this quotation which might foreshadow future events?

5. Cite specific statements which reveal the author's viewpoint toward laws of the revolutionary government.

6. (a) Who was the third witness who denounced Darnay? *(b)* Find at the end of Chapter VII specific statements which foreshadowed the identity of this witness.

CHAPTER X
The Substance of the Shadow

"I, Alexandre Manette, unfortunate physician, native of Beauvais, and afterwards resident in Paris, write this melancholy paper in my doleful cell in the Bastille, during the last month of the year, 1767. I write it at stolen intervals under every difficulty. I design to secrete it in the wall of the chimney, where I have slowly and laboriously made a place of concealment for it. Some pitying hand may find it there, when I and my sorrows are dust.

"These words are formed by the rusty iron point with which I write with difficulty in scrapings of soot and charcoal from the chimney, mixed with blood, in the last month of the tenth year of my captivity. Hope has quite departed from my breast. I know from terrible warnings I have noted in myself that my reason will not long remain unimpaired, but I solemnly declare that I am at this time in the possession of my right mind—that my memory is exact and circumstantial—and that I write the truth as I shall answer for these my last recorded words, whether they be ever read by men or not, at the Eternal Judgment Seat.

"One cloudy moonlight night, in the third week of December (I think the twenty-second of the month) in the year 1757, I was walking on a retired part of the quay by the Seine at an hour's distance from my place of residence in the Street of the School of Medicine, when a carriage came along behind me, driven very fast. As I stood aside to let that carriage pass, a head was put out at the window, and a voice called to the driver to stop.

"The carriage stopped as soon as the driver could rein in his horses, and the same voice called to me by my name. I answered. The carriage was then so far in advance of me that two gentlemen had time to open the door and alight before I came up with it. I observed that they were both wrapped in cloaks, and appeared to conceal themselves. As they stood side by side near the carriage door, I also observed that they both looked of about my own age, or rather younger, and that they were greatly alike, in stature, manner, voice, and—as far as I could see—face too.

" 'You are Doctor Manette?' said one.

" 'I am.'

" 'Doctor Manette, formerly of Beauvais,' said the other; 'the young physician, originally an expert surgeon, who within the last year or two has made a rising reputation in Paris?'

" 'Gentlemen,' I returned, 'I am that Doctor Manette of whom you speak so graciously.'

" 'We have been to your residence,' said the first, 'and being informed that you were probably walking in this direction, we followed, in the hope of overtaking you. Will you please to enter the carriage?'

"The manner of both was imperious, and they both moved, as these words were spoken, so as to place me between themselves and the carriage door. They were armed. I was not.

" 'Gentlemen,' said I, 'pardon me; but I usually inquire who does me the honor to seek my assistance, and what is the nature of the case to which I am summoned.'

"The reply to this was made by him who had spoken second. 'Doctor, your clients are people of condition. As to the nature of the case, our confidence in your skill assures us that you will ascertain it for yourself better than we can describe it. Enough. Will you please to enter the carriage?'

"I could do nothing but comply. They entered after me—the last springing in, after putting up the steps. The carriage turned about, and drove on at its former speed.

"I repeat this conversation exactly as it occurred. I have no doubt that it is, word for word, the same. I describe everything exactly as it took place.

"The carriage left the streets behind, passed the North Barrier, and emerged upon the country road. At two thirds of a league from the Barrier—I did not estimate the distance at that time, but afterwards when I traversed it—it struck out of the main avenue, and presently stopped at a solitary house. We all three alighted, and walked to the door of the house. It was not opened immediately, in answer to the bell, and one of my conductors struck the man who opened it, with his heavy riding glove, across the face.

"There was nothing in this action to attract my particular attention, for I had seen common people struck more commonly than dogs. But, the other of the two struck the man in like manner; the look and bearing of the brothers were so exactly alike that I then first perceived them to be twin brothers.

"From the time of our alighting at the outer gate—which one of the brothers had opened to admit us, and had relocked—I had heard cries proceeding from an upper chamber. I was conducted to this chamber, the cries growing louder as we ascended the stairs, and I found a patient in a high fever of the brain, lying on a bed.

"The patient was a woman of great beauty, not much past twenty. Her hair was torn and ragged, and her arms were bound to her sides with sashes and handkerchiefs. I noticed that these bonds were all portions of a gentleman's dress. On one of them, a fringed scarf, I saw the armorial bearings of a noble, and the letter E.

"Her eyes were dilated and wild, and she constantly uttered piercing shrieks, repeating the words: 'My husband, my father, and my brother!' An instant she would pause, then repeat the cry, then count up to twelve and say, 'Hush!' There was no variation in the order, or the manner.

" 'How long,' I asked, 'has this lasted?'

"To distinguish the brothers, I will call them the elder and the younger; by the elder I mean him who exercised the most authority. The elder replied, 'Since last night.'

" 'She has a husband, a father, and a brother?'

" 'A brother.'

" 'I do not address her brother?'

"He answered with great contempt, 'No.'

" 'She has some recent association with the number twelve?'

"The younger brother impatiently rejoined, 'With twelve o'clock!'

" 'See, gentlemen,' said I, 'how useless I am. If I had known what I was to see, I could have come provided. As it is, time must be lost. There are no medicines in this lonely place.'

"The younger said haughtily, 'There is a case of medicines here,' brought it from a closet, and put it on the table.

"I opened some of the bottles, smelled them, and put the stoppers to my lips. If I had wanted to use anything save narcotic medicines that were poisons in themselves, I would not have administered any of those.

" 'Do you doubt them?' asked the younger brother.

" 'You see, monsieur, I am going to use them,' I replied.

"I made the patient swallow, with great difficulty, and after many efforts, the dose that I desired to give. I then sat down by the side of the bed. There was a timid and suppressed woman in attendance—wife of the man downstairs—who had retreated into a corner.

"I had sat by the side of the bed for half an hour, with the two brothers looking on, before the elder said:

" 'There is another patient.'

"I was startled, and asked, 'Is it a pressing case?'

" 'You had better see,' he carelessly answered; and took up a light.

"The other patient lay in a back room across a second staircase, which was a species of loft over a stable. On some hay on the ground, with a cushion thrown under his head, lay a handsome peasant boy of not more than seventeen. He lay on his back, teeth set, right hand clenched on his breast, and eyes glaring straight upward. I could not see where his wound was, as I kneeled over him; but I could see that he was dying of a wound from a sharp point.

"'I am a doctor,' said I. 'Let me examine it.'

"'I do not want it examined,' he answered; 'let it be.'

"It was under his hand, and I soothed him to let me move his hand away. The wound was a sword thrust, received from twenty to twenty-four hours before, but no skill could have saved him if it had been looked to without delay. He was then dying fast. As I turned my eyes to the elder brother, I saw him looking down at this handsome boy whose life was ebbing out, as if he were a wounded bird, or a hare, or rabbit; not at all as if he were a fellow creature.

"'How has this been done, monsieur?' said I.

"'A crazed young common dog! A serf! Forced my brother to draw upon him, and has fallen by my brother's sword—like a gentleman.'

"There was no touch of pity, sorrow, or kindred humanity in this answer. The speaker seemed to acknowledge that it was inconvenient to have that different order of creature dying there, and was incapable of any compassion for him.

"The boy's eyes had slowly moved to him as he had spoken, and they now slowly moved to me.

"'Doctor, they are very proud, these nobles; but we common dogs are proud too, sometimes. They plunder us, outrage us, beat us, kill us; but we have a little pride left, sometimes. She—have you seen her, Doctor?'

"I said, 'I have seen her.'

"'She is my sister, Doctor. They have had their shameful rights, these nobles, in the modesty and virtue of our sisters, many years, but we have had good girls among us. She was a good girl, betrothed to a good young man. We were all tenants of his —that man's who stands there.'

"It was with greatest difficulty that the boy gathered force to speak; but his spirit spoke with dreadful emphasis.

"'We were so robbed by that man who stands there—taxed by him without mercy, obliged to work for him without pay, to grind our corn at his mill, to feed scores of his tame birds on our wretched crops—I say we were so robbed, and hunted, and were made so poor that our father told us it was a dreadful thing to bring a child into the world, and that what we should most pray for was that our women might be barren and our miserable race die out!'

"I had never before seen the sense of being oppressed, bursting forth like a fire until I saw it in the dying boy.

"'Nevertheless, Doctor, my sister married. He was ailing at that time, poor fellow, and she married her lover that she might tend and comfort him in our cottage. She had not been married many weeks, when that man's brother saw her and admired her, and asked that man to lend her to him—for what are husbands among us! My sister was good and virtuous, and hated his brother with a hatred as strong as mine. What did the two then, to persuade her husband to use his influence with her, to make her willing?'

"The boy's eyes slowly turned to the looker-on, and I saw in the two faces that all he said was true. The two opposing kinds of pride confronting one another, I can see, even in this Bastille; the gentleman's, negligent indifference; the peasant's, passionate revenge.

"'You know, Doctor, that it is among the rights of these nobles to harness us common dogs to carts, and drive us. They so harnessed and drove him. You know that it is among their rights to keep us in their grounds all night, quieting the frogs, in order that their noble sleep may not be disturbed. They kept him out in the unwholesome mists at night, and ordered him back into his harness in the day. But he was not persuaded. No! Taken out of harness one day at noon, to feed—if he could find food—he sobbed twelve times, once for every stroke of the bell, and died on her bosom.'

"Nothing human could have held life in the boy but his determination to tell all his wrongs. He forced back the gathering shadows of death, as he forced his clenched right hand to remain clenched, and to cover his wound.

"'Then with that man's permission and even with his aid, his brother took her away; in spite of what I know she must have told his brother—and what that is, will not be long unknown to you, Doctor, if it is now—his brother took her away—for his pleasure and diversion, for a little while. I saw her pass me on the road. When I took the tidings home, our father's heart burst. I took my young sister—for I have another—to a place beyond the reach of this man. Then I tracked the brother here, and last night climbed in—a common dog, but sword in hand—

"'She heard me, and ran in. I told her not to come near us till he was dead. He came in and first tossed me some pieces of money; then struck at me with a whip. But I, though a common dog, so struck at him as to make him draw. Let him break into as many pieces as he will the sword that he stained with my common blood; he drew to defend himself—thrust at me with all his skill for his life.'

"My glance had fallen, but a few moments before, on the fragments of a broken sword, lying among the hay. That weapon was a gentleman's. In another place, lay an old sword that seemed to have been a soldier's.

"'Now, lift me up, Doctor; lift me up. Where is he?'

"'He is not here,' I said, supporting the boy, and thinking that he referred to the brother.

"'He! Proud as these nobles are, he is afraid to see me. Where is the man who was here? Turn my face to him.'

"I did so, raising the boy's head against my knee.

"'Marquis,' said the boy, 'in the days when all these things are to be answered for, I summon you and yours, to the last of your bad race, to answer for them. I mark this cross of blood upon you, as a sign that I do it. I summon your brother, the worst of the bad race, to answer for them separately. I mark this cross of blood upon him, as a sign that I do it.'

"Twice, he put his hand to the wound in his breast, and with his forefinger drew a cross in the air. He stood for an instant with the finger yet raised, and, as it dropped, he dropped with it, and I laid him down dead.

"When I returned to the bedside of the young woman, I found her raving in precisely the same order and continuity. I knew that this might last for many hours, and that it would probably end in the silence of the grave.

"This lasted twenty-six hours from the time when I first saw her. I had come and gone twice, and was again sitting by her, when she began to falter. I did what little could be done to assist that opportunity, and by-and-by she sank into a lethargy, and lay like the dead. I called the woman to assist me to compose her figure and the dress she had torn. It was then that I knew her condition to be that of one in whom the first expectations of being a mother have arisen; it was then I lost the little hope I had had of her.

"'Is she dead?' asked the Marquis, coming booted into the room from his horse.

"'Not dead,' said I; 'but like to die.'

"'What strength there is in these common bodies!' he said, looking down at her with some curiosity.

"'There is prodigious strength,' I answered him, 'in sorrow and despair.'

"He first laughed at my words, and then frowned at them. He moved a chair with his foot near to mine, ordered the woman away, and said in a subdued voice:

"'Doctor, finding my brother in this difficulty with these hinds, I recommended that your aid be invited. Your reputation is high, and, as a young man with your fortune to make, you are probably mindful of your interest. The things you see here, are things to be seen, and not spoken of.'

"I listened to the patient's breathing, and avoided answering. 'Do you honor me with your attention, Doctor?'

"'Monsieur,' said I, 'in my profession, communications of patients are always received in confidence.' I was guarded in my answer, for I was troubled in my mind.

"Her breathing was difficult to trace. There was life, and no more. Looking round, I found both the brothers intent upon me.

"She lingered for a week. Toward the last I could understand some few syllables that she said to me, by placing my ear close to her lips. She asked me where she was, and I told her; who I was, and I told her. It was in vain that I asked her for her family name. She faintly shook her head upon the pillow, and kept her secret, as the boy had done.

"I had no opportunity of asking her any question, until I had told the brothers she could not live another day. Until then, one or other of them had always jealously sat behind the curtain at the head of the bed when I was there. But when it came to that, they seemed careless what communication I might hold with her; as if—the thought passed through my mind—I were dying too.

"As often as I caught the younger brother's eyes, their expression reminded me that he disliked me deeply, for knowing what I knew from the boy. He was smoother and more polite to me than the elder; but I saw this. I also saw that I was an incumbrance in the mind of the elder, too.

"My patient died, two hours before midnight—at a time, by my watch, answering almost to the minute when I had first seen her. I was alone with her, when her forlorn young head drooped and all her earthly sorrows ended.

"The brothers were waiting in a room downstairs, impatient to ride away. I had heard them, striking their boots with their riding whips, and loitering up and down.

"'At last she is dead?' said the elder, when I went in.

"'She is dead,' said I.

"'I congratulate you, my brother,' were his words as he turned round.

"He now gave me a rouleau of gold. I took it but laid it on the table. I had resolved to accept nothing.

"'Pray excuse me,' said I. 'Under the circumstances, no.'

"They exchanged looks, but bent their heads to me as I bent mine to them, and we parted without another word.

"I am weary, weary, weary—worn down by misery. I cannot read what I have written with this gaunt hand.

"Early in the morning, the rouleau of gold was left at my door in a little box, with my name on the outside. From the first, I had anxiously considered what I ought to do. I decided, that day, to write privately to the Minister, stating the nature of the two cases to which I had been summoned, and the place to which I had gone; in effect, stating all the circumstances. I knew what the immunities of the nobles were, and I expected that the matter would never be heard of; but I wished to relieve my own mind. I had kept the matter a profound secret, even from my wife; and this, too, I resolved to state in my letter. I had no apprehension whatever of my real danger; but I was conscious that there might be danger for others, if others were compromised by possessing the knowledge that I possessed. The letter was before me just completed, when I was told that a lady waited, who wished to see me. . . .

"I am growing more and more unequal to the task I have set myself. It is so cold, so dark, my senses are so benumbed, and the gloom upon me is so dreadful.

"The lady presented herself as wife of the Marquis St. Evrémonde. I connected the title by which the boy had addressed the elder brother, with the initial letter embroidered on the scarf, arriving at the conclusion that I had seen that nobleman very lately.

"She had in part suspected, and in part discovered, the main facts of the cruel story, of her husband's share in it, and my being resorted to. She did not know that the girl was dead. Her hope had been, she said in great distress, to show her, in secret, a woman's sympathy.

"She had reasons for believing that there was a young sister living, and her greatest desire was to help that sister. I could tell her nothing but that there was such a sister; beyond that, I knew nothing.

"She was a good, compassionate lady, and not happy in her marriage. How could she be! The brother distrusted and disliked her, and his influence was all opposed to her; she stood in dread of him, and in dread of her husband too. When I handed her down to the door, there was a child, a pretty boy from two to three years old, in her carriage.

" 'For his sake, Doctor,' she said, pointing to him in tears, 'I would do all I can to make what poor amends I can. He will never prosper in his inheritance otherwise. I have a presentiment that if no other innocent atonement is made for this, it will one day be required of him. What I have left to call my own—it is little beyond the worth of a few jewels—I will make it the first charge of his life to bestow on this injured family, if the sister can be discovered.'

"She kissed the boy, and said, 'It is for thine own dear sake. Thou wilt be faithful, little Charles?' The child answered her bravely, 'Yes!' I kissed her hand, and she went away. I never saw her more.

"As she had mentioned her husband's name in the faith that I knew it, I added no mention of it to my letter. I sealed my letter, and delivered it myself that day.

"That night, the last night of the year, toward nine o'clock, a man in a black dress demanded to see me, and softly followed my servant, Ernest Defarge, into the room where I sat with my wife—O my wife, beloved of my heart! My fair young English wife! 'An urgent case in the Rue St. Honoré,' he said. It would not detain me. He had a coach in waiting.

"When I was clear of the house, a black muffler was drawn tightly over my mouth from behind, and my arms were pinioned. The two brothers crossed the road from a dark corner, and identified me with a single gesture. The Marquis took from his pocket the letter I had written, showed it me, burned it in the light of a lantern that was held, and extinguished the ashes with his foot. Not a word was spoken. I was brought here, to my living grave.

"If it had pleased God to put it in the hard heart of either of the brothers, in all these frightful years, to grant me any tidings of my dearest wife—so much as to let me know by a word whether alive or dead—I might have thought that He had not quite abandoned them. But now I believe that the mark of the red cross is fatal to them, and that they have no part in His mercies. And them and their descendants, to the last of their race, I, Alexandre Manette, unhappy prisoner, do this last night of the year 1767, in my unbearable agony, denounce to the times when all these things shall be answered for. I denounce them to heaven and to earth."

A terrible sound arose when the reading of this document was done. Little need to show how the Defarges had not made the paper public with the other captured Bastille memorials and had kept it, biding their time. Little need to show that this detested family name was wrought into the fatal register. The man never trod ground whose virtues and services would have sustained him in that place that day, against such denunciation.

And all the worse for the doomed man

that the denouncer was a well-known citizen, his own attached friend, the father of his wife. One of the frenzied aspirations of the populace was, for imitations of the questionable public virtues of antiquity, and for sacrifices and self-immolations on the people's altar. Therefore when the President said—else had his own head quivered on his shoulders—that the good physician of the Republic would deserve better still of the Republic by rooting out an obnoxious family of aristocrats, and would doubtless feel a sacred glow and joy in making his daughter a widow and her child an orphan, there was wild excitement, patriotic fervor, not a touch of human sympathy.

"Much influence around him, has that Doctor?" murmured Madame Defarge, smiling to The Vengeance. "Save him now, my Doctor, save him!"

At every Juryman's vote, there was a roar. Another and another. Roar and roar.

Unanimously voted. At heart and by descent an aristocrat, an enemy of the Republic, a notorious oppressor of the People. Back to the Conciergerie, and Death within four-and-twenty hours!

WHAT DO YOU SAY?

1. (a) What is the significance of the chapter title? *(b)* How was the word "shadow" brought into earlier chapters?

2. (a) Who were the twin brothers? *(b)* Which one have you met earlier in the novel?

3. (a) What does the chapter explain about the cause of Doctor Manette's imprisonment? *(b)* How does the chapter help you understand Madame Defarge's bitterness toward the aristocratic class?

4. (a) In the last paragraph of the letter, what does Doctor Manette mean by his statement that he denounces "to the times when all these things shall be answered for"? *(b)* How does Madame Defarge interpret this statement?

5. Was Doctor Manette aware of Charles Darnay's relationship to the Marquis St. Evrémonde? Give evidence supporting your answer.

CHAPTER XI
Dusk

The wife of the innocent man thus doomed to die fell under the sentence, as if she had been mortally stricken. But so strong was the voice within her, representing that she of all the world must uphold him in his misery, that it quickly raised her, even from that shock.

The Judges having to take part in a public demonstration out of doors, the Tribunal adjourned. The quick noise and movement of the court's emptying itself had not ceased, when Lucie stood stretching out her arms toward her husband, with nothing in her face but love and consolation.

"If I might touch him! If I might embrace him once! Oh, good citizens, if you would have so much compassion for us!"

There was but a jailer left, with two of the men who had taken him last night, and Barsad. The people had all poured out to the show in the streets. Barsad proposed, "Let her embrace him; it is but a moment." They passed her over the seats in the hall to a raised place, where he, by leaning over the dock, could fold her in his arms.

"Farewell, darling of my soul. My parting blessing on my love. We shall meet again, where the weary are at rest!" They were her husband's words, as he held her.

"I can bear it, dear Charles. I am supported from above; don't suffer for me. A parting blessing for our child."

"I send it to her by you, say farewell to her by you."

Her father had followed her, and would have fallen on his knees to them, but Darnay seized him, crying:

"No, no! What have you done that you should kneel to us! We know now what a struggle you underwent when you suspected my descent, and when you knew it. We thank you with all our hearts, and all our love and duty. Heaven be with you!"

Her father's only answer was to draw his

hands through his white hair, and wring them with a shriek of anguish.

"It could not be otherwise," said the prisoner. "Be comforted, and Heaven bless you!"

As he was drawn away, his wife released him, and stood looking after him with her hands touching one another in the attitude of prayer, and with a radiant look upon her face, in which there was even a comforting smile. As he went out at the prisoners' door, she turned, laid her head lovingly on her father's breast, tried to speak to him, and fell at his feet.

Then Sydney Carton came and took her up. Only her father and Mr. Lorry were with her. His arm trembled as it raised her, and supported her head. Yet, there was an air about him that was not all of pity—that had a flush of pride in it.

"Shall I take her to a coach? I shall never feel her weight." He carried her to the door, and laid her tenderly down in a coach. Her father and their old friend got into it, and he took his seat beside the driver.

When they arrived at the gateway where he had paused not many hours before, he lifted her again, carried her up the staircase, and laid her on a couch, where her child and Miss Pross wept over her.

"Don't recall her to herself," he said softly; "she is better so. Don't revive her while she only faints."

"Oh, Carton, Carton, dear Carton!" cried little Lucie, throwing her arms round him, in a burst of grief. "Now that you have come, I think you will do something to help mamma, something to save papa!"

He bent over, laid her blooming cheek against his and looked at her unconscious mother.

"Before I go," he said, and paused—"I may kiss her?"

It was remembered afterwards that when he bent down and touched her face with his lips, he murmured some words. The child, who was nearest to him told them afterwards, and told her grandchildren when she was a handsome old lady, that she heard him say, "A life you love."

When he had gone into the next room, he turned on Mr. Lorry and her father, and said to the latter:

"You had great influence but yesterday, Doctor Manette; let it at least be tried. These Judges are very friendly to you, are they not?"

"I had the strongest assurances that I should save him," he returned in great trouble, and very slowly.

"Try them again. The hours are few and short, but try."

"I intend to try. I will not rest a moment."

"That's well. I have known such energy as yours do great things before now—though never," he added, with a smile and a sigh together, "such as this. Of little worth as life is when we misuse it, it is worth that effort. It would cost nothing to lay down if it were not."

"I will go," said Doctor Manette, "to the Prosecutor and the President straight, and to others whom it is better not to name. But stay! There is a celebration in the streets, and no one will be accessible until dark."

"Well! It is a forlorn hope at best, not much forlorner for being delayed till dark. I should like to know how you speed; though, mind! I expect nothing! When are you likely to have seen these dread powers, Doctor Manette?"

"Immediately after dark, I should hope. Within an hour or two from this."

"It will be dark soon after four. Let us stretch the hour or two. If I go to Mr. Lorry's at nine, shall I hear what you have done, either from our friend or from yourself?"

"Yes."

"May you prosper!"

Mr. Lorry followed Sydney to the outer door, and, touching him on the shoulder, caused him to turn.

"I have no hope," said Mr. Lorry, in a sorrowful whisper.

"Nor have I."

"If any one or all of these men were disposed to spare him, I doubt if they durst spare him after the demonstration in the court."

"And so do I. I heard the fall of the ax in that sound."

Mr. Lorry leaned his arm upon the doorpost, and bowed his face upon it.

"Don't despond," said Carton, very gently; "don't grieve. I encouraged Doctor Manette in this idea, because I felt that it might one day be consolatory to her. Otherwise, she might think 'his life was wantonly thrown away or wasted,' and that might trouble her."

"Yes, yes, yes," returned Mr. Lorry, drying his eyes, "you are right. But he will perish; there is no real hope."

"Yes. He will perish; there is no real hope," echoed Carton. And walked with a settled step, downstairs.

WHAT DO YOU SAY?

1. Who would you say is the main character in this chapter? Why?

2. Why do you think Dickens titled the chapter "Dusk"?

3. In kissing Lucie, Carton repeats the phrase "A life you love." Where and in what context has this phrase occurred earlier in the story?

4. Why does Carton encourage Doctor Manette to attempt to obtain Charles Darnay's release even though he feels the attempt is doomed to failure?

CHAPTER XII
Darkness

Sydney Carton paused in the street. "At Tellson's Banking House at nine," he said, musing. "Shall I do well, in the meantime, to show myself? I think so. It is best these people should know there is such a man as I here; it is a sound precaution, may be a necessary preparation. But care! Let me think it out!"

Checking his steps, he took a turn or two in the already darkening street, and traced the thought in his mind to its possible consequences. His first impression was confirmed. "It is best," he said, finally resolved, "that these people should know there is such a man as I here." And he turned his face toward Saint Antoine.

Defarge had described himself, that day, as keeper of a wine shop in Saint Antoine. It was not difficult for one who knew the city well to find his house without asking any question. Having ascertained its situation, Carton dined at a place of refreshment and fell sound asleep after dinner. For the first time in many years he had no strong drink. Last night he had dropped the brandy slowly down on Mr. Lorry's hearth like a man who had done with it.

It was as late as seven o'clock when he awoke refreshed, and went out into the streets again. As he passed along toward Saint Antoine, he stopped at a shop window where there was a mirror, and slightly altered the disordered arrangement of his loose cravat, and his coat collar, and his wild hair. This done, he went on direct to Defarge's, and went in.

There happened to be no customer in the shop but Jacques Three of the restless fingers and the creaking voice. This man, whom he had seen upon the Jury, stood drinking at the little counter, in conversation with the Defarges, man and wife. The Vengeance assisted in the conversation, like a regular member of the establishment.

As Carton walked in, took his seat, and asked—in very indifferent French—for a small measure of wine, Madame Defarge cast a careless glance at him, and then a keener, and then a keener, and then advanced to him herself, and asked him what it was he had ordered.

He repeated what he had already said.

"English?" asked Madame Defarge, inquisitively. He answered, in his former strong foreign accent, "Yes, madame, yes. I am English!"

Madame Defarge returned to her counter to get the wine, and, as he took up a Jacobin journal[1] and feigned to pore over it, he heard her say, "I swear to you, like Evrémonde!"

Defarge brought him the wine, and gave him Good evening.

"How?"

"Good evening."

"Oh! Good evening, citizen," filling his glass. "Ah! and good wine. I drink to the Republic."

Defarge went back to the counter and said, "Certainly, a little like." Madame sternly retorted, "I tell you a good deal like." Jacques Three pacifically remarked, "He is so much in your mind, madame." The Vengeance added, with a laugh, "And you are looking forward with so much pleasure to seeing him once more tomorrow!"

Carton followed the lines of his paper, with a slow fore-finger, and a studious, absorbed face. They were all leaning on the counter close together, speaking low. After a silence, during which they all looked toward him without disturbing his attention, they resumed their conversation.

"It is true what madame says," observed Jacques Three. "Why stop? There is great force in that. Why stop?"

"Well, well," reasoned Defarge, "but one must stop somewhere. After all, the question is still where?"

"At extermination," said madame.

"Magnificent!" croaked Jacques Three. The Vengeance, also, highly approved.

"Extermination is good doctrine, my wife," said Defarge, rather troubled. "But this Doctor has suffered much; you observed his face when the paper was read."

"I observed his face!" repeated madame, contemptuously and angrily. "Yes. I observed his face to be not the face of a true friend of the Republic."

"And you observed, my wife," said Defarge, in a deprecatory manner, "the anguish of his daughter."

"I observed his daughter," repeated madame; "yes, more times than one. I observed her today, and other days. I observed her in the court, and in the street by the prison. Let me but lift my finger—!" She seemed to raise it and let it fall as if the ax had dropped.

"The citizeness is superb!" croaked the Juryman.

"She is an angel!" said The Vengeance, and embraced her.

"As to thee," pursued madame, implacably, addressing her husband, "if it depended on thee—which, happily, it does not—thou would'st rescue this man even now."

"No!" protested Defarge. "But I would leave the matter there. I say, stop there."

"See you," said Madame Defarge, wrathfully. "For crimes as tyrants and oppressors, I have this race a long time on my register, doomed to destruction and extermination. Ask my husband, is that so."

"It is so," assented Defarge, without being asked.

"In the beginning of the great days, when the Bastille falls, he finds this paper of today, and brings it home; in the middle of the night when this place is clear and shut, we read it, here on this spot. Ask him, is that so."

"It is so," assented Defarge.

"That night I tell him, when the paper is read through and the lamp is burnt out, that I have a secret to communicate. Ask him, is that so."

"It is so," assented Defarge again.

"I communicate to him that secret. I tell him, Defarge, I was brought up among the fishermen of the seashore, and that peasant family so injured by the two Evrémonde brothers, as that Bastille paper describes, is my family. Defarge, that sister of the mortally wounded boy was my sister, that husband was my sister's husband, that unborn child was their child, that brother was my

---

1. *Jacobin* (jak'ə bin) *journal,* a periodical published by the members of the radical political club organized during the revolution; in current usage the term refers to anyone who holds radical political views.

brother, that father was my father, and that summons to answer for those things descends to me! Ask him, is that so."

"It is so," assented Defarge once more.

"Then tell Wind and Fire where to stop," returned madame; "but don't tell me."

Customers entered, and the group was broken up. The English customer paid for what he had had, perplexedly counted his change, and asked, as a stranger, to be directed towards the National Palace. Madame Defarge took him to the door, and put her arm on his, in pointing out the road. The English customer was not without reflections then, that it might be a good deed to seize that arm, lift it, and strike under it sharp and deep.

But he went his way, and was soon swallowed up in the shadow of the prison wall. At the appointed hour he emerged from it to present himself in Mr. Lorry's room again, where he found the old gentleman walking to and fro in restless anxiety. He said he had been with Lucie until just now, and had only left her for a few minutes, to come and keep his appointment. Her father had not been seen since toward four o'clock. She had hopes that his mediation might save Charles, but they were very slight. He had been more than five hours gone; where could he be?

Mr. Lorry waited until ten; but, Doctor Manette not returning, and he being unwilling to leave Lucie any longer, it was arranged that he should go back to her, and come to the Banking house again at midnight. In the meanwhile, Carton would wait alone by the fire for the Doctor.

He waited, and the clock struck twelve; but Doctor Manette did not come. Mr. Lorry returned, found no tidings of him, and brought none. Where could he be?

They were discussing this question, when they heard him on the stairs. The instant he entered the room, it was plain that all was lost.

Whether he had really been to anyone, was never known. As he stood staring at them, they asked him no question, for his face told them everything.

"I cannot find it," said he, "and I must have it. Where is it?"

His head and throat were bare, and, as he spoke, he took his coat off, and let it drop on the floor.

"Where is my bench? I can't find it. Time presses: I must finish those shoes."

They looked at one another, and their hearts died within them.

"Come, come!" said he, in a whimpering miserable way; "let me get to work. Give me my work." Receiving no answer, he tore his hair. "Don't torture a poor forlorn wretch," he implored them, "but give me my work!"

Lost, utterly lost!

It was so clearly beyond hope to try to restore him—that—as if by agreement—they each soothed him to sit down before the fire, with a promise that he should have his work presently. He sank into the chair, and brooded. As if all that had happened since the garret were a dream, Mr. Lorry saw him shrink into the exact figure that Defarge had had in keeping.

Affected as they both were by this spectacle of ruin, it was not a time to yield to emotions. His lonely daughter, bereft of her final reliance, appealed to them both too strongly. They looked at one another with one meaning in their faces. Carton was the first to speak:

"The last chance is gone; it was not much. Yes; he had better be taken to her. But before you go, will you, for a moment, steadily attend to me? Don't ask me why I make the stipulations I am going to make, and exact the promise I am going to exact; I have a reason—a good one."

"I do not doubt it," answered Mr. Lorry. "Say on."

The figure in the chair was all the time rocking itself to and fro, and moaning. Carton stooped to pick up the coat. As he did so, a small case fell on the floor. Carton took it up, and there was a folded paper in it. "We should look at this!" he said. Mr. Lorry nodded. He opened it, and exclaimed, "Thank God!"

"What is it?" asked Mr. Lorry, eagerly.

"A moment! Let me speak of it in its place. First," he put his hand in his coat, and took another paper from it, "that is the certificate which enables me to pass out of this city. You see—Sydney Carton, an Englishman?

"Keep it for me. I shall see him tomorrow, you remember, and I had better not take it into the prison."

"Why not?"

"I don't know; I prefer not to do so. Now, take this paper that Doctor Manette has carried about him. It is a similar certificate, enabling him and his daughter and her child, at any time, to pass the Barrier and the frontier. You see?"

"Yes!"

"Perhaps he obtained it as his last and utmost precaution against evil, yesterday. Put it up carefully with mine and your own. Now, observe! I never doubted until within this hour or two that he had, or could have, such a paper. It is good, until recalled. But it may be soon recalled, and, I have reason to think, will be."

"They are not in danger?"

"They are in great danger—danger of denunciation by Madame Defarge. I know it from her own lips. Since then, I have seen the spy. He confirms me. He knows that a wood sawyer, living by the prison wall, has been rehearsed by Madame Defarge as to his having seen her"—he never mentioned Lucie's name—"making signs and signals to prisoners. It is easy to foresee that the pretence will be the common one, a prison plot, and that it will involve her life—and perhaps her child's—and perhaps her father's—for both have been seen with her at that place. Don't look so horrified. You will save them all."

"Heaven grant I may, Carton! But how?"

"I am going to tell you how. It will depend on you, and it could depend on no better man. This new denunciation will certainly not take place until after tomorrow. You know it is a capital crime to mourn for, or sympathize with, a victim of the Guillotine. She and her father would unquestionably be guilty of this crime, and this woman would wait to add that strength to her case, and make herself doubly sure. You follow me?"

"So attentively, and with so much confidence in what you say, that for the moment I lost sight," touching the back of the Doctor's chair, "even of this distress."

"Your preparations have been completed to return to England. Early tomorrow have horses ready, so that they may be in starting trim at two o'clock in the afternoon."

"It shall be done!" His manner was so fervent and inspiring that Mr. Lorry caught the flame and was as quick as youth.

"You are a noble heart. Did I say we could depend upon no better man? Tell her, tonight, what you know of her danger as involving her child and her father. Dwell upon that, for she would lay her own fair head beside her husband's cheerfully." He faltered for an instant; then went on as before. "For the sake of her child and her father, press upon her the necessity of leaving Paris, with them and you, at that hour. Tell her that it was her husband's last arrangement. Tell her that more depends upon it than she dare believe, or hope. You think that her father, even in this sad state, will submit himself to her; do you not?"

"I am sure of it."

"I thought so. Quietly and steadily have all these arrangements made in the courtyard here, even to the taking of your own seat in the carriage. The moment I come to you, take me in, and drive away."

"I understand that I wait for you under all circumstances?"

"You have my certificate in your hand with the rest, you know, and will reserve my place. Wait for nothing but to have my place occupied, and then for England!"

"Why, then," said Mr. Lorry, grasping his

eager but so firm and steady hand, "it does not all depend on one old man, but I shall have a young and ardent man at my side."

"By the help of heaven you shall! Promise me solemnly that nothing will influence you to alter the course on which we now stand pledged to one another."

"Nothing, Carton."

"Remember these words tomorrow: change the course, or delay in it—for any reason—and no life can possibly be saved, and many lives must inevitably be sacrificed."

"I will remember them. I hope to do my part faithfully."

"And I hope to do mine. Now, good-by!"

Though he said it with a grave smile of earnestness, and though he even put the old man's hand to his lips, he did not part from him then. He helped him so far to arouse the rocking figure before the dying embers, as to get a cloak and hat put upon it, and to tempt it forth to find where the bench and work were hidden that it still moaningly besought to have. He walked on the other side of it and protected it to the courtyard of the house where the afflicted heart—so happy in the memorable time when he had revealed his own desolate heart to it—outwatched the awful night. He entered the courtyard and remained there for a few moments alone, looking up at the light in the window of her room. Before he went away, he breathed a blessing toward it, and a farewell.

WHAT DO YOU SAY?

1. What directions did Sydney Carton give Mr. Lorry?

2. *(a)* What was Sydney Carton's object in going to the wine shop? *(b)* What were the Defarges discussing when Carton entered the wine shop? *(c)* Explain their difference of opinion regarding Charles Darnay, citing preceding events and statements.

3. What effect does the verdict have on Doctor Manette?

CHAPTER XIII
Fifty-Two

In the black prison of the Conciergerie the doomed of the day awaited their fate. They were in number as the weeks of the year. Fifty-two were to roll that afternoon to the boundless everlasting sea. Before their cells were quit of them, new occupants were appointed; before their blood ran into the blood spilled yesterday, the blood that was to mingle with theirs tomorrow was already set apart.

Two score and twelve were told off. From the Farmer-General of seventy, whose riches could not buy his life, to the seamstress of twenty, whose poverty and obscurity could not save her.

Charles Darnay, alone in a cell, had sustained himself with no flattering delusion since he came to it from the Tribunal. In every line of the narrative he had heard, he had heard his condemnation. He had fully comprehended that no personal influence could possibly save him, that he was virtually sentenced by the millions.

Nevertheless, it was not easy, with the face of his beloved wife fresh before him, to compose his mind to what it must bear. His hold on life was strong, and it was very, very hard, to loosen; by gradual efforts and degrees unclosed a little here, it clenched the tighter there; and when he brought his strength to bear on that hand and it yielded, this was closed again. But all this was at first. Next followed the thought that much of the future peace of mind enjoyable by the dear ones depended on his quiet fortitude. So by degrees he calmed into the better state, when he could raise his thoughts much higher, and draw comfort down.

Before dark on the night of his condemnation, he had traveled thus far on his last way. Being allowed to purchase the means of writing, and a light, he sat down to write until such time as the prison lamps should be extinguished.

He wrote a long letter to Lucie, showing her that he had known nothing of her father's imprisonment, until he had heard of it from herself, and that he had been as ignorant as she of his father's and uncle's responsibility for that misery, until the paper had been read. He had already explained to her that his concealment from herself of the name he had relinquished was the one condition—fully intelligible now—that her father had attached to their betrothal. He entreated her, for her father's sake, never to seek to know whether her father had become oblivious of the existence of the paper, or had had it recalled to him—for the moment, or for good—by the story of the Tower, on that old Sunday under the dear old plane tree in the garden. If he had preserved any definite remembrance of it, there could be no doubt he had supposed it destroyed with the Bastille, when he had found no mention of it among the relics of prisoners there, which had been described to all the world. He besought her to console her father, by impressing him with the truth that he had done nothing for which he could justly reproach himself, but had uniformly forgotten himself for their joint sakes. Next to her preservation of his own last grateful love and blessing, and her overcoming of her sorrow, to devote herself to their dear child, he adjured her, as they would meet in heaven, to comfort her father.

To her father himself, he wrote in the same strain; but, he told her father that he expressly confided his wife and child to his care. He told him this, very strongly, with the hope of rousing him from any despondency or dangerous retrospect toward which he foresaw he might be tending.

To Mr. Lorry, he commended them all, and explained his worldly affairs. That done, with many added sentences of grateful friendship and warm attachment, all was done. He never thought of Carton. His mind was so full of the others, that he never once thought of him.

He had time to finish these letters before the lights were put out. When he lay down on his straw bed, he thought he had done with this world. He awoke in the somber morning, unconscious where he was or what had happened, until it flashed upon his mind, "This is the day of my death!"

Thus had he come through the hours, to the day when the fifty-two heads were to fall. And now, while he was composed, and hoped that he could meet the end with quiet heroism, a new action began in his waking thoughts, which was very difficult to master.

He had never seen the instrument that was to terminate his life. How high it was from the ground, how many steps it had, where he would be stood, how he would be touched, whether the touching hands would be dyed red, which way his face would be turned, whether he would be the first, or might be the last; these and many similar questions, in no wise directed by his will, obtruded themselves over and over again. Neither were they connected with fear; he was conscious of no fear. Rather, they originated in a strange besetting desire to know what to do when the time came; a desire gigantically disproportionate to the few swift moments to which it referred.

The hours went on as he walked to and fro, and the clocks struck the numbers he would never hear again. Nine gone forever, ten gone forever, eleven gone forever, twelve coming on to pass away. Twelve gone forever.

He had been apprized that the final hour was Three, and he knew he would be summoned some time earlier, as the tumbrils jolted slowly through the streets. He resolved to keep Two before his mind, as the hour, and so to strengthen himself that he might be able to strengthen others.

Walking regularly to and fro with his arms folded on his breast, a very different man from the prisoner who had walked to and fro at La Force, he heard One struck away from him, without surprise. Devoutly thankful to heaven for his recovered self-possession, he thought, "There is but another now," and turned to walk again.

Footsteps in the stone passage outside the door. He stopped. The lock turned. Before the door opened, a man said in a low voice in English: "He has never seen me here. Go in alone; I wait near. Lose no time!"

The door was quickly opened and closed, and there stood before him quiet, with the light of a smile on his features, and a cautionary finger on his lip, Sydney Carton.

There was something so bright and remarkable in his look that, for the first moment, the prisoner misdoubted him to be an apparition. But he spoke, and it was his voice; he took the prisoner's hand, and it was his real grasp.

"Of all the people upon earth, you least expected to see me?" he said.

"I could not believe it to be you. I can scarcely believe it now. You are not —a prisoner?"

"No. I am accidentally possessed of a power over one of the keepers here, and in virtue of it I stand before you. I come from her—your wife, dear Darnay."

The prisoner wrung his hand.

"I bring you a request from her."

"What is it?"

"A most earnest, pressing, and emphatic entreaty, addressed to you in the voice so dear to you."

The prisoner turned his face partly aside.

"You have no time to ask me why I bring it, or what it means; I have no time to tell you. You must comply with it—take off those boots you wear, and draw on these of mine."

There was a chair against the wall of the cell, behind the prisoner. Carton had already, with the speed of lightning, got him down into it and stood over him, barefoot.

"Draw on these boots of mine. Quick!"

"Carton, there is no escaping from this place; it never can be done. You will only die with me. It is madness."

"It would be madness if I asked you to escape; but do I? Change that cravat for this of mine, that coat for this of mine. While you do it, let me take this ribbon from your hair, and shake out your hair like this of mine!"

With a strength both of will and action, that appeared quite supernatural, he forced all these changes upon him. The prisoner was like a young child in his hands.

"Carton! Dear Carton! It is madness. It cannot be accomplished, it has been attempted, and has always failed. I implore you not to add your death to the bitterness of mine."

"Do I ask you, my dear Darnay, to pass the door? When I ask that, refuse. There are pen and ink and paper on this table. Is your hand steady enough to write?"

"It was when you came in."

"Write what I shall dictate. Quick, friend, quick!"

Bewildered, Darnay sat down at the table. Carton, with his right hand in his breast, stood close beside him.

"Write exactly as I speak."

"To whom do I address it?"

"To no one." Carton still had his hand in his breast.

"Do I date it?"

"No."

The prisoner looked up, at each question. Carton, standing over him with his hand in his breast, looked down.

" 'If you remember,' " said Carton, dictating, " 'the words that passed between us, long ago, you will readily comprehend this when you see it. You do remember them, I know.' " He was drawing his hand from his breast.

"What is it in your hand?"

"You shall know directly. Write on; there are but a few words more." He dictated again. " 'I am thankful that the time has come, when I can prove them.' " As he said these words with his eyes fixed on the writer, his hand slowly and softly moved down close to the writer's face.

The pen dropped from Darnay's fingers on the table, and he looked about him vacantly.

"What vapor is that?" he asked.

"Vapor?"

"Something that crossed me?"

"I am conscious of nothing; there can be nothing here. Take up the pen and finish. Hurry, hurry!"

As if his memory were impaired, or his faculties disordered, the prisoner made an effort to rally his attention. As he looked at Carton with clouded eyes and with an altered manner of breathing, Carton looked steadily at him.

"Hurry, hurry!"

The prisoner bent over the paper once more.

"'If it had been otherwise'"; Carton's hand was again watchfully and softly stealing down; "'If it had been otherwise'"; the hand was at the prisoner's face; "'I should but have had so much the more to answer for.'" Carton saw the pen trailing off into unintelligible signs. The prisoner sprang up with a reproachful look, but Carton's hand was firm at his nostrils. For a few seconds he struggled with the man who had come to lay down his life for him; but, within a minute or so, he was stretched insensible on the ground.

Quickly, Carton dressed himself in the clothes the prisoner had laid aside, combed back his hair, and tied it with the ribbon the prisoner had worn. Then, he softly called, "Come in!" and the spy presented himself.

"See?" said Carton, as he kneeled beside the insensible figure, putting the paper in the breast; "is your hazard very great?"

"Mr. Carton," the spy answered, "my hazard is not *that,* if you are true to the whole of your bargain."

"Don't fear me. I will be true to the death."

"You must be, Mr. Carton, if the tale of fifty-two is to be right. Being made right by you in that dress, I shall have no fear."

"Have no fear! I shall soon be out of the way of harming you, and the rest will soon be far from here, please God! Now, get assistance and take me to the coach."

"You?" said the spy nervously.

"Him, man, with whom I have exchanged. You go out at the gate by which you brought me in?"

"Of course."

"I was weak and faint when you brought me in; I am fainter now you take me out. The parting interview has overpowered me. Such a thing has happened here, often. Quick! Call assistance!"

"You swear not to betray me?" said the trembling spy.

"Man, man!" returned Carton, stamping his foot. "You waste precious moments now? Take him yourself to the courtyard you know of, place him in the carriage, show him to Mr. Lorry, tell him to give him no restorative but air, and to remember my words and his promise of last night, and drive away!"

The spy withdrew, and Carton seated himself at the table. The spy returned immediately, with two men.

"How, then?" said one of them, contemplating the fallen figure. "So afflicted to find that his friend has drawn a prize in the lottery of Sainte Guillotine?"

"A good patriot," said the other, "could hardly have been more afflicted if the aristocrat had drawn a blank."

They raised the unconscious figure, placed it on a litter they had brought to the door, and bent to carry it away.

"The time is short, Evrémonde," said the spy, in a warning voice.

"I know it well," answered Carton. "Be careful of my friend, I entreat you, and leave me."

"Come, then, my children," said Barsad. "Lift him, and come away!"

The door closed, and Carton was left alone. Straining, he listened for any sound that might denote suspicion or alarm. There was none. Keys turned, doors clashed, foot-

Ronald Searle

steps passed along distant passages; no cry was raised, or hurry made. Breathing more freely in a little while, he sat down at the table, and listened again until the clock struck Two.

Sounds that he was not afraid of, for he divined their meaning, then began to be audible. Several doors were opened in succession, and finally his own. A jailer, with a list in his hand, looked in, merely saying, "Follow me, Evrémonde!" and he followed into a large dark room. He could but dimly discern the others who were brought there to have their arms bound. Some were lamenting, but these were few. The great majority were silent and still, looking fixedly at the ground.

As he stood by the wall in a dim corner, while some of the fifty-two were brought in after him, a young woman, with large patient eyes, rose from the seat where he had observed her sitting, and came to speak to him.

"Citizen Evrémonde," she said, "I am a poor little seamstress, who was with you in La Force."

He murmured for answer: "True. I forget what you were accused of?"

"Plots. Though the just heaven knows I am innocent of any. Is it likely? A poor weak creature like me?"

The forlorn smile with which she said it so touched him that tears started from his eyes.

"I am not afraid to die, but I have done nothing. I am not unwilling to die, if the Republic which is to do so much good to us poor will profit by my death; but I do not know how that can be, Citizen Evrémonde."

As the last thing on earth that his heart was to warm and soften to, it warmed and softened to this pitiable girl.

"I heard you were released, Citizen Evrémonde. I hoped it was true?"

"It was. But I was again taken and condemned."

"If I may ride with you, Citizen Evrémonde, will you let me hold your hand? I am not afraid, but I am little and weak, and it will give me more courage."

As the patient eyes were lifted to his face, he saw a sudden doubt in them, and then astonishment. He pressed the work-worn young fingers, and touched his lips.

"Are you dying for him?" she whispered.

"And his wife and child. Hush! Yes."

"Oh, you will let me hold your brave hand, stranger?"

"Hush! Yes, my poor sister; to the last."

Shadows are falling in that same hour of the early afternoon, on the Barrier with the crowd about it, when a coach going out of Paris drives up to be examined.

"Who goes here? Whom have we within? Papers!"

The papers are handed out and read.

"Alexandre Manette. Physician. French. Which is he?"

This is he; this helpless old man pointed out.

"Apparently the Citizen-Doctor is not in his right mind? The Revolution-fever has been too much for him?"

Greatly too much for him.

"Lucie. His daughter. French. Which is she?"

This is she.

"Apparently. Lucie, wife of Evrémonde; is it not?"

It is.

"Hah! Evrémonde has an assignation elsewhere. Lucie, her child. English. This is she?"

She and no other.

"Kiss me, child of Evrémonde. Now, thou hast kissed a good Republican; something new in thy family; remember it! Sydney Carton. Advocate. English. Which is he?"

He lies here in this corner of the carriage.

"Apparently the English advocate is in a swoon?"

It is hoped he will recover in the fresher air. He is not in strong health, and has separated sadly from a friend who is under the displeasure of the Republic.

"Is that all? Jarvis Lorry. Banker. English. Which is he?"

"I am he. Necessarily, being the last."

It is Jarvis Lorry who has replied to all the previous questions. It is Jarvis Lorry who has alighted and stands with his hand on the coach door, replying to a group of officials. They leisurely walk around the carriage and leisurely mount the box, to look at what little luggage it carries on the roof; the country people press nearer to the coach doors and greedily stare in; a little child, carried by its mother, has its arm held out that it may touch the wife of an aristocrat who has gone to the Guillotine.

"Behold your papers, Jarvis Lorry, countersigned."

"One can depart, citizen?"

"One can depart. Forward, postilions!"

"I salute you, citizens.—And the first danger passed!"

These are again words of Jarvis Lorry, as he clasps his hands, looks upward. There is terror in the carriage; there is the heavy breathing of the insensible traveler.

"Are we not going too slowly? Can they not be induced to go faster?" asks Lucie, clinging to the old man.

"It would seem like flight, my darling. I must not urge them too much; it would rouse suspicion."

"Look back, and see if we are pursued!"

"The road is clear. So far, we are not pursued."

Out of the open country, in again among dye works, tanneries, and the like. Have these men deceived us, and taken us back by another road? Is not this the same place twice over? Thank heaven, no. A village. Look back, and see if we are pursued! Hush! the posting house.

Leisurely, our four horses are taken out; leisurely, the coach stands in the little street; leisurely, the new horses come; leisurely, the new postilions follow. All the time, our overfraught hearts are beating at a rate that would far outstrip the fastest gallop of the fastest horses ever foaled.

At length the new postilions are in their saddles. We are through the village. Suddenly the horses are pulled up, almost on their haunches. We are pursued?

"Ho! Within the carriage there. Speak then!"

"What is it?" asks Mr. Lorry, looking out at window.

"How many did they say?"

"I do not understand you."

"—At the last post. How many to the Guillotine today?"

"Fifty-two."

"I said so! A brave number! My fellow citizen here would have it forty-two. Hi forward! Whoop!"

The night comes on. He moves; he is beginning to revive; he thinks they are still together; he asks him, by his name, what he has in his hand. O pity us, kind heaven, and help us! Look out, look out, and see if we are pursued.

The wind is rushing after us, the clouds are flying after us, and the whole wild night is in pursuit of us; but, so far, we are pursued by nothing else.

WHAT DO YOU SAY?

1. What earlier clues are related to Carton's actions in this chapter?

2. What rôle does John Barsad play in the deception? Why?

3. What is the significance of the letter which Carton dictates to Darnay?

AUTHOR'S CRAFT

Empathy

Have you ever shouted at a football game, jumped up and down and pushed your neighbor as you helped your team get the football across the goal line? If you have, you were experiencing a response called ***empathy,*** which means "feeling into." Your muscles were responding automatically to what was happening in front of you. You were "getting into the spirit of the thing." When you slide into home base with the batter, help land the punch that knocks out the boxer, or scream with the heroine when the villain's hands close around her throat, you are actually taking part in the emotions of these "performers," that is, you are experiencing ***empathy.***

These examples of empathy are all taken from forms of action happening in front of you. But empathy is not restricted to a situation where the action is "live" or actually happening before your eyes. You can shiver or laugh or cry or otherwise physically react in response to images which printed words evoke. When you enter fully, through imagination, into the feelings of a character in fiction, you experience an ***empathic response.*** If, for example, you recoiled with Mr. Lorry when he saw the bloody grindstone in the courtyard, if you held your breath while Sydney Carton was exchanging places with Charles Darnay, if you breathed more quickly during the Darnays' escape from Paris, you were experiencing empathy.

Be alert to the many empathic responses you will find yourself experiencing in the next two chapters.

CHAPTER XIV
The Knitting Done

Madame Defarge held darkly ominous council with The Vengeance and Jacques Three. Not in the wine shop did Madame Defarge confer with these ministers, but in the shed of the wood sawyer, erst a mender of roads.

"But our Defarge," said Jacques Three, "is undoubtedly a good Republican? Eh?"

"My husband, fellow citizen, is a good Republican and a bold man. But my husband is so weak as to relent toward this Doctor."

"It is a great pity," croaked Jacques Three.

"See you," said madame, "I care nothing for this Doctor, I. He may wear his head or lose it. But, the Evrémonde people are to be exterminated, and the wife and child must follow the husband and father."

Madame Defarge cast down her eyes, and reflected a little.

"The child also," observed Jacques Three, with a meditative enjoyment of his words, "has golden hair and blue eyes. And we seldom have a child there. It is a pretty sight!"

"In a word," said Madame Defarge, coming out of her short abstraction, "I cannot trust my husband in this matter. I feel, since last night, that I dare not confide to him the details of my projects; also I feel that if I delay, there is danger of his giving warning, and then they might escape."

"That must never be," croaked Jacques Three.

"In a word," Madame went on, "my husband has not my reason for pursuing this family to annihilation; I have not his reason for regarding this Doctor with sensibility. I must act for myself, therefore. Come hither, citizen."

The wood sawyer, who held her in mortal fear, advanced with his hand to his red cap.

"Touching those signals, little citizen," said Madame Defarge, sternly, "that she made to the prisoners; you are ready to bear witness to them this very day?"

"Aye, aye," cried the sawyer. "Every day, in all weathers, from two to four, always signaling, sometimes with the little one, sometimes without."

"Clearly plots," said Jacques Three. "Transparently!"

"There is no doubt of the Jury?" inquired Madame Defarge, letting her eyes turn to him with a gloomy smile.

"Rely upon the patriotic Jury, dear citizeness. I answer for my fellow Jurymen."

"Now, let me see," said Madame Defarge, pondering again. "Can I spare this Doctor to my husband?"

"He would count as one head," observed Jacques Three. "We really have not heads enough; it would be a pity."

"He was signaling with her when I saw her," argued Madame Defarge; "I cannot speak of one without the other; and I must not be silent, and trust the case wholly to him, this little citizen here. For I am not a bad witness."

The Vengeance and Jacques Three vied with each other in protestations that she was the most admirable and marvelous of witnesses.

"He must take his chance," said Madame Defarge. "No, I cannot spare him! You are engaged at three o'clock; you are going to see the batch of today executed—

"I," said madame, "am equally engaged at the same place. After it is over—say at eight tonight—come to me, and we will give information against these people."

The wood sawyer said he would be proud to attend the citizeness. The citizeness looking at him, he became embarrassed, evaded her glance as a small dog would, and hid his confusion over the handle of his saw.

Madame Defarge beckoned the Juryman and The Vengeance and expounded her further views to them thus:

"She will now be at home, mourning and grieving, in a state of mind to impeach the justice of the Republic. She will be full of sympathy with its enemies. I will go to her."

"What an admirable woman!" exclaimed Jacques Three, rapturously. "Ah, my cherished!" cried The Vengeance.

"Take my knitting," said Madame Defarge, "and have it ready for me in my usual seat. Go there, straight; there will be a greater concourse than usual today."

"I willingly obey the orders of my Chief," said The Vengeance, kissing her cheek. "You will not be late?"

"I shall be there before the commencement."

"And before the tumbrils arrive. Be sure you are there, my soul," said The Vengeance, calling after her, for she had already turned into the street, "before the tumbrils arrive!"

Madame Defarge slightly waved her hand, to imply that she heard, and might be relied upon to arrive in good time, and so went round the corner of the prison wall.

There were many women at that time, upon whom the time laid a dreadfully disfiguring hand; but there was not one among them more to be dreaded than this ruthless woman, now taking her way along the streets. Imbued from her childhood with a brooding sense of wrong, and an inveterate hatred of a class, opportunity had developed her into a tigress. She was absolutely without pity.

It was nothing to her that an innocent man was to die for the sins of his forefathers; she saw, not him, but them. It was nothing to her that his wife was to be made a widow and his daughter an orphan; that was insufficient punishment, because they were her natural enemies and her prey, and as such had no right to live. To appeal to her was made hopeless by her having no sense of pity, even for herself.

Such a heart Madame Defarge carried under her rough robe. Carelessly worn, it was a becoming robe enough, in a weird way, and her dark hair looked rich under her coarse red cap. Lying hidden in her bosom was a loaded pistol. Lying hidden at her waist was a sharpened dagger. Thus accoutered, and walking with confident tread, Madame Defarge took her way along the streets.

When the journey of the traveling coach had been planned out last night, the difficulty of taking Miss Pross in it had engaged Mr. Lorry's attention. It was not merely desirable to avoid overloading the coach, but it was of the highest importance that the time occupied in examining it and its passengers, should be reduced to the utmost; since their escape might depend on the saving of only a few seconds. Finally, he had proposed, after anxious consideration, that Miss Pross and Jerry, who were at liberty to leave the city, should leave at three o'clock in the lightest wheeled conveyance known to that period. Unencumbered with luggage, they would soon overtake the coach, and, passing it and preceding it on the road, would order its horses in advance, and greatly facilitate its progress during the precious hours of the night when delay was most to be dreaded.

Seeing in this arrangement the hope of rendering service in that pressing emergency, Miss Pross hailed it with joy. She and Jerry had beheld the coach start, had known who it was that Solomon brought, had passed some ten minutes in tortures of suspense, and were concluding their arrangements to follow the coach, even as Madame Defarge, taking her way through the streets, drew nearer and nearer to the else-deserted lodging in which they held their consultation.

"What do you think, Mr. Cruncher," said Miss Pross, "of our not starting from here? Another carriage having already gone from here today, it might awaken suspicion."

"My opinion, miss," returned Mr. Cruncher, "is as you're right. Likewise would you do me the favor, miss, to take notice o' two promises and wows wot it is my wishes fur to record in this here crisis? First," said Mr. Cruncher, who was all in a tremble, "them poor things well out o' this, never no more will I do it, never no more!"

"I am quite sure, Mr. Cruncher," returned Miss Pross, "that you never will do it again, whatever it is."

"No, miss," returned Jerry. "Second: them poor things well out o' this, and never no more will I interfere with Mrs. Cruncher's flopping! I go so far as to say, miss, morehover," proceeded Mr. Cruncher, as from a pulpit—"and let my words be took down and took to Mrs. Cruncher through yourself—that wot my opinions respectin' flopping has undergone a change, and that wot I only hope with all my heart as Mrs. Cruncher may be a-flopping at the present time."

"If ever we get back to our native land," said Miss Pross, "you may rely upon my telling Mrs. Cruncher as much as I may be able to remember and understand of what you have so impressively said. Now, pray let us think! My esteemed Mr. Cruncher, let us think!"

Still Madame Defarge came nearer and nearer.

"If you were to go before," said Miss Pross, "stop the vehicle, and wait somewhere for me; wouldn't that be best?" Mr. Cruncher thought it might be.

"By the cathedral door," said Miss Pross. "Would it be much out of the way, to take me in, near the great cathedral door between the two towers?"

"No, miss," answered Mr. Cruncher.

"Then, like the best of men," said Miss Pross, "go to the posting house straight, and make that change."

"I am doubtful," said Mr. Cruncher, hesitating, "about leaving of you, you see."

"Have no fear for me. Take me in at the cathedral, at three o'clock, or as near it as you can, and I am sure it will be better than our going from here. Bless you, Mr. Cruncher! Think—not of me, but of the lives that may depend on us!"

This exordium, and Miss Pross' two hands in quite agonized entreaty clasping his, decided Mr. Cruncher. With an encouraging nod or two, he went out to alter the arrangements, and left her to follow as she had proposed.

Miss Pross got a basin of cold water and began laving her eyes, which were swollen and red. Haunted by feverish apprehensions, she constantly looked round to see that there was no one watching her. In one of those pauses she recoiled for she saw a figure standing in the room.

The basin fell to the ground broken, and the water flowed to the feet of Madame Defarge.

Madame Defarge looked coldly at her and said, "The wife of Evrémonde; where is she?"

It flashed upon Miss Pross' mind that the doors were all standing open, and would suggest the flight. Her first act was to shut them. She then placed herself before the door of the chamber which Lucie had occupied.

Madame Defarge's eyes followed her through this rapid movement. Miss Pross too was a determined woman and she measured Madame Defarge with her eyes.

"You shall not get the better of me. I am an Englishwoman," said Miss Pross.

Madame Defarge looked at her scornfully, but still with something of Miss Pross' own perception that they two were at bay. She saw a tight, hard, wiry woman before her. She knew full well that Miss Pross was the family's devoted friend; Miss Pross knew full well that Madame Defarge was the family's malevolent enemy.

"On my way yonder," said Madame Defarge, "where they reserve my chair and my knitting for me, I am come to make my compliments to her in passing. I wish to see her."

"I know your intentions are evil," said Miss Pross, "and depend upon it, I'll hold my own against them."

Each spoke in her own language; neither understood the other's words; both were very watchful, and intent to deduce from look and manner, what the unintelligible words meant.

"It will do her no good to keep herself concealed from me at this moment," said Madame Defarge. "Good patriots will know what that means. Let me see her. Do you hear?"

"If those eyes were bed winches," returned Miss Pross, "and I an English four poster, they shouldn't loose a splinter of me. No, you wicked woman; I am your match."

"Woman imbecile and piglike!" said Madame Defarge, frowning. "I demand to see her. Stand out of the way and let me go to her!"

"I little thought," said Miss Pross, "that I should ever want to understand your nonsensical language; but I would give all I have to know whether you suspect the truth."

Neither of them for a single moment released the other's eyes. Madame Defarge now advanced one step.

"I am a Briton," said Miss Pross, "I am desperate. The longer I keep you here, the greater hope there is for my Ladybird. I'll not leave a handful of that dark hair upon your head, if you lay a finger on me!" Her courage brought the irrepressible tears into her eyes.

This was a courage that Madame Defarge so little comprehended as to mistake for weakness. "Ha, ha!" she laughed, "you poor wretch! I address myself to that Doctor." Then she called out, "Citizen Doctor! Wife of Evrémonde! Child of Evrémonde!"

Perhaps the following silence, perhaps some latent disclosure in the expression of Miss Pross' face, whispered to Madame Defarge that they were gone. Three of the doors she opened swiftly, and looked in.

"Those rooms are all in disorder, there has been hurried packing, there are odds and ends upon the ground. There is no one in that room behind you! Let me look."

"Never!" said Miss Pross, who understood the request as perfectly as Madame Defarge understood the answer.

Madame Defarge made at the door. Miss Pross, on the instinct of the moment, seized her round the waist in both her arms, and held her tight. It was in vain for Madame Defarge to struggle and to strike; Miss Pross, with the vigorous tenacity of love, always so much stronger than hate, clasped her tight, and even lifted her from the floor in the struggle. The two hands of Madame Defarge buffeted and tore her face; but, Miss Pross, with her head down, held her round the waist, and clung to her with more than the hold of a drowning woman.

Soon Madame Defarge's hands ceased to strike, and felt at her encircled waist. "It is under my arm," said Miss Pross, in smothered tones, "you shall not draw it. I am stronger than you, I bless heaven for it. I'll hold you till one or other of us faints or dies!"

Madame Defarge's hands were at her

bosom. Miss Pross looked up, saw what it was, struck at it, struck out a flash and a crash, and stood alone—blinded with smoke.

All this was in a second. As the smoke cleared, leaving an awful stillness, it passed out on the air, like the soul of the furious woman whose body lay lifeless on the ground.

Miss Pross passed the body and ran down the stairs to call for help. Happily, she bethought herself of the consequences in time to check herself and go back. It was dreadful to go in again; but she did go in, to get the bonnet and other things she must wear. These she put on, out on the staircase, first shutting and locking the door and taking the key. She sat down on the stairs to breathe and to cry, then got up and hurried away.

By good fortune she had a veil on her bonnet, or she could hardly have gone along the streets without being stopped, for the marks of griping fingers were deep in her face, her hair was torn, and her dress was clutched and dragged a hundred ways. Crossing the bridge, she dropped the door key in the river.

Arriving at the cathedral, she thought, what if she were stopped at the gate, sent to prison, and charged with murder! In the midst of these fluttering thoughts, the escort appeared, took her in, and took her away.

"Is there any noise in the streets?" she asked him.

"The usual noises," Mr. Cruncher replied, surprised by the question and by her aspect.

"I don't hear you," said Miss Pross. "What did you say?"

"I'll nod my head," thought Mr. Cruncher, amazed, "at all events she'll see that." And she did.

"I feel," said Miss Pross, "as if there had been a flash and a crash, the last thing I should ever hear in this life."

"Blest if she ain't in a queer condition!" said Mr. Cruncher, more and more disturbed. "Wot can she have been a-takin', to keep her courage up? Hark! There's the roll of them dreadful carts! You can hear that, miss?"

"I hear nothing"—seeing that he spoke to her.

"If she don't hear the roll of those dreadful carts, now very nigh their journey's end," said Mr. Cruncher, glancing over his shoulder, "it's my opinion that indeed she never will hear anything else in this world."

And indeed she never did.

WHAT DO YOU SAY?

1. (a) For what purpose does Madame Defarge decide to visit Lucie on the day of the execution? *(b)* How do her comments about her own husband reinforce earlier events and statements?

2. What plans did Mr. Lorry make for the escape?

3. (a) What do the events of this chapter reveal about Miss Pross' character? *(b)* What strong emotion does Miss Pross' part in the struggle represent? *(c)* Madame Defarge's?

4. What hope do we have that Jerry has undergone a change in his ways?

CHAPTER XV
The Footsteps Die Out Forever

Along the Paris streets the death carts rumble, hollow and harsh. Six tumbrils carry the day's wine to La Guillotine.

Of the riders in the tumbrils, some observe all things on their last roadside, with an impassive stare; others, with a lingering interest in the ways of life and men. Some, seated with drooping heads, are sunk in silent despair. Several close their eyes, and think. Only one, a miserable creature, of a crazed aspect, is so made drunk by horror that he sings and tries to dance. Not one appeals by look or gesture to the pity of the people.

A guard of horsemen riding abreast of the tumbrils are asked some question. It would seem to be always the same question, for it is always followed by a press of people toward the third cart. The horsemen abreast of that cart frequently point out one man in it with their swords. He stands at the back of the tumbril with his head bent down, to converse with a mere girl who sits on the side of the cart, and holds his hand. Here and there in the long street of St. Honoré cries are raised against him. If they move him at all, it is only to a quiet smile, as he shakes his hair a little more loosely about his face. He cannot easily touch his face, his arms being bound.

On the steps of a church, awaiting the coming up of the tumbrils, stands the spy. He looks into the first of them; not there. He looks into the second; not there. He asks himself, "Has he sacrificed me?" His face clears as he looks into the third.

"Which is Evrémonde?" says a man behind him.

"That. At the back there."

The man cries, "Down, Evrémonde! To the Guillotine all aristocrats! Down, Evrémonde!"

"Hush, hush!" the spy entreats him, timidly.

"And why not, citizen?"

"He is going to pay the forfeit; it will be paid in five minutes more. Let him be at peace."

But the man continuing to exclaim, "Down, Evrémonde!" Evrémonde for a moment turns toward him. Evrémonde sees the spy, looks attentively at him, and goes his way.

The clocks are on the stroke of three. Seated, as in a garden of public diversion, are a number of women, busily knitting. On one of the foremost chairs, stands The Vengeance, looking about for her friend. "Thérèse!" she cried, "Who has seen her? Thérèse Defarge! Bad Fortune!" cries The Vengeance, stamping her foot in the chair, "and here are the tumbrils! Evrémonde will be dispatched in a wink, and she not here!"

The tumbrils begin to discharge their loads. Crash!—A head is held up, and the knitting women who scarcely lifted their eyes to look at it a moment ago when it could think and speak, count One.

The second tumbril empties and moves on; the third comes up. Crash!—And the knitting women, never faltering or pausing in their work, count Two.

The supposed Evrémonde descends, and the seamstress is lifted out next after him. He has not relinquished her patient hand in getting out, but still holds it as he promised.

He gently places her with her back to the crashing engine that constantly whirs up and falls, and she looks into his face and thanks him.

"But for you, dear stranger, I should not be so composed, for I am naturally a poor thing, faint of heart; nor should I have been able to raise my thoughts to Him who was put to death, that we might have hope and comfort here today. I think you were sent to me by heaven."

"Or you to me," said Sydney Carton. "Keep your eyes upon me, dear child, and mind no other object."

"I mind nothing while I hold your hand. I shall mind nothing when I let it go, if they are rapid."

"They will be rapid. Fear not!"

"You comfort me so much! I am so ignorant. Am I to kiss you now? Is the moment come?"

"Yes."

She kisses his lips; he kisses hers; they solemnly bless each other. The spare hand does not tremble as he releases it. She goes next before him—is gone; the knitting women count Twenty-two.

"I am the Resurrection and the Life, saith the Lord; he that believeth in me, though he were dead, yet shall he live; and whosoever liveth and believeth in me shall never die."

The murmuring of many voices, the upturning of many faces, the pressing on of many footsteps in the outskirts of the crowd, so that it swells forward in a mass, like one great heave of water, all flashes away. Twenty-three.

Ronald Searle

They said of him, about the city that night, that it was the peacefullest man's face ever beheld there. Many added that he looked sublime and prophetic.

One of the most remarkable sufferers by the same ax—a woman—had asked at the foot of the same scaffold, not long before, to be allowed to write down the thoughts that were inspiring her. If he had given an utterance to his, and they were prophetic, they would have been these:

"I see Barsad and Cly, Defarge, The Vengeance, the Juryman, the Judge, long ranks of the new oppressors who have risen on the destruction of the old, perishing by this retributive instrument. I see a beautiful city and a brilliant people rising from this abyss, and, in their struggles to be truly free, in their triumphs and defeats, through long long years to come, I see the evil of this time and of the previous time of which this is the natural birth, gradually making expiation for itself and wearing out.

"I see the lives for which I lay down my life, peaceful, useful, prosperous, and happy, in that England which I shall see no more. I see her with a child upon her bosom, who bears my name. I see her father, aged and bent, but otherwise restored, and faithful to all men in his healing office, and at peace. I see the good old man, so long their friend, in ten years' time enriching them with all he has, and passing tranquilly to his reward.

"I see that I hold a sanctuary in their hearts, and in the hearts of their descendants, generations hence. I see her, an old woman, weeping for me on the anniversary of this day. I see her and her husband, their course done, lying side by side in their last earthly bed, and I know that each was not more honored in the other's soul than I was in the souls of both.

"I see that child who bore my name, a man winning his way up in that path of life which once was mine. I see him winning it so well that my name is made illustrious by the light of his. I see the blots I threw upon it faded away. I see him, foremost of just judges and honored men, bringing a boy of my name, with a forehead that I know and golden hair, to this place—then fair to look upon, with not a trace of this day's disfigurement—and I hear him tell the child my story, with a tender and a faltering voice.

"It is a far, far better thing that I do than I have ever done; it is a far, far better rest that I go to than I have ever known."

WHAT DO YOU SAY?

1. *(a)* What is Barsad's reaction to the citizen who cries "Down, Evrémonde"? *(b)* What could have prompted his reaction?

2. *(a)* How did Sydney Carton at last find life's fulfillment? What sentences provide the best evidence? *(b)* What did Sydney Carton say to Lucie earlier in the novel that provided a clue to his eventual sacrifice?

3. You have seen throughout the story Dickens' own views on tyranny, oppression, and injustice. Can you find, in this last chapter, a statement, or statements, which summarize this view?

KNOW YOUR WORDS

Appropriate adjectives

Which of the descriptive words in the first list below apply to the items in the second list? Number to 20, and opposite each number write the letter of the matching item. A letter may be used more than once, and you may have reason to use more than one letter for a number. Use your glossary or a dictionary for help.

After you have had a chance to justify your work—or make corrections—during discussion, write a paragraph recounting an episode in the novel using some of the descriptive words. You may change the form of the words.

1. anonymous	*a.* Jarvis Lorry
2. arrogant	*b.* Jerry Cruncher
3. compassionate	*c.* Miss Pross
4. conventional	*d.* Lucie Manette
5. cognate	*e.* Doctor Manette
6. cynical	*f.* Charles Darnay
7. dissipated	*g.* Sydney Carton
8. eccentric	*h.* Mr. Stryver
9. expiatory	*i.* John Barsad
10. feckless	*j.* Madame Defarge
11. grotesque	*k.* The Marquis
12. gruff	*l.* The Jacquerie
13. heroic	*m.* The Roadmender
14. insidious	*n.* St. Antoine
15. persecuted	*o.* Wine
16. presumptuous	*p.* Relation of the revolution to the theme of resurrection
17. squalid	
18. symbolic	
19. vapid	*q.* Sydney Carton's death
20. vindictive	

TIMETABLE for Book the Third

1792

Book the Third opens.

In France the king's "office" is abolished.

Henceforth (January 1) the property of French émigré noblemen shall be confiscated, and the émigrés shall be treated as enemies subject to the death penalty.

Charles Darnay is arrested and imprisoned in Paris.

Lucie follows her husband to Paris.

The September Massacres occur.

1793

Louis XVI is executed (January); Marie Antionette is executed (October).

The French Revolution has a Reign of Terror (ending in the summer of 1794).

Darnay is freed, retried and condemned, then rescued. The escape from France is carried out.

1799

The French Revolution ends after ten years.

1812

Charles Dickens is born.

1837

Thomas Carlyle's The French Revolution *is published.*

1859

A Tale of Two Cities *is published.*

1870

Charles Dickens dies.

UNIT 6 REVIEW

1. The plot of *A Tale of Two Cities* contains three strands: the Manettes, the Evrémondes, and the revolutionists. At what point do these strands become most critically entangled?

2. Dickens uses many contrasts. What are some of the most striking?

3. (a) What would you list as the most important symbols in the novel? (b) What does Sydney Carton symbolize?

4. (a) What does Dickens imply about mob behavior? (b) What scenes both in France and in England best illustrate this?

5. In what ways does the French Revolution show how one extreme can produce another?

6. What does Madame Defarge represent?

7. Where does Dickens use humor in the novel?

8. To what extent does Dickens "take sides" in the novel?

SUGGESTED READING

AUSTEN, JANE, *Pride and Prejudice.* (Dodd • Dolphin) Finding husbands for five daughters can lead to rather humorous situations, but the author also uses her novel to comment on the British society of the times.

BOYD, JAMES, *Drums.* (Scribner) Sent to England by his father, young James Fraser meets John Paul Jones and comes to take an active part in the American Revolution.

BRONTE, CHARLOTTE, *Jane Eyre.* (Dodd • Dolphin) A partly autobiographical novel of a young English girl's attempt to find love and happiness.

CATHER, WILLA, *My Antonia.* (Knopf • Riverside Literature Series) In this story of a young Bohemian girl, the author creates unforgettable characters and a realistic picture of life on the Nebraska prairie.

DICKENS, CHARLES, *Oliver Twist.* (Dodd • Dolphin) In this novel, Dickens tells the story of a boy trained by criminals to be a pickpocket and of his efforts to escape from his life of crime.

DUMAS, ALEXANDRE, *The Count of Monte Cristo.* (Grosset) In this adventure-packed tale, Edmund Dantes, a young sailor, is unjustly imprisoned and, after his escape, attempts to avenge the wrongs done to him. *The Three Musketeers.* (Dodd • Pyramid Books) This story concerns the adventures of D'Artagnan and his three friends against the historical background of the colorful French court of Louis XIII.

FREEDMAN, BENEDICT AND NANCY, *Mrs. Mike.* (Coward-McCann • Bantam Books) Sixteen-year-old Katherine O'Fallon leaves her Boston home to marry Sergeant Mike Flanagan of the Canadian mounted police and together they face the rugged life of Northern Canada.

HILTON, JAMES, *Goodbye, Mr. Chips.* (Little • Bantam Books) Mr. Chipping, a retired English schoolteacher, reminisces on his experiences with three generations of schoolboys at Brookfield School. *Lost Horizon.* (Morrow • Riverside Literature Series) A young Englishman narrates the story of four people and their experiences in the mysterious land of Shangri-la.

HUDSON, WILLIAM HENRY, *Green Mansions.* (Modern Library • Bantam Books) Romance and mystery are combined in the story of a young South American, and the unusual girl he discovers in the jungle.

HUGO, VICTOR, *The Hunchback of Notre Dame.* (Dodd) The famous cathedral of Paris provides the background for the tale of a faithful and devoted cripple and his attempts to shield a beautiful French girl from the fury of a mob.

JOHNSTON, MARY, *To Have and to Hold.* (Houghton) After fleeing from an English nobleman, an English girl travels to America where she marries a rough settler and attempts to adjust to a new way of life.

LLEWELLYN, RICHARD, *How Green Was My Valley.* (Macmillan) The narrator, Huw Morgan, recalls his childhood in a Welsh mining town before the smoke and dirt of industrialization had driven him away.

PATTON, FRANCES GRAY, *Good Morning, Miss Dove.* (Dodd) When the elderly Miss Dove is carried away to a doctor, the citizens of the town remember with affection their experiences in her classroom.

• paperback

At Random, the final unit in *Outlooks Through Literature,* is different from any other unit in your book. It is an anthology within an anthology. Its keynote is variety. Here you will find examples of the different types of literature you have studied throughout the year—poetry, short stories, a biographical sketch, and two plays written for television. These various types of literature include selections which vary in tone, mood, style, time, and place. The characters drawn vary in personality, viewpoint, and in their worth as individuals. Studying these selections will enable you to review, reapply, and extend what you have learned about plot, characterization, setting, and elements of style. In addition, two other types of literature are introduced—the essay and the speech.

Unit 7

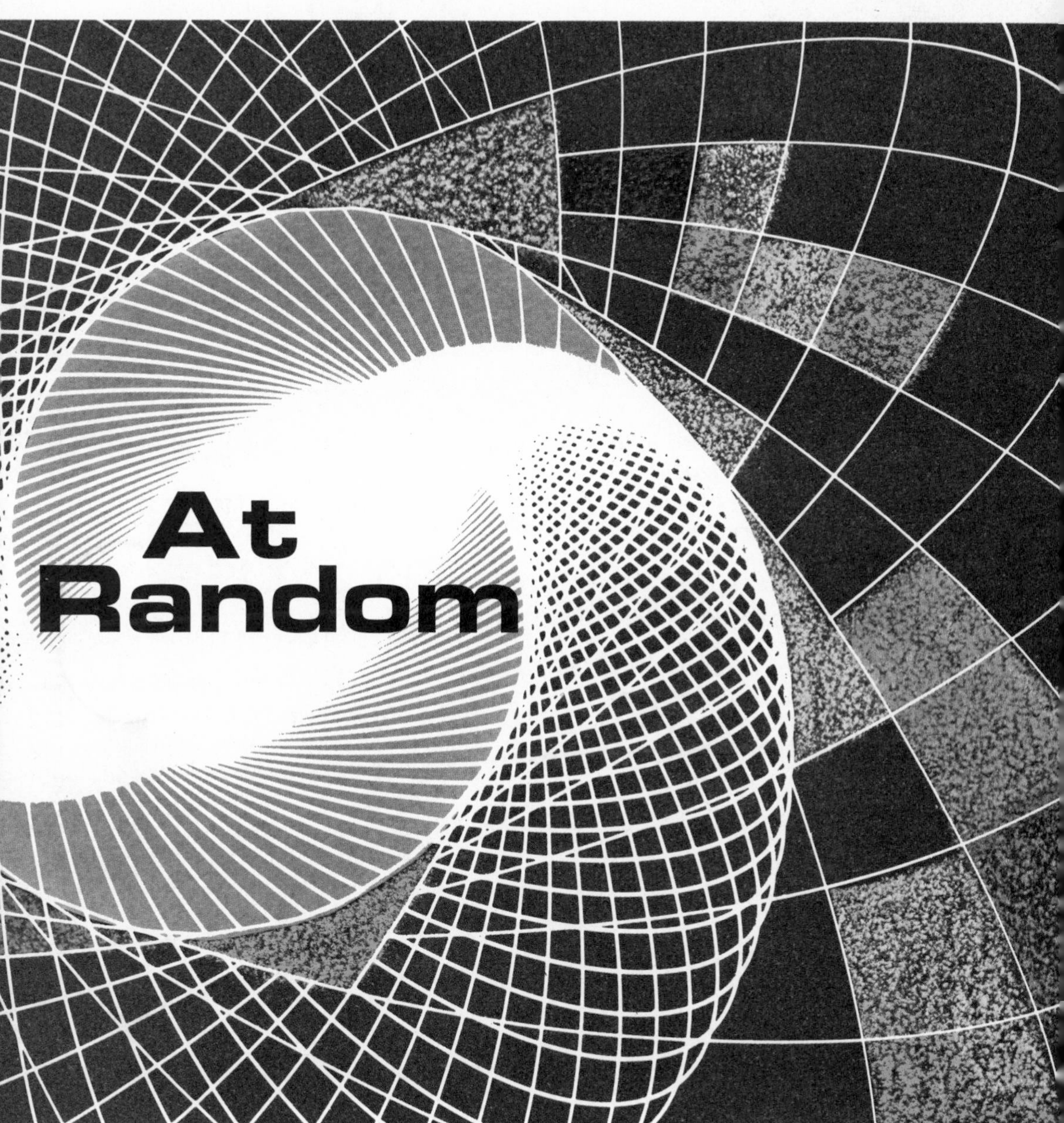

You have not yet discussed in this book the essay as a type of literature. That is because it is often very difficult to find a borderline between the essay and other prose types of literature. Sometimes the essay is so like a short story, it is difficult to tell which is which. At other times the essay may be a character sketch, a kind of biography. The only requirements for an essay are: a writer has something he wishes to say, and, he says it interestingly. Perhaps the best identifying mark of an essay is that it is personal. It reveals the feelings and mood as well as the point of view of its author. In the essay that follows, Arnold Bennett expresses his personal feeling on the subject of the relationship of literature to life.

TRANSLATING LITERATURE INTO LIFE

ARNOLD BENNETT

Lo, a parable! A certain man, having bought a large, elaborate, and complete manual of carpentry, studied it daily with much diligence and regularity. Now there were no cupboards in his house; his dining-table consisted of an arrangement of orange boxes, and he had scarcely a chair that was not a menace to the existence of the person who sat upon it. When asked why he did not set to work, and, by applying the principles of the manual, endeavor to improve the conditions of his life and of the lives of his wife and children, he replied that he was a student, and he plunged more deeply than ever into the manual of carpentry. His friends at length definitely came to the conclusion that though he was an industrious student, he was also a hopeless fool.

By which I wish to indicate that there is no virtue in study by itself. Study is not

"Translating Literature into Life" from ***Things That Have Interested Me*** by Arnold Bennett.

an end, but a means. I should blush to write down such a platitude, did I not know by experience that the majority of readers constantly ignore it. The man who pores over a manual of carpentry and does naught with it is a fool. But every book is a manual of carpentry, and every man who pores over any book whatever and does naught else with it is—deserving of an abusive epithet. What is the object of reading unless something definite comes of it? You would be better advised to play billiards. Where is the sense of reading history unless you obtain from it a clearer insight into actual politics and render yourself less liable to be duped by the rhetoric of party propaganda? Where is the sense of reading morals unless your own are improved? Where is the sense of reading biography unless it is going to affect what people will say about *you* after your funeral? Where is the sense of reading poetry or fiction unless you see more beauty, more passion, more scope for your sympathy, than you saw before?

If you boldly answer: "I only read for pleasure," then I retort that the man who drinks whisky might with force say: "I only drink whisky for pleasure." And I respectfully request you not to plume yourself on your reading, nor expect to acquire merit thereby.

But should you answer: "I do try to translate literature into life," then I will ask you to take down any book at random from your shelves and conduct in your own mind an honest inquiry as to what has been the effect of that particular book on your actual living. If you can put your hand on any subsequent period, or fractional moment, of your life and say: "I acted more wisely then, I wasn't such a dupe then, I perceived more clearly then, I felt more deeply then, I saw more beauty then, I was kinder then, I was more joyous then, I was happier then, than I should have been if I had not read that book"—if you can honestly say this, then your reading of that book has not been utterly futile. But if you cannot say this, then the chances are that you have been studying a manual of carpentry while continuing to sit on a three-legged chair and to dine off an orange box.

You say: "I know all that. But it is not so easy to translate literature into life." When I think of the time I have wasted in reading masterpieces, I stand aghast.

The explanation is simple. Idleness, intellectual sloth, is the explanation. Self-conceit is the explanation. If you were invited to meet a great writer, you would brace yourself to the occasion. You would say to yourself: "I must keep my ears open, and my brain wide-awake, so as to miss nothing." You would tingle with your own bracing of yourself. But you—I mean "we"—will sit down to a great book as though we were sitting down to a ham sandwich. No sense of personal inferiority in us? No mood to resolve! No "tuning up" of the intellectual apparatus! But just a casual, easy air, as if saying to the book: "Well, come along, let's have a look at you!"

What is the matter with our reading is casualness, languor, preoccupation. We don't give the book a chance. We don't put ourselves at the disposal of the book. It is impossible to read properly without using all one's engine-power. If we are not tired after reading, common sense is not in us. How should one grapple with a superior and not be out of breath?

But even if we read with the whole force of our brain, and do nothing else, common sense is still not in us, while sublime conceit is. For we are assuming that, without further trouble, we can possess, coördinate, and assimilate all the ideas and sensations rapidly offered to us by a mind greater than our own. The assumption has only to be stated in order to appear in its monstrous absurdity. Hence it follows that something remains to be done. This something is the act of reflection. Reading without subsequent reflection is ridiculous; it is equally a proof of folly and of vanity.

Further, it is a sign of undue self-esteem

to suppose that we can grasp the full import of an author's message at a single reading. I would not say that every book worth reading once is worth reading twice. But I would say that no book of great and established reputation is read till it is read at least twice. You can easily test the truth of this by reading again any classic; assuredly you will discover in it excellencies which had previously escaped you.

To resume and finish: Open a great book in the braced spirit with which you would listen to a great man. Read with the whole of your brain and soul. Tire yourself (would you not tire yourself at tennis?). Reflect. After an interval, read again. By this process, and by no other, will a book enter into you, become a part of you, and reappear in your life.

I have been consulted about the practice of making notes. Well, I do not care to offer counsels of perfection. My advice is simply to keep a pencil handy and to write down on a small sheet of paper (or in the inside back-cover if the book belongs to you) the number of the page on which anything has struck you, together with the merest hint, in half a dozen words, of what it was. If you do this, by the time you have finished the book, you will have automatically constructed a table and page-index of its salient points. It is well, of course, to write on the papers the title and author of the work, the name of the edition, and the date of perusal. A collection of these small sheets of paper would constitute a souvenir of one's reading. At the end of each year one might advantageously spend a few shillings in having the year's harvest bound. Say you have read a hundred books. A hundred uniform leaves would make a respectable volume, whose interest and utility I need not insist upon. A row of such volumes would really amount to the secret history of one's life.

WHAT DO YOU SAY?

1. In reading an essay one looks for the author's main viewpoint, or ***thesis.*** What sentence of Bennett's best expresses his central idea?

2. The author's first paragraph does not directly state his thesis. What is the purpose of this "parable"?

3. In your own words explain at least four things Mr. Bennett says reading should do for the reader.

4. What does the author say about reading books twice?

5. What suggestions does Bennett make about note-taking?

6. Frankness and sincerity are necessary qualities of a good essayist. Select several sentences or passages that demonstrate the author's strong feeling on the subject.

7. In your estimation, does the essayist in this essay fulfill the qualifications of having something to say and saying it interestingly? Defend your answer.

8. Why is the author's title a good one?

ARNOLD BENNETT

Born in Staffordshire in 1867, Arnold Bennett began his career as a clerk in his father's law office. After a family dispute, he left home at the age of nineteen to work as a solicitor's clerk in London. He read widely and he had done some writing when, at the suggestion of a friend, he submitted one of his short stories for publication and won a prize for it. He left his job to become sub-editor of a magazine called ***Woman*** for which he wrote beauty tips and advice to the lovelorn. He later became a free-lance writer, producing in tremendous quantity book and play reviews, short stories, and novels.

His intense interest in what he was writing at the moment, his common sense and perfect frankness, his kindness and sense of beauty all contributed to his success as a writer.

At the time of his death in 1931 he had achieved literary and financial success. Among his best known works are ***The Old Wives' Tale*** and ***Clayhanger,*** both of which present a realistic picture of the people of Staffordshire.

Often, during times off from work as a British civil service employee stationed at Gibraltar, John D. Stewart has roamed the Andalusian plains studying the great vultures that live in Spain. Here, in a descriptive essay, he describes the fascinating habits of these birds.

VULTURE COUNTRY

JOHN D. STEWART

Spain is the stronghold of the vultures. There are four listed species in Europe, two common and two rare; if they are anywhere, they are in Spain. The bearded vulture and the black survive there, the Egyptian flourishes, and the great griffon swarms. The further south you go the more numerous they become, until you reach the hot grazing plains of Andalusia.[1] There, summer and winter through, they hang in hordes in the roofless sky, for Andalusia is the vulture country.

There are three essential qualities for vulture country: a rich supply of unburied corpses, high mountains, a strong sun. Spain has the first of these, for in this sparsely populated and stony land it is not customary, or necessary, to bury dead animals. Where there are vultures in action such burial would be a self-evident waste of labor, with inferior sanitary results. Spain has mountains, too, in no part far to seek; and the summer sun is hot throughout the country. But it is hottest in Andalusia, and that is the decisive factor.

The sun, to the vulture, is not just something which makes life easier and pleasanter, a mere matter of preference. His mode of life is impossible without it. Here in Andalusia the summer sun dries up every pond and lake and almost every river. It drives the desperate frogs deep into the mud cracks and forces the storks to feed on locusts. It kills the food plants and wilts the fig trees over the heads of the panting flocks. Andalusia becomes like that part of ancient Greece, "a land where men fight for the shade of an ass."

All animals, both tame and wild, weaken in these circumstances, and the weakest go to the wall and die. The unpitying sun glares down on the corpses and speeds their putrefaction, rotting the hide and softening the sinews and the meat, to the vulture's advantage. But the sun plays a still greater part in his life. Its main and vital function, for him, is the creation of thermal currents in the atmosphere, for without these he would be helpless.

The vulture must fly high—high enough to command a wide territory, for, except at times of catastrophe, dead animals are never thick on the ground. His task is to soar to ten thousand feet, more or less, two or three times in a day, and to hang there and keep constant survey. A male griffon weighs up to sixteen pounds, so that to hoist himself up to that necessary viewpoint would call for fifty-three thousand calories, the equivalent of fifty pounds of meat. To find and eat three times his own weight in a day is clearly impossible; a short cut must be made. In the dawn of any day, in Andalusia, you may see the vulture discovering that short cut.

The eagles, buzzards, kites, and falcons

---

1. ***Andalusia,*** a plain-like region in the southern Spanish province of Seville.

are already on the wing, quartering the plain fast and low, seeking reptiles and small game. But the vulture sits on a crag and waits. He sees the sun bound up out of the sierra, and still he waits. He waits until the sun-struck rocks and the hard earth heat up and the thermal currents begin to rise. When the upstream is strong enough, he leaps out from the cliff, twists into it, and without one laborious wing-beat, spirals and soars.

By the time the vulture reaches his station, a half hour later and maybe more, the sun is blazing down on the plain and betraying every detail to his telescopic eye, and the updraft is strengthening as the day approaches its zenith. His ceiling for this day is fixed by two factors. One is the strength and buoyancy of his chosen thermal, which will vary with the strength of the sun and the behavior of the upper winds. But the more important factor, for it fixes his horizontal bearings as well, is the distribution of neighboring vultures in the sky, his colleagues and competitors.

He cocks his head from side to side and checks their various positions. There they hang, dotted across the clear sky at intervals of a mile or so—at the corners of one-mile squares. Height and lateral distances all adjusted, the vulture settles, circling slowly on his invisible support, and begins his long and lonely vigil.

This griffon vulture, which I select from the four species as being by far the most prevalent and typical, is almost sure to be a male. The female rarely leaves her nest from early March, when she lays her rough white egg, until August, when her huge poult is fledged and flying. The father has to feed and carry for all three.

At first glance, from below, he appears as one great wing, ten feet from tip to tip and two feet broad. His tail is square and very short, which is all it needs to be, for there are no sharp or sudden quirks in his flight that would call for a strong rudder. His movements are premeditated, stressless, and leisurely, for his energy must be conserved at all costs and never wasted on aerobatics.

The vulture's head and neck, too, protrude very little in front of his wing plane, and this distinguishes his flight silhouette from the eagle's. His neck is, in fact, some two feet long, but since it is bare—and must be bare—he folds it back into his collar to keep it warm. His head, apart from its nakedness, is like an eagle's; his yellow claws, which never kill and rarely carry, are shorter and not so strong. His plumage is a uniform sandy color, faded and tattered by work and waiting and, perhaps, by old age. It is relieved only by his coffee-colored ruff and the broad black primary wing feathers fingering the air.

The vulture sails in silence, for no vocal signals could serve him at such a distance from his fellows. He croaks, growls, and whistles only in his family circle, and at his feasts. He circles by almost imperceptible adjustments of his wing planes, aided by slight twists of his tail. But his head is in constant and active movement. He swivels it from one side to the other, bringing each eye in turn to bear on the earth. Then he bends his neck to right or left to check on one of his neighbors to north, south, east, or west.

The whole vulture network is interdependent. Each vulture can give and receive two signals or, as the scientists call them, "visual stimuli." Circling means "Nothing doing"; dropping, or its resultant hole in the sky, calls "Come here!" Like all other vultures, he rests reassured by the first and is rapidly and relentlessly drawn by the second.

It is demonstrable how, with a special density of nerve endings on his retina, the vulture can see a small animal from a great height. Many other birds—gannets, for example—have the same propensity. Their eyesight is surprising only when we compare it with the poor standards of our own.

But a mystery remains: how does the bird know that the animal is dead? The sense of smell is to be ruled out straightway. It is impossible that it would operate at such a distance, even allowing for the upward current of air. Birds are not, generally, well endowed in this respect, and in the vulture's case this may be especially fortunate.

No book, no expert, could answer this question for me, and I carried it through the vulture country for years, the one tantalizing imponderable, the broken link. Then, one hot afternoon, I lay down beside an old swineherd in the shade of a cork oak on the foothills overlooking the great plain of La Janda. For fifty years, he told me, he had watched pigs on that plain—the pigs, yes, and the vultures. I put my problem to him.

The swineherd's theory is not to be proved, but it is a wise one and I shall hold it until I find a better. No, he said, it is not the white belly skin that distinguishes the dead animals. White fur may fix the vulture's eye, but it does not offer him evidence of death. All herds and flocks, said the old man, lie down together and at one time. They have their place and their hour of rest. When a vulture sees an animal lying alone and apart, he is bound to notice it. The next time he crosses, the same image strikes his eye and startles him again. Over and over again he marks it and waits and watches; but now, alerted, he watches it more closely.

The next day the animal is still there; his attention is fixed upon it now; so he circles a little lower, his eye riveted, seeking the slightest movement of limb or lung. He sees none, but he continues to wait, said the old man. It takes him two days, at least, to confirm death. He goes on circling, but lower. He becomes more engrossed, and more sure. The other vultures note his behavior and move over a little in the sky. Every time he falls, they move closer. Now he is very low. He seeks the heaving of the flanks or eye movements; he sees neither. At some point, perhaps, he receives a visual stimulus in some death sign—the protruding tongue or the wide and whitened eye. Then he falls quickly, landing heavily at a little distance from the corpse.

The swineherd and I watched the first vulture land. We watched him sidling and circling the dead goat, standing erect to see better, wing tips trailing, naked neck stretched to the full, head swiveling rapidly to bring alternate eyes to bear. He hopped closer and paused, peering intently. If he could smell, even as well as we, his doubts would have been over. But he stood there, irresolute, famished yet fearful, with his bill open and his wings ready for use.

Then a big shadow swept across the brown grass, and the vulture glanced upwards. His involuntary signal had been answered, and a tall column of vultures wheeled overhead. He hopped to close quarters, stretched forward, pecked the corpse, and leapt back. He watched it for a second more; no movement. Then he croaked once, as though to bless himself, and threw himself on the body. He struck his heavy beak into the flank, flapped for balance, and thrust backwards with feet and wings to strip the hide from the ribs and belly.

Almost immediately there were eight more vultures at the corpse, and we saw that all of them sought and fought for the same place. Their aim was to penetrate, their object the viscera. Watching them thrusting their long necks deep into the belly cavity and withdrawing them befouled and bloodstained, I saw why those necks must be bare. Yes, said the swineherd, and that is the one part the vulture cannot reach to clean. His mate may clean it for him later, for pure greed, but if he had feathers there he would have maggots in them.

Now sixteen more vultures swept down, landing heavily in their haste and flap-hopping to the feast—the second square

from the sky pattern. The corpse was covered, submerged in a heaving, struggling mass of broad brown wings. A new column wheeled above us, circling lower. There should be twenty-four up there, I reckoned. There were twenty-three.

The latecomers landed on nearby trees, including ours, and their weight bent thick limbs to the ground. From points four miles distant, we could expect thirty-four more, and at the height of the carnival I counted just short of one hundred birds.

A mule lasts two hours, said the old man, and an ox, three. This goat became bones in the sun in half an hour.

As the hundred fed, or hoped and waited, many more vultures circled high above, assessing the situation and the prospects and treasuring their altitude. Toward the end, when the feasters scattered and exposed the small skeleton, the watchers flapped and drifted wearily away to resume their distant stations. But they had fulfilled their function. They had marked the spot and drawn the Egyptian vultures and the kites.

Now the little Egyptian vultures landed daintily and dodged nimbly through the throng of giants. They are bare on the face and throat only, with well-feathered head and neck, and so, perforce, they are cleaner feeders. The dirty work has been done; now the long and delicate beak comes into play. The Egyptian vultures attack the skull, the large joints, and the crevices of the pelvic girdle—all parts inaccessible to the griffon's heavy beak. They extract brains, membranes, and the spinal cord, and clip out tendons and ligaments. They dodge out through the encircling griffons with their spoils, gobble them swiftly, and dance back for more. The griffons, gorged with meat and panting in the sun, pay them scant attention.

Finally, when all but the whistling kites have left the scene, comes the great solitary bearded vulture, the fierce lammergeier.[2] His whole head is feathered, so he despises carrion. He lives aloof from all the rest of the vulture tribe, but they serve his interests, so he keeps them within sight. The old swineherd calls him *Quebrantahuesos*[3]—the bone smasher—and Aeschylus[4] noted him, long ago, for the same behavior. The lammergeier seizes the largest bones, carries them high, in his claws, and drops them on the rocks. Then he swoops down and rakes out the marrow.

Like an eagle, he can kill as well as carry with his claws, and he has not the true vulture's patient, soaring habit. He attacks flocks and herds and carries off the lambs and kids and piglets. After his work has been done nothing will remain except an empty skull and some small bones, which the ants and carrion beetles pick and polish.

Our griffon, first on the scene, will not be the first to leave it. He is sure to have

2. ***lammergeier*** (la′mėr gī′ėr). 3. ***Quebrantahuesos*** (kü brän′tä hwā′sōs). 4. ***Aeschylus*** (es′ki lus), a Greek dramatist who lived from 525-456 B. C.

gorged himself with his advantage. Crop, throat, and neck distended, he squats back on his tail, with his wings spread to steady him and his beak hanging open. From time to time he chokes and belches and gags, and it is an hour, maybe, before the meat subsides in him.

When he is ready, the griffon runs and leaps across the plain, thrashing heavily with his big wings, and labors into the air. He finds a thermal, circles in it to his altitude, then slips sideways and sweeps gently across the sierra to his distant nest.

The griffon vultures are gregarious in nesting, with colonies throughout the mountains at fairly regular intervals of thirty miles. They are said to pair for life. Certainly they return every year to the same nest. In January they begin to repair the nest, a broad and battered saucer of strong branches, topped with twigs and grass. They are careless builders, and many nests have bare rock protruding in them. No attempt is made to cover it. The egg is laid in late February and incubated for forty days. The new chick is bare and blue-skinned and looks as though he might become a dragon, but soon he sprouts white down and begins to assert the characteristics of his race. In a month he is voracious, and by the end of April he will demand four pounds of meat every day. Before he is fledged he will need eight pounds. Providentially, his demands coincide with the heyday of death.

When the male vulture arrives at the nest he settles on a nearby ledge, vomits, and sorts out the result with his beak. The female helps with this assessment, feeding herself hungrily on the larger relics. Then she offers her gape and crop to her cowering, whistling infant. The chick gobbles madly. With vultures it can never be "little and often," for animals dine irregularly, as they must, so the birds, young and old, must gorge to the neck when opportunity offers. That is their instinct and their nature.

A male vulture with family responsibilities cannot rest for long. Now that his load is delivered and eaten, he is likely to be the hungriest of the family. This, too, is as it should be, for the hunger sends him out and up again, however little daylight may remain, to circle in the sky until the sunset reddens the sierra.

Time was when the summer drought killed thousands of beasts every year and the floods of winter hundreds more. Nowadays there are fewer casualties, but the vultures still have a fairly constant food supply in the charnel gorges, which lie below most mountain villages.

Grazalema, Arcos, Casares,[5] and a hundred more were built, for protection from the raiding Moors,[6] on the edge of the precipice. All dead and dying animals, as well as all the garbage of the town, are simply pushed over the cliff and left to the birds. There is a bird in Andalusia for every class and size of refuse. From the escarpment you can watch all the scavengers of the air, soaring below you or fighting on the feast. The great black vulture may be here, the griffon and Egyptian for sure, and two kinds of kites. The cunning ravens and carrion crows wait on the outskirts, dashing in to snatch their choice. Clouds of choughs and jackdaws[7] wheel and cry above them.

There is a new feeding ground in the unfenced highways of Andalusia. As motor traffic increases, these offer more and more dead dogs, cats, kids, pigs, and rabbits. If you are abroad at dawn, it is a common thing to run down a vulture intent on scraping a dead dog off the asphalt. Even so, with an apparently limitless population of these great birds, each looking for some thirty pounds of meat every day, one wonders how they flourish.

Their wonderful feeding system has, it seems to me, one fatal flaw. They can signal

---

*5. **Grazalema, Arcos, Casares.*** Grazalema and Arcos are cities of Cadiz, the southernmost province of Spain; Casares is a province in the central part of Spain. *6. **Moors,*** a dark-skinned North African people who conquered Spain in the eighth century A. D. *7. **choughs*** (chufs) ***and jackdaws,*** small birds which are similar to crows in appearance.

"Food here," but not how much. At the feast which I have described only some succeeded in feeding at all, and only two or three ate their fill. A majority came the distance and lost their height for little or for nothing.

In Africa, also vulture country, there is no such difficulty, for there all the game is big game, and every funeral is worth attending. It may be that some of our Andalusian vultures go there in the winter. Certainly our vulture population increases here, but that is because the vultures from further north crowd in as the heat decreases and the air currents weaken in their homelands. Fortunately, there is a seasonal food supply ready for them all, for it is the time of birth, with all its failures and fatalities. After the winter storms, too, the torrents offer up their toll of corpses. And in winter, each bird has only himself to feed. But you would not doubt, if you knew the constant panic for food which dominates him summer and winter alike, that the vulture leads a competitive and anxious life. He has strong forces for survival. It is held—and we know it to be true of eagles—that the vulture has a very long life. If this longevity is a fact, then the solitary chick each year may add up to a good replacement rate.

The nest is inaccessible, and the hen guards it constantly against the only possible natural enemy—other vultures or raptors. So the survival rate must be high, as is proved by the evident increase toward saturation point.

At times, lying on my back on the plain with binoculars trained on the sky, I have seen vultures circling in two or three layers, each one high above the other. What can this mean? A hungry duplication, or triplication, hopelessly covering the same feeding ground and using the only available thermals? Or the opposite—idle and well-fed reserves standing by for surplus?

No one can tell me. But here in the vulture country there are no birds more spectacular, more fascinating to watch and to study. In time we may find out the last of their secrets. I lie on the plains and keep on watching them. And they, I know, keep on watching me.

WHAT DO YOU SAY?

1. *(a)* What three essential qualities does the Andalusian countryside offer that vultures need? *(b)* In what ways does the sun help the vulture survive?

2. How do the various parts of the anatomy, or "build," of the vulture fit him for the life he must lead?

3. *(a)* What was the swineherd's theory of how a vulture can detect a dead animal from a great height? *(b)* According to this theory what steps does a vulture take to make certain an animal is dead? *(c)* Why is it that a vulture should not risk a trip to the ground for nothing?

4. *(a)* How do vultures help one another in "coöperative" living? *(b)* In what ways are the various kinds of vultures helpful to human beings?

5. *(a)* In this essay, the author has chosen a subject interesting to him, has described his experiences, and at the same time has given us insight into his own personality. What have you learned about the author from his essay? *(b)* How does the author feel about vultures in general? Are they necessary? What purpose do they serve?

6. *(a)* What in your estimation is particularly interesting about the style and tone of this author? *(b)* Is it simple and direct, flowery, emotional? Quote lines to support your answer.

7. What is the author suggesting in the last sentence of his essay?

GRANDMA

BY

RAY BRADBURY

She was a woman with a broom or a dustpan or a washrag or a mixing spoon in her hand. You saw her cutting piecrust in the morning, humming to it, or you saw her setting out the baked pies at noon or taking them in, cool, at dusk. She rang porcelain cups like a Swiss bell ringer, to their place. She glided through the halls as steadily as a vacuum machine, seeking, finding, and setting to rights. She strolled but twice through any garden, trowel in hand, and the flowers raised their quivering fires upon the warm air in her wake. She slept quietly and turned no more than three times in a night, as relaxed as a white glove to which, at dawn, a brisk hand will return. Waking, she touched people like pictures, to set their frames straight.

But, now . . . ?

"Grandma," said everyone. "Great-grandma."

Now it was as if a huge sum in arithmetic were finally drawing to an end. She had stuffed turkeys, chickens, squabs, gentlemen, and boys. She had washed ceilings, walls, invalids, and children. She had laid linoleum, repaired bicycles, wound clocks, stoked furnaces, swabbed iodine on ten thousand grievous wounds. Her hands had flown all around about and down, gentling this, holding that, throwing baseballs, swinging bright croquet mallets, seeding black earth, or fixing covers over dumplings, ragouts, and children wildly strewn by slumber. She had pulled down shades, pinched out candles, turned switches, and—grown old. Looking back on thirty billions of things started, carried, finished and done, it all summed up, totaled out; the last decimal was placed, the final zero swung slowly into line. Now, chalk in hand, she stood back from life a silent hour before reaching for the eraser.

"Let me see now," said Great-grandma. "Let me see. . . "

With no fuss or further ado, she traveled the house in an ever-circling inventory, reached the stairs at last, and, making no special announcement, she took herself up three flights to her room where, silently, she laid herself out like a fossil imprint under the snowing cool sheets of her bed and began to die.

Again the voices:

"Grandma! Great-grandma!"

The rumor of what she was doing dropped down the stair well, hit, and spread ripples through the rooms, out doors and windows and along the street of elms to the edge of the green ravine.

"Here now, here!"

The family surrounded her bed.

"Just let me lie," she whispered.

Her ailment could not be seen in any microscope; it was a mild but ever deepening tiredness, a dim weighting of her sparrow body; sleepy, sleepier, sleepiest.

As for her children and her children's children—it seemed impossible that with such a simple act, the most leisurely act in the world, she could cause such apprehension.

"Great-grandma, now listen—what you're doing is no better than breaking a lease. This house will fall down without you. You must give us at least a year's notice!"

Great-grandma opened one eye. Ninety years gazed calmly out at her physicians like a dust-ghost from a high cupola window in a fast-emptying house.

"Tom . . . ?"

The boy was sent, alone, to her whispering bed.

"Tom," she said, faintly, far away, "in the Southern Seas there's a day in each man's life when he knows it's time to shake hands with all his friends and say good-by and sail away, and he does, and it's natural—it's just his time. That's how it is today. I'm so like you sometimes, sitting through Saturday matinees until nine at night when we send your dad to bring you home. Tom, when the time comes that the same cowboys are shooting the same Indians on the same mountaintop, then it's best to fold back the seat and head for the door, with no regrets and no walking backward up the aisle. So, I'm leaving while I'm still happy and still entertained."

Douglas was summoned next to her side.

"Grandma, who'll shingle the roof next spring?"

Every April for as far back as there were calendars, you thought you heard woodpeckers tapping the housetop. But no, it was Great-grandma somehow transported, singing, pounding nails, replacing shingles, high in the sky!

"Douglas," she whispered, "don't ever let anyone do the shingles unless it's fun for them."

"Yes'm."

"Look around come April, and say, 'Who'd like to fix the roof?' And whichever face lights up is the face you want, Douglas. Because up there on that roof you can see the whole town going toward the country and the country going toward the edge of the earth and the river shining, and the morning lake, and birds on the trees down under you, and the best of the wind all around above. Any one of those should be enough to make a person climb a weather vane some spring sunrise. It's a powerful hour, if you give it half a chance. . . ."

Her voice sank to a soft flutter.

Douglas was crying.

She roused herself again. "Now, why are you doing that?"

"Because," he said, "you won't be here tomorrow."

She turned a small hand mirror from herself to the boy. He looked at her face and himself in the mirror and then at her face again as she said, "Tomorrow morning I'll get up at seven and wash behind my ears; I'll run to church with Charlie Woodman; I'll picnic at Electric Park; I'll swim, run barefoot, fall out of trees, chew spearmint gum . . . Douglas, Douglas, for shame! You cut your fingernails, don't you?"

"Yes'm."

"And you don't yell when your body makes itself over every seven years or so, old cells dead and new ones added to your fingers and your heart. You don't mind that, do you?"

"No'm."

"Well, consider then, boy. Any man saves fingernail clippings is a fool. You ever see a snake bother to keep his peeled skin? That's about all you got here today in this bed is fingernails and snake skin. One good breath would send me up in flakes. Important thing is not the me that's lying here, but the me that's sitting on the edge of the bed looking back at me, and the me that's downstairs cooking supper, or out in the garage under the car, or in the library reading. All the new parts, they count. I'm not really dying today. No person ever died that had a family. I'll be around a long time. A thousand years from now a whole township of my offspring will be biting sour apples in the gumwood shade. That's my answer to anyone asks big questions! Quick now, send in the rest!"

At last the entire family stood, like people seeing someone off at the rail station, waiting in the room.

"Well," said Great-grandma, "there I am. I'm not humble, so it's nice seeing you standing around my bed. Now next week there's late gardening and closet-cleaning and clothes-buying for the children to do. And since that part of me which is called, for convenience, Great-grandma, won't be here to step it along, those other parts of me called Uncle Bert and Leo and Tom and Douglas, and all the other names, will have to take over, each to his own."

"Yes, Grandma."

"I don't want any Halloween parties here tomorrow. Don't want anyone saying anything sweet about me; I said it all in my time and my pride. I've tasted every victual and danced every dance; now there's one last tart I haven't bit on, one tune I haven't whistled. But I'm not afraid. I'm truly curious. Death won't get a crumb by my mouth I won't keep and savor. So don't you worry over me. Now, all of you go, and let me find my sleep. . . ."

Somewhere a door closed quietly.

"That's better." Alone, she snuggled luxuriously down through the warm snowbank of linen and wool, sheet and cover, and the colors of the patchwork quilt were bright as the circus banners of old time. Lying there, she felt as small and secret as on those mornings eighty-some-odd years ago when, wakening, she comforted her tender bones in bed.

A long time back, she thought, I dreamed a dream, and was enjoying it so much when someone wakened me, and that was the day when I was born. And now? Now, let me see . . . She cast her mind back. Where was I? she thought. Ninety years . . . how to take up the thread and the pattern of that lost dream again? She put out a small hand. *There* . . . Yes, that was it. She smiled. Deeper in the warm snow hill she turned her head upon her pillow. That was better. Now, yes, now she saw it shaping in her mind quietly, and with a serenity like a sea moving along an endless and self-refreshing shore. Now she let the old dream touch and lift her from the snow and drift her above the scarce-remembered bed.

Downstairs, she thought, they are polishing the silver, and rummaging the cellar, and dusting in the halls. She could hear them living all through the house.

"It's all right," whispered Great-grandma, as the dream floated her. "Like everything else in this life, it's fitting."

And the sea moved her back down the shore.

RAY BRADBURY

While still in high school, Ray Bradbury began writing science fiction stories and publishing them in his own magazine, ***Futuria Fantasia,*** which ran for four issues. After graduation, Bradbury worked at several jobs, choosing only those which allowed him time to write. In 1942, he decided to devote himself completely to writing and his short stories, radio dramas, and television plays have since been widely acclaimed both by critics and by the general public.

Though his reputation is based largely on his skill as a science fiction writer, Bradbury also shows facility in creating distinct and realistic characters as is seen in the sketch, "Grandma."

WHAT DO YOU SAY?

1. (a) From the many activities of a lifetime, enumerated in the story, what can you infer about the character traits of Grandma? *(b)* What was her general outlook on life?

2. (a) What analogy, or comparison, does Grandma use with Tom to explain her dying? *(b)* What analogy does she use to explain it to Douglas?

3. When Grandma says "No person ever died that had a family" is she implying that without children a person's life is useless? Explain.

4. (a) Of what poem in Unit 3 does this sketch remind you? *(b)* How do the viewpoints in the two selections differ?

5. The author of "Grandma" has used much figurative language in his descriptions. Cite several specific examples of similes, metaphors, and personification. You may wish to review the "Author's Craft" on page 233.

6. (a) Although "Grandma" is really fiction, what elements of a character sketch does it have? *(b)* How does it fit the qualifications for an essay?

LIBERTY OR DEATH!

PATRICK HENRY

Speeches

Delivered to the Second Virginia Convention on March 23, 1775.

Not all great literature was originally written to be read—some literature was written to be heard. Appreciating good literature may well include being a good listener. The idea that how a thing is said is often as important as what is said applies equally to the written and spoken word. Style and tone in a speech are as important as in an essay or a short story. Often a good test of the written word is to read it aloud to see how it sounds.

The four selections that follow should, ideally, be heard for one to appreciate fully their exact meaning and mood. Like essayists, the speakers had something to say and said it convincingly and with individual style.

SIR, we have done everything that could be done to avert the storm which is now coming on. We have petitioned; we have remonstrated; we have supplicated; we have prostrated ourselves before the throne, and have implored its interposition to arrest the tyrannical hands of the ministry and Parliament. Our petitions have been slighted; our remonstrances have produced additional violence and insult; our supplications have been disregarded; and we have been spurned with contempt from the foot of the throne!

In vain, after these things, may we indulge the fond hope of peace and reconciliation. There is no longer any room for hope. If we wish to be free, if we mean to preserve inviolate those inestimable privileges[1] for which we have been so long contending, if we mean not basely to abandon the noble struggle in which we have been so long engaged, and which we have pledged ourselves never to abandon until the glorious object of our contest shall be obtained—we must fight. An appeal to arms and to the God of Hosts is all that is left us!

They tell us, sir, that we are weak—unable to cope with so formidable an adversary. But when shall we be stronger? Will it be next week, or next year? Will it be when we are totally disarmed, and when a British guard shall be stationed in every house?[2] Shall we gather strength by irres-

---

1. *those inestimable privileges,* a reference to the rights that the Colonists had claimed, such as the right to levy their own taxes rather than to have the British Parliament do so. **2. *when a British guard . . . every house.*** One of the "Intolerable Acts" passed by the British Parliament to punish the Colonists for the Boston Tea Party was the quartering of British soldiers in their homes.

olution and inaction? Shall we acquire the means of effectual resistance by lying supinely on our backs, and hugging the delusive phantom of hope until our enemies shall have bound us hand and foot? Sir, we are not weak, if we make a proper use of those means which the God of nature hath placed in our power. Three millions of people, armed in the holy cause of liberty, and in such a country as that which we possess, are invincible by any force which our enemy can send against us.

Besides, sir, we shall not fight our battles alone. There is a just God who presides over the destinies of nations, and who will raise up friends to fight our battles for us. The battle, sir, is not to the strong alone; it is to the vigilant, the active, the brave. Besides, sir, we have no election.[3] If we were base enough to desire it, it is now too late to retire from the contest. There is no retreat but in submission and slavery! Our chains are forged! Their clanking may be heard on the plains of Boston![4] The war is inevitable—and let it come! I repeat it, sir, let it come!

It is in vain, sir, to extenuate the matter. Gentlemen may cry, Peace, peace—but there is no peace. The war is actually begun! The next gale that sweeps from the north will bring to our ears the clash of resounding arms! Our brethren are already in the field! Why stand we here idle? What is it that gentlemen wish? What would they have? Is life so dear, or peace so sweet, as to be purchased at the price of chains and slavery? Forbid it, Almighty God! I know not what course others may take; but as for me, give me liberty or give me death!

---

3. ***election,*** choice. 4. ***Our chains . . . Boston,*** a reference to the "Intolerable Acts" which, at that time, were being put into effect in Boston.

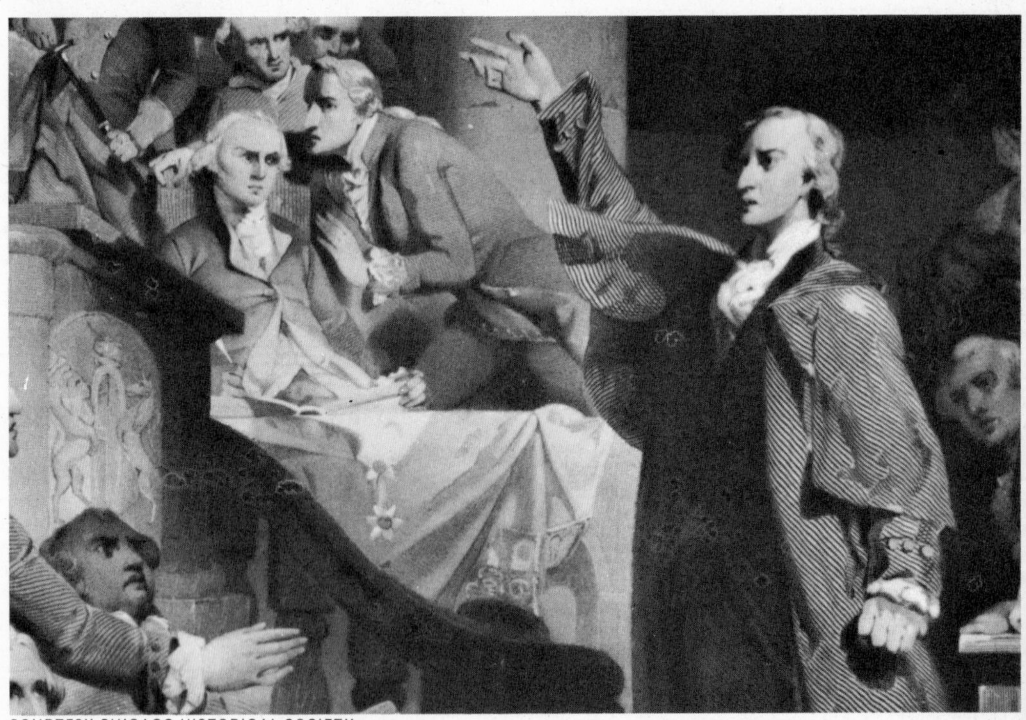

COURTESY CHICAGO HISTORICAL SOCIETY

GETTYSBURG ADDRESS

Delivered by Abraham Lincoln at the dedication of Gettysburg National Cemetery on November 19, 1863.

Fourscore and seven years ago our fathers brought forth on this continent a new nation, conceived in liberty, and dedicated to the proposition that all men are created equal.

Now we are engaged in a great civil war, testing whether that nation, or any nation so conceived and so dedicated, can long endure. We are met on a great battlefield of that war. We have come to dedicate a portion of that field as a final resting place for those who here gave their lives that that nation might live. It is altogether fitting and proper that we should do this.

But, in a larger sense, we cannot dedicate, we cannot consecrate, we cannot hallow this ground. The brave men, living and dead, who struggled here, have consecrated it far above our poor power to add or detract. The world will little note, nor long remember, what we say here, but it can never forget what they did here. It is for us, the living, rather, to be dedicated here to the unfinished work which they who fought here have thus far so nobly advanced. It is rather for us to be here dedicated to the great task remaining before us—that from these honored dead we take increased devotion to that cause for which they gave the last full measure of devotion; that we here highly resolve that these dead shall not have died in vain; that this nation, under God, shall have a new birth of freedom; and that government of the people, by the people, for the people, shall not perish from the earth.

Abraham Lincoln.

THE FOUR FREEDOMS

FRANKLIN D. ROOSEVELT

Delivered before Congress on January 6, 1941.

In the future days, which we seek to make secure, we look forward to a world founded upon four essential freedoms.

The first is freedom of speech and expression—everywhere in the world.

The second is freedom of every person to worship God in his own way—everywhere in the world.

The third is freedom from want—which, translated into world terms, means economic understandings which will secure to every nation a healthy peacetime life for its inhabitants—everywhere in the world.

The fourth is freedom from fear—which, translated into world terms, means a world-wide reduction of armaments to such a point and in such a thorough fashion that no nation will be in a position to commit an act of physical aggression against any neighbor—anywhere in the world.

That is no vision of a distant millennium. It is a definite basis for a kind of world attainable in our own time and generation. That kind of world is the very antithesis of the so-called new order of tyranny which the dictators seek to create with the crash of a bomb.

To that new order we oppose the greater conception—the moral order. A good society is able to face schemes of world domination and foreign revolutions alike without fear.

Since the beginning of our American history we have been engaged in change—in a perpetual peaceful revolution—a revolution which goes on steadily, quietly adjusting itself to changing conditions—without the concentration camp or the quick-lime in the ditch.[1] The world order which we seek is the coöperation of free countries, working together in a friendly civilized society.

This Nation has placed its destiny in the hands and heads and hearts of its millions of free men and women; and its faith in freedom under the guidance of God. Freedom means the supremacy of human rights everywhere. Our support goes to those who struggle to gain those rights or keep them. Our strength is in our unity of purpose.

To that high concept there can be no end save victory.

1. *quick-lime in the ditch,* a method used by the Nazis to dispose of the bodies of their victims.

PHOTOS OF JOHN GLENN FROM WIDE WORLD PHOTOS

A NEW ERA

BY JOHN H. GLENN, JR.

Lieutenant Colonel, United States Marine Corps

Delivered at a Joint Session of Congress, Washington, D.C., February 26, 1962

Mr. Speaker, Mr. President, Members of the Congress, I am only too aware of the tremendous honor that is being shown us at this joint meeting of the Congress today. When I think of past meetings that involved heads of state and equally notable persons, I can only say I am most humble to know that you consider our efforts to be in the same class.

This has been a great experience for all of us present and for all Americans, of course, and I am certainly glad to see that pride in our country and its accomplishments is not a thing of the past.

I still get a hard-to-define feeling inside when the flag goes by—and I know that all of you do, too. Today as we rode up Pennsylvania Avenue from the White House and saw the tremendous outpouring of feeling on the part of so many thousands of our people I got this same feeling all over again. Let us hope that none of us ever loses it.

The flight of *Friendship 7* on February 20 involved much more than one man in the spacecraft in orbit.

I can think of many people who were involved in this, but I think of none more than just a few sitting in the front row right up here.

I'd like to have them stand up. If my parents would stand up, please. My dad and mother.

My wife's mother is there. I don't believe Dr. Castor is there right now but—Mrs. Castor.

I guess Dr. Castor is up there in the third row, I'm told here. There he is.

My son and daughter, Dave and Lynn. And the real rock in our family, my wife Anne. I'm real proud of her.

There are many more people, of course, involved in our flight in *Friendship 7;* many more things involved, as well as people. There was the vision of Congress that established this national program of space exploration. Beyond that, many thousands of people were involved, civilian contractors and many subcontractors in many different fields; many elements—civilian, civil service and military, all blending their efforts toward a common goal.

To even attempt to give proper credit to all the individuals on this team effort would be impossible. But let me say that I have never seen a more sincere, dedicated, and hard-working group of people in my life.

From the original vision of the Congress to consummation of this orbital flight has been just over three years. This, in itself, states eloquently the case for the hard work and devotion of the entire Mercury team. This has not been just another job. It has been a dedicated labor such as I have not seen before. It has involved a cross cut of American endeavor with many different disciplines coöperating toward a common objective.

Friendship 7 is just a beginning, a successful experiment. It is another plateau in our step-by-step program of increasingly ambitious flights.

The earlier flights of Alan Shepard and Gus Grissom, who are over here, were stepping stones. Their efforts were stepping stones toward my flight in *Friendship* 7 and my flight in that spacecraft will, in turn, provide additional information for use in striving toward future flights some of the other gentlemen you see here will take part in.

Scott Carpenter here, who was my backup on this flight; Walt Schirra, Deke Slayton, and one missing member, who is still on his way back from Australia, where he was on the tracking station, Gordon Cooper. A lot of direction is necessary for a project such as this, and the Director of Project Mercury since its inception has been Dr. Robert Gilruth, who certainly deserves a hand here.

I have been trying to introduce Walt Williams. I do not see him here. There he is up in the corner.

As well as being Associate Director of Mercury, Walt has the unenviable position of being Operational Director. He is a character, no matter how you look at him. He says hold the count occasionally, and poor weather and one thing and another.

With all the experience we have had so far, where does this leave us?

These are the building blocks upon which we shall build much more ambitious and more productive portions of the program.

As was to be expected, not everything worked perfectly on my flight. We may well need to make changes —and these will be tried out on subsequent 3-orbit flights, later this year, to be followed by 18-orbit, 24-hour missions.

Beyond that, we look forward to Project Gemini—a two-man orbital vehicle with greatly increased capability for advanced experiments. There will be additional rendezvous experiments in space, technical and scientific observations—then, Apollo orbital, circumlunar and finally, lunar landing flights.

What did we learn from the *Friendship* 7 flight that will help us attain these objectives?

Some specific items have already been covered briefly in the news reports. And I think it is of more than passing interest to all of us that information attained from these flights is readily available to all nations of the world.

The launch itself was conducted openly and with the news media representatives from around the world in attendance. Complete information is released as it is evaluated and validated. This is certainly in sharp contrast with similar programs conducted elsewhere in the world and elevates the peaceful intent of our program.

Data from the *Friendship 7* flight is still being analyzed. Certainly, much more information will be added to our storehouse of knowledge.

But these things we know. The Mercury spacecraft and systems design concepts are sound and have now been verified during manned flight in space. We also proved that man can operate intelligently in space and can adapt rapidly to this new environment.

Zero G or weightlessness—at least for this period of time—appears to be no problem. As a matter of fact, lack of gravity is a rather fascinating thing.

Objects within the cockpit can be parked in midair. For example, at one time during the flight, I was using a hand-held camera. Another system needed attention; so it seemed quite natural to let go of the camera, take care of the other chore in the spacecraft, then reach out, grasp the camera and go back about my business.

It is a real fascinating feeling, needless to say.

There seemed to be little sensation of speed although the craft was traveling at about 5 miles per second—a speed that I, too, find difficult to comprehend.

In addition to closely monitoring onboard systems, we were able to make numerous outside observations.

The view from that altitude defies description.

I had listened earlier to Alan and Gus both describe this and was eagerly looking forward to it, and in their wildest use of adjectives they didn't describe what it's like even.

Nor can I describe it.

The horizon colors are brilliant and sunsets are spectacular.

It is hard to beat a day in which you are permitted the luxury of seeing four sunsets.

I think after all of our talk of space, this morning coming up from Florida on the plane with President Kennedy, we had the opportunity to meet Mrs. Kennedy and Caroline before we took off. I think Caroline really cut us down to size and put us back in the proper position. She looked up, upon being introduced, and said, "Where is the monkey?"

All this, and I didn't get a banana pellet on the whole ride.

Seriously, though, I feel we are on the brink of an area of expansion of knowledge about ourselves and our surroundings that is beyond description or comprehension at this time.

Our efforts today and what we have done so far are but small building blocks in a huge pyramid to come.

Questions are sometimes raised regarding the immediate payoffs from our efforts. What benefits are we gaining from the money spent? The real benefits we probably cannot even detail. They are probably not even known to man today. But exploration and the pursuit of knowledge have always paid dividends in the long run—usually far greater than anything expected at the outset.

Experimenters with common, green mold, little dreamed what effect their discovery of penicillin would have.

The story has been told of Disraeli, Prime Minister of England at the time, visiting the laboratory of Faraday, one of the early experimenters with basic electrical principles. After viewing various demonstrations of electrical phenomena, Disraeli asked, "But of what possible use is it?" Faraday replied, "Mister Prime Minister, what good is a baby?"

That is the stage of development in our program today—in its infancy. And it indicates a much broader potential impact, of course, than even the discovery of electricity did. We are just probing the surface of the greatest advancements in man's knowledge of his surroundings that has ever been made, I feel. There are benefits to science across the board. Any major effort such as this results in research by so many different specialties that it is hard to even envision the benefits that will accrue in many fields.

Knowledge begets knowledge. The more I see, the more impressed I am—not with how much we know—but with how tremendous the areas are that are as yet unexplored.

Exploration, knowledge, and achievement are good only insofar as we apply them to our future actions. Progress never stops. We are now on the verge of a new era, I feel.

Today, I know that I seem to be standing alone on this great platform—just as I seemed to be alone in the cockpit of the *Friendship 7* spacecraft. But I am not. There were with me then—and with me now—thousands of Americans and many hundreds of citizens of many countries around the world who contributed to this truly international undertaking voluntarily and in a spirit of cooperation and understanding.

On behalf of all of those people, I would like to express my and their heartfelt thanks for the honors you have bestowed upon us here today.

We are all proud to have been privileged to be part of this effort, to represent our country as we have. As our knowledge of the universe in which we live increases, may God grant us the wisdom and guidance to use it wisely.

Thank you.

ASSOCIATED PRESS WIREPHOTO

WHAT DO YOU SAY?

1. The four speeches you have just read have what ideas in common?

2. In what way does the idea of "unfinished work" appear in each speech?

3. Each of the four speeches was delivered for a different purpose. Some of the purposes of speeches might be classified as follows: to convince, to inspire, to instruct, to entertain. Which of these purposes would you attribute to each of the four speeches?

4. What is the tone of each speech? Is it forceful, sincere, sympathetic, bitter, happy, sad, thoughtful, amused, inspired, sarcastic?

5. The style of each of the four speeches is very different from the others. From what you have learned of an author's style, describe in your own words a few characteristics of style of each of the four speeches. You may wish to refer to the "Author's Craft" on page 451.

6. What advantages and disadvantages does the writer of a speech have over the writer of an essay?

Biography

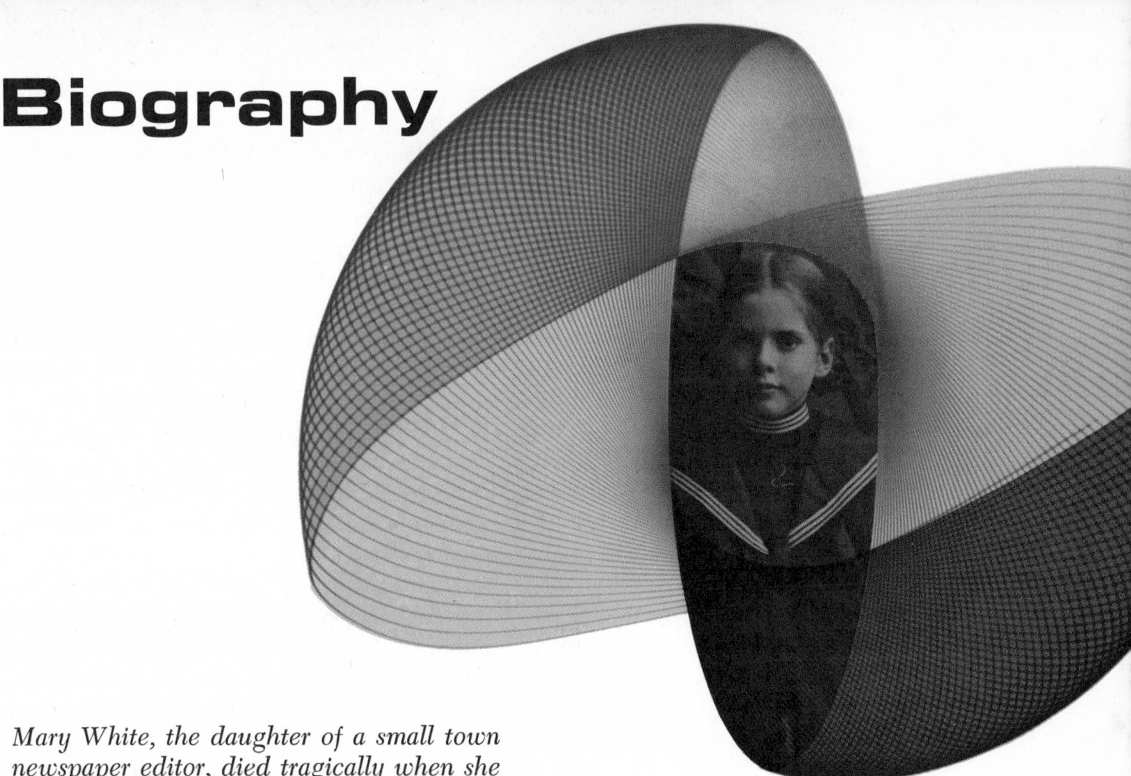

Mary White, the daughter of a small town newspaper editor, died tragically when she was sixteen. This sketch of her brief life, which her father wrote as an editorial, has become famous.

MARY WHITE

WILLIAM ALLEN WHITE

The Associated Press reports carrying the news of Mary White's death declared that it came as the result of a fall from a horse. How she would have hooted at that! She never fell from a horse in her life. Horses have fallen on her and with her – "I'm always trying to hold 'em in my lap," she used to say. But she was proud of few things, and one was that she could ride anything that had four legs and hair. Her death resulted not from a fall, but from a blow on the head which fractured her skull, and the blow came from the limb of an overhanging tree on the parking.

The last hour of her life was typical of its happiness. She came home from a day's work at school, topped off by a hard grind with the copy on the high-school *Annual,* and felt that a ride would refresh her. She climbed into her khakis, chattering to her mother about the work she was doing, and hurried to get her horse and be out on the dirt roads for the country air and the radiant fields of the spring. As she rode through the town at an easy gallop she kept waving at passers-by. She knew everyone in town. For a decade the little figure with the long pigtail and the red hair-ribbon has been familiar on the streets of Emporia, and she got in the way of speaking to those who nodded at her. She passed the Kerrs, walking the horse, in front of the Normal Library, and waved at them, passed another friend a few hundred feet farther on, and waved at her. The horse was walking, and as she turned into North Merchant Street she took off her cowboy hat, and the horse swung into a lope. She passed the Tripletts and waved her cowboy hat at them, still moving gaily north on Merchant Street. A *Gazette* carrier passed—a high-school boy friend—and she waved at him, but with her bridle hand; the horse veered quickly, plunged into the parking where the low-hanging limb faced her, and, while she still looked back, waving, the blow came. But she did not fall from the horse; she slipped off, dazed a bit, staggered, and fell in a faint. She never quite recovered consciousness.

But she did not fall from the horse, neither was she riding fast. A year or so ago she used to go like the wind. But that habit was broken, and she used the horse to get into the open to get fresh, hard exercise, and to work off a certain surplus energy that welled up in her and needed a physical outlet. That need has been in her heart for years. It was back of the impulse that kept the dauntless little brown-clad figure on the streets and country roads of this community and built into a strong, muscular body what had been a frail and sickly frame during the first years of her life. But the riding gave her more than a body. It released a gay and hardy soul. She was the happiest thing in the world. And she was happy because she was enlarging her horizon. She came to know all sorts and conditions of men. Charley O'Brien, the traffic cop, was one of her best friends. W. L. Holtz, the Latin teacher, was another. Tom O'Conner, farmer-politician, and the Rev. J. H. J. Rice, preacher and police judge, and Frank Beach, music master, were her special friends, and all the girls, black and white, above the track and below the track, in Pepville and Stringtown, were among her acquaintances. And she brought home riotous stories of her adventures. She loved to rollick; persiflage was her natural expression at home. Her humor was a continual bubble of joy. She seemed to think in hyperbole and metaphor. She was mischievous without malice, as full of faults as an old shoe. No angel was Mary White, but an easy girl to live with, for she never nursed a grouch five minutes in her life.

With all her eagerness for the out-of-doors, she loved books. On her table when she left her room were a book by Conrad, one by Galsworthy, *Creative Chemistry* by E. E. Slosson, and a Kipling book. She read Mark Twain, Dickens, and Kipling before she was ten—all of their writings. Wells and Arnold Bennett particularly amused and diverted her. She was entered as a student in Wellesley in 1922, was assistant editor of the high-school *Annual* this year, and in line for election to the editorship of the *Annual* next year. She was a member of the executive committee of the high-school Y.W.C.A.

Within the last two years she had begun to be moved by an ambition to draw. She began as most children do by scribbling, in her schoolbooks, funny pictures. She bought cartoon magazines and took a course—rather casually, naturally, for she was, after all, a child with no strong purposes—and this year she tasted the first fruits of success by having her pictures accepted by the high-school *Annual*. But the thrill of delight she got when Mr. Ecord, of the Normal *Annual*, asked her to do the cartooning for that book this spring, was too beautiful for words. She fell to her work with all her enthusiastic heart. Her drawings were accepted, and her pride—always repressed by a lively sense of the ridiculousness of the figure she was cutting—was a really gorgeous thing to see. No successful artist ever drank a deeper draft of satisfaction than she took from the little fame her work was getting among her schoolfellows. In her glory, she almost forgot her horse—but never her car.

For she used the car as a jitney bus. It was her social life. She never had a "party" in all her nearly seventeen years—wouldn't have one; but she never drove a block in the car in her life that she didn't begin to fill the car with pickups! Everybody rode with Mary White—white and black, old and young, rich and poor, men and women. She liked nothing better than to fill the car full of long-legged high-school boys and an occasional girl, and parade the town. She never had a "date," nor went to a dance, except once with her brother Bill, and the "boy proposition" didn't interest her—yet. But young people—great spring-breaking, varnish-cracking, fender-bending, door-sagging carloads of "kids"—gave her great pleasure. Her zests were keen. But the most fun she ever had in her life was acting as chairman of the committee that got up the big turkey dinner for the poor folks at the county home; scores of pies, gallons of slaw, jam, cakes, preserves, oranges, and a wilderness of turkey were loaded in the car and taken to the county home. And, being of a practical turn of mind, she risked her own Christmas dinner by staying to see that the poor folks actually got it all. Not that she was a cynic; she just disliked to tempt folks. While there, she found a blind colored uncle, very old, who could do nothing but make rag rugs, and she rustled up from her school friends rags enough to keep him busy for a season. The last engagement she tried to make was to take the guests at the county home out for a car ride. The poor she had always with her and was glad of it. She hungered and thirsted for righteousness, and was the most impious creature in the world. She joined the Congregational Church without consulting her parents; not particularly for her soul's good. She never had a thrill of piety in her life, and would have hooted at a "testimony." But even as a little child she felt the Church was an agency for helping people to more of life's abundance, and she wanted to help. She never wanted help for herself. Clothes meant little to her. It was a fight to get a new rig on her; but eventually a harder fight to get it off. She never wore a jewel and had no ring but her high-school class ring, and never asked for anything but a wrist watch. She refused to have her hair up, though she was nearly seventeen. "Mother," she protested, "you don't know how much I get by with, in my braided pigtails, that I could not with my hair up." Above every other passion of her life was her passion not to grow up, to be a child. The tomboy in her, which was big, seemed to loathe to be put away forever in skirts. She was Peter Pan, who refused to grow up.

Her funeral yesterday at the Congregational Church was as she would have wished it; no singing, no flowers save the big bunch of roses from her brother Bill's Harvard classmen—heavens, how proud that would have made her!—and the red roses from the *Gazette* force—in vases at her head and feet. A short prayer, Paul's beautiful essay on "Love" from the thirteenth chapter of First Corinthians, some remarks about her democratic spirit by her friend, John H. J. Rice, pastor and police judge, which she would have deprecated if she could, a prayer sent down for her by her friend, Carl Nau, and, opening the service, the slow, poignant movement from Beethoven's "Moonlight Sonata," which she loved, and, closing the service, a cutting from the joyously melancholy first movement of Tchaikovsky's *Pathetic Symphony,* which she liked to hear in certain moods on the phonograph; then the Lord's Prayer by her friends in the high school.

That was all.

For her pallbearers only her friends were chosen: her Latin teacher, W. L. Holtz; her high-school principal, Rice Brown; her doctor, Frank Foncannon; her friend, W. W. Finney; her pal at the *Gazette* office, Walter Hughes; and her brother Bill. It would have made her smile to know that her friend, Charley O'Brien, the traffic cop, had been transferred from Sixth and Commercial to the corner near the church to direct her friends who came to bid her good-by.

A rift in the clouds in a gray day threw a shaft of sunlight upon her coffin as her nervous, energetic little body sank to its last sleep. But the soul of her, the glowing, gorgeous, fervent soul of her, surely was flaming in eager joy upon some other dawn.

CULVER PICTURES, INC.

WHAT DO YOU SAY?

1. *(a)* Review the "Author's Craft" on page 177. What qualities of the character sketch does this selection demonstrate? *(b)* "Mary White" is sometimes classified as an essay. In what ways does it qualify as an essay?

2. *(a)* What is the tone of this sketch? *(b)* How do you think this tone might have affected the way ***Gazette*** readers would remember Mary?

3. In which sentences do you think White best shows his love for Mary?

4. *(a)* White reveals many characteristics of his daughter. Which ones stand out in your mind? *(b)* What particular traits made her popular? *(c)* Would any of her traits have tended to make her unpopular?

5. What were Mary's tastes in books and music?

6. What funeral arrangements were especially suitable?

WILLIAM ALLEN WHITE

William Allen White was born and died in Emporia, Kansas. Except for time spent in college and on the ***Kansas City Star,*** he lived his whole life in Emporia. He once said that he had worked most of his life within a thousand feet of his birthplace. Kansans respected him as an honest, friendly, neighborly man. As owner and publisher of the ***Emporia Gazette*** he became one of America's most famous small town editors. He was regarded as an important liberal spokesman for the Middle West. Although he published sixteen books, including short stories, novels, biographies, and political essays, he is, perhaps, best remembered for his columns in the ***Gazette.***

WHEN I WAS ONE AND TWENTY

A. E. HOUSMAN

When I was one-and-twenty
  I heard a wise man say,
"Give crowns and pounds and guineas
  But not your heart away;
Give pearls away and rubies
  But keep your fancy free."
But I was one-and-twenty
  No use to talk to me.

When I was one-and-twenty
  I heard him say again,
"The heart out of the bosom
  Was never given in vain;
'Tis paid with sighs a plenty
  And sold for endless rue."
And I am two-and-twenty,
  And oh, 'tis true, 'tis true.

A. E. HOUSMAN

Alfred Edward Housman was born in 1859 and died in 1936. The last half of his life he spent as a Latin professor—first at University College, London, later at Cambridge. Although he became a leading classical scholar, he is more widely known as a poet. In both fields of accomplishment he was a perfectionist, having no patience with mistakes in his own work or in the work of others. He published only two slim volumes of poetry during his lifetime; a third was published by his brother, Laurence, after Alfred's death. All his other poems he destroyed.

(Discussion questions for this and next two poems on page 634.)

OH, PLEASE DON'T GET UP!

BY OGDEN NASH

There is one form of life to which I unconditionally surrender,
Which is the feminine gender.
Like lightning and thunder, women are awe-inspiring phenomena,
And they have a custom which many men might well adopt, which is to gird themselves in devices that reduce or at least repress their abdomena,
And they have a traditional rite which is handed down from mother to daughter,
Which is that they always have to wash their face with cold cream instead of water.
Also, I think there must be some great difference in the way men and women are built,
Because women walk around all day wearing shoes that a man would break his neck the first step he took in them because where a man's shoe has a heel a woman's shoe has a stilt,
So I often wonder who started this rumor about woman being the clinging vine and man the mighty oak or elm,
And I have an idea that the phrase "weaker sex" was coined by some woman to disarm some man she was preparing to overwhelm,
Because certainly a man shod like a woman would just have to sit down all day, and yet my land!
Women not only don't have to sit, but prefer to stand,
Because their pleasure in standing up is exquisite,
As everybody knows who has ever watched a woman pay a call or a visit,
Because at first they will sit in a chair,
And their heart may be in the highlands, but it certainly isn't there,
And their conversation is unspontaneous,
And their topics are trifling and miscellaneous,
But finally, after an uncomfortable while,
Their faces brighten with the well-I-must-be-running-along-now smile,
And they get to their feet and the front door,
And the Old Mother of Waters surges over the levee with a roar,
Because the proportions of feminine social chitchat are constant, always;
One part of sitting down in the sitting room to four parts standing up saying good-by in foyers and hallways,
Which is why I think that when it comes to physical prowess,
Why woman is a wow, or should I say a wowess.

OGDEN NASH

Born in 1902 in Rye, New York, Ogden Nash received his education at a private school in Rhode Island and attended Harvard University. For the next several years he worked for a New York publishing company. His first two volumes of verse, ***Hard Lines*** and ***Free Wheeling,*** were published in 1931. Since that time several more volumes, including ***The Face is Familiar*** and ***Family Reunion,*** have been published, and his poems have appeared in the ***New Yorker*** and the ***Saturday Evening Post.***

Nash's specialty is light verse with exaggerated, unexpected rhythms, and forced, ridiculous rhymes. From sheer nonsense to satire on human foibles, he applies his unorthodox language patterns to a wide variety of situations and subjects.

freddy the rat perishes

BY DON MARQUIS

At night, archy, who is a cockroach, climbs up on the typewriter in the newspaper office and writes reports to the boss, a newspaper columnist.

listen to me there have
been some doings here since last
i wrote there has been a battle
behind that rusty typewriter cover
in the corner
you remember freddy the rat well
freddy is no more but
he died game the other
day a stranger with a lot of
legs came into our little circle a tough looking kid
he was with a bad eye

who are you said a thousand legs
if i bite you once
said the stranger you won t ask
again he he little poison tongue said
the thousand legs who gave you hydrophobia
i got it by biting myself said
the stranger i m bad keep away
from me where i step a weed dies
if i was to walk on your forehead it would
raise measles and if
you give me any lip i ll do it

they mixed it then
and the thousand legs succumbed
well we found out this fellow
was a tarantula he had come up from
south america in a bunch of bananas
for days he bossed us life
was not worth living he would stand in
the middle of the floor and taunt
us ha ha he would say where i
step a weed dies do
you want any of my game i was
raised on red pepper and blood i am
so hot if you scratch me i will light
like a match you better
dodge me when i m feeling mean and
i don t feel any other way i was nursed
on a tabasco bottle if i was to slap
your wrist in kindness you
would boil over like job[1] and heaven
help you if i get angry give me
room i feel a wicked spell coming on

last night he made a break at freddy
the rat keep your distance
little one said freddy i m not
feeling well myself somebody poisoned some
cheese for me i m as full of
death as a drug store i
feel that i am going to die anyhow
come on little torpedo come on don t stop
to visit and search then they
went at it and both are no more please
throw a late edition on the floor i want to
keep up with china we dropped freddy
off the fire escape into the alley with
military honors

archy

1. *job* (jōb), a Biblical figure who was afflicted with boils.

DON MARQUIS

After working as a reporter and as an editorial writer, in 1912 Don Marquis became a newspaper columnist. It was in his column for the *New York Sun,* that archy the cockroach, and his friend, mehitabel the cat, first made their appearance. The author of numerous essays, novels, and short stories, Marquis once remarked, "It would be one on me if I should be remembered longest for creating a cockroach character." Ironically, his statement appears to have come true, and people everywhere continue to enjoy the antics and adventures of archy the cockroach.

WHAT DO YOU SAY?

"When I Was One and Twenty"

1. What advice does the wise man give the youth on the two occasions?

2. *(a)* How do you know the youth failed to heed the advice? *(b)* What happened to him between the ages of 21 and 22?

3. Would the speaker in this poem agree with the following lines by Alfred Tennyson? Explain.

> 'Tis better to have loved and lost
> Than never to have loved at all.

4. What contrast in tone do you find between this poem and "Grandma"?

"Oh, Please Don't Get Up"

1. *(a)* What is the tone of this poem; critical, satirical, or just humorous? *(b)* Does this tone necessarily reflect Nash's real attitude toward the "weaker sex"?

2. What examples are there of exaggerated comparison and contrast?

3. *(a)* Are you likely to find "wowess" in a dictionary? *(b)* What effect does the word give?

4. *(a)* What feminine foibles has Nash used for comment? *(b)* In your opinion what other foibles might he also have selected?

"freddy the rat perishes"

1. Why do you suppose there is a lack of capitals and punctuation in archy's typewriting?

2. What might be a reason for the irregularity of the lines?

3. Where did the battle archy describes take place?

4. *(a)* Who were the first two contestants? *(b)* What happened?

5. *(a)* Why did freddy decide to take on the tarantula? *(b)* What was the outcome?

6. What did archy want with a late edition?

THE WAYFARER

BY STEPHEN CRANE

The wayfarer,
Perceiving the pathway to truth,
Was struck with astonishment.
It was thickly grown with weeds.
"Ha," he said,
"I see that no one has passed here
In a long time."
Later he saw that each weed
Was a singular knife.
"Well," he mumbled at last,
"Doubtless there are other roads."

WHAT DO YOU SAY?

1. *(a)* Who is the wayfarer? *(b)* What does the pathway he perceives lead to? *(c)* Why is he astonished at the appearance of the pathway? *(d)* What conclusion does he draw?

2. *(a)* What does the wayfarer discover about the weeds? *(b)* What final decision does he come to? *(c)* Summarize what the poem says literally.

3. This poem is called an ***allegorical*** poem; that is, it uses symbols to imply a meaning not actually stated in the literal words of the poem. (See the Author's Crafts on pages 73, 95, and 544.) The series of actions in the poem are really figurative. For example, who is the wayfarer, a particular kind of person or just anybody?

4. *(a)* What are the "weeds" in the pathway to truth? *(b)* Why is the wayfarer astonished at the weeds?

5. What lines indicate that the pathway to truth is little traveled?

6. *(a)* What did the wayfarer later discover each weed to be? *(b)* What is the poet suggesting in this figure of speech?

7. How does the wayfarer react when he discovers the pathway to truth is a difficult one?

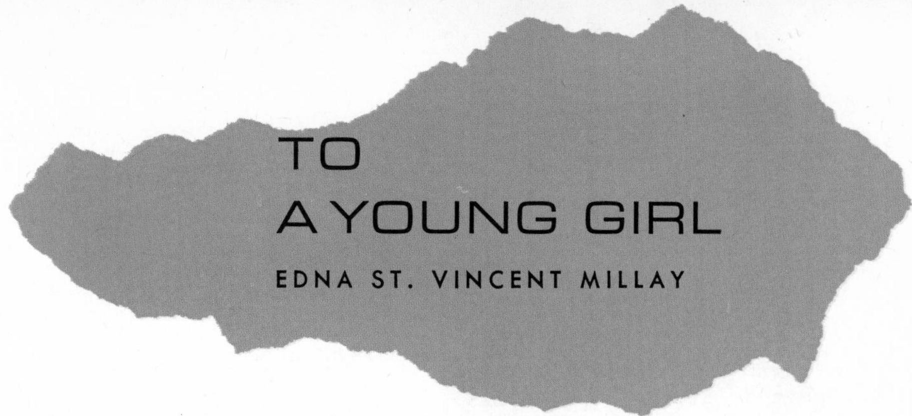

TO A YOUNG GIRL

EDNA ST. VINCENT MILLAY

Shall I despise you that your colourless tears
Made rainbows in your lashes, and you forgot to weep?
Would we were half so wise, that eke a grief out
By sitting in the dark, until we fall asleep.

I only fear lest, being by nature sunny,
By and by you will weep no more at all,
And fall asleep in the light, having lost with the tears
The colour in the lashes that comes as the tears fall.

I would not have you darken your lids with weeping,
Beautiful eyes, but I would have you weep enough
To wet the fingers of the hand held over the eye-lids,
And stain a little the light frock's delicate stuff.

For there came into my mind, as I watched you winking the tears down,
Laughing faces, blown from the west and the east,
Faces lovely and proud that I have prized and cherished;
Nor were the loveliest among them those that had wept the least.

WHAT DO YOU SAY?

1. (a) Who, does the author feel, is wiser, the one who weeps or the one who ekes a grief out sitting in the dark? *(b)* What line tells you?

2. How do the colourless tears cause rainbows?

3. (a) What is the girl's usual nature? *(b)* What does the author fear? *(c)* What does the girl stand to lose if she weeps no more?

4. In stanza three, the author states how much she would like the girl to weep. Explain what is meant in these lines.

5. (a) In stanza four the author recalls faces she has known. Which were the loveliest, those who had wept the least or those who had wept some? *(b)* Explain in your own words the author's attitude toward showing emotion.

In the first three lines of this poem, the poet is saying that knowledge, or wisdom, may come from many unlikely sources. The "fig" and the "grape" are figurative expressions for knowledge. Lines 4-6 introduce the speaker as a girl who is about to illustrate through her own experience the significance of the first three lines. Her story begins with line 7.

What tree may not the fig be gathered from?
The grape may not be gathered from the birch?
It's all you know the grape, or know the birch.
As a girl gathered from the birch myself
Equally with my weight in grapes, one autumn,
I ought to know what tree the grape is fruit of.
I was born, I suppose, like anyone,
And grew to be a little boyish girl
My brother could not always leave at home.
But that beginning was wiped out in fear
The day I swung suspended with the grapes,
And was come after like Eurydice
And brought down safely from the upper regions;
And the life I live now's an extra life
I can waste as I please on whom I please.
So if you see me celebrate two birthdays,
And give myself out as two different ages,
One of them five years younger than I look–

One day my brother led me to a glade
Where a white birch he knew of stood alone,
Wearing a thin head-dress of pointed leaves,
And heavy on her heavy hair behind,
Against her neck, an ornament of grapes.
Grapes, I knew grapes from having seen them last year.

One bunch of them, and there began to be
Bunches all round me growing in white birches,
The way they grew round Leif the Lucky's German[1];
Mostly as much beyond my lifted hands, though,
As the moon used to seem when I was younger,
And only freely to be had for climbing.
My brother did the climbing; and at first
Threw me down grapes to miss and scatter
And have to hunt for in sweet fern and hardhack;
Which gave him some time to himself to eat,
But not so much, perhaps, as a boy needed.
So then, to make me wholly self-supporting,
He climbed still higher and bent the tree to earth
And put it in my hands to pick my own grapes.
"Here, take a tree-top, I'll get down another.
Hold on with all your might when I let go."
I said I had the tree. It wasn't true.
The opposite was true. The tree had me.
The minute it was left with me alone
It caught me up as if I were the fish
And it the fishpole. So I was translated
To loud cries from my brother of "Let go!
Don't you know anything, you girl? Let go!"
But I, with something of the baby grip
Acquired ancestrally in just such trees
When wilder mothers than our wildest now
Hung babies out on branches by the hands
To dry or wash or tan, I don't know which,
(You'll have to ask an evolutionist)—
I held on uncomplainingly for life.
My brother tried to make me laugh to help me.
"What are you doing up there in those grapes?
Don't be afraid. A few of them won't hurt you.
I mean, they won't pick you if you don't them."
Much danger of my picking anything!
By that time I was pretty well reduced
To a philosophy of hang-and-let-hang.
"Now you know how it feels," my brother said,
"To be a bunch of fox-grapes, as they call them,
That when it thinks it has escaped the fox
By growing where it shouldn't—on a birch,
Where a fox wouldn't think to look for it—
And if he looked and found it, couldn't reach it—
Just then come you and I to gather it.
Only you have the advantage of the grapes
In one way: you have one more stem to cling by,
And promise more resistance to the picker."

One by one I lost off my hat and shoes,
And still I clung. I let my head fall back,
And shut my eyes against the sun, my ears
Against my brother's nonsense; "Drop," he said,
"I'll catch you in my arms. It isn't far."
(Stated in lengths of him it might not be.)

---

1. ***Leif the Lucky's German.*** With Leif Ericsson's Viking crew was a German who lived with Leif's family in Greenland. When they reached what may have been North America, he was overjoyed to find grapes, a fruit unknown in Greenland.

"Drop or I'll shake the tree and shake you
down."
Grim silence on my part as I sank lower,
My small wrists stretching till they showed
the banjo strings.
"Why, if she isn't serious about it!
Hold tight awhile till I think what to do.
I'll bend the tree down and let you down
by it."
I don't know much about the letting down;
But once I felt ground with my stocking
feet
And the world came revolving back to me,
I know I looked long at my curled-up
fingers,
Before I straightened them and brushed the
bark off.
My brother said: "Don't you weigh
anything?
Try to weigh something next time, so you
won't
Be run off with by birch trees into space."

It wasn't my not weighing anything
So much as my not knowing anything—
My brother had been nearer right before.
I had not taken the first step in knowledge;
I had not learned to let go with the hands,
As still I have not learned to with the heart,
And have no wish to with the heart—nor
need,
That I can see. The mind—is not the heart.
I may yet live, as I know others live,
To wish in vain to let go with the mind—
Of cares, at night, to sleep; but nothing
tells me
That I need learn to let go with the heart.

WHAT DO YOU SAY?

Lines 7-18

1. In lines 7-13, the background for the story the girl is about to relate is given. What is this background?

2. *(a)* In lines 14-18, the girl speaks of having an extra life. What happened to the first one? *(b)* How old was the girl at the time of her experience? *(c)* Lines 12 and 13 contain an ***allusion.*** To what is the author alluding? (See Author's Craft on page 380.)

Lines 19-30

3. *(a)* Where did the girl's brother take her? *(b)* What did she see there?

4. *(a)* To what does the poet compare the birch and the grapes? *(b)* Are the grapes in the birch trees completely out of reach, somewhat out of reach, or easily accessible?

Lines 31-40

5. Trace the actions of the brother.

Lines 41-91

6. What happens in lines 41-91?

7. What is the advantage, expressed in line 70, that the girl has over the grapes?

8. What are the "banjo strings" in line 80?

Lines 92-103

9. What is "the first step in knowledge"?

10. What is the difference between letting go with the mind and letting go with the heart?

11. *(a)* What is the poet's attitude toward letting go with the mind? *(b)* Toward letting go with the heart?

12. Reread the entire poem, including the headnote, and state in your own words the central idea of the poem.

Drama

GORE VIDAL

VISIT TO A SMALL PLANET

Characters

KRETON	GENERAL POWERS
ROGER SPELDING	AIDE
ELLEN SPELDING	PAUL LAURENT
MRS. SPELDING	SECOND VISITOR
JOHN RANDOLPH	PRESIDENT OF PARAGUAY

ACT I

Stock Shot[1]*: The night sky, stars. Then slowly a luminous object arcs into view. As it is almost upon us, dissolve to*[2] *the living room of the Spelding house in Maryland.*

Superimpose card: "THE TIME: THE DAY AFTER TOMORROW"[3]

The room is comfortably balanced between the expensively decorated and the homely. Roger Spelding is concluding his TV broadcast. He is middle-aged, unctuous, resonant. His wife, bored and vague,

1. ***Stock Shot,*** standard scene. 2. ***dissolve to,*** one picture fades out as another fades in. 3. ***"The Time: . . . Tomorrow."*** These words appear over the scene.

knits passively while he talks at his desk. Two technicians are on hand, operating the equipment. His daughter, Ellen, a lively girl of twenty, fidgets as she listens.

SPELDING *(Into microphone)*. . . . and so, according to General Powers . . . who should know if anyone does . . . the flying object which has given rise to so much irresponsible conjecture is nothing more than a meteor passing through the earth's orbit. It is not, as many believe, a secret weapon of this country. Nor is it a space-ship as certain lunatic elements have suggested. General Powers has assured me that it is highly doubtful there is any form of life on other planets capable of building a space-ship. "If any traveling is to be done in space, we will do it first." And those are his exact words. . . . Which winds up another week of news. *(Crosses to pose with wife and daughter)* This is Roger Spelding, saying good night to Mother and Father America, from my old homestead in Silver Glen, Maryland, close to the warm pulse-beat of the nation.

TECHNICIAN. Good show tonight, Mr. Spelding.

SPELDING. Thank you.

TECHNICIAN. Yes sir, you were right on time.

Spelding nods wearily, his mechanical smile and heartiness suddenly gone.

MRS. SPELDING. Very nice, dear. Very nice.

TECHNICIAN. See you next week, Mr. Spelding.

SPELDING. Thank you, boys.

Technicians go.

SPELDING. Did you like the broadcast, Ellen?

ELLEN. Of course I did, Daddy.

SPELDING. Then what did I say?

ELLEN. Oh, that's not fair.

SPELDING. It's not very flattering when one's own daughter won't listen to what one says while millions of people . . .

ELLEN. I always listen, Daddy, you know that.

MRS. SPELDING. We love your broadcasts, dear. I don't know what we'd do without them.

SPELDING. Starve.

ELLEN. I wonder what's keeping John?

SPELDING. Certainly not work.

ELLEN. Oh, Daddy, stop it! John works very hard and you know it.

MRS. SPELDING. Yes, he's a perfectly nice boy, Roger. I like him.

SPELDING. I know. I know: He has every virtue except the most important one: he has no get-up-and-go.

ELLEN *(Precisely)*. He doesn't want to get up and he doesn't want to go because he's already where he wants to be on his own farm which is exactly where *I'm* going to be when we're married.

SPELDING. More thankless than a serpent's tooth is an ungrateful child.[1]

ELLEN. I don't think that's right. Isn't it "more deadly . . ."

SPELDING. Whatever the exact quotation is, I stand by the sentiment.

MRS. SPELDING. Please don't quarrel. It always gives me a headache.

SPELDING. I never quarrel. I merely reason, in my simple way, with Miss Know-it-all here.

ELLEN. Oh, Daddy! Next you'll tell me I should marry for money.

SPELDING. There is nothing wrong with marrying a wealthy man. The horror of it has always eluded me. However, my only wish is that you marry someone hard-working, ambitious, a man who'll make his mark in the world. Not a boy who plans to sit on a farm all his life, growing peanuts.

ELLEN. English walnuts.

SPELDING. Will you stop correcting me?

ELLEN. But, Daddy, John grows walnuts . . .

John enters, breathlessly.

JOHN. Come out! Quick! It's coming this way. It's going to land right here!

SPELDING. *What's* going to land?

JOHN. The space-ship. Look!

SPELDING. Apparently you didn't hear my

---

1. ***More thankless . . . an ungrateful child.*** How sharper than a serpent's tooth it is to have a thankless child. (From Shakespeare's ***King Lear,*** Act I, Scene 4).

broadcast. The flying object in question is a meteor not a space ship.

John has gone out with Ellen. Spelding and Mrs. Spelding follow.

MRS. SPELDING. Oh, my! Look! Something *is* falling! Roger, you don't think it's going to hit the house, do you?

SPELDING. The odds against being hit by a falling object that size are, I should say, roughly, ten million to one.

JOHN. Ten million to one or not it's going to land right here and it's *not* falling.

SPELDING. I'm sure it's a meteor.

MRS. SPELDING. Shouldn't we go down to the cellar?

SPELDING. If it's not a meteor, it's an optical illusion . . . mass hysteria.

ELLEN. Daddy, it's a real space ship. I'm sure it is.

SPELDING. Or maybe a weather balloon. Yes, that's what it is. General Powers said only yesterday . . .

JOHN. It's landing!

SPELDING. I'm going to call the police . . . the army!

Bolts inside.

ELLEN. Oh look how it shines!

JOHN. Here it comes!

MRS. SPELDING. Right in my rose garden!

ELLEN. Maybe it's a balloon.

JOHN. No, it's a space ship and right in your own backyard.

ELLEN. What makes it shine so?

JOHN. I don't know but I'm going to find out.

Runs off toward the light.

ELLEN. Oh, darling, don't! John, please! John, John come back!

Spelding, wide-eyed, returns.

MRS. SPELDING. Roger, it's landed right in my rose garden.

SPELDING. I got General Powers. He's coming over. He said they've been watching this thing. They . . . they don't know what it is.

ELLEN. You mean it's nothing of ours?

SPELDING. They believe it . . . *(Swallows hard)* . . . it's from outer space.

ELLEN. And John's down there! Daddy, get a gun or something.

SPELDING. Perhaps we'd better leave the house until the army gets here.

ELLEN. We can't leave John.

SPELDING. I can. *(Peers nearsightedly)* Why, it's not much larger than a car. I'm sure it's some kind of meteor.

ELLEN. Meteors are blazing hot.

SPELDING. This is a cold one . . .

ELLEN. It's opening . . . the whole side's opening! *(Shouts)* John! Come back! Quick. . . .

MRS. SPELDING. Why, there's a man getting out of it! *(Sighs)* I feel much better already. I'm sure if we ask him, he'll move that thing for us. Roger, you ask him.

SPELDING *(Ominously)*. If it's really a man?

ELLEN. John's shaking hands with him. *(Calls)* John darling, come on up here . . .

MRS. SPELDING. And bring your friend . . .

SPELDING. There's something wrong with the way that creature looks . . . if it is a man and not a . . . not a monster.

MRS. SPELDING. He looks perfectly nice to me.

John and the visitor appear. The visitor is in his forties, a mild, pleasant-looking man with side-whiskers and dressed in the fashion of 1860. He pauses when he sees the three people, in silence for a moment. They stare back at him, equally interested.

VISITOR. I seem to've made a mistake. I *am* sorry. I'd better go back and start over again.

SPELDING. My dear sir, you've only just arrived. Come in, come in. I don't need to tell you what a pleasure this is . . . Mister . . . Mister . . .

VISITOR. Kreton . . . This *is* the wrong costume, isn't it?

SPELDING. Wrong for what?

KRETON. For the country, and the time.

SPELDING. Well, it's a trifle old-fashioned.

MRS. SPELDING. But really awfully handsome.

KRETON. Thank you.

MRS. SPELDING *(To husband)*. Ask him about moving that thing off my rose bed.

Spelding leads them all into living room.

SPELDING. Come on in and sit down. You must be tired after your trip.

KRETON. Yes, I am a little. *(Looks around delightedly)* Oh, it's better than I'd hoped!

SPELDING. Better? What's better?

KRETON. The house . . . that's what you call it? Or is this an apartment?

SPELDING. This is a house in the State of Maryland, U.S.A.

KRETON. In the late 20th century! To think this is really the 20th century. I must sit down a moment and collect myself. The *real* thing!

He sits down.

ELLEN. You . . . you're not an American, are you?

KRETON. What a nice thought! No, I'm not.

JOHN. You sound more English.

KRETON. Do I? Is my accent very bad?

JOHN. No, it's quite good.

SPELDING. Where *are* you from, Mr. Kreton?

KRETON *(Evasively)*. Another place.

SPELDING. On this earth of course.

KRETON. No, not on this planet.

ELLEN. Are you from Mars?

KRETON. Oh dear no, not Mars. There's nobody on Mars . . . at least no one I know.

ELLEN. I'm sure you're teasing us and this is all some kind of publicity stunt.

KRETON. No, I really am from another place.

SPELDING. I don't suppose you'd consent to my interviewing you on television?

KRETON. I don't think your authorities will like that. They are terribly upset as it is.

SPELDING. How do you know?

KRETON. Well, I . . . pick up things. For instance, I know that in a few minutes a number of people from your Army will be here to question me and they . . . like you . . . are torn by doubt.

SPELDING. How extraordinary!

ELLEN. Why did you come here?

KRETON. Simply a visit to your small planet. I've been studying it for years. In fact, one might say, you people are my hobby. Especially, this period of your development.

JOHN. Are you the first person from your . . . your planet to travel in space like this?

KRETON. Oh my no! Everyone travels who wants to. It's just that no one wants to visit you. I can't think why. *I* always have. You'd be surprised what a thorough study I've made. *(Recites)* The planet, Earth, is divided into five continents with a number of large islands. It is mostly water. There is one moon. Civilization is only just beginning. . . .

SPELDING. Just beginning! My dear sir, we have had. . . .

KRETON *(Blandly)*. You are only in the initial stages, the most fascinating stages as far as I'm concerned . . . I do hope I don't sound patronizing.

ELLEN. Well, we are very proud.

KRETON. I know and that's one of your most endearing, primitive traits. Oh, I can't believe I'm here at last!

General Powers, a vigorous product of the National Guard, and his Aide enter.

POWERS. All right folks. The place is surrounded by troops. Where is the monster?

KRETON. I, my dear General, am the monster.

POWERS. What are you dressed up for, a fancy-dress party?

KRETON. I'd hoped to be in the costume of the period. As you see I am about a hundred years too late.

POWERS. Roger, who is this joker?

SPELDING. This is Mr. Kreton . . . General Powers. Mr. Kreton arrived in that thing outside. He is from another planet.

POWERS. I don't believe it.

ELLEN. It's true. We saw him get out of the flying saucer.

POWERS *(To Aide)*. Captain, go down and look at that ship. But be careful. Don't touch anything. And don't let anybody else near it. *(Aide goes)* So you're from another planet.

KRETON. Yes. My, that's a very smart uniform but I prefer the ones made of metal, the ones you used to wear, you know: with the feathers on top.

POWERS. That was five hundred years ago . . . Are you *sure* you're not from the Earth?

KRETON. Yes.

POWERS. Well, I'm not. You've got some pretty tall explaining to do.

KRETON. Anything to oblige.

POWERS. All right, which planet?

KRETON. None that you have ever heard of.

POWERS. Where is it?

KRETON. You wouldn't know.

POWERS. This solar system?

KRETON. No.

POWERS. Another system?

KRETON. Yes.

POWERS. Look, Buster, I don't want to play games: I just want to know where you're from. The law requires it.

KRETON. It's possible that I could explain it to a mathematician but I'm afraid I couldn't explain it to you, not for another five hundred years and by then of course *you'd* be dead because you people do die, don't you?

POWERS. What?

KRETON. Poor fragile butterflies, such brief little moments in the sun. . . . You see *we* don't die.

POWERS. You'll die all right if it turns out you're a spy or a hostile alien.

KRETON. I'm sure you wouldn't be so cruel.

Aide returns; he looks disturbed.

POWERS. What did you find?

AIDE. I'm not sure, General.

POWERS *(Heavily)*. Then do your best to describe what the object is like.

AIDE. Well, it's elliptical, with a fourteen-foot diameter. And it's made of an unknown metal which shines and inside there isn't anything.

POWERS. Isn't anything?

AIDE. There's nothing inside the ship: No instruments, no food, nothing.

POWERS *(To Kreton)*. What did you do with your instrument board?

KRETON. With my what? Oh, I don't have one.

POWERS. How does the thing travel?

KRETON. I don't know.

POWERS. You don't know. Now look, Mister, you're in pretty serious trouble. I suggest you do a bit of coöperating. You claim you travelled here from outer space in a machine with no instruments . . .

KRETON. Well, these cars are rather common in my world and I suppose, once upon a time, I must've known the theory on which they operate but I've long since forgotten. After all, General, we're not mechanics, you and I.

POWERS. Roger, do you mind if we use your study?

SPELDING. Not at all. Not at all, General.

POWERS. Mr. Kreton and I are going to have a chat. *(To Aide)* Put in a call to the Chief of Staff.

AIDE. Yes, General.

Spelding rises, leads Kreton and Powers into next room, a handsomely furnished study, many books and a globe of the world.

SPELDING. This way, gentlemen.

(Kreton sits down comfortably beside the globe which he twirls thoughtfully. At the door, Spelding speaks in a low voice to Powers) I hope I'll be the one to get the story first, Tom.

POWERS. There isn't any story. Complete censorship. I'm sorry but this house is under martial law. I've a hunch we're in trouble. *(He shuts the door. Spelding turns and rejoins his family)*

ELLEN. I think he's wonderful, whoever he is.

MRS. SPELDING. I wonder how much damage he did to my rose garden . . .

JOHN. It's sure hard to believe he's really from outer space. No instruments, no nothing . . . boy, they must be advanced scientifically.

MRS. SPELDING. Is he spending the night, dear?

SPELDING. What?

MRS. SPELDING. Is he spending the night?

SPELDING. Oh yes, yes, I suppose he will be.

MRS. SPELDING. Then I'd better go make up the bedroom. He seems perfectly nice to me. I like his whiskers. They're so very ... comforting. Like Grandfather Spelding's. *She goes.*

SPELDING *(Bitterly).* I *know* this story will leak out before I can interview him. I just know it.

ELLEN. What does it mean, we're under martial law?

SPELDING. It means we have to do what General Powers tells us to do. *(He goes to the window as a soldier passes by)* See?

JOHN. I wish I'd taken a closer look at that ship when I had the chance.

ELLEN. Perhaps he'll give us a ride in it.

JOHN. Traveling in space! Just like those stories. You know: intergalactic drive stuff.

SPELDING. *If* he's not an impostor.

ELLEN. I have a feeling he isn't.

JOHN. Well, I better call the family and tell them I'm all right.

He crosses to telephone by the door which leads into hall.

AIDE. I'm sorry, sir, but you can't use the phone.

SPELDING. He certainly can. This is my house ...

AIDE *(Mechanically).* This house is a military reservation until the crisis is over: Order General Powers. I'm sorry.

JOHN. How am I to call home to say where I am?

AIDE. Only General Powers can help you. You're also forbidden to leave this house without permission.

SPELDING. You can't do this!

AIDE. I'm afraid, sir, we've done it.

ELLEN. Isn't it exciting!

Cut to study.

POWERS. Are you deliberately trying to confuse me?

KRETON. Not deliberately, no.

POWERS. We have gone over and over this for two hours now and all that you've told me is that you're from another planet in another solar system ...

KRETON. In another dimension. I think that's the word you use.

POWERS. In another dimension and you have come here as a tourist.

KRETON. Up to a point, yes. What did you expect?

POWERS. It is my job to guard the security of this country.

KRETON. I'm sure that must be very interesting work.

POWERS. For all I know, you are a spy, sent here by an alien race to study us, preparatory to invasion.

KRETON. Oh, none of my people would *dream* of invading you.

POWERS. How do I know that's true?

KRETON. You don't, so I suggest you believe me. I should also warn you: I can tell what's inside.

POWERS. What's inside?

KRETON. What's inside your mind.

POWERS. You're a mind reader?

KRETON. I don't really read it. I hear it.

POWERS. What am I thinking?

KRETON. That I am either a lunatic from the earth or a spy from another world.

POWERS. Correct. But then you could've guessed that. *(Frowns)* What am I thinking now?

KRETON. You're making a picture. Three silver stars. You're pinning them on your shoulder, instead of the two stars you now wear.

POWERS *(Startled).* That's right. I was thinking of my promotion.

KRETON. If there's anything I can do to hurry it along, just let me know.

POWERS. You can. Tell me why you're here.

KRETON. Well, we don't travel much, my people. We used to but since we see everything through special monitors and recreators, there is no particular need to travel. However, *I* am a hobbyist. I love to gad about.

POWERS *(Taking notes).* Are you the first to visit us?

KRETON. Oh, no! We started visiting you long before there were people on the planet. However, we are seldom noticed on our trips. I'm sorry to say I slipped up, coming in the way I did . . . but then this visit was all rather impromptu. *(Laughs)* I am a creature of impulse, I fear.

Aide looks in.

AIDE. Chief of Staff on the telephone, General.

POWERS *(Picks up phone)*. Hello, yes, sir. Powers speaking. I'm talking to him now. No, sir. No, sir. No, we can't determine what method of power was used. He won't talk. Yes, sir. I'll hold him here. I've put the house under martial law . . . belongs to a friend of mine, Roger Spelding, the TV commentator. Roger Spelding, the TV . . . What? Oh, no, I'm sure he won't say anything. Who . . . oh, yes, sir. Yes, I realize the importance of it. Yes, I will. Good-by. *(Hangs up)* The President of the United States wants to know all about you.

KRETON. How nice of him! And I want to know all about him. But I do wish you'd let me rest a bit first. Your language is still not familiar to me. I had to learn them all, quite exhausting.

POWERS. You speak *all* our languages?

KRETON. Yes, all of them. But then it's easier than you might think since I can see what's inside.

POWERS. Speaking of what's inside, we're going to take your ship apart.

KRETON. Oh, I wish you wouldn't.

POWERS. Security demands it.

KRETON. In that case *my* security demands you leave it alone.

POWERS. You plan to stop us?

KRETON. I already have . . . Listen.

Far-off shouting. Aide rushes into the study.

AIDE. Something's happened to the ship, General. The door's shut and there's some kind of wall all around it, an invisible wall. We can't get near it.

KRETON *(To camera)*. I hope there was no one inside.

POWERS *(To Kreton)*. How did you do that?

KRETON. I couldn't begin to explain. Now if you don't mind, I think we should go in and see our hosts.

He rises, goes into living room. Powers and Aide look at each other.

POWERS. Don't let him out of your sight.

Cut to living room as Powers picks up phone. Kreton is with John and Ellen.

KRETON. I don't mind curiosity but I really can't permit them to wreck my poor ship.

ELLEN. What do you plan to do, now you're here?

KRETON. Oh, keep busy. I have a project or two . . . *(Sighs)* I can't believe you're real!

JOHN. Then we're all in the same boat.

KRETON. Boat? Oh, yes! Well, I should have come ages ago but I . . . I couldn't get away until yesterday.

JOHN. Yesterday? It only took you a *day* to get here?

KRETON. One of *my* days, not yours. But then you don't know about time yet.

JOHN. Oh, you mean relativity.

KRETON. No, it's much more involved than that. You won't know about time until . . . now let me see if I remember . . . no, I don't, but it's about two thousand years.

JOHN. What do we do between now and then?

KRETON. You simply go on the way you are, living your exciting primitive lives . . . you have no idea how much fun you're having now.

ELLEN. I hope you'll stay with us while you're here.

KRETON. That's very nice of you. Perhaps I will. Though I'm sure you'll get tired of having a visitor under foot all the time.

ELLEN. Certainly not. And Daddy will be deliriously happy. He can interview you by the hour.

JOHN. What's it like in outer space?

KRETON. Dull.

ELLEN. I should think it would be divine!

Powers enters.

KRETON. No, General, it won't work.

POWERS. What won't work?

KRETON. Trying to blow up my little force field. You'll just plough up Mrs. Spelding's garden.

Powers snarls and goes into study.

ELLEN. Can you tell what we're *all* thinking?

KRETON. Yes. As a matter of fact, it makes me a bit giddy. Your minds are not at all like ours. You see we control our thoughts while you . . . well, it's extraordinary the things you think about!

ELLEN. Oh, how awful! You can tell *everything* we think?

KRETON. Everything! It's one of the reasons I'm here, to intoxicate myself with your primitive minds . . . with the wonderful rawness of your emotions! You have no idea how it excites me! You simply seethe with unlikely emotions.

ELLEN. I've never felt so sordid.

JOHN. From now on I'm going to think about agriculture.

SPELDING *(Entering)*. You would.

ELLEN. Daddy!

KRETON. No, no. You must go right on thinking about Ellen. Such wonderfully *purple* thoughts!

SPELDING. Now see here, Powers, you're carrying this martial law thing too far . . .

POWERS. Unfortunately, until I have received word from Washington as to the final disposition of this problem, you must obey my orders: no telephone calls, no communication with the outside.

SPELDING. This is unsupportable.

KRETON. Poor Mr. Spelding! If you like, I shall go. That would solve everything, wouldn't it?

POWERS. You're not going anywhere, Mr. Kreton, until I've had my instructions.

KRETON. I sincerely doubt if you could stop me. However, I put it up to Mr. Spelding. Shall I go?

SPELDING. Yes! *(Powers gestures a warning)* Do stay, I mean, we want you to get a good impression of us . . .

KRETON. And of course you still want to be the first journalist to interview me. Fair enough. All right, I'll stay on for a while.

POWERS. Thank you.

KRETON. Don't mention it.

SPELDING. General, may I ask our guest a few questions?

POWERS. Go right ahead, Roger. I hope you'll do better than I did.

SPELDING. Since you read our minds, you probably already know what our fears are.

KRETON. I do, yes.

SPELDING. We are afraid that you represent a hostile race.

KRETON. And I have assured General Powers that my people are not remotely hostile. Except for me, no one is interested in this planet's present stage.

SPELDING. Does this mean you might be interested in a *later* stage?

KRETON. I'm not permitted to discuss your future. Of course my friends think me perverse to be interested in a primitive society but there's no accounting for tastes, is there? You are my hobby. I love you. And that's all there is to it.

POWERS. So you're just here to look around . . . sort of going native.

KRETON. What a nice expression! That's it exactly. I am going native.

POWERS *(Grimly)*. Well, it is my view that you have been sent here by another civilization for the express purpose of reconnoitering prior to invasion.

KRETON. That *would* be your view! The wonderfully primitive assumption that all strangers are hostile. You're almost too good to be true, General.

POWERS. You deny your people intend to make trouble for us?

KRETON. I deny it.

POWERS. Then are they interested in establishing communication with us? trade? that kind of thing?

KRETON. We have always had communication with you. As for trade, well, we do not trade . . . that is something peculiar only to your social level. *(Quickly)* Which I'm not criticizing! As you know, I approve of everything you do.

POWERS. I give up.

SPELDING. You have no interest then in . . . well, trying to dominate the earth.

KRETON. Oh, yes!

POWERS. I thought you just said your people weren't interested in us.

KRETON. *They're* not, but *I* am.

POWERS. You!

KRETON. Me . . . I mean I. You see I've come here to take charge.

POWERS. Of the United States?

KRETON. No, of the whole world. I'm sure you'll be much happier and it will be great fun for me. You'll get used to it in no time.

POWERS. This is ridiculous. How can one man take over the world?

KRETON *(Gaily)*. Wait and see!

POWERS *(To Aide)*. Grab him!

Powers and Aide rush Kreton but within a foot of him, they stop, stunned.

KRETON. You can't touch me. That's part of the game. *(He yawns)* Now, if you don't mind, I shall go up to my room for a little lie-down.

SPELDING. I'll show you the way.

KRETON. That's all right. I know the way. *(Touches his brow)* Such savage thoughts! My head is vibrating like a drum. I feel quite giddy, all of you thinking away. *(He starts to the door; he pauses beside Mrs. Spelding)* No, it's not a dream, dear lady. I shall be here in the morning when you wake up. And now, good night, dear, wicked children . . .

He goes as we fade out.

ACT II

Fade in on Kreton's bedroom next morning. He lies fully clothed on bed with cat on his lap.

KRETON. Poor cat! Of course I sympathize with you. Dogs *are* distasteful. What? Oh, I can well believe they do: yes, yes, how disgusting. They don't ever groom their fur! But you do *constantly*, such a fine coat. No, no, I'm not just saying that. I really mean it: exquisite texture. Of course, I wouldn't say it was *nicer* than skin but even so. . . . What? Oh, no! They *chase* you! Dogs chase you for no reason at all except pure malice? You poor creature. Ah, but you *do* fight back! That's right! give it to them: slash, bite, scratch! Don't let them get away with a trick. . . . No! Do dogs really do that? Well, I'm sure *you* don't. What . . . oh, well, yes I completely agree about mice. They *are* delicious! (Ugh!) Pounce, snap and there is a heavenly dinner. No, I don't know any mice yet . . . they're not very amusing? But after all think how you must terrify them because you are so bold, so cunning, so beautifully predatory! *(Knock at door)* Come in.

ELLEN *(Enters)*. Good morning. I brought you your breakfast.

KRETON. How thoughtful! *(Examines bacon)* Delicious, but I'm afraid my stomach is not like yours, if you'll pardon me. I don't eat. *(Removes pill from his pocket and swallows it)* This is all I need for the day. *(Indicates cat)* Unlike this creature, who would eat her own weight every hour, given a chance.

ELLEN. How do you know?

KRETON. We've had a talk.

ELLEN. You can *speak* to the cat?

KRETON. Not speak exactly but we communicate. I look inside and the cat coöperates. Bright red thoughts, very exciting, though rather on one level.

ELLEN. Does kitty like us?

KRETON. No, I wouldn't say she did. But then she has very few thoughts not connected with food. Have you, my quadruped criminal? *(He strokes the cat, which jumps to the floor)*

ELLEN. You know you've really upset everyone.

KRETON. I supposed that I would.

ELLEN. Can you really take over the world, just like that?

KRETON. Oh, yes.

ELLEN. What do you plan to do when you *have* taken over?

KRETON. Ah, that is my secret.

ELLEN. Well, I think you'll be a very nice President, *if* they let you of course.

KRETON. What a sweet girl you are! Marry him right away.

ELLEN. Marry John?

KRETON. Yes. I see it in your head *and* in his. He wants you very much.

ELLEN. Well, we plan to get married this summer, if father doesn't fuss too much.

KRETON. Do it before then. I shall arrange it all if you like.

ELLEN. How?

KRETON. I can convince your father.

ELLEN. That sounds awfully ominous. I think you'd better leave poor Daddy alone.

KRETON. Whatever you say. *(Sighs)* Oh, I love it so! When I woke up this morning I had to pinch myself to prove I was really here.

ELLEN. We were all doing a bit of pinching too. Ever since dawn we've had nothing but visitors and phone calls and troops outside in the garden. No one has the faintest idea what to do about you.

KRETON. Well, I don't think they'll be confused much longer.

ELLEN. How do you plan to conquer the world?

KRETON. I confess I'm not sure. I suppose I must make some demonstration of strength, some colorful trick that will frighten everyone . . . though I much prefer taking charge quietly. That's why I've sent for the President.

ELLEN. The President? *Our* President?

KRETON. Yes, he'll be along any minute now.

ELLEN. But the President just doesn't go around visiting people.

KRETON. He'll visit me. *(Chuckles)* It may come as a surprise to him, but he'll be in this house in a very few minutes. I think we'd better go downstairs now. *(To cat)* No, I will not give you a mouse. You must get your own. Be self-reliant. Beast!

Dissolve to the study. Powers is reading book entitled: "The Atom and You." Muffled explosions off-stage.

AIDE *(Entering)*. Sir, nothing seems to be working. Do we have the General's permission to try a fission bomb on the force field?

POWERS. No . . . no. We'd better give it up.

AIDE. The men are beginning to talk.

POWERS *(Thundering)*. Well, keep them quiet! *(Contritely)* I'm sorry, Captain. I'm on edge. Fortunately, the whole business will soon be in the hands of the World Council.

AIDE. What will the World Council do?

POWERS. It will be interesting to observe them.

AIDE. You don't think this Kreton can really take over the world, do you?

POWERS. Of course not. Nobody can.

Dissolve to living room. Mrs. Spelding and Spelding are talking.

MRS. SPELDING. You still haven't asked Mr. Kreton about moving that thing, have you?

SPELDING. There are too many *important* things to ask him.

MRS. SPELDING. I hate to be a nag but you know the trouble I have had getting anything to grow in that part of the garden . . .

JOHN *(Enters)*. Good morning.

MRS. SPELDING. Good morning, John.

JOHN. Any sign of your guest?

MRS. SPELDING. Ellen took his breakfast up to him a few minutes ago.

JOHN. They don't seem to be having much luck, do they? I sure hope you don't mind my staying here like this.

Spelding glowers.

MRS. SPELDING. Why, we love having you! I just hope your family aren't too anxious.

JOHN. One of the G.I.'s finally called them, said I was staying here for the week-end.

SPELDING. The rest of our *lives,* if something isn't done soon.

JOHN. Just how long do you think that'll be, Dad?

SPELDING. Who knows?

Kreton and Ellen enter.

KRETON. Ah, how wonderful to see you again! Let me catch my breath.... Oh, your minds! It's not easy for me, you know. So many crude thoughts blazing away! Yes, Mrs. Spelding, I will move the ship off your roses.

MRS. SPELDING. That's awfully sweet of you.

KRETON. Mr. Spelding, if any interviews are to be granted you will be the first. I promise you.

SPELDING. That's very considerate, I'm sure.

KRETON. So you can stop thinking *those* particular thoughts. And now where is the President?

SPELDING. The President?

KRETON. Yes, I sent for him. He should be here. *(He goes to the terrace window)* Ah, that must be he. *(A swarthy man in uniform with a sash across his chest is standing bewildered, on the terrace. Kreton opens the glass doors)* Come in, sir, come in, Your Excellency. Good of you to come on such short notice. *(Man enters)*

MAN *(In Spanish accent).* Where am I?

KRETON. You *are* the President, aren't you?

MAN. Of course I am the President. What am I doing here? I was dedicating a bridge and I find myself...

KRETON *(Aware of his mistake).* Oh, dear! *Where* was the bridge?

MAN. Where do you think, you idiot, in Paraguay!

KRETON *(To others).* I seem to've made a mistake. Wrong President. *(Gestures and the man disappears)* Seemed rather upset, didn't he?

JOHN. You can make people come and go just like that?

KRETON. Just like that.

Powers looks into room from the study.

POWERS. Good morning, Mr. Kreton. Could I see you for a moment?

KRETON. By all means.

He crosses to the study.

SPELDING. I believe I am going mad.

Cut to study. The Aide stands at attention while Powers addresses Kreton.

POWERS. ... and so we feel, the government of the United States feels, that this problem is too big for any one country, therefore we are turning the whole affair over to Paul Laurent, the Secretary-General of the World Council.

KRETON. Very sensible. I should've thought of that myself.

POWERS. Mr. Laurent is on his way here now. And I may add, Mr. Kreton, you've made me look singularly ridiculous.

KRETON. I'm awfully sorry. *(Pause)* No, you can't kill me.

POWERS. You were reading my mind again.

KRETON. I can't really help it, you know. And such *black* thoughts today, but intense, very intense.

POWERS. I regard you as a menace.

KRETON. I know you do and I think it's awfully unkind. I do mean well.

POWERS. Then go back where you came from and leave us alone.

KRETON. I'm afraid I can't do that just yet ... *Phone rings, the Aide answers it.*

AIDE. He's outside? Sure, let him through. *(To Powers)* The Secretary-General of the World Council is here, sir.

POWERS. *(To Kreton).* I hope you'll listen to *him.*

KRETON. Oh, I shall, of course. I love listening.

The door opens and Paul Laurent, middle-aged and serene, enters. Powers and his Aide stand to attention. Kreton goes forward to shake hands.

LAURENT. Mr. Kreton?

KRETON. At your service, Mr. Laurent.

LAURENT. I welcome you to this planet in the name of the World Council.

KRETON. Thank you sir, thank you.

LAURENT. Could you leave us alone for a moment, General?

POWERS. Yes, sir.

Powers and Aide go. Laurent smiles at Kreton.

LAURENT. Shall we sit down?

KRETON. Yes, yes I love sitting down. I'm afraid my manners are not quite suitable, yet.

They sit down.

LAURENT. Now, Mr. Kreton, in violation of all the rules of diplomacy, may I come to the point?

KRETON. You may.

LAURENT. Why are you here?

KRETON. Curiosity. Pleasure.

LAURENT. You are a tourist then in this time and place?

KRETON *(Nods)*. Yes. Very well put.

LAURENT. We have been informed that you have extraordinary powers.

KRETON. By your standards, yes, they must seem extraordinary.

LAURENT. We have also been informed that it is your intention to . . . to take charge of this world.

KRETON. That is correct. . . . What a remarkable mind you have! I have difficulty looking inside it.

LAURENT *(Laughs)*. Practice. I've attended so many conferences. . . . May I say that your conquest of our world puts your status of tourist in a rather curious light?

KRETON. Oh, I said nothing about *conquest*.

LAURENT. Then how else do you intend to govern? The people won't allow you to direct their lives without a struggle.

KRETON. But I'm sure they will if I ask them to.

LAURENT. You believe you can do all this without, well, without violence?

KRETON. Of course I can. One or two demonstrations and I'm sure they'll do as I ask. *(Smiles)* Watch this. *(Pause: Then shouting. Powers bursts into room)*

POWERS. Now what've you done?

KRETON. Look out the window, your Excellency. *(Laurent goes to window. A rifle floats by, followed by an alarmed soldier)* Nice, isn't it? I confess I worked out a number of rather melodramatic tricks last night. Incidentally, all the rifles of all the soldiers in all the world are now floating in the air. *(Gestures)* Now they have them back.

POWERS *(To Laurent)*. You see, sir, I didn't exaggerate in my report.

LAURENT *(Awed)*. No, no, you certainly didn't.

KRETON. You were skeptical, weren't you?

LAURENT. Naturally. But now I . . . now I think it's possible.

POWERS. That this . . . this gentleman is going to run everything?

LAURENT. Yes, yes I do. And it might be wonderful.

KRETON. You *are* more clever than the others. You begin to see that I mean only good.

LAURENT. Yes, only good. General, do you realize what this means? We can have one government . . .

KRETON. With innumerable bureaus, and intrigue. . .

LAURENT *(Excited)*. And the world could be incredibly prosperous, especially if he'd help us with his superior knowledge.

KRETON *(Delighted)*. I will, I will. I'll teach you to look into one another's minds. You'll find it devastating but enlightening: all that self-interest, those *lurid* emotions . . .

LAURENT. No more countries. No more wars . . .

KRETON *(Startled)*. What? Oh, but I like a lot of countries. Besides, at this stage of your development you're supposed to have lots of countries and lots of wars . . . innumerable wars . . .

LAURENT. But you can help us change all that.

KRETON. *Change* all that! My dear sir, I am your friend.

LAURENT. What do you mean?

KRETON. Why, your deepest pleasure is violence. How can you deny that? It is the whole point to you, the whole point to my hobby . . . and you are my hobby, all mine.

LAURENT. But our lives are devoted to *controlling* violence, and not creating it.

KRETON. Now, don't take me for an utter fool. After all, I can see into your minds. My dear fellow, don't you *know* what you are?

LAURENT. What are we?

KRETON. You are savages. I have returned to the dark ages of an insignificant planet simply because I want the glorious excitement of being among you and revelling in your savagery! There is murder in all your hearts and I love it! It intoxicates me!

LAURENT *(Slowly)*. You hardly flatter us.

KRETON. I didn't mean to be rude but you did ask me why I am here and I've told you.

LAURENT. You have no wish then to . . . to help us poor savages.

KRETON. I couldn't even if I wanted to. You won't be civilized for at least two thousand years and you won't reach the level of my people for about a million years.

LAURENT *(Sadly)*. Then you have come here only to . . . to observe?

KRETON. No, more than that. I mean to regulate your past times. But don't worry: I won't upset things too much. I've decided I don't want to be known to the people. You will go right on with your countries, your squabbles, the way you always have, while I will *secretly* regulate things through you.

LAURENT. The World Council does not govern. We only advise.

KRETON. Well, I shall advise you and you will advise the governments and we shall have a lovely time.

LAURENT. I don't know what to say. You obviously have the power to do as you please.

KRETON. I'm glad you realize that. Poor General Powers is now wondering if a hydrogen bomb might destroy me. It won't, General.

POWERS. Too bad.

KRETON. Now, your Excellency, I shall stay

in this house until you have laid the groundwork for my first project.

LAURENT. And what is that to be?

KRETON. A war! I want one of your really splendid wars, with all the trimmings, all the noise and the fire . . .

LAURENT. A war! You're joking. Why at this moment we are working as hard as we know how *not* to have a war.

KRETON. But secretly you want one. After all, it's the one thing your little race does well. You'd hardly want me to deprive you of your simple pleasures, now would you?

LAURENT. I think you must be mad.

KRETON. Not mad, simply a philanthropist. Of course I myself shall get a great deal of pleasure out of a war (the vibrations must be incredible!) but I'm doing it mostly for you. So, if you don't mind, I want you to arrange a few incidents, so we can get one started spontaneously.

LAURENT. I refuse.

KRETON. In that event, I shall select someone else to head the World Council. Someone who *will* start a war. I suppose there exist a few people here who might like the idea.

LAURENT. How can you do such a horrible thing to us? Can't you see that we don't want to be savages?

KRETON. But you have no choice. Anyway, you're just pulling my leg! I'm sure you want a war as much as the rest of them do and that's what you're going to get: the biggest war you've ever had!

LAURENT *(Stunned)*. Heaven help us!

KRETON *(Exuberant)*. Heaven won't! Oh, what fun it will be! I can hardly wait! *(He strikes the globe of the world a happy blow as we fade out)*

ACT III

Fade in on the study, two weeks later. Kreton is sitting at desk on which a map is spread out. He has a pair of dividers, some models of jet aircraft. Occasionally he pretends to dive bomb, imitating the sound of a bomb going off. Powers enters.

POWERS. You wanted me, sir?

KRETON. Yes, I wanted those figures on radioactive fall-out.

POWERS. They're being made up now, sir. Anything else?

KRETON. Oh, my dear fellow, why do you dislike me so?

POWERS. I am your military aide, sir: I don't have to answer that question. It is outside the sphere of my duties.

KRETON. Aren't you at least happy about your promotion?

POWERS. Under the circumstances, no, sir.

KRETON. I find your attitude baffling.

POWERS. Is that all, sir?

KRETON. You have never once said what you thought of my war plans. Not once have I got a single word of encouragement from you, a single compliment . . . only black thoughts.

POWERS. Since you read my mind, sir, you know what I think.

KRETON. True, but I can't help but feel that deep down inside of you there is just a twinge of professional jealousy. You don't like the idea of an outsider playing your game better than you do. Now confess!

POWERS. I am acting as your aide only under duress.

KRETON *(Sadly)*. Bitter, bitter . . . and to think I chose you especially as my aide. Think of all the other generals who would give anything to have your job.

POWERS. Fortunately, they know nothing about my job.

KRETON. Yes, I do think it wise not to advertise my presence, don't you?

POWERS. I can't see that it makes much difference, since you seem bent on destroying our world.

KRETON. I'm not going to destroy it. A few dozen cities, that's all, and not very nice cities either. Think of the fun you'll have building new ones when it's over.

POWERS. How many millions of people do you plan to kill?

KRETON. Well, quite a few, but they love this sort of thing. You can't convince me they don't. Oh, I know what Laurent says. But he's a misfit, out of step with his time. Fortunately, my new World Council is more reasonable.

POWERS. Paralyzed is the word, sir.

KRETON. You don't think they like me either?

POWERS. You *know* they hate you, sir.

KRETON. But love and hate are so confused in your savage minds and the vibrations of the one are so very like those of the other that I can't always distinguish. You see, we neither love nor hate in my world. We simply have hobbies. *(He strokes the globe of the world tenderly)* But now to work. Tonight's the big night: first, the sneak attack, then: boom! *(He claps his hands gleefully)*

Dissolve to the living room, to John and Ellen.

ELLEN. I've never felt so helpless in my life.

JOHN. Here we all stand around doing nothing while he plans to blow up the world.

ELLEN. Suppose we went to the newspapers.

JOHN. He controls the press. When Laurent resigned they didn't even print his speech. *(A gloomy pause)*

ELLEN. What are you thinking about, John?

JOHN. Walnuts. *(They embrace)*

ELLEN. Can't we do anything?

JOHN. No, I guess there's nothing.

ELLEN *(Vehemently)*. Oh! I could kill him!

Kreton and Powers enter.

KRETON. Very good, Ellen, *very* good! I've never felt you so violent.

ELLEN. You heard what I said to John?

KRETON. Not in words, but you were absolutely bathed in malevolence.

POWERS. I'll get the papers you wanted, sir.

Powers exits.

KRETON. I don't think he likes me very much but your father does. Only this morning he offered to handle my public relations and I said I'd let him. Wasn't that nice of him?

JOHN. I think I'll go get some fresh air. *(He goes out through the terrace door)*

KRETON. Oh, dear! *(Sighs)* Only your father is really entering the spirit of the game. He's a much better sport than you, my dear.

ELLEN *(Exploding)*. Sport! That's it! You think we're sport. You think we're animals to be played with: well, we're not. We're people and we don't want to be destroyed.

KRETON *(Patiently)*. But *I* am not destroying you. You will be destroying one another of your own free will, as you have always done. I am simply a . . . a kibitzer.

ELLEN. No, you are a vampire!

KRETON. A vampire? You mean I drink blood? Ugh!

ELLEN. No, you drink emotions, our emotions. You'll sacrifice us all for the sake of your . . . your vibrations!

KRETON. Touché. Yet what harm am I really doing? It's true I'll enjoy the war more than anybody; but it will be *your* destructiveness after all, not mine.

ELLEN. You could stop it.

KRETON. So could you.

ELLEN. I?

KRETON. Your race. They could stop altogether but they won't. And I can hardly intervene in their natural development. The most I can do is help out in small, practical ways.

ELLEN. We are not what you think. We're not so . . . so primitive.

KRETON. My dear girl, just take this one household: your mother dislikes your father but she is too tired to do anything about it so she knits and she gardens and she tries not to think about him. Your father, on the other hand, is bored with all of you. Don't look shocked: he doesn't like you any more than you like him . . .

ELLEN. Don't say that!

KRETON. I am only telling you the truth. Your father wants you to marry someone important; therefore he objects to John while you, my girl . . .

ELLEN *(With a fierce cry, Ellen grabs vase to throw).* You devil! *(Vase breaks in her hand)*

KRETON. You see? That proves my point perfectly. *(Gently)* Poor savage, I cannot help what you are. *(Briskly)* Anyway, you will soon be distracted from your personal problems. Tonight is the night. If you're a good girl, I'll let you watch the bombing.

Dissolve to study: Eleven forty-five. Powers and the Aide gloomily await the war.

AIDE. General, isn't there anything we can do?

POWERS. It's out of our hands.

Kreton, dressed as a Hussar with shako, enters.

KRETON. Everything on schedule?

POWERS. Yes, sir. Planes left for their targets at twenty-two hundred.

KRETON. Good . . . good. I myself, shall take off shortly after midnight to observe the attack first-hand.

POWERS. Yes, sir.

Kreton goes into the living room where the family is gloomily assembled.

KRETON *(Enters from study).* And now the magic hour approaches! I hope you're all as thrilled as I am.

SPELDING. You still won't tell us who's attacking whom?

KRETON. You'll know in exactly . . . fourteen minutes.

ELLEN *(Bitterly).* Are we going to be killed too?

KRETON. Certainly not! You're quite safe, at least in the early stages of the war.

ELLEN. Thank you.

MRS. SPELDING. I suppose this will mean rationing again.

SPELDING. Will . . .will we see anything from here?

KRETON. No, but there should be a good picture on the monitor in the study. Powers is tuning in right now.

JOHN *(At window).* Hey look, up there! Coming this way!

Ellen joins him.

ELLEN. What is it?

JOHN. Why . . . it's *another* one! And it's going to land.

KRETON *(Surprised).* I'm sure you're mistaken. No one would dream of coming here. *He has gone to the window, too.*

ELLEN. It's landing!

SPELDING. Is it a friend of yours, Mr. Kreton?

KRETON *(Slowly).* No, no, not a friend . . .

Kreton retreats to the study; he inadvertently drops a lace handkerchief beside the sofa.

JOHN. Here he comes.

ELLEN *(Suddenly bitter).* Now we have two of them.

MRS. SPELDING. My poor roses.

The new Visitor enters in a gleam of light from his ship. He is wearing a most futuristic costume. Without a word, he walks past the awed family into the study. Kreton is cowering behind the globe. Powers and the Aide stare, bewildered, as the Visitor gestures sternly and Kreton reluctantly removes shako and sword. They communicate by odd sounds.

VISITOR *(To Powers).* Please leave us alone.

Cut to living room as Powers and the Aide enter from the study.

POWERS *(To Ellen).* Who on earth was that?

ELLEN. It's another one, another visitor.

POWERS. Now we're done for.

ELLEN. I'm going in there.

MRS. SPELDING. Ellen, don't you dare!

ELLEN. I'm going to talk to them. *(Starts to door)*

JOHN. I'm coming, too.

ELLEN *(Grimly).* No, alone. I know what I want to say.

Cut to interior of the study, to Kreton and the other Visitor as Ellen enters.

ELLEN. I want you both to listen to me . . .

VISITOR. You don't need to speak. I know what you will say.

ELLEN. That you have no right here? That you mustn't . . .

VISITOR. I agree. Kreton has no right here. He is well aware that it is forbidden to interfere with the past.

ELLEN. The past?

VISITOR *(Nods)*. You are the past, the dark ages: we are from the future. In fact, we are *your* descendants on another planet. We visit you from time to time but we never interfere because it would change *us* if we did. Fortunately, I have arrived in time.

ELLEN. There won't be a war?

VISITOR. There will be no war. And there will be no memory of any of this. When we leave here you will forget Kreton and me. Time will turn back to the moment before his arrival.

ELLEN. Why did you want to hurt us?

KRETON *(Heart-broken)*. Oh, but I didn't! I only wanted to have . . . well, to have a little fun, to indulge my hobby . . . against the rules of course.

VISITOR *(To Ellen)*. Kreton is a rarity among us. Mentally and morally he is retarded. He is a child and he regards your period as his toy.

KRETON. A child, now really!

VISITOR. He escaped from his nursery and came back in time to you . . .

KRETON. And *every*thing went wrong, everything! I wanted to visit 1860 . . . that's my *real* period but then something happened to the car and I ended up here, not that I don't find you nearly as interesting but . . .

VISITOR. We must go, Kreton.

KRETON *(To Ellen)*. You did like me just a bit, didn't you?

ELLEN. Yes, yes I did, until you let your hobby get out of hand. *(To Visitor)* What is the future like?

VISITOR. Very serene, very different . . .

KRETON. Don't believe him: it is dull, dull, dull beyond belief! One simply floats through eternity: no wars, no excitement . . .

VISITOR. It is forbidden to discuss these matters.

KRETON. I can't see what difference it makes since she's going to forget all about us anyway.

ELLEN. Oh, how I'd love to see the future . . .

VISITOR. It is against . . .

KRETON. Against the rules: how tiresome, you are. *(To Ellen)* But, alas, you can never pay us a call because you aren't born yet! I mean where we are you are not. Oh, Ellen, dear, think kindly of me, until you forget.

ELLEN. I will.

VISITOR. Come. Time has begun to turn back. Time is bending.

He starts to door. Kreton turns conspiratorially to Ellen.

KRETON. Don't be sad, my girl. I shall be back one bright day, but a bright day in 1860. I dote on the Civil War, so exciting . . .

VISITOR. Kreton!

KRETON. Only next time I think it'll be more fun if the *South* wins!

He hurries after the Visitor.

Cut to clock as the hands spin backwards. Dissolve to the living room, exactly the same as the first scene: Spelding, Mrs Spelding, Ellen.

SPELDING. There is nothing wrong with marrying a wealthy man. The horror of it has always eluded me. However, my only wish is that you marry someone hard-working, ambitious, a man who'll make his mark in the world. Not a boy who is content to sit on a farm all his life, growing peanuts . . .

ELLEN. English walnuts! And he won't just sit there.

SPELDING. Will you stop contradicting me?

ELLEN. But, Daddy, John grows walnuts . . .

John enters.

JOHN. Hello, everybody.

MRS. SPELDING. Good evening, John.

ELLEN. What kept you, darling? You missed Daddy's broadcast.

JOHN. I saw it before I left home. Wonderful broadcast, sir.

SPELDING. Thank you, John.

John crosses to window.

JOHN. That meteor you were talking about, well, for a while it looked almost like a space ship or something. You can just barely see it now.

Ellen joins him at window. They watch, arms about one another.

SPELDING. Space ship! Nonsense! Remarkable what some people will believe, *want* to believe. Besides, as I said in the broadcast: if there's any traveling to be done in space we'll do it first.

He notices Kreton's handkerchief on sofa and picks it up. They all look at it, puzzled, as we cut to stock shot of the starry night against which two space ships vanish in the distance, one serene in its course, the other erratic, as we fade out.

WHAT DO YOU SAY?

Act I

1. What is the time?

2. (a) How would you describe the place? *(b)* How would you describe the space ship?

3. What characters are introduced, and what are their relationships to one another?

4. (a) What are the clues to Mrs. Spelding's character? *(b)* What kind of woman is she?

5. What are the main interests of Roger Spelding?

6. How is Kreton dressed?

7. What is going on in the Spelding house at the time John announces that the space ship is going to land?

8. (a) Why has Kreton come to visit earth? *(b)* What is his attitude toward earth people? *(c)* What does Powers suspect of Kreton? *(d)* In what ways are the earth people at a disadvantage with Kreton? *(e)* What clues show that Kreton was an "odd" person on his own planet?

Act II

1. What various reactions do the other characters show toward Kreton?

2. (a) In Kreton's mind what is the status of earth's "civilization"? *(b)* How far have earth people progressed compared with his own people?

3. (a) By what powers can Kreton conquer the world? Bring peace if he wishes? *(b)* What are his plans?

Act III

1. (a) As Act III opens what is the relationship of Powers to Kreton? *(b)* What is Powers' feeling about his "promotion"?

2. What leads up to Ellen's throwing a vase at Kreton?

3. (a) At what point does the play's crisis come, where the action can go either way? *(b)* During the crisis how are the reactions of the Spelding family members typical of their characters as earlier established?

4. (a) How is the plot resolved? *(b)* What do you make of the fact that the earth people and the visitors part in the end without apparently having changed each other?

5. Why are the stock shots at the end and at the beginning of the play the same?

6. What is the serious point behind the satire in this play?

GORE VIDAL

Gore Vidal wrote his first novel, ***Williwaw,*** in 1946 while he was a nineteen-year-old first mate of an army freighter in the Aleutians. Since then he has written novels, plays, and poems in impressive number. Though he has experimented with style and theme, and his work has ranged from realism to allegory, his main view is that human relationships are important but at the same time irrelevant in our impersonal universe. This outlook pervades the satirical ***Visit to a Small Planet.***

THE MOTHER

PADDY CHAYEFSKY

Characters

OLD LADY
DAUGHTER
BOSS
SON-IN-LAW
NEGRO WOMAN
SISTER
MRS. GEEGAN
MRS. KLINE
BOOKKEEPER
PUERTO RICAN GIRL

ACT I

Fade in: Film—a quick group of shots showing New York in a real thunderstorm—rain whipping through the streets—real miserable weather.

Dissolve to: Close-up of an old woman, aged sixty-six, with a shock of gray-white hair, standing by a window in her apartment, looking out, apparently deeply disturbed by the rain slashing against the pane.

We pull back to see that the old woman is wearing an old kimono, under which there is evidence of an old white batiste nightgown. Her gray-white hair hangs loosely down over her shoulders. It is early morning, and she has apparently just gotten out of bed. This is the bedroom of her two-and-a-half-room apartment in a lower-middle-class neighborhood in the Bronx. The bed is still unmade and looks just slept in. The furniture is old and worn. On the chest of drawers there is a galaxy of photographs and portrait pictures, evidently of her various children and grandchildren. She stands looking out the window, troubled, disturbed.

Suddenly the alarm, perched on the little bed table, rings. Camera moves in for close-up of the alarm clock. It reads half past six. The old lady's hand comes down and shuts the alarm off.

Cut to: Close-up of another alarm clock, ringing in another apartment. It also reads half past six; but it is obviously a different clock, on a much more modern bed table. This one buzzes instead of clangs. A young woman's hand reaches over and turns it off.

Camera pulls back to show that we are in the bedroom of a young couple. The young woman who has turned the clock off is a rather plain girl of thirty. She slowly sits up in bed, assembling herself for the day. On the other half of the bed, her husband turns and tries to go back to sleep.

SON-IN-LAW *(From under the blankets)*. What time is it?

DAUGHTER *(Still seated heavily on the edge of the bed)*. It's half past six.

SON-IN-LAW *(From under the blankets)*. What did you set it so early for?

DAUGHTER. I wanna call my mother. *(She looks out at the window, the rain driving fiercely against it)* For heaven's sake, listen to that rain! She's not going down today, I'll tell you that, if I have to go over there and chain her in her bed. . . . *(She stands, crosses to the window, studies the rain.)* Boy, look at it rain.

SON-IN-LAW *(Still under the covers)*. What?

DAUGHTER. I said, it's raining.

She makes her way, still heavy with sleep, out of the bedroom into the foyer of the apartment. She pads in her bare feet and pajamas down the foyer to the telephone table, sits on the little chair, trying to clear her head of sleep. A baby's cry is suddenly heard in an off room. The young woman absently goes "Sshh." The baby's cry stops. The young woman picks up the receiver of the phone and dials. She waits. Then . . .

DAUGHTER. Ma? This is Annie. Did I wake you up?. . . I figured you'd be up by now. . . . Ma, you're not going downtown today, and I don't wanna hear no arguments . . . Ma, have you looked out the window? It's raining like . . . Ma, I'm not gonna let you go downtown today, do you hear me?. . . I don't care, Ma . . . Ma, I don't care . . . Ma, I'm coming over. You stay there till . . . Ma, stay there till I come over. I'm getting dressed right now. I'll drive over in the car. It won't take me ten minutes . . . Ma, you're not going out in this rain. It's not enough that you almost fainted in the subway yesterday . . . Ma, I'm hanging up, and I'm coming over right now. Stay there . . . all right, I'm hanging up . . .

She hangs up, sits for a minute, then rises and shuffles quickly back up the foyer and back into her bedroom. She disappears into the bathroom, unbuttoning the blouse of her pajamas. She leaves the bathroom door open, and a shaft of light suddenly shoots out into the dark bedroom.

SON-IN-LAW *(Awake now, his head visible over the covers)*. Did you talk to her?

DAUGHTER *(Off in bathroom)*. Yeah, she was all practically ready to leave.

SON-IN-LAW. Look, Annie, I don't wanna tell you how to treat your own mother, but why don't you leave her alone? It's obviously very important to her to get a job for herself. She wants to support herself. She doesn't want to be a burden on her children. I respect her for that. An old lady, sixty-six years old, going out and looking for work. I think that shows a lot of guts.

The daughter comes out of the bathroom. She has a blouse on now and a half-slip.

DAUGHTER *(Crossing to the closet)*. George, please, you don't know what you're talking about, so do me a favor, and don't argue with me. I'm not in a good mood. *(She opens the closet, studies the crowded rack of clothes)* I'm turning on the light, so get your eyes ready. *(She turns on the light. The room is suddenly bright. She blinks and pokes in the closet for a skirt, which she finally extracts)* My mother worked like a dog all her life, and she's not gonna spend the rest of her life bent over a sewing machine. *(She slips into the skirt)* She had one of her attacks in the subway yesterday. I was never so scared in my life when that cop called yesterday. *(She's standing in front of her mirror now, hastily arranging her hair)* My mother worked like a dog to raise me and my brother and my sister. She worked in my old man's grocery store till twelve o'clock at night. We owe her a little peace of mind, my brother and my sister and me. She sacrificed plenty for us in her time. *(She's back at the closet, fishing for her topcoat)* And I want her to move out of that apartment. I don't want her living alone. I want her to come live here with us, George, and I don't want any more arguments about that either. We can move Tommy in with the baby, and she can have Tommy's room. And that reminds me—the baby cried for a minute there. If she cries again, give her her milk because she went to sleep without her milk last night. *(She has her topcoat on now and is already at the door to the foyer)* All right, I'll probably be back in time to make your breakfast. Have you got the keys to the car?... *(She nervously pats the pocket of her coat)* No, I got them. All right, I'll see you. Good-by, George...

She goes out into the foyer.

SON-IN-LAW. Good-by, Annie...

Off in some other room, the baby begins to cry again, a little more insistently. The husband raises his eyebrows and listens for a moment. When it becomes apparent that the baby isn't going to stop, he sighs and begins to get out of bed.

Dissolve to: The old lady standing by the window again. She is fully dressed now, however, even to the black coat and hat. The coat is unbuttoned. For the first time, we may be aware of a black silk mourning band that the old lady has about the sleeve of her coat. Outside, the rain has abated considerably. It is drizzling lightly now. The old lady turns to her daughter, standing at the other end of the bedroom, brushing the rain from her coat. When the old lady speaks, it is with a mild, but distinct, Irish flavor.

OLD LADY. It's letting up a bit.

DAUGHTER *(Brushing off her coat)*. It isn't letting up at all. It's gonna stop and start all day long.

The old lady starts out of her bedroom, past her daughter, into her living room.

OLD LADY. I'm going to make a bit of coffee for myself and some Rice Krispies. Would you like a cup?

The daughter turns and starts into the living room ahead of her mother.

DAUGHTER. I'll make it for you.

OLD LADY. You won't make it for me. I'll make it myself.

She crowds past the daughter and goes to the kitchen. At the kitchen doorway, she turns and surveys her daughter.

OLD LADY. Annie, you know, you can drive somebody crazy, do you know that?

DAUGHTER. I can drive somebody crazy! *You're* the one who can drive somebody crazy.

OLD LADY. Will you stop hovering over me like I was a cripple in a wheel chair. I can make my own coffee, believe me. Why did you come over here? You've got a husband and two kids to take care of. Go make coffee for them, for heaven's sakes.

She turns and goes into the kitchen, muttering away. She opens a cupboard and extracts a jar of instant coffee.

OLD LADY. I've taken to making instant coffee, would you like a cup?

The daughter is standing on the threshold of the kitchen now, leaning against the doorjamb.

DAUGHTER. All right, make me a cup, Ma.

The old lady takes two cups and saucers out and begins carefully to level out a teaspoonful of the instant coffee into each. The daughter moves into the kitchen, reaches up for something in the cupboard.

DAUGHTER. Where do you keep your saccharin, Ma?

The old lady wheels and slaps the daughter's outstetched arms down.

OLD LADY. Annie, I'll get it myself! *(She points a finger into the living room)* Go in there and sit down, will you? I'll bring the cup in to you!

The daughter leans back against the doorjamb, a little exasperated with the old lady's petulant independence. The old lady now takes an old teapot and sets it on the stove and lights a flame under it.

OLD LADY. You can drive me to the subway if you want to do something for me.

DAUGHTER. Ma, you're not going downtown today.

OLD LADY. I want to get down there extra early today on the off-chance that they haven't given the job to someone else. What did I do with that card from the New York State Employment Service?...

She shuffles out of the kitchen, the daughter moving out of the doorway to give her passage. The old lady goes to the table in the living room on which sits her battered black purse. She opens it and takes out a card.

OLD LADY. I don't want to lose that. *(She puts the white card back into her purse)* I'm pretty sure I could have held onto this job, because the chap at the Employment Service called up the boss, you see, over the phone, and he explained to the man that I hadn't worked in quite a number of years...

DAUGHTER *(Muttering)*. Quite a number of years...

OLD LADY. ... and that I'd need a day or so to get used to the machines again.

DAUGHTER. Did the chap at the Employment Service explain to the boss that it's forty years that you haven't worked?

OLD LADY *(Crossing back to the kitchen)*. ... and the boss understood this, you see, so he would have been a little lenient with me. But then, of course, I had to go and faint in the subway, because I was in such a hurry to get down there, you know, I didn't even stop to eat my lunch. I had brought along some sandwiches, you see, cheese and tomatoes. Oh, I hope he hasn't given the job to anyone else...

The old lady reaches into the cupboard again for a bowl of sugar, an opened box of Rice Krispies, and a bowl. The daughter watches her as she turns to the refrigerator to get out a container of milk.

DAUGHTER. Ma, when are you gonna give up?

The old lady frowns.

OLD LADY. Annie, please...

She pours some Rice Krispies into the bowl.

DAUGHTER. Ma, you been trying for three weeks now. If you get a job, you get fired before the day is over. You're too old, Ma, and they don't want to hire old people...

OLD LADY. It's not the age...

DAUGHTER. They don't want to hire white-haired old ladies.

OLD LADY. It's not the age at all! I've seen plenty old people with white hair and all, sitting at those machines. The shop where I almost had that job and he fired me the other day, there was a woman there, eighty years old if she was a day, an old crone of a woman, sitting there all bent over, her machine humming away. The chap at the Employment Service said there's a lot of elderly people working in the needle trades. The young people nowadays don't want to work for thirty-five, forty dollars a week, and there's a lot of old people working in the needle trades.

DAUGHTER. Well, whatever it is, Ma . . .

OLD LADY *(Leaning to her daughter)*. It's my fingers. I'm not sure of them any more. When you get old, y'know, you lose the sureness in your fingers. My eyes are all right, but my fingers tremble a lot. I get excited, y'know, when I go in for a tryout, y'know. And I'll go in, y'know, and the boss'll say: "Sit down, let's see what you can do." And I get so excited. And my heart begins thumping so that I can hardly see to thread the needle. And they stand right over you, y'know, while you're working. They give you a packet of sleeves or a shirt or something to put a hem on. Or a seam or something, y'know. It's simple work, really. Single-needle machine. Nothing fancy. And it seems to me I do it all right, but they fire me all the time. They say: "You're too slow." And I'm working as fast as I can. I think, perhaps, I've lost the ability in my fingers. And that's what scares me the most. It's not the age. I've seen plenty of old women working in the shops.

She has begun to pour some milk into her bowl of cereal; but she stops now and just stands, staring bleakly down at the worn oilcloth on her cupboard.

DAUGHTER *(Gently)*. Ma, you worked all your life. Why don't you take it easy?

OLD LADY. I don't want to take it easy. Now that your father's dead and in the grave I don't know what to do with myself.

DAUGHTER. Why don't you go out, sit in the park, get a little sun like the other old women?

OLD LADY. I sit around here sometimes, going crazy. We had a lot of fights in our time, your father and I, but I must admit I miss him badly. You can't live with someone forty-one years and not miss him when he's dead. I'm glad that he died for his own sake—it may sound hard of me to say that—but I am glad. He was in nothing but pain the last few months, and he was a man who could never stand pain. But I do miss him.

DAUGHTER *(Gently)*. Ma, why don't you come live with George and me?

OLD LADY. No, no, Annie, you're a good daughter. . . .

DAUGHTER. We'll move Tommy into the baby's room, and you can have Tommy's room. It's the nicest room in the apartment. It gets all the sun . . .

OLD LADY. I have wonderful children. I thank God every night for that. I . . .

DAUGHTER. Ma, I don't like you living here alone . . .

OLD LADY. Annie, I been living in this house for eight years, and I know all the neighbors and the store people, and if I lived with you, I'd be a stranger.

DAUGHTER. There's plenty of old people in my neighborhood. You'll make friends.

OLD LADY. Annie, you're a good daughter, but I want to keep my own home. I want to pay my own rent. I don't want to be some old lady living with her children. If I can't take care of myself, I just as soon be in the grave with your father. I don't want to be a burden on my children . . .

DAUGHTER. Ma, for heaven's sakes . . .

OLD LADY. More than anything else, I don't want to be a burden on my children. I pray to God every night to let me keep my health and my strength so that I won't have to be a burden on my children . . . *(The teapot suddenly hisses. The old lady looks up)* Annie, the pot is boiling. Would you pour the water in the cups?

The daughter moves to the stove. The old lady, much of her ginger seemingly sapped out of her, shuffles into the living room. She perches on the edge of one of the wooden chairs.

OLD LADY. I been getting some pains in my shoulder the last week or so. I had the electric heating pad on practically the whole night. . . . *(She looks up toward the windows again)* It's starting to rain a little harder again. Maybe, I won't go downtown today after all. Maybe, if it

clears up a bit, I'll go out and sit in the park and get some sun.

In the kitchen, the daughter pours the boiling water into each cup, stirs.

DAUGHTER *(To her mother, off in the living room).* Is this all you're eating for breakfast, Ma? Let me make you something else . . .

Dissolve to: A park bench. The old lady and two other old ladies are seated, all bundled up in their cheap cloth coats with the worn fur collars. The second old lady is also Irish. Her name is Mrs. Geegan. The third old lady is possibly Jewish, certainly a New Yorker by intonation. Her name is Mrs. Kline. The rain has stopped; it is a clear, bright, sunny March morning.

OLD LADY. . . . Well, it's nice and clear now, isn't it? It was raining something fierce around seven o'clock this morning.

MRS. GEEGAN *(Grimacing).* It's too ruddy cold for me. I'd go home except my daughter-in-law's cleaning the house, and I don't want to get in her way.

MRS. KLINE. My daughter-in-law should drop dead tomorrow.

MRS. GEEGAN. My daughter-in-law gets into an awful black temper when she's cleaning.

MRS. KLINE. My daughter-in-law should grow rich and own a hotel with a thousand rooms and be found dead in every one of them.

MRS. GEEGAN *(To the old lady).* I think I'll go over and visit Missus Halley in a little while, would you like to go? She fell down the stairs and broke her hip, and they're suing the owners of the building. I saw her son yesterday, and he says she's awful weak. When you break a hip at that age, you're as good as in the coffin. I don't like to visit Missus Halley. She's always so gloomy about things. But it's a way of killing off an hour or so to lunch. A little later this afternoon, I thought I'd go to confession. It's so warm and solemn in the church. Do you go to Saint John's? I think it's ever so much prettier than Our Lady of Visitation. Why don't you come to Missus Halley's with me, Missus Fanning? Her son's a sweet man, and there's always a bit of fruit they offer you.

OLD LADY. I don't believe I know a Missus Halley.

MRS. GEEGAN. Missus Halley, the one that fell down the stairs last week and dislocated her hip. They're suing the owners of the building for forty thousand dollars.

MRS. KLINE. They'll settle for a hundred, believe me.

MRS. GEEGAN. Oh, it's chilly this morning. I'd go home, but my daughter-in-law is cleaning the house, and she doesn't like me to be about when she's cleaning. I'd like a bottle of beer, that's what I'd like. Oh, my mouth is fairly watering for it. I'm not allowed to have beer, you know. I'm a diabetic. You don't happen to have a quarter on you, Missus Fanning? We could buy a bottle and split it between us. I'd ask my son for it, but they always want to know what I want the money for.

OLD LADY *(Looking sharply at Mrs. Geegan).* Do you have to ask your children for money?

MRS. GEEGAN. Oh, they're generous. They always give me whenever I ask. But I'm not allowed to have beer, you see, and they wouldn't give me the twenty-five cents for that. What do I need money for anyway? Go to the movies? I haven't been to the movies in more than a year, I think. I just like a dollar every now and then for an offering at mass. Do you go to seven o'clock novena, Missus Fanning? It's a good way to spend an hour, I think.

OLD LADY. Is that what you do with your day, Missus Geegan? Visit dying old ladies and go to confession?

MRS. GEEGAN. Well, I like to stay in the house a lot, watching television in the

afternoons, with the kiddie shows and a lot of dancing and Kate Smith and shows like that. But my daughter-in-law's cleaning up today, and she doesn't like me around the house when she's cleaning, so I came out a bit early to sit in the park.
The old lady regards Mrs. Geegan for a long moment.

MRS. KLINE. My daughter-in-law, she should invest all her money in General Motors stock, and they should go bankrupt.
A pause settles over the three old ladies. They just sit, huddled, their cheeks pressed into the fur of their collars. After a moment, the old lady shivers noticeably.

OLD LADY. It's a bit chilly. I think I'll go home. *(She rises)* Good-by, Missus Geegan . . . Good-by, Missus . . .
The other two old ladies nod their good-bys. The old lady moves off screen. We hold for a moment on the remaining two old ladies, sitting, shoulders hunched against the morning chill, faces pressed under their collars, staring bleakly ahead.
Dissolve to: Door of the old lady's apartment. It opens, and the old lady comes in. She closes the door behind her, goes up the small foyer to the living room. She unbuttons her coat and walks aimlessly around the room, into the bedroom and out again, across the living room and into the kitchen, and then out of the kitchen. She is frowning as she walks and rubs her hands continually as if she is quite cold. Suddenly she goes to the telephone, picks it up, dials a number, waits.

OLD LADY *(Snappishly).* Is this Mister McCleod? This is Missus Fanning in Apartment 3F! The place is a refrigerator up here! It's freezing! I want some steam! I want it right now! That's all there is to it! I want some steam right now!
She hangs up sharply, turns—scowling—and sits heavily down on the edge of a soft chair, scowling, nervous, rocking a little back and forth. Then abruptly she rises, crosses the living room to the television set, clicks it on. She stands in front of it, waiting for a picture to show. At last the picture comes on. It is the WPIX station signal, accompanied by the steady high-pitched drone that indicates there are no programs on yet. She turns the set off almost angrily.

She is beginning to breathe heavily now. She turns nervously and looks at the large ornamental clock on the sideboard. It reads ten minutes after eleven. She goes to the small dining table and sits down on one of the hard-back chairs. Her black purse is still on the table, as it was during the scene with her daughter. Her eyes rest on it for a moment; then she reaches over, opens the purse, and takes out the white employment card. She looks at it briefly, expressionlessly. Then she returns it to the purse and reclasps the purse. Again she sits for a moment, rigid, expressionless. Then suddenly she stands, grabs the purse, and starts out the living room, down the foyer, to the front door of her apartment—buttoning her coat as she goes. She opens the door, goes out.

Camera stays on door as it is closed. There is the noise of a key being inserted into the lock. A moment later the bolts on the lock shift into locked position. Hold.

Fade out.

ACT II

Fade in: Film. Lunchtime in the needle-trade district of New York—a quick montage of shots of the streets, jammed with traffic, trucks, and working people hurrying to the dense little luncheonettes for their lunch.

Dissolve to: Interior of the Tiny Tots Sportswear Co., Inc., 137 West Twenty-seventh Street, on the eighth floor. It is lunchtime. We dissolve in on some of the women operators at their lunch. They are seated at their machines, of which there are twenty—in two rows of ten, facing each other. Not all of the operators eat their lunch in: about half go downstairs to join the teeming noontime crowds in the oily little restaurants of the vicinity. The ten-or-so women whom we see—munching their sandwiches and sipping their containers of coffee and chattering shrilly to one another—all wear worn house dresses. A good proportion of the operators are Negro and Puerto Rican. Not a few of them are gray-haired, or at least unmistakably middle-aged.

The rest of the shop seems to consist of endless rows of pipe racks on which hang finished children's dresses, waiting to be shipped. In the middle of these racks is a pressing machine and sorting table at which two of the three men who work in the shop eat their lunch. At the far end of the loft—in a corner so dark that a light must always be on over it—is an old, battered roll-top desk at which sits the bookkeeper, an angular woman of thirty-five, differentiated from the hand workers in that she wears a clean dress.

Nearby is the boss, a man in his thirties. He is bent over a machine, working on it with a screw driver. The boss is really a pleasant man; he works under the illusion, however, that gruffness is a requisite quality of an executive.

Somehow, a tortured passageway has been worked out between the racks leading to the elevator doors; it is the only visible exit and entrance to the loft.

As we look at these doors, there is a growing whirring and clanging announcing the arrival of the elevator. The doors slide reluctantly open, and the old lady enters the shop. The elevator doors slide closed behind her. She stands surrounded by pipe racks, a little apprehensive. The arrival of the elevator has caused some of the people to look up briefly. The old lady goes to the presser, a Puerto Rican.

OLD LADY. Excuse me, I'm looking for the boss.

The presser indicates with his hand the spot where the boss is standing, working on the machine. The old lady picks her way through the cluttered pipe racks to the bookkeeper, who looks up at her approach. The boss also looks up briefly at her approach, but goes back to his work. The old lady opens her purse, takes out the white card, and proffers it to the bookkeeper. She mutters something.

BOOKKEEPER. Excuse me, I can't hear what you said.

OLD LADY. I said, I was supposed to be here yesterday, but I was sick in the subway I—fainted, you see and . . .

The boss now turns to the old lady.

BOSS. What? . . . What? . . .

OLD LADY. I was sent down from the . . .
BOSS. What?
OLD LADY *(Louder)*. I was sent down from the New York State Employment Service. I was supposed to be here yesterday.
BOSS. Yes, so what happened?
OLD LADY. I was sick, I fainted in the subway.
BOSS. What?
OLD LADY *(Louder)*. I was sick. The subway was so hot there, you see—there was a big crush at a Hundred and Forty-ninth Street . . .
BOSS. You was supposed to be here yesterday.
OLD LADY. I had a little trouble. They had my daughter down there and everything. By the time I got down here, it was half past five, and the fellow on the elevator—not the one that was here this morning—another fellow entirely. An old man it was. He said there was nobody up here. So I was going to come down early this morning, but I figured you probably had the job filled anyway. That's why I didn't come down till now.
BOSS. What kind of work do you do?
OLD LADY. Well, I used to do all sections except joining and zippers, but I think the fellow at the Employment Service explained to you that it's been a number of years since I actually worked in a shop.
BOSS. What do you mean, a number of years?
OLD LADY *(Mumbling)*. Well, I did a lot of sewing for the Red Cross during the war, y'know, but I haven't actually worked in a shop since 1916.
BOSS *(Who didn't quite hear her mumbled words)*. What?
OLD LADY *(Louder)*. Nineteen sixteen. October.
BOSS. Nineteen sixteen.
OLD LADY. I'm sure if I could work a little bit, I would be fine. I used to be a very fast worker.
BOSS. Can you thread a machine?

The old lady nods.

He starts off through the maze of pipe racks to the two rows of machines. The old lady follows after him, clutching her purse and the white card, her hat still sitting on her head, her coat still buttoned. As they go up the rows of sewing machines, the other operators look up to catch covert glimpses of the new applicant. The boss indicates one of the open machines.

BOSS. All right. Siddown. Show me how you thread a machine.

The old lady sets her purse down nervously and takes the seat behind the machine. The other operators have all paused in their eating to watch the test. The old lady reaches to her side, where there are several spools of thread.

OLD LADY. What kind of thread, white or black? . . .

BOSS. White! White!

She fumblingly fetches a spool of white thread and, despite the fact she is obviously trembling, she contrives to thread the machine—a process which takes about half a minute. The boss stands towering over her.

BOSS. Can you sleeve?

The old lady nods, desperately trying to get the thread through the eye of the needle and over the proper holes.

BOSS. It's a simple business. One seam. *He reaches into the bin belonging to the machine next to the one the old lady is working on and extracts a neatly tied bundle of sleeve material. He drops it on the table beside the old lady.*

BOSS. All right, make a sleeve. Let's see how you make a sleeve.

He breaks the string and gives her a piece of sleeve material. She takes it, but is so nervous it falls to the floor. She hurriedly bends to pick it up, inserts the sleeve into the machine, and hunches into her work—her face screwed tight with intense concentration. She has still not unbuttoned her coat, and beads of sweat begin to appear on her brow. With painstaking laboriousness, she slowly moves the sleeve material into the machine. The boss stands, impatient and scowling.

BOSS. Mama, what are you weaving there, a carpet? It's a lousy sleeve, for Pete's sake.

OLD LADY. I'm a little unsure. My fingers are a little unsure . . .

BOSS. You gotta be fast, Mama. This is week work. It's not piecework. I'm paying you by the hour. I got twenny dozen cottons here, gotta be out by six o'clock. The truckman isn't gonna wait, you know . . . Mama, Mama, watch what you're doing there . . . *(He leans quickly forward and reguides the material)* A straight seam, for heaven's sake! You're making it crooked . . . Watch it! Watch it! Watch what you're doing there, Mama . . . All right, sew. Don't let me make you nervous. Sew . . . Mama, wadda you sewing there, an appendicitis operation? It's a lousy sleeve. How long you gonna take? I want operators here, not surgeons . . .

Through all this, the terrified old lady tremblingly pushes the material through the machine. Finally she's finished. She looks up at the boss, her eyes wide with apprehension, ready to pick up her purse and dash out to the street. The boss picks up the sleeve, studies it, then drops it on the table, mutters.

BOSS. All right, we'll try you out for a while . . .

He turns abruptly and goes back through the pipe racks to the desk. The old lady sits, trembling, a little slumped, her coat still buttoned to the collar. A middle-aged Negro woman, sitting at the next machine over her lunch, leans over to the old lady.

NEGRO WOMAN *(Gently)*. Mama, what are you sitting there in your hat and coat for? Hang them up, honey. You go through that door over there.

She points to a door leading into a built-in room. The old lady looks up slowly at this genuine sympathy.

NEGRO WOMAN. Don't let him get you nervous, Mama. He likes to yell a lot, but he's okay.

The tension within the old lady suddenly bursts out in the form of a soft, staccato series of sighs. She quickly masters herself.

OLD LADY *(Smiling at the Negro woman).* I'm a little unsure of myself. My fingers are a little unsure.

Cut to: The boss, standing by the desk. He leans down to mutter to the bookkeeper.

BOSS *(Muttering).* How could I say no, will you tell me? How could I say no?...

BOOKKEEPER. Nobody says you should say no.

BOSS. She was so nervous, did you see how nervous she was? I bet you she's seventy years old. How could I say no? *(The telephone suddenly rings)* Answer...

The bookkeeper picks up the receiver.

BOOKKEEPER *(On the phone).* Tiny Tots Sportswear...

BOSS *(In a low voice).* Who is it?

BOOKKEEPER *(On phone).* He's somewhere on the floor, Mister Raymond. I'll see if I can find him...

BOSS *(Frowning).* Which Raymond is it, the younger one or the older one?

BOOKKEEPER. The younger one.

BOSS. You can't find me.

The bookkeeper starts to relay this message, but the boss changes his mind. He takes the receiver.

BOSS. Hello, Jerry? This is Sam... Jerry, for heaven's sake, the twenty dozen just came at half past nine this morning... Jerry, I told you six o'clock; it'll be ready six o'clock... *(Suddenly lowers his voice, turns away from the bookkeeper, embarrassed at the pleading he's going to have to go through now)* Jerry, how about that fifty dozen faille sports suits... Have a heart, Jerry, I need the work. I haven't got enough work to keep my girls. Two of them left yesterday... Jerry, please, what kind of living can I make on these cheap cottons? Give me a fancier garment... It's such small lots, Jerry. At least give me big lots... *(Lowering his voice even more)* Jerry, I hate to appeal to you on this level, but I'm your brother-in-law, you know.... Things are pretty rough with me right now, Jerry. Have a heart. Send me over the fifty dozen failles you got in yesterday. I'll make a rush job for you... please, Jerry, why do you have to make me crawl? All right, I'll have this one for you five o'clock...I'll call up the freight man now. How about the failles? ... Okay, Jerry, thank you, you're a good fellow... All right, five o'clock. I'll call the freight man right now... Okay...

He hangs up, stands a moment, sick at his own loss of dignity. He turns to the bookkeeper, head bowed.

BOSS. My own brother-in-law...

He shuffles away, looks up. The old lady, who had gone into the dressing room to hang up her coat and hat, comes out of the dressing room now. The boss wheels on her.

BOSS. Watsa matter with you? I left you a bundle of sleeves there! You're not even in the shop five minutes, and you walk around like you own the place! *(He wheels to the other operators)* All right! Come on! Come on! What are you sitting there? Rush job! Rush job! Let's go! Five o'clock the freight man's coming! Let's go! Let's go!

Cut to: The bedroom of the daughter's and son-in-law's apartment. The bed has been made, the room cleaned up. The blinds have been drawn open, and the room is nice and bright. The son-in-law sits on one of the straight-back chairs, slumped a little, surly, scowling. The daughter sits erectly on the bed, her back to her husband, likewise scowling. Apparently, angry words have passed between them. The doorbell buzzes off. Neither of them moves for a moment.

Then the daughter rises. At her move, the son-in-law begins to gather himself together.

SON-IN-LAW. I'll get it.

The daughter moves—in sullen, quick silence—past him and out into the foyer. The son-in-law, who has started to rise, sits down again.

In the hallway, the daughter pads down to the front door of the apartment. She is wearing a house dress now and house slippers. She opens the door. Waiting at the door is an attractive young woman in her early thirties, in coat and hat.

DAUGHTER. Hello, Marie, what are you doing here?

SISTER. Nothing. I just came by for a couple of minutes, that's all. I just brought the kids back to school. I thought I'd drop in for a minute, that's all. How's George?

She comes into the apartment. The daughter closes the door after her. The sister starts down the hallway.

DAUGHTER. You came in right in the middle of an argument.

The son-in-law is now standing in the bedroom doorway.

SON-IN-LAW *(To the sister)*. Your sister drives me crazy.

SISTER. Watsa matter now?

DAUGHTER *(Following her sister up the foyer)*. Nothing's the matter. How's Jack? The kids?

The two women go into the bedroom, the son-in-law stepping back to let them in.

SISTER. They're fine. Jack's got a little cold, nothing important. I just took the kids back to school, and I thought I'd drop in, see if you feel like going up to Fordham Road, do a little shopping for a couple of hours. *(To the son-in-law)* What are you doing home?

SON-IN-LAW. It's my vacation. We were gonna leave the kids with my sister, drive downna Virginia, North Carolina, get some warm climate. But your crazy sister don't wanna go. She don't wanna leave your mother... *(Turning to his wife)* Your mother can take care of herself better than we can. She's a tough old woman.... How many vacations you think I get a year? I don't wanna sit in New York for two weeks, watching it rain.

SISTER. Go ahead, Annie. Me and Frank will see that Mom's all right.

DAUGHTER. Sure, you and Frank. Look, Marie, I was over to see Mom this morning...

SON-IN-LAW. Half past six she got up this morning, go over to see your mother.

DAUGHTER. After what happened yesterday, I decided to put my foot down. Because Mom got no business at her age riding up and down in the subways. You know how packed they are. Anyway, I called Mom on the phone, and she gave me the usual arguments. You know Mom. So anyway, I went over to see her, and she was very depressed. We talked for about an hour, and she told me she's been feeling very depressed lately. It's no good Mom living there alone, and you know it, Marie. Anyway, I think I finally convinced her to move out of there and come and live over here.

SON-IN-LAW. You didn't convince me.

DAUGHTER. George, please...

SON-IN-LAW. Look, Annie, I like your mother. We get along fine. We go over visit her once, twice a week, fine. What I like about her is that she doesn't hang all over you like my mother does.

DAUGHTER. This is the only thing I ever asked you in our whole marriage...

SON-IN-LAW. This is just begging for trouble. You know that in the bottom of your heart...

DAUGHTER. I don't wanna argue any more about it...

SISTER. Look, Annie, I think George is right, I think...

The daughter suddenly wheels on her sister, a long-repressed fury trembling out of her.

DAUGHTER *(literally screaming)*. You keep

outta this! You hear me? You never cared about Mom in your whole life! How many times you been over there this week? How many times? I go over every day! Every day! And I go over in the evenings too sometimes!

The sister turns away, not a little shaken by this fierce onslaught. The daughter sits down on the bed again, her back to both her husband and sister, herself confused by the ferocity of her outburst. The son-in-law looks down, embarrassed, at the floor. A moment of sick silence fills the room. Then without turning, but in a much lower voice, the daughter goes on.

DAUGHTER. George, I been a good wife to you. Did I ever ask you for mink coats or anything? Anything you want has always been good with me. This is the only thing I ever ask of you. I want my mother to live here with me where I can take care of her.

The son-in-law looks up briefly at his wife's unrelenting back and then back to the floor again.

SON-IN-LAW. All right, Annie. I won't argue any more with you about it.

SISTER. I guess I better go because I want to get back in the house before three o'clock when the kids come home from school.

Nobody says anything, so she starts for the door. The son-in-law, from his sitting position, looks up briefly at her as she passes, but she avoids his eyes. He stands, follows her out into the foyer. They proceed silently down the foyer to the doorway. Here they pause a minute. The scene is conducted in low, intense whispers.

SON-IN-LAW. She don't mean nothing, Marie. You know that.

SISTER. I know, I know . . .

SON-IN-LAW. She's a wonderful person. She'd get up at three o'clock in the morning for you. There's nothing she wouldn't do for her family.

SISTER. I know, George. I know Annie better than you know her. When she's sweet, she can be the sweetest person in the world. She's my kid sister but many's the time I came to her to do a little crying. But she's gonna kill my mother with all her sacrifices. She's trying to take away my mother's independence. My mother's been on her own all her life. That's the only way she knows how to live. I went over to see my mother yesterday. She was depressed. It broke my heart because I told Jack; I said: "I think my mother's beginning to give up." My mother used to be so sure of herself all the time, and yesterday she was talking there about how maybe she thinks she is getting a little old to work. It depressed me for the rest of the day . . .

SON-IN-LAW. Marie, you know that I really like your mother. If I thought it would work out at all, I would have no objection to her coming to live here. But the walls in this place are made out of paper. You can hear everything that goes on in the next room, and . . .

SISTER. It's a big mistake if she comes here. She'll just dry up into bones inside a year.

SON-IN-LAW. Tell that to Annie. Would you do that for me, please?

SISTER. You can't tell Annie nothing. Annie was born at a wrong time. The doctor told my mother she was gonna die if she had Annie, and my mother has been scared of Annie ever since. And if Annie thinks she's gonna get my mother to love her with all these sacrifices, she's crazy. My mother's favorite was always our big brother Frank, and Annie's been jealous of him as long as I know. I remember one time when we were in Saint John's school on Daly Avenue—I think Annie was about ten years old, and . . . oh, well, look, I better go. I'm not mad at Annie. She's been like this as long as I know her. *(She opens the door)* She's doing the worst thing for my mother, absolutely the worst thing. I'll see you, George.

SON-IN-LAW. I'll see you.

The sister goes out, closing the door after her. The son-in-law stands a moment. Then, frowning, he moves back up the foyer to the bedroom. His wife is still seated as we last saw her, her back to the door, her hands in her lap—slumped a little, but with an air of rigid stubbornness about her. The son-in-law regards her for a moment. Then he moves around the bed and sits down beside his wife. He puts his arm around her and pulls her to him. She rests her head on his chest. They sit silently for a moment.

Dissolve to: Interior, the shop. The full complement of working operators are there, all hunched over their machines, and the place is a picture of industry. The women chatter shrilly with each other as they work. A radio plays in the background. Occasionally, one of the operators lifts her head and bellows out: "Work! Work! Jessica! Gimme some work!"... The bookkeeper, Jessica, scurries back and forth from her desk to the sorting table—where she picks up small cartons of materials, bringing them to the operators—and back to her desk.

Dissolve to: The old lady and her immediate neighbor, the Negro woman, both bent over their machines, sewing away. The motors hum. The two women move their materials under the plunging needles. The old lady hunches, intense and painfully concentrated, over her work. They sew in silent industry for a moment. Then . . .

OLD LADY *(Without daring to look up from her work).* I'm getting the feel back, you know?

NEGRO WOMAN *(Likewise without looking up).* Sure, you're gonna be all right, Mama.

OLD LADY. I used to be considered a very fast operator. I used to work on the lower East Side in those sweatshops, y'know. Six dollars a week. But I quit in October, 1916, because I got married and, in those days, y'know, it was a terrible disgrace for a married woman to work. So I quit. Not that we had the money. My husband was a house painter when we got married, which is seasonal work at best, and he had to borrow money to go to Atlantic City for three days. That was our honeymoon.

They lapse into silence. A woman's shrill voice from farther down the row of machines calls out: "Work! Hey, Jessica! Bring me some work!" The two women sew silently. Then . . .

OLD LADY. I got a feeling he's going to keep me on here. The boss, I mean. He seems like a nice enough man.

NEGRO WOMAN. He's nervous, but he's all right.

OLD LADY. I've been looking for almost four weeks now, y'know. My husband died a little more than a month ago.

NEGRO WOMAN. My husband died eighteen years ago.

OLD LADY. He was a very sick man all his life—lead poisoning, you know, from the paints. He had to quit the trade after a while, went into the retail grocery business. He was sixty-seven when he died, and I wonder he lived this long. In his last years, the circulation of the blood in his legs was so bad he could hardly walk to the corner.

NEGRO WOMAN. My big trouble is arthritis. I get terrible pains in my arms and in my shoulders sometimes.

OLD LADY. Oh, I been getting a lot of pains in my back, in between my shoulder blades.

NEGRO WOMAN. That's gall bladder.

OLD LADY. Is that what it is?

NEGRO WOMAN. I had that. When you get to our age, Missus Fanning, you gotta expect the bones to rebel.

OLD LADY. Well, now, you're not such an old woman.

NEGRO WOMAN. How old do you think I am?

OLD LADY. I don't know. Maybe forty, fifty.

NEGRO WOMAN. I'm sixty-eight years old.

For the first time, the old lady looks up. She pauses in her work.

OLD LADY. I wouldn't believe you were sixty-eight.

NEGRO WOMAN. I'm sixty-eight. I got more white hair than you have. But I dye it. You oughtta dye your hair too. Just go in the five-and-ten, pick up some kind of hair dye. Because most people don't like to hire old people with white hair. My children don't want me to work no more, but I'm gonna work until I die. How old do you think that old Greek woman over there is?

OLD LADY. How old?

NEGRO WOMAN. She's sixty-nine. She got a son who's a big doctor. She won't quit working either. I like working here. I come in here in the morning, punch the clock. I'm friends with all these women. You see that little Jewish lady down there? That's the funniest little woman I ever met. You get her to tell you some of her jokes during lunch sometime. She gets me laughing sometimes I can hardly stop. What do I wanna sit around my dirty old room for when I got that little Jewish woman there to tell me jokes all day? That's what I tell my children.

The old lady turns back to her sewing.

OLD LADY. Oh, I'd like to hear a couple of jokes.

At this moment there is a small burst of high-pitched laughter from farther down the rows of machines. Camera cuts to long shot of the rows of operators, singling out a group of three Puerto Rican girls in their twenties. One of them has apparently just said something that made the other two laugh. A fourth Puerto Rican girl, across the table and up from them, calls to them in Spanish: "What happened? What was so funny?" The Puerto Rican girl who made the others laugh answers in a quick patter of high-pitched Spanish. A sudden gust of laughter sweeps all the Puerto Rican girls at the machines. Another woman calls out: "What she say?" One of the Puerto Rican girls answers in broken English.

PUERTO RICAN GIRL. She say, t'ree week ago, she make a mistake, sewed the belts onna dress backward. Nobody found out. Yesterday, she went in to buy her little girl a dress inna store. They tried to sell her one-a these dresses . . . *(A wave of laughter rolls up and down the two rows of operators)* She say, the label onna dress say: "Made in California."

They absolutely roar at this.

Close-up: The old lady joining in the general laughter. She finishes the sleeve she has been working on. It is apparently the last of the bunch. She gathers together in front of her the two dozen other sleeves she has just finished and begins to tie them up with a black ribbon. She lifts her head up and—with magnificent professionalism—calls out.

OLD LADY. Work! Work! . . .

Camera closes down on the bundle of sleeves she has tied together with the black ribbon.

Dissolve to: The same bundle of sleeves. We pull back and see it is now being held by the boss. He is frowning down at them. At his elbow is standing one of the Puerto Rican girls. She is muttering in broken English.

PUERTO RICAN GIRL. So what I do? The whole bunch, same way . . .

BOSS *(Scowling)*. All right, all right. Cut them open, resew the whole bunch . . .

PUERTO RICAN GIRL. Cut! I didn't do! I can't cut, sew, five o'clock the truckman . . . I gotta sew them on the blouse. Take two hours . . .

BOSS. All right, all right, cut them open, sew them up again . . .

The girl takes the bundle of sleeves and shuffles away. The boss turns, suddenly deeply weary. He goes to the desk.

BOSS *(To the bookkeeper)*. The old lady come in today, she sewed all the sleeves for the left hand. She didn't make any rights. All lefts . . .

BOOKKEEPER. So what are you gonna do? It's half past four.

BOSS. Call up Raymond for me.

The bookkeeper picks up the phone receiver, dials. The boss looks up and

through the pipe racks at the old lady, sitting hunched and intense over her machine, working with concentrated meticulousness. The boss's attention is called back to the phone by the bookkeeper. He takes the phone from her.

BOSS *(In a low voice)*. Jerry? This is Sam. Listen. I can't give you the whole twenty dozen at five o'clock. . . . All right, wait a minute, lemme . . . All right, wait a minute. I got fifteen dozen on the racks now . . . Jerry, please. I just got a new operator in today. She sewed five dozen sleeves all left-handed. We're gonna have to cut the seams open, and resew them . . . Look, Jerry, I'm sorry, what do you want from me? I can get it for you by six . . . Jerry, I'll pay the extra freight fee myself . . . Jerry . . . Listen, Jerry, how about those fifty dozen faille sport suits? This doesn't change your mind, does it . . . Jerry, it's an accident. It could happen to anyone . . . *(A fury begins to take hold of the boss)* Look, Jerry, you promised me the fifty dozen fai . . . Look, Jerry, you know what you can do with those fifty dozen failles? You think I'm gonna crawl on my knees to you? *(He's shouting now. Every head in the shop begins to look up)* You're a miserable human being, you hear that? I'd rather go bankrupt than ask you for another order! And don't come over to my house no more! You hear? I ain't gonna crawl to you! You hear me? I ain't gonna crawl to you! . . .

He slams the receiver down, stands, his chest heaving, his face flushed. He looks down at the bookkeeper, his fury still high.

BOSS. Fire her! Fire her! Fire her!

He stands, the years of accumulated humiliation and resentment flooding out of him.

Fade out.

ACT III

Fade in: Interior of a subway car heading north to the Bronx during the rush hour—absolutely jam-packed. The camera manages to work its way through the dense crowd to settle on the old lady, seated in her black coat and hat, her hands folded in her lap, her old purse dangling from her wrist. She is staring bleakly straight ahead of herself, as if in another world. The train hurtles on.

Dissolve to: Interior of the old lady's apartment—dark—empty. Night has fallen outside. The sound of a key being inserted into the lock. The bolts unlatch, and the door is pushed open. The old lady enters. She closes the door after herself, bolts it. She stands a moment in the dark foyer, then shuffles up the foyer to the living room. She unbuttons her coat, sits down by the table, places her purse on the table. For a moment she sits. Then she rises, goes into the kitchen, turns on the light.

It takes her a moment to remember what she came into the kitchen for. Then, collecting herself, she opens the refrigerator door, extracts a carton of milk, sets it on the cupboard shelf. She opens the cupboard door, reaches in, extracts the box of Rice Krispies and a bowl. She sets the bowl down, begins to open the box of cereal. It falls out of her hands to the floor, a number of the pebbles of cereal rolling out to the floor. She starts to bend to pick the box up, then suddenly straightens and stands breathing heavily, nervously wetting her lips. She moves out of the kitchen quickly now, goes to the table, sits down again, picks up the phone, and dials. There is an edge of desperation in her movements. She waits. Then . . .

OLD LADY. Frank? Who's this, Lillian? Lillian, dear, this is your mother-in-law, and I . . . oh, I'm sorry, what? . . . Oh, I'm sorry . . . Who's this, the baby sitter? . . . This is Missus Fanning, dear—Mister Fanning's mother, is he in? . . . Is Missus Fanning in? . . . Well, do you expect them in? I mean, it's half past six. Did they eat their dinner already? . . .Oh, I see. Well, when do you . . . Oh, I see . . . No, dear, this is Mister Fanning's mother. Just tell him I called. It's not important. *She hangs up, leaving her hand still on the phone. Then she lifts the receiver again and dials another number. She places a smile on her face and waits. Then . . .*

OLD LADY. Oh, Marie, dear, how are you . . . this is Mother . . . Oh, I'm glad to hear your voice . . . Oh, I'm fine . . . fine. How's Jack and the kids? . . . Well, I hope it's nothing serious . . . Oh, that's good . . . *(She is mustering up all the good humor she has in her)* Oh my, what a day I had. Oh, wait'll I tell you. Listen, I haven't taken you away from your dinner or anything . . . Oh, I went down to look for a job again . . . Yes, that's right, Annie was here this morning . . . how did you know? . . . Oh, is that right? Well, it cleared up, you know, and I didn't want to just sit around, so I went down to this job, and I got fired again . . . The stupidest thing, I sewed all left sleeves . . . Well, you know you have to sew sleeves for the right as well as the left unless your customers are one-armed people . . . *(She is beginning to laugh nervously)* Yes, it's comical, isn't it? . . . Yes, all left-handed . . . *(She bursts into a short, almost hysterical laugh. Her lip begins to twitch, and she catches her laughter in its middle and breathes deeply to regain control of herself)* Well, how's Jack and the kids? . . . Well, that's fine . . . What are you doing with yourself tonight? . . . *(A deep weariness seems to have taken hold of her. She rests her head in the palm of her free hand. Her eyes are closed)* Oh, do you have a baby sitter? . . . Well, have a nice time, give my regards to your mother-in-law . . . No, no, I'm fine . . . No, I was just asking . . . No, no, listen, dear, I'm absolutely fine. I just come in the house, and I'm going to make myself some Rice Krispies, and I've got some rolls somewhere, and I think I've got a piece of fish in the refrigerator, and I'm going to make myself dinner and take a hot tub, and then I think I'll watch some television. What's tonight, Thursday? . . . Well, Groucho Marx is on tonight . . . No, no, I just called to ask how everything was. How's Jack and the kids? . . . That's fine, have a nice time . . . Good-by, dear . . . *She hangs up, sits erectly in the chair now. Her face wears an expression of the most profound weariness. She rises now and shuffles with no purpose into the center of the dark room, her coat flapping loosely around her. Then she goes to the television set, turns it on. In a moment a jumble of lines appear, and the sound comes up. The lines clear up into Faye and Skitch Henderson engaging each other in very clever chitchat. The old lady goes back to a television-viewing chair, sits down stiffly—her hands resting on the armrests—and expressionlessly watches the show. Camera comes in for a close-up of the old lady, staring wide-eyed right through the television set, not hearing a word of the chitchat. She is breathing with some difficulty. Suddenly she rises and almost lurches back to the table. She takes the phone, dials with obvious trembling, waits . . .*

OLD LADY. Annie? Annie, I wonder if I could spend the night at your house? I don't want to be alone . . . I'd appreciate that very much . . . All right, I'll wait here . . .

Dissolve to: Interior of the old lady's bedroom. The son-in-law, in his hat and jacket, is snapping the clasps of an old valise together. Having closed the valise, he picks it off the bed and goes into the living room. The old lady is there. She is seated in one of the straight-back chairs by the table, still in her coat and hat, and she is talking to the daughter—who can be seen through the kitchen doorway, reaching up into the pantry for some of her mother's personal groceries.

OLD LADY. . . . Well, the truth is, I'm getting old, and there's no point in saying it isn't true. *(To her son-in-law as he sets the valise down beside her)* Thank you, dear. I always have so much trouble with the clasp. . . . Did you hear the stupid thing I did today? I sewed all left-handed sleeves. That's the mark of a wandering mind, a sure sign of age. I'm sorry, George, to put you to all this inconvenience . . .

SON-IN-LAW. Don't be silly, Ma. Always glad to have you.

OLD LADY. Annie dear, what are you looking for?

DAUGHTER *(In the kitchen)*. Your saccharin.

OLD LADY. It's on the lower shelf, dear. . . . This isn't going to be permanent, George. I'll just stay with you a little while till I get a room somewheres with some other old woman . . .

DAUGHTER *(In the kitchen doorway)*. Ma, you're gonna stay with us, so, for heaven's sakes, let's not have no more arguments.

OLD LADY. What'll we do with all my furniture? Annie, don't you want the china closet?

DAUGHTER. No, Ma, we haven't got any room for it . . .

OLD LADY. It's such a good-looking piece. What we have to do is to get Jack and Marie and Frank and Lillian and all of us together, and we'll divide among the three of you whatever you want. I've got that fine set of silver—well, it's not the best, of course, silver plate, y'know—it's older than you are, Annie. *(To her son-in-law)* It was a gift of the girls in my shop when I got married. It's an inexpensive set, but I've shined it every year, and it sparkles. *(To her daughter in the kitchen)* Yes, that's what we'll have to do. We'll have to get all of us together one night and I'll apportion out whatever I've got. And whatever you don't want, well, we'll call a furniture dealer . . . *(To her son-in-law)* . . . although what would he pay me for these old things here? . . . *(To her daughter)* Annie, take the china closet . . . It's such a fine piece . . .

DAUGHTER. Ma, where would we put it?

OLD LADY. Well, take that soft chair there. You always liked that chair . . .

DAUGHTER. Ma . . .

OLD LADY. There's nothing wrong with it. It's not torn or anything. The upholstery's fine. Your father swore by that chair. He said it was the only chair he could sit in.

DAUGHTER. Ma, let's not worry about it now. We'll get together sometime next week with Marie and Lillian.

OLD LADY. I want you to have the chair . . .

DAUGHTER. Ma, we got all modern furniture in our house . . .

OLD LADY. It's not an old chair. We just bought it about six years ago. No, seven . . .

DAUGHTER. Ma, what do we need the . . .

OLD LADY. Annie, I don't want to sell it to a dealer! It's my home. I don't want it to go piece by piece into a second-hand shop.

DAUGHTER. Ma . . .

SON-IN-LAW. Annie! we'll take the chair!

DAUGHTER. All right, Ma, the chair is ours.

OLD LADY. I know that Lillian likes those lace linens I've got in the cedar chest. And the carpets. Now these are good carpets, Annie. There's no sense just throwing them out. They're good broadloom. The first good money your father was making we bought them. When we almost bought that house in Passaic, New Jersey. You ought to remember that, Annie, you were about seven then. But we bought the grocery store instead. Oh, how we scraped in that store. In the heart of the depression. We used to sell bread for six cents a loaf. I remember my husband said: "Let's buy a grocery store. At least we'll always have food in the house." It seems to me my whole life has been hand-to-mouth. Did we ever not worry about the rent? I remember as a girl in Cork, eating boiled potatoes every day. I don't know what it all means, I really don't . . . *(She stares rather abstractedly at her son-in-law)* I'm sixty-six years old, and I don't know what the purpose of it all was.

SON-IN-LAW. Missus Fanning . . .

OLD LADY. An endless, endless struggle. And for what? For what? *(She is beginning to cry now)* Is this what it all comes to? An old woman parceling out the old furniture in her house . . . ?

She bows her head and stands, thirty years of repressed tears torturously working their way through her body in racking shudders.

DAUGHTER. Ma . . .

The old lady stands, her shoulders slumped, her head bowed, crying with a violent agony.

OLD LADY *(The words tumbling out between her sobs).* Oh, I don't care . . . I don't care . . .

Hold on the old lady, standing, crying.

Dissolve to: Film. Rain whipping through the streets of New York at night—same film we opened the show with—a frightening thunderstorm.

Dissolve to: The old lady's valise, now open, lying on a narrow single bed. We pull back to see the old lady—in a dress, but with her coat off—rummaging in the valise for something. The room she is in is obviously a little boy's room. There are a child's paintings and drawings and cutouts Scotch-taped to the wall, and toys and things on the floor. It is dark outside, and the rain whacks against the window panes. The old lady finally extracts from out of the valise a long woolen nightgown and, holding it in both arms, she shuffles to the one chair in the room and sits down. She sets the nightgown in her lap and bends to remove her shoes. This is something of an effort and costs her a few moments of quick breathing. She sits, expressionless, catching her breath, the white nightgown on her lap, her hands folded on it. Even after she regains her breath, she sits this way, now staring fixedly at the floor at her feet.

Hold.

Dissolve to: The window of the child's bedroom. It is daylight now, and the rain has stopped. The cold morning sun shines thinly through the white chintz curtains. The camera pulls slowly back and finally comes to rest on the old lady sitting just as we saw her last, unmoving, wrapped in thought, the white nightgown on her lap, her hands folded. From some room off, the thin voice of a baby suddenly rises and abruptly falls. The old lady looks slowly up.

Then she bends and puts her shoes on. She rises, sets the nightgown on the chair from which she has just risen, moves with a slight edge of purpose down the room to the closet, opens the door, reaches in, and takes out her coat. She puts it on, stands a moment, looking about the room for something. She finds her hat and purse sitting on the chest of drawers. She picks them up. Then she turns to the door of the room and carefully opens it. She looks out onto the hallway. Across from her, the door to her daughter's and son-in-law's bedroom stands slightly ajar. She crosses to the door, looks in. Her daughter and son-in-law make two large bundles under their blankets. For a moment she stands and surveys them. Then the daughter turns in her bed so that she faces her mother. Her eyes are open; she has not been asleep. At the sight of her mother in the doorway, she leans upon one elbow.

OLD LADY *(In an intense whisper).* Annie, it just wasn't comfortable, you know? I just can't sleep anywheres but in my own bed, and that's the truth. I'm sorry, Annie, honest. You're a fine daughter, and it warms me to know that I'm welcome here. But what'll I do with myself, Annie, what'll I do? . . .

The daughter regards her mother for a moment.

DAUGHTER. Where are you going, Ma, with your coat on?

OLD LADY. I'm going out and look for a job. And, Annie, please don't tell me that everything's against me. I know it. Well, I'll see you, dear. I didn't mean to wake you up . . .

She turns and disappears from the doorway. The daughter starts quickly from the bed.

DAUGHTER. Ma . . .

She moves quickly across the room to the door of the hallway. She is in her pajamas. She looks down the hallway, which is fairly dark. Her mother is already at the front door, at the other end.

DAUGHTER. Ma . . .

OLD LADY. I'm leaving the valise with all my things. I'll pick them up tonight. And please don't start an argument with me, Annie, because I won't listen to you. I'm a woman of respect. I can take care of myself. I always have. And don't tell me it's raining because it stopped about an hour ago. And don't say you'll drive me home because I can get the bus two blocks away. Work is the meaning of my life. It's all I know what to do. I can't change my ways at this late time.

For a long moment the mother and daughter regard each other. Then the daughter pads quietly down to the old lady.

DAUGHTER *(Quietly).* When I'm your age, Ma, I hope I'm like you.

For a moment the two women stand in the dark hallway. Then they quickly embrace and release each other. The old lady unbolts the door and disappears outside, closing the door after her. The daughter bolts it shut with a click. She turns and goes back up the dark foyer to her own bedroom. She goes in, shuffles to the bed, gets back under the covers. For a moment she just lies there. Then she nudges her sleeping husband, who grunts.

DAUGHTER. George, let's drop the kids at your sister's for a week or ten days and drive down to Virginia. You don't want to spend your one vacation a year sitting in New York, watching it rain.

The son-in-law, who hasn't heard a word, grunts once or twice more. The daughter pulls the blankets up over her shoulders, turns on her side, and closes her eyes. Fade out.

WHAT DO YOU SAY?

ACT I

1. *(a)* What conflicts can you cite in Act I? *(b)* Between what two characters is the main conflict? *(c)* How is it dramatically suggested by camera action at the opening of the act?

2. Whom is the Old Lady mourning?

3. What clues reveal the social-economic class to which the characters belong?

4. *(a)* What does the Son-in-law say would happen to the Old Lady if she were to move in with his family? *(b)* What does the Daughter say would happen to her if she got a job? *(c)* How does the Old Lady want to live? *(d)* What makes the Old Lady decide to go for the job after all?

ACT II

1. *(a)* While the Sister is in the apartment, what do you learn about the character of both the Daughter and the Old Lady? *(b)* What additional information do you get about the cause of the conflict between them?

2. *(a)* What kind of man is the Boss? *(b)* How does the Old Lady's work affect his production problem? *(c)* How is the Daughter's prophecy in Act I fulfilled?

ACT III

1. *(a)* At the beginning of Act III what state of mind prompts the Old Lady to make the telephone calls? *(b)* What is the significance of the sequence of her calls? *(c)* Of what prophecy by the Son-in-law in Act I are you reminded?

2. *(a)* The last scene parallels the first part of Act I. What are the similarities? The differences? *(b)* What discoveries have the Old Lady and the Daughter made about themselves and about each other? *(c)* Has the Daughter won any kind of "victory"? Explain.

3. *(a)* What do you think of the Old Lady's final decision? *(b)* Had she surrendered and retired to live with the Daughter, what might have resulted?

PADDY CHAYEFSKY

Paddy Chayefsky, born in 1923, grew up in New York during the depression. He attended high school in the Bronx and, later, City College of New York. During the war he enlisted in the army, was sent over-seas, and was injured in a landmine explosion. While in the hospital he wrote two plays, a musical comedy which was presented in London and a movie script which was later produced for the army.

After the war, he began writing for radio and later for television. His first-hand knowledge of ordinary people living ordinary lives has provided the material for his venture into dramatic writing for television. Critics have both praised and condemned his natural "tape-recording" use of dialogue. He moved from television to writing for the stage, and his plays from both media have been made into movies. His ***Television Plays (1955)*** included ***Marty,*** which in a movie version won an Academy Award.

Short Stories

THE WALTZ

DOROTHY PARKER

Why, thank you so much. I'd adore to.

I don't want to dance with him. I don't want to dance with anybody. And even if I did, it wouldn't be him. He'd be well down among the last ten. I've seen the way he dances; it looks like something you do on St. Walpurgis Night.[1] Just think, not a quarter of an hour ago, here I was sitting, feeling so sorry for the poor girl he was dancing with. And now *I'm* going to be the poor girl. Well, well. Isn't it a small world?

And a peach of a world, too. A true little corker. Its events are so fascinatingly unpredictable, are not they? Here I was, minding my own business, not doing a stitch of harm to any living soul. And then he comes into my life, all smiles and city manners, to sue me for the favor of one memorable mazurka. Why, he scarcely knows my name, let alone what it stands for. It stands for Despair, Bewilderment, Futility, Degradation, and Premeditated Murder, but little does he wot. I don't wot his name, either; I haven't any idea what it

1. ***Saint Walpurgis*** (väl pủr'gis) ***Night,*** the night of April 30, when witches were supposed to consort with the devil.

is. Jukes,[2] would be my guess from the look in his eyes. How do you do, Mr. Jukes? And how is that dear little brother of yours, with the two heads?

Ah, now why did he have to come around me, with his low requests? Why can't he let me lead my own life? I ask so little—just to be left alone in my quiet corner of the table, to do my evening brooding over all my sorrows. And he must come, with his bows and his scrapes and his may-I-have-this-ones. And I had to go and tell him that I'd adore to dance with him. I cannot understand why I wasn't struck right down dead. Yes, and being struck dead would look like a day in the country, compared to struggling out a dance with this boy. But what could I do? Everyone else at the table had got up to dance, except him and me. There I was, trapped. Trapped like a trap in a trap.

What can you say, when a man asks you to dance with him? I most certainly will *not* dance with you, I'll see you in hell first. Oh, yes, *do* let's dance together—it's so nice to meet a man who isn't a scaredy-cat about catching my beri-beri. No. There was nothing for me to do, but say I'd adore to. Well, we might as well get it over with. All right, Cannonball, let's run out on the field. You won the toss; you can lead.

Why, I think it's more of a waltz, really. Isn't it? We might just listen to the music a second. Shall we? Oh, yes, it's a waltz. Mind? Why, I'm simply thrilled. I'd love to waltz with you.

I'd love to waltz with you. I'd love to waltz with you, I'd love to have my tonsils out, I'd love to be in a midnight fire at sea. Well, it's too late now. We're getting under way. *Oh.* Oh, dear. Oh, dear, dear, dear. Oh, this is even worse than I thought it would be. I suppose that's the one dependable law of life—everything is always worse than you thought it was going to be. Oh, if I had had any real grasp of what this dance would be like, I'd have held out for sitting it out. Well, it will probably amount to the same thing in the end. We'll be sitting it out on the floor in a minute, if he keeps this up.

I'm so glad I brought it to his attention that this is a waltz they're playing. Heaven knows what might have happened, if he had thought it was something fast; we'd have blown the sides right out of the building. Why does he always want to be somewhere that he isn't? Why can't we stay in one place just long enough to get acclimated? It's this constant rush, rush, rush, that's the curse of American life. That's the reason that we're all of us so—*Ow*! Don't *kick*, you idiot; this is only second down. Oh, my shin. My poor, poor shin, that I've had ever since I was a little girl!

Oh, no, no, no. Goodness, no. It didn't hurt the least little bit. And anyway it was my fault. Really it was. Truly. Well, you're just being sweet, to say that. It really was all my fault.

I wonder what I'd better do—kill him this instant, with my naked hands, or wait and let him drop in his traces. Maybe it's best not to make a scene. I guess I'll just lie low, and watch the pace get him. He can't keep this up indefinitely—he's only flesh and blood. Die he must, and die he shall, for what he did to me. I don't want to be of the over-sensitive type, but you can't tell me that kick was unpremeditated. Freud[3] says there are no accidents. I've led no cloistered life, I've known dancing partners who have spoiled my slippers and torn my dress; but when it comes to kicking, I am Outraged Womanhood. When you kick me in the shin, *smile*.

Maybe he didn't do it maliciously. Maybe it's just his way of showing his high spirits. I suppose I ought to be glad that one of us is having such a good time. I suppose I ought to think myself lucky if he brings me back alive. Maybe it's cap-

---

2. ***Jukes,*** a New York state family with a record of crime and low moral standards. 3. ***Freud*** (froid), an Austrian physician who developed a theory and technique of psychoanalysis. He lived from 1856 to 1939.

tious to demand of a practically strange man that he leave your shins as he found them. After all, the poor boy's doing the best he can. Probably he grew up in the hill country, and never had no larnin'. I bet they had to throw him on his back to get shoes on him.

Yes, it's lovely, isn't it? It's simply lovely. It's the loveliest waltz. Isn't it? Oh, I think it's lovely, too.

Why, I'm getting positively drawn to the Triple Threat here. He's my hero. He has the heart of a lion, and the sinews of a buffalo. Look at him—never a thought of the consequences, never afraid of his face, hurling himself into every scrimmage, eyes shining, cheeks ablaze. And shall it be said that I hung back? No, a thousand times no. What's it to me if I have to spend the next couple of years in a plaster cast? Come on, Butch, right through them! Who wants to live forever?

Oh. Oh, dear. Oh, he's all right, thank goodness. For a while I thought they'd have to carry him off the field. Ah, I couldn't bear to have anything happen to him. I love him. I love him better than anybody in the world. Look at the spirit he gets into a dreary, commonplace waltz; how effete the other dancers seem, beside him. He is youth and vigor and courage, he is strength and gayety and—*Ow!* Get off my instep, you hulking peasant! What do you think I am, anyway—a gangplank? *Ow!*

No, of course it didn't hurt. Why, it didn't a bit. Honestly. And it was all my fault. You see, that little step of yours—well, it's perfectly lovely, but it's just a tiny bit tricky to follow at first. Oh, did you work it up yourself? You really did? Well, aren't you amazing! Oh, now I think I've got it. Oh, I think it's lovely. I was watching you do it when you were dancing before. It's awfully effective when you look at it.

It's awfully effective when you look at it. I bet I'm awfully effective when you look at me. My hair is hanging along my cheeks, my skirt is swaddled about me, I can feel the cold damp of my brow. I must look like something out of the Fall of the House of Usher.[4] This sort of thing takes a fearful toll of a woman my age. And he worked up his little step himself, he with his degenerate cunning. And it was just a tiny bit tricky at first, but now I think I've got it. Two stumbles, slip, and a twenty-yard dash; yes, I've got it. I've got several other things, too, including a split shin and a bitter heart. I hate this creature I'm chained to. I hated him the moment I saw his leering, bestial face. And here I've been locked in his noxious embrace for the thirty-five years this waltz has lasted. Is that orchestra never going to stop playing? Or must this obscene travesty of a dance go on until hell burns out?

Oh, they're going to play another encore. Oh, goody. Oh, that's lovely. Tired? I should say I'm not tired. I'd like to go on like this forever.

I should say I'm not tired. I'm dead, that's all I am. Dead, and in what a cause! And the music is never going to stop playing, and we're going on like this, Double-Time Charlie and I, throughout eternity. I suppose I won't care any more, after the first hundred thousand years. I suppose nothing will matter then, not heat nor pain nor broken heart nor cruel, aching weariness. Well. It can't come too soon for me.

I wonder why I didn't tell him I was tired. I wonder why I didn't suggest going back to the table. I could have said let's just listen to the music. Yes, and if he would, that would be the first bit of attention he has given it all evening. George Jean Nathan[5] said that the lovely rhythms of the waltz should be listened to in stillness and not be accompanied by strange gyrations of the human body. I think that's what he said. I think it was George Jean Nathan. Anyhow, whatever he said and whoever he was and whatever he's doing

---

4. ***"The Fall of the House of Usher,"*** a gruesome short story by Edgar Allan Poe. 5. ***George Jean Nathan,*** a noted American drama critic.

now, he's better off than I am. That's safe. Anybody who isn't waltzing with this Mrs. O'Leary's cow[6] I've got here is having a good time.

Still, if we were back at the table, I'd probably have to talk to him. Look at him —what could you say to a thing like that! Did you go to the circus this year, what's your favorite kind of ice cream, how do you spell cat? I guess I'm as well off here. As well off as if I were in a cement mixer in full action.

I'm past all feeling now. The only way I can tell when he steps on me is that I can hear the splintering of bones. And all the events of my life are passing before my eyes. There was the time I was in a hurricane in the West Indies, there was the day I got my head cut open in the taxi smash, there was the night the drunken lady threw a bronze ashtray at her own true love and got me instead, there was that summer that the sailboat kept capsizing. Ah, what an easy, peaceful time was mine, until I fell in with Swifty, here. I didn't know what trouble was, before I got drawn into this *danse macabre.*[7] I think my mind is beginning to wander. It almost seems to me as if the orchestra were stopping. It couldn't be, of course; it could never, never be. And yet in my ears there is a silence like the sound of angel voices. . . .

Oh, they've stopped, the mean things. They're not going to play any more. Oh, darn. Oh, do you think they would? Do you really think so, if you gave them fifty dollars? Oh, that would be lovely. And look, do tell them to play this same thing. I'd simply adore to go on waltzing.

---

6. ***Mrs. O'Leary's cow.*** According to popular belief, the great Chicago fire of 1871 was started when Mrs. O'Leary's cow kicked over a lantern in the cow barn. 7. ***danse macabre*** (däNs' mə kä'brə), a dance of death. In this dance a figure of death, usually represented by a skeleton, leads the living to the grave.

WHAT DO YOU SAY?

1. What elements contribute to the humor of this selection?
2. To what sport does the speaker compare her dancing experience?
3. What is the major satire in this selection?

DOROTHY PARKER

American humorist and satirist, Dorothy Parker, was born in 1893 in West End, New Jersey. Following her education at private New England schools, she worked as a drama critic and, later, as a book critic. Her first book, a volume of poetry entitled ***Enough Rope,*** was published in 1927, and it proved so successful that Miss Parker turned to free-lance writing.

Caustic wit, demonstrated in "The Waltz," was Dorothy Parker's forte. Her humor is brittle and sharp, but her merciless glimpses into life reveal a special kind of truth about people and human relationships.

There were the two oak stumps, knee high to a not-too-tall man and cut quite squarely across. They became to the two children objects of wonder. They had seen the two trees cut but had run away just as the trees fell. They hadn't thought of the two stumps, to be left standing there; hadn't even looked at them. Afterwards Ted said to his sister Mary, speaking of the stumps: "I wonder if they bled, like legs, when a surgeon cuts a man's leg off." He had been hearing war stories. A man came to the farm one day to visit one of the farm-hands, a man who had been in the World War and lost an arm. He stood in one of the barns talking. When Ted said that, Mary spoke up at once. She hadn't been lucky enough to be at the barn when the one-armed man was there talking, and was jealous. "Why not a woman or a girl's leg?" she said, but Ted said the idea was silly. "Women and girls don't get their legs and arms cut off," he declared. "Why not? I'd just like to know why not?" Mary kept saying.

It would have been something if they had stayed, that day the trees were cut. "We might have gone and touched the places," Ted said. He meant the stumps. Would they have been warm? Would they have bled? They did go and touch the places afterwards, but it was a cold day and the stumps were cold. Ted stuck to his point that only men's arms and legs were cut off, but Mary thought of automobile

accidents. "You can't think just of wars. There might be an automobile accident," she declared, but Ted wouldn't be convinced.

They were both children, but something had made them both in an odd way old. Mary was fourteen and Ted eleven, but Ted wasn't strong and that rather evened things up. They were the children of a well-to-do Virginia farmer named John Grey in the Blue Ridge country in Southwestern Virginia. There was a wide valley called the "Rich Valley" with a railroad and a small river running through it and high mountains in sight, to the north and south. Ted had some kind of a heart disease, a lesion, something of the sort, the result of a severe attack of diphtheria when he was a child of eight. He was thin and not strong but curiously alive. The doctor said he might die at any moment, might just drop down dead. The fact had drawn him peculiarly close to his sister Mary. It had awakened a strong and determined maternalism in her.

The whole family, the neighbors on neighboring farms in the valley, and even the other children at the schoolhouse where they went to school recognized something as existing between the two children. "Look at them going along there," people said. "They do seem to have good times together, but they are so serious. For such young children they are too serious. Still, I sup-

BROTHER DEATH

SHERWOOD ANDERSON

pose, under the circumstances, it's natural." Of course, everyone knew about Ted. It had done something to Mary. At fourteen she was both a child and a grown woman. The woman side of her kept popping out at unexpected moments.

She had sensed something concerning her brother Ted. It was because he was as he was, having that kind of a heart, a heart likely at any moment to stop beating, leaving him dead, cut down like a young tree. The others in the Grey family, that is to say, the older ones, the mother and father and an older brother, Don, who was eighteen now, recognized something as belonging to the two children, being, as it were, between them, but the recognition wasn't very definite. People in your own family are likely at any moment to do strange, sometimes hurtful things to you. You have to watch them. Ted and Mary had both found that out.

The brother Don was like the father, already at eighteen almost a grown man. He was that sort, the kind people speak of, saying: "He's a good man. He'll make a good solid dependable man." The father, when he was a young man, never drank, never went chasing the girls, was never wild. There had been enough wild young ones in the Rich Valley when he was a lad. Some of them had inherited big farms and had lost them, gambling, drinking, fooling with fast horses and chasing after the women. It had been almost a Virginia tradition, but John Grey was a land man. All the Greys were. There were other large cattle farms owned by Greys up and down the valley.

John Grey, everyone said, was a natural cattle man. He knew beef cattle, of the big so-called export type, how to pick and feed them to make beef. He knew how and where to get the right kind of young stock to turn into his fields. It was the blue-grass country. Big beef cattle went directly off the pastures to market. The Grey farm contained over twelve hundred acres, most of it in blue-grass.

The father was a land man, land hungry. He had begun, as a cattle farmer, with a small place, inherited from his father, some two hundred acres, lying next to what was then the big Aspinwahl place and, after he began, he never stopped getting more land. He kept cutting in on the Aspinwahls who were a rather horsey, fast lot. They thought of themselves as Virginia aristocrats, having, as they weren't so modest about pointing out, a family going back and back, family tradition, guests always being entertained, fast horses kept, money being bet on fast horses. John Grey getting their land, now twenty acres, then thirty, then fifty, until at last he got the old Aspinwahl house, with one of the Aspinwahl girls, not a young one, not one of the best-looking ones, as wife. The Aspinwahl place was down, by that time, to less than a hundred acres, but he went on, year after year, always being careful and shrewd, making every penny count, never wasting a cent, adding and adding to what was now the Grey place. The former Aspinwahl house was a large old brick house with fireplaces in all the rooms and was very comfortable.

People wondered why Louise Aspinwahl had married John Grey, but when they were wondering they smiled. The Aspinwahl girls were all well educated, had all been away to college, but Louise wasn't so pretty. She got nicer after marriage, suddenly almost beautiful. The Aspinwahls were, as everyone knew, naturally sensitive, really first class but the men couldn't hang onto land and the Greys could. In all that section of Virginia, people gave John Grey credit for being what he was. They respected him. "He's on the level," they said, "as honest as a horse. He has cattle sense, that's it." He could run his big hand down over the flank of a steer and say, almost to the pound, what he would weigh on the scales or he could look at a calf or a yearling and say, "He'll do," and he would do. A steer is a steer. He isn't supposed to do anything but make beef.

There was Don, the oldest son of the Grey family. He was so evidently destined to be a Grey, to be another like his father. He had long been a star in the 4H Club of the Virginia county and, even as a lad of nine and ten, had won prizes at steer judging. At twelve he had produced, no one helping him, doing all the work himself, more bushels of corn on an acre of land than any other boy in the State.

It was all a little amazing, even a bit queer to Mary Grey, being as she was a girl peculiarly conscious, so old and young, so aware. There was Don, the older brother, big and strong of body, like the father, and there was the younger brother Ted. Ordinarily, in the ordinary course of life, she being what she was—female—it would have been quite natural and right for her to have given her young girl's admiration to Don but she didn't. For some reason, Don barely existed for her. He was outside, not in it, while for her Ted, the seemingly weak one of the family, was everything.

Still there Don was, so big of body, so quiet, so apparently sure of himself. The father had begun, as a young cattle man, with the two hundred acres, and now he had the twelve hundred. What would Don Grey do when he started? Already he knew, although he didn't say anything, that he wanted to start. He wanted to run things, be his own boss. His father had offered to send him away to college, to an agricultural college, but he wouldn't go. "No. I can learn more here," he said.

Already there was a contest, always kept under the surface, between the father and son. It concerned ways of doing things, decisions to be made. As yet the son always surrendered.

It is like that in a family, little isolated groups formed within the larger group, jealousies, concealed hatreds, silent battles secretly going on—among the Greys, Mary and Ted, Don and his father, the mother and the two younger children, Gladys, a girl child of six now, who adored her brother Don, and Harry, a boy child of two.

As for Mary and Ted, they lived within their own world, but their own world had not been established without a struggle. The point was that Ted, having the heart that might at any moment stop beating, was always being treated tenderly by the others. Only Mary understood that—how it infuriated and hurt him.

"No, Ted, I wouldn't do that."

"Now, Ted, do be careful."

Sometimes Ted went white and trembling with anger, Don, the father, the mother, all keeping at him like that. It didn't matter what he wanted to do, learn to drive one of the two family cars, climb a tree to find a bird's nest, run a race with Mary. Naturally, being on a farm, he wanted to try his hand at breaking a colt, beginning with him, getting a saddle on, having it out with him. "No, Ted. You can't." He had learned to swear, picking it up from the farm-hands and from the boys at the country school. "Hell!" he said to Mary. Only Mary understood how he felt, and she had not put the matter very definitely into words, not even to herself. It was one of the things that made her old when she was so young. It made her stand aside from the others of the family, aroused in her a curious determination. "They shall not." She caught herself saying the words to herself. "They shall not."

"If he is to have but a few years of life, they shall not spoil what he is to have. Why should they make him die, over and over, day after day?" The thoughts in her mind did not become so definite. She had resentment against the others. She was like a soldier, standing guard over Ted.

The two children drew more and more away, into their own world and only once did what Mary felt come to the surface. That was with the mother.

It was on an early Summer day and Ted and Mary were playing in the rain. They were on a side porch of the house, where the water came pouring down from the eaves. At a corner of the porch there was a great stream, and first Ted and then Mary dashed through it, returning to the porch with clothes soaked and water running in streams from soaked hair. There was something joyous, the feel of the cold water on the body, under clothes, and they were shrieking with laughter when the mother came to the door. She looked at Ted. There was fear and anxiety in her voice. "Oh, Ted, you know you mustn't, you mustn't." Just that. All the rest implied. Nothing said to Mary. There it was. "Oh, Ted, you mustn't. You mustn't run hard, climb trees, ride horses. The least shock to you may do it." It was the old story again, and, of course, Ted understood. He went white and trembled. Why couldn't the rest understand that was a hundred times worse for him? On that day, without answering his mother, he ran off the porch and through the rain toward the barns. He wanted to go hide himself from everyone. Mary knew how he felt.

She got suddenly very old and very angry. The mother and daughter stood looking at each other, the woman nearing fifty and the child of fourteen. It was getting everything in the family reversed. Mary felt that but felt she had to do something. "You should have more sense, Mother," she said seriously. She also had gone white. Her lips trembled. "You mustn't do it any more. Don't you ever do it again."

"What, child?" There was astonishment and half anger in the mother's voice.

"Always making him think of it," Mary said. She wanted to cry but didn't.

The mother understood. There was a queer tense moment before Mary also walked off, toward the barns, in the rain. It wasn't all so clear. The mother wanted to fly at the child, perhaps shake her for daring to be so impudent. A child like that to decide things—to dare to reprove her mother. There was so much implied—even that Ted be allowed to die, quickly, suddenly, rather than that death, danger of sudden death, be brought again and again to his attention. There were values in life, implied by a child's words: "Life, what is it worth? Is death the most terrible thing?" The mother turned and went silently into the house while Mary, going to the barns, presently found Ted. He was in an empty horse stall, standing with his back to the wall, staring. There were no explanations. "Well," Ted said presently, and, "Come on, Ted," Mary replied. It was necessary to do something even perhaps more risky than playing in the rain. The rain was already passing. "Let's take off our shoes," Mary said. Going barefoot was one of the things forbidden Ted. They took their shoes off and, leaving them in the barn, went into an orchard. There was a small creek below the orchard, a creek that went down to the river and now it would be in flood. They went into it and once Mary got swept off her feet so that Ted had to pull her out. She spoke then. "I told Mother," she said, looking serious.

"What?" Ted said. "Gee, I guess maybe I saved you from drowning," he added.

"Sure you did," said Mary. "I told her to let you alone." She grew suddenly fierce. "They've all got to—they've got to let you alone," she said.

There was a bond. Ted did his share. He was imaginative and could think of plenty of risky things to do. Perhaps the mother spoke to the father and to Don, the older brother. There was a new inclination in the family to keep hands off the pair, and the fact seemed to give the two children new room in life. Something seemed to open out. There was a little inner world created, always, every day, being re-created, and in it there was a kind of new security. It seemed to the two children—they could not have put their feelings into words—that, being in their own created world, feeling a security there, they could suddenly look out at the outside world, and see, in a new way, what was going on out there in the world that belonged also to others.

It was a world to be thought about, looked at, a world of drama too, the drama of human relations, outside their own world, in a family, on a farm, in a farmhouse.... On a farm, calves and yearling steers arriving to be fattened, great heavy steers going off to market, colts being broken to work or to saddle, lambs born in the late Winter. The human side of life was more difficult, to a child often incomprehensible, but after the speech to the mother, on the porch of the house that day when it rained, it seemed to Mary almost as though she and Ted had set up a new family. Everything about the farm, the house and the barns got nicer. There was a new freedom. The two children walked along a country road, returning to the farm from school in the late afternoon. There were other children in the road but they managed to fall behind or they got ahead. There were plans made. "I'm going to be a nurse when I grow up," Mary said. She may have remembered dimly the woman nurse, from the county-seat town, who had come to stay in the house when Ted was so ill. Ted said that as soon as he could—it would be when he was younger yet than Don was now—he intended to leave and go out West... far out, he said. He wanted to be a cowboy or a bronco-buster or something, and, that failing, he thought he would be a railroad engineer. The railroad that went down through the Rich Valley crossed a corner of the Grey farm, and, from the road in the afternoon, they could sometimes see trains, quite far away, the smoke rolling up. There was a faint rumbling noise, and on clear days they could see the flying piston rods of the engines.

As for the two stumps in the field near the house, they were what was left of two oak trees. The children had known the trees. They were cut one day in the early Fall.

There was a back porch to the Grey house—the house that had once been the seat of the Aspinwahl family—and from the porch steps a path led down to a stone spring house. A spring came out of the ground just there, and there was a tiny stream that went along the edge of a field, past two large barns and out across a meadow to a creek—called a "branch" in Virginia, and the two trees stood close together beyond the spring house and the fence.

They were lusty trees, their roots down in the rich, always damp soil, and one of them had a great limb that came down near the ground, so that Ted and Mary could climb into it and out another limb into its brother tree, and in the Fall, when other trees, at the front and side of the house, had shed their leaves, blood-red leaves still clung to the two oaks. They were like dry blood on gray days, but on other days, when the sun came out, the trees flamed against the distant hills. The leaves clung, whispering and talking when the wind blew, so that the trees themselves seemed carrying on a conversation.

John Grey had decided he would have the trees cut. At first it was not a very definite decision. "I think I'll have them cut," he announced.

"But why?" his wife asked. The trees meant a good deal to her. They had been planted, just in that spot, by her grandfather, she said, having in mind just a certain effect. "You see how, in the Fall, when you stand on the back porch, they are so nice against the hills." She spoke of the trees, already quite large, having been brought from a distant woods. Her mother had often spoken of it. The man, her grandfather, had a special feeling for trees. "An Aspinwahl would do that," John Grey said. "There is enough yard, here about the house, and enough trees. They do not shade the house or the yard. An Aspinwahl would go to all that trouble for trees and then plant them where grass might be growing." He had suddenly determined, a half-formed determination in him suddenly hardening. He had perhaps heard too much of the Aspinwahls and their ways. The conversation regarding the trees took place at the table, at the noon hour, and Mary and Ted heard it all.

It began at the table and was carried on afterwards out of doors, in the yard back of the house. The wife had followed her husband out. He always left the table suddenly and silently, getting quickly up and going out heavily, shutting doors with a bang as he went. "Don't, John," the wife said, standing on the porch and calling to her husband. It was a cold day but the sun was out and the trees were like great bonfires against gray distant fields and hills. The older son of the family, young Don, the one so physically like the father and apparently so like him in every other way, had come out of the house with the mother, followed by the two children, Ted and Mary, and at first Don said nothing, but, when the father did not answer the mother's protest but started toward the barn, he also spoke. What he said was obviously the determining thing, hardening the father.

To the two other children—they had walked a little aside and stood together watching and listening—there was something. There was their own child's world. "Let us alone and we'll let you alone." It wasn't as definite as that. Most of the definite thoughts about what happened in the yard that afternoon came to Mary Grey long afterwards, when she was a grown woman. At the moment there was merely a sudden sharpening of the feeling of isolation, a wall between herself and Ted and the others. The father, even then perhaps, seen in a new light, Don and the mother seen in a new light.

There was something, a driving destructive thing in life, in all relationships between people. All of this felt dimly that day—she always believed both by herself and Ted—but only thought out long afterwards, after Ted was dead. There was the farm her father had won from the Aspinwahls—greater persistence, greater shrewdness. In a family, little remarks dropped from time to time, an impression slowly built up. The father, John Grey, was a successful man. He had acquired. He owned. He was the commander, the one having the power to do his will. And the power had run out and covered, not only other human lives, impulses in others, wishes, hungers in others . . . he himself might not have, might not even understand . . . but it went far beyond that. It was, curiously, the power also of life and death. Did Mary Grey think such thoughts at that moment? . . . She couldn't have. . . . Still there was her own peculiar situation, her relationship with her brother Ted, who was to die.

Ownership that gave curious rights, dominances—fathers over children, men and women over lands, houses, factories in cities, fields. "I will have the trees in that orchard cut. They produce apples but not of the right sort. There is no money in apples of that sort any more."

"But, Sir . . . you see . . . look . . . the trees there against that hill, against the sky."

"Nonsense. Sentimentality."

Confusion.

It would have been such nonsense to think of the father of Mary Grey as a man without feeling. He had struggled hard all his life, perhaps, as a young man, gone without things wanted, deeply hungered for. Someone has to manage things in this life. Possessions mean power, the right to say "Do this" or "Do that." If you struggle long and hard for a thing it becomes infinitely sweet to you.

Was there a kind of hatred between the father and the older son of the Grey family? "You are one also who has this thing—the impulse to power, so like my own. Now you are young and I am growing old." Admiration mixed with fear. If you would retain power it will not do to admit fear.

The young Don was so curiously like the father. There were the same lines about the jaws, the same eyes. They were both heavy men. Already the young man walked like the father, slammed doors as did the father. There was the same curious lack of delicacy of thought and touch—the heaviness that plows through, gets things done. When John Grey had married Louise Aspinwahl he was already a mature man, on his way to success. Such men do not marry young and recklessly. Now he was nearly sixty and there was the son—so like himself, having the same kind of strength.

Both land lovers, possession lovers. "It is my farm, my house, my horses, cattle, sheep." Soon now, another ten years, fifteen at the most, and the father would be ready for death. "See, already my hand slips a little. All of this to go out of my grasp." He, John Grey, had not got all of these possessions so easily. It had taken much patience, much persistence. No one but himself would ever quite know. Five, ten, fifteen years of work and saving, getting the Aspinwahl farm piece by piece. "The fools!" They had liked to think of themselves as aristocrats, throwing the land away, now twenty acres, now thirty, now fifty.

Raising horses that could never plow an acre of land.

And they had robbed the land too, had never put anything back, doing nothing to enrich it, build it up. Such a one thinking: "I'm an Aspinwahl, a gentleman. I do not soil my hands at the plow."

"Fools who do not know the meaning of land owned, possessions, money—responsibility. It is they who are second-rate men."

He had got an Aspinwahl for a wife and, as it had turned out, she was the best, the smartest and, in the end, the best-looking one of the lot.

And now there was his son, standing at the moment near the mother. They had both come down off the porch. It would be natural and right for this one—he being what he already was, what he would become—for him, in his turn, to come into possession, to take command.

There would be, of course, the rights of the other children. If you have the stuff in you (John Grey felt that his son Don had) there is a way to manage. You buy the others out, make arrangements. There was Ted—he wouldn't be alive—and Mary and the two younger children. "The better for you if you have to struggle."

All of this, the implication of the moment of sudden struggle between a father and son, coming slowly afterwards to the man's daughter, as yet little more than a child. Does the drama take place when the seed is put into the ground or afterwards when the plant has pushed out of the ground and the bud breaks open, or still later, when the fruit ripens? There were the Greys with their ability—slow, saving, able, determined, patient. Why had they superseded the Aspinwahls in the Rich Valley? Aspinwahl blood also in the two children, Mary and Ted.

There was an Aspinwahl man—called "Uncle Fred," a brother to Louise Grey—who came sometimes to the farm. He was a rather striking-looking, tall old man with a gray Vandyke beard[1] and a mustache, somewhat shabbily dressed but always with an indefinable air of class. He came from the county-seat town, where he lived now with a daughter who had married a merchant, a polite courtly old man who always froze into a queer silence in the presence of the sister's husband.

The son Don was standing near the mother on the day in the Fall, and the two children, Mary and Ted, stood apart.

"Don't, John," Louise Grey said again. The father, who had started toward the barns, stopped.

"Well, I guess I will."

"No, you won't," said young Don, speaking suddenly. There was a queer fixed look in his eyes. It had flashed into life—something that was between the two men: "I possess". . ."I will possess." The father

1. *Vandyke beard,* a pointed beard patterned after that worn by Anthony Van Dyke, a Flemish painter (1599-1641).

wheeled and looked sharply at the son and then ignored him.

For a moment the mother continued pleading.

"But why, why?"

"They make too much shade. The grass does not grow."

"But there is so much grass, so many acres of grass."

John Grey was answering his wife, but now again he looked at his son. There were unspoken words flying back and forth.

"I possess. I am in command here. What do you mean by telling me that I won't?"

"Ha! So! You possess now but soon I will possess."

"I'll see you in hell first."

"You fool! Not yet! Not yet!"

None of the words, set down above, was spoken at the moment, and afterwards the daughter Mary never did remember the exact words that had passed between the two men. There was a sudden quick flash of determination in Don—even perhaps sudden determination to stand by the mother—even perhaps something else—a feeling in the young Don out of the Aspinwahl blood in him—for the moment tree love superseding grass love—grass that would fatten steers. . . .

Winner of 4H Club prizes, champion young corn-raiser, judge of steers, land lover, possession lover.

"You won't," Don said again.

"Won't what?"

"Won't cut those trees."

The father said nothing more at the moment but walked away from the little group toward the barns. The sun was still shining brightly. There was a sharp cold little wind. The two trees were like bonfires lighted against distant hills.

It was the noon hour and there were two men, both young, employees on the farm, who lived in a small tenant house beyond the barns. One of them, a man with a harelip, was married and the other, a rather handsome silent young man, boarded with him. They had just come from the midday meal and were going toward one of the barns. It was the beginning of the Fall corn-cutting time and they would be going together to a distant field to cut corn.

The father went to the barn and returned with the two men. They brought axes and a long cross-cut saw. "I want you to cut those two trees." There was something, a blind, even stupid determination in the man, John Grey. And at that moment his wife, the mother of his children . . . There was no way any of the children could ever know how many moments of the sort she had been through. She had married John Grey. He was her man.

"If you do, Father . . ." Don Grey said coldly.

"Do as I tell you! Cut those two trees!" This addressed to the two workmen. The one who had a harelip laughed. His laughter was like the bray of a donkey.

"Don't," said Louise Grey, but she was not addressing her husband this time. She stepped to her son and put a hand on his arm.

"Don't."

"Don't cross him. Don't cross my man." Could a child like Mary Grey comprehend? It takes time to understand things that happen in life. Life unfolds slowly to the mind. Mary was standing with Ted, whose young face was white and tense. Death at his elbow. At any moment. At any moment.

"I have been through this a hundred times. This is the way this man I married has succeeded. Nothing stops him. I married him; I have had my children by him.

"We women choose to submit.

"This is my affair, more than yours, Don, my son."

A woman hanging onto her things—the family, created about her.

The son not seeing things with her eyes. He shook off his mother's hand, lying on his arm. Louise Grey was younger than her husband, but, if he was now nearing sixty, she was drawing near fifty. At the moment she looked very delicate and fragile. There was something, at the moment, in her bearing . . . Was there, after all, something in blood, the Aspinwahl blood?

In a dim way perhaps, at the moment the child Mary did comprehend. Women and their men. For her then, at that time, there was but one male, the child Ted. Afterwards she remembered how he looked at that moment, the curiously serious old look on his young face. There was even, she thought later, a kind of contempt for both the father and brother, as though he might have been saying to himself—he couldn't really have been saying it—he was too young: *"Well, we'll see. This is something. These foolish ones—my father and my brother. I myself haven't long to live. I'll see what I can, while I do live."*

The brother Don stepped over near to where his father stood.

"If you do, Father . . ." he said again.

"Well?"

"I'll walk off this farm and I'll never come back."

"All right. Go then."

The father began directing the two men who had begun cutting the trees, each man taking a tree. The young man with the harelip kept laughing, the laughter like the bray of a donkey. "Stop that," the father said sharply, and the sound ceased abruptly. The son Don walked away, going rather aimlessly toward the barn. He approached one of the barns and then stopped. The mother, white now, half ran into the house.

The son returned toward the house, passing the two younger children without looking at them, but did not enter. The father did not look at him. He went hesitatingly along a path at the front of the house and through a gate and into a road. The road ran for several miles down through the valley and then, turning, went over a mountain to the county-seat town.

As it happened, only Mary saw the son Don when he returned to the farm. There were three or four tense days. Perhaps, all the time, the mother and son had been secretly in touch. There was a telephone in the house. The father stayed all day in the fields, and when he was in the house was silent.

Mary was in one of the barns on the day when Don came back and when the father and son met. It was an odd meeting.

The son came, Mary always afterwards thought, rather sheepishly. The father came out of a horse's stall. He had been throwing corn to work horses. Neither the father nor the son saw Mary. There was a car parked in the barn and she had crawled into the driver's seat, her hands on the steering wheel, pretending she was driving.

"Well," the father said. If he felt triumphant, he did not show his feeling.

"Well," said the son, "I have come back."

"Yes, I see," the father said. "They are cutting corn." He walked toward the barn door and then stopped. "It will be yours soon now," he said. "You can be boss then."

He said no more and both men went away, the father toward the distant fields and the son toward the house. Mary was afterwards quite sure that nothing more was ever said.

What had the father meant?

"When it is yours you can be the boss." It was too much for the child. Knowledge comes slowly. It meant:

"You will be in command, and for you, in your turn, it will be necessary to assert.

"Such men as we are cannot fool with delicate stuff. Some men are meant to command and others must obey. You can make them obey in your turn.

"There is a kind of death.

"Something in you must die before you can possess and command."

There was, so obviously, more than one kind of death. For Don Grey one kind and for the younger brother Ted, soon now perhaps, another.

Mary ran out of the barn that day, wanting eagerly to get out into the light, and afterwards, for a long time, she did not try to think her way through what had happened. She and her brother Ted did, however, afterwards, before he died, discuss quite often the two trees. They went on a cold day and put their fingers on the stumps, but the stumps were cold. Ted kept asserting that only men get their legs and arms cut off, and she protested. They continued doing things that had been forbidden Ted to do, but no one protested, and, a year or two later, when he died, he died during the night in his bed.

But while he lived, there was always, Mary afterwards thought, a curious sense of freedom, something that belonged to him that made it good, a great happiness, to be with him. It was, she finally thought, because having to die his kind of death, he never had to make the surrender his brother had made—to be sure of possessions, success, his time to command—would never have to face the more subtle and terrible death that had come to his older brother.

WHAT DO YOU SAY?

1. *(a)* What similarities do you see in the relationship between Ted and Mary and the relationship between the two brothers in "The Scarlet Ibis"? *(b)* What other similarities do you find in the two stories?

2. In what respects is Don like his father? Find lines that support your answer.

3. Describe the conflicts between these characters: *(a)* Mary and her mother, *(b)* Don and his father, *(c)* the father and the mother, *(d)* John Grey and the Aspinwahl "blood."

4. *(a)* What does Mary understand about Ted that the others do not? *(b)* Are the other members of the family concerned about keeping Ted alive for their sake or his? Explain.

5. Explain why Don's death was more "subtle and terrible" than Ted's.

6. *(a)* Describe success as it applied to John Grey. *(b)* What is the author implying that one must sacrifice for this kind of success? *(c)* Quote lines to explain how the author feels about John Grey's success.

7. *(a)* Despite the protests of Don and the mother, John Grey persists in his decision to have the trees cut down. What is his major reason? *(b)* Whose side in the controversy does the author seem to be on? How do you know?

8. What symbols has the author used for death? For the aging father?

9. What is the author's purpose in personifying the trees?

10. Discuss the appropriateness of the title.

SHERWOOD ANDERSON

One thread of Sherwood Anderson's life seems to have been revolt. He completed only one year of high school. Later he attended, but briefly, a prep school. Though he subsequently did well as a businessman, suddenly in middle age he abandoned both business career and family. From his native Ohio he returned to Chicago and, among distinguished literary contemporaries, continued with renewed energy to explore in writing his questions about American life. In his most famous novel, ***Winesburg, Ohio,*** he gives the lonely, inarticulate Midwesterner a voice in protesting abuses by the Machine Age of the 1920's. Anderson's short stories reflect his troubled, deep concern for understanding of human relationships.

A LESSON IN DISCIPLINE

BY

TERESA FOLEY

We were a terrible class. Every class likes to remember that it was pure hellion, but the thirty of us who started under Miss Gallagher at the Down School near the Buick garage really were terrible. We came along just when the argument between the phonics people and the associationists[1] was at its height. We went at reading for three years by the word-recognition method and then in the fourth grade the teacher insisted that we learn to read all over again by sounds. We were also caught in the controversy over manuscript and cursive writing. And we hit the crisis in arithmetic.

In the beginning of the fifth grade, we were forbidden to use brackets in finding the lowest common denominator. We had to go click-click to an equivalent fraction instead, seeing all the pieces of pie in our heads. This meant that nobody at home (Who had Gestaltists[2] in their families?) could help us any more. But, willing sneaks, we drew brackets with furtive fingers on our pants legs.

Child-centered psychology burgeoned in our town at this time. We were allowed to do some ridiculous things in school because we wanted to. When our parents heard about them, they were furious at first. Then they decided that the school must know what it was doing, and they let us do the same things and worse at home. Finally, like beer chasers after an evening of Mickey Finns,[3] came comic books and television.

"A Lesson in Discipline" by Teresa Foley. Reprinted from ***Harper's Magazine,*** December 1956 by permission of the author.

1. ***phonics people and the associationists.*** Phonics people are educators who believe that reading should be taught by the analysis of speech sounds as opposed to the associationists who believe that reading should be taught by having the children relate words to objects and to their own experiences.
2. ***Gestaltists*** (gə shält′ists), a school of contemporary psychology which believes that the personality of an individual should be studied and analyzed as a whole rather than as separate parts.
3. ***Mickey Finns,*** alcoholic beverages to which a narcotic has been added.

Every year for six years we grew stupider and lazier and fresher and more obnoxious. No one ever separated any of us, or kept any of us back, or adulterated us with new blood. We were a terrible package, referred to by certain members of the PTA as "Les Misérables."[4]

Then came the seventh year and Miss Barracombie.

She was new to the school that year, so we did not have the usual case studies on her from previous classes. Her looks might have given us a clue, but we had always known amateur, experimental teachers so we did not recognize the career teacher when we saw her. She was perhaps fifty, tall, square-shouldered, and erect; neither feminine nor mannish, merely healthy and strong. Her face was handsome but not pretty. She had no subtle expressions: she smiled outright, she frowned outright, or she concentrated. Her voice was not harsh but had a peculiar carrying quality, vibrating longer than most. Eugene Kent took off his hearing-aid after the first day.

She greeted us that day as no teacher ever had. No talk of adjustment here, no plea for growth, no challenge to find ourselves. She said:

"My name is Virginia Barracombie and it will be Miss Barracombie to you indefinitely. One of these days you will meet someone from the last school in which I taught. The worst that he tells you about me will be true. It's a far cry from child to man, and it's not through games that we get there. You and I are bound together in a contract for one year. I teach; you learn. Behave yourselves and pay attention and this will be one of the good years of your lives. You have a minute to prepare yourself with ruler, compass, pencil, and paper for a review of the meaning and use of decimals."

It was the shock treatment all right—but with economy, with the clarity of piano keys struck singly, above all with authority. We had neither the opportunity nor the mind to look across the aisles at each other until recess. We were at work in the first five minutes—we, who always had a period in which to get ready to get ready. It was a blow to our unit pride, but we were less cohesive after the long summer and temporarily distracted from getting together on what to do about it.

We thought at first that we were just going along with her in a momentary tolerance. She was novelty, and among teachers that was hard to find. Then we found ourselves bound in a work routine. At that point some of us tried to bolt.

In its reactions to Miss Barracombie the class divided into four groups. Several of the nicer girls and a couple of the boys who had strict scholastic accountability to professional parents went into her camp almost immediately when they saw that she was systematic, skillful, and just. Another group, whose names and faces are always hard to remember, went along with her because they sensed that she was a stronger personality; that balking would be tiring, involve exposure of weakness, and end in failure. These two groups accounted for perhaps two-thirds of the class. In the remaining third were the Idiot rebels and the Hard-nut rebels.

The Idiots moved in first, without seeing where they were going. For example:

Idiot: "Do we *have* to put our names on our compositions?" (looking around at the other Idiots for appreciative laughter).

Miss B.: "You don't *have* to."

Idiot: (Next day after papers had been passed back) "I didn't get my paper back. I haven't no grade."

Miss B.: "Did you expect one?"

Idiot: "You said we didn't *have* to put our names on them."

Miss B.: "That's right. You don't *have* to walk around with your eyes open, either."

The Idiot sat down, uneasily. That after-

---

4. *Les Misérables* (lā mē'zér ä'bl). The title of a novel by Victor Hugo, a nineteenth century French writer, the term literally means the miserable or wretched people.

noon his name was up with the absentees who had to make up the composition.

The Idiots were beaten from the start. She was indifferent to petty annoyances, and they did not dare try big ones.

The Hard-nuts, the long-time class heroes, waited more patiently, seeking their own ground. Their particular dragon in the case of Miss Barracombie was her good sense, which forced an antagonist to assume a role so foolish as to threaten his status among his classmates. This forced the Hard-nuts to try to operate outside the teaching periods, in the rather limited areas of truancy, ground rules, and personal relationships.

It was difficult to challenge her with truancy because there our parents were solidly on her side, and besides, the occasional absence or trumped-up tardiness of an individual did little to alter the steady civilizing routine. As for opportunities on the school grounds, Miss Barracombie supervised only in her turn, and was by some unexpected quirk more lenient than any of the other teachers, letting us proceed at games considerably rougher than we wished to be playing.

The worst of the Hard-nuts was Lennie Sopel. He was big and tough and bearded already, very much in the know about engines, baseball statistics, and older women. He had a way of muttering wisecracks half under his breath when girls recited. At first they reached only to people in the surrounding seats. Then one day as Lila Crocker went down the aisle, Lennie said in a loud whisper that shook the room like an east wind,

"Oh, man. I wish I had that swing in my backyard!"

Miss Barracombie stopped listening to a girl at the study table. The girl stopped talking. Lila fled to the waste basket and back to her seat, her face scarlet.

The room became as silent as a tomb in a pyramid.

Miss Barracombie looked at Lennie for a long time, and he locked eyes with her, ready for a showdown.

"What are you thinking about, Lennie?" she asked at last, rather softly for her.

"Nothin'." He could say that one word as though it were the nastiest in the language. "Absolutely nothin'."

"Well, I'm thinking about something," she said, still calm and relaxed. "You come in at three and I'll tell you about it. In the meantime, stand up."

"What for? What'd I do?"

"Stand up, please."

Lennie hesitated. Again it was one of her simple inescapable requests. He slid out into the aisle and stood up.

Miss Barracombie went back to her work with the girl at the table. Lennie started to sit down once, but she gave him a steady eye and he straightened up again. He had to stand by his seat throughout the rest of the afternoon. We kept looking at him, waiting for him to say something; Lennie couldn't seem to think of anything to say.

She kept him after school forty-five minutes every day for six months. He never spoke out of turn again in class and he never missed a session with her. It seemed a heavy punishment for one remark, and we couldn't get over either her giving it or his taking it. When we asked him what he had to do, all he would say was, "Nothin'. She just gives me hell."

"For forty hours, Lennie?"

"Who's countin'? And whose business?"

Then one day Alice Rowe gave us the lowdown. She had been helping in the inner office when the intercom was open to Miss Barracombie's room.

"She's teaching him to read."

Nobody would believe her. Lennie's in seventh grade, everybody said. He knows how to read.

"No, he doesn't," Alice said. "I heard him stumbling over the littlest words up there. Who's ever heard him read in class?"

We tried to remember when we had

heard Lennie read. He was a transfer to us in the fourth grade, and there hadn't been much oral reading since then.

"How does he do his other work?" we asked.

"Who says he does?"

No wonder Lennie couldn't fight her. She taught him in secret the one thing he needed to have to give up cheating and pretending.

The truth was, no rebellion had a chance with her. She wasn't mean and she never struck anybody (although our parents queried us over and over again on this point, wanting, we thought, to be able to say, "Of course, she has order! She whips them"). No situation could come up that she would not know how to handle efficiently and without damage to her single drive: she would teach; we would learn.

Whatever we studied, we mastered. Of course, she knew the ones of us who could not connect with the main lines she was trolling, but she put out other lines for them and they mastered, too. Nobody was free not to learn. We were free to fail, but somehow a failure was not a separate thing, only a step in learning. She never assumed that we had achieved. She probed and exposed until she read it in the blood. A week later when we were not expecting it, she would check again. She was the only teacher whose grades on our report cards we never questioned. Nor would we let our indignant parents go to her. She knew.

This was no love affair between the class and Miss Barracombie, however. She was businesslike and not tender with us. She encouraged no intimacies, and the thought of confiding in her as we had in Miss Tondreau who used to love us in the third grade was wholly ridiculous. We were just different with her. When our special teachers came and Miss Barracombie left the room, Eugene Kent would replace his hearing aid, and we would be at once on the Plain of Esdraelon,[5] stalking a world of enemies. By the end of the period our specials would be limp and distraught.

We did no better left on our own. If Miss Barracombie stepped out of the room—something she wisely did rarely—we would have the ceiling. After all, we had been indulged for years. Thirty near-simians don't slough that off in a few stretching months. We had never been convinced that discipline comes from within, and when the restraining presence was removed we reverted to the barbarians that we were.

Miss Barracombie never mentioned our behavior with other teachers or when she was out of the room, although the specials must have complained bitterly. It seemed to be part of her code that she was responsible when she was with us and others were responsible when they took us. We liked that. Miss Barracombie did not lecture or make us feel guilty. There was nothing to lecture or feel guilty about. We behaved. We learned. We had to: it was the contract.

But the final lesson we learned from Miss Barracombie was one she did not try to teach us. It was during the last period. We were in the midst of a discussion on the use of quotation marks. The intercom box pinged on the wall and the principal said:

"A telegram has just arrived for you, Miss Barracombie. Will you send a boy down for it?"

She sent Herbert Harvey Bell. He was in the corner seat by the door. He went out running because she knew exactly how long it took to get to the office and back and he did not want to answer for loitering.

He returned with the telegram, gave it to her, and took his seat.

She opened the envelope calmly and neatly so as not to tear the inside sheet. Still reading it, she turned about slowly so that her back was toward the class. Her hands lowered. We could see that she was no longer looking at the telegram but at

5. ***Plain of Esdraelon*** (ez drə ē'lən), a valley in Palestine which, several times in history, has served as a battlefield.

the bulletin board. She did not turn back to us. She kept looking at something on the board.

Then before the alerted, somehow apprehensive eyes of the class, Miss Barracombie began to grow smaller. It was in her shoulders first. They began to narrow, to go forward. Her back curved. Her head dropped. We waited, not knowing what to do. Herbert Harvey Bell seemed to feel the most responsible. He looked around at all of us with a question in his wide, stunned eyes. We had nothing for him. Herbert Harvey pulled himself up from his seat and ran across the hall to the teacher there.

Lennie Sopel had started down from his seat, but when he saw the other teacher, Mrs. Hamilton, coming, he turned and went back up the aisle.

Mrs. Hamilton went up to Miss Barracombie and peered into her face. Then she bent to the telegram still in her hands.

"Oh, my dear," she said and put her arm around Miss Barracombie. Miss Barracombie did not move. Her shoulders were gone, melted into her narrow back.

Mrs. Hamilton turned her in the direction of the door. Our teacher put both hands across her face and, huddled and small, walked out like a child under Mrs. Hamilton's arm.

No one breathed or moved. A few minutes later Mrs. Hamilton looked into our room.

"Miss Barracombie has lost someone dear to her, boys and girls. Try to finish the period quietly."

No one came near us for the rest of the afternoon, not even to dismiss us. But we did not behave as we usually did when left alone. Most of us took out our composition notebooks and pens. Some just sat there.

We were frightened—a little sad for Miss Barracombie, of course—but mainly frightened, and frightened for ourselves. If she could be struck down, who was so tall, so erect, with all things under control, what could not happen to the rest of us who never had any control on the inside, who had to be made by others to hold our shoulders back?

We were the best we had ever been until the bell rang that day. For a moment we could see our connection with adults. Through a maze of equivalent fractions and common denominators we could see other people, huddled and shrinking, being led out of strange rooms. And their faces were ours.

WHAT DO YOU SAY?

1. What are some of the reasons the thirty students during six years "grew stupider and lazier and fresher and more obnoxious"?

2. (a) What qualities make Miss Barracombie a competent teacher? *(b)* Describe her appearance. *(c)* What is her attitude toward her students? *(d)* What is her single drive? *(e)* Which paragraph do you think best shows her manner of managing a class? *(f)* What insights does she have in handling problem students? Give examples. *(g)* In what varied ways does she make sure students will learn? *(h)* How do the students respond?

3. (a) What happens after the principal announces that the telegram has arrived? *(b)* What are the reactions of Miss Barracombie and of the students?

4. (a) Why are the students frightened? *(b)* What understanding do they gain "for a moment"?

COMPOSITION GUIDE

DON OTTO

Reading literature should provoke a response. You will find that many times you will have something to say on the subject about which you have been reading. The composition lessons that follow will give you a chance to respond. If you really try this year to improve your ability to communicate your ideas, when school closes you will be a better conversationalist, a better thinker, a better reader, and a better writer.

These composition lessons are all related to the reading you will do this year. Some of them are based on experimenting with writing the type of literature you are studying; for example, when you are reading *Romeo and Juliet,* you are invited to try writing a one-act play. Other compositions are centered on having you express your ideas about the selections in a unit; thus, after reading certain short stories or poems you explain your reactions to the ideas they advance.

There are sixteen of these composition lessons, each divided into two assignments. Many of the lessons also contain a third optional assignment for ambitious students or students particularly interested in writing. In most lessons Assignment 1 is a composition of a paragraph or two, and Assignment 2 is a longer paper of the same type. This means that each lesson gives you two chances to practice the same kind of writing.

Like even the most experienced professional writer, you will need advice and information to help you in your writing. Your teacher and your classmates can offer valuable criticism of your work. Your language textbook and your dictionary are fine sources of information about the technical aspects of writing. Use them frequently. The better acquainted you become with your language text and your dictionary, the more you will advance in the craft of writing.

Printed below are the titles of the lessons in the composition guide and the units in the text which they are designed to accompany.

One: Comparison and Contrast	Unit 1: The Short Story
Two: Explaining Things	
Three: Expressing Opinions	
Four: Writing Incidents	Unit 2: Biography and Autobiography
Five: Writing Description	Unit 3: A Book of Poetry
Six: Interpreting Poetry	
Seven: News Stories	Unit 4: Romeo and Juliet
Eight: Character Sketches	
Nine: One-Act Plays	
Ten: Using Reference Materials	Unit 5: Classical Heritage
Eleven: Expressing Ideas	
Twelve: Writing Explanations	Unit 6: A Tale of Two Cities
Thirteen: Interpretation	
Fourteen: Book Reviews	
Fifteen: Writing Essays	Unit 7: At Random
Sixteen: Interpretation	

LESSON ONE: *Comparison and Contrast*

ASSIGNMENT 1. *Based on "The Adventure of the Speckled Band" and "The Cask of Amontillado," pages 3-26.*

Two men walking down the street linked together by a pair of handcuffs may look much alike; yet one is the prisoner, the other the representative of law and order. The prisoner has his good qualities, although the fact that we see him in his position as prisoner emphasizes his faults; and the faults of the representative of the law are hidden by the good qualities he exhibits as guardian of law and order. Such matters of degree and detail mark the differences between characters in stories. Can you identify such differences, or do you immediately classify characters simply as either heroes or villains?

Jot down notes emphasizing the differences between Sherlock Holmes and Dr. Roylott. Now list some ways in which these two men are similar. (Why, for example, is Dr. Roylott so dangerous an opponent for a clever detective?) Develop these notes into a composition of no more than two paragraphs, using one paragraph to explain the differences between the two men and one to develop ways in which they are similar.

If you would like to try your skill at a more difficult assignment, write a composition comparing and contrasting Fortunato and Montresor. For information on what kinds of individuals these two men were, you will have to read between the lines. Obviously, you cannot trust anything Montresor says about Fortunato, nor can you rely on his opinions of himself. Use the actions and the utterances of the men as clues to character.

Before you begin to write, review in your language text the qualities that a good paragraph must have. After you have written a first draft of your composition, read it over carefully. Is it well organized? Can you improve the structure of any of the sentences? Are there any errors in grammar or spelling? Revise accordingly. Remember revision is an important part of writing.

ASSIGNMENT 2. *Based on "The Adventure of the Speckled Band," "The Cask of Amontillado," "Bargain," "Most Dangerous Game," and "An Underground Episode," pages 3-57.*

When you tell a friend about a book you have really enjoyed, you may begin by comparing it in some respects with a story you both know and like. Pointing out similarities and differences is also an excellent device to use in writing compositions, since it is one of the best ways of making an idea clear to the reader.

Listed below are several questions bearing on the short stories you have read. Choose one of them and write a composition giving your ideas on the subject. Make up your own title.

1. What is a "hero"? *(Point out similarities and differences between the boy in "An Underground Episode," Rainsford, and Sherlock Holmes. Which comes closest to your idea of a hero?)*
2. What are the disadvantages and advantages of using a narrator in a short story? *(The authors of "The Speckled Band," "The Cask of Amontillado," and "Bargain" use a narrator to tell the story. In "The Most Dangerous Game" and "An Underground Episode" the author tells his own story, using the third person point of view.)*
3. In what different ways may a narrator function? *(Compare and contrast the rôles played by Dr. Watson, Montresor, and Al.)*
4. Which story has a plot most like that of "The Cask of Amontillado"? *(Consider the motives of the characters and the basic idea.)*
5. How does the conflict in "An Underground Episode" differ from that of the other stories?

Because you will probably need several paragraphs to develop your idea, make an outline before beginning to write your first draft. An outline will help you avoid repetition and channel your separate thoughts into logical groups. Consult your language text to find out how to go about making an outline of the type needed.

LESSON TWO: *Explaining Things*

ASSIGNMENT 1. *Based on "The Life and Death of a Western Gladiator," "After You, My Dear Alphonse," "The Necklace," and "Indian Burial," pages 58-85.*

Whether talking or writing we spend much of our time explaining things. You may explain to a stranger how to find the post office. A recipe in a cookbook explains how to prepare a certain casserole. An article in a magazine explains a writer's viewpoint on foreign policy. An editorial in a newspaper explains why the paper supports a certain candidate for office. Even in fiction certain kinds of explanation are necessary if the reader is to understand the story.

One type of explanation concentrates on stating facts. You have become accustomed to this type of writing in your science texts or in some magazines—one devoted to aeronautics, for example. While not much fiction is so filled with facts as "The Life and Death of a Western Gladiator," Dean Doner points out in the article entitled "Fact and Fiction" (page 84) that many stories contain a hard core of factual material.

Write one or (at most) two paragraphs on one of the topics listed below. Draw on factual material from the stories you have studied in class, supplementing it with your own knowledge if necessary. Try to present your facts in a logical order. Make your explanation so clear your classmates will have no difficulty in grasping the facts you are presenting.

1. The Reasons Few Rattlesnakes Reach Maturity.
2. The Life Cycle of a Rattlesnake.
3. The Habitat of Rattlesnakes.
4. The Rattlesnake's Methods of Protecting Himself.
5. Sioux Burial Customs.

ASSIGNMENT 2. *Based on "After You, My Dear Alphonse," "The Necklace," "Indian Burial," "The Scarlet Ibis," and "A Reading Problem," pages 64-110.*

Your second assignment in this lesson is to explain an idea; this is a somewhat different problem from organizing and stating facts. In writing such a paragraph, it is often well to begin with a topic sentence. Review in your language text the functions of a topic sentence. Review also the various ways in which a paragraph may be developed: through the use of similarities and differences, details, examples, and reasons.

Listed here are several topic sentences which suggest ideas drawn from one of the stories you have studied. Choose one of the sentences and write a paragraph developing the idea it summarizes.

1. Mrs. Wilson has some stereotyped impressions about Negroes.
2. Sometimes it is better to admit one has made a mistake rather than to conceal it.
3. Faith in himself can help a person to accomplish seemingly impossible tasks.
4. Doodle's death was to a large extent the result of his brother's pride.
5. The humor in "A Reading Problem" stems largely from exaggerated characterizations.

When you have finished writing, read your paragraph carefully. If possible, read it aloud. Sometimes you can detect faults in sentence structure and usage from the sound. Examine your paragraph for sentences that are not clear. Does the paragraph really explain the topic sentence? Does it stick to the point? Read your paragraph to a classmate and ask him whether he thinks your explanation is easy to understand. Revise your paragraph accordingly.

LESSON THREE: *Expressing Opinions*

ASSIGNMENT 1. *Based on "The Third Ingredient," "By the Waters of Babylon," and "The Fifty-first Dragon," pages 111-135.*

A good story may cause the reader to react automatically. At first he may want to say simply that he likes the story; next he may identify what he likes about it; eventually, though, he may want to challenge or affirm what the author seems to be saying about life or about human nature. The stories named above are apt to lead you to weighing the author's ideas, since in each of them the author indirectly comments upon one or more aspects of life.

Listed below are quotations from these stories. Choose one and write a paragraph agreeing or disagreeing with the idea expressed.

1. Figuratively (let us say), some people are Bosoms, some are Hands, some are Heads, some are Muscles, some are Feet, some are Backs for burdens ("The Third Ingredient," page 115).
2. It is better to lose one's life than one's spirit ("By the Waters of Babylon," page 124).
3. Truth is a hard deer to hunt. If you eat too much truth at once, you may die of the truth ("By the Waters of Babylon," page 128).
4. . . . life is not a matter of theories. Life is a matter of facts. It calls on the young and the old alike to face these facts, even though they are hard and sometimes unpleasant ("The Fifty-first Dragon," page 134).
5. There isn't any such thing as a magic word ("The Fifty-first Dragon," page 134).

ASSIGNMENT 2. *Based on "The Third Ingredient," "By the Waters of Babylon," "The Fifty-first Dragon," and "The Slip-over Sweater," pages 111-143.*

If you are to persuade others that your opinion is to be taken seriously, you must present your facts clearly, give examples to enforce your position, and organize your arguments logically. Write several paragraphs defending or opposing one of the following statements:

1. O. Henry's use of coincidence strengthens (weakens) the humor in his story.
2. The situation Benét describes is (is not) believable.
3. The narrator of "By the Waters of Babylon" is (is not) justified in disobeying the laws of the People of the Hills.
4. Confidence in one's ability to perform a task is (is not) the most important element in success.
5. Shan's attitudes toward Jo-Anne Burton and Grace Hinton reveal (do not reveal) that he is quite immature.
6. Jo-Anne Burton is (is not) a more convincing character than Grace Hinton.
7. Shan's actions are (are not) typical of the average high-school boy.

OPTIONAL ASSIGNMENT

Why not try to write a short story or an anecdote on your own? Review the "Author's Craft" articles on pages 19, 26, 35, 50, and 95, learning from them how authors handle problems of plot, character, setting, and symbol. When you have studied these references, think through what you are going to tell, make a few notes, outline the plot, and then write. Simply tell the most interesting story you can, whether it is fact or fiction. Write about the people and the life around you. Usually your story will have these elements:

1. A chief character the reader can like.
2. A goal the character wants to reach.
3. A problem he has to solve or an obstacle he must overcome to reach this goal.
4. Some personality trait or characteristic within the chief character that enables him to achieve (or, perhaps, causes him to fail to achieve) his goal.

LESSON FOUR: *Writing Incidents*

ASSIGNMENT 1. *Based on selection from George Rogers Clark, "No Feeling of Falling," and "The Great Day," pages 151-181.*

One of the tasks confronting the biographer is making the characteristics of the person about whom he is writing clear. To do this he often includes anecdotes or incidents. In writing about George Rogers Clark, Walter Havighurst needed to convey the idea that Clark was a spirited man able to face any circumstance with cool courage. The biographer accomplishes this by citing Clark's words to the fiddler: "Strike up the music! . . . On with the dance. The horses are not yet ready" (page 152). A similar problem confronts the writer of an autobiography. Thus Helen Keller shows her unhappiness and temper tantrums as a child by describing the fate of her new doll.

Each of the topic sentences below mentions a characteristic possessed by a certain person. Develop a paragraph from the sentence by using an incident that makes the person mentioned a real individual. You are free to change the sentence in any way you wish, or to develop a paragraph from a sentence of your own. Consult your language book on how to develop a paragraph of this type. Remember to revise your first draft carefully before making a final copy. As you work to improve your skill in writing, don't overlook the importance of painstaking revision.

1. My father is the most patient man I have ever known.
2. My older brother is famous in the family for his absent-mindedness.
3. Our next-door neighbor has an explosive temper.
4. There is an air of perpetual mourning about my aunt.
5. The stranger was notable for his unfailing courtesy.

ASSIGNMENT 2. *Based on selections in "Biography and Autobiography," pages 148-211.*

In the "Author's Craft" on page 209 you read of the important part selection and condensation play in writing a good biography or autobiography. Helen Keller is exercising this skill when in the account of her early life she passes lightly over the events of many days to focus attention on the miraculous day on which she learned the mystery of language. She makes this event clear by telling the incident at the well.

Think back over your own early years. Select an incident that stands out in your memory. Why is this incident significant? Do you remember it with fear, or joy, or the sense of discovery? What mood surrounds it? What details of sight or sound or taste or feeling make it vivid? Write a composition of several paragraphs recounting this incident. Select words that will recapture how you felt as well as relate what actually happened.

OPTIONAL ASSIGNMENT

After sampling the autobiographies of others, you may decide that you would like to try writing your own autobiography. After all, here is a subject you know better than anyone else. It requires no research. The information, except for the bare facts of your earliest years, is stored in your memory.

Writing your autobiography will probably seem a less difficult task if you think of it as a series of chapters, each chapter centering on some important aspect of your life. (The composition you have written for Assignment 2 might serve as one chapter.) Remember what you have learned about what makes a biography good. Select only the high points of your life. Use incidents to show character and to develop action.

LESSON FIVE: *Description*

ASSIGNMENT 1. *Based on the group of poems entitled "People," pages 214-233.*

The poems in the section entitled "People" offer fleeting impressions of various individuals. Few of the portraits are complete in the way a police description would be complete, with all the measurements and shapes and colors spelled out. Instead, the portraits in verse are often single impressions or a series of impressions. They are like quick looks that catch one or two of the most distinctive characteristics of the subject. Some of the poems, like "The Poet at Seven," show us an individual at only one period of his life; others, like "The Ballad of William Sycamore," give us glimpses of a character at various times in his life.

Which character most interested you? Was it the dashing Allen-a-Dale? Was it Melora Vilas, using a tin basin for a mirror? Or was it the old flute player? Choose an individual that seemed like a real person to you. Jot down all the impressions of his personal appearance and of his character that the poet gives you. Then put your imagination to work to round out the portrait. Write a composition of from one to three paragraphs describing this individual as you imagine him.

ASSIGNMENT 2. *Based on the group of poems entitled "Nature," pages 234-243.*

Poets who are describing some aspect of the outdoors also make use of groups of impressions: recalled sounds, glimpses of things, remembered scents, and the feeling of heat, of cold, or of damp. In "Stars" Sara Teasdale makes the reader see "a heaven full of stars" more vividly than most of us do: their colors emerge—they are "White and topaz/And misty-red"; their twinkling is suggested by the fact that they have "beating/Hearts of fire." She mentions the spicy scent of the pines, and contrasts the stillness of the trees with the far-off movement of the stars. Through use of such sense impressions she creates a vivid picture of a starry night.

Since all the details the poet includes must help build up a particular mood or atmosphere, the poet exercises great care in choosing details. In "God's World" Edna St. Vincent Millay is writing of the overwhelming beauty of nature; therefore each sense impression must build up this idea. John Masefield in "A Wanderer's Song" wishes to emphasize the call of far places. His poem is rich with movement and sound: the foresail yanks at the sheet, the anchorage is windy and tossing, the sea clucks and sucks, the wind sings and the gulls mew. Every impression speaks of putting to sea.

Think of a moment when you were suddenly and vitally aware of your surroundings. What sights do you remember? What sounds? Is a fragrance or an odor a part of your remembrance? What is your general impression as you recall the moment—tranquillity, fear, majesty, beauty, stillness, solemnity? Write a single paragraph that captures your feeling at that time and place.

OPTIONAL ASSIGNMENT

You have discovered that you can do fairly well in writing a prose impression of a person or a place. Now attempt an impressionistic picture in verse. From your study of the poems in this chapter and of the "Author's Craft" article on sensory imagery (page 239), you have learned the necessity of using fresh, sharp images. In writing your poem you may use either rhymed or unrhymed verse. The important thing is to select the right phrases to describe your impression and to create a particular tone.

LESSON SIX: *Interpreting Poetry*

ASSIGNMENT 1. *Based on the groups of poems entitled "Principles" and "Visions," pages 244-274.*

What is Sara Teasdale saying in "There Will Come Soft Rains"? Is the poem merely a catalogue of treasured sights and sounds—the smell of the ground after rain, the twittering of swallows, the snowy white of blossoming trees—or does the author use these impressions to develop her theme? The best way of finding out whether you really understand the meaning of a poem is to write your own interpretation of it. Forcing yourself to find words to pin down your ideas will clarify your thinking.

Select one of the poems from the sections entitled "Principles" and "Visions." Read and reread the poem until every line is clear to you and fits into the idea of the poem as a whole. Then write one paragraph explaining the meaning of the poem.

ASSIGNMENT 2. *Based on "The Rime of the Ancient Mariner," pages 257-274.*

If we are to understand "The Rime of the Ancient Mariner," we must do more than grasp the underlying idea; we must also react to the impressions of sight and sound and feeling which Coleridge has woven into the poem. Only by imagining the arctic cold and the tropic heat, seeing the sails of the specter ship and hearing the ghostly carols of the dead men, can we come under the spell which the poet creates and sense the illusion in which the story of the Mariner takes form.

Select one of the topics listed below. Glance through the poem for allusions to this subject. Then write a composition of not more than 300 words explaining how Coleridge treats this subject.

1. The polar regions and the tropics. *(What details are emphasized in Coleridge's description of the polar regions? Of the tropics? What references are there to color, sound, motion? How is the contrast between the two regions developed?)*
2. The spectral ship. *(What is unusual about its appearance? Its movement? At what time of day does it come? Who does the ship carry for crew? What impression does it create?)*
3. Coleridge's use of sound. *(The poem is rich in the imagery of the sounds of the natural world. What impressions do you gain of the sounds of the moving ship, the wind, the ice? There are also ghostly or supernatural sounds. How do these contrast with the natural sounds?)*
5. The Mariner's home port. *(What details are the same when the Mariner leaves and when he returns? What things are different? What is the tone of the stanza describing his departure? What impression do the stanzas describing his return create?)*

If you prefer, you may write a composition tracing the steps through which Coleridge develops the spiritual meaning of the Mariner's experience: his crime, his physical punishment, his spiritual torture, and his expiation for his crime.

When you have thought over your topic, jot down notes covering the points you wish to include. Convert these notes into a simple outline before you begin to write. Your language text will furnish information on making an appropriate outline.

LESSON SEVEN: *News Stories*

ASSIGNMENT 1. *Based on* Romeo and Juliet, Act I, *pages 283-304.*

The street fights in Verona in the opening scene in *Romeo and Juliet,* followed as they were by the stern proclamation of the Prince, must have been the biggest news of the day for the local citizens. Although these events took place before the advent of newspapers, you can be sure that in one way or another all Verona heard the news before nightfall.

Suppose Verona had had a newspaper and that you were a reporter for this paper. Imagine that you had happened upon the fight and the subsequent proclamation. Your job would then be to write a news story about the event for your paper. Write such a story, explaining in three or four paragraphs the exciting happenings in your town. Consult your language text for information on the order in which information is given in a news story.

ASSIGNMENT 2. *Based on* Romeo and Juliet, Act I *to* Act III, Scene 1, *pages 283-327.*

Even though the news of the Prince's proclamation was carried throughout Verona by word of mouth only, most of the citizens probably received a fairly accurate idea of the proclamation and the reasons the Prince had for issuing it. The situation as regards reports of the duels between Tybalt and Mercutio and between Tybalt and Romeo would have been far different. Think of the rumors that must have sped through the town! Is Mercutio, kinsman of Prince Escalus, really dead? Who killed him? Is Tybalt dead also? How many have been killed? Is Romeo dead at Tybalt's hand? Is Romeo banished? Who provoked the fight?

Again imagine yourself a reporter for the Verona newspaper. This time your assignment is far more difficult, for you are to write an account of an event at which you were not present—the quarrel described in Act III, Scene 1. Since the scraps of information floating around town seem contradictory, you decide the only way to arrive at the facts of the case is to interview someone who has first-hand knowledge of the situation. Who is the best source of information?

When you have decided on the person you wish to interview, consider his relationship to the participants in the fights. Does he have connections with either of the feuding families? If so, would such a connection affect his report of what happened?

Write your account in much the same way you would write an ordinary news story, placing important facts first and details later. Be sure that your story accurately reflects the point of view of the character you are interviewing. Use actual lines from the play as his quoted statements, or, if you wish, write a paraphrase of pertinent lines, enclosing them in quotation marks as if they were direct quotations of the speaker. Before writing, review the rules for punctuation of direct quotations in your language text. Your interview may follow the following plan:

I. The most important statement made by the person interviewed, a brief identification of him, and a summary of the events of which the interview treats.
II. Other information given by the person interviewed, both direct quotations and material summarized by the interviewer.
III. A further explanation of who the person interviewed is and his relationship to the events.

OPTIONAL ASSIGNMENT

Imagine you are the society reporter of the Verona newspaper attending the ball of the Capulets. You will be particularly interested in getting the names of some of the important guests. You will probably note carefully how Lady Capulet and her daughter Juliet are dressed. You may observe what is served at the supper. And you will be very eager to pick up any scrap of real news—for example, the presence of Montagues at the ball—that you can subtly hint at in your article.

LESSON EIGHT: *Character Sketches*

ASSIGNMENT 1. *Based on* Romeo and Juliet, Acts I-IV, *pages 283-352.*

Before you had read very far in *Romeo and Juliet,* you probably had a strong picture in your mind of each major character. Some of these mental images, interestingly enough, strongly resembled people you have seen in the movies or on television. From the list below select three characters that you visualize clearly. Decide what movie, stage, or television personality you would cast for each one. Then write a composition of three paragraphs naming your candidates to play these three parts and explaining why you think these actors fit the rôles you have assigned them.

Romeo	The Nurse
Juliet	Friar Laurence
Mercutio	Capulet
Tybalt	Paris
Benvolio	Lady Capulet

ASSIGNMENT 2. *Based on* Romeo and Juliet, Acts I-V, *pages 280-365.*

In the Author's Craft on characterization (page 35) you studied the ways open to the writer of short stories to reveal character. Some of these ways are not available to the dramatist. Because in a play the author never speaks directly to the reader, he cannot insert passages of narration to describe a character or tell the reader what sort of person this individual is. The dramatist must rely exclusively on dialogue to develop character. The reader must learn through careful reading of the dialogue to figure out the characteristics of the various individuals he meets. A character's own words reveal much about his temperament, his philosophy, and his attitude toward others. The way in which one character greets another, for instance, may indicate something of the speaker's habits of courtesy, his education, his social position, and his aggressiveness—or lack of it. The statements others make about this character add to your knowledge of him. However, the character's actions are probably the most important source of information about him.

With these ideas in mind, consider the following characters from *Romeo and Juliet:*

Mercutio	Juliet
Benvolio	The Nurse
Tybalt	Lady Capulet
Romeo	Friar Laurence
Paris	The Prince of Verona

Choose the character who interests you most, or the one you believe you understand best. Then prepare to write a composition of no more than 300 words describing this character. Go through the play again, studying carefully everything the character says and does and everything the other characters say about him. Make brief notes of all details, and write out quotations that are particularly significant in explaining the kind of person this character really is. (Your language text will give you some ideas on various ways of taking notes.) Before you begin writing, use an outline to get your ideas in proper order. (Your language text will be of help to you here too.)

In writing your character sketch try to present as complete and well-rounded a portrait as possible. What hints does the play give you about this character's physical appearance? How does he move? What do his speech and his manner show about his upbringing and education? What are his good qualities? What are his faults? Use brief quotations from the drama to help make your ideas clear. End your composition with a short paragraph giving your total impression of the character.

You will find it interesting to compare your interpretation of a character with the compositions of students who have written about the same individual. If you find your ideas and those of your classmates do not agree, be prepared to produce evidence from the play in support of your opinion.

LESSON NINE: *One-Act Plays*

ASSIGNMENT 1. *Based on* Romeo and Juliet, *pages 280-365.*

In working out the previous assignment, you discovered that the dramatist is limited in the methods open to him for describing character. Another difficulty the writer of stage plays must face is that he can include only scenes that can be acted out on a platform. Review the story of "The Most Dangerous Game" (pages 36-50). What scenes in it could not be staged? Could this story be successfully converted to a movie? What is one essential difference between a movie and a stage play?

Try your hand at converting the indicated portion of one of the short stories named below into the first scene of a one-act play. First give the setting. Then tell what characters are on the stage when the curtain rises. Remember to note the entrances and exits of characters. Studying the form of *Romeo and Juliet* will show you how the dialogue itself is printed in a drama (note that quotation marks are not used) and how entrances and exits are indicated.

1. The Cask of Amontillado (page 21 to page 22, column 1, paragraph 10). *(Poe has written much of the dialogue for you. How are you going to convey the ideas expressed in the first four paragraphs: the fact that it is carnival time, Montresor's real opinion of Fortunato, Fortunato's pride in himself as a connoisseur of wine? Is introducing a new character a possibility?)*
2. Bargain (page 28 to page 30, column 1, paragraph 6). *(Remember you are to include the events on these pages in only one scene. Where will you stage it? Add any necessary dialogue to prepare for later events?)*
3. A Reading Problem (page 101, column 1, paragraph 2 to page 103, excluding the last line of column 2). *(Develop the scene in which Emily meets the Gerlashes. Where are they? What do they say that the audience needs to know? How can the dialogue reveal this to be a humorous story?)*
4. The Third Ingredient (page 114, column 2, paragraph 8 to page 116). *(What is the setting? What information must be put into the dialogue to prepare for later events in the play?)*

When you have finished writing, select some of your classmates to read the scene aloud, while you time the reading. (Of course, adding action will make the scene a little longer.) Is the scene long enough to warrant pulling the curtain? Do the personalities of the characters come through at all? Can you see the beginnings of the plot? Is necessary background information included? On a separate piece of paper explain how you would revise the scene to make it more satisfactory.

ASSIGNMENT 2. *Based on* Romeo and Juliet, *pages 280-365.*

Your first try at writing a dramatic version of a short story has probably taught you a great deal about the difficulties of converting fiction into drama. For your second assignment do one of the three things listed below.

1. Using as a guide the criticism of the scene you have written, rewrite the scene.
2. Write a one-act play based on "After You, My Dear Alphonse." Confine the action to one setting—the kitchen. Most of the dialogue is given, but you will want to describe the setting in detail as well as indicate how lines should be delivered.
3. Write a complete one-act play based on one of the stories listed in Assignment 1. (This is a difficult task and should not be attempted unless you are willing to spend a lot of time on it.) First think over the plot and figure out how it can be arranged in no more than three scenes. This will probably necessitate changing the setting of certain action. In an outline in which your main points are the scenes, jot down the action each scene must include. Be careful to cover all essentials. Then begin to write.

LESSON TEN: *Using Reference Materials*

ASSIGNMENT 1. *Based on "Orpheus and Eurydice," "Perseus and Medusa," and "Perseus and Andromeda," pages 374-380.*

In reading the myth of Perseus and Medusa, you came upon the name *Minerva*. Undoubtedly you knew that Minerva is a goddess; further, on page 373, she is identified as the Goddess of Wisdom. How much more do you know about this great figure of classic times? *Minerva* is the name by which the Romans knew her; what name did the Greeks use? What is the famous legend of her birth? How is she usually pictured? What attributes in addition to wisdom did she possess? What great city is named for her?

Write a paragraph giving the most important and interesting facts about Minerva or one of the other gods and goddesses listed below:

Jupiter	Venus
Juno	Mercury
Mars	Diana
Vulcan	Ceres
Apollo	Neptune

You will find information in unabridged dictionaries, encyclopedias, and books of mythology. Consult at least three sources. List the information from each source on a separate card or piece of paper. Then jot down in outline form the information you intend to use and the order in which you will present it. If you find that your sources differ on certain facts, qualify your statements by writing, "Some authorities say . . ." or "Sources differ on . . ." or similar remarks. List the names of the sources you have used at the end of your paper.

ASSIGNMENT 2. *Based on "The Surprise," "The Flight of Aeneas," and "In the House of Circe," pages 382-401.*

For almost three thousand years Homer's tales of the Trojan War and of the wanderings of Odysseus have fascinated writers and readers alike. John Masefield is only one of many twentieth-century writers who have retold the story Homer tells in *The Iliad.* Scholars had tried to discover the exact location of Homer's Troy for over two thousand years. Then in the nineteenth century, Heinrich Schliemann used the details Homer himself gives in describing Troy to locate the ruins of Priam's city. Since Schliemann's discovery of Troy, archaeologists of many nations have searched the islands and the shores of the Mediterranean for sites described by Homer.

What interests you more—the tales of the gods and heroes of ancient Greece and Rome or the efforts made by scholars and archaeologists to discover the history that underlies the legends? Choose the subject below about which you would like to know more and write a composition no longer than 300 words. Make an outline before you begin writing.

1. The Judgment of Paris. *(What was inscribed on the Golden Apple? What goddesses vied for it? How is this legend related to both the cause and the outcome of the Trojan War?)*
2. Odysseus (Ulysses). *(Where did he come from? What part did he play in the Trojan War? What were some of his most famous adventures on his homeward journey? What are his outstanding characteristics?)*
3. Aeneas. *(What were some of the important things that happened to Aeneas after he left Troy? What great city was, according to legend, founded by his descendants?)*
4. The Trojan War. *(How did it start? Who were the leaders on each side? How was the war waged? What was the outcome?*
5. Schliemann's Discovery of Ancient Troy. *(Where is this city? How did Schliemann locate it? What did he find?)*
6. The Palace of Agamemnon. *(King Agamemnon was the leader of all the Greek forces. Where is his palace located? What have archaeologists discovered there?)*

If you choose one of the first four topics, you may use the same types of reference you used for Assignment 1. In writing on topics 5 or 6, consult encyclopedias or books of archaeology.

LESSON ELEVEN: *Expressing Ideas*

ASSIGNMENT 1. *Based on "The Prophecy of Socrates," "The Death of Socrates," and "The Educated Man," pages 403-407.*

Socrates said ". . . those of us who think that death is an evil are in error." Although his words were spoken over two thousand years ago, the idea they convey is as true today as it was in ancient Athens. Through the centuries in every country men have reasoned as Socrates did and have died bravely for their religion, their king, or their country.

In studying the observations Socrates made about life and death, think how the ideas he sets forth relate to the life of men today. Read carefully the following examples of Socrates' wisdom:

1. . . . the detractors of the city . . . will say that you killed Socrates, a wise man; for they will call me wise, even although I am not wise, when they want to reproach you.
2. I would rather die having spoken after my manner, than to speak in your manner and live.
3. For neither in war nor yet at law ought I or any man to use every way of escaping death.
4. The difficulty . . . is not to avoid death, but to avoid unrighteousness.
5. If you think that by killing men you can prevent someone from censuring your evil lives, you are mistaken.
6. No evil can happen to a good man, either in life or after death.

Use one of these statements as the subject of a paragraph. First explain in your own words what the statement means. Then illustrate the truth of the statement by citing an example from your own acquaintance or from modern history of a person who has lived according to this principle or whose reputation illustrates its truth.

ASSIGNMENT 2. *Based on "Classical Heritage," pages 370-445.*

The literature of Greece and Rome illustrates the ideals of the people as embodied in the lives of heroes. Ulysses was one of the greatest heroes of ancient Greece. What qualities make him a hero? The Romans looked on Aeneas as a great hero. What heroic qualities do you find in him? Creon was a tragic figure. What flaws of character kept him from heroic stature?

Look back over this chapter with the character of the classic hero in mind. List the characteristics of each hero. Locate specific incidents that show the hero possesses the traits you attribute to him. Then, after considering all the heroes, decide which characteristics are essential to the classic idea of the hero. Write an essay of no more than four paragraphs in which you present these characteristics and use appropriate examples from the selections to illustrate them. You may use the following outline as a guide:

TITLE: Portrait of a Hero *(or a title of your own choice)*

I. Introduce your paper by summarizing the most significant traits of a hero of classic times.
II. Describe each trait and illustrate it with examples from the selections you have read.
III. Compare and contrast the hero of ancient times with the concept of a hero today.

OPTIONAL ASSIGNMENT

Whom do you consider an educated man? Do your ideas agree with those of Isocrates, or is your concept of an educated man different from his? Write a composition in which you briefly explain Isocrates' ideas in your own words and then voice your opinions on the subject, pointing out similarities and differences in viewpoint.

LESSON TWELVE: *Writing Explanations*

ASSIGNMENT 1. *Based on* A Tale of Two Cities, Book the First, *pages 450-472.*

In the first chapters of a novel the author must supply any background the reader needs to understand the plot of the novel and comprehend why the characters act as they do. Furnishing this background material, or *exposition,* is particularly important in a historical novel like *A Tale of Two Cities.* Dickens devotes the brilliant first chapter of this novel entirely to an overview of the general conditions in France and England in 1775—not a single character is introduced. Then in Chapters II-VI he goes into more detail on the specific background of the story, at the same time introducing some of the characters.

What did you learn in these chapters to convince you that the period Dickens is describing was "the worst of times"? Did you find any evidence it was "the best of times"? Using the information Dickens gives you as subject matter, write one or two paragraphs on one of the following subjects or on some other topic drawn from Book the First of the novel.

1. Hazards of an English Highway in 1775.
2. A Description of a Poor Section of Paris.
3. The Condition of the Poor in Paris.
4. The Mood of the Poor of Paris.

ASSIGNMENT 2. *Based on* A Tale of Two Cities, Book the Second, *Chapters I-V, pages 473-492.*

Tellson's Bank by Temple Bar was certainly different in its physical appearance from most banks today. In fact, you would probably not recognize it as a bank at all. In the first place, the disreputable figures of Jerry Cruncher and his son just outside the door would blind your twentieth-century eyes to the fact that this was a reputable place of business. If you persevered in believing this was a bank and opened the creaky door, the crowded, dingy inside would probably convince you that this establishment had no reputation and no stability. Yet Mr. Lorry accepted Tellson's as a first-rate bank, as did thousands of other Englishmen and Frenchmen at the end of the eighteenth century.

This ordinary world of banks and courts and shops that Jarvis Lorry and Lucie Manette and Charles Darnay knew was almost unbelievably different from the world we know today. These individuals would be bewildered and lost in the civilization we take for granted.

Select one of the characters named above or another you have met in *A Tale of Two Cities.* Imagine this character has suddenly awakened this morning in modern London, or, if you wish, in your own community. Can you imagine his first sensations of surprise at the changes in environment? In order to do so, you will have to compare the late-eighteenth-century world with that of the twentieth century. This will require you to look closely at the world we live in today.

After you have prepared notes listing some of the surprises in store for the character in his new situation, arrange his experiences in the order in which he would encounter them. Use an outline to help you arrange them in chronological order. Then, in three or four paragraphs, write an account of the character's first day, or his first morning, or even the first hour after he leaves the house to walk in your world. If you wish, you may give your story a title like "The Awakening." You may write your composition in either a humorous or a serious vein.

LESSON THIRTEEN: *Interpretation*

ASSIGNMENT 1. *Based on* A Tale of Two Cities, Book the Second, *Chapters III-XII, pages 478-514.*

When you read a short story or a novel, you are sometimes surprised to find yourself liking a character that you would expect to dislike. You may say to a friend, "I like him but I don't know why." The reason why may be hidden in the author's skill as a word craftsman; his own attitude toward the character is implied in the way he writes about him and in turn is reflected in your attitude. Sometimes the reader does not adopt the author's reaction toward a character. This frequently happens with regard to novels written in the past: although the author's tone tells us clearly that he regards his heroine as the best and most beautiful of young women, we may look on her as sentimental or spineless. Fashions in personality change as surely as fashions in clothes.

An author's attitude toward a character he has created may be just as complex as your feeling for a classmate. You may dislike the way the classmate dresses but admire the way he performs in Latin class. Think a moment about Dickens' attitude toward Sydney Carton. What aspects of Carton's behavior does he disapprove? What does he find to like in Carton? Judging from what you have learned up to this point in the novel, what is his predominant attitude toward this man?

Select Sydney Carton or one of the characters listed below as the subject for a brief composition. Reread the parts of the novel in which this character appears, paying particular attention to words and sentences which indicate the author's attitude toward him. Then write a paragraph explaining the way in which Dickens seems to regard this individual. If your attitude disagrees with that of the author, add a second paragraph in which you state your own reactions and the reasons you feel as you do.

Miss Pross	John Barsad
Jerry Cruncher	Roger Cly
Lucie Manette	

ASSIGNMENT 2. *Based on* A Tale of Two Cities, Book the First *and* Book the Second, *pages 450-544.*

The careful reader can discover an author's attitude not only toward the characters he has created but also toward the setting in which he places them and the events which he sets in motion. In the first chapter of *A Tale of Two Cities* we catch glimpses of the emotional attitude, or tone, with which Dickens regards the turbulent time in which his novel is set. As the novel unfolds, Dickens not only builds up little by little a picture of various institutions and situations in England and France, but also in various ways expresses his attitude toward them. Choose one of the topics below and write a composition of no more than 300 words. Jot down your ideas in outline form before you begin to write.

1. Dickens' Attitude Toward British Business. *(What is Dickens' attitude toward Tellson's Bank? Cite phrases or sentences that make this attitude clear. In what way do you think this attitude toward Tellson's indicates Dickens' feeling about British business methods in general? Reread the first part of Chapter 1,* Book the Second, *to discover material for your composition.)*
2. Dickens' Attitude Toward the Law Courts. *(Do you think cases were actually conducted in the manner Dickens describes or that Dickens' description reflects his own feeling? Is Dickens merely telling a story, or is he also working for certain reforms? Explain your answer. Reread* Book the Second, *Chapters II-III before you begin writing.)*
3. Dickens' Attitude Toward the French Revolution. *(Does Dickens feel the French Revolution is justified? What is his attitude toward the mob as it storms the Bastille, burns the château, kills Foulon? Cite words and phrases to justify your answer. To substantiate your opinion reread* Book the First, *Chapter V, and* Book the Second, *Chapters VII, XIII, XVIII, XIX, and XX.)*

LESSON FOURTEEN: *Book Review*

ASSIGNMENT 1. *Based on* A Tale of Two Cities, Book the First, Book the Second, and Book the Third, *Chapters I-IX, pages 473-572.*

As you read the chapter entitled "The Game Made" (pages 567-572), you were doubtless aware that Sydney Carton has reached a momentous decision. Do you know what that decision is? At a much earlier point in the novel Charles Darnay decides to go to Paris in an attempt to save the life of an old family servant. Is this a decision that, judging from Darnay's character, you would expect him to make? Still earlier in the story, when Charles Darnay, in asking to marry Lucie wishes to tell Doctor Manette his real name, Doctor Manette refuses to hear him. Is this decision in line with the doctor's character, or is it a device Dickens uses to build suspense? There are many other decisions in the novel which, like these, have a definite effect on the plot.

Choose one of the characters who plays an important part in the novel. Jot down the decisions this individual makes in the course of the story. Then consider carefully the various aspects of this individual's character. Do the decisions grow naturally from his character? Can you suggest actions that would have been more in keeping? When you are confident you know the individual well, write a paragraph or two describing his character and explaining why the decisions he makes are, or are not, in keeping with his character as Dickens develops it.

ASSIGNMENT 2. *Based on* A Tale of Two Cities, pages 446-603.

In the previous assignment you did one of the things that a book review demands: you looked critically at one aspect of the novel—in this case, character—and explained whether in your opinion the author has created a human being who acts in a believable and consistent manner. Criticism is an essential element of the book review. A book review is not a summary of the plot of a novel; it is an expression of opinions and judgments of various aspects of a literary work.

Write a book review of about 300 words on *A Tale of Two Cities.* The following outline may help you cover the most important points:

I. Introduction. *(Summarize your general opinion of the novel. What did you find outstanding? What did you dislike?)*

II. Setting. *(How important is the setting to the development of the story? Are time and place vividly described? Is there too much or too little description? Is the background information interesting in itself? If so, what makes it so? If not, why not?)*

III. Characters. *(Do the characters seem like real people? Which individuals stand out in your mind? Why? Are there more characters than the story needs?)*

IV. Plot. *(Do the incidents develop naturally out of the situations in which the characters find themselves? Is the rôle of chance, or coincidence, overdrawn? Would the omission of some incidents or the inclusion of others have made the novel more interesting? Be specific about the scenes you would omit and those you would add.)*

V. Conclusion. *(Is the ending convincing? Would it have been a better novel if the ending had been different? How would you have changed it?)*

OPTIONAL ASSIGNMENT

You probably have a favorite novel that you would like to recommend to your classmates. If you were a salesman trying to persuade them to buy copies of the book, what one feature would you emphasize: a particular character, the theme, the suspense, the humor? Write a sales talk of no more than 100 words in which you present the most important reason for buying the book. Try your talk out on the class, or post it on the bulletin board.

LESSON FIFTEEN: *Writing Essays*

ASSIGNMENT 1. *Based on "Translating Literature into Life," pages 606-608.*

In the headnote preceding "Translating Literature into Life," you read that this selection by Arnold Bennett is an essay. You learned also that the distinguishing mark of an essay is that it expresses personal opinions. One of the most interesting things about essays is the insights they give into the minds of writers—their ideas, enthusiasms, prejudices, ways of reasoning, and habits of thought.

Arnold Bennett in "Translating Literature into Life" expresses his ideas on the values to be gained from reading. You may agree heartily with these ideas, you may totally disagree, or you may accept some of his ideas and reject others. Select one of the quotations from the essay listed below. Write a single paragraph explaining briefly the meaning of the quotation and why you agree or disagree with it.

1. Study is not an end, but a means.
2. What is the object of reading unless something definite comes of it? . . . If you boldly answer: "I only read for pleasure," then I retort that the man who drinks whiskey might with force say: "I only drink whiskey for pleasure."
3. What is the matter with our reading is casualness, languor, preoccupation. We don't give the book a chance.
4. If we are not tired after reading, common sense is not in us.
5. Reading without subsequent reflection is ridiculous; it is equally a proof of folly and vanity.
6. . . . it is a sign of undue self-esteem to suppose that we can grasp the full import of an author's message at a single reading.

ASSIGNMENT 2. *Based on selections from "Vulture Country" through "Wild Grapes," pages 609-638.*

An essay may be long or short; it may be serious or humorous; it may be written on any subject. Essays may vary as much from one another as "Translating Literature into Life" differs from "Vulture Country." The former is made up almost entirely of opinions; the latter contains many facts; yet because both emphasize an author's point of view, both are considered essays.

Listed below are several subjects for essays. On one of these topics, or on any other topic you prefer, write an essay of no more than 400 words. Some subjects necessarily require a serious approach; others may be treated seriously, humorously, or satirically. Be careful to keep the same tone throughout the essay.

1. Bird Watching. *(How do bird watchers operate? What is the fascination of bird watching? Are bird watchers a particular type of people?)*
2. The Opening of the Hunting Season. *(How does the world look as you start out? How do you feel?)*
3. Note to Patrick Henry. *(Can you explain to Patrick Henry that for nearly two hundred years Americans have held to the ideas he expressed? How do we show our love of liberty today?)*
4. These Honored Dead. *(What do we owe them—these men who have died for their country? How do we make sure that "these dead shall not have died in vain"?)*
5. I Advance Freedom. *(What can you do to advance one of the freedoms Roosevelt writes of?)*
6. Why I'd Like to Be an Astronaut.
7. Popularity. *(Is it important? What causes some people to be popular? Mary White's father speaks of her happiness. Are happiness and popularity synonymous?)*
8. Growing up. *(Both "To a Young Girl" and "Wild Grapes" are concerned with aspects of growing up. What does growing up mean to you?)*

OPTIONAL ASSIGNMENT

Try your skill at writing a humorous verse in which, like Ogden Nash, you hold forth on a custom or fashion that annoys you.

LESSON SIXTEEN: *Interpretation*

ASSIGNMENT 1. *Based on* Visit to a Small Planet, *pages 639-657.*

Visit to a Small Planet first appeared several years ago as a television play. If you had watched it, you would probably have been caught up in the excitement of the space-ship's landing, the appearance of Kreton, the converging of the military men on the Spelding home. Your attention would have been so riveted on what was happening that when the story ended you might have classified it as merely "another space play." However, after reading and talking about the play, you realize that it is more than escape literature. In it Gore Vidal has some important things to say about the citizens of the small planet, Earth. Write one paragraph, or at most two, explaining the serious ideas that underlie this suspenseful tale.

ASSIGNMENT 2. *Based on* The Mother, *"The Waltz," "Brother Death," and "A Lesson in Discipline," pages 658-698.*

Think a moment about some of the stories you read in the first unit in your textbook; for example, "The Most Dangerous Game." Almost from the outset you were aware that the plot concerned a conflict between two powerful men–Rainsford and Zaroff. And when you read the last line of the story–"He had never slept in a better bed, Rainsford decided"–you knew exactly how the conflict had been resolved.

The stories in "At Random" are of a different type. As in many modern short stories, idea rather than plot is emphasized. Because such stories may leave you with unanswered questions, you may feel that the story has no real ending; and in a certain sense this is true. The thinking continues after the reading is completed. It is up to the reader to probe the ideas presented and to satisfy himself as to their validity.

Listed below are some questions that might be raised by selections in this chapter. Select one which you would like to explore. Write a composition of as many paragraphs as you find necessary to develop your answer clearly and thoughtfully.

1. Is the Old Lady in *The Mother* a stubborn and ungrateful character, or is she wiser than her children?
2. The common, ordinary people presented in *The Mother* are generally ungrammatical, sometimes poor, but all of them are kind. Why then, is there so much sorrow in the play?
3. In "Brother Death," through describing the differences between the Greys and the Aspinwahls, Sherwood Anderson sketches in two attitudes toward life. What is good about each of these attitudes?
4. Sherwood Anderson implies in "Brother Death" that conflict between father and son is inevitable. Do you agree?
5. Must all individuals who succeed in life face "the subtle and terrible death" that overcomes Don Grey?
6. What produces "the curious sense of freedom" that surrounds Ted?
7. Why is discipline imposed from within more valuable than discipline commanded by others?
8. What is the most valuable gift a teacher can impart to students?

OPTIONAL ASSIGNMENT

(For Boys Only) In "The Waltz" Dorothy Parker takes off on boys who can't dance. If you can unfold a tale of woe embracing the opposite viewpoint, try writing a male version of "The Waltz," using Miss Parker's technique of what is thought and said by the dancer.

GLOSSARY OF LITERARY TERMS

ACTION, the happenings, or series of events, in a narrative.

ALLEGORY, a narrative in which the underlying meaning is different from the surface meaning.

ALLITERATION, repetition of consonant sounds at the beginnings of words or accented syllables.

ALLUSION, a brief and sometimes indirect reference to a person, place, event, or work of art.

APOSTROPHE, a figure of speech in which an absent person, an abstract quality, or an inanimate object is addressed directly.

ASSONANCE, the repetition of vowel sounds within a sentence or a line of poetry.

ATMOSPHERE, an emotional quality often developed through the handling of the setting.

AUTOBIOGRAPHY, a type of literature which gives an account of a person's life or part of a person's life written by the individual himself.

BALLAD, a narrative song or poem handed down orally from generation to generation. (See *Literary Ballad*).

BIOGRAPHY, a type of literature which gives an account of a person's life written by another person.

CHARACTER, a fictional personality created by an author.

CHARACTER SKETCH, a type of biography which presents aspects of a person's character and personality; may be actual or fictional.

CHARACTERIZATION, the techniques used by an author in creating a character.

CLASSIC, of the highest grade or quality; excellent; first-class.

CLIMAX, the decisive action or turning-point in a series of events in a narrative.

COMEDY, a play in which the conflicts are designed to amuse or entertain the audience without arousing deep emotional feelings; also, a play which has a happy ending.

CONFLICT, an interplay between opposing forces, a central element in most plots.

CRITIC, a judge of defects and merits in literature or in other arts; one who analyzes the various elements of a literary work.

DIALOGUE, the direct presentation of conversation between two or more characters.

DRAMA, a type of literature written to be acted out by actors on a stage.

EMPATHY, entering into the feelings or motives of the characters.

EPIC, a long narrative poem originally handed down orally from generation to generation; dealing with national heroes and events of great importance in the life of a country.

ESSAY, a type of literature which reflects the author's personal feelings on a particular subject.

EXTENDED METAPHOR, a metaphor in which the main image, or comparison, is extended and developed through several lines or through an entire poem.

FICTION, prose writings that tell about people and happenings which have been created by an author.

FIGURATIVE LANGUAGE, using words out of their literal meaning to create a specific image in the mind of a reader.

FIGURES OF SPEECH, specific literary devices for achieving the effects of figurative language such as similes or metaphors.

FORESHADOWING, implication by the author of events to come later in a narrative.

IMAGERY, the use of vivid, concrete, sensory details.

IRONY, 1) *verbal irony,* expression in which the ordinary meaning of the words is the opposite of the thought in the speaker's mind. 2) *irony of situation,* an event contrary to what would naturally be expected.

LEGEND, a traditional story which has been passed down through the ages. A legend is fictional but is often popularly accepted as history.

LITERARY BALLAD, a narrative poem written by a specific author in imitation of a folk ballad.

LYRIC, a short poem or a brief passage in a longer poem which expresses intense personal emotion.

METAPHOR, a figure of speech involving an implied comparison of two unlike things.

MYTH, a traditional story connected with the religion of a people, frequently to explain some happening in nature or some specific belief.

MYTHOLOGY, a complete group of closely connected myths.

NARRATIVE, any writing which concerns a series of happenings or events.

NARRATOR, the person who tells the story, usually a character.

NOVEL, a type of fiction which uses the same elements as a short story but longer and more complex.

ONOMATOPOEIA, words used in such a way that the sound of the words imitates the sound of the thing spoken about.

PARADOX, a statement which is basically true but which seems to say two different things.

PERSONIFICATION, a figure of speech in which an abstract quality or an inanimate object is given the characteristics or qualities of a human being.

PLOT, the pattern of events in a story, play or poem.

POETRY, a type of literature which communicates feeling and thought through the careful arrangement of words for their sounds, rhythm, and meaning.

PROSE, the ordinary form of spoken or written language; language not arranged into verses.

POINT OF VIEW, see *Viewpoint.*

REPETITION, the deliberate repeating of any word, phrase, sentence, or idea for the sake of effect.

RHYME, the repetition of similar sounds in at least the final syllables of two or more words.

RHYTHM, the recurrent beat or stress in the sound of poetry (or prose). The pattern may be regular, irregular, or broken, depending on the effect the writer wishes to achieve.

SATIRE, the use of sarcasm or irony to ridicule an idea, custom, or a habit.

SENSORY IMAGERY, images which have a special appeal to one or more of the senses such as sight, hearing, smell, touch, taste, and feeling.

SETTING, the place and time in which events of a narrative take place.

SHORT STORY, a type of prose fiction involving conflict, characters, situation and scene and setting forth the action in the form of a plot.

SIMILE, a figure of speech involving a comparison between two unlike things by the use of the words *like* or *as.*

SPEECH, a literary work written to be spoken before an audience.

STAGE DIRECTIONS, a dramatist's written directions as to how scenes are to be set and how the play is to be produced.

STYLE, the distinctive use of language by a given author.

SYMBOLISM, the use of a person, place, event, or object which represents something else, frequently an abstract quality or idea.

THEME, the main idea of a literary work; also a subject which recurs in the same work or in a different work.

TONE, the author's attitude toward his material as expressed in his work; the overall mood of a literary work.

TRAGEDY, a narrative writing in which the main character or characters suffer disaster after a serious and significant struggle but face their downfall with dignity and in such a manner as to attain heroic stature. The term is usually applied to plays of this nature.

TRAGIC FLAW, the flaw of character in a tragic hero which brings about his downfall.

TRANSLATION, changing from one language into another; also the literary version resulting from the process of translation.

VERSE, often used as a synonym for poetry; also a single line of poetry.

VIEWPOINT, the opinion of an author toward his characters, events, and settings as expressed in the literary work itself.

GLOSSARY

PRONUNCIATION KEY

The pronunciation of each word is shown just after the word, in this way: **ab bre vi ate** (ə brē/vi āt). The letters and signs used are pronounced as in the words below. The mark / is placed after a syllable with primary or strong accent, as in the example above. The mark / after a syllable shows a secondary or lighter accent, as in **ab bre vi a tion** (ə brē/vi ā/shən).

Some words, taken from foreign languages, are spoken with sounds that otherwise do not occur in English. Symbols for these sounds are given at the end of the table as "Foreign Sounds."

a	hat, cap
ā	age, face
ã	care, air
ä	father, far
b	bad, rob
ch	child, much
d	did, red
e	let, best
ē	equal, see
ėr	term, learn
f	fat, if
g	go, bag
h	he, how
i	it, pin
ī	ice, five
j	jam, enjoy
k	kind, seek
l	land, coal
m	me, am
n	no, in
ng	long, bring
o	hot, rock
ō	open, go
ô	order, all
oi	oil, voice
ou	house, out
p	paper, cup
r	run, try
s	say, yes
sh	she, rush
t	tell, it
th	thin, both
ŦH	then, smooth
u	cup, butter
u̇	full, put
ü	rule, move
ū	use, music
v	very, save
w	will, woman
y	young, yet
z	zero, breeze
zh	measure, seizure

ə represents:
a in about
e in taken
i in pencil
o in lemon
u in circus

FOREIGN SOUNDS

Y as in French du. Pronounce ē with the lips rounded as for English ü in **rule.**

œ as in French peu. Pronounce ā with the lips rounded as for ō.

N as in French bon The N is not pronounced, but shows that the vowel before it is nasal.

H as in German ach. Pronounce k without closing the breath passage.

ETYMOLOGY KEY

<	from, derived from, taken from
?	possibly
abl.	ablative
accus.,	accusative
cf.	compare
dial.	dialect
dim.	diminutive
fem.	feminine
gen.	genitive
lang.	language
masc.	masculine
neut.	neuter
pp.	past participle
ppr.	present participle
pt.	past tense
ult.	ultimately
var.	variant

LANGUAGE ABBREVIATIONS

AF	Anglo-French (= Anglo-Norman, the dialect of French spoken by the Normans in England, esp. 1066-c. 1164)
Am.E	American English (word originating in the United States)
Am.Ind.	American Indian
Am.Sp.	American Spanish
E	English
F	French
G	German
Gk.	Greek (from Homer to 300 A.D.)
Gmc.	Germanic (parent language of Gothic, Scandinavian, English, Dutch, German)
HG	High German (speech of Central and Southern Germany)
Hindu.	Hindustani (the commonest language of India)
Ital.	Italian
L	Latin (Classical Latin 200 B.C.-300 A.D.)
LG	Low German (speech of Northern Germany)
LGk.	Late Greek (300-700)
LL	Late Latin (300-700)
M	Middle
ME	Middle English (1100-1500)
Med.	Medieval
Med.Gk.	Medieval Greek (700-1500)
Med.L	Medieval Latin (700-1500)
MF	Middle French (1400-1600)
MHG	Middle High German (1100-1450)
MLG	Middle Low German (1100-1450)
NL	New Latin (after 1500)
O	Old
OE	Old English (before 1100)
OF	Old French (before 1400)
OHG	Old High German (before 1100)
Pg.	Portuguese
Scand.	Scandinavian (one of the languages of Northern Europe before Middle English times; Old Norse unless otherwise specified)
Skt.	Sanskrit (the ancient literary language of India, from the same parent language as Persian, Greek, Latin, Germanic, Slavonic, and Celtic)
Sp.	Spanish
VL	Vulgar Latin (a popular form of Latin, the main source of French, Spanish, Italian, Portuguese, and Rumanian)

OTHER ABBREVIATIONS

adj.	adjective
adv.	adverb
Anat.	anatomy
Ant.	antonym
Brit.	British
conj.	conjunction
E	Eastern
esp.	especially
interj.	interjection
n.	noun
pl.	plural
prep.	preposition
pron.	pronoun
sing.	singular
SW	Southwestern
Syn.	synonym
U.S.	United States
v.	verb

---

a bash (ə bash′), *v.* embarrass and confuse; make uneasy and somewhat ashamed: *The shy girl was abashed when she saw the room filled with strangers.*

ab duct (ab dukt′), *v.* carry off (a person) unlawfully and by force; kidnap. [< L *abductus,* pp. of *abducere* < *ab-* away + *ducere* lead] **—ab duc′tion,** *n.*

ab hor (ab hôr′), *v.,* **-horred, -hor ring.** shrink away from with horror; feel disgust or hate for; detest: *Some people abhor snakes.* [< L *abhorrere* < *ab-* from + *horrere* shrink, bristle with fear] **—ab hor′rer,** *n.*

ab hor rence (ab hôr′əns or ab hor′əns), *n.* a feeling of very great hatred; horror; disgust.

a bide (ə bīd′), *v.,* **a bode** or **a bid ed, a bid ing.** **1.** stay; remain: *"Though much is taken, much abides."* **2.** dwell; continue to live (in a place). **3.** put up with; endure; tolerate: *A good housekeeper cannot abide dirt.* **abide by, a.** accept and follow out. **b.** remain faithful to; fulfill: *You must abide by your promise.*

a bom i na ble (ə bom′ə nə bəl or ə bom′nə bəl), *adj.* **1.** disgusting; hateful; loathsome. **2.** very unpleasant; distasteful.

ab scond (ab skond′), *v.* go away suddenly and secretly; go off and hide: *The dishonest cashier absconded with the bank's money.* [< L *abscondere* < *ab-* away + *condere* store] **—ab scond′er,** *n.*

ab so lu tion (ab′sə lü′shən), ***n.*** **a freeing or freedom from guilt and punishment for sin; forgiveness.** A person who confesses and is sorry for his sins and promises to do penance, is granted absolution by a priest.

ab solve (ab solv′ or ab zolv′), *v.,* **-solved, -solving.** **1.** declare (a person) free from sin, guilt, or blame. **2.** set free (from a promise or duty). [< L *absolvere* < *ab-* from + *solvere* loosen]

ab sorp tion (ab sôrp′shən or ab zôrp′shən), *n.* great interest (in something).

ab stract ed (ab strak′tid), *adj.* lost in thought; absent-minded. **—ab stract′ed ly,** *adv.*

ab strac tion (ab strak′shən), *n.* being lost in thought; absence of mind.

ac cede (ak sēd′), *v.,* **-ced ed, -ced ing.** **1.** give in; agree (*to*): *Please accede to my request.* **2.** become a party (*to*): *Our government acceded to the treaty.* [< L *accedere* < *ad-* to + *cedere* come]

ac ces si ble (ak ses′ə bəl), *adj.* **1.** that can be entered or reached. **2.** easy to get at; easy to reach or enter: *A telephone should be put where it will be accessible.*

ac cli mate (ə klī′mit or ak′lə māt), *v.,* **-mat ed, -mat ing.** *Esp. U.S.* accustom or become accustomed to a new climate, surroundings, or conditions. [< F *acclimater* < *à* to (< L *ad-*) + *climat* climate (< L *clima*)]

ac cord (ə kôrd′), *n.* agreement; harmony: *Their opinion of war was in accord with his.* [< OF *acorder* < VL *acchordare* bring into harmony < L *ad-* to + *chorda* string]

ac cost (ə kôst′ or ə kost′), *v.* speak to first; come up and speak to; address: *A ragged beggar accosted him, asking for money.* [< F *accoster* < Ital. < LL *accostare* < L *ad-* to + *costa* side, rib]

ac count a bil i ty (ə koun′tə bil′ə ti), *n.* state of being responsible; liable to be called to account: *Each person has an accountability for his own work.*

ac cou ter (ə kü′tər), *v.* equip; array: *Knights were accoutered in armor.* [< F *accoutrer*]

ac cou tre ments (ə kü′tər mənts), *n.pl. Esp. Brit.* **1.** a soldier's equipment with the exception of his weapons and clothing. **2.** personal equipment; outfit.

ac crue (ə krü′), *v.,* **-crued, -cru ing.** come as a growth or result: *Ability to think will accrue to you from good habits of study.*

ac curs ed (ə kėr′sid or ə kėrst′), *adj.* **1.** damnable; detestable; hateful. **2.** under a curse.

acetic acid, a very sour, colorless acid, present in vinegar. *Formula:* CH_3COOH

ac quit (ə kwit′), *v.,* **-quit ted, -quit ting.** **1.** declare (a person) not guilty (*of* an offense): *The jury acquitted the innocent man of the crime.* **2.** set free or release (from a duty, an obligation, etc.). **3. acquit oneself,** do one's part; behave.

ac quit tal (ə kwit′əl), *n.* **1.** a setting free by declaring not guilty; discharge; release. **2.** performance (of a duty, obligation, etc.).

a dieu (ə dü′ or ə dū′), *interj., n., pl.* **a dieus** or **a dieux** (ə düz′ or e dūz′). good-by; farewell. [< F *à dieu* to God]

ad ju ra tion (aj′ů rā′shən), *n.* solemn command; earnest appeal.

ad jure (ə jür′), *v.,* **-jured, -jur ing.** ask earnestly or solemnly: *I adjure you to speak the truth.* [< L *adjurare* < *ad-* to + *jurare* swear]

ad mon ish (ad mon′ish), *v.* **1.** advise against something; warn: *The policeman admonished him not to drive too fast.* **2.** reprove gently: *The teacher admonished the student for his careless work.* **3.** recall to a duty overlooked or forgotten; remind. [< *admonition*]

➔ **admonish.** *Of,* not *against,* is used after this rather formal word for warn: *John admonished them of the impending peril.*

ad mon i to ry (ad mon′ə tô′ri or ad mon′ə tō′ri), *adj.* admonishing; warning.

a do (ə dü′), *n.* stir; bustle. [ME *at do* to do]

a dul ter ate (ə dul′tər āt), *v.,* **-at ed, -at ing.** make lower in quality by adding inferior or impure materials: *adulterate milk with water.* [< L *adulterare,* ult. < *ad-* to + *alter* other, different]

ad vent (ad′vent), *n.* coming; arrival.

ad ver si ty (ad vėr′sə ti), *n., pl.* **-ties.** **1.** condition of unhappiness, misfortune, or distress. **2.** stroke of misfortune; unfavorable or harmful thing or event.

ad vo cate (ad′və kit or ad′və kāt), *n.* **1.** person who pleads or argues for: *an advocate of peace.* **2.** lawyer who pleads in a low court. [< L *advocare* < *ad-* to + *vocare* call]

Ae a cus (ē′ə kus).

ae gis (ē′jis), *n.* shield or breastplate used by the Greek god Zeus or by his daughter Athena. Also, **egis.** [< L < Gk. *aigis*]

Ae ne as (i nē′əs).

a er o bat ics (ãr′ô bat′iks), ***n.*** **performance of stunts, as nose dives, etc., in an airplane, glider, or the like.**

af fect[1] (ə fekt′), *v.* **1.** have an effect on; act on; influence: *Disease affects the body.* **2.** touch the heart of; stir the emotions of. [< L *affectus,* pp. of *afficere* < *ad-* to + *facere* do]

af fect[2] (ə fekt′), *v.* pretend to have or feel: *He affected ignorance of the fight, but we knew that he had seen it.* [< F < L *affectare* strive for < *ad-* to + *facere* do]

➔ **affect, effect.** Since little or no distinction is made in pronouncing the first vowel of these words, the spelling is likely to be confused. Except in some obsolete and technical uses, *affect* is always a verb: *The new rules affect the behavior of the entire student body. He affects a taste for imported clothes. Effect* is most commonly a noun, meaning result: *The effect of the explosion was visible for miles around. Effect* is also a verb in formal English, meaning most commonly bring about: *The School Spirit Club effected a marked change in the students' attitude toward sports.*

< = from, taken from; cf., compare; dial., dialect; dim., diminutive; pp., past participle; ppr., present participle; pt., past tense; ult., ultimately; var., variant; ?=possibly.

af fi da vit (af′ə dā′vit), *n.* statement written down and sworn to be true. An affidavit is usually made before a judge or notary public. [< Med.L *affidavit* he has stated on oath]

af flict (ə flikt′), *v.* cause pain to; trouble greatly; distress: *be afflicted with troubles.* [< L *afflictus,* pp. of *affligere* < *ad-* upon + *fligere* dash]

af fright (ə frīt′), *Archaic.* —*v.* frighten; terrify.

af ter deck (af′tər dek′ or äf′tər dek′), *n.* deck toward or at the stern of a ship.

ag ate (ag′it), *n.* a variety of quartz with variously colored stripes or clouded colors. [< F *agathe* < L *achates* < Gk.]

ag ile (aj′əl), *adj.* moving quickly and easily; active; lively; nimble: *An acrobat has to be agile.* [< L *agilis* < *agere* move]

al ba tross (al′bə trôs or al′bə tros), *n.* any of various large web-footed sea birds related to the petrel, that can fly long distances. [var. of obsolete *alcatras* frigate bird < Sp. < Pg. *alcatraz* < Arabic *al-qādus* the bucket < Gk. *kados* < Phoenician]

Albatross (30 in. long)

Al be marle (al′be märl)

A leu tian Islands (ə lü′shən), chain of many small islands SW of Alaska, belonging to the United States. 1000 pop.

a light (ə līt′), *v.,* **a light ed** or (*Poetic*) **a lit, a light ing.** get down; get off: *alight from a horse.*

al ka li (al′kə lī), *n., pl.* **-lis** or **-lies.** any salt or mixture of salts that neutralizes acids. Some desert soils contain much alkali. [< MF *alcali* < Arabic *al-qalī* the ashes of saltwort (a genus of plants)]

ag i tate (aj′ə tāt), *v.,* **-tat ed, -tat ing. 1.** move or shake violently. **2.** disturb; excite (the feelings or the thoughts of): *She was much agitated by the news of her brother's illness.* **3.** argue about; discuss vigorously. **4.** keep arguing about and discussing a matter to arouse public interest: *agitate for a shorter working day.*

ag nos tic (ag nos′tik), *n.* person who believes that nothing is known or can be known about the existence of God or about things outside of human experience. —*adj.* of agnostics or their beliefs. [< Gk. *agnostos* < *a-* not + *gnostos* (to be) known]

al lo cate (al′ə kāt), *v.,* **-cat ed, -cat ing. 1.** assign or allot (a share, portion, etc.). **2.** locate. [< Med.L *allocare* < L *ad-* to, at + *locus* place]

al lot (ə lot′), *v.,* **-lot ted, -lot ting. 1.** divide and distribute in parts or shares: *The profits have all been allotted.* **2.** give as a share; assign: *The teacher allotted work to each student.* [< OF *aloter* < *a-* to (< L *ad-*) + *lot* lot < Gmc. Akin to *lot.*]

al ter ca tion (ôl′tər kā′shən or al′tər kā′shən), *n.* an angry dispute; quarrel: *The two teams had an altercation over the umpire's decision.*

Am a zon (am′ə zon or am′ə zən), *n.* the largest river in the world, flowing from the Andes Mountains in NW South America across Brazil into the Atlantic. 3900 mi.

am bi gu i ty (am′bə gū′ə ti), *n., pl.* **-ties. 1.** possibility of two or more meanings. **2.** word or expression that can have more than one meaning.

a mends (ə mendz′), *n. sing. or pl.* payment for loss; satisfaction for an injury; compensation.

a men i ty (ə men′ə ti or ə mē′nə ti), *n., pl.* **-ties.** pleasant feature.

A mon til la do (ä′mon tə lä′dō)

am o rous (am′ə rəs), *adj.* **1.** inclined to love. **2.** in love. **3.** showing love; loving. **4.** having to do with love or courtship. [< OF *amorous* < *amour* love < L *amor*]

a ne mic (ə nē′mik), *adj.* having insufficiency of red corpuscles or of hemoglobin in the blood.

an e mom e ter (an′ə mom′ə tər), *n.* instrument for measuring the velocity or pressure of the wind. [< Gk. *anemos* wind + E *-meter*]

an i mos i ty (an′ə mos′ə ti), *n., pl.* **-ties.** violent hatred; ill will; active dislike or enmity.

Anemometer

an nals (an′əlz), *n. pl.* **1.** a written account of events year by year. **2.** historical records; history. [< L *annales* (*libri* books) annual record < *annus* year]

an no Dom i ni (an′ō dom′ə nī), *Latin.* in the year of our Lord; any year since the birth of Christ. *Abbrev.:* A.D.

a non (ə non′), *adv.* **1.** in a little while; soon. **2.** at another time; again. [OE *on ān* into one, *on āne* in one, at once]

a non y mous (ə non′ə məs), *adj.* **1.** by or from a person whose name is not known or given: *An anonymous book is one published without the name of the author.* **2.** having no name; nameless. [< Gk. *anonymos* < *an-* without + (dialectal) *onyma* name] —**a non′y mous ly,** *adv.*

an tag o nist (an tag′ə nist), *n.* one who fights, struggles, or contends with another: *The knight defeated each antagonist.*

an tith e sis (an tith′ə sis), *n., pl.* **-ses** (-sēz). the direct opposite: *Hate is the antithesis of love.* [< L < Gk. *antithesis* < *anti-* against + *tithenai* set]

a pos tro phize (ə pos′trə fīz), *v.,* **-phized, -phiz ing.** stop in a speech, poem, etc., and address some thing or absent person, usually with emotion.

a poth e car y (ə poth′ə ker′i), *n.,pl.* **-car ies. 1.** person who prepares and sells drugs and medicines; druggist. **2.** *Brit.* formerly, a person who prescribed medicines and sold them. [< LL *apothecarius* warehouseman< L *apotheca* storehouse < Gk. *apotheke* < *apo-* away + *tithenai* put]

ap pel la tion (ap′ə lā′shən), *n.* name; title.

ap per tain (ap′ər tān′), *v.* belong as a part; pertain; relate: *The control of traffic appertains to the police.*

ap point ments (ə point′mənts), *n.* furniture; equipment.

ap por tion (ə pôr′shən or ə pōr′shən), *v.* divide and give out in fair shares; distribute according to some rule: *The father's property was apportioned among his children after his death.* [< obsolete F *apportionner,* ult. < L *ad-* to + *portio* portion]

ap prize (ə prīz′), *v.,* **-prized, -priz ing.** appraise. Also, **apprise.**

aq ui line (ak′wə līn or ak′wə lin), *adj.* curved like an eagle's beak; hooked: *an aquiline nose.* [< L *aquilinus* < *aquila* eagle]

ar bi trar y (är′bə trer′i), *adj.* based on one's own wishes, notions, or will; not going by rule or law: *A good judge tries to be fair and does not make arbitrary decisions.* —**ar′bi trar′i ly,** *adv.* —**ar′bi trar′i ness,** *n.*

ar bi trate (är′bə trāt), *v.,* **-trat ed, -trat ing.** give a decision in a dispute; act as arbiter: *arbitrate between two persons in a quarrel.* [< L *arbitrari* < *arbiter.*]

ar bu tus (är bū′təs), *n.* a trailing plant growing in E North America, that has clusters of fragrant, pink or white flowers very early in the spring.

ar mo ri al (är mô′ri əl or är mō′ri əl), *adj.* having to do with coats of arms or heraldry.

ar raign (ə rān′), *v.* bring before a law court for trial: *The tramp was arraigned on a charge of stealing.*

ar rest (ə rest′), *v.* stop; check: *Filling a tooth arrests decay.*

ar ro gant (ar′ə gənt), *adj.* too proud; haughty.

ar thri tis (är thrī′tis), *n.* inflammation of a joint or joints. [< L < Gk. *arthritis* < *arthron* joint]

as cer tain (as′ər tān′), *v.* find out; determine. [< OF *acertener* < *a-* to + *certain* certain < L *certus* sure]

As cle pi us (as klē′pi əs), *n.* Greek god of medicine and healing, identified with the Roman god Aesculapius.

as per i ty (as per′ə ti), *n.* roughness; harshness; severity. [< OF *asprete* < L *asperitas* < *asper* rough]

as sail (ə sāl′), *v.* set upon vigorously with arguments, abuse, etc. [< OF *asalir* < VL *adsalire* < L *ad-* at + *salire* leap]

as sert (ə sėrt′), *v.* **1.** state positively; declare. **2.** insist on (a right, a claim, etc.); defend.

as sess (ə ses′), *v.* figuratively, to appraise; evaluate.

as sev er a tion (ə sev′ər ā′shən), *n.* a solemn declaration; emphatic assertion.

as sid u ous (ə sij′ü əs), *adj.* careful and attentive; diligent. [< L *assiduus* < *assidere* sit at. See ASSESS.] **—as sid′u ous ly,** *adv.*

as sig na tion (as′ig nā′shən), *n.* appointment for a meeting, often an illicit meeting of lovers.

as sim i late (ə sim′ə lāt), *v.,* **-lat ed, -lat ing. 1.** absorb; digest: *The girl reads so much that she does not assimilate it all. The human body will not assimilate sawdust.* **2.** make or become like (people of a nation, etc.) in customs and viewpoint: *Swedes assimilate readily in this country.* [< L *assimilare* < *ad-* to + *similis* like]

As syr i an (ä sir′i′ən)

as tra khan or **as tra chan** (as′trə kən), *n.* the curly furlike wool on the skin of young lambs from Astrakhan.

as tute (əs tüt′ or əs tūt′), *adj.* shrewd; crafty; sagacious: *Many lawyers are astute.*

a thwart (ə thwôrt′), *adv.* crosswise; across from side to side.

a tone ment (ə tōn′mənt), *n.* a making up for something; giving satisfaction for a wrong, loss, or injury; amends. [< *at onement* a being at one, i.e., in accord; *onement* < ME *onen* unite, ult. < OE *ān* one]

at tain (ə tān′), *v.* arrive at; reach: *attain years of discretion.*

at test (ə test′), *v.* **1.** declare to be true or genuine; certify. **2.** bear witness; testify: *The handwriting expert attested to the genuineness of the signature.*

at trib ute (at′rə būt), *n.* **1.** a quality considered as belonging to a person or thing; a characteristic: *Kindness is an attribute of a good teacher.* **2.** an object considered appropriate to a person, rank, or office; symbol: *The eagle was the attribute of Jupiter.*

at tune (ə tün′ or ə tūn′), *v.,* **-tuned, -tun ing.** tune; put in tune.

au di tor (ô′də tər), *n.* person who examines and checks business accounts.

au gu ry (ô′gū ri), *n., pl.* **-ries. 1.** art or practice of foretelling the future by the flight of birds, the appearance of the internal organs of sacrificed animals, thunder and lightning, etc. **2.** rite or ceremony performed by an augur.

au ro ral (ô rô′rəl or ô rō′rəl), *adj.* of the aurora borealis or the aurora australis.

aus pi cious (ôs pish′əs), *adj.* **1.** with signs of success; favorable. **2.** fortunate. **—aus pi′cious ly,** *adv.*

a venge (ə venj′), *v.,* **a venged, a veng ing. 1.** get retribution for: *The Indian will avenge the murder of his brother by killing the murderer.* **2.** take vengeance on behalf of: *The clan avenged their slain chief.* **3.** get revenge. [< OF *avengier* < *a-* to (< L *ad-*) + *vengier* < L *vindicare* punish < *vindex* champion] **—a veng′er,** *n.*

a verse (ə vėrs′), *adj.* opposed; unwilling: *She was averse to fighting.*

a ver sion (ə vėr′zhən or ə vėr′shən), *n.* **1.** a strong or fixed dislike; antipathy. **2.** thing or person disliked.

➔ **aversion.** Either *to* or *for* follows *aversion: He has an aversion to moving fast and working hard. We'll eat alone; they have an aversion for fried shrimp.*

a vi a trix (ā′vi ā′triks or av′i ā′triks), *n.* a woman airplane pilot.

av o ca tion (av′ə kā′shən), *n.* something that a person does besides his regular business; minor occupation; hobby: *Mr. Brown is a lawyer, but writing stories is his avocation.*

a vow (ə vou′), *v.* declare frankly or openly; confess; admit; acknowledge: *He avowed that he could not sing.*

a vun cu lar (ə vung′kū lər), *adj.* **1.** of an uncle. **2.** like an uncle. [< L *avunculus* mother's brother, dim. of *avus* grandfather]

back gam mon (bak′gam′ən or bak′gam′ən), *n.* game for two played on a special board with pieces moved according to the throw of dice. [< *back,* adj. + *gammon* game; because the men are sometimes set back]

bade (bad or bād), *v.* *Archaic.* invite, command.

➔ **Bade** is used chiefly in formal and literary English: *The king bade her remain.*

bail iff (bāl′if), *n.* officer of a court who has charge of prisoners while they are in the courtroom. [< OF *baillif* < *baillir* govern < *bail* guardian, manager < L *bajulus* carrier]

bal sam (bôl′səm), *n.* something that heals or soothes.

bal us ter (bal′əs tər), *n.* a support for a railing. [< F *balustre* < Ital. < L < Gk. *balaustion* pomegranate blossom; from the shape]

bal us trade (bal′əs trād′), *n.* row of balusters and the railing on them. < F *balustrade* < *balustre.* See BALUSTER.]

Baluster and balustrade

ban dy (ban′di), *v.,* **-died, -dy ing,** *adj.* **—***v.* **1.** throw back and forth; toss about. **2.** give and take; exchange: *To bandy words with a foolish person is a waste of time.*

bar ba rous (bär′bə rəs), *adj.* **1.** not civilized; savage. **2.** cruelly harsh; brutal. [< L < Gk. *barbaros* foreign, apparently originally, stammering]

ba ro ni al (bə rō′ni əl), *adj.* suitable for a baron; splendid; stately; magnificent.

bar ris ter (bar′is tər), *n.* lawyer in England who can plead in any court. [< *bar* + *-ster*]

bar ter (bär′tər), *v.* **1.** trade by exchanging one kind of goods for other goods without using money. **2.** exchange. **3.** give (away) without an equal return.

base (bās), *adj.,* **bas er, bas est,** *n.* **—***adj.* **1.** morally low; mean; selfish; cowardly: *To betray a friend is a base action.* **2.** fit for an inferior person or thing; menial; unworthy: *No needful service is to be looked at as base.*

< = from, taken from; cf., compare; dial., dialect; dim., diminutive; pp., past participle; ppr., present participle; pt., past tense; ult., ultimately; var., variant; ?=possibly.

bas-re lief (bä′ri lēf′ or bas′ri lēf′), *n.* carving or sculpture in which the figures project only slightly from the background.

bas tion (bas′chən or bas′ti ən), *n.* a projecting part of a fortification made so that the defenders can fire at attackers from as many angles as possible.

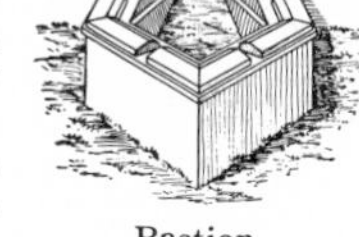
Bastion

ba tiste (bə tēst′), *n.* a fine, thin, cotton cloth. [< F *Baptiste,* probably from name of maker]

bat tle ment (bat′əl mənt), *n.* wall for defense at the top of a tower or wall, with indentations through which soldiers could shoot.

bay ber ry (bā′ber′i or bā′bər i), *n., pl.* **-ries.** a North American shrub with clusters of grayish-white berries coated with wax. The leaves of the shrub are aromatic, and candles made from the wax of the berries burn with a pleasant fragrance.

bay ou (bī′ü), *n., pl.* **-ous.** *U.S.* a marshy inlet or outlet of a lake, river, or gulf in the southern United States. [Am.E; < Louisiana F < Choctaw *bayuk* small stream]

be daub (bi dôb′), *v.* **1.** smear with something dirty or sticky. **2.** ornament in a gaudy or showy way.

be deck (bi dek′), *v.* adorn; decorate.

be foul (bi foul′), *v.* make dirty; cover with filth.

be get (bi get′), *v.,* **be got** or (*Archaic*) **be gat, be got ten** or **be got, be get ting.** **1.** become the father of. **2.** cause to be; produce: *Hate begets hate.* [ME *begete(n), begite(n),* alteration of earlier unrecorded *beyiten* (OE *begitan*) under the influence of *get(n)* get (< Scand. *geta*)] **—be get′ter,** *n.*

be girt (bi gėrt′), *adj.* surrounded; encircled.

be grimed (bi grīmd′), *adj.* made grimy; soiled and dirty.

be hest (bi hest′), *n.* command; order. [OE *behǣs* promise]

Benét, Stephen Vincent (bə-nā′)

be numb (bi num′), *v.* **1.** make numb. **2.** stupefy.

ber i ber i (ber′i ber′i), *n.* disease affecting the nerves, accompanied by weakness, loss of weight, and wasting away. It occurs in tropical countries and is probably caused by lack of vitamin B in the diet.

be seech (bi sēch′), *v.,* **-sought** or **-seeched, -seech ing.** ask earnestly; beg.

be set ting (bi set′ing), *adj.* habitually attacking: *Laziness is a loafer's besetting sin.*

be shrew (bi shrü′), *v. Archaic.* call down evil upon; curse mildly.

bes tial (bes′chəl or best′yəl), *adj.* **1.** beastly; brutal; vile. **2.** of beasts. [< L *bestialis* < *bestia* beast]

be strewn (bi strün′), *adj.* scattered about. *—v.* a pp. of **bestrew.**

be stride (bi strīd′), *v.,* **-strode** or **-strid, -strid den** or **-strid, -strid ing.** **1.** get on or sit on (something) with one leg on each side. One can bestride a horse, a chair, or a fence. **2.** stand over with one leg on each side.

bide (bīd), *v.,* **bode** or **bid ed, bid ing.** bear; endure; suffer.

bier (bēr), *n.* a movable stand on which a coffin or dead body is placed. [OE *bēr* < *beran* bear]

bi lin gual (bī ling′gwəl), *adj.* able to speak one's own language and another equally or almost equally well.

bil let (bil′it), *n.* **1.** a thick stick of wood. **2.** bar of iron or steel. [< F *billette,* dim. of *bille* log, tree trunk]

bi zarre (bə zär′), *adj.* odd; queer; fantastic; grotesque. [< F < Sp. *bizarro* brave < Basque *bezar* beard]

blad der (blad′ər), *n.* **1.** a soft, thin bag in the body that receives urine from the kidneys. **2.** anything like this. A football has a hollow rubber bladder that can be blown up with air. [OE *blǣdre*]

blas phe my (blas′fə mi), *n., pl.* **-mies.** abuse or contempt for God or sacred things.

blight (blīt), *n.* anything that causes destruction or ruin. *—v.* **1.** cause to wither or decay. **2.** destroy; ruin.

blind (blīnd), *n.* anything that conceals an action or purpose.

blun der buss (blun′dər bus), *n.* a short gun with a wide muzzle. It is no longer used.

bode[1] (bōd), *v.,* **bod ed, bod ing.** be a sign of; indicate beforehand: *Dark clouds boded rain.*

Boer War, (bôr, bōr, or bür), war between Great Britain and the Boers of South Africa, lasting from 1899 to 1902.

bole (bōl), *n.* trunk of a tree. [< Scand. *bolr*]

boll (bōl), *n.* a rounded seed pod or capsule of cotton or flax. [var. of *bowl*]

Bor deaux (bôr dō′), *n.* a red or white wine.

bos om (bůz′əm or bü′zəm), *n.* **1.** the upper, front part of the human body; breast. **2.** heart, thoughts, affections, desires, etc.

boun ty (boun′ti), *n., pl.* **-ties.** a reward: *The State government gives a bounty of one dollar for each wolf killed.*

bow el (bou′əl), *n.* **1.** part of the bowels; intestine. **2.** Usually, **bowels,** *pl.* tube in the body into which food passes from the stomach; intestines. **3. bowels,** *pl.* **a.** the inner part: *Miners dig for coal in the bowels of the earth.*

bow er (bou′ər), *n.* **1.** shelter of leafy branches. **2.** summerhouse or arbor.

Bra bant (brə bant′ or brä′bənt), *n.* region in the S Netherlands and N Belgium. It was formerly a duchy.

brace (brās), *n., v.,* **braced, brac ing.** *—n.* pair; couple: *a brace of ducks.* *—v.* give strength or firmness to; support.

brag gart (brag′ərt), *n.* boaster. *—adj.* boastful.

bran (bran), *n.* the broken coat of the grains of wheat, rye, etc., separated from the flour. [< OF]

breach (brēch), *v.* break through; make an opening in: *The enemy's fierce attack finally breached the wall.*

breadth (bredth or bretth), *n.* **1.** how broad a thing is; distance across; width. **2.** spaciousness; extent. [ME *bredethe* < *brede* breadth, OE *brǣdu* < *brād* broad]

brev i ty (brev′ə ti), *n., pl.* **-ties.** shortness; briefness. [< L *brevitas* < *brevis* short]

brig and (brig′ənd), *n.* man who robs travelers on the road; robber; bandit. [< OF < Ital. *brigante* < *brigare*]

broach (brōch), *v.* **1.** open by making a hole: *broach a barrel of cider.* **2.** begin to talk about: *broach a subject.* [< OF *broche* < L *broccus* projecting]

broad loom (brôd′lüm′), *adj.* woven on a wide loom in one color: *a broadloom carpet.*

bro gan (brō′gən), *n.* a coarse, strong shoe. [< Irish, Scotch Gaelic *brōgan,* dim. of *brōg* shoe]

brood (brüd), *v.* dwell on in thought: *For years he brooded vengeance.*

bru tal (brü′təl), *adj.* coarse and savage; like a brute.

Bru tus (brü′təs), *n.* **Marcus Junius,** 85-42 B.C., Roman political leader and one of the men who killed Julius Caesar.

buf fet (buf′it), *v.*, **-fet ed, -fet ing.** **1.** strike with the hand or fist. **2.** knock about; strike; hurt: *The waves buffeted him.* **3.** fight or struggle against: *He reached home exhausted from buffeting the storm.* [< OF *buffet,* dim. of *buffe* blow]
bump er (bump′ər), *n.* cup or glass filled to the brim.
bung (bung), *n.* stopper for closing the hole in the side or end of a barrel, keg, or cask.
buoy an cy (boi′ən si or bü′yən si), *n.* tendency to rise.
bur geon (bėr′jən), *v., n.* bud; sprout. [< OF *burjon,* apparently < Gmc.]
bur row (bėr′ō), *n.* hole dug in the ground by an animal for refuge or shelter. Rabbits live in burrows. —*v.* dig a hole in the ground: *The mole quickly burrowed out of sight.*

cab i net (kab′ə nit or kab′nit), *n.* group of advisers chosen by the head of a nation to help him with the administration of the government. Each member of the cabinet of the President of the United States administers a department of the government.
cache (kash), *n.* a hiding place to store food or supplies. [< F *cache* < *cacher* hide]
ca dav er ous (kə dav′ər əs), *adj.* pale and ghastly.
ca dence (kā′dəns), *n.* **1.** fall of the voice. **2.** rising and falling sound; modulation.
ca jole (kə jōl′), *v.*, **-joled, -jol ing.** persuade by pleasant words, flattery, or false promises; coax. [< F *cajoler*]
Cal cut ta (kal kut′ə), *n.* seaport in E India.
cal i ber or **cal i bre** (kal′ə bər), *n.* amount of ability: *The president of a railroad or a big factory should be a man of large caliber.*
cal li o pe (kə lī′ə pi; *also* kal′i ōp), *n.* a musical instrument having a series of steam whistles played by pushing keys.
ca lotte (kə lot′), *n.* a close cap without visor or brim; a plain skullcap.
Cam bridge (kām′brij), *n.* **1.** city in SE England. **2.** university located there.
can dor (kan′dər), *n.* speaking openly what one really thinks; honesty in giving one's view or opinion.
cant (kant), *n.* the peculiar language of a special group, using many strange words: *thieves' cant.* —*adj.* peculiar to a special group: *a cant phrase.*
can tan ker ous (kan tang′kər əs), *adj.* hard to get along with because ready to make trouble and oppose anything suggested; ill-natured.
cape (kāp), *n.* point of land extending into the water.
ca pit u late (kə pich′ů lāt), *v.*, **-lat ed, -lat ing.** surrender on certain terms or conditions.
cap stan (kap′stən), *n.* machine for lifting or pulling that revolves on a vertical shaft or spindle. Sailors hoist the anchor on some boats by turning the capstan.
cap tious (kap′shəs), *adj.* hard to please; faultfinding. [< L *captiosus* < *capere* take]
car a pace (kar′ə pās), *n.* shell on the back of a turtle, lobster, crab, etc.
ca reen (kə rēn′), *v.* **1.** lean to one side; tilt; tip: *The ship careened in the strong wind.* **2.** cause to lean to one side: *The strong wind careened the ship.*
car i ca ture (kar′ə kə chür or kar′ə kə chər), *n., v.*, **-tured, -tur ing.** —*n.* **1.** picture, cartoon, description, etc., that ridiculously exaggerates the peculiarities or defects of a person or thing. **2.** a very poor imitation. —*v.* make a caricature of. [< F < Ital. *caricatura* < *caricare* overload, exaggerate]

car nage (kär′nij), *n.* slaughter of a great number of people. [< F < Ital. *carnaggio* < L *caro* flesh]
car riage (kar′ij), *n.* manner of holding the head and body; bearing: *She has a queenly carriage.*
car ri on (kar′i ən), *n.* **1.** dead and decaying flesh. **2.** rottenness; filth.
cat a comb (kat′ə kōm), *n.* Usually, **catacombs,** *pl.* an underground gallery forming a burial place. [< LL *catacumbae,* pl. < *cata* (< Gk. *kata*) *tumbas* (< Gk. *tymbos*) among the tombs]

Famous catacombs of Rome, probably formed for the burial of Christians between the 2nd and 4th centuries A.D.

caul (kôl), *n.* membrane sometimes covering the head of a child at birth. It was supposed to bring good luck and to safeguard against drowning. [< OF *cale* a kind of little cap]
caus tic (kôs′tik), *adj.* sarcastic; stinging; biting: *The director's caustic remarks made the actors very angry.*
cau tion ar y (kô′shən er′i), *adj.* warning; urging to be careful.
cav al cade (kav′əl kād′ or kav′əl kād), *n.* procession of persons riding on horses or in carriages.
ce ler i ty (sə ler′ə ti), *n.* swiftness; speed.
cen sure (sen′shər), *n., v.*, **-sured, -sur ing.** —*n.* act of blaming; expression of disapproval; criticism. —*v.* express disapproval of; find fault with; blame; criticize [< L *censura* < *censere* appraise]
cess pool (ses′pül′), *n.* any filthy place.
chafe (chāf), *v.*, **chafed, chaf ing.** rub to make warm: *She chafed her cold hands.*
cha grin (shə grin′), *n.* a feeling of disappointment, failure, or humiliation.
chaise (shāz), *n.* a lightweight carriage. One kind usually has a folding top.
champ (champ), *v.* bite and chew noisily.
chap ar ral (chap′ə ral′), *n.* in the southwestern United States, a thicket of low shrubs, thorny bushes, etc. [Am.E; < Sp. *chaparral* < *chaparro* evergreen oak]
char nel (chär′nəl), *n.* charnel house. —*adj.* **1.** of or used for a charnel. **2.** like a charnel; deathlike; ghastly.
charnel house, place where dead bodies or bones are laid.
char y (chãr′i), *adj.*, **char i er, char i est.** careful: *A cat is chary of wetting its paws.*
chaste (chāst), *adj.* **1.** pure; virtuous. **2.** decent; modest. **3.** simple in taste or style; not too much ornamented. [< OF < L *castus* pure. Doublet of CASTE.]
châ teau (sha tō′), *n., pl.* **-teaux** (-tōz′). **1.** a French castle. **2.** a large country house.
Chayefsky (chī əf′ski)
cher ish (cher′ish), *v.* **1.** hold dear; treat with affection; care for tenderly: *A mother cherishes her baby.* **2.** keep in mind; cling to: *For many years the old woman cherished the hope that her wandering son would come home.* [< F *chériss-,* stem of *cherir* < *cher* dear < L *carus*]
chintz (chints), *n.* a cotton cloth printed in patterns of various colors and often glazed.
chol er (kol′ər), *n.* an irritable disposition; anger. [< L < Gk. *cholera* cholera, apparently < *chole* bile]
chor tle (chôr′təl), *v.* chuckle or snort with glee. [blend of *chuckle* and *snort;* coined by Lewis Carroll]
chouse (chous), *v.* to cheat; trick; defraud.
chron i cle (kron′ə kəl), *n.* record of happenings in the order in which they happened.

< = from, taken from; cf., compare; dial., dialect; dim., diminutive; pp., past participle; ppr., present participle; pt., past tense; ult., ultimately; var., variant; ?=possibly.

cir cuit (sėr′kit), *n.* a going around; a trip around: *It takes a year for the earth to make its circuit of the sun.*

cir cum scribe (sėr′kəm skrīb′ or sėr′kəm skrīb), *v.*, **-scribed, -scrib ing.** **1.** surround. **2.** limit; restrict: *A prisoner's activities are circumscribed.* [< L *circumscribere* < *circum* around + *scribere* write]

cit a del (sit′ə dəl or sit′ə del), *n.* fortress commanding a city.

civil service, public service concerned with affairs not military, naval, legislative, or judicial.

clan gor (klang′gər or klang′ər), *n.* continued clanging.

clap trap (klap′trap′), *n.* empty talk or an insincere remark made just to get attention or applause.

cleat (klēt), *n.* strip of wood or iron fastened across anything for support or for sure footing. A gangway has cleats to keep people from slipping.

cleave (klēv), *v.*, **cleft** or **cleaved** or **clove, cleft** or **cleaved** or **clo ven, cleav ing.** **1.** split; divide. **2.** pass through; pierce; penetrate.

cloy (kloi), *v.* **1.** weary by too much, too sweet, or too rich food. **2.** weary by too much of anything pleasant.

co a ti (kō ä′ti), *n., pl.* **-tis.** a small mammal somewhat like a raccoon, living in Central and South America. It has a long body and tail and a flexible snout.

cob bler (kob′lər), *n.* *U.S.* a fruit pie baked in a deep dish, usually with a crust only on top.

cock ade (kok ād′), *n.* knot of ribbon or a rosette worn on the hat as a badge.

cock chaf er (kok′chāf′ər), *n.* a large European beetle that destroys plants.

codg er (koj′ər), *n.* *Informal.* a queer or peculiar person.

co er cion (kō ėr′shən), *n.* **1.** use of force; compulsion; constraint. **2.** government by force.

cog i tate (koj′ə tāt), *v.*, **-tat ed, -tat ing.** think over; consider with care; meditate; ponder.

co gnac (kōn′yak or kon′yak), *n.* kind of French brandy.

cog nate (kog′nāt), *adj.* **1.** related by family or origin. English, Dutch, and German are cognate languages. **2.** having a similar nature or quality. —*n.* person, word, or thing related to another by having a common source. German *Wasser* and English *water* are cognates. [< L *cognatus* < *co-* together + *gnatus* born]

co her ent (kō hēr′ənt), *adj.* logically connected; consistent in structure and thought: *A sentence that is not coherent is hard to understand.* **—co her′ent ly,** *adv.*

co he sive (kō hē′siv), *adj.* sticking together; tending to hold together. **—co he′sive ly,** *adv.* **—co he′sive ness,** *n.*

col lect ed (kə lek′tid), *adj.* under control; not confused or disturbed; calm. **—col lect′ed ly,** *adv.*

col on nade (kol′ə nād′), *n.* series of columns set the same distance apart.

com mis er ate (kə miz′ər āt), *v.*, **-at ed, -at ing.** feel or express sorrow for; sympathize with; pity. [< L *commiserari* < *com-* + *miser* wretched]

com mis sar y (kom′ə ser′i), *n., pl.* **-sar ies.** **1.** store handling food and supplies in a mining camp, lumber camp, army camp, etc. **2.** an army officer in charge of food and daily supplies for soldiers. **3.** deputy.

com mis sion (kə mish′ən), *n.* doing; performance: *People are punished for the commission of crimes.* —*v.* give authority to; give (a person) the right or power (to do something).

com mons (kom′ənz), *n.pl.* food: *The poor orphans were kept on short commons.*

com pas sion ate (kəm pash′ən it), *adj.* desiring to relieve another's suffering; deeply sympathetic.

com pa tri ot (kəm pā′tri ət; *esp. Brit.* kəm pat′ri ət), *n.* a fellow countryman.

com pel (kəm pel′), *v.*, **-pelled, -pel ling.** **1.** force: *Rain compelled them to stop.* **2.** cause or get by force: *A policeman can compel obedience.* [< L *compellere* < *com-* + *pellere* drive]

com pen sate (kom′pən sāt), *v.*, **-sat ed, -sat ing.** **1.** make an equal return to; give an equivalent to. **2.** balance by equal weight, power, etc.; make up (*for*).

com pla cent (kəm plā′sənt), *adj.* pleased with oneself; self-satisfied: *The winner's complacent smile annoyed some people.*

com pli ance (kəm plī′əns), *n.* act of complying; act of doing as another wishes; act of yielding to a request or command.

com ply (kəm plī′), *v.*, **-plied, -ply ing.** act in agreement with a request or a command: *We should comply with the doctor's request.*

com pose (kəm pōz′), *v.*, **-posed, -pos ing.** get (oneself) ready; put in proper state: *compose oneself to read a book.*

com pro mise (kom′prə mīz), *v.*, **-mised, -mis ing,** *n.* —*v.* **1.** settle (a dispute) by agreeing that each contestant will give up a part of what he demands. **2.** put under suspicion; put in danger: *You will compromise your good name if you go around with thieves and liars.* [< n.] —*n.* settlement of a dispute by a partial yielding on both sides.

con cede (kən sēd′), *v.*, **-ced ed, -ced ing.** give (what is asked or claimed); grant; yield: *He conceded us the right to walk through his land.*

con cep tion (kən sep′shən), *n.* thought; idea; impression.

con cert ed (kən sėr′tid), *adj.* arranged by agreement; planned or made together; combined: *a concerted attack.*

Con ci er ge rie (coɴ′cē ər gė′rē)

con course (kon′kôrs, kong′kôrs, kon′kōrs, or kong′kōrs), *n.* crowd.

con dole (kən dōl′), *v.*, **-doled, -dol ing.** express sympathy; sympathize: *The widow's friends condoled with her at the funeral.*

con done (kən dōn′), *v.*, **-doned, -don ing.** forgive; overlook.

con du cive (kən dü′siv or kən dū′siv), *adj.* helpful; favorable: *Exercise is conducive to health.*

con fes sor (kən fes′ər), *n.* priest who has the authority to hear confessions.

con fine (kon′fīn), *n.* Usually, **confines,** *pl.* boundary; border; limit: *These people have never been beyond the confines of their own valley.*

con firm (kən fėrm′), *v.* **1.** prove to be true or correct; make certain: *confirm a rumor.* **2.** strengthen; make firmer: *A sudden storm confirmed my decision not to leave.*

con fla gra tion (kon′flə grā′shən), *n.* a big fire: *A conflagration destroyed most of the city.* [< L *conflagratio, -onis* < *conflagrare* < *com-* up + *flagrare* burn]

con found (kon found′ or kən found′ *for* **1.** kon′found′ *for* 2), *v.* **1.** surprise and puzzle. **2.** damn. *Confound* is used as a mild oath. [< OF *confondre* < L *confundere* < *com-* together + *fundere* pour]

con front (kən frunt′), *v.* **1.** meet face to face; stand facing. **2.** face boldly; oppose.

con geal (kən jēl′), *v.* **1.** freeze. **2.** thicken; stiffen.

con i cal (kon′ə kəl), *adj.* cone-shaped; like a cone.

con jec ture (kən jek′chər), *n.* **1.** formation of an opinion admittedly without sufficient evidence for proof; guessing. **2.** a guess.

con junc tion (kən jungk′shən), *n.* act of joining together; union; combination: *A severe illness in conjunction with hot weather has left the baby very weak.*

con ju ra tion (kon′jü rā′shən), *n.* *Archaic.* a solemn appeal.

con nois seur (kon′ə sėr′), *n.* expert; critical judge: *He is a connoisseur of antique furniture.*

con sol a to ry (kən sol′ə tô′ri or kən sol′ə tō′ri), *adj.* consoling; comforting.

con sol i date (kən sol′ə dāt), *v.*, **-dat ed, -dat ing.** **1.** unite; combine; merge: *The three banks consolidated and formed a single, large bank.* **2.** make secure; strengthen: *The army spent a day in consolidating its gains by digging trenches.* **3.** make or become solid.

con sort (kən sôrt′), *v.* **1.** associate: *Do not consort with thieves.* **2.** agree; accord. [< F < L *consors, -ortis* sharer < *com-* with + *sors* lot]

con spir a tor (kən spir′ə tər), *n.* person who conspires; plotter: *Conspirators planned to kill the king.*

con spir a to ri al (kən spir′ə tô′ri əl or kən spir′ə tō′ri əl), *adj.* having to do with conspiracy or conspirators.

con spire (kən spīr′), *v.*, **-spired, -spir ing.** **1.** plan secretly with others to do something wrong; plot. **2.** act together: *All things conspired to make her birthday a happy one.*

con sta ble (kon′stə bəl or kun′stə bəl), *n.* a police officer; policeman.

Con stan ti no ple (kon′stan tə nō′pəl), *n.* a former name of **Istanbul,** a city in Turkey.

con sti tute (kon′stə tüt or kon′stə tūt), *v.*, **-tut ed, -tut ing.** **1.** make up; form: *Seven days constitute a week.* **2.** set up; establish: *Courts are constituted by law to give out justice.*

con strain (kən strān′), *v.* force; compel.

con straint (kən strānt′), *n.* a holding back of natural feelings; forced or unnatural manner.

con strict (kən strikt′), *v.* draw together; contract; compress: *A rubber band constricts what it encircles.*

con sume (kən süm′), *v.*, **-sumed, -sum ing.** **1.** use up: *A student consumes much of his time in studying.* **2.** destroy; burn up. **3.** spend; waste (time, money, etc.)

con sum ma tion (kon′sə mā′shən), *n.* completion; fulfillment.

con tem plate (kon′təm plāt), *v.*, **-plat ed, -plat ing.** **1.** look at for a long time; gaze at. **2.** think about for a long time; study carefully. [< L *contemplari* survey < *com-* + *templum* restricted area marked off for the taking of auguries]

con ten tion (kən ten′shən), *n.* argument; dispute; quarrel.

con tig u ous (kən tig′ū əs), *adj.* adjoining; near. [< L *contiguus* < *com-* + *tag-*, root of *tangere* touch. Related to *contact.*]

con tin gen cy (kən tin′jən si), *n.*, *pl.* **-cies.** a happening or event depending on something that is uncertain; possibility: *The explorer carried supplies for every contingency.*

con tra band (kon′trə band), *n.* **1.** goods imported or exported contrary to law; smuggled goods. **2.** trading contrary to law; smuggling.

con tract (kən trakt′), *v.* draw together; make or become narrow; shorten; make or become smaller; shrink: *Wrinkling your forehead contracts your brows.*

con trive (kən trīv′), *v.*, **-trived, -triv ing.** **1.** invent; design: *contrive a new kind of engine.* **2.** plan; scheme; plot: *contrive a robbery.* **3.** manage: *I will contrive to be there by ten o'clock.* [< OF *controver* < *con-* (< L *com-*) + *trover find* < L *turbare* stir up < *turba* commotion]

con ven tion al (kən ven′shən əl), *adj.* depending on conventions; customary: *"Good morning" is a conventional greeting.*

con ver sant (kən vėr′sənt or kon′vər sənt), *adj.* familiar by use or study; acquainted.

con vert (*v.* kən vėrt′; *n.* kon′vėrt), *v.* change; turn: *These machines convert cotton into cloth.*

con vex (kon veks′ or kon′veks), *adj.* curved out, like the outside of a circle or sphere. The crystal of a watch is slightly convex. [< L *convexus* vaulted, probably < *com-* around + *vac-* bend (related to *vacillare* totter, sway)]

con vey ance (kən vā′əns), *n.* thing that carries people and goods; vehicle.

con viv i al (kən viv′i əl), *adj.* fond of eating and drinking with friends; jovial; sociable.

cop pice (kop′is), *n.* copse.

copse (kops), *n.* a thicket of small trees, bushes, shrubs, etc.

cor rob o rate (kə rob′ə rāt), *v.*, **-rat ed, -rat ing.** make more certain; confirm: *Witnesses corroborated the policeman's statement.* [< L *corroborare* strengthen < *com-* + *robur* oak]

cos mop o lite (koz mop′ə līt), *n.* a cosmopolitan person. [< Gk. *kosmopolites* < *kosmos* world + *polites* citizen < *polis* city]

cos mos (koz′məs or koz′mos), *n.* the universe thought of as an orderly, harmonious system; opposite of chaos.

couch (kouch), *v.* **1.** lay on a couch. **2.** lie down on a couch.

coun sel (koun′səl), *n.*, *v.*, **-seled, -sel ing** or *esp. Brit.* **-selled, -sel ling.** —*n.* **1.** act of exchanging ideas; act of talking things over. **2.** advice: *A wise person gives good counsel.* **3.** lawyer or group of lawyers. Each side of a case in court has its own counsel. **4. keep one's own counsel,** keep still about one's ideas and plans; not tell one's secrets. —*v.* **1.** give advice to; advise. **2.** recommend: *He counseled acting at once.*

coun se lor (koun′sə lər or koun′slər), *n.* lawyer.

coun ter feit (koun′tər fit), *v.* resemble closely. —*n.* copy made to deceive or defraud and passed as genuine.

coun ter pane (koun′tər pān′), *n.* an outer covering for a bed; bedspread.

coun ter part (koun′tər pärt′), *n.* person or thing closely resembling another: *This twin is her sister's counterpart.*

coun ter plot (koun′tər plot′), *n.*, *v.*, **-plot ted, -plot ting.** plot to defeat another plot.

coun ter sign (koun′tər sīn′), *v.* sign (something already signed by another) to confirm it.

cour ti er (kôr′ti ər or kōr′ti ər), *n.* **1.** person often present at the court of a king, prince, etc.; court attendant. **2.** person who tries to win the favor of another by flattering and pleasing him.

court ly (kôrt′li or kōrt′li), *adj.*, **-li er, -li est.** suitable for a king's court; polite; elegant.

cov ert (kuv′ərt), *adj.* secret; hidden; disguised: *covert glances.* —*n.* thicket in which animals hide.

cra vat (krə vat′), *n.* **1.** necktie. **2.** neckcloth; scarf. [< F *cravate,* special use of *Cravate* Croat]

< = from, taken from; cf., compare; dial., dialect; dim., diminutive; pp., past participle; ppr., present participle; pt., past tense; ult., ultimately; var., variant; ?=possibly.

cre do (krē′dō or krā′dō), *n., pl.* **-dos.** creed. [< L *credo* I believe. Doublet of CREED.]
crone (krōn), *n.* a withered old woman. [< MDutch *croonje* < OF *carogne* carcass, hag. Doublet of CARRION.]
crop (krop), *n.* baglike swelling of a bird's food passage where food is prepared for digestion.
cross bow (krôs′bō′ or kros′bō′), *n.* a medieval weapon with a bow and a grooved stock in the middle to direct the arrows, stones, etc.

Man using a crossbow

Cro ta lus a trox (crä′tə ləs ā′trox)
croup (krüp), *n.* inflammation or diseased condition of the throat and windpipe characterized by a hoarse cough and difficult breathing. [< *croup,* v., ? blend of *croak* and *whoop*]
crown (kroun), *n.* a former British silver coin, worth 5 shillings.
cu bit (kū′bit), *n.* an ancient measure of length, about 18 to 22 inches. [< L *cubitum* elbow, cubit]
cud (kud), *n.* mouthful of food that cattle and similar animals bring back into the mouth from the first stomach for a slow, second chewing.
cud dy (kud′i), *n.* a pipe for smoking.
cu li nar y (kū′lə ner′i or kul′ə ner′i), *adj.* having to do with cooking.
cull (kul), *v.* **1.** pick out; select: *The lawyer culled important facts from the mass of evidence.* **2.** pick over; make selections from.
cul ti vat ed (kul′tə vāt′id), *adj.* cultured; refined.
cu po la (kū′pə lə), *n.* a rounded roof; dome.
cu rate (kūr′it), *n. Esp. Brit.* clergyman who is an assistant to a pastor, rector, or vicar.
cut ler (kut′lər), *n.* person who makes, sells, or repairs knives, scissors, and other cutting instruments. [< F *coutelier* < *coutel* small knife < L *cultellus,* dim. of *culter* knife]
cy cle (sī′kəl), *n.* period of time or complete process of growth or action that repeats itself in the same order: *The seasons of the year—spring, summer, autumn, and winter—make a cycle.*
cyn ic (sin′ik), *n.* person inclined to believe that the motives for people's actions are insincere and selfish.
cy press (sī′prəs), *n.* an evergreen tree of the South, with hard wood and dark leaves.
czar (zär), *n.* emperor. It was the title of the former emperors of Russia. Also, **tsar, tzar.** [< Russian *tsar* < Old Church Slavic < Gothic < L *Caesar* Caesar]
Czech o slo va ki a (chek′ə slō vä′ki ə or chek′ə slō vak′i ə), *n.* country in central Europe. 13,564,000 pop.; 49,355 sq. mi. *Capital:* Prague.

Dan a üs or **Dan a us** (dan′ā əs), *n.* in Greek legend, a king of Argos.
dank (dangk), *adj.* unpleasantly damp; moist; wet: *The cave was dark, dank, and chilly.* [ME. Cf. Swedish *dank* marshy spot.]
Dar dan (där′dan)
d'Aul nais (dōl nā′)
de ba cle (dā bä′kəl or di bak′əl), *n.* disaster; overthrow; downfall.
de bauch (di bôch′), *v.* lead away from duty, virtue, or morality; corrupt morally; seduce: *Bad companions had debauched the boy.* —*n.* **1.** excessive indulgence in sensual pleasures; excess in eating or drinking. **2.** bout or period of debauchery.
de cap i tate (di kap′ə tāt), *v.,* **-tat ed, -tat ing.** cut off the head of; behead. [< LL *decapitare* < L *de-* + *caput* head] **—de cap′i ta′tion,** *n.*
de cep tive (di sep′tiv), *adj.* **1.** deceiving. **2.** meant to deceive. **—de cep′tive ly,** *adv.* **—de cep′tive ness,** *n.*
de duce (di düs′ or di dūs′), *v.,* **-duced, -duc ing.** **1.** infer from a general rule or principle; reach (a conclusion) by reasoning. **2.** trace the course, descent, or origin of. [< L *deducere* < *de-* down + *ducere* lead]
de duc tion (di duk′shən), *n.* inference from a general rule or principle. A person using deduction reasons from general laws to particular cases.
def er ence (def′ər əns), *n.* a yielding to the judgment or opinion of another; courteous submission.
def er en tial (def′ər en′shəl), *adj.* showing deference; respectful. **—def′er en′tial ly,** *adv.*
de fi cien cy (di fish′ən si), *n., pl.* **-cies.** lack or absence of something needed or required; incompleteness.
de fin i tive (di fin′ə tiv), *adj.* **1.** conclusive; final. **2.** limiting; defining. **—de fin′i tive ly,** *adv.* **—de fin′i tive ness,** *n.*
deg ra da tion (deg′rə dā′shən), *n.* a degrading.
de hy dra tion (dē′hī drā′shən), *n.* removal of water from a chemical compound or from vegetables, fruits, etc.
deign (dān), *v.* condescend; think fit: *So great a man would never deign to notice us.*
del e gate (del′ə gāt), *v.,* **-gat ed, -gat ing.** **1.** appoint or send (a person) as a delegate: *Each club delegated one member to attend the State meeting.* **2.** give over (one's power or authority) to another as agent or deputy: *The States delegated the control of foreign affairs to the federal government.* [< L *delegatus,* pp. of *delegare* < *de-* + *legare* send with a commission]
de lude (di lüd′), *v.,* **-lud ed, -lud ing.** mislead; deceive. [< L *deludere* < *de-* (to the detriment of) + *ludere* play]
de lu sive (di lü′siv), *adj.* misleading; deceptive; false.
de ment ed (di men′tid), *adj.* insane; crazy. [< L *dementare* < *demens* mad < *de-* out of + *mens* mind]
de mesne (di mān′ or di mēn′), *n.* **1.** house and land belonging to a lord and used by him. **2.** domain; realm. [< AF *demesne,* a respelling of OF *demeine* domain. Doublet of DOMAIN.]
de mon stra ble (di mon′strə bəl or dem′ən strə bəl), *adj.* capable of being proved.
de mur (di mėr′), *n.* an objection.
de note (di nōt′), *v.,* **-not ed, -not ing.** be the sign of; indicate: *A fever usually denotes sickness.*
de nounce (di nouns′), *v.,* **-nounced, -nounc ing.** **1.** condemn publicly; express strong disapproval of. **2.** inform against; accuse: *He denounced his own brother to the military police as a spy.* [< OF *denoncer* < L *denuntiare* < *de-* + *nuntius* messenger] **—de nounc′er,** *n.*
den si ty (den′sə ti), *n., pl.* **-ties.** dense condition or quality; having parts very close together; compactness; thickness: *The density of the forest prevented us from seeing more than a little way ahead.*
de nun ci a tion (di nun′si ā′shən), *n.* **1.** public condemnation; expression of strong disapproval. **2.** act of informing against; accusation.
de plete (di plēt′), *v.,* **-plet ed, -plet ing.** empty; exhaust: *Because the traveler's funds were depleted, he went home.*
de plor a ble (di plôr′ə bəl or di plōr′ə bəl), *adj.* to be deplored; regrettable; lamentable.

hat, āge, cãre, fär; let, ēqual, tėrm; it, īce; hot, ōpen, ôrder; oil, out; cup, pu̇t, rüle, ūse; th, thin; ᴛʜ, then; zh, measure; ə represents *a* in about, *e* in taken, *i* in pencil, *o* in lemon, *u* in circus.

de plore (di plôr′ or di plōr′), *v.*, **-plored, -plor ing.** be very sorry about; regret deeply; lament.

de pos i to ry (di poz′ə tô′ri or di poz′ə tō′ri), *n. pl.* **-ries.** place where a thing is put for safekeeping; storehouse.

dep re cate (dep′rə kāt), *v.*, **-cat ed, -cat ing.** express strong disapproval of; plead against; protest against: *Lovers of peace deprecate war.* [< L *deprecari* plead in excuse, avert by prayer < *de-* + *precari* pray]

dep re ca to ry (dep′rə kə tô′ri or dep′rə kə tō′ri), *adj.* **1.** deprecating. **2.** *Informal.* apologetic.

de ride (di rīd′), *v.*, **-rid ed, -rid ing.** make fun of; laugh at in scorn; ridicule with contempt.

de sign ed ly (di zīn′id li), *adv.* purposely; intentionally.

des patch (dis pach′), *v.*, *n.* dispatch.

de spoil (di spoil′), *v.* rob; plunder.

de spond (di spond′), *v.* lose heart, courage, or hope. —*n. Archaic.* despondence. [< L *despondere* < *de-* + *spondere* lose heart]

de spond ent (di spon′dənt), *adj.* without courage or hope; discouraged; dejected.

des pot ism (des′pət iz əm), *n.* tyranny; oppression.

des tine (des′tən), *v.*, **-tined, -tin ing. 1.** set apart for a particular purpose or use; intend: *The prince was destined from birth to be a king.* **2.** cause by fate: *My letter was destined never to reach him.*

des ul to ry (des′əl tô′ri or des′əl tō′ri), *adj.* jumping from one thing to another; unconnected; without aim or method.

de ten tion (di ten′shən), *n.* act of keeping in custody; confinement: *A jail is used for the detention of persons who have been arrested.*

de vice (di vīs′), *n.* a mechanical invention used for a special purpose; machine; apparatus: *a device for lighting a gas stove.*

de vise (di vīz′), *v.*, **-vised, -vis ing.** think out; plan; contrive; invent: *The boys devised a scheme for earning money during the summer vacation.*

dex ter i ty (deks ter′ə ti), *n.* **1.** skill in using the hands. **2.** skill in using the mind; cleverness.

di a be tes (dī′ə bē′tis or dī′ə bē′tēz), *n.* disease in which the digestive system is unable to absorb normal amounts of sugar and starch.

di a bet ic (dī′ə bet′ik or dī′ə bē′tik), *adj.* **1.** of or having to do with diabetes. **2.** having diabetes. —*n.* person having diabetes.

di a bol ic (dī′ə bol′ik), *adj.* devilish; like the Devil; very cruel or wicked; fiendish. [< LL *diabolicus* < Gk. *diabolikos* < *diabolos.*]

dif fer en ti ate (dif′ər en′shi āt), *v.*, **-at ed, -at ing.** make different.

din gle (ding′gəl), *n.* a small, deep, shady valley. [origin uncertain]

diph the ri a (dif thēr′i ə or dip thēr′i ə), *n.* a dangerous, infectious disease of the throat, usually accompanied by a high fever and formation of membranes that hinder breathing.

dirge (dėrj), *n.* a funeral song or tune. [contraction of L *dirige* direct (imperative of *dirigere*), first word in office for the dead]

dirk (dėrk), *n.* dagger. —*v.* stab with a dirk.

dis cern (də zėrn′ or də sėrn′), *v.* perceive; see clearly; distinguish; recognize. [< F < L *discernere* < *dis-* off + *cernere* separate]

dis com fit (dis kum′fit), *v.* embarrass greatly; confuse; disconcert.

dis com pose (dis′kəm pōz′), *v.*, **-posed, -pos ing.** disturb the self-possession of; make uneasy; bring into disorder.

dis con cert ed (dis′kən sėr′tid), *adj.* disturbed; confused.

dis con so late (dis kon′sə lit), *adj.* without hope; forlorn; unhappy; cheerless.

dis cord (dis′kôrd), *n.* **1.** difference of opinion; disputing; disagreement. **2.** harsh, clashing sounds. [< OF

dis course (*n.* dis′kôrs, dis′kōrs; *v.* dis kôrs′ or dis kōrs′), *n.*, *v.*, **-coursed, -cours ing.** —*n.* **1.** a formal speech or writing: *Lectures and sermons are discourses.* **2.** conversation; a talk. —*v.* **1.** speak or write formally. **2.** converse; talk. [< F *discours* < Med.L < L *discursus* < *dis-* in different directions + *currere* run]

dis par age ment (dis par′ij mənt), *n.* something that lowers a thing or person in worth or importance.

dis patch (dis pach′), *v.* **1.** send off to some place or for some purpose: *He dispatched a messenger to tell the king what had happened.* **2.** give the death blow to; kill. —*n.* **1.** a written message, such as special news or government business. **2.** a putting to death; a killing. Also, **despatch.** [< Ital. *dispacciare* hasten or Sp. *despachar*]

dis perse (dis pėrs′), *v.*, **-persed, -pers ing.** spread in different directions; scatter: *The crowd dispersed when the policeman came.*

dis place ment (dis plās′mənt), *n.* act of displacing.

dis po si tion (dis′pə zish′ən), *n.* **1.** habitual ways of acting toward others or of thinking about things; nature: *a cheerful disposition, a selfish disposition.* **2.** act of putting in order or position; arrangement: *the disposition of soldiers in battle.* **3.** disposal.

dis praise (dis prāz′), *v.*, **-praised, -prais ing,** express disapproval of; speak against; blame.

dis pro por tion ate (dis′prə pôr′shən it or dis′prə pōr′shən it), *adj.* out of proportion; lacking in proper proportion.

Dis rae li (diz rā′li), *n.* **Benjamin,** 1804-1881, Earl of Beaconsfield, English statesman and novelist, twice prime minister.

dis rep u ta ble (dis rep′ū tə bəl), *adj.* **1.** having a bad reputation. **2.** not respectable.

dis sem ble (di sem′bəl), *v.*, **-bled, -bling.** conceal one's motives, etc.; be a hypocrite. —**dis sem′bler,** *n.*

dis sim u la tion (di sim′ū lā′shən), *n.* act of dissembling; hypocrisy; pretense; deceit.

dis si pat ed (dis′ə pāt′id), *adj.* indulging too much in evil or foolish pleasures; dissolute.

dis so ci ate (di sō′shi āt), *v.*, **-at ed, -at ing.** break the connection or association with; separate: *When the honest man discovered that his companions were thieves he dissociated himself from them.*

dis so lute (dis′ə lüt), *adj.* living an evil life; very wicked; lewd; immoral.

dis tem per (dis tem′pər), *n.* **1.** sickness of the mind or body; disorder; disease. **2.** disturbance.

dis tend (dis tend′), *v.* stretch out; swell out; expand: *The balloon was distended to the bursting point.*

dis till (dis til′), *v.*, **-tilled, -till ing.** heat (a liquid or other substance) and condense the vapor given off. Water obtained by distilling dirty water is clean and pure because the steam given off contains no impurities.

dith y ramb (dith′ə ram or dith′ə ramb), *n.* **1.** a Greek choral song in honor of Dionysus. **2.** poem that is full of wild emotion, enthusiasm, etc. **3.** any speech or writing like this. [< L < Gk. *dithyrambos*]

< = from, taken from; cf., compare; dial., dialect; dim., diminutive; pp., past participle; ppr., present participle; pt., past tense; ult.. ultimately; var., variant; ?=possibly.

di verge (də vėrj′ or dī vėrj′), *v.*, **-verged, -verg ing.** move or lie in different directions from the same point; branch off: *Their paths diverged at the fork in the road.* [< LL *divergere* < *dis-* in different directions + *vergere* slope]
di vert (də vėrt′ or dī vėrt′), *v.* **1.** turn aside: *A ditch diverted water from the stream into the fields.* **2.** amuse; entertain: *Music diverted him after a hard day's work.* [< F *divertir* < L *divertere* < *dis-* aside + *vertere* turn]
div i dend (div′ə dend), *n.* **1.** money to be shared by those to whom it belongs. If a company makes a profit, it declares a dividend to the owners of the company. **2.** share of such money. [< L *dividendum* (thing) to be divided]
di vine (də vīn′), *v.*, **-vined, -vin ing.** find out or foretell by inspiration, by magic, or by guessing; predict. [< OF < L *divinus* of a deity < *divus* deity]
di vin i ty (də vin′ə ti), *n., pl.* **-ties.** study of God, religion, and divine things; theology.
doff (dof or dôf), *v.* take off; remove: *He doffed his hat as the flag passed by.* [contraction of *do off*]
dole ful (dōl′fəl), *adj.* sad; mournful; dreary; dismal. **—dole′ful ly,** *adv.*
Dolopes (dō lō′pās)
dol or ous (dol′ər əs or dō′lər əs), *adj.* mournful; sorrowful.
dom i cile (dom′ə səl or dom′ə sīl), *n.* house; home; residence.
dom i nant (dom′ə nənt), *adj.* **1.** most influential; controlling; ruling; governing. **2.** rising high above its surroundings; occupying a commanding position: *A dominant cliff rose at the bend of the river.*
do min ion (də min′yən), *n.* territory under the control of one ruler or government.
don (don), *v.*, **donned, don ning.** put on (clothing, etc.). [contraction of *do on*]
door jamb (dôr′jam′ or dōr′jam′), *n.* the upright piece forming the side of a doorway.
dos si er (dos′i ā or dos′i ər), *n.* collection of documents or papers about some subject. [< F]
dote (dōt), *v.*, **dot ed, dot ing.** **1.** be weak-minded and childish because of old age. **2. dote on** or **upon,** be foolishly fond of; be too fond of.
draft (draft or dräft), *n.* Usually, **draught. a.** act of drinking: *He emptied the glass at one draft.* **b.** amount taken in one drink.
dram (dram), *n.* **1.** a small weight. In apothecaries' weight, 8 drams make one ounce; in avoirdupois weight, 16 drams make one ounce. **2.** fluid dram.
draught (draft or dräft), *n., v., adj.* draft.
drawl (drôl), *n.* a slow, lazy way of talking. [apparently related to *draw*] **—drawl′er,** *n.*
dregs (dregz), *n.pl.* the most worthless part: *Thieves and murderers are the dregs of humanity.*
duc at (duk′ət), *n.* a gold or silver coin formerly used in some European countries. Its value varied, being at most about $2.30.
dun (dun), *n., adj.* dull, grayish brown. [OE *dunn,* ? < Celtic]
dupe (düp or dūp), *n., v.*, **duped, dup ing.** *—n.* person easily deceived or tricked. *—v.* deceive; trick. [< F < L *upupa* hoopoe (a bird)]
du ra tion (dü rā′shən or dū rā′shən), *n.* length of time; time during which anything continues.
du ress (dü res′, dū res′, dür′es, or dūr′es), *n.* compulsion. A person cannot be legally forced to fulfill a contract signed under duress.
durst (dėrst), *v.* a pt. of **dare.**
ec cen tric (ek sen′trik), *adj.* out of the ordinary; odd; peculiar.
ec cle si as tic (i klē′zi as′tik), *n.* clergyman.
e dict (ē′dikt), *n.* a public order or command by some authority; decree.
ef fect (ə fekt′), *n.* **1.** whatever is produced by a cause; something made to happen by a person or thing; result. **2.** power to produce results; force; validity. *—v.* produce as an effect; make happen; get done; bring about.
ef fec tu al (ə fek′chü əl), *adj.* producing the effect desired; capable of producing the effect desired: *Quinine is an effectual preventive of malaria.*
ef fem i nate (ə fem′ə nit), *adj.* lacking in manly qualities; showing weakness or delicacy that is not manly. [< L *effeminatus,* pp. of *effeminare* make a woman of < *ex-* + *femina* woman]
ef fete (i fēt′), *adj.* no longer able to produce; worn out; exhausted.
ef fi ca cy (ef′ə kə si), *n., pl.* **-cies.** power to produce a desired effect or result; effectiveness.
e go tism (ē′gə tiz əm or eg′ə tiz əm), *n.* **1.** excessive use of *I, my,* and *me;* habit of thinking, talking, or writing too much of oneself. **2.** self-conceit. **3.** selfishness. [< *ego* + *-t-* + *-ism*]
e jac u late (i jak′ū lāt), *v.*, **-lat ed, -lat ing.** say suddenly and briefly; exclaim.
e jac u la tion (i jak′ū lā′shən), *n.* something said suddenly and briefly; exclamation.
eke (ēk), *v.*, **eked, ek ing.** *Archaic* and *Dialect.* increase; enlarge; lengthen.
e late (i lāt′), *v.*, **e lat ed, e lat ing.** put in high spirits; make joyful or proud. [< L *elatus* < *ex-* out, away + *latus,* pp. to *ferre* carry]
e lic it (i lis′it), *v.* draw forth: *elicit a reply, elicit applause, elicit the truth.* [< L *elicitus,* pp. of *elicere* < *ex-* out + *lacere* entice]
el lipse (i lips′), *n.* oval having both ends alike.
el lip ti cal (i lip′tə kəl), *adj.* shaped like an ellipse; of an ellipse.
e lude (i lüd′), *v.*, **e lud ed, e lud ing.** **1.** slip away from; avoid or escape by cleverness, quickness, etc.: *The sly fox eluded the dogs.* **2.** escape discovery by; baffle: *The cause of cancer has eluded all research.* [< L *eludere* < *ex-* out + *ludere* play]
em bas sy (em′bə si), *n., pl.* **—sies.** a special errand; important mission; official message.
em bez zle ment (em bez′əl mənt), *n.* theft of money, securities, etc., entrusted to one's care.
e mit (i mit′), *v.*, **e mit ted, e mit ting.** give off; send out; discharge: *The sun emits light and heat. Volcanoes emit lava. The trapped lion emitted roars of rage.*
em pan el (em pan′əl), *v.*, **-eled, -el ing** or *esp. Brit.* **-elled, -el ling.** put on a list for duty on a jury.
em u late (em′ū lāt), *v.*, **-lat ed, -lat ing.** try to equal or excel: *The proverb tells us to emulate the industry of the ant.* [< L *aemulari* < *aemulus* striving to equal]
en am ored (en am′ərd), *adj.* **1.** very much in love, very fond; charmed: *The enamored prince gave up his throne to marry the beautiful peasant girl.* **2. enamored of,** in love with; very fond of; charmed by.
en camp (en kamp′), *v.* **1.** make a camp: *It took the soldiers only an hour to encamp.* **2.** stay in a camp: *They encamped all night.* **3.** put in a camp: *They were encamped in tents.* **—en camp′ment,** *n.*
en com pass (en kum′pəs), *v.* surround completely; shut in on all sides; encircle: *The atmosphere encompasses the earth.*

en cum ber (en kum′bər), *v.* **1.** hold back (from running, doing, etc.); hinder; hamper: *Heavy shoes encumber anybody in the water.* **2.** weigh down; burden: *The farm was encumbered with a heavy mortgage.*

en due (en dü′ or en dū′), *v.*, **-dued, -du ing.** provide with a quality or power; furnish; supply: *The wisest man is not endued with perfect wisdom.*

en gen der (en jen′dər), *v.* bring into existence; produce; cause: *Filth engenders disease.*

en join (en join′), *v.* order; direct; urge: *Parents enjoin good behavior on their children.*

en mi ty (en′mə ti), *n.*, *pl.* **-ties.** the feeling that enemies have for each other; hate.

en nui (än′wē), *n.* a feeling of weariness and discontent from lack of occupation or interest; boredom.

en sure (en shür′), *v.*, **-sured, -sur ing.** make sure or certain: *Careful planning and hard work ensured the success of the party.*

en trails (en′trālz or en′trəlz), *n.pl.* the inner parts of a man or animal.

en treat (en trēt′), *v.* ask earnestly; beg and pray; implore: *The captives entreated the savages not to kill them.*

en treat y (en trēt′i), *n.*, *pl.* **-treat ies.** an earnest request; prayer: *The savages paid no attention to their captives' entreaties for mercy.*

en try (en′tri), *n.*, *pl.* **-tries.** thing written or printed in a book, list, etc. Each word explained in a dictionary is an entry.

en vi ron (en vī′rən), *v.* surround; enclose. [< OF *environner* < *environ* around < *en-* in (< L *in-*) + *viron* circle]

ep i thet (ep′ə thet), *n.* a descriptive expression; adjective or noun, or even a clause, expressing some quality or attribute: *In "crafty Ulysses" and "Richard the Lion-Hearted" the epithets are "crafty" and "the Lion-Hearted."*

ep och (ep′ək; *esp. Brit.* ē′pok), *n.* **1.** period of time; era. **2.** period of time in which striking things happened.

e quiv a lent (i kwiv′ə lənt), *adj.* equal in value, measure, force, effect, meaning, etc.: *Nodding your head is equivalent to saying yes.* —*n.* something equivalent.

er ro ne ous (ə rō′ni əs), *adj.* wrong; mistaken; incorrect: *the erroneous belief that the earth is flat.*

erst (ėrst), *adv. Archaic.* formerly; long ago.

erst while (ėrst′hwīl′), *adj. Archaic.* former; past.

es carp ment (es kärp′mənt), *n.* a steep slope; cliff.

es cutch eon (es kuch′ən), *n.* **blot on the escutcheon,** disgrace to honor or reputation.

es sence (es′əns), *n.* that which makes a thing what it is; necessary part or parts; important feature or features: *Kindness is the essence of politeness.*

es teem (es tēm′), *v.* have a very favorable opinion of; regard highly: *We esteem courage.* —*n.* a very favorable opinion; high regard: *Courage is held in esteem.*

eu ca lyp tus (ū′kə lip′təs), *n.*, *pl.* **-tus es, -ti** (-tī). a very tall tree that grows in Australia and elsewhere. It is valued for its timber and for an oil made from its leaves.

ev a nesce (ev′ə nes′), *v.*, **-nesced, -nes cing.** disappear gradually; fade away; vanish. [< L *ēvanescere* < *ex-* out + *vanescere* vanish < *vanus* insubstantial]

e ven tide (ē′vən tīd′), *n. Poetic.* evening.

e vince (i vins′), *v.*, **e vinced, e vinc ing.** show that one has (a quality, trait, etc.). [< L *evincere* < *ex-* out + *vincere* conquer]

e voke (i vōk′), *v.*, **e voked, e vok ing.** call forth; bring out: *A good joke evokes a laugh.* [< L *evocare* < *ex-* out + *vocare* call]

ev o lu tion (ev′ə lü′shən), *n.* theory that all living things developed from a few simple forms of life or from a single form.

ew er (ū′ər), *n.* a wide-mouthed water pitcher: *The ewer and basin are on the washstand.*

ex act (eg zakt′), *v.* demand and get; force to be paid: *If he does the work, he can exact payment for it.*

ex e cra tion (ek′sə krā′shən), *n.* a curse: *The mob shouted angry execrations.*

ex em pla ry (eg zem′plə ri or eg′zəm pler′i), *adj.* **1.** worth imitating; being a good model or pattern: *exemplary conduct.* **2.** serving as an example; typical.

ex em pli fy (eg zem′plə fī), *v.*, **-fied, -fy ing.** show by example; be an example of: *The knights exemplified courage and courtesy.*

ex or cise (ek′sôr sīz), *v.*, **-cised, -cis ing.** drive out (an evil spirit) by prayers, ceremonies, etc.

ex or di um (eg zôr′di əm or ek sôr′di əm), *n.*, *pl.* **-di ums, -di a** (-di ə). the beginning.

ex pe di ent (eks pē′di ənt), *adj.* fit for bringing about a desired result; desirable or suitable under the circumstances. [< L *expediens, -entis,* ppr. of *expedire* to free from a net, set right < *ex-* out + *pes* foot]

ex pe di tious (eks′pə dish′əs), *adj.* quick; speedy; efficient and prompt. —**ex′pe di′tious ly,** *adv.*

ex pi a tion (eks′pi ā′shən), *n.* a making amends for a wrong, sin, etc.; atonement: *He made a public apology in expiation of his error.*

ex pi a to ry (eks′pi ə tô′ri or eks′pi ə tō′ri), *adj.* intended to expiate; expiating; atoning.

ex plic it (eks plis′it), *adj.* clearly expressed; distinctly stated; definite: *He gave such explicit directions that everyone understood them.* [< L *explicitus,* pp. of *explicare* unfold, explain < *ex-* un- + *plicare* fold]

ex pound (eks pound′), *v.* **1.** make clear; explain; interpret. **2.** set forth or state in detail.

ex qui site (eks′kwi zit or eks kwiz′it), *adj.* **1.** very lovely; delicate: *Those violets are exquisite flowers.* **2.** of highest excellence; most admirable: *She has exquisite taste and manners.*

ex tant (eks′tənt or eks tant′), *adj.* still in existence: *Some of Washington's letters are extant.*

ex tem po rize (eks tem′pə rīz), *v.*, **-rized, -riz ing.** compose offhand; make for the occasion: *The campers extemporized a shelter for the night.*

ex ten u ate (eks ten′ū āt), *v.*, **-at ed, -at ing.** make (guilt, a fault, offense, etc.) seem less; excuse in part: *His foreign bringing-up extenuates his faulty pronunciation.*

ex trac tion (eks trak′shən), *n.* descent; origin.

fa bled (fā′bəld), *adj.* told about in fables, legends, or myths.

fac et (fas′it), *n.* aspect; phase.

fa cil i tate (fə sil′ə tāt), *v.*, **-tat ed, -tat ing.** make easy; lessen the labor of; help forward; assist: *A vacuum cleaner facilitates my housework.*

fa cil i ty (fə sil′ə ti), *n.*, *pl.* **-ties. 1.** power to do anything easily, quickly, and smoothly. **2.** something that makes an action easy; aid; convenience: *Ropes, swings, and sand piles are facilities for play.*

fag got (fag′ət), *n.*, *v. Esp. Brit.* fagot.

fag ot (fag′ət), *n.* bundle of sticks or twigs tied together: *He built the fire with fagots.*

faille (fīl or fāl), *n.* a soft, ribbed silk or rayon cloth.

fal la cious (fə lā′shəs), *adj.* **1.** deceptive; misleading. **2.** logically unsound; erroneous: *It is fallacious reasoning to base a general rule on just two or three instances.*

< = from, taken from; cf., compare; dial., dialect; dim., diminutive; pp., past participle; ppr., present participle; pt., past tense; ult., ultimately; var., variant; ?=possibly.

fare (fãr), *v.*, **fared, far ing.** **1.** get along; do: *If you fare well, you have good luck or success.* **2.** turn out; happen: *It will fare hard with the thief if he is caught.*
far ri er (far′i ər), *n. Esp. Brit.* **1.** blacksmith who shoes horses. **2.** a horse doctor; veterinarian.
fath om a ble (faᴛʜ′əm ə bəl), *adj.* that can be measured.
fawn (fôn), *v.* **1.** cringe and bow; act slavishly: *Many flattering relatives fawned on the rich old man.* **2.** of dogs, etc., show fondness by crouching, wagging the tail, licking the hand, etc.
feck less (fek′lis), *adj.* futile; ineffective.
feign (fān), *v.* put on a false appearance of; make believe; pretend: *Some animals feign death when in danger.*
fell (fel), *adj.* cruel; fierce; terrible: *a fell blow.*
fel on (fel′ən), *n.* person who has committed a serious crime; criminal: *Murderers and thieves are felons.*
fer ret (fer′it), *v.* hunt; search: *The detectives ferreted out the criminal.*
fi as co (fi as′kō), *n., pl.* **-cos** or **-coes.** failure; breakdown.
fie (fī), *interj.* for shame! shame! [< OF]
fil a ment (fil′ə mənt), *n.* a very fine thread; very slender, threadlike part.
fi nesse (fə nes′), *n.* **1.** delicacy of execution; skill: *That artist shows wonderful finesse.* **2.** the skillful handling of a delicate situation to one's advantage; craft; stratagem: *A shrewd diplomat must be a master of finesse.*
fi nite (fī′nīt), *adj.* having limits or bounds; not infinite: *Death ends man's finite existence.*
fis sion (fish′ən), *n.* the splitting that occurs when the nucleus of an atom under bombardment absorbs a neutron. Nuclear fission releases tremendous amounts of energy when heavy elements, especially plutonium and uranium, are involved.
flam beau (flam′bō), *n., pl.* **-beaux** (-bōz) or **-beaus.** a flaming torch.
flank (flangk), *n.* **1.** side of an animal or person between the ribs and the hip. **2.** the far right or left side of an army, fleet, etc.
foal (fōl), *v.* give birth to (a foal). [OE *fola*]
foi ble (foi′bəl), *n.* a weak point; weakness: *Talking too much is one of her foibles.*
for ay (fôr′ā or for′ā), *n.* a raid for plunder.
for bear[1] (fôr bãr′), *v.,* **-bore, -borne, -bear ing.** **1.** hold back; keep from doing, saying, using, etc.: *The boy forbore to hit back because the other boy was smaller.* **2.** be patient; control oneself. [OE *forberan*]
fore close (fôr klōz′ or fōr klōz′), *v.,* **-closed, -clos ing.** take away the right to redeem (a mortgage). When the conditions of a mortgage are not met, the holder can foreclose and have the property sold to satisfy his claim.
fore most (fôr′mōst or fōr′mōst), *adj.* **1.** first. **2.** chief; leading; most notable.
fore or dain (fôr′ôr dān′ or fōr′ôr dān′), *v.* ordain beforehand; predestine.
forge (fôrj or fōrj), *n., v.,* **forged, forg ing.** —*n.* place with fire where metal is heated very hot and then hammered into shape. A blacksmith uses a forge. —*v.* make or write (something false).
for ger y (fôr′jər i or fōr′jər i), *n., pl.* **-ger ies.** something made or written falsely to deceive.
form (fôrm), *n. Brit.* grade in school.
for sooth (fôr süth′), *adv. Archaic.* in truth; indeed.
for swear (fôr swãr′), *v.,* **-swore, -sworn, -swear ing.** renounce on oath; swear or promise solemnly to give up.

forte (fôrt or fōrt), *n.* something a person does very well; strong point: *Cooking is her forte.*
fort night (fôrt′nīt or fôrt′nit), *n.* two weeks.
foy er (foi′ər or foi′ā), *n.* an entrance hall.
Fran cis can (fran sis′kən), *n.* member of a religious order founded by Saint Francis in 1209.
fra ter nal (frə tėr′nəl), *adj.* **1.** brotherly. **2.** having to do with a fraternal order.
fraught (frôt), *adj.* loaded; filled: *A battlefield is fraught with horror.*
fray (frā), *n.* a noisy quarrel; fight. [var. of *affray*]
free lance, writer, artist, etc., who sells his work to anyone who will buy it.
fri ar (frī′ər), *n.* member of certain religious orders of the Roman Catholic Church.
friv o lous (friv′ə ləs), *adj.* lacking in seriousness or sense; silly: *Frivolous behavior is out of place in church.* [< L *frivolus*] —**friv′o lous ly,** *adv.*
frond (frond), *n.* a divided leaf of a fern, palm, etc.
fru gal (frü′gəl), *adj.* **1.** avoiding waste; saving; tending to avoid unnecessary spending: *A frugal housekeeper buys and uses food carefully.* **2.** costing little; barely sufficient: *He ate a frugal supper of bread and milk.* [< L *frugalis* < *frugi* temperate]

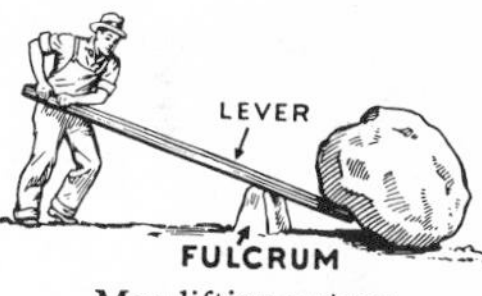

Man lifting a stone with a lever

ful crum (ful′krəm), *n., pl.* **-crums, -cra** (-krə). support on which a lever turns or is supported in moving or lifting something.
func tion ar y (fungk′shən er′i), *n., pl.* **-ar ies,** *adj.* official.
fur tive (fėr′tiv), *adj.* **1.** done stealthily; secret: *a furtive glance into the forbidden room.* **2.** sly; stealthy; shifty: *The thief had a furtive manner.* [< L *furtivus* < *fur* thief] —**fur′tive ly,** *adv.* —**fur′tive ness,** *n.*

Gabelle, Thé ophile (gə bel′ tā′ō fēl′)
gad (gad), *v.,* **gad ded, gad ding.** move about restlessly; go about looking for pleasure or excitement.
gai ter (gā′tər), *n.* a covering for the lower leg or ankle, made of cloth, leather, etc.
gall (gôl), *n.* **1.** a bitter, yellow, brown, or greenish liquid secreted by the liver and stored in the gall bladder; bile of animals. **2.** gall bladder. **3.** anything very bitter or harsh.
gam ut (gam′ət), *n.* the entire range of anything: *In one minute I ran the gamut of feeling from hope to despair.*
gan net (gan′it), *n.* a large, fish-eating sea bird somewhat like a pelican, but with long, pointed wings and a shorter tail.
gaol er (jāl′ər), *n. Brit.* jailer.
gape (gāp or gap), *n. zool.* the width of the open mouth.
gar ble (gär′bəl), *v.,* **-bled, -bling.** make unfair or misleading selections from (facts, statements, writings, etc.); omit parts of, often in order to misrepresent: *Foreign newspapers gave a garbled account of the President's speech.*
gar goyle (gär′goil), *n.* spout for carrying off rain water, ending in a grotesque head that projects from the gutter of a building.

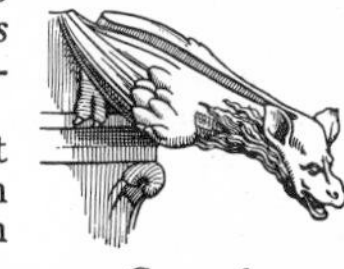
Gargoyle

gar ish (gãr′ish), *adj.* unpleasantly bright; glaring; showy; gaudy.

gar ru lous (gar′ə ləs or gar′ū ləs), *adj.* **1.** talking too much about trifles. **2.** using too many words.
gaunt (gônt or gänt), *adj.* very thin and bony; with hollow eyes and a starved look; *Hunger and suffering make people gaunt.*
Gem i ni (jem′ə nī), *n.pl.* **1.** a northern constellation in the zodiac containing two bright stars. **2.** the third sign of the zodiac. The sun enters Gemini about May 21.
gen der (jen′dər), *n.* **1.** in many languages, the grouping of nouns into a series of classes, such as masculine, feminine, neuter, etc. **2.** *Informal.* sex. [< OF *gendre* < L *genus* kind, sort]
ges tic u la tion (jes tik′ū lā′shən), *n.* gesture.
Gi bral tar (jə brôl′tər), *n.* seaport and fortress on a high rock at the southern tip of Spain.
gin seng (jin′seng), *n.* a low plant with a thick, branched root.
gird (gėrd), *v.,* **girt** or **gird ed, gird ing.** put a belt or girdle around.
glean (glēn), *v.* gather little by little or slowly.
glow er (glou′ər), *v.* stare angrily; scowl.
glut ton ous (glut′n əs), *adj.* greedy about food; having the habit of eating too much.
glyc er in (glis′ər in), *n.* a colorless, syrupy, sweet liquid obtained from fats and oils, used in ointments, lotions, antifreeze solutions, and explosives.
graft[1] (graft or gräft), *v.* transfer (a piece of skin, bone, etc.) from one part of the body to another so that it will grow there permanently.
graft[2] (graft or gräft), *U.S.* —*n.* **1.** method of getting money dishonestly. **2.** money dishonestly taken or obtained.
Gram o phone (gram′ə fōn), *n.* *Trademark* type of sound-recording machine.
graph ic (graf′ik), *adj.* lifelike; vivid.
graph ite (graf′īt), *n.* a soft, black form of carbon with a metallic luster, used for lead in pencils, for lubricating machinery, etc.
grap ple (grap′əl), *v.,* **-pled, -pling,** *v.* **1.** seize and hold fast; grip or hold firmly. **2.** struggle; fight.
grease wood (grēs′wu̇d′), *n.* a stiff, prickly shrub with narrow leaves, growing in alkaline regions in the W United States. [Am.E]
gre gar i ous (grə gãr′i əs), *adj.* **1.** living in flocks, herds, or other groups: *Sheep and cattle are gregarious.* **2.** of or having to do with a flock or crowd.
griz zled (griz′əld), *adj.* **1.** grayish; gray. **2.** gray-haired.
groin (groin), *n.* the hollow on either side of the body where the thigh joins the abdomen.
gross (grōs), *adj.* **1.** very bad; easy to see: *She makes gross errors in pronouncing words.* **2.** coarse; vulgar: *Her manners are too gross for a lady.* —**gross′ly,** *adv.*
gro tesque (grō tesk′), *adj.* odd or unnatural in shape, appearance, manner, etc.; fantastic; queer.
grov el (gruv′əl or grov′əl), *v.,* **-eled, -el ing** or *esp. Brit.* **-elled, -el ling.** lie face downward, crawl at someone's feet; humble oneself.
guile (gīl), *n.* crafty deceit; craftiness; sly tricks.
guin ea (gin′i), *n.* a former English gold coin worth 21 shillings, so-called because originally made of gold from Guinea.
gum bo (gum′bō), *n.* **1.** a heavy sticky mud. **2.** something notably sticky or gummy. **3** mixture.
gy ra tion (jī rā′shən), *n.* circular or spiral motion; whirling; rotation.
gyve (jīv), *n., v.,* **gyved, gyv ing.** fetter; shackle, especially for the leg.
hack ney (hak′ni), *n., pl.* **-neys,** *adj., v.,* **-neyed, -ney ing.** —*adj.* hired; let out, employed, or done for hire.
hack neyed (hak′nid), *adj.* used too often; commonplace: *"White as snow" is a hackneyed comparison.*
hap less (hap′lis), *adj.* unlucky; unfortunate.
har bor (här′bər), *v.* keep or nourish in the mind.
hard hack (härd′hak′), *n.* shrub of the rose family with clusters of small pink, purple, or white flowers and woolly leaves and branches.
hare lip (hãr′lip′), *n.* deformity caused when parts of the lip fail to grow together before birth. —**hare′-lipped′,** *adj.*
Har vard (här′vərd), *n.* university for men in Cambridge, Massachusetts. Harvard College was founded in 1636 and is the oldest college in the United States.
hasp (hasp or häsp), *n.* clasp or fastening for a door, window, trunk, box, etc.; especially, a hinged metal clasp that fits over a staple or into a hole and is fastened by a peg, padlock, etc. [var. of OE *hæpse*]
hav er sack (hav′ər sak), *n.* bag used by soldiers and hikers to carry food.
he ma tox ic (hē mə tok′sik), *adj.* **1.** pertaining to or causing blood poisoning. **2.** destructive to red blood corpuscles.
hem lock (hem′lok), *n.* **1.** *Esp. Brit.* a poisonous plant with spotted stems, finely divided leaves, and small white flowers. It belongs to the same family as the carrot. **2.** poison made from it.
her ald (her′əld), *n.* **1.** person who carries messages and makes announcements; messenger. *Herald* is often used as the name of a newspaper. **2.** forerunner; harbinger: *Dawn is the herald of day.* —*v.* bring news of; announce.
he red i tar y (hə red′ə ter′i), *adj.* **1.** coming by inheritance: *"Prince" is a hereditary title.* **2.** transmitted or caused by heredity: *Color blindness is hereditary.*
her e sy (her′ə si), *n., pl.* **-sies.** belief different from the accepted belief of a church, school, profession, etc.
her pe tol o gy (hėr′pə tol′ə ji), *n.* branch of zoology dealing with reptiles. [< Gk. *herpeton* reptile (< *herpein* creep) + E *-logy*]
hew (hū), *v.,* **hewed, hewed** or **hewn, hew ing.** cut with an ax, sword, etc.: *He hewed down the tree.*
hi a tus (hī ā′təs), *n., pl.* **-tus es** or **-tus.** an empty space; gap; space that needs to be filled.
hie (hī), *v.,* **hied, hie ing** or **hy ing.** hasten; go quickly. [OE *hīgian*]
hind (hīnd), *n.* *Archaic* or *Brit. Dialect.* **1.** a farm worker. **2.** peasant.
hire ling (hīr′ling), *n.* **1.** person who works only for money, without interest or pride in the task. **2.** person hired to do whatever another orders him to do.
hoar frost (hôr′frôst′, hōr′frôst′, hôr′frost′, or hōr′frost′), *n.* white frost.
ho mo ge ne ous (hō′mə jē′ni əs, hō′mə jēn′yəs, hom′ə jē′ni əs, or hom′ə jēn′yəs), *adj.* composed of similar elements or parts. [< Med.L < Gk. *homogenes* < *homos* same + *genos* kind]
hone (hōn), *n., v.,* **honed, hon ing.** —*n.* a fine-grained whetstone on which to sharpen cutting tools, especially razors. —*v.* sharpen on a hone.
hop vine (hop′vīn), *n.* the hop, a twining vine whose cones, "hops," are used to flavor malt liquor and in medicines.
host[1] (hōst), *n.* person who receives another at his house as his guest.

< = from, taken from; cf., compare; dial., dialect; dim., diminutive; pp., past participle; ppr., present participle; pt., past tense; ult., ultimately; var., variant; ?=possibly.

host² (hōst), *n.* a large number; multitude: *As it grew dark, a few stars appeared, then a host.*

hov el (huv′əl or hov′əl), *n.* house that is small, mean, and unpleasant to live in.

hu mane (hū mān′), *adj.* kind; merciful; not cruel or brutal.

hus band ry (huz′bənd ri), *n.* careful management; thrift.

hus sar (hu̇ zär′), *n.* a European light-armed cavalry soldier.

hutch (huch), *n.* **1.** hut. **2.** box; chest; bin.

hy dra (hī′drə), *n., pl.* **-dras, -drae** (-drē). **1. Hydra,** in Greek mythology, a monstrous serpent having nine heads, each of which was replaced by two heads after being cut off unless the wound was cauterized. The Hydra was slain by Hercules. **2.** any persistent evil.

hy dro pho bi a (hī′drə fō′bi ə), *n.* an infectious disease of dogs and other flesh-eating mammals that causes convulsions, frothing at the mouth, and madness; rabies.

i bis (ī′bis), *n., pl.* **i bis es** or (*esp. collectively*) **i bis.** a long-legged wading bird like a heron. The ancient Egyptians regarded the ibis as sacred. [< L < Gk. < Egyptian]

Ibis (about 3½ ft. long)

i dol a try (ī dol′ə tri), *n., pl.* **-tries.** **1.** worship of idols. **2.** worship of a person or thing; great love or admiration; extreme devotion.

ill-fat ed (il′fāt′id), *adj.* sure to have a bad fate or end.

il lus tri ous (i lus′tri əs), *adj.* very famous; great; outstanding: *Washington and Lincoln are illustrious Americans.* [< L *illustris* lighted up, bright] **—il lus′tri ous ly,** *adv.* **—il lus′tri ous ness,** *n.*

im bue (im bū′), *v.,* **-bued, -bu ing.** fill; inspire: *He imbued his son's mind with the ambition to succeed.*

im mac u late (i mak′ū lit), *adj.* **1.** without a spot or stain; absolutely clean. **2.** without sin; pure.

im meas ur a ble (i mezh′ər ə bəl or i māzh′ər ə bəl), *adj.* too vast to be measured; boundless.

im mi nent (im′ə nənt), *adj.* likely to happen soon; about to occur: *The black clouds, thunder, and lightning show that a storm is imminent.* [< L *imminens, -entis,* ppr. of *imminere* overhang] **—im′mi nent ly,** *adv.*

im mod er ate (i mod′ər it), *adj.* not moderate; too much; going too far; extreme; more than is right.

im mo late (im′ə lāt), *v.,* **-lat ed, -lat ing.** **1.** kill as a sacrifice. **2.** sacrifice.

im pale (im pāl′), *v.,* **-paled, -pal ing.** **1.** pierce through with anything pointed; fasten upon anything pointed: *The butterflies were impaled on pins stuck in a sheet of cork.* **2.** torture or punish by thrusting upon a pointed stake.

im part (im pärt′), *v.* **1.** give a share in; give: *The furnishings imparted an air of elegance to the room.* **2.** communicate; tell: *I will impart a secret to you.*

im peach (im pēch′), *v.* **1.** call in question: *impeach a person's honor or accuracy.* **2.** charge with wrongdoing; accuse.

im pe cu ni ous (im′pi kū′ni əs), *adj.* having little or no money; penniless; poor.

im ped i ment (im ped′ə mənt), *n.* hindrance; obstruction.

im pend ing (im pen′ding), *adj.* likely to happen soon; threatening; about to occur.

im per cep ti ble (im′pər sep′tə bəl), *adj.* **1.** very slight; gradual. **2.** that cannot be perceived or felt.

im per il (im per′əl), *v.,* **-iled, -il ing** or *esp. Brit.* **-illed, -il ling.** put in danger.

im pe ri ous (im pēr′i əs), *adj.* haughty; arrogant; domineering; overbearing.

im per turb a ble (im′pər tėr′bə bəl), *adj.* not capable of being excited or disturbed.

im pet u ous (im pech′ü əs), *adj.* acting hastily, rashly, or with sudden feeling.

im pi e ty (im pī′ə ti), *n., pl.* **-ties.** **1.** lack of piety or reverence for God; wickedness. **2.** lack of dutifulness or respect. **3.** an impious act.

im pinge (im pinj′), *v.,* **-pinged, -ping ing.** hit; strike: *Rays of light impinge on the eye.*

im pi ous (im′pi əs), *adj.* not pious; not having or not showing reverence for God; wicked; profane.

im pla ca ble (im plā′kə bəl or im plak′ə bəl), *adj.* that cannot be placated, pacified, or appeased; relentless. **—im pla′ca bly,** *adv.*

im ply (im plī′), *v.,* **-plied, -ply ing.** indicate without saying outright; express indirectly; suggest: *Silence often implies consent.*

im pon der a ble (im pon′dər ə bəl), *adj.* without weight that can be felt or measured: *Faith and love are imponderable forces.* —*n.* something imponderable.

im port (*v.* im pôrt′, im pōrt′, im′pôrt, or im′pōrt; *n.* im′pôrt or im′pōrt), *v.* mean; signify: *Tell me what your remark imports*—*n.* **1.** meaning: *What is the import of your remark?* **2.** importance. [< L *importare* < *in-* in + *portare* carry]

im por tune (im′pôr tün′, im′pôr tūn′, or im pôr′chən), *v.,* **-tuned, -tun ing.** ask urgently or repeatedly; trouble with demands.

im pos ture (im pos′chər), *n.* deception; fraud.

im pru dence (im prü′dəns), *n.* lack of prudence; imprudent behavior.

im pru dent (im prü′dənt), *adj.* not prudent; rash; not discreet. **—im pru′dent ly,** *adv.*

im pu ni ty (im pū′nə ti), *n.* freedom from punishment, injury, or other bad consequences: *If laws are not enforced, crimes are committed with impunity.*

im pute (im pūt′), *v.,* **-put ed, -put ing.** consider as belonging; attribute; charge (a fault, etc.) to a person; blame: *I impute his failure to laziness.*

in ad vert ent (in′əd vėr′tənt), *adj.* not done on purpose; caused by oversight. **—in′ad vert′ent ly,** *adv.*

in an i mate (in an′ə mit), *adj.* lifeless.

in aus pi cious (in′ôs pish′əs), *adj.* with signs of failure; unfavorable; unlucky.

in cep tion (in sep′shən), *n.* a beginning; commencement. [< L *inceptio, -onis* < *incipere* begin < *in-* on + *capere* take]

in cite (in sīt′), *v.,* **-cit ed, -cit ing.** urge on; stir up; rouse. [< L *incitare,* ult. < *in-* on + *ciere* cause to move] **—in cit′er,** *n.*

in clem ent (in klem′ənt), *adj.* **1.** rough; stormy. **2.** severe; harsh: *an inclement ruler.*

in cli na tion (in′klə nā′shən), *n.* **1.** tendency: *an inclination to become fat.* **2.** preference; liking: *a strong inclination for sports.* **3.** slope; slant: *the inclination of a roof.*

in cog ni zant (in kog′nə zənt), *adj.* not cognizant; unaware or unconscious;—with *of.*

in co her ence (in′kō hēr′əns), *n.* **1.** lack of logical connection. **2.** disconnected thought or speech.

in co her en cy (in′kō hēr′ən si), *n., pl.* **-cies.** incoherence.

---

hat, āge, cãre, fär; let, ēqual, tėrm; it, īce; hot, ōpen, ôrder; oil, out; cup, pu̇t, rüle, ūse; th, thin; ᴛʜ, then; zh, measure; ə represents *a* in about, *e* in taken, *i* in pencil, *o* in lemon, *u* in circus.

in com mode (in′kə mōd′), *v.*, **-mod ed, -mod ing.** inconvenience; trouble. [<L *incommodare* < *incommodus* < *in-* not + *commodus* convenient]

in com mo di ous (in′kə mō′di əs), *adj.* **1.** not roomy enough. **2.** inconvenient; uncomfortable.

in con stant (in kon′stənt), *adj.* not constant; changeable; fickle. **—in con′stant ly,** *adv.*

in con ti nent (in kon′tə nənt), *adj.* without self-restraint. [< L *incontinens, -entis*]

in cor po rate (in kôr′pə rāt), *v.*, **-rat ed, -rat ing.** **1.** make (something) a part of something else; join or combine (something) with something else: *We will incorporate your suggestion in this new plan.* **2.** unite or combine so as to form one body.

in cum bent (in kum′bənt), *adj.* resting (on a person) as a duty: *She felt it incumbent upon her to answer the letter at once.*

in cum brance (in kum′brans), *n.* encumbrance.

in cur (in kėr′), *v.*, **-curred, -cur ring.** run or fall into (something unpleasant); bring (blame, punishment, danger, etc.) on oneself.

in dict ment (in dīt′mənt), *n.* a formal accusation; especially, the legal accusation presented by a grand jury.

in dis crim i nate (in′dis krim′ə nit), *adj.* not discriminating; with no feeling for differences: *He is an indiscriminate reader and likes both good books and bad ones.* **—in′dis crim′i nate ly,** *adv.*

in do lent (in′də lənt), *adj.* lazy; disliking work.

in ef fa ble (in ef′ə bəl), *adj.* not to be expressed in words; too great to be described in words.

in es ti ma ble (in es′tə mə bəl), *adj.* too good, great, valuable, etc., to be measured or estimated.

in ex o ra ble (in ek′sə rə bəl), *adj.* relentless; unyielding; not influenced by prayers or entreaties: *The forces of nature are inexorable.*

in ex tri ca ble (in eks′trə kə bəl), *adj.* that cannot be disentangled or solved. [< L *inextricabilis*]

in fal li bil i ty (in fal′ə bil′ə ti), *n.* absolute freedom from error.

in fa mous (in′fə məs), *adj.* **1.** deserving or causing a very bad reputation; shamefully bad; extremely wicked. **2.** having a very bad reputation; in public disgrace: *A traitor's name is infamous.*

in fa my (in′fə mi), *n., pl.* **-mies.** **1.** very bad reputation; public disgrace: *Traitors are held in infamy.* **2.** shameful badness; extreme wickedness.

in fer (in fėr′), *v.*, **-ferred, -fer ring.** find out by reasoning; conclude.

in fi del (in′fə dəl), *n.* **1.** person who does not believe in religion. **2.** person who does not accept a particular faith. Mohammedans call Christians infidels. **3.** person who does not accept Christianity.

in firm (in fėrm′), *adj.* **1.** weak; feeble. **2.** not firm; not stable.

in frac tion (in frak′shən), *n.* a breaking of a law or obligation; violation.

in fuse (in fūz′), *v.*, **-fused, -fus ing.** **1.** pour in; put in: *The captain infused his own courage into his soldiers.* **2.** inspire.

in ge nu i ty (in′jə nü′ə ti or in′jə nū′ə ti), *n., pl.* **-ties.** skill in planning, inventing, etc.; cleverness.

in grained (in grānd′ or in′grānd′), *adj.* deeply and firmly fixed; thoroughly imbued: *ingrained honesty.*

in her ent ly (in hēr′ənt li or in her′ənt li), *adv.* by its own nature; essentially.

in iq ui ty (in ik′wə ti), *n., pl.* **-ties.** a wicked or unjust act.

in no va tion (in′ə vā′shən), *n.* **1.** change made in the established way of doing things. **2.** making changes; bringing in new things or new ways of doing things.

in quis i tive (in kwiz′ə tiv), *adj.* curious; asking many questions. **—in quis′i tive ly,** *adv.*

in scru ta bil i ty (in skrü′tə bil′ə ti), *n.* a being inscrutable.

in scru ta ble (in skrü′tə bəl), *adj.* that cannot be understood; so mysterious or obscure that one cannot make out its meaning; incomprehensible.

in sen sate (in sen′sāt or in sen′sit), *adj.* unfeeling: *insensate cruelty.*

in sen si ble (in sen′sə bəl), *adj.* not able to feel anything; unconscious.

in sin u a tion (in sin′ū ā′shən), *n.* an indirect suggestion against someone.

in so lence (in′sə ləns), *n.* bold rudeness; insulting behavior or speech.

in so lent (in′sə lənt), *adj.* boldly rude; insulting.

in stinct (in′stingkt), *n.* natural feeling, knowledge, or power, such as guides animals; unlearned tendency: *An instinct leads birds to fly.*

in stinc tive (in stingk′tiv), *adj.* of or having to do with instinct; caused or done by instinct; born in an animal or person, not learned.

in te grate (in′tə grāt), *v.*, **-grat ed, -grat ing.** bring together (parts) into a whole.

in ten si fy (in ten′sə fī), *v.*, **-fied, -fy ing.** make or become intense or more intense; strengthen; increase.

in tent (in tent′), *adj.* very attentive; having the eyes or thoughts earnestly fixed on something; earnest: *an intent look.*

in ter cede (in′tər sēd′), *v.*, **-ced ed, -ced ing.** plead or beg in another's behalf: *Friends of the condemned man interceded with the governor for a pardon.*

in ter ces sion (in′tər sesh′ən), *n.* act or fact of interceding.

in ter change (in′tər chānj′), *n.*, a giving and taking; exchanging.

in ter course (in′tər kôrs or in′tər kōrs), *n.* communication; dealings between people; exchange of thoughts, services, feelings, etc.: *Airplanes, good roads, and telephones make intercourse with different parts of the country far easier than it was 50 years ago.*

in ter de pend ent (in′tər di pen′dənt), *adj.* dependent each upon the other.

in ter ga lac tic (in tər gə lak′tik), *adj.* situated or taking place in the vast spaces between galaxies.

in ter im (in′tər im), *n.* meantime; time between. *—adj.* for the meantime; temporary. [< L *interim* in the meantime < *inter* between]

in ter lace (in′tər lās′), *v.*, **-laced, -lac ing.** cross over and under each other; weave together; intertwine: *Baskets are made by interlacing reeds or fibers.*

in ter ment (in tėr′mənt), *n.* act of putting a dead body into a grave or tomb; burial.

in ter pose (in′tər pōz′), *v.*, **-posed, -pos ing.** interfere in order to help; intervene.

in ter po si tion (in′tər pə zish′ən), *n.* an interposing.

in ter stel lar (in′tər stel′ər), *adj.* among the stars.

in ti ma tion (in′tə mā′shən), *n.* indirect suggestion; hint: *A frown is often an intimation of disapproval.*

in to na tion (in′tō nā′shən or in′tə nā′shən), *n.* manner of sounding words.

in tro spec tion (in′trə spek′shən), *n.* examination of one's own thoughts and feelings. [< L *introspectus,* pp. of *introspicere* < *intro-* into + *specere* look]

< = from, taken from; cf., compare; dial., dialect; dim., diminutive; pp., past participle; ppr., present participle; pt., past tense; ult., ultimately; var., variant; ?=possibly.

in tu i tion (in′tü ish′ən or in′tū ish′ən), *n.* perception of truths, facts, etc., without reasoning: *By experience with all kinds of people Mr. Jones had developed great powers of intuition.* [< LL *intuitio, -onis* a gazing at < L *intueri* < *in-* at + *tueri* look]

in un da tion (in′un dā′shən), *n.* an overflowing; flood.

in val u a ble (in val′ū ə bəl or in val′ū bəl), *adj.* priceless; very precious; valuable beyond measure. **—in val′u a bly,** *adv.*

in vest (in vest′), *v.* **1.** use (money) to buy something that is expected to produce a profit, or income, or both: *He invested his money in stocks, bonds, and land.* **2.** invest money: *Learn to invest wisely.* **3.** clothe; cover; surround: *Darkness invests the earth at night.* [< L *investire* < *in-* in + *vestis* clothing]

in vet er ate (in vet′ər it), *adj.* long and firmly established: *Cats have an inveterate dislike of dogs.*

in vi o late (in vī′ə lit or in vī′ə lāt), *adj.* not violated; uninjured; unbroken; not profaned.

in vo ca tion (in′və kā′shən), *n.* act of calling upon in prayer; appeal for help or protection: *A church service often begins with an invocation to God.*

i o ta (ī ō′tə), *n.* a very small quantity: *There is not an iota of truth in the prisoner's story.* [< L < Gk. *iota.* Doublet of JOT]

ir i des cent (ir′ə des′ənt), *adj.* displaying colors like those of the rainbow. **—ir′i des′cent ly,** *adv.*

ir rel e vant (i rel′ə vənt), *adj.* not to the point; off the subject: *A question about arithmetic is irrelevant in a music lesson.* **—ir rel′e vant ly,** *adv.*

ir re li gion (ir′i lij′ən), *n.* **1.** lack of religion. **2.** hostility to religion; disregard of religion.

ir re press i ble (ir′i pres′ə bəl), *adj.* that cannot be repressed or restrained.

ir res o lute (i rez′ə lüt), *adj.* not resolute; unable to make up one's mind; not sure of what one wants; hesitating: *Irresolute persons make poor leaders.* **—ir res′o lute ly,** *adv.* **—ir res′o lute ness,** *n.*

Isocrates (ī so′ crə tēs′)

Is ra el ite (iz′ri əl īt), *n.* Jew; Hebrew; descendant of Israel. *—adj.* of or having to do with Israel or the Jews.

is su ance (ish′ü əns), *n.* an issuing; issue.

is sue (ish′ü), *v.,* **-sued, -su ing,** *n.* *—v.* **1.** send out; put forth: *The government issues money and stamps.* **2.** come out; go out; proceed: *Smoke issues from the chimney.* **3.** be published. **4.** put into public circulation; publish. **5.** emerge. **6.** result or end *(in)*: *The game issued in a tie.*

Ith a ca (ith′ə kə), *n.* a small island W of Greece, the home of Odysseus.

jack al (jak′ôl or jak′əl), *n.* person who does drudgery for another.

jal ou sie (zhal′ü zē′), *n.* a window shade or shutter made of horizontal slats set at an angle; Venetian blind. [< F *jalousie,* literally, jealousy < *jaloux* jealous]

jas mine or **jas min** (jas′mən or jaz′mən), *n.* shrub or vine with clusters of fragrant flowers. There are yellow, white, and red jasmines.

jaunce (jôns or jäns), *v. Archaic.* probably, to prance.

jit ney (jit′ni), *n., pl.* **-neys.** *U.S. Slang.* automobile that carries passengers for a small fare. It usually travels along a regular route.

jo cose (jō kōs′), *adj.* jesting; humorous; playful. [< L *jocosus* < *jocus* jest] **—jo cose′ly,** *adv.*

kib itz er (kib′it sər), *n. Informal.* person who gives unwanted advice; meddler. [Am.E; < Yiddish]

ki mo no (kə mō′nə), *n., pl.* **-nos.** a woman's loose dressing gown. [< Japanese]

kin dred (kin′drid), *n.* **1.** family or relatives. **2.** family relationship; connection by birth or marriage. *—adj.* **1.** related: *kindred tribes.* **2.** like; similar: *We are studying about dew, frost, and kindred facts of nature.*

kine (kīn), *n. pl. Archaic* or *Dialect.* cows; cattle. [earlier *kyen,* formed after pattern of *oxen* < OE *cȳ,* pl. of *cū* cow]

kite (kīt), *n.* hawk with long pointed wings.

Swallow-tailed kite (about 2 ft. long)

lack a dai si cal (lak′ə dā′zə kəl), *adj.* languid; listless; dreamy; weakly sentimental. [< *lackaday*] **—lack′a dai′si cal ly,** *adv.*

la con ic (lə kon′ik), *adj.* using few words; brief in speech or expression; concise.

La Guar di a Airport (lə gwär′di ə or lə gär′di ə), a major domestic and international airport, in the Borough of Queens in New York City.

La Janda (lä hən′də)

lance (lans or läns), *v.,* **lanced, lanc ing. 1.** pierce with a lance. **2.** cut open with a lancet: *The dentist lanced the gum so that the new tooth could come through.*

lank (langk), *adj.* long and thin; slender; lean: *a lank boy.*

la tent (lā′tənt), *adj.* present but not active; hidden; concealed: *latent germs of disease, latent powers, latent ability.* [< L *latens, -entis,* ppr. of *latere* lie hidden]

lat er al (lat′ər əl), *adj.* of the side; at the side; from the side; toward the side. A lateral branch of a family is a branch not in the direct line of descent.

lat i tude (lat′ə tüd or lat′ə tūd), *n.* **1.** distance north or south of the equator, measured in degrees. **2.** place or region having a certain latitude: *Polar bears live in the cold latitudes.*

lave (lāv), *v.,* **laved, lav ing.** *Poetic.* wash; bathe.

le Coeur-Hardy, Ga waine (lə kėr-härdi gä′wān)

lees (lēz), *n. pl.* dregs; sediment. [< F *lie* < Celtic]

lee way (lē′wā′), *n.* convenient room or scope for action.

Les Amoureuses (lās ä′mu rœs′)

le sion (lē′zhən), *n.* **1.** injury; hurt. **2.** a diseased condition. [< L *laesio, -onis* injury < *laedere* to strike]

lest (lest), *conj.* for fear that; that ——not; in order that ——not: *Be careful lest you fall from that tree.*

leth ar gy (leth′ər ji), *n., pl.* **-gies. 1.** drowsy dullness; lack of energy; sluggish inactivity. **2.** an unnatural sleep. [< L < Gk. *lethargia* < *lethargos* forgetful < *lethe* forgetfulness + *argos* lazy]

lev ee (lev′i), *n.* U.S. bank built to keep a river from overflowing. There are levees along the lower Mississippi River.

lev i tate (lev′ə tāt), *v.,* **-tat ed, -tat ing.** rise or float in the air.

lev i ta tion (lev′ə tā′shən), *n.* a levitating.

li ba tion (lī bā′shən), *n.* **1.** a pouring out of wine, water, etc., as an offering to a god. **2.** wine, water, etc., offered in this way. [< L *libatio, -onis* < *libare* pour out]

lib er al (lib′ər əl or lib′rəl), *adj.* **1.** generous: *a liberal donation.* **2.** broad-minded; not narrow in one's ideas: *a liberal thinker.*

lib er al i ty (lib′ər al′ə ti), *n., pl.* **-ties.** generosity.

---

hat, āge, cãre, fär; let, ēqual, tėrm; it, īce; hot, ōpen, ôrder; oil, out; cup, pu̇t, rüle, ūse; th, thin; ᴛʜ, then; zh, measure; ə represents *a* in about, *e* in taken, *i* in pencil, *o* in lemon, *u* in circus.

li cense (lī′səns), *v.*, **—censed, —cens ing.** give a license to; permit by law: *A doctor is licensed to practice medicine.*

lief (lēf), *adv.* willingly.

liege (lēj), *n.* lord having a right to the homage and loyal service of his vassals.

lieu (lü), *n.* **1.** place; stead. **2. in lieu of,** in place of; instead of. [< F < L *locus*]

li queur (li kėr′ or li kūr′), *n.* a strong, sweet, highly flavored alcoholic liquor.

lit ur gy (lit′ər ji), *n., pl.* **-gies.** form of public worship. Different churches use different liturgies.

lo co mo tion (lō′kə mō′shən), *n.* act or power of moving from place to place. Walking and flying are common forms of locomotion. [< L *loco* from a place + E *motion*]

lode (lōd), *n.* a course, path, road, also a waterway, a canal, a drain.

loft y (lôf′ti or lof′ti), *adj.*, **loft i er, loft i est.** exalted; dignified; grand: *lofty aims.*

loin (loin), *n.* Usually, **loins,** *pl.* part of the body between the ribs and the hipbones. The loins are on both sides of the backbone.

loll (lol), *v.* recline or lean in a lazy manner: *loll on a sofa.*

lon gev i ty (lon jev′ə ti), *n.* long life. [< L *longaevitas* < *longaevus* long-lived < *longus* long+ *aevum* age]

lot ter y (lot′ər i), *n., pl.* **-ter ies.** scheme for distributing prizes by lot or chance. In a lottery a large number of tickets are sold, some of which draw prizes.

low er (lou′ər), *v.* look dark and threatening. frown; scowl. Also, **lour.** [ME *loure* (*n*)]

lu cra tive (lü′krə tiv), *adj.* bringing in money; profitable. [< L *lucrativus* < *lucrari* to gain < *lucrum* gain]

lu gu bri ous (lü gü′bri əs or lü gū′bri əs), *adj.* sad; mournful. [< L *lugubris* < *lugere* mourn] **—lu gu′bri ous ly,** *adv.*

lu rid (lür′id), *adj.* terrible; sensational; startling: *lurid crimes.* [< L *luridus*]

lust ful (lust′fəl), *adj.* **1.** desiring indulgence of sex; sensual; lewd. **2.** *Archaic.* lusty.

Lyd i a (lid′i ə), *n.* an ancient country in W. Asia Minor, famous for its wealth and luxury.

Lyd i an (lid′i ən), *adj.* of Lydia, its people, or their language.

lyre (līr), *n.* an ancient stringed musical instrument somewhat like a small harp. [< OF < L < Gk. *lyra*]

Lyre player

mack i naw (mak′ə nô), *n.* kind of short coat made of heavy woolen cloth.

mag got (mag′ət), *n.* legless larva of any of various kinds of flies, often living in decaying matter.

mag nan i mous (mag nan′ə məs), *adj.* **1.** noble in soul or mind; generous in forgiving; free from mean or petty feelings or acts. **2.** showing or arising from a generous spirit: *a magnanimous attitude toward a conquered enemy.* [< L *magnanimus* < *magnus* great + *animus* spirit] **—mag nan′i mous ly,** *adv.*

mal a dy (mal′ə di), *n., pl.* **-dies.** sickness; illness; disease.

ma lev o lence (mə lev′ə ləns), *n.* the wish that evil may happen to others; ill will; spite.

ma lev o lent (mə lev′ə lənt), *adj.* wishing evil to happen to others; showing ill will; spiteful.

ma lign (mə līn′), *v.* speak evil of; slander: *You malign a generous person when you call him stingy.*

ma lig nant (mə lig′nənt), *adj.* **1.** very evil; very hateful; very malicious. **2.** very harmful.

man grove (mang′grōv), *n.* a tropical tree that sends down many branches that take root and form new trunks. Mangroves grow in swamps along the banks of rivers.

ma ni a (mā′ni ə), *n.* **1.** kind of insanity characterized by great excitement and sometimes violence. **2.** unusual fondness; craze. [< L < Gk. *mania* madness]

ma ni a cal (mə nī′ə kəl), *adj.* insane; raving.

man tle (man′təl), *n.* anything that covers like a mantle: *The ground had a mantle of snow.*

Man tu a (man′chü ə), *n.* city in N Italy.

mar quis (mär′kwis), *n.* nobleman ranking below a duke and above an earl or count.

mar qui sette (mär′kə zet′ or mär′kwə zet′), *n.* a very thin fabric with square meshes, made of cotton, silk, or rayon and often used for window draperies.

ma son (mā′sən), *n.* Often, **Mason.** member of the world-wide secret society of Freemasons.

match coat (mach′kōt), *n.* a kind of mantle or wrap worn by American Indians, orig. of fur, but afterward of coarse woolen cloth, called "matchcloth," sold to them by traders.

ma ter nal (mə tėr′nəl), *adj.* of or like a mother; motherly.

Maugham (môm), *n.* (**William**) **Somerset,** born 1874, English author of plays, novels, and short stories.

maw (mô), *n.* **1.** mouth. **2.** throat. **3.** stomach.

ma zur ka or **ma zour ka** (mə zėr′kə or mə zür′kə), *n.* a lively Polish dance. [< Polish *mazurka,* woman of *Mazovia* in Poland]

me di ate (*v.* mē′di āt; *adj.* mē′di it), *v.*, **-at ed, -at ing,** **1.** be a go-between; act in order to bring about an agreement between persons or sides. **2.** effect by intervening; settle by intervening. **3.** be a connecting link between.

me di a tion (mē′di ā′shən), *n.* a mediating; effecting an agreement; friendly interference.

me di e val (mē′di ē′vəl or med′i ē′vəl), *adj.* **1.** belonging to or having to do with the Middle Ages (the years from about 500 A.D. to about 1450 A.D.). **2.** like that of the Middle Ages.

mel o dra ma (mel′ə drä′mə or mel′ə dram′ə), *n.* a sensational drama with exaggerated appeal to the emotions and, usually, a happy ending.

mel o dra mat ic (mel′ə drə mat′ik), *adj.* of, like, or suitable for melodrama; sensational and exaggerated.

mem bra nous (mem′brə nəs or mem brā′nəs), *adj.* **1.** of or like membrane. **2.** characterized by the formation of a membrane. In **membranous croup,** a membrane forms in the throat and hinders breathing.

me nag er ie (mə naj′ər i or mə nazh′ər i), *n.* place where animals are kept. [< F *ménagerie,* literally, management of a household]

mer can tile (mėr′kən til or mėr′kən tīl), *adj.* of merchants or trade; commercial: *a mercantile firm, mercantile law.* [< F < Ital. *mercantile* < *mercante* merchant]

mer cu ri al (mər kūr′i əl), *adj.* sprightly; quick.

mere (mēr), *n. Poetic* or *Dialect.* lake; pond. [OE]

met a bol ic (met′ə bol′ik), *adj.* having to do with metabolism.

me tab o lism (mə tab′ə liz əm), *n.* processes of building up food into living matter and using living matter until it is broken down into simpler substances or waste matter, giving off energy.

< = from, taken from; cf., compare; dial., dialect; dim., diminutive; pp., past participle; ppr., present participle; pt., past tense; ult., ultimately; var., variant; ?=possibly.

met a mor pho sis (met′ə môr′fə sis), *n., pl.* **-ses** (-sēz). a noticeable or complete change of character, appearance, or condition. [< L < Gk. *metamorphosis,* ult. < *meta-* over + *morphe* form]

me te or o log i cal (mē′ti ər ə loj′ə kəl), *adj.* having to do with the atmosphere and weather; having to do with meteorology.

me tic u lous (mə tik′ū ləs), *adj.* extremely or excessively careful about small details. [< L *meticulosus* < *metus* fear]

mew (mū), *n.* cage. *—v.* shut up in a cage; conceal; confine. [< OF *mue* < *muer* molt < L *mutare*]

mid wife (mid′wīf′), *n., pl.* **-wives.** woman who helps women in childbirth.

mill (mil), *v.* grind into powder or pulp.

mil len ni um (mə len′i əm), *n., pl.* **mil len ni ums, mil len ni a** (me len′i ə). a period of righteousness and happiness. [< NL < L *mille* thousand + *annus* year]

mill er (mil′ər), *n.* moth whose wings look as if they were powdered with flour.

min is ter (min′is tər), *v.* **1.** act as a servant or nurse; be of service: *She ministers to the sick man's wants.* **2.** be helpful; give aid; contribute. **3.** *Archaic.* furnish; supply.

Mi nos (mī′nəs or mī′nos), *n.* in Greek legend: **a.** a king and lawgiver of Crete who became a judge in Hades. **b.** his grandson, who built the Labyrinth at Crete and kept the Minotaur in it.

mis cre ant (mis′kri ənt), *adj.* having very bad morals; base.

mode[1] (mōd), *n.* manner or way in which a thing is done.

mode[2] (mōd), *n.* style, fashion, or custom that prevails; the way most people are doing.

mod i cum (mod′ə kəm), *n.* a small or moderate quantity. [< L *modicum,* neut., moderate < *modus* measure]

mod i fi ca tion (mod′ə fə kā′shən), *n.* partial alteration or change: *The teacher recommended six modifications in my essay.*

mod u late (moj′ů lāt), *v.,* **-lat ed, -lat ing.** regulate; adjust; vary; soften; tone down.

mold er (mōl′dər), *v.* turn into dust by natural decay; crumble; waste away. Also, *esp. Brit.* **moulder.**

mo ly (mō′li), *n., pl.* **mo lies.** a fabulous herb with a milk-white flower and a black root, having magic properties. Hermes gave Odysseus moly to counteract the spells of Circe.

mon i tor (mon′ə tər), *n.* a screen or receiver used by television personnel to view the picture being picked up by a camera or being broadcast.

mon sieur (mə syœ′), *n., pl.* **mes sieurs** (ma syœ′). Mr.; sir. [< F *monsieur,* earlier *mon sieur* my lord]

mon tage (mon tazh′), *n.* in motion pictures, the use of a rapid succession of pictures, especially to suggest a train of thought.

Mo ra vi a (mô rā′vi ə or mō rā′vi ə), *n.* region in central Czechoslovakia.

mor i bund (môr′ə bund or mor′ə bund), *adj.* dying. [< L *moribundus* < *mori* die]

mor tar[1] (môr′tər), *n.* mixture of lime, sand, and water, or of cement, sand, and water, for holding bricks or stones together.

mor tar[2] (môr′tər), *n.* a very short cannon for shooting shells or fireworks at high angles.

mot ley (mot′li), *n., pl.* **-leys.** suit of more than one color worn by clowns.

mu nif i cent (mū nif′ə sənt), *adj.* extremely generous. [< *munificence*] **—mu nif′i cent ly,** *adv.*

Muse (mūz), *n.* one of the nine Greek goddesses of the fine arts and sciences.

mus ket eer (mus′kə tēr′), *n.* soldier armed with a musket.

mut ton (mut′ən), *n.* meat from a sheep. [< OF *moton* < Med.L *multo* ram < Celtic]

Myr mi don (mėr′mə don), *n.* in Greek mythology, a member of a warlike people of ancient Thessaly who accompanied Achilles, their king, to the Trojan War.

myr tle (mėr′təl), *n.* *U.S.* a low, creeping evergreen vine with blue flowers; periwinkle.

nan ny (nan′i), *n., pl.* **—nies.** *Brit.* a nurse for children.

Na po le on I (nə pō′li ən or nə pōl′yən), 1769-1821, Napoleon Bonaparte, general of the French army who made himself emperor of the French in 1804. He conquered a large part of Europe, but was defeated at Waterloo in 1815, and exiled to the island of St. Helena.

nar cot ic (när kot′ik), *n.* drug that produces drowsiness, sleep, dullness, or an insensible condition, and lessens pain by dulling the nerves. Opium is a powerful narcotic. *—adj.* having the properties and effects of a narcotic.

nat u ral ize (nach′ə rəl īz or nach′rəl īz), *v.,* **ized, -iz ing.** admit (a foreigner) to citizenship. After living in the United States for a certain number of years, an immigrant can be naturalized if he passes a test.

naught (nôt), *n.* nothing.

ne ces si tate (nə ses′ə tāt), *v.,* **-tat ed, -tat ing.** make necessary: *His broken leg necessitated an operation.*

neg li gent (neg′lə jənt), *adj.* **1.** neglectful; given to neglect; showing neglect. **2.** careless; indifferent.

Nem e sis (nem′ə sis), *n., pl.* **-ses** (-sēz). **1.** the Greek goddess of vengeance. **2. nemesis, a.** just punishment for evil deeds. **b.** person who punishes another for evil deeds.

neth er (neᴛʜ′ər), *adj.* lower. [OE *neothera*]

net tle (net′əl), *n., v.,* **-tled, -tling.** *—n.* kind of plant having sharp leaf hairs that sting the skin when touched. *—v.* sting the mind of; irritate; provoke; vex.

net work (net′wėrk′), *n.* any netlike combination of things: *a network of vines, a network of railroads.*

ni ce ty (nī′sə ti), *n., pl.* **-ties. 1.** exactness; accuracy; delicacy: *Television sets require nicety of adjustment.* **2.** a fine point; small distinction; detail.

night shade (nīt′shād′), *n.* any of various plants somewhat like the potato and the tomato. The **black nightshade** has white flowers and black, poisonous berries. The **deadly nightshade,** or belladonna, has red berries.

ni ter (nī′tər), *n.* potassium nitrate, obtained from potash, used in making gunpowder; saltpeter.

noc tur nal (nok tėr′nəl), *adj.* of the night; in the night: *Stars are a nocturnal sight.*

no mad (nō′mad or nom′ad), *n.* wanderer.

no ta ble (nō′tə bəl), *adj.* worthy of notice; striking; remarkable: *a notable event, a notable man, a notable book, a notable painter.*

no to ri ous (nō tô′ri əs or nō tō′ri əs), *adj.* **1.** well-known because of something bad; having a bad reputation: *The notorious thief was sent to prison for his many crimes.* **2.** well-known.

no ve na (nō vē′nə), *n., pl.* **-nas, -nae** (-nē). in the Roman Catholic Church, a religious exercise consisting of prayers or services on nine days, or sometimes nine corresponding days in consecutive months: *a novena of nine first Fridays.* [< Med.L *novena,* ult. < L *novem* nine]

nox ious (nok′shəs), *adj.* very harmful; poisonous: *Fumes from the exhaust of an automobile are noxious.* [< L *noxius* < *noxa* hurt < *nocere* to hurt]

nu cle us (nü′kli əs or nū′kli əs), *n., pl.* **-cle i** or **-cle us es.** **1.** a beginning to which additions are to be made. **2.** a central part or thing around which other parts or things are collected.

nup tial (nup′shəl), *adj.* of marriage or weddings. —*n.* **nuptials,** *pl.* a wedding; the wedding ceremony.

oa kum (ō′kəm), *n.* a loose fiber obtained by untwisting and picking apart old ropes, used for stopping up the seams or cracks in ships.

ob lit er ate (əb lit′ər āt), *v.,* **-at ed, -at ing.** remove all traces of; blot out; destroy: *The heavy rain obliterated the footprints.*

ob scene (əb sēn′), *adj.* offending modesty or decency; impure; filthy; vile.

ob se quies (ob′sə kwiz), *n. pl.* funeral rites or ceremonies; stately funeral.

ob se qui ous (əb sē′kwi əs), *adj.* polite or obedient from hope of gain or from fear; servile; fawning: *Obsequious courtiers greeted the king.*

ob sti na cy (ob′stə nə si), *n., pl.* **-cies.** stubbornness; being obstinate.

ob trude (əb trüd′), *v.,* **-trud ed, -trud ing.** put forward unasked and unwanted; force.

of fal (ôf′əl or of′əl), *n.* garbage; refuse.

om nip o tent (om nip′ə tənt), *adj.* having all power; almighty.

om ni pres ent (om′nə prez′ənt), *adj.* present everywhere at the same time.

om nis cient (om nish′ənt), *adj.* knowing everything; having complete or infinite knowledge.

om niv o rous (om niv′ə rəs), *adj.* **1.** eating every kind of food. **2.** eating both animal and vegetable food: *Man is an omnivorous animal.* **3.** taking in everything.

o pi ate (ō′pi it or ō′pi āt), *n.* **1.** drug that contains opium and so dulls pain or brings sleep. **2.** anything that quiets.

op tion (op′shən), *n.* **1.** right or freedom of choice. **2.** a choosing; choice.

or a cle (ôr′ə kəl or or′ə kəl), *n.* answer of a god to some question. It often had a hidden meaning that was hard to understand.

or dain (ôr dān′), *v.* order; fix; decide; appoint; establish as a law.

ore (ôr or ōr), *n.* rock, sand, or dirt containing metal.

or gy (ôr′ji), *n., pl.* **-gies.** **1.** a wild, drunken revel. **2.** period of uncontrolled indulgence.

or i son (ôr′ə zən or or′ə zən), *n. Archaic* or *Poetic.* prayer.

o sier (ō′zhər), *n.* **1.** *Esp. Brit.* kind of willow tree. **2.** *Esp. Brit.* a tough, flexible branch or twig of this tree. Osiers are woven into baskets.

os ten si ble (os ten′sə bəl), *adj.* apparent; pretended; professed: *Her ostensible purpose was borrowing sugar, but she really wanted to see the new furniture.*

out crop (out′krop′), *n.* **1.** a coming to the surface of the earth: *the outcrop of a vein of coal.* **2.** part that comes to the surface: *The outcrop that we found proved to be very rich in gold.*

o ver lay (ō′vər lā′), *n.* something laid over something else; layer or decoration; covering.

pa cif ic (pə sif′ik), *adj.* peaceful; calm; quiet.

pal at a ble (pal′ə tə bəl), *adj.* agreeable to the taste; pleasing. —**pal′at a bly,** *adv.*

pa la tial (pə lā′shəl), *adj.* like a palace; fit for a palace; magnificent.

pa lav er (pə lav′ər or pə lä′vər), *v.* **1.** talk. **2.** talk fluently or flatteringly.

pall (pôl), *n.* a dark, gloomy covering: *A pall of smoke shut out the sun from the city.* [OE *pæll* < L *pallium* cloak]

pal lid (pal′id), *adj.* lacking color; pale: *a pallid complexion.*

pal lor (pal′ər), *n.* lack of color from fear, illness, death, etc.; paleness. [< L]

pal met to (pal met′ō), *n., pl.* **-tos** or **-toes.** any of several kinds of palm trees with fan-shaped leaves, abundant on the SE coast of the United States.

pal pa ble (pal′pə bəl), *adj.* **1.** readily seen or heard and recognized; obvious: *a palpable error.* **2.** that can be touched or felt.

par a ble (par′ə bəl), *n.* a short story used to teach some truth or moral lesson: *Jesus taught in parables.*

Par a guay (par′ə gwā or par′ə gwī), *n.* country in central South America, between Bolivia, Brazil, and Argentina.

par a mour (par′ə mür), *n. Archaic.* lover.

par ish (par′ish), *n.* district that has its own church and clergyman.

par ox ysm (par′ək siz əm), *n.* **1.** a severe, sudden attack: *a paroxysm of coughing.* **2.** fit; convulsion: *a paroxysm of rage.* [< Med.L < Gk. *paroxysmos,* ult. < *para-* + *oxynein* render acute]

par ri cide (par′ə sīd), *n.* person who kills his parent. [< F < L *parricida,* earlier *paricida* < unrecorded *parus* kinsman + *-cida* killer]

par ry (par′i), *v.,* **-ried, -ry ing,** *n., pl.* **-ries.** —*v.* ward off; turn aside; evade (a thrust, stroke, weapon, question, etc.). —*n.* act of parrying; avoiding.

pa tri arch (pā′tri ärk), *n.* **1.** person thought of as the father or founder of something. **2.** a venerable old man.

pa tron (pā′trən), *n.* **1.** person who gives his approval and support to some person, art, cause, or undertaking. **2.** a guardian saint or god.

pau per (pô′pər), *n.* a very poor person; person supported by charity.

pawn (pôn), *n.* an unimportant person or thing used by someone for his own purpose.

pel let (pel′it), *n.* a little ball of mud, paper, food, medicine, etc.; pill.

pel vis (pel′vis), *n., pl.* **-ves** (-vēz), the basin-shaped cavity formed by the hipbones and the end of the backbone.

pen ance (pen′əns), *n.* punishment borne to show sorrow for sin, to make up for a wrong done, and to obtain pardon.

pend ing (pen′ding), *adj.* waiting to be decided or settled: *while the agreement was pending.* —*prep.* while waiting for; until: *Pending his return, let us get everything ready.*

pen sive (pen′siv), *adj.* **1.** thoughtful in a serious or sad way. **2.** melancholy. [< OF *pensif* < *penser* think < L *pensare* weigh, ponder < *pendere* weigh]

pen u ry (pen′ū ri), *n.* great poverty.

Pen zance (pen zəns′)

per ceive (pər sēv′), *v.,* **-ceived, -ceiv ing.** **1.** be aware of through the senses; see, hear, taste, smell, or feel. **2.** take in with the mind; observe: *I perceived that I could not make him change his mind.*

< = from, taken from; cf., compare; dial., dialect; dim., diminutive; pp., past participle; ppr., present participle; pt., past tense; ult., ultimately; var., variant; ?=possibly.

per cept (pėr′sept), *n.* **1.** that which is perceived. **2.** understanding that is the result of perceiving.
per cep ti ble (pər sep′tə bəl), *adj.* that can be perceived.
per cep tion (pər sep′shən), *n.* act of perceiving: *His perception of the change came in a flash.*
per cept u al (pėr sep′chü əl), *adj.* pertaining to perception; involving perception. See perception.
per chance (pər chans′ or pər chäns′), *adv. Archaic* or *Poetic.* perhaps.
per coon (pər kün′), *n.* a flowering plant with roots that yield a yellow dye.
per force (pər fôrs′ or pər fōrs′), *adv.* by necessity; necessarily. [< F *par* by + *force*]
per i pa tet ic (per′ə pə tet′ik), *adj.* walking about; traveling from place to place.
per jured (pėr′jərd), *adj.* guilty of perjury.
per ju ry (pėr′jər i), *n., pl.* **-ries.** act of swearing that something is true which one knows to be false.
per ni cious (pər nish′əs), *adj.* **1.** that will destroy or ruin; causing great harm or damage: *Gambling is a pernicious habit.* **2.** fatal.
per pet u ate (pər pech′ü āt), *v.,* **-at ed, -at ing.** make perpetual; keep from being forgotten: *The Washington Monument was built to perpetuate the memory of a great man.*
per plex (pər pleks′), *v.* trouble with doubt; puzzle; bewilder.
per se cute (pėr′sə kūt), *v.,* **-cut ed, -cut ing.** **1.** treat badly; do harm to again and again; oppress. **2.** punish for religious reasons. **3.** annoy: *persecuted by silly questions.* [< *persecution*] **—per′se cu′tor,** *n.*
Per seph o ne (pər sef′ə nē), *n.* in Greek mythology, the daughter of Zeus and Demeter, who was carried off by Hades, the king of the lower world, and made his queen, but allowed to spend part of each year on the earth. The Latin equivalent is **Proserpina,** often Anglicized as **Proserpine.**
per se ver ance (pėr′sə vēr′əns), *n.* a sticking to a purpose or an aim; never giving up what one has set out to do.
per si flage (pėr′sə fläzh), *n.* light, joking talk.
per son i fy (pər son′ə fī), *v.,* **-fied, -fy ing.** **1.** be a type of; embody: *Satan personifies evil.* **2.** regard or represent as a person. We often personify the sun and moon, referring to the sun as *he* and the moon as *she.*
per vert (pər vėrt′), *v.* lead or turn from the right way or from the truth: *Reading silly stories perverts our taste for good books.* [< L *pervertere* < *per-* to destruction + *vertere* to turn] **—per vert′er,** *n.*
pe ti tion (pə tish′ən), *n.* **1.** a formal request to a superior or to one in authority for some privilege, right, benefit, etc.: *The people signed a petition asking the city council for a new sidewalk.* **2.** in law, a written application for an order of court or for some action by a judge. *—v.* ask earnestly; make a petition to: *They petitioned the mayor to use his influence with the city council.*
pet u lant (pech′ů lənt), *adj.* peevish; subject to little fits of bad temper; irritable over trifles. [< L *petulans, -antis,* ult. < *petere* seek. aim at]
pha lanx (fā′langks or fal′angks), *n., pl.* **pha lanx es, pha lan ges** (fə lan′jēz). **1.** in ancient Greece, a special battle formation of infantry fighting in close ranks with their shields joined and long spears overlapping each other. **2.** a compact or closely massed body of persons, animals, or things. **3.** number of persons united for a common purpose. **4.** any bone in the fingers or toes. [< L < Gk.]
phi lan thro pist (fə lan′thrə pist), *n.* person who shows his love for mankind by practical kindness and helpfulness to humanity.
phlox (floks), *n.* plant with clusters of showy flowers in various colors.
phoe nix (fē′niks), *n.* a mythical bird, the only one of its kind, said to live 500 or 600 years, to burn itself on a funeral pile, and to rise again from the ashes, fresh and beautiful, for another long life. Also, **phenix.**
pig iron, crude iron as it first comes from the blast furnace or smelter, usually cast into oblong masses called pigs.
pike[1] (pīk), *n.* a long wooden shaft with a sharp-pointed metal head; spear. Foot soldiers used to carry pikes. [< F *pique* < *piquer* pierce < *pic* a pick < Gmc.]
pike[2] (pīk), *n.* a sharp point; spike.
pil lage (pil′ij), *v.,* **-laged, -lag ing.** rob with violence; plunder: *Pirates pillaged the towns along the coast.*
pil lar (pil′ər), *n.* a slender, upright structure; column. Pillars are usually made of stone, wood, or metal and used as supports or ornaments for a building. Sometimes a pillar stands alone as a monument.
pil lo ry (pil′ə ri), *n., pl.* **-ries,** frame of wood with holes through which a person's head and hands were put. The pillory was formerly used as a punishment, being set up in a public place where the crowd could make fun of the offender.

Man in a pillory

pine (pīn), *v.,* **pined, pin ing.** **1.** long eagerly; yearn. **2.** waste away with pain, hunger, grief, or desire.
pith (pith), *n.* an important or essential part: *the pith of a speech.*
plain tive (plān′tiv), *adj.* mournful; sad. [< OF *plaintif,* ult. < L *planctus* complaint]
plane[1] (plān), *n.* any flat or level surface.
plane[2] (plān), *n.* plane tree.
plume (plüm), *v.,* **plumed, plum ing.** **1.** furnish with plumes. **2. plume oneself on,** be proud of.
ply (plī), *v.,* **plied, ply ing.** **1.** work with; use: *The dressmaker plies her needle.* **2.** work busily or steadily.
poign ant (poin′ənt or poin′yənt), *adj.* **1.** very painful; piercing: *poignant suffering.* **2.** keen; intense.
poise (poiz), *v.,* **poised, pois ing.** **1.** balance: *Poise yourself on your toes.* **2.** hold or carry evenly or steadily: *The athlete poised the weight in the air before throwing it.*
Po lo ni us (pə lō′ni əs), *n.* pompous old man who is the father of Ophelia in Shakespeare's *Hamlet.*
pol troon (pol trün′), *n.* a wretched coward. [< F < Ital. *poltrone* < *poltro* lazy, originally, bed]
Pont-Neuf (pôɴ nœf)
po rous (pô′rəs or pō′rəs), *adj.* full of pores or tiny holes; permeable by water, air, etc.
por rin ger (pôr′ən jər or por′ən jər), *n.* a small dish from which soup, porridge, bread and milk, etc., can be eaten.
por tend (pôr tend′ or pōr tend′), *v.* indicate beforehand; be a portent of: *Black clouds portend a storm.*
por ten tous (pôr ten′təs or pōr ten′təs), *adj.* indicating evil to come; ominous; threatening.
post (pōst), *n.* one of a series of fixed stations along a route for furnishing relays of men and horses for carrying letters, etc., and supplying service to travelers by post horse, post chaise, etc. *—v.* send by post; mail: *post a letter.*

pos ter i ty (pos ter′ə ti), *n.* **1.** generations of the future: *If we burn up all the coal in the world, what will posterity do?* **2.** all of a person's descendants.

pos til ion or **pos til lion** (pōs til′yən or pos til′-yən), *n.* man who rides one of the horses drawing a carriage. [< F *postillon*]

poult (pōlt), *n.* a young turkey, esp. before sex can be determined; also, less commonly, a young chicken, pheasant, grouse, or the like.

poul tice (pōl′tis), *n., v.* **-ticed, -tic ing.** —*n.* a soft, moist mass of mustard, herbs, etc., applied to the body as a medicine. —*v.* put a poultice on.

pre car i ous (pri kãr′i əs), *adj.* not safe or secure; uncertain; dangerous; risky: *A soldier leads a precarious life.*

pre cept (prē′sept), *n.* rule of action or behavior; maxim: "*If at first you don't succeed, try, try again*" *is a familiar precept.*

pre cip i tate (pri sip′ə tāt), *v.* **-tat ed, -tat ing.** **1.** hasten the beginning of; bring about suddenly: *precipitate a war.* **2.** throw headlong; hurl: *precipitate a rock down a cliff.* —**pre cip′i tate ly,** *adv.*

pre cip i tous (pri sip′ə təs), *adj.* hasty; rash.

pre clude (pri klüd′), *v.,* **-clud ed, -clud ing.** shut out; make impossible; prevent. [< L *praecludere* < *prae-* before + *claudere* to shut]

pre co cious (pri kō′shəs), *adj.* **1.** developed earlier than usual: *This very precocious child could read well at the age of four.* **2.** developed too early.

pre ëmp tion or **pre-emp tion** (pri emp′shən), *n.* the act or right of purchasing before others or in preference to others.

pre judge (prē juj′), *v.,* **-judged, -judg ing.** judge beforehand; judge without knowing all the facts.

prel ude (prel′ūd or prē′lüd), *n.* anything serving as an introduction; preliminary performance: *the organ prelude to a church service.*

pre med i tate (prē med′ə tāt), *v.,* **-tat ed, -tat-ing.** consider or plan beforehand: *The murder was premeditated.* [< L *praemeditari* < *prae-* before + *meditari* meditate]

pre pos ter ous (pri pos′tər əs or pri pos′trəs), *adj.* contrary to nature, reason, or common sense; absurd; senseless: *It would be preposterous to shovel coal with a teaspoon.* —**pre pos′ter ous ly,** *adv.*

pres age (pri sāj′), *v.,* **pre saged, pre sag ing.** **1.** give warning of; predict: *Some people think that a circle around the moon presages a storm.* **2.** have or give prophetic impression (of). [< L *praesagium,* ult. < *prae-* before + *sagus* prophetic]

pre scribe (pri skrīb′), *v.,* **-scribed, -scrib ing.** order; direct: *Good citizens do what the laws prescribe.*

pre sen ti ment (pri zen′tə mənt), *n.* a feeling or impression that something is about to happen; vague sense of approaching misfortune; foreboding. [< MF *presentiment,* ult. < L *prae-* before + *sentire* to sense]

pre sump tu ous (pri zump′chü əs), *adj.* acting without permission or right; too bold; forward.

prev a lent (prev′ə lənt), *adj.* widespread; in general use; common: *Colds are prevalent in the winter.*

pre var i cate (pri var′ə kāt), *v.,* **-cat ed, -cat ing.** turn aside from the truth in speech or act; lie. [< L *praevaricari* make a sham accusation, ult. < *prae-* before + *varicus* straddling < *varus* crooked]

pri mor di a (prī môr′di ə), *n., pl.* the earliest part or stage; beginning; origin.

prise (prīz), *v.,* **prised, pris ing.** prize.

prith ee (priᴛʜ′i), *interj.* *Archaic.* I pray thee.

privy council, group of personal advisers to a ruler.

prize (prīz), *v.,* **prized, priz ing.** *Esp. Brit.* raise or move by force; pry. Also, **prise.**

pro cliv i ty (prō kliv′ə ti), *n., pl.* **-ties.** tendency; inclination. [< L *proclivitas,* ult. < *pro-* forward + *clivus* slope]

pro cure (prə kūr′), *v.,* **-cured, -cur ing.** **1.** obtain by care or effort; get: *A friend procured a position in the bank for my brother.* **2.** bring about; cause: *procure a person's death.*

pro di gious (prə dij′əs), *adj.* **1.** very great; huge; vast: *The ocean contains a prodigious amount of water.* **2.** wonderful; marvelous.

prof fer (prof′ər), *v.* offer; offer for acceptance: *We proffered regrets at having to leave so early.*

prof li gate (prof′lə git), *n.* person who is very wicked or extravagant.

prog nos tic (prog nos′tik), *n.* **1.** indication; sign. **2.** forecast; prediction. [< Med.L *prognosticus* < Gk. *prognostikos* foretelling, ult. < *pro-* before + *gignoskein* recognize]

pro logue or **pro log** (prō′lôg or prō′log), *n.* speech or poem addressed to the audience by one of the actors at the beginning of a play.

pro mis cu ous (prə mis′kū əs), *adj.* mixed and in disorder: *a promiscuous heap of clothing on your closet floor.* —**pro mis′cu ous ly,** *adv.*

prom on to ry (prom′ən tô′ri or prom′ən tō′ri), *n., pl.* **-ries.** a high point of land extending from the coast into the water; headland. [< Med.L *promontorium,* var. of L *promunturium* < *pro-* forward + *mons* mountain]

prop a gate (prop′ə gāt), *v.,* **-gat ed, -gat ing.** increase in number: *Trees propagate themselves by seeds.*

pro pen si ty (prə pen′sə ti), *n., pl.* **-ties.** a natural inclination or bent; inclination: *Most boys have a propensity for playing with machinery.*

pro pi tious (prə pish′əs), *adj.* **1.** favorable: *propitious weather for our trip.* **2.** favorably inclined; gracious.

prop o si tion (prop′ə zish′ən), *n.* **1.** what is offered to be considered; proposal: *The tailor made a proposition to buy out his rival's business.* **2.** statement. *Example:* "All men are created equal." **3.** problem to be solved: *a proposition in geometry.* **4.** *U.S. Informal.* person or thing to be dealt with. [< L *propositio, -onis* a setting forth < *proponere* < *pro-* forth + *ponere* put, place]

pro sce ni um (prō sē′ni əm), *n., pl.* **-ni a** (-ni ə). **1.** part of the stage in front of the curtain. **2.** curtain and the framework that holds it.

pro scribe (prō skrīb′), *v.,* **-scribed, -scrib ing.** **1.** put outside of the protection of the law; outlaw. **2.** forbid to come into a certain place; banish. [< L *proscribere* < *pro-* openly, publicly + *scribere* write]

pro scrip tion (prō skrip′shən), *n.* a being proscribed.

pro te id (prō′ti id), *n., adj.* protein.

pro tein (prō′tēn or prō′ti in), *n.* a complex compound containing nitrogen that is a necessary part of the cells of animals and plants. Meat, milk, cheese, eggs, and beans contain protein.

pro tract (prō trakt′), *v.* draw out; lengthen in time: *protract a visit.*

prov erb (prov′ėrb), *n.* a short wise saying used for a long time by many people.

prov i dent (prov′ə dənt), *adj.* having or showing foresight; careful in providing for the future: *Provident men lay aside money for their families.*

< = from, taken from; cf., compare; dial., dialect; dim., diminutive; pp., past participle; ppr., present participle; pt., past tense; ult., ultimately; var., variant; ?=possibly.

prov i den tial (prov′ə den′shəl), *adj.* fortunate: *Our delay seemed providential, for the train we had planned to take was wrecked.*

pro vin cial (prə vin′shəl), *adj.* belonging or peculiar to some particular province or provinces rather than to the whole country; local: *provincial English, provincial customs.*

pro vi so (prə vī′zō), *n., pl.* **-sos** or **-soes.** sentence or part of a sentence in a contract, or other agreement, that states a condition; condition: *Tom was admitted to the eighth grade with the proviso that he was to be put back if he failed any subject.*

prow ess (prou′is), *n.* **1.** bravery; daring. **2.** brave or daring acts. **3.** unusual skill or ability.

prox y (prok′si), *n., pl.* **prox ies.** a writing authorizing a proxy to act or vote for a person.

pseu do nym (sü′də nim), *n.* name used by an author instead of his real name. Mark Twain is a pseudonym for Samuel Langhorne Clemens.

pule (pūl), *v.,* **puled, pul ing.** cry in a thin voice, as a sick child does; whimper; whine.

pul sa tion (pul sā′shən), *n.* **1.** beating; throbbing. **2.** a beat; throb. **3.** vibration; quiver.

pun cheon (pun′chən), *n.* **1.** a large cask for liquor. **2.** slab of timber, or a piece of a split log, with the face roughly smoothed.

punc til i ous (pungk til′i əs), *adj.* very careful and exact.

purge (pėrj), *v.,* **purged, purg ing,** **1.** wash away all that is not clean from; make clean. **2.** become clean.

pur loin (pėr loin′), *v.* steal.

pur vey or (pėr vā′ər), *n.* person who supplies provisions.

pu tre fac tion (pū′trə fak′shən), *n.* decay; rotting.

Pyr rhus (pir′əs), *n.* 318?-272 B.C., king of Epirus in Greece from 300 to 272 B.C. He invaded Italy.

qua drille (kwə dril′), *n.* a square dance for four couples that has five parts or movements.

quad ru ped (kwod′rů ped), *adj.* having four feet.

quan da ry (kwon′də ri or kwon′dri), *n., pl.* **-ries.** state of perplexity or uncertainty; dilemma.

quar ter (kwôr′tər), *v.* cut the body of (a person) into quarters, especially as a punishment.

quash (kwosh), *v.* put down completely; crush: *quash a revolt.*

quat rain (kwot′rān), *n.* stanza or poem of four lines.

quib ble (kwib′əl), *v.,* **-bled, -bling.** evade the point or the truth by twisting the meaning of words.

quick lime (kwik′līm′), *n.* a white, alkaline substance obtained by burning limestone and used for making mortar; unslaked lime.

quince (kwins), *n.* a hard, yellowish acid fruit, used for preserves.

rad i cal (rad′ə kəl), *adj.* favoring extreme changes or reforms; extreme.

ra gout (ra gü′), *n.* a highly seasoned stew of meat and vegetables.

ran cor (rang′kər), *n.* bitter resentment or ill will; extreme hatred or spite.

rank[1] (rangk), *n.* row or line, especially of soldiers, placed side by side.

rank[2] (rangk), *adj.* **1.** large and coarse: *rank grass.* **2.** growing richly. **3.** having a strong, bad smell or taste: *rank meat, rank tobacco.*

rap tor (rap′tər), *n.* a bird of prey of the same family as the hawk, eagles, vultures, and owls.

rar i ty (rãr′ə ti), *n., pl.* **-ties.** something rare: *A man over a hundred years old is a rarity.*

raze (rāz), *v.,* **razed, raz ing.** tear down; destroy completely. Also, **rase.**

Reading (red′ing, re′ding)

realm (relm), *n.* **1.** kingdom. **2.** region or sphere in which something rules or prevails.

re cal ci trant (ri kal′sə trənt), *adj.* resisting authority or control; disobedient.

re cant (ri kant′), *v.* **1.** take back formally or publicly; withdraw or renounce (a statement, opinion, purpose, etc.). **2.** renounce an opinion or allegiance: *Though he was tortured to make him change his religion, the prisoner would not recant.*

re cep ta cle (ri sep′tə kəl), *n.* any container or place used to put things in to keep them conveniently.

re cip i ent (ri sip′i ənt), *n.* person or thing that receives something: *The recipients of the prizes had their names printed in the paper.*

reck on ing (rek′ən ing or rek′ning), *n.* **1.** settlement of an account. **2.** bill, especially at an inn or tavern.

rec om pense (rek′əm pens), *v.,* **-pensed, -pensing,** *n.* —*v.* pay (a person); pay back; reward. —*n.* payment; reward; return; amends.

re count (ri kount′), *v.* tell in detail; give an account of: *He recounted all the happenings of the day.*

re cur (ri kėr′), *v.,* **-curred, -cur ring.** come up again; occur again; be repeated: *Leap year recurs every four years.*

re dress (ri dres′), *v.* set right; repair; remedy.

re dun dan cy (ri dun′dən si), *n., pl.* **-cies.** more than is needed.

re fec to ry (ri fek′tə ri), *n., pl.* **-ries.** a room for meals, especially in a monastery, convent, or school.

re frac to ry (ri frak′tə ri), *adj.* hard to manage; stubborn; obstinate: *Mules are refractory.*

reg i men (rej′ə men or rej′ə mən), *n.* set of rules or habits of diet, exercise, or manner of living intended to improve health, reduce weight, etc.

reg i ment (rej′ə mənt), *n.* unit of an army consisting of several companies of soldiers organized into one large group, usually commanded by a colonel.

re it er ate (rē it′ər āt), *v.,* **-at ed, -at ing.** say or do several times; repeat (an action, demand, etc.) again and again: *The boy did not move though the teacher reiterated her command.*

re join (ri join′), *v.* answer; reply.

re join der (ri join′dər), *n.* an answer to a reply; response.

re lapse (ri laps′), *n.* falling or slipping back into a former state, way of acting, etc.: *He seemed to be getting over his illness but had a relapse.*

rel e gate (rel′ə gāt), *v.,* **-gat ed, -gat ing.** **1.** send away, usually to a lower position or condition. **2.** send into exile; banish.

re lent (ri lent′), *v.* become less harsh or cruel; be more tender and merciful.

re lin quish (ri ling′kwish), *v.* give up; let go: *The small dog relinquished his bone to the big dog.*

rel ish (rel′ish), *n.* liking; appetite; enjoyment: *The hungry boy ate with a great relish.*

re mit (ri mit′), *v.,* **-mit ted, -mit ting.** **1.** refrain from carrying out; refrain from exacting; cancel: *The king remitted the prisoner's punishment.* **2.** send back, especially to prison.

---

hat, āge, cãre, fär; let, ēqual, tėrm; it, īce; hot, ōpen, ôrder; oil, out; cup, pu̇t, rüle, ūse; th, thin; ᴛʜ, then; zh, measure; ə represents *a* in about, *e* in taken, *i* in pencil, *o* in lemon, *u* in circus.

re mon strance (ri mon′strəns), *n.* protest; complaint.
re mon strate (ri mon′strāt), *v.*, **-strat ed, -strat ing.** object; protest: *The teacher remonstrated with the boy about his low marks.*
re mote (ri mōt′), *adj.*, **-mot er, -mot est.** **1.** far away; far off: *a remote country.* **2.** out of the way; secluded: *a remote village.* **3.** slight; faint: *I haven't the remotest idea what you mean.* **—re mote′ly,** *adv.*
re nas cence (ri nas′əns or ri nā′səns), *n.* **1.** revival; new birth; renewal. **2.** a being renascent.
ren der (ren′dər), *v.* **1.** cause to become; make: *An accident has rendered him helpless.* **2.** give; do: *She rendered us a great service by her help.*
re nounce (ri nouns′), *v.*, **-nounced, -nounc ing.** declare that one gives up; give up entirely; give up: *He renounces his claim to the money.*
re nun ci a tion (ri nun′si ā′shən), *n.* a giving up of a right, title, possession, etc.; renouncing.
rep a ra ble (rep′ə rə bəl), *adj.* that can be repaired or remedied.
re past (ri past′ or ri päst′), *n.* meal; attractive meal; food.
re pose (ri pōz′), *n.*, *v.*, **-posed, -pos ing.** *—n.* **1.** rest; sleep: *Do not disturb her repose.* **2.** peace; calmness. *—v.* **1.** lie in a grave. **2.** be supported. **3.** depend; rely (on).
re press (ri pres′), *v.* **1.** prevent from acting; check: *She repressed an impulse to cough.* **2.** keep down; put down: *The dictator repressed the revolt.*
re proof (ri prüf′), *n.* words of blame or disapproval; blame.
re pulse (ri puls′), *v.*, **-pulsed, -puls ing.** **1.** drive back; repel. **2.** refuse to accept; reject: *She coldly repulsed him.*
req ui site (rek′wə zit), *adj.* required by circumstances; needed; necessary: *the qualities requisite for a leader, the number of votes requisite for election.*
re sent ment (ri zent′mənt), *n.* the feeling that one has at being injured or insulted; indignation.
res er voir (rez′ər vwär or rez′ər vôr), *n.* anything to hold a liquid: *A fountain pen has an ink reservoir.*
res i due (rez′ə dü or rez′ə dū), *n.* what remains after a part is taken; remainder: *Mr. Smith's will directed that after the payment of all debts and $10,000 to his brother the residue of his property should go to his son. The syrup had dried up, leaving a sticky residue.*
re sorb (rē sôrb′), *v.* to swallow or suck in again; to reabsorb.
re sort (ri zôrt′), *v.* **1.** go; go often: *Many people resort to the beaches in hot weather.* **2.** turn for help: *resort to violence.*
re spec tive (ri spek′tiv), *adj.* belonging to each; particular; individual: *The classes went to their respective rooms.*
re spec tive ly (ri spek′tiv li), *adv.* as regards each one in his turn or in the order mentioned: *Bob, Dick, and Tom are 16, 18, and 20 years old, respectively.*
res pite (res′pit), *n.* time of relief and rest; lull: *A thick cloud brought a respite from the glare of the sun.*
res tive (res′tiv), *adj.* restless; uneasy.
re stor a tive (ri stôr′ə tiv or ri stōr′ə tiv), *n.* something that restores health and strength.
re sult ant (ri zul′tənt), *adj.* resulting.
re tain er (ri tān′ər), *n.* fee paid to secure services: *This lawyer receives a retainer before he begins work on a case.*
re tal i a tive (ri tal′i ā′tiv), *adj.* disposed to retaliate; retaliatory.
re tal i a to ry (ri tal′i ə tô′ri or ri tal′i ə tō′ri), *adj.* returning like for like, especially evil for evil.
ret i cent (ret′ə sənt), *adj.* disposed to keep silent or say little; not speaking freely; reserved in speech.
ret i cule (ret′ə kūl), *n.* a woman's small handbag.
ret i na (ret′ə nə), *n.*, *pl.* **-nas, -nae** (-nē). layer of cells at the back of the eyeball that is sensitive to light and receives the images of things looked at.
re tort (ri tôrt′), *v.* **1.** reply quickly or sharply. **2.** return in kind; turn back on: *retort insult for insult or blow for blow.*
ret ri bu tion (ret′rə bū′shən), *n.* a deserved punishment; return for evil done, or sometimes for good done.
re trib u tive (ri trib′ū tiv), *adj.* paying back; bringing or inflicting punishment in return for some evil, wrong, etc.
ret ro spect (ret′rə spekt), *n.* survey of past time, events, etc.; thinking about the past.
re vere (ri vēr′), *v.*, **-vered, -ver ing.** love and respect deeply; honor greatly; show reverence for. [< L *revereri* < *re-* back + *vereri* stand in awe of, fear]
re ver sion (ri vėr′zhən or ri vėr′shən), *n.* return to a former condition, practice, belief, etc.; return.
re ver sion al (ri vėr′zhən əl or ri vėr′shən əl), *adj.* of, having to do with, or involving a reversion.
re vile (ri vīl′), *v.*, **-viled, -vil ing.** call bad names; abuse with words: *The tramp reviled the man who drove him off.*
Rhadamanthus (rad a man′thus)
rhet o ric (ret′ə rik), *n.* **1.** art of using words in speaking or writing. **2.** mere display in language.
rheum (rüm), *n.* a watery discharge, such as mucus, tears, or saliva.
right eous (rī′chəs), *adj.* **1.** doing right; virtuous; behaving justly. **2.** morally right or justifiable: *righteous indignation.*
rig or (rig′ər), *n.* strictness; severity; harshness: *the rigor of a long, cold winter.*
rig or ous (rig′ər əs), *adj.* very severe; harsh; strict: *the rigorous discipline in a prison.*
rime (rīm), *n.* rhyme.
rind (rīnd), *n.* the firm outer covering (of oranges, melons, cheeses, etc.). The bark of a tree or plant may be called the rind.
rogue (rōg), *n.* a tricky, dishonest, or worthless person; rascal.
ro guer y (rō′gər i), *n.*, *pl.* **-guer ies.** playful mischief.
roof tree (rüf′trē′ or ruf′trē′), *n.* the horizontal timber along the top of the roof.
ro sa ry (rō′zə ri), *n.*, *pl.* **-ries.** string of beads for keeping count in saying a series of prayers.
rou leau (rü lō′), *n.* a roll of coins put up in paper.
rub ber (rub′ər), *v. Slang.* stretch the neck or turn the head to look at something.
Rue St. Honoré (rə sant hō′nō rā′)
rue ful (rü′fəl), *adj.* **1.** sorrowful; unhappy; mournful: *a rueful expression.* **2.** causing sorrow or pity: *a rueful sight.*
ruff (ruf), *n.* collar of specially marked feathers or hairs on the neck of a bird or animal.
run a gate (run′ə gāt), *n. Archaic.* runaway.
ruse (rüz or rüs), *n.* trick; stratagem.
rus tic (rus′tik), *n.* a country person. [< L *rusticus* < *rus* country]

< = from, taken from; cf., compare; dial., dialect; dim., diminutive; pp., past participle; ppr., present participle; pt., past tense; ult., ultimately; var., variant; ?=possibly.

sac cha rin (sak′ə rin), *n.* a very sweet substance obtained from coal tar, used as a substitute for sugar.
sac ra men tal (sak′rə men′təl), *adj.* especially sacred.
sac ris tan (sak′ris tən), *n.* person in charge of the sacred vessels, robes, etc., of a church.
sa gac i ty (sə gas′ə ti), *n., pl.* **-ties.** keen, sound judgment; mental acuteness; shrewdness.
sa li ent (sā′li ənt or sāl′yənt), *adj.* standing out; easily seen or noticed; prominent; striking: *the salient features in a landscape, the salient points in a speech.*
sal vage (sal′vij), *v.,* **-vaged, -vag ing.** save from fire, shipwreck, etc.
San ta ya na (sän′tə yä′nə), *n.* **George,** born 1863, American philosopher, poet and essayist.
sa pi ent (sā′pi ənt), *adj.* wise; sage. [< L *sapiens, -entis,* ppr. of *sapere* be wise] **—sa′pi ent ly,** *adv.*
sa ti ate (sā′shi āt), *v.,* **-at ed, -at ing.** **1.** feed fully; satisfy fully. **2.** weary or disgust with too much.
sa vor (sā′vər), *v.* enjoy the savor of; perceive or appreciate by taste or smell.
scav en ger (skav′ən jər), *n.* animal that feeds on decaying matter. Vultures are scavengers.
Schirra (zhə rä′)
scone (skōn or skon), *n.* a thick, flat cake.
score (skôr or skōr), *n.* group or set of twenty.
scrag (skrag), *v.,* **scragged, scrag ging.** *—n.* a lean, bony part. A scrag of mutton is the neck.
scru ple (skrü′pəl), *n.* **1.** a feeling of doubt about what one ought to do: *No scruple ever holds him back from prompt action.* **2.** a feeling of uneasiness that keeps a person from doing something.
scul ler y (skul′ər i or skul′ri), *n., pl.* **-ler ies.** *Esp. Brit.* a small room where the dirty, rough work of a kitchen is done.
scur vy (skėr′vi), *adj.,* **-vi er, -vi est.** low; mean; contemptible: *a scurvy fellow, a scurvy trick.*
scythe (sīᴛʜ), *n.* a long, slightly curved blade on a long handle, for cutting grass, etc.
sear (sēr), *adj.* dried up; withered.
sedge (sej), *n.* a grasslike plant that grows in wet places.
seer (sēr), *n.* person who foresees or foretells future events; prophet.
Seine (sān), *n.* river flowing from E France into the English Channel. Paris is on the Seine. 480 mi.
seis mic (sīz′mik or sīs′mik), *adj.* of earthquakes.
sem a phore (sem′ə fôr or sem′ə fōr), *n., v.,* **-phored, -phor ing.** *—n.* apparatus for signaling.
sep ul cher (sep′əl kər), *n.* place of burial; tomb.
se pul chral (sə pul′krəl), *adj.* **1.** of sepulchers or tombs. **2.** of burial: *sepulchral ceremonies.* **3.** deep and gloomy; dismal; suggesting a tomb.
se ques tra tion (sē′kwes trā′shən or si kwes′trā′shən), *n.* the seizing and holding of property until legal claims are satisfied.
sere (sēr), *adj.* sear. [var. of *sear*]
Seriphus (sə rī′fəs)
ser vil i ty (sėr vil′ə ti), *n., pl.* **-ties.** attitude or behavior fit for a slave; servile yielding.
shak o (shak′ō), *n., pl.* **shak os.** a high, stiff military hat with a plume or other ornament.
shank (shangk), *n.* the part of the leg between the knee and the ankle.
sheath (shēth), *n., pl.* **sheaths** (shēᴛʜz). case or covering for the blade of a sword, knife, etc.

Shako

sheathe (shēᴛʜ), *v.,* **sheathed, sheath ing.** put (a sword, etc.) into a sheath.
sher ry (sher′i), *n., pl.* **-ries.** a strong wine made in S. Spain. It varies in color from pale yellow to brown.
shirk (shėrk), *v.* avoid or get out of doing (work, a duty, etc.).
shiv er (shiv′ər), *v.* break into small pieces: *He shivered the mirror with a hammer.*
shrive (shrīv), *v.,* **shrove** or **shrived, shriv en** or **shrived, shriv ing.** *Archaic.* hear the confession of, impose penance on, and grant absolution to.
si dle (sī′dəl), *v.,* **-dled, -dling.** move sideways.
sig nal ly (sig′nəl i), *adv.* remarkably; strikingly.
si gnior (sē′nyōr), *n.* signor.
si gnor (sē′nyōr), *n. Italian.* **1.** Mr.; sir. **2.** gentleman.
silt (silt), *n.* very fine earth, sand, etc., carried by moving water and deposited as sediment.
sim i an (sim′i ən), *adj.* like or characteristic of an ape or monkey. *—n.* ape; monkey.
sin ew (sin′ū), *—n.* a tough, strong band or cord that joins muscle to bone; tendon.
sin gu lar (sing′gū lər), *adj.* **1.** extraordinary; unusual: *"Treasure Island" is a story of singular interest to boys.* **2.** strange; queer; peculiar: *The detectives were greatly puzzled by the singular nature of the crime.*
si phon (sī′fən), *n.* a bent tube through which liquid can be drawn over the edge of one container into another at a lower level by air pressure.
slake (slāk), *v.,* **slaked, slak ing.** satisfy (thirst, revenge, wrath, etc.).
sledge (slej), *n.* sled; sleigh.
sleuth (slüth), *v.* to track or trail as a detective does.
sling er (sling′ər), *n.* fighter armed with a sling.
sloth (slōth or slôth), *n.* unwillingness to work or exert oneself; laziness; idleness.
slough (sluf), *v.* **1.** drop off; throw off; shed. **2.** be shed or cast; drop or fall: *A scab sloughs off when new skin takes its place.*
slov en ly (sluv′ən li), *adj.,* **-li er, -li est,** untidy, dirty, or careless in dress, appearance, habits, work, etc.
Soc ra tes (sok′rə tēz), *n.* 469-399 B.C., famous Athenian philosopher.
So ho (sō hō′ or sō′hō), *n.* district in London containing many restaurants.
so journ (*v.* sō jėrn′ or sō′jėrn; *n.* sō′jėrn), *v.* stay for a time: *The Israelites sojourned in the land of Egypt.* *—n.* a brief stay.
sol der (sod′ər), *v.* mend; repair; patch.
so lic it (sə lis′it), *v.* ask earnestly; try to get: *The tailor sent around cards soliciting trade.*
so lic i tor (sə lis′ə tər), *n.* lawyer. In England, a solicitor prepares a case, and a barrister pleads it.
so lil o quy (sə lil′ə kwi), *n., pl.* **-quies.** speech made by an actor to himself when alone on the stage. It reveals his thoughts and feelings to the audience, but not to the other characters in the play.
som no lent (som′nə lənt), *adj.* sleepy; drowsy. [< L *somnolentus* < *somnus* sleep]
so no rous (sə nô′rəs or sə nō′rəs), *adj.* **1.** giving out or having a deep, loud sound. **2.** full and rich in sound.
so phis ti cal (sə fis′tə kəl), *adj.* **1.** clever but misleading; based on false or unsound reasoning. **2.** using clever but misleading arguments; reasoning falsely.
Soph o cles (sof′ə klēz), *n.* 495?-406? B.C., a famous Greek tragic poet.

hat, āge, cãre, fär; let, ēqual, tėrm; it, īce; hot, ōpen, ôrder; oil, out; cup, pu̇t, rüle, ūse; th, thin; ᴛʜ, then; zh, measure; ə represents *a* in about, *e* in taken, *i* in pencil, *o* in lemon, *u* in circus.

sor did (sôr′did), *adj.* caring too much for money; meanly selfish; mean; low; base.

sor rel (sôr′əl or sor′əl), *adj.* reddish-brown. —*n.* **1.** a reddish brown. **2.** a reddish-brown horse. [< OF *sorel* < *sor* yellowish-brown]

sou (sü), *n.* a former French coin.

sov er eign (sov′rən), *n.* king or queen; supreme ruler; monarch.

sparse (spärs), *adj.*, **spars er, spars est.** thinly scattered; occurring here and there.

sphere (sfēr), *n.* **1.** place or surroundings in which a person or thing exists, acts, works, etc. **2.** range; extent; region.

spleen (splēn), *n.* **1.** a ductless gland at the left of the stomach in man, and near the stomach or intestine in other vertebrates. **2.** bad temper; spite; anger.

spo rad ic (spə rad′ik), *adj.* appearing or happening at intervals in time: *sporadic outbreaks.*

spo rad i cal ly (spə rad′ik li), *adv.* here and there; now and then; separately.

spright ly (sprīt′li), *adj.*, **-li er, -li est.** lively; gay.

sprite (sprīt), *n.* elf; fairy; goblin.

squab (skwob), *n.* a very young bird, especially a young pigeon.

squal id (skwol′id), *adj.* filthy; degraded; wretched.

stake (stāk), *n.* money risked; what is staked.

stance (stans), *n.* position of the feet of a player when making a stroke in golf or other games.

stat ute (stach′üt), *n.* law; decree; formally established rule.

stile (stīl), *n.* steps for getting over a fence or wall.

stint (stint), *n.* limit; limitation: *That generous man gives without stint.*

stip u la tion (stip′ū lā′shən), *n.* condition in an agreement or bargain.

stoke (stōk), *v.*, **stoked, stok ing.** poke, stir up, and feed (a fire); tend the fire of (a furnace).

stol id (stol′id), *adj.* hard to arouse; not easily excited; showing no emotion; seeming dull.

strait (strāt), *n.* **straits,** *pl.* difficulty; need; distress.

Strand (strand), *n.* an important street in London.

strat a gem (strat′ə jəm), *n.* scheme or trick for deceiving the enemy; trick; trickery.

stra tum (strā′təm or strat′əm), *n.*, *pl.* **stra ta** or **stra tums.** layer of material; especially, one of several parallel layers placed one upon another.

strin gent (strin′jənt), *adj.* strict; severe.

stu por (stü′pər or stū′pər), *n.* a dazed condition; loss or lessening of the power to feel.

sub ju gate (sub′jü gāt), *v.*, **-gat ed, -gat ing.** subdue; conquer.

sub se quent (sub′sə kwənt), *adj.* coming after; following; later: *subsequent events.*

sub sid ence (səb sīd′əns or sub′sə dəns), *n.* act or process of subsiding.

sub si dy (sub′sə di), *n.*, *pl.* **-dies.** grant or contribution of money, especially one made by a government.

sub stan tial (səb stan′shəl), *adj.* real; actual.

sub tle (sut′əl), *adj.* **1.** faint; mysterious: *a subtle smile.* **2.** sly; crafty; tricky: *a subtle scheme to get some money.* **3.** skillful; clever; expert. [< OF *soutil* < L *subtilis,* originally, woven underneath]

suc cor (suk′ər), *n.*, *v.* help; aid.

suite (swēt), *n.* a connected series of rooms to be used by one person or family.

sun dry (sun′dri), *adj.* several; various.

su per e rog a to ry (sü′pər ə rog′ə tô′ri or sü′pər-ə rog′ə tō′ri), *adj.* unnecessary; superfluous.

su per flu ous (sù pėr′flü əs), *adj.* **1.** more than is needed. **2.** needless.

su per scribe (sü′pər skrīb′), *v.*, **-scribed, -scrib-ing.** write (words, letters, one's name, etc.) above, on, or outside of something.

su per sede (sü′pər sēd′), *v.*, **-sed ed, -sed ing.** **1.** take the place of; cause to be set aside; displace: *Electric lights have superseded gas lights in most homes.* **2.** fill the place of; replace.

su pine (*adj.* sü pīn′; *n.* sü′pīn), *adj.* lazily inactive; listless. —**su pine′ly,** *adv.*

sup pli cate (sup′lə kāt), *v.*, **-cat ed, -cat ing.** beg humbly and earnestly.

sup pli ca tion (sup′lə kā′shən), *n.* **1.** a supplicating. **2.** a humble and earnest request or prayer.

sur feit (sėr′fit), *n.* too much; excess: *A surfeit of food makes one sick.* —*v.* overfeed.

sur mise (sər mīz′), *v.*, **-mised, -mis ing.** guess.

sur name (sėr′nām′), *n.* a last name; family name.

Sur rey (sėr′i), *n.* county in SE England.

sus tain (səs tān′), *v.* **1.** keep up; keep going. **2.** supply with food, provisions, etc.

swab (swob), *v.*, **swabbed, swab bing.** clean with a swab; apply a swab to: *swab a person's throat.*

swart (swôrt), *adj.* dark; swarthy.

swathe (swāᴛʜ), *v.*, **swathed, swath ing,** wrap up closely or fully: *swathed in a blanket.*

swoon (swün), *v.* faint.

syl van (sil′vən), *adj.* of the woods; in the woods.

sym bol (sim′bəl), *n.* something that stands for or represents something else.

sym bol ic (sim bol′ik), *adj.* used as a symbol: *A lily is symbolic of purity.*

sym met ri cal (si met′rə kəl), *adj.* having symmetry; well-proportioned.

sym me try (sim′ə tri), *n.*, *pl.* **-tries.** a regular, balanced arrangement on opposite sides of a line or plane, or around a center or axis.

tab er nac le (tab′ər nak′əl), *n.* a Jewish temple.

taint (tānt), *v.* give a taint to; spoil.

tal low (tal′ō), *n.* the hard fat from sheep, cows, etc., used for making candles and soap.

tan gi ble (tan′jə bəl), *adj.* **1.** capable of being touched or felt by touch: *A chair is a tangible object.* **2.** real; actual; definite: *The good will of a business is not so tangible as its buildings and stock.*

ta ran tu la (tə ran′chù lə), *n.*, *pl.* **-las, -lae** (-lē). a large, hairy spider whose bite is painful, if not dangerous.

tar pau lin (tär pô′lən), *n.* canvas, or other coarse strong cloth, made waterproof.

taw ny (tô′ni), *adj.*, **-ni er, -ni est.** brownish yellow: *A lion has a tawny skin.*

tech ni cal (tek′nə kəl), *adj.* of or having to do with a mechanical or industrial art or applied science: *This technical school trains engineers, chemists, and architects.*

tem per (tem′pər), *v.* bring or be brought to a proper or desired condition by mixing or preparing. Steel is tempered by heating it and working it till it has the proper degree of hardness and toughness.

te nac i ty (ti nas′ə ti), *n.* stubbornness; persistence.

ten don (ten′dən), *n.* a tough, strong band or cord of tissue that joins a muscle to a bone or some other part; sinew.

ter mi nate (tėr′mə nāt), *v.*, **-nat ed, -nat ing.** **1.** bring to an end; put an end to: *terminate a partnership.* **2.** come to an end: *His contract terminates soon.*

< = from, taken from; cf., compare; dial., dialect; dim., diminutive; pp., past participle; ppr., present participle; pt., past tense; ult., ultimately; var., variant; ?=possibly.

ter res tri al (tə res′tri əl), *adj.* of the earth; having to do with the earth.

Thames (temz), *n.* river flowing from SW England into the North Sea. London is on the Thames. 210 mi.

the o lo gian (thē′ə lō′jən or thē′ə lō′ji ən), *n.* person skilled or trained in theology.

the ol o gy (thi ol′ə ji), *n., pl.* **-gies.** **1.** study of the nature of God and His relations to man and the universe. **2.** study of religion and religious beliefs.

ther mal (thėr′məl), *adj.* of or having to do with heat.

ther mo graph (thėr′mō graf), *n.* a self-registering thermometer.

Thes pi an (thes′pi ən), *adj.* of or having to do with the drama or tragedy; dramatic; tragic. —*n.* actor or actress. [< *Thespis*, Greek poet]

thews (thüz), *n. pl.* **1.** muscles. **2.** sinews.

thrall dom or **thral dom** (thrôl′dəm), *n.* bondage; slavery.

thwart (thwôrt), *v.* oppose and defeat; keep from doing something.

tim or ous (tim′ər əs), *adj.* easily frightened; timid.

toc sin (tok′sən), *n.* **1.** alarm sounded on a bell; warning signal. **2.** bell used to sound an alarm.

tol er a ble (tol′ər ə bəl), *adj.* able to be borne or endured.

to paz (tō′paz), *n.* a crystalline mineral that occurs in various forms and colors.

tou ché (tü shā′), *adj.* Literally, touched; esp. by a fencing opponent's weapon; hence, scored on in argument; used to acknowledge a home thrust.

tox ic (tok′sik), *adj.* poisonous; of poison; caused by poison.

trace (trās), *n.* either of the two straps, ropes, or chains by which an animal pulls a wagon, carriage, etc.

trac ta ble (trak′tə bəl), *adj.* easily managed or controlled; easy to deal with; docile.

tran scend ent (tran sen′dənt), *adj.* surpassing ordinary limits; excelling; superior; extraordinary.

tran si tion (tran zish′ən), *n.* a change or passing from one condition, place, thing, activity, topic, etc., to another.

tran si to ry (tran′sə tô′ri or tran′sə tō′ri), *adj.* passing soon or quickly; lasting only a short time.

trans port (trans′pôrt or trans′pōrt), *n.* **1.** a carrying from one place to another: *Trucks are much used for transport.* **2.** ship used to carry men and supplies.

trans verse (trans vėrs′, tranz vėrs′, trans′vėrs, or tranz′vėrs), *adj.* lying across; placed crosswise; crossing from side to side: *transverse beams.*

trav ail (trav′āl), *n.* **1.** toil; labor. **2.** trouble; hardship.

trav erse (trav′ərs or trə vėrs′), *v.,* **-ersed, -ersing.** pass across, over, or through.

trav es ty (trav′is ti), *n., pl.* **-ties.** any treatment or imitation that makes a serious thing seem ridiculous.

tre ble (treb′əl), *v.,* **-bled, -bling.** make or become three times as much.

trench ant (tren′chənt), *adj.* **1.** sharp; keen; cutting: *trenchant wit.* **2.** clear-cut; distinct: *in trenchant outline against the sky.*

trep i da tion (trep′ə dā′shən), *n.* nervous dread; fear; fright.

tri bu nal (tri bū′nəl or trī bū′nəl), *n.* court of justice; place of judgment.

trib u tar y (trib′ū ter′i), *n., pl.* **-tar ies.** stream that flows into a larger stream or body of water.

tri col or (trī′kul′ər), *adj.* having three colors.

trip li cate (trip′lə kāt), *v.,* **-cat ed, -cat ing.** make threefold; triple.

Triptolemus (trip tol′ē mus).

triv i al (triv′i əl), *adj.* **1.** not important; trifling; insignificant. **2.** *Archaic.* not new or interesting; ordinary.

tri um vi rate (trī um′və rit or trī um′və rāt), *n.* any group of three.

troll (trōl), *v.* fish (for) with a moving line.

trou ba dour (trü′bə dôr, trü′bə dōr, or trü′bə-dür), *n.* one of the lyric poets of S France, E Spain, and N Italy from the 11th to the 13th centuries.

trus tee (trus tē′), *n.* person responsible for the property or affairs of another person, of a company, or of an institution.

tum brel or **tum bril** (tum′brəl), *n.* cart that carried prisoners to be executed.

turn key (tėrn′kē′), *n., pl.* **-keys.** person in charge of the keys of a prison; keeper of a prison.

tus sle (tus′əl), *v.,* **-sled, -sling,** *n.* struggle; wrestle; scuffle.

tu te lage (tü′tə lij or tū′tə lij), *n.* instruction.

twain (twān), *n., adj. Archaic* or *Poetic.* two.

tyr an nous (tir′ə nəs), *adj.* acting like a tyrant; cruel or unjust; arbitrary; tyrannical.

un a bashed (un′ə basht′), *adj.* not embarrassed, ashamed, or awed.

un a vail ing (un′ə vāl′ing), *adj.* not successful; useless.

un com pro mis ing (un kom′prə mīz′ing), *adj.* unyielding; firm.

unc tu ous (ungk′chü əs), *adj.* soothing, sympathetic, and persuasive.

un due (un dü′ or un dū′), *adj.* **1.** not fitting; not right; improper. **2.** too great; too much.

un hal lowed (un hal′ōd), *adj.* not made holy; not sacred.

un im peach a ble (un′im pēch′ə bəl), *adj.* free from fault; blameless.

un kempt (un kempt′), *adj.* neglected; untidy. [< *un-*[1] + OE *cembed* combed, pp. of *cemban* < *camb* comb]

un mit i gat ed (un mit′ə gāt′id), *adj.* unqualified or absolute: *an unmitigated fraud.*

un right eous (un rī′chəs), *adj.* wicked; sinful; unjust. [OE *unrihtwīs*] —**un right′eous ness,** *n.*

un sa vor y (un sā′vər i or un sāv′ri), *adj.* morally unpleasant; offensive.

ur chin (ėr′chən), *n.* **1.** a small boy. **2.** a mischievous boy. **3.** a poor, ragged child.

u su rer (ū′zhə rər), *n.* person who lends money at an extremely high or unlawful rate of interest.

u surp (ū zėrp′ or ū sėrp′), *v.* seize and hold (power, position, authority, etc.) by force or without right.

ut ter (ut′ər), *v.* put (forged checks, counterfeit money) into circulation. —**ut′ter er,** *n.*

val et (val′it or val′ā), *n.* servant who takes care of a man's clothes, helps him dress, etc.

val i date (val′ə dāt), *v.,* **-dat ed, -dat ing.** support by facts or authority; confirm.

va lise (və lēs′), *n.* a traveling bag to hold clothes, etc.

van quish (vang′kwish), *v.* conquer; defeat; overcome.

vap id (vap′id), *adj.* without much life or flavor; tasteless; dull. [< L *vapidus*]

---

hat, āge, cãre, fär; let, ēqual, tėrm; it, īce; hot, ōpen, ôrder; oil, out; cup, pu̇t, rüle, ūse; th, thin; ᴛʜ, then; zh, measure; ə represents *a* in about, *e* in taken, *i* in pencil, *o* in lemon, *u* in circus.

va por (vā′pər), *n.* **1.** steam from boiling water; moisture in the air that can be seen; fog; mist. **2.** a gas formed from a substance that is usually a liquid or a solid.
var i a ble (vãr′i ə bəl), *adj.* apt to change; changeable; uncertain: *variable winds.*
var i a tion (vãr′i ā′shən), *n.* a varying in condition, degree, etc.; change.
vast (vast or väst), *adj.* very great; immense: *Texas is a vast State. A billion dollars is a vast amount of money.* [< L *vastus*] **—vast′ness,** *n.*
veg e tate (vej′ə tāt), *v.,* **-tat ed, -tat ing.** live with very little action, thought, or feeling.
ve he mence (vē′ə məns), *n.* forcefulness; violence; strong feeling.
ve he ment (vē′ə mənt), *adj.* having or showing strong feeling; caused by strong feeling; eager; passionate. **—ve′he ment ly,** *adv.*
ven er a ble (ven′ər ə bəl), *adj.* worthy of reverence; deserving respect because of age, character, or associations: *a venerable priest, venerable customs.*
ves per (ves′pər), *n.* evening.
ves tige (ves′tij), *n.* a slight remnant; trace: *Ghost stories are vestiges of a former widespread belief in ghosts.*
vex (veks), *v.* **1.** anger by trifles; annoy; provoke. **2.** disturb; trouble.
vi al (vī′əl), *n.* a small glass bottle for holding medicines or the like; bottle.
vi and (vī′ənd), *n.* **viands,** *pl.* articles of choice food.
vict ual (vit′əl), *n.* Usually, **victuals,** *pl. Informal* or *Dialect.* food.
vie (vī), *v.,* **vied, vy ing.** strive for superiority; contend in rivalry; compete. [< F *envier* challenge < L *invitare* invite]
vil lain ous (vil′ən əs), *adj.* **1.** very wicked. **2.** extremely bad; vile.
vin di cate (vin′də kāt), *v.,* **-cat ed, -cat ing.** **1.** clear from suspicion, dishonor, hint, or charge of wrongdoing, etc.: *The verdict of "Not guilty" vindicated him.* **2.** defend successfully against opposition; uphold; justify: *The heir vindicated his claim to the fortune.*
vin dic tive (vin dik′tiv), *adj.* **1.** feeling a strong tendency toward revenge; bearing a grudge: *He is so vindictive that he never forgives anybody.* **2.** showing a strong tendency toward revenge: *Vindictive acts rarely do much good.*
vin tage (vin′tij), *n.* the wine from a certain crop of grapes: *The finest vintages cost much more than others.*
vir gin (vėr′jən), *n.* a maiden; a pure, unmarried woman.
vir u lent (vir′ū lənt or vir′ə lənt), *adj.* very poisonous or harmful; deadly: *a virulent form of a disease.*
vis age (viz′ij), *n.* face.
vis cer a (vis′ər ə), *n. pl. of* **vis cus** (vis′kəs). the soft inside parts of the body. The heart, stomach, liver, intestines, kidneys, etc., are viscera.
vi sion ar y (vizh′ən er′i), *adj., n., pl.* **-ar ies.** *—adj.* not practical; dreamy: *Ruth is a visionary girl; she spends her time daydreaming.* *—n.* person who is not practical; dreamer.
vis ta (vis′tə), *n.* **1.** view seen through a narrow opening or passage: *The opening between the two rows of trees afforded a vista of the lake.* **2.** such an opening or passage itself: *a shady vista of elms.*
vi tal (vī′təl), *adj.* **1.** necessary to life: *Eating is a vital function. The heart is a vital organ.* **2.** very necessary; very important; essential: *An adequate army is vital to the defense of a nation.*
vogue (vōg), *n.* the fashion: *Hoop skirts were in vogue many years ago.*
vo ra cious (və rā′shəs), *adj.* eating much; greedy in eating; ravenous.
vor tex (vôr′teks), *n., pl.* **-tex es** or **-ti ces.** whirl of activity or other situation from which it is hard to escape: *The two nations were unwillingly drawn into the vortex of war.*
vul ner a ble (vul′nər ə bəl), *adj.* **1.** capable of being wounded or injured; open to attack: *Achilles was vulnerable only in his heel.* **2.** sensitive to criticism, temptations, influences, etc.: *Most people are vulnerable to ridicule.*

waist coat (wāst′kōt′ or wes′kət), *n. Esp. Brit.* a man's vest.
ward (wôrd), *n.* person under the care of a guardian or of a court.
warp (wôrp), *v.* **1.** bend or twist out of shape: *This floor has warped so that it is not level.* **2.** mislead; pervert: *Prejudice warps our judgment.*
wel ter weight (wel′tər wāt′), *n.* boxer or wrestler weighing between 135 and 147 pounds.
wench (wench), *n.* **1.** girl or young woman. **2.** a woman servant.
wend (wend), *v.* **wend ed** or (*Archaic*) **went, wend ing.** **1.** direct (one's way): *We wended our way home.* **2.** go.
whet (hwet), *v.,* **whet ted, whet ting.** **1.** sharpen by rubbing: *whet a knife.* **2.** make keen or eager; stimulate: *The smell of food whetted my appetite.*
whip stock (hwip′stok′), *n.* handle of a whip.
Wil ton (wil′tən), *n.* a kind of velvety carpet.
winch (winch), *n.* a machine for lifting or pulling, turned by a crank.
win now (win′ō), *v.* sort out; separate; sift: *winnow truth from falsehood.*
with al (wiᴛʜ ôl′ or with ôl′), *Archaic.* *—adv.* with it all; as well; besides; also: *The lady is rich and fair and wise withal.*
wont (wunt or wōnt), custom; habit: *He rose early, as was his wont.*
wreak (rēk), *v.* **1.** give expression to; work off (feelings, desires, etc.): *The cruel boy wreaked his bad temper on his dog.* **2.** *Archaic.* avenge.
wretch ed (rech′id), *adj.* very unsatisfactory; miserable: *a wretched hut.* **—wretch′ed ness,** *n.*

Yale (yāl), *n.* university for men at New Haven, Connecticut. It was founded in 1701.
yeast y (yēs′ti), *adj.* light or trifling; frivolous.
yeo man (yō′mən), *n., pl.* **-men.** *Archaic.* a servant or attendant of a lord or king.
yoke (yōk), *n., v.,* **yoked, yok ing.** *—n.* rule; dominion: *Slaves are under the yoke of their masters.* *—v.* put a yoke on; fasten with a yoke.
yond (yond), *adj., adv. Archaic* or *Dialect.* yonder.
yon der (yon′dər), *adj.* situated over there; being within sight, but not near: *He lives in yonder cottage.*

zeal (zēl), *n.* eager desire; earnest enthusiasm: *A good citizen feels zeal for his country's welfare.*
zeal ous (zel′əs), *adj.* full of zeal; eager; earnest; enthusiastic: *The children made zealous efforts to clean up the house for the party.* [< Med.L *zelosus* < L *zelus* zeal < Gk. *zelos*]
zest (zest), *n.* keen enjoyment; relish: *The hungry man ate with zest.*

< = from, taken from; cf., compare; dial., dialect; dim., diminutive; pp., past participle; ppr., present participle; pt., past tense; ult., ultimately; var., variant; ?=possibly.

INDEX OF AUTHORS AND TITLES

Names of authors are in capital letters; titles of selections are italicized.

6 7 8 9 10 11 12 13 14 15 16 17 18 19 20 21 22 23 24 25 D 72 71 70